D1509391

AUG -- 2009

DATE DUE

DEC 1 1 2009	
MAR 3 1 2010 APR 0 7 2012	
AUG 1 5 2012	
SEP 1 9 2012	
WITHDRAWN	

The Library Store   #47-0106

WINNETKA-NORTHFIELD
PUBLIC LIBRARY DISTRICT
WINNETKA, IL
847-446-7220

THE OFFICIAL HISTORY OF THE
OLYMPIC GAMES AND THE IOC

Iconic Cathy Freeman, Australian Aborigine 400m champion at Sydney.
(© Getty Images/Powell)

The Official History of the Olympic Games and the IOC

Athens to Beijing, 1894–2008

DAVID MILLER

MAINSTREAM
PUBLISHING

EDINBURGH AND LONDON

For Michèle and Max, Gavin and Ygraine

Copyright © David Miller, 2008
All rights reserved
The moral right of the author has been asserted

First published in Great Britain in 2003 by
MAINSTREAM PUBLISHING COMPANY (EDINBURGH) LTD
7 Albany Street
Edinburgh EH1 3UG

ISBN 9781845961596

No part of this book may be reproduced or transmitted in any form or by any
means without written permission from the publisher, except by a reviewer who
wishes to quote brief passages in connection with a review written for insertion in
a magazine, newspaper or broadcast

Copyright permissions cleared by the author.
The author has tried to trace all copyright details but
where this has not been possible the publisher will be pleased to
make necessary arrangements at the earliest opportunity

The views of the author are not necessarily those of the IOC President and the Executive Board

A catalogue record for this book is available from the British Library

Typeset in Stone
Printed and bound in Great Britain by
Butler and Tanner Ltd, Frome

Contents

Foreword

The path of the modern Olympic Games has seldom been easy and there have expectedly been many controversies and many crises, one or two of which threatened the continuation of the Games or the authority of the International Olympic Committee itself. There have been in the past lengthy debates about definitions of amateurism, professionalism and eligibility; more recently and urgently about the contents of the programme; about the division of income, once minimal, latterly substantial and still happily so; about the virtues or otherwise of sponsorship, which invaluably helps to sustain global activities in the development of sport; about halting the scourge of drugs; about the structure of the IOC itself.

The many high-profile doping revelations in 2007 might make some observers think that we are losing the battle. I disagree. The fact that so many instances of unfair play were revealed, and that more athletes admitted responsibility, tells us that we are on the right track. Illegal betting also presents a formidable threat to the credibility of sport and must be tackled in the same aggressive way in which we are fighting against doping.

I am proud of what we in the Olympic Movement have achieved in the past few years. We have kept the Olympic Games unique and manageable, while producing excellent Winter Games in Turin. We have delivered record revenues to assist athletes and sports organisations the world over through our Solidarity Fund, promoting sport throughout society. We have brought Olympic values to life every day.

The Olympic Games do not just happen. Though they legally belong to the IOC, founded by Baron Pierre de Coubertin in 1894 as a re-creation of the ancient games of Greece, they are the complex product of a benevolent sporting partnership between the IOC, the 205 national Olympic committees and their competitors, the international sports federations and, fourth, a succession of host cities. The IOC is dedicated, under the terms of its Charter, to ensuring that the Games are an outstanding celebration embracing the youth of the world, currently every two years alternately for Summer and Winter sports. We must find new ways to engender the interest of young people in the thrill of active sports to help reduce the threat to their well-being from alarming obesity rates in developed countries. We must make the education of youth through sport as relevant today as it was in de Coubertin's time. The creation of our Youth Olympic Games can go some way towards that.

The IOC hopes that Beijing 2008 will realise its potential as a spectacular Olympic Games. The dialogue surrounding Beijing will likely increase in volume. A remarkable amount of effort and dedication has been focused on an array of social and political issues in China. This is natural. It is positive proof that we live in a world in which citizens are concerned to express what they believe is best for the common good.

Many books have been written about the IOC or the Games. David Miller's history relates the parallel evolution of the two, the administration and the event, analysing the influence of each upon the other, and is a valuable informative work.

Jacques Rogge
President of the International
Olympic Committee

Preface

Sport provides motivation for people in different ways, whether performers or spectators, whether emotionally, actively or philosophically. It has motivated me all my life, since I first read about Jesse Owens when aged ten, since I was coached as a teenager by Emmanuel McDonald Bailey, twice Olympic 100m finalist, and onwards throughout my 52 years as a journalist.

Sport is by no means always pure, but it does encapsulate in microcosm the virtues of human nature, and while I do not believe that peace, per se, is the business of sport, sport at its best, by its existence, can help define the objectives of humanity. It seems to me appropriate, for instance, that sport should be providing a tiny arm of life-support amid the turmoil of the Middle East. The Peres Centre for Peace in Tel Aviv finds commitment and conviction when bringing its moral message to the peoples of Palestine and Israel in the tortuous attempt to integrate these warring nations. It was a touching moment at a conference in December 2007 to witness, on stage in Monte Carlo, the meeting of Professor Manuel Hassassian, Palestinian ambassador to the United Kingdom, and Galeb Magadla, Israeli minister for sport, shaking hands and giving their unqualified support to the objectives of the Sports Department of the Peres Centre. This exceptional venture unites some 5,000 children from more than 12,000 families from two historically alien nations, introducing them to interdenominational coaching and competition in a unique project. Sport's own objectives must be the pursuit of sport, but simultaneously it can be a vehicle, a tool, for direct action by governments and NGOs in searching for a better world. That is something of which sport, and the Peres Centre, can be proud. A percentage of royalties from this book will be donated to the Centre.

As an adolescent I was a would-be Olympian, then a professional bystander as journalist and author. We who nowadays cover an Olympic Games are a privileged few thousand, beneficiaries of the technological advance by which it is possible for a single writer to see all the action, hear all the post-event quotations and read all the biographical backgrounds without ever moving from a seat in the main press centre. The subsidy from the IOC to each journalist for this facility is calculated at $15,000 per head, a figure that few journalists acknowledge when criticising the IOC for its commercial activities.

When Juan Antonio Samaranch, the then President, suggested in 1997 that I should write a history of the International Olympic Committee, the initial intention was that it should be a volume making available to the ordinary reader, as opposed to the specialist or academic, the affairs of the governing body of the Olympic Games. There is, and has been, so much misinformation about the function of the IOC. However, it seemed to me that it would be preferable to try to relate, I think for the first time, the parallel evolution and history of both the administrators and the competitors. A work of such complexity, single-handed, was a daunting task, especially in the wake of the IOC's formal three-volume history, *1894–1994, The International Olympic Committee: One Hundred Years*, covering some 1,100 pages and assembled by such a learned group of historians: Dr Karl Lennartz, director of the Carl and Liselotte Diem Archives; Yves-Pierre Boulogne, Honorary Professor at the University of Paris-Val de Marne, Cretil; Otto Schanz, Associate Professor at the Universitié des Sciences Humaines, Strasbourg; Fernand Landry and Magdeleine Yerlès, professors of the Université Laval, Quebec; Norbert Müller, Professor of Johannes Guttenberg University, Mainz; and all of this under the editorial direction of the late and esteemed Raymond Gafner, IOC member from Switzerland. This has been a continual source of reference, as have, among many, the works of Ian Buchanan and Stan Greenberg of Britain, Americans Allen Guttmann, John Lucas, Bill Mallon and David Wallechinsky, Wolf Lyberg of Sweden, Roberto Quercentani of Italy, and Erwin Roth's extended publication by OSB of *A Hundred Years of the Modern Games*.

Dr Jacques Rogge, new President in 2001, maintains his predecessor's enthusiastic support, as does Kevan Gosper, head of the IOC Press Commission. I have been especially grateful to those who have kindly read the manuscript, to eradicate my various errors and omissions: including HM King Constantine of the Hellenes, whose grandfather Crown Prince Constantine was effectively co-founder of the modern Games, and Richard Pound, ex-Olympian, Montreal QC and pillar of the IOC.

Deciding to give each chapter a first-person reminiscence in order to bring an individual flavour, I have had to find comments from some 20 deceased Olympic champions and leading IOC figures, together with original contributions from over 50 of the living, and the collaboration of the latter has been most rewarding. Such contributions are marked in the text with an asterisk. I am grateful to the following IOC members, Thomas Bach, Anita DeFrantz, the late Nikos Filaretos, Kevan Gosper, Zhen-liang Hé, Paul Henderson, Arne Ljungqvist, the late Keba M'baye, Ser Miang Ng, Denis Oswald, Richard Pound, Sam Ramsamy, Vitaly Smirnov, Walter Tröger and Mario Vazquez Raña, for their introductions, and not least to the President for his Foreword. Tireless researchers at the Olympic Museum Picture Library were Alexandra Mandl and Fernando Scippa. My computer-literate assistant, Susan Buck, worked as diligently on this updated edition as on the first, as did all-embracing Mainstream editor Ailsa Bathgate.

David Miller

INTRODUCTION

Maintaining Relevance

Carolina Kluft of Sweden, Olympic heptathlon champion

'The Olympic Games are special because of their history and tradition: the flame, the rings and the emotional experience of being part of it, together with all nations and all the varying events, different people all equal as competitors, loving sport. The Games also have a social and political relevance. Yet when you're out there on the track, everything is so focused. If you need an extra incentive, it's right there: the sight of the flame.

As a child, I was never in front of the television but outside playing, so I was not particularly conscious of the Games. Growing up in a small village, with not much to choose from, it was mostly football that we played. I didn't have my first encounter with track and field until I was about 12. I was never motivated by a desire to be successful; for me it was always just about having fun and being with my friends, simply training or competing, driven by a wish to improve.

When I took part in my first Junior World Championships aged 17 in Athens, there was not so much an expectation of what the future might bring as the pleasure of being there, being involved. I don't even remember who my main rivals were, just the experience of trying to discover how far I could go. To become number one was never my motivation. All I've wanted is to be at the peak of my own ability, the unity of body and brain. Nowadays, of course, I know more about my sport, but when I was young I never consulted statistics; I competed because it was exhilarating. I love training for its own sake, the satisfaction of improving. And I've learned so much from other people, other countries.

The Olympics are a lesson in life, yet sport is only a small part of my life – though admittedly a very important part right now. The objective is to be happy, to be in harmony with your surroundings. I don't want to put pressure on myself, in sport, to the point where I become unhappy. I want to live a life that feels meaningful. When I'm older and look back, I want to see the memories, the people, the experiences, not the medals. Life is so much more than a gold medal. Yes, that can be a great feeling, an adventure, but the world has bigger issues than competing on the track. There are things I want to do beyond that – charitable work that I do privately, something I was involved in before I became a full-time athlete. These two worlds have nothing to do with each other. I have a foster child in Africa. I've been there reporting for the Swedish media, hoping to persuade people to open their eyes, to realise that not everyone has it as good as we do, to try to do my best to make things better for many children. In doing this, I've realised that sport is important for connecting people, enabling you to do something not just for yourself.

Winning the heptathlon in Athens in 2004 was hard, I did have pressure – from the Swedish public, from people around me – but I tried just to keep focused. In the Village, I observed the reactions of those who had won and those who had lost, either smiling or not, heads up or heads down. I think the way you handle success or failure is important, because I want to be the same person whether I win or lose, to be happy even if I'm not succeeding. I think I am still worth the same either way.

Am I intense? Yes, I can switch on and switch off. When I'm on the track, all other thoughts disappear. I'm focused, taking energy from the crowd, from the flame, from the sensation of being part of the Olympics, attempting to achieve something good. When I go to jump, I push all the energy into that one moment. I can hear music inside myself, special lyrics; I can hear my own voice. I know that maybe I look angry, because everything else is shut out in order to do my best. When I've jumped, successfully or not, I switch off, because otherwise all my energy would be gone in two jumps.

Between jumps, I like to chat with other girls, to cheer for them. Yes, of course – to enjoy being there with them, part of the atmosphere, relaxed. I love the relationship with the crowd, and I want to cheer the other girls to do better. A world record is never something I'm aiming at; I put records aside. As long as I've done as well as I could, I'm satisfied, though if I knew I was on course for a record I would run for it – as I did in the Junior Championships in 2002. Not setting a record will never make me unhappy.

I'll be as focused as ever if I defend my Olympic title this year [2008], always assuming I'm fit, though maybe I'll decide instead to switch to the individual long jump or triple jump event. I'm interested in a fresh challenge, and I will have made up my mind after the European Indoor at Valencia in March. I went to Osaka last year to defend my world title totally free of injury for the first time. My training preparation was good. Sure, there was some pressure, but I was able to achieve my personal best performance and break the European record. I never think more than one tournament ahead.

The exposure of Marion Jones is tragic for sport and for her. I think she loved sport, and now her life is destroyed; her victories will be forgotten. I hope people will understand that what she did was not worth it, that it's not right to jeopardise your reputation, to be unfair in competition. That's not acceptable. It has really upset me. I'm very much against doping, and I'd wanted to trust Marion as a shining star, so her end is very bitter for everyone. We must keep sport clean, which is the way to be happy.'*

(Photograph © IOC/Kishimoto. Asterisk denotes first-person interview with the author.)

Slowly to climb the steps from the road at Lausanne beside Lake Geneva, through the tranquil landscaped gardens towards the Olympic Museum, past the bronze statues of legendary Olympians Paavo Nurmi and Emil Zátopek, is to gain some small sense of ancient mythological Olympia. Can this modern version of this unique brand of human activity, so dependent upon the dedication of athletes to the pursuit of excellence, survive for another century, Baron Pierre de Coubertin having set the ball rolling 114 years ago? Can it survive, indeed, for even another 20? Amid exploitation on so many fronts, by governments bidding to host the Games and not least by athletes greedy for financial success, Olympic Games need that abstract quality of integrity at every level, without which de Coubertin's concept, his idealism, will perish. Competitors such as Carolina Kluft give us hope, reminding us that the Games are about competing *with* rivals, not seeking to surpass them by any means. In today's cynical world, Kluft's attitude seems to some to be too good to be true, yet her aura of friendship within her attempt to excel is profoundly sincere, in the tradition of illustrious past champions such as Jesse Owens and Fanny Blankers-Koen. Without the continuation of athletes who cherish the Olympic ethic, there can be no future. Kai Holm, an IOC member from Denmark, president of the International Masters (veteran) Games and a man without any private agenda within the Olympic Movement, has a stark message: 'This wonderful century-old idealistic body, created for altruistic patronage of sport and of young competitors, is now obsolete. The world changes, and unless we do the same within the IOC, unless we adapt, we have no chance of surviving another 100 years.' There are some within the Olympic Movement who do not wish to hear, immune to the views of younger IOC athlete members such as Pernilla Wiberg, four times Olympic Alpine skier yet too shy to try to force her hand on essential revision.

The Greeks glorified sport between 750 BC and 450 BC, though Euripides viewed athletics as worthless and Plato and Aristotle decried the allegiance of athletics and professionalism, claiming that it produced 'violence and disharmony'. With Greek culture overtaken by Roman vulgarity, and this in turn by puritanical Christianity, the Olympics died by decree of Emperor Theodosius in AD 393 and with it the ancient ethics of competitive physical strife. Revived by French aristocrat Pierre de Coubertin in 1894, after an inauspicious start the modern Games became the most illustrious sporting event of the twentieth century, proclaimed by Nelson Mandela for 'reaching areas far beyond any sphere of political influence, doing more to unify nations than any politician has ever done'. Their history has, however, been dogged by intermittent crises: variously threatened by administrative incompetence, by a long-running conflict between the old amateur concept and increasingly irresistible professionalism, by two World Wars, by constant political manipulations including three damaging boycotts between 1976 and 1984, by rampant commercialisation that latterly has been simultaneously essential but harmful, by alleged gigantism in the escalation of sports and competitor numbers, by corrupt practices in the host-city bidding process, by an alarming increase in the resort to performance-enhancing drugs, and not least by the reluctance of the IOC to adapt by the inclusion of sports that appeal to the modern generation of young people. Today, the Games are as threatened as ever by human frailty, and within a maelstrom of problems the energetic, modest, if at times dogmatic Jacques Rogge, the IOC's second President to come from Belgium, wrestles to call his members, and some aspects of the Games, to order.

Olympic spirit. Jesse Owens and rival Lutz Long of Germany in friendly conference during the long jump, 1936. (© IOC/Ruebelt)

'The lesson of sport is that competition is only possible when played within the rules' – Zulu leader Mangosuthu Buthelezi, on meeting Keba M'Baye's South African Mission in 1991: (l–r) Fekrou Kidane, Lamine Ba, Kevan Gosper, Mangosuthu Buthelezi, Keba M'Baye, François Carrard, Henry Adefope, Jean-Claude Ganga. (© IOC/Locatelli)

The Games are distinguished and separated from other sport, as Richard Pound, prominent member for 30 years from Canada, describes in his book *Inside the Olympics*, 'by their branding': defined by their motto 'Citius, Altius, Fortius' – swifter, higher, stronger – the Games being based on symbolism and rituals, key to the brand image which captures public acclaim not least from its global audience of television and sponsors. Unless the IOC can now protect that image, propagated by de Coubertin – sport allied to discipline and fair play, and built around the platform of organised athletics, cycling, rowing, swimming and tennis in the latter part of the nineteenth century among the leading industrial nations – the uniqueness of the Games will be lost.

Ser Miang Ng, IOC Executive Board (EB) member from Singapore, reflects: 'The Games are not a simple sports event where you win, you lose, go home and that's it. It's something more noble: the magic of the torch runs through communities, the mood is so contagious. Because of success, the Games have exceeded their original scope.' During negotiations in 1991 for the re-introduction of South Africa to the Olympics, Mangosuthu Buthelezi, chief of the Zulus, observed: 'Sport coaches people for higher office and does so in such a way that the checks and balances which are there in democracy are made to work because people want them to work. The lesson sport has for us is that competition is only viable when it is played within the rules.' Phil Coles, Australian member and three-time Olympian canoeist, treasures the experience of the Games:

> More should be done to promote the IOC's moral message – through the Olympic Museum, through our education programmes. Ninety-nine per cent of the athletes in the three Olympic Villages I experienced were fine people setting an example to any society, and I wish we could rub off more of our ethic on young people . . . there's so much brotherhood. In Canberra, we have an Iraqi single-sculler training for Beijing because it would be impossible for him at home.

Phil Coles of Australia, three-time Olympic canoeist: 'there's so much brotherhood'. (© IOC)

The famed actor Robin Williams, enlisted to help promote Olympic ethics, recalls: 'Many of my favourite Olympic memories are not gold-medal situations but inspiring instances of humanity that transcended political borders, obstacles and languages, and unified people.'

Chief Dan George, a Native American who was part of the threatened ethnic culture that his people of southern Alberta successfully attempted to protect prior to the Calgary Winter

Games of 1988, perceptively wrote in his book *My Spirit Soars*: 'There is a longing among all peoples to have a sense of purpose and worth. To satisfy that common longing in all of us, we must respect each other. Young people are the pioneers of new ways. Since they face too many temptations, it will not be easy for us to know what is best.' There was an echo of this in the *Los Angeles Times* during the Salt Lake City Winter Games of 2002, when the respected commentator Randy Harvey wrote: 'We haven't advanced that far through the Olympics in pursuit of a more perfect civilisation, but the important thing is that we have the vehicle that enables us to keep trying.' He went on to say that it would be the concept of ideals, often unreached, or not even reached for, that would keep him coming back: memories of Elana Mayer, a white South African, and Derartu Tulu, the black Ethiopian victor, embracing and circling the track after the women's 10,000m in 1992, the first year of South Africa's return; of Kerri Strug vaulting with a badly sprained ankle in 1996 because her US team believed they needed her points; of Austrian Hermann Maier winning the Alpine super-G three days after an horrific crash in 1998. There are dozens more such examples that the author could give: Gabriele Andersen-Scheiss, Swiss marathon runner, wilfully staggering, half-insensible, to the finish in LA; Guam's first-ever Olympic competitor, Judd Bankert, finishing out of sight and unknown in the 10km biathlon in Calgary after mortgaging his house to be there; Martinho de Araujo, an East Timorese weightlifter who had trained for Sydney with a bucket of concrete on each end of a pole; Glory Alozie of Nigeria, 100m hurdles silver medal winner in Sydney, persuaded by friends to run in memory of her fiancé, who had been run down and killed three weeks earlier; Esther Kim, American taekwondo competitor, who donated her qualification place for Sydney to her friend and rival Kay Poe, injured during the trials; Joey Cheek, American speed skater, who, emulating Norwegian Johann Olav Koss at the Lillehammer Winter Games, donated to charity his medal bonuses in Turin, saying, 'It's empowering to think of somebody other than yourself – I skate around the ice in tights, it's not that big a deal.'

Joey Cheek of America, 2006 speed skating champion and charity benefactor. (© IOC/Kishimoto)

Cheek put his finger on the true moral pulse of the Games. When Robert Badinter, former French Minister of Justice, was appointed to the new Ethics Commission in 1999 following the Salt Lake scandal, he spelt out some disregarded truths: 'Given that loyalty, fair play, respect for others and their dignity, and the rejection of all racist, sexist or nationalistic discrimination are fundamental to the Olympic Games, they convey a global ethical message, particularly for the young . . . the Olympic Movement has an ethical dimension which must be clearly defined, firmly guarded and scrupulously protected.' Simultaneously, in the Netherlands' daily newspaper *NRC*, Ruud Stokvis, sociologist from Amsterdam University, had observed:

> There is no other organisation that has such a generalised and strong relationship with the population of the whole world as the IOC, nor one which has proved to be so enduring . . . a majority of the world's people attach more importance to the Olympic Games than to meetings of the UN General Assembly . . . the League of Nations, which preceded the UN, lasted just 20 years. The durability of the IOC is partly due to the system of co-option by which it recruits its members. This is unquestionably not a democratic system, but it has not been proved that democratic appointment procedures are the best for all organisations. Companies have never seriously started adopting them . . . the IOC has succeeded, in spite of all, in organising the Games every four years. A more representative organisation would have failed long before.

The mystical quality that can surround an Olympic medal is one of the reasons why at any world championship in any sport many victors will say that their major ambition is to compete at the Olympic Games. The negative side of the elevation of Olympic prestige above all else is, of course, the chauvinism that it can promote. Contemplating the seemingly unending celebration of America's 174 medals in 1984 and the prospect of a five-day national tribute tour, Joe Gurgan reflected in the *LA Times*: 'Another week to teach our children the wrong lesson, not only about the nature of the Olympic Games but also the essence of sport.' Not all understand this. Even sober leader articles in *The Times* and the *Daily Telegraph* of Britain prior to the start of the Sydney Games suggested that 'Olympism' was humbug: or, in other words, that much of the IOC Charter was an archaic waste of time, irrelevant to contemporary sport. The motto of the Games, that 'the most important thing is not winning but taking part, the essential thing in life is not conquering but fighting well' was stated by *The Times* to bear no relation to what happened in the arena, which was all about fame, money and spectacle. 'Olympics yes, Olympism no,' opined the *Telegraph*, claiming that the Charter's principles were fundamental but irrelevant. Olympism was a 'fig-leaf that was always bogus'. Try telling that to Kip Keino, Kenyan track hero, who on the proceeds of his Olympic fame runs an orphanage for some hundred children in the Rift Valley. Or to Alex Gilady, IOC member from Israel:

> It's important to understand that for those coming from a small country, the ambition is not so much to climb the medals table but just to get a medal of any colour. This is sufficient to fuel the Olympic flame for the next four years . . . while there are 70 countries who may win medals, the other 130 are merely looking forward to the opening ceremony, to show the world that they exist. 'This is who we are.' For a tiny delegation, it may be for 15 or 20 seconds that they have the attention of the whole world.

Alex Gilady, Israeli member: the opening ceremony is a chance for small nations to show the world they exist. (© IOC/Lopez)

Can Rogge, a unifier intent on fulfilling the aims of the IOC's moral transformation implanted seven years ago, following the corruption scandal involving Salt Lake City, secure the future of this noble institution, hold the reins of galloping commercialism, stifle rampant drug abuse and overcome the reluctance of international federations to adjust to a programme relevant to youth? In many ways, Rogge is similar to Lord Killanin, IOC leader prior to Juan Antonio Samaranch (President 1980–2001): diligent, without ostentation, someone from a smaller country free from heavy political or financial agendas, one who is occasionally willing to seek compromise. As a past Olympian and chairman of the Coordination Commission for both Sydney 2000 and, until he became President, for Athens 2004, he knows the ropes. He believes the Games are safe 'because they are created by desire, and we, the IOC, just have to manage them properly'. Easier said than done. He is not part-revolutionary as was Samaranch. Pound relates the story of Samaranch discussing administration with Manfred Ewald, Sports Minister of the former German Democratic Republic, Ewald asserting that there were two elements in officialdom – power and glory – and that he did not mind who had the glory so long as he had the power. 'No,' Samaranch countered, 'you do not understand. The power *is* the glory.' Rogge quests not for glory, yet the power to persuade the members at a Session, the IOC's annual administrative gathering, can prove elusive.

An orthopaedic surgeon, Rogge is both fortified and to a degree confined by his professional exactitude. He says, self-effacingly:

> I think I have some modest credit, some influence for instance on judging in figure skating and gymnastics. We have improved the refereeing in boxing, introduced video replays in fencing and taekwondo – subjective judgement has been vastly improved in a whole range of sports. And I think there's some merit in having achieved greater financial security. When I took over we had reserves of $100 million. Today it stands at $320 million, so we've tripled our protection, which would allow us to survive a Games cancellation.

Protection is one thing, but the President needs, as already stated, to make the programme more relevant to youth, restore public credibility – the latest horror involving Sydney's multiple medal winner Marion Jones – and, possibly most important of all, rationalise the structure of the IOC itself.

Marques Juan Antonio Samaranch hands responsibility of sustaining IOC reforms to Dr Jacques Rogge: 'we just have to manage [the Games] properly'. (© IOC/Locatelli)

A constitutional flaw has developed at the heart of the IOC, in particular in relation to revision of the programme, compounding the difficulties for the President. This is that the IOC membership is no longer wholly independent, dispassionate and, under the stipulation of the Charter, politically, geographically, racially and financially neutral, pursuing only the best interests of the Olympic Games. So many members now have vested interests and private agendas. Some of the older members are acutely aware of this. 'At present, we have 15 ex-officio members from international federations, 15 from national Olympic committees and 15 athletes, and I have some serious doubts about this structure alongside the 70 who are conventionally elected,' Shun-ichiro Okano of Japan, elected in 1990, past president of the Japanese Football Association, says. 'I'm not sure that we can maintain a body in which members are supposed to be devoting themselves specifically to IOC themes. Yes, we do need to listen to the athletes, but, to be honest, they lack experience, especially in administration, so I think we need some change to the Charter.' Toni Khoury, member from Lebanon, also questions the present format:

> What happens if I try to act according to the regulations of the Charter? In my opinion, one of the problems is that decisions are now being taken by the IOC's [un-elected] staff, they're directing things, IOC members are losing control, forfeiting their responsibility. The Charter asks for each member to present every year a report from their country. This is no longer happening.

Anita DeFrantz from America, candidate for the presidency in 2001, adds:

> Democratisation arrived under President Samaranch – without IOC funding I would not have been able to function [prior to Samaranch's presidency, members paid a subscription and financed their own travel – for example, Killanin would not have been able to travel to Melbourne in 1956 as an ordinary member had he not been funded by Aspro, of which he was a director]. But with democratisation came the notion of representation, in ways that haven't been there in the past. Over the last ten years, there has increasingly

developed the notion that members are there representing something else, rather than representing the Olympic Movement itself in their country. It's been a significant shift.

The much-criticised self-elected IOC, founded through the initiative of de Coubertin, a minor French nobleman, together with an initial small band of disciples, had run an often tortuous path through a turbulent century. Thirty years ago, the IOC verged on bankruptcy. Since then, however, the Games have expanded exponentially to a point where there now are over 10,500 competitors in an event with billion-dollar funding. Central to expansion, through substantial contracts in the sale of television rights and sponsorship programmes, remains the perceived ideology of a continuing link with ancient Greek heritage. To maintain this, members are supposed to be representing the interests of the Olympic Games in their country rather than vice-versa.

Under the regime of Samaranch, the IOC became within itself the entire 'Olympic Movement', embracing the often-fractious international sports federations and the national Olympic committees, in the name of unity. As Ching-Kuo Wu of Taiwan (in Olympic-speak Chinese Taipei), an international architect involved in the creation of Milton Keynes new town in Britain and the recently elected president of international boxing, observes: 'Under Killanin, there was a Tripartite Commission involving the IOC, the federations and NOCs. Now the IOC has itself become the tripartite commission.' Samaranch's expansion, sensing the ever-present vulnerability of the IOC, inadvertently risked destroying its original coherence. He had been trapped by history's advance, compromising the IOC's abstract virtue: that essence of moral identity which cements any enduring private club. Yet how could there be a private club in so public an arena? The unity that Samaranch achieved, a voluntary amalgamation held together more by money than ideals, has still not lost its potential fragility. On the one hand the IOC, now directed by Rogge, is a paternal oligarchy dispensing vast funds around Olympic sports (approaching 90 per cent of its income), while on the other the Association of National Olympic Committees (ANOC) and the two collective organisations of summer and winter federations – the Association of Summer Olympic International Federations (ASOIF) and the Association of International Olympic Winter Sports Federations (AIOWF) – are democratically based yet without executive power, other than through the vote of their members elected to the IOC. They were the creation of Samaranch, specifically designed to neutralise the rebellious Thomas Keller, president in the '80s of the General Association of International Sports Federations (GAISF), who questioned IOC authority in the Games. The restructure introduced by Commission 2000, the temporary body nominated to revise the IOC following the Salt Lake scandal, attempted to establish a stable equation, but introduced one that is now prone to stalemate, as Rogge was to discover for the first time in December 2002 (see Chapter LXXI).

Any serious loss of stability, such as that of 1999, can open the gates to an external commercial takeover at any time. The ex-officio election of 45 members, while supposedly generating unity on the one hand – it makes no sense, as Samaranch realised, for any multinational company not to have representation on the Board of prime movers – at the same time produces a kind of impasse, in which members with private agendas may protect their own interests and resist change. For example, with the election to membership at the Session in Guatemala 2007 of Patrick Baumann, secretary-general of international basketball, there are now five Swiss in the IOC, including Sepp Blatter (football), René Fasel (ice-hockey), Gian-Franco Kasper (skiing) and Denis Oswald (rowing and president of ASOIF). Honourable men all, but over-representing a single country, highlighting the need to ensure that all members should be uniformly dedicated first and foremost to the interests of the IOC rather than, perhaps, to specialised objectives.

There is one potential confusion, however, that the IOC has resisted: a demand by the European Commission that Europe should be deemed a single country with all medals amalgamated under a European flag. Following Athens 2004, the then European Commission president, Romano Prodi, said he hoped that in Beijing member state teams 'will carry the flag of the European Union alongside their own national flag'. Such a proposal is rejected out of hand by the IOC. 'It's not acceptable,' Rogge states, recalling that the notion first emerged at a meeting between Jacques Delors and Samaranch in 1992, the European Union having acquired representational participation as part of the opening ceremony at the Albertville Winter Games. 'Prodi disregarded the history and tradition of the Games, that people want national teams and national heroes, national identity,' Rogge says. 'I'm sorry – there's no European identity, no common culture or language.' Breathe again.

If Rogge can win that one, what about recapturing the allegiance of youth? Sebastian Coe, double Olympic champion and leader of the 2012 Games in London, has an oft-told, worrying anecdote. Taking his children to the track and field World Championships in Paris in 2005, and keen to impress upon them the privilege of being there at such an event, his elder daughter, aged eleven, responded that there were 'probably not even three in my class who know the World Championships are happening'. Coe further recalls that when the Laureus Sports Awards committee were discussing the election of a new member of their academy, some had not even heard the name of Tony Hawke, million-dollar prizewinner in skateboarding, yet Coe's ten-year-old son urged him: 'Get me his autograph, I've got his poster!' Such are the trends of youth.

Irma Zandl, a trends forecaster in America, claims: 'The Olympics has lost its soul. I hear no buzz about the Olympics any more; to many Americans, particularly younger people, the Olympics aren't relevant. Put simply, they aren't cool.' In Australia, speaking to Melbourne's daily paper *The Age*, John Coates, NOC president, reflected: 'Some of our structured sports are not what interests young people these days, and analysis shows that Olympic audiences on television are becoming older.' He quoted a survey that reveals more American children surfed the Internet than watched television. Rogge's answer, his idea having simmered for some while, is the introduction of a Youth Olympic Games every four years in opposition to what he terms 'the tyranny of the screen'. The Youth Games, aimed at children between 14 and 18, was approved at the Guatemala Session in 2007. 'Unless the Games can change people's habits, the world is heading for a major health crisis, and the IOC has to look at the long-term future,' Rogge said. 'In Europe, young people spend more than 20 hours a week in front of a screen – instant messaging, video games, the PC and television. In my generation, these were 20 hours devoted to physical activity. The dilemma of sport is that it is very popular, yet the practice of sport is in decline, with more watchers than movers.' Richard Pound, ever the idiosyncratic thinker, questions whether the Games will reach the obese and disaffected.

And the solution is not exclusively a matter of ploughing more money into sports training and preparation at national level. In Germany, the price of 169 medals gained at four consecutive Games, Nagano–Sydney–Salt Lake City–Athens, was $6 million per medal, a massive social investment. In Japan, in response to declining success, there is a national restoration project ongoing in search of more medals that will prove equally expensive. Yet national investment is unlikely to be productive unless there is a broad base to the pyramid beneath the elite peak. In Britain, £4 billion was invested over ten years from 1994 on grass-roots sports development, but it was indicative of the lack of amenities in the public education sector that four-fifths of their Olympic medals in 2004 came from competitors educated at independent (private) schools, where there was a greater emphasis on sport.

It is symptomatic that IOC members disagree on what should be the prime objective: grass-roots or elitism? The question lies at the heart of the Games' maxim: taking part. 'Without mass sport, the Olympic Movement is a river without a source,' Zhen-liang He of China, past Vice-President, says. 'In my first speech at a Session, in 1983, I spoke about the importance of sport-for-all, and Samaranch answered that this was not the IOC's province, yet within a year he established a working group for Mass Sport, appointing me as vice-chairman.' Peter Tallberg, Finnish member and five-time Olympian, stands at the opposite pole. 'Besides being worried about rising costs, my concern is maintenance of the Games at their performance level, that is elite sport, not descending towards sport-for-all, something quite different. The Games are for the best.' Patrick Chamunda, of Zambia, from the IOC's Sport-For-All Commission, questions this view. 'The IOC's past focus has been purely elite, that being their main source of income, but mass sport is an area we need to develop.' The same from Syed Ali from Pakistan, sitting on the same Commission: 'Olympic Solidarity [the IOC's donation fund] was created to further every talent . . . in many countries sport is not given government assistance . . . if young performers don't have facilities, how can we tell if they are worthy for Solidarity funding?' Lamine Diack from Senegal, president of international athletics, touches on the pulse of the developing world:

> *All* sports can be developed in Africa, never mind from where they originate, we can develop any sport in the right circumstances, with an influx of coaches and administrators who know the sport – mountain bike, for instance, fencing. We have the raw human materials to achieve anything. The kids are there! We [Senegal] had two fencers who qualified for Athens.

So, what should be the IOC's programme for the future, making the Games relevant for the twenty-first century, recognising perhaps that youngsters are not forever going to be throwing the discus, whatever that event's noble heritage? Ottavio Cinquanta from Italy, Executive Board member and president of international skating, stresses that the IOC must adjust to public attitudes: 'Compared with 60 years ago, television permits the spectator often to be in a better position to judge the interest of a sport,' he observes. 'Viewers can see details better than those who have paid for tickets in row 27. Administrators cannot any longer determine the validity of a sport solely on the basis of their own experience.' And Richard Carrión, Puerto Rican banker, key negotiator on IOC commercial deals and potential successor to Rogge, concedes:

> Where youth has so many alternatives, I believe the programme should be a central theme at our Congress in 2009 [an intermittent gathering of all arms of the Olympic Movement in conjunction with the annual Session]. We've already seen how snowboarding changed the dynamics of the Winter Games. It is increasingly

difficult for physical sports to compete with video games, with the Internet and television, to create the mindset in young people of the need to find a balance between mind and body.

Richard Carrión, presidential candidate who believes the programme should be a central theme at the 2009 Congress. (© IOC/Juilliart)

Who succeeds Rogge could be a crucial factor in the IOC's survival over the next 20 years, so multiple are the current demands. Besides Carrión there is Thomas Bach, German lawyer, Olympic fencing champion, key figure in commissions and seemingly being groomed by Rogge; Hein Verbruggen of Holland, another favoured under Rogge's reign but with a complex CV as former president of discredited cycling; and Sergei Bubka of Ukraine, pole vaulting legend, ambitious, shrewd and inscrutable.

'If it was possible that we could decide, for the Games of 1992 under Samaranch, to change our principle from amateurism to professionalism,' Sheikh Ahmad, president of the Olympic Council of Asia, says, 'then 15 years later we must consider which are the best sports for the programme. We have a responsibility to embrace different cultures. We should design the Congress in Copenhagen specifically to address this. [Puzzlingly, the programme is not at the time of writing a core issue for 2009.] What I'm suggesting is not just a dream, we're already achieving it in our continent.'

The Emir of Qatar (centre) with Jacques Rogge and Sheikh Ahmad of Kuwait, president of the Olympic Council of Asia (left): 'We have a responsibility to embrace different cultures.' (© IOC/Juilliart)

Sheikh Ahmad, regrettably, has insufficient support from fellow members to help push through the adjustment sought by Rogge since he took office but effectively stalled under the influence of international federations who wilfully resist change that might put their own sport at risk.

Rogge, immediately conscious of the crisis upon his election in 2001, called an Extraordinary Session in 2002, only to find himself blocked by the members (see Chapter LXXII). At that time, Franco Carraro of Italy was indecisively in charge of the Programme Commission, insufficiently briefed on this Session, while Richard Pound – having made his peace with Rogge after being roundly defeated by him in the presidential election the previous year – had been appointed to chair a financially effective Review Commission, aimed at streamlining costs. Following this initial rejection in 2002, Rogge established that the programme would be reviewed at the conclusion of every Games: in spite of which there was no movement following Athens, and in a heated debate at the Session of 2005 in Singapore nothing was achieved bar the removal of baseball and softball (post-2008), no proposed new sport gaining the necessary majority. The situation remained still unresolved after Turin 2006 and then Guatemala 2007. In seven years . . . zero, bar two eliminations. As Pound elaborates in his Olympic biography: 'We need the Programme Commission to come up with a matrix, showing how the Executive Board measures the sports that have been recommended. That's the Commission's job, but their report was so riddled with errors . . . when considering rugby, or golf, or karate.' Behind the resistance of some federations is the genuine fear that without Olympic participation, and accompanying financial subsidy, their sport would all but disappear. As Craig Reedie, member from Britain, comments:

> In Singapore, the Executive Board seemed to become obsessed with the process of the decision, rather than the principle that was at stake. If two sports were removed and then not replaced, how could we convince the public what we were playing at? . . . I'm sitting there thinking what we might have done in London in seven years' time had we included rugby sevens and golf, having an 80,000-capacity stadium at Twickenham and some of the best golf courses in Britain within 25 miles.

Another part of the problem, given that Rogge has instituted a cap of around 10,500 competitors and 28 Summer sports, is that some sports, notably athletics and swimming, account for almost a third of the medals at a Summer Games, while all the rest share two-thirds. 'We must analyse these details and make adjustments if we're to find a new formula,' Ching-Kuo Wu says. 'Some sports are definitely not universal and are never seen on certain continents.'

Rogge seeks to rationalise pedestrian administration:

> Nothing was introduced in Singapore because of the two-thirds majority rule. A difficulty is that some federations want to add events within their sport – women in weightlifting, wrestling and boxing. Our stipulation is a limit of 300 events: if a federation wants to add an event, they must remove another. It's a possibility that space could be created by reducing events in athletics, swimming and gymnastics, but that only takes us halfway.

Why not increase the self-imposed limit on 28 sports, asks Ung Chang, member from North Korea?

It would be good to have at least 30 sports, and I think the number could go up to 32 without them being a financial burden on organising cities. The income would increase. We should look at the spread of certain contemporary sports, and we already know which are the most popular, such as rugby, golf, cricket and softball, a women's sport.

Ung Chang from North Korea: 'It would be good to have at least 30 sports [on the programme].' (© IOC/Locatelli)

Issa Hayatou from Cameroon, president of the African Football Confederation (CAF), coincidentally believes that FIFA should allow their Olympic tournament to be open, without an age restriction. 'Football should be presented at the Games in the best possible way, with revision of the qualifying arrangements. This would mean effectively staging the World Cup every two years, but Sepp Blatter, the president, quite recently proposed a two-yearly tournament. I believe there is no risk to the World Cup in elevating the Olympic tournament.' Of those who would like to dispose of tennis, because of fluctuating entry from the professional ranks, Franceso Ricci Bitti from Italy, international president, asserts: 'The Olympic Games needs tennis more than tennis needs the Games – unlike, say, gymnastics or swimming, which are to a degree dependent on the Games. Most of our top professionals are ambitious to take part, just look at those who have carried their national flag at the opening ceremony: Sabatini, Ivanisevic, Kuerten, Federer.'

What the author finds surprising is that the IOC will not be utilising the advent of the Youth Games to get a foot in the door for new sports, a heaven-sent opportunity to appeal to youth without, for the moment, any risk to established sports. Yet Rogge insists: 'We're going to start with established federations, though many of them know they have to adapt for the Youth Games. There will be mixed-sex relays in athletics and swimming, freestyle BMX cycling, mixed doubles for tennis players eliminated in the first round. We definitely have skateboarding in mind for the future.' But when? Pernilla Wiberg acknowledges that younger members should be more forthright in pressing the diehards to consider new ways.

The IOC needs to utilise goodwill wherever it still exists, and nowhere is this more important than in the field of drugs. Many members are aware that so much of the time in the battle with cheating chemists the authorities are, so to speak, skiing off piste, unsure what they may next encounter. On the other hand, the existing regulations are sufficiently clear-cut for no athlete ever to be confident that, if resorting to drugs, they can permanently evade detection. Nor can they plead excuses. 'A competitor cannot maintain the stance that he or she didn't know about supplements in certain drugs,' HRH the Prince of Orange, member from Netherlands, insists. 'Such claims are totally empty. Every athlete has the opportunity to discover and understand the details.' In response to the largely spurious notion that malicious 'plants' can be made, the Prince's emphasis on the athlete's own responsibility is echoed by Alexander Popov, renowned swimmer member from Russia. 'I do believe that there is much more need for both moral and practical education,' he says. 'Athletes need to know what exactly is the content of any medicine they take. When I was competing, if I had a drink in my kitbag, I wouldn't touch it if the bag was out of my sight for a second, that's how careful you have to be.' The Athletes Commission is itself increasingly hardline – and alarmed. IOC member Dr Rania Elwani from Egypt, accomplished swimmer who was semi-finalist in two freestyle sprints in Sydney 2000, speaks for many when she says: 'On the Commission, we consider that the guilty should receive a four-year ban, thereby missing the next Games . . . we sense that there are now more athletes using drugs, that the number of the guilty is increasing.' Her view is vigorously backed by Wiberg: 'It's wretched that as soon as some young competitor achieves something special, there is immediate public scepticism about what they might be taking.' Randhir Singh from India, secretary-general of OCA, is concerned with lax officialdom: 'National federations with athletes testing positive should [themselves] be suspended.'

Issa Hayatou from Cameroon, President of the African Football Confederation (AFC), considers the Olympic tournament should be at full-strength on a par with the World Cup. (© IOC/Locatelli)

The Prince of Orange from the Netherlands: athletes' claims of ignorance are 'empty'. (© IOC/Lopez)

Alexander Popov of Russia: there is a need for 'moral and practical education'. (© IOC/Juilliart)

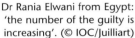

Dr Rania Elwani from Egypt: 'the number of the guilty is increasing'. (© IOC/Juilliart)

Randhir Singh from India: 'national federations with athletes testing positive should themselves be suspended'. (© IOC)

The influence of government involvement is illustrated by Arne Ljungqvist, Swedish chairman of the IOC Medical Commission. 'Once a government has ratified the WADA Convention, then that country will not be able to host a major competition of a sport whose international federation is not in compliance with the WADA Code. And that sport would therefore be disqualified from the Olympics.' Gunilla Lindberg from Sweden, Vice-President, points to the anomaly that can occur when an athlete suspended by an international federation appeals to the Court of Arbitration for Sport (CAS), 'which then revokes that suspension by an authority specifically attempting to make the sport clean, and which had believed that CAS would be on its side. Sometimes our penalties are more severe for what someone does to their own body than they are in ordinary life for assault against someone else's.' Tamás Aján from Hungary, weightlifting president who struggles to stem his sport's wanton abuse, suggests that out-of-competition testers should have special passports not requiring visas, so that they may randomly enter a country for unannounced surveillance, but he is also concerned that some federations are simply not bothered. 'When WADA invited every Olympic federation and many other non-Olympic IFs to a seminar, only 11 from the Olympic programme bothered to send a representative. In weightlifting, we delegate over 30 per cent of our annual budget to testing.'

Yet if honourable athletes are alarmed at the state of things, it is vital that the World Anti-Doping Agency (WADA), extensive though its vigilance may be in coordinating out-of-competition testing worldwide, is fully supported at government level. WADA was launched in February 1999, an initiative of the IOC to create an independent testing agency, funded initially by them with $25 million. The significance of the launch had been lost amid the furore of the Salt Lake scandal, breaking in December 1998. Pound's ambition had been to create an organisation in line with competitors' desire – a belief that 'the Olympics are about character, not chemistry' – his determination magnified when Dr Robert Voy, medical officer of USOC from 1983 to 1989, made a sworn affidavit to a US district court that use of performance-enhancing drugs was common among American Olympic competitors.

Robert Ctvrtlik, member from USA, pinpoints the financial issue:

> Testing is expensive and invasive; we're expecting so much of athletes to cooperate when the majority are innocent. We need to look at partnering with governments, to tap into their research budgets. The budget of WADA is $27 million per annum – that's a quarter of the research budget of one major pharmaceutical company . . . to get at the problem, you have to have governments looking at this as a national health issue.

Regulation, however, can be equivocal. Els van Breda Vriesman, Netherlands member and president of international hockey, observes:

> Look at Holland, where it's legal to use drugs but not to traffic in them. That's ridiculous. In Spain, when the police suddenly became involved, there was sharp reaction among competitors. Only governments and the country's judicial system can properly get on top of the crisis. As we saw in the Tour de France, as soon as the French and Swiss police intervened, competitors became frightened. There's a powerful difference between a prison sentence and a fine. Athletes don't want their families to be exposed to the police, while they can live with a two-year ban from the IAAF or the Cycling Union.

Beating the cheats. Richard Pound has borne the weight of attempting to ensure that 'the Olympics are about character, not chemistry'. (© IOC/Locatelli)

Damage to the credibility of track and field in particular has been in the news for more than 40 years, dating back to suspicion about shot putters and hammer throwers in the 1950s, misgivings that progressed arm-in-arm, so to speak, with the climb in record performances. Much of the damage comes not only from straightforward positive tests but by insinuation and assumption: as when Denise Lewis, British winner of the heptathlon in Sydney, joined forces with Dr Ekkart Arbeit, former East German coach prominently involved for two decades in the systematic drug programme supervised by the state for sports competitors and subsequently barred in Australia and South Africa. The concern was not whether Lewis might be taking drugs but that her professional association with Arbeit persuaded the passive UK Athletics board to accept his registration. David Hemery, Olympic champion in 1968 and former president of UK Athletics, the British governing body, called it 'an astonishing choice on Denise's part'. Rogge considered her action 'unwise'. One of the female athletes that Arbeit had trained previously, Heidi Kreiger, European shot put champion, became so hormonally disorientated by a diet of steroids that she underwent a sex-change operation in 1997.

The tide of public cynicism continued to rise with events in 2003 surrounding famous American champions Carl Lewis and Marion Jones – the latter having divorced C.J. Hunter, the positive-tested shot put world champion who had pronounced that she too was a cheat. Jones had by now begun a relationship with Tim Montgomery, then 100m world record holder, and together they had embarked on a coaching consultation with Charlie Francis, former coach of Ben Johnson, infamously disqualified at the Seoul Games. Francis was suspended within his own country, Canada, and the IAAF demanded explanation from his two new sprinters: none was forthcoming. Under pressure from her alarmed sponsors Nike, Jones withdrew from her connection with Francis. At the same time there was a bombshell for Lewis, for so many years having proclaimed himself clean, when Dr Wade Exum, former director for drug-control within the US Olympic Committee, released documents proving that Lewis and others had tested positive at the US trials for the Seoul Games but that the tests had been waived, allowing Lewis, and also Joe DeLoach and Andre Phillips, respective winners of the 200m and 400m hurdles, to compete instead of being suspended. Lewis had finished second to Johnson in the 100m, upgraded to gold when Johnson tested positive. It should be noted that the herbal supplement from China that Lewis had been taking, the source of ephedrine, contained a percentage that, under subsequent revision by the Medical Commission, would not have constituted a positive test (see Chapters LV, LVIII, LXI and LXV).

The covert 'blind eye' of officialdom can be almost as damning as the expediency and greed of competitors, evident over many years in the USA and latterly in Britain, with that nation's defence of IAAF 400m world champion Christine Ohuruogu in Osaka 2007, she having missed three tests and thereby incurring a life ban from the Olympics. Pleas for her support, Britain being so bereft of champions, included that from UK Athletics chairman Ed Warner, stressing she had never tested positive. But if you don't take the tests, you won't – which is the point of the rule. Opportunism is flying in the face of principle, though Ohuruogu's appeal for Olympic reinstatement was upheld in November by the appeals committee, overturning the automatic ban imposed by the BOA under their bylaw introduced in 1992. The BOA was to review its subsequent procedure. While circumstantial evidence dictated that Ohuruogu's lapses had been inadvertent, suggesting genuine innocence – and rank stupidity – her controversial acquittal left deep misgivings in a sport fighting for survival. Similar scepticism existed when Michael Rasmussen of Denmark was barred from the 2007 Tour de France for missing two tests, thereby under the regulations of the Cycling Union becoming ineligible. As an example of what should be done, the international rowing federation (FISA) banned three Russian rowers from the World Championships in Munich for admission of unnamed self-injected substances, the regulation designed specifically to obstruct medication without supervision, for competitors' own protection.

When confronting the drugs issue, successive presidents of the IOC find themselves in much the same situation as Canute, legendary king of ancient Britain, who proved to his courtiers that he lacked the power to command the waves. Twenty years ago, the author on occasion had the ear of the then President, Samaranch, and suggested several times that long-term anxiety should not be about conversion from the age-old concept of amateurism to modern professionalism – a debate at its climax in 1987 – but the consequence of this conversion: the resort to drugs when driven by greed. And so it has proved. Yet Jacques Rogge, along with those doggedly clinging to the wreckage of de Coubertin's idealism, is not giving up the fight, however daunting the odds. The revelation in the late autumn of 2007 that Marion Jones, having lived on the precipice of suspicion for more than seven years, had lied as wilfully as Judas has not frozen his blood. The President insists:

> As a sports lover, I'm disappointed, but I don't see it as wholly damaging. Be it Ben Johnson or now Jones, the testing system in all its guises is proving that it's efficient. Admittedly and alarmingly, Jones was not exposed by testing but by circumstantial evidence. The second arm of anti-doping is to call in judicial powers, as the FBI did with the Bay Area Laboratory Co-operative [BALCO] case, which indirectly brought her down. It is a progressive process, and the Jones incident will have a determining future effect, just as the Johnson case led to out-of-competition testing, non-existent at the time. The Festina Team case in the Tour de France has confirmed the belief that sport alone cannot fight without government support alongside WADA. I recognise that the public will be thinking, 'Just one more case, we always had suspicion', but they must be confident that the combination of WADA and government intervention can work.

At the time of writing [February 2008] neither the IOC nor the IAAF had yet agreed on what principle should guide retroaction regarding the record books for Sydney, Athens and respective World Championships, reluctant to upgrade the medals of those finishing behind Jones (who had by now incurred a prison sentence of six months) – the IOC being no longer bound by a three-year limit but having the power to go back eight years to amend results. Upgrading the women's 100m for Sydney would mean the gold medal going to Ekatarini Thanou, the Greek runner-up who, immediately prior to the Athens Games, missed a scheduled test together with her teammate Kostas Kenteris, the pair involved in a mysterious alleged motorcycle accident and subsequently withdrawing from the Games (see Chapter LXXII). The prolonged case against the pair, for making false statements and seeking fabricated certificates from medical staff, was postponed to June 2008, and in late 2007, when confronting the dilemma, Rogge confined himself to stating, 'The problem is one of two issues, moral and juridical. We have to discuss the matter and await the opinion of the IAAF, and it may take the Executive Board till well into the new year to come to a conclusion.'

Fools' gold: Thanou (GRE), 2nd; Jones (USA) 1st; Ottey (JAM) 4th; Ferguson (BAH) 8th; Lawrence (JAM) 3rd, rivals in a discredited 100m at Sydney. (© IOC/Nagaya)

At its meeting of December 2007, the Executive Board, while disqualifying Jones from all events contested by her in 2000 and 2004, deferred decision on medal adjustment while awaiting developments in the BALCO investigation by US authorities. Jones had already returned her medals.

Rogge's positive view, contrary to public cynicism, stems partially from events at Athens and then Turin's Winter Games. The drugs bust of 26 positive tests in Athens he regards as confirmation of WADA efficiency:

> There are two sides of the coin. Being a strong proponent of credibility, I also believe in revealing the facts without window dressing. Between the first Winter Games at Chamonix in 1924 and Nagano '98, the IOC found only five cases of doping. What we did following Nagano was drastically to step up the number of tests at Salt Lake City, which led to seven positives, together with the disciplinary action against the Austrian team coach Mayer. At Sydney, we had 12 positives and I decided we should double the tests for Athens, the positives rising from 12 to 26. The increase in testing between Nagano and Turin was almost double, and it will be almost the same between Sydney and Beijing, an increase in testing of over 90 per cent. At Moscow in 1980, there were zero positives, which was not credible, and by now we are far more effective, though the situation is by no means ideal.

How desirable was the involvement of Italian police during the Turin Games that led to life bans for some Austrian competitors (see Chapter LXXVI)? Rogge answers:

> Before the Games, we contacted Italian lawyers, because we were worried about the possibility of athletes serving jail sentences under national law. I discussed this with Prime Minister Berlusconi, saying this didn't mean we did not want to know. The Italian authorities promised to amend their laws, to re-align with the philosophy of WADA, which is to criminalise dealers, while athletes are disciplined only by their sports bodies. [Italy has subsequently done this.] When we heard that Mayer, though banned, was staying with some members of the Austrian team outside the Village and therefore beyond our control, we knew that action was needed. On the wider front, our point of view is that if an athlete is guilty, operating alone and not part of a network, this is not damaging for society in the way it is with a dealer trading drugs. It is not reasonable to ask governments to investigate a relatively small number of athletes in the relation to the whole of society.

If Ben Johnson's exposure 20 years earlier had not scared contemporary fellow abusers, it was to be hoped that the abyss into which Marion Jones fell might do so. In 1988, a survey revealed that young aspirants would happily consume the same additives as Johnson, irrespective of health hazards, if it might make them rich and famous. Jones's prison sentence is another matter. The truth emerged because she had lied to federal investigators during a 2003 investigation into BALCO (see Chapter LXXVI), the San Francisco-based laboratory in the drug-trafficking trade, of whom she had been a well-documented client. Now, aged 31 and appearing in court charged with perjury, she admitted taking steroids in 2000–01, though disingenuously still insisted she had believed it was flaxseed oil, and acknowledged that the drug – tetrahydrogestrinone, known as THG or 'the clear' – raised her performance standards. In tears outside the court she was contrite. 'I have been dishonest, I have let down my family, my country and myself . . . I lied because I panicked, to protect my coach at the time, it was an incredibly stupid thing to do, to break the law, and I have to take full responsibility.' So consistent had been her lying during seven years that there was little justification for grief among even her closest admirers. In a formal statement as president of IAAF, Lamine Diack was unrestrained in his condemnation:

> I am deeply disappointed that an athlete with Marion Jones's immense natural ability gave in to the corrupt, get-rich-quick spin of a dope dealer like Victor Conte [head of BALCO]. If she had trusted her own natural gifts and allied them to self-sacrifice and hard work, I sincerely believe she could have been an honest champion. Now, instead, she will be remembered as one of the biggest frauds in sporting history. It is a tragedy, and I'm glad that Marion Jones is aware not only of the damage that her action caused herself and her loved ones, but also her fans, her country and her sport of athletics, both in the USA and all over the world.

Marion Jones: 'one of the biggest frauds in sporting history.' (© IOC)

Conte, by now administering a company called Scientific Nutrition for Advanced Coaching (SNAC) from the same Californian building as BALCO, was unrepentant concerning his earlier activities, claiming that besides Jones there were several thousand competitors utilising drugs at Sydney and then Athens. 'There is a level playing field,' he asserted, 'but it's not the one people want.' He further alleged that it was simple for some athletes to evade the testing system in out-of-the-way countries by intermittently missing a single test and then waiting the necessary 18 months to become free to miss another, and that many national governing bodies were willing to indulge in a cover-up. The IOC might counter by saying, 'Well, he would say that, wouldn't he?', but his allegations are disturbing. So, too, is the hackneyed view of Don Talbot, Australian swimming coach, who, despite maintaining an anti-drug stance, renewed the suggestion that penalisation should be removed, his defence of this argument being that there was too much money at stake. 'Maybe it [legalisation] needs to be looked at,' Talbot suggested, in an interview with the *Sun-Herald* in Australia. This simplistic view tends to be justified by suspicion of past abuse about which nothing now can be done: the world sprints records set by Florence Griffith Joyner at the Seoul Games alongside Johnson – she having later died from an epileptic seizure at the age of 38 – and the earlier records of Marita Koch (GDR) and Jarmila Kratochvilova (Czechoslovakia), though there is no clinical evidence that these athletes cheated. Yet if the disease had continued to flourish – Linford Christie of Britain, 100m champion at Barcelona '92, who subsequently tested positive for nandrolone; Michelle Smith de Bruin (Ireland), with three swimming golds at Atlanta '96 but subsequently banned for four years; Tim Montgomery, et al. – Rogge's claim that the net is gradually closing is gaining confirmation. The IOC was nonetheless left holding the hot potato of Jones's guilt: Jamaica, for instance, claiming that the Sydney 100m gold medal should now be awarded to Tanya Lawrence, who finished third behind Jones and Thanou, while additionally Merlene Ottey – who tested positive for nandrolone in 1999 but was subsequently cleared – would become eligible for elevation to the bronze medal.

Aside from the controversies that surround predominantly black sprinters, it is worth a detached observation that notions of geographic advantage by blacks over whites in sprinting, first and most beautifully illustrated by the immortal Jesse Owens, as a generalisation is misleading, even if 53 athletes to have run inside ten seconds all are black and no white runner has reached the Olympic 100m final since 1980, the year of the Moscow boycott and won by Allan Wells (GBR). The reality is that such advantage, supposing it may exist genetically, is confined to races from West Africa and their descendants in the USA, the West Indies, Europe and elsewhere. Black runners from East Africa, for instance, are technically gifted at distance running, probably on account of high-altitude habitat. Genetic characteristics have more to do with inherited adaptation to geophysical, dietary and climatic condition rather than simply the irrelevant and emotive question of race. As a teenage sprinter at the August bank holiday Games in 1956, warming up in the centre of the White City track in London alongside Jamaican Olympic legend Mal Whitfield, the author marvelled at his liquid suppleness and flexibility. Black sprinters are indeed a gift to the Games.

The succession of John Fahey, former Premier of the state of New South Wales, as president of WADA in November 2007 in place of Richard Pound provoked speculation over whether he would be as uncompromising in his pursuit of cheats as the often provocative Canadian had been. Fahey has no background in sport, other than his prominent role in the election of Sydney

in 1993 as host city for 2000. He emerged as a late alternative to the long-term favourite Jean-François Lamour, French Sports Minister involved in Paris's failed bid for 2012, himself an Olympic double fencing champion and vice-president of WADA. Lamour, with the backing of influential IOC figures, seemed to be a shoe-in. With the emergence of Fahey, Lamour suddenly and controversially resigned, making covert suggestions of a Commonwealth liaison to oust him. Rogge expressed regret at Lamour's decision, paying tribute to his anti-doping work in France, while Pound vigorously denied that such engineering had taken place. A later vain move by aggrieved Europeans, to postpone the election and institute the Olympian Guy Drut of France as interim chairman, surrounded the event in disagreeable controversy. Fahey's sole candidacy then made for a straightforward decision by representatives of 17 governments and the Council of Europe that comprise WADA's foundation board. Acclaimed at home for having attained the highest level of international sporting appointment by an Australian, Fahey manned the ramparts by asserting that 'zero tolerance must remain'. He rebutted Talbot's legalisation notion, upholding sport's fundamental ethic of being true and fair. He will need vigorously to pursue the signing of governments' allegiance to the WADA code, an often protracted process depending on domestic law administration but guaranteeing a shared responsibility with WADA that is paramount.

Formerly for 20 years the most influential figure within the IOC after President Samaranch, Pound's own role had now become unspecific. Would he become chairman of the Court of Arbitration for Sport (CAS) in succession to the deceased Judge Keba M'Baye of Senegal? Pound had confirmed that he was no longer a candidate for IOC presidency, having been defeated in 2001 by Rogge, but felt that as a lawyer he might be an appropriate figure for CAS. The other nomination for the post, by the Executive Board, was a Swiss lawyer Robert Brinner. Pound's renowned outspokenness might once again count against him, as it had in 2001. It would be remembered, for instance, that he had invoked criticism by the Ethics Commission for comments he had made about Lance Armstrong, seven-time winner of the Tour de France. Pound remained unrepentant about his accusation of lack of vigilance by the international Cycling Union (UCI) and its former president Hein Verbruggen. Rogge suggested to the author, in late 2007, that there might be a tendency to prefer an independent chairman of CAS, though a sports background was essential.

If host bidding cities had run out of control in the '80s and '90s in their 'generosity' towards voting IOC members, their conduct had become no less worryingly exaggerated, if different, by 2007 at the time of the election for the Winter Games of 2014. Sochi, from Russia's Black Sea coast, and Pyeongchang, in a second successive bid from South Korea, had each spent enough to build, say, a small town in Albania or Somalia, reaching a point where extravagance could be considered immoral. The irony was that cities were partly given cause by IOC members' exclusion from visiting, following regulations post-Salt Lake: the alternative option being extravagant publicity. The IOC appeared less inclined to take a grip on this excess than on athletes' cheating. The author's interviews with more than half the membership over the past four years revealed that 50 per cent were in favour of visiting being restored so that they would be able to see for themselves, the honest majority offended by the public perception that they were open to bribery which, if indeed intended, could take place at any hotel or airport anywhere in the world. Shun-ichiro Okano of Japan amusingly observed: 'Once, I asked a companion, who was a managing director, whether he could make a decision about whether to employ someone by looking at their photograph. "No," he said. "You have to meet them!" It's the same principle with bidding cities.' Kai Holm, member from Denmark, is more adamant:

> Those members on the floor now have no real idea what's going on, so how do they gauge the Evaluation Commission's report? They're influenced by outside facts. Let them see what's going on, let them go to bidding cities, if they wish, but in groups on specific dates under IOC direction. In my view, you should only have a vote on the Winter Games if your country sent competitors to the previous Games.

Francesco Ricci Bitti from Italy, president of international tennis, bites the bullet: 'We have lost the plot. Jacques and the EB have to get a grip. The Ethics Commission stops us going to countries, though if we did go again in the future we would have to be careful.'

Fifteen years ago, the author wrote an official biography of Samaranch entitled *Olympic Revolution*, portraying the extensive changes undergone, the majority of them for the better, during Samaranch's first 12 years in office. By an irony, that first revolution would indirectly and partially be the cause of a second revolution, precipitated by the scandal during which both he and the IOC might have disappeared from sight. The wealth achieved from the sale of television rights since the 1972 Munich Games and from sponsorship marketing since LA set the pattern in 1984 had helped generate a mood of extravagance, especially among host bidding cities from 1984 onwards, sucking into a web of intrigue that 15 per cent of the IOC membership which was regrettably a willing party to abuse. Confronted with this crisis, controversially refusing to resign and being almost unanimously requested to continue by the members, Samaranch had assembled a second revolution, involving an entire restructure of IOC regulations and ethics, which stemmed the torrent of criticism and gave the Olympic Movement its springboard for recovery.

It had been Samaranch's exploitation of television rights that inadvertently helped lead to scandal. Addressing the Session of 1986, prior to the vote on a turbulent campaign for 1992, he revealed understandable euphoria at the galaxy of thirteen cities contending for the two Games, Summer and Winter. His satisfaction revealed his sheltered viewpoint, however, as disapproval was already rampant about the $50 million collectively spent on promotion by the candidates. Their thirst was partially driven by publicity for the contest on television, culminating in the televised declaration of the vote – introduced by Samaranch and invaluable free advertising. The Games were suddenly popular but not wholly for the right reasons. The President had furthered the element of showbusiness that would become the vehicle of misuse and ultimately abuse. By the time of the bidding in 1991 for the Winter Games of 1998, Nagano of Japan alone spent an estimated $66 million in securing victory – and subsequently destroyed most of the records of their expenditure. Six IOC members were expelled following investigations in 1999, one offender had died, four resigned and five others were warned (see Chapter LXVIII).

Initiating a more serious commercial approach to a candidate's bid back in the '80s had been Horst Dassler, energetic leader of sport manufacturers Adidas: he denigrated by many as the arch commercial manipulator, though to a degree a benefactor, providing subsidised equipment for many nations, if not without self-interest. In the '60s, he had conducted an advertising war

with rivals Puma, run by his uncle Rudi, utilising well-rewarded Olympic stars who wore Adidas running spikes. Dassler was believed to have helped organise the success of Seoul, in 1981, when winning the vote for 1988, yet he would write in the IOC magazine *Olympic Review* that elite sport had lost its ethical value, 'which it owes to the Olympic ideal'. The irony is that the money-driven motives of Olympic sport in the late twentieth century were closer to the Ancient Greek model on which de Coubertin had based his re-creation. Indeed, de Coubertin represented an inherent contradiction: on the one hand, an advocate of the gentlemanly English school system, on the other a pursuer of the social Darwinism that was intellectually in vogue in middle-class Europe, the development of the strong at the expense of the weak. In the latter aspect he was closer to disciplinarian mass-gymnastics in Germany than the playing fields of Eton School. His ardent disciple Avery Brundage (President 1952–72) would vigorously, almost blindly, pursue the ethics of the latter.

There are many who wish Rogge to retract on the exclusion of visiting, the ban almost unanimously reconfirmed at the Extraordinary Session in 2002. 'It would be preferable, in order for members to reach their judgement from what they had seen,' Shagdarjav Magvan, member from Mongolia, says. 'We have to fine-tune the system, because some of us are already able to visit bidding cities on unrelated international events, perhaps through inter-governmental relations, and this provides a contradiction for the Ethics Commission.' Chiharu Igaya from Japan agrees: 'I support this totally. When the ban was introduced, I spoke against it. If you accept it, you're putting in doubt your own honesty. Nobody can buy my honesty. There are many positive aspects [to visiting], such as assessing traffic conditions, adequacy of the Village, timings to venues and so on. You cannot fully assess simply on the Evaluation report.' Denis Oswald, often a cautious compromiser, says: 'I think the argument has some merit. In 1999, we had to send out a strong message. Nowadays, when you have some little-known new bidders such as Sochi, you need to search for fresh information. I think collective trips on certain dates would be acceptable under strict rules.' Gian-Franco Kasper, president of skiing, adds: 'The number of experts [on the Evaluation Commission] for the past two Games was sufficient. The problem is whether their report gets to the truth, for example why was Sestriere [mountain resort] not right for Turin? These things ought to be stated, not just put into nice words.'

Denis Oswald of Switzerland, adroit compromiser: 'I think the argument [for visits] has some merity.' (© IOC)

Expenditure by a bidding city is effectively beyond the IOC's control: whether heads of state should continue to be permitted inclusion in the cities' presentations to the Session is another matter, and Gunilla Lindberg is one who strongly opposes the practice. Tony Blair of Britain and Jacques Chirac of France were both present for the London and Paris presentations in 2005 in Singapore, Vladimir Putin for Russia and Moo-Hyun Roh for South Korea at the Guatemala Session in 2007. Was political pressure on the IOC members, for a sporting appointment, reaching an unacceptable level? Rogge said guardedly, following Guatemala: 'The Executive Board will assess the bidding process, and the presence of heads of states is something we will review.'

Sochi had reportedly spent more than Nagano in 1991, many uncommitted IOC members feeling that the election had been an auction, yet two-thirds of them had been willing to accept, so to speak, the highest bid. 'Putin bought the 2014 Olympics,' ran the headline of Agence France Press. The money available for Sochi surpassed imagination, with Oleg Deripaska, Russian oligarch with global business ambitions and reputedly worth $18 billion, being a committed backer: not merely to help finance the Games but, with Putin's approval, to expand his land and property interests within Moscow's long-term planning for the expansion of the Sochi tourist region. A difficulty for Rogge was that he remained committed to the principle of a geographically open bidding process, to remain unimpeded by continental rotation as operated, up to the present time, by FIFA: thereby encouraging strong, ambitious contenders willing to speculate exorbitantly.

For better or worse, the pattern was now established that would encourage oil-rich cities of the Middle East to venture into the Olympic arena – such as Doha of Qatar, its imagination given impetus by the success of an extravagant Asian Games in late 2006. Doha's entry as candidate for the Olympic Games of 2016 was a plus and a minus: the success of its Asian Games emphasised that the IOC must take note of the forces of the Gulf's oil, of China's and Indian's population power, of Asian sporting culture and a willingness to embrace fresh sports, but the idea that a tiny nation devoid of sporting heritage could just buy its way into the Olympic rings was alien to many in the Olympic Movement. The Asian Games may have raised Doha's profile on the global map, but is the city really equipped to rival such as Chicago, Tokyo, Madrid and Rio for 2016, when the native population of this tiny sheikdom is 150,000, swollen by half-a-million foreign workers? A disagreeable element of Qatar's ride up the prestige escalator is its attempt to purchase for itself an effective international team of foreign mercenaries in sports such as weightlifting, athletics and football: Bulgarians for weightlifting, Kenyans for track and field, Brazilians and Africans for football. 'It's a concern, and we're resisting,' Rogge says. 'There must be legitimate reasons to change nationality – marriage, conventional migration, these cannot be challenged. The problem is paying money for fake nationality. The IOC demands three years' residence unless this is mutually waived by both NOCs. Buying from the "market" is unacceptable, and IFs are tightening their rules.'

Reservation about the eligibility of a city such as Doha as Olympic host has no bearing on the continuing importance of minorities as competitor participants, a fundamental ethic of the Games. There were few global headlines arising from Athens for windsurfer Gal Fridman, marksman Ahmed Almaktoum, tennis players Fernando Gonzalez and Nicolás Massú, taekwondo winner Shih Hsin Chen or 400m hurdler Felix Sanchez, but they shared an unrepeatable achievement: they had all won their country's first gold medal at a Games, coming respectively from Israel, the United Arab Emirates, Chile, Chinese Taipei and the Dominican Republic. 'We

are all excited, all the people of Israel, I think also all of the Jewish people,' Israeli President Moshe Katsav said. And there were those who won no medal but nonetheless earned distinction for countries with little sporting prestige. Friba Razayee, the first Afghan woman in history to take part in an Olympic event, went out in the first round of the women's judo 70kg division, losing to Cecilia Blanco of Spain in 42 seconds. She was one of three Afghan women in Athens, the others being Robina Muqimyar in the 100m and Neema Suratger, who carried the flag in the opening ceremony. 'It was a proud moment for all three of us, to proclaim the rights of Afghan women as other women around the world have done,' Suratger said, having organised a clandestine school for girls during the reign of the Taliban. Afghanistan had returned to the Games only in 2004, having been banned since 1992 because of the oppression of women, allowed neither education nor sport, under the previous regime.

And if it's not a handful from oppressed nations who are breaking the mould, it is other small-time athletes who are upholding the principle of universality – such as Arturo Kinch, the one-man team from Costa Rica at the Turin Winter Games, having qualified for a fifth time. The youngest of 11 children, aged 23 he had taken part in the downhill at Lake Placid in 1980 before he went to college in Colorado. In Turin, aged 49 and having buried his father two weeks earlier, he was 41st in the Nordic cross-country 15km: his best yet. Taking time off from his job in customer relations with United Airlines in Denver to compete in the necessary five qualifying races, sometimes housed by friendly Norwegians, had cost him some $15,000 out of his own pocket.

None should underestimate the impact that one Olympic competitor can make within a small nation. Listen to Dr Robin Mitchell, member from Fij:

> The Solidarity programme makes such a huge difference – for NOCs, for national federations. Look at Nauru, lying on the equator between the Solomon and Gilbert islands. At one time it was similar to the Gulf States, rich from phosphate deposits. Then the wealth ran out, long before there was a national Olympic committee. The island took up weightlifting, and with Solidarity support they produced a Pacific champion and a silver medallist in the World Championships. National pride overflowed. In a region that struggles to survive in international sport, something like that can change a small country.

Dr Robin Mitchell from Fiji: 'The Solidarity programme makes such a huge difference.' (© IOC/Juilliart)

A coincidental problem for host-city logistics is that small countries inevitably have a high official/competitor ratio. In Athens, teams from Panama, the Ivory Coast, Senegal and Afghanistan, for example, had two 'blazers' for every tracksuit, no fewer than 45 delegations having more officials than athletes. 'Accreditation regulations stipulate that a maximum of half the team can be officials,' Rogge says, 'but the problem of small countries, represented in only three or four sports, is that a single athlete in one sport may need both coach and doctor, requiring special dispensation.' The highest ratio among major countries in Athens were the USA, with 538 blazers to 549 tracksuits, and Russia, with 351 to 458. Lower down the scale, Australia were 236 to 490 and Britain 116 to 270.

A continuing minority issue, though one increasingly corrected, is the proportional participation of women. It had been asserted by chauvinist de Coubertin that 'feminine applause as reward' was due to male competitors; by the turn of the twentieth century, much of the Sydney Games belonged to mothers, sisters and daughters. There were a shoal of new events for women, including such formerly male preserves as weightlifting and pole vaulting – a massive cultural shift. Four years earlier, women's team sports had made their mark in soccer, softball and basketball. By then, 42 per cent of competitors were women, compared with 28 per cent 24 years earlier in Munich and 26 per cent in Barcelona. Progress had certainly moved swiftly since the first sports bra was, allegedly, invented in 1977. Expansion had been long overdue, though still restricted in the Middle East and parts of Asia and Africa where prejudice has religious or social derivation. In Ireland, Archbishop McQuaid pronounced that women undressing beside the track would be an occasion of sin for male viewers, his sexually repressed disapproval, accepted by sports administrators to avoid confrontation with the Catholic Church, seriously impeding the development of women's sport.

None better represented the emancipation of women's sport than the heroic performance of Cathy Freeman in Sydney, everyone able to identify with her achievement in winning the 400m. When an individual additionally bears the burden of a moral sub-theme – the emancipation of an ethnic race following 200 years of domination by white colonialists, for whom the occasion is also an opportunity to assuage collective guilt – then attention is magnified. Freeman was not just running one lap but acting as a symbol, for her country and indeed for the world. It had been the same for Native American Jim Thorpe in 1912, slave descendant Jesse Owens and subjugated Kee-Chung Sohn of Japanese-occupied Korea at the Berlin Olympics, by African-American Wilma Rudolph in 1960 and Native American Billy Mills in 1964, by human rights activists Tommie Smith and John Carlos in 1968, and liberated South African Josiah Thugwane in 1996. Freeman knew everything about subjugation, disenfranchisement and white supremacy. Her grandmother Alice Sibley had been sent to a penal colony after being snatched off the streets aged eight. So it was hardly a surprise that over a weekend in which Steve Redgrave of Britain had won his fifth gold in rowing in consecutive Games, Michael Johnson of America had swept to a repeat victory in the men's 400m and Haile Gebrselassie of Ethiopia had won an epic 10,000m, Freeman should be almost the only talk in town. Few champions have reacted to victory with more dignity:

> I'd had an Olympic dream for 15 years, of running a lap of honour with both flags, Australian and Aborigine . . . the message is simple – celebration for Australia but especially indigenous people. Much was said about my lighting the cauldron at the opening ceremony, but for

me the race was always more important. With the flame, I recognised the honour, but I was so focused on the race that I could have lit the flame even if they'd asked me to do it naked, in pink high heels and a yellow wig. I wouldn't have noticed.

Cathy Freeman, iconic Sydney champion, who'd had a dream for 15 years – a lap of honour with both flags, Australian and Aborigine. (© Getty Images/Fordter)

If the Millennium Games at Sydney were a turning point in Olympic history, there are concerns for the IOC beyond those already mentioned: the inflexibility in the programme, drug abuse and the unofficially shifting constitution of IOC membership. All of these conspire to produce a fourth problem: potentially declining finance upon which the power of the Olympic Movement now depends. How long will the appetite of television companies and sponsors, interdependent, be sustainable? Broadcast revenue (US) for the Summer Games has grown from $101 million in 1980 to $1.7 billion by 2008. The sponsorship programme has grown from $96 million for TOP I to $866 million for TOP VI, for Turin/Beijing, and is projected to surpass $1 billion for TOP VII, Vancouver/London. Yet there are indications, post-Athens and post-Turin, that the market may be shrinking. 'The existing pattern of the TV networks is going to change,' Juan Antonio Samaranch Jr from Spain forecasts. 'They're not going to be able to rely so much on advertising revenue. They will need to find other sources, and we must investigate what they will be and start adapting ourselves. The way our "property" is valued will alter.' Francisco Elizalde from Philippines, former member of the Marketing Commission, agrees. 'I fear there could be a serious drop in revenue post-2012, especially relevant to time-zone coverage.

Within the IOC we might be thinking we're eternal, but we have to keep our ear to the ground. Track and field has become a secondary sport in the USA. The IOC cannot be complacent, supposing they're OK because they're running the greatest show on earth.' Gross global broadcast revenue might have increased by 2008 to $3 billion, NBC and the European Broadcasting Union having raised their contribution a further 35 per cent through to 2012, but these figures have been achieved prior to knowing audiences for Beijing and London. An unspoken anxiety is what General Electric, themselves a TOP sponsor and owners of NBC, will do post-Beijing. There is said to be unrest within GE about the equity of NBC's valuation at $40 billion. Concurrently, for the first time in two decades, the IOC has selected a city, Sochi, without first having concluded television contracts. Network television, under threat from new technology, has stayed its hand, especially following depressed advertising revenue rates for Turin. It is rumoured that ESPN's 24-hour sport network may enter future bidding, but clearly the Olympic Movement, and all that it supports in global sport, is facing an uncertain future, with doubts about which way the American economy is going to turn. The golden years in which, for example, VISA, the credit-card giant, enjoyed an annual growth rate of 16 per cent when becoming a TOP sponsor are probably over, though there could be a counter upturn from the mushrooming markets of China and India. 'The TOP sponsorship is largely American at present because it is largely American companies who are multinational,' Timothy Fok, billionaire member from Hong Kong, observes. 'Yet consider the Beijing Partners, a second-category level of sponsors who are contributing more to 2008 than TOP. The IOC must look beyond merely the next four years, at the true globalisation of the Games.' It is estimated that this year China will become the world's second largest advertising market, their Games estimated to contribute up to 0.4 percentage GDP growth and the generation of 1.3 million new jobs in building. Simultaneously, global business gloats at the prospect of enticing China's 1.36 billion consumers. Despite anxiety among some about a six-year doubling of IOC staff/administrative costs ($40 million), Carrión is confident that expanding TV rights from China can swell to, say, $400 million, offsetting any US decline: this, plus rising fees from other developing countries enabling future Games to be financed from IOC surplus-fund interest, the overrun dispersed within the Olympic Movement.

Francisco Elizalde from Philippines (left) studies the financial figures with Richard Carrión. (© IOC/Locatelli)

Timothy Fok, Hong Kong billionaire who believes the IOC must look at the 'true globalisation of the Games'. (© IOC/Locatelli)

Administrative extravagance by over-ambitious host cities has long been the Movement's bugbear, especially since the time of the Montreal Games of 1976 and the building of a main stadium for which the tax bill for local residents was finally closed only in 2006. The truth is, unacknowledged by the ever scandal-hungry media, that most cities benefit from the Olympic experience, even including Athens in 2004, supposedly undersize and underfunded for a Games costing $7 billion. In fact, Montreal generated revenue of $430 million against operational costs of $207 million, making a profit: it was capital expenditure by the city, charged against the Games' budget, that for 30 years drew negative publicity. Seoul '88 cost $3 billion but helped transform the South Korean economy and global perception of the country; Barcelona '92 covered only a third of its $10 billion investment, but tourism numbers thereafter doubled, and structurally and visually the city was transformed. Sydney 2000 largely covered its $2.25 billion costs for a Games that did immense service in repairing the IOC's damaged reputation. In *The Times* (London), author Bill Bryson wrote: 'I invite you to suggest a more successful event anywhere in the peacetime history of mankind.' Assessing the Athens Games, a 2006 report from Hellenic Olympic Properties (HOP) undermined many doomsayers:

> Hosting the Games was a catalyst for significant improvements in infrastructure . . . with a hugely improved road and public transport system, better hotel accommodation and a new image for tourism. The Games left Athens with a new sea-front in Faliron, Hellinikon and Agios Kosmas . . . of twenty-two Olympic venues, HOP has completed six tenders, helping to ensure revenue is generated for transformation to further use, including museums, shopping centres and amusement parks. The Main Press Centre (MPC) will become the Ministry of Health, the weightlifting centre a university campus. Additionally, unemployment has fallen.

Beijing's budget is estimated at $5.6 billion, but a reported further $26 billion in city development, including the transport system, will be spent as China seeks to challenge American economic supremacy. In parallel with this, efforts of undisclosed dimension and cost have been made in a bid to ensure that China leads the medals table, having finished third in Athens – a huge leap from their tiny re-entry onto the stage in 1984. Having competed in only 14 of the 28 sports in Sydney, the number rose to 26 in Athens, and they won medals in 20 events. When Xiang Liu won the 110m hurdles in Athens, China's first-ever men's track and field gold, Xinhua News Agency claimed he had ended '108 years of national humiliation' in the Games. Chinese historians routinely describe the nineteenth century as one of humiliation by Western powers. Now the challenge, to appease future historians, is how to improve the country's condemned record in human rights. The issue of 'free Tibet' will not go away, and many of the 20,000 invading foreign journalists will not be slow to highlight this controversy. China will be under microscopic investigation, including NBC's unprecedented 24-hour round-the-clock coverage approaching 2,000 hours. The IOC steadfastly refuses to be drawn on human rights issues, Rogge stating: 'We cannot intervene, these are matters between nations' political leaders, we can only call for respect for human rights, and I have clearly asked this of Chinese leaders and noticed there has been some progress in freedom of expression.'

There can be no doubt that Beijing will be a benchmark: more so than, say, the re-establishment of Germany's international reputation in 1972, or the business/economic emergence of Japan and South Korea in 1964 and 1988 respectively. Beijing could help sustain the 112-year-old magic of the Games, or could highlight ills that threaten its future. It was ever thus, for the Olympic Movement all but collapsed several times, nearly so between the second and fourth Games of Paris and London. Criticism of de Coubertin in America was rife, led by James Sullivan, organiser of the third Games at St Louis. He wanted to create a new body, supposedly one that would extend American influence within the new Olympic Movement. Sir Theodore Cook, British IOC member, recorded in his *The Sunlit Hours: A Record of Sport and Life* that 'the IOC is an inept organisation, and its leader flounders in his inability to accept practical suggestions'. In spite of these disparaging comments, the IOC held together thanks in part to efficient leadership in Britain and Sweden respectively by Robert de Courcy-Laffan and Viktor Balck, by William Sloane, American doctor of philosophy who separated himself from the strictures of

Victor Balck of Sweden, a pillar upon whom Pierre de Coubertin leaned. (© IOC)

Sullivan, and by the equally loyal Willibald Gebhardt from Germany. Balck was a pillar upon whom de Coubertin increasingly leaned. Ahead of his time, Balck was conscious of likely trends, and at the IOC Congress at Le Havre in 1897 was already suggesting that IOC membership should include representatives from international federations and that the programme should be constantly reviewed. Congresses are staged intermittently: at that in Brussels in 1905, 29 NOCs sent a total of 120 delegates. It was this mounting collective interest that helped the IOC survive the disarray of 1904 in St Louis.

Today, the IOC is facing an equally crucial Congress in 2009. If the Games of Vancouver and London are to prosper uninhibitedly – London by 2007 well ahead of planning in its seven-year schedule, with an unspectacular main stadium moderate in cost but capable of downsizing subsequently – it is essential that the President and his members grasp some nettles in Copenhagen if they are to preserve the glories of a unique institution.

Nelson Mandela congratulates Sam Ramsamy on South Africa's post-apartheid Olympic re-emergence in 1991. (© IOC/Locatelli)

CHAPTER I

Foundation

Baron Pierre de Coubertin of France, second IOC President, 1896–1925

'*In this year, 1894, and in this city of Paris, whose joys and anxieties the world shares so closely that it has been likened to the world's nerve centre, we were able to bring together the representatives of international athletics, who voted unanimously for the restoration of a 2,000-year-old idea, which today, as in the past, still quickens the human heart – for it satisfies one of its most vital and, whatever may have been said on the subject, one of its most noble instincts. In the temple of science, these delegates heard echoing in their ears a melody also 2,000 years old, reconstituted by an eminent archaeologist through the successive labours of several generations. And in the evening, electricity transmitted everywhere the news that Hellenic Olympism had re-entered the world after an eclipse of centuries.*

The Greek heritage is so vast, Gentlemen, that all those who, in the modern world, have conceived physical exercise under one of its multiple aspects have been able legitimately to refer to Greece, which contained them all. Some have seen it as training for the defence of one's country, others as the search for physical beauty and health through a happy balance of mind and body, and yet others as that healthy drunkenness of the blood which is nowhere so intense and so exquisite as in bodily exercise.

At Olympia, Gentlemen, there was all that, but there was something more, which no one has yet dared to put into words – because since the Middle Ages a sort of discredit has hovered over bodily qualities and they have been isolated from qualities of the mind.

This has been an immense error, the scientific and social consequences of which it is almost impossible to calculate. After all, Gentlemen, there are not two parts to a man, body and soul: there are three, body, mind and character. Character is not formed by the mind, but primarily by the body. The men of antiquity knew this and we are painfully relearning it.

The adherents of the old school groaned when they saw us holding our meetings in the heart of the Sorbonne: they realised that we were rebels and that we would finish by casting down the edifice of their worm-eaten philosophy. It is true, Gentlemen: we are rebels, and that is why the press, which has always supported beneficent revolutions, has understood and helped us.

I lift my glass to the Olympic idea, which has traversed the mists of the ages like an all-powerful ray of sunlight and returned to illumine the threshold of the twentieth century with a gleam of joyous hope.' (From an address to the Inaugural Congress, Paris 1894)

(Photograph © IOC)

He was short, some 1.62 metres or 5 ft 3 in., with a handlebar moustache that was his dominant feature. Pierre de Coubertin was less a sportsman than an educationalist, not a politician but an amateur sociologist, rather a philosopher than a teacher. Above all, he was a moral leader, a liberal, with both an acute sense of history and a vision of the future that was controversially way ahead of his time, especially within France. He was preoccupied during his adolescence and early adulthood with the mental and moral condition of the French in the aftermath of defeat in the Franco-Prussian War of the 1870s. He had read *Tom Brown's Schooldays*, an acclaimed book by Thomas Hughes, which reflected the muscular Christianity of Dr

Thomas Arnold and was quoted by contemporary French philosophers, such as Hippolyte Taine in his *Notes sur L'Angleterre*. Arnold had become headmaster of Rugby School in 1828 and had been less concerned with academic vigour than with creating an environment for the emergence of a generation of men of character, courage and self-determination. De Coubertin was convinced that the introduction of a system of school sports, student self-government and postgraduate athletic associations, so effectively operating in Britain, might strengthen the democratic society of France and reinvigorate the moral discipline of those enlisting in the French Army.

Though de Coubertin was little active in sport, confining

Pierre de Coubertin, aged six. (© IOC/Le Jeune)

and preserved until the second century AD. The truce is widely mentioned in ancient records and its reinstitution was to be unavailingly advocated over 2,850 years later, first by Eric von Frenckell of Finland and then by Juan Antonio Samaranch at the time of the Bosnian war.

The celebration of the Games continued under Aethlius, the first King of Elis, son of Zeus and Protogenia. It is alleged that from Aethlius's name came the title 'athlete'. The site of Olympia lies in the north-west Peloponnese, which was presided over by the town of Elis, where the Greeks, settlers who followed the ancient Achaeans, created their religious sanctuary. The first record of athletic activity at Olympia is dated 776 BC because the available Olympic victor list commences from that year, though archaeological evidence confirms the presence of religious activity long before that. The winner of the 'Stade' race, the sprint, in that first year was Coroebus of Elis. From Stade comes the word 'stadium', the distance being the length of a running track, which is said to be the length that Hercules could walk while holding one breath – almost 200 metres. The four-year period between each Games was an 'Olympiad', and the festival progressively included, besides the *stade*, the *diaulus* (400m), the *dolichus* (4.5km) and, by 708 BC, wrestling and the pentathlon, the latter consisting of running, discus, jumping, javelin and wrestling. By 688 BC, boxing was added, then chariot racing, and in 648 BC the *panchratium*, a combination of wrestling and boxing.

At the time of the Greek–Persian Wars, 510–450 BC, great fame descended upon Olympia and Hellenic lands, and from Olympia spread the exposition not only of sport but also of Greek classical art. Plato (427–347 BC) first visited Olympia when he was 70 and by that time the town had become an essential part of the experience for every person of education. In the fourth century BC, King Philip of Macedon was booed at the Games when it was believed he was preparing to invade Greece, and it was at Olympia in 324 BC, during the 114th Olympiad, that Alexander the Great declared that all Greeks would be united under his shield.

Throughout most of the period the athletes ran naked, apparently in order to be able to compete more freely without obstructive tunics. Though the prize for winners was a branch of wild olive, there were also more valued gifts and indeed sums of money. For obscure reasons, women were barred, even as spectators, and indeed could only visit the sacred precinct of Olympia when the Games were not being staged. The fame of champions in those far-off times exceeded even the acclaim poured upon contemporary winners by the media waterfall, for ancient Olympic champions carried not only the mark of victory but also an aura of beauty and perfection, of mental grace and pure conscience, and were considered to have achieved the greatest feat any man could witness. Champions more lauded than any in the twentieth century included Leonidas of Rhodes, who won the three running events in four consecutive Olympiads, 164–152 BC, and 12 Olympic titles in all – a triumph surpassing that of Carl Lewis. Then, as now, huge crowds gathered from around the known world to watch the festival: from Italy, Egypt, Libya, Ionia and the Caucasus.

The glory of Greece was not to last for ever. Decline set in as athleticism was replaced by the virtues of academia. Socrates was criticised for his contribution to this trend. Slowly the culture of Greece was overrun by the march of the Roman Empire. Stadia were converted into arenas in which slaves might fight for their lives. The opposition was no longer admired opponents but wild animals. The final blow to sporting glory was the spread of Christian asceticism, the perceived virtue of fasting and privation. The Games ended in 393 AD by decree of Emperor

himself to recreational riding, fencing and rowing, he travelled to England for the first time in 1883, at the age of 20, visiting several schools – Eton, Harrow, Wellington, Winchester, Rugby and Marlborough, and the more important Jesuit Catholic schools – and universities, including Oxford and Cambridge. The visit confirmed and justified de Coubertin's objectives, and five years later he published the results of his studies on the British educational system, substantially a reflection of Arnold's principles. In the 1880s, school sport competitions had belatedly begun in Paris. For the first time schools were playing soccer. The Racing Club de France was founded. Yet de Coubertin's vision was already ultra-national. Only a grand project of international breadth would capture the public imagination. He realised, too, that such a project must be formalised, and thus began his ambition to revive the Olympic Games.

De Coubertin's philosophical inspiration can be traced back to the stage of ancient Greek tradition: indeed to the thirteenth century BC and the religious ceremonies and games that were held in Olympia, sanctuary of Greek gods, with its altar to Rhea, Mother of the Earth. The legends of these times – of Zeus fighting his father Kronos, the child-eater; of Apollo defeating Hermes; of Hercules, a victor, stipulating that the games be known as 'Olympic' – were transmitted orally until, in the eighth century BC, the poet Homer recorded them in written form in his epics *Iliad* and *Odyssey*, still read almost 3,000 years later in many languages. They reveal the emergence of athletic competition in the festival context of the ancient world. Though Homer's tales were written 500 years after the events, they show that athletes competed for prestige under stipulated regulations and in front of huge crowds – and that there were substantial prizes for the winners.

Imperative in the conduct of the Games was the remarkable institution of a truce, said to have originated in 884 BC: an agreement for the cessation of any war involving Greece and free passage for competitors, the clause carved on a bronze disc

Theodosius – the last of 320 Games of Antiquity. Olympia was overrun by barbarians, the statue of Zeus was purloined by Turks, his temple set on fire by the Goths, the valley flooded by the River Cladeus. The riches of the past were gone.

Following the post-Roman religious asceticism of the Middle Ages, the seeds of ancient Greek culture in the shape of sport, individual and collective, began to take root again in the sixteenth century. Robert Dover (1575–1652), an English lawyer, sportsman and anti-Puritan, had organised the Cotswolds Games. There had been circus-style athletics events in Poland entitled 'Olympic Competitions', and similarly in Ramlösa, Sweden, under the auspices of Gustav Schartau, a professor in Lund. In 1844, enthusiasts from Quebec organised the 'Olympic Games of Montreal', with competition in 28 events. In England in 1850, Dr William Brookes founded the Much Wenlock Olympian Society, progenitor of the Much Wenlock Games, which were an alliance of sport and art, encouraging harmony between the aristocracy and working classes. In Greece, Panagiotis Soutsos, a poet, recommended an Olympic revival, which prompted Evangelis Zappas, a wealthy patriotic tradesman, to support such a proposal, and an Olympic Games, so called, were staged in 1859.

In 1884, Georges de Saint-Clair, an all-round sportsman who had earlier translated *Tom Brown's Schooldays* into French, became secretary-general of the Racing Club de France, where he instilled the British principle of a multi-sports club. From here arose in 1887, in conjunction with the Stade Francais, the Union des Sociétés Français de Course à Pied (Union of French Running Clubs). French sport was clearly expanding, thereby providing a platform for de Coubertin's slowly flowering ambition.

Though de Coubertin was a lone intellectual with few friends, a man driven by a single passion, he inevitably needed close associates to help add momentum to his project. Foremost among these as he furthered his intention to create a committee designed to be responsible for physical education in schools were Jules Simon and Father Henri Didon.

Simon, a Republican reformer, was a man of convictions as powerful as de Coubertin's, both of them determined liberal democrats. Simon was 74, de Coubertin 25, and de Coubertin looked upon the older man as his spiritual adviser. In Father Didon, however, de Coubertin found a disciple. Didon's view was that chivalry was an essential element of sport and that sport was educational. If de Coubertin gave Didon a fresh outlook on developing society, the monk gave to him a spirituality that strengthened his resolve.

The Comité pour la Propagation des Exercises Physiques was inaugurated in 1888, consisting of five members, though de Coubertin was the fulcrum. The Comité was short on public support, but de Coubertin was able to publish informative essays in newspapers and magazines and slowly the Comité attracted attention: an assembly room was arranged at the Sorbonne.

Three years later, 1891, the association organised its first athletic championships: Didon as honorary president announcing to the members that their motto was to be '*Citius, Altius, Fortius*' – faster, higher, stronger – the basis of sport and to become the motto of de Coubertin's ultimate creation. Later the same year de Coubertin also fulfilled a request from the government to stage a conference on physical education. Octogenarian Dr Brookes, acclaimed for his progressive work in England, was invited to attend the conference but his age

Dr William Brookes, founder in 1850 of the Much Wenlock Olympian Society, progenitor of the Much Wenlock Games that formed part of de Coubertin's inspiration from England. (© IOC)

The Dominican Father Didon, friend and mentor, co-founder with Pierre de Coubertin of the Comité pour la Propagation des Exercises Physiques. (© IOC)

prevented him, so the following year de Coubertin travelled to Much Wenlock where a special athletics event was staged in his honour.

As ideas began to be realised, de Coubertin needed foreign colleagues to help substantiate his international concept. Foremost among these would be William Milligan Sloane, son of a Scottish Presbyterian pastor, born in Richmond, Ohio, in 1850, and later of New York where he took a degree at Columbia University. Subsequently he taught Classics at Newell Institute, Pittsburgh, then moved to Berlin to study ancient history and gained a doctorate in Leipzig in ancient Arabian poetry. Additionally, he was secretary to the American Ambassador in Germany, George Bancroft, who helped develop in him a proclivity for sport, which Sloane retained upon returning to work at Princeton and then Columbia universities. It was in his role as president of the Ivy Collegiate Faculty Committee on Athletic Sports that de Coubertin sought his allegiance on a visit to the States in 1889. In 1892, Sloane visited Paris to attend rowing and football competitions involving French, American and English teams. De Coubertin outlined his plan and Sloane set about attempting to convince a sceptical, traditionally insular American audience of its virtues. De Coubertin returned to the States in 1893 on a promotional visit during the finalisation of his plans for a sports congress in Paris the following year. Reaction, however, remained lukewarm: only Professor Sloane was keen to attend.

Liberal educationalist. The founder (seated third left) at Ecole Monge, 1887–8. (© IOC/David)

Charles Herbert was born in India in 1846, his entire family bar himself slaughtered in the Cawnpore Massacre of 1857, a bloody uprising against British rule. He returned to live in England, becoming in 1883 honorary secretary of the Amateur Athletic Association created three years earlier. He then met de Coubertin, who appointed him 'Commissioner for England and the British Colonies' in the preparation for the Congress. Though Herbert was doubtful about the project, it was through him that de Coubertin would direct his efforts to ensure the presence of a British team at the inaugural Games of 1896. Herbert himself would not attend, unable to afford the journey.

Viktor Gustav Balck, who was to become known as the 'Father of Swedish sport', was an initially cautious but eventually committed disciple, fired by de Coubertin's ideological objective. Born in 1844, the son of a shopkeeper, Balck had joined the merchant navy at the youthful age of 12, switching to the royal navy in 1859 and subsequently joining the Karlsberg Military Academy. Here he became involved in sports and in 1891 joined the staff of the Stockholm Central

Institute of Gymnastics, run by the Ministry of War. Rising to major, then colonel, by 1907 he was head of the Institute, having vigorously popularised all branches of currently conventional games in Sweden. In 1875 he had founded the Stockholm Gymnastics Association and was equally influential in the development of rowing and ice skating, promoting strong links with England. Though elected as an inaugural member of the new Olympic Committee, he was unable to attend the Congress at the Sorbonne, but he ensured that Sweden was represented, by one Frederic Bergh. At short notice, he was only able to persuade one athlete to compete in Athens but was himself one of seven members to attend the Session there. Balck was of immense significance, as evidenced by his extensive correspondence with de Coubertin, some 100 missives being exchanged between 1894 and 1921. Balck was also instrumental in founding the International Skating Union.

While de Coubertin was on the one hand a reforming democratic liberal, he was also alert to the social prejudices of the day, aware that the presence, on the sporting committee he was about to create, of titled noblemen would enhance credibility: much as it does in the present day with charitable organisations. Arthur Oliver Villiers Russel, second Baron Ampthill, was born in 1869 in Rome, where his father was British Ambassador. His grandfather, the Earl of Clarendon, was at the time Minister of Foreign Affairs. Russel was to make his name at Eton and then New College, Oxford, becoming president of both the Oxford (political debating) Union and the Boat Race Club. De Coubertin had met him on his visit to Eton and immediately envisioned this young sportsman as an inaugural member of what was to be the International Olympic Committee. Although Ampthill made little direct intervention in de Coubertin's campaign, the prestige of his involvement was undoubtedly beneficial.

So, too, was that of Karl August Willibald Gebhardt, who had qualified as a chemist at the Friedrich-Wilhelm University in Berlin before moving to the United States to work on physiological chemistry between 1890 and 1893. At school, Gebhardt had been a fencer. He was concerned with the social aspects of overcrowded cities in relation to their inhabitants'

IOC founding members. Standing (r–l): Dr Willibald Gebhardt (GER), Jiri Guth-Jarkovski (TCH), Ferenc Kemeny (HUN), Viktor Balck (SWE). Seated: Pierre de Coubertin (FRA), Demetrius Vikelas (GRE), Gen. de Butovski (RUS). (© IOC/Meyer)

physical well-being, was an advocate of healthy sport as a fundamental right and hence became a natural disciple of de Coubertin's. Gebhardt regarded Germany's entrenchment in the traditions of gymnastics as too nationalistic and became involved in the second 'General Exhibition of Sport, Games and Gymnastics' in Berlin in 1895. He was enthusiastic about Germany's participation in what were to be the inaugural Games in Athens, even creating a special committee to campaign for this. He would become the first German member of the IOC and it was his energy that drew Germany committedly into the innovative venture.

Jiri Guth-Jarkovski, a Bohemian-Czech, met de Coubertin in 1891 in Paris. Later he became a professor of philosophy at a university in Prague. He was of modest origins, and for a while a headmaster of a provincial grammar school, but his importance to de Coubertin was his contact with provincial Austrian aristocracy. Impecunious and unable to attend the Congress in 1894, Guth-Jarkovski was nonetheless a vital point of contact for de Coubertin in central Europe.

So too, in western Russia/Ukraine, was General Alexei Dimitrievic Butovski, who worked at the Military Academy in St Petersburg before being transferred to the Ministry of Education, with responsibility for sport in schools. Sport hardly existed in Russia in the 1880s and so Butovski made a survey of PE teaching elsewhere in Europe, his knowledge and experience becoming part of de Coubertin's jigsaw.

Ernest Callot was president of French gymnastics and became a member of de Coubertin's 'propagation of PE' committee. As de Coubertin's domestic right-hand man, he was known as the 'second Frenchman' – in time appointed as the IOC's treasurer.

Wishing the Olympic idea to be truly international, de Coubertin enlisted Leonard Albert Cuff of Christchurch, New Zealand, founder member of the New Zealand Amateur Athletic Association. During a visit to Europe, Cuff had joined Herbert at events organised by the Racing Club de France and, although he was unable to attend the Congress of 1894, de Coubertin made him an honorary member of the IOC, thereby embracing the South Pacific continent.

De Coubertin never doubted that only in an international context could the re-creation of the Olympic Games be successful. His conviction had been increased when American competitors came to Paris in 1891 for a series of events. Newspaper articles, pamphlets and speeches flowed from him. In *Une Campagne de 21 Ans* he argued that if German archaeologists could excavate the relics of Olympia, France could recreate Olympia's grand style. He further advanced this proposal at a lecture at the Sorbonne in 1892.

In February 1893, the Racing Club de France met with associates in London, then in July staged international athletics championships at the Pré Catelan. The time was not right to include other sports. De Coubertin was concerned about the respectability of rowing and cycling, the latter prosperous in France but disregarded in Britain because of its professional background. Following the intervention of the French Embassy in London, the Union des Sociétés Francais de Sports Athlétiques (USFSA) was able to sign a convention with the committee of Henley Royal Regatta, guardian of sporting puritanism, which was responsible in Britain for the issuing of a Certificate of Virtue.

In August, de Coubertin submitted to USFSA his preparatory programme for the Congress, entitled 'Paris International Congress for the Study and Propagation of Amateur Exercises'. Sloane and Herbert were to help coordinate the programme and to be joint hosts at the Sorbonne.

In January 1894, de Coubertin wrote to foreign sports clubs, seeking to extend cooperation, in both theory and practice. This was much more difficult than he had supposed: individual sports suspected dilution of their own importance in an amalgamated event, though in the invitation to the Congress de Coubertin had underplayed the main objective: the re-creation of the Games. By May, few replies had been received at 20 Rue Oudinot, his Paris home, which had become the office for the Congress. A second appeal, with a reply card, drew barely a dozen foreign replies; the Congress would be primarily a French affair, though King Constantine II, nowadays an honorary IOC member, believes that his grandfather, Crown Prince Constantine, was unofficially present in Paris at the time.

In June 1894, the Congress opened at the Sorbonne, an institution rootedly opposed to sport. The opening ceremony began with the 'Hymn to Apollo', which had just been discovered in Delphi, transcribed and re-orchestrated by Théodore Reinach and Gabrielle Fauré. There was no fanfare announcement to the 79 delegates and sports associations present from 12 countries, the debate edging by degrees towards its climax delivered by de Coubertin.

The Congress voted to re-establish the Olympic Games; to create an organisation to guide their destiny, the 'Comité International des Jeux Olympiques'; and to provide a definition of amateurism. Fourteen individuals, some not in attendance, were selected as members of the newly named committee and Demetrius Vikelas of Greece was appointed President, since it had been determined that the first Games were to be held in Athens. The emergence of Vikelas and the selection of Athens are both surrounded in a degree of mystery (see Chapter II). At this stage it was intended that the President should be from the host country for the four years prior to each Games. Father Didon's motto was officially accepted and two commissions were created: the first to address the question of amateurism, chaired by Michel Gondinet of the Racing Club, the second to mastermind the Games, under Vikelas.

The unofficial first executive meeting of the IOC was held at 4 Rue Babylon, the Paris apartment of Vikelas, immediately following the Congress. In attendance were Dr Sloane, Callot and de Coubertin. These four approved the first three host cities: in addition to Athens in 1896, Paris in 1900 and a US city in 1904. De Coubertin and Sloane were designated second and third respective Presidents, with de Coubertin acting as

The founder as leisurely oarsman. (© IOC)

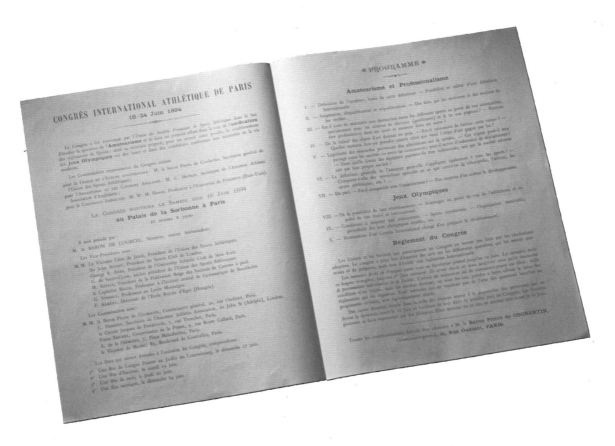

The programme for the Paris International Athletics Congress. (© IOC)

Secretary-General. As de Coubertin was to write in his *Memoires*:

> Opposition to my ideas? Ironical remarks? Or total indifference? No, not a bit of it! The audience applauded. They liked my ideas. They wished me good luck. Yet to be honest, probably no one had understood me. What I had said was totally incomprehensible to the whole audience. The committee was to be a self-recruiting body, with the same type of management structure as that for the Henley Regatta. But it was already composed of three concentric circles: a small core of earnest and hard-working members; a nursery of willing members ready to be taught; finally a façade of more or less useful people whose presence satisfied national pretentions at the same time as it gave prestige to the committee as a whole.

The latter group presumably consisted of the dukes, comtes and generals who, inadvertently over the next half century of social evolution, would induce as much criticism as acclaim for this perceived oligarchy.

None of that was apparent at the time to its altruistic founder. He wanted members to be trustees of the Olympic idea, as indeed they should still be. They would be selected for their knowledge of sport and their national standing, since, by de Coubertin's principle of delegation in reverse, an IOC member

De Coubertin's manuscript defining the role of the IOC. (© IOC)

33

was to be an ambassador to his own country and not of his country to the IOC.

In July 1894, the first *Bulletin* of the IOC was published. This was to be the main source of information of the Olympic Movement. It would appear sporadically, at various times under other titles, including the *Olympic Review* of today. The Congress, it was said, 'was a development of international significance for the sporting world'.

The Commission for the Olympic Games met three times and unanimously approved the *Bulletin*'s report, while the Committee on Amateurism rejected outright the regulations of the English Amateur Rowing Association, which prohibited manual workers from being amateurs. The minutes referred to their proposal as a 'challenge to democracy'. Later in the year, a tireless de Coubertin would publish his thesis on professionalism.

Following the resounding success at the Sorbonne, de Coubertin now had to persuade the Greek government to undertake the hosting of the inaugural Games. Worried about their possible refusal on financial grounds, he travelled to Athens. He found the majority of the government opposed to the idea, concerned about financial loss on a project which the majority of the population thought meaningless. Much work lay ahead, de Coubertin supplying plans, cost estimates and a brochure at his own expense. When finally the Greek Olympic Committee decided to accept the task, and being optimistic of their success, they lost interest in de Coubertin and his initiative, and intended to take the credit for themselves. How many innovators have suffered the same fate?

Modern priestesses arrive for the lighting of the Olympic flame at the Temple of Hera, Olympia, site of the Ancient Games.
(© IOC/Drakopoulou)

CHAPTER II

Greek Mentor

Demetrius Vikelas of Greece, first IOC President, 1894–96

'Look always higher and further from the spot where you stand. This is the only way to progress and diminishes the risk of falling. In order to go further, always ensure that you take small, solid steps, never seek to stretch your legs more than the width of your natural stride. Always follow the programme that you have set yourself.

My friend Pierre de Coubertin, with fine imagination, last year initiated the formation of an International Olympic Committee, for the prospect of renewing the ancient Olympic Games of Greece, but now in the modern context of contemporary sport. Quite unexpectedly, I received through Baron de Coubertin's influence a request from the Pan-Hellenic Gymnasium Club to represent them at this international congress which was to take place at the Sorbonne. I duly attended the congress and was astonished to find myself proposed and elected as president of this new sports committee. I then claimed Greece's rights with regard to the re-establishment of a Greek institution. As Victor Hugo put it, the civilised world has a common grandmother in Ancient Greece. Here was the source of my request that the restored Olympic Games be inaugurated on our Greek soil. It must be said that Crown Prince Constantine was of considerable assistance and influence behind the scenes.

Because of financial restrictions that necessarily exist in Athens at this time, it is my conviction that these Olympic Games must remain simple as well as being properly serious. Should there by chance be any excess of income over expenditure from the Games, then I consider that this should be used by Greece for the benefit of Greek athletes at future Games and to help erect new gymnasia for Greek students. Sport is important in the process of education, a fact that has been much in the mind of Baron de Coubertin following his visits to study the wide range of sport that exists in schools in England. The practice of sport is important for body and mind, and should be especially so for Greeks with such an ancient tradition. The monuments of Ancient Greece testify to our history of sport and there can be no doubt that the organisation of this new festival will beneficially bring foreigners to Greece. Not only may there be financial profit from that but also the moral and cultural profit that will come from exchange with other civilisations.' (From an address to the Greek Students' Association, April 1895)

(Photograph © IOC)

Demetrius Vikelas was born in 1835 on the island of Syros. His childhood was spent there and in Constantinople (latterly Istanbul), his family being refugees during the Greek War of Independence. Aged 16, he joined two of his uncles in London, working in their cereal trading firm, 'Melas Brothers', from which position he acquired financial security. Simultaneously studying at the University of London, he became fluent not only in English but also German, Italian and French. Additionally, he studied botany and architecture, published a collection of his own poems and wrote widely on education in both England and Greece in both languages. He contributed to the foundation of a Greek school in London and began his extensive work on the translation of several of Shakespeare's plays, notably *Macbeth* and *Hamlet*. Aged 30, he married a wealthy Greek heiress and travelled extensively, living in Athens from the 1870s and also in Paris and London. His

literary fame was assured with the publication of *Loukis Laris*, a novel on the War of Independence that was translated into 11 languages. A short work, *From Nikopolis to Olympia*, relating to a journey in Greece, extolled the virtues of tourism. In 1879, he had become a member of the board of the 'Society for the Encouragement of Greek Studies'. His life was marred by his wife's mental illness, which caused them to live predominantly in Paris for her treatment until the time of her death in 1894. It was his presence in Paris that facilitated his formative attendance at the Sorbonne. Here was a man as passionate about his country as was de Coubertin about the value of sport.

An aura of uncertainty, regarding the IOC's foundation, surrounds Vikelas: how and why did he become the first President, having no background in sport, and indeed how did Athens come to be chosen as the inaugural host city? Vikelas was a man of substance: the most academic and educated of all the Presidents, yet also a rich man from his family business and held in esteem in several European countries, such were his literary credentials and profound knowledge of his mother country.

The uncertainty regarding Vikelas centres on the initiative for the nomination of Athens: whether this came from him or de Coubertin, concerning which the records are conflicting; also unclear is which of the two men had the stronger influence in persuading a reluctant Greek government to accept the responsibility.

The uncovering of the mystery, and such it is, owes much to the research of the historian David C. Young, whose study of archive material leads him to believe that Vikelas was the more significant figure in the period between the creation of the IOC at the Sorbonne Congress in 1894 and the staging of the first Games. The notes and memoirs of both men, and the minutes of relevant Congress meetings, are contradictory, leaving us with doubt about the perceived historical reputation of de Coubertin as the cornerstone, the inspiration and the architect of all that the Olympic Games were subsequently to become.

The mystery hinges on a telegram sent by King George I of Greece to de Coubertin on 21 June 1894, two days before what is accepted as the date of the decision to award the Games to Athens. The telegram read: 'With deep feeling toward Baron de Coubertin's courteous petition, I send him and the members of the Congress, with my sincere thanks, my best wishes for the revival of the Olympic Games. George.' The problem, historically, is that the telegram arrived between a meeting of the Congress on 19 June, at which de Coubertin first lodged the proposal for Athens, and the meeting on 23 June, at which Vikelas, in his own records, claims to have initiated the idea of Athens in preference to either London or Paris.

From this one fact, the date of the King's telegram, arise several questions. Had the choice of Athens been planned in advance, through clandestine contacts with Crown Prince Constantine, an avid supporter of the re-creation of the Games? Was Vikelas, within less than three months of becoming involved in de Coubertin's ideological and ambitious concept, also manoeuvred into position by secret planning, so as to be able, through his own position of prestige, to persuade, as IOC President, the Athens authorities to accept responsibility? Indeed, was Vikelas in the event the more powerful tool in the establishment of the Games of Athens, with all its mythology and ancient background, or was he simply the place-man shrewdly envisaged by de Coubertin as the figure around whom a Greek Games could be constructed? Adding to the sense of intrigue is the further fact that private notes of Vikelas record that he was made aware, following the meeting of 19 June and prior to the King's telegram, that a telegram from de Coubertin 'was immediately sent to Athens'. We do not know the message it contained and if there was advance collaboration between de Coubertin and Crown Prince Constantine – or even, conceivably, between Vikelas and Constantine, through mutual close friends in Athens – this would not have been recorded. Direct contact by de Coubertin with Constantine would have been difficult: his first visit to Greece was not until November 1894.

It is, therefore, debatable which of the two IOC figures was more involved in directing the inaugural Games towards the country that is regarded as the mother of European civilisation. The more one reflects upon it, however, the abrupt emergence of Vikelas in February 1894, to become a guiding hand from the supposedly alien world of academia, inevitably arouses speculation.

It was in February that Vikelas had received a letter from a

Members of the IOC and Athens organising committee. Seated (l–r): Prince Georgios, Crown Prince Constantine, Prince Nikolaos. Standing: Georgios Streit, Col. Kokides, Jiri Guth-Jarkovski (IOC), Demetrius Vikelas (IOC President), Alexei de Butovski (IOC), Dr Willibald Gebhardt (IOC), Viktor Balck (IOC). (© IOC/Meyer)

friend, Alexander Phokianos, requesting him to deputise for him as representative of the Pan-Hellenic Gymnasium Club of Athens at the Congress at the Sorbonne. We must ask with what motivation? Allegedly surprised and reluctant, Vikelas had nonetheless accepted when learning that the promoter of the Congress was de Coubertin, of whose ideals and objectives we know he had some knowledge. He would later say, in a lecture delivered in Paris the following spring: 'Imagine my amazement, Gentlemen, when participants took the floor to propose me as President. Me, president of a sports committee!' Vikelas also chaired the commission to study the staging of the Games.

The twists that preceded his selection and the nomination of Athens are genuinely a riddle. Vikelas's private records proclaim himself as the one who proposed Athens on the final plenary session of the Congress on 23 June. David Young considers the proposal was accepted by acclamation, yet there must be doubts about the accuracy of Vikelas's memory. He says that the idea occurred to him on 22 June, yet the minutes of the Session on 19 June contradict this, recording that the majority choice was initially for London, that de Coubertin then proposed Athens, that the floor continued to press for London and that the matter was then deferred by de Coubertin. The absence of Charles Herbert, delegate from the British Amateur Athletic Association, undermined debate on London, nonetheless the minutes are clear on the majority opinion: that the Games should first be in London and then in Paris in 1900. The sentiment for London is confirmed in a German publication of 1894 and it remains puzzling that this fact has tended to be ignored for the past 110 years.

De Coubertin's own records are conflicting, one of his notes, as researched by Young, stating:

> After consulting with M. Vikelas about the resources which the Greek capital might present, we resolved, he and I, to propose it as the first site. I still keep this note from the Greek delegate dated 19 June – 'Dear Baron de Coubertin, I did not see you after our session to tell you how touched I was by your proposal to start with Athens. I'm sorry that I could not support you more warmly.'

Notwithstanding the contradictions, the improbable election of

Vikelas, almost as though by prior arrangement, must lead us to speculate on the likelihood of clandestine dealings. De Coubertin had spent years making contacts, eliciting friends in high places, studiously building intellectual and moral support for his objective. The puzzle remains why Vikelas, if part of a pre-arranged plan, was seemingly unaware of some of the details. It would clarify the situation were the contents of de Coubertin's telegram to Greece known. With Constantine himself having nurtured hopes to stage an Olympics in Athens in 1892, the incentive for him to have been involved in private negotiations with de Coubertin is obvious. The original intention of de Coubertin had been to stage the first Games in Paris in 1900, but he realised that six years between the creation of the principle and the event itself was too long. Crown Prince Constantine's grandson, King Constantine II, who was deposed in 1973, considers that the enlistment of an unwitting Vikelas by de Coubertin is highly probable. 'I suspect that de Coubertin, the Crown Prince and King George must have collaborated,' King Constantine reflects. 'They will have agreed privately that Athens should be the inaugural city, which would explain the King's telegram when informed of the decision by de Coubertin in Paris. At the same time, de Coubertin and my grandfather will have planned the election of Vikelas, in order to exploit his prestige to help convince the Greek government to accept the Games.'

Getting the administration under way for 1896 was not easy. Among the complications was the death of Vikelas's wife, while de Coubertin was preparing for his marriage. There was also trenchant opposition from Greek Prime Minister Charilaos Tricoupis, who stated that the government could not possibly host the Games on account of an economic crisis arising from earthquake and flood disasters in Turkey and Cyprus that precluded the construction of necessary facilities. Thus, when Vikelas arrived in Athens in October, he was confronted with the prospect of rejection, and indeed it was reported in Paris that he had failed. But such reports took no account of the latent influence of Constantine. There had been successful modern Games staged in Athens in 1870, 1875 and 1889 under the direction of an 'Olympic committee' – otherwise known as the 'Zappeion Commission', in honour and memory of Evangelis Zappas, patron of many exhibitions and of those Games. This committee had, however, fallen into abeyance. The job of Vikelas, and de Coubertin, was now to overcome the resistance in Athens, with Constantine's assistance. The problem was sufficiently severe for alternative sites to have been considered.

Vikelas and de Coubertin set about convincing the Greeks of the value of fulfilling their task, though David Young seeks to suggest that the greater part of the burden was borne by Vikelas, de Coubertin being preoccupied with his impending wedding. Indeed, such was de Coubertin's disillusionment at this time that in January 1895 he would submit his resignation from the IOC, Vikelas declining to accept it.

A few months earlier, however, de Coubertin had addressed a select audience in the Athens salon of the literary society 'Parnassus', where he detected a reassuring interest among professional tradesmen, who stood to gain by the influx of many visitors. De Coubertin was careful to stress that the re-creation of the Games was not a restoration of antiquity, but a modern search for 'a balance between body and soul, an admirable compromise between the two forces vying for control over man'. There was no need to be nostalgic about the good old days, he told them: 'Modern sport is both more and less than sports in Antiquity. Modern sport has more perfected equipment, but has less philosophy and lacks an elevated goal:

the entire political and religious framework surrounding the celebration of youth.'

De Coubertin's preoccupation was the philosophy as much and more than the practice of his project. Undoubtedly, he left to Vikelas much of the responsibility to untangle the Athenian political intrigues. An indication of the burden placed upon Vikelas is that de Coubertin returned to Athens for the Games only 12 days before the opening ceremony.

Constantine's influence was therefore of particular significance. He was the patron of the Pan-Hellenic Gymnastics Club, his brothers both honorary members, and it was he who now created an organising committee under his own chairmanship and whose discreet work in the background gradually nudged the city towards an acceptable state of preparedness. It was all very well for de Coubertin, with his vision of symbolism and plans for opening and closing ceremonies, but what would happen in between? And where would the money come from?

The ceremonies and athletic events would be staged in the Pan-Athenean Stadium, built around 300 BC, used for the Games of 1870, but urgently in need of reconstruction. According to the newspaper *Alithea* (Truth) of 14 May 1877, George I donated the site of the stadium to the conceived 'Olympic Committee' to assist the renovation planned, but unfulfilled, by Evangelis Zappas. The King had purchased the land eight years earlier from a resident German architect. A delegation was sent to Alexandria to seek assistance from George Averoff, a prosperous Greek merchant and generous benefactor.

Statue of the first Olympic sponsor, George Averoff, at the entrance to the Pan-Athenean Stadium, for which he funded the rebuilding. (© IOC/Meyer)

His donation of almost a million drachmas effectively saved de Coubertin's dream. Without a stadium there could have been no Games. Thanks to Averoff's generosity, there was also sufficient money ultimately to construct a shooting gallery, a velodrome and even a pier for the spectators at the swimming events in Piraeus Bay. The funding of the Games was officially recorded as: donations, 332,756 drachmas; Averoff gift, 920,000; stamp sales, 400,000; tickets and souvenir medallions, 200,000; government subsidy, 400,000. In recognition of Averoff's contribution, a statue in white marble by the sculptor Georgeos Vroutos was erected at the stadium entrance and unveiled on the eve of the Games. Modest and shy, Averoff was not present at the Games.

The reconstruction of the stadium – initially rebuilt in 200 AD by Herodes Atticus, then left to disintegrate again until excavated in 1870 – was remarkably accomplished in a short time, supervised by the architect Anastas Metaxas. Hundreds of labourers worked round the clock to clear the site and renovate the terraces with white marble, the seating capacity approaching 70,000. A sand running track was constructed under the direction of Charles Perry, groundsman at Stamford Bridge football ground in London, who was given too little time and inadequate materials: the track was 333 metres with exceedingly sharp turns, which reduced sprinters almost to a walk, causing abandonment of the 200 metres. Races were run clockwise in those days. There was no swimming pool, just a primitive area of Zea beach. It was spring and it was cold, the sea temperature about 13°C (55°F), storms preventing the staging of rowing and sailing events. Tennis courts were hastily arranged at the Temple of Zeus.

Ideology was no use without the necessary supporting logistics and this included the loyalty of affiliated countries in sending their teams. In 1896 there were no effective international federations to govern specific sports and in many countries one national sports federation would be at odds with another. De Coubertin would be dependent on Willibald Gebhardt in Germany, Vice-President of the IOC Viktor Balck in Sweden, Ferenc Kemeny in Hungary and on Sloane in America to galvanise local enthusiasm among competitors. In Britain and, embarrassingly, in France, de Coubertin found less support. In spite of a campaign against Gebhardt in Germany, accusing him of an anti-German stance, he created in December 1895 a 'committee for German participation in Athens', second to the Hellenic NOC created the previous January. He was encouraged by Prince Ernst zu Schillingsfürst, the son of the Chancellor of the German Empire. So enthusiastic was Gebhardt that he was recruited to the IOC.

The Thomas Cook travel agency had been nominated by de Coubertin to arrange the travel of foreigners to Athens and they began to arrive well in advance of the Games. There were no formally official teams prior to the spread of national Olympic committees, most teams being randomly gathered. William Sloane organised an American team primarily from Princeton, Harvard and the Boston Athletic Association, gathering a total of 13 competitors, the prominent New York Athletic Club being uninterested in representation. The five from Boston were financed by a wealthy stockbroker, Arthur Burnham, and the Governor of Massachusetts, Oliver Ames. In total there would be 245 male athletes from 14 countries, all but 81 from Greece. France and Germany sent 19 competitors each, the USA 13, Great Britain 8, no other country more than 4, most travelling at their own expense for a programme that had 9 sports and 43 events. Only the first- and second-placed winners were to receive prizes: a silver medal, crown of olive branches and a diploma for the winner; a bronze medal, laurel crown and diploma for the runner-up. Jules Chaplain, a French sculptor,

designed the medals, which were to be awarded on the last day by King George I.

At the recommendation of Professor Michel Bréal, a French classical scholar and friend of de Coubertin, there was to be a symbolic race in commemoration of the Battle of Marathon, 490 BC, in which the outnumbered Athenians slew 20,000 Persians. According to legend, an Athenian messenger, Pheidippides, ran from Marathon to Athens to announce 'rejoice, we have conquered' before falling dead – the distance calculated to be approximately 25 miles or 40 kilometres.

Forty thousand people attended the opening ceremony, the 75th anniversary of independence from Turkey, with more than that number taking vantage points on surrounding hills. In front of assembled competitors, the King and Queen arrived, he in military uniform, she in a white dress. Prince Constantine gave an opening address, inaudible to most in the era before loudspeakers. Then the King rose to declare: 'I hereby proclaim the opening of the first International Olympic Games at Athens.' Cannons were fired, pigeons were released, followed by a rendering of the Olympic Hymn written by Costas Palamas, the national poet, to music composed by Spyros Samaras. This would be formally adopted only at the IOC Session of 1958 in Tokyo. The audience demanded an encore. To the sound of trumpets, the competitors arrived.

Among the dignitaries present was Father Henri Didon. He had been to Olympia and been photographed at the ruins of the Temple of Zeus. On Easter Day, the day of the opening ceremony, he proclaimed in Athens:

> I was eager to associate myself with this development of physical effort, of which Greece has given us such a perfect example and which must increasingly be part of the education of man. I wanted to teach the young people who are entrusted to me to take part in this movement of international union, which seems to be a first step towards the fraternity of peoples, and a moral unity that Jesus was the first to formulate as the great goal of the spiritual kingdom of which He is the head, the initiator and the unshakeable support.

The founder hones his technique against Monsieur Vienne at the School of Utilitarian Sports. (© IOC)

Subsequently de Coubertin wrote:

> The nineteenth century has seen the awakening of a taste for athletics everywhere; at its dawn in Germany and Sweden, at its noonday in England, at its sunset in France and America . . . could it be otherwise, but that sportsmen of diverse nationalities should begin to meet each other on common ground . . . [thus] the revival of the Olympic Games became possible, indeed I may even say, necessary.

> For many years I had studied the school life of English and American youth. Although we may criticise on many points the teaching which public schools afford in England, there can be no reasonable doubt about their providing a strong and vigorous education of body and character. To the merits of this education we may ascribe a large share in the prodigious and powerful extension of the British Empire in Queen Victoria's reign. It is worthy of note that this development began at the same time as the United Kingdom school reforms of 1840. In these reforms, physical games and sports held the most prominent place. In France, on the contrary, physical inertia was till recently considered an indispensable assistant to the perfection of intellectual powers. Games were supposed to kill study. Regarding the development of youthful character, the axiom that a close connection exists between force of will and strength of body never entered anyone's mind . . . all my researches convinced me that at the close of the century that had witnessed its rise, athletics already ran a great danger of degenerating if energetic influence were not brought to bear upon it . . . of all measures towards this end, only one seemed to me practicable, namely the establishment of a periodic contest, to which sporting societies of all nationalities would be invited to send their representatives, and the placing of these meetings under the only patronage which could invest them with a halo of greatness and glory – the patronage of classical antiquity. To do that was to re-establish the Olympic Games . . . the idea of the revival came triumphantly to the front.

One of the few disagreements between de Coubertin and Vikelas during the latter's term of presidency concerned future Games. Those of Athens having been relatively successful, the Greeks, predictably, wished to claim the credit, and indeed the Games themselves, as their own. They wished all future Games to be staged in Athens; ironic in view of the difficulty there had been in persuading them to be inaugural hosts. De Coubertin knew that the Games must be global and therefore itinerant. Though Vikelas agreed, his loyalty to his country persuaded him to lobby in favour of a permanent Greek home. As a compromise, he proposed interim Games in Athens, an idea rejected by de Coubertin. With the next Games scheduled for Paris, the presidency transferred to de Coubertin – prior to this acting as the IOC's Secretary-General – under the principle that the President should be from the host country during the preceding four years. Vikelas even called unilaterally for an Olympic Congress to discuss the proposal, but de Coubertin held firm and Vikelas handed over the insignia of office and shortly afterwards resigned his membership of the IOC.

He resumed his travelling, supporting Greece in its ongoing conflict with Turkey, but above all being an active educationalist, initiating a congress on education in Athens in 1904. The following year, under the persuasion of friends, he was the delegate of Greece to the Olympic Congress in Brussels and managed to establish the Intermediate Games of Athens 1906 – an event de Coubertin reluctantly acknowledged but refused to attend. Though continuing as close friends, the relationship between the two men who were more than 30 years apart in age had become strained, de Coubertin considering that his trust in the older man had not been wholly reciprocal – especially in the light of the Greeks effectively ignoring the degree to which his efforts had granted them the opportunity to reclaim their historical position. When he returned home to Paris, his new wife confronted him with the cruel question: 'Why was it that not one time did they mention your name at any ceremonies?' Monique Berlioux, IOC Director-General under Presidents Brundage and Killanin, recalled in her book *Olympica*: 'The name of de Coubertin was not mentioned once by [Greek] journals or officials.'

Vikelas died in July 1908 – philanthropist, literary zion, passionate nationalist. His mark on Olympic history had been greater than is nowadays recognised.

CHAPTER III

Athens (I) 1896

Spyridon Louis of Greece, inaugural Olympic marathon champion

'The day before the race, a decrepit old horse and cart pulled some of us from Marusi, my home village, to Marathon. It was raining and the journey took almost five hours. It had rained and even hailed in the night, and as a result we were shaking with cold; the people of Marathon kindly lent us their jackets. That evening, the mayor plied us liberally to get us warm again, to keep our strength up for the race. "Is there anything else you want?" he asked. "Yes!" we cried in unison, "bring us some more wine, please." That rainy Thursday, we celebrated in a way that probably no other athletes have ever done before a competition. What did we know about abstaining during training?

The next morning, when the foreign runners were being massaged by their helpers, I said to my companions, "Let's do a couple of laps round the village square to stretch our legs a bit!" In that way, we wore in the new shoes which the people of Marusi had bought for us. They were good and cost about 25 drachmas a pair – at the time an enormous sum for shoes.

At eleven, there was milk and two eggs for each man. At two, we were in the street, ready to start. After some way, my future father-in-law, standing by the roadside, offered me a beaker of wine and an Easter egg. I slurped down the wine, felt much stronger, and quickly caught up with my colleague Christovoulos. The crowds were shouting "Go, Louis, go!" That spurred me on. A policeman who shouted "The only ones in front of you are foreigners" had to ride a brisk trot on his horse to keep up with me. A few hundred metres in front was the American. I thought: "I'll show him what's what", and stepped up the pace. It was enough. Vasilakos overtook him too and I said, "Let's run together." But Vasilakos was exhausted and couldn't keep up, so I left him and came up behind the Frenchman. He did his best, but suddenly collapsed. He was all in. Once I was past him, I realised that the front runner, the Australian, was there. Everyone was bellowing: "Catch him, Louis. You've got to beat him. Hellas! Hellas!" Ambition took hold of me. I lengthened my stride and it did the trick. He was a tough lad, but I closed on him. When I caught up with him after 34 kilometres, an officer shot his pistol in the air and everyone cheered. For 500 metres we ran side by side. I kept watching him from the corner of my eye, I didn't let him gain a foot of ground. At last he got short of breath and fell further and further back.' (Interview at the Berlin Olympics, 1936)
(Photograph © IOC)

Performances at the inaugural Games were poor, even by standards of the time, primarily because of the absence of proper infrastructure and the haphazard nature of the foreign entries, most of them personally paying their expenses, some no more than tourists. Although 34 countries had taken the initiative to revive the Games, only 14 were represented. Invitations had been sent out only the previous December, leaving little time for planning. The college-dominated American team, for example, though clearly the strongest, was without many of the country's top competitiors, such as Luther Cary, 100m record holder. The French, with the largest contingent after the hosts, who provided the majority, were unsuccessful except in cycling and fencing. All except three of the Germans competed only in gymnastics, in which they were dominant.

Newspapers reported there were 20,000 foreign visitors.

George Robertson from Oxford University, who had decided to enter the shot put and unfamiliar discus event primarily on account of being a Greek scholar, questioned this figure. 'I doubt if visitors and competitors together totalled more than 1,000, partly because of the preposterous prices at which agents advertised accommodation. My friend E.H. Flack [an Australian member of the London Athletic Club who won the 800m and 1,500m] and I hired a furnished flat, fed at Greek restaurants and lived for a fortnight on £4.' Nonetheless, there was a festive air, the city decorated with flowers and flags, illuminated at night, with thousands of Athenians singing and dancing into the early hours. It was even said that the police had to be on alert for illegal ticket sales, the main stadium always being crowded.

If for nothing else, the first Games were remarkable for an act of sportmanship unsurpassed at any future time. After 150 laps

Athens – the awards ceremony. (© IOC)

Alfréd Hajós of Hungary (aka Guttman) champion swimmer in open sea – 'My will to live completely overcame my desire to win.' (© IOC/Meyer)

of the 100-kilometre cycle track race, the opponents of Léon Flameng of France had all retired after being lapped, bar Georgios Kolettis of Greece, who was far behind and was then halted by a mechanical defect. Flameng, seeing his rival's predicament, dismounted and waited for the Greek to be given a new cycle and to continue. At the finish, Flameng won by six laps and was warmly applauded. How much sporting morality has changed in a century.

In the 87-kilometre road race, from Athens to Marathon and back, Aristidis Konstantinidis of Greece crashed and injured himself on the return half, received treatment and continued on a cycle borrowed from a helper. In the Athens suburbs, after swerving to avoid a spectator, he again crashed into a wall and further injured himself, but continued to victory, dirty and bloodstained, on a cycle borrowed from a spectator. His journey took him 3 hours 22 minutes 31 seconds.

The eight Hungarian competitors were inconspicuous apart from a swimmer, Alfréd Hajós, aged 18 – though it became apparent some years later that his name was in fact Guttman. In the resulting confusion of records, he changed his name by deed poll to Hajós, and as such it now appears. At the Games in Paris in 1924 he was awarded the silver medal for architecture in the art competition: the second person to have won Olympic awards in both sporting and cultural fields. The first was Walter Winans, an Anglo-American who was awarded a cultural medal in 1912, having been also ninth in pistol shooting. De Coubertin was always intent on simultaneous cultural exhibitions and awards, though inevitably they gained little of the attention showered on sport. Such cultural prizes continue to this day. There will be an exhibition in Athens in the spring of 2004 under the title of 'Sport and Art', with prizes in two categories: sculpture and graphic art. Having won the 100m at Athens, Hajós covered himself in grease for the 1,200m; for which the competitors were taken out to sea in three small launches and then left to contend with a heavy swell as they headed back to shore and the finishing line. Several had to be saved from drowning. 'My will to live completely overcame my desire to win,' Hajós related. He learned to swim when young, after his father had drowned in the Danube.

James Bernard Connolly, like other colleagues at Harvard

University, was refused leave of absence, but set out with the rest of the team by boat and then across Europe by train, thereby ending his university career. He became the first winner of the new Games when he cleared, in what was then still known as the hop, step and jump, 13.71m (44 ft 11 in.). In later Games he would have been disqualified for taking two hops with his preferred left leg before the final jump. With no interim announcements, he had to ask if he was in the lead and was told 'by a metre'. In later life, becoming a journalist and author, he declined an Honorary Doctorate from Harvard.

The Americans were to start a subsequent trend by winning all but three of the twelve athletic events, the exceptions being the marathon, the 800m and 1,500m, the latter pair won by the Australian Edwin Flack, who had taken a month's holiday from accountancy in London. Francis Lane, Thomas Burke and Thomas Curtis, three Americans, won the three heats of the 100m – the first placed two from each qualifying for the final four days later, Lane thereby being the winner of the Games' first race. Curtis chose not to start in the final, saving himself for the 110m hurdles, the next race. Burke, the only runner using a 'horizontal' crouch start, with hands on the starting line, was fastest in the heats and repeated the slowish time, 12.0 seconds, in the final to win by two metres. Curtis duly won the hurdles, defeating Grantley Goulding of Britain – who had been boastful of his prospects prior to the race by wearing previous medals pinned to his waistcoat. With the other two finalists failing to appear, Grantley did have the distinction of being the only man or woman to finish last in a still-surviving Olympic event and take a silver medal.

One of the tourist competitors was John Boland, an Irish barrister visiting a friend. Being also a tennis enthusiast, he decided to try his luck. He won both the singles, defeating

Kasdaglis of Greece, and the doubles with Fritz Traun of Germany – joint third place in the latter going to the ad hoc pair of Flack and Robertson. Such was the amateurish, as opposed to amateur, level of these Games, Boland was actually unaware that he had become Olympic champion.

The discus, a classic discipline evolved by the Greeks, was, to their immense disappointment, won almost inadvertently by Robert Garrett, a Princeton student, who had begun training only two weeks before leaving America, with an irregular implement fashioned by a friend. His Greek rivals were favoured, but, finding the official implement lighter and pleasantly aerodynamic, Garrett beat Panoyotis Paraskevopoulos by 20 centimetres – to much cheering by Bostonian supporters. American triumphalism at the Games began early.

There were several multiple winners: Paul Masson (FRA), with three cycling events; Hermann Weingärtner (GER), four placings in gymnastics; and Carl Schuhmann (GER) winning not only three gymnastic events but also a wrestling title. John and Sumner Paine (USA), in military and free pistol respectively, became the first brothers to win Olympic gold medals.

Marathon champion and national hero Spyridon Louis leads the medal winners' parade at the closing ceremony. (© IOC)

The United States delegation gather beneath their flag. (© IOC)

Excited by the prospect of the marathon reviving national pride in past glory, the Greeks eagerly awaited the event, with only four foreigners among the seventeen starters. Two preliminary Greek trials had been staged, Spyridon Louis prominent in the second. Born 23 years earlier, a descendant of combatants of the War of Independence, he worked on his father's small farm, regularly delivering spring water by mule to Athens. When a pupil of Theophilos Voreas, later a philosopher and theologian, Louis had declined the chance of further education. During a period of military service, he had impressed Major Papadiamantopoulos, for whom he was groom, with his running: on one occasion covering 20 kilometres in under two hours in the early morning, having accidentally left his sword, compulsory for parade, at home during weekend leave. 'My horse is nothing compared to you,' the Major had said, and with the announcement of the race's inclusion, Louis was an immediate volunteer.

The four foreigners – Albin Lermusiaux (FRA), third in the 1,500m, Edwin Flack (AUS), Arthur Blake (USA), second to Flack in the 1,500m, and Gyula Kellner (HUN) – were all unaccustomed to the distance and began too fast. Although Lermusiaux led by a huge distance at the halfway stage, he subsequently got cramp and dropped out, Flack doing likewise after another five kilometres and being taken back to Athens by carriage. Blake, hallucinating, had toppled into a ditch and only Kellner survived. Flack, following discussion with the British Ambassador, was accompanied by the Embassy butler, wearing a bowler hat and riding a bicycle. At one village, Lermusiaux, when still leading, prematurely had a garland placed over his shoulders when passing through an arch erected by the villagers. Accompanying horse-drawn carts carrying doctors, officials and time-keepers, together with a guard of cavalry officers, kicked up such a dust that the runners found it difficult to breathe. It was after 32 kilometres that Louis caught up with Flack, finally going in front four kilometres later.

Early reports of foreign leaders had dismayed a packed and expectant crowd at the main stadium, but now came news for the assembled 70,000 that their man was ahead. As Louis entered the arena, the scene was one of pandemonium. Women removed their jewellery to throw at his feet. A mounted band followed him into the stadium and the two Crown Princes, Constantine and George, ran alongside him to the finishing line. 'It seemed that all of Greek Antiquity entered the stadium with him,' de Coubertin recalled. 'This was one of the most extraordinary spectacles in my memory.'

Averoff had allegedly promised the hand of his daughter in marriage to the winner. Fortunately for him – or her? – Louis was already betrothed to Heleni, a Marousi girl. He was, however, promised by other Athenians the gift of free suits, free shaves and free meals for life. The only sombre note was Kellner's allegation that Dimitri Velokas, who had finished third, had taken a lift in a carriage for part of the route. The Greek, unable to deny it, was stripped of his award, his singlet ripped off his back. Kellner was then awarded third place. Local euphoria was such, however, that an official remarked to de Coubertin: 'I see that your internationalism does not kill national spirit – it strengthens it.' The tone had been set for the coming century.

The King gave a breakfast party the next day, playing leap-frog and mimic baseball with competitors in a park: the Royal Family never one to stand on dignity. In what would become a classic example for future Games, a country boy had emerged from obscurity, motivated by the abstract concept of self-fulfilment. Asked for his wish by the King, he requested a horse and cart with which to carry his water barrels.

There was an unusual interlude at the prizegiving. George Robertson, later a QC, related:

I had composed an ode in Aeolic Greek of the kind that Pindar used to sell to Olympic champions. The King heard of it, but the committee would not allow it to be recited, as they had refused other Greeks such requests. So the King arranged with me that, when he gave the signal, the ode should be delivered. He was so pleased with his victory over the committee that he gave me both an olive branch and a laurel branch, which was some consolation for my failure in the discus.

Leon Stukelj of Slovenia, formerly Yugoslavia, heir to Germany's inaugural Olympic gymnastics champions of 1896 – Alfred Flatow, Hermann Weingärtner and Carl Schuhmann – personified de Coubertin's moral philosophy of *mens sana in corpore sano* (healthy mind, healthy body) and lived to be 100.

CHAPTER IV

Visionary

Baron Pierre de Coubertin of France, second IOC President, 1896–1925

'. . . *circumstances obliged us to deal with the second Olympiad quite differently from the first. It was essential to scatter the competitions, in terms of location and date. There was no point in trying to group sports and festivals together to create a "Two-week Olympic Event", the brilliance of which would always be overshadowed by the neighbouring World's Fair. We had not considered the problematic side of choosing the year 1900.*

As had been my custom before, I assumed all responsibility for all the advertising, telegrams, correspondence, etc. In approaching each of the associations whose assistance we were soliciting, we stated: "Every year, you organise a major athletics event. In 1900, would you simply give that event an international character, with greater solemnity than usual? In return, we will exempt you from having to provide the prizes, which means significant saving" . . . *A real obstacle arose, in the name of the Union des Sociétés Français de Sports Athlétiques (USFSA)* [of which de Coubertin was in fact Secretary-General], *who managed to persuade the Racing Club and the Stade Francais to reject our proposals – stating they would reserve support only for organisation made by the city of Paris or by the government. The reason was that USFSA, which was angling for government subsidy, was trying to rid itself of the counts and marquises by whom it was apparently encumbered. One member wrote to me in provocative and nasty terms: "Your inferiority is that you have no ribbons* [civic honours] *to hand out"* . . . *I had stupidly thought that the federations, whose regulations we would be applying and to whom we would leave the formation of the juries and the running of the contests, would find these responsibilities sufficient reward to interest them. Good heavens, I had forgotten the decorations! In France, what madness on my part! A vast intrigue developed. Charles de la Rochefoucauld, head of the organising committee, resigned early in 1899. I was harassed "in the name of patriotism" in order that French athleticism could be presented "united and without division". I gave in, and I was wrong* . . .

It is clear that sport is gradually spreading over the whole world and taking the place of unhealthy amusements and evil pleasures in the lives of young men . . . *In 1900, it was still only among real sportsmen that the sporting spirit existed instinctively. The general public had no idea of it at all. On all sides were heard expressions of mistrust regarding the Games "organised by that band of incompetents in Paris", as Sloane put it.*

The days continued to pass, nothing concrete was being achieved. No money, no stadium, no grounds . . . *most politicians of the time* . . . *considered Olympism a totally superfluous, eccentric neologism. Six years later, at a banquet, the word Olympism still brought a incredulous, disdainful smile to the lips of ministers* . . .

A great deal of goodwill was shown [in 1900]. *The athletes did their best. Interesting results were achieved, but with nothing Olympic about them. According to one of our IOC colleagues, "Our idea had been used, but it had been torn to shreds in the process." It proved that we should never allow the Games to become dependent on or be taken over by a big fair, where their philosophical value vanishes into thin air and their educational merit becomes nil. Unfortunately, the alliance we had concluded was more indissoluble than we thought. In 1904 and 1908, for budgetary reasons, we were unable to sever our relations with exhibitions. It was not until 1912 that the break was finally completed, in Sweden.'* (From collected papers)
(Photograph © IOC)

It could rationally be argued that there were *no* Olympic Games in 1900. Stretching from May almost to November, with no official opening or closing ceremonies, with both amateur and professional events staged in a programme of almost total disarray, with many competitors even unaware for some years afterwards that they had become 'Olympic champions' and with de Coubertin no more than involved on the fringe, being conspicuously present only at the track and field events at the Bois de Boulogne, the alleged festival in conjunction with the World Exhibition was no more than a minor Paris sideshow. The city's publicity announced only an 'International Meeting of Physical Exercises and Sports'; to an embarrassing degree the

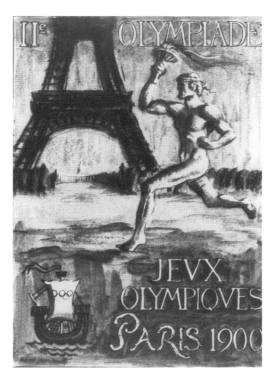

Graceful symbol of a disorganised Games – designed and produced after the Games were concluded. (© IOC)

ideology of de Coubertin had been discarded, if not forgotten. Contestants were from a mere 19 nations.

While history has retrospectively bestowed upon de Coubertin the virtue of having founded the world's most acclaimed sporting event, the four years from 1896 to 1900, and indeed the next eight years or so, found him frantically treading water and often close to drowning, as he attempted to keep afloat his altruistic philosophy that was as much to do with education as sport. Of Paris in 1900, he said to a friend: 'It's a miracle that the Olympic Movement survived that celebration. We made a hash of our work.' Only the depth of his conviction, not to say that of his private fortune, which he all but exhausted in pursuit of his dream, enabled him to ignore the sceptics and continue down a lonely and sometimes hostile road.

Pierre de Frédy, Baron de Coubertin, was born at 20 Rue Oudinot in Paris on 1 January 1863, the son of an old Italian family that had lived for nearly 500 years in France. One of his ancestors had served as chamberlain to King Louis XI, from whom was received the de Coubertin title and armorial bearings in 1477. De Coubertin's grandfather, Julien-Bonaventure Frédy de Coubertin, was made hereditary baron during the reign of Louis XVIII and the family settled in Normandy. His mother, Agathe Marie Marcelle Gigoault de Crisenoy, was descended from aides of William the Conqueror. Tradition would have seen young Pierre seeking a military career.

Aged 12, he was an inaugural student at a new Jesuit college, Externat St Ignace, in Paris, where he remained for seven years, his parents intending a sober, conventional schooling. An able student, the boy earned a place at the French Military Academy, but quickly resigned. As a child, he had witnessed the humiliating defeat of France by Prussia in 1870, Emperor Napoleon III being captured together with most of the French

Army and the provinces of Alsace and Lorraine being annexed. The offspring of one of France's old aristocratic families acquired a desire not for revenge but for the re-education of his nation, so that it might rediscover its dignity.

His early instinct was for a study of literature, history and sociology. He was involved in sport as a boy only informally, indulging in leisurely rowing, fencing and boxing. Although he entered law school in 1884, in deference to his father, he remained there less than a year. By his early 20s, he had become addicted to educational reform, submitting papers to the Society for the Advancement of Political Science. Besides his celebrated revival of the Olympic Games, he was responsible for a universal history in four volumes, his total publications covering some 60,000 pages.

Early mentors had led him to the social theories of Frederic LePlay, a contemporary philosopher preoccupied with the class divisions that threatened French society. De Coubertin's vision of an improved society was liberal in the sense of classic nineteenth-century liberalism: that of the development of the individual. Aligned with this was the conviction that belief in nationality was a basis of individual identity, yet when his Olympic Movement came to be founded, his International Olympic Committee evolved into what was partially a contradiction: a contest between individuals, who had, however, been strictly selected by national representation. It would be ironic for its creator that this contradiction was to cause controversy throughout the mounting fame of the Games during the next century: the usurping of individual achievement in the listing of national medals tables.

'Nothing in ancient history inspired more reverie in me than Olympia,' de Coubertin said, though in the restoration of the Olympic ideal he was following in the footsteps of others throughout the nineteenth century. De Coubertin and one of his successors as President of the IOC, Avery Brundage, calculatedly proclaimed 'Olympism' as a form of religion, believing that it might override political and religious differences between nations: a philosophy that was simultaneously pure but over-simplistic. Although the Games over the next century were to fulfil de Coubertin's ambitions more than he might have dared hope, successfully dampening the flames of religious conflict and drawing together competitors from politically opposed nations – Communist–Capitalist, East–West, China–Formosa (later Taiwan), North and South Korea, Iran–Iraq – his philosophy would never be a match for extreme despotic regimes or paranoid governments. Moreover, his own liberalism possessed its flaws. He was slow-witted, or naive, in failing to understand the class differences that so defined the amateurism of British sport, which had provided for him the supreme example of physical education; and at the same time he remained largely immune to the interests and emancipation of women at the turn of the century – never mind his determined proclamation: 'I shall burnish a flabby and cramped youth, its body and its character, by sport: by its risks, even its excesses, all this to be for everyone, with no discrimination on account of birth, caste, financial standing or occupation.' So distorted, however innocently, were de Coubertin's aristocratic social perceptions, that he was horrified at the prospect of women appearing undignified by sweating in public.

In exercising noble sentiments, de Coubertin was therefore a slightly remote amateur from a privileged world, driven by motives which, in spite of his inexhaustible goodwill, he did not fully comprehend.

De Coubertin and his IOC colleagues were ahead of their time in

The Baron and Mlle Marie Rothan on their wedding day. (© IOC)

their concept of the possibilities of international sport, both as an end in itself and as a platform for global fraternity, even though they were operating within a society which was evolving at a pace never previously witnessed, driven by the communication inventions of telephone, radio, railway and motor car. Yet, to gather people, even once every four years, from the corners of the globe to take part in *sport* was esoteric to a degree that some found absurd.

In spite of his elation at the founding of the IOC and the staging of the inaugural Games, de Coubertin was regarded by critics and envious rivals as, variously, a social freak, a snob, or merely a nuisance. Following the relative success of the Games in Athens – an opportunity initially scorned by the Greek government – an ungracious Greek press accused de Coubertin of being a thief, 'trying to strip Greece of one of its historic jewels', according to the history of John J. MacAloon, *This Great Symbol*. The Greeks, not excluding a more moderate King George, wished to re-acquire an event now proven to possess modern viability. Momentum was given to their cause by articles in the *New York Times* and *The Times* of London, supporting the notion of continuation in Athens. De Coubertin then increased his unpopularity with the Greeks by alleging that their motive was financial profit.

As they sought to institutionalise the Games in Athens, the Greek government was encouraged by the King, who suggested to de Coubertin that Athens should become the permanent home. De Coubertin pretended not to understand and politely wrote in reply that the next Games would be in Paris. Prince Constantine, recognising the financial implications of monopolising the Games, now persuaded his father of the impossibility; even though Prime Minister Deliyannis had passed a law decreeing that the Games belonged to Greece. Following the Athens Games, Vikelas had organised a meeting

of IOC members, without de Coubertin, at which was discussed the principle of interim Games in Athens every alternate two years. De Coubertin adopted an attitude mainly of dignified silence, even though he was pained that the Greeks regarded him 'only as a superfluous figure, whose presence reminded them that the new Olympic Games were a foreign invention, and wished to forget the initiative that France had taken to resurrect the Games. Most of those with whom I worked in 1894–5 avoided me'. On his objective he held firm, however. In a letter to the King he said, having succeeded Vikelas in the presidency:

> I wish to make my first act a message of thanks, addressed in the person of its august sovereign to the whole of Greece. Two years ago, at the Paris Congress, your majesty deigned to address to me a telegram of encouragement. I now venture to recall to your majesty that my wishes have been fulfilled and that the Olympic Games have been reinstated. In presiding over its reinstatement, your majesty gave my colleagues and me the right to count on your further goodwill in the future.

At the closing banquet in Athens, de Coubertin had confirmed the next Games would be in Paris. At the dawn of the new century, a re-emerging France seemed the perfect host country for this wilful ideologist. In November 1896, in a report on the Athens Games for *Century* magazine, he signed himself as 'Founder of the Games, Baron Pierre de Coubertin', suggested that the proposal for interim Pan-Hellenic Games could be accepted and planned a Congress for July 1897 at which the possibility of a permanent Greek home would be buried.

While conscious that too frequent a staging of an Olympic Games would dilute their significance – the long-term secret of a unique success – he realised that momentum needed to be maintained during each Olympiad in order to foster allegiance. Hence the Congress at Le Havre, his summer home, a tranquil sea port chosen for its lack of political significance. Conveniently, Greek attention unavoidably turned towards a war with Turkey, as a consequence of which there were no Greek representatives at Le Havre. In spite of some support at the Congress for returning to Athens, de Coubertin was able to persuade his IOC colleagues and others in attendance that their destiny must be Paris for 1900 and thereafter a moving global festival, with his stated preference for an American city, possibly New York, in 1904. Paris appealed to the 59 participants, only 12 of whom were from abroad – comparative figures at the Sorbonne in 1894 had been 78 and 20 – the initial belief being that the World Fair and the newly constructed Eiffel Tower would add glamour to their sporting convention. How wrong they were to be.

If discussion at Le Havre had rolled lightly over the issues of organisation in Paris, it soon emerged that the problems were profound. De Coubertin's hope that USFSA might coordinate the administration floundered in November 1898, when USFSA announced its rejection of a 'private' sports meeting. Adding to the hostility was the request by American contributors to the Fair to build an arena 'suitable for American sportsmen'. As the Games progressively slid into the arms of the Exhibition and its organiser, Alfred Picard, all thoughts of a dignified sports festival dissolved. Picard was resentful of being given responsibility for sport and personally antagonistic towards de Coubertin. In February 1899, he nominated Daniel Merillon, president of the national shooting federation, which was a

member of the USFSA, as director-general of the sporting contests.

In April 1899, de Coubertin resigned as nominal secretary-general of the USFSA – a position he had retained only in a vain attempt to bolster national solidarity – and Vicomte de la Rochefoucauld resigned as head of de Coubertin's nascent organising committee, which in turn voted to dissolve itself, only 12 months before the opening of the Games. In a desperate attempt to sustain the loyalty of foreign countries, de Coubertin went on a European tour, while back home the proposed sites for different sports changed almost by the week. The direction under Merillon was bizarre: rowing was bracketed under 'lifesaving', skating and fencing were assigned to the 'cutlery' department, while track and field were categorised under 'provident societies'. To compound de Coubertin's anxieties, the previous year Jacques, his first-born son, had suffered a stroke when left too long in the sun, which rendered him severely retarded. Grief-stricken, de Coubertin's concentration and judgement were doubtless compromised.

Distortion of de Coubertin's ideology increased with the listing of professional events. Other anxieties came with the French Foreign Minister protesting at the prospect of Germans being allowed to compete, while Sloane, IOC member of the

United States, though opposing his country's request to build its own competition arena, threatened to withdraw the American team unless there was more information on logistics.

Ironically, it was because de Coubertin was not in control that the Paris Games featured the entry of women. The Games would include women's golf and tennis, with five countries sending female competitors: Bohemia (later Czechoslovakia), France, Great Britain, Switzerland and the United States. There is debate about who was the first women's champion. Charlotte Cooper of Britain, who defeated Hélène Prévost of France 6–4, 6–2 in the tennis singles, and won the mixed doubles on the same day with Reginald Doherty, beating Prévost and Harold Mahoney, is credited with the first gold medal. However, Walter Teutenberg, a German historian, discovered that Countess de Pourtalès was one of the crew on the Swiss yach *Lerina* which was victorious prior to Cooper. Margaret Abbott of America won the women's golf, but in the multiple confusion which surrounded the Games, this and cricket, soccer, rugby and polo were regarded as unofficial demonstration sports. Coincidentally, de Pourtalès's husband – she was born American – Count Hermann Alexander is regarded as the first-born future Olympic participant of European origin, on 31 March 1847. There were no national teams and no Village, the competitors staying in hotels.

Professor William Sloane, though a loyal disciple of de Coubertin, threatened to withdraw the US team because of Parisian incompetence. (© IOC)

Charlotte Cooper of Britain, the first Olympic women's champion, winner of the tennis singles and the mixed doubles with Reginald Doherty. (© IOC)

CHAPTER V

Paris (II) 1900

E. Ion Pool of Britain, marathon runner

'*The marathon turned out a dismal fiasco. The whole conduct of the race on the part of the responsible organisers, beginning with the tardy date of the announcement sent abroad, down to the smallest details of providing, or rather failing to provide, for the conveniences of contestants on the appointed day, and the entire absence of precautions to ensure fair play, can only be characterised by a single word: Preposterous, with a capital P. Add to this the non-sporting demeanour of the French populace and it will not be necessary to cite fully the extent of the troubles that variously beset the foreign runners. At best it proved a steeplechase, with bicycles and cars for obstacles. Twenty-five miles really is too far for a steeplechase, but that was a mere incidental. Suffice to say that when the three first finishers in last year's London to Brighton race found it necessary to retire within four miles and Arthur Newton, that well-known long distance record breaker in the United States, who was unwise enough to finish, took almost longer than walking time to complete the distance, it shows that everything was very, very wrong. I could a further tale unfold . . . but no matter.*' (From an interview in *South London Harriers* magazine) (Olympic Poster © IOC)

Anxieties abroad during preparations prior to the Games were nothing compared to the problems that arose as soon as the teams, especially the American team, arrived in Paris. The competitors soon discovered that the sporting festival that they had come to participate in had merely been shoehorned in as a sideshow in the five-month-long international exposition taking place concurrently. Nowhere was the word 'Olympic' to be seen, any reference to the Games appearing only as 'Paris Championships' or 'The Great Exhibition meeting of 1900'. Far worse than this, however, was the decision by the French organisers to revert to their original intention of opening the Games, and scheduling later competition, on a Sunday. When that intention had originally been apparent, Princeton and Pennsylvania universities, led by Caspar Whitney, IOC member, had threatened a boycott if competition was not moved from the Sabbath. 'No first-class American club or team holds meets on a Sunday,' Whitney asserted. Yet the French had allowed themselves to be manoeuvred into a cleft stick. Saturday, 14 July, scheduled for the opening, was Bastille Day, so that they found themselves obliged to revert to their original plans. Hostility from the Americans was predictable and widespread. However, US officials' moral indignation at the prospect of Sunday competition nonetheless gave them no authority over amateur competitors. While Robert Garrett of Princeton, discus hero of 1896, refused to compete on Sunday, as did his university

colleagues and those from Michigan and Syracuse, unity proved elusive. Members of the Penn squad decided to compete, leading to recriminations among the Americans more emotional than those directed against the French. Whitney charged that those competing on Sunday were 'unscrupulous mug hunters' and published back home a shaming list of names.

The novelist Hjalmar Boyesen had stated, following the Games in Athens, that Olympic victories had made the American nation confident in its physical superiority. There was clear evidence in the attitude of the universities that the Americans, subjectively or otherwise, regarded the Games as something of a religious crusade: an attempt to identify athletic prowess with cultural, religious and political principles, the same muscular Christianity that was present in Britain. However, in Paris, a conflicting principle arose among some of the American athletes: that victory would establish a reputation as the boldest and strongest people in the world. It was therefore unsurprising that five of Penn's thirteen competitors decided they would shrug off the moral censure and go for glory. Four of them would be victorious. Irving Baxter won the high jump and pole vault, Walter Tewksbury the 400m hurdles, George Orton – a Canadian posing as an American – the 2,500m steeplechase, and Alvin Kraenzlein the 60m, the 110 and 200m hurdles and the long jump.

Kraenzlein, with his four individual gold medals, a feat yet to

Kraenzlein was the first to perfect the technique of the trailing-leg in hurdles. (© IOC)

Alvin Kraenzlein of America, the first all-star champion, victorious in four events and at the centre of a religious controversy. (© IOC)

be surpassed in track and field at one Games and all of them confirmed as Olympic records, was doubly famous, or infamous, on account of the Sabbath controversy. In the long jump he was scheduled to compete against his arch rival and the current world record holder Myer Prinstein, from the staunchly Methodist Syracuse. The problem for Prinstein was that the qualifying round was on a Saturday and the final on Sunday, when he declared he would not compete out of religious solidarity even though he was Jewish. On the Saturday, Prinstein led with 7.17m (23 ft 6 in.), which regulations at the time permitted to be carried forward to the following day. He did not expect Kraenzlein to jump on Sunday and was dismayed when his rival did so, surpassing his mark by 1cm. When he learned of Kraenzlein's victory, he challenged the Penn star to a jump-off on the Monday. Kraenzlein refused and Prinstein's Syracuse colleagues had to restrain him from assaulting the victor.

With or without his opportunist attitude, Kraenzlein had become the first truly Olympian figure of modern times. In spite of the wretchedly uneven grass track at Pré Catalan in the Bois de Boulogne – the French having declined to desecrate their beloved park with a cinder track – he set world records of 7 seconds for the short sprint, 15.4 and 25.4 seconds for the respective hurdles, and with 7.18m (23 ft 7 in.) won the long jump. At one time or another that year, Kraenzlein held six world records. Above all, he was recognised as the athlete who revolutionised hurdling, with his introduction of the style of leading with one leg over the hurdle, rather than jumping with both legs tucked up as most competitors then did. He was, also, the dandy of the 55-man American team, strolling around central Paris, when not competing, in jaunty cap, Eton collar and silk cravat. He had taken leave of dental school at Penn and following his athletic triumphs declared that he had run his last race and would devote himself 'to something more serious'.

Hardly that: he became an itinerant track coach, going to Germany to prepare their team for the Berlin Games of 1916 – which in the event were cancelled – and then to Cuba.

The nearest challenge to Kraenzlein as individual star of the Games came from Ray Ewry (USA), whose supremacy lay in a technique unattempted, and indeed virtually unknown, to modern performers: the standing jump. Some of his achievements remain remarkable even when considered today. He remains the all-time record holder for individual victories, with ten between 1900 and 1908 (including the unofficial intermediary Games of 1906 in Athens). In Paris, he took with ease the standing high jump (1.65m/5 ft 5in.), long jump (3.21m/10 ft 6 in.) and triple jump (10.58m/34 ft 8 in.), each time ahead of Irving Baxter, a member of the Sioux tribe and the first part-Native American competitor.

Ewry was visible proof of de Coubertin's philosophy that sport and health went hand in hand. As a child, he had suffered from rheumatic fever and had regained his strength and mobility through running and jumping. His medical history makes his performances all the more exceptional: no run-up, stationary feet flat on the ground, everything dependent on the spring of coiled muscles. Away from the track, Ewry was a far cry from the extrovert Kraenzlein – a hydraulics engineer for the New York City water department. In Paris, denied even a firm take-off platform – soggy grass instead – he won all three titles on a single day, 16 July.

The plateau of French disorganisation was achieved in the marathon. Press coverage was all but non-existent, many sports received no mention at all, and confusion regarding names and nationalities of medal winners continued for years afterwards. A case in point was Michel Theato, the winner of the marathon, supposedly French, but actually born in Luxembourg, though the record books, in his case, remained unchanged. The favourite for the race was Arthur Newton of America. When he reached the finish, after covering a circuitous maze of twisting Paris streets, he believed himself the winner – only to discover that three Frenchmen and a Swede had finished ahead of him. Newton claimed he had taken the lead halfway through the race and thereafter had not been passed by any other runner, and that he had indeed passed Theato on the way. Because of scheduling errors and maladministration, the course had been obstructed at several points, proper marshalling was non-existent and, if the truth be told, there was little proof of exactly which course every runner had run. Theato, a baker's delivery boy, knew some of the backstreets better than any taxi driver and was presumed by rivals to have taken advantage of convenient and undetected shortcuts. How else could he have finished, in the 90°F (32°C) heat, more than an hour in front of the widely heralded Newton? One of the other Frenchmen, Emile Champion, also presumably knew the fast route, because he finished only four and a half minutes behind Theato's 2 hrs 59 mins 45 secs. Dick Grant of America, who finished sixth, attempted a lawsuit against the IOC, claiming to have been run over by a cyclist when about to overtake Theato – who remained unaware for some years that he had won an Olympic title.

Emile Champion (FRA) was runner-up in a chaotic marathon, allegedly knowing a faster route than some of the others. (© IOC)

In spite of minority participation by Britain, never mind the proximity of the event, the 800 and 1,500m titles from Athens were retained by Alfred Tysoe and Charles Bennett respectively, the latter, a railway engine driver, in a world record of 4:06.2, a couple of strides ahead of Henri Deloge of France. The Americans took 17 of the 23 track and field titles. With 10.8 in a preliminary heat of the 100m, Frank Jarvis of Princeton became the first to run under 11 seconds in the Olympics: exceptional because the Americans were running on grass for the first time. Tewksbury, runner-up to Jarvis (11.0) in the final, had equalled Jarvis's record in his semi-final. The favourite,

Arthur Duffey of Georgetown University, collapsed halfway in the final with a torn hamstring. Two years later, Duffey was to run 100 yards in 9.6 seconds, a world record that would last 24 years.* Because of haphazard organisation there were few spectators: nearly fewer still when discus throwers, including the defending champion Garrett, repeatedly hurled the implement into the crowd, the eventual winner being Rudolph Bauer of Hungary. Unsurprisingly, the hammer, staged between an avenue of trees, regularly got caught in the branches, Americans taking the first three places. Characteristic of the chaos was the pole vault: changed from Sunday to Monday to enable Americans to take part, then changed back again during their absence at church and nonetheless won by another American – Baxter. Following further protests, the event was re-staged on the Monday, this time to be won by American Dan Horton, a church attendee, who was declared fresh Olympic champion. A few days later, however, the French changed their minds yet again, declared Baxter re-instated as champion and offered Horton a compensation prize of an umbrella.

To add to all the confusion, the French staged events for non-amateurs, with victory prize money of 250 French francs. Perhaps most bizarre of all incidents in these Games was that of the pairs rowing final. Hermanus Brockmann, cox to the Dutch crew in the heats, was thought to be too heavy and was replaced, when winning the final, by an unknown French boy of ten or younger, considered to have been the youngest ever competitor. The gymnastics was dominated by Sweden; the fencing, lasting more than five weeks, was intolerably haphazard, with no information regarding venues and competitors arriving to find no opponents. There was no boxing, wrestling or weightlifting. Although an alleged four million people passed through the turnstiles of the exhibition, there were estimated to be never more than a thousand spectators at any Olympic event.

At the conclusion of what had been, by any estimation, the most dismal celebration of de Coubertin's idealistic objectives, the overriding element to emerge was an American identification of national superiority with Olympic victory, never mind the conflict of that attitude with de Coubertin's perception of Olympism: of not conquering but of fighting well.

---

*At that time Great Britain and the US raced domestically at imperial distances, not metric. Thus, 100m = 109+ yards; 200m and 220 yards are approximately equal; also 400m = 440 yards, the latter being one lap of the old mile track. Four metric laps = 1,600m, therefore the 1,500m race starts 100m round the first bend.

CHAPTER VI

American Farce

James E. Sullivan, secretary, US Amateur Athletic Union

'*America must be given the absolute credit of carrying to a success these Games, the like of which will never again be equalled until the Olympic Games are brought back to America, as America has set a standard that certainly will be hard for other countries to follow. The Department of Physical Culture was notified that it was the desire of the IOC that all sports that were to be given under the auspices of the Louisiana Purchase Exposition must bear the name "Olympic". The different governing bodies of America appreciated the great good that the Games would do to all organised amateur sport in America and cooperated cheerfully toward making the year's sports a gigantic success.*

Owing to the conditions in America, particularly for athletics, and the advanced stage we are now in, the Games were held for many classes . . . We have had in St Louis under the Olympic banner handicap athletics meets, inter-scholastic meets, Turners' mass exercises, baseball, gymnastics, lacrosse, swimming, basketball, one of the best rowing regattas ever contested, bicycle championships, roque tounaments, fencing, a special week for the Olympic YMCA championships, tennis, golf, archery, wrestling, boxing, as well as the Olympic Games that decided the world's championships at track and field sports.

The Department received over 4,000 entries for the Games, and when we include the team competitions and mass exercises, the number that participated during the year was close to 9,000. The Olympic Games, [track and field only] *from 29 August to 3 September brought together in the stadium the greatest athletes in the world. Never before in America or any other country were such contests witnessed. When one looks over the list of winners and then the list of eligible men, there are perhaps two men living today who were not in the stadium who could have won Olympic honours . . . The results of the Olympic Games proved conclusively what has often been claimed: that the colleges of America will furnish the champion athletes of the future.*' (From *Spalding's Official Athletic Almanac*)
(Photograph © IOC)

James Sullivan should have been a Hollywood publicity agent. The long-running conflict that Pierre de Coubertin faced between ideology and reality, between his vision for the future and that of his contemporaries at home and abroad, was to persist long after the fragmented affair that passed for an Olympic Games in Paris. Indeed, many of the mistakes of 1900, worst of all involvement with a commercial exposition, were to plague the third Olympic Games. It seemed that the Frenchman's sporting altruism was damned. Also exposed was the extent to which this benevolent, aristocratic, liberal philosopher was out of his depth when it came to handling the private agendas and mean objectives and envies of the majority, who lacked or indeed scorned his sense of history, past and future. It was cruel for de Coubertin that, having gained such admiration for American enterprise and progress, his advocacy of the US as third hosts was to be so wretchedly betrayed. Only the man's remarkable perseverance, and the loyalty of a handful of disciples in Britain, Sweden, Germany and Czechoslovakia, were to sustain his sporting bequest to mankind.

The idea of taking the Games to America had been there since the inaugural Congress at the Sorbonne, with de Coubertin's affection for the New World implanted prior to that. He had returned to the United States in 1893 to attend Chicago's Columbian Exposition as an official representative of the French Ministry of Education, following which he had visited San Francisco and New Orleans before spending three weeks at Princeton University. Professor Sloane, his host, arranged a dinner party in New York for American sports administrators to hear de Coubertin speak about his theories and objective. They were largely unimpressed: particularly James E. Sullivan, secretary of the Amateur Athletic Union.

Sullivan and de Coubertin took an immediate dislike to each other, Sullivan exhibiting that element of national introspection and gross self-confidence that was to characterise some of America's less happy international decisions throughout the coming century. Sullivan, also head of the US Department of Physical Culture, was to work at the US pavilion at the World Fair in Paris, at which time he conceived the idea of extending, independently, an 'Olympic Games' at the Buffalo Exposition of 1901. He was a competent administrator, adroit at public relations, and was motivated by the shambles in Paris. Towards

James Sullivan (second from right), egocentric chairman of the third Games, with his organising committee. (© IOC)

One of a few benefits of a commercialised Games: modern mobilisation of transport for the judges. Rear: Hugh MacGrath, George Hench; front: A.E. Johnson, Charles Lucas. (© IOC)

the end of 1900, he mounted a campaign of criticism against de Coubertin, finding an echo among some of the international sports federations and de Coubertin's enemies in France. Sullivan the commoner denounced de Coubertin the aristocrat when stating: 'The Baron or his associates have no longer any power to name the place at which Olympic Games or international athletics events of any character shall be held.'

In November 1900, the *New York Sun* prematurely informed its readers that the Games of 1904 would be held in Chicago, and interest in the burgeoning Midwest city was further heightened by an article in the *Chicago Tribune* the following May. So much so that William Harper, president of the University of Chicago, formed a committee, chaired by lawyer Henry J. Furber, to study the question of bidding for the Games. However, St Louis, with government-backed rescheduling, from 1903 to 1904, of its Centenary Exposition in celebration of the Louisiana Purchase, was lurking as a rival alternative.

The IOC were delighted to find themselves with two potential host candidates. At its fourth Session, staged in Paris in May 1901, the IOC, encouraged by de Coubertin, unanimously voted in favour of Chicago. Sloane, who by existing regulations would have become IOC President with the election of an American city, prior to the vote had persuaded de Coubertin to accept the presidency for a further ten years to consolidate the still fragile Olympic Movement.

A thirst for the Games by American cities, however far their concept might stray from de Coubertin's, was symptomatic of the extraordinary rate of development and accompanying wealth of the country during what was referred to as the 'Age of Optimism'. In the 35 years since the end of the Civil War, America had become a massive industrial power, domestically and internationally. It may seem trifling today, but there were already 8,000 registered automobiles at the dawn of the internal combustion engine. There was, moreover, that insatiable get-up-and-go attitude that has characterised the nature of a nation born of immigrant peoples, often persecuted refugees, who possess the will to make a better life. We do not yet know, but maybe there is a gene that actually contains this will-power, an inherited belief that America and Americans have some inalienable power to do anything they set their minds to do. Without real justification, they believed at the beginning of the

twentieth century that it was their right to host the Olympic Games, thereby to add another page to mounting pride in their pervasive achievements. Chicago, with a population of more than a million, was to a degree the heart of industrial America, a view that was supported in their Olympic bid by President Theodore Roosevelt – a President who, for some, was disarmingly preoccupied with sport as opposed to political priorities.

Pride was no less evident in the southern Midwest. The acquisition in 1803 of 2,000,000,000 square kilometres (800,000 square miles) of French territory, for which President Thomas Jefferson paid Napoleon I a bargain $15 million, had become the jewel of the south, notwithstanding the outcome of the Civil War. Although the cotton capital of America did not send a representative to Paris for the IOC Session, an awareness quickly developed that hosting an Olympic Games would be an added attraction to their Exposition and that if Chicago would not relinquish their hosting of the event, then St Louis would create its own rival sports festival.

St Louis, Missouri, nestling in the bowl of the Mississippi River, was then the fourth-largest city in the United States. It was now on a collision course with Chicago. De Coubertin had been adamantly opposed to allowing the Games once more to become involved in a trade fair, and Chicago's promise of sponsorship – there is nothing new in life! – of $200,000 from local business had made the northern city by far the more attractive. A letter of support from Roosevelt in August 1902 seemed to underline the wisdom of the IOC's decision. Yet there was uneasy equilibrium. Furber, heading Chicago's 'Olympic Games Association', was becoming disenchanted by the size of the task, while Sullivan was beginning to sense his own opportunity for self-promotion by siding with the opposition from St Louis. In October 1902, the St Louis officials requested a meeting with Furber to place before him their position. The IOC was now in a quandary. They could not afford to have St Louis staging a rival unauthorised event, with the possibility that Chicago might be a financial failure, nor did they wish to become subsidiary to the Louisiana Exposition; never mind that it could offer competitors larger souvenir prizes and by now had the express support of Roosevelt, switching horses. The worst prospect was for Chicago to cancel their event at the last minute and for there to be no Games. The IOC met informally again in

Paris in December 1902, with de Coubertin now convinced that St Louis was the less harmful of two unattractive choices, and by a vote of fourteen to two, with five abstentions (a partial postal vote), the Games were switched to St Louis. Equally reluctantly, de Coubertin wrote to Walter Liginger, president of the Amateur Athletic Union, suggesting that Sullivan should oversee the administration.

This was the best of a bad job and for de Coubertin close to humiliation: so much so that he decided not to attend this staging of his reinvented festival. Initially, he announced in March 1904 that he would be present at the closing ceremony in November and was awaiting transport facilities and

Ferenc Kemeny (standing, centre), who kept de Coubertin informed of events in St Louis, seen here with Hungarian NOC committee members and, sitting, competitors Géza Kiss and Zóltán Halmay. (© IOC)

documents, but instead he and his family spent a vacation in Bayreuth. His disenchantment temporarily seemed absolute. No Session was held in St Louis and the IOC was represented only by Kemeny of Hungary and Gebhardt of Germany. A satisfactory explanation of de Coubertin's absence was never given. It surely cannot have been on account of travel, to which he was accustomed, though the distance certainly had an effect on many Europeans, who also had an unfamiliar notion of what was ignorantly still regarded as the 'Wild West'. Yet there were other factors. There was as yet little idea of competitors being organised under the umbrella of a national team, the club ethic was still paramount – most notably in the United States. The outcome was that the St Louis event was almost exclusively American. A mere 13 nations were represented and of the 687 competitors 432 were Americans. In a way, however unconventionally by IOC principles, Sullivan's administration was effective. He staged more than 40 different events, Olympic or otherwise, and by his own count attracted nearly 10,000 participants. Many events, of course, such as lacrosse, bore no relation to the Olympic Games.

If the manner of the realisation of the Games of 1904 was regrettable, the most reprehensible act was the staging of what were termed the 'Anthropology Days' – events for so-called 'primitive' peoples variously drawn from Indian tribes, the Cocopas from Mexico, Ainus from Japan, Pygmies from Africa, Moros from Philippines, Turks and Patagonians. This grotesque exhibition of aboriginies was a blight upon American social history, justified by Sullivan as a scientific demonstration of the ability of alleged savages. De Coubertin, kept informed of events by Kemeny, was appalled. 'That outrageous charade will lose any appeal when black, red and yellow men learn to run, jump and throw, and leave the white men behind them,' he observed with rare prescience.

With there being no Session at St Louis, the sixth Session was held in a banqueting suite at the Mansion House in London in June, put at the disposal of the IOC by the Lord Mayor and under the patronage of King Edward VII. With the withdrawal by Berlin of its candidature, Rome was elected as host for the Games of 1908. That would involve another about-turn.

CHAPTER VII

St Louis (III) 1904

Emil Breitkreutz of America, Olympic 800m bronze medal winner

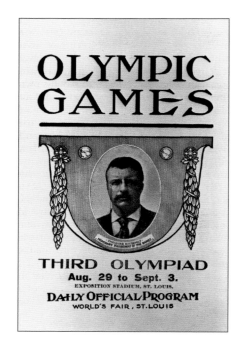

'*Although "Meet me in St Louis" may have become a popular musical injunction, as a clarion call to the world's athletes in 1904 it fell flat. In Europe, distance lent no enchantment to the Olympic view. Of the few foreign teams' competitors, most could be counted on the fingers of one hand, though the two-man throwing contingent from Greece was supplemented by ten Hellenic hopefuls from the local Greek community, who entered for the marathon in an attempt to repeat the 1896 victory of their compatriot, Spyridon Louis. Also in the marathon were two Africans, who worked at one of the concessions of the Louisiana Purchase Exposition, or "World's Fair". This commercial get-together was the peg on which the Games were hung, but, as in Paris in 1900, sport and business did not prove ideal running mates. The Olympic Games were once again relegated to the status of a trade-fair sideshow. They were held in the grounds of the Exhibition site and I can vouch for the consequent conflict of interests. Most of the athletes had never been near a world's fair and naturally wanted to see the sights. Take my own case. As an engineering student, I was keenly interested in the engineering exhibits and must admit that these attracted me more than some of the Olympic tussles.*

The night before my 800m race I felt in no condition to run. Shortly after reaching St Louis with the Milwaukee AC team, I was taken ill with stomach trouble. I lost about 4 lb in weight and on the eve of the race felt distinctly groggy. By the next afternoon, however, I had recovered and took my place with about a dozen others at the starting line on the back stretch of the track, which was three laps to the mile. I always used the crouch start, and as I liked to avoid the jams on the first bend I shot into the lead. I was ahead at 400 metres in 53 seconds – much too fast for my condition – and as we entered the home straight I was still in front. Then I heard the cheers for Lightbody. That was the last I remember until I came to, after collapsing, while being led off the track. I learned that Lightbody had won in 1:56 – the first Olympic time under two minutes – but I was in no mood to care. For the next few hours I had a blinding headache and it was not until 8 p.m. that I tottered from the dressing-room. There are conflicting records of the times for second and third places. Having blacked out near the tape, I cannot state for certain how I finished, but one photograph shows Howard Valentine, from New York AC, about five yards behind Lightbody, with myself about a yard further back. Such a protracted programme was bound to cause a flagging of interest in the Olympic section of the Fair. An international flavour in competition was completely lacking.' (Adapted from *The Olympic Games, 1904*, by Charles J.P. Lucas) (Olympic Poster © IOC)

For the third time, a modern Olympic Games was a near disaster, its reputation in terms of performance rescued only by a small handful of champions. Evidence that the rest of the world did not care is there in some reported figures: 525 of the 687 competitors were American-based, 41 were from Canada, the US won 80 of the 99 gold medals contested and 242 of the 279 medal total. Canada, Germany, Hungary, Austria, Britain, Greece, Switzerland, France and Cuba were the only other countries to win medals. The Games were effectively a college or club tournament, with New York AC beating Chicago AA for the 'track and field team title', a points table being published. All the Americans wore the uniforms of their club rather than their country. Some

outstanding American champions from eastern states did not bother to attend.

Event discipline was loose, to say the least. In the 400m track race there were no heats, 13 competing in the final. The track measured a third of a mile and only two track and field events were won by non-Americans: Etienne Desmarteau of Canada in the now discontinued weight throw and Irishman Tom Kiely in the all-round ten events, the first decathlon. Rowing was staged over a course which included a turn; swimming was competed over imperial distances.

Lifting the Games to a level of genuine accomplishment was James Davies Lightbody from Chicago, a mere 18 years old, of Scottish descent, originally a sprinter but here dominant in the

Event definitions at St Louis were loose. Was Julius Lenhart of Austria, gymnastics champion in team and individual combined exercises, more body-builder than athlete? (© IOC)

middle-distance track events. On 29 August, he won the steeplechase, 2,590m, in 7:39.6; on 1 September, the 800m in 1:56; and on 3 September, the 1,500 m in 4:05.4, a world record surpassing that of Charles Bennett of Britain in Paris four years earlier. Lightbody gained a silver medal with Chicago behind New York in the only ever four-mile team race.

Prior to his victory, in no way was he considered to be a steeplechaser, never previously having run more than two miles in any event. Against him were Bernard Gallagher of Kansas, a former intercollegiate two-mile champion, and Arthur Newton of New York, due to run in the marathon, plus the Irish champion John Daly. At the end of the first lap, Daly led by 10 yards, with Lightbody another 20 yards behind the trailing pack. On the second lap, Daly increased his lead to 40 yards, but the only one wholly to clear the water jump was Lightbody. Over the fourth and fifth laps, Daly's lead was steadily cut back and Lightbody, with easy stride, moved to the front ahead of Newton to win by 30 yards.

For the 800m, in which there were 13 starters, track and weather conditions were ideal. The favourites were Johannes Runge of Germany, with a previous fast time, and Howard Valentine, the US champion, with Peter Deer, a Canadian Indian, also highly rated. Once again, few gave Lightbody a chance. The early leader was Harvey Cohn, of Greater New York Irish AC, followed by Emil Breitkreutz and Runge. At the back, loping along as though the distance was much longer, came Lightbody. Cohn continued to set the early pace and was challenged by William Verner. At the halfway mark these two

had been overtaken by Breitkreutz and Runge. Lightbody did not begin to make his effort until the last 200 metres, his steady long stride contrasting with the shorter action of the rest. Only a few yards separated the four leading runners as they made for the tape, with the crowd rising to its feet. Over the final 30 yards, his hands clenched and face a picture of determination, Lightbody came through to win by barely a stride in an Olympic record of 1:56.0, while behind him Valentine and Breitkreutz desperately fought for the silver medal.

The conclusion of Lightbody's triumph, the 1,500m, was no less stylish and emphatic. The field included many of the competitors from the 800m. Together with his Chicago colleagues, Verner and Lacey Hearn, he toyed with the field. Once more he waited until the end of the final back straight before making his move to win in world record time, Verner and Hearn taking silver and bronze. Runge could manage only fifth place.

The recording of winners, medals and times at St Louis was entirely erratic. A major omission was that of Tom Kiely of Ireland, comfortable winner of the all-round event. He received his gold medal, still held by his family in Ireland, but the result was not listed officially in Olympic records until intervention in 1954 by Ferenc Mezö of Hungary. The 35-year-old Kiely had apparently been offered a free trip to St Louis to represent Britain – Ireland then having no team – but had chosen to pay his own way. Five years earlier Kiely had briefly held the world record for the hammer. Uniquely, this first staging of what would be called the decathlon, took place in a single day. In St Louis, the ten events included, rather than the 400m and 1,500m, an 800-yard walk and the mile. Kiely won three of the events to defeat Adam Gunn of the US by 129 points (6,036 to 5,907).

There were three other triple winners in what was effectively an American festival. Archie Hahn of Milwaukee took the 60m in 7.0, the 100m in 11.0 and the 200m in 21.6, an Olympic record. In the latter, Nathaniel Cartmell, William Hogenson and Fay Moulton all false started and under the rules of the day were penalised with a two-yard handicap. Hahn won easily by three yards. Harry Hillman dominated the 400m, a somewhat chaotic final run without lanes over one and a quarter laps, in an Olympic record of 49.2. He then took the 200m low-hurdles in 24.6 and the 400m hurdles in 53.0. He was denied a world record in the latter because he knocked over one hurdle and the hurdles were below standard height. In third place George Poage, who had come sixth in the 400m flat, became the first black Olympic medal winner.

Memories of the marathon lingered, though for the wrong reasons. In the intense heat, William Garcia, a local runner, suffered a cerebral haemorrhage, was discovered motionless beside the road, and nearly died. Course supervision was negligible, some runners being pursued into fields by stray dogs. No water was available until 12 miles from the finish. Most bizarre of the entries was a 5 ft Cuban postman, Felix Carvajal, who raised money for the journey by passing round the hat in Havana. Nonetheless, he is said to have arrived penniless, having gambled his takings while he hitch-hiked to St Louis, arriving only just in time for the start – which was delayed while somebody cut off his trousers to the knees. Two black Africans, Lentauw and Yamasani, Zulus who were part of the Boer War exhibit at the Fair, were entered, as were the three previous years' winners of the Boston Marathon, John Lordon, Michael Spring and Thomas Hicks. The last was to prove the winner – though by roundabout and unconventional means, amid which Carvajal provided coincidental entertainment, chatting to spectators, pausing to pick an apple or two and then having to stop for stomach cramps to subside.

Myer Prinstein (USA) gains consolation in the long jump, following controversial defeat four years earlier. (© IOC)

Many of the 31 starters were overcome by the heat and the dust thrown up by the accompanying automobiles – a comparatively recent invention – of judges and friends following on unmade roads. After ten miles or so, Fred Lorz (USA) obtained a lift in a truck until the truck broke down. He then continued to run, arrived first in the stadium and was acclaimed and congratulated by President Roosevelt. The medal ceremony was already under way when the British-born Hicks tottered into the stadium. Seven miles from the finish, Hicks, reduced almost to a walk along with leaders Sam Mellor and Arthur Newton, had been given a bracing drink of cognac, strychnine and eggs. From there on, he continued in the lead, to cross the line in 3:28:53. Now the hoax pulled by Lorz became apparent. He was banned for life, though was competing again after only a year, winning the Boston Marathon the following year, officialdom having relented. Hicks' winning time was the worst in Olympic history.

Myer Prinstein had the belated satisfaction, following the controversy in Paris, of winning the long jump and also the triple jump, though in the absence of the world record holder, Peter O'Connor of Ireland, in the former. Prinstein also finished fifth in both 60m and 400m. Ray Ewry repeated his three victories of Paris in the standing jumps. The most gold medals of these Games, five, were won by Anton Heida (USA), in gymnastics, together with one silver. Another remarkable achievement in gymnastics was made by George Eyser, who won several medals even though one of his legs had been amputated, his wooden leg thumping noisily.

The swimming pool, an asymmetric lake used in the Fair, was without lanes, and starting signals were given from a raft, which occasionally sank. Compared with other sports, it was internationally represented, the leading figures being Zóltán Halmay of Hungary and Emil Rausch of Germany, each winning two golds; Rausch also took a bronze.

The 18-year-old James Lightbody (USA), one of the few to give St Louis distinction, with his triple victories at 800m, 1,500m – a world record – and, in his first ever race, the steeplechase. (© IOC)

CHAPTER VIII

Back to Athens, on to London

The Rev. Robert S. de Courcy-Laffan of Britain, IOC member, 1897–1927

'It's inevitable that in work like this [organising a Games] *many mistakes should be made, that there should have been many moments when it was impossible to satisfy the demands of everyone . . . the work could not possibly have been done unless we had met from our foreign colleagues a great measure of tolerance and forbearance and readiness to excuse all manner of shortcomings. It has been because they have so nobly and disinterestedly worked with us in the organisation that these Games have attained the success which they have. Let me say to our foreign visitors that we hope and intend, that when your turn comes to organise an Olympic Games, to try to repay you the kindness and courtesy which you have shown to us.*

Do not let us forget that these Olympic Games in London are only an episode in a great Movement and a great life. The first revival took place at Athens in 1896. What is 12 years in the life of a Movement that sets before it those great ideals: of perfect physical development, of a new humanity, the spreading all over the world of that spirit of sport which is the spirit of the truest chivalry, and the drawing together of all the nations of the Earth in the bonds of peace and mutual amity? You cannot expect that an ideal such as that can be carried out in a year or in a decade or possibly even a century. You are at the beginning of one of those world movements which is going to develop itself long after those of us who are here have departed. You have seen the beginning of something of which no man can foresee the ultimate results.

I am well aware that there are those who will laugh at this ideal. I should have laughed at it myself 12 years ago. I came to the Olympic Movement prepared to scoff, and I remain to admire, and I hope I shall remain to work . . . I must warn those who organise future Olympiads that they must be prepared for times of trial.' (From an address to the concluding banquet of the 1908 Games in London) (Photograph © IOC)

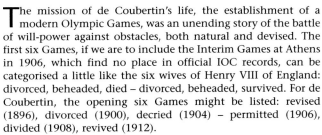

The mission of de Coubertin's life, the establishment of a modern Olympic Games, was an unending story of the battle of will-power against obstacles, both natural and devised. The first six Games, if we are to include the Interim Games at Athens in 1906, which find no place in official IOC records, can be categorised a little like the six wives of Henry VIII of England: divorced, beheaded, died – divorced, beheaded, survived. For de Coubertin, the opening six Games might be listed: revised (1896), divorced (1900), decried (1904) – permitted (1906), divided (1908), revived (1912).

When the Greeks had sensed that what they came to regard, in 1896, as their *own* Olympics were slipping from their grasp, they had passed a law decreeing that every four years they would organise an Interim Games. With the war against Turkey concluded, the Greeks were agitating, at the Session in Brussels in 1905, for such a Games to take place the following year, supported in their aim by Crown Prince Constantine.

This presented de Coubertin with a dilemma. While he recognised the historic heritage of Greece, he remained adamant that the Games should travel the globe. Reluctantly, he had shown some sympathy towards the Athens plan at the Session

in Paris four years earlier and now momentum was gathering behind the Greeks. With his confidence in the long-term future of the IOC strengthened by the creation of the British Olympic Association, under the direction of de Courcy-Laffan, and with the satisfactory conclusion of differences with Germany, de Coubertin ceded to the wish of the Greeks, the IOC sanctioning the title for 1906 of 'Athens International Olympic Games'.

Against the background of disregard exhibited towards him by the Greeks in 1896, it was unsurprising that de Coubertin was absent from the event in 1906, acknowledging that they were formally sanctioned but preferring to attend instead an 'Olympic Arts Exhibition' in Paris. Some members of the IOC did visit the Games in Athens and were rumoured to have considered voting de Coubertin out of office. Their suggestion of making Constantine honorary President of the IOC, to his embarrassment, was swiftly vetoed by de Coubertin, who also ensured that all subsequent references to the Games of 1906 were titled 'unofficial'.

The Greeks attempted to organise Interim Games for 1910 and 1914, and indeed those for 1914 appeared as scheduled in de Coubertin's *Review Olympique*, with William Sloane, IOC founder member from America, promising to send a team. These Games never occurred. Those of 1906 were relatively successful, attracting big crowds and performances of international calibre; as much was admitted in the first edition of de Coubertin's memoirs. Yet, while he was generous towards Demetrius Vikelas, the inaugural IOC President, for his passionate support of the Greek cause and the opening Games, he strangely avoided acknowledgement of the earlier revival of interest in Olympic Games by Evangelis Zappas and the fact that there had been quasi-Games organised by Zappas prior to 1896. When he wished, de Coubertin could be a selective historian.

The Interim Games, from 22 April to 2 May, attracted 826 competitors, including 6 women, from 20 countries. For the first time there was an official American team – as opposed to a random collegiate team – a US Olympic committee having been established two years earlier; and also for the first time a team from Finland, for whom Verner Järvinen won the first of his country's many gold medals in the Greek-styled discus. A rare double victory was that of the American Paul Pilgrim, a member of the winning New York AC relay team in St Louis, who won the 400m and 800m, a feat not matched for the next 70 years until Alberto Juantorena did likewise in Montreal. For the hosts, the event was a major success. Their competitors came third in the medal rankings behind France and the United States, just ahead of Great Britain and Italy. Though relegated to the sidelines of official records, the Greeks had done far more to enhance the durability of the IOC and the Olympic Games in 1906 than they had at the inaugural Games of 1896; a fact quietly admitted by some of de Coubertin's colleagues.

Whatever the opinions regarding Athens 1906, it was during these Games that Italy revealed that Rome would be unable to

The Interim Games, though unrecognised by the IOC, had some distinguished performances, not least by standing jumper Ray Ewry (USA), multiple champion from Paris and St Louis. (© IOC)

be host in 1908 as the country had been temporarily impoverished by the eruption of Vesuvius. Britain, with its newly created NOC, was invited to step into the breach. Though there were only two years remaining in hand, Lord Desborough accepted the task on behalf of the British Olympic Association. For the third time, the Games would coincide with a major trade fair; the difference between London and the previous near-disasters in Paris and St Louis was that the organisers of the scheduled Franco-British Exhibition were powerful advocates of the Olympic Movement and intended to make the Games the centrepiece of the festival.

The economic success of the Games was, therefore, not a factor for the city, and indeed the British organising committee were opposed to any idea of government or municipal assistance. Britain at the start of the twentieth century was proud of its already well-established reputation for the organisation of prominent sporting events: the Derby horse race, Henley Royal Regatta, the FA Cup final and the All-England (Wimbledon) Tennis Championships. It was a valuable bonus when the Exhibition offered to provide a new main stadium, to be built at Shepherd's Bush, later known as the White City Stadium, seating 68,000 people.

The preparatory work for the Games was daunting, there being 21 separate competitions. Apart from physical labour, books of separate rules needed to be translated into French and German, the different events scheduled, the definition of amateurism for each sport to be clarified and, for the British, the complicated transfer of measurement to the metric system from the imperial. Nonetheless, satisfactory progress had been made by the time of the IOC Session at The Hague in May 1907. Here it was decided that champions should be awarded a gold medal and, controversially, that judging should be exclusively under British management with the power to appoint foreign assistants where it was thought necessary.

This step was supported by de Coubertin – who had just been re-elected as President for ten years – though the British in fact fell so far short of their perceived tradition of impartiality that de Coubertin came to be embarrassed by the decision. It was taken in spite of the fact that by now, only 11 years after the inaugural Games, the individual federations were demanding the creation of a unifying international council for the standardisation of rules and judging. De Coubertin had thought this dangerous, stating:

Scenic panorama at Henley, symbolic of Britain's sports organisation. (© IOC)

'Sports federations have developed from utilitarianism to domination, from the role of secretary to that of policeman. They care less to encourage than to order and forbid. To make their power felt seems to be their leaders' last word.'

There was also no doubting de Coubertin's influence regarding the position of women in sport. At the Session in Brussels in 1905, 'Sports for women' was on the agenda, but de Coubertin had the item postponed 'for another more suitable occasion'. At The Hague, their involvement must have been debated, as it was agreed that figure skating should be included in the programme for London. At the Berlin Session of 1909, when Viktor Balck proposed a standard programme for future Games, there was not a word concerning women, though a year later it was agreed to include women's gymnastics, tennis and swimming for Stockholm in 1912.

As an alternative site to Rome, there was no better time for London to be host. Lord Desborough, the organising chairman, personified the halcyon Edwardian era. The reign of King Edward VII, from the death of Queen Victoria in 1901 to his own in 1910, and the remaining years before the horrors of the First World War were regarded as the golden age of Britain: an era of peace, wealth and unrivalled style at that time. The country basked under the leadership of the new Liberal Prime Minister, Herbert Asquith, and of a King who delighted his subjects by returning the monarchy to Buckingham Palace in London, instead of the more remote retreats of his mother. In every sense, London was a reassuring setting for the 21 visiting national teams that would assemble.

In spite of this background of elegance and wealth, the Games were to encounter a flood, almost literally, of difficulties. The weather was consistently miserable, apart from the day of the marathon when it was baking hot. The All-England Club, hosting the tennis event at Wimbledon, had to transfer play indoors. Ticket prices were pitched too high, so that attendances were often poor, forcing the organisers to reduce the cost of

admission to the main stadium; nationalism clouded the opening ceremony; and rampant prejudice by British judging officials created a rift between the hosts and the Americans which was to last long afterwards.

Such was the King's interest that he remained for two hours following the opening ceremony to observe some of the early events. In the march-past of the national teams, Ralph Rose, a shot putter and the American flag-bearer, had declined to dip the Stars and Stripes to the King, in protest at the absence of the Stars and Stripes from among the flags flying around the stadium. Also missing was the Swedish flag – causing some Swedes to decide to quit the Games – and that of Finland, the Russian Ambassador having demanded that the Finns should march behind the flag of the Tsarist regime. (This the Finns refused to do four years later in Stockholm, short-stepping as they entered the stadium, so that there was a pronounced gap between them and the Russians.) On the first Sunday, at a service in St Paul's Cathedral, the Bishop of Pennsylvania's sermon contained a phrase that became symbolic of the Games: 'What is important in these Olympic Games is not so much to

Enthusiastic royal patronage. Queen Alexandra presents a consolation trophy to disqualified marathon winner, Dorando Pietri (ITA). (© IOC)

Lord Desborough of Taplow (right), London's organising chairman, together with Albert, Prince of Wales, and his tutor Mr Hansell. (© IOC)

win as to take part.' This has been inaccurately attributed to de Coubertin, who in fact merely expanded upon it when speaking at a reception given by the Liberal government, when he said: 'What is important in life is not victory but the battle. What matters is not to have won, but to have fought well.' This fundamental ethic of the Games, relevant to the thousands who do take part as opposed to the handful who are champions, has been widely mocked by those who regard victory as everything; not least the Americans initially, but by the end of the twentieth century by many others too.

Though the Games of London had their divisions, de Coubertin considered they had substantially directed his ideological venture down the right road. The British had, so to speak, reinvented the wheel for sports administration, helping to raise the Olympic Games above other international events, even if henceforth there would need to be serious reappraisal of the regulations for judging and scoring events.

CHAPTER IX

London (IV) 1908

Dorando Pietri of Italy, disqualified Olympic marathon hero

'*I knew that I had formidable adversaries but I didn't let that put me off. I was going to run my race without worrying about other people's tactics. I relied a lot on my lungpower and can assure you that when I attack the uphill parts of a course, I seem to have four lungs and not two. It was predicted I would lose – the articles in the newspapers and all the stories about the Americans had told me that, but I wanted to prove myself. I was determined that the people who had selected me for this Olympiad would not regret their choice . . .*

After about 16 kilometres, two Englishmen, Price and Lord, were in the lead, with me and Charles Hefferon of South Africa about 50 metres back. By 32 kilometres [20 miles], Hefferon and I had gone into the lead. When I passed Hefferon after 40 kilometres, nearing the finish, he looked at me with such a sad expression and then gave up the challenge. Now I was first. I could have slowed down but I was seized by a fury to go ever faster. I pushed myself until I had no one else challenging me. With the road ahead of me clear, I could not put a brake on myself. The runners passed between lines of spectators on both sides. In my frenzy I could not see them, but I heard them. I looked straight in front to search for something that I could not yet see because the road made a lot of turns. Suddenly, after another bend, my heart gave a jump. I saw a grey mass in front that seemed a bastion with the bridge beflagged. It was the stadium. And after that, I remember little . . .

Later I discovered that no one had ever run a marathon so fast before. Hayes of America, who was six months younger, took half a minute longer. Only 27 of the runners, less than half of those who had started, managed to finish. It seems that Queen Alexandra, who had taken great interest in the race, was moved by my misfortune, because the following day she presented me with an inscribed silver cup, "In remembrance of the marathon race from Windsor to the stadium, 24 July 1908. From Queen Alexandra."' (From newspaper interviews provided by the Italian National Olympic Committee) (Photograph © IOC)

By one of those quirks of sporting history it was in 1908 that the distance of the marathon race was determined in a bizarre manner. Queen Alexandra, who took close interest in the Games, requested that the race should begin beneath the windows of the royal nursery in Windsor Castle grounds. A course of approximately 26 miles was laid out, but, with a final circumference of the track inside the stadium, the exact distance became 26 miles 385 yards, or 42.195km. Thus it remained, becoming formally established internationally by the then International Amateur Athletics Federation (IAAF) 16 years later.

In London, an immense crowd, more than a quarter of a million people, assembled along the course, with an estimated 90,000 in a stadium designed to accommodate little more than two-thirds that number. The weather, quixotically, was hot and humid. A mile or so after the halfway stage, two men were well ahead of the field, effectively unchallenged for the gold medal: the 22-year-old Dorando Pietri from Reggio, Italy, and Charles Hefferon from South Africa. The British contingent, over-eager to make their mark in front of the home crowd, had already prematurely burned off their endurance. With eight miles remaining, Hefferon led Pietri by over three minutes, and over the next two miles extended this to almost four minutes. Then Pietri began to close. Two miles from the stadium, Hefferon,

taking a drink, developed cramps and Pietri accelerated. Some way back, three Americans, John Hayes, Joseph Forshaw and Alton Welton, were making their late but well-judged move.

Ill-fated marathon winner Dorando Pietri (ITA) in confident form mid-race. (© IOC)

A mile from the stadium, Pietri overtook Hefferon, but as he entered the stadium it was evident to the huge crowd that he was a spent figure, almost unconscious. He began to circle the track in the wrong direction. Re-directed by officials, he collapsed. Many of the crowd, which included the Queen, were calling for him to be assisted, unaware that would mean disqualification. By now, another runner had arrived, not Hefferon, but Hayes, who had overtaken him at the stadium entrance. Dorando, as he would become known to one and all, continued to stagger, weaving his way along the track, intermittently collapsing. Possibly having in mind the tale of Pheidippides, alleged runner of the original marathon bringing news of victory over the Persians to Athens, at which point he fell dead to the ground, officials including a Dr Bulger, megaphone in one hand (but not, as has been reported, Sir Arthur Conan Doyle, later creator of Sherlock Holmes), part-carried Dorando across the line. The Italian flag was raised, while Hayes, all but ignored, had trotted across the line unaided. Dorando was borne away on a stretcher, the Americans lodging a protest at the assistance he had received. The protest was backed by Lord Desborough, an exemplary sportsman, and, although the race officials myopically considered that Dorando should have been declared the winner, the protest was upheld and Hayes was declared champion. Dorando was fit enough to return to the stadium the following day and was presented with his compensatory cup by the Queen. Such did Dorando's celebrity become that he and Hayes, a sales clerk at Bloomingdale's department store in New York, were invited to turn professional. They ran many subsequent races, Dorando winning the two most prominent.

An ailing Pietri is illegally assisted towards the finishing line at White City. (© IOC)

A coincidental benefit from the constant bickering that arose between the British and Americans at these Games was that newspaper stories, which on account of human nature tend to revel in disputes, spread to all corners of the globe. The worst of the rows occurred in the final of the 400m on the track. The four contestants were three Americans plus a single Briton, Lt Wyndham Halswelle, a 26 year old who had served in the Boer War. In the semi-final he had set an Olympic record of 48.4 seconds and, therefore, was the clear favourite. Yet, in a free-for-all race run without lanes, British officials were concerned about

the potential in the final for team tactics to be used by the Americans to thwart a lone rival. William Robbins leapt into the lead and was over 10 metres in front after 200 metres. Entering the home straight, he was overtaken by Halswelle and John Carpenter. When Halswelle accelerated in an attempt to pass Carpenter on the outside, the American veered to the right to obstruct him. British officials had been staged around the track and several immediately started shouting 'foul', one of them breaking the tape to prevent Carpenter doing so. John Taylor, from the University of Pennsylvania, was physically hauled off the track. For half an hour there was chaos, with Americans protesting against the disqualification of Carpenter by the Amateur Athletic Association, which had taken statements from race officials and from Halswelle. Not one American official or runner had been asked to testify. The disqualification stood and a re-run was ordered for two days later, now with strings stretched out to mark the lanes. Taylor and Robbins refused to run, so Halswelle was left to circle the track on his own in a

The first famous judging row. On the left, John Carpenter (USA), 400m winner, was disqualified by over-eager home officials, his compatriots refusing to take part in a re-run, thereby allowing Wyndham Halswelle (GBR) to run a solo victory. (both © IOC)

sedate 50 seconds while the Americans fumed on the sidelines: the only walkover in Olympic track history. Dismayed by the fracas, Halswelle retired from sport, returned to military duty and died fighting in France in 1915. The scandal, as it was viewed by the Americans, was actively instrumental in the formation four years later of the International Amateur Athletic Federation (IAAF), which, like all international federations, would take upon itself the responsibility of regularising its own sport.

Another of America's many protests was at the staging of Sunday events. Forrest Smithson, in winning the high hurdles in a world record of 15.0 – improving on Kraenzlein by a fifth of a second – allegedly carried a Bible in his left hand, though the only evidence of this gimmick was provided by a clearly contrived subsequent photograph.

Because the working classes could not afford entry prices at many events, attendances were often below capacity, though consistently good compared with the three previous Games. The standard of competition, too, was of regular international calibre; not least by the Irish, whose many medal winners would have made them a leading nation had they been competing for the country of their birth rather than Britain. In track and field, in which America led with fifteen victories, ahead of Britain with eight, Irishmen won four titles with three second places: gold medals for Robert Kerr of Canada in the 200m; John Flanagan (USA), retaining his hammer title for the second time; Tim Ahearne (GBR), winning the triple jump; and Martin Sheridan (USA) retaining the discus. Con Leahy (GBR), Dennis Horgan (GBR) and Matt McGrath (USA) took second place in the high jump, shot and hammer respectively.

Halswelle apart, the outstanding track performer was Mel Sheppard, with his double 800/1,500m victories. At the longer distance, the favourite was Harold Wilson, the world record holder with 3:59.8, but down the final straight Sheppard found reserves for a sprint which carried him to the front to win by a stride, in an Olympic record of 4:03.4. For the two-lap race, Ian Fairbairn-Crawford of Britain altruistically set an early fast pace in the hope of over-stretching Sheppard to the advantage of Theodore Just, the number one Briton. Sheppard was not to be misled, however. He ran his own race by taking the lead after 500 metres and with perfect judgement set a world record of 1:52.8, well clear of Lunghi of Italy, with Just back in fifth place and Fairbairn-Crawford failing to finish.

A champion of London unsung outside his own country of Hungary was the swimmer Zóltán Halmay, something of an all-round sportsman. He played ice hockey in winter and won championships in speed skating, but his favoured sport had always been swimming. He had competed in the Games of Paris, with two second places and a third, and at St Louis, with two victories. At the Interim Games of 1906 he had gained a first and second. For the trip to London, by now aged 27, Halmay was additionally the Hungarian team leader and this had restricted the preparations of a holder of three world records. With Hungary leading by almost ten metres in the 4 x 200m relay, victory seemed a formality with Halmay to complete the final leg. Mid-way through the last 100 metres, he was gripped with cramp and started to flounder, losing his sense of direction. Despite being in severe pain, however, and showing great will-power he managed to hold on to give Hungary second place behind Britain. With second place in the 100m freestyle, he took his Olympic tally to nine medals and may rightfully be said to have been the first swimming star of Olympic history.

At St Louis, Halmay had twice defeated Charles Daniels of America, but the tables had been reversed in 1906 and were again now in London. They became friends and when Halmay suffered serious illness following the Second World War, regular medical and food parcels from Daniels to Budapest provided succour to the ailing former champion.

Unique to London was the staging of figure skating at a summer Games: held at Prince's Skating Rink in Knightsbridge, arranged, in the tenor of the times, by the Duchess of Bedford, and scheduled in October on a rink 16m by 62m, long after other events because refrigeration could then not cope with summer temperatures. The event coincided with Russia's first appearance at a Games – with a team of seven competitors – and provided them with their first gold medal, by Nikolai Panin, who defeated two British entries.

The women's event was won by Madge Syers. Six years earlier she had caused a sensation by becoming the first woman to enter the World (Open) Championships and, shockingly,

Ray Ewry (USA) remained undefeated over three official Games in any standing jump, with a total of eight victories. (© IOC)

finishing second behind Ulrich Salchow (of technical fame); thereby causing the authorities to ban women from international competition. Syers did take part in the British championships of 1903 and 1904, though . . . defeating her husband. She was the unanimous first choice of the judges in 1908, ahead of Elsa Rendschmidt of Germany.

For Ray Ewry, the Games concluded an exceptional sequence. In three Games, he had been undefeated in any standing jump, now winning once more the high and long jumps, which together with the triple jump in 1900–04 (absent in 1908) gave him a total of eight Olympic victories. He had also two victories in the Interim Games of 1906.

If Ewry was unchallengeable, there was further American dissent in the tug-of-war event, in which they protested that British teams – which took the first three places – were wearing illegal boots with steel cleats and heels. The rules had been defined by the British Olympic Association and they rejected the American appeal, asserting that these were regulation police boots, all three teams – City of London, Liverpool and Metropolitan K Division – being police teams. The Americans, in regular street shoes, decided to compete against Liverpool but made no effort, in a show of contempt for what they regarded as unsportsmanlike behaviour. Matthew Halpin, the American team manager, then withdrew his team.

No medals were awarded in the cycling 1,000m sprint. Of the four finalists, Ben Jones and Clarence Kingsbury of Britain suffered punctures, while Maurice Schilles of France and Victor Johnson (GBR) adopted such delaying tactics, finishing outside the time limit, that the race was declared void. France made a humiliating debut in the first football tournament, entering two teams both of which were trounced by Denmark. The A team lost 17–1, Sven Neilson scoring a record 10 goals, the B team 9–0. Alberto Braglia of Italy won the first of two successive all-

John Douglas, middleweight champion, part of Britain's clean sweep of victories in boxing, rowing, sailing and tennis. (© IOC)

round gymnastic titles, while J.W.H.T. Douglas, a renowned 'stonewall' cricketer, became the only Test batsman to win an Olympic gold medal, defeating R.L. 'Snowy' Baker of Australia in the middleweight boxing division. Douglas represented England subsequently in 23 Test matches, 1911–25. Baker was a rare multiple sportsman, representing Australia in five different sports including swimming, fencing and equestrianism. Oscar and Alfred Swahn of Sweden became the first father and son to win gold medals, in shooting, while Ivan Osiier, a Danish fencer, and Norwegian yachtsman Magnus Konow, began Olympic careers, though unplaced, which continued until the next Games in London 40 years later.

The Games, in every sense, belonged to Britain, with 145 medals to 47 by the United States, though the latter had won 15 of the 27 track and field events, setting all three of the world records. The British had won every gold medal in boxing, rowing, sailing and tennis. The Americans returned home to continue their tirade of criticism, even lodging a protest 'against the British attitude towards American protests'. Severely stung by this attitude, the British replied with the formal publication of a book, *Replies to Criticisms of the Olympic Games*: the old-fashioned and traditional response to the young and boastful. James Sullivan, the US *chef-de-mission*, had claimed: 'their aim was to beat the Americans, their conduct was unsportsmanlike and unfair'. This polarisation in attitudes and temperament would continue for many years. These were the first Games in which entries were only by nations, rather than individuals; which emphasised the element of nationalism that over the next century would regularly be a cause of controversy. It certainly was this time.

Florence 'Madge' Seyers (GBR) won the British figure skating championships as the first woman entrant, aged 20, in 1920 – and was promptly banned. At the London Games she won the inaugural Olympic title and, with brother Edward, the pairs. (© IOC)

CHAPTER X

Enchantment

Viktor Gustav Balck of Sweden, inaugural IOC member

'"The Olympic Games . . ." how often were these words echoed throughout the year of 1912. Simultaneously, the patriotic feelings of all Swedes made their hearts tremble with expectation or joy. This was a year of honour for Sweden.

We need such years. Not only in order to secure the respect of foreign nations but also in order to teach us that hard work, even strain, is necessary when it comes to national interests – above all to teach us to realise the full extent of our own competence and capability and thus believe in ourselves. It is true that even in Sweden many voices were raised saying it would be unwise to take on such expensive and hazardous organisation as an international competition in Stockholm. Yet how can it be possible to achieve a victory if you do not dare to enter the battle? Sweden won a memorable though almost surprising victory.

The Olympic Games may now be just a memory, but what a beautiful and shining memory, with the sun illuminating our capital and the magnificent new stadium – a stadium filled with thousands of spectators, all jubilantly awaiting the strenuous competition among competitors who had arrived from all corners of the world. The gaze of the civilised world was fixed upon us in these days and weeks. The foreign visitors also had great expectations and made demands of us, too, and it was a difficult duty we had taken on. It had been given to us as a sign of confidence and appreciation, based on the respect we had won thanks to our performances at earlier Games.

Sweden performed its duties with honour, raising our reputation among other nations. Yet the most important factor was one that occurred outside the competition, namely the contribution of all in Sweden to a unity never seen and felt before. When had we ever witnessed such enthusiasm among the population? The importance of sport was raised to a degree that even I had never dared to expect. Even well-known sceptics now seem to have understood the possibility and the importance of international contacts through sport.' (From Viktor Balck's memoirs) (Photograph © IOC)

Demetrius Vikelas, whose impact upon the Olympic stage had been so brief but significant over four short years, died on 7 July 1908. In his tribute in *Olympic Review* that September, de Coubertin stressed the virtues of the first IOC President, 'who was one of the most noble figures of contemporary Hellenism', referring to a great writer and cultured man, who, like others in Europe at that time, 'was an apostle of popularisation in education for all'. He had been a devoted husband and had withstood the terrible blow of his wife's long illness, while professionally he had united 'a pagan wisdom with Christian virtues'.

At the Session in Berlin the following year, Sweden was elected as host of the Vth Olympic Games, largely on account of the representations of Col Viktor Balck, who immediately became chairman of the Swedish organising committee. Germany had withdrawn the candidacy of Berlin, partially out of altruism, so that Stockholm might be elected unopposed, but also on the informal understanding that they would be the choice for 1916. Sweden was particularly favoured on account of its agreement to reduce the Games from twelve to eight days, the Swedish NOC aligning itself with de Coubertin, who wished to reduce the number of events there had been in London –

twenty, which had included racquets, rugby and three women's sports – tennis, archery and skating. A proposal in Berlin to reduce the Games merely to track and field, swimming, gymnastics and wrestling had been rejected, however, as was another from Germany that there should be international judges with final jurisdiction for all events. Many of the members agreed with Balck, who said that there would be insufficient time to train enough international judges and that Swedish officials would be satisfactorily impartial; an international jury would be necessary only for appeal.

At the Session of 1910 in Luxembourg, a number of important innovations were introduced including individual registration for the Games only by an official Olympic form bearing the athlete's signature; and the acceptance of gymnastics, tennis and swimming as women's events. The agreement to increase the number of events for women would mean a rise in the number of female athletes from 36 in 1908 to 55. It did not meet with approval from all sides and James Sullivan, for example, remained adamantly against the growth of women's sports in America. There was also a debate in Luxembourg on the possibility of organising winter sports during the Stockholm Games – a foretaste of things to come –

The Stockholm organising committee provided in 1912 the most coherent Games so far. Viktor Balck, cornerstone of the IOC's early years, and J. Sigfrid Edström, later to become IOC President, are seated second and fourth left. (© IOC)

plus concern was voiced about random exploitation of the title 'Olympic Games' in connection with different events by some international federations.

In every sense, the sun shone for Stockholm. The organisation, under the direction of Balck and his Secretary-General, J.S. Hellström, was flawless and additionally enjoyed the practical interest of the Crown Prince. Stockholm was untroubled neither by any association with a world fair, nor by the political wrangles that had tainted the event in London, where a further distraction had been demonstrations by suffragettes.

The sports logistics for Stockholm were organised under the direction of J. Sigfrid Edström, chairman of the NOC. In addition to the regular sports – track and field, swimming, fencing, gymnastics and wrestling – football, equestrian competitions, shooting, rowing, yachting, lawn tennis and the modern pentathlon were added; the latter a concession to de Coubertin, who viewed its five component events (swimming, fencing, shooting, riding and running) as the essential disciplines in the training of a military officer. In the inaugural competition there was disagreement on the issue of horses, the Swedes wishing each competitor to bring his own horse – which some did – but being obliged to make horses available for others, this eventually becoming standard practice: leaping onto an unknown mount! Clarence von Rosen, a Swedish count, was responsible for the inclusion for the first time of equestrianism, ten nations entering the team and individual competitions. The Swedes were to win both, outperforming Germany and America. Boxing, in contrast, was off the programme as the sport was banned in Sweden at the time, but it was subsequently ever-present in the Games.

In Stockholm the number of participating countries, from all five continents, rose from 22 to 28, the number of competitors from just over 2,000 to 2,437. This increase from London revealed the momentum that the Olympic Movement was gathering. A magnificent new stadium of arches, vaults and towers, accommodating 22,000, was designed by Torben Grut and for nearly a century would remain the scene of world record performances on those evenings of perfect, tranquil Scandinavian summers. The original track was laid by Charles Perry, the Englishman responsible for those of 1896 and 1908.

There were a number of innovative features at the Games: semi-automatic electrical timing; an unofficial photo-finish

On-track. Avery Brundage, future IOC autocrat, finished sixth in Stockholm's subsequently discontinued pentathlon. (© IOC)

camera, which was critical in the result of the 1,500m; special apparatus for measuring the height of the cross-bar in high jump and pole vault; chalked lanes on the track; special platforms for umpires; a daily results paper published in three languages; attachés for each foreign team to ease communications; an alphabetical parade of nations at the opening ceremony. The Swedes sought to maximise their income in every way and a postcard company paid for the rights to photograph and publish, the following day, scenes of victories and champions.

The Stockholm Games placed de Coubertin and the IOC in a position of unrivalled prestige. By now the maverick Sullivan had fallen into step in America, the Interim Games in Athens had faded through lack of funds and the formerly exclusive oarsmen and cyclists had joined rank. Nonetheless, in his opening speech to the Swedish parliament, with the Crown Prince in the chair, de Coubertin found it necessary to speak of his resentment 'at unjustified and mischievous opposition', which the IOC had faced for many years, adding that even in Stockholm he could 'find traces of a last ditch which a belated hostility sought to dig beneath our feet'. The only obvious hiccup existed when the German gymnastic federation, Deutsche Turnerschaft, under the leadership of chairman Ferdinand Goetz, refused to participate, in opposition to DRAFOS (the German National Association for the Olympic Games), which was financed by the Reich. In place of Turnerschaft, a squad of students, prospective gymnastic teachers, was sent instead. On the political front, Russia and

Austria continued their haughty protest against the presence of Finland and Bohemia respectively, though it was a vain gesture in the face of the unifying influence exercised by sport.

Sweden had embraced the full spectrum of de Coubertin's ideology, with a simultaneous cultural programme alongside the sports festival, including receptions at the Skansen nature museum, where groups were guided in their mother tongue by well-known scientists. The cultural highlight of the Games occurred on 14 July, when the main stadium was transformed into an amusement park and a Swedish men's chorus of 3,000 entertained the visitors prior to a fireworks display across the city. In every way, the Games were a triumph. Reality had replaced ideology: an Olympic spirit had taken shape. While there was no Olympic Village, the Americans residing on the transatlantic liner in which they had arrived, at every venue there was fraternisation among competitors and not necessarily those from the same sport. That network of cross-referencing between officials of different sports and nations had begun to take shape. Stockholm presented to the world not only glamour but also a framework for the future. This was a significant milestone in the early history of the Olympics. Sweden, a neutral country, had presented a Games that were fun and fair in their judging. Philip Noel-Baker, of Britain, who would win a 1,500m silver medal eight years later, when recalling these Games, wrote:

> We were young, we were comfortable enough, there were no complaints to worry the manager of the team. The moment we walked out of our hotel, we found that Stockholm had a powerful attraction that was all its own: grass and roses at almost every turn, the lovely waterfront, bathed as I remember every day in glittering sun, the Royal palaces, the Skansen national park, not least the forest, then close around the city. We went to Stockholm as British athletes: we came home Olympians, with a new vision which I never lost.

For de Coubertin, seen here with J. Sigfrid Edström, IAAF President, and his daughter, the Stockholm Games were the apotheosis of his dream. (© IOC)

Balck, von Rosen and Edström could indeed be proud.

In his closing speech, declaring that the Games had been an enchantment, de Coubertin said:

> A great people [Germany] has received the torch of the Olympiad from your hands in Sweden and has thereby undertaken to preserve and, if possible, to quicken its precious flame . . . may the VIth Olympiad contribute, like its illustrious predecessor, to the general welfare and betterment of humanity. May it be prepared in the fruitful labour of peaceful times.

How far from the mark his words were to prove to be. There were those present who would perish in the coming years.

In his memoirs, de Coubertin would say of Stockholm: 'The perfect running of the organisers' machinery was beyond all praise.' This Swedish characteristic would remain unchanged, and it amounts almost to negligence that the IOC has subsequently never seen fit to grant Sweden the honour of staging either its first Winter Games or another Summer Games.

If there was one blight upon the year it lay in the continuing disinclination to treat seriously the rights of women. Although de Coubertin, aesthetically cultural and sensitive, won a gold medal in Stockholm in the artistic events with his anonymously entered poem 'Ode to Sports', he remained opposed to the further inclusion of women. Revealing his colours in *Olympic Review* that summer, he wrote:

> The question of admitting women to the Olympic Games is not settled. It could not be settled negatively just because that was how it was resolved in Antiquity, nor could it be resolved positively simply because female competitors were accepted in swimming and tennis in 1908 and 1912. The discussion is still open. It is as well that too prompt a decision was not taken. A solution will be found naturally at the Paris Congress in two years' time that will give the Olympiad its definitive characteristics. In what direction? We're not in a position to predict, but we are not afraid to give our support to the negative side. We consider that the Olympic Games should be reserved for men. Can one grant women access to all Olympic competitions? No? . . . Then why allow them access to only a few and forbid them access to others? There are not only women tennis players and swimmers. There are also women fencers, horse riders and in America there have been women rowers. Tomorrow, there will probably be women runners, or even women football players. If such sports are played by women, would they constitute a proper spectacle to offer the audience that an Olympiad brings together? We do not think this may be claimed to be so.

Meanwhile, Edström initiated the foundation of the International Amateur Athletic Federation. This organisation, too, would be prejudicial towards the emancipation of women.

The indefatigable Balck would remain a member of the IOC for another eight years. He lived to see the first cancellation of a Games, because of the First World War, before handing over his responsibilities in 1920 to another born leader, J. Sigfrid Edström. Aged 80, Balck was present when the Games returned to Paris in 1924. He died in 1928.

CHAPTER XI

Stockholm (V) 1912

Jim Thorpe of America, Olympic decathlon champion (arguably the greatest all-round sportsman of the twentieth century at American football, baseball, and track and field)

'*Pop Warner, the coach at Carlisle College, always said I could do more with a football than any man he'd ever seen. But he also thought I was lazy. Maybe he was right. I played for fun. I always have, ever since I was a kid. But I'll tell you one day when I was trying.*

We were playing at West Point in 1912. We'd won all our games that season except for a 0–0 tie. We were really keyed up for the army. They were looking for us, too. They were the number-two team in the country and they were out to stop me. It was a rough game from the beginning. Our fullback got into a fight with an army player and was thrown out of the game in the first quarter. I got mad then. We moved close to their goal line and they gave me the ball. Three of the army players hit me, one after the other, and they were still hanging on to me when I dragged them across for a touchdown.

That slowed them up a little. We got the ball again, I threw a pass to our right halfback and we made another touchdown. The army was supposed to have a great defence that year but they couldn't stop us. Their right halfback, Dwight Eisenhower, was hard to get away from but mostly they just tried to bang you as you went through. The third quarter was the most exciting of my career. Their captain, Devore, was sent out for slugging. A few minutes later I was out, the left shoulder felt funny and I couldn't move for a minute. But I got back and those West Point people gave me a nice hand. That was when we opened up. We lined up on our own ten-yard line. I got the ball, went wide and cut back. Guys were diving at me and I was running as hard as I could, with them bumping me and sliding off. All of a sudden, I was across the line and the crowd was on its feet. But one of our players was offside. Well, we lined up once more and I did it again. Ninety-five yards. That was my biggest thrill. We beat them 27–6 and I got 22 of our points.' (From Esquire's *Great Men and Moments in Sport*)
(Photograph © IOC)

Jim Thorpe was a phenomenon, even more so when considered with hindsight, yet the man who caught major public attention at the time, especially in Stockholm, was Hannes Kolehmainen from neighbouring Finland: the first in a succession of inimitable Finnish distance runners over the next 70 years. He won the 5,000m and 10,000m and the cross-country race, while in his 3,000-metre leg of the team race, in which Finland was eliminated in the first round, he set a world record of 8:36.9. His triumphs were distinguished not just by his athleticism but also by his manner, as he was a generous, smiling and modest winner. His 5,000m duel with Jean Bouin of France provided one of the most memorable of all races prior to the First World War, on the first Olympic occasion this distance was competed.

Kolehmainen, a bricklayer from an athletic family, had won the 10,000m two days previously; this was his fourth race in as many days. From the start, it became a battle between two men as he and Bouin endlessly disputed the lead, each in vain attempting to break free. At the bell for the last lap, the entire crowd was on its feet. On the final bend Bouin held off yet another surge by the Finn, but some 20 metres from the tape Kolehmainen edged in front, to win by a tenth of a second in a world record of 14:36.6. Both Bouin and George Hutson of Great Britain, half a minute behind in third place, were killed in action two years later.

Finland at the time was within the jurisdiction of Russia, whose detested colours they were obliged to accept as their flag for the Games: one of few political controversies. As Kolehmainen was congratulated on his magnificent victory he reflected: 'I would almost rather not have won than see that flag up there.' He had improved the world record by over 24 seconds.

Jim Thorpe's fame in twentieth-century sport was as much due to an act of official infamy as for his own multi-faceted brilliance. In Chapter XVI of his *History of the Olympics*, written in collaboration with Thomas Collison, he said:

In that glorious Swedish summer of 1912, Thorpe not only won the later discontinued pentathlon, assured of the gold medal – unless he fell over in the 1,500m – after four of the five events, he also completed a unique double by winning the decathlon too, ahead of Hugo Wieslander of Sweden, by a withering 598 points, and came fourth and seventh respectively in the open high jump and long jump events. When handing him a bronze bust made in his honour, the King commented: 'Sir, you are the greatest athlete in the world.' This was undoubtedly true then, and some would say for all time. The disarmingly informal Thorpe – whose father was half Sac-and-Fox Indian and half Irish, whose mother was half Potawatomi Indian and half French – is said to have replied: 'Thanks, King.' But six months later he was robbed of his medals and consigned to humiliation.

Hannes Kolehmainen, first of Finland's line of Olympic middle-distance champions, defeats Jean Bouin of France in the 5,000m. (© IOC)

Man-made axioms always throw the first stone at violation of regulations. Man himself is never as hard as his rules. By enforcing rules, he is only adhering to a statement of belief to which he committed himself in the past. Once written, rules are the hardest things in the world to get off the book. Rules are like steamrollers – there is nothing they won't do to flatten the man that stands in their way.

Thorpe won the decathlon, including five of the individual ten events (here the discus), and four of the pentathlon's five events. 'The greatest athlete in the world,' said the King. (© IOC)

The *Worcester Telegram* of Massachusetts reported that Thorpe had earlier received some piffling reward, a handful of dollars for playing semi-pro baseball in North Carolina in 1909–10. In reply to charges by the Amateur Athletic Union, Thorpe did not deny it, but ingenuously stated: 'I did not play for the money . . . but because I like to play ball. I was not wise in the ways of the world . . . that it would make me a professional . . . I'm very sorry to have it all spoiled in this way . . . and hope that the AAU will not be too hard in judging me.'

They were indeed unduly severe in punishing him. The AAU 'apologised' to the IOC for allowing him to compete and deleted all his records from the books; the IOC gave his gold medals to Wieslander and to Ferdinand Bie of Norway in the pentathlon. The bust of King Gustav V and a chalice from Tsar Nicholas of Russia, presented for his decathlon victory, were returned to the IOC. Wieslander and Bie accepted the medals with reluctance. Thorpe went on to fulfil a top-flight role in American football and major league baseball, yet by 1932 he was too broke even to buy a ticket for the Games in Los Angeles. Near penniless, living in a caravan park in California, he died in 1953.

Undoubtedly, this greatest of all Olympians was a victim of racial prejudice, not least, it must be suspected, by Avery Brundage, later IOC President, who had come sixth in the pentathlon and a dilatory fifteenth in the decathlon. Though the AAU posthumously reinstated him as an amateur in 1973, the IOC stubbornly rejected representations for a pardon. 'Ignorance is no excuse,' stated Brundage when President. Lord

Jim Thorpe (USA), of Native American, Irish and French extraction, the greatest all-round athlete-footballer-baseballer of the twentieth century. (© IOC)

Killanin likewise declined to act as President and it was left to Juan Antonio Samaranch to hand replica medals to members of Thorpe's family in 1982. For the man christened Wa Tho Huck, or 'Bright Path', honour was finally restored.

Arnold Strode-Jackson, an Oxford undergraduate in his second year, was one of the last of that breed of Edwardian gentlemen-amateurs, a runner whose concept of training was diligent relaxation: walking or a bit of golf. Between races in Stockholm, he would sit in the shade at the lawn tennis courts to feast his eyes upon Mademoiselle Marguerite Broquedis of France, the eventual singles winner and, he observed, 'one of the most delectable sights ever to appear on court'. Feeling less than in top form following the heats of the 1,500m, he concluded that the best preparation for the final was quietly to go to bed.

There were 14 runners contending the final, including Melvin Sheppard, the defending champion; the world record holder, Abel Kiviat of America; and the mile world record holder, John Jones; plus the able Philip Noel-Baker of Britain. Strode-Jackson possessed priceless talent for middle-distance running besides innate athleticism. He had the tactical sense to watch the leaders and stay in touch, and also possessed immeasurable courage: in the First World War he would be awarded the Distinguished Service Order four times and at 27 became the youngest acting brigadier-general in the British Army. In Stockholm, Kiviat led into the final lap, followed by Jones and Norman Taber, with Jackson and Sheppard on their heels. Into the finishing straight an American 1–2–3 seemed probable, but in the last 30 metres Strode-Jackson swept by on the outside to win by a stride from Kiviat, in an Olympic record of 3:56.8. Only by the evidence of the photo-finish camera, the first instance of its use, was Kiviat awarded second place ahead of his compatriot Norman Taber.

Sheppard was also defending his London title in the 800m, in which six of the eight finalists were Americans. One of his challengers, Hanns Braun from Munich – who was fortunate to avoid disqualification in a collision with Donnel Young (USA) in a heat of the 400m, in which he took the silver medal by a foot or so behind Charles Reidpath (USA) – was as graceful a runner as he was sculptor. He could not, however, penetrate American dominance, four of them breaking the existing world record. James Meredith fought Sheppard all the way to the line, getting the verdict by a tenth of a second in 1:51.9. The youthful Meredith, considered an outsider, had been instructed, ironically, by US coaches to set the pace for Sheppard. Braun,

surviving three years in the trenches of Picardy, would die in a fighter aircraft in the last months of the war.

Uninterrupted sunshine added to the enjoyment and success of Stockholm; though not, once again, for the marathon runners, half of whom were forced to retire before the finish, with Francisco Lazaro of Portugal collapsing and dying in hospital the following day. Among those falling by the way was Tatu Kolehmainen, older brother of Hannes and an early leader. South Africans Christian Gitsham and Kenneth McArthur led over the final stages, but at a refreshment stand two miles from the stadium, Gitsham stopped for water, believing McArthur, immigrant son of an Irish father and a former pedestrian-powered postman, would wait for him. But no, McArthur forged ahead to victory.

Swimming produced the first of its characters who would move on to other forms of entertainment: Duke Paoa Kahanamoku from Honolulu, so named in honour of the visiting Duke of Edinburgh, at the time of his birth. His world record in the 100m freestyle, when defending his Stockholm title at Antwerp four years later, was part of an Olympic career which spanned 12 years and brought him three gold and two silver medals. He could be viewed in Stockholm relaxing on a surf board in the hotel pool, a pastime he was to popularise.

The swimming was by now fully international, with 18 nations and 313 contestants entered, including the inaugural women. They were granted one individual event and a relay, Fanny Durack of Australia winning the 100m freestyle while wearing a long woollen swimming costume with a skirt and a rubber cap covered with a cloth bandanna, like a nurse's cap. The male selectors having refused to nominate her, the New South Wales Ladies Amateur Swimming Association had raised the funds to send her and rival Mina Wylie, who took the silver medal. Durack's winning time of 1:22.2 was the same as that of Alfréd Hajós when winning the inaugural men's race 16 years earlier. Crowds flocked to the women's events, Swedish women taking seven of the first eight places in platform diving.

Oscar Swahn, member of an outstanding Swedish medal-winning shooting family. (© IOC)

A new event, the initiative being de Coubertin's, was the modern pentathlon, objections to its inclusion having been overcome. The five events of shooting, swimming, fencing, cross-country riding and cross-country running represented the supposed essential disciplines of a military officer, spread over five days. Mental endurance has always been as much a factor as physical, with every fencer, for instance, having to face every other rival. Sweden were dominant in the event, taking six of

The face of a well-run Games: Stockholm's timekeepers. (© IOC)

the front seven positions, the sequence only punctured by the sixth-placed George Patton, later of Second World War fame. Also seriously prominent, and popular, for the second time was football, with 11 teams all from Europe. Denmark and Britain were clearly stronger than the rest, disputing the final in front of 25,000 spectators, with Britain winning 4–2, watched by the entire Swedish Royal Family. The British captain, Vivian Woodward, from an era when amateurs could still hold their own alongside professionals, was a legendary centre-forward

with Tottenham Hotspur and later Chelsea, his shooting being a feature of these Games.

The same rise in status could be claimed by gymnastics, with heavy entries for five days of competition conducted in brilliant sunshine in the main stadium. As a prelude of things to come half a century later, the Scandinavian women, in their colourful costumes, stole the show and represented something of the free spirit of the democratic northern nations.

Women's impact. An impressive gymnastics event in Stockholm established female sporting credibility (the Swedish team performing here), as did the first-ever swimming race, the 100m freestyle (from left): Fanny Durack (AUS) who was sent by public subscription, first; Wilhelmina Wylie (AUS) funded by friends, second; Jennie Fletcher (GBR) who worked a 70-hour week in a factory, third. (© both IOC)

CHAPTER XII

War-torn

Comte Henri de Baillet-Latour of Belgium, third IOC President, 1925–42

'My dear friend, I have been to find out what the war-time rail connections between Brussels and Amsterdam are like. Unfortunately they are very bad and, although I would have been delighted to meet you, I give up the idea of taking the trip. We may talk on the telephone, which is working normally. I will be at home on the 9th and 10th and you may call me or let me know when I can get hold of you.

I'm expecting Diem [Carl Diem of Germany, organiser of the impending Winter Games of 1940] *to settle any day the Garmisch business. The answers of the international federations, except for shooting, weightlifting and canoeing, are at hand. All so far are in favour of the Helsinki Games continuing, except equestrian sports and rowing, on account of the difficulties of sending over horses and boats. Cycling and fencing are doubtful.*

A few colleagues have also already expressed their opinion, but it is too early to know what the result of my circular letter in October will be. Anyhow, I am happy to say that Brundage has written that America has given up the idea to volunteer to stage the Games if Helsinki has to give them up. I sincerely hope the situation of Finland will be stabilised in a few days because I am afraid these Games might be the last ones. I am very pessimistic on the whole. The present war is not a war, and if it goes on like it is at the moment, every country will be ruined by the onset of mobilisation, with everything stopped, business, trade etc., even for the neutrals. The Soviets will be the only winners. Misery and poverty everywhere will help Bolshevik propaganda now that Stalin rules from the Baltic States to Siberia . . . Now Poland has lost 13 million of its population to the Bolsheviks, who are killing those unfortunate landowners and establishing Soviet rule everywhere. England has not even objected after the failure of the effort made to have Stalin on the side of the Allies. People at large in every country are against war but every country is ruled by a minority of madmen, who are living in hope that Germany or England can be wiped from the map. This means extermination by exhausting every possible resource of the world and a return to barbarism.' (Letter to Vice-President J. Sigfrid Edström, November 1939)
(Photograph © IOC)

It is remarkable that the Olympic Games, dependent on global collaboration, should have survived the calamities of two world wars. The IOC responsibilities of de Baillet-Latour bridged the two, the experience of the first doing little to prepare him for the second. Aware of Germany's growing militarism, de Coubertin had naively considered in 1909 that, if Berlin were to be awarded the 1916 Games, war might be averted; Kaiser Wilhelm was known to enjoy power but to be averse to war. Only slightly less naive was de Baillet-Latour before the Second World War. The election of Germany for 1916 would prove in the event to have been a futile gesture, notwithstanding that German delegates had been confident of staging the Games because any war 'would be short-lived'.

Germany had long affiliated itself to the ancient Olympic ideal. Prior to the unification of Germany in 1871, there had been planned an archaeological expedition to Olympia to excavate the ancient stadium. This finally took place in 1875, revealing the ruins of the Temple of Zeus and Hera. With the financial backing of the Reichstag, the ancient Olympic site was laid bare and this venture had helped to give impetus to de Coubertin's ideological crusade. As the IOC began to gather momentum at the beginning of the twentieth century, Willibald Gebhardt, the German IOC member, formulated plans for an Olympic Games, the 'German Imperial Board for the Olympic Games' being created to further this project, raising money and securing a location. A German bid was disregarded in 1908, but the following year Berlin had announced its candidacy for 1912. Such was their commitment, they became assured hosts for 1916, following the preference for Stockholm for the Vth Games.

At the Session of 1913 in Lausanne, the IOC was dazzled by the range of Berlin's preparations, to the extent that fears of an impending war were barely considered. In line with its thoroughness on the military front, Germany was additionally ensuring that its Olympic team would show a huge improvement on 1912. A four-man exploratory team had been sent to the United States to study American training methods, the party consisting of Carl Diem, secretary-general of the Imperial Board,

Lt Walter von Reichenau from the Ministry of War, Joseph Wartzer, a leading German coach, and Martin Berner, a writer-journalist. Arising from their tour of US universities and military academies, they hired Alvin Kraenzlein, former Olympic champion, to take charge of German track and field. Promotional parades were staged in Germany and the opening of the new stadium in Berlin by Kaiser Wilhelm was declared to be 'the greatest athletics exhibition Europe has ever witnessed'. The IOC and de Coubertin sat back in uncalculating awe, their self-satisfaction further buoyed by their own presentation at the Session of the newly devised five-ringed Olympic flag, designed by de Coubertin. He had adapted the five rings from a plinth in Delphi commemorating the first Olympic flame in 1936, to signify the unity of the five continents, the interlaced rings of blue, black and red at the top and yellow and green beneath selected because at least one of these colours was included in the member nations' flags. The rings were to signify the harmonisation of mankind, on a white background symbolising peace.

At the same time the Session self-righteously confirmed the condemnation and disqualification of Jim Thorpe for professionalism and required him to return his medals. The glorious guillotine wielded in the name of amateurism was showing the way forward.

Whatever the ominous portents in Europe, the Olympic flag was soon flying elsewhere: over Alexandria on the occasion of the Pan-Egyptian Games in 1914, the following year at San Francisco, during an exhibition dedicated to the Olympic Movement, and the year after in South America, thanks to de Coubertin's tireless campaigning. The Olympic bandwagon, up and running, was not to be halted.

At the Congress of 1914 in Paris, celebrating the 20th anniversary of the IOC's foundation, far from the Germans withdrawing at a time of impending crisis, the programme for 1916 was finalised and the Olympic flag unveiled in Europe for the first time. Yet in the midst of the Congress, on 28 June, a Serbian assassin shot and killed Archduke Franz Ferdinand, heir to the Austro-Hungarian throne, in the Bosnian capital of Sarajevo. Within a month, Austria-Hungary declared war on Serbia and shortly afterwards Germany aligned themselves by declaring war on Russia and France. Germany invaded neutral Belgium and Britain immediately formed a military triumvirate with the Belgians and French. In spite of these events, de Coubertin continued to refuse to consider the cancellation of the Berlin Games, decreeing that even if an Olympiad was not celebrated it would, like the ancient Games, maintain its number.

In the face of this intransigence, Theodore Cook from the British Olympic committee demanded the expulsion of German IOC members. When this was rejected, Cook resigned in protest. He was not alone in his anxiety. A few days before Germany declared war, Kraenzlein and his staff sailed for America. The Germans, confident that conflict would be brief, continued with their Olympic preparations. In November 1914, two months after the battle of the Marne, the IOC members met unofficially in Lyons, at the champagne factory of de Polignac, the French member, without German representation. At this meeting recommendations for moving the Games to an alternative site were resisted. It seems bizarre, nearly a century later, that the IOC should have remained so inert. Indeed, at the Congress they were busy still discussing domestic issues, such as the confining of individual entries to countries having a national Olympic committee and the inclusion of further sports only for those with an international federation. Amateurism, it was

decided, should be defined by each international federation for its own sport. The interest of Antwerp in staging a Games was noted and, with a proposal from Norway to include skiing in the Olympic programme, there was debate, encouraged by Germany, Austria, Switzerland and Canada, for the creation of a Winter Games.

The first concession, or rather safeguard, that de Coubertin deigned to make regarding the war concerned the IOC offices. It had been an original stipulation that the IOC's registered office should be moved each four years to the country staging the next Games. Fearing that the Germans might attempt to make a move to put this into effect, de Coubertin decided unilaterally, in 1915, to install the IOC's headquarters in a country outside the world conflict, namely at Lausanne in Switzerland. On 10 April, at the Lausanne Town Hall, signatures were exchanged establishing the IOC's administration and archives in that town, de Coubertin writing to Godefroy de Blonay, the IOC member in Switzerland, to apologise for omitting to warn him of this minor but important *coup d'etat*. There then arose the question of de Coubertin's own situation. Though already 51 when

Pierre de Coubertin in army uniform during IOC 'leave of absence' for the First World War. (© IOC)

hostilities began, de Coubertin enlisted in the army, disillusioning those who believed him to be a pacifist. Considering it incorrect for a neutral, altruistic organisation such as the IOC to be presided over by a soldier, he requested de Blonay to assume temporary presidential duties. Rejected for active service on account of his age, he was delegated to present the face of French morale at secondary schools, to further the mood of patriotic solidarity behind those at the front. Meanwhile, the German Imperial Olympic committee continued with its preparations. In the United States there was

Baron Godefroy de Blonay, together with his wife, St Moritz 1928. He was the first president of the Swiss NOC, deputy President of the IOC during de Coubertin's absence on war-time duty – and strangely later ignored as possible successor. (© IOC)

disbelief and offers of alternative hosting arrived from Chicago, Cleveland, Newark, New York, Philadelphia and San Francisco. But in a letter to Associated Press, de Coubertin said:

> The IOC has not the right to withdraw the celebration of the Olympic Games from the country to which the celebration was given without consulting that country. The VIth Olympic Games remain and will remain credited to Berlin but it is possible they will not be held. In olden times it happened that it was not possible to celebrate the Games but they did not for this reason cease to exist.

Ultimately, the Berlin Games of 1916 were cancelled by default. In 1915, the war had become a gruesome stalemate and by summer the following year the stadium was deserted and any thought of the Games had been abandoned, never mind that the Imperial Board had selected the team which it was believed would bring fresh glory to the country. A rapid consequence of the conflict was that, with the simultaneous Bolshevik revolution of 1917, the 'bourgeois sport' of the IOC and its Olympic Games was rejected in formerly Tsarist Russia. In a counter-movement, the emerging Union of Soviet Socialist Republics created Red Sports International, under the aegis of which the multi-sport Spartakiads would be staged in Moscow. Such was the gulf in ideology that the IOC would find no need to defend its rights and sanctions within the new and isolated regime. A fictional Russian NOC continued.

It could be said that de Coubertin's determination to fulfil the staging of the Berlin Games at almost any cost was due to idealism rather than perversity: that he recognised the immense potential of German allegiance to sport. In that sense he was saddened by its cancellation, whatever the appalling, overriding cause of this. However, immediately the guns were silenced, he summoned his members to Lausanne in 1919 in an attempt to determine a fresh host for the Olympiad of 1920. Baron Edouard de Laveley, president of the Belgian NOC, had made a preliminary bid for a Games in Antwerp at the Session in Budapest in 1911. Initially the intention had been to stage the Games in Brussels, the capital, but by 1914, when the decision for 1920 should have been made, Antwerp was preferred, the

decision being delayed by the outbreak of war. Shortly after the Armistice in 1918, de Coubertin had sounded out the Belgian government on whether they might host the Games of either 1920 or 1924. When an Antwerp provisory committee pledged financial support, the choice the following April was straightforward, even though Antwerp had been devastated, with much of its road and rail network destroyed and now under repair. It was a noble gesture by the Belgians, so soon after their suffering and with little more than a year in which to receive the rest of the world for a major sporting festival. For Belgium now to accommodate not only the sporting events but also the social and ceremonial occasions was a task that would have been beyond them without an immense sense of national pride. Incredibly, the Olympic stadium was officially inaugurated in the spring of the following year.

Inevitably there would not be the standard of excellence created in Stockholm eight years earlier. King Albert of the Belgians, who was to lose his life in a mountaineering accident in 1934, was in attendance with Queen Elizabeth and Cardinal Mercier, the latter holding a Requiem Mass of remembrance in Antwerp Cathedral for those who had lost their lives in active service. It was observed that the marching of the teams, as colourful as it had been eight years earlier, was also a good deal smarter. Involuntarily, many had learned to march during the interim years. If the marching was brisk, the track was not; the slow and heavy surface, reflected in many of the performances, worsened whenever it rained.

Pierre de Coubertin with King Albert of Belgium and Comte Henri de Baillet-Latour at the Antwerp Games. (© IOC)

The enemies – Germany, Austria-Hungary and Turkey – were not invited, yet in spite of many difficulties there were to be a record number of competitors, 2,607 and 29 countries. New Zealand competed separately for the first time, rather than as part of an Australasian team, as did Argentina and Brazil. This was all a reflection of mankind's instinct for self-preservation and continuity. Finland would be present independently, winning as many gold medals in track and field as the United States. Amidst the renewal of old, interrupted friendships there was also sadness. Hannes Kolehmainen, winner of the marathon but now overshadowed by Paavo Nurmi, discovered that his 5,000m rivals, Jean Bouin of France and George Hutson of Britain, as previously mentioned, had both died in action.

Victor Boin of Belgium takes the Olympic Oath. (© IOC)

Glad to be alive, European athletes in particular were disinclined to complain about the spartan nature of some of the accommodation, food and washing facilities, the hard bunks and hay-filled pillows of converted schoolrooms. Some of the larger countries contrived to convert the playgrounds of the schools where they were housed into leisure areas, including open-air dance halls. Yacht races took place at Östend on the North Sea coast, shooting at the army camp of Beverloo, some 60 kilometres east. The *Echo de Paris* reported that 'not even at Verdun were so many rifle shots heard'.

The crowds predominantly were small, but for everyone, competing or watching, the new Olympic flag, raised for the first time at a Games, was symbolic of renewed hope. One night the flag was removed by souvenir hunters, quickly arrested but pardoned for their misdemeanour. For the first time the Olympic Oath was sworn at the opening ceremony, in this instance by Victor Boin, a Belgian fencer, later a sports journalist and founder of Association International de Presse Sportif. He had won medals in water polo in 1908 and 1912 and now was to gain a silver in the épée team event.

The previous year, in consolidating the affairs of the IOC, de Coubertin had appointed Jiri Guth-Jarkovski, IOC member in Czechoslovakia, as Secretary-General. Another dimension of the IOC was thus placed in unwavering loyal hands.

Duke Paoa Kahanamoku, nobleman and legendary swimmer from Hawaii, who introduced the overarm crawl stroke, would retain his 100m freestyle title in Antwerp and later gain silver in 1924. (© IOC)

CHAPTER XIII

Antwerp (VII) 1920

Comments from Suzanne Lenglen of France, Olympic tennis champion (the most dramatic, possibly the most accomplished, ever of all women players)

'*Nothing is so fine as wine for the nerves, for the strength, for the morale. A little wine tones up the system just right. One cannot always be serious, there must be some sparkle too . . .*

'*When I am asked a question I endeavour to give a frank answer. If I know I'm going to win, what harm is there in saying so? Should I fail, no one suffers but myself. Never in my life have I failed to say to someone, perhaps to my mother or father, that I would win . . .*

'*Some* [of the crowd] *are in love with me, others are contented with friendship, while a large percentage are attracted by the reflected glory which comes to them from the association with so famous a personage. They like the limelight even when not directed full upon themselves. I distribute my attentions and smiles with royal impartiality. It is what is expected by the public . . .*

'*But of course, my little one . . . I have been careless this week, n'est ce pas?* [responding to her father's praise for hitting only four unforced errors in four matches] *. . .*

'*Willing oneself to win is good psychology, and good tennis requires good psychology. I never for a minute permit myself to entertain doubt. Confidence is not egotism. If your mind is in doubt, your muscles will be also. When you are wavering, the nerves will not convey to the muscles the exact impulse which must be imparted. Everything in the world is a blank to you except that exact spot where the ball must go . . . without the will to win, which allows no doubts, you cannot expect to be a consistent winner . . .*

'*I never had a wicked service. My forehand drive is not nearly as powerful as Miss* [Helen] *Wills', but I've always been able to place the ball within inches of where I wanted it.*' (From *The Goddess and the American Girl* by Larry Engelmann, OUP) (Photograph © IOC)

The most committed competitors at Antwerp were probably those of the Japanese team, numbering 15, who raised sufficient funds to travel halfway round the world to Belgium, but ran out of money for the return journey. They appealed, successfully, to the Mitsubishi and Mitsui companies to get them home again.

Travel was no less problematic for the American team, who crossed the Atlantic on the *Princess Matioka*, an ancient freighter unhappily known as the 'death ship', having been used to ferry home American casualties from the First World War. Abysmal conditions on board led to protests and near-revolt, and tempers did not improve when the team arrived at the Belgian port and found that they were expected to continue to live on board. Dan Ahearn, veteran world record holder in the triple jump led a brief mutiny. Unsurprisingly, therefore, team spirit was less than it might have been, though this did not prevent the United States from leading the medals table. If they perceived their achievements as being moderate, most other nations considered that beating the Americans in their event constituted success.

Having gained independence in 1917, Finland was for the first time competing under its own flag and marked the occasion by challenging the Americans, winning as many gold medals in track and field. In all, they won an exceptional 34 medals with a team of only 60. While a surprise victory was that of Hannes Kolehmainen, returning from his triumphs of 1912 to win the marathon, his place as national hero was claimed by Paavo Nurmi. Although he lost his first Olympic final, the 5,000m, to Joseph Guillemot, a French war veteran gassed in the trenches, Nurmi was to win nine gold and three silver medals in a career that stretched from Antwerp to Helsinki in 1952, when he carried the flame into the Olympic arena, and was to include 29 world records, from 1,500m to 20km. The son of a carpenter who had died when he was young, Nurmi was shy, taciturn, almost aloof, yet was to set new standards in ferocious fitness training, the results of which he was to reveal to the world now for the first time with the diversity of his range.

Oddly, he was to misjudge that first final, permitting revenge by the French for Kolehmainen's legendary defeat of Bouin eight years previously. Nurmi, taking the lead after the third lap, appeared to have the race in hand until Guillemot sprinted past him in the finishing straight to win by more than four seconds in 14:55.6, a time well outside Kolehmainen's world record.

Three days later, Nurmi exacted his own revenge. It was no surprise to those at home who were aware of his rare capabilities. The previous year, while on army duty, he had run the whole of a 20km march carrying full equipment. For the 10,000m in Antwerp he ran a cagey race, allowing James Wilson, a Scot, to make the early pace and going to the front himself with only two laps remaining. Guillemot briefly overtook him, but Nurmi accelerated for a clear victory. In defence of the Frenchman, it must be said that, with the race scheduled for an early evening start, he had eaten a normal lunch, only to be told that the race had been advanced at the request of the King, and the precipitous start left him near to vomiting. In the subsequent 8,000m cross-country race, Guillemot suffered further misfortune, injuring his ankle in a rut and being obliged to retire. Nurmi swept to two further gold medals, this being also a team event.

For the first time in six Games, conditions were cool for the marathon, resulting in fast times in spite of the course being a shade longer than normal. Few expected that Kolehmainen, now living in America, could win. After about a third of the race, he joined Christian Gitsham, second at Stockholm, at the front and together they reached the halfway stage. Thereafter, with Gitsham handicapped by a damaged shoe, Kolehmainen drew ahead, holding off a challenge by Jüri Lossman of Estonia to win by some 70 yards.

Albert Hill of Great Britain, who had served for three years in France, was 35 by the time of these Games and his double victory at 800m and 1,500m was the more acclaimed because his selection at the shorter distance had been in some doubt up to a week before departure on account of strained shin muscles in his left leg. He managed to persuade the selectors that he was fit to attempt both distances and their agreement was to be well rewarded. Hill regarded his victory in the 800m as the finest of his career. After his war experiences, he abstained from drinking unclean water in the school accommodation provided and largely confined himself to light lager; the tea, he recorded, being undrinkable. He and a friend also took to dining at an adjacent hotel.

The worst incident of Hill's Games was to arise in the first of his seven races in eight days, when it was learned that all the

leading runners had been placed in the same heat of the 800m. The Belgian officials, in a perverse bid for fair play, had decided that this would level the competition and no amount of protest could change their minds as the programmes were already printed. In the event, the first three in Hill's heat would take the first three places in the final, though in a different order. Bevil Rudd of South Africa, who had already won the 400m in a slowish 49.6, his blatant smoking and drinking habits seemingly being no impediment, was the favourite. He was a heroic survivor of the war, an officer in some of the first-ever tank battles who had once managed to escape with his life after his tank broke down between the lines. Hill, much experienced, planned to shadow Rudd and the number-one American, Earl Eby. Rudd's habit was to make his attempted break 300 metres out, and he did so this time, entering the home straight some four yards clear. Then he began to stiffen and a relaxed Hill went by to take the tape by a yard from Eby. In seventh place was Adriaan Paulen of Holland, who was later to become president of the IAAF.

The final of the 1,500m was run in a downpour and on a soggy track. The main threat was expected to come from Joie Ray of America but his threat never materialised. It became something of a team race, with Philip Noel-Baker tailing Hill, altruistically fending off the foreign challenge. Hill gained the easiest of victories four or five yards clear of Noel-Baker, who was to become a Member of Parliament in later life and won the Nobel Peace Prize in 1959 for his work on disarmament.

The sprints, predictably on such a track, were not the fastest, and the short sprint was marred at the start by confusion over the starter's instructions in French. Charley Paddock was the favourite. His starting procedure was always to place his hands far in front of the starting line and slowly to withdraw them to the correct position. He was admonished by the assistant starter, so that Loren Murchison supposed that there would be a re-call when the starter said 'Pret'. When the gun then fired, Murchison

War veteran Albert Hill (GBR) leads the field home for 800/1,500m double victory. (and above right) (both © IOC)

was on his haunches and left ten yards adrift. Jackson Scholz and Morris Kirksey, the other two of four US finalists, led at halfway, but Paddock came through to win by a tenth of a second with his renowned finishing leap across the line: a gimmick that was of more benefit to photographers than his performance, for any technician would tell him he lost time in the air. Poor Murchison finished last.

The swimming events saw the first women's Olympic multi-medal star. Etheda Bleibtrey, who had suffered from polio as a child, won all three events in world record time: 100m and 300m freestyle and relay. The previous year, such was the hypocrisy of Victorian morality that existed in America, she had been arrested for swimming 'naked' at a public beach: she had removed her stockings. The death of James Sullivan had, however, removed the obstacle to American women's participation in the Olympics.

Etheda Bleibtrey (USA) (left), the first multi-medal swimming star, pictured with rivals Violet Walrond (NZL), Jane Gylling (SWE), Frances Schroth, Irene Guest (USA), and Constance Jeans (GBR). (© IOC)

American Norman Ross was also a triple winner, at 400m and 1,500m freestyle and the relay, being disqualified in the 100m freestyle for impeding an Australian. That was the race in which Duke Kahanamoku, successfully defending his Stockholm title, beat the world record, with 1:00.4. In the resulting re-swim Kahanamoku's time was a second slower but the order remained the same.

Pua and Warren Kealoha from Hawaii became the first brothers to win gold medals in swimming at the same Games. At the age of 14 years, 119 days, Aileen Riggin of the US became, at that time, the youngest individual Olympic champion, in the diving, though Nils Skoglund of Sweden, three months younger, nearly displaced her, missing the gold medal in the men's discontinued plain high-diving event by half a point.

Hero of the rowing was Jack Kelly, a Philadelphia bricklayer. He had earlier been refused entry for the Diamond Sculls at Henley because the Vespa Boat Club of which he was a member was accused of professionalism. Poetic justice was now done when Kelly defeated the Diamond winner, Jack Beresford, in the single sculls. Though both men were so exhausted at the finish of a race won by a single second that they could scarcely acknowledge each other, a short while later Kelly doubled his

tally with Paul Costello in the double sculls with a clean-cut victory over Italy. Kelly's son, John Jnr, would take bronze 36 years later at Melbourne, while his daughter Grace married Prince Rainier of Monaco.

Nedo Nadi of Italy was exceptional in fencing, winning five gold medals. What might he have achieved but for the war? At Stockholm he had won the foil, and now he took also the sabre and all three team events. In shooting, Oscar Swahn of Sweden, team champion of 1908 and 1912, took the team silver medal in the running-deer event at the age of 72 years and 280 days, a record to this day, and his sixth Olympic medal. Ugo Frigerio of Italy did not merely win both the walking events, 3,000m and 10,000m, but also proved himself an exceptional technician. Basking in the attention, he had even provided sheet music for the band leader in the middle of the field as requested accompaniment during the shorter race, at one stage pausing to correct their tempo.

Eddie Eagan of the USA, who became a renowned professional boxing administrator, took the light-heavyweight crown, while 12 years later he was a member of the team which took the four-man bobsleigh title: the only man to have won gold medals at both Summer and Winter Games. Almost as an aside, the inimitable Suzanne Lenglen of France, to this day regarded by some as the finest woman player of all time, notwithstanding the likes of Martina Navratilova, Steffi Graf and the Williams sisters, Venus and Serena, lost only nine games in the ten sets required to win the women's singles tennis title, the final against against Dorothy Holman (GBR). She also took the mixed doubles with Max Decugis, defeating Kitty McKane and Max Woosnam (GBR). Of the 77 women at the Games, she was the unquestioned star as well as the most eccentric. Being French, she even managed to warm the attitude of de Coubertin towards women.

The inimitable Suzanne Lenglen of France lost only nine games while winning the ladies' tennis singles. (© IOC)

Two winter sports were staged, ice hockey and figure skating, 10 nations entering 85 contestants. Walter and German-born Ludowika Jakobsön of Finland, in pairs skating, became the first husband and wife gold medal winners, while the incomparable Gillis Grafström of Sweden, who did more than any before or since to advance his sport, took the men's figure skating title.

CHAPTER XIV

Expansion

Anita DeFrantz of America, Olympic rowing bronze medal winner, first female IOC Vice-President, 1996–2000

'The role of women in sports has generally been portrayed in negative terms. The focus has been on their exclusion rather than on their participation. History shows us that women have always been involved in sport, though varying cultures have dealt differently with women's role. There can be no denying that women have a key function in sports development. In the twentieth century, people who care about equal opportunity will insist that women assume their position as full partners.

Women did not compete in the inaugural Games of 1896, though it was not from a lack of desire to do so. At the 1900 Paris Games, 12 women competed. The numbers may have been small, but their presence reflected the increasing role of women in sport and in society. It is humbling to consider the courage and determination of the women who were competing in swimming and diving, in archery, tennis and sailing in the early Olympic days.

A landmark was the creation of the Fédération Sportive Féminine Internationale by the French sportswoman Alice Milliat. The FSFI staged a series of women's competitions between 1922 and 1934. The success of these so-called "Women's Olympics" led the IOC to include women's track and field for the first time on the programme of the Games in 1928.

By the time of the Millennium Games in Sydney 2000, all but two sports, wrestling and boxing, would be open to women. While women did not compete in Sydney in baseball, softball was open for women exclusively. At Salt Lake City 2002, women were eligible to compete in every sport on the programme, though ski jumping did not yet have a women's event – therefore qualification would require the same standards as for men. The programme for Athens 2004 includes women's wrestling.

Female competitors have immeasurably enriched the Olympic Movement. Try to imagine the Games without Sonja Henie, Babe Didrikson, Fanny Blankers-Koen, Wilma Rudolph, Katarina Witt, Derartu Tulu, Nawal El Moutawakel, Ludmila Tourischeva and Fu Mingxia. The lesson of the first quarter of the twenty-first century will be that women's sports leaders will significantly enhance the sporting environment.

In 1981, Juan Antonio Samaranch fulfilled his commitment to bring women to the policy-making table with the election of two women members. By the turn of the century there would be 13. Among the recommendations of the Centennial Congress of 1994 was the increased involvement of women at all levels. In 1996, the IOC resolved that by the year 2000 women should comprise at least 10 per cent of all policy-making committees throughout the Olympic Movement. This target was met, while available data revealed that 130 NOCs had at least one woman on their executive, and in 31 of these NOCs more than 20 per cent of the members were women. Two-thirds of Olympic international federations had at least one woman on the executive.

To expand the reach of sport in the twenty-first century, more women will be needed in every function, yet it has been a remarkable journey for us during an Olympic century. There is a saying that women hold up one half of the sky. In sport, they do not yet hold up a quarter. The Olympic Movement is committed to the idea that sport belongs to all. In increasing numbers, we will reach for and hold up our share of the sky.'*

(Photograph © IOC/Locatelli)

The four years between Antwerp and the Games of Paris 1924 were among the most significant in the history of the IOC. There was the creation of the Executive Board; the foundation of a Bureau des Fédérations Internationales Sportives, forerunner of today's General Association of International Sports Federations (GAISF); a major advance in the sporting franchise of women under the influence of Alice Milliat's movement; a distant, principled resistance to potential takeover by Bolshevik emulators; and the foundation of the Winter Olympic Games. The inter-relation of all these factors meant that by the time de Coubertin was approaching his retirement, the roots of his once-fledgling Olympic Movement were now penetrating deep into the social structure of most countries around the world.

Nine cities, four in America and five in Europe, had lodged an interest in the Games of 1924 prior to the Session at Lausanne in 1921. It was de Coubertin's ambition that the

Games should return to Paris, under a more attractive guise than had been possible 24 years earlier. The lingering economic downturn following the war would make it difficult for European teams to cross the Atlantic, yet sport itself was expanding rapidly throughout European nations, especially with the development of individual sports' world championships. With clandestine negotiations, de Coubertin managed to establish a mood in which Amsterdam, one of the contenders, would be assured of the 1928 Games if Paris were to be elected for 1924. This he achieved, with the United States and Netherlands strongly supporting Paris, for which Aristide Briand, the French Prime Minister, promised substantial financial backing. Thus for the first time two future sites were elected simultaneously.

Germany, Austria, Hungary and the new Soviet Union would be not be invited to these Games, and the IOC voted not to replace deceased German IOC members. With his ingrained idealism/blindness, de Coubertin campaigned for the inclusion of the German team for Paris, but was unable to persuade his unsurprisingly embittered colleagues. There would, however, be newcomers: Ireland, competing separately from Britain for the first time, Poland and Romania. There had been Polish competitors at previous Games but always in the teams of other nations.

Also established was that each international federation would supervise its own sport in Paris, thereby relieving the host organising committee of that responsibility. By now the international federations were beginning to feel their power, the need to coordinate in debate and to establish their own representative bodies. In athletics, football and swimming in particular, the level of self-importance was accelerating and with it an as yet unspoken challenge to the IOC. Despite these changes, the new administrative regulations for Paris would not wholly remove complaints of unfair decisions, notably in boxing.

Though de Coubertin remained the figurehead, the affairs of the IOC were increasingly being decided among the rank and file. In a futile attempted rebuff against human nature, the Congress voted to abolish the chauvinistic nations' points table. Such legislation was doomed: the medals table would always be avidly perused, the more so in Paris where records of every kind were to be established. There would be 44 nations competing compared with 29 in Antwerp (although there were three fewer sports, 17 instead of 19) and 3,072 participants, setting 6 world and 15 Olympic records in track and field, with many others in swimming.

Back in 1900, Viktor Balck of Sweden, a charter member of the IOC, had helped create the Nordic Games, first held the following year near Stockholm with entries from Sweden, Norway and Denmark. An informal proposal in 1897 by Balck to de Coubertin recommending Winter Games had been rebuffed. Thereafter the Nordic event had taken place every four years, primarily regional though attracting entries from elsewhere in Europe.

Following the First World War and the rapid expansion of Alpine sports among Swiss, Austrians, Italians and French, the momentum for establishing a Winter Olympics had become hard to resist, never mind that the Nordic countries were strongly proprietorial about their event and that de Coubertin was disapproving. Figure skating and ice hockey had been included in the Summer Games in Antwerp and at the 1921 Congress – simultaneous with the Session – the debate on a special IOC report outlining the issue was energetic. France, Switzerland and Canada, the latter having had an ice hockey league for 34 years, supported the proposal, the Nordic countries

were opposed – believing, not without reason, that the more dramatic Alpine events would wrest attention from their own competition. J. Sigfrid Edström, prominent IOC member from Sweden, and later to become President, was in a difficult position, but marginally supported the proposal. There was a danger of the IOC being divided and the Marquis de Polignac of France offered a compromise: 'The Congress suggests to the IOC that in all countries where Olympic Games are held and where it is also possible to organise winter sports competitions, such competitions should be put under the patronage of the IOC and arranged in accordance with the rules of the relevant international federations.' With Edström's passive approval, it was agreed that France would stage a 'Winter Sports Week'. The Nordic countries, though dismayed that they would not be inaugural hosts of such an event, could not but fall in line. In 1926 the French event, having been staged at Chamonix, was retrospectively granted the title of 'Winter Olympic Games'.

The attitude of de Coubertin towards women in sport was, as already stated, contradictory. Initially he was utterly opposed to their involvement, ceding to their admission only reluctantly. In his report on the Antwerp Games, in reference to their swimming events, he acknowledged merely that 'they have excelled, beating their previous records'. On one hand, he had consistently campaigned against the difference in educational programmes for girls and boys and deplored the fact that certain careers were barred to women. On the other, in his memoirs towards the end of his life, he mentioned none of the winners of the few women's sports, events that were regarded, condescendingly, as 'appropriate' – being free of violent or 'inappropriate' physical action, such as tennis, golf, archery, ice skating, fencing and swimming. His equivocal attitude was all the more odd because France was among the leaders in the liberation of women's interests. In 1917, however, when their first national championship was staged for women in track and field, a shot put competitor, Violette Gouraud-Morris, did the cause a disservice when it was learned she had had her breasts removed in the interest of improving her performance.

Such championships catalysed the creation of the first national women's sports federation under the presidency, from 1919, of Alice Milliat. A childless widow, her sport was rowing.

Uneasy accord. Alice Milliat, a reluctantly accepted agent provocateur for the inclusion of women's sports, seated with J. Sigfrid Edström (second from right), president of IAAF, and the referees' committee during track and field events at Amsterdam, 1928. (© IOC)

Indignant at the refusal to admit women to all events in Antwerp, she founded the FSFI, which planned to stage its own four-yearly cycle of 'Women's Olympic Games'. The first of these was held in Paris in 1922, with 65 women from 5 nations (Britain, France, Germany, Switzerland and the USA) competing in 11 events and setting 18 world records, with attendances reaching 20,000. The appropriation of the term 'Olympic' infuriated the IOC, which condemned Milliat's initiative at the Session in Rome in 1923.

The reservations maintained by de Coubertin – the perceived vulgarity of female exertion in public, let alone alleged impairment to childbearing – served only to provoke counter-propaganda in answer to such publications by de Coubertin as *The Crisis of Marriage and the New Woman in the United States* in 1920. Edström, however, was more pragmatic. Under the old adage, if you can't beat them, join them – and there was no way the increasingly militant women were going to be defeated – he led a move within the International Amateur Athletic Federation to embrace responsibility for women's track and field. Thus, in a sense, Milliat won and lost in the same breath, for her sport, now recognised, moved wholly into the domain of male control. It should be remembered that under a British/Swedish initiative the international swimming federation (FINA) had admitted women to the programme for 1912. Yet it would be another four years before a limited number of women's track and field events were admitted and a further 20 years before they were granted a more extended programme.

Whether it was for reasons of finance, travel, fatigue or his advancing years, de Coubertin unexpectedly advocated at the Lausanne Session the establishment of an Executive Board. His colleagues were largely unaware that the 58-year-old idealist had exhausted the family fortune by his selfless subsidy of the IOC's administrative expenses. Indeed he was close to financial ruin. With uncomplaining reticence, he had said: 'We have always run on very few resources – it is becoming necessary for us to publicise our cause. It would be a good idea to set up an "Olympic extension fund".' It was unanimously agreed to establish the Executive Board, de Coubertin's excuse being that he was about to make an extended trip abroad and the IOC's business needed handling effectively in his absence. There was an immediate, unanimous election of the following: President – Godefroy de Blonay (Switzerland); members – Edström, Guth-Jarkovski (Secretary-General); de Polignac (France), de Baillet-Latour (Belgium). They were to assume their responsibilities immediately, meeting at least twice a year, and it was the Board which recommended first that 'women were to be accepted as Olympic athletes in those sports in which they could compete' and, second, that the various international federations should integrate responsibility for women's sport.

The Board, from the moment of its inception, was to play an increasingly important role in the IOC's operation: giving advice on policy for members attending the Sessions, its brief including the handling of IOC's finances, responsibility for incoming correspondence, dealing with disputes, responsibility for the archives, maintenance of IOC regulations and preparation of the agenda for Sessions. Such was its immediate influence that it created divisions in the long-standing friendship between de Blonay, its new President, and de Coubertin.

Perhaps unwisely, de Coubertin had not devised to have himself included as an Executive Board member, an omission he was to regret. In a pained letter to de Blonay, he was to write: 'The Board was constituted to administer the IOC during my absence, not to reform it.' As a sign of the mounting influence of de Blonay, he was appointed IOC Vice-President – there was

Jiri Guth-Jarkovski from Prague, at that time capital of Bohemia, a devoted de Coubertin disciple and Secretary-General of the inaugural Executive Board. (© IOC)

at the time only the one – at the Session in Paris in 1922. Yet he had himself been absent from the Board's first meeting in 1921. The election of Edström to the Board was indicative of his significance and influence as president of the major federation, the IAAF, for he had been an IOC member barely a year, whereas it had been de Blonay who had taken IOC affairs under his wing during wartime.

Besides the anomaly of his mixed attitude towards women – an echo of the British Victorian male's sexual repression? – de Coubertin was divided on the social front, in the matter of distinction between privileged aristocracy and the working classes. While eagerly enlisting aristocratic IOC members, it was essential, in his view, that the underprivileged should benefit from reform of education, that there should be 'workers' universities'. In a pamphlet in 1921, *Les Universitiés Ouvrières*, he had written: 'These ought to be the instruments of equalising culture and free from all restraint . . . the direction must be left to the students . . . this is a point of view which penetrates with great difficulty into the heads of the privileged.' In order to force educational changes, to free students from authority, he was a revolutionary.

The Bolshevik revolution clearly formed a potential threat to the relatively privileged world of the IOC. Inequality still governed in many countries, not least America, where African-Americans had been barred from professional boxing until 1908 and continued to be excluded from American football and

baseball until the 1940s. In college track and field, African-Americans were rare. The ethical position of the IOC was to support the promotion of unity and comradeship among all, but it remained critically restricted by dogmatic attitudes towards amateurism.

Following the First World War, labour leaders became increasingly interested in competitive sport, and in Lucerne in 1920 there emerged the 'Socialist Workers' Sports International' (SWSI), which would gather two million members. In parallel, in Moscow in 1921, there developed Red Sport International (RSI), an intended arm of the proletarian revolution. Yet SWSI and RSI were, with typical communist conflicting principles, firmly opposed to each other and this disharmony, together with the isolationism of the USSR, served to protect the Olympic Movement from damaging infiltration. The first unofficial workers' festival was staged in Prague in 1921 and by 1925 the SWSI had organised respective 'Workers' Olympics' in summer and winter sports, the former at Frankfurt, drawing over 100,000 spectators – to which the RSI was not invited. A further 'Workers' Olympics' took place in 1931 in Vienna, drawing 250,000 spectators and 80,000 competitors from 23 countries. These festivals were rooted in Marxist ideology, but so introspective was the administration, so increasingly oppressive the government and also so minimal the international reporting of the events, that they presented little threat to the now stabilised IOC. While de Coubertin showed some enthusiasm for communication with these groups, proposing a meeting with the workers' union in 1921, his IOC colleagues varied between apathetic and hostile. De Baillet-Latour was vigorously opposed.

By 1921, the damage to railway lines in France had largely been repaired and, although the national debt had soared, there were signs of economic recovery, with unemployment close to zero. There were, however, certainly difficulties in the preparation for the Winter Games in Chamonix. While a small mountain resort with a population of 3,000 was accustomed to handling 2,000 visitors, it was likely now to be inundated by ten times that number. Beds had to be placed in the corridors, ballrooms and billiard halls of the Chamonix hotels, and private citizens were requested to open their homes. None of this would be sufficient, however, and special daily excursion trains were scheduled to allow nearby Alpine towns to accommodate the overflow. There would be 16 nations represented at these first Winter Games, though women were only admitted for figure skating. They would not be permitted to endanger themselves by skiing until 1948 and speed skating (even more dangerous!) in 1960.

Weather hazards are part and parcel of a Winter Games. Two days before Christmas in 1924, there was not a snowflake to be seen in Chamonix. By the following morning, there was more than a metre, and thousands of cubic metres had to be shovelled from the skating rink as there were no efficient snow ploughs in

those days. Yet a week before the opening, on 25 January, rain had turned the stadium into a lake. Mercifully a hard frost overnight allowed the opening ceremony to proceed untroubled. The 16 inaugural countries who would take part in 14 events were: Austria, Belgium, Canada, Czechoslovakia, Finland, France, Great Britain, Hungary, Italy, Latvia, Norway, Poland, Sweden, Switzerland, United States and Yugoslavia. Norway and Finland were to win four gold medals each, Austria two, with Canada, Switzerland, Sweden and the USA sharing the other four. Although losses ran to several million francs, crowds had exceeded 3,000 on most days, including thousands who had entered with free tickets, and even the Nordics had to admit that the inaugural Winter Games had been a success.

Undoubtedly the Summer Games in Paris were a monument to Coubertin's 30-year initiative. As Gertude Stein observed: 'Paris was where the twentieth century was.' In whatever medium of art, theatre, music and indeed sport, Paris was a world leader. Those who took up residence in the city included Colette, Jean Cocteau, Hemingway, F. Scott Fitzgerald, Ezra Pound, James Joyce, Stravinsky, Erik Satie, Picasso and Miro. Where else would anyone want to be?

It was not quite thus for some of the competitors. As in Chamonix, though for far higher numbers, demand for accommodation exceeded availability. Vladimir Stoytchev and Kroum Lekarski, Bulgarian equestrians, having travelled with their horses for a week by train from Sofia, then had to hunt for their own lodgings and stabling, though the organising committee had established a bureau to marshal accommodation in both hotels and private residences at tolerable prices. The French built the first Olympic Village, but residence was not obligatory in what was not much more than an odd assembly of huts; many teams preferred the comfort of hotels. Transportation to events was lengthy and inadequate. Restaurants serving the Village were also inconveniently distant. The relative success of the Games was undermined by the renovated main stadium being at Colombes, far from the centre of the city. Renovation work was, however, completed in good time, with seating for 20,000 and standing room for an additional 40,000. Electric bells summoned competitors from the warm-up area prior to events.

Whatever the negative aspects, the Games attracted over 500,000 paying spectators and a record 30 countries shared in the winning medals. Among the visitors was the Prince of Wales, subsequently the uncrowned King Edward VIII of Britain, and Benjamin Spock, gold medal winner in the US rowing eight, who was later to become an authority on parenthood. Additionally there was HRH Tafari Makonnen, heir-apparent of Abyssinia (later Ethiopia), descendant of Solomon and Sheba, no king or heir-apparent having ever previously left that country.

CHAPTER XV

Chamonix (I) 1924

Arnold Clas Thunberg of Finland, Olympic speed skating champion

'*I was in good shape before the Games and very optimistic. I'd been training hard all winter in Helsinki, always outdoors because there were no sports halls in those days. I set off in December by boat to Szczecin [Stettin] in Poland and then on by train to Berlin, where I could train in a big indoor hall. Early in January, I moved to Davos to continue training, staying with a Norwegian family because the hotels were too expensive and the Finnish Olympic committee had no money for hotels. They even had no money for a manager or uniform for our speed skating team. All the managers were involved with the ski team. Nobody could speak German or English and there were problems with the food, though the ski team had brought their own.*

A week before the Games in a practice competition, I won the 500m and 1,500m, and was second at 5,000m and 10,000m. Three days later we moved to Chamonix, only to find there was no snow and no ice, making training, therefore, impossible.

My training was for longer distances and in the opening 500m final I was tied in third place. The next day conditions were good and I won the 1,500m, even though Roald Larsen from Norway set a hard target in the first round. In the 5,000m, I was able to win quite comfortably ahead of my colleague Julius Skutnabb. On the way to the track for the 10,000m, Skutnabb asked me if I would allow him to win. I was in a good mood, so I was happy to agree. After 20 laps or so, Skutnabb called out – we were skating in the same pair together – "Don't forget what you promised." Skutnabb won and I was really pleased to make this gesture.

The prize-giving was in a very nice and expensive hotel, we had to wear dinner jackets, but our team could only afford to stay there one night. The American and Canadian teams formed a lane in our honour as we came downstairs and I was invited to compete in the USA the next winter. When we arrived home, there were 10,000 people waiting to greet us at the railway station. People nicknamed me "Nurmi on ice", but I never much liked that. He was Nurmi, I was Thunberg. But he gave me some good hints, among them adding dancing to my training. I used to dance alone with a cushion for an hour a day.' (From conversations with his friend Ingmar Björkman) (Olympic Poster © IOC)

Arnold Lunn, a travel agent, and other 'mad' Englishmen had begun Alpine skiing as a sport in the early part of the twentieth century. Local shepherds at Saas Fe used to throw stones at them at they careered down the slopes on what were regarded as workmen's snowdrift footwear. Alpine events were not introduced into the Olympic Games until after the Second World War. There had been downhill races in Kitzbühl, Austria, and Crans-Montana, Switzerland, before the First World War, organised by Lunn, who also invented the slalom, but skiing in the early Olympic years was strictly Nordic.

Predictably, there was an unrivalled champion from Norway in the skiing, the 29-year-old Thorleif Haug winning the 18 and 50km events as well as the Nordic combination. For all but the supremely fit – which has always included a huge section of the population of Scandinavia – the prospect of Nordic skiing, especially uphill, is almost that of being consigned to damnation, so unrelentingly severe are the demands. Such was Norway's command that they took the first four places in the 50km, and three days later four of the first five in the 18km. The interloper, for the bronze medal, was Tipani Niku of Finland, and Scandinavians, indeed, took the first 11 places in this race.

With Haug first, Norway also took the first four places in the combined event, this being the amalgamation – nowadays – of the ski jumping on the normal (small) hill and their 15km performance (18km until 1952). Jumping was only split into two, 70m and 90m, in 1964. At Chamonix, the jump was on the large hill, and Haug took an individual bronze medal. Fifty years later, however, with Haug long dead, his compatriot Thoralf Strömstad, who had won the combined silver medal, unearthed, together with historian Jacob Vaage, an error in the points calculation. This placed Anders Haugen of America correctly above Haug. The medal was presented to the Norwegian-born American, by now 83, by Haug's daughter at a special ceremony in Oslo.

The feature of figure skating was less that the inimitable Gillis Grafström of Sweden 'retained' the gold medal he had won during the Summer Games of Antwerp, than the appearance of an 11 year old in the women's event. Sonja Henie had missed the initial registration and was squeezed into the entries at the last minute because of the non-appearance of a Norwegian male figure skater. Grafström was to enhance his own fame, subsequently, by becoming coach to this young superstar. In

The 11-year-old Sonja Henie from Norway made her debut in figure skating, finishing eighth and last: the beginning of a spectacular career that would carry her to Hollywood. (© IOC/Couttet)

Speed skaters Julius Skutnabb (left) and his Finnish colleague Arnold Clas Thunberg, who 'gave' him the gold medal in their 10,000m final. (© IOC)

Chamonix, however, young Henie came eighth and last. Prior to the competition, Herma Planck-Szabó, of Austria, who would be the first women's Winter Games victor, had said contemptuously: 'I do not like to compete against children, but it can well happen.' Henie was to demonstrate maturity far beyond her years.

Grafström was a clear victor in the men's event, but there was evidence of the prejudiced judging that was to afflict the sport throughout history. The Czech judge voted for the Czech, the two Austrian judges for the Austrian, and the other four, none of them Swedish, for Grafström.

Although Thunberg, with three gold medals, one silver and one bronze, was as much or more of a star at these Games than Haug, the distinction of being the first gold medal winner of the

first Winter Games fell to speed skater Charles Jewtraw of the United States. Jewtraw proved that a poor background is not always a handicap. He came from Lake Placid, where his father was caretaker of the speed skating rink. His winning 500m time, 44.0, was three-fifths outside the world record, but a fifth ahead of Norwegian Oskar Olsen. Returning to Lake Placid in search of a job during the Depression, Jewtraw was put to work sweeping floors.

Although enthusiasts had been devising toboggan-type bobsleighs for more than 40 years, the sport's own federation had not been formed until the previous year, a set of rules only being adopted a few days before the Games. There was only one inaugural event, the four-man, and this was won by a convincing margin of three seconds by a Swiss quartet of Eduard Scherrer, Alfred Neveu, Alfred Schläppi and Heinrich Schläppi. Britain was second and Belgium gained their only medal in third place.

With east- and west-coast leagues both professional, it was difficult for Canada to find a strong amateur team for ice hockey. At Antwerp, the Winnipeg Falcons comfortably won the title, and now this was retained by the Toronto Granite club, even more one-sidedly than four years earlier, scoring 110 goals to 3 in their 5 matches: the closest being 6–1 against the US in the final, watched by the largest crowd of the Games, which overspilled on to the roofs and even chimney-tops of nearby houses. Britain took the bronze. The last event of significance at Chamonix was the founding of the international ski federation.

CHAPTER XVI

Paris (VIII) 1924

Paavo Nurmi of Finland, multiple Olympic track champion

'*When the Finnish team stopped in Hamburg to rest and train on the journey to Paris in 1924, the discipline was almost military. The team leader was an army captain. Team members were shut in the hotel garden and the captain took the keys with him. We decided to sneak away to sample the nightlife and the pleasures of St Pauli. Caught on our return, the captain locked us in our rooms and stopped our per diem* [daily] *pocket money allowance. Later, after Ritola and I had won our gold medals, the captain decided to restore the per diem, backdated.*

We lived in a house near to the Colombes stadium, on the edge of the city. On the evening after I'd won the 1,500m and 5,000m on the same day, I went dancing at a nightclub in Montmartre. One of the Finnish journalists was surprised to see me there, but dancing was a good way of winding down after a hard day's running on the track.

If I'd been aware of present training methods, I would have run better, especially in 1920–6. As a youngster I had no idea of correct training, but that applied to most of the others as well. The exceptions may have been Hannes and Tatu Kolehmainen, who had programmes mailed to them from the US by their brother, William. Mostly prior to 1920 there was not much sense in my training. It was not until military service that I trained regularly and began to progress.

At school, I had speed and stamina in games, so perhaps I had more talent than boys usually have. Also, I started my working life early, pushing heavy carts as an errand-boy on the hilly streets of Turku, which strengthened my legs. I was greatly inspired by the victories of Hannes in 1912 and a few days later bought my first pair of sneakers at the age of 15, starting racing occasionally two years later. In the early years, I was terribly slow and scared of a last lap finishing kick. I decided to do something about it and after a couple of years I had such a spurt I was afraid of no one. A runner must be rid of all fear at the starting line. Without finishing speed, he cannot feel himself secure. You have to be able to sprint for at least one full lap in the 5,000m and 10,000m.

My success in 1924 was based on excellent fitness. Six months beforehand I had decided to take part in all the Olympic races between 1,500m and 10,000m. The team leaders, worried that I would be taxing myself, told me to forget about the 10,000, though I still think I would have been fit enough to win that race as well. On his way to the top, a runner must have ambition together with iron will. Money does not make a runner, but a deep desire from within.' (From an interview with journalist and friend Kauko Niemelä in 1971, two years before Nurmi's death)
(Photograph © IOC)

If Nurmi's pervasive dominance in these Games was to be punctured, it might happen at the shortest of his distances, the 1,500m. It was here that there were rivals who might possibly challenge him, particularly apparent after the 800m. The winner of this was Douglas Lowe, one of the gentlemen-amateurs from Cambridge University, who seldom trained more than twice a week and rarely in winter. He was one of those who excelled on natural talent. Favourite for the 800m was Henry Stallard, the British first-string, but besides having a strained foot, he set too fast an early pace and was spent after the first 600 metres. Lowe, with a controlled finishing burst, won by barely a yard from Paul Martin of Switzerland, with Stallard collapsing as he crossed the line in fourth place behind Schuyler Enck (USA). In spite of his limiting injury, Stallard qualified for the 1,500m final.

What was it that distinguished Nurmi, that made him supreme even in the company of another great Finnish runner, Ville Ritola, whose own magnificence was almost drowned in

Nurmi's wake? The background is well known: one of twelve children of a poor family whose carpenter father had died when he was twelve, obliging him while still a boy to take menial jobs to help support the family. So withdrawn was he that hardly anyone knew him intimately, later not even his own son. He had few friends and though he was to make a small fortune, first outside the regulations through his running, then by investment of those funds and subsequently a successful building company and menswear shop, he lived and died inexplicably a bitter man, feeling that life had given him less than he deserved, when indeed it had given him so much. Olympic historian Wolf Lyberg of Sweden, however, relates that he could at other times be charming.

He was a driven man and his means of expression, from the time he joined an athletic club at 17, was his sport. He was solitary and uncommunicative, training alone to a self-devised programme in which the content and timing was calculated to the last degree: the first example of the benefits to be obtained

Ville Ritola of Finland, himself already champion in these Games for the steeplechase and 10,000m, is outpaced by his compatriot, the legendary Paavo Nurmi, in the 5,000m. (© IOC)

by interval training, mixing endurance and speed work, which would become fashionable 50 years or more later. He carried a stopwatch, uniquely even in competition, discarding it towards the conclusion of a race, thrown on to the grass, when satisfied he was on schedule. Paris was to be his apotheosis, with five gold medals, requiring seven races in six days, to add to his three in Antwerp; all in addition to his 22 world records between 1921 and 1931.

The previous April, Nurmi had fallen during a cross-country run, damaging his knee, which for two months restricted his training. This served only to harden his already obsessive ambition – which had been magnified by the refusal of the Finnish selectors to nominate him for the 10,000m, with the inference that Ritola was his superior. To prove his point, Nurmi ran an unofficial trial race at 10,000m, in a world record time that could not be ratified except in his own mind. In the first week of the Games, however, Ritola, who had returned to Helsinki from his home in America specially to prepare for Paris, stole a march on his rival by winning the 3,000m steeplechase and the 10,000m, breaking his own world record in the latter by 12 seconds, yet some 17 seconds slower than Nurmi's earlier unofficial time – rivalry echoed later by the Ovett–Coe saga.

Now came one of the most remarkable days not merely in Nurmi's career but in Olympic history. Intending, possibly, to break Nurmi's dominance, the IAAF had scheduled the finals of the 1,500m and the 5,000m within half an hour of each other; relenting, in the face of Finnish protest, by expanding the gap to 55 minutes. In preparation for this, Nurmi had staged a dress rehearsal three weeks previously at a home meeting, running the two distances an hour apart and setting world records in both. All were aware, therefore, that the 1,500m could be primarily a race for second place.

Lowe, at 22, was six years younger than Nurmi, but his ambitious challenge was over by the end of the first lap. From the gun, Nurmi set out to bury the field at a pace no one else could sustain and at one point led by more than 30 metres, discarding his stopwatch and coasting over the final lap to preserve some strength for an hour later. Nonetheless, he set an Olympic record of 3:53.6, while behind him Stallard and Wilhelm Schärer battled it out for the silver, the valiant, injured Stallard yielding by three strides. Nurmi had covered the first 500 metres faster than would either Herb Elliott or Jim Ryun when setting their world records in 1960 and 1967 respectively.

At the finish, ignoring the crowd, retrieving his sweater and stopwatch, he disappeared for brief relaxation.

And so to the 5,000m. Ritola and Edvin Wide of Sweden set a hard pace, intending to exploit any fatigue that Nurmi might be feeling. But no. The running phenomenon stayed on their heels, then took the lead at the halfway mark. Doggedly Ritola hung on to him, two metres down. Nurmi accelerated into the last lap and when Ritola tried to pass in the finishing straight, Nurmi accelerated again to win by a stride, again in an Olympic record of 14:31.2.

If this had been a majestic double performance, the following day witnessed something as remarkable, though different. Paris was gripped in a heatwave, only partially relieved by thunderstorms, and at the time of the 10,000m cross-country, the temperature touched 35°C (95°F). Only 15 of the 38 starters would finish the course, many in a state of extreme distress. Ambulance men could barely cope with the demands. A Spaniard and four Swedes collapsed and were rushed to hospital, others had to be carried from the track as they tottered towards the finishing line, some in the wrong direction. And Nurmi? He arrived at the stadium, unruffled and barely out of breath, some 500 metres ahead of Ritola and indeed far less distraught than some of those in the crowd – conditions that led to the abandonment of such an event in summertime. Ritola, in second place, arrived groggily in the stadium almost a minute and a half later, Earle Johnson of America another minute after that. Three finishers were required for team medals and Heikki Liimatainen, the third Finn, arrived delirious; 30 metres short of the line he stopped and started to run the wrong way, finally walking across the line as the crowd verbally directed him. A London correspondent cabled: 'Nurmi runs as though pre-ordained, the embodiment of grace.' He went on to take his fifth gold medal in the 3,000m team race, finishing eight seconds ahead of second-place Ritola.

In heatwave conditions, Nurmi pulverises the field in the cross-country ahead of Edvin Wide (SWE, No. 746), and Ritola (FIN, No. 329). (© IOC)

If Nurmi was an enigma, Harold Abrahams, the British winner of the 100m, was a paradox: a self-proclaimed amateur from the old regime who embraced the same professional attitude as Nurmi, going so far as to employ Sam Mussabini, an Arab-French professional coach. Abrahams, the youngest of six children of a Lithuanian Jewish immigrant, was privately scorned by some of his contemporaries and senior Fellows of his college at Cambridge University. Born in 1899, educated at Repton public school, pushed by his older brothers – one of them, Sidney, competed in the long jump at Stockholm – he was regarded as betraying the ethics of his time. As much a driven man as Nurmi, Abrahams was thick-skinned throughout his 78 years. He ignored the resentment and headed for fame: his response to the class and racist undertones in the criticism of which he was well aware. It was strange that, as a later administrator, fulsomely exploiting his fame for professional ends, he should become a predatory guardian of the amateur ethic as treasurer of the national federation.

Abrahams was fortunate that Eric Liddell, whose manner in every way was quite the reverse, should be removed from his path in Paris by his rival's religious convictions. Contrary to the script of *Chariots of Fire*, the celebrated film portrayal of these Games, Liddell, a Divinity student at Edinburgh University, decided six months beforehand – not, as in the film, on the cross-channel ferry the previous week – that he could not compete in the 100m, the final of which was scheduled for Sunday. Instead he would concentrate on the 200m and 400m. Liddell won a sprint double five years running in the Scottish Championships, and set a British 100 yards record in 1923 of 9.7 seconds which would last for 35 years. He would have been someone for Abrahams to fear; never mind the precision of the latter's preparation with Mussabini, who shortened Abrahams' stride and calculated every yard of the course – more evidence of an attitude allegedly 'unbecoming' of a gentleman.

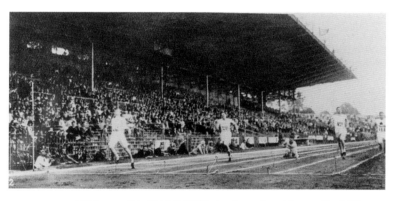

Missionary Eric Liddell (GBR), having refused to run the 100m on a Sunday, streaks to victory in the 400m ahead of Horatio Fitch (USA) and Guy Butler (GBR). (© IOC)

To Abrahams' credit he three times equalled the Olympic record of 10.6, the first time in the second round and again, though getting a bad start, in the semi-final, in which he finished ahead of both the Americans in his race – the defending champion, Charlie Paddock, and Chester Bowman. The final, run four hours later, saw the following line-up: Paddock, Scholz and Murchison (all USA), Abrahams, Bowman (USA) and Porritt (NZL), later chairman of the IOC Medical Commission. Abrahams got away well, but Scholz was level at 50 metres. Neck and neck, they lunged to the finish, where Abrahams, his chest thrust forward and both arms back, got the decision by two tenths of a second, with Arthur Porritt, later his country's Governor-General, taking the bronze in the same time as Bowman and Paddock.

Abrahams, the first European to win the title, had been spared participation by the selectors in the long jump, in which

he held the British record of 7.38m (24 ft 2½ in.) that would survive until 1956. In the 200m he was to come last behind Scholz, Paddock and Liddell. The day before the semi-finals and final, Paddock had suffered a loss of confidence. This was partially relieved by a light-hearted dinner with Douglas Fairbanks, Mary Pickford and Maurice Chevalier, but in the last three strides of the final he was overtaken by Scholz, who equalled the Olympic record of 21.6. If ever one race made a life, it was the Paris 100m for Abrahams.

While Abrahams was winning on a Sunday, Liddell was preaching at the Scottish Kirk in Paris. Like Lowe, Liddell was something of an inspired amateur, also representing Scotland at rugby. His style – arms flailing, knees high, head rolling – was as unconventional, and theoretically restricting, as that of Abrahams' was precise, yet his performance in the 400m final was inspired. Never previously having beaten 49 seconds, Liddell won his semi-final in 48.2. Unexpectedly, he now seemed to have a chance over his less-favoured distance. Drawn in the outside lane, with the disadvantage of his rivals being 'blind', he made an electrifying start, covering the first 200 metres in 22.2, only 0.3 seconds slower than he had run the final of the 200m. Incredibly, he even increased his lead over the second half of the race comfortably to beat Horatio Fitch (USA) in an Olympic record of 47.6. Josef Imbach (SUI) and John Taylor (USA) fell, such was the pace. A year later, having been received as a hero in Edinburgh, Liddell returned to China, where he had been born, to join his father as a missionary. He died of a brain tumour during the Japanese occupation in 1945. All he had earned from Paris was enduring honour and acclaim.

The world long jump record was broken, but not in the long jump competition. Robert LeGendre was irritated that William DeHart Hubbard was preferred for the US long jump squad and was determined that he would out-jump him in the pentathlon, staged for the last time. He not only did so, with 7.76m (25 ft 5 in.), but also took the pentathlon bronze medal behind Eero Lehtonen of Finland. Hubbard, meanwhile, became the first black athlete to win an individual gold medal, with 7.44m (24 ft 5 in.). Hubbard had prospered as an athlete through the patronage of Len Barringer, a white businessman, who engineered his entry to the University of Michigan. His victory in Paris was synonymous with black culture and status in Paris during the jazz age led by singer/dancer Josephine Baker and Sidney Bechet.

The American team was quartered not in the organisers' assembly of huts masquerading as a Village, but on the outskirts of the city, where the cuisine, allegedly, was anything but French. This made little if any difference to one of the most famous swimmers of all time, Johnny Weissmuller, exceptional in his range of distances. From the age of 15 he had trained under William Bachrach of Illinois Athletic Club, who had demanded he should train without races to perfect his style; that the records would then come. The reward would be 67 world records, from 50 yards to 800m; and his performances in Paris, and four years later in Amsterdam, led swimming to become a major Olympic sport. In Paris he became the first man to swim the Olympic 100m in under a minute, with 59.0, ahead of defending champion Duke Kahanamoku – preventing the latter's third successive victory – though Weissmuller had lowered the world record to 57.4 the previous February: a time that would endure for ten years. The same day he also won gold in the 4 x 200m relay and a bronze in water polo. Two days earlier he had won the 400m.

Born in Romania, his immigrant father had worked as a coal miner, dying of tuberculosis before his son made history. In between races, Weissmuller charmed the crowds with stunt

Johnny Weissmuller (USA) (centre) wins the 'race of the Games', the 400m freestyle from Arne Borg (SWE) (right) and Andrew Charlton (AUS). (© IOC)

Uruguay, with the first of four Olympic and World Cup football titles. (© IOC)

Gymnastics champion Leon Stukelj (YUG), the first man to perform the inverted crucifix on rings. (© IOC)

diving and on one occasion he had to be summoned to the start when chatting to a group of female friends. It was Weissmuller who perfected the crawl, amply demonstrated in the record-breaking 400m victory by a metre from Arne Borg of Sweden and Andrew Charlton of Australia – the latter a teenage sensation who, in the 1,500m freestyle, beat Borg by almost 36 seconds.

Tennis was included for the last time for 64 years, Americans Vincent Richards and Helen Wills winning the respective singles against home favourites Henri Cochet and Julie Vlasto. Norris Williams, partnering Hazel Wightman – of Wightman Cup fame – to win the mixed doubles, was a survivor from the *Titanic* 12 years earlier.

The present-day format of gymnastics began, for separate apparatus as well as combined exercises, for individuals and teams. Floor exercises had yet to appear, competition was for men only and Leon Stukelj of Yugoslavia – competing for the first time as a nation following independence from Austria, and composed entirely of Slovenes – took the all-round title.

Uruguay, the first entry from South America, won the football tournament, a prelude to this tiny country's emergence as a major football force. The United States led the medals table with 45 gold, followed by Finland with 14 and France 13. A comparison of Finland's population of 3 million against America's of 105 million demonstrated the exceptional level of fitness and sporting prowess in the little Nordic nation.

CHAPTER XVII

Passing the Baton

Baron Pierre de Coubertin of France, second IOC President, 1896–1925

'. . . my first concern is the belief of others that, now sport has become part of our social habits, there is no risk of it being discarded again. A grave mistake. Sport is a physical discipline sustained by an enthusiastic addiction to unnecessary effort. It is therefore not natural to man, who always tends to follow the line of least resistance. At the moment, sport is upheld by fashion: an irresistible force, but soon spent. This infatuation which we did so much, my friends and I, to bring about 40 years ago because it gave us a handy lever, will disappear as it came. Surfeit will kill it. On that day, what will remain? Does the individual man feel the need for sport? No. The fuss that has been made about some champions does not create this need. It will assert itself only when the champion himself ceases to care whether people look at him or not.

This, then, is one direction in which to work – less advertising, less restrictive organisations, less intolerant unions and top-heavy hierarchies. Instead, to make all forms of sport available, as nearly cost-free as possible, to all citizens, is one of the duties of modern local government. That is why I have campaigned for the restoration of the municipal gymnasium of the ancient world, to be accessible to all without regard to opinions, belief or social rank, and placed under the direct and sole authority of the city. In that way only will a healthy sporting generation be created.

Another utopian notion is to imagine that sport can be officially united with moderation, in the name of science. Sport cannot be made timid and cautious without its vitality being compromised. It needs the freedom of excess. Daring for the sake of daring, and without necessity – in this way our body rises above its animal nature . . .

You would be astonished were I to pass over the famous amateur question. It used not to be insoluble. Before the war, a little goodwill would have been enough to solve it. Today it is more complicated because the high cost of living has transformed the picture, public opinion is not disposed to let sport become a pastime of the rich . . . we should ensure that in each federation the current ruling is honourably enforced, though we are far from this goal . . . a lot of cheating and lying goes on, the repercussion of a moral decline.

Sport has grown up within a society in which the lust for money is threatening to rot to its marrow . . . the imposition of an individual oath on all participants will be the best way of bringing sport within the realm of honour again . . . the renewed Olympism will be the force best able to undertake this task of purification, provided people stop wanting to turn the Olympic Games into world championships. It is because they are imbued with this idea that some technicians are forever trying to destroy the Olympic Constitution, in order to seize a power which they think they are fitted to exercise absolutely. If modern Olympism has prospered, it is because it has had at its head an independent council that no one has ever subsidised and which, since it is self-recruiting, is free from all electoral meddling and does not allow itself to be influenced by nationalistic passions or by the weight of corporate interests. With a supreme council composed of delegates of national Olympic committees or the international federations, Olympism would have died within a few years . . . may harmony reign between the three powers – IOC, NOCs and IFs.

The hour has come to raise a pedagogic edifice whose architecture is more fitted to the needs of the day . . . my fellow workers and friends will continue their ascent of the hill on which we hope to raise a temple, while an immense fair is being organised on the plain. The temple will endure, while the fair will pass away. Fair or temple – sportsmen must make their choice. They cannot expect to frequent both one and the other.' (Retirement speech to the Olympic Congress, 29 May 1925, Prague Town Hall) (Photograph © IOC)

At the age of 61, de Coubertin realised full well it was time for him to pass the baton. His confidence in stepping back from his life's work and leaving future development in the hands of colleagues had been enhanced by the institution of the Executive Board. This by now had become the agenda-forming body that guided the rank and file IOC members, though by no means necessarily controlling them. When issues became heated, the pressure could be removed at annual Sessions by referring matters to the Executive Board 'for study'. The Executive Board also formed a buffer between the members and power-seeking sections of the NOCs and IFs. At the time of the Congress in Prague in 1925, the immediate matters of concern were those of amateurism and the disputes arising from this vexed debate in tennis and football. Taking the broader view as always, de Coubertin considered it his responsibility to address the Congress on the long-term moral obligations of the IOC, as evidenced in the address quoted here: prescient to an extreme. It was up to the Executive Board to thrash out the details with the respective tennis and football federations, the ILTF and FIFA. At the heart of the dispute with these two bodies was the question of compensation to competitors for 'broken time': in other words, for loss of earnings for blue-collar workers while away from work. The IOC itself was not without sympathy. Comte de Clary of France was in favour of such compensation, but J. Sigfrid Edström, the increasingly influential leader of the IAAF, was heavily opposed. Compensation was outvoted at Prague, but athletes were allowed reimbursement for expenses for up to 15 days. Government-funded training was explicitly forbidden. The concept of 'fair play' was debated and a declaration was instituted to be signed by the NOC, the relevant national federation and the athlete, stating: 'I, the undersigned, declare on my word of honour that I am an amateur, in accordance with the Olympic rules on amateurism.' At the same time, an amateur was freshly defined as 'one who devotes himself to sport for sport's sake without deriving from it, directly or indirectly, the means of existence. A professional is one who derives the means of existence entirely or partly from sport.' The continuing class bias was unresolved. There were, for instance, and would continue to be, many school teachers in Britain employed at public (in fact, private) schools, not for their ability to impart the subtleties of Latin or chemistry, but because of their eminence as coaches in the sporting arena, some of whom were admired Olympic performers. Scandinavian representatives mooted the idea of eligibility being left to the discretion of each international federation, but the good sense of this went unobserved for another half-century.

Comte Henri de Baillet-Latour, third President of the IOC, courteous Belgian banker, faithful disciple of de Coubertin, sport's anti-feminist, anti-Bolshevist. (© IOC)

The election of de Coubertin's successor at the 1925 Session took place on 28 May. Absentee members had sent postal votes, some of them voting for de Coubertin on the assumption that he would stand again. In the first round, the 40 votes were divided thus: de Baillet-Latour 17, de Coubertin 11, de Blonay 6, de Clary 4, de Polignac 1, with one invalid. In the second round, confined to those present and thereby excluding the wasted postal votes for de Coubertin, de Baillet-Latour received 19 of the 27 votes cast, thus becoming the IOC's third President.

The oddity of the election was the poor result for Godefroy de Blonay, the Swiss member, who had been deputy President during the war while de Coubertin was a non-combatant officer in the army. He had had a close relationship with de Coubertin, but this had waned after the war when de Blonay had irritated the founder by over-reaching what he personally regarded as the responsibilities of the new Executive Board. There may have been a reluctance to offend de Coubertin by favouring de Blonay, whereas de Baillet-Latour had never been anything but a faithful disciple. Elected to the IOC in 1903, he had been acclaimed by de Coubertin for 'ensuring that Belgium's participation in the Olympic Games is a credit to his country and his sovereign'. Aside from this, de Coubertin had wanted de Baillet-Latour to organise the Congress in Brussels in 1905, and when Antwerp came to be chosen as emergency host city after the war for the Games of 1920, de Baillet-Latour's energy as president of the organising committee had been exemplary. Becoming president of the Belgian NOC in 1923, he had, by 1925, 22 years of Olympic experience. His first term of office was to be for eight years.

Henri de Baillet-Latour was born on 1 March 1876, son of Comte Ferdinand de Baillet-Latour, former Governor of the Province of Antwerp, and of Countess Caroline d'Oultremont de Duras. After studying at the University of Louvain, he went into the diplomatic service. An accomplished horseman, he was to become the president of the exclusive Jockey Club de Bruxelles.

While de Coubertin had always striven to remain above petty politics and the manoeuvres of the jealous, de Baillet-Latour's presidency, which would last 17 years, was to be regularly enmeshed – in spite of his devotion to maintaining Olympic ideals – in ground-floor controversies. He was no philosopher and was more entrenched in the manners and attitudes of the aristocracy than his predecessor. While de Coubertin, the educationalist, had remained open-minded on many philosophical issues, his successor was, for example, opposed to any liaison with the workers' sporting movement and anything that smelled of Bolshevism. This pedantry led de Baillet-Latour to several defeats on policy: notably on the Olympic football tournament in Amsterdam, with broken-time payments, and the introduction of women's track and field events in spite of his committed resistance. He was among those who, following the 'distress' of the women's 800m finalists in 1928, joined the chorus for a return to the ancient Greek custom of male-only competition; only to be rebuked by Lady Heath of the English WAAA, who reminded the men that women were already proving themselves equal in the fields of commerce and science. However, de Baillet-Latour's inherent courtesy enabled him to ride his reverses and suffer no loss of respect. He was less assertive towards his contemporaries than de Coubertin had been and was to prove an administrator notable for the thoroughness of his organisation.

By 1925, the Fédération Sportive Féminine Internationale, led by Alice Milliat, had become quite strident, buoyed by the success of its 'Women's Olympics' in 1922 at the Stade Pershing in Paris, a second staging of which was planned for 1926. The

IAAF had voted in 1924 to sanction women's track and field but not to advocate its inclusion in the Olympic Games. With the FSFI continuing to press, Edström met Milliat, agreeing to leave the FSFI in control of women's events, in return for which they would omit the title 'Olympic' from their event. However, in April 1926 the IOC bowed to the inevitable, accepting the IAAF's recommendation to permit the admission of women to a restricted number of track and field events. Also to be admitted was women's gymnastics, though only for team competition, with track and field limited to 100m, 800m, 4 x 100m relay, high jump and discus. This compared poorly with the 13 events contested under FSFI at Gothenburg in 1926. British women were so incensed at the limitation to five events at Amsterdam that their association, the WAAA, boycotted the 1928 Games. However, women finally had their foot in the Olympic door.

Edström attended the congress of FSFI – which now had 23 member federations – during the Olympics in Amsterdam, Milliat being a reciprocal guest at the IAAF congress, presenting her federation's demands. The misogyny of de Coubertin and some of his contemporaries was gradually being dissolved. The former President had been privately attacked at the Prague Congress by the Czechoslovak Women's Sports Federation and by Britain. The last stand of de Coubertin against women had been to preside over an official report that decreed that women should be provided with 'a healthy, persevering and beautiful body . . . a creative factor in the family and in society in general' but should refrain from practising violent sports and 'should not pursue records'. It was agreed that 'it is women who should preside over women's physical education, so that femininity is not imperilled'.

The amateur clause adopted in Prague was more restrictive than that which was operated by the ILTF. Tennis had been a cause of contention at the Olympic tournament in Paris in 1924 and this now deepened at the ILTF general assembly in March 1926. The federation demanded a seat on the IOC; the right to be actively involved in the organisation of the event (as opposed to controlling the rules); the exclusive application of its own amateur definition; and dispensation from any requirement to drop any events from its normal programme. The ILTF was advised by de Baillet-Latour that the tennis tournament for the 1928 Games would be cancelled if it did not revise its position, and was given a deadline of the end of 1926. This was ignored, the ILTF stating it would discuss the situation at the following year's general assembly. Hoping to avert a rift, de Baillet-Latour suggested deferring the controversy to the next IOC Congress but the ILTF remained resolute. The IOC therefore regretted that:

> . . . because the IOC does not allow the re-qualification of professional athletes, the ILTF has forbidden all its members to take part in the Games at Amsterdam. In the attempt to maintain Olympic amateurism at the Olympic Games, and in its determination to keep them open for all qualified amateurs, the IOC points out by way of reminder that only amateurs whose qualification is in compliance with the Olympic rules are eligible.

When the ILTF failed to attend further consultation meetings, the Executive Board decided to recommend to the 1926 Session in Lisbon that tennis should not be included in the programme. In Brussels in 1927, the Executive Board minuted that the ILTF remained anxious to be included in the 1928 Games, but the impasse continued, so that their eligibility became impossible. Tennis would remain absent from the Olympic programme for 60 years.

From early days, the presence of football was an important element in the financing of any Games, attracting as it did sizeable crowds. Furthermore, it was evident that exclusion of football would drive FIFA towards creating its own rival world championship, though it was obvious to anyone with common sense that this would happen anyway. In the meantime, Jules Rimet of France, president of FIFA, was invited for negotiations with the Executive Board in Paris in August 1927. The IOC's

Jules Rimet, French president of FIFA, and founder of the World Cup, reluctantly withdrew from the Olympic Games over the issue of compensation for loss of earnings, banned by the IOC. (© FIFA)

newly defined position on amateurism, from Prague 1925, was explained by de Baillet-Latour in an attempt to find a mutually acceptable compromise settlement. The Executive Board accepted new FIFA rules, on broken time, on condition that compensation for loss of earnings be paid not to the athlete but to his employer. This device enabled the letter of the IOC's rules still to be respected. However, Edström and Brigadier Reginald Kentish of Britain, Executive Board members, refused to agree to the compromise. The Executive Board was accused of exceeding its brief and the disgruntled four individual British associations – England, Scotland, Northern Ireland and Wales, all older than the world governing body – withdrew from FIFA. The Executive Board reconvened, countered the accusation that it had exceeded its powers on the grounds that, between Sessions, it could take binding decisions, and attempted to clarify its acceptance of the FIFA regulations – determined at its own congress of 1926 – that players not granted a paid holiday would be compensated for loss of earnings out of its own resources, so as to create equality of opportunity. An uneasy compromise, which undoubtedly contravened the IOC's own definition of amateur status, allowed the 1928 football tournament to survive. Irrespectively, FIFA's 'Jules Rimet Cup' was inaugurated two years later for their first World Championship.

At the Executive Board meeting in March 1926, Edström surprised his colleagues by announcing that the international ski federation (FIS) had retrospectively decided a month earlier to call the Winter Games of Chamonix in 1924 the 'International Olympic Winter Sports', and this no doubt provoked the IOC at their Session in Lisbon in 1926 to settle on the title 'First Olympic Winter Games'. At the IOC Congress in Prague, it had been decided to continue with a four-yearly cycle of winter events, though without determining where should be host city for 1928. What had been agreed was that the country of the summer host city should have the option of additionally staging the winter Games.

In 1921, Amsterdam had been selected as summer host for 1928, having failed in its previous bids for 1912 and 1924. Los Angeles had also been a contender for 1928, but the Netherlands was thought to be politically expedient, having been neutral in the First World War. Yet by the time of the Prague Congress doubts had arisen about Dutch capability to provide facilities for the summer event, so there was little possibility that they might be delegated to stage both. Discussions between Dutch and French Olympic committees provisionally agreed for a return to Chamonix. This was controversially criticised from the sidelines by de Coubertin, insisting that 'the celebration of the Games is awarded to a city, not a country, and cannot be split under any pretext'. This in turn invoked criticism from nations lacking the physical environment to hold both events. The controversy was further complicated by the French government refusing to grant their NOC's request for two million francs for the preparation of a team for 1928. Ultimately the decision was taken to stage the winter Games at St Moritz in neutral Switzerland, influenced by awareness of the political issue surrounding the return of German athletes, who would be competing for the first time since 1912. Even ten years after the War, some hostility remained towards German readmission, the Belgian NOC voting against it.

The programme for St Moritz remained limited, with only thirteen events for men and two for women. Curling was omitted, having been a demonstration event at Chamonix, though St Moritz had become by now a well-established centre for all ice/snow events. A special pavilion for VIPs, seating 400, and a 5,000-seat grandstand for spectators were constructed as well as the world's then highest ski jump, with a vertical height of 310 feet.

In almost every aspect the St Moritz Games would prove beneficial to both the Alpine city and the Olympic Movement;

though the IOC only narrowly overcame a problem over the sale of newsreel rights, which re-emerged at the time of the summer Games. It was during these Games that Sir Arnold Lunn, the Alpine skiing innovator and a council member of the FIS, persuaded his colleagues to include downhill and slalom racing experimentally in international competition. It would be another 20 years before they appeared on the Olympic programme, but another door had been opened for what was to become a major Olympic spectacle. Competition at St Moritz was invigorated by the entry for the first time of competitors from Japan, Mexico, the Netherlands and Romania.

The Dutch, who had been among the original supporters of de Coubertin's revivalist movement, might be a small nation but historically played a major role in the evolution of Europe's modern civilisation. Their canal and dyke method of land reclamation from the sea had been spectacular and in the seventeenth century they had matched the British, Spanish and French in the breadth of their global sea-faring commercial expansion. Amsterdam was among the most beautiful of European cities, the cycling and skating Dutch were among the most physically active of races and were determined that the Amsterdam Games would be a celebration of their national culture and industry. A 40,000 capacity stadium, requiring 4,500 piles driven into the ground to provide the foundation, was the showpiece – containing a 400m track, the now standardised distance, encircled by a cycling track. For the first time, there was a large results board and a flame burning, though this had not been ferried from Olympia. Fortunately for the Dutch, the worldwide economic recession, epitomised by the Wall Street crash a year later, had not yet hardened, and this was the interim period between the destructions of the First World War and the emergence of Adolf Hitler's National Socialist Party, which fed on the humiliation and poverty created in Germany by the effects of the Treaty of Versailles in 1919. Hitler would not gain absolute power for another four and a half years, but in Amsterdam, with its substantial Jewish population, there was latent unease at the rise of Fascism. Although a German team would be prominently present in Amsterdam, together with their wartime allies, Austria, Hungary and Bulgaria, the Soviet Union and Chinese remained absent.

Illness prevented de Coubertin being present in Amsterdam, but General MacArthur, *chef-de-mission* of the US team, declared the Games 'a model for all future Olympics'.

Jacob Thams (NOR) experiences the world's then highest ski jump at St Moritz. (© IOC)

Queen Wilhelmina of the Netherlands awarding medals at Amsterdam. (© IOC)

CHAPTER XVIII

St Moritz (II) 1928

William Fiske of America, youngest Olympic bobsleigh champion driver

'Pilot Officer W.L.M. Fiske, RAF, the first American serving as an officer in the RAF to lose his life in action against the enemy in this war, died on Saturday from wounds received in combat with German bombers on Friday. Pilot Officer Fiske, who was 29 years old, came to England shortly before the outbreak of war to enlist and, after training, was gazetted acting Pilot Officer in March. He became a member of a fighter squadron and had taken part in several successful fights and was reported to have destroyed a number of enemy aircraft. After the successful conclusion of Friday's fight, he landed his machine safely. It was found he was badly hurt and he was taken to hospital.

William Fiske was a member of a well-known American banking family. He was a partner in the New York firm Dillon, Read and Co. In the United States he was known as "William Fiske III". He was a champion toboggan rider and a winner several times of the Cresta Run course record at St Moritz. Fearless and tough, he was equally popular in business circles on both sides of the Atlantic as on the toboggan track, and more recently among his RAF colleagues. In 1938 he married Rose, daughter of the late Mr D.C. Bingham, Coldstream Guards, killed in action in 1914, and of Lady Rosabelle Brand, who married secondly in 1916 Lt Col J.C. Brand, who died in 1929. Mrs Fiske was formerly the wife of the Earl of Warwick.' (Obituary, *The Times*, London, 19 August 1940)

'A very gallant gentleman, Billy Fiske, has given his life for us. As a racing motorist, as a bobsleigh rider, as a flier he was well known, but as a Cresta rider he was supreme. Taking some years to become first-class, his fame eventually was legendary. No record he did not break, no race he did not win, he was the supreme artist of the Run. Never did he have a fall, he was in a class by himself. An American citizen, blessed with this world's goods, of a family beloved by all who knew them, with a personal charm that made all worship him, he elected to join the Royal Air Force and fight our battles. We thank America for sending us the perfect sportsman. Many of us would have given our lives for Billy, instead he has given his for us. The memory of him will live long in the Alps, where he had his greatest successes; in the hearts of his friends it will endure forever.' (Lt Col J.T.C. Moore-Brabazon, MP, *The Times*, London, 20 August 1940)
(Photograph © IOC/Roebett)

Although winter sports were a leisure activity rapidly developing strands of serious competition, the degree to which certain events remained amateur is apparent from the bobsleigh competition staged at this socially up-market tourist resort. Three members of the winning US team, Geoffrey Mason, Richard Parke and Nion Tucker, were selected when answering an advertisement in the Paris edition of the *New York Herald Tribune*. None had ever boarded a bobsleigh before. They won after barely three weeks' practice and Mason never rode in a bobsleigh again. For the first and only time, teams were composed of five rather than four men. William Fiske, the US driver, was the then youngest Winter gold medal winner at the age of 16 years, 260 days, while the 42-year-old Tucker was the oldest competitor at these Games. Americans also took the silver medal, while the skeleton toboggan race on the Cresta Run, unique to Games that are staged at St Moritz, saw brothers Jennison and John Heaton of America take first and second with David, Earl of Northesk of Britain, third.

Billy Fiske was born into a wealthy New York banking family in June 1911 and the family background opened many opportunities for him, including those of sport. He was already a veteran of the Cresta by the time of the St Moritz Games, combining fearlessness with accurate judgement. He won the major trophy of the Cresta Run from 1935, when 23, to 1938. In 1932, he carried the US flag at the Lake Placid Games and his driving was even more spectacular in victory than four years earlier. Fiske declined the captaincy of the overall US team for the Garmisch Games (1936) in protest at the treatment of Jews, the US speed skater Irving Jaffee, double winner at Lake Placid, being a good friend. After the outbreak of war he joined the 601 Squadron based at Tangmere, Sussex, known to outsiders as 'the millionaires' mob' because of their carefree manner, and he was recorded as having made six hits on German craft in the one-month spell in a Hurricane before his death. With his cockpit on fire, he had landed back at base, but died of shock from his burns.

Although the future inclusion of Alpine skiing events had been assured, traditional Nordic events remained the present objective – though under continuous threat from perverse meteorological patterns, disrupted by the warming Föhn wind from the south. On the morning of the 50km race, the temperature was -17°C when the skiers made their first wax tests: determined by the state of the snow and critical to success. Within a few hours the temperature had risen to +25°C, never mind the altitude of 1,850 metres (6,000 ft), and the course had become like brooks in springtime. A quarter of the skiers were forced to retire, in what were transparently unfair circumstances. Three Swedes, Per Erik Hedlund, Gustaf Jonsson and Volger Andersson, took the medals with times more than an hour slower than four years previously in Chamonix. The following day, to compound the problem, it rained and an entire day's events had to be postponed. This was followed by a hard night frost that rescued the Games but came too late to save competitors in the 10,000m speed skating, which had begun on the day of rocketing temperatures. By the time seven of the ten entrants had completed their heats, the ice had turned to cheese and it was impossible to continue. Irving Jaffee was in the lead by a tenth of a second from Bernt Evensen of Norway. The event was halted and rescheduled to recommence the following day, when the conditions were as bad or worse. With some of the Norwegians now departed, a re-run was impossible, Jaffee was regarded as the winner, but officially the race is regarded as not having taken place. In other speed skating events, Clas Thunberg of Finland added two gold medals to the three gold, one silver and one bronze he had won in Chamonix, in the shortest race of which, the 500m, there was the unique occurrence of Thunberg and Evensen being tied for first place, in an Olympic record of 43.4. No silver medal was awarded, with third place for the bronze medal tied by John Farrell (USA), Jaako Friman (FIN) and Roald Larsen (NOR) on 43.6.

The major news item of these Games, transferring sport from the back to the front page, was that of Sonja Henie, the 15-year-old Norwegian, winning the first of what was to be three successive Olympic figure skating titles. With her interpretation of Tchaikovsky's 'The Dying Swan', she brought a new dimension to figure skating. Following the experience gained at Chamonix, she had finished second in the World Championships two years later. In 1927, the Championships were staged on her home rink in Oslo, where the judging aroused controversy, not for the last time in a subjective sport. Three of the five judges were Norwegian, all of them voting for Henie, the other two Austrian and German, voting for Herma Planck-Szabó. This provoked the International Skating Union to rule that there should be only one judge per country. So outstanding, however, was Henie in St Moritz, that she was placed first by six of the seven judges: the American judge voting for the American competitor, Beatrix Loughran, who came third.

Despite an injured and swollen knee, Gillis Grafström of Sweden, now 34, retained his men's figures title. Such was the perfection of his style that he narrowly held off the challenge of Willy Böckl of Austria and Robert von Zeebroeck of Belgium, whose more muscular approach embracing jumps appealed to some judges. Grafström was the Fred Astaire of the ice, for whom skating was always more of an art form than a competition. He often trained four or five times a day, starting at 6 a.m. and liked to be left undisturbed. He was happiest in a near-empty stadium watched by a few schoolchildren, yet had the temperament to remain focused when skating for a gold medal, even though he had to be persuaded to enter both the Olympic Games and the World Championships. From 1928 until his death in 1938 at the age of 45, he lived in Berlin, where he had married Cecile Mendelsohn-Bartholdy, a great-granddaughter of the composer Felix. An architect, he was a noted collector of art and skating memorabilia.

Gillis Grafström, a Fred Astaire on ice, retains his men's figures title. (© IOC)

Sonja Henie, by now 15, stuns the opposition in the first of her three Olympic figure skating titles. (© IOC)

Realising that Canada, the defending champions, and again represented by the national champions from Toronto, were so superior in ice hockey, the organisers scheduled a draw in which Canada proceeded immediately to the final round, while the other ten nations were divided into three pools; the winners of these then joined Canada in the final round robin. The sense of this was apparent when Canada beat Sweden 11–0, Great Britain 14–0 and Switzerland 13–0.

In spite of the weather, the Games had been an organisational, visual and commercial success. Japan, Holland, Romania and Mexico had made their Winter Games debuts, and the social desirability of St Moritz had further risen.

CHAPTER XIX

Amsterdam (IX) 1928

Percy Williams of Canada, Olympic double sprint champion

'*At King Edward High School in Vancouver, like everyone else I took physical education. You had to do something; I got pushed into track. Somebody told Bob Granger, a well-known track coach, that there was this kid at King Ed who could run and he came up to watch me and we got talking. It was a bit of a lonely drag, training for a year just for a couple of track meets, but with Bob Granger, he just took over.*

I had some unexpected success at the Olympic trials in Hamilton. Most of the others trained at American colleges but I was able to win both the short sprints. I couldn't quite understand why at the time but winning the 100m put me on the boat for Amsterdam.

Bob missed the boat because he hadn't got the fare but my mother helped canvass in Vancouver to raise the money and he left on the next boat. Because he was late arriving in Amsterdam – we'd hoped to practise sprint starts on board – Bob devised makeshift training in the hotel room, placing a mattress against the wall as a buffer. The hotel management didn't think much of that but the practice got me in the mood. Most of the other finalists seemed much bigger and stronger but Bob just said to me: "Keep calm, it's only another Sunday school race." He made me wear three tracksuits over four sweaters in the warm-up, so that I'd be really warm and loose. It was a bit of a shock for everyone, me included, when I won. So now I'm supposed to be the world's 100m champion. Crushed apples. No more fun in running now.

I never really looked the part of an athlete, even at my peak, at 5 ft 6 in. tall, 130 lb, but a few days later I was able to win the 200m. Not so bad. Telegrams galore. The girls' team sent flowers to me. Hot dog! All my rivals, Paddock, Wykoff and the rest, they all congratulated me. I knew Bob would be pleased. Whatever I'd done had been through my coach. Granger was everything. Everything. On the way back to the hotel with Doral Pilling, our javelin thrower, there was a bit of a mob around the entrance. We asked what the fuss was about and someone said, "We're waiting for the Canadian sprinter, Williams, to come out of the hotel." We stood around waiting for him, too, and talking to people. It was more fun that way.

At the first British Empire Games in Hamilton two years later, I won the 100m in spite of having a slightly torn muscle and the problem was still there at the Olympics in Los Angeles, when I was captain of the Canadian team. I went out in the semi-final of the 100m. I was not too bothered. I was glad to be done with track, with public appearances. I never did much like running, anything I accomplished I did because of the determination of Bob Granger. I always thought it was a lot of hogwash to say that you ran for your flag and country. I was just out there to beat the guy beside me.*' (An amalgamation of newspaper interviews)
(Photograph © IOC)

With some assistance from the British Empire, a fact largely overlooked by the IOC at the end of the twentieth century, the Olympic Movement spread the sporting ethic around the globe. Here in Amsterdam were Uruguay winning the football tournament; Argentina taking two gold medals and two silver in the boxing and a gold in swimming; a Chilean runner coming second in the marathon; India winning the hockey against the hosts in front of 50,000 people; Mikio Oda winning the triple jump for Japan, which also gained a gold in swimming; Ibrahim Moustafa of Egypt a winner in Greco-Roman wrestling; Silvio Cator of Haiti second in the long jump; Sid Atkinson of South Africa winning the high hurdles, with compatriot George Weightman-Smith breaking the world record in the semi-final; and Edward Morgan of New Zealand taking

boxing's welterweight title. Truly the Games had become universal.

On the other hand, the glory of these Games belonged primarily to Finland. This was the last hurrah of their middle- and long-distance dynasty, a dominance that had become the wonder of the athletic world. Now they were first and third in the 1,500m with Harri Larva and Eino Purje; first and second in the 5,000m, with Ville Ritola and Paavo Nurmi; first and second in the 10,000m, Nurmi and Ritola; took all three places in the steeplechase, with Toivo Loukola, Nurmi and Ove Andersen; and third in the marathon, with Martti Marttelin. The Finns themselves and analysts elsewhere attributed their phenomenal success to a characteristic which they term *sisu*: a quality that is a combination of will-power and endurance and in part could

Emerging East. Mikio Oda (JPN) takes Asia's first individual Olympic gold in the triple jump. (© IOC)

explain their exceptional fortitude in the hazards of their winter war against the Soviet Union in 1940. Nurmi was by now 31 and his presence on Amsterdam's new 400m track was a relief to his country's enthusiasts and officials, for in the previous two seasons he had been on the soft pedal, his exceptional training schedule taking its toll on his limbs. Now he was revived. Finland's victory in all track events from 1,500m upwards would not be matched until 60 years later by Kenya.

The ninth and last of Nurmi's gold medals came in the 10,000m, the event in which his glory had begun eight years earlier. After only a third of the race, it became dominated by him, Ritola and Edvin Wide of Sweden, the latter falling back with seven laps remaining. From there on Nurmi trailed Ritola, surging past in the finishing straight to win by a couple of strides in a new Olympic record of 30:18.8.

The order of the two Finns was reversed in the 5,000m, Nurmi unable to retain his title from Paris, both of them running outside the record established then by Nurmi. The same three men as in the 10,000m drew clear, but this time it was Ritola who moved in front on the final bend to win comfortably from a tiring Nurmi in 14:38.0, Wide finishing several strides astern of Nurmi. A day later, Nurmi again had to be content with second place, this time in the steeplechase, in which he was a total novice, never previously having negotiated a hurdle. There had been the unusual sight of seeing him fall headlong in the water jump during the heats, and the final was to be the last Olympic appearance for both him and Ritola. Indeed, Ritola dropped out exhausted a lap and a half from the finish, but Nurmi hung on, in his fifth race in seven days, for a silver medal way behind his compatriot Loukola, who had resorted to running as rehabilitation from tuberculosis and was now busy setting a world record of 9:21.8.

Nurmi had remained taciturn to the last in his uneasy relationship with Ritola. When winning the 10,000m, he had shunned photographers and Ritola and walked off the track without a smile; though conversely he had been gracious to a Frenchman, Lucien Duquesne, who helped Nurmi to his feet when he had fallen at the water jump, Nurmi pacing him for the remainder of that race and inviting him to break the tape

first – which Duquesne equally sportingly declined to do.

US supremacy in track and field was sharply interrupted. The first shock arrived with the 100m victory of Percy Williams, a little-known 19-year-old high school student from Vancouver. He immediately caught public attention when equalling the Olympic record of 10.6 in the second round, though his time was matched in both semi-finals by American Bob McAllister, ahead of Williams, and by Jack London, a Briton from Guyana and the first Briton to employ starting blocks. Williams had hitch-hiked across Canada to compete in the national trials, working as a waiter in the city to cover his expenses. He was anything but favourite for the final, yet, calmly surviving two false starts, led from first to last, holding off the challenge of London and Georg Lammers of Germany. McAllister pulled a tendon and finished last. In the final of the 200m Helmut Kornig of Germany, who had equalled the Olympic record of 21.6 in the heats, was passed 50 metres out by Williams and Walter Rangeley of Britain. In his eighth race in four days, Williams won by a clear tenth of a second. Showered with material rewards on his return home, he remained unimpeded by the vigilant watchdogs of amateurism.

Emerging Canada. Percy Williams, 19-year-old student from Vancouver, unheralded 100m champion. (© IOC)

Americans Frank Cuhel and Morgan Taylor, the world record holder, could do nothing in the 400m hurdles to hold off the quality of Lord Burghley, who set an Olympic record of 53.4. David Burghley, heir to the Marquis of Exeter, had been eliminated in the heats of the high hurdles four years earlier. He had furthered his fame at home, a year before Amsterdam, by completing a circuit of Trinity College Great Court – where the soothing sound of the fountain in the centre, echoed by the ancient buildings, is at night one of the most soporific sounds to be heard anywhere – within the time it takes the college clock to toll twelve. This feat was corrupted in the film *Chariots of Fire* by being attributed to Harold Abrahams, while Burghley's hurdles victory was portrayed as being performed in Paris.

In the 800m there was another memorable British victory, the event attracting added interest due to a race two years earlier at Stamford Bridge when Dr Otto Peltzer of Germany had broken the 14-year-old world record while competing against Douglas Lowe, the champion from Paris: a record then improved by Lloyd Hahn of America and in turn by Séra Martin of France. Peltzer, in Amsterdam, was injured and eliminated in the semi-finals. Lowe, however, showed himself to be a champion of champions, running away from a star-studded field to win by a second in an Olympic record of 1:51.8. Second was Erik Bylehn of Sweden, with Hahn, whom Lowe had left wallowing on the final bend, finishing fifth and Martin sixth. Lowe, with innate sympathy, wrote to Peltzer in commiseration, though a month later in Berlin he beat the German narrowly in a fine race to substantiate the worthiness of his Olympic victory.

A pointer towards the future, though half a century or more

Emerging women. Elizabeth Robinson (USA) wins the inaugural 100m, Canadians Fanny Rosenfeld and Ethel Smith taking silver and bronze. (© IOC)

Emerging Africa. Mohamed El Ouafi, Algerian-born Frenchman, marathon champion. (© IOC)

away, was the marathon victory of Mohamed El Ouafi, an Algerian-born Frenchman, pathfinder of North Africa's great distance runners, who had finished seventh in Paris. He and Miguel Plaza Reyes of Chile, sixth in Paris, moved into second and third place three kilometres from the finish behind Kanematsu Yamada of Japan, El Ouafi then racing ahead to win from Reyes by almost half a minute. El Ouafi was randomly shot dead while sitting in a Paris café, poverty-stricken at the age of 61.

A perceived misfortune overtook the women's five track and field events, condescendingly included following lengthy prejudiced debate among their arbiters . . . the men. At the finish of the 800m, many collapsed at the finishing line, and why not, it might be asked, for a similar reaction occurs occasionally to this day among the men. The affected dismay among male officials, with professed concern for the functional well-being of the female form, resulted in this race being omitted from the Games until 1960. The winner on this occasion was Lina Radke of Germany, in a world record of 2:16.8. She and her compatriots, Marie Dollinger and Elfriede Wever, ran as a team, the latter two as pacemakers for Radke, whose winning time, nearly a second ahead of Hitomi Kinue of Japan – world record holder in both 200m and long jump, neither of them included at Amsterdam – would survive for 16 years.

The first woman to win an Olympic track race, Anni Holdmann of Germany, had not survived the 100m second-round heats. The final was won by a 16 year old from Illinois, Elizabeth Robinson, whose talent had been spotted when she was running for the bus. Amsterdam was only her fourth track outing and her victory was distinguished by equalling the world record of 12.2. There was also a popular victory in the high jump by Ether Catherwood of Canada, who cleared 1.59m (5 ft 2 in.).

American swimmers fared better than their athletes. The already legendary Johnny Weissmuller improved his own Olympic record by four tenths of a second to 58.6 in the 100m freestyle, more than a second ahead of István Bárány of Hungary, in spite of choking on accidentally inhaled water on the turn. Yoshiyuki Tsuruta and Katsuo Takaishi emphasised Japan's emergence by taking the 200m breaststroke gold and 100m freestyle bronze respectively. Four years later, Weissmuller made his Hollywood debut in *Tarzan, the Ape-Man*.

Albina Osipowich of America won the women's 100m freestyle with an Olympic record of 1:11.0, plus a share in the 4 x 100m relay. At the tender age of 12, she was the youngest winner of two gold medals in history. The continuing rivalry between Arne Borg of Sweden and Andrew Charlton of Australia took an odd turn in the absence of Weissmuller, who decided not to defend his 400m title. Concentrating on each other, they battled furiously over the final length of the pool, Charlton just getting the touch ahead of Borg – only to discover that Alberto Zorilla of Argentina, whom they had ignored, had taken the gold medal with an Olympic record of 5:1.6, albeit 11 seconds behind Borg's world record. Borg went on to win the 1,500m freestyle, leading from start to finish to beat Charlton with an Olympic record of 19:51.8. In an eight-year spell up to 1929, Borg set 32 world records, his 1,500m time of 19:7.2 surviving for 11 years.

The mounting appeal of football – its first World Cup still two years away – was evident from a total audience of more than a quarter of a million. Uruguay beat Argentina 2–1 in the final, Italy taking the bronze medals by whipping Egypt 11–3. India won the first of six consecutive hockey titles. Richard Allen, their goalkeeper, did not concede a single goal, the Netherlands losing the final 3–0. Britain, who had taken the game to the sub-continent, notably to Calcutta in the nineteenth century, were no longer in the frame. Dhyan Chand, an army captain and later national coach, inspirationally led his team to three of their Olympic gold medals.

Equestrianism was notable for the fading influence of Sweden, all-powerful at Stockholm and then in Antwerp, but now taking only two bronze medals. Dominant were the Dutch, winning the three-day event – and Lt Charles Ferdinand Pahud de Mortanges the individual title – and the Germans likewise in dressage, Carl von Langen the individual winner. Capt. Frantisek Ventura of Czechoslovakia had the distinction of winning the show-jumping without a single fault in the entire competition, in which Spain won the team event. Ibrahim Moustafa of Egypt became the first non-European to take a Greco-Roman event when winning the light-heavyweight wrestling title.

Sven Thofelt of Sweden, who was to become the doyen of his sport over three consecutive Games and subsequent officialdom, won the modern pentathlon ahead of his compatriot Bo

Sven Thofelt (SWE) begins an extended Olympic career when winning the modern pentathlon individual title from compatriot Bo Lindman and Helmut Kahl (GER). (© IOC)

Lindman, his forte being the 300m swimming section. Crown Prince Olav, later King of Norway, set a first as a royal winner of a gold medal when he competed as a crew member in the six-metre yachting class. His son, Crown Prince Harald, was to compete without comparable success from 1964 to 1972.

The Swiss were predominant in gymnastics, winning five of the seven gold medals available and Georges Miez being the all-round champion, though the Netherlands won the first of the women's team events. Although they won only bronze medals, Harry, Percy and Frank Wyld of Britain became the first three brothers, together with Frank Southall, to win medals in the same event at the same Games, finishing behind Italy and Netherlands in the 4,000m cycle pursuit.

Lina Radke (GER), the eventual champion, leads Kinue Hitomi (JAP) in her heat of the inaugural women's 800m – the final of which, with some runners collapsing with exhaustion, caused the event's omission until 1960. (© IOC)

CHAPTER XX

Beating the Crash

Denis Oswald of Switzerland, Olympic oarsman, president of FISA (rowing), IOC Executive Board member

'*A few years ago, a world champion and Olympic medal-winning rower had his house destroyed by fire. Most notably lost in the blaze were all the sporting medals the athlete had won during his career. He asked me to what extent and at what price these medals could be replaced, and then added: "If it's too complicated, then forget about the World Championship medals, but let's try to replace the Olympic medals at least."*

This reaction rightly reflects the special prestige enjoyed by the Olympic Games. For an athlete, participation in the Games represents the ultimate goal of his or her sporting career. An Olympic medal is more valued than a World Championship medal, even if, in fact, both competitions are of a similar level and the opponents are identical.

In the eyes of the public, too, the Games seem to have a special aura. Many people who are not particularly interested in sport and do not usually follow competitions, nonetheless watch Olympic events on television and show an interest in the results, just because "it's the Olympic Games".

The exceptional prestige associated with the Olympic Games stems from several factors: the rarity of the event, as they only happen once every four years, their established place in history with their antique origins and tradition, and especially their universal and multi-sport nature. Indeed, the Olympic Games transcend sports. The Games create a link between different sports and unite them in a common competition, with shared rules and identical rewards. They appear as a unit. A wrestling champion is crowned in the same manner as the winner of the 100m. He is the best in his field, as are all other Olympic champions. The Olympic Games imply a universal acknowledgement of athletic performance, whatever the discipline. It is no longer a matter of sport, but of universal sport.

This principle also appears within the national Olympic teams, as these encompass all disciplines and unite all the athletes from one country into one single group. The Games thus create bridges between athletes of different sports who often only know each other through their shared Olympic experience.

This transcendence of sports can only be achieved if all sports are united, whether they be more or less known, lend themselves more or less to media coverage and be more or less important. The allegedly small sports therefore also have a role to play within this context. Their inclusion is what makes the Olympic Games and gives them their unique and universal character. They bring an added value to this event and distinguish and separate it from a football World Cup or a World Athletics Championships. Moreover, they are often associated with moral and educational values, and these contribute to the perception of an enriched Olympic Games.

The allegedly lesser sports can therefore be seen, in reality, as essential founding stones of the Olympic edifice and contribute to making the Games a universal and unique event, above and beyond mere sport.'*

(Photograph © IOC/Locatelli)

At the turn of the eighteenth century, Lake Placid was an area of farming land granted to African-Americans who had gained their freedom. John Brown, the famous abolitionist, owned a farm outside Lake Placid and was buried there in 1859 after he was hanged in Virginia for his assault on the US arsenal at Harper's Ferry. By then Lake Placid was becoming a cultural and sporting haven, attracting mountain climbers and artists from the big cities who came to relax in the tranquil summertime of the Adirondacks, and in 1895 Dr Melvil Dewey founded the Lake Placid Club to exploit the growing tourist trade. Dewey was librarian of New York State, but he made his minor mark on history by expanding his club, in the winter of 1904–5, to incorporate winter sports activities. Skis, unavailable in America, were imported from Norway and enthusiastic members began skiing and tobogganing and skating on Mirror Lake. It was Dewey's son, Godfrey, who would mount the bid to stage the Winter Games of 1932 at the resort little known outside the eastern seaboard.

By 1921, Lake Placid had both a ski jump and a speed skating rink, and the local ski association had become America's dominant winter sports organisation, but it would nevertheless be a challenge to convince the IOC that this still minor resort could stage a Winter Games. One factor in the resort's favour was that in 1923 the Summer Games of 1932 were awarded to Los Angeles and it was still unofficial practice of the IOC, where possible, to stage both Games in the same country. However, other winter sites closer to southern California, such as Lake Tahoe and Denver, were also interested in hosting the Games, as were Montreal and Oslo. Godfrey Dewey, by now secretary of his father's club, formed a bid committee in 1928, having persuaded the town and, more importantly, Franklin D. Roosevelt, the Governor of New York, that it was a worthy venture. The following year Dewey's delegation sailed to France and thence to Switzerland, and on 10 April they were able to convince the IOC that their bid was serious and well-qualified.

Besides Roosevelt, who coordinated a supporting State Commission, there was valuable backing from Avery Brundage, who had recently been elected president of the American Olympic Committee (AOC). Brundage directed himself towards the provision of training facilities for the home team and of equipment for the host city.

The size of the task to which Lake Placid had committed itself was daunting. There would be several hundred contestants and a predicted daily inundation of 8,000 spectators to what was little more than a large village. A bobsleigh-run and a main stadium were required, not to mention facilities for ice hockey and other sports. New York State agreed to fund the bob-run, at $125,000, and a German designer was hired for the construction. Controversy raged over the felling of trees, protected in the Adirondack forests by state law, and constitutional 'amendment' was required before much of the work could go ahead.

As the time of the Games approached, the economic situation, both domestic and global, became critical following the Wall Street crash of Black Friday, 25 October 1929. The total cost of the Games was estimated at more than a million dollars. The town of North Elba, the administration of which embraced Lake Placid, created a $200,000 bond issue, but this was nowhere near enough to meet expenses, even with the addition of moderate ticket sales. In the end the State legislature bore the main burden, extending to over half a million dollars.

If the budget strings were tight at home, so were those in Europe, and the prospect of travel to America dissuaded many countries from attending. Brundage negotiated with shipping and rail companies to reduce fares by 20 per cent for foreigners

travelling to the Games – including the Summer Games – while President Herbert Hoover agreed to exempt foreigners from visa fees, which at the time were strict and expensive. To add to the organisers' worries, there was little snowfall in January and temperatures during an exceptional heatwave climbed to 10°C (50°F), melting what snow there was and thawing the ice rinks. Happily, however, temperatures dropped in time and a storm deposited fresh snow.

With Hoover declining to open the Games, Roosevelt, his rival in the forthcoming presidential election, jumped at the chance, using the occasion, broadcast nationwide by NBC and Columbia networks, as a campaign-stop on his election trail. For good measure, his wife Eleanor took a ride down the newly constructed bob-run.

While the Depression restricted the scope and the attendances at Lake Placid, it posed a far more serious threat of disruption to the summer event at Los Angeles, a six-day train journey away on the other side of the continent. By the summer of 1932, a quarter of the US workforce, some 13 million people, were unemployed. National output had dropped by a third and there were bread queues in the streets. In Sacramento, California's capital city, protestors marched in opposition to the Olympics. 'Groceries not Games,' declared the banners. Rejecting the further request that he should open the Summer Games, Hoover exclaimed: 'It takes some gall to expect me to be part of it.'

The situation was little better in Europe. Germany had been brought to its knees by inflation on top of post-First World War reparations and the growing Nazi party was already clamouring for unity with Austria. Italy was likewise reeling and in Britain unemployment had reached almost three million. Elsewhere, Japan's GNP had dropped by almost a half.

The man of the moment would prove to be William Garland. At the 1920 IOC Session in Antwerp, Garland had had the

Franklin D. Roosevelt (second from left), hat in hand, declares the Lake Placid Winter Games open. (© IOC)

Dr Karl Ritter von Halt (right) leads a team from inflation-racked, Nazi-gripped Germany. (© IOC)

foresight to make the first bid for LA to host the Games in 1928. In Antwerp, however, Paris still appeared as the frontrunner for 1924 and there were already plans for Amsterdam four years later. Such was the impression that Garland made in Antwerp, though, that he was elected to the IOC by postal vote in 1921, and on his return to the US he ensured that the Memorial Coliseum in LA, previously commissioned, was now built. At the Session in Rome in 1923, Garland was therefore in a strong position to renew his bid. With Paris and Amsterdam already in the pipeline, the IOC was happy to grant LA the Games nine years in advance and did so by acclamation without search for an alternative candidate.

The debate regarding female participation continued at an Executive Board meeting in 1929. For all his magnanimity in other areas, de Baillet-Latour remained more steadfastly opposed to women's involvement in the Games than even de Coubertin and vowed that only aesthetic sports should be permitted for women. Absurdly, this included swimming, one of the most muscularly violent of all sports, but, because it takes place in water, hypocritically sensitive male eyes would not be confronted by the sight of ladies pouring with sweat: they would instead merely elegantly drip cool water. As a challenge to IOC bigotry, Gustavus Kirby, an American member of the IAAF, threatened to withdraw the American men's track and field team if women were excluded from the Los Angeles Games. He was indirectly motivated by the ambitions of his daughter, an only child, to make her mark internationally in equestrianism.

The IOC's reticence about the inclusion of women was appearing increasingly archaic. In 1930, the FSFI had staged its third World Women's Games, as they were now called, in Prague, with competitors from 17 nations taking part in 12 track and field disciplines, in addition to basketball and handball. Kirby had been present in Prague and sent a written recommendation to any doubters assembled at the Session in Barcelona in 1931. His stance did not go unrecognised and the IOC voted to retain women's track and field events at LA – with 80m hurdles and javelin added, alongside fencing, gymnastics, skating and swimming, though the 800m was to be withdrawn. By coincidence, the retention of track and field would assist the emergence of Mildred 'Babe' Didrikson, the first female track and field superstar.

So, the women were going to be present, but not the legendary Paavo Nurmi. Shortly before the opening ceremony, the IAAF ruled that the fabulous Finn was a professional on account of financial rewards he had received and he was therefore barred from competition. The disgruntled Finns threatened to withdraw but did not follow through. Also absent for the first time since 1900 would be the footballers. The issue of amateurism continued to rage – as it would for another half century – and remained impossibly confused, the more so after blurred definitions emerged from the Congress of 1925. When the IOC ruled, at the Berlin Session of 1930, an absolute ban on broken-time payments – accepted by FIFA for the Games in Amsterdam – FIFA promptly withdrew. FIFA was not particularly bothered. Their own World Cup had just begun for the first time in Uruguay and, anyway, who in California cared about football?

Pride and enthusiasm had been unrestrained among Californians when William Garland had returned with his prize in 1923. A $1 million bond issue had been approved to underwrite the Games and the Coliseum had been enlarged to a

William May Garland (right), mastermind of the Los Angeles Games, takes IOC President de Baillet-Latour (centre) and US Vice President Charles Curtis on a tour of facilities. (© IOC)

100,000 capacity. The world seemed good – until 1929 and the arrival of soup kitchens. By 1930, the economic situation was desperate. Who could afford now to cross oceans and continents?

Addressing the Session in Berlin, Garland told the IOC that LA was prepared to feed, house and transport every competitor for two dollars a day, and in order to do so they were specially building a competitors' village. Within this, each NOC would have its own dining room, with its own cook if so wished. In conjunction with reduced steamship and rail fares, European teams might thus make a month's round trip for $500 a head, a third of what had been expected. As a result of this splendid innovation, the Village being sited on Baldwin Hills with cooling Pacific breezes, only a few minutes from the main stadium, European teams reconsidered their hesitancy. Primarily on account of the Village, competitors from 37 countries would be able to attend the Games. The Village additionally was to have its own hospital, fire department, independent policing and a security fence. At a stroke, the Americans had through necessity created the environment of competitor cohabitation that thereafter was to be a basic ethic of Olympic competition. The women, meanwhile, were given exclusive occupation of the grand Chapman Park Hotel on Wiltshire Boulevard.

Having turned the financial corner, LA, in conjunction with Hollywood, set about creating the best-appointed and most glamorous Games there had yet been. Gala functions would fill the ballrooms and banquet halls of the Biltmore and other plush hotels; the Coconut Grove would be packed with visitors every night. The release of the first Tarzan film with Johnny Weissmuller added a special touch of glamour. Mary Pickford and Douglas Fairbanks, Olympic junkies for the past decade, broadcast invitations to a worldwide audience to come and have fun and entertained many visitors, including athletes, at their sumptuous Regency mansion. Other stars such as Marlene Dietrich and Buster Keaton joined the social jamboree and the Games were front-page news before they had even begun.

Not only did LA now possess one of the world's foremost

Competitors relax in their purpose-built, zephyr-cooled Olympic Village. (© IOC)

President de Baillet-Latour fills the tank of his luxurious loaned limousine. (© IOC)

stadiums, with a new crushed-peat running track, but there was also a 10,000-seat swimming stadium; the State Armoury, where fencing took place; a further 10,000-capacity auditorium for boxing, wrestling and weightlifting; plus a wooden track within the Pasadena Rose Bowl, specially constructed for cycling. No previous Olympics had equalled the programme for art competitions, staged at the LA Museum of History, Science and Art. What had seemed might become a nightmare was in the event a bubbling success. No effort had been spared in the precision of detail. There was photo-finish equipment for the track, accurate to one-hundredth of a second but used only to determine close finishes. There was a three-tiered victory stand and medal ceremonies included the raising of respective national flags. A reflection of the financial difficulties of the time, in an era when IOC members paid all their own expenses, was that only 18 of the 66 members, 3 of these Americans, were present at LA.

More than a million spectators over the two weeks paid nearly two million dollars to attend the events. Perhaps for the first and last time until the Games were again staged in LA 52 years later, they had made a profit, contrary to every expectation. One source of income was a new three-cent postage stamp depicting a runner, for which the model was Alfred Leconey, anchorman of the winning sprint relay team in 1924. For the closing ceremony of this milestone in Olympic history there was a crowd of 87,000, many competitors and spectators having returned home earlier for reasons of economy. As the sun dipped below the horizon, a chorus of a thousand voices filled the air with the strains of 'Aloha'. The Games had indeed fulfilled the maxim displayed on the scoreboard at the opening ceremony, an act repeated ever since: 'The most important thing in the Olympic Games is not to win but to have taken part . . . the essential thing is not to have conquered but to have fought well.'

CHAPTER XXI

Lake Placid (III) 1932

Sonja Henie of Norway, three-times Olympic figure skating champion

'*I was given my first pair of skates for Christmas when I was eight. I'd never before put on skates and I was in a real hurry to go out and join my older brother Leif. I took several spills that morning but even the aches and pains and bruises were fun. My father thought I showed some promise and decided to get me an instructor.*

Until the Olympic Winter Games of 1928, figure skating had been rather stiff and pedantic in its competitive form. The free skating programmes, the part of each contestant's performance that is left to invention and taste, had been little more than a series of school figures and minor stunt figures strung together. I'm sure that my introduction of a dance pattern into my free skating programme at St Moritz had a great deal to do with my winning that Olympic title. It gave form and flow to the sequence of orthodox spins and jumps. Since then skaters have come to build their free skating programme to a large extent on dance choreography.

The Games at Lake Placid turned out to be a disappointment for all Norwegians; weather conditions, and so of competition, were in a state of constant change and therefore troublesome. It was some relief for us that the figure skating events went well . . . the field was strong and the victory equivalently gratifying. I felt I had really achieved something.

The 1932 Games left Europeans with few good memories. It was utterly unlike Garmisch-Partenkirchen in 1936, where the scene of competition was at the centre, the burning point. Too many outsiders at Lake Placid reduced the Games as a whole to tameness. The flurry of packing trunks, making adieus and boarding trains out of that beautiful if distressing spot – on account of the wretched weather – in the Adirondack Mountains was accomplished more quickly than usual.

From a young age, it had been my ambition to move into films. Many dancers are actresses and they prepare for their acting career by dancing. I did the same. I did not wish or intend ever to give up skating. It meant too much to me and I believe it is as beautiful and entertaining as dancing. But I wanted new experiences, to carry my career another step forward. I did miss the thrill of competition but the main thing I cared about was to skate, no matter to what end. I skated more after retirement from competition than I ever did before and with greater variety. In working things out for films, I learned new tricks and figures that I did not think possible before. Most important for me, though, was that I could at last present to the public my ideas of dancing on skates, about which I had a dream as a child.' (From her autobiography, *Wings on my Feet*)
(Photograph © Getty Images)

Born in Oslo in 1912, Sonja Henie was the second child of wealthy parents, her mother's family being in shipping, her father's in the fur trade. The girl had both inherited and acquired advantages. Wilhelm, her father, was himself a champion cyclist and an accomplished speed skater and cross-country skier, while an imposing family house in Oslo, a mountain hunting lodge and a summer seaside villa provided the comfort and opportunity for the self-indulgence that would help a precocious child become one of the most famous Olympic figureheads.

Owner of the first automobile, allegedly, and the first private plane in Norway, Wilhelm indulged his daughter's every wish. It is, therefore, unsurprising that she grew up selfish and with few friends, her every breath devoted to training and the advancement of her ambitions. At nine, she had been national figure skating champion. Between the ages of twelve and sixteen – prior to the Games at St Moritz – she studied, and also met,

Anna Pavlova, becoming equally dedicated to her sport. Though she was to remain officially amateur until 1937, by which point she had won ten World Championships and three Olympic titles, she was already famously rich, in the manner of Suzanne Lenglen – that equally famous and formidable amateur in tennis. It is one of the mysteries of their time that they were able to evade the scrutiny of the trenchant official disciples of amateurism.

Adored worldwide for her grace and originality as Olympic champion, transforming the concept of her sport, and subsequently under contract to Darryl F. Zanuck at a reported $125,000 per picture, Henie was less than revered in her native Norway, particularly as a result of her imprudent friendship with Adolf Hitler. At a skating exhibition in Berlin in 1935, she wantonly courted his approval with a Nazi salute, receiving in return his autographed picture in a silver frame. This was regarded as a national disgrace in a country later occupied by Hitler's invading forces.

Karl Schäfer of Austria pushes defending champion Gillis Grafström into second place in men's figures. (© IOC)

Jack Shea achieves a 500/1,500m speed skating double in controversial 'heats' racing.
(© IOC)

The unanimous choice of all seven judges in Lake Placid, from the USA, Austria, Canada, Finland, France, Great Britain and Norway, Henie was far ahead of her nearest contestants, Fritzi Burger of Austria and Maribel Vinson of America. The men's title, by an almost similar margin, went to Karl Schäfer of Austria – only Finland and Britain placing him second – ahead of Gillis Grafström, the Swedish champion of the past two Games. A blunder by the 38-year-old Grafström on a compulsory figure early in the competition was recovered with his usual panache, but he could not reclaim his gold. He had been disconcerted by a collision with a badly placed movie camera.

Hosting their first Winter Games, the United States were more dominant than in previous years, earning six gold medals, four silver and two bronze from the fourteen events – nine more than their aggregate hitherto. Their success, however, was largely due to them exercising 'local' rules in speed skating, leading to open, free-for-all massed starts, rather than the European system of successive pairs measured against the clock. Also, as a result of the weather and the Depression, there was a sharp drop in entries, of both individuals and countries, and more than half of those attending were from the USA and Canada.

So incensed was Clas Thunberg, the multiple former champion from Finland, at the adopted form of racing in heats of five or six, that he refused to compete. The system was to prove disastrous for the Europeans, America and Canada winning ten of the twelve available medals. The Europeans insisted on traditional starts being restored for the World Championships, which were to take place on the same rink immediately after the Games, and for future Winter Games. To prove the point Ivar Ballangrud of Norway, 5,000m speed skating champion in 1928, won three titles in the Championships, having managed only one silver medal, for the

10,000m, in the Games. The 500m and 1,500m races both went to Jack Shea, a 21-year-old local boy who had taken the oath at the opening ceremony an hour or two before the three qualifying heats of the 500m (see also Chapter LXXI). Five of the six finalists, unsurprisingly, were North American, Shea winning by five yards from the defending Bernt Evensen of Norway and equalling the latter's Olympic record in the irregular racing format. In the 1,500m, Herbert Taylor (USA) fell on the final bend, enabling Shea comfortably to beat Alex Hurd of Canada.

The Adirondacks had their mildest winter in 117 years, according to the Albany weather bureau. For the first time in history the Hudson River did not freeze until the end of February. As a result, the Americans were obliged to import truckloads of snow from across the Canadian border and for the only time, so far, the final run of the four-man bobsleigh event took place the day after the closing ceremony. There were a number of accidents on the course, which had been financed by some 5,000 tourists contributing ten dollars a head to go down the run with the help of an instructor. For the first time there was also a two-man event, plus the novelty of Edward Eagan, a lawyer from Denver, being a member of America's winning four-man team. Eagan, who had been born into a poor family and made good through attendance at Yale, Harvard and then Oxford, became the only person to win a gold medal in both summer and winter Games, having won the light-heavyweight boxing title at Antwerp in 1920. Eagan was a member of the team driven by Billy Fiske, winner four years earlier with his ad-hoc team drawn from advertisements, one of whom, Clifford Gray, a 40-year-old songwriter and British citizen, was now competing again, together with Jay O'Brien, 48-year-old chairman of the US bobsleigh committee. The two-man event was won by the Stevens brothers, Hubert and Curtis, who were

Billy Fiske leads the American bobsleigh team to a successful defence of its title. From left: Zahn Werner of Germany, bronze winner, presents the trophy to Fiske, Edward Eagan, Clifford Gray and Jay O'Brien (© IOC)

The Canadian ice-hockey squad that retained the title, their fourth. (© IOC)

local residents. They had heated their runners with blowtorches prior to each run, a practice now illegal.

Thaw and rain caused the ski jumpers to finish in a pool of water, not the best preparation when waiting for their second jump on the exposed tower in soaking clothes. Three Norwegians, Birger Ruud, Hans Beck and Kaare Wahlberg, took the medals, Ruud out-jumping Beck, the reigning world champion, on his second leap. Canada retained their ice hockey title, their fourth, though only on goal average after three periods of overtime against the United States in the final game.

These slightly ravaged Games had been marked by demonstration speed skating events for women, who would have to wait another 28 years for inclusion on the full programme, and by Mollie Phillips, a British skater, being the first woman to carry her nation's flag at the opening ceremony.

CHAPTER XXII

Los Angeles (X) 1932

Mildred 'Babe' Zaharias (née Didrikson) of America, double Olympic track and field champion

'Going over the hurdles, I bent my front leg more than you're supposed to, on account of having practised over those hedges at home. And I didn't throw the javelin quite the way they said you should. I told the [US team] coach I was sorry but I wasn't going to change. My own coach, Col McCombs, told me to stick to my natural style.

It was a wonderful thrill to march into the stadium on the opening day, but to tell you the truth I couldn't enjoy the ceremonies after we got out there. We all had to wear special dresses and stockings and white shoes. That was the first time I'd ever worn stockings in my life, and as for the shoes, they were really hurting my feet.

The javelin took place that first day, but not until late afternoon when shadows were coming up over the stadium and it was turning cool. Warming up, I was watching the German girls because they were supposed to be the best. They'd been taught to loosen up by throwing into the ground. I'd been told this was the way to practise but could never agree. It seemed to me this gave you the wrong motion. I always thought you should warm up with the same swing you used in competition.

They had a little flag stuck in the ground to show how far the new Olympic record was. It was a German flag because a German girl had just set the inaugural record – some distance short of my own best. When my turn came, what with the cool air and my lack of warm-up, I wasn't loosened properly. Yet the javelin kept on going to set a new Olympic record of 143 ft 4 in. (43.68m). In practice, I'd been close to 150 ft, but I tore a muscle in my shoulder making that first throw and in my last two turns people thought I wasn't trying.

Two days later we had the hurdles heats, another first-time event. The new best was 12.2 seconds. My personal record, which I'd set a couple of weeks before, was 11.9. I beat both those marks in my heat with 11.8. In the finals the next day, I was so anxious again to set a record that I jumped the gun. A second time, and I would have been disqualified, so I held back, and it wasn't until the fifth hurdle that I caught up and just beat Evelyne Hall of Chicago. In horse racing, you'd say I won by a nose, Even with the late start, it was a world record of 11.7.

I needed to win the high jump to make a clean sweep of my three events [women were restricted to competing in only three individual events in track and field athletics]. Jean Shiley and I were better than we'd ever been, the bar climbing to 5 ft 5 in. [1.65m], nearly two inches higher than we'd jumped in the trials. We both cleared it and now I'd beaten the world record in two of my events. There was still first place to be settled. They raised the bar another three-quarters of an inch. We both missed, so they dropped the bar down to 5 ft 5 in. Jean made her jump, I made mine. They weren't used to seeing my Western roll and under the rules of the day your feet had to cross the bar first. If your head went over first, it was a "dive" and didn't count. They suddenly ruled that I'd "dived" and the rule cost me my first-place tie. A picture proves my feet in fact went over just ahead of me. I'd been jumping the same way all afternoon – all year for that matter. I told the judges so, but they just said: "If you were diving before, we didn't see it. We saw it this time."' (Adapted from her autobiography, *This Life I've Led*)

(Didrikson (centre) with Jean Shiley (left) and Eva Dawes, photograph © IOC)

Opinion on 'Babe' Didrikson's character was divided, such was her extreme self-confidence. On the one hand, this phenomenal sportswoman, the most devastating all-rounder that has ever lived, was the 19-year-old darling of these Games, on the other it was alleged that her team colleagues were collectively praying for Shiley to win the high jump. Evelyne Hall was reported as saying, years later: 'We were very highly strung and we put a lot of pressure on Jean to beat this obnoxious girl.' When accused of not trying in her second and third attempts at the high jump, Didrikson had responded: 'I didn't need to.' Once, partnering a man at golf, she had said at the first tee: 'You'd better play first, it's the only time you will.'

Her father was a Norwegian ship's carpenter who had sailed many times round Cape Horn. From childhood onwards she challenged boys for physical supremacy. She was never known to possess a doll and devised weightlifting exercises in the back yard with a broomstick and her mother's flat-irons. In contradiction to such a tomboy image, her lack of femininity haunted her for much of her life. At 18, she *quit* boxing, declaring, 'I'm a lady.' She excelled at baseball, football, basketball and handball, and was above average at lacrosse, tennis, fencing, skating, shooting, cycling and billiards. In

Phenomenon Mildred 'Babe' Didrikson (USA) battles for the 80m hurdles title with compatriot Evelyne Hall and wins by a whisker in the same time. (both © IOC)

addition to her sporting prowess, she could type at more than 80 words to the minute, played the harmonica, was a smooth ballroom dancer and a dab hand at cards. It is perhaps, therefore, unsurprising that such a figure would be resented.

As a teenager, she won three consecutive national basketball titles with the Dallas Cyclones, at 17 reached 296 feet (90.22m) in the Baseball Throwing Championships, pitched for the Brooklyn Dodgers and once struck out the legendary Di Maggio in front of a crowd of 72,000. In the trials for Los Angeles at Evanston, Illinois, she won five of eight events, setting three world records in the process. Even so, it was as a golfer that she earned her greatest fame. Going round in 95 the first time she picked up a club, after three lessons she shot 83. In a career that went from amateur to professional, she won the World Championships and the US Women's Open three times each, the latter for the last time in 1954, only two years before she died of cancer at the age of 43.

It is an irony of the 1932 Games that while Didrikson was

almost certainly penalised incorrectly in the high jump, denying her a shared gold medal, she should instead have been tied for the hurdles. These Games saw the official introduction of the photo-finish camera, used only on an experimental basis, but it was mostly too slow in film development for effective use. A week after the hurdles final, it became evident from the photographs that Evelyne Hall was at least equal with Didrikson. Without use of this they had incorrectly been given the same world record time.

The 1932 LA Games were a success, though there had been much pessimism in advance on account of the Depression and low demand for tickets. Interest only lifted immediately prior to the opening when Hollywood stars such as Douglas Fairbanks, Mary Pickford, Charlie Chaplin, Clara Bow and Marlene Dietrich voluntarily joined a publicity drive. For the competitors, many of whom from Europe had endured a five-day trek by train across the continent from New York – hopping off at brief stops every few hundred miles to limber up – the radiant sunshine and clean air enjoyed in the first-ever Olympic Village, high on a plateau overlooking the Pacific, was a balm for most ills. The opening ceremony attracted the largest officially recorded attendance in sports history at that time, with 101,000 spectators filling the extended LA Coliseum, and some of the loudest cheers greeted Chun Liu Cheng, the first and sole Chinese competitor bearing the flag of the then half a billion people. He failed to survive the first round of both sprints, but such was the climate and the impeccable new track that in track and field events Olympic records fell like pheasants before Christmas.

It was a feature of the Games that Finland's dominance of distance races, so pervasive in 1924 and 1928, was now broken, and not just because of the absence of the banned Nurmi, who had been said to have the lowest heartbeat and the highest asking price of any athlete in the world. He had to sit in the stands with Bing Crosby, the Marx Brothers and the rest. Controversy followed Finland on to the track, though not in the 10,000m, which turned into a duel between Janusz Kusocinski of Poland and Volmari Iso-Hollo of Finland. These two shadowed each other until the last lap, over which the Pole sprinted clear for an Olympic record of 30:11.4, five seconds outside Nurmi's world record. The 5,000m was more heated and was one of those occasions when good manners on the part of the Americans came to the fore. With three laps to go, Ralph Hill, best of the home runners, had joined Lauri Lehtinen, the

Lauri Lehtinen sustains Finland's middle-distance tradition when defeating Ralph Hill (USA) in the 5,000m at the end of a controversial finishing sprint. (© IOC)

Finnish world record holder, and his compatriot Lauri Virtanen at the front, and excitement mounted as Hill overtook Virtanen. Down the finishing straight Hill attempted to pass Lehtinen, first on the outside, then the inside, but each time the Finn moved across to block him. Lehtinen won by less than a stride and both runners were credited with an Olympic record time of 14:30.0. Raucous booing greeted the outcome and was only subdued by the announcer pleading: 'Please remember, these people are our guests.' US officials declined to protest.

The 1,500m saw another absentee, as world record holder Jules Ladoumegue of France had also been banned for professionalism, but nonetheless the race boasted famous names of the future: Jack Lovelock (NZL) and Glenn Cunningham (USA). At the bell, Cunningham and Philip Edwards of Canada led by five or six strides but coming off the final bend Luigi Beccali of Italy overtook both of them, followed by John Cornes of Britain. Beccali set an Olympic record time of 3:51.2 with Finland nowhere to be seen. This was one of 12 gold medals for Italy, second only to the 41 of the United States.

The marathon was won by Juan Carlos Zabala of Argentina, aged 20. He established and held an early lead for three-quarters of the race, at which point he was overtaken by Virtanen, already bronze medal winner in the 10,000m and 5,000m. Zabala narrowly regained the lead and there were three other runners circling the track within the stadium – Samuel Ferris (GBR), Armas Thoivonen (FIN) and Duncan Wright (GBR) – before an exhausted Zabala collapsed across the finishing line. This was a welcome reward for a troubled Argentinean team, which had gone on strike in the Village against a dictatorial *chef-de-mission* and later came to blows on the ship on the way home. The ringleaders were reportedly sent to prison, including Santiago Lovell, winner of the heavyweight boxing title.

If trying to predict the outcome of the 800m prior to the final, few would have put money on Tommy Hampson, a 24-year-old British teacher, who had never beaten 1:52, let alone approached the world record of 1:50.0 of Ben Eastman of America, who in LA had decided to concentrate on the 400m. Hampson, however, had prepared for the race on the bold assumption that the winner would have to beat 1:50, a time then regarded with the same awe as the four-minute mile would be in later years. He reckoned he must aim at two quarter miles (400m) of around 55 seconds each and this he stunningly achieved, to record a world record of 1:49.7. 'My inspiration the whole way down the finishing straight was the thought of Winnie, my fiancée, just when I thought my legs wouldn't get me there,' Hampson said.

Now for a trick question. Who broke a world record and finished second? The 400m hurdles final contained not only Morgan Taylor (USA), world record holder and champion of 1924, and Lord Burghley, champion of 1928, but also Glenn Hardin (USA), who had equalled the Olympic record in the first semi-final, a feat matched by Bob Tisdall in the second. This was only Tisdall's seventh race at the distance, his entry with the Irish team being almost experimental – as his training, without hurdles, had been. Since arriving in LA, Tisdall had been sleeping for 15 hours a day to recover from the arduous journey but now, such was his strength, he was well clear of the field at the final obstacle. Surprised by the absence of challenge, he relaxed, knocked down the hurdle, stumbled but recovered and still held his lead to beat Hardin by two-tenths of a second. Under the rules then applying, however, his world record of 51.7 was discounted by the falling hurdle, Hardin being given the record at 51.85.

Eddie Tolan and Ralph Metcalfe lined up for the final of the 100m as joint favourites: Metcalfe having won the trials, Tolan

Irish outsider Bob Tisdall outpaces famous rivals, Americans Glen Hardin and Morgan Taylor, to win the one-lap hurdles, Hardin finishing second with a world record. But how? (© IOC)

having set an Olympic record of 10.4 in the second round. Neck and neck they fought over the last 20 metres, with the impression being given that Metcalfe had won. Delayed viewing of the finish camera persuaded the judges that Tolan was the winner but reassessment of that photograph years later suggests that in fact it should have been Metcalfe, both setting a new record time of 10.3. Fate was to frown upon Metcalfe again in the 200m, also won by Tolan in an Olympic record of 21.2, when faulty track marking led to Metcalfe digging his starting holes a metre behind where he should have been, this costing him the silver medal behind compatriot George Simpson. Absent from the event was world record holder James Carlton of Australia, who had suddenly retired to a monastery to become a monk.

Japanese men suddenly emerged as the best swimmers in the world at LA, though not without intense preparation. Four of them won individual events; three broke Olympic records; and their 800m relay quartet improved the Olympic mark by an astonishing 38 seconds. Kusuo Kitamura, who won the 1,500m freestyle, was only 14; Masaji Kiyokawa, the 100m backstroke champion, was 16; and Yasuji Miyazaki, the 100m freestyle winner, was 17. In every one of the men's races, all three Japanese reached the final and the Japanese won 11 of the 16 medals.

Had it not been for Clarence 'Buster' Crabbe, the Japanese might have won all five races. Crabbe, another future Hollywood Tarzan, took the 400m freestyle in a record 4:48.4, coming from two lengths behind at halfway to beat Jean Taris of France, the world record holder, by a tenth of a second. Chuhei Nambu added to Japan's growing reputation by winning the triple jump and taking bronze in the long jump, while colleagues Kenichi Oshima and Shuhei Nishida won bronze and silver respectively in the triple jump and pole vault.

There was much speculation over whether Jules Noël of France should have won the discus. The formal result showed that he came fourth behind John Anderson of America, who took gold. Unfortunately for Noël, at the moment of by far his longest throw the judges were busy watching the pole vault and no one knew for sure where his throw had landed. A consolation throw then proved to be in vain. Duncan MacNaughton of Canada won the high jump, though only by unusual persistence. Studying at the University of Southern California, his request to compete in the US trials was rejected, as was his request to Canada. After repeated pleas he was allowed to take part in the Canadian championships and won the event, but was still excluded from the Olympic team. He nevertheless turned up in the Olympic Village, yet again demanding a place. The Canadian committee's patience exhausted, they yielded, and he became the first man to break America's monopoly of this event since the modern Games began.

Italy provided the largest number of immigrant spectators and a huge gathering excitedly watched the University of Pisa eights crew give the University of California a battle royal over the 2km rowing course at Long Beach. Italy led by a metre approaching the line only for a final heave to give the US victory by 30 centimetres. In the singles sculls, Henry Pearce of Australia successfully defended his title. The previous year he had won the Diamond Sculls at Henley by six lengths.

In a rare display of self-discipline, Ivar Johansson, a Swedish policeman, won the middleweight freestyle wrestling event, then shed five kilos in less than a week to win the Greco-Roman welterweight title. Culinary control was also exhibited by Attilio Pavesi of Italy in the 100km cycling lasting two-and-a-half hours: on his handlebars he carried soup, water, a dozen bananas, cheese sandwiches and some cold spaghetti, together with two spare tyres around his neck. He defeated his compatriot Guglielmo Segato by more than a minute. By winning the individual three-day equestrian event, Charles Ferdinand Pahud de Mortanges of the Netherlands became the first horseman to win four Olympic gold medals, following earlier titles in Paris and Amsterdam.

It was an unhappy Games for the 69 competitors of the Brazilian team, who, unfinanced, had set off in a government-supplied cargo ship carrying coffee, the sale of which en route

Cool in the pool. Johan Oxenstierna of Sweden, eventual modern pentathlon winner, relaxes with team colleagues after his swim victory. (© IOC)

was to fund their trip. Regrettably, there was a world glut of coffee, sales were negligible and only 24 competitors could afford to land at Los Angeles – where their water polo team lost 7–3 to Germany, lost their tempers, insulted the referee and were disqualified. The winners were Hungary, who included a record 18–0 victory over Japan. India's hockey team, having paid its way by playing exhibition matches across Europe, won the title for the third time, including a 24–1 record score over the United States in which Roop Singh scored 12 goals and Dhyan Chand seven. These had been an outstandingly successful Games with 1.25 million spectators, a $1 million surplus and in both mood and performance this festival exceeded all others.

Celebrity gathering: Duke Kahanamoku (left), initiator of overarm crawl in swimming, Paavo Nurmi (with boater) and Douglas Fairbanks (second right), patron of the LA Games. (© IOC)

CHAPTER XXIII

Veiled Evil

Carl Diem of Germany, IOC member

'*Germany is facing the task of organising a counterpart to the enormously successful Games held in Los Angeles two years ago. Firstly the Games are – without a doubt – the united world championships of all 15 sporting disciplines which they cover. However, this does not entirely exhaust the concept of an Olympic Festival. The Games are intended to be more than just united world championships. They are designed to be a festival of youth culture. They are linked with art competitions in painting, sculpture, music, literature and architecture, which together embrace various classes in conjunction with their sub-divisions. Alongside the prescribed ceremonies, the organising country is also asked to arrange a number of arts events suited to the solemnity and significance of the occasion.*

Germany will devote itself to the three resulting assignments with assiduousness. The first is, of course, to provide a competent sports performance itself at the Games and to be a dogged but courteous opponent to the competitors who will be flocking to Germany from 50 Olympic countries. The present status of our international sports achievements shows that there is still a lot to be done in this field.

The second assignment consists of technical preparation work, extension of the different sports facilities, such as the huge stadium in Grunwald, the rowing course at Grünau, the sailing course on Müggelsee and in Kiel, and the joint residence of all the Olympic contestants in the Village at Döberitz. Then there is the extension of the winter sports facilities, the ski jump, the bob run and the ice skating stadium in Garmisch-Partenkirchen.

The third part, however, comprises the artistic concept of the festival in its whole range, and thus the real character of the event. It is precisely in this shaping of the festival in Germany that the world is hoping for a significant achievement. The will of the founder of the Olympic Games was that they should be a festival of physical strength, a cult of beauty, a service to the community of the peoples of the world: all these three interwoven into a firm bond. The Olympic Torch is designed to shine through the centuries, a signal of peaceful understanding between nations, with the aim of arousing more and more enthusiasm for the ideal of humanity throughout the world.' (From an interview with *Berliner Tageblatt*, February 1934)
(Photograph © IOC)

How sincere sound these words of a genuine sports administrator, yet, perhaps unintentionally, how ultimately misleading. After the cancellation of the Berlin Games of 1916 on account of the First World War, re-approval for Germany had been a while in coming. At the Session in Berlin in 1930 their representatives, especially Theodore Lewald, one of their three IOC members, had worked diligently to press their case. When the decision for Los Angeles had been taken nine years prior to 1932, many cities hastened to bid for 1936 but no decision was taken in Paris in 1924, nor at any of the next six Sessions as Budapest, Buenos Aires, Lausanne and Rome jostled for attention. In their own city in 1930, the Germans made a strong impression and by the time of the Session next year in Barcelona the candidates were effectively reduced to two: Barcelona and Berlin. Only 20 members were present, so a postal ballot was agreed upon, the result of which was in favour of Berlin by 43–16. The German Olympic committee had declared that it wished also to stage the Winter Games at Garmisch-Partenkirchen, but this decision was deferred, finally being confirmed by the IOC in 1933. Garmisch had been favoured on account of its proximity to the largely populated and nearby cities of Munich and Innsbruck, and the proximity of the Zugspitze, Germany's tallest mountain. Moreover, Bavaria was home to the Nationalist Socialist Party, with Munich its headquarters and Nuremberg hosting the annual conventions.

With its introverted preoccupation with sport, the IOC had granted its favour to the unstable centrist coalition of the Weimar Republic under the chancellorship of Heinrich Brüning. The Nazi ogre for the moment remained in the wings, though the threat was nonetheless evident. The following year, Bruno Malitz, Nazi spokesman, condemned modern sport because it was infested with 'Frenchmen, Belgians, Polacks and Jew-Niggers', and on 19 August, *Der Volkische Beobachter* editorialised that the Olympic Games should be confined to white athletes. A month later, Karl Ritter von Halt, German IOC member since 1929, president-to-be of the organising committee for Garmisch and under pressure from colleagues to determine the attitude of Adolf Hitler's National Socialists towards the plans for hosting

Dr Karl Ritter von Halt, president of the Garmisch-Partenkirchen Winter Games organisation, greets Adolf Hitler. (© IOC/Ruebelt)

the Olympic Games, requested an audience with Hitler himself. This was refused on the grounds of Hitler's election campaign, but von Halt received the following statement: 'The German National Socialist party will place no difficulties in the way of staging international competitions such as the Olympic Games, *nor will it oppose the participation of coloureds in these competitions* [author's italics].' Von Halt sent a copy of this supposed reassuring news to the IOC and the committee's doubts were, and regrettably would continue to be, dispelled, whatever the evidence to the contrary. It required no more than moderate perception to recognise that the assurances they were receiving were anything but the truth.

On 30 January 1933, Hitler and his National Socialists were elected to power, one week after the first meeting of the Berlin organising committee under Lewald's presidency, the committee's secretary being Carl Diem, another stalwart of German sport. A contributing factor to the complexity of events over the next three years was that Lewald, born in 1860, was half Jewish. He had been the Reich's cultural representative for the world fairs in Chicago, Paris and St Louis, had been responsible for the finances of German Olympic teams, had administered the financial preparations of Berlin 1916 and, following the First World War, had devoted his energies exclusively to sport, being elected to the IOC in 1926. Despite Lewald's acknowledged status, once Hitler was in power, he soon came under attack from Joseph Goebbels, head of propaganda, and was forced to resign from the National Committee for Physical Exercise. Diem, of upper middle-class background, had risen to prominence through the German Sports Authority for Athletics (DSBA). Though not of Jewish origin, his wife was, and he was denounced in Goebbels' propaganda newspaper *Der*

Angriff (The Attack) and other Nazi press for being 'a white Jew', on account of his association with Deutsch Hochscule für Leibesübungen – the German Sports University – which had several Jews in its faculty. By May 1933 the *New York Times* was questioning the wisdom of holding a Games in Berlin.

Two months earlier, Lewald had been granted an audience with Hitler, seeking to confirm the Chancellor's support for the financing of the Games previously guaranteed by the Weimar government under the presidency of von Hindenburg. Hitler, having swiftly recognised the potential publicity value of a successful Games, and encouraged by Goebbels, responded positively. Almost immediately, however, there was a move to oust Lewald and Diem from the organising committee and replace them with Hans von Tschammer und Osten, effectively the new sports minister. This did provoke immediate reaction from de Baillet-Latour. In May he wrote to the three German IOC members, reminding them of IOC statutes and urging them to inform Hitler of the protocol in organisation of a Games under the IOC Charter, namely: 'That the Games are given to a city, not a country, that they have no political, racial, national or denominational character, that the organising committee is directly responsible to the IOC, and that if these conditions are not met the Games will be transferred.' A written guarantee that they would observe the IOC's regulations was demanded from the German government, to be provided in time for the Session in Vienna in June that year. Had de Baillet-Latour been more sensitive he would have recognised that the three German members, whatever their private beliefs, had been placed in an intolerable position. Any dissention voiced by them towards the newly aggressive policies of the National Socialists would pose a risk to their own careers. Von Halt, in his reply, went so far as to extol the 'national revolution' currently taking place, though Hitler backed down and assured the IOC President that the appointed officials would not be superseded by von Tschammer.

Preserving the office of Lewald and his colleagues was one thing. A matter of far greater public concern was the issue of Germany's attitude towards Jewish potential members of their own team and their continuing eligibility. Under the direction of von Tschammer, the newly appointed Reichssportführer, the reorganisation of sports federations and clubs was carried out and Jews, widely referred to as 'non-Aryans', were excluded from all sports organisations. Additionally, the management of domestic sport was expanded to embrace government and armed forces officials for the purpose of implementing Nationalist Socialist ideology, totally opposed to every Olympic ideal. Within this structure, Lewald and his colleagues were powerless to show dissent.

By the time of the IOC Session in Vienna, the Jewish issue was already reaching a crescendo, yet General Charles Sherrill, one of the three American members and one of the twenty-eight attending at Vienna, felt able to write to the American Jewish Congress, stating: 'Be assured that I will stoutly maintain the American principle that citizens are equal under all laws.' He and William Garland, his compatriot member, questioned, together with de Baillet-Latour, the three German IOC members, Lewald, von Halt and Adolf von Mecklenburg, about Jewish participation. Although von Halt, a Nazi Party member, resisted the idea, the IOC insisted upon a further guarantee from Berlin that Jews did have this right. Receiving this guarantee, de Baillet-Latour sank further into his state of appeasement.

The IOC is seen clearly to have been equivocal on the Jewish issue. J. Sigfrid Edström, for instance, had written to Avery Brundage: 'I'm not at all in favour [of the persecution] but I fully understand that an alteration had to take place . . . a great part of the German nation was led by the Jews and not by the Germans themselves. Even in the USA, the day may come when you will have to stop the activities of the Jews. They are intelligent and unscrupulous.'

Amid this controversy the Vienna Session had re-elected de Baillet-Latour as President for a further eight-year term by a substantial majority. The only other candidate was Godefroy de Blonay. For whatever reason, de Baillet-Latour had demanded a secret ballot. As a post-script to the worldwide recession, it became apparent by the following year that the IOC's bank, Banque d'Escompte Suisse, was bankrupt, but the IOC was able to remain financially stable.

At the Session in Athens in 1934, concern about Nazi assurances was expressed by Lord Aberdare, British IOC member, and by Garland, who questioned the German government's pledges. They received an almost reflex reply from Lewald and von Halt: 'It goes without saying that Germany's pledges last year to admit to the German team those of non-Aryan origin will be strictly observed.'

If the IOC was appeased, however, America was not. Samuel Untermyer, member of the Anti Defamation League, demanded a boycott and in December the Athletics Union voted to postpone acceptance of the official invitation to Berlin. Within six months, the campaign reached a crescendo and Brundage found it necessary to publish a pamphlet, 'Fair Play for American Athletes', claiming Americans were being manipulated for a foreign cause. In this there was some truth, for there was indeed political collaboration between Communist and Jewish groups to resist any Nazi activity.

De Baillet-Latour's myopia continued as the months passed and in retrospect defies comprehension, though he was actively misled by some of his colleagues, and not just those in Germany, who were at the mercy of national propaganda. In August 1935, an equivocal Sherrill, known anti-Communist and suspected anti-Semite, was received by Hitler during a European tour. Hitler denied awareness of assurances given in 1933 on Jewish participation and said this could only apply to guest teams but not to German Jews. When Sherrill warned of the risk of withdrawal of the Games, Hitler stated that in that case there would merely be 'German Olympic Games'. Alarmed, Sherrill suggested that de Baillet-Latour should personally confront Hitler. This recommendation became all the more urgent, when, on 15 September, Hitler proclaimed the Nuremberg Laws, which defined Jews as 'sub human' and were followed by widespread persecutions. No Jew could be a German citizen or, under threat of imprisonment, marry a German.

In November, de Baillet-Latour was received by Hitler, the latter well briefed on de Baillet-Latour's aversion to calls for a boycott which were mounting in America. There is no record of their conversation. Incredibly, after the meeting the IOC President felt able to write to the American members to state that he had been reassured that Jewish German athletes could continue to train. How could this Belgian aristocrat have been fooled by cosmetic promises?

Ernest Jahncke, an American IOC member, remained unconvinced by de Baillet-Latour's reassurances. In November 1935, when requested by de Baillet-Latour and Lewald to join the campaign resisting an American boycott, his forthright reply, which he simultaneously had published in the *New York Times*, said:

> . . . I do not doubt that you have received all sorts of assurances from the Nazi sports authorities . . . they have been lavish with their promises . . . the fact is that they have dissolved Catholic sports clubs, have denied

Ernest Jahncke, American IOC member expelled for his support of the American-Jewish sympathy boycott campaign against Berlin, seen here presenting winners' medals to Andrew Libano and Gilbert Gray (USA) for Star-class yachting in 1932. (© IOC)

> Jewish athletes opportunity to train for competition in trials which is equivalent to excluding them as a group from the German team. Let me beseech you to seize your opportunity to take your rightful place in the history of the Olympics alongside de Coubertin instead of Hitler.

Predictably, de Baillet-Latour was not pleased, accused Jahncke in his reply of going 'over the limit' and asserted that the Honorary Life President (de Coubertin) had the same view as the IOC members whom Jahncke had criticised. 'You have also misled the public at large, which is not aware that you know very little of Olympic things and nothing at all about the XIth Olympiad's problems, as you have never been present at any of the meetings of the Committee.' In December, at a congress of the American Athletic Union, those opposing a boycott won the day, the decision being taken to send an American team to Berlin, though by a majority of only 3 votes out of 114.

Jahncke, regarded as a traitor by his IOC colleagues, was asked to resign but he refused. The IOC's blind, unshakeable trust in Germany's right to host the Games come what may, led, however, to a unanimous decision, by 49 votes to nil to expel him at the Session immediately prior to the Berlin Games. It might be said that the IOC's attitude in 1936 was in principle no different from that in 1980, when they were to stand firm in staging the Moscow Games, but by most criteria the circumstances must be regarded as crucially different. The 1980 boycott would be political expediency during the Cold War; in 1936, the campaign then was essentially humanitarian. If the IOC were theoretically free to allow themselves to believe Hitler's lies, they should, at the least, have granted Jahncke, and those who thought similarly, the right to hold an alternative view. Many prominent Americans other than Jews had been part of the boycott movement: congressmen, churchmen of all denominations, journalists, artists and writers. A Gallup poll in 1935 showed 43 per cent of the American population in favour of a boycott and the movement was also strongly supported in Britain and Canada. So extreme was Brundage's campaign to counter the boycott movement that he was accused privately by some of being anti-Semitic.

Although global disgust at Hitler's formalised wave of oppression against German Jews partially subsided following the American decision to send a team, there was a further meeting between de Baillet-Latour and the Führer in Garmisch prior to the opening ceremony. De Baillet-Latour first advised Hitler that he was confined by protocol to a single sentence when pronouncing the Games open and that there should be no political propaganda. Hitler was given a sheet of paper on which was written the sentence 'I declare the Winter Olympic Games of Garmisch-Partenkirchen open', to which Hitler is said to have replied sarcastically: 'I shall do my best to learn the sentence by heart.' There was a further point of confrontation. Although it had been agreed that offensive signs and directions were to be removed, the IOC was confronted by public notices outside toilets at the arenas stating: 'No dogs or Jews.' When de Baillet-Latour protested about this, he was reproved by Hitler, who said it was not normal when visiting a friend's house to tell him how he should behave. The IOC President retorted: 'Excuse me, Mr Chancellor, but when the Olympic flag is raised over the arenas, it is no longer Germany but Olympia, and in Olympia we are the masters.' Within hours, the signs were removed.

Behind the scenes, the National Socialists were planning their imminent occupation of the de-militarised Rhineland in breach of the Locarno Treaty.

Because the whole Olympic exercise was regarded by Hitler, Goebbels, Göring and the rest as a splendid propaganda opportunity, the facilities for public attendance at the Winter Games exceeded anything provided hitherto. For instance, the ski jump competition, with its 43m tower, had a viewing arena accommodating 75,000. With a further 50,000 watching from surrounding vantage points, the event, in which Birger Ruud of Norway successfully defended his title, was witnessed by a larger

Hitler, Hermann Göring, Air Minister, and von Halt (IOC) at the Garmisch-Partenkirchen opening ceremony. (© IOC/Wilmkes)

sporting crowd than could be contained anywhere but the Maracana Stadium, Rio de Janeiro, or Hampden Park, Glasgow.

For the first time, Alpine skiing was on the programme, though confined to a combined event of downhill and slalom for both men and women. Its inclusion added fuel to the fires of amateur eligibility, as, at its Oslo Session the previous year, the IOC had overruled the decision of the FIS, the international ski federation, which had decreed that professional instructors could be regarded as amateurs for competition. Austria and Switzerland therefore withdrew, which led to Germany dominating the event.

Those present for the first time at the Winter Games included Australia, Bulgaria, Liechtenstein, Spain and Turkey. For his attendance at the opening ceremony, Hitler had an SS bodyguard totalling 6,000, while von Halt in his opening address stated: 'We want to show the world that, faithful to the order of our Führer, we can stage a Winter Games that is a true festival of peace and sincere understanding among peoples.' To ensure that this understanding was not ruptured by prying foreign photographers, they received no credentials, making the press dependent on distribution from German photographers. The organising committee wrote news 'briefings' in five languages to manipulate the message reaching the outside world. The most prominent news story, that of Sonja Henie's third gold medal in figure skating, much assisted in giving the Games an upbeat image. As the token selection as the only Jew, Rudi Ball, a member of the bronze medal winning German ice hockey team four years earlier, retained his place in a competition bizarrely won by Britain with the help of borrowed Canadians, most of them born in Britain.

For a largely uninquisitive outside world, the Games of Garmisch were thus a grand sporting festival, fulfilling Hitler's wish for Nazi culture to play a supporting role to Nazi militarism. The Nazi ideology was an echo of traditional attitudes from the past century and the gymnastics world of Deutsche Turnerschafte, with its collective non-competitive but disciplined exercise, which simultaneously portrayed fitness and subordination. Hitler accepted an invitation in 1933 to be guest of honour at a grand Turnfest in Stuttgart, where he was impressed with the athletic parades to martial music. His vision of a racially purified population was partially based on the belief that Aryans were the descendants of ancient Greeks, whose blond characteristics had been corrupted by intermarrying with lesser races. When the Olympic flame passed through Vienna on its way to Berlin, greeted by ecstatic crowds shouting 'Sieg Heil!',

Hitler's motorcade arrives at Garmisch-Partenkirchen. (© IOC)

the *New York Times* noted: 'The Olympic torch is more like a firebrand than a symbol of the welding flame of international sport. It is only a flare illuminating dark shapes and bewildering prospects.' The flame, far from being the historic emblem that many suppose, was actually the suggestion of Lewald in 1928, his proposal being that the flame be lit from the sun's rays in Olympia and thence carried to the host city. The enactment of this symbolic rite, authorised in 1934, took place for the first time at the Berlin Games, a relay of 3,000 runners bearing the torch from Olympia through Greece, Bulgaria, Yugoslavia, Hungary, Austria and Czechoslovakia and into Germany.

While the occupation of the Rhineland went unchallenged in March 1936, preparations for the Summer Games in Berlin proceeded in parallel with comparable efficiency. These were to be the first Games broadcast on radio and television, the latter on a closed-circuit system within Germany with a daily six-figure audience for events from the four main Olympic sites. Continuing the cosmetic notion of an 'open' Games, Hitler personally requested Helène Mayer, the country's leading woman fencer and Olympic champion in 1928 who was living in America, to return for qualifying events. She would finish second in the foil to another Jew, Ilona Elek of Hungary. By contrast, Gretel Bergmann, Germany's leading high jumper, was excluded on the grounds that, in spite of winning the trials, she was not a member of an 'official' sports club. Other Jews, invited for trials from the Makkabi and similar Jewish clubs, were likewise ignored even when they had earned selection. George Messersmith, American Consul in Berlin, reported that a tearful Lewald admitted to him in November 1935 that he had lied when claiming in 1933 that there would be no discrimination.

The preparation of the German team, meanwhile, was more professional than any previous: metaphorically and literally. They had been given a year to train full time at camps in the Black Forest. If this was a sign of trends yet to come, so was the situation in the shooting events. In 1932 at Los Angeles, nine competitors had come under suspicion of receiving cash prizes at previous events, an occurrence seemingly so widespread that the IOC provocatively agreed to a reinstatement clause: marksmen would be eligible provided they had received no cash prize since August 1934. The issue of amateurism was, and always would be, a total mess.

To further Hitler's intention of maximising the promotion of Germany, the main stadium in Berlin, originally planned for 1916, was expanded to accommodate 110,000 spectators, while the open-air swimming and diving pool seated 18,000. The transport system, ferrying competitors from the excellently appointed men's Village – later to be used as an officers' club – and the special guest houses for over 300 women competitors, was near faultless. The electrical timing and photo-finish cameras were the most proficient yet used, the public address system audible to the point of intimidation, the Unter den Linden, Kurfürstendan and every main street were lined with huge swastika banners, every café and restaurant had a radio blaring military music or proclamations of fealty to the Chancellor. Some 150,000 visiting foreigners could not fail to be impressed unless they paused to consider the ulterior motive of the extravagance on view.

The opening ceremony was more like a coronation than a sports celebration, an ear-splitting fanfare greeting the arrival of the Führer prior to the march-past of the teams of 4,000 athletes from 49 nations. All were supposed to grant Hitler an acknowledging 'Heil'. The French did, to massive cheers. The British did not, keeping their right arm lowered and giving merely the conventional eyes-right. Brownshirts and Blackshirts were to be seen everywhere in the crowd; overhead hovered the

Hindenburg zeppelin. Protocol had been breached prior to the opening ceremony when Rudolph Hess, Hitler's deputy, and von Tschammer und Osten had addressed the Session, and now conventionalists were further dismayed when Spyridon Louis, the original marathon winner who had been invited to Berlin, presented Hitler with a symbolic olive branch – an ironic gesture considering that other champions of 1896 such as gymnast Alfred Flatow (horizontal bar) would be among those murdered in the 'final solution'. What further irony, too, that, 11 months before his death, the voice of de Coubertin should echo round the stadium, a recording proclaiming the eternal message of the importance not in winning but of taking part. The wisdom of Avery Brundage, subsequent fifth President of the IOC, would often be questioned, seldom more so than for his pronouncement following the Games: 'Fulfilling the visions of

Dr Theodore Lewald (right), president of the German organising committee, whose position, being half-Jewish, had been under continual threat, accompanies Adolf Hitler and IOC President de Baillet-Latour (left) into the Berlin stadium, 1936. (© IOC/H. Kutschera)

its founder, once again this great quadrennial celebration has demonstrated that it is the most effective influence towards international peace and harmony yet devised.' Brundage would always declare that the boycott movement had been nothing but Jewish propaganda, motivated by disapproval of the government 'that had nothing to do with the organisation or content of the Games'.

We must presume that he never read the editorials of Goebbel's propaganda newspaper *Der Angriff*, which labelled Jesse Owens and other Americans as 'black auxiliaries', of whom Baldour von Schirach, the Nazi youth leader would say: 'The Americans ought to be ashamed of themselves for letting their medals be won by negroes. I myself would never shake hands with one of them.' For many, the chance to shake Owens' hand, the author among them at Montreal in 1976, was a moment of privilege.

Towards the end of the Games, de Baillet-Latour, having also turned a Nelsonian eye toward much that was lamentable, attended a dinner given by Hitler and found himself sitting next to von Schirach's wife. She remarked how well the festival of 'peace and reconciliation' was going. With unexpected foresight, de Baillet-Latour replied: 'Madam, may God preserve you from your illusions. If you ask me, we shall have war within three years.'

CHAPTER XXIV

Garmisch-Partenkirchen (IV) 1936

Birger Ruud of Norway, Olympic ski jump champion

'*A common goal, a dream for all good skiers, is to defend Norwegian colours in international competition on foreign snow. This is to everybody the most inspiring challenge and one of the greatest privileges. Yes, I think it is even more important than winning one of the top honours at Holmenkollen, Oslo's renowned ski jump park. As young boys we followed the first Winter Olympic Games in Chamonix in the newspapers. All our idols were down there and they achieved results which impressed the whole ski-conscious world. Their success made us happy and proud. They filled us with eagerness to be just as capable. In our dreams we saw how Thorleif Haug and the other famous Norwegians had succeeded and imagined ourselves as one of the big boys during our daily time on skis, fantasising that we too could be champions.*

What do the Olympics mean to the individual? Enjoyment and exhilaration for many, disappointment and too much sweat for others. However, everybody has the same aim: an objective which inspires us and makes us strong, and which requires self-discipline and sacrifice. Therefore, the Games are healthy and worthy competition for the world's youth.

Can we take the liberty of believing that this goal will continue to motivate us? Yes we can, hoping that it will last for all time. However, in these major international sports events, nobody knows how they will function in the future, in which form and in what conditions. At this time [1945] this picture is still very unclear. We need careful leadership. The Olympic Games were once an event for peace. Time has shown us the benefits and the rewards attainable, but also some of the pitfalls. As competition became keener and keener, the demands on the athletes grew bigger and bigger. The concept of being an amateur differed very strongly from one country to another. This made competition on equal terms difficult. We should also not forget that some countries use the Games for unhealthy propaganda, which has nothing to do with the ideals of the Olympic Movement. Let us hope that the difficulties can be solved and that young people competing in sport can meet around the Olympic flame in the mood in which we want this flame to burn.' (From the archives of the Olympic Museum at Königsberg)
(Photograph © IOC)

Alpine skiing at last arrived on the Olympic scene at the combined villages of Garmisch and Partenkirchen, a short drive south of Munich and within easy access for more spectators than had ever previously attended a Winter Games. Sir Arnold Lunn, who had organised the first racing contest downhill in 1911, subsequently devised the slalom event – a race with 'chicanes', as in motor racing, marked by pairs of poles in the snow. And he had finally persuaded the IOC and overcome Scandinavian objections towards the big-dipper sport. It was quite a contrast to the then traditional Nordic version and it was therefore quite ironic that Norwegians should figure prominently in the competition for the first two events, the combined embracing downhill and slalom for both men and women.

Birger Ruud, successfully defending his ski jump title from 1932, proceeded to enter, and win, the combined downhill section. Travelling on business, he had regularly raced in Alpine events in Germany, Austria and Switzerland, and was now assisted by the exclusion from the Games of ski instructors, deemed professional by the IOC. He was the winner of the

Birger Ruud (NOR) successfully defends his ski-jump title. (© IOC)

downhill by more than three seconds but, coming sixth in the slalom, finished one place outside the medals. While at the top station of the downhill, he had shrewdly used an independent telephone line to obtain details of softer conditions at the bottom of the course and critically changed his wax accordingly. The combined winner was Franz Pfnür, a cabinet maker from Bavaria: second in the downhill and first in both runs in the slalom. Silver medal winner was Gustav Lantschner of Germany, a prominent member of the Nazi Party. In the women's combined, Laila Schou Nilsen of Norway, an outstanding speed skater and tennis player, was fastest on the downhill by four seconds, but could only place eighth in the slalom, having a six-second penalty for missing a gate. This was still sufficient for her to take bronze behind Christel Cranz of Germany. Though only 16, Nilsen held five world speed skating records and had entered the skiing because of the absence of her speciality.

Sonja Henie won her third figure skating title in a row to add to her ten World Championship titles. As she intended to leave immediately afterwards for a legitimately professional life in Hollywood, she was under intense emotional pressure in the bid to remain undefeated. At the conclusion of the compulsory figures she was only 3.6 points ahead of Cecilia Colledge, the 15-year-old British girl, and became visibly distressed when the scores were announced. Colledge, however, was distracted at the start of her free programme, when the wrong music was initially played, and Henie, tenaciously skating at her peak even though last on the ice of the 26 contenders, ensured her success. Colledge was second and Vivi-Anne Hultén of Sweden third. Within a year, Henie's salary was way into six figures and five years later she took US citizenship. After two earlier failures she married Niels Onstad, a childhood friend, but was to die at 57 of leukaemia. She was said by then to be worth nearly $50 million.

A peerless Henie gains her third figures title. (© IOC)

Arrival of Alpine events. Christel Cranz (GER) and Laila Schou Nilsen (NOR), respectively first and third in the inaugural women's combined (downhill and slalom). (both © IOC)

The men's figures title went to Karl Schäfer of Austria, the unanimous choice of all seven judges. To maintain the prejudice without which no figure skating competition would be complete, the Hungarian judge placed two Hungarians second and third, none of the other judges ranking them above seventh. The others duly awarded Ernst Baier of Germany the silver medal. Baier was close to achieving a rare double. In the pairs he won the gold medal with Maxi Herber, his being the best two-event placing ever; Herber was the youngest gold medal winner of these Games at 15 years 128 days.

For the concluding event of the Games, the ski jump, won by Ruud, there was a crowd of 125,000 people, trains leaving Munich at ten-minute intervals throughout the night. The Nazis had successfully brought sport to the people and people to sport. They were soon to demonstrate a more evil competence in the compulsory transportation of people.

CHAPTER XXV

Berlin (XI) 1936

Jesse Owens of America, quadruple Olympic track and field champion

'*I wanted no part of politics. I wasn't in Berlin to compete against any one athlete. The purpose of the Olympics was to do your best. As I'd learned long ago from Charles Riley, my coach at school, the only victory that counts is the one over yourself. I'd prepared for this moment for eight years. One mistake could ruin it all. So, why worry about Hitler? When we lined up for the 100m final, I knew that the next ten seconds was maybe the climax of my life.*

I was very fortunate as a kid, meeting individuals who took an interest in me. True, I had talent, but talent is like a stream, it will run downhill in a rush and perhaps be self-destructive unless it is properly guided. Thanks to my coach in my senior year at high school I was able to break world records. That Olympic year was the fulfilment of my dreams. Everything just came together right. Winning the 100m was the most memorable moment of all – to be known as the world's fastest human being.

That business with Hitler [who allegedly refused to shake hands with Owens] *didn't bother me. I didn't go there to shake hands. What I remember most was the friendship I struck up with Lutz Long, the German long jumper. He was my strongest rival, yet it was he who advised me to adjust my run-up in the qualifying round and thereby helped me to win. Our friendship was important to me. We corresponded regularly until Hitler invaded Poland and then the letters stopped. I learned later that Lutz was killed in the war but afterwards I started corresponding with his son and in this way our friendship was preserved.*

When I also won the 200m and the long jump, it dawned on me that I had moved into a different aura – one that only a handful of people are lucky enough to experience. It's a tremendous feeling when you watch your flag fly above the others. For me that was another fulfilment of the dream and I couldn't forget the country that brought me there. I owe everything to the Olympics, which I see as the greatest movement in the world. I never fail to be moved by the sight of some 10,000 men and women singing, living and playing together. Where else can you see so much discipline, so much determination? Every night they come back to the Village as individuals, yet as the flame dies on the final day you'll see them all looking around for the friends they have made. They embrace and dance together. It's the only occasion when the young people of the world are brought together in this way. Maybe they can't speak the other's language but they can live together. Yet at the same time you cannot do away with nationalism, you cannot do away with a man's country or flag and the respect he has for it.

I knew prejudice even after I became an Olympic champion. I'd gone over there and defied a man who changed the shape of the world but that didn't matter, I still had to sit in the back of the bus. Thankfully things began to change with Dr Martin Luther King and others even before him. In the 1930s, the black people of America had no image they could relate to. Then along came two people – Joe Louis and Jesse Owens. Because of what we did, cracks began to appear in the door. It was Dr King who opened the books of justice.

Maybe people remember one or two points you make, maybe they pass them on to their sons. That's immortality, I think – your ideas being passed from father to son, and on and on. The road to the Olympics does not lead to any particular country or city. It goes far beyond Moscow or Ancient Greece or Nazi Germany. The road to the Olympics leads, in the end, to the best within us.' (Abridgement of Owens' speeches and press interviews)
(Photograph © IOC)

Jesse Owens would have been a milestone figure of twentieth-century athleticism even without the racist element of the Berlin Games. Owens was a naturally extraordinary athlete, so supreme that even at his peak he appeared almost not to be trying – the secret of spontaneous muscle relaxation by an American of African descent. The coincidence of his achievements at a time of mounting Nazi triumphalism served to accentuate the unparalleled beauty of his deeds.

The youngest of ten children born in 1913 in Alabama, the grandson of slaves, Owens' family moved before he was a teenager to Cleveland, where a schoolteacher at enrolment misheard him giving his initials J.C. – for James Cleveland – and entered the name Jesse. It would somehow later add to his aura.

From early coaching by Charles Riley, a benevolent PE teacher, Owens was already exceptional by the age of 15, long jumping 7m or nearly 23 ft. Entering Ohio State University, his deeds accelerated. On 25 May 1935, aged 21, at Ann Arbor, Michigan, he recorded the greatest single day by an athlete in history – and this with a sore back. In less than an hour he broke five world records and equalled a sixth. In the 100 yards, his 9.4 equalled the record. A leap of 8.13m (26 ft 8 in.) beat the existing world record by six inches: his only jump of the day that was to stand for 25 years. In a straight 220 yards he improved the record with 20.3, simultaneously lowering the record for the shorter 200m. Finally he similarly broke two records in one over the 220 yards low hurdles.

At 18, he had not gained selection for the Games in LA, but Berlin was to be his apotheosis, a monumental affront to the warped philosophy of the hosts. The cultural snub came not just from Owens. Ten of the sixty-six men in the US track and field team were black and between them they were to win seven gold medals, three silver and three bronze, which would exceed the track total of any other nation and all of their colleagues.

Owens did not start as favourite for the 100m in Berlin, never mind that he already shared the world record of 10.2 with Charlie Paddock and Ralph Metcalfe, the latter the silver medallist four years earlier. The previous year Owens had lost several times to both Metcalfe and Eulace Peacock of Temple University, simultaneously having to handle private pressures due to the birth out of wedlock of a daughter to his high school sweetheart whom he subsequently married. Despite the threat of racist insults, Owens found himself a hero in Berlin even before the first of his twelve events, including heats, in seven days, such was his fame abroad already. His was the last of the

12 first-round heats, in which he equalled the Olympic record of 10.3; then, with an illegal following wind, recording 10.2 in the second round. It was a cool and cloudy day for the semi-finals and final; he clocked 10.4 in the former and Metcalfe 10.5. For the final, Owens made one of his better starts, Metcalfe almost stumbling. Owens was away like the wind, uncatchable. Though Metcalfe closed on him slightly before the finish, he could not get nearer than a tenth of a second as Owens again equalled the Olympic record, despite a sodden track. Martinus Osendarp of the Netherlands took the bronze.

A story which gathered momentum at the time was that Hitler, present in the main tribune throughout the first day, had declined to shake hands with Owens after his success on the second day, refusing to concede to the acclaim being bestowed on an African-American athlete scorned by the Nazis. The truth was slightly different. Germany had never won a gold medal in track and field and so national delight overflowed when Hans Woellke, the blondest of Aryans, won the first title of the Games in the shot put. Then his countryman Gerhard Stöck took gold in the javelin, while later Tilly Fleischer and Louise Krüger won gold and silver in the women's javelin. All these athletes were led to the tribune to be greeted and saluted by the Führer, as were the three Finnish medal winners in the 10,000m. With evening approaching, Hitler then departed, thereby being absent for the award of medals in the high jump, the winner of which, it was evident, would be the African-American Cornelius Johnson. If Hitler had snubbed anyone it was Johnson. Overnight, de Baillet-Latour sent word to Hitler that, as guest of honour, he must receive all medal winners or none and that those he wished specially to congratulate should be met privately. Hitler decided on the latter, so the question of greeting Owens never arose.

The superiority of Owens in the 200m was to be even greater than in the short sprint. In both first and second rounds he set an Olympic record of 21.1, a time equalled in the semi-final by Mack Robinson. In the final, run on a cold, damp evening, Robinson was briefly level with Owens, but off the bend Owens was moving clear, finishing four yards in front and improving his Olympic record to 20.7.

Now came the long jump. Though in some ways this was the event in which he was strongest, Owens had his closest shave during his acquisition of four gold medals, equalling Kraenzlein

Moral symbol. Supreme stylist. Jesse Owens effortlessly wins the 100m, the first of a then unique four titles. (© IOC)

Owens coasts through a 200m heat. (© IOC)

in 1900. Whether through nerves or due to misinformation, he only qualified, narrowly, on his third jump. Believing that competitors were still warming up, he had run through on a testing approach, only to discover that it had been recorded as a no-jump. On his second attempt, he fouled. It is here, if legend is to be believed, that he had his first close contact with Long, a blond and able German upon whom the Nazi leaders had pinned their faith. They believed he was the man to halt the meteoric 'black auxiliary'. Long, however, was a man of magnanimity. Drawing Owens to one side, he advised him to move back his run-up mark at least a foot to ensure that he gained the minimum qualifying distance. Thereby – if Owens' recollection is strictly correct and not enhanced by romance – Long contributed to a fabled achievement and to his own defeat.

Whether the story is true or not, with the previous year's world record of 8.13m (26 ft 8¼ in.) momentarily irrelevant, Owens cleared the 7.16m (23 ft 6 in.) qualifying distance by a mere centimetre. There followed a titanic battle in the final round. First, Long leaped 7.84m (25 ft 8⅔ in.), a European record. Owens surpassed him by an inch. In the first attempt of their last three jumps, both fluffed. On his second, Long matched Owens' earlier distance, tying the new Olympic record. In response Owens cleared 7.92m (26 ft) with his penultimate jump, then extended this to 8.06m (26 ft 5½ in.) with his final leap. First to congratulate him was Long, though the acclaim from the crowd, the majority of them seemingly immune to official racist policy, echoed in the vast stadium. The friendship established on that field of play between Owens and Long became entrenched, the two corresponding until the outbreak of war, during which Long was killed in the Battle of St Pietro in 1943. Owens subsequently corresponded with Long's son until he himself died of lung cancer on 31 March 1980: the end of a tale of two of the most gentlemanly of sportsmen.

In Berlin there remained for Owens the matter of the sprint relay, which was to cast a shadow over American successes. This was a title continuously held by the US subsequent to their semi-final disqualification in the inaugural race of 1912. For some while, the quartet, working under the guidance of coaches, was Sam Stoller, Marty Glickman, Frank Wykoff and Foy Draper. In a practice individual race at the Olympic Village, this order seemed to have been confirmed, the only doubt being the possible inclusion of Metcalfe in place of Draper. Questioned on whether Owens ought to be included, Lawson Robertson, the relay coach, had stated that Owens had 'enough glory already'. Yet on the morning of the heats the runners were assembled and told that Stoller and Glickman would be replaced by Owens and Metcalfe. It was a coincidental fact that Draper and Wykoff were from the University of Southern California where the coach was Dean Cromwell – now assistant to Robertson. The second coincidence was that Stoller and Glickman were the only two Jews on the US track squad. The switch was never satisfactorily explained, though the coaches argued that the Germans were about to reveal new unheralded sprinters, something that never materialised. The composition of the US team, Owens–Metcalfe–Draper–Wykoff, was all the more odd considering Draper was the slowest of the six candidates. Rumour suggested that Brundage, head of the US Olympic committee, had ordered the change to avoid having Jews on the winning podium. Confronted with this, Brundage unconvincingly asserted that the selection had long been determined. Glickman had protested against the decision, though Brundage's stance was supported by Owens, who said it had been stated during trials in New York that the four fastest in Berlin would be nominated. Draper's inclusion, however, belies that argument. It is likely

that any four from the six would have won, in the event the US setting a world record of 39.8, ahead of Italy, with Germany third. Thus Owens gained his fourth gold and Wykoff became a member of three consecutive winning relay teams, each with a world record. This record would survive for 20 years.

If Owens claimed the greater glory of these Games, there were many other events of comparable athletic distinction. Those who had filled the first five places of the 1,500m metres four years earlier all qualified for the final now: Beccali (ITA), who had set an Olympic record; Cornes (GBR); Edwards (CAN); Cunningham (USA); and Ny (SWE). None were to win. After one lap, John Cornes was leading from Fritz Schaumburg, the German champion, with Glenn Cunningham and Ny hard on their heels. Close behind them were Luigi Beccali and Jack Lovelock of New Zealand – the latter an esteemed 27 year old, a former amateur boxer whose running career had been previously interrupted when breaking a leg in university rugby. At the bell, the order was now Ny, Cunningham, Lovelock and Beccali, though Ny was soon to fade. Down the final back straight Lovelock surged to the front, way before his usual finishing sprint over the last 50 metres. His early kick, a tactic which the former Rhodes Scholar at Oxford and current medical student had been studying, left the rest floundering. Suddenly he had a lead of two or three strides and a desperate Cunningham, try as he might, could do little about it. Lovelock held his lead to win by some four yards in a world record of 3:47.8, Cunningham himself surpassing the previous record with 3:48.4, Beccali taking the bronze in 3:49.2: two seconds faster than when he had previously won the title. It was truly a great race. Tragically, Lovelock fell from a horse in 1940 and the head injuries he incurred left him with recurrent dizziness. In 1949 he toppled from a railway platform when working as a physician in Brooklyn and was killed by an oncoming train.

The marathon, so often an event of special drama, was

Jack Lovelock of New Zealand (black vest) bides his time prior to out-sprinting Glenn Cunningham (USA) and Luigi Beccali (ITA) to win the 1,500m. (© IOC)

notable in part for an example of heartless exploitation. Korea at this time was occupied by imperialist Japan, whose two entrants were both Korean: Kee-Chung Sohn and Seong-Yong Nam, but forced to run under the imposed names of Kitei Son and Shoryu Nan. The favourite was Juan Carlos Zabala, the Argentine defending champion who had been busy training in Germany, and he was expected to be challenged primarily by Finnish runners. On a warm day, Ernest Harper of Great Britain soon emerged as a contender. Zabala established an early lead and after 15km was almost two minutes ahead, though by halfway this had dropped to less than a minute. Trailing him were Harper and Sohn, the latter an improbably short, bent figure, his will-power obscured behind Asian impassivity. Behind them lay the three Finns. At 28km, Sohn and Harper overhauled Zabala, who, exhausted by his early pace, soon dropped out. The Finns, in contrast, now discovered they had held back too long and were being challenged for third place by Nam. Out in front, Sohn was pulling away from Harper, who was handicapped by blisters. Sohn, entering the stadium alone, won by over two minutes in an Olympic best time of 2:29:19.2. Harper bravely held on for the silver and Nam took the bronze, one and two minutes respectively ahead of Erkki Tamila and Vaïnö Muinonen. When two Japanese flags were raised during the medals ceremony, Sohn and Nam lowered their heads in shame. For autograph hunters, Sohn wilfully signed his name in Korean and back home was regarded as a national hero among his oppressed people.

Kee-Chung Sohn of Korea (left), obliged to run during Japanese occupation under the name Kitei Son, defeated Ernest Harper (GBR, No. 265) by two minutes when winning the marathon.
(© IOC)

The standard of results throughout was unprecedented: those for athletics in the outstanding Games of 1932 were surpassed in 15 events out of 29 and equalled in 3. One of the former was the

pole vault, which became an endurance contest lasting nearly 12 hours on account of 25 competitors qualifying for the final. As the contest moved to a climax under floodlights, it had become a battle between two Americans, Earle Meadows and Bill Sefton, and two Japanese, Shuhei Nishida and Sueo Oe. George Varoff, a Ukrainian immigrant from San Francisco, who had recently set a world record of 4.43m (14 ft 6½ in.), had then failed to qualify in the US trials. The four medal contenders all cleared 4.25m, then all missed at 4.35m. On his second attempt, Meadows cleared for a new Olympic record, Sefton was placed fourth on the failure countback and Nishida and Oe, declining a jump-off, tossed for silver and bronze, Nishida winning.

Finland revived its long-distance reputation by taking all three places in the 10,000m, though the crowd's sympathy lay with Kohei Murakoso, a diminutive Japanese who set such a severe early pace that by 6km he had burned off all but the Finns and James Burns of Britain. Repeatedly the Finns, Salminen, Askola and Iso-Hollo, would pass him, only for Murakoso to grind his way back to the front. So it was till the final lap, when the Finns sprinted clear. Murakoso clung on for fourth place ahead of Burns, only ten seconds behind Salminen, the winner. Gunnar Höckert won the 5,000m with an Olympic record of 14:22.2, some 18 metres ahead of world record holder Lauri Lehtinen. Salminen, well-placed for another medal, tripped two laps out and finished sixth.

A 6 ft tall, 18-year-old farm girl from Fulton, Missouri, was the first star of the women's events. Helen Stephens, who had already become a sensation over 50 yards in school meetings, now won her wind-assisted heat by 10 metres, and though her 11.5 time in the 100m final was also wind-assisted and ineligible as an improvement on her own world record, she thrashed Stella Walsh (Stanisława Walasiewicz), the defending champion, by two metres. Taken to meet Hitler afterwards, she firmly declined his overt sexual advances. Stephens added a gold in the sprint relay when Germany, leading by a distance, dropped the baton at the final takeover. Her winning 100m time, incidentally, had been half a second faster than the first men's champion of 1896.

Stella Walsh (Stanisława Walasiewicz) (POL) (far left), defending 100m champion, qualifies in her heat, only to be defeated in the final by 18-year-old Helen Stephens (USA), seen relaxing with Owens. (both © IOC)

Japanese and Americans dominated the men's swimming events and Holland the women's. Outstanding was Hendrika Mastenbroek, who won three gold medals and a silver. The men's 100m freestyle, however, produced a surprise with Ferenc Csik of Hungary winning from an outside lane in 57.6 ahead of

1932 and now gold again, and all without one leg, cut off just below the knee when he was run down by a tram in Budapest at the age of 11. Winner also of a European 1,500m freestyle title, he was murdered on the street by an occupying Soviet soldier in 1946.

Hendrika Mastenbroek of Holland, accompanied by trainer Mama Braun, reflects on her 100m freestyle victory (left), and celebrates relay triumph with Willemijntje den Ouden (far left), Katerina Wagner (second from right) and Johanna Selbach (far right). (both © IOC)

There were complaints that the equestrian three-day event course, during which three horses died and only 27 out of 50 entrants finished the course, was too severe. The deaths ended the team chances of Denmark, Hungary and America. Ludwig Stubbendorff, on the aptly named Nurmi, rode splendidly to win the individual title for Germany and additionally the team title, though only on account of the bravery of his colleague Konrad von Wangenheim. During the cross-country section, von Wangenheim's horse stumbled, throwing him and breaking his collar-bone. The rider remounted and completed the circuit without a fault. The next day the horse fell again and there were fears that it had broken its neck. The moment the horse moved, however, von Wangenheim remounted and continued, to ensure a German victory.

three Japanese. Adolf Kiefer (USA) gave a particularly impressive performance, lopping nearly three seconds from the 100m backstroke record. Most remarkable of all was Oliver Halassy of Hungary in water polo: silver medal winner in 1928, gold in

The medals table was led by Germany with 89: 33 gold, 26 silver and 30 bronze. It was the first time America had been dislodged from the top.

CHAPTER XXVI

Post-War Austerity

J. Sigfrid Edström of Sweden, IOC President, 1942–52

'The world has started to breathe more freely now that the war in Europe has ended. It is of course a catastrophe that hundreds of thousands of lives have been sacrificed, historic buildings of inestimable value destroyed, irreplaceable monuments gone forever. Let us hope that through united efforts we can repair and rebuild a better world. Let us hope that in this vital job the Olympic Movement will also have an important role to fulfil for the benefit of humanity. May the Olympic flame, once again burning, help restore for future generations the hope and the happiness to live, and the will to work hard.

I well know that each of you will do his best to assist in this enormously valuable work for our Movement and I'm aware that all of you are awaiting advice on how this job should be done. I have therefore set up five points which, in my opinion, are important and which I recommend you begin as soon as possible:

- *Organise and encourage in your own country the culture of physical exercise and formal sport.*
- *Try to assist reorganisation in consultation with the national federations.*
- *Invite your NOCs to start work immediately.*
- *Try to find funds to assist the re-start of training, thus preparing athletes for future Olympic Games.*
- *Everything seems to indicate that the War in the far east with Japan will be over within two years or less. We may therefore conclude, perhaps, that the next Games could be organised in 1948. Furthermore, let me say that the IOC under my leadership may be convened at a meeting in London as early as spring next year. It is therefore important for each of you to take steps for it to possible to be present at this meeting.*

Let me also inform you of the result of my proposal to install a second Vice-President. The majority of the votes forwarded to me have agreed and I have the honour and pleasure to inform you that I declare Mr Avery Brundage as the second Vice-President of the IOC.' (A letter to members, June 1945)
(Photograph © IOC)

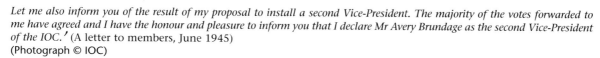

The Second World War made it impossible to stage any Olympic Games between 1936 and 1948. In spite of this inactivity, they were difficult years for the IOC: a period in which two IOC Presidents died and in which, but for the will-power of a veteran Swede, the cherished achievement of de Coubertin might almost have become a coincidental victim of the fray.

De Coubertin remained tenaciously loyal to his search for ethical human existence and in 1936, after negotiations with the IOC Executive Board, the City of Lausanne had agreed to finance an Olympic Museum, to which de Coubertin had left his artefacts, manuscripts and collections, other than a portion which were bequeathed to the International Olympic Institute directed by Carl Diem in Berlin. Lausanne also granted their most famous citizen the Freedom of the City in 1937. Besides assuming financial responsibility for the museum, the city had additionally responded to de Coubertin's unpublicised but by now serious personal financial difficulties. He had given to the Olympic Movement not only a life's work but also the backing of his private fortune and was now almost destitute. Francis

Messerli, secretary of the Swiss NOC, suggested to other NOCs that they set up a fund in recognition of de Coubertin's 50 years of work towards educational reform. His written documents ran to some 60,000 pages. Many NOCs, IFs, IOC members, governments and heads of state donated a total of over 50,000 Swiss francs to the 'Pierre de Coubertin Fund', the most substantial donations coming from the governments of Japan, Germany, Greece and Czechoslovakia, from FIFA and from the NOCs of Italy, Sweden and Brazil. So impoverished was de Coubertin that in 1936 he had had to relinquish even his small apartment in Lausanne, moving alone into lodgings in Geneva. He died from a heart attack on 2 September 1937, sitting on a bench while taking a walk in the Parc de la Grange. This was a month after his last act of public dedication to his cause: a message of support to the organisers of the first Asian Games, recommending them to familiarise all Asians with the notions of Olympism and Hellenism.

It was in recognition of a life's work that 49 of his IOC colleagues had nominated him, during the Oslo Session of 1935, for the Nobel Peace Prize, dispatching their signatures to the

Nobel Committee in Oslo. The Norwegian sports press had already proposed him for the prize seven years earlier, though he had declined the nomination, saying that only personalities who had fought politically for peace should be considered. He was never to receive the award, perhaps partially because the nomination was backed by Germany in an unsuccessful attempt to prevent the prize being awarded to Carl von Ossietzky, an opponent of the Nazi regime who was interned in a concentration camp. It was strange that this altruistic paragon of educational reform should never have received public support in his native France, where he had more often encountered opposition than enthusiasm. Only after his death would the opportunist French seek to claim the freehold of his initiative and inspired magnanimity.

Few of those to whom he was a hero knew of his endurance of a blighted family life. He had married Marie Rothan in 1895 and for a while all was well until their first-born, Jacques, became retarded when suffering sunstroke as a baby after being left too long in the sun. A guilt-ridden Marie subsequently overwhelmed their daughter to the extent that she suffered an emotionally disturbed life. Devoting themselves additionally to the welfare of two nephews, Pierre and Marie were further distraught when both were killed at the front in the First World War; thus, with the event of his own death, ended centuries of the de Coubertin line. His grave is at the Bois de Vaux in Lausanne, close to the IOC's headquarters, and, by decree of his will, his heart is buried at Olympia.

Shortly before his death, de Coubertin had written to von Tschammer, the Reichssportführer, requesting that he establish

an Olympic Studies Centre to maintain and advance his educational work. In 1938, with government support, the International Olympic Institute was founded in Berlin, with Carl Diem, who had attended the entombment of de Coubertin's heart, as director of his intellectual legacy. In the spring of 1939 the Greek parliament voted to create an Olympic Academy in Olympia but this intention would not be fulfilled until after the war.

The founder would live to see neither that nor, indeed, a year after his death, the effective end of the women's international sports movement, the FSFI. The IAAF, declaring itself the sole body responsible for women's athletics, had called for the dissolution of the FSFI during its own congress at the time of the Berlin Games. The scheduled fifth World Women's Games of 1938 in Vienna were cancelled, in their place being the first Women's European Athletics Championships under the aegis of the IAAF. With the 200m, long jump and shot put being added to the women's programme at the IOC Session in Cairo in 1938, the FSFI had become increasingly irrelevant.

In 1936 the respective Games of 1940 had been awarded to Tokyo and Sapporo in an innovative and romantic move to the Far East. With the arrival of the Sino-Japanese war in 1937, the IOC requested confirmation of Japan's intentions. The Japanese NOC delayed reply, while government preparation on 16 sites for the Games continued, but eventually the IOC was forced to switch venues to Helsinki and St Moritz. The decision regarding St Moritz was complicated by the refusal of the international ski federation, backed by the Swiss, to compete in Alpine events because of the IOC's refusal to admit skiing instructors as amateurs. As a consequence, the IOC switched again, from St Moritz to Garmisch. Helsinki and Garmisch continued with respective preparations until November 1939 – two months after Germany's invasion of Poland in September – and May 1940, the Finns having to withdraw following the eastern invasion by the Soviet Union.

Amid all this was the further complication of Hitler's grandiose plan for a new world sports order, of permanent Olympic Games to be staged in Germany. For the return to Garmisch it had been proposed to stage a 'skiing day' with 10,000 participants, which would include a lengthy speech by Hitler in open breach of Olympic regulations. So in awe,

Comte Henri de Baillet-Latour, IOC President, addresses mourners at Ancient Olympia (above), prior to the internment of de Coubertin's heart, at the founder's decree, by Crown Prince Paul of Greece (right). (both © IOC)

seemingly, was de Baillet-Latour, the President, that he wrote to Diem, upon cancellation of the Games: 'How sad it is to think that the wonderful work you have done to give the Vth Olympic Winter Games an even more impressive character than was the case in 1936 has now been in vain. The Skiing Day would have been an unforgettable experience for all those fortunate enough to be present.' It defies belief that de Baillet-Latour and his colleagues should have thought it suitable to return without question to Garmisch in spite of Germany's recent seizure of Bohemia and Moravia.

At the 1939 Session in London, the two Games for 1944 had been granted to London and Cortina, the other candidates being respectively Athens, Budapest, Helsinki and Lausanne, and St Moritz and Oslo. With the continuation of the war, these in turn had to be cancelled. As late as February 1942, Lord Aberdare wrote to Edström that 'the extension [of the War] could make it difficult to organise the 1944 Games', writing further in the autumn that the Games would not be possible 'even if the War is over at the beginning of 1943'.

The cancellations avoided a continuing problem. At the Cairo Session in 1938, the conflict with the FIS over the eligibility of ski instructors had re-arisen, the Norwegian president of the FIS having threatened to resign if the IOC did not accept the FIS decision that instructors were eligible. Cruising down the Nile on a steamer, the IOC had had three options for the scheduled Games in Sapporo: abandon the Winter Games, postpone them until 1944, or stage them without skiing. The decision taken was to exclude skiing but, while this might possibly have been acceptable to the Japanese, the position was highly controversial if the Games were to be held in the Alpine resort of St Moritz. Initially, St Moritz organisers planned for skiing as a 'demonstration sport', then changed their minds. At the Session in London in 1939, the IOC stood on its dignity, reaffirming that they alone had the right to interpret the rules and decide on the programme, that a host organising committee should fulfil the approved programme. With the failure to reach agreement with St Moritz, the Games were duly switched to Garmisch but the problem would remain until after the war was ended. A compromise would be reached at the 1946 Session in Lausanne, unsatisfying though it was, that instructors were eligible so long as they received no payment after October 1946. Partial pregnancy was apparently acceptable.

The advent of war, and Germany's occupation of the Low Countries, inevitably compromised de Baillet-Latour's ability as a Belgian to maintain communications with IOC members. This was more easily done by Vice-President Edström, who was from neutral Sweden. The IOC was indeed fortunate that Edström, though nearly 70, was still energetic, for there were clear signs of German moves to usurp the IOC's authority. In the winter of 1940–1, Diem, von Halt and von Tschammer visited de Baillet-Latour, ostensibly for reasons of social goodwill but actually to explain Hitler's takeover plans for international sport. Diem even appeared at the IOC's headquarters in Lausanne with the apparent intention of taking control shortly after de Baillet-Latour suffered a stroke in his sleep and died during the night of 6 January 1942. Diem's appearance in Lausanne was foiled by the fact that Lydia Zanchi, the IOC secretary since 1927, kept essential documents locked in the cellar.

Though probably unrelated, de Baillet-Latour's death occurred soon after hearing that his son had been killed in an air crash while training with Free Belgian Forces in the United States. The passing of the President committed Edström, now interim President, to extend his efforts in holding the organisation

Madame Lydia Zanchi, secretary at the IOC office in Lausanne, thwarted an attempted German takeover during the Second World War by hiding essential documents in the cellar. (© IOC)

together. He did so, in spite of postal and cable communication difficulties, to the extent that members were in touch more frequently than some of the 73 had ever been beforehand. With some exceptions, he upheld a promise to send a circular of IOC and other news three to four times a year. This included, in January 1943, the news of the death of the last of the 13 founding members, Jiri Guth-Jarkovski of Czechoslovakia.

J. Sigfrid Edström was born in Gothenburg on 21 November 1870, educated there and in Zurich as a civil engineer, also becoming fluent in English, French and German, spoken and written, with some knowledge of Russian. He had been a useful sprinter, achieving 11 seconds for the 100m, and after attending the 1904 Games in St Louis he had devoted his spare time at home to sports administration, being founder of the national sports federation and vice-president of the 1912 Games in Stockholm. There he founded the IAAF, serving as its first president until he retired in 1946, when he was elected President of the IOC.

He had served on the IOC Executive Board since its creation in 1921. In every sense he was conservative, as devoted as Brundage to the nineteenth-century definition of amateurism, and, like de Coubertin and de Baillet-Latour, resistant to the involvement of women in the Olympics. He was, however, a man of immense energy and unfailing attention to detail – having, together with Viktor Balck, made such a success of the Stockholm Games – and would apply the same diligence when leading the IOC. Having become acting President in 1942, at the age of 71, he made the arduous and dangerous journey to the United States by courier plane to discuss the protection and the future of the IOC with Brundage, who, as stated, he immediately proposed for the inaugural position of second Vice-President. He himself had become Vice-President upon the death of Godefroy de Blonay in 1937.

Away from the war zones, travelling was not impossible for neutrals – or for Germans. Lewald, for instance, was able to holiday in Switzerland, while von Halt made trips to Paris and Sweden. It had been possible, moreover, in June 1944, to celebrate in Lausanne the 50th anniversary of the IOC's foundation. The only IOC members present were von Halt and Stephan Tchapratchikov of Bulgaria, who was predominantly resident in Berlin. Also present was Carl Diem, as Director of the International Olympic Institute, and delegates of the Swiss NOC, together with the widows of de Coubertin and de Blonay. Absent with apologies were de Baillet-Latour's widow and J. Sigfrid Edström.

In August 1945, Edström, Brundage and Lord Aberdare, comprising the first post-war Executive Board meeting, met in London to discuss the revival of the Games. Though Aberdare was sceptical, the enthusiasm of Brundage – who had received special permission to travel on the *Queen Elizabeth*, while it was

Three IOC Presidents: Henri de Baillet-Latour of Belgium (left), who died in 1942, his successor J. Sigfrid Edström of Sweden (right) and Avery Brundage study global relations. (© IOC)

still requisitioned for military transport – and of the acting President carried the day. Possible candidates for 1948 were discussed, those interested being Lake Placid and St Moritz for the winter, Athens, Baltimore, Lausanne, London, Los Angeles, Minneapolis and Philadelphia for the summer. A mail ballot was proposed with agreement that, if London was selected, the Board would recommend St Moritz for the winter. The first post-war Session was scheduled for Lausanne the following year. Edström reported that Otto Mayer, a 46-year-old Swiss, had been appointed Chancellor of the IOC Secretariat.

The following February it was announced that London was the overwhelming favourite in the ballot, the Lord Mayor of London having already promised commitment. At that year's Session in Lausanne, Edström was elected as fourth IOC President, never mind that he was now nearly 76. He had been so, de facto, for nearly five years. Of the 73 members from the London Session of 1939, only 51 remained, and 13 new

members were co-opted. Other decisions taken included the acceptance of the compromise of the FIS eligibility of instructors for skiing; rejection of petitions for the inclusion on the programme of archery, baseball, gliding, team handball, polo, roller-skating, table tennis and volleyball; and the transfer of the International Athletic Institute from Berlin to Lausanne. Thus ended Diem's official activity for the IOC.

The St Moritz Session prior to the Games was preoccupied by heated and lengthy debate concerning the Ligue Internationale de Hockey sur Glace (LIHG), formed in 1908. The LIHG was the recognised international federation for ice hockey. The problem arose when the American Athletics Union (AAU), the governing body of a number of amateur sports in the United States and a member of the LIHG, had expelled a number of commercial teams. These teams subsequently formed the American Hockey Association (AHA), which had also applied for LIHG recognition. In January 1948, two teams, the AHA and the AAU (NOC-approved), headed for St Moritz. Neither would withdraw, notwithstanding that at the Stockholm Session an amateur oath had been approved which declared: 'I, the undersigned, declare on my honour, that I am an amateur according to the rules of the international federation governing my sport . . . that I am eligible in all respects for participation in the Olympic Games.' When the St Moritz Session decreed that the LIHG was no longer recognised, that ice hockey was to be removed from the programme and that the local organising committee was censured for accepting the AHA team, the Swiss responded by threatening to cancel the Games, stating that ice hockey, the best-attended and most financially profitable of any sport, must be reinstated. The IOC relented, agreeing to restore ice hockey provided AHA results were excluded from the tournament and medal calculations. Brundage, his dedication to the amateur ethic and the AAU itself on the line, was in a frenzy but the Swiss organising committee defied the IOC and the AHA team competed, eventually finishing fourth. A year later the AHA would be disqualified for non-affiliation to the Olympic Movement. The LIHG's recognition was withdrawn by the IOC.

The division of Summer and Winter Games as separate administrations came to be the post-war pattern. Although Switzerland had been isolated from, even if surrounded by, the Second World War, the country had suffered economically, no area more than its tourist trade. Many hotels and restaurants had been forced to close, so that the advent of the Winter Games at St Moritz provided a welcome financial boost from 20,000 spectators and more than 2,000 competitors, officials and media.

Neither Germany nor Japan were invited to participate, the official reason being that no government existed to whom the invitation could be sent. Lord Aberdare had minuted a protest at the prospect of Germany being involved in any potential Games as early as 1944, Brundage and Edström tactically side-stepping the issue through the absence of political recognition. With the fall of the Third Reich, von Halt and his fellow NOC officials had been interned in Buchenwald by the Russians and in spite of IOC representations von Halt remained captive for five years. A steadfast IOC continued to recognise the membership of both von Halt and the other German member, Duke Adolph-Friedrich von Mecklenburg. Indeed, food parcels and clothing were sent to their families. Greta, von Halt's wife, assured the IOC that he had always rejected Hitler's policies and loyal discretion was likewise accorded to Diem. Germany's allies – Austria, Bulgaria, Hungary, Italy and Romania – did send teams, though they were unwelcome guests, with allegations of former Nazis being included amongst selections. Of the involuntary Soviet allies in the Cold War only Poland and Czechoslovakia were present. Newcomers were Chile, Denmark, Iceland, South Korea and Lebanon.

If the IOC had been insensitive in the 1930s to the persecution of Jews, they were now sensitive to retaining contact within the new Communist network. As for the Soviet Union, in 1946 it was decreed that their sports federations would have to become affiliated to an NOC before an IOC member could be elected from the USSR. A move in this direction began with the USSR's participation at that year's European Athletics Championships in Oslo. However, in Executive Board discussions the following year, it was agreed there was not the time for the formation of a Soviet NOC prior to the Games of 1948, even though by the end of 1947 the Soviets were affiliated in basketball, football, weightlifting and wrestling. There would, oddly, be no problem with the Soviet bloc over amateurism, regarding which Brundage, Lord Burghley and the rest continued to ride their high horse. Soviet assurances on amateur idealism obscured a rampant policy of full-time training for 'civil servant' international sportsmen.

King George VI welcomes IOC President Edström and members Lord Burghley (left) and Viscount Portal at Wembley, London. (© IOC)

There was a strange moral anomaly within the Session at St Moritz when Count Clarence von Rosen of Sweden sent a letter of resignation. On the one hand, von Rosen was known, from correspondence with Brundage, to be cynically sceptical about news of the holocaust that was gradually emerging, yet he pedantically drew to the IOC's attention the undemocratic regulation of the international equestrian federation (FEI) that competitors must hold a commissioned military rank. The Belgian president of the FEI, Gaston de Trannoy, said the matter should be referred to the FEI, not the IOC. The interpretation of von Rosen became all the more relevant when the Swedish team that competed in London was disqualified after winning the gold medal on the basis that a Sgt Gehnäll Persson had been temporarily promoted to second lieutenant for the duration of the Games: the giveaway being that Persson rode wearing his sergeant's cap. France were promoted to gold medal winners, though in 1950 the FEI duly democratised its regulations.

Those attending the Games of 1948 mostly accepted, even admired, the capacity of the British, in their condition of post-war deprivation which included food and clothes rationing, still to put on a show under the wartime adage 'make do and mend'. The British had agreed to hosting as a further illustration of their commitment to basic freedoms. Staging the Games was doubly difficult in the light of the election of a socialist government whose priorities understandably lay elsewhere.

In spite of handicaps borne by many countries, the entry of over 4,000 competitors from 59 countries was the highest yet. A temporary running track was laid at Wembley Stadium and the surrounding halls that had been built for the 1924 Empire Exhibition were now utilised for other sports. With over 80,000 spectators on most days at Wembley, the Games even made a marginal profit on a gross expenditure totalling a moderate three-quarters of a million pounds.

CHAPTER XXVII

St Moritz (V) 1948

Åke Seyffarth of Sweden, Olympic speed skating champion

'It was a loss for me that my best years would probably have been during the Second World War, when of course there were no Games. I'd been originally a cyclist and only started my career as a skater in 1939–40. By the time of St Moritz my form was not so good, I'd had some accidents during cycle races and nobody gave me much of a chance, particularly as I had no experienced international Olympic coach. Yet my cycling had given me one important asset – that was the strength of my leg muscles. I'd been hoping to achieve a time of around 2:15 for the 1,500m, but managed only 2:18.1 behind Sverre Farstad of Norway, for a silver medal. People had warned me that I had no chance of beating Liaklev of Norway in the 5,000m, in which I came seventh, and I had decided not to bother with the 10,000m as I was too tired and stiff.

The Swedish team had no masseur and I could not sleep. Then at the last minute I was persuaded to have a go. I started only because I wished to show goodwill. For a long while in the race I thought they were giving me wrong intermediate times just to encourage me. I knew that there were so many good skaters to come later, so I just ran on without any particular ambition. After 7,000 metres, I had some pains but overcame them. Then I heard Prince Berthol, who was himself a good skater, shouting at me "Go on, you'll win the gold." I thought to myself that a prince could not make a joke about such things, so it stimulated me, and it was only later that I discovered I had a ten-second advantage over the Finn who came second. It was a real surprise, but so rewarding.' (From an interview with *Idrottsbladet*)
(Åke Seyffarth (centre), photograph © IOC/Roebett)

The presence of Åke Seyffarth was typical of the St Moritz Games. The war had interrupted the training and development of a generation that by 1948 should have reached maturity, meaning that veterans such as Seyffarth were still sufficiently competitive to fill the gap in many instances. He was the world record holder, on 8:13.7, for the 5,000m but was advised that he would have little chance at this distance against Reidar Liaklev. Nonetheless, he might have gained a medal, even gold, had he not lost time on the final lap due to a minor collision with a Swedish photographer, who had encroached on to the ice to steal a picture of a possible unprecedented victory.

Seyffarth's performance in the 10,000m was, in the circumstances, exceptional. Though apparently unaware of his own blistering speed, he covered the first 5,000 metres in 9:20, and his winning 10,000m time of 17:26.3 was only two seconds outside the Olympic record. His triumph in St Moritz, the first ever in speed skating by Sweden, heightened his reputation at home and enabled him to become one of the first commercially successful Swedish sports stars when opening an equipment store. In a sport dominated in 1948 by the Scandinavians, the Soviet Union was not yet present. Failing conspicuously in a championship in Sweden the same year, all their coaches and officials had been dismissed on the orders of Stalin, to be replaced by KGB officials devoid of any sporting experience.

Almost the oldest of events was the toboggan, or skeleton

The veteran Åke Seyffarth, Sweden's first Olympic speed skating champion, became one of the first commercially successful sports stars. (© IOC/Ruebelt)

race, staged on the unique Cresta Run and so far only ever held three times in the history of the Games – in 1928, now in 1948 and again in 2002. Linking the first two was the American John Heaton, second behind his first-placed brother Jennison on the previous occasion and now silver-medal winner again, 20 years later, at the age of 39. The Cresta epitomised the elite ambience of St Moritz, the Tobogganing Club having the most distinguished membership of any sporting organisation in Europe other than, perhaps, the Royal Yacht Squadron at Cowes. The winner this time, and anything but blue-blooded, was a rough-hewn young Italian, Nino Bibbia, who had grown up just across the border and whose father ran the local fruit and veg shop. Regular practice had given him intimate experience of the frightening course, including Shuttlecock, often a disastrous bend for others. Discounting what appeared a close shave on one run, Bibbia said: 'I still had two fingers of space between the top of the bank and my toboggan – that's enough.'

Nino Bibbia (ITA), son of a local greengrocer, wins the second-ever Olympic staging on the Cresta Run of the skeleton race. (© IOC)

Those of increasing years may have dominated some events, but not figure skating, where two teenagers, Dick Button of America, 18, and Barbara-Ann Scott of Canada, a year older, took the prizes. Button, a Harvard freshman, introduced an acrobatic revolution in his sport, thrilling the crowds with the first public performance in Europe of the double axel. Like Scott, he practised 20 hours a week but had omitted the double axel from the European Championships in Prague immediately prior to the Games. Repeated perfect landings in subsequent training convinced him now to risk the innovation. 'The cravenness of backing away from something because of the pressure of an Olympic Games repulsed me,' he wrote in his autobiography 'and once I had made up my mind, I could not divert the steps that culminated in the double axel.' Successfully achieving the jump, he was given a perfect 6 by one judge, to gain America's first gold medal in men's figure skating. Eight of the nine judges had placed him first, except needless to say the Swiss, who voted for the local Hans Gerschwiler, the silver medal winner.

In 1947 Scott had won the World Championships, following which the Mayor of her home town, Ottawa, had given her the keys to a new car. Protests from the IOC led to her returning the gift. The only impediment to her victory in St Moritz came from a melting, rutted surface caused by warm winds. In fur-trimmed all-white, she was a fitting successor to the balletic Henie. Taking Henie's example, Scott immediately turned professional . . . and re-collected her car.

Richard Button, introducing a dramatic jumping technique, wins America's first figures title. (© IOC)

Henri Oreiller of France was a well-known rally and motor-racing driver besides being a daredevil skier, seemingly immune to hazards. In Alpine skiing, officially baptised as a full sport at St Moritz, he proceeded to win the men's downhill and combination, and a bronze medal in the special slalom. An almost suicidal downhill run gave him victory by more than four seconds, a huge margin, over Franz Gabl of Austria. His headlong bravery has been matched probably only by Franz Klammer in 1976. Halfway down he had survived a near fall, regaining his balance on only one ski. He was later to meet his

Dare-devil Henri Oreiller of France, renowned motor racing driver, confirmed his risk-taking nerve in the downhill, one of his three Alpine medals. (© IOC)

death when driving a Ferarri in a race at Montlhery, not far from Paris, in 1962.

An old stager who in normal times would probably not have been there was the 36-year-old Birger Ruud, now coach to the Norwegian national team. Having won the Nordic combined in all four previous Winter Games, the Norwegians were shocked when Heikki Hasu and Martti Huhtala, both of Finland, took first and second place with a Swede third. Nonetheless, Norway remained confident for the jump, which they had also won consistently since it began in 1924. Ruud, who had taken the gold in both 1932 and 1936, was interned throughout the German occupation. Finding that the jump hill was deeply rutted and that experience would be vital, he decided at the last moment to include his own name among the entries. The winner was to be Petter Hugsted, with a huge second jump, but in a Norwegian clean sweep Ruud distinguished himself with the silver medal. Though beaten by future world champion Matti Pietikainen of Finland in distance, Ruud's style marks

proved decisive. Norwegian dominance in Nordic skiing, however, was interrupted by Sweden, which finished one–two–three over 18km, with Nils Karlsson claiming gold in the 15km.

Following the lengthy ice hockey dispute, the US team of AHA not surprisingly lost 5–4 to Switzerland, as the AAU team loudly cheered the Swiss. Undeterred, the AHA then inflicted misery on the Italians, winning by 31–1. Many matches were marred by rutted ice on the open rink on warmer days, whereas on those days when it snowed, the puck tended to get lost. The tournament was reduced to a contest essentially between Canada, Czechoslovakia and Switzerland, and Canada were gold medal winners again, though only on goal average. The Czechs took the silver medal, one of their best players being Jaroslav Drobny, who combined his career with tennis. He was to defect when criticised by the Communist press in Prague after defeat at Wimbledon, for allegedly being 'bourgeois'.

John Heaton (USA), second in the Cresta Run in 1928 behind his brother Jennison, repeats the feat 20 years later at the age of 39. (© IOC)

Barbara-Ann Scott (CAN), 19-year-old figures champion. A year earlier she had 'earned' a motor car, but been obliged to surrender it. Now she immediately turned professional – and re-collected it. (© IOC)

CHAPTER XXVIII

London (XIV) 1948

Fanny Blankers-Koen of the Netherlands, quadruple Olympic track and field champion

'*I had competed at Berlin in 1936, when I was 18, in the high jump and the relay, finishing sixth and fifth. There were only six relay lanes and the last German girl dropped the baton! During the war, there were a few local meetings and quite often I was competing against men. I was able to break four world records during the war in the high jump, long jump, the hurdles and the 100 yards.*

I was very happy when I heard that London was going to organise the next Games, though by then I was married with two children, a boy of seven and a girl of two. I had kept up my competitive training and before the Games had set up another world record in the 100m of 11.5.

The race that stands out most in my mind is the hurdles against Maureen Gardner, who, like me, later married her coach, Geoff Dyson. I recall every detail of the heats and the final. On the day of the heats I went to the warm-up track behind Wembley Stadium, already an Olympic champion from the 100m, yet nobody could have felt less like a champion. My legs were trembling. I'd never been so nervous before a race and was even turning away the children wanting autographs, who normally didn't bother me. I went through my warm-up as usual but was not concentrating properly, waiting for my first glimpse of Maureen, whom I'd never seen before. I was aware she had a best time of 11.2, and though earlier that year I had set a world record of 11.0, I knew from experience how things could go wrong. Maureen arrived by car and made a big impression when I saw that she had bought her own hurdles. Someone who does that really must be first class, I thought. There were no other hurdles available on the training track, so, finding courage, I asked if I could borrow hers before my first race. We shook hands and I noticed she was as nervous as I was.

I was to see just how good she was when she touched a hurdle in her semi-final and lost her balance but still managed to qualify in third place. People started to tell me it was going to be easy, but Jan, my husband, was cautious. He decided that I should withdraw from the long jump qualifying round the following morning, prior to the hurdles final in the afternoon, and concentrate on the hurdles because he recognised how dangerous was my rival. I hardly slept that night, turning over in my mind again and again Jan's words "concentrate on the hurdles".

I was drawn in the next lane to Maureen, which was helpful, but on one of the few occasions in my career I made a poor start and was a yard down after ten metres. Yet, I then briefly hurdled as I'd never hurdled before and soon I was almost level with Maureen – going so fast that I was too close to the fifth hurdle, hit it and lost my balance. From there it was a struggle again, with my rhythm gone to pieces. Even so, I felt I had passed Maureen before the finish, but was not sure about Shirley Strickland, who seemed level with me at the line. I was jolted soon after the finish when I heard the British national anthem being played, momentarily thinking Maureen must have won, but the band was playing because the Royal Family had just arrived.

Arriving back at the Hook of Holland, I was nervous going through customs. What about my new coat? Yet having left home a nobody, I now discovered I was public property. When the train arrived at the station in Amsterdam, there was a horse-drawn carriage waiting for me, with four horses.

When I retired, I became a housewife. When I was running, we'd help each other with starting blocks and so on. Now they all have individual sponsors. Poof! I think I've had more fun.'*
(Photograph © IOC)

Fanny Blankers-Koen is one of the foremost figures in Olympic history. Circumstances magnified her achievement. Firstly, her country had endured Nazi occupation, during which she had contrived to maintain the highest athletic standards. Secondly, by the time she competed in London in 1948 she was 30 and a mother. Such was the perception of motherhood in the mid-twentieth century that it was almost by definition a disqualification from athletic excellence. Though Blankers-Koen came to London as the current holder of seven world records – about which a largely uninformed British audience knew little – there was public incredulity that such a person could be a serious contender. How spectacularly Blankers-Koen was to change social attitudes as she galloped to four gold medals within the space of nine days. Only in the 80m hurdles was she seriously challenged. The margin of her victory in the 200m – staged for the first time – is the largest ever achieved in an Olympic sprint victory by man or woman: 0.7, ahead of Audrey Williamson of Britain. But for the advice of her husband and coach, she would surely also have won the long jump, in which the winner, Olga Gyarmati of Hungary, was almost two feet, or well over half a metre, behind Fanny's world record of 6.25m (20 ft 6¼ in.).

Her tour de force began with the 100m and she immediately silenced the doubters with the fastest first round of 12.0, winning the final on a muddy track in 11.9, with Dorothy Manley of Britain yards adrift on 12.2, the same time as recorded by a youthful Shirley Strickland of Australia. The story of the hurdles is told in her own words above; that of the 200m is one of emotional discipline over her self-doubt, again on a wet track and by a huge margin. Her anchor leg in the relay was a final flourish, overtaking the runners of Britain, Canada and Australia to set her name in the headlines for all time. In track and field, if not in other ball games, she had surpassed the legendary Babe Didrikson.

Few runners at any distance have approached an Olympic Games with a longer string of consecutive victories than Harrison Dillard, a boyhood admirer of Jesse Owens, with whom he had become friendly. The run ended, however, when the world record holder in the 110m hurdles struck three hurdles in the US trials and failed to finish. His participation in London

Fanny Blankers-Koen of Holland, with a then unique four gold medals, was pressed only in the 80m hurdles, seen here leading Maureen Gardner (GBR), silver and Shirley Strickland (AUS), bronze. Her 200m victory in rain and mud was the widest ever for this event. (© IOC/Ruebelt) (© IOC)

was nonetheless ensured by having come third in the 100m, and for the final at Wembley he was there alongside world record holder Henry Norwood Ewell (10.2) and 100 yards record holder Mel Patton (9.3). The 30-year-old Ewell had won the trials. Also on the starting line were Lloyd LaBeach of Panama, joint record holder with Ewell, and Emmanuel McDonald Bailey and Alastair McCorquodale, both of Britain – Bailey born in Trinidad and McCorquodale a Scottish rugby player. Against all expectation, Dillard led from the gun, and though Ewell thought he had edged it at the tape and began to celebrate, the photo-finish camera ruled in favour of Dillard – equalling the Olympic record of 10.3, with LaBeach third, Panama's only Olympic medal winner.

Dillard's absence from the high hurdles did not prevent a clean sweep by the US, led by Bill Porter with an Olympic record of 13.9. Patton, meanwhile, compensated for his disappointment in the short sprint by taking the 200m by no more than the width of his chest from Ewell, with LaBeach again third and Herb McKenley of Jamaica, considered by many the favourite, squeezed into fourth place. McKenley, uniquely, was a finalist in both short sprints and the 400m, the latter being his major event. Yet in this he found himself outrun by a British-Jamaican doctor, Arthur Wint, representing his country of birth, Jamaica. Wint had joined the Royal Air Force, as had McDonald Bailey, likewise remaining in London afterwards to acquire medical qualification. Wint had narrowly lost the 800m to the American Mal Whitfield, but had never been beaten at the shorter distance by McKenley.

Arthur Wint (JAM, No. 122) breasts the tape a fraction ahead of compatriot Herb McKenley, with Mal Whitfield (USA, No. 136), double 800m champion, taking the bronze. (© IOC)

The only tactic known to the gazelle-like McKenley was to run from the gun as though the hounds of hell were after him and hope that his anaerobic capacity would last the distance without collapse. Predictably, he was still ahead of Wint into the home straight, only to fade, Wint coming through to win by a fifth of a second in an Olympic record of 46.2, with Whitfield third. Jamaica's team for the four-lap relay, strongly fancied with Wint, McKenley and the impressive George Rhoden, failed to finish when Wint pulled up with cramp on the third leg. In the 400m hurdles, won in an Olympic record time of 51.1 by Roy Cochran (USA), Duncan White of Sri Lanka (then Ceylon) in second place gained his country's first and as yet only ever medal.

If knowledge of Blankers-Koen had been limited beforehand, even less was known about Emil Zátopek. Making his first overseas flight to Oslo for the 1946 European Championships, he had finished fifth behind the veteran Sydney Wooderson of Britain in the 5,000m. 'What I learnt in Oslo,' he said, 'was that you must know how to run tactically and that you must preserve your power for the finish.' The next year he ran the eighth all-time fastest 3,000m, 'but I still didn't feel capable of Olympic victory'. Arriving at the Uxbridge men's Village, Zátopek trained quietly, played his guitar and insisted on taking part in the opening ceremony during a heatwave, even though the 10,000m was the following day. Ordered to return to the Village, he slipped back one place among the marching nations, mingled with the Danes and defiantly re-appeared in the arena. With his coach, he had devised a scheme for checking his 71-second even-lap schedule. If he was going too fast, the coach in the stand would raise a white scarf: too slow, a red one. Two months before the Games, the rapidly emerging Czech had come within two seconds of the 10,000m world record of Finnish Viljo Heino, which stood at 29:35.8. It was expected that Heino might be hard pressed by this phenomenal new runner, who submitted himself daily to a training regime never previously attempted. In the main event of the opening day, Zátopek took over the lead from Heino after eight laps – a red scarf – and continued at such a pace that the field was soon broken, Heino and his compatriot Heinström dropping out with exhaustion. Zátopek lapped every runner bar two, creating such confusion among the judges that the bell for the final lap was rung one lap too soon. The metronomic Zátopek was not misled, continuing for two laps and an Olympic record of 29:59.6, some half a minute slower than Heino's best, but 48 seconds and 300 metres ahead of the redoubtable Frenchman, Alain Mimoun.

A double in the 5,000m was well within Zátopek's capacity but he unnecessarily drained himself in his heat with an irrelevant fight for first place with Erik Ahlden of Sweden. This, and his 10,000m effort, left him tired for the final, in which he was 50 metres adrift of Gaston Reiff of Belgium at the bell. Nevertheless, he set off in vain pursuit over the sodden track, rousing the crowd as he drew closer and closer to Reiff. Reiff accelerated only just in time, to narrowly sustain his lead and win by not much more than a stride in an Olympic record of 14:17.6. Zátopek would later confide that he had never considered himself a possible winner and was 'running for the bronze', which in fact went to Willem Slijkhuis of Holland. Zátopek's last lap was run in 60 seconds, an exceptional pace for that era. He also confided that he had managed to make an out-of-hours, prohibited visit to the women competitors' university accommodation to show his 10,000m medal to Dana Ingrova, the Czech javelin thrower who was soon to become his wife.

The makeshift London Games were conspicuous for exceptional performers – not least Robert Mathias, who, in only his third competition, became the youngest winner of the decathlon. It was only five months earlier that he had taken up the event on the advice of a coach, gaining Olympic selection three months after that. He was an outstanding all-round athlete, excelling at both American football and basketball, but his path to victory in London was to be fraught with problems. In the shot put, he forfeited his best throw by unknowingly walking out of the front of the circle, a regulation about which he had not been told, and nearly blew his chance with a below-average performance in the high jump. At the conclusion of the first day's five events he was lying third behind Enrique Kistenmacher of Argentina and Ignace Heinrich of France. Wretched weather delayed the start of the second day and in the second event, the discus, the mark for his best throw, some 44 metres, was temporarily 'lost' when the marker fell over. There

The legendary Emil Zátopek, seen here in the lead, smashed records and competitors' hearts, but in this 5,000m of 1948, Gaston Reiff of Belgium, lying third behind Erik Ahlden (SUI), out-sprinted Zátopek in the home straight. (© IOC)

followed a half-hour search in the gloom. As there were no floodlights at Wembley, the lines for the penultimate event, the javelin, had to be illuminated by motor car headlights and the 1,500m was finally concluded at 10.30 in the evening, an exhausted youngster having the second slowest time among the first eight but beating Heinrich by 165 points with a total of 7,139 (6,628 by contemporary tables). His mother, father and two brothers, having travelled 6,000 miles, were there in the near-darkness to share his triumph.

At this time Sweden was the heartland of middle-distance running, though Gunder Hägg and Arne Andersson, their two finest, as professionals had been banned. The favourite for the 1,500m was Lennart Strand, joint world record holder with

There being no floodlights at Wembley, the best discus throw of 17-year-old decathlon champion Robert Mathias (USA), was temporarily 'lost' in the gloom. The javelin event had to be illuminated by motor-car headlights. (© Getty Images)

Hägg. Marcel Hansenne of France led for just over two laps during a downpour, but was then overtaken by three Swedes, Henry Eriksson, Strand and Gösta Bergkvist. Eriksson had never beaten Strand but Strand hated the rain and Eriksson was able to sustain a three-yard lead over him coming off the final bend.

The drama of the marathon 40 years earlier, with the famous Dorando, was to be repeated. On one of the few hot days of the fortnight, Etienne Gailly of Belgium was the first to re-enter Wembley Stadium at the finish but he was in pitiful condition. Totally exhausted and near to collapse, he shuffled his way around the track, reducing an anguished crowd to near silence. The 21-year-old Belgian paratrooper had taken the lead for the second time, just ahead of Delfo Cabrera of Argentina, a mile from the stadium, and had entered 200 yards ahead, but on the final lap of the track he was overhauled first by Cabrera and then by Tom Richards of Britain. Mindful of history and Dorando's disqualification, no one made a move to assist Gailly, who with great presence of mind forced himself to the finish to take the bronze medal – so dehydrated that he was unable to attend the medal ceremony.

Fencing attracted its largest entry at any Games and lasted until late evening throughout 13 days. The French were outstanding, with Jehan Buhan not losing a fight in the individual foil final and helping his team to ensure the double of individual and team gold. The cycling events at Herne Hill in South London also finished late; so late on the last day, because officials had not calculated for sprint cyclists remaining almost motionless as they jockeyed with rivals for a tactical break, that the 2,000m tandem final took place in near darkness, again because there were no floodlights. Reg Harris of Britain, wounded in the Western Desert in the war but world champion in 1947, lost the 1,000m sprint to Mario Ghella of Italy and was again second in the tandem (now discontinued), when he and Alan Bannister lost the decisive third race to Ferdinando Terruzi and Renato Perona of Italy by less than a foot. The competitors were by now all but invisible to any remaining spectators, journalists using matches and torches to file their reports from unilluminated booths.

New records were set in eight of the swimming events and equalled in another, the US making a clean sweep in the six men's events, with fifteen of its eighteen representatives reaching the finals. American monopoly was punctured by Greta Andersen of Denmark in the women's 100m freestyle. She would turn professional and later swim the English Channel six times, with a record crossing of 13 hours and 14 minutes in 1964.

The boxing entry was the biggest for 24 years and remained unusually sporting in the light of persistent incompetence by judges and referees through lack of experience during the wartime period. Argentina, Hungary and South Africa each won two weights, Czechoslovakia and Italy one each. László Papp of Hungary began an illustrious career with the middleweight title, winning and successfully defending the light-middle title in the next two Games before becoming Hungary's first professional and winning the European Championship. Victories by Turkey in Greco-Roman wrestling were unexpected, their forté being freestyle, limited technique being compensated by strength.

There were 17 teams for the football tournament, Sweden and Yugoslavia reaching the final. This saw the start of half a century of distinguished performances by both the thinly populated Sweden and multi-ethnic Yugoslavs. Sweden won 3–1

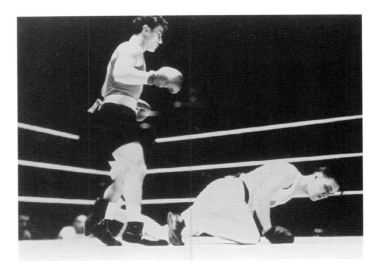

A run of three successive Olympic victories by László Papp of Hungary began with his middleweight knockout of John Wright of Britain. (© Getty Images)

to bring their goal tally to 22, one of the more remarkable being by Henry Carlsson in the semi-final against Denmark. With the Danish goalkeeper caught out of position, Gunnar Nordahl, one of three brothers in the Swedish team, caught the ball inside the goal behind the line, having stepped there to avoid being offside.

In six Games since the introduction of the modern pentathlon Sweden had never lost the gold medal and now won again. Willie Grut, son of the designer of the Stockholm stadium in 1912, rode a faultless round in riding, was first of 45 competitors in fencing with 28 victories, came fifth in shooting, won the swimming four seconds ahead of the second best and was eighth in the concluding cross-country. No other competitor has ever led in three of the five events. Heikki Savolainen of Finland won his fifth gymnastics bronze medal on the pommel horse and his first gold in the combined team exercises at the age of 40, the event being transferred from the open Wembley Stadium to an indoor hall because of continual bad weather.

The rowing was staged at Henley, the course widened to accommodate three craft instead of two, as at the annual Royal Regatta. Jack Kelly Junior, who had won the Diamond Sculls the previous year, failed to emulate his father's single sculls victory of 1920 when eliminated in the semi-finals. The winner was Mervyn Wood of Australia, the current Diamonds holder. Durward Knowles, competing for Britain in the regatta at Torbay, subsequently participated in the next six Games for the Bahamas and made it an eighth at Pusan in 1988. Paul and Hilary Smart of America were unusual father-and-son winners of the Star class. Second in the individual equestrian dressage event was André Jousseaume of France, aged 54 and one of the outstanding horsemen of all time: in five Games spanning 24 years he finished fifth three times in the individual event, in addition to silver and bronze medals and team gold and silver in 1932 and 1936 respectively.

CHAPTER XXIX

Enter the Soviets

Vitaly Smirnov of Russia, IOC Vice-President, 2001–05

'The development of sport and its fomal organisation in the Soviet Union, and later within the Russian Federation, reflects the difficult evolutionary course travelled by our country. During the twentieth century, it had occasion to go through several socio-economoic upheavals and each of them affected the life of people living on this huge territory.

The socialist revolution in October 1917 brought with it the ideology of the confrontation of classes. So almost all sports activities between 1917 and the Second World War were available and possible within the working-class movement; though during that period there were very few who nowadays we would call "sportsmen". The situation, and the politics, changed after 1945. The Communist Party and the government under Josef Stalin recognised the significance of international sport. The slogan of that time – "We won the war, we should win in sport!" – reflected the new reality, the new political geography in eastern Europe and the necessity to demonstrate the advantages of the socialist system with major sports victories. So the Soviet Union began to take part, from 1945 onwards, in international competition.

The best athletes of that time began to receive financial subsidies from the state. The dimension of the grants was very modest for most, at the level of a living wage, though it gave the opportunity to dedicate time to training. Professionalism as such was not admitted. At the same time the state invested substantially in children's and youth sports, in sports education and science, in building training centres and sports facilities all over the USSR. With the money from the state budget, there was created a system of preparing young athletes and sports personnel that served as an example for many countries.

Russian life was to change at the end of the 1980s. At first some athletes – ice hockey and tennis players, for example – were given permission to go abroad. Then, with the disintegration of the USSR, everyone gained the chance to go anywhere. The new Russian state could no longer afford to pay subsidies and so many went abroad, sometimes without the agreement of their national sports federation.

The situation had been brought more or less under control by the start of the twenty-first century. Nowadays, any athlete who wants to sign a contract with a foreign club must obtain a transfer from the national federation. Many sports people – figure skaters, tennis, ice hockey, handball, volleyball players, etc. – live and train abroad but form part of the Russian national teams. At the same time there are not too many sportsmen who could be called real professionals within the country. The exceptions, perhaps, are in football and basketball. Though sports federations and clubs are trying to find sponsors, most of the finance comes from the state budget. The federal budget is used to cover preparation of national teams for international competitions, the regional budget for development of sport at local level. There is still no real market economy in the country and that is why it is difficult to speak of open professionalism in Russian sport. That is something for the future.'*

(Photograph © IOC/Imsand)

If the Second World War changed the face of the globe politically, economically and socially, it also had a massive further impact upon the Olympic Games, bringing to them the full force of the systematic organisation and planning within the huge multicultural, amalgamated Communist nation of the USSR. For the next 45 years, sport was to offer Soviet citizens one of the few opportunities for foreign travel and the broadening of human experience; not to mention material rewards in a country where most endured a fairly spartan existence. Vitaly Smirnov witnessed the whole cycle of sporting evolution among Russia and its satellite allies in the second half of the twentieth century. He was a young administrator when Stalin first initiated the regimentation of national coaching and the study of sports science in the pursuit of political propaganda through sport.

Early after the war, J. Sigfrid Edström told Brundage that he believed Communist countries should be invited to take part in the Olympic Games, though he was reluctant to have Communists elected to the IOC Executive Board. The USSR was invited to participate in London in 1948 but declined on the grounds that its competitors were not ready. Soviet observers, however, attended the Games and took note. Within two years, Soviet athletes had made rapid advances, performing impressively at the European Athletics Championships of 1950. The same year, no doubt for expedient reasons, the Soviets released German IOC member Karl von Halt from prison. The following year, at the IOC Session in Vienna, the Soviet Union

133

applied for and was granted IOC recognition, though both Edström and Brundage were concerned about the uncertain amateur status of Soviet competitors. With the belligerence that was to characterise their sporting negotiations through four decades, the USSR simultaneously demanded acceptance of Russian as an official IOC language, a seat on the Executive Board and the expulsion of Spain. When their demands were rejected, they re-applied, conceding to IOC regulations. However, Stalin demanded that the recently created NOC of the USSR unilaterally 'announce' its own IOC member, Konstantin Andrianov, who was told to travel to Vienna and present himself. Edström was furious at this attempted breach of IOC protocol but, when tempers had calmed, Andrianov was elected in 1951.

Confronted by Brundage on the question of state-sponsored training and payment subsidies, Andrianov insisted that these arrangements were no longer 'routine', claiming that most athletes were either students or government employees in the civil service or armed forces. The IOC could do nothing but accept these assurances, though they increasingly became aware of talented elderly students and military officers on permanent sports leave.

In June 1952, the USSR announced it would be competing at Helsinki, though they demanded that their team, together with those from subordinated Eastern European nations, should be housed in a separate Olympic Village. The Finnish hosts reluctantly agreed. Nonetheless, the USSR brought only competitors known to be politically correct. Those of independent thought, such as Estonian-born Soviet decathlon champion Heino Lipp, were left behind.

If Edström was vaguely uneasy about the admission of the USSR, there could no doubting the eagerness of Brundage to recall Germany to the fold, or at least the newly created Federal Republic. Brundage saw West Germany as a potential ally in his thinly veiled disapproval of Jewish/Communist practices. In

An ageing President Edström was 'uneasy' about the admission of the Soviet Union to the Olympic arena in time for the Games of 1952. (© IOC)

September 1949, West Germany's NOC was created. President was Adolf von Mecklenburg, with Carl Diem as honorary secretary, though by 1951 von Mecklenburg had resigned office in favour of von Halt. The IOC gave provisional recognition at the 1950 Session in Copenhagen. The Executive Board subsequently recommended that Germany should not be allowed to participate at the Winter Games of Oslo but the suggestion was ignored. A controversy within a controversy was that some IOC members resented the continuing acceptance of von Halt, a former Nazi, never mind that von Halt had assured friends that he would not attend the Winter Games in Norway, where antagonism lingered towards the Germans. And there was a further problem: the widely unrecognised East German Democratic Republic (GDR) also formed an NOC in April 1951.

Formal recognition of the Federal NOC was granted at the 1951 Session in Vienna and there was indignation from socialist nations at the rejection of the GDR. Several IOC members, including Lord Exeter, suggested recognition of both if they would agree to form a single team for Olympic participation, a proposal welcomed by Brundage. Such a merger for the Games would seemingly favour the Federal NOC with its more powerful economic background. The GDR, however, were reluctant to sacrifice their autonomy. At a private meeting with their Western counterparts they demanded equal representation if there were to be a single NOC. At a subsequent Executive Board meeting, the GDR committee agreed to a joint team but this was denounced by the government in Berlin and rescinded. A further Executive Board meeting was called for Copenhagen in February 1952, immediately prior to the Winter Games. Absurdly, the GDR contingent arrived in the Danish capital but inexplicably failed to reach the conference room where Edström and the West German delegation were awaiting them. The IOC continued to stretch out a helping hand by stating at the Session prior to the Winter Games: 'It is necessary to form a special commission of West and East representatives to organise a single German team for the Games in Helsinki. In this commission there should be three representatives of each under the chairmanship of Dr Karl von Halt, as member of the IOC. The German team shall be selected at a special try-out . . . irrespective of whether they are resident in East or West.' Continued reluctance by the GDR to cooperate meant that it was impossible for their competitors to be coordinated in any team for Helsinki.

The case of the two Chinese committees was to prove even more problematic than that of Germany, the opposing factions being even more recalcitrant. Edström, therefore, proposed that both the People's Republic and Formosa (Taiwan) should be barred from the Summer Games in Helsinki.

The Chinese NOC had originally been recognised in 1922, the first lone competitor appearing in 1932 in Los Angeles. Following the Communist uprising in 1949, and the flight of Chiang Kai-shek to Taipei, the mainland Communists re-organised sport within an All-China Athletic Federation, requesting recognition from the IOC and an invitation from Helsinki. By 1952 nothing had been heard from Taiwan. Meanwhile the Finnish government recognised only the People's Republic.

After the revolution, the majority of 'nationalist' NOC officials had fled to Taipei. One of the three IOC members, Yi-tung Shou, elected in 1947, had sided with Mao Tse-tung's coup and remained in Beijing and the other two, Chen-ting Wang and Xiang-Xi Kong, had gone to Hong Kong and New York respectively. When Eric von Frenckell, Finland's IOC member, reported to the Session in Oslo that the All-China Athletic Federation had requested an invitation, backed by the Chinese

Embassy in Stockholm, Lord Burghley pointed out that the People's Republic was not affiliated to the IAAF and the IOC then requested clarification on which IFs *did* have the People's Republic as a registered member. The IOC's formal position was that the recognised Chinese NOC was the former nationalist body now in Formosa-Taiwan. The idea that they could transport with them the mainland NOC was patently ridiculous. On the other hand, the United States was opposed to the acceptance of the People's Republic, as they were allies of North Korea in the ongoing peninsula war. In a not unreasonable telegram to Helsinki from the People's Republic team, en route in Leningrad, they claimed to be the legitimate Chinese representatives and had received an invitation which they had accepted. At the Helsinki Session, von Frenckell recommended that both 'countries' should be allowed to attend, though nothing had been heard from Chinese IOC members since 1948. When told that Yi-tung Shou was indeed alive and living in Beijing, Edström demanded his presence. He arrived three days later with an interpreter but then beat a retreat to the Embassy, leaving the Session to decide in his absence between two proposals: no Chinese team, or two teams. The second was carried by 29 votes to 22. In a continuation of a farcical episode, a 50-strong People's Republic team arrived ten days after the opening ceremony, five days before the close, while Formosa-Taiwan decided to boycott the event on account of the presence of the team from the People's Republic. In the end one mainland competitor took part, in the 100m freestyle swimming.

Amid the obscurantism of the Chinese, the arrogance of the USSR and the perversity of the German Democratic Republic, other IOC decisions over the four years following the London Games were largely pushed into the background. One of these was the election, at the Session in Rome in 1949, of Melbourne as host for the Summer Games in 1956, with the slightly irritating provision, on account of Australian equestrian quarantine regulations, for the equestrian events to be staged in Stockholm. There had been thirteen candidate cities, including eight American. The choice for the Winter Games was Cortina D'Ampezzo in the Italian Alps, the other candidates being Colorado Springs and Lake Placid. The abundance of American candidates on this occasion led the IOC to take the decision four years later that a candidate city would only be accepted if first ratified by its NOC.

At the Copenhagen Session of 1950, Miklos Horthy, Jr, the son of a prominent Hungarian fascist, who had taken refuge after the war at the Vatican where he was granted asylum, refused to resign for failing to meet the IOC's requirement of residing in his own country and was excluded as a lapsed member; as was, for the same reason, the Italian member and Fascist Giorgio Vaccaro, who had fled to Argentina. Under regulation of the Charter, after missing four consecutive Sessions, Enrique Barboza Baeza of Chile, Miguel Idigoras Fuentes of Guatemala, Comte de Vallelano of Spain – 18 in a row since 1934 – and Rechid Atabinen of Turkey were also excluded as lapsed members. The NOC of Israel was recognised.

The award of the Winter Games to Oslo had taken place at the Session of 1947 in Stockholm, Oslo being preferred to Cortina and Lake Placid on the first ballot, thus becoming both the first capital city and first Scandinavian city with that honour. The practice of dividing Winter and Summer between different countries had arisen with the election of London for 1948, London advocating Oslo for the winter event. Oslo declined on that occasion, being absorbed in post-war restoration, but subsequently resubmitted their bid for 1952. Their prospects for 1952 were enhanced by Lake Placid having already staged a Winter Games and being

considered an economic handicap for European teams – which provided the bulk of competitors – only seven years after the war, while Cortina remained in the shade as Italy was still viewed as a Nazi ally. Such sentiments endured in the run up to 1952 and indeed beyond.

It was highly appropriate that the Winter Games should for the first time take place in Scandinavia, the spiritual home of winter sport, cross-country skiing being a way of life long before the reinvention of the Olympic ideal and ice skating being the commonest of national sports. Norwegians are sentimentalists and these Games saw the first winter innovation of the Olympic flame, beginning its journey not from the slopes of Olympia but from Morgedal, a small village in the south where Sondre Norheim had pioneered skiing and ski jumping in the nineteenth century. The flame was in fact ignited in the hearth of his original home, at the start of its 220-kilometre journey to Oslo.

There had been some confusion concerning ice hockey at Oslo, following the fracas in the tournament in 1948. The international federation demanded that the main rink have an artificial surface to ensure the best conditions but the Norwegians were reluctant to embark on such an expensive project when it was not sure if the competition would take place. At the IOC Session of 1950 in Copenhagen, a special commission was appointed to deal with the LIHG issue and after some weeks a report was submitted stating that LIHG had revised its rules 'in a manner which justifies the hope that ice hockey can be restored to the programme'. The compromise was that the US team for 1952 was to be selected by a joint committee of the AHA and USOC, plus two professionals from the National Hockey League. Bitterness remained within the Amateur Athletic Union, which ironically accused Brundage of siding with the professionals, but hockey was back in the Games. Added to the programme for Oslo was the giant slalom for both men and women and the Nordic 10km for women.

When Edström was elected the IOC's fourth President in 1948 at 75, an age which none of his predecessors had reached, there was no discussion regarding his term of office: normally eight years under the Charter. Edström had stated in 1949 that he wished to retire the following year but was persuaded to remain in office until the Helsinki Games. Throughout this time he lobbied transparently for Brundage as his successor. Opposition to Brundage was largely clandestine, there being some who would never forgive him for opposing the boycott campaign of 1934–6. He in turn was paranoid about those who disagreed with him. Brundage's overriding virtue was his dedication to the cause of de Coubertin, never mind his own muddled, sometimes contradictory philosophy, and he was the nomination of the Executive Board. Those opposed to this self-made Chicago building-contractor millionaire, on the grounds of snobbery and anti-Americanism, wished to keep the presidency in Europe. Prince Axel of Denmark, backed by Porritt and Andrianov of the Soviet Union, proposed Lord Burghley, president of the IAAF. In a secret ballot, Brundage was the winner by 30 votes to 17 with 2 abstentions. For the next 20 years the dogmatic Brundage was to attempt to rule the Olympic Movement by unilateral diktat. His inaugural address in Lausanne a week after the Helsinki Games was a predictable sermon. On amateurism. Listening as ever was that other traditionalist and strict financial critic Reginald Alexander, increasingly harassed white IOC member from Kenya and former mayor of Nairobi. During 18 months of Mao-mao atrocities, Alexander slept in a chair backed against the front door with a gun across his knees.

Reginald Alexander, contentious white IOC member from Kenya, was a strong supporter of Brundage on traditional amateurism, and an accountant with strict views on commercial deals. (©IOC/Pi)

Helsinki had originally been offered the Games in 1940, and now in 1952, amid a troubled world, they would be conducted in an atmosphere of characteristic northern serenity. The quiet, reserved Finns staged the best of Games, parliament having granted more than a million dollars for renovation of facilities and construction of an Olympic Village. The Olympic stadium was increased in capacity to 70,000, that of the swimming pool to 8,000, the latter with special heating. With the Village built in 1940 now occupied, a new one was required and was ready a year early. The nursing school accommodated female competitors. With hotels having occupancy for only 4,000 guests, accommodation was organised for a further 100,000 visitors in private homes, schools, military barracks and camping grounds. By now, there was already anxiety about the growth in numbers, Brundage having recommended a reduction in men's gymnastics, rowing and walking, and women's track and field. Nevertheless, the programme from London was retained, indeed increased in women's gymnastics and weight divisions in boxing. Preliminary rounds in team games were staged prior to the official start of the Games. Competing for the first time were the Bahamas, Dutch Antilles, Ghana, Guatemala, Hong Kong, Indonesia, Israel, Nigeria, Saarland (for the only time), Thailand and Vietnam.

At the opening ceremony in the smallest city ever to be host – population under 400,000 – there was the usual expectation for entry of the final torchbearer. When he appeared through the tunnel, the crowd erupted with emotion, thunderous applause accompanying his lap of the track. Finland had never forgiven Edström, Brundage and the IOC for allowing the IAAF to ban Paavo Nurmi, as revered a national figure as Sibelius, from the Games of 1932 on the grounds of professionalism: something that from the end of the First World War was unspoken, unseen but common practice among front-line runners. Now the 55-year-old Nurmi was given his final fling. Having lit the stadium flame, he then passed the torch to

Hannes Kolehmainen, his famous forerunner – the two having seventeen Olympic medals between them – who ascended the stadium tower by lift to ignite a second flame. The specially erected tower was 72.71 metres high to commemorate the Olympic javelin record of Matti Järvinen in 1932.

Finnish hero Paavo Nurmi, a controversial choice in the view of the IOC, lights the Helsinki flame to rapturous applause. (© IOC)

While Helsinki appeared a sea of tranquillity, there was evident tension in the Cold War sporting confrontation – Orwell's 'war without bullets' – between the United States and the Soviet Union. This rivalry was amplified by the daily press recording of national medal tallies. Bob Mathias of America, retaining his decathlon title, remarked that defeating the Soviet Union was not the same as 'beating some friendly country like Australia'. The Soviet presence inspired the American men's track and field squad to win 14 gold medals, to none by the Soviets. Performances all round were high, with 17 Olympic records broken in 22 track and field events. Yet Soviet dominance in women's athletics and in gymnastics gave them an overall lead in medals until the last day of competition, in which the USA overhauled them with medals from swimming, basketball and boxing. The IOC's attempt to bar the blatant nationalistic recording of the medal count inevitably proved impossible. The indignity for the USSR was that it was obliged, following American success, to dismantle the board at the entrance to its isolationist village which proudly proclaimed the daily medal rankings.

The Games were distinguished by sporting achievement – 'the big-hearted Olympics' Carl Diem called them – and a turning point in the IOC's evolution. From this moment, the Games would become ever larger and costlier – Helsinki had a record 69 nations – leaving some hosts in debt, thereby discouraging others from bidding. The IOC was also heading, with the emergence of the USSR, towards another impasse: the double standard of false state amateur and supposedly genuine 'Western' amateur.

CHAPTER XXX

Oslo (VI) 1952

Jeanette Altwegg of Britain, Olympic figure skating champion

'*My memories of the Games in Oslo are conditioned to a degree by those from my first involvement at St Moritz four years earlier. They came immediately after the war; the experience, the ambience was new to everybody after a long interval without competition and every participant was something of an unknown quantity. As an avid student and admirer of the legends of Greek mythology and all the stories of the ancient Games, it was with huge excitement, and indeed awe, that I had arrived to compete in the beautiful setting of St Moritz. At that time, I was unburdened by expectation, my own or other people's, merely indulging in the sheer joy of being there. I was thrilled to have come third. Arriving in Oslo was an entirely different matter. This was much more serious combat, a more severely disciplined environment. There was nothing carefree about it anymore and yet there are elements from those weeks in Oslo that will remain with me for ever.*

The cold, pristine night air, so silent and peculiar to Norway, was something that made one's spine and one's mind tingle. Arriving on the ice for competition, with that night silence exchanged for the music of one's skating programme – there is nothing to describe that special, wonderful prickling feeling as you sense the climax of your career is approaching. Yes, this is it, this is the Olympics. And you are going to prove to your coach, to your parents, to your country and to yourself that you can do it. Oslo was truly the peak of my career, one that I can never forget, yet a feeling that is difficult to describe.'*

(Olympic Poster © IOC)

The Winter Games of Oslo, the first to take place in a Scandinavian country, were without major dramas, yet contained sinister evidence of an evil that would come to threaten fundamental philosophies over the next half-century. When everybody had packed up and gone home, abandoned ampules and syringes were discovered in the Olympic Village, irrefutable evidence that some athletes were experimenting with, indeed resorting to, performance-enhancing pharmaceuticals. The evidence was lightly ignored at the time: to everybody's cost. Another seven Winter and Summer Games took place before anabolic steroids, the most offensive of drugs, were banned.

A more positive aspect of the Oslo Games was the thirst of the Norwegian public for international competition and their unsullied sportsmanship in welcoming champions of every race – a phenomenon that was again to be so apparent in Lillehammer 42 years later. More than 560,000 spectators watched the record number of 30 nations throughout 11 days of competition, in mostly glorious weather. When Arnfinn Bergmann of Norway won the esteemed jumping title on the large hill at Holmenkollen, there were 103,432 paying spectators, the largest recorded crowd ever for either Winter or Summer Games, more even than LA and Sydney. Bergmann narrowly won from his compatriot Torbjörn Falkanger, with Karl Holmström of Sweden third. This brought Norway's total of medals since the inauguration of the Winter Games in 1924 to 14 out of 18 in the ski jump events, yet thereafter their success in this speciality would markedly decline as the Finns, Austrians, East Germans, Japanese and others improved.

If Holmenkollen was the scene of national celebration, the Norwegians' handling of the less favoured Alpine skiing events evoked little approval from those dependent on good facilities. The Alpine disciplines drew the largest number of entries but were poorly administered at Norefjell, some 100 kilometres from Oslo. Dangerously sited trees were only removed from the women's downhill course on the morning of the race.

Given the Norwegians' jaundiced view of Alpine skiing and their early opposition between the wars to the IOC's wish to introduce this sport, it was ironic that Stein Eriksen, a Norwegian, should win the demanding giant slalom. A debonair stylist, akin to later heroes such as Franz Klammer and Alberto Tomba, he was the first of only five skiers from a non-Alpine country to have won an Alpine event Olympic gold medal. It

Stein Eriksen of Norway, debonair stylist, wins the giant slalom by a wide margin. (© IOC)

Hjalmar Andersen of Norway, triple speed skating champion. (© IOC/Ruebelt)

could be said, indeed, that he was the first superstar of the Winter Olympics, widely celebrated beyond his own land. He finished almost two and four seconds respectively ahead of Austrians Christian Pravda and Toni Spiss, then went off to become a professional instructor successively in Michigan, California, Colorado, Vermont and Utah. With local knowledge of Norefjell, he could or should have doubled with victory in the slalom, but after setting the fastest time on the first run he was beaten by Othmar Schneider of Austria by an aggregate 1.2 seconds.

In the blue-riband downhill event, Eriksen finished sixth behind Tuscan restaurateur Zeno Colò, while in the women's events, Andrea Mead-Lawrence from Vermont, aged 19, achieved a double in the slalom and giant slalom, recovering from a fall in her first round in the former, to record the fourth fastest time and surpassing everyone else by two seconds or more on the second. The downhill went to Trude Jochum-Beiser of Austria.

The Scandinavians took all but six of the twenty-four medals for mens' skiing, and the similarity of skiing to running cross-country was emphasised in the 18km Nordic event, which was won by Hallgeir Brenden of Norway, who subsequently won two national steeplechase titles. Martin Stokken, a colleague in the second-placed relay team, had been fourth in the 10,000m track race in London behind Emil Zátopek. A competitor later in 1952 in Helsinki, Stokken was one of the few to have competed in a Winter and Summer Games in the same year. Scandinavian cross-country dominance was apparent in the 18km in Oslo, with Norway, Sweden and Finland occupying the first 17 places. On the same day that Brenden won the 18km, Hjalmar Andersen won the 1,500m speed skating and Simon Slåttvik

won the Nordic combined – a triple Norwegian success that provoked such celebrations throughout Oslo that it was almost impossible to obtain service in any of the hotels.

A brief blot on the landscape of happy home nationalism had been the selection of Finn Hodt as one of Norway's speed skaters. He had been convicted as a Nazi collaborator after fighting for the Germans on the Eastern front. The Norwegian Olympic committee overruled his nomination by their own skating union and the matter was forgotten when Hjalmar Andersen became a focal point of domestic celebration when winning all three speed skating titles at 1,500m, 5,000m and 10,000m on consecutive days.

Dick Button, having introduced the double axel when winning the figure skating at St Moritz, now distinguished his retention of his title with his revelationary triple loop, a technique never previously performed in competition. He would probably have won again even without it, but this was a competitor of courage, nervous though he was about its introduction. David Wallechinsky, in his comprehensive statistical and anecdotal record *Complete Book of the Winter Olympics*, quotes from Button's autobiography:

> I forgot in momentary panic which shoulder should go forward and which back. I was extraordinarily conscious of the judges, who looked so immobile at the rinkside. But this was it . . . height was vital. Round and around again, in a spin which took only a fraction of a second to complete before it landed on a clean, steady back edge. I pulled away breathless, excited and overjoyed.

He was a unanimous choice among the nine judges and shortly afterwards turned professional.

Although Jeanette Altwegg had been marked first by the British judge in 1948 – surprise, surprise – several had placed her fourth or fifth when she gained the bronze medal and her victory in Oslo was dependent on her technique in the compulsory figures, for she came only fourth in the free skating. Chief of her rivals was Tenley Albright, a future winner. The US judge in Oslo maintained a warped system by ranking Altwegg fourth and Albright first, whereas six of the nine judges placed Altwegg first. She thus won Britain's first skating gold medal since Madge Syers in 1908, when the event was included in the

Summer Games. Altwegg was one of few to scorn professionalism, instead working at the Pestalozzi Village for orphaned children in Switzerland.

Ice hockey, having recovered its administrative dignity after the eligibility arguments of 1948, was nonetheless involved in controversy, this time on the rink. The US team was singularly rough, to the demonstrative criticism of Norwegian spectators. By tying with Canada, once again champions, in their final pool game, the Americans were accused by the Soviet press of bourgeois capitalist cheating. The tie lifted the US from fourth place to the silver medal, while the Canadians, represented in Oslo by the Edmonton Mercurys, had accumulated Winter Games statistics over thirty-two years of thirty-seven wins, one loss and three ties for five titles in six Games. West Germany marked their return to the Games by winning both the two- and four-man bobsleigh events. However, such was the weight of their four-man team, an aggregate 472 kg (1,041 lb), that the international federation was thereafter obliged to introduce regulations to restrict weight in the interest of equality of competition.

Jeanette Altwegg, Britain's only champion in women's figures since Madge Syers at the Summer Games of 1908. (© IOC)

Andrea Mead-Lawrence (USA), double winner at slalom and giant slalom, shows the aggression of mind and muscle that the founder and his contemporaries considered 'inelegant' for women. (© IOC)

CHAPTER XXXI

Helsinki (XV) 1952

Emil Zátopek of Czechoslovakia, Olympic triple long-distance champion

'*In our family I had a good reputation . . . as a fast messenger. Even my teacher knew that and used to send me to bring him a ham sandwich. I also have happy memories of our grey Chinese geese, which were wonderful houseguards. Our postman dared to deliver the mail only to our garden gate. Once he had his trousers nearly torn off by them when he overstepped the boundary. I became very friendly with the geese because they loved to run and fly. I used secretly to open the gate to let them out and then start to run like mad down the road, calling them after me. They joyfully followed and I could hear the patter of their feet, a humming sound overhead and, suddenly, with necks outstretched, there they were airborne. Like this they accompanied me for several hundred metres to the end of our street, and they must have enjoyed the fun as much as I did because they made a habit of waiting at our garden gate for me to return from school. My mother was worried that the geese were not fattening quickly. When she learned about our fun and games, she soon put a stop to it, saying: "Geese are for fattening and laying eggs, not to take part in athletic events."*

Once, the boys from our street measured out a kilometre circuit around our houses. They challenged everyone to run the distance without stopping. I was running and running, without any difficulty, and I was the only one who finished the third lap. The boys stared at me and one of them said: "You were running like Nurmi!" It was the first time I ever heard his name.

I was 14 when I left my family and started to work in the Bata shoe factory in Zlin. Often I felt very lonely. After my working hours I started to run one or two kilometres. Just for the pleasure of it. By the time I was 18 I still didn't know the length of an athletics track. In 1941, our department supervisor forced me to run in a race through Zlin. I did it with reluctance but I finished second. People were applauding during the race and that affected me. All of a sudden I felt more important than normally. And that's how it all started.

I discovered a good athletic club and before I realised, running had become the centre of my life. After the war, I was already Czechoslovak record holder at 5km and 10km. All of a sudden I had become eligible for selection for the Olympic Games in London. I didn't want to lose this chance. I was practising even during the night with interval running – which at that time was a very unusual schedule. I was driven by the thought that I would meet the best in the world but the main motivation was not to make a disgrace of myself.

As an Olympic beginner, I finished very well in London. A gold and silver medal helped me to step up among the sports stars and they opened the doors to sporting society and a wider public. This woke in me an admiration for Olympic ideals and increased my ambition. I achieved that in Helsinki. The Olympic games in Sydney will be the gateway to the new century. Let's hope that this marvellous world event will sustain sport's motivation, the principles of fair play and the warmth of worldwide friendship.'* (From a conversation with the author shortly before Zátopek's death in 2000)
(Photograph © IOC/Roebelt)

After protesting against the Soviet tanks that rolled into Prague in 1968 to quell the democratic movement led by Premier Alexander Dubcek and student martyr Jan Palac, who sacrificially burned himself to death, Emil Zátopek was dismissed as a senior army officer and consigned for six years to pushing a shovel in the Bohemian uranium mines. He had dared to suggest that the Soviet Union should be banned from the Olympic Games in Mexico City. Still largely unknown, however, suppressed at the time by the state-controlled media, is the courageous act that nearly cost him his Olympic place in 1952, or worse. Then the hottest name in world sport, he arrived in Helsinki three days after the rest of the team – a seemingly ordinary occurrence. Among a tide of young athletes striving to

emulate the national hero was Stanislav Jungwirth, a gifted young 1,500m runner. His father, however, an anti-Communist activist, was a political prisoner and as a result Jungwirth was omitted from the Olympic team. Zátopek instantly stated: 'If he does not go, neither do I.' Both stayed behind in Prague. Such was Zátopek's global prestige, and the national expectation, that within 48 hours the Communist authorities relented and the two departed for Helsinki. Though Jungwirth narrowly missed the final, he would come sixth four years later and break the world record in 1957.

Zátopek was a phenomenon not just for his records and medals, but also for his extreme modesty. His will-power burned intensely, yet outwardly he was throughout his life so gently unassuming that it was difficult to correlate the man and the athlete. 'I was not very talented, I never imagined I would succeed,' he says of his early days, working as a plastics-chemistry technician in the shoe factory in Zlin. His parents discouraged him from running, his father, a carpenter, in particular. 'Working in the garden is enough if you want exercise,' young Emil was told.

Under German occupation sport was restricted, crowds forbidden for any kind of gathering. In 1941, aged 19, Zátopek's 1,500m time was 4:20, something bettered by British schoolboys for the longer mile. Improving slowly, in 1944 he was having to borrow some tennis shoes to continue running. Nonetheless, he broke the national records for 2,000m, 3,000m and 5,000m. Sceptical sports editors in Bohemian Prague telephoned to check the news being sent from rival Moravia. Even as the Soviet tanks bombarded Zlin and German trucks beat a vain retreat westwards, Zátopek was busy improving those records. Experts questioned the rolling head, the tortured arm action. What they did not notice was the perfect leg cadence.

For Helsinki, Zátopek was pressing 30 and the year began badly. Running with a virus to bolster a minor meeting, he became seriously ill. The team doctor said he should rest for three months or he risked damaging his heart. There were only six weeks left before Helsinki. He provocatively decided to cure himself: with tea and fresh lemons. 'By the time I arrived, I was healthy again,' he recalled. 'I was the record holder and defending champion for 10km, so I didn't feel too worried, even if not in peak condition.' Up in the stands, the legendary Nurmi and Kolehmainen were watching the 25-lap event. There was the usual early jockeying for position but, as in London, Zátopek was to dominate the race from the seventh lap onwards, his relentless even pace eventually destroying Gordon Pirie of Britain, whose training schedule was equally Herculean. By halfway, Pirie was out of contention and a surge in the 18th lap left Alain Mimoun of France unable to respond. Forging onwards alone, Zátopek improved his Olympic record in London by no less than 42.6 for a time of 29:17, with the gallant Mimoun again second, *only* 15 seconds behind, with the first six all inside the old record.

On to the 5,000m. The heats had been conducted tranquilly, though it was evident when Herbert Schade of Germany beat Reiff's Olympic record by over two seconds that the final was going to be no easy matter. Zátopek finished second in his heat, encouraging Aleksandr Anufriyev of the USSR to finish ahead of him with the aid of a friendly shove – an irrelevant moment of political correctness. 'It was,' Zátopek would later reflect on the final, 'the best finish I ever had, and against great rivals: Schade, who was favourite, Mimoun, Pirie and Chataway of Britain. I'd calculated to win on the last lap, but when three of them went past me, I thought it was all over.' After 2km, Zátopek took the lead from Schade, who was running at the front out of fear. 'Herbert, do a couple of laps with me,' Zátopek said, side by side, remarkably attempting to ease the pressure on someone he knew could beat him. Schade ignored him, to his own eventual cost. Such was Zátopek's nature that he would regularly chat with rivals, not out of gamesmanship, but unaffected sportsmanship. Lap by lap the five potential medal winners – Schade, Zátopek, Mimoun, Chataway, Pirie – wove their tense pattern, the lead repeatedly changing. At the bell, Zátopek narrowly led Schade, and down the final back-straight Chataway, Mimoun and Schade all went past him. Into the final bend, Zátopek made his critical move, running wide, and as he did so the unfortunate Chataway caught his foot on the kerb and fell, with Zátopek, Mimoun and Schade now separated by no more than a stride. 'I was experienced enough to know that

the sprint by the other three in the back straight would produce quick fatigue,' Zátopek said. 'After Chataway fell, Schade gave up and I knew Mimoun could not last, so it gave me a chance for a second kick.' Zátopek was two yards clear at the line in an Olympic record of 14:06.6 – the first to achieve the 5km/10km double since Kolehmainen – while Chataway courageously picked himself up to finish fifth behind Pirie in the same time. Meanwhile, Zátopek's wife, Dana, was busy winning the women's javelin with a record 50.47m (165 ft 7 in.).

Zátopek is said to have suggested to enquirers that he would attempt to win a medal in the marathon in order to reassert male authority in the household, though that may have been in jest, for at home in Prague, Dana was the more assertive figure. Although he had never run the distance before, Zátopek was not too concerned at the marathon's prospects. 'It is not a very difficult race,' he recalled. 'Other races are all about speed, while the marathon is about aerobic rate of recovery. Jim Peters of Britain was favourite, but running without control. In the marathon, control is everything. Having the one-hour record, I felt I might do all right.' His tactic was to shadow Peters, who began fast, Zátopek and Gustav Jansson of Sweden keeping pace with him. Shortly before halfway, the three of them now running together, Zátopek enquired of Peters whether the pace was fast enough. Peters, knowing he himself was near exhaustion, replied archly that it was too slow, perhaps hoping Zátopek might push ahead and then burn himself out. In the event, Peters dropped out with cramp after 20 miles and Zátopek pulled clear of Jansson, running the last five miles or so on his own, chatting happily with the crowd and duty policemen. He entered the stadium to a tumultuous ovation, was chaired by the still-celebrating Jamaican four-lap relay team and was signing autographs before Reinaldo Gorno of Argentina entered the stadium in second place. Zátopek had taken more than six minutes off the previous Olympic best, though he was over two

The phenomenal Emil Zátopek leads Jim Peters of Britain – early front runner who dropped out after 20 miles – during the marathon, entering the stadium for his unique treble triumph two and a half minutes ahead of the field. (© IOC/Ruebelt) (© IOC)

minutes outside the world best recently established by Peters. His third victory in the Games, together with his demeanour, created a fame that would endure for all time.

The Helsinki Games saw the first appearance of a team from the Soviet Union. In the pre-Bolshevik era before 1917, a few Russians had competed, exclusively from the upper social strata, together with some from the Baltic states. Soviet affiliation had been granted in 1948, but Josef Stalin had decreed that participation must be as winners; that defeat by Western capitalists was not allowed. Coaches had spent four years analysing Western techniques. 'Sport,' said Petr Sobolov, secretary-general of the Soviet Olympic committee, 'will be a weapon in the fight for peace and for the promotion of friendship among all people' – a propaganda phrase that was to be heard many times. They were to win no gold medals in men's track and field, compared with 14 by the United States, but Soviet presence brought a new dimension. 'There were many more pressures on American athletes because of the Russians,' said Robert Mathias, who retained his decathlon title with a massive world record of 7,887 points (7,592 by current tables). 'They were in a sense the real enemy. You just loved to beat 'em. You just had to. The feeling ran through the entire team.'

If a single event dramatised the US–Soviet rivalry, it came in the 3,000m steeplechase, in which the favourite was world record holder Vladimir Kazantsev. The leading American, Horace Ashenfelter, an FBI agent, had a best time some 18 seconds slower. An inspired Ashenfelter led after the first kilometre, was overhauled by Kazantsev 200 metres out, but at the final water jump Kazantsev stumbled, with Ashenfelter winning in world record time.

A widely fancied contender for the men's 1,500m was Roger Bannister of Britain, together with Werner Lueg of Germany, who already shared the world record with Gunder Hägg and Lennart Strand. Bannister's training, however, had been geared to a heat and final but such was the large entry to the event that the IAAF were obliged to introduce a semi-final round, which threw Bannister's energy reserves. Here was someone who would have benefited from Pirie's endurance training. Bannister was unimpressive in his semi-final, beaten into second place by the little-known Josef Barthel of Luxembourg. In the final, the leader at the end of the third lap was Rolf Lamers of Germany, from Lueg. It was here, in the last back straight, that Bannister attempted his characteristic kick from 300 metres out but the tank was empty. While Lueg held off Bannister and Patrick El Mabrouk of France, Barthel and the unheralded Robert McMillen (USA) had stolen through from the back of the field and were at Lueg's shoulder with 50 metres remaining. With arms raised triumphantly, the little Luxembourger thrust himself ahead of the American and the German for one of the biggest upsets of all time, in an Olympic record of 3:45.1: Luxembourg's first and still its only Summer Olympic gold medal. It took some time for the band to locate the score for the anthem of the Grand Duchy.

An unhappy Bannister had trailed home fourth. Few knew that ten days previously, in a last time trial before leaving for Finland, together with Chataway at Motspur Park in south London, Bannister had recorded one of the most impressive runs of his career: three quarters of a mile (1,320 yards) in 2:52.9, almost four seconds faster than the unofficial world record by Arne Andersson in 1945. Renowned worldwide for breaking the four-minute barrier two years later, Bannister by his own admission was not really a miler, but a half-miler who could sustain his pace for another lap and a bit. This was why the 1,500m was more suited to him than the mile. The very next morning after the trial run, however, he had read that there were to be semi-finals in Helsinki. Bannister was a genuine amateur, combining medical studies – he was to become an acclaimed neurologist – with limited training. He knew in an instant that the extra race would leave him at a huge disadvantage compared to tougher rivals prepared on severe interval running. He further knew that he would not compete in another Games, so his disappointment at the result was profound, never mind that the first eight runners had surpassed Jack Lovelock's previous Olympic record of 3:47.8. 'I felt great admiration for Josef Barthel as he climbed the Olympic rostrum,' Bannister wrote in his autobiography *First Four Minutes*:

> He was a worthy victor, tougher as well as faster than the rest of us. I knew his happiness must be without limit . . . I had found new meaning in the Olympic words that the important thing was not the winning but the taking part . . . and felt no bitterness at the outcome of my own race. My only chance to win an Olympic title was over . . . any attempt to explain away a disappointment is taken as an admission of failure. Barthel's triumph was to me symbolic of the Olympic spirit that safeguards the Games from harmful influences.

Werner Lueg (GER), eventual third, leads Josef Barthel (LUX, No. 406), unprecedented winner of the 1,500m. Bob McMillen (USA), silver winner, and Roger Bannister (GBR, No. 177), fourth, and Patrick El Mabrouk (FRA), fifth, trail Barthel, who receives his country's only gold medal from Prince Jean of Luxembourg. (both © IOC)

In another surprise result, in the men's 100m, Lindy Remigino (USA) was doubly grateful for the invention of the photo-finish camera in one of the closest finals in history. In the American trials he was placed fourth, but re-examination of the pictures led to him being reinstated as third, for a place in the team. Favourites for the final were the consistent Emmanuel McDonald Bailey of Britain and Herbert McKenley of Jamaica, world record holder at 400m, who had entered the short sprint for starting practice. It was McKenley's finishing burst, however, which gave the impression that he had won, and indeed initially he was congratulated by Remigino, who was convinced that he had been passed. There in the picture, almost abreast, was a line of four: McKenley in lane two, Remigino, Dean Smith (USA) and Bailey, all with the same hand-timing of 10.4. Remigino got the decision by one inch on electrical timing of 10.79, with McKenley 10.80, Bailey

10.83 and Smith 10.84. McKenley, coincidentally, is the only man ever to qualify for the final of all three of the shortest Olympic races.

It was an exceptional Games for Jamaica's sprinters. In addition to McKenley's silver medal, George Rhoden, he and Arthur Wint finished first, second and fifth respectively in the 400m; Wint again came second to the inimitable Mal Whitfield in the 800m; Leslie Laing was fifth in the 200m; and the four of them set a world record of 3:03.9 ahead of the Americans in the four-lap relay.

There are Olympic champions who are commendable for more than merely the numeric dimension of their victory. At the age of eight, Walter Davis (USA) had contracted polio and spent five years in a wheelchair; until a few years before his Olympic appearance he had been unable to walk without the aid of crutches. Yet by 1952 he had grown to more than two metres – probably the tallest competitor ever to win an individual event – and became high jump champion with an Olympic record of 2.04m (6 ft 8 in.) – his own height.

In women's track and field, the US managed victory only in the sprint relay. Australians Marjorie Jackson and Shirley Strickland were the stars, Jackson winning both the short sprints, equalling the world record in the 100m – with Strickland third and lowering Walasiewicz's 17-year-old world record in a semi-final of the 200m with 23.4. Strickland set a world record in the 80m hurdles, defender Fanny Blankers-Koen hitting the first two hurdles and failing to finish.

Marjorie Jackson, Australian double sprint star. (© IOC)

Boxing was conspicuous in several ways. Floyd Patterson (USA) and Ingemar Johansson (SWE), each destined to become world professional heavyweight champion, had contrasting results. Patterson won the middleweight title, knocking out his last three opponents and taking only 74 seconds to eliminate Vasile Tita of Romania in the final. Red Smith, the famed

American columnist, wrote of him: 'Patterson has faster hands than a subway pickpocket and they cause more suffering.' Johansson, strangely, was disqualified for not trying in the heavyweight final against Ed Sanders (USA). His silver medal was withheld until 1983. Patterson might never have won, and his professional career therefore been more uncertain, but for the introduction of two new weights, light-middle and light-welter. The former allowed the entry of László Papp of Hungary, who had won the middleweight title in London and was now able to make the lighter weight. Otherwise he would have provided a strong challenge to Patterson. In the end it was Johansson who, nearly seven years later, would take the heavyweight title from Patterson.

Dominant in swimming were the American men and Hungarian women, with the Soviet Union relatively nowhere, their failure unexpectedly matched by the Japanese, who had had high expectations: Hironashin Furuhashi, the favourite, finished last in the 400m freestyle. Hungarian women took four of the five titles. In the 100m freestyle, 0.3 seconds covered the first five swimmers, led by Katalin Szöke. Both diving titles were won by Pat McCormick. When Jean Boiteux of France won the men's 400m freestyle, his elated father, complete with jacket and beret, leapt into the pool to embrace him.

Károly Takács of Hungary retains his rapid-fire pistol title with his 'wrong', and only, left hand. (© IOC)

Hungary won the football tournament, beating Yugoslavia 2–0 in the final: the beginning of one of the most distinguished sequences in the game by one of the most accomplished of all teams including such players as Grosics in goal, Bozsik and Hidegkuti in midfield, Puskas, Kocsis and Czibor in attack. Károly Takács of Hungary retained his rapid-fire pistol title, shooting with his wrong, left, and only, hand.

CHAPTER XXXII

Wayward Fanaticist

Avery Brundage of America, fifth IOC President, 1952–72

'. . . Now that the Olympic Movement has reached maturity, and more than 80 countries eagerly participate, it is not easy to imagine the difficulties faced by Baron Pierre de Coubertin 60 years ago. At that time, there was little interest in sport in most countries, there were no organisations to handle the Games, no national Olympic committees, few international federations, there were no accepted rules and regulations, there was no money, there was only an idea. It is difficult, therefore, to overestimate the importance of this enthusiastic support, which came not from any of the larger and richer countries at this crucial time but from tiny Greece.

In that ancient era . . . culture was both physical and mental. In the contests, beauty and grace, intangible things, were esteemed as much as strength, speed and agility. Honour was held above all. The events were staged in a beautiful natural park. The finest sculptures in the world adorned the grounds. Music and poetry greeted the ears of the athletes, elegance and taste surrounded them. It was in this enlightened atmosphere that the Games developed.

Of all the significant ideas which evolved in this momentous period of the world's history, none is more important than that which the IOC are pledged to guard and cherish . . . Sport, which must be spontaneous and without restraint, could be practised only by free and independent men, so the ancient Olympic Games were confined to Greeks. Only civilised men who appreciated and respected the high ideals of sport could take part.

Despite the bounties of nature, the developments of science and the teachings of philosophy and religion, we still have not learned how to live together in peace. After thousands of years, politics have not succeeded in establishing a peaceful world. The Egyptians, Persians and Romans, Alexander, Caesar and Napoleon have attempted to establish peace by force. All have failed. So has religion.

Sport teaches respect for the rules, which must be fair and just. Sportsmen make them so . . . the Olympic Movement has now been accepted in all quarters of the globe and the youth of all countries heed the admonition pronounced at the Olympic closing ceremony "that the Olympic torch may be carried on with ever greater eagerness, courage and honour for the good of humanity throughout the ages". One must be amazed that such an idealistic enterprise has prospered in the commercial atmosphere that prevails today. It is testimony to the innate good in man and to the desire for a world ruled by honesty and good sportsmanship, where all have an equal opportunity, where victory depends on ability and hard work, on personal skill and efficiency, and where the reward is based upon merit.

The Olympic truce covering the ancient Games was respected throughout the Hellenic world. We have extended the Games to the entire world. Perhaps we can also extend the truce. Perhaps sport, the twentieth-century religion, with its message of fair play, will succeed where other agencies have failed.' (From an address to the 49th Session, Mexico City, 1953)
(Photograph © IOC)

Avery Brundage was despotic, a moralistic bulldozer, fanatical defender of de Coubertin's legacy, loyal to close friends (who were few and occasionally undeserving), prominent engineer/building contractor and self-made millionaire, champion of public virtue and philandering husband. His presidency, which was to last for 20 years, varied in style between that of godparent and bully, so it was unsurprising that his nickname was 'Slavery Bondage'. He was the best and occasionally the worst friend that the Olympic Movement could have, for his obsessive commitment to the past, to traditional sporting ideals of the nineteenth century and what he perceived as de Coubertin's philosophy, blinded him to the changes of an evolving society, almost all of which operated at a financial level out of sight and far below his acquired standard of living. Nobody could have had better intentions, yet such were his

dogmatic and eventually isolated beliefs that by the end of his presidency, when he was in his ninth decade, his attitudes jeopardised the very institution that was the most cherished aspect of his life, above and beyond family and friends.

He was born on 28 September 1887 in Detroit, the industrial heart of Michigan, the elder of two sons of Charles Brundage, a stonemason, who deserted the family which had moved to Chicago when Avery was six. His secondary education took place at Crane Manual Training School and he went on to study civil engineering at the University of Illinois. During his youth he acquired a taste for and knowledge of literature and art, his eventual wealth enabling him to collect Asian antiques which after his death were bequeathed, some 3,000 pieces, to the M.H. Young Memorial Museum of San Francisco. By the age of 28 he had founded his own building construction company, was sufficiently shrewd to survive the financial crash 14 years later and subsequently shifted his attention to dealing in shares and property: the personification of the American fairy tale of newspaper-boy to millionaire, belligerently proud that every penny had been earned.

At the age of 25, Brundage gained selection for the Olympic Games in Stockholm. There he took sixth place in the pentathlon and, in a rare moment of weakness, about which he was self-critical, dropped out in the final discipline of the decathlon; the latter won by the later-disqualified Jim Thorpe. Brundage would remain pedantically unforgiving thereafter in his attitude towards Thorpe, while he personally moved by degrees through the ranks of officialdom of the Amateur Athletic Union (seven terms as president) and the US Olympic Committee (president for 25 years) towards ultimate power within the IOC, to which he was controversially elected in 1936 as replacement for Ernest Jahncke. After only one year he was appointed to the Executive Board and immediately after the Second World War was manoeuvred into place by President Edström as new second Vice-President, becoming first Vice-President the following year. In 1927, then 40, he married Elizabeth Dunlap, a musician three years younger.

Brundage was to spare no effort or personal expense in his travels in pursuit of sustaining his, and essentially de Coubertin's, version of the Olympic ideal. His conviction had deepened when attending the memorial ceremony at Olympia in 1938 to mark the entombment there of de Coubertin's heart. This bred in him a sense of missionary status. 'Sport is recreation,' he said, 'it is a pastime or a diversion, it is play, it is action for amusement. It is the opposite of work.' One of the first incidents that roused his barely hidden fury was when he received information in the mid-1950s that Wes Santee, the world's fastest miler, had been receiving hundreds of dollars in expenses per track meeting, at a time when the AAU's allowance was $15 a day.

Unknown at this time, coincidentally, was that Brundage had taken a Finnish mistress, Lilian Wähämäk Dresden, who had borne him, in California in 1951 and 1952, two sons, Avery and Gregory. Brundage provided a house and a trust fund of half a million dollars for their care, without, however, ever formally acknowledging his paternity. Lilian Dresden was only one of many affairs during his lifetime.

It was impossible not to be impressed by the diligence of the new President as he tackled, head-on, right or wrong, those he considered to be wandering from the rightful path of Olympism. Inflexibility led him to fall out with many over the issues of eligibility, commercialism, nationalism, politics and racism; never mind that he was spending some $75,000 a year out of his own pocket on travel and IOC administration. A particular obstacle was his resolute interpretation of Rule 26 of the Charter, concerning eligibility. His allegiance to the myth of amateurism, perpetuated by the English upper-middle class, was set in concrete and, although the Charter would be modified in 1962, to allow NOCs the possibility of making broken-time payments to competitors for the support of 'dependents suffering hardships', Brundage remained adamant that nothing but evil lay down this path.

On the other hand, his propaganda for the true cause was inexhaustible. He had been present for the inaugural Pan-American Games in 1951 in Buenos Aires and was there again for the second celebration at Mexico City in 1955; even though, in spite of being a founder member, he regarded them as imitative and lacking any link with classical antiquity. This attitude epitomised his lack of understanding of the small fry of the sporting world. It is the association of the Pan-Am Games with Olympic ideals that, for the majority of competitors who

President Avery Brundage and his first wife Elizabeth Dunlap, a musician, on the occasion of his 80th birthday. (© IOC)

never reach the Olympics, enhances their more modest involvement in the regional event. Being hostage to his own prejudices, he did nothing to intervene when, during the second staging of the Mediterranean Games in 1955 in Barcelona, Arab hostility and the threat of a boycott obliged the Spanish to withdraw the invitation to Israel, with its recognised NOC. 'We cannot become involved in a matter of this kind,' Brundage asserted. 'Those who organise regional games are quite within their rights to include or exclude any country.' Where now his principle of universalism? Sad to say, he was supported in his view by Lord Burghley.

In 1951, the GDR had been denied approval of its NOC at the time Federal Germany was accepted. Karl von Halt set about campaigning for a unified team, all the more difficult in the face of the Cold War, though he was encouraged by a close relationship with Dr Heinz Schöbel, leader of the GDR body, who persistently sought to ingratiate himself with Brundage. Moreover, the GDR was strongly supported by Andrianov of the USSR. Approval was again refused at the 1954 Session in Athens, some IOC members motivated by constant abuse in the East German press. The vote was 31–14 and the GDR would have to wait another year until the Session in Paris. By then the GDR was integrated within the Warsaw Pact, signed on 14 May 1955, and sports officials within the GDR committee had become less aggressive. Prior to the meeting in Paris, Brundage questioned Schöbel about whether or not theirs was a political organisation. Schöbel insisted it was not but was told the condition for acceptance was the creation of a unified team for 1956 under the following agreement: a common flag, uniform and national emblem; joint accommodation; chef-de-mission from the NOC with the higher number of competitors; national anthem from the country of the gold medal winner; no national anthem for victory by a mixed team. Brundage was able to claim: 'We have succeeded in something where the politicians have failed – there will be a joint German team here in Cortina and in Melbourne.' Circumstances favoured West German selection, with a ratio of nearly three-to-one in both teams.

The Sessions of the IOC had never been the same after the election of USSR members Konstantin Andrianov and Aleksei Romanov, in 1951 and 1952 respectively. For the next 40 years, until the break-up of the Warsaw Pact in 1989–90, the Communist bloc took their cue from the Soviet members. It was observed that whenever either of them made a proposal, the other Communist members dutifully rose, one by one, to parrot their approval. Despite itself, the IOC had become internally politicised. Brundage might resist for all his worth – protesting in 1953, for instance, about special prolonged training camps for Polish boxers – only to be dismissed by the Communists as 'a lackey of imperialist ideology'. He knew that the leading Soviet football teams were professional in all but name, as were those in Hungary and elsewhere, hence the dominance of Eastern bloc teams in the Olympic tournament, but there was no way to penetrate the smokescreen.

Contradictorily, Brundage was impressed, following an invited tour of the USSR in 1954 – for which he paid – by the efficiency of the Soviet sporting production line, reporting that he had seen 'the greatest mass army of athletes the world has ever known – there are four million specialists in track and field alone'. Brundage saw only what he wanted to see as the tentacles of Communism crept ever inwards. In 1956, General Vladimir Stoytchev of Bulgaria, equestrian competitor of the 1920s and Communist only by necessity, was elected to the Executive Board; subsequently, at the conclusion of his term, his place was taken by Andrianov. Between times, the Soviets would please themselves: they had arrived for the Oslo Games without having registered their team, 'the invitations having arrived while our sports director was on holiday'. And this was their first Winter Games!

General Vladimir Stoytchev of Bulgaria became the first Communist member of the Executive Board: aristocrat by birth, Communist by obligation, military equestrian by profession.
(© IOC)

Unlike the Germans, the Chinese had no representatives who were cronies of Brundage and, therefore, neither camp – mini-nationalists from Formosa/Taiwan, nor the mainland People's Republic – had any side door through which to exert influence. At the Athens Session of 1954, the IOC recognised a new NOC formed in Beijing under the title 'Olympic Committee of the Republic of China', despite the existence of the already recognised

NOC in Taiwan, the Session narrowly voting to accept both bodies. In November that year both NOCs were invited to attend the Games in Melbourne. With the People's Republic immediately accepting, the nationalists in consequence declined – but then changed their minds, which in turn persuaded the Communists to change theirs. The All-China Athletic Federation declared from Beijing that 'The Chinese people and the Chinese athletes cannot tolerate this scheme of artificially splitting China.' The IOC's dilemma was accentuated by the political-economic strategies of global diplomacy: the United States aligned against the isolationist People's Republic, which was supported in principle by the rest of the Communist world. Formal White House approval of Taiwan inflamed the controversy with which the IOC grappled. At the Cortina Session, Yi-tung Shou, the People's Republic of China member – who the previous year had criticised Brundage at the Paris Session, demanding the exclusion of Taiwan – protested that his statement in Paris had been omitted from the minutes. He was advised firmly that the recording of political speeches was not part of IOC protocol. Prior to the Melbourne Games, the Excutive Board learned that both Chinas had registered their teams. Taiwan protested that Beijing had attempted, in radio broadcasts, to tempt Taiwanese competitors to participate in selection competitions in Beijing. The Taiwanese felt insulted when, on arrival in Melbourne, they found that their flag had inadvertently been raised in the Village over the quarters of the Communist team. So, in the wilful oriental contest of face-saving, nobody took part, the losers as ever being the athletes. Amid all the political wranglings concerning the USSR, the Germanies and the two Chinese, another political serpent, that of racial segregation, reared its threatening head. In 1955, the international boxing federation raised the question of apartheid within South Africa, where 'coloured, i.e. black, boxers are not authorised to meet white boxers. It seems to us that this is in contravention of the principles of the Olympic Charter'. A time bomb was ticking.

The IOC nonetheless evolved. At the Session of 1953 in Mexico City, simultaneous translation was provided for the first time in English, French and Spanish. From 1948, stenographers had made notes on debates but lack of finance had restricted this practice. Then, from 1954, Sessions were taped for the purpose of record. Also in 1954, Rule 24 regarding NOCs was established: that they must consist of representatives from at least five sports federations, themselves affiliated to the corresponding international federation. From 1955, the introduction of a new member to the IOC was accompanied for the first time by an oath:

> Recognising the responsibilities that go with the great honour of serving as (one of the) representative(s) of the international Olympic committee in my country, I, . . . bind myself to promote the Olympic Movement to the best of my ability and to guard and preserve its fundamental principles as conceived by Baron Pierre de Coubertin, keeping myself as a member free from all political, sectarian and commercial influence.

It was increasingly to prove an oath as fragile as that taken by the athletes. The same year, the Hellenic NOC announced that the Olympic Academy had been established in Olympia. In 1956, it was agreed that no more than 16 teams would be allowed to compete in any team event, the international federations were to organise qualifying competitions which would not be counted as 'Olympic events'. More ominously, accounts showed that the IOC had resources of only 130,000

Swiss francs, reckoned to be insufficient to meet obligations in the immediately forthcoming years.

Cortina D'Ampezzo, basking in an Alpine ampitheatre in northern Italy, was originally part of the Venetian Republic but was annexed to the Tyrol in the early sixteenth century, passed into Austrian control during the Napoleonic Wars and remained so until reoccupied by Italy in 1915. There had been no winter sport as such until the early twentieth century when skating, elementary bobsleighing and ice hockey were introduced. Count Alberto Bonacossa began the campaign to host the Winter Games there following the success of Chamonix in 1924. A prominent skier and figure skater, he became an IOC member in 1925 and, after prolonged negotiations supported by CONI (the Italian NOC), Cortina was awarded the Games of 1944 during the London Session of 1939. Following the Second World War, Bonacossa renewed his efforts, initially bidding for 1952 for which Cortina was outvoted at Stockholm in 1947 by Oslo, 18–9. Two years later Cortina was the overwhelming choice for 1956.

After Bonacossa's death in 1953, CONI delegated authority to an organising committee led by Italy's IOC members Giorgio de Stefani and Count Paolo Thaon di Revel. The programme was to be identical to Oslo, with the addition of a men's 30km cross-country and a women's 3 x 5km relay. The Soviet Union's request for the inclusion of women's speed skating was rejected.

Cortina boasted few existing facilities and had to build a new main rink stadium, the seats rising almost vertically with an open view of the Dolomites and accommodating 7,500 spectators, temporary seats doubling this capacity. The old ski jump was replaced and there was a new 6,000-seat stadium for cross-country. The bob run had been rebuilt in 1948 and subsequent World Championships had proved its satisfactory standard. All events except speed skating were within a close distance of the town, this event being held at Lake Misurina, 15

Self-made millionaire and royalty. IOC President Brundage alongside HRH the Duke of Edinburgh at Melbourne's opening ceremony. (© IOC/Jay)

kilometres distant, in ideal conditions free of wind. Financing came predominantly from the country's football lottery. At the opening of the Games by President Giovanni Gronchi, the oath was taken for the first time by a woman, Giuliana Chenal-Minuzzo, downhill bronze medal winner in 1952.

The first Winter Games outside television broadcasts proved to be a godsend for an organisation heading for bankruptcy, though within 20 years television would become a threatening ogre. In 1955, a meeting of the Executive Board and

international federations had discussed possible future profits, the international federations avariciously looking at their share. Brundage, strangely for a self-made man, was sceptical, taking the view that it was for organising committees to negotiate with television companies under IOC guidelines, but that the IOC itself should not contaminate its moral stance by a commercial partnership. Nonetheless, the IOC's right to a television rights fee was recognised, even if Brundage felt it proper to state, 'We in the IOC have done well without television for 60 years and will do so for the next 60 years.'

To meet IOC requirements, the Melbourne organising committee produced a film and arranged for domestic television transmission from the main stadium of Melbourne Cricket Cround (MCG) and other venues for no more than a nominal payment, there being only 5,000 receiving sets. This was the first 'national' television broadcast of a Games.

Another, reluctant, first was the staging of one sport in a different country. Because of Australian animal quarantine regulations, it was impossible to temporarily import horses, and the decision had to be taken, in breach of the Charter, to accept the hospitality of Stockholm for staging the equestrian events from 10–17 June. Except for the cross-country section of the three-day event, the 29 competing countries rode in the Olympic stadium of 1912, the host country winning three of the six titles.

Shortly after the end of the Second World War, it became the ambition of the so-called 'Victorian Olympic Council (VOC)' to bring the Olympics to Melbourne. There had been earlier suggestions in Melbourne's *Argus* for an Australian hosting as far back as the inaugural Games. Perth had been proposed for the 1920s and Sydney for the 1930s with the anticipated completion of the Harbour Bridge. A leading figure in the Melbourne bid was Sir Frank Beaurepaire, winner of three silver and three bronze medals in the Games of 1908, 1920 and 1924. He had developed a tyre business under the brandname 'Olympic', became president of the VOC and persuaded the city council to create a bid committee. With air travel now so sufficiently developed that it was possible to reach Australia from Europe or America within 30 hours, a bid had become realistic when presented in Rome in 1949. Melbourne won on the fourth ballot, defeating Detroit by a single vote.

There followed extended deliberation over the main venue, alternatives to Melbourne Cricket Ground being promoted. The Victoria state, however, balked at the cost of a new second stadium. Robert Menzies, the Premier, became involved, the ultimate decision being that the national government would pay half the construction costs for the Games, including modification of MCG, the swimming pool and the velodrome, the balance to be met jointly by Victoria and Melbourne city council. The situation was further eased when the state housing department agreed to fund a low-grade public housing project that would be used for the Village. It required a personal visit in April 1955 by Brundage, who castigated the organisers for inactivity during a labour dispute, to ensure that MCG and other sites were finished on time.

If there was mild chaos in Melbourne, that was nothing compared with what was happening elsewhere in the world immediately prior to the Games in Australia's 'winter' summer. Tensions rose in the Middle East when the USA and Britain withdrew their offer to to help Egypt with the construction of the Aswan Dam as a result of Egypt's connections to the Soviet bloc. In July 1956 President Nasser then announced the nationalisation of the Suez Canal Company and asserted Egyptian control of the waterway linking the Mediterranean and Indian Ocean. In October, Israel, Britain and France began an unwise and quickly aborted land, sea and air attack on Egypt. After a furious response from the US, the United Nations negotiated the ceasefire, which was humiliating for both Britain and France. Egypt, having suffered heavy losses and with the Canal blocked by sunken vessels, demanded that Britain and France be banned from the Games. When the IOC refused, Egypt, Lebanon and Iraq withdrew in the first Olympic political boycott. Others would join them.

On 23 October, anti-Soviet resentment spilled onto the streets in Budapest with hundreds and thousands demanding the withdrawal of Soviet troops. The puppet Communist government restored former premier Imre Nagy, ousted in 1955, as an attempt at appeasement, and in a malevolent ploy Soviet forces left Budapest on 31 October – for four days. On the morning of 4 November, planes and tanks returned to plunder the city, imprisoning Nagy and the government, killing more than 10,000 citizens, with János Kádár, a stooge of Soviet President Nikita Khrushchev, being installed. Heartrendingly, by this time the Hungarian Olympic team was already in Czechoslovakia en route to Melbourne. Many wished to return to the bloody street fighting, but were unable to cross the border and were forced to continue on to Melbourne. A group of Hungarian coaches and officials found themselves on a passenger liner to Australia unaware of what was happening at home.

The double crisis for the Games, which a record number of countries had been expected to attend, resulted in others joining the boycott by Arabs. The Netherlands withdrew, sending a gift of 100,000 guilders to aid victims in Hungary. Spain and Switzerland joined them, the Swiss changing their minds, but too late to get flights to Australia. Otto Mayer, IOC Chancellor, was dismayed: 'It is a disgrace that Switzerland, a neutral nation and the country where the IOC has its headquarters, should set such a shameful example of political interference with the Olympic ideal.' Also withdrawn, besides both Chinas, were Ghana, Guatemala, Malta and Panama. Brundage stated:

> We are dead set against any country using the Games for political purposes, whether right or wrong. The Olympics belong to the people. They are contests for individuals and not of nations. In antiquity there was an Olympic truce and all warfare stopped during the period of the Games, but now after 2,000 years of civilisation, we stop the Games and continue our wars.

Brundage had it slightly wrong: the truce had been a promise of safe passage for those attending and returning from Olympia. The Session in Melbourne issued a formal press release, reminding the world of the ancient truce that had existed for nearly 1,200 years, stating:

> On behalf of the tens of millions of supporters of the Olympic Movement throughout its 89 member countries, the IOC wishes to draw attention to this fact and to the friendly atmosphere of goodwill which prevails among athletes, officials and spectators from more than three-score different nations, some of which do not even maintain diplomatic connections, yet are observing the amateur sport rules of fair play here in Australia during the Games of the XVI Olympiad.

If there were absentees, there were also new participants: Ethiopia, Fiji, Kenya, Liberia, Uganda, Malaya and North Borneo, the latter two later amalgamated as Malaysia. Cambodia made its first appearance in Stockholm. The 67 countries sent 3,547 competitors, the lowest number since 1932.

Giuliana Chenal-Minuzzo takes the Olympic oath at Cortina D'Ampezzo. (© Constantini)

At an opening ceremony presided over by HRH the Duke of Edinburgh, Hungary's team was cheered to the echo as it marched in an assortment of uniforms and civilian clothes, new uniforms without the Communist logo not having been ready for all. The lighting of the flame was by Ron Clarke, a young runner who had already set a world junior mile record and was to become a multiple world record holder. In performing the ceremony his uplifted arm was burned, though the 103,000 spectators at MCG were unaware of his ordeal. The oath was taken by John Landy, the famous sub-four miler.

Ron Clarke, the Australian whose Olympic career never matched his record-breaking, carries the flame at Melbourne's opening ceremony. (© IOC/Jay)

CHAPTER XXXIII

Cortina D'Ampezzo (VII) 1956

Anton 'Toni' Sailer of Austria, Olympic triple Alpine champion

'The Games then were different from nowadays; everybody's become so preoccupied with what they're doing themselves. In those days I had time to go and watch some of the ice hockey, make a visit to the ski jumping, or go and support colleagues in the cross-country events. I had the time. Yet the Games, then as now, were the biggest sporting competition we had, the most important.

A chance for three gold medals? I never imagined that. My dream had begun when I was 12, following the Winter Games in St Moritz. There was such a great tradition for Alpine skiing in Austria, from the time of the foundation of our Ski Club in 1903 and through the growing fame of the Hahnenkahm race. I was too young to compete at Oslo in 1952, I then broke my leg the following year and by the time it came to Cortina I was just hoping that I might win one gold medal. The first event, the giant slalom, was my favourite and the previous year I'd won every race except one. I knew I would be challenged by my colleague Molterer but on the day I was able to beat him with something to spare. Yet you should never expect anything when racing, least of all in the Olympics. You cannot win if you are not ready to lose. In the slalom, I was the fastest over both races and therefore able to win a second title, though I remember that "Chic" Igaya of Japan was very elegant, a real stylist with the coolness you need in the Games, and if I'd faltered he would have been the winner.

The downhill came last – the course was bumpy, icy and it was very cold. I had a problem when one of my ski straps broke just before the start. I had a bit of time in hand, maybe ten minutes or so, but none of our coaches had a spare and there were not many other people around. Then an old friend of mine came out of one of the huts near the start, realised the crisis and gave me his. Even that was damaged and I was lucky to finish. If it had not been the Olympic Games, I wouldn't have raced. Yes, I suppose the three medals did change my life in a way, but not that much. It's hard to say. Critics can quickly put you in your place. I remember one of them who had come to watch me saying that after four or five minutes of following the event, he became so engrossed that he had forgotten all about me. Either way, I would probably still have become a singer and involved in films. That was something I enjoyed, making around 30 films, love stories and so on. That was something different.'

(Photograph © DPA)

During the six previous Winter Games, no one had achieved in any sport the heights of fame that Anton Sailer did now. Bred at Kitzbühl, that mecca of Austrian skiing, the 20 year old won all three Alpine events by exceptional margins: the giant slalom by 6.2 seconds, the slalom by 4.0 and the downhill by 3.5. He not only became the fifth Winter competitor to win three gold medals in a single Games – the others having been Thorleif Haug, Clas Thunberg, Ivar Ballangrud and Hjalmar Andersen, all Scandinavians – but also did so with such elegance, technique and speed that everyone marvelled at his versatility. Travel agents gleefully rubbed their hands at the unprecedented publicity for winter resorts.

His assault upon history began with the giant slalom. Before the event, every competitor was presented with a souvenir picture of Ilio Colli, a local skier who had died when colliding with a tree, fracturing his skull, and after whom the course was now named. 'Hardly encouraging for competitors to be handed a death notice before the start,' observed Sailer laconically. His compatriot Andreas Molterer, the sixth starter, was acclaimed as a likely winner with the fast time of 3:06.3, but he reminded everybody that 'Toni', as Sailer was known to all, was yet to come. Sailer's time when his turn came, sweeping swallow-like through the gates, was an astonishing 3:00.1, six seconds and more ahead of Molterer and the rest. Walter Schuster, with 3:07.2, made it a clean sweep for Austria.

Sailer's superiority in the slalom was no less impressive, achieving the fastest time on both runs and being way ahead of Chiharu Igaya of Japan, Asia's first Alpine medal winner, who took the silver, and Stig Sollander of Sweden. Igaya was later to become an IOC member and was elected to the Executive Board.

Sailer already held the course record for the downhill, the third leg of his unique bid, but prior to the start he discovered that one of the safety straps, securing ski to boot, had snapped. Fortunately, the trainer of the Italian team came to his aid shortly before Sailer was due at the gate. So formidable was the course on the day that nearly half the starters failed to finish and eight concluded their race in hospital. Sailer's control was such that he corrected his one serious misjudgment on the way down and finished a handsome three and a half seconds in front of Raymond Fellay of Switzerland, with Molterer taking the bronze.

In the women's Alpine events, the Swiss had the edge over

Toni Sailer of Austria, first of the triple Alpine champions in a single Games. (© IOC)

their fierce neighbour-rivals. Madeleine Berthod, the favourite, beat her compatriot Frieda Dänzer by almost five seconds in the downhill while Renée Colliard, on her first appearance in the Swiss team, took the slalom ahead of Regina Schöpf of Austria with Yevgeniya Sidorova (URS) third. Austria had the consolation of further medals from Josefine Frandl and Dorothea Hochleitner behind Ossi Reichert of Germany in the giant slalom, with Berthod in fourth place.

American figure skaters all but excluded the rest of the fields in the individual events. Tenley Albright, who had suffered polio as a child, had recently badly injured her right ankle, cutting it with her left skate in a fall during practice. Her father, a surgeon from Massachusetts in whose footsteps she would later follow, arrived in time to patch her up. In Cortina, skating with the confidence of someone who had been silver medal winner four years earlier, she was awarded first place by ten of the eleven judges, the exception being the American, giving it to her compatriot Carol Heiss, who took the silver medal with ten second-place votes. Albright has related what an impact the Games made upon her life, emotionally and professionally.

Former polio victim Tenley Albright remarkably rose to become figures champion. (© IOC/Ruebelt)

The Village of this tiny town in the Dolomites was overrun by the Games, yet the people embraced the happy mayhem. There were no shuttle buses to the events in those days and one morning a group of us were standing waiting for a taxi to get to a practice session. A car slowed, we all jumped in and told the driver to take us to the stadium. It wasn't until we tried to pay him that we realised he was a resident on the way to work. His act of unassuming generosity made us all feel at home. Since then, every time I enter an Olympic Village I experience that cross-cultural unity that *is* the Olympics. The Games give a message to young people – if they have poured themselves into something, it will have an application to whatever they do later. Taking part in the Olympics really prepared me for the feel of general surgery in a way that I could have no idea of at the time – for doing everything the best I could, the need for intense concentration, the importance of planning your time and being efficient, the multidimensional element.

The outcome of the pairs' event was as disputed as Albright's victory was clear-cut. Elizabeth 'Sissy' Schwarz and Kurt Oppelt of Austria and Frances Dafoe and Norris Bowden of Canada both received four first-place votes, the Austrians then winning with five second-place votes to the Candians' three. The Italian crowd, given the nation's perennial love of children, had taken the German pair to their hearts, on account of the 12-year-old Marika Kilius, partnered by Franz Ningel. When the Germans were placed fourth, the judges were bombarded with a shower of oranges. For Sissy Schwarz the occasion had not been the joy it is for many. 'I wish I could say it was,' she recalls, 'but not at all. We were never expected to win. The Canadians had been world champions the year before in Vienna. I had fallen prior to the Games and we felt we were coming to collect a medal if we could. To be second would have been wonderful for us. It was only three months later we began to realise what we had done. We never earned a penny as amateurs and after three years in [professional] shows I only had a good car and a small bank account.'

A revelation in 1956, perhaps predictably, was the exemplary preparation of Soviet competitors, especially in ice hockey. In a few years, a scientific approach to coaching, programme planning and physical conditioning had lifted their performances dramatically. Their hockey team was disciplined, coordinated and scrupulously correct – in a tournament notorious for foul play – and in the final they beat Canada 2–0, which pushed the Canadians into bronze medal position, for they had also lost to the United States. Soviet domination in speed skating provided another shock. Yevgeni Grischin won the 500m and 1,500m titles in world record times – the latter record shared with joint gold medal winner Yuri Mikhailov – while Boris Schilkov took the 5,000m with an Olympic record and Oleg Gontscharenko the bronze, as he did also in the 10,000m behind Sigvard Ericsson (SWE) and Knut Johannesen (NOR). The records had confirmed the surface at Lake Misurina, at an altitude of 1,755 metres, as being one of the fastest ever. Grishin, incidentally, had been a member of the Soviet cycling team in Helsinki four years earlier.

Norwegian pride was left depending upon cross-country events. Hallgeir Brenden retained his 18km title – in Cortina reduced to 15km – while Sixten Jernberg took the 50km freestyle event plus two silver medals and a bronze. Here again, however, Soviet strength was apparent: four in the top seven behind Jernberg, four in the top six of the 30km behind Veikko

Scandinavian pride is rescued on cross-country events by Sixten Jernberg (SWE), winner of the 50km freestyle in addition to three other medals. (© IOC) (right © IOC/Ruebelt)

Hakulinen of Finland and a runaway victory in the 4 x 10km relay ahead of Finland and Sweden.

Finland dominated the ski jumping, taking gold and silver with Antti Hyvärinen and Aulis Kallakorpi – a disaster for Norway who had won every 90m event since 1924. Franz Kapus of Switzerland led his four-man bobsleigh team to victory at the age of 46. Lamberto Dalla Costa, who had never raced anywhere but Cortina, expectedly won the two-man event with Giacomo Conti, with fellow locals Eugenio Monti and Renzo Alvera

taking the silver. Monti had driven the Italian four-man bob to another silver.

Cortina set landmarks in the history of Olympic Winter sport. It was the first Winter Games to have been televised, even if in black-and-white. And the Soviets, with a total of 16 medals at the head of the unofficial table, had established a questionable tradition of dominance by totalitarian countries, which ultimately would be interpreted 30 years later as counter-productive to the interests of the Olympic Movement.

CHAPTER XXXIV

Melbourne (XVI) 1956

Al Oerter of America, four times Olympic discus champion, 1956–68

'Only when I walked on to the field at the Melbourne Cricket Ground did I realise what the Olympic Games really meant. Here were the best of the best in what I had chosen to do, in the best of environments. I had never dreamed of being an Olympian as a child, yet once I entered the ring for my first throw at Melbourne it was as if I had arrived at a place where I'd wanted to be all my life. When the name of Rome was flashed on the scoreboard at the closing ceremony, I then began my preparation for those Games. To win, while satisfying, was not the motivating force that drove me towards the next Games, rather it was the challenge of working at ever increasing levels again to be with the best.

I'm proud to have won four gold medals in four Games but what I remember most are those days when the Games were three or four years in the future and I was clearing the throwing ring of snow to complete a training session that would place me one more day closer to my goal. In 1956 I was very young and not expected to do anything against experienced veterans such as Consolini [Adolfo, the Italian winner in 1948] *and Fortune* [Gordien, US world record holder], *but I was given marvellous advice from the team coach Elvin Drake. While I was waiting for the event to start, he said: 'Look, kid, I think you've ability, but don't get involved with the others, get your first throw under your belt, stay on your own.' I was as scared as any athlete had ever been, yet at the first attempt I made my winning throw.*

At Rome, I almost defeated myself. My colleague Rink Babka had been reaching world-record distance regularly in training. When I went for my first throw and dipped my hand in the resin, it was a sticky mess, I couldn't get it off, threw well below my best and was really under pressure. Before my fifth throw, Rink, who seemed to have the gold in his pocket, came over to say that I was too anxious and was leading with my upper body instead of trailing. My next throw took the lead – if it wasn't for Rink I wouldn't have won.

Six days prior to the final in Tokyo, working with the team coach at the training ground in a muddy ring, I tore a muscle in my ribcage. Being focused, I blocked it out, threw again . . . and badly tore a disc cartilage. I was advised that was the end of my defence but I'd trained for four years and refused to accept the situation. For the qualifying round, my back was frozen with ice packs. The Czech world record holder, Ludvik Danek, or one of my colleagues Jay Silvester or David Weill, ought to have won, but I did it with my fifth throw – reverting to a training sequence with a slower turn.

By 1968 in Mexico City, I was much too old! The rest of the world had passed me by and I was even lucky to make the team. My best of the year was 20 feet behind the leaders such as Silvester, now the world record holder. Yet I sensed things might not be the same in Mexico City. When we entered the field, it was still raining after a delayed start because of lightning, which unnerved the others, huddled under umbrellas. I managed to find a good grip on my third throw and reached 212 ft 6 in. [64.78m, an Olympic record, five feet further than Oerter had ever thrown before], *which undermined the rest.'**
(Photograph © IOC)

Melbourne was to provide the Soviet Union with their first gold medals for men in track and field, both by the same man, Vladimir Kuts, a Ukrainian sailor, who bemused and overpowered the field in both the 10,000m and 5,000m with his confusing tactics and immense endurance, setting Olympic records in both. Two months earlier Kuts had broken the 10,000m world record by 12 seconds, yet that followed an earlier defeat in England by Gordon Pirie of Britain at 5,000m. A fascinating duel was forecast for both distances, with possible intervention at the longer distance from József Kovács of Hungary. On the opening day, Kuts sped into the lead in the 10,000m, Pirie tugging at his heels. After five laps Kuts put in a

sprint but by the end of the lap Pirie had closed the gap. Intermittently, Kuts would now run wide into the second lane, inviting Pirie to take the lead but Pirie declined to do so. At halfway, leading the field by 100 metres, the two of them were close to Zátopek's Olympic record of 14:06.6 for the shorter distance, testimony to the sport's rate of progress. Another five laps and Kuts made another sprint, raising his lap time by five seconds. Pirie stuck to him. With five laps remaining, Kuts came almost to a standstill, obliging Pirie to move in front. But only briefly. In the next lap Kuts surged in front once again to open a gap once more of 100 metres. Pirie was a broken man, slipping back eventually to finish eighth, with Kovács taking the silver medal some seven seconds behind Kuts' Olympic record of 28:45.6. The first five all beat Zátopek's record. 'He murdered me,' Pirie said. The Hungarian Kovács refused to congratulate the Soviet victor. Three days before the race, Kuts had banged his chest in a minor car accident, but made no mention of the pain.

> I could see from Pirie's shadow on the grass that he was sticking behind me, step by step. I was sure Pirie was running with ease and made my first spurt, but at the end of the fifth lap his shadow was again next to mine. Who was the hunter and who was the prey? At halfway, in 14:06.6, the battle still lay ahead. I had to have a look at his face to know how he was finding it. Suddenly I slowed down so much I almost came to a stop. At last Gordon came alongside and I had a look at the tired, limp figure. Fatigue was spelt all over his face. I realised that this was the moment for the decisive spurt.

Pirie had nothing if not guts and despite his bitter experience was determined still to challenge Kuts for the 5,000m, having set his world record against him. The Ukrainian, however, was in irresistible form and five days later he immediately went to the front, was never led, again erasing Zátopek's Olympic record – but not Pirie's world time – by almost half a minute. Future record breaker Derek Ibbotson of Britain took the bronze, Kuts emulating the 'double' of Kolehmainen in 1912 and Zátopek in 1948, which would not be repeated until 1972. Sadly, Kuts was to die after a series of heart attacks, at the age of 48 in 1975, doubtless over-extended by a damaging Soviet training regime.

Vladimir Kuts, record-breaking Soviet and double long-distance champion at Melbourne, waves his delight at the finish of the 10,000m and leaves Gordon Pirie of Britain holding on for the silver medal in the 5,000m.(© IOC/Warlow) (© IOC)

Alain Mimoun of France was 36 by the time of Melbourne. Three times in the two previous Games he had taken silver medals behind Zátopek on the track and now, belatedly like Zátopek, had set his sights on the marathon. Born in Algeria, Mimoun had left his native village aged 18 and joined the French Army, yet his real career had always been running. In 1954, he had been cured of chronic sciatica on a pilgrimage to the Basilica of St Theresa of Lisieux and thereafter began his preparation for Melbourne, partially in the hope that the year-cycle would prove appropriate for a Frenchman: the marathons of 1900 and 1928 had been respectively won by Theato and El Ouafi of France. For the first half of the race Mimoun was among the leading pack, then he opened a lead of almost a minute, which he held all the way to the finish ahead of Franjo Mihalic of Yugoslavia. An ageing Zátopek came home sixth, duly to congratulate his old rival. 'Better than a medal,' Mimoun reflected.

Although Bobby Joe Morrow of America achieved the first sprint treble – 100m, 200m and relay – since Owens 20 years earlier, his victory in the 100m, in the same time as his colleague Thane Baker in second place, was a relatively slow 10.5 into a strong head wind. Jack Davis (USA) for the second time shared a Games' record without a gold medal: by now the holder of the 110m hurdles world record with 13.4, he lost a photo-finish decision to colleague Lee Calhoun, both with an Olympic record of 13.5.

A drama unseen by the crowd took place in the jury room following the 3,000m steeplechase. The fancied Ernst Larsen of Norway and world record holder Sándor Rozsnói had led on the final bend. As Rozsnói ran wide to clear a hurdle, Christopher Brasher, of Britain, who had never previously won a major event and had only just made the team, zipped between the two of them to forge in front and win by over two seconds ahead of Rozsnói in an Olympic record of 8:41.2, six seconds better than Brasher had ever run before. Then came an announcement that Brasher had been disqualified, allegedly for elbowing Larsen as they cleared the fourth-last hurdle. Brasher had to press his NOC to lodge a protest. Rozsnói, Larsen, third, and Heinz Laufer of Germany, fourth, all sportingly supported Brasher's protest, Larsen saying he considered the incident irrelevant. Three hours later the Jury of Appeal unanimously re-instated Brasher for Britain's first track and field gold medal since 1936. Two years earlier he had paced the first two laps in Bannister's celebrated mile record and he later founded the London Marathon.

Within a short time of Bannister's four-minute mile, John Landy of Australia, a marvellously fluent young runner, had improved the record, though subsequently losing to Bannister over a mile in a memorable British Empire Games in Vancouver that same year. Subsequently eight other runners had broken four minutes and five of them – Brian Hewson (GBR), Laszlo Tabori and Istvan Roszavölgyi (world record holder) of Hungary, Ron Delany (IRE) and Gunnar Nielsen (NOR) – were there for the 1,500m in Melbourne, though Delany had almost been omitted by the selectors following two defeats by Hewson. The heats saw the elimination of Josef Barthel, the holder, Roszavölgyi and Michel Jazy of France, silver medal winner four years later and future mile record holder. Such was the composition of one of the greatest four-lap fields ever assembled for an Olympic final that the last lap began with less than three strides separating the entire field. Hewson led from Merv Lincoln of Australia, with Delany boxed at the back, though seemingly relaxed. Steadily Delany moved past those ahead of him until he delivered a final sprint in the finishing straight. For him it was an unprecedented performance, running the last lap in 53.8, setting an Olympic record of 3:41.2, comfortably clear of Klaus Richtzenhain of the GDR, who shared the same time as third-placed Landy.

The previous year, Roger Moens of Belgium had finally beaten the German Rudolf Harbig's 17-year-old 800m record but was injured and absent from Melbourne, where the final was expected to be a duel between US rivals Thomas Courtney and Arnie Sowell, and indeed these two were pressing each other round the last bend. Down the finishing straight, Courtney moved to the third lane to avoid rough cinders in the inner

The surprise victory of Ronnie Delany, Irish winner of the 1,500m, is celebrated in the National Gallery of Ireland by James Hanley, member of the Royal Hibernian Academy. (Reproduced courtesy of the National Gallery of Ireland)

the 200m, Cuthbert repeated her victory over Stubnick, this time equalling Jackson's four-year-old record with 23.4.

Shirley Strickland, by now Mrs de la Hunty and a mother, successfully defended her 80m hurdles title with an Olympic record of 10.7 and shared a sprint relay victory with Cuthbert, Norma Croker and Fleur Mellor in a world record 44.5, ahead of Britain and the USA, thus ending her three-Games career with a total of three gold, one silver and three bronze medals. Years later, a rediscovered photo-finish picture showed that in 1948 she was third and not fourth in the 200m ahead of Audrey Patterson (USA).

The Australians had deliberately arranged the programme so that swimming, in which they held the highest hopes, would provide the climax of the Games. The 5,500 seats at the new complex were sold out months beforehand, the public queuing to pay even to watch the training. The reward was eight gold, four silver and two bronze medals, compared with two, four and five respectively for the Americans who had previously dominated. Especially satisfying was Australian success in all the men's and women's freestyle events. In the men's and women's 100m, Australia made a clean sweep. Behind this triumph was a 12-week training camp, from July, supervised by the latest physiologists and coaches. It was a professional approach that the Australians were to repeat 44 years later in Sydney.

Jon Hendricks led John Devitt and Gary Chapman in the men's sprint with an Olympic record of 55.4 – Hendricks's 56th win in 57 races over three years. Dawn Fraser, the youngest of eight children, set a world record in the women's event of 1:02.0 ahead of Lorraine Crapp, the favourite, and Faith Leech. This was the start of an exceptional and often controversial career for Fraser. Her rivalry with Crapp would be intense, each of them further breaking the record and Fraser going on to defend her title in Olympic record time at the next two Games. In the 400m freestyle, she came second to Crapp's world record of 4:54.6.

Murray Rose, born in England but brought up in Australia, took the men's 400m freestyle, aged 17, with a burst in the third

lanes, at which point Derek Johnson of Britain sped between the Americans and into the lead. Courtney retaliated, clawed his way back and lunged at the line abreast of Johnson, unaware which of them had won. So distraught was Courtney that the medal ceremony had to be delayed. He had beaten Johnson by a tenth of a second in an Olympic record of 1:47.7. Johnson, with Brasher and Bannister, was the last of what might be termed old-fashioned, part-time amateurs in the mould of *Chariots of Fire*.

Olympic achievement is so often as much about inspiration as perspiration and never more so than with the 20-year-old Al Oerter, the discus champion from West Babylon, New York state. In each of his four historic victories at consecutive Games, he had to beat the current world record holder. What distinguishes the Games is the infrequency of the four-year cycle and therefore the requirement, in order to be the best of the best, to deliver on the day. Consecutively beaten into second place were world record holders Gordien (USA) in Melbourne, Babka (USA) in Rome and Danek (CZE) in Tokyo, while Silvester (USA) could finish only fifth in Mexico City. Oerter on his first throw in Melbourne achieved the best of his career thus far, 56.36m (184 ft 11 in.), had the best three throws of the competition and was so surprised by his success he almost fell off the medal podium.

The home audience was agog at the sprint double of an 18-year-old girl from Sydney, Betty Cuthbert. In the first round of the 100m she broke Marjorie Jackson's four-year-old Olympic record with 11.4, lost the semi-final to Christa Stubnick of the GDR, but reversed that in the final to win by half a stride. In

Confident, controversial Dawn Fraser heralded a dramatic development in women's swimming with a 100m freestyle world record at the start of her three-Games epic. (© IOC)

quarter, which threw off Tsuyoshi Yamanaka of Japan. The highlight of the men's events was the 1,500m freestyle in which George Breen of America had set a world record in the qualifying round, surpassing the existing record of Rose. In the final, Breen, Rose and Yamanaka were level at the halfway stage, with Rose then forging ahead. In the last 100 metres, Yamanaka was close to catching him.

Joaquin Capilla Pérez, a Mexican architect, had the rare distinction of improving his medal position in three successive Games when winning the platform diving. His forward one and a half somersault with double twist on his final dive was decisive in the defeat of Gary Tobian (USA). In 1948 he had taken the bronze behind Americans Sammy Lee and Bruce Harlan, and in 1952 had been runner-up to Lee.

Despite the bloodshed in Budapest, the Hungarian team had made its way to Melbourne, where a number of competitors defected in preference to returning to a Moscow-imposed dictatorship. Unsurprisingly, the Hungarians underperformed compared with four years earlier. Equally unsurprising was the tenor of their water polo semi-final against the Soviet team, the match degenerating into a confrontation of verbal and physical spite. With the Hungarians leading 4–0, the Soviets began taunting them with shouts of 'Fascists'. The referee had to

The Hungarian water polo team, refugees from Budapest's bloodshed, won a predictably rugged penultimate match against the Soviet Union on their way to claiming the title, some of them refusing to return home. (© IOC)

suspend five players at one point for punching and kicking, and there was blood in the water when Valentin Prokopov head-butted Ervin Zador of Hungary, splitting his eyebrow. At this point the Soviet team decided to forfeit the match when the Swedish referee called matters to a halt.

One who did return to Hungary, and with a proud distinction that still stands, was László Papp. Defeating José Torres of America in the light-middleweight boxing final, he became the first fighter in Olympic history to win three gold medals at successive Games: the middleweight title in 1948, beating Johnny Wright (GBR), and light-middleweight in 1952, defeating Theunis van Schalkwyk (RSA). Papp's achievement captured the imagination of the local spectators and it was indeed a worthy victory against Torres, Puerto Rican-born, who would subsequently become professional world lightweight champion. There were many ex-patriate Hungarians in the crowd and they raised the roof when their man came close to knocking out Torres in the second round. Guarding his 30 years carefully, Papp took no risks, tactically out-boxing Torres in the third.

The 18-year-old Vyacheslav Ivanov of Russia won the first of three successive single sculls titles with a devastating finishing sprint over the final tenth of the race, which carried him past Stuart Mackenzie of Australia, the leader. Jumping up and down in his euphoria following the presentation ceremony, Ivanov threw his medal in the air and saw it disappear into the waters of Lake Wendouree. Although he dived in to search repeatedly, he failed to find it, as did professional divers. The IOC presented him with a replacement. John Kelly Junior, son of the 1920 winner, took the bronze.

The longest span in Olympic competition by a woman in any sport until this time was achieved by Ellen Müller-Preiss of Austria when finishing seventh in the individual foil behind champion Gillian Sheen of Britain. Twenty-four years earlier Müller-Preiss had won the title in Los Angeles, then went on to take the bronze at both Berlin and London. Sheen, the only British fencer ever to win a gold medal, won on classic technique at the beginning of an era which saw the advance of a new athleticism. Subsequently, Kerstin Palm, a Swedish fencer, competed in seven Games, 1964–88.

It had been a fine Games in the southern hemisphere. Australians had won 13 gold medals, their best yet, while 36 Olympic and 11 world records were broken. The Soviet Union claimed a socialist victory with 98 medals, 37 of them gold, ahead of America's 74 and 32 respectively.

CHAPTER XXXV

Arrival of Television

Kevan Gosper of Australia, Olympic track silver medal winner, IOC Vice-President, 1999–2003

'*The closing ceremony at Melbourne went down in history. John Wing, an unknown Australian boy of Chinese descent, had written to Sir Wilfred Kent Hughes, chairman of the organising committee, suggesting that, instead of marching in teams, the athletes should mingle as they liked, waving to the public. "The march I have in mind is different from that in the opening ceremony and will make these Games even greater," wrote Wing. "Instead, there will be only one team. What more could anybody want than the world as one nation. You can do it in a small way." That is what happened.*

Despite Cold War anxieties, and the aftermath of Suez and the crushed Hungarian uprising, I did not see any tensions between teams in the Village. There was the over-stated "blood-in-the-water" story of the water polo match between USSR and Hungary but otherwise relations everywhere were calm and friendly. The compelling interest lay in USA–Soviet rivalry.

The Games marked the arrival of television in Australia. Few could afford home sets, so viewers gathered around store windows to watch the black-and-white transmissions.

Though the Games have changed dramatically since then, when I was running for my country – and nothing in sport can compare with this singular experience – they essentially remain the same: athletes from every race, culture and religion mixing in the Village, bringing all nations together, millions around the world watching together at home. It is still about being the best in the world.

In the mid-twentieth century, Melbourne was still hostage to the tyranny of distance, which had so constrained Australians with regard to global travel, other than when our young people were sent overseas to fight other nations' wars, or by travelling media men and a small cadre of foreign students. It was a big effort to get to Australia from almost anywhere. Antiquated pictures from that time show a flying boat, with the caption boasting "these fast-flying aircraft enable visitors to reach Australia within three to four days"! Isolation reflected the mainstream Australian way of life and the Olympics in Melbourne provided the first real connection with the international community. Most of all, we were left with a sense of "can do" national pride and rewarded with renewed self-confidence. And all this through Olympic sport.

A generation later would start on the long path of bringing the Games back to Australia, this time to Sydney, and the IOC President would announce to the world at the closing ceremony that they were "the best Games ever". The successful outcome in 2000, as in 1956, was simply a demonstration of the social relevance and heartfelt love of sport within every Australian. And to represent Australia at an Olympic Games continues to be the dream of every young Australian athlete.'*

(Photograph © IOC/Locatelli)

While athletes like Vladimir Kuts were making breathtaking advances centre-stage at Melbourne, there were equally striking long-term political manoeuvres taking place behind the scenes. Avery Brundage was all too aware of the growing phenomenon of bloc-building, which was likely to become more pronounced as the Games gained wider prominence. In a circular to IOC members in January 1954, he had written: 'There must be no blocs and there must be no nationalism in the IOC.' At that year's Session in Athens, the members reaffirmed their independence: that they were ambassadors of the IOC to their country and not vice-versa. Yet the USSR was like a dog with a bone – it would not let go of what it perceived as a way of establishing its own version of democracy. Brundage's treasured platform of ideologies was increasingly becoming a husting for opportunistic politicians.

Shortly before the Session of 1959 in Munich, the USSR proposed the wholesale reorganisation of the IOC. The new body would consist of: the current members (then 64 in number); the presidents of affiliated NOCs; and the presidents of affiliated international federations. The effect of this would have been to triple the size of the IOC and dramatically increase the influence of the Communist bloc and Third World countries. The plan was analogous to Nikita Khrushchev's recent proposals for reformation of the UN.

As a sop to the more powerful nations it was proposed that they should carry two votes on decision-making. Predictably, however, the proposal foundered. Four years earlier, Konstantin Andrianov had demanded that the Executive Board should be increased to nine members and that there should be a third Vice-President. He failed on the first count, lacking a two-thirds

Lord Burghley (GBR), later the Marquis of Exeter, seen here winning the 400m hurdles in 1928. As IOC member he argued that Formosa-Taiwan could be accepted only by altering the name of its NOC. (© IOC)

vote, but succeeded on the second. A year later, General Vladimir Stoytchev of Bulgaria became the first Communist to serve on the Executive Board. Four years later Andrianov succeeded Stoytchev, another four before he succeeded Lord Burghley as second Vice-President.

Relations between the two Chinas and the IOC continued to ride on a knife edge. Brundage and Yi-tung Shou continued to exchange distant insults and Shou eventually tendered his resignation in 1958. The issue was debated once more at the Session of 1959 and Douglas Roby, US member, suggested that Taiwan continue to be recognised providing they change their name from 'Chinese National Olympic Committee'. With the People's Republic member having resigned, there was no limb on which their Soviet supporters could reintroduce them into the argument.

After heated debate, the following compromise, suggested by Lord Burghley, was reached by a vote of 48–7: 'The Chinese Olympic committee having its seat in Taipei will be notified that it can no longer be recognised under this name because it does not administer sport in China. The [present] name will be stricken from the official list. If the IOC is presented with a request for recognition under another name, the IOC will reconsider.' This rational ruling by a sports body met with open hostility in the press, especially in pro-Taiwan America. It was alleged that Formosa-Taiwan had been expelled, which was only half true, and the blame was inevitably placed upon Brundage. The US State Department joined the condemnation of what it called 'a politically discriminatory act designed in effect to exclude the free Chinese athletes from participation'. Brundage responded that the IOC 'does not deal with governments' and added that the vote had been nearly unanimous. Henry Cabot Lodge, US Ambassador to the UN, called for a revision of the decision. The IOC and Brundage were unavoidably out of their depth, the Formosa Straights currently being one of the world's troublespots, the people's Republic of China having fired on the nationalist islands of Quemoy and Matsu. To a US audience, the IOC's action appeared to be expelling a victim in order to appease an aggressor.

Brundage attempted to back-track, stating:

> By its vote of 28 May, the IOC neither expelled nor evicted the Nationalist Chinese Committee from the Olympic Movement and we deplore this error of

interpretation which was widely broadcast. The sole purpose of the IOC's action was to identify the athletes eligible to participate in the Games under the control of the Olympic Committee of Taiwan.

In a further compromise, the IOC authorised officials of Taiwan, which had no Winter Games competitors, to attend the Squaw Valley Games because they had been invited prior to decertification. India, fearful of offending the People's Republic, consequently withdrew. Taiwan, marching under the enforced title of 'Formosa', paraded an additional banner, 'Under Protest'.

On the German front, all was calm if not wholly quiet. The agreement for Melbourne, of a single team, was maintained for the Games in Rome. Heinz Schöbel and his GDR colleagues pressed to have their 'provisional' status upgraded but the IOC resisted and was still able to mediate with both NOCs for a combined team under a single flag and anthem. For Brundage, who had successfully suggested that the two teams use a black-red-and-gold flag bearing the Olympic rings instead of the GDR's hammer-and-calipers, the sight of the joint team marching into Rome's Olympic stadium was a moment of triumph. Giovanni Gronchi, the Italian State President, remarked to Brundage at the opening ceremony that the achievement by the IOC was a miracle. 'In sport, we can do such things,' Brundage boasted.

The ticking time bomb of apartheid was now becoming more audible. Although it had no bearing upon IOC affairs, the first action to be taken against Afrikaaner separatism occurred in football in the African Nations Cup of 1957, when South Africa was suspended prior to its semi-final against Ethiopia on account of the national federation's refusal to field a mixed team. In 1960, there was the first formal anti-apartheid meeting between CAF, the African football confederation, and South Africa's non-racial football governing body. It was all very well for Brundage to claim that the IOC would never permit a breach of the Charter's first rule – no country and no individual to be discriminated against on the grounds of race, religion or politics – but the IOC could not conceivably uphold South Africa's Olympic participation in the face of the antagonism of the largest and most united continent, whatever the indifference of some members to South Africa's own internal discrimination. For some years Brundage had been friendly with Reginald Honey, IOC member in South Africa, and had repeatedly asserted that the Games were not to be shaped by politics. By degrees, however, this would increasingly become the situation. In 1959, Alexei Romanov drew attention to South Africa's segregation policy, in answer to which Honey insisted that his NOC 'is bona fide and that all the athletes of our country are eligible to participate in the Games', that there was no discrimination against non-white competitors and that the absence of non-whites from South African Olympic teams, thus far, was due to performance levels among non-whites falling short of international standard. This argument, though supported by Sir Arthur Porritt of New Zealand in his capacity as president of the 1958 Commonwealth Games in Cardiff, was undermined by the fact that even the South African team for that competition was all-white. The participation of an all-white team in Rome would rapidly drive the growing anti-apartheid movement into fresh and wider action.

At the 1959 Session, Guru Dutt Sondhi of India questioned also the level of colour discrimination in Rhodesia. As with South Africa, Brundage chose to accept assurances by white

Reginald Honey, IOC member from South Africa, trod a tightrope in perversely attempting to bridge the moral gulf between his government's racist apartheid regime and continuing national Olympic membership. (© IOC)

Rhodesians that there was 'no problem'. Significant evidence from Brazil and other nations that their black footballers had not been allowed to compete in South Africa, however, could not be ignored and Brundage promised that the South African issue would be properly investigated following the Rome Games. The time-honoured IOC policy of procrastination on controversial issues was inevitably doomed to failure on this hyper-sensitive racial matter of apartheid, protest by no means confined to Africa.

There were other matters away from the nationalistic front. At the Sofia Session of 1957, Rome's organising committee requested permission to schedule athletic events over the whole two weeks but Burghley, as IAAF president, said that this would diminish public interest. On the other hand, as a means of restricting competitor numbers, Burghley proposed the introduction of qualifying performances where a country wished to enter more than one competitor for a single event. It was agreed at Sofia that there should be a minimum of 15 sports on the Summer programme, with permission for any organising committee to withdraw an event if there were entries from fewer than 12 countries, and that for any sport to become recognised it must be practised in a minimum of 25 countries. At the same Session, Sir Philip Noel-Baker was acclaimed for receiving the Nobel Peace Prize.

Monique Berlioux, former Olympic swimmer and sports journalist in France, who initially had been appointed to work on the IOC's *Bulletin*, was promoted to Director of Press and Public Relations, alongside the newly appointed Technical Director, Artur Takac of Yugoslavia. Berlioux would later become Brundage's confidante, and by degrees, as controller of administration during his absence while travelling or at home in San Francisco, the quasi-President.

Meanwhile the clandestine scourge of professionalism, an ailment without cure, continued unofficially to mock the President. At the Session of 1957 in Sofia, the IOC again considered amateurism. In America and elsewhere, in the mood of enlightened social conscience that had followed the Second World War, there was concern about the principle and definition of 'broken-time' payment to athletes taking time off work to prepare for major sporting events. Many other than Brundage felt that competitors deserved, when representing their country, some reimbursement for lost wages, and the principle was viewed with sympathy by realistic NOCs. Reality, however, was not a quality widely to be found among older IOC members, who now half-heartedly revised Rule 26 on Eligibility:

> Competitors will *not* be regarded as amateur if they participate for money, or goods easily converted into money, or prizes exceeding $40 [then £14]; coach for payment (excluding schoolmasters); receive financial benefit to help them compete; receive unauthorised expenses; declare an intention to become professional following the Games; cease work in order to train for more than 30 days.

These principles, never mind how patently impractical the last three might be, were in tune with the view expressed, for example, before the Melbourne Games by the Duke of Edinburgh: that Britain did not want to send a team of 'temporary civil servants'. That sounded nice in the drawing rooms of Britain and the chandelier-hung mansions of Bellevue Avenue, Newport, Rhode Island, but was not much help to honourable working men such as Don Thompson of Britain, who was to win the 50km walk at the Rome Games after months of preparing himself for the humidity by exercising in his overheated bathroom. André Chassaignon, a French sports editor, severely attacked Brundage at the time of the Rome Games under the headline 'The Olympic flag is the Symbol of a Lie'. An irate Brundage sued for defamation and was awarded by a French court the derisory damages of $200. For the avoidance, coincidentally, of another embarrassment, it had been decided in Sofia that the IOC should abandon the practice of members assembling in the centre of the arena during the opening ceremony: an athletic exercise that was occasionally beyond the dignified scope of the more elderly.

Most significant of all innovations, however, was the advent of the new era of big business, with the signing by CONI, the Italian NOC, of a $394,000 contract with Columbia Broadcasting System (CBS) for American television rights to the Rome Games, with a further two-thirds as much from Eurovision, plus $50,000 paid by CBS for the Winter rights to Squaw Valley. For an organisation that was hitherto surviving precariously on membership fees and contributions from host cities, not to mention the administrative subsidies paid out of his own pocket from Brundage – in a similar manner to de Coubertin – this truly was a financial windfall.

Brundage, however, found himself in a dilemma: on the one hand having an entrenched view against commercialisation, on the other being all too aware of the IOC's annual four-figure deficit and its duty in principle to accept what it was rightly owed in its proprietorial position as owner of the Games. In 1959, Lord Burghley had proposed a 5 per cent tax on spectator tickets to help generate income, 3 per cent of this to go to the local organising committee and 2 per cent to the IOC. Burghley further threatened that if this was rejected, the IAAF, for which the Olympic Games represented its world championships, would establish separate independent championships. Nonetheless, Brundage had doggedly refused to contemplate this step. With Rome's organising committee he had less influence, and so Guilio Onesti, president of CONI, went ahead with a rights sale. Following the Games, CONI offered the IOC 5 per cent of the fee, which was accepted. Live broadcasts by Radiotelevisione Italiana (RAI) had reached almost all Western Europe and, by Intervision link, much of Eastern Europe. CBS reached the whole of North America and NHK of Japan flew home daily videotapes from Rome. Thus the Games were watched on screen in 21 countries.

Alexander Cushing, a prominent New York lawyer and enthusiastic skier, was so taken by Squaw Valley, following a visit in 1947, that he purchased nearly 600 acres, raised half a million dollars and moved his family west to create a ski resort. Discovering that USOC was to bid for the Winter Games for 1960, he instantly spied a chance for development of his venture, never mind that its site on the California–Nevada state line, close to Lake Tahoe, was devoid of the kind of facilities required for Olympic competition. In spite of this, the Governor of California and the state's two senators coordinated to create a $1million fund for site development, if Cushing could secure USOC approval. When Cushing first met USOC officials in 1955, Squaw Valley boasted one chair-lift and one motel. Though he was up against such familiar winter sports centres as Aspen in Colorado, Sun Valley in Idaho and Lake Placid, the appeal of Squaw Valley's scenic beauty won official backing. Having cleared that hurdle, there seemed little likelihood that Squaw Valley, with its Squaw Peak rising to nearly 9,000 feet, would be preferred to either St Moritz or the supposed favourite, Innsbruck. Yet, impressed by Cushing's promise to restore the 'Olympic ideal' within an untarnished environment, in June 1955 Squaw Valley won the vote over Innsbruck on the second ballot by 32–30. Now all that was required was a new $4 million stadium for opening and closing ceremonies plus figure skating and ice hockey, not to mention a new sewage treatment plant. In no time, the projected cost had risen from $2.4 million to $8 million. Along the way, the environmental factor in what was intended to be an intimate Games got lost. Walt Disney was hired as director of ceremonies, Hollywood razzmatazz upstaged scenic beauty and the business of entertainment took the foreground. The Scandinavians became worried about the problem of thin air on a cross-country course 12 miles out of town, at 6,000 feet above sea level. Consumed by rising costs, the organising committee decided not to build a bobsleigh course. The international bobsleigh federation's protests were ignored, so they staged their own World Championships at Cortina two weeks beforehand. By the time of the opening, Squaw Valley's bill had risen to $15 million, with the inclusion of artificially refrigerated outdoor rinks, electronic timing, a computerised results service by IBM, plus Disney's lavish imagination for the ceremonials.

In spite of a profusion of problems, Squaw Valley, the first

Queen Federika of Greece arrives for the Games at Rome railway station with, to her right, Crown Prince Constantine and Princess Sophia: the former to win a yachting gold medal, the latter his reserve crew and later to marry the future King of Spain. (© IOC)

purpose-built Winter Games venue, was considered a success. South Africa took part for the first and last time for 34 years, and the biathlon and speed skating for women made their first appearance, the biathlon the successor to the military patrol event.

Rome had been the final site of the Ancient Games until terminated by decree of Emperor Theodosius in AD 393. Thus the Summer Games would find themselves in a historically natural home, following the near misses of the past half-century: denied the chance in 1904, forced to relinquish them in 1908 and 1944. The Eternal City was finally elected at Paris in 1955, defeating Lausanne by a vote of 35–24. Backed by financing from the football lottery, Totocalcio, CONI was to invest over $50 million in a Games that had a grace all of its own, with 12 venues – designed or improved by architect Pier Luigi Nervi – presenting events to spectators, both live and on television, in glorious surroundings. Mussolini's Stadio Olympico was updated, the Foro Italico site also accommodating swimming and diving venues. Basketball took place at the modern Palazetto dello Sport, gymnastics at the ancient Baths of Caracalla, wrestling under the arches of the ancient Basilica di Massenzio. The Pope was able to observe the rowing at Lake Albano from the terrace of his home. The Village was constructed across the Tiber in a new neighbourhood, new bridges over the river linking it to the stadiums. Amid this magnificence, these were a Games gratifyingly free of any immediate political hostility. Morocco, Sudan, San Marino and Tunisia made their first appearance.

CHAPTER XXXVI

Squaw Valley (VIII) 1960

Heidi Biebl of Germany, Olympic downhill champion

'*In 1960, when I won the women's downhill, the Olympic Games were also the world championships, so I became Olympic and world champion the same day. I didn't realise at the time of my victory what it meant to win such a competition, though I gradually became aware that this success had as many disadvantages as advantages. On the one hand, I was offered the opportunity to run a ski school, combined with a hotel and sports centre, but on the other, the pressure from the public was very demanding. People expected me to win and win. Besides that, not only did I not receive any financial reward but I also still suffer severe health problems because in the 1960s nobody took care of the medical side of sport. I can't really tell if the gold medal changed my life, but I can assure anyone it is not easy to be in the public eye. Yet to become Olympic champion is something very special, more than anything because you know that you made a small part of history.*

It was a wonderful race day, with blue sky and bright sunshine. Snow conditions on the piste were ideal. I went up to the start on the T-bar with a fellow competitor from Switzerland, Anne Marie Waser. Arriving there, I tried to keep away from the bustle of the crowd, to make sure I would be able to gather all the concentration I needed for the race. I was just as nervous as for any other race. My thoughts were not about the possibility of victory, just about the course and getting down as smoothly and as fast as possible. Some insiders already considered me the winner but on that day many competitors could have won because the standard was very level. After my run I had the fastest time so far but was left waiting anxiously until the last competitor skied through. Only gradually did I begin to realise that I was champion. What was most important to me was to be able to contact my mother back home in Bavaria from a radio broadcasting box. I had become aware just how perfect, how special a day it was, all the elements coming together at one moment.'*

(Photograph © IOC/Roebelt)

The chief rival to Heidi Biebl was Penny Pitou from New Hampshire, who had made a name for herself by qualifying for her high school student men's team and finishing fifth in the state slalom championship before being barred as a girl. At 19, she was one of the favourites on Squaw Valley's 'home slope', though more for the two slalom events than the downhill. The latter included a so-called 'Airplane Turn', a hard-packed mound that lifted racers into a jump as they negotiated a near right-angle bend. Several competitors fell foul of this turn, including Pitou but she managed to recover her balance and temporarily held the lead with the early fastest time of 1:38.6. However, she had to settle for the silver medal when Biebl came down a full second faster, with Traudl Hecher of Austria in third place, split seconds behind Pitou. In the giant slalom three days later, Pitou again came second, this time behind Yvonne Rüegg of Switzerland. In the slalom, Pitou was wholly out of luck, falling on the second run. The winner, Anne Heggtveit of Canada, finished an exceptional 3.3 seconds ahead of Betsy Snite (USA) and seven seconds faster than Barbara Henneberger of Germany, a margin only ever bettered by the 1936 combined winner Christel Cranz of Germany. Heggtveit is another whose life,

before and after victory, was conditioned by the Olympic environment:

The spirit of the Olympic Movement was a fundamental part of my upbringing. My dad, Halvor, though named for the 1936 cross-country team, had been unable to take part. He nurtured my love of skiing, introducing me to Alpine competition at the age of six. The 1948 Games opened the eyes of an enthusiastic nine year old to the possibilities of international competition. I was fascinated by Gretchen Fraser's win in the slalom event and captivated by Barbara-Ann Scott's homecoming to Ottawa with her gold medal from figure skating. From that moment on I had my own Olympic dream, my Olympic goal. Commitment, dedication, tenacity and the ability to accept new challenges, lessons from my Olympic experience, gave me the confidence to tackle other obstacles: a university education undertaken as an adult and the forging of a new vocation in risk management. Carrying the Olympic flag into the stadium in the opening ceremony of the Calgary Games in 1988 was as emotional as standing on the podium in 1960. A special thread is woven through the fabric of my day-to-day activities, remnants of my experience of the Olympic Movement.

Heavy snow caused the postponement of the men's downhill for three days and made the choice of ski wax a matter of critical importance. Not for Jean Vuarnet of France, who in his downhill victory became the first Olympic gold medal winner to use metal skis. He is also said to have inaugurated the aerodynamically effective position of the crouch.

The more technical slalom events were dominated by the Austrians. Ernst Hinterseer won the slalom ahead of compatriot Matthias Leitner and took bronze in the giant slalom behind his colleague Josef Stiegler, with Roger Staub of Switzerland the victor.

Women's speed skating featured in the Games for the first time, the Soviet Union triumphantly challenging the more traditional countries. Lydia Skoblikova won both 1,500m and 3,000m titles, the former in world record time, the latter by a margin of two and a half seconds over compatriot Valentina Stenina. Skoblikova missed a bronze medal by half a second in the 1,000m, her colleagues Klara Guseva and Tamara Rylova coming first and third either side of Helga Haase of Germany. Elwira Seroczynska of Poland fell at the final bend while holding the fastest time. Haase had already won the 500m, in the inaugural Olympic final, ahead of Natalya Donchenko of the Soviet Union.

The events took place on the first refrigerated speed skating rink in the world. Yevgeni Grishin (URS) for the second successive Olympic final equalled his world record time of 40.2

Carol Heiss from New York was runner-up as a 16-year-old figure skater, but four years later, having vowed to her mother who was dying of cancer that she would be Olympic champion, fulfilled that dream in Squaw Valley. (© IOC)

and was the first to successfully defend his 500m title. He would have improved the record had he not stumbled in the finishing straight. Knut Johannesen of Norway beat the 10,000m world record by 46 seconds, the widest margin achieved in the twentieth century.

Carol Heiss from New York had come second in the figure skating of 1956 at the age of 16, subsequently beating Tenley Albright, the gold medal winner, two weeks later to win the World Championship. Shortly after that her mother died of cancer and Carol vowed to win an Olympic gold in her honour. At Squaw Valley, all nine judges placed Heiss first, ahead of an up-and-coming Dutch girl, Sjoukje Dijkstra.

Highly dramatic, even for non-Americans, was the ice hockey tournament. Prior to arriving at Squaw Valley, the US team had been unimpressive on a preparatory tour but in their opening match against Czechoslovakia they scored four goals in the final period to win 7–5, having trailed 4–3 in the first two periods. They continued successfully, defeating joint-favourites Canada 2–1 and then gained their first victory over the Soviet Union in a tense affair. To win their first title they had to survive a final seventh match against their opening opponents and by now were match-weary. The Czechs led 4–3 after two periods but a squad somehow revitalised in the third period shot six goals to win 9–4: a rare moment. The Canadians had scored more goals and conceded fewer but their defeat by their neighbours had proved decisive. The novelty of the Americans' final game was a seeming thaw in the Cold War when the Soviet captain, Nikolai Sologubov, arrived at the US locker room before the final period with canisters of oxygen which clearly were instrumental in the late revival.

Knut Johannesen (NOR) lopped 46 seconds off the speed skating 10km world record. (© IOC/Ruebelt)

CHAPTER XXXVII

Rome (XVII) 1960

Herb Elliott of Australia, Olympic 1,500m champion

'*The Olympic Games of 1956 in Melbourne changed my life. At that time I was a schoolboy athlete of above natural ability but, for the moment, no world beater. After watching the opening ceremony and the remorseless victories of Vladimir Kuts in the 5km and 10km events, it inspired me to commit the next four years of my life to developing my natural aptitude to its utmost. With the 1960 Olympics in Rome as my goal, I left my family home in order to be with Percy Cerutti, my coach, and I went through four years of training, growing and maturing that utterly changed my life for the better – physically and spiritually. The win in the 1,500m in Rome is now inextricably part of the way in which I am perceived and treated by those around me. Without these two Olympic Games, I would be a different person. The training changed my perception of myself, the Games changed the way others perceived me . . . There was so much pressure on me for that particular race – for all sorts of reasons, even just the wish to gain the sense of relief once I had actually done it. It has to be the most significant thing that happened in my athletic career.*

Working with Percy was something unique, getting used to his unrelenting drive, the need for the runner to combine mind and spirit, releasing the power that they could impose on the body. Achieving this was beyond imagination. Yet, in a sense he didn't drive, he was all carrot rather than stick, nothing difficult, just a matter of listening to him and mostly fulfilling the training regime on my own.

It was Landy and Bannister who created my fascination with the mile. When I wrote to Landy while still at school, asking for training ideas, he wrote back and I was able to relate with someone far greater than I was. His acknowledgement of me gave me thus an unspoken responsibility.

Yes, my greatest satisfaction was Rome, yet the pressures of the Olympics are greater than anything. You're waiting four years, aware of your weaknesses, knowing you can bugger it up on the day, thinking "Why am I doing this, imposing this terrible test on myself?" I'd have been happy just to win in Rome, but Percy insisted on winning with excellence. The strategy was to sit around for a couple of laps, looking at the field, and then to go for it.

A few weeks after the race, I realised I was sick to death of running, didn't enjoy it any more. I'm glad to be remembered the way I am: for having been an athlete, I'm happy with whatever that was – something a bit different, someone who could be relied on to produce a bloody good performance every time that I performed. I like to be thought of as a reasonable, decent sort of person.'

(Photograph © popperfoto.com)

It is rare that any sportsman dominates the rivals of his era to the extent that Herb Elliott did. Born in Perth, Western Australia, in 1938, his natural talent together with the perceptive coaching of the 66-year-old Percy Cerutti – the young runner acquiring a fanaticism in his application that began to match that of the older man – combined to produce an exceptional runner, mentally schooled by Cerutti to make Olympic victory unforgettable by establishing a world record.

Elliott's eminence was well-established before Rome. At the Commonwealth (formerly British Empire) Games in Cardiff, Wales, in 1958, he had won the half-mile (880 yards) and the mile, and in the same year had established world records for the 1,500m, with 3:36.0, and for the mile with 3:54.5. He arrived at the Rome final unbeaten at either 1,500m or a mile and his victory now would extend that sequence to 44 races. There was

never much doubt, among rivals or the public, that he would win, only about how he would do so. The manner of the achievement took the breath away.

Those who came to the line included three who, in different circumstances, might have earned acclaim: Michel Jazy of France, István Rószavölgyi of Hungary and Dan Waern of Sweden. Instead, they were to be lost beyond the fringe of Elliott's shadow. At the start, Elliott remained near the back and it was not until they were two-thirds of the way through the blue-riband event that he made his move to the front, overtaking Michel Bernard of France. There was agreement that if he was on schedule for a world record he would receive a signal from Cerutti in the stands – though coaching during an event is forbidden. As Elliott took the lead, still unsure at this stage whether any of the others remained within range, Cerutti,

All-time great. Herb Elliott (AUS) en route to his shattering world record for the 1,500m – and youthful premature retirement. (© IOC)

Barefoot Abebe Bikila of Ethiopia heralds the African breakthrough when winning the Rome marathon. Another African, Rhadi ben Abdesselem of Morocco, was second. (© IOC)

though being restrained by officials from encroaching close to the track, waved a white towel. From this moment, Elliott was in a world of his own, running as though alone on the sand dunes, not in front of a 90,000 audience spellbound in expectation. Here was a stunning demonstration of mind over matter. He ran the last lap in a blistering 55 seconds, winning by a daunting 20 metres and taking four-tenths of a second off his previous world record for a time of 3:35.6. Never had there been such a margin. Jazy and Rószavölgyi, collecting compensation medals in his wake, conceded that they had been outclassed. Waern was fourth, more than four seconds adrift. Elliott was the first Australian to take the title since Edwin Flack in the inaugural Games and his time was almost a minute faster. Elliott had once said that he never studied his opponents; on this day it was almost as though he did not know they were there. His decision to retire at his moment of glory, unbeaten at the age of only 22, was an act of public relations without parallel.

The Italians imaginatively scorned the use of their new Olympic arena for the marathon, beginning and ending the race for the first time away from the main stadium: the 69 starters commencing amid chaotic crowd scenes beneath Capitol Hill and finishing in the cool of the evening moonlight along the Appian Way. The organisers were doubly rewarded for their originality with a world best performance, achieved by the first Olympic champion from Ethiopia, Abebe Bikila, herald of an imminent revolution by runners from Africa. The barefooted Bikila was a member of the Imperial Guard of Emperor Haile Selassie, his father had fought against the invading troops of Mussolini in 1935. To add to the novelty of Bikila's emergence, it was only his third race over the distance and his first outside his own country. Before the race was half over, two runners had pulled clear, Bikila being joined by Rhadi ben Abdesselem of Morocco. On and on they ran along the route illuminated by

flares before a crowd of tens of thousands. A mile from the finish, at the Arch of Constantine, Bikila inexorably moved into the lead to win by over 25 seconds in 2:15:16.2, with Barry Magee of New Zealand, a protégé of the renowned coach Arthur Lydiard, taking the bronze medal behind ben Abdesselem. Bikila was the first of a line of distinguished Ethiopian athletes whose statues would be erected at the national stadium.

Magee was in good company and not just in the marathon. There were two other distinguished students of Lydiard, whose influence on the development of training practices was to spread worldwide over the next decade. Competing in the 800m and 5,000m respectively were Peter Snell and Murray Halberg. For a nation of less than three million to produce three such men in one Games was indeed a distinction. For Halberg, his victory in Rome was the climax of a battle against misfortune. For ten years, he had struggled to overcome a serious rugby injury incurred at the age of 17. Blood clotting from a damaged shoulder had even threatened his life and ultimately left him with a withered left arm. In order to recover his fitness, he had turned to running, and by 1958 had become sufficiently established to win the three-mile title at the Commonwealth Games. He had developed his basic speed to a degree that enabled him to break four minutes for the mile the same year but under Lydiard had also gained the stamina essential for the 5,000m.

The early stages of the race in Rome were led by Kazimierz Zimny of Poland, intense daytime heat sapping the strength of most of the contenders. Such was Halberg's preparation that he was unworried and initially content to be at the back of the field. After 2km he had moved up to fifth, carefully watching the leading moves between Zimny and two East Germans, Hans Grodotzki and Friedrich Jahncke. The tactic planned with Lydiard was for Halberg to strike earlier than is normal for potential winners in the twelve-and-a-half-lap race. He made his move with just over three laps remaining, opening a gap of ten metres, doubled over the next lap with a further surge of 61 seconds. In the final lap it seemed as if he might have over-reached himself as Grodotzki cut back the lead. Alerted by the roar of the crowd to the danger behind him, Halberg clung on, eyes almost closed with the effort when at the point of exhaustion. He reached the tape with four strides to spare before collapsing on the infield. His last lap of 73 had been the slowest in the race but he had done what mattered. Grodotzki took second and Zimny third. Halberg was the first New Zealand track winner since Lovelock in 1936.

The triumph of Peter Snell, Halberg's young compatriot aged 22 – the same age as Elliott – had taken place half an hour earlier. Snell arrived as an unknown, though notice should have been taken of the fact that he had defeated Elliott over this shorter distance. The favourites, however, were Roger Moens of Belgium, the world record holder but by now 30, and the hugely talented George Kerr of Jamaica. The 800m is one of the more difficult events for which to train, requiring as it does the combination of a sprinter's anaeorobic speed and oxygen-fuelled aerobic stamina. Lydiard was a believer in sheer strength, as exemplified by Snell. The draw for the final, from the inside, was Matuschewski (GDR), Moens, Wägli (SUI), Kerr, Schmidt (FRG), and Snell on the outside. For the first time since the Games began, there was no American in an 800m final. Wägli presumptuously took the lead, going through the first lap in 52.3, but predictably faded after the third bend, Moens taking up the pace followed by the fluid Kerr. Entering the final straight, Moens remained in the lead, seemingly about to achieve the climax of a notable career. Glancing to his right to guage the proximity of Kerr, he was fatally caught off guard as the bludgeoning Snell came through on the kerb to inch his way into the lead. An agonised Moens, glancing left, had nothing left with which to respond and Snell was the winner, lowering Courtney's four-year-old Olympic record by more than a second with 1:46.3. Kerr took the bronze. Snell had run the perfect race, totally expended, his face blurred with pain as he crossed the line. 'Who won?' he asked Moens. 'You did,' said a dejected Moens.

For the first time since 1928, the United States failed to win either of the men's two short sprints and in the relay were disqualified in the final for a faulty change. Although earlier that summer both Armin Hary of West Germany and Harry Jerome of Canada had become the first men to record 10.0, the favourite among many for the 100m was Ray Norton, the American who had gained the sprint double at the previous year's Pan-Am Games. Also fancied was American Dave Sime. In the second round in Rome, Hary set an Olympic record of 10.2, beating Sime in the process. Peter Radford of Britain, who had suffered childhood illness, won the first semi-final, Jerome failing to finish; Hary beating Sime and Norton in the other. There were three false starts in the final, one of them by Hary, who had a controversial reputation for rising late into the 'set' position and moving almost instantly into his start in anticipation of the gun, prior to the introduction of the electronic false start mechanism. This time he managed a near-legitimate flyer, led after two strides and, although Sime came back strongly in the last quarter, Hary sustained his lead to become the first 100m champion from a non-English-speaking country, again recording 10.2, the same time as Sime. Radford took the bronze.

Successful white sprinters were becoming increasingly rare, yet Radford had set a 200m world record of 20.5 early that summer, a time matched by Stonewall Johnson and Norton in the US trials. Appalling seeding in the semi-finals found the three record holders and home favourite Livio Berruti thrown together. Radford was the one who failed to qualify and Berruti, running in his hallmark dark glasses, took the gold, equalling the world record ahead of Lester Carney (USA). Berruti was the first sprinter from outside North America to have won this event.

Another young man to defy handicap and achieve Olympic success was Rafer Johnson, from Kingsburg, California. In a childhood accident Johnson's leg had been crushed and lacerated when caught in a conveyor belt. He was lucky in fact not to lose it and for a year afterwards he walked on crutches. Though he set a decathlon Olympic record of 8,392 points, he still found it difficult to walk in spiked shoes. The spice of the competition was that locked together throughout were he and Chuan-Kwang Yang, a member of the aboriginal Takasago people of Taiwan. The two were colleagues and trained together at the University College of Los Angeles but in Rome they were rivals representing their separate nations. Yang, second, was Taiwan's first Olympic medal winner.

There were ten women's events in track and field and the USSR won six of them, yet the undoubted heroine was a young African-American whose status as Olympic champion astonishingly defied the circumstances of her childhood. Wilma Rudolph from Tennessee had been the prematurely born 20th child of her father's 22, had suffered pneumonia, polio and scarlet fever, the legacy of which was the brace she wore on her left leg until she was 11. However, massage of the leg by her mother and siblings helped restore her to normal health and after further gradual physical development from playing basketball, by the age of 16 she had become an accomplished sprinter and qualified for the US team in Melbourne, where she earned a bronze medal in the relay. By 1960 she was the favourite for the 100m and few have so emphatically lived up to expectations. In the semi-final, she equalled Shirley de la Hunty's world record of 11.3 and in the final was out on her own, way ahead of Dorothy Hyman of Britain, in a wind-assisted 11.0. In the 200m she set an Olympic record of 23.2 in the heats, three-tenths outside her own world record, and took the final with ease ahead of Jutta Heine of Germany.

The 800m was reintroduced after 28 years and once more provoked misguided doubts about women's capacity for this longer event, a number of them finishing in visible distress and Dixie Willis of Australia collapsing 150 metres from the finish when leading the final. Clearly, however, the problem lay with training rather than ability. Ludmila Shevtsova from the USSR equalled her own world record of 2:04.3 with a late burst past Brenda Jones of Australia.

Iolanda Balas of Romania, who had finished fifth in Melbourne, was to establish an exceptional dominance of the high jump over a decade, becoming the first to clear six feet and 14 times improving the world record. Her leap of 1.91m (6 ft 3¼ in.) remained unbeaten for ten years and in Rome she was no less than 14 centimetres ahead of Jaroslawa Józwiakowska of Poland with an Olympic record of 1.85m (6 ft ¾ in.).

American swimmers, having slumped in Melbourne with *only* five gold medals, revived themselves in Rome, where they won eleven and broke five world records. This time it was the Australians who experienced setbacks . . . but not in the men's 100m freestyle. The final of this was without two of the favourites: Jeff Farrell (USA), who had been unable to qualify because of appendicitis, and Jon Hendricks (AUS), unwell in the semi-final. The race produced one of the most contested outcomes of all time. Of the six judges concerned with first and second place, three claimed that John Devitt of Australia had won, the other three that Lance Larson of America had won. Larson thought he had won, and indeed Devitt congratulated him, Larson's late burst appearing to carry him past Devitt in the last few metres. Moreover, unofficial electronic timing showed Larson the winner by six-hundredths of a second, only for the chief judge to overrule all evidence and opinions and make Devitt the winner. Hand timing gave both the Olympic record atmosphere with their lighted newspapers under the huge dome, with six Italians competing in the finals for ten of the gold medals. When Franco de Piccoli, a powerful southpaw heavyweight, took less than two minutes to knock out Andrei Abramov, the Soviet European champion, the stadium was in danger of being set alight. For those looking for class, it was provided by Clay, later to adopt the Muslim faith and the name Muhammad Ali. Though only 18, he was already professional in

The 18-year-old Cassius Clay (USA) threw his light-heavyweight gold medal into the Ohio River when mugged by a white gang on his return home. He had defeated Zbigniew Pietrzykowski (POL), right, Anthony Madigan (AUS) and Giulio Saraudi (ITA) gaining bronze medals. (© Getty Images)

John Devitt (AUS) was controversially judged to have fractionally defeated Lance Larson (USA), the more probable winner of the 100m freestyle. Manuel dos Santos (BRA) took bronze. (© IOC)

of 55.2 (Devitt being world record holder on 54.6). American protests, at the time and subsequently, proved in vain.

The outstanding swimmer of the competition was Christine von Saltza of America, a descendant of Prussian/Swedish nobility, aged 16, who won three gold medals, two of them relays, and a silver. In the latter, the 100m freestyle, she could do nothing to prevent Dawn Fraser of Australia becoming the first woman to defend an Olympic swimming title, in an Olympic record of 1:01.2. Fraser was undefeated at this distance since the previous Games. She duly celebrated, supposing she was free the following day, when in fact she was scheduled for a medley relay heat. A row with the team management erupted and the fiery Fraser found herself ostracised by the rest of the team; they lost the final to the USA. Ingrid Krämer, of Germany, 17, won both springboard and platform diving events: the first non-American to take the springboard title since it was first included in 1920 and the first in the platform since the same year.

For many famous performers, the Olympic Games have provided a vault into the professional world. Cassius Clay arrived in Rome for the light-heavyweight boxing tournament as though he were an established old hand. He took to Village life as a duck to water, the most gregarious sportsman there has ever been, willing to talk to one and all about anything they wished but more especially about his own impending victory. So captivating was his self-promotion that people tended to tolerate, indeed admire, his many extravagances, though not all of white America. Boxing took place in the elegant Palazzo dello Sport and Italian spectators, wise in the fight game, added to the

skill and style. Against Zbigniew Pietrzykowski of Poland, three-times European champion, Clay boxed two calculated defensive rounds, accelerating at the end of the second with a flow of hooks to the head, then in the third unleashing a string of counter-punches from which Pietrzykowski only just managed to stay on his feet. On return home to Louisville, Kentucky, Clay discovered that, despite becoming Olympic champion, little had changed. Threatened by a white gang in a café, the man who was to earn more than $60 million survived an unscheduled bloody fight, but in disgust and dismay threw his gold medal into the Ohio river. Four years later he would defeat Sonny Liston to gain the title he had promised. Clement Quartey of Ghana became the first black African to win an Olympic boxing medal when beaten in the light-welterweight final by Bohumil Nemecek of Czechoslovakia.

It was rare throughout the first half of the twentieth century for yachting to make Olympic news, but in the historic setting of the Bay of Naples, Paul Elvstrøm of Denmark, by winning the Finn class, gained his fourth successive gold medal in consecutive Games, following Finn victories at Helsinki and Melbourne and Firefly in 1948. Crown Prince Constantine of Greece, grandson of the co-founder, who was to become King Constantine II, was at the helm of *Nirefs* when winning the Dragon class: the first medal for Greece since the standing long jump victory of Constantin Tsiklitiras in 1912. Peter Lunde of Norway contributed to an unusual Olympic record when winning the Flying Dutchman event. His father, also Peter, had

Boris Shakhlin (URS), Ukrainian multiple gymnastics medal winner with four gold, two silver and a bronze. (© IOC)

Italian brothers Raimondeo and Piero d'Inzeo uniquely take gold and silver in equestrian showjumping. (© IOC)

won a silver medal in 5.5m in 1952 and his grandfather, Eugene, a gold in 6m in 1924: the only father, son and grandson to have won Olympic medals. America had dominated rowing eights since 1920 but now trailed home fifth behind Germany, Canada, Czechoslovakia and France. The events were viewed from a distance by the Pope from his summer home at Castel Gandolfo, overlooking the course on Lake Albano.

Cycling was the scene of tragedy when Knud Enemark Jensen of Denmark collapsed during the 100km road race and died on the way to hospital. Here was evidence of the encroaching threat to sporting morality from drugs, as the post-mortem revealed Jensen to be heavily positive, though nobody knows whether the dose of Ronicol was voluntarily consumed or administered by a third party, perhaps a coach. In the light of this event the international cycling federation became the first to introduce drug testing.

India suffered their first loss in field hockey since they entered the competition in 1928, defeated by Pakistan in a tense and occasionally bad-tempered final by the only goal. Behind them lay 30 victories and no defeats, with an aggregate score of 197–8. Pakistan's winning goal came from Naseer Ahmad in the 12th minute.

Aladár Gerevich of Hungary won his sixth successive gold medal at the age of 50 in the sabre team fencing event. He had already won team gold medals in 1932, 1936, 1948, 1952 and 1956. Additionally, one of the finest swordsmen in the history of the sport, he had won sabre gold in 1948, silver in 1952 and bronze in 1936, plus a bronze in team foil in 1952, for a total of ten medals.

In a brilliantly conceived and conducted Games, with 83 nations present, qualifying standards in some sports had risen so steeply that some champions of 1956 had been unable to attend in order to defend their titles.

CHAPTER XXXVIII

Anti-Apartheid Flame

Sam Ramsamy of South Africa, anti-apartheid campaigner, IOC Executive Board member

'*South Africans first competed in the Olympic Games in 1904 – unofficially – a team of Boers entering the tug-of-war and two Zulus running in the marathon. In 1908, an official team included only white members. Ultimately, anti-apartheid protests forced South Africa's exclusion from 1964, thereafter black South Africans thwarting attempts by the government to re-enter via by the back door.*

In 1988, President Samaranch created the Apartheid and Olympic Commission [see Chapter LIX], setting in motion South Africa's return. In March 1992, a visit to the then president of the African National Congress, Nelson Mandela, who was recuperating in the Kruger National Park after years of imprisonment, provided the final endorsement for participation in Barcelona, Mandela stating it would accelerate the demise of apartheid.

The months approaching the Games were fraught with difficulties – no anthem, no flag, another massacre – but eventually a team of 95 athletes representing 17 sports took part, South Africa returning home with two silver medals. We had to overcome the opposition from some quarters that participation was inappropriate before the democratic elections of 1994. However, the urge to be there prevailed, as this was the first event to signal the end of South Africa's isolation. Re-acceptance into the Olympic fold opened the door for participation in non-Olympic sports such as cricket and rugby.

There was an agreement between President Samaranch and Nelson Mandela that South Africa would be allowed to include its development squad at Barcelona as observers and to march in the opening ceremony. The welcome roar as we entered was extraordinary. Mandela was occupying one of the Heads of State seats – another first for the world, long before he became Head of State. He spent three days with us and his visit to our accommodation at the Olympic Village was something precious and memorable, a great crowd converging to see him.'*

(Photograph © IOC/Imsand)

At the Session prior to the Rome Games, Avery Brundage was re-elected by acclamation to another four-year term as IOC President. Armand Massard of France and Lord Burghley of Britain continued as first and second Vice-Presidents. Brundage remained king of the castle but he and his colleagues soon had to confront the most challenging problem of his 20 years in the hot-seat: the apartheid regime of South Africa.

The first African to formally compete in the Games had been Ali Mohamed Hassanein of Egypt, a fencer at Stockholm in 1912. The first African to win a gold medal had been Mohamed El Ouafi, marathon winner in 1928 when representing France. North-of-Sahara nations had long been involved in many sports: indeed Angelo Bolanaki, a Greek IOC member resident in Egypt, had attempted to organise IOC-sponsored regional games in Alexandria in 1927. The bid failed and the first All-Africa games, sponsored by the French – Les Jeux de l'Amitié – took place in Madagascar in 1960, followed by games at Abidjan, Ivory Coast (1961), and Dakar, Senegal (1963), attended by Brundage and Comte Jean de Beaumont of France. Shortly afterwards, Brundage nominated Sir Adetokunbo Ademola, a noted Nigerian lawyer, to become the first African member of the IOC.

The South African dilemma should not have come as a surprise, however. In 1950, the Norwegians had warned that they were prepared to exclude all-white South Africa from the 1952 Winter Games in Oslo. There had also been the Soviet protest at the Session of 1959 in Munich, Reginald Honey deceitfully responding by saying that all South African competitors were guaranteed a passport: all white competitors, that was. Since then the IOC had been pussy-footing around the issue, the Executive Board having stated in 1960: 'The South African Olympic Association has made every reasonable effort to implement the undertaking given in 1959, to ensure that no competitor of requisite calibre was excluded from the South African team.' Really?

By 1962, African militancy was being headed by Chief Abraham Ordia of Nigeria, representing the newly formed South African Non-Racial Olympic Committee (SANROC), based in London under the leadership of a well-known academic and poet, Dennis Brutus, and an emigrant teacher and swimming coach from Natal, Sam Ramsamy. SANROC had no serious connection with sport, being a wholly political arm of black African protest, funded by Czechoslovakia and other Communist sources. Within days of its formation, it applied to the IOC for recognition, stating it would withdraw if the recognised South African NOC were to amend its racial policy.

Sir Adetokunbo Ademola, Nigerian lawyer, became the first black African member of the IOC amid anti-apartheid struggles. (© IOC)

Dr Arthur, later Lord, Porritt of New Zealand became chairman of the inaugural Medical Commission, formed in 1961, following the drug-related death at Rome of Knud Jensen, Danish cyclist. (© IOC)

This latter demand was, however, impossible, since the apartheid regime was government-initiated.

The IOC Session of 1963 was scheduled for Nairobi but had to be switched to Baden-Baden when the Kenyan government refused to allow South African delegates into the country. Kenya's action was in line with the policy adopted at an Addis Ababa conference of black African states. In Baden-Baden, Frank Braun of the South African NOC told the Session that apartheid was not something that should be the concern of the IOC and that non-whites could indeed train together with whites, could compete outside South Africa and that all who were qualified would be selected. Unimpressed, the Session demanded confirmation from the NOC of its support for IOC regulations and for it to ensure that by the end of the year the Pretoria government had changed its stance – otherwise South Africa would be barred from both Games in 1964.

Early that year the NOC informed the IOC: 'The resolution taken at Baden-Baden was communicated to our government, which has declined to consider a change in policy of the nature contemplated in the resolution.' This left the Executive Board with no option. While it was accepted that the NOC was 'willing to include non-white athletes in its Olympic team' it had not, as required, disassociated itself from its government's racial policy, and so it was given a further ultimatum: a deadline of 16 August to meet the IOC's demands or to be barred from the Tokyo Games. The Executive Board's decision was communicated to the Session prior to the Winter Games in Innsbruck, Ryotaro Azuma instructing that no invitation be sent to South Africa. In June, the IOC was again advised by the NOC that non-white athletes would be allowed to join the Tokyo team, but, with the ultimatum otherwise ignored, South Africa inevitably would be absentees.

The other shadow looming ever larger over the Games was the spectre of performance-enhancing drugs. Throughout history man and woman have resorted to medicine, to herbs and chemicals that might enhance mental and physical performance in war, love and more latterly sport. Small quantities of arsenic were a known stimulant, as was, for example, opium.

The relevance of stimulants in sport had become dramatically apparent for the first time with the death of Knud Jensen, the Danish cyclist in the 100km cycling final of the Rome Olympics. In the light of Jensen's death, the Session at Athens in 1961 reviewed the problem of doping and the application of penalties in cases of breaches of the rules. Brundage reported on a discussion with representatives of the international federation of sports medicine (FIMS), considering it important to collaborate with this body. The IOC therefore created a Medical Commission, with Dr Porritt of New Zealand in the chair. Others on the Commission were Ryotaro Azuma of Japan, Joaquim Ferreira Santos of Brazil, Josef Gruss of Czechoslovakia and Augustin Sosa of Panama. The Commission was recommended to collaborate with Professor La Cava of Italy, a prominent member of the FIMS.

Evidence of drug abuse was already widespread. In 1962, Austria was the first state to legislate against doping, instituting severe penalties for competitors and their clubs. This trend was followed in Belgium, France and Italy. In 1963, a Council of Europe Commission, attempting to establish international agreement on effective action, formulated a definition of doping.

At the 1964 Session in Tokyo, Bo Ekelund of Sweden recommended the introduction of blood tests for the detection of offenders. Porritt responded that the Medical Commission believed it was premature to consider blood testing as an effective solution. He proposed that the Session adopt the following three steps: a formal declaration condemning the use of drugs; provision for sanctions against NOCs or individuals directly or indirectly promoting the use of drugs; a request to NOCs that athletes should be prepared to submit to testing at any time; and the following addition to individual application forms: 'I do not use drugs, and hereby declare that I am prepared to submit to any examination that may be thought necessary.' The text did not meet with general approval and the Executive Board was delegated to produce a more precise version that would be appended to the eligibility rules.

Alongside concern about drugs was the question of

biologically ineligible women competitors. Coincidentally or otherwise, the Tokyo Games would see the final appearance of the abnormally muscular throwing-event Soviet sisters, Tamara and Irina Press, the latter a pentathlon winner, and the towering Romanian high-jumper, Iolanda Balas, all of whom won gold medals and immediately retired. Ewa Klobukowska of Poland, bronze winner in the 100m, became the first woman to fail a sex test the following year. In 1968, however demeaning for normal women, gender verification was introduced.

Patronage of regional games was a principle approved by the IOC, especially Brundage. In 1954, under the initiative of Indian Prime Minister Nehru, the first Asian Games had been celebrated in Manila. These games would be without political incident until the hosting of the event in Jakarta, Indonesia, in 1962, where the government denied visas to Israel and Taiwan, the Indonesian NOC failing to protest. G.D. Sondhi, IOC member from India, persuaded the Executive Board to declare that these Games were not IOC-sponsored Asian Games but should be known as the 'Jakarta Games'. This provoked local fury, a mob attacking the Indian Embassy in Jakarta and the hotel where Sondhi was staying. In consequence, the IOC suspended the Indonesian NOC in February 1963. This rebuke in turn provoked President Sukarno, Indonesia's dictator, to create that autumn what he grandly called 'The Games of the New Emerging Forces' (GANEFO). Sukarno was reflecting the mood of the Bandung Conference of 1955, a Third World gathering designed for unification against alleged 'imperialist aggressors' – which of course included the IOC. Backing for Sukarno came from Beijing, the People's Republic of China being glad to embarrass the IOC, with additional support coming from Cambodia, Iraq, Mali, North Korea, North Vietnam, Pakistan, the United Arab Republic (Egypt/Syria) and the Soviet Union.

At this time the People's Republic was a member of neither the IAAF nor FINA (swimming) and these federations warned their member countries not to compete in GANEFO under pain of suspension from the Tokyo Games. The IOC agreed a compromise: participating nations at GANEFO could send to Tokyo athletes who had not competed at Jakarta. Indonesia and North Korea both chose to ignore this, sending teams that included barred competitors. When they were refused admission by the Japanese organisers, both withdrew their entire teams. North Korea returned home even though only six of their 180-strong team were barred. The expulsion of the Indonesian NOC had been revoked when it had declared it was ready to abide by the rules. By a narrow squeak the Tokyo Games had escaped a major embarrassment.

Early in 1960, a major earthquake in Chile had resulted in a heavy death toll. As a gesture of solidarity, the French NOC had sponsored the journey of three Chilean competitors to the Rome Games, while CONI had offered to finance the accommodation of the entire team. These spontaneous actions inspired Comte de Beaumont to propose, at the Session in Athens the following year, a formal means of financial assistance for any affiliated country (no one was better positioned: the IOC's entire resources rested in de Beaumont's personal bank, a situation of serious conflict). The idea was met with caution, as it was considered that the IOC's resources were insufficient to implement such a proposal. At the next Session in Moscow, de Beaumont announced that an examining commission had decided to call itself the International Olympic Aid Committee. Another year on, and he was reporting activity to the Executive Board, where there was divided opinion. The suggestion that cities bidding to host the Games be approached with requests for donations was irately opposed by Vice-President Massard.

Brundage, too, took the view that the aid committee should concentrate on educational rather than financial assistance and for the time being the committee was obliged to drop the word 'Olympic' from its name and headed notepaper. It would be another nine years before de Beaumont's initiative would become properly established.

For all Brundage's immense energy, the workload was becoming ever greater. Some of the weight was carried by the Chancellor, Otto Mayer, owner of a Lausanne jewellers, whose brother Albert was a Swiss IOC member. Mayer was aided by Lydia Zanchi, a part-time secretary, but the numerous controversies were proving too much for him and he felt compelled to resign in 1964, admitting: 'The whole concept of amateurism has changed so completely during the 18 years I have been chancellor that there must be some changes made in Olympic ideas of what constitutes an amateur today.'

Otto Mayer, IOC Chancellor, resigned because of amateur eligibility confusion. (© IOC)

The 1964 Session in Tokyo confirmed the appointment of Eric Jonas, a Swiss, as Secretary-General, the title of Chancellor being abolished, with Marc Hodler – president of international skiing and IOC member – becoming Honorary Treasurer. However, the new Secretary-General never gained Brundage's confidence and was succeeded within a year by Johann Westerhoff, a retired Dutch general. Westerhoff realised the impossibility of running the IOC with two part-time employees and considered a staff of at least ten was necessary. This would require a move to larger premises than the Villa Mon Repos, which had been made available by the city of Lausanne since 1922, serving as both IOC headquarters and, formerly, residence for de Coubertin and his wife. The city made possible a move to the present Chateau de Vidy.

Imperceptibly, the IOC was becoming less a club, more a business. It would have seemed strange to that pillar of the former, J. Sigfrid Edström, who died in March, 1964. Though hardly a multinational in financial terms, the IOC's assets had by now tolerably increased to nearly half a million Swiss francs, thanks to a half share in the television rights fees for Tokyo and Innsbruck, the respective other halves going to the international federations represented at the Summer and Winter Games. Tokyo, incidentally, also witnessed a breakthrough for colour television, if of limited broadcast.

Avery Brundage attracted media attention by design it seemed. Prior to the Innsbruck Games, he questioned whether the Winter event should be allowed to continue. His justification was obsessive concern with the regulations on amateurism and his conviction that they must be applied as stipulated in the Charter. Ironically, there would have been no Games in the Austrian capital of the Tyrol but for 3,000 soldiers of the Austrian Army, who were required to deliver, by road, train, helicopter and their own backs, some 40,000 cubic metres of snow from the Brenner Pass and other slopes, in order that competition still might take place on the Alpine and Nordic runs. Artificial snow-making machines were imported from the United States as workers laboured around the clock to preserve the thawing bob and luge runs. The cause of the problem was the Föhn, a seasonal warm, dry wind from the south.

The success of the first big-city Winter Games was imperative to Innsbruck, which had invested $30 million in the promotion of its sports facilities and those at satellite centres such as Igls, Seefeld and Axamer Lizum, the latter 15 kilometres from Innsbruck where a new ski area was created to accommodate the Alpine events, Nordic races being held at Seefeld. A new skating stadium was constructed in the city, where a 50-foot screen was erected to obscure the only remaining bomb-damaged building. The decentralisation of the Games led to criticism. The distant sub-centres and an out-of-town Village meant that competitors seldom had time to visit the host city, where only skating and hockey were staged. Yet with massive worldwide publicity from 34 television networks and more than a thousand radio and newspaper outlets, excluding agencies, the organisers would not be left dissatisfied. Austria was already the second biggest manufacturer of ski equipment behind West Germany and the largest exporter, so with a clean sweep of Alpine events by Toni Sailer, the local hero, PR promotion was immense.

In statistics alone they would be the most successful Winter Games yet, with more than half a million spectators attending a record number of 34 events. For the first time the ski jump competition was divided into 70m and 90m events. Mongolia and India competed in the Games for the first time. With investment of more than two million dollars, IBM were again present, following their invaluable contribution at Squaw Valley. At Cortina in 1956, figure skating results had taken hours to compile: now it was done in seconds.

At the Session prior to the Games, the NOCs of Algeria, Congo, Nigeria and Sierra Leone were recognised, bringing to 114 the number of nations within the IOC, while Grenoble was elected in preference to Banff, Canada, as host for the Winter Games of 1968.

There is a natural tendency to proclaim each successive Games the best yet. This had indeed been true in a way of Melbourne for its friendship and of Rome for its style, and for everyone who was there, not least Brundage, it was true of Tokyo in 1964. These were the first Games granted to Asia. The Japanese expediently viewed the occasion as an opportunity to gain attention for the industrial post-war miracle they were busy creating, especially in the electronics field. More than this, the Tokyo Games were also a triumph of administrative efficiency and open hospitality.

The earliest interest by Tokyo as hosts was back in 1931, when

an invitation was extended for the IOC to visit the city. In 1936, when London withdrew from consideration for 1940, Tokyo was preferred to Helsinki by a vote of 36–27. However, by the next year Japan and China were at war and Tokyo withdrew. A further bid was made in the early 1950s but it was not until the Session of 1958 that Tokyo lodged its formal bid for 1964, being elected the following year in preference to Brussels, Vienna and Detroit.

In Tokyo harbour, there were passenger liners accommodating 1,600 spectators. In a city already known for its congestion, the organising committee employed 21,000 cars and 6,000 buses. These were merely logistical records in a Games that had 93 nations, 10 more than the record in Rome, and 163 events as against 150. With the liberation of Africa, 14 countries made their first appearance. Germany began the Games as one team and ended as two, East and West, the IOC having agreed in the interim to recognise both for future Games. Northern Rhodesia began the Games under their traditional flag, but by the closing ceremony, having now acquired the independent name of Zambia, paraded under a new flag.

Daigoro Yasukawa, president of the organising committee, with Avery Brundage at Tokyo's opening ceremony. (© IOC)

At the Session prior to the Games, Avery Brundage was re-elected a second time for a further four-year term, Lord Burghley (who would become Marquis of Exeter), his only rival, withdrawing during the course of voting. At 77, Brundage was already seen as being representative of an organisation out of touch with contemporary life. The IOC had managed without television for 60 years, he had stated, and could do for another 60 years. Yet his commitment remained undiluted. 'The Olympic Movement is a twentieth-century religion, a religion with universal appeal which incorporates all the basic values of other religions,' he had stated at the Session. 'Christians, Muslims, Hindus, Buddhists and atheists all respect its basic principles of common honesty, mutual regard, fair play and good sportsmanship, which are the essence of all religion.'

CHAPTER XXXIX

Innsbruck (IX) 1964

Eugenio Monti of Italy, double Olympic bobsleigh champion

'The most exciting Games for me would be 1968. Finally, I won an Olympic title! In 1956, at Cortina, I had taken the silver medal, in both two-man and four-man events. The winner there of the two-man was Lamberto [Dalla Costa], who never raced anywhere else and knew the course so well. The driver of the winning four-man team was Franz Kapus of Switzerland, who was to give me such a lot of help. He quit after 1956 and went to work in St Moritz. In 1960 at Squaw Valley there were no events, because the Americans wouldn't build a run.

For the Games at Innsbruck, I was physically at a low ebb. I'd been busy building a ski lift at Cortina and was almost too tired to compete in the Games. Quite a lot of fuss has been made about the fact that in the two-man event I provided Tony Nash and Robin Dixon of Britain with a bolt from my sled, which enabled them to repair theirs and win the event, while I came third together with Sergio Siorpaes. As far as I was concerned, Tony and Robin would have done the same for me.

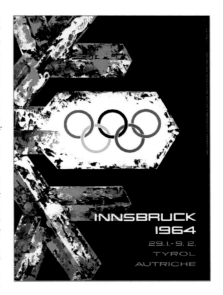

Four years later, it was a desperately close thing in the two-man. After four runs we had exactly the same time as Horst Floth and 'Peppi' Bader in Germany I. It was thought that both teams would be awarded a gold medal but under the rules first place goes to the team with the fastest single run – and that was us. It had been a very difficult two days because on the first day we were racing in the evening, waiting for the run to freeze, and on the second day we then had to start at 4 a.m., before it melted again. It was difficult to get any sleep. At the World Championships the previous year, Sergio, my brake-man, broke his arm in the two-man and missed the Games. Luciano De Paolis, who was very strong, took his place, though there was no expectation that we would win. In the four-man, because of the thaw, the race was confined to two runs and we just beat the Austrians.

I only began racing in 1954 at the age of 26; I hadn't been interested in bob events, skiing was my favourite and I'd won a couple of Italian championships in slalom and giant slalom. Before the Olympic Games in Oslo in 1952, I'd crashed and broken both my knees and then switched to the bob run. Fear? You can't have fear, or you don't compete! Driving is a particular skill, something that has to be done with feeling, through the seat of your pants as much as technique, just like Formula 1. Nowadays there is not much difference driving a two-man or a four-man. With the new sleds, you can go where you want. In those days, the four-man was much steadier, quieter, and you needed a day's adjustment when switching to the two-man.'*

(Olympic Poster © IOC)

Self-effacing to a degree, Eugenio Monti is a modest hero, never mind that in major championships, including the Olympics, he won eleven titles, eight at two-man and three at four-man between 1957 and 1968, with additionally three silver and two bronze medals. There would presumably have been more but for the absence of bobsleigh in 1960, yet his total of six Olympic medals, two of each hue, is nonetheless a record for his sport. It is an odd twist that in 1964, in the presence of such a supreme contender, the two bobsleigh titles should, for the first time, go to countries which did not possess bob runs.

Monti's gesture to the British pair for the final run of the two-man event was typical of the man. Tony Nash and Robin Dixon sped down the run to push Sergio Zardini and Romano Bonagura, the second Italian pair, into silver medal position by twelve-hundredths of a second, with Monti and Siorpaes squeezed into third. For his sportsmanship, Monti was awarded the Pierre de Coubertin Fairplay Trophy. In the four-man run, Monti and his colleagues were well-beaten into third place behind Austria by a quartet of bachelors from Montreal on the first occasion Canada had entered.

Luge, that form of tobogganing in which the competitor lies backwards, heading feet-first down the mountain – as opposed to head-first in the Cresta Run – made its debut at Innsbruck, though considered by many to be too dangerous. Sadly and swiftly this view was given substance when, on a trial run, the Polish-born British racer, Kazimierz Skrzypesci flew out of the main bend, hit and injured two policemen, crashed into a tree and died in hospital. Josef Fleishmann and Josef Lenz of Germany were later severely injured in the pairs. The incidents resulted in over-hanging lips being constructed at each bend.

Eugenio Monti of Italy, king of the bobsleigh, won two silver in 1956, two bronze in these Games and two gold in 1968. Here with Sergio Siorpaes on the way to two-man bronze. (© IOC)

Lydia Skoblikova of the Soviet Union had won all four distances at the speed skating World Championships of 1963 at Karuizawa, Japan. There was scheduled to be a showdown at Innsbruck with her compatriot Inga Voronina, who had dominated the World Championships in 1962, but Voronina, still recovering from serious illness, was an absentee, allowing Skoblikova to become the first person to win four gold medals in a single Winter Games. Irina Yegorova topped the leader board with 45.4 for the 500m until overhauled by Skoblikova in an Olympic record of 45.0. Skoblikova proceeded to set an Olympic record at 1,000m and 1,500m, and to win the 3,000m by a margin of two and a half seconds: thus becoming also the first to win six gold medals in total.

All-powerful speed skater Lydia Skoblikova (URS) becomes the first to win four gold medals in a single Winter Games: 500m, 1,000m, 1,500m and 3,000m. (© IOC)

There was never much doubt that the powerful Sjoukje Dijkstra of Holland, already twice world champion, would take the figure skating title. She did so with masterful jumps and the decision of the nine judges was unanimous. The men's champion, Manfred Schnelldorfer, a convert from roller skating, gained the verdict over Alain Calmar of France, the latter receiving two first-place marks. Most acclaimed, from the figures rink, were probably Lyudmila Belousova and her husband, Oleg Protopopov, the mercurial pairs champions, though their victory over Marika Kilius and Hans-Jürgen Bäumler of Germany was close: the Germans received four first-place marks to their five. Two years later, the German pair were required to return their silver medals when it was claimed they had signed a professional contract prior to the Games. The medals were eventually restored to them by the IOC in 1987.

Austria's women bolstered home pride by taking all three medals in the downhill, Christl Haas being the winner more than a second ahead of Edith Zimmerman and Traudl Hecher, with Heidi Biebl, champion at Squaw Valley, in fourth place. It was less happy for the Austrians elsewhere. Christine and Marielle

More was to be heard of Austria's Karl Schranz, runner-up in Innsbruck's giant slalom. (© IOC/Ruebelt)

Goitschel, French sisters from Val d'Isère, commanded the gates. Marielle was fastest over the first run of the slalom ahead of Christine, who overtook her on the second run for respective gold and silver; and the two repeated but reversed the act two days later, Marielle winning the giant slalom nearly a second ahead of her sister with Haas a disappointed fourth. In the slalom and the giant slalom, Jean Saubert took bronze and silver respectively. The Alpine events witnessed a further death. Ross Milne, a 19-year-old Australian, was killed during practice when he hit a tree.

On the first occasion on which there were two ski jumping

events – normal hill being added to the large – two Norwegians and a Finn shared the six medals. Veikko Kankkonen of Finland won the normal hill ahead of Toralf Engan and Torgeir Brandtzäg of Norway. As there were three attempts, Kankkonen finished in front when his second and third jumps surpassed his poor first attempt. On the large hill, Engan pushed his two rivals down a peg.

Nordic events were staged at Seefeld, Soviet women in the ascendant with Klaudia Boyarskikh winning both individual events, the 5km and the now-discontinued 10km, and successfully anchoring the 3 x 5km relay. In men's events the

35-year-old Sixten Jernberg of Sweden regained the 50km title he had won in 1956 and with victory in the 4 x 10km relay was celebrating a total of nine medals at three Games, a record which would not be surpassed for 28 years.

The Soviet Union won the ice hockey with victory in all seven matches. It was a narrow squeak over Canada in the last, however, when a win for Canada would have placed them first. The Canadians did indeed lead 2–1 but their eventual defeat enabled Sweden and Czechoslovakia to claim silver and bronze. In a Winter Games dominated by the Soviet Union, for the first and only time Switzerland failed to gain a single medal.

François Bonlieu, idiosyncratic Frenchman, beat the Austrians, including Schranz, on their own piste to win the giant slalom. Nine years later he was murdered on the street in Cannes. (© IOC)

CHAPTER XL

Tokyo (XVIII) 1964

Billy Mills of America, Olympic 10,000m champion

'*Being half Lakota Sioux Indian and half white, both cultures rejected me, but I found another culture called sport. Sport accepted me on equal terms. I became a distance runner and made the US Olympic team for the Games in Tokyo. My mum died when I was seven and my dad when I was twelve. My dad taught me many things, most of all that your life is a gift from God and what you do with it is your gift back to Him – that one must have a passion in life, a spiritual focus. He introduced me to the concept of the Olympic Games and explained that in Greek mythology Olympic champions are chosen by the Gods. I remember reading about Buster Charles, a Native American who came fourth in the decathlon in 1932, following in the tradition of Jim Thorpe. I remember my dad telling me what Socrates said: that with achievement comes honour and with honour comes responsibility.*

In my freshman year at college, when I was among the top five all-American runners, and again in my final year, competing in the AAU championships, when we had our photograph taken, each time the photographer asked me, "You, the dark-skinned guy", to get out of the photo. I was weary of this discrimination and back at my college I opened the window on the eighth floor. I was broken and I was about to jump. But then I heard my dad's voice saying "Don't." And I remembered his words about visualising an Olympic victory, "Believe, believe, believe."

For 1964 I made the team for the marathon and then had to meet the Olympic qualifying time. Six days later I achieved the qualifying time for the 10km, running the six miles. This was a big breakthrough, as I had not rested between the two races. My qualifying time put me among the top eight in the world and I went to Tokyo knowing I had done this even so close to running a marathon. Now I had endurance, speed and I could visualise, repeatedly, being among the best in the world with one lap to go.

Halfway through the final of the 10km in Tokyo, however, I realised "I'm within seconds of my best time for three miles and there are still three to go!" As a result I lost my focus, I was looking for a place to quit on the in-field, where no one knew me, but then on the curve into the finishing straight at halfway I could see my wife, Patricia, sitting 30 or 40 rows back. We'd made a commitment together, I couldn't let go now.

Into the last lap I was at Clarke's shoulder, together with Gammoudi. Clarke was going to be boxed in as he started his kick. He pushed me into the third lane and I nearly stumbled. Again I could have quit, could have settled for third place. Then the visualisation over four years of this one moment in time was there in my head and as we came off the final bend I could hear the roar of the crowd, and yet strangely at the same time a silence in which my own voice was saying "I can win, I can win." Years later Ron Clarke was joking with me that in defeat he had helped to make me famous, but I told him I had been following a passion of my youth and that he was, on the day, up against insurmountable odds.'*
(Photograph © IOC)

The two long-distance events at Tokyo were notable in several ways, not just on account of the unexpected triumph of Billy Mills in the longer one. First, the races were a double defeat for the magnificent Australian world record holder of both the 10,000m and its equivalent six miles. Ron Clarke was the overwhelming favourite for the opening race on the track, the last time that this event would be run without heats. Such challenge as there was would come, it was expected, from Mohamed Gammoudi of Tunisia, Halberg of New Zealand, the defending 5km champion, or the defending 10km champion from Russia, Bolotnikov. No American had ever won the race or even come close since it was introduced in 1912. Mills, at 26, had never run the distance faster than a minute outside Clarke's record.

Thirty-eight runners set off, an entry that was far too large. The lapped runners in the final stages proved an impediment to the leaders – Clarke in particular, as it happened. After 5km, Mills, almost a stranger, was still there with the leaders, though Clarke's repetitive surges on intermittent laps had burned off all other pursuers except Gammoudi, Mamo Wolde of Ethiopia and Koichi Tsuburaya, the home favourite. These five stayed together until Wolde fell back with one kilometre remaining. Clarke's record stood at 28:15.6 and, since neither Gammoudi nor Mills had ever broken 29 minutes, the conclusion was obvious.

On the penultimate lap, incredibly, Mills moved to the front and this provoked Clarke to make his final effort at the bell.

Here the real problem started. Clarke found himself boxed in by a straggler glued to the inside lane, who refused to move out and make way in the conventional manner, and by Mills on the outside, who likewise refused to give way. Clarke gave Mills a shove but, as Mills half-staggered to the right, Gammoudi, close behind, nipped between Mills and Clarke to take a ten-metre lead. Clarke went after him amid a crescendo of noise. As the two of them entered the finishing straight, Clarke just ahead, Gammoudi gave it his last shot with victory seemingly beckoning. In the final 40 metres, however, Mills, with unimagined reserves, pounded his way past the other stragglers and the two leaders to cross the line a stride and a half in front. By what might be termed an act of God, he had run 45 seconds faster than he had ever run before, setting an Olympic record of 28:24.4.

Gammoudi, too, had improved his personal best by 47 seconds in claiming the silver medal, a second ahead of poor Clarke, disconsolately left with the bronze. A Japanese finishing judge was even reduced to asking Mills who he was. An orphan from South Dakota, he had attended the Haskell Institute for Native Americans in Kansas and in the weeks prior to the Games, while he was preparing in the Village, not a single newsman had so much as spoken to him. A year later, however, Mills was to beat Clarke's six-mile world record by six seconds and was honoured by the Sioux tribe.

Ron Clarke, multiple long-distance record-breaker, suffered a shock defeat in the 10,000m in Tokyo, and four years later was overcome (above) by the heat and altitude of Mexico City.
(© Getty Images)

There was even less joy in the 5,000m for the unfortunate Clarke, who again led for much of the race, for which he and Gammoudi were again the favourites (though the world record for this distance still belonged to Kuts). Also in the hunt, in the mind of the pundits, was Michel Jazy, on account of his speed over shorter distances: the following year he would break the mile record that was currently held by Snell. Robert Schul of America, though an outsider, had strong credentials, having set a world record for two miles two months before the Games and twice having beaten four minutes for the mile. But did he have the stamina?

Jazy took over the lead from Clarke at the 4km mark then gave way to Bill Dellinger, the other American. By now all the contenders were feeling the additional strain of the soft cinder track made muddy by earlier heavy rain. Into the final lap, the leading bunch consisted of Jazy, Harald Norpoth of Germany, Clarke, Dellinger and an up-and-coming Kenyan, Kipchoge Keino. Into the final bend, Jazy still held the lead, convinced he was the winner, yet in an instant he was overcome with fatigue, his strength evaporating. Jazy was possibly the victim of excessive domestic praise, which had produced in the runner an absence of nerve for competitive crisis. He ran now as if already awaiting the ultimate acclaim and was unable to cope with the climax. Schul's finishing kick was leading him inexorably to the front and when the troubled Jazy glanced back in anxiety it was now Schul's turn to be convinced of victory. Down the final straight Jazy was overhauled by Schul and then Norpoth and in the last metres by Dellinger, missing a bronze medal by mere hundredths of a second. 'Capitulation de Jazy' said the headline in L'Équipe. The luckless Clarke had faded to ninth.

In 1960, Peter Snell was an unknown 21 year old when he arrived in Rome and proceeded to win the 800m in record time. Returning to New Zealand, he had extended his rigorous training under Arthur Lydiard, enhancing his stamina, and in a single week in 1962 had improved the world records for the mile and 800m, the former held by Herb Elliott. By 1964 he looked a positive Charles Atlas in physique and he was the first in a line of two-lap runners to emerge during the next decade who were dependent on muscular power, culminating with Alberto Juantorena of Cuba and, less emphatically, Steve Ovett of Britain.

Snell's pulse rate was now down to 42, only a fraction above that of the legendary Nurmi, and he toyed with the idea of attempting the double in Tokyo. 'The 1,500m is the glamour race,' he had observed and his training prior to Tokyo was geared to the longer distance. No one had won the double since Albert Hill of Britain in 1920, at a time of much less severe competition.

But for his confidence in his physical form, Snell might have been unnerved by the semi-final times in the 800m. Having himself won the first in 1:46.9, only half a second outside his own Olympic record, he then watched George Kerr of Jamaica, third behind him in Rome, and Wilson Kiprugut of Kenya

Power-fanatic New Zealander Peter Snell, having improved Elliott's mile world record, achieves the 800/1,500m double, here winning the latter way ahead of Josef Odlozil (TCH) and compatriot John Davies. (© IOC)

jointly break the record with 1:46.1 in the second semi. Snell tried to convince himself that the new record holders would thereby have diminished their chances.

At the end of the first lap of the final, Snell found himself boxed behind Kiprugut and had to drop back in order to make his challenge running wide. His strength duly came to his aid as he surged down the home straight for a new record of 1:45.1, a whole second faster than the previous day's record. Kiprugut tripped on the heel of a fading Kerr 50 yards out but managed to take bronze behind Bill Crothers of Canada – Kenya's first Olympic medal in any sport.

Snell's 1,500m victory was a simpler affair, though it was his sixth race in eight days. Conveniently, his heat was the slowest, though his semi-final, which he won, was the fastest by almost three seconds in 3:38.8. In the final he experienced a moment of good fortune, or rather sportsmanship. With just over a lap remaining and lying in third place, he again found himself boxed in. Indicating with a touch that he intended to move into the second lane, he was allowed a fraction of space by John Whetton of Britain to do so and in an instant Snell was gone. So emphatic was his lead that, glancing over his shoulder on the final bend, he was able to ease off and still finish one and a half seconds ahead of Josef Odlozil of Czechoslovakia, with his compatriot John Davies taking the bronze.

For the defence of his marathon title Abebe Bikila lost his appendix and found some shoes – the former only six weeks before the race in Tokyo. Whether or not he was more comfortable than when running barefoot, it turned out to be a most one-sided affair. Contenders included Clarke, who was running his fourth race in a week and, no doubt motivated by early disappointments, took an early lead. Bikila, perhaps waiting to become accustomed to the feel of socks, did not join the leaders until after the 7km mark. More seriously, he was probably waiting to judge his fitness, having only returned to training three weeks previously.

Soon after the halfway mark, by which time Clarke and another early leader, Jim Hogan of Ireland, had faded, Bikila felt himself strong enough to forge ahead on his own, astonishingly to win with a world best time of 2:12:11.2, over four minutes ahead of Basil Heatley of Britain – the previous fastest – becoming the first successful Olympic marathon defender. Heatley gained the silver medal by overtaking Tsuburaya of Japan on the final lap of the track inside the stadium, in front of a capacity crowd. Bikila was so euphoric that it mattered not if the band could not find the score for the Ethiopian national anthem . . . and played the Japanese anthem instead. Tsuburaya had been regarded as the home country's best hope for a gold medal and though his bronze, Japan's first track and field medal for 28 years, made him a national hero, he remained consumed by a sense of failure. Immediately ordered by his army superiors to train for the next Games in Mexico, he sustained injury, was hospitalised and realised on release that his ability had gone. Shortly before the Games in Mexico he took his own life.

The extraordinary Bob Hayes from Florida, all muscle and power and little style, thunderously reasserted American supremacy in the 100m. In the semi-final, with a following wind, he ran an 'illegal' 9.9, and was a runaway winner of the final in 10.0, equalling the world record held by Armin Hary, Harry Jerome and Horacio Estevez. How could someone with pigeon toes go so fast? Enrique Figuerola of Cuba and Jerome led off the blocks and were still ahead after 30 metres, only to be overhauled by Hayes' rolling, seemingly unbalanced stride. His huge winning margin over Figuerola was a fifth of a second, Figuerola being the first Cuban to win an Olympic track and field medal. So robust was Hayes that he was one of the few

champion sprinters successfully to convert to professional football and spent nine years playing for the Dallas Cowboys.

Al Oerter maintained his fairy-tale sequence for America in the discus, with his third successive win, again with an Olympic record, equalling the three successive hammer victories of American John Flanagan in 1900–08.

While Mills was pounding his way to stardom, Mary Rand (formerly Bignal), was simultaneously winning the women's long jump with a world record of 6.76m (22 ft 2¼ in.), thereby giving Britain a double in conjunction with Lynn Davies, winner of the men's event. Back home, Queen Elizabeth II was said to be so astonished that a woman could leap such a distance that she had it marked in chalk on the carpet in the corridor at Windsor Castle.

Four years earlier in Rome, Rand had been shy and nervous, but now she was a picture of composure. Indeed, shortly before leaving for Tokyo she had said that she would like the world record *as well as* the gold medal. 'Somehow it seems to me that you make history more by being the first woman over 22 feet,' she said, conveniently overlooking that most of the world does not talk in feet and inches. Nonetheless, she did exceed that distance – though she had to check in the book in her kit bag when it was announced metrically – becoming Britain's first woman Olympic athletics champion.

Favourites for the men's event were Ralph Boston (USA), the defending champion, and world record holder Igor Ter-Ovanesian of Russia. However, cold, wet conditions aided the Welshman, Davies, who only qualified for the final with his last jump. In the fifth round of the final, Davies was still lying third, but, taking advantage of a brief drop in the wind, achieved his best-ever jump with 8.07m (26 ft 5¾ in.).

There was a rare instance of abject failure in the men's javelin. Terje Pedersen of Norway had astonished the world five weeks before the Games when exceeding 100 yards (91.72m; 300 ft 11 in.), yet in Tokyo was more than 20 metres short of this, victory going to Pauli Nevala of Finland with 82.66m (271 ft 1½ in.).

Wyomia Tyus, a 19 year old from Georgia, produced a rare improvement from 11.5 to 11.2 in the second round of the women's 100m to equal Wilma Rudolph's world record, and in the final was a surprise victor over her arch-rival and teammate Edith Maguire; though Maguire realised her potential with victory in the 200m in record time ahead of Irena Kirszenstein, an 18 year old from Poland who would compete in five Games (later as Mrs Szewinska), winning seven medals in five events. In Tokyo, Kirszenstein also finished second to Rand in the long jump and was in the winning short sprint relay team.

In the first staging of the women's 400m, Dan Sin Kim of North Korea, the world record holder, was prevented from competing and the unexpected winner was Betty Cuthbert of Australia, making a renaissance eight years after Melbourne. Second was Ann Packer of Britain, who set a British record. She touched a peak – again in the absence of world record holder Kim – to claim the 800m with an Olympic record of 2:01.1.

Since 1956, the dominant figure of women's gymnastics had been Larissa Latynina, a Ukrainian Soviet, and now she claimed another six medals to bring her career total to eighteen: her gold medal in the combined team plus two silver and two bronze giving her a gross of nine gold, five silver and four bronze. Yet for the premier prize, the all-round title, she was pushed into second place by an equally exceptional woman, Vera Cáslavská, a 22 year old from Prague, who had already won a silver medal in Rome. Cáslavská was notable for her femininity and charm and, though she was not to surpass Latynina – her amalgamation of medals over two Games being well short of the Ukrainian's seven

Vera Cáslavská from Prague, impeccable stylist, takes the all-round individual gymnastics title ahead of favourite Larissa Latynina (URS) and Polina Astakhova (URS), Alexandru Siperco of Romania (IOC) presenting the medals. (© IOC)

gold and four silver – the impact of her style was as emphatic. In men's gymnastics, Boris Shakhlin, also a Ukrainian, capped a three-Games sequence of excellence in Tokyo by bringing his total medals to fourteen: seven, five and two.

Dawn Fraser, by now regarded as the aunty of swimming, distinguished herself once more. And in different ways. She not only improved the 100m freestyle record to 59.5 but, at 27, was also the oldest to have won the event and the first male or female to win three consecutively. Moreover, earlier that year, when driving home from a social function, her mother had been killed, her sister knocked unconscious and she had been hospitalised with a chipped vertebrae. Seven months later, remarkably, she was again at her peak. Still there, too, was that streak of irreverence. She ignored instructions to miss the opening ceremony and when

From strength to strength. Dawn Fraser (AUS) improves her 100m freestyle record; at 27 she was the oldest to win the event. (© IOC)

competition was finished went on a night-time escapade in which a flag was stolen from the Emperor's palace. She was arrested and subsequently discharged, the Emperor graciously allowing the flag to be retained, but she was suspended by a self-righteous Australian swimming union for four years.

The new swimming pool was one of the finest of venues, in which Don Schollander, an 18-year-old Yale student, set a new standard by winning four gold medals: 100m and 400m freestyle and both relays. Americans having won 14 gold medals in 26 track and field events, they also won 16 in 22 swimming events. The only European gold went to Galina Prozumenschchikova (URS) with a world record in the women's 200m breaststroke. With his Olympic record in the 100m and world record in the 400m, Schollander became the first swimmer to take first place in the individual medal ranking of a Games.

Don Schollander, 18-year-old from Yale, uniquely won four golds in the pool. Here he takes the 400m freestyle ahead of Frank Wiegand (GER) and Allan Wood (AUS). (© IOC)

Judo as a sport had been invented in 1882 by Jigoro Kano and for 80 years it had predominantly been the preserve of the Japanese. In 1961, Japanese confidence had been undermined when Anton Geesink of Holland had won the World Championship open-weight category, defeating Akio Kaminaga the favourite. For the home Games, Kaminaga was the nation's prime hope for honour and success, though the public was uneasily aware of the potential of this young Dutchman twenty centimetres taller and five kilos heavier. An almost religious reverence greeted the start of their final bout. After nine minutes, one of Kaminaga's attacks failed – an inner thigh throw – Geesink adroitly exploiting his opponent's momentum to his own advantage, getting a hold on the floor and sustaining it for 30 seconds. When the bell sounded his victory, the silence was broken by the inrushing sound of a thousand drawn breaths, followed by polite Asian applause.

An American boxer describing himself as 'a skinner from a Philadelphia slaughterhouse', who only made the team as a late replacement for Buster Mathis, took the heavyweight gold medal. His name was Joe Frazier. Knocking out his first three opponents, he won a split decision in the final over Hans Huber, a German bus driver, in spite of having a damaged right hand. Six years later, with Muhammad Ali having been stripped of his world professional title, Frazier claimed the vacancy with a win over Jimmy Ellis.

Anton Geesink (NED) stuns the Japanese and their judo open-weight favourite Akio Kaminaga. (© IOC)

France were gold-less until, in the equestrian events, Pierre Jonquères d'Oriola came to their rescue on Lutteur. At 41, d'Oriola regained the individual jumping title he had won 12 years earlier, for France's only victory.

The football tournament had begun against the background of a major disaster in the qualifying round, when 328 people had died, with 500 injured, during a match in Lima between Peru and Argentina. Only the final between Hungary and Czechoslovakia – Eastern European state-amateur professionals – was of presentable class, Hungary winning 2–1.

The Japanese were able to celebrate the triumph of their women's volleyball team following a frightening training programme. The squad was selected from nearly 1,300 women from the Dai Nippon spinning mill at Kaizuku. They worked from 8 a.m. to 3.30 p.m. each day, then went to the gymnasium for eight hours of unremitting training. This continued every day of the week for a whole year. The captain, Masae Kasai, is said to have chosen her place on the team in preference to marriage. They defeated the Soviet Union, gaining one of the highest television audiences of the Games.

Joe Frazier (USA), late replacement in the team for Buster Mathis, defeats West German Hans Huber for the super-heavyweight gold medal, six years prior to gaining the world professional title. (© IOC)

CHAPTER XLI

Reformist's Advent

Juan Antonio Samaranch of Spain, IOC President, 1980–2001

'Sports competitions were not Baron de Coubertin's only aim. He wanted to create an educational movement that would ensure for sport its proper place among other activities, those of youth in particular. To attach a symbol to this educational movement, he thought of crowning it with a multi-sport competition inspired by the ancient Greek games at Delphi, Corinth, Nemea and Olympia. In this way Olympia became the symbol of a Movement that has never ceased growing, despite two World Wars.

The Games represent the apex of a pyramid of international competition. Prior to the apex there is a host of international federations' events, and before that, at the base, the whole edifice of national competitions that are the mainspring of world sport. However, the IOC is restricting its activities more and more to the organisation of the Olympic Games, becoming increasingly remote from the organisation of worldwide sport, and is moving away from many international organisations that have been created to organise competition.

The relation between the IOC and IFs rests solely on a basis of respect, to such an extent that, apart from the Olympic Games and approved regional games, the IFs come little if at all under IOC jurisdiction. Therefore, the IOC is viewed merely as a praiseworthy, venerable but rather remote committee, and the Olympic Movement, which is so much more than the Games, remains in many cases restricted to that competition. This is a big mistake. While the IFs have no wish to be controlled, the IOC itself determines the limits of its own power. Naturally, it is not the IOC's job to supervise sports development everywhere in the world. Nevertheless, it should give moral backing and instil the Olympic ideal in all sports, from the highest level down to schools, youth movements and universities.

This is the spirit that de Coubertin tried to convey to us: that the Olympic Games should be the culmination of all sports. In the perpetual struggle to defend the ideological purity of the Movement, much energy has been consumed and structures which might have evolved have remained unchanged. History will render justice to those who were wise and strong enough to maintain the path of an ideal, yet the continued implementation of such ideas in a format that was acceptable 50 years ago but is debatable today may lead to a crisis . . .

What is important for us is to remember that it is up to us to ensure the continuity of the great work of education that sport has entrusted to us. The IOC must occupy the position that is its due through its undoubted merits: that is to say, it must remain the supreme authority in world sport. We believe that it is its duty to do so if it does not want to run the risk of seeing other bodies emerge, which are merely waiting to take its place at the head of sport – a position that belongs to the IOC by right and by history, and to it alone.' (From a Spanish magazine article published soon after his election to the IOC)
(Photograph © IOC)

These words from a relatively new IOC member, elected in 1966, were prescient sentiments regarding an organisation that had just experienced two of its more turbulent years. The inter-related issues of the anti-apartheid struggle in South Africa and the Black Power movement in America were increasingly intruding into world sport, and Olympic sport in particular, while at the same time the tide of commercialism was simultaneously taxing the administrators. The passage of Avery Brundage during his extended presidency had never been tranquil; now he was confronted by problems that were beyond reasonable control. The antennae of Juan Antonio Samaranch, even at this early stage of his IOC career, unerringly detected the new trends that, without the most attentive guidance, could throw the IOC off the rails.

Infiltration of the Olympic Games by external forces with vested interests had long been a phenomenon but a fresh one of particular significance had emerged at the beginning of the 1960s. Bavarian brothers Adolph and Rudolph Dassler, a pair of shoemakers, had appeared, metaphorically and literally, in the starting blocks. They had been partners, only to become rivals – Adolph founding Adidas and Rudolph creating Puma. Each promoted his range by providing complimentary shoes to athletes. Rudolph staged a coup when stealing from Adidas, by cash incentive, Armin Hary – the German who swept to victory, and fame for Puma, in the Rome final. The response from Adidas was to enlist Bob Hayes of America, who took advantage of a virtual auction before winning the title in Tokyo with an alleged payout from Adidas of $8,000. By the time of the Games in Mexico City, the endorsement fees available to top athletes from one or other of the spikes rivals had reached five-figure sums,

179

Shoe buy-out. Jim Hines, 100m champion in Mexico City, and rivals parade for the cameras the familiar stripes, an endorsement that gave Adidas a near-global monopoly. (© IOC)

the two companies collectively spending, in hand-outs and free goods, a gross amount approaching a million dollars in order to gain 'air time' on worldwide television exposure.

With an alleged four-fifths of the most prominent athletes lured into the Adidas camp, the endorsement policy had taken the company into the red. Adolph's son Horst sought consultation with Brundage to discuss the mutual dilemma faced by the sport and the manufacturers. Brundage stated, naively, that all was well: the IAAF was about to introduce a regulation permitting only neutral shoes for major meetings. It was, of course, a plan doomed even before it was put on paper and the so-termed corruption of competitors, together with the massive growth of Adidas and to a lesser degree Puma, in both the sport and leisurewear markets, would continue unimpeded.

Moreover, it was no secret. The French weekly *L'Express* commented that only the ignorant believed that they would watch genuine amateurs in the forthcoming Games of 1968. Wherever you looked, there was, according to the terms of the Charter, infringement of regulations. Marika Kilius and Hans-Jürgen Bäumler, the West German figure skating pairs silver medal winners in 1964, had signed a film contract prior to the Games. Suspension was demanded, though not by their own IF, but in order to silence the debate the skaters returned their medals to the IOC – who were left in a quandary, as the third- and fourth-place couples, theoretically entitled to promotion, had all turned professional.

The blatant abuse of the principles he held dearest made Brundage livid. IOC press releases threatening retribution only partially eased his ire. 'Alpine skiing does not belong in the Olympic Games,' pronounced one such communiqué prior to the Grenoble Games. To the French Minister of Sport, Colonel Marceau Crespin, he protested: 'I hear that half the skiers on the French team don't live up to our definition of amateurism.' Crespin replied: 'You have been misinformed, Monsieur. No one in the French ski team lives up to your definition.'

The IOC and its President were trapped within a convoluted web of avaricious forces. With the television rights fees, plus the endorsement fees pouring out of the shoe companies, there was a three-way market. The IOC, despite its stance on amateurism for the competitors, needed its then modest share of the television income merely to administer, together with the host

organising committee, the preparation and function of the Games. The shoe, and in particular the ski, manufacturers wanted exposure on television for the leisure market. The athletes, understandably, wanted their cut as vehicles of the whole exercise.

Following the Innsbruck Games of 1964, relations between Brundage and the international ski federation (FIS) sank to near zero. The FIS eligibility commission had promised there would be no brand names on skis for 1968, but their own Council rejected this. Marc Hodler, FIS president, made the tenuous promise, impossible to uphold, that skiers would not allow themselves to be photographed with their skis; many were, however, under contract with the manufacturers specifically to do so.

Perversely, Grenoble had been chosen as host city in preference to Banff in Canada, in spite of requiring an expenditure of $100 million to provide for a ten-day event spread over many sub-centres. Brundage fumed that this was 'altogether out of proportion'; a factor which, in conjunction with ski commercialism, persuaded him, unilaterally and unavailingly, to threaten termination of the Winter Games. The decision of the FIS shortly before the Games, aware that many of their national federations were dependent on manufacturers' sponsorship, to renege on the promise to remove advertisements, was the last straw. There was nothing the IOC could do. It was common knowledge that the ski industry was waiting to spring into personalised production if and when Jean-Claude Killy of France won his expected gold medals. From this he might, and indeed did, make a fortune from endorsements. So furious was Brundage with what he regarded as betrayal, collectively, by both IFs and FIS in particular and by the NOCs, that he refused to attend or present medals at Grenoble's Alpine events.

The IOC's dilemma was severe. By 1967, the mounting administrative costs from huge expansion threatened financial crisis. Within two Olympiads, its annual outgoings had increased seven-fold, from 36,000 Swiss francs in 1960 to 266,000 by 1966. The share of income from the $200,000 and $30,000 from Mexico City and Grenoble respectively would ease the situation, though Brundage acceded reluctantly to the new

Jean-Claude Killy predictably made his fortune with his Alpine treble, equally predictably infuriating Brundage. (© IOC)

windfall, stating in a circular to members in 1967: 'We have gone into business – with all the attendant problems. One can already observe the change, however subtle, in our activities and I am not convinced that it is something that we should welcome. The IOC's vocation has never been that of a commercial undertaking.' Nevertheless, advance television payments for the Games of Munich in 1972 would allow the IOC to bridge the period 1968–72 without incurring debt. At an Executive Board meeting in 1966, Hodler, chairman of the IOC's finance commission, had proposed that television rights income be divided as follows: the first million dollars equally between the IOC, IFs and NOCs; of the second million, the local organising committee to receive a third, and the IOC/IFs/NOCs two-ninths each; from the third million, two-thirds to the organising committee, one-ninth each to the other three – the proposal to be effective from 1972.

Embarrassment from the anti-apartheid campaign continued. At the 1965 Session in Madrid, Giulio Onesti reported that 80 NOCs were supporting the IOC policy (of exclusion), but that Reginald Honey, South Africa's member, was indignant at having been barred from a meeting to which he claimed 'South Africa has been invited'. African NOCs considered it contradictory that while South African sportsmen were banned their officials could attend meetings. As a result, the South African NOC was suspended the following year. However, by then Frank Braun, representing SANOC, was singing a different tune, saying SANOC would send a non-racial team to Mexico City, selected by a non-racial committee. This mood of conciliation was promptly contradicted on return home; Braun's comments to the *Johannesburg Star* commending those who did not 'pander to Afro-Asians'.

In spite of SANOC having appointed an alleged 'mixed' selection committee, and the IOC deciding to send in 1967 its own enquiry commission comprising Killanin (Ireland), Ademola (Nigeria) and Secretary-General Westerhoff, patience in black Africa was running thin. In December 1966, 32 African states gathering in Bamako, Mali, had formed the Supreme Council of Sport in Africa (SCSA), resolving to obtain South Africa's expulsion and simultaneously warning of a boycott should South Africa participate at Mexico City. Much now depended on the 1967 Session in Tehran, though the enquiry commission led by Killanin had not yet made its visit. Braun

persisted in Tehran with the assurance that there would be a mixed South African team. Jean-Claude Ganga, representing the SCSA, protested provocatively: 'We do not wish that the blacks of Africa appear like costumed apes, presented at a fair and then, when the fair is over, sent back to their cages.' The Killanin-led visit spent ten days on tour and, though encountering some obvious evidence of social apartheid, nonetheless felt able to produce a nebulous report in January 1968, concluding that SANOC's proposals were 'an acceptable basis for a multi-racial team'.

Brundage promptly but naively stated that the IOC had struck a blow against apartheid and that the South African government had been sidestepped by a 'multi-racial committee'. Within two days Algeria and Ethiopia announced their intention to boycott and by the conclusion of the Grenoble Games the Organisation of African Unity's 32 nations called for the same action. Brundage's initial indifference to this threat shifted when Caribbean, Islamic and Communist countries joined the tide, especially when the USSR joined them. Yet at the Session in Grenoble, by a vote of 36 to 25, South Africa was re-admitted, never mind the assurance from Dennis Brutus of London-based SANROC, then living in exile in Lausanne, that 'South Africa will not be participating in Mexico.' In France, *Le Monde* labelled Brundage and the IOC as racist.

With hostile global opinion gathering, and with the Mexican organisers in evident panic, Brundage flew to South Africa hoping to persuade SANOC now to withdraw voluntarily. Braun retorted that 'I would rather be shot in Mexico City than hanged in Johannesburg.'

Meanwhile, Artur Takac, the IOC's Technical Director, was asked by Pedro Ramirez-Vazquez, president of the organising committee – later an IOC member and designer of the Olympic Museum in Lausanne – to visit Lord Exeter, influential Executive Board member and staunch defender of South Africa, to press upon him the reality of the current danger to the Games. Takac, knowledgeable talker that he is, finding Exeter relaxed over a jigsaw puzzle in his London flat overlooking Hyde Park, attempted at length to persuade him of the extent of the crisis. 'But I doubt whether I made much impact since his view was rooted somewhere in the undergrowth of the manner in which the British Empire had formerly flourished,' Tarak says. Lady Exeter, however, advised her husband of the wisdom of the visitor's advice. Takac moved on for similar talks with leading IOC members around Europe. An Executive Board meeting on 20 April, though warned by Brundage that, if South Africa were barred, 'we are abandoning 20 million people', decided that, despite the Grenoble decision, South Africa should not be present in Mexico; that it was not sensible to seek an Extraordinary Session, but that the IOC members, not the Executive Board, should be final arbiters. By postal poll, the membership now voted forty-seven to sixteen, with eight abstentions, to withdraw South Africa's invitation.

By comparison, the Cold War issue over East and West Germany was less complicated. With the building of the Berlin Wall and its mined extension along the entire border, the East's desire for separation from Bonn intensified. In 1965, at the Session in Madrid, the IOC granted the GDR the right to enter a separate team in 1968, though both German teams were to fly the same flag carrying the Olympic Rings and would have the same uniforms and anthem. The following year, Heinz Schöbel of the GDR was elected IOC member and at the 1968 Session in Mexico City the IOC gave unqualified recognition of the GDR NOC under its own flag. Thus, with the Grenoble Games, there began the era of two German teams.

Jean-Claude Ganga, anti-apartheid protagonist from Congo: 'We do not wish that the blacks of Africa appear like costumed apes.'
(© IOC/Strahm)

At the Session in Tehran in 1967, Arthur Porritt announced that the new Medical Commission was ready for the application of tests for anabolic steroids and other stimulants, and for gender testing for women. The first list of prohibited substances included alcohol, amphetamines and ephedrine, cocaine, vaso-dilaters, opiates and cannabis. There was additionally a list of synthetic derivatives of steroids and details of their damaging effects, such as jaundice and impotence in men, hirsuitism and menstrual disruption in women. With Porritt's retirement to a position as adviser, Prince de Mérode of Belgium became the Commission's chairman. Within a short time of his appointment there occurred one of the most conspicuous instances of the danger of drug abuse, with the death on the 13th stage of the Tour de France of Tommy Simpson of Britain. Climbing the notorious Mont Ventoux, Simpson twice collapsed with exhaustion and died in hospital at Avignon.

Sex-testing was introduced to eliminate fraud. Once a certificate was obtained following the 1968 Games, no further confirmation was required. Dora Ratjen, fourth in the 1936 high jump, confessed in the 1950s that she was actually Herman and had been forced by the Nazi administration to impersonate a woman for three years. Of 640 females tested in 1968, none was disqualified.

Though the prospects for Grenoble itself and in the long term for the Winter Games had seemed threatened, in the event the spectacular nature of some of the competition drew public attention back to the essence of the Olympic Movement: intense, elite competition under the gaze of a now global audience.

Grenoble had been chosen in 1964, victorious over Calgary by 27 votes to 24. The downside of the location would be the transport problems caused by long distances separating different venues and the fact that many competitors understandably preferred to be housed at those venues rather than at a central Village. By the following year, the IOC was doubting the organisers' decision to stage the events at six sub-centres throughout the Dauphine region, only skating events and ice hockey being in the host city. The others were Chamrousse/Val d'Isère for Alpine skiing, Autrans for cross-country, St Nizier for ski jumping, Alpe D'Huez for bobsleigh, Villard de Lans for luge. There would be three separate Villages.

When Mexico City was elected, at the Session of 1963 in Baden-Baden, as host for 1968, it was not just domestic unrest that caused concern about the ability of the first non-industrialised city to handle such a major task. There was alarm, especially among coaches and physiologists, about the durability of athletes in distance events and even the long-term threat to health, at an altitude of 2,240m (7,400 ft). Brundage dismissed the alarm saying: 'The Olympics belong to all countries of the world, be they hot or cold, wet or dry, in the east, west, north or south or at high or low altitude. The Games were not instituted to break records.'

No previous Games had been above 200m altitude. It was already evident that there was a difference in capacity in responding to high-class competition between those who lived and trained at altitude and those resident at sea level. Several countries undertook physiological tests and the conclusions of the British Olympic Association in particular brought a proposal by the IOC that competitors should spend a minimum of four weeks, during the three months prior to the Games, acclimatising at high altitude. To offset anxieties, and costs, the Mexicans offered to pay for two weeks, being able to afford this on account of Village costs being under three dollars per person per day.

Certainly the altitude would have a bearing on longer races, most notably on the fancied Jim Ryun of America in the 1,500m, where he was no match for the altitude-based Kip Keino from the Rift Valley in Kenya. Another ailing sea-level favourite was Ron Clarke of Australia, and there has been speculation that the serious heart problems he suffered in later life were a legacy of his unavailing efforts in Mexico City. At the shorter explosive distances, and in other track and field events, of course, the altitude was a bonus: notably to Bob Beamon with his incredible record in the long jump and Dick Fosbury in the high jump. No less than 252 competitors surpassed previous Olympic records in quantifiably measured sports, with 24 world records also improved.

Beamon and short-distance champions Jim Hines, Tommie Smith and Lee Evans were representatives of the mounting dominance in the Games of African-Americans. There had been the possibility that they might not be present. All of them had to weigh up whether the reward of possible personal achievement in Mexico, once they returned home to social segregation – as opposed to legal segregation in South Africa – was more important than any moral stance.

Leading a campaign for African-Americans to boycott the Games, for the advancement of civil rights, was Harry Edwards, who had once been a track star with San José State College of California. Social conscience had persuaded Edwards to abandon sport and take a degree in sociology at Cornell University, where he wrote his thesis on 'The Black Muslim Movement and Malcolm X'. In 1966, he had returned to San José to teach sociology and mobilise black athlete protest. In 1967, he formed the Olympic Project for Human Rights (OPHR). Enthusiastic supporters included Evans and Smith. Far-fetched objectives were the removal of Brundage as head of the IOC, the exclusion of South Africa, a minimum of two African-American coaches among those for the US track team, African-American representation on USOC and de-segregation of the hidebound New York Athletic Club. However, with the approach of the Games, athletes had to face the bottom line: abandonment of years of devotion to attaining their individual Olympic dream and with it, undoubtedly, material reward. Encouraging them to remain loyal to their sport was one who had suffered as much as any from prejudice and segregation: Jesse Owens. 'There is no place in the athlete's world for politics,' he declared. The stance of Owens was, on the other hand, at odds with public outrage over the murder on 4 April 1968 of Martin Luther King.

In the event, the athletes would remain loyal to themselves and their sport. Their loyalty to fellow black Americans would be expressed a different way. 'We voted on a boycott and it was almost unanimous that we go,' Lee Evans said. 'But it was also unanimous that we make some kind of protest at the Games.'

Social unrest was not confined in 1968 to Africa/South Africa or American black ghettos. The Prague Spring of Czechoslovakia's democracy-seeking Alexander Dubcek had been snubbed by a Soviet invasion that was an echo of Budapest in 1956. In mute symbolism, student Jan Palac fatally set fire to himself in Wenceslas Square. The legendary Emil Zátopek also protested and was ousted from the Communist Party, and his military post as colonel, and was banished to menial labouring jobs. Norway's IOC member Jan Staubo cabled Brundage, urging the suspension of the Soviet Union, to which the President replied: 'If participation in sport is to be stopped every time the politicians violate the laws of humanity, there will never be any international contests.' True enough.

In Paris and London student agitation was threatening

governments and embassies. It was little different in Mexico City, where students rallied throughout the summer in protest against what was considered disproportionate expense for a sporting festival in a country of widespread poverty. By September, a month before the opening, the demonstrations were so vigorous that tanks were stationed outside the university and the main Olympic stadium. The number of students and teachers on strike approached half a million. Only the army stood between stability and civil war. Artur Takac's secretary, sent on a mission to the stadium, close to the University, did not return. She was only released by army security upon representation to the Games organising committee. On 2 October, ten days before the opening ceremony, troops surrounded the Plaza de las Tres Culturas where 10,000 people had gathered. At a given signal, the army opened fire. With some of the students also armed in preparation, a battle raged. It was officially announced that 35 had died, but from figures compiled by hospitals and clinics, the figure was 267 dead and 1,200 injured. With opposition crushed, President Diaz Ordaz felt confident to announce that there would be no interference with the Games or those taking part. Even in the face of such an appalling massacre, the full extent of which they did not know at the time, the IOC had no option but to continue.

Artur Takac, the IOC's Technical Director, masterminded Mexico City's preparations. (© IOC/Nett)

Pedro Ramirez-Vazquez, president of the organising committee, and Avery Brundage either side of Gustavo Diaz Ordaz, state president, who uncompromisingly put down student riots days before the opening ceremony. (© IOC)

Quelling the protests was doubly important to the government. In two years' time, Mexico was also scheduled to host the high-profile football World Cup and could afford no disruption of the Games. These two events were seen as an opportunity to realign the international view of a largely peasant country that had languished as a Third World nation since the ill-starred revolution of 1910. Out of sight of the city's slums, home to millions, much had been done in preparation under the organising chairmanship of architect Pedro Ramirez-Vazquez. A Village for 5,000 had been constructed south of the capital close to a new Sports Palace accommodating 22,000. There was a new velodrome next to the Sports Palace and a magnificent new main stadium, the Azteca, privately financed and designed as much for the football of 1970. Rowing and canoeing were at the tourist site of Xochimilco, famous for its

floating gardens, while gymnastics were at the renovated National Auditorium in Chapultepec. Outlay was calculated at $180 million and about a third of that was specifically allocated to sport construction. Besides $56 million directly from the government, income included $6.4 million from television rights, ABC of America alone paying $4.5 million. There was no doubt that the legacy in construction, housing and communications was a permanent benefit to the city, though it had required arduous attention to detail by Takac and others to bring the sports administration and the logistics up to scratch. In his autobiography, *Sixty Olympic Years*, Takac related:

> Twelve months before the Games we found chaos: no properly qualified judges or referees, no programme, no announcers, no knowledge of procedure. We had to deliver an ultimatum: that if Cesar Moreno, a young PE professor who understood the job, was not immediately appointed a year beforehand, then I and Adriaan Paulen, the IAAF council member from Holland, who was technical adviser, would be on the first plane back home . . . I put an idea to Moreno that PE students should study for officiating at an athletics meeting. Thus we had 400 students, aged 19 or 20, who had passed the referee's and judge's examination . . . it was from this contribution that I came to understand how important a successful Games was to the whole of Mexico and to its image in the world.

As a result of such dedication from comparatively anonymous figures such as Takac and Moreno, the Mexico Games were a fine success; from the moment that Enriqueta Basilio, a hurdler, became the first woman to light the Olympic flame. Another female first was by Janice Romary, a fencer, carrying the American flag at an opening ceremony.

For a man of business it was strange that Brundage was never able to understand how essential collaboration was between the three arms of the Movement, how the IOC could never hope to stand in isolation, how the Games were ultimately as much or even more financially dependent in practical terms upon the individual sports bodies and those who provided the competitors than upon the IOC as rights holders. In 1965, Giulio Onesti had convened a meeting attended by 68 NOCs. This was a turning point in the coordination of NOCs. Onesti, together with Raoul Mollet, president of the Belgian NOC, had planned such a gathering for the Tokyo Session the previous year, but had been warned by Brundage that a permanent organisation of NOCs 'is fraught with many dangers'. Brundage feared that it would lead to a system of one-country-one-vote within the IOC, thereby ceding majority rule to the Communists and the Third World, as in the UN.

A committee established by the NOCs in 1965 consisted of Onesti, Andrianov (USSR), de Clark Flores (Mexico), Korenthin (Mali), Duncan (Britain), Ganga (Congo), Gemayel (Lebanon), Takeda (Japan), Weir (Australia), Weyman (Switzerland) and Wilson (USA). The primary objectives were to secure the right to 25 per cent of television income and the transfer of the issue of eligibility/amateurism from the IOC to the IFs.

When a third assembly of NOCs took place at the Session of 1967 in Tehran, Brundage's agitation reached a peak. 'The meeting of NOCs with the Executive Board was loaded with dynamite . . . we were on the edge of a precipice . . . one slip and we could have been over the edge.' He found it particularly objectionable that Ganga, blatantly political, was among what he regarded as the opposition that was consistently out-manoeuvring him. In 1966 he had written to Andrianov: 'The only reason for the negative attitude of the Executive Board towards an organisation of NOCs is the fact that the majority of NOCs do not want and will not participate in such an organisation.' How wrong he was to be proved, with 78 NOCs attendant in Tehran. The IOC had formed a sub-committee to deal with NOC affairs but this would be overrun, and, at the Session in Mexico City the following year, the Permanent General Assembly of NOCs was formally created with Onesti as president. Brundage's ruse of bringing Onesti inside the IOC's exclusive stockade, in 1964, had failed.

A month after the Tehran Session, the IFs formed the General Association of International Sports Federations (GAISF) under the initiative of Berge Phillips (swimming), Roger Coulon (wrestling) and Thomas Keller (rowing), though the IAAF felt itself powerful enough to remain independent of GAISF. Brundage had warned the IFs that they were forming an association 'that intended to handle matters that are not of their competence'. Wrong again. Keller was the new GAISF president, Coulon its secretary, and they were all too conscious of their moral power. Through the 1970s, their membership would expand rapidly, and under Keller's leadership would come to consider the IOC as the lesser body. There was indeed the danger that Brundage perceived, though it would fall to Samaranch, the next President but one, to handle this issue. Killanin as President successfully fended off attempted interventions by UNESCO, and at the Congress in Varna, 1973, only temporarily put a break on Keller's opposition from GAISF.

For Brundage, time was running out, but not quite yet. Reginald Alexander of Kenya advised him that at 80, and already President for 16 years, there was only one way to go, and that was down. Why not retire at the top? Brundage, typically, shrugged off the advice. Alexander and others asked Killanin if he would stand against Brundage in the election in 1968 but Killanin, ever-cautious, backed off. Opposed only by Comte Jean de Beaumont, Brundage was re-elected yet again by a wide margin. The campaign of de Beaumont had included a proposal for at least one woman to be elected to the IOC but, even in the second half of the twentieth century, this was not a matter that moved the minds of the IOC.

Lee Evans (USA), 400m champion in world record time, anchors the four-lap relay victory. Resisting the US boycott movement among black athletes, he voted to go 'but make some kind of protest at the Games'. (© IOC)

CHAPTER XLII

Grenoble (X) 1968

Jean-Claude Killy of France, triple Olympic Alpine champion, IOC member

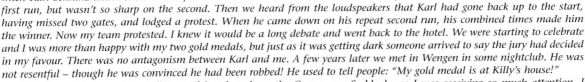

'I'd had such a terrific season in 1967 that I hesitated about going to Grenoble. I'd had 23 wins in 30 races, including all the downhills, and I felt that there was no chance I could ski as well again – no way that I could guarantee even one gold medal. I was intending to retire after Grenoble, yet felt it would be bad to do so when not feeling on top of the world. The summer beforehand, I discussed the situation with Mark McCormack, my agent. It was my first meeting with McCormack and he said, "Whether you win or not, you'll still be the best there's been."

By August, I'd decided I would go and was not too concerned about the World Cup that winter, concentrating exclusively on preparing for the Games. During the build-up, however, everything started to go wrong, I couldn't win a race and at that stage I would happily have accepted a single gold.

When the downhill came round, I won it by only eight-hundredths of a second, it was such a lucky win. Having had everything running against me, that night I thought to myself it would be a surprise if I did not win the next two events.

After I'd won the giant slalom and we came to the slalom, I realised something was amiss when Karl Schranz didn't show at the finish on the second slalom run. I'd had the fastest first run, but wasn't so sharp on the second. Then we heard from the loudspeakers that Karl had gone back up to the start, having missed two gates, and lodged a protest. When he came down on his repeat second run, his combined times made him the winner. Now my team protested. I knew it would be a long debate and went back to the hotel. We were starting to celebrate and I was more than happy with my two gold medals, but just as it was getting dark someone arrived to say the jury had decided in my favour. There was no antagonism between Karl and me. A few years later we met in Wengen in some nightclub. He was not resentful – though he was convinced he had been robbed! He used to tell people: "My gold medal is at Killy's house!"

Having won three medals, I discovered just how huge the Games are. Suddenly, as I was receiving so much attention, I decided I ought to get out of Grenoble. The army offered me a helicopter and when I approached the chopper the police saluted me. Why would they salute a jerk like me? Soon I began to discover the answer. The postman was arriving every four or five hours with thousands of telegrams.

Yes, success in the Games did make everything easier. My aim beforehand had been to travel the world a bit, make some money and then go back and run Dad's ski shop. But I'd signed a contract with McCormack. I was now a citizen of the world. I worked for 120 different companies, appeared in a Hollywood movie, two television series and countless ads. If I went to the Bahamas or to Fifth Avenue, I was recognised. Yet hard work was the foundation for it all, you can't be successful if you don't work.

The Games didn't change me at all, I'm still the same guy, not fond of crowds or cocktail parties, I still have the same few friends, I haven't bought a big house or a big boat. On the other hand, life is undoubtedly easier for an Olympic champion. You never get a speeding ticket! Many doors are opened to you. The Olympic Games changed my life. But not me, I hope.'*

(Photograph © IOC)

The obsessive yet doomed attempt by Avery Brundage to purge the Games of the commercial interests that threatened to submerge them only served to heighten the fame that surrounded Jean-Claude Killy in 1968. It was ironic that the campaign by the IOC President should serve to publicise the very festival that he sought to abolish.

Jean-Claude Killy had had the advantage of ideal surroundings in childhood, growing up in Val d'Isère in the Savoy Alps, but his mother deserted the family, obliging his father to send him to boarding school. By the age of 15, Killy was a member of the French ski team. He then served in the army in Algeria and, in spite of a bacterial illness, qualified for all three Alpine events at Innsbruck, where he came fifth in the giant slalom but failed to finish in the other two. From this point his career climbed rapidly and by the time of Grenoble he was carrying the weight of heavy domestic expectations.

For the opening downhill, his run was little more than a kneecap ahead of his colleague Guy Périllat, 1:59.85 as against 1:59.93. His perceived main rival, Karl Schranz of Austria, was fifth.

The abuse, for that palpably is what it was, of Brundage's attempted strictures, was instant. A friend of Killy's, emblazoned with commercial logos, raced on to the finishing pan to embrace him and when Killy's skis were formally confiscated by attendants to prevent any ostentatious display of the manufacturer's name the friend adroitly displayed the same ski brand. Brundage was a drowning preacher, Killy an ad man's Pied Piper. He went on to take the giant slalom comfortably – staged for the first time with a combination of two runs on separate days rather than by a single run – by more than two seconds and was then poised for the triple trump.

To heighten the drama, the slalom was beset with controversy. The bad weather would have caused postponement but for the fact it was the penultimate day of the Games and officialdom did not want a last-day conflict with the ski jumping. The piste was shrouded in fog. Only once did the sun break through – conveniently at the moment of the first of Killy's two runs. This enabled him to post the fastest time, rivals suffering the frustration of waiting to start when the mists eased. After Killy's second run – as the first starter – his combined time looked vulnerable. Häkon Mjön of Norway surpassed it, but had missed two gates. Then came Schranz, already a veteran boasting every honour bar Olympic gold. From causes never satisfactorily defined, Schranz missed gates 18 and 19 of the 69 covering the course and skidded to a halt. He claimed that a security policeman had crossed the piste at gate 21, just ahead of him. Accompanied by three witnesses, Schranz returned to the starting gate to demand a re-run. This was granted by the British referee. Now Schranz recorded a time that carried him into the lead and he was declared the winner. The French immediately lodged a protest – claiming that, at Gates 18 and 19, Schranz could not have seen the alleged policeman at Gate 21 because of the fog – while Schranz was busy giving a celebration press conference. A lengthy meeting of the jury of appeal, wrestling with contentions either that the policeman had acted deliberately to distract Schranz or that indeed he was imaginary, finally voted 3–2 against Schranz. Killy had delivered and the party back home ran for 48 hours. Days later the amateur/professional debate continued to rage when Killy appeared on the front page of *Paris-Match* wearing his three medals and was allegedly rewarded with a car for his collaboration, an allegation he denied.

It was some compensation for Austria that their women had been first, third and fourth in their downhill event, Olga Pall having a margin over Isabelle Mir of France rather more comfortable than Killy's: almost half a second. An absentee from this race was the Austrian reigning world champion, Erica Schinegger. Medical testing prior to the Games had revealed her

Jean-Claude Killy negotiates a gate as adroitly as he did the amateur regulations and Brundage's attempted purge. (© IOC)

Eugenio Monti achieves his ultimate reward with double gold, here with double partner Luciano De Paolis between Germans Horst Floth and Pepi Bader (silver) and Romanians Ion Panturu and Nicolae Neagoe (bronze). (© IOC)

saliva to contain only male hormones: Schinegger was a man, not a woman, her organs having grown internally. She/he subsequently had corrective surgery.

Nancy Greene of Canada won the giant slalom by a substantial margin over Annie Famose of France and came second to Marielle Goitschel of France in the slalom by the slenderest of margins, twenty-nine-hundredths of a second. For Greene, this was her third Games, the giant slalom her last chance of victory, and in an adroit manoeuvre her coaches arranged for her to arrive at the gate only a short time before her start to reduce anxiety. The ploy worked.

A Games dogged by dispute had another in the women's single luge. The defending East German, Ortrun Enderlein, led the field, with her colleagues Anna-Maria Müller and Angela Knösel respectively second and fourth. Furtive behaviour at start and finish aroused suspicion and investigation revealed that they had been illegally heating their sled runners over an open fire to increase their speed. All three were disqualified amid vain protest of a capitalist plot, the winner being Erica Lechner of Italy; and, to make the East Germans even more miserable, their western neighbours Christa Schmuck and Angelika Dünhaupt claimed silver and bronze.

The bobsleigh run at Alpe D'Huez, thought to be dangerous, was the scene of ultimate reward for Eugenio Monti, nine-time world champion – seven in the two-man, twice in the four-man – who had never secured an Olympic title. After four runs in the two-man, Monti and Luciano De Paolis shared an identical cumulative time with Horst Floth and Pepi Bader in *Germany I*. Italy got the verdict with the fastest single run, following an initial ruling that both teams should be awarded gold medals. At the age of 40, the oldest gold medal winner of the Games, Monti had reached his zenith. Victory in the four-man came after only two runs, the event being reduced because of the prospect of a thaw. Monti and his colleagues had a margin over Austria of nine-hundredths of a second.

Peggy Fleming of the US, the youngest champion of the Games at 19, had been world figures champion the previous year, was the favourite now and won with relative ease. Her acclaim was magnified by the media's proclivity for stereotypical glamour. Fleming looked nice and graced the television screen. Women's issues had not yet infiltrated the thinking of the sports press. She was simply the male media's ideal of the female Olympian and coverage of her success, placed first by all nine judges, gave less attention to her technical or athletic superiority over Gabrielle Seyfert (GDR), the silver medal winner, than to her appearance.

Unusually in speed skating, no one gained more than one victory. In the women's 500m, three Americans tied for the silver medal in identical time – Jennifer Fish, Dianne Holum and Mary Meyers – behind Ludmila Titova of the Soviet Union, whose colleague Tatyana Sidorova had set a world record of 44.7 six days earlier but could now finish only ninth. Carolina Geijssen set an Olympic record of 1:32.6 in the 1,000m, three-tenths ahead of Titova to become Holland's first skater to win an Olympic gold medal. Franco Nones of Italy became the first cross-country medal holder from a country outside Scandinavia or the USSR when winning the 30km.

The inimitable Protopopovs, Ludmila and Oleg, spectacularly defend their pairs title. (© IOC)

Glamorous champion Peggy Fleming (USA), the focus of photographers more for her figure than her figures. (© IOC)

CHAPTER XLIII

Mexico City (XIX) 1968

Kip Keino of Kenya, Olympic legend, IOC member

'*I'd had some problems back home in Kenya, serious cramps in my stomach. When I arrived in Mexico, I was taken to see a doctor with the German team, who diagnosed that I had gallstones. He told me that I should not run, that I was risking my health by competing. But I had come to Mexico to represent my country, to win a medal for Kenya, and I was determined to do that. In my first race, the final of the 10,000m, the pain was really bad, so bad that I stumbled off the track and fell, though I managed to pick myself up and finish.*

The next day I did not feel so good, but was still determined to compete in the 5,000m, to win that medal. The semi-final was fairly comfortable, I was running easily again but in the middle of the final the pain returned. I kept going and fortunately it disappeared. I think I would have won but for a mistake that I made together with my colleague Naftali Temu. I found I had plenty of energy and should have made my finishing burst earlier, but Temu and I simultaneously tried to accelerate into the second lane and collided, giving Gammoudi of Tunisia his chance. It was our mistake and I was just behind him at the line.

My stomach was now really bad and both the Kenyan team doctor and the German told me I ought not to run in the 1,500m, which involved three races, but I told them my name was not to be removed from the starting list. I knew Jim Ryun was the best because he held the world record but I felt I had a chance. I'd been able to get a measure of him in the semi-final.

The pain was there again before the final. The bus from the Village was caught in traffic, so I jumped out and jogged the last couple of kilometres to the stadium. I was so tense and focused that I put the pains to the back of my mind. I was trying to relax with gentle exercises in the warm-up, in two minds about how I should run – whether to go slowly behind the field, or from the front. It was said that we had a plan for Ben Jipcho to make the pace, so as to extend Ryun, but really I ran my own race after Ben had given us a very fast first lap. I wanted to open a big gap ahead of Ryun and I continued fast into the third lap, even though I was now in serious pain. I do not know where I got the physical strength from to keep going but we were proud of our country and ready to sacrifice everything for a medal.

That evening I was not feeling at all well and the following day the German doctor gave me some tablets that made things a little better. When I returned home, I continued with medicine for more than two months and eventually was OK, though I occasionally still have some bother today. I tried my level best in Mexico and I'm happy with what happened.'*
(Photograph © IOC)

There are two views of the Games staged in Mexico City at an altitude of nearly 2,240m (7,400 ft): that it was an ill-advised choice by the IOC which deprived several notable competitors of their true heritage; alternatively that it opened the way for those from high altitude countries like Kenya and Ethiopia to reveal their talent and the physiological characteristics that arise in such geographic locations. Additionally, the first Games at altitude produced several world records, notably in the men's long jump, that would not be approached for many years at 'normal' sea level. Kenya and Ethiopia were to win nine medals at distances from 1,500m to the marathon. The greatest controversy in the middle and long distances surrounded the record-breaking Ron Clarke of Australia, and the rivalry between American protégé Jim Ryun and the equally spectacular though less heralded Kip Keino of Kenya.

Ryun had commanded worldwide headlines as a 19 year old in 1966 when breaking the mile and half-mile records. Across the South Atlantic, the son of a goat herdsman, who as a boy had thought nothing of trotting 20 miles to and from school, had been carving the foundations of an equally formidable career. At 19 he had joined the police and his early racing had consisted, rather like a tyre with a slow puncture, of running until the oxygen ran out. Competing in the three miles at the Commonwealth Games of 1962 in Perth, Australia, and using a lengthy stride more appropriate for goat pasture than a cinder track, he had led into the last lap only to finish 11th. In a preview of their Olympic meeting, over 1,500m at sea level in Los Angeles in 1967, Keino had lost to Ryun's finishing kick, the American surpassing Herb Elliott's record with a spectacular 3:33.1. Keino had learned much, tactically, from this race. Ryun might have the pace, but Keino had pace *plus* endurance. Returning to Kenya, he ran a double of mile and three miles in one day, the former in 3:53.1, the third-fastest in history.

Prior to arriving in Mexico City, both runners had endured problems: Ryun a viral infection and failure to qualify in the US trials at Lake Tahoe for the 800m, initially having had in mind an attempted emulation of Peter Snell's double. In Oslo, meanwhile, competing against Clarke over 5,000m, Keino had encountered the first, and potentially devastating, symptoms of his gall bladder infection.

The altitude debate was encapsulated at the outset of the Games by the outcome of the 10,000m, in which the first five were all from high-altitude countries or those who had trained at altitude. Clarke epitomised the plight of the lowlanders, struggling to stay with the leaders at a pace two minutes slower than his world record. Though still in touch two laps out, he took two minutes eighteen seconds to run the last two laps, finishing sixth, collapsing across the line and requiring oxygen in a state of semi-consciousness. Twenty minutes later he was still motionless. Christopher Brasher, former steeplechase champion, angrily wrote in the British *Observer*: 'I feel like throttling the whole of the IOC.'

During the first eight kilometres there had been eleven different leaders. One kilometre later, Keino was seen to collapse but his ailment had nothing to do with thin air. There were four runners left in contention for the medals: Temu; Mohamed Gammoudi, defeated by Billy Mills four years earlier; Mamo Wolde of Ethiopia; and Clarke, the latter about to wilt. Gammoudi, reared in the high North African central desert, had trained rigorously in the Pyrenees. It was Temu, with a 24th lap of sub-65, who led the late charge for the line, but it was Wolde in front by a fraction at the bell. In a desperate final lap, Temu got the verdict by a stride from Wolde, with Gammoudi third.

Kip Keino, affable and courageous Kenyan, who used his fame to create an orphanage. (© IOC)

Brian Corrigan, the Australian team physician, had thought Clarke was going to die. 'I had difficulty even in seeing,' Clarke later recalled, 'but I had to finish, it was a matter of pride.' So, too, was it for Keino. Having stumbled onto the in-field, he had been automatically disqualified yet struggled to his feet to finish the race. Mere gallstones were not going to halt his ambition.

Before the 5,000m came the steeplechase. If Temu had previously been little-known, Amos Biwott, aged 20, was even less so. Heedless of style, form or tactics, clearing the hurdles as though they were a succession of high jumps, he led his heat by 30 metres after half a lap and his time of 8:49.4 was some eight

seconds faster than anyone had ever run at altitude before. Advised by the Kenyan coach of his imprudence, Biwott hung back in the final, allowing Gaston Roelants of Belgium and others to make the pace. Ben Kogo of Kenya led at the bell, only for Biwott to surge through after the last hurdle to win by a couple of strides in 8:51.0, with George Young (USA) third.

The next day came the 5,000m and another African sweep of the medals, with sixth and eighth place also claimed by Africans. Clarke had recovered sufficiently to run, but was never in the frame. Now was the moment for Gammoudi's revenge for the 10,000m. Taking the lead after 4km, he had to fight off the challenge of Temu and finally Keino; the latter, as he has related, bungling his finishing kick in a slow race. Gammoudi's winning time of 14:05.0 was almost 50 seconds outside Clarke's world mark and 25 seconds beyond Kuts' 12-year-old Olympic record. For Keino, the ultimate race remained.

Ryun had been advised by Jack Daniels, a friend and physiologist, to try to conserve his anaerobic strength and, if possible, to make it a slow race, to avoid the fate of Clarke. 'How I prayed for a slow pace,' Ryun was to recall. The Kenyans were to give him no chance. From the gun, Jipcho was off like the proverbial hare with a blistering opening lap of 56, Keino hard on his heels and the other ten finalists in anxious pursuit. The 28-year-old Keino, running the most courageous race of the century, was not going to allow his gall bladder to subject him to the further venom of Ryun's finishing kick. As Jipcho seemed fractionally to ease in the second lap, Keino forged to the front, going through the 800m in an unbelievable 1:55, which every expert witness calculated unsustainable. But no. Through the third lap Keino held the pace, passing the bell at 2:53 – an incredible five seconds ahead of Ryun's world record pace for the longer mile. Ryun by now was more than 30 yards adrift and knew he must do something. Soon. He made the effort and hauled himself past Jipcho but the oxygen debt was too great. Into the last back straight he was still trailing by seven or eight strides, hoping in vain for the crack in Keino's armour that would never appear. The debilitated Keino not only won by a margin greater than Elliott in Rome, some 20 metres, but also in an Olympic record of 3:34.9, inferior only to Ryun's sea-level record of 3:33.1. Keino's Olympic time would not be lowered for 16 years. The pains had erupted once more in the final straight, 'but I said to myself that I had to finish'.

As Ryun collapsed into a chair, the leading marathon runners were arriving under a scorching sun, led by Mamo Wolde, already bronze winner in the 10,000m and successor to his twice-triumphant compatriot Abebe Bikila, who this time had dropped out before the halfway stage. The 36-year-old Wolde, who had made his Olympic debut 12 years earlier in the middle distances, had raised the tempo mid-race together with Temu, who then faded after 30km to finish 19th. Wolde won by more than three minutes from Kenji Kimihara of Japan. Sadly, Bikila was paralysed in a road accident the following year and died five years later at the age of 41.

For the first time in the 72 years of the modern Games, there was an all-black final of the men's 100m: in finishing order, Jim Hines (USA), Lennox Miller (JAM), Charles Greene (USA), Pablo Montes (CUB), Roger Bambuck (FRA), Mel Pender (USA), Harry Jerome (CAN) and Jean-Louis Ravelomanantsoa (MAD). Four months earlier Hines had become the first to go under ten seconds, with 9.9 in the AAU championships in California, but he had lost eight of twelve meetings with Greene, who had equalled his record. In the final in Mexico, Hines had the best start of his life, shared the lead with Greene at halfway and pulled away over the last 20 metres to win in an electronically timed 9.95, regarded as superior to his hand-timed record of 9.9. Ravelomanantsoa's 10.2 in eighth place would have won any Olympic final up to 1960.

In the first all-black final of the Olympic 100m, Jim Hines (USA), the first man to have gone under ten seconds, leads Lennox Miller (JAM, No. 536), silver, and Charles Greene (USA, No. 275), bronze. (© Getty Images)

John Carlos and Tommie Smith, 20-something world record holders in the sprints, were founder members of the 'Olympic Project for Human Rights' initiated by Harry Edwards. Carlos was from Harlem. Smith was the seventh of twelve children of a black sharecropper from Clarksville, Texas, who had taken his family from the cotton fields to the migrant labour camps of California. If Carlos was the extrovert, Smith, near-illiterate, was shy and circumspect, yet socially aware, having experienced the race riots of Birmingham, Alabama. The spontaneous emotions of the two men were about to burst upon the watching world as they raced to triumph in the 200m.

Each won his semi-final heat in the identical time of 20.1, 0.2 off the world record currently held by Carlos. They should have taken 1–2 in the final, but Carlos, momentarily glancing at Smith in the last few strides, allowed Peter Norman of Australia to split them, Smith having improved the record to 19.83.

Vince Matthews, Ronald Freeman, Lawrence James and Lee Evans, America's world record breaking 4-lap relay team, echo the clenched-fist Black Power salute of expelled 200m colleagues Tommie Smith and John Carlos, as they lead out Kenya and Germany after the medal presentation. (© Getty Images)

As they mounted the victory podium, Smith wearing a black scarf around his neck, the two of them shared left- and right-hand gloves supplied by Smith's wife, the pentathlete Denise Paschal. As the band played the US anthem, they raised clenched, gloved fists and stared fixedly at the ground. 'It was not a gesture of hate, but frustration,' Smith said. Memory of their action would long outlive the purity of their athleticism. The US Olympic committee was appalled by this exhibition of racial dissent, though less so than the IOC Executive Board, which pompously demanded that the two be expelled from the Village. Particularly incensed were Brundage and the Marquis of Exeter, the former Olympic champion. The athletes were duly sent home, supposedly in disgrace. Yet sympathy was widespread. Had their gesture been any more political or offensive than that of many non-Germans in 1936 who gave a straight-armed salute in feigned respect for Adolf Hitler? (There is confusion on this issue, because the official Olympic salute and that of the Nazis was at that time identical.) Carlos responded with the claim that the Olympic Movement itself was political. 'Why do you have to wear the uniform of your country, why do they play national anthems, why do the Americans have to beat the Russians?' he asked. 'Why can't everyone wear the same colours and just numbers to tell them apart? What happened to the Olympic ideal of man against man?' These were questions which Brundage, Exeter and others preferred not to address. Coincidentally, in 1982, Peter Ueberroth, head of the organising committee, appointed Carlos to promote the LA Games in 1984.

Lee Evans was already the world record holder for 400m and the outright favourite for the Olympic event, but he was also a close friend and teammate of Smith and Carlos at San José State University and, like Smith, he was a former migrant labourer from California. His instinct was to return home with his expelled colleagues, but he relented when Carlos told him it made more sense to race. In the event, even allowing for the advantages of altitude, it was to be one of the finest of all one-lap races.

The draw for the final favoured Evans' more dangerous compatriot rival, Larry James, who was drawn inside him and, thus, had him in view. Evans knew, therefore, it had to be flat out all the way, but as they came into the final straight James was in his peripheral vision to his left. Faint though he felt, Evans held on, lowering his record by sixteen-hundredths to 43.86, with James almost a tenth of a second behind and their colleague Ron Freeman in third place. On the victory podium, all three wore black berets, though were careful to remove them during the national anthem, then waved them provocatively when the band halted. Brundage fumed in vain.

The thin air at altitude was a significant advantage for an anaerobic event such as the 400m, even more so for jumping, as proved devastatingly by Bob Beamon. Speculation was rife that something special would happen, but attention focused on Ralph Boston of America and Igor Ter-Ovanesian of the Soviet Union, joint world record holders at 8.35m (27 ft 4¾ in.) and respective silver and bronze winners four years earlier behind Lynn Davies of Britain – also present. Beamon, however, was in prime physical shape at 21, a relative lightweight for 6 ft 3 in., with critical sprinting ability from both power and length in the femur (thigh bone). Yet in the qualifying round, Beamon, just like Owens in 1936, was in some trouble, with two foul jumps. Boston, with the same benevolence as Lutz Long had shown to Owens, told Beamon to pull back his take-off mark. This he did, his third jump of 8.19m (26 ft 10½ in.) carrying him two feet or so more than he needed. Tension was added to the final by a delay while Artur Takac, the IOC's Technical Director, removed a clutter of shoes placed down the runway by jumpers as checkmarks but also so that their shoe brands would be highlighted by television coverage. As Adriaan Paulen of the IAAF inspected the runway, Boston turned to him in good humour, saying 'Hurry up, old man, Christmas is coming.'

The first to record a legal jump was Beamon. Three before him had fouled. Now came a landmark moment in the history of sport. Beamon launched into his approach, 19 strides, a perfect take-off and there he was soaring up and away, feet stretched out at waist level. 'That's 28 feet,' Boston said to Davies as they went to the pit for a closer look. Beamon was dancing around agitatedly; he, too, knew it was special. But there was a delay, a problem in the pit. Early in the day, Takac had told the stadium's technical engineer to add 40 centimetres to the marking device. Paulen had agreed that this should be plenty. Yet the jump was still beyond the capacity of the measuring system, and an old-fashioned steel tape used by building surveyors had to be fetched. The judge stretched the tape from the marker point to the board. The watching Paulen was uncompromising: 'Jesus, we must re-measure, something is wrong.' He and Takac stretched out the tape again. There was no error. At last the distance flashed on the scoreboard. Beamon had not merely surpassed the 28-foot mark, but also the 29-foot mark, with a leap of 8.90m (29 ft 2½ in.). Momentarily, Beamon could not adjust to reality, being unfamiliar with the metric system, until Boston explained to him just what he had done. Davies muttered to Boston: 'What's the point in going on? We'll all look silly.'

If Beamon had shattered conventional concepts, in distance, so too did Dick Fosbury, an American high jumper, in style. By a study of physics and engineering, he had deduced that, rather than attempting to clear the bar by either the straddle, with one foot following the other, or the western roll, in which both feet cleared the bar together – the whole body more or less horizontal and all of it above the bar at the same time – it was geometrically/ergonomically expedient to clear the bar

It was not just alliteration that made famous the Fosbury Flop. Innovatively landing on his neck, Dick Fosbury revolutionised the high jump. (© Getty Images)

backwards. By thus rolling in an arc, with the head and feet vertically below the hips at the peak of the arc, on opposite sides of the bar, it was possible never to raise the centre of gravity to the height at which the bar was set. Presto! The only minor disadvantage, of course, was that he landed on the back of his neck. Fosbury, indeed, had compressed a couple of vertebrae when devising his new technique at high school in the mid-1960s, none of the schools being able to afford foam landing pits. He survived this injury of initiative and indeed 30 years later was still as full of laughter as ever. The final became a contest between three: him, Edward Caruthers and Valentin Gavrilov, a Russian Soviet. With the bar raised to 2.24m (7 ft 4 ¼ in.), Olympic record height, Caruthers and Gavrilov failed three times, Fosbury twice. With a huge crowd on the final day captivated by the novelty of his display, Fosbury made his final attempt, almost exceeding the two-minute preparation margin. Leaping forward, pivoting on his right leg and rising like a rolling, half-opened jackknife, he made it. The Fosbury Flop had become history. Soon it was standard technique.

Thin air also assisted the short track events. The first seven in the 400m hurdles beat the previous Olympic record, yet David Hemery (GBR) made even them look second class as he won by a huge margin of nearly a second, with a world record of 48.1. Gerhard Hennige of Germany was second, John Sherwood (GBR) third. Hemery led from the second hurdle and received his medal from the Marquis of Exeter, winner 40 years earlier.

If Hemery's performance was of truly Olympian status, so was that of the incredible Al Oerter, winning his fourth consecutive discus title. All season, Oerter, by now a computer company executive and 32 years old, had lagged behind his compatriot Jay Silvester, the new world record holder. In the final, there was a halt during rain and on resumption, in spite of a wet throwing circle and heavy humidity, Oerter exceptionally achieved his best-ever throw of 64.78m (212 ft 6½ in.) – each of his Olympic titles having been won with an Olympic record. The silver

Bob Beamon (USA) looks as astonished as everyone else as he soars to his historic long-jump world record of 8.90m (29 ft 2½ in.). (© IOC)

At the age of 32, in a rain-soaked throwing circle, Al Oerter (USA) wins his remarkable fourth successive discus title.
(© Getty Images)

medal was taken by Lothar Milde (GDR), with Silvester fifth: proof of a unique element of the Games being the mental ability to deliver on one day in four years, often one day in a lifetime.

The women's 100m was as much notable for the girl who came third, Irena Szewinska (Kirszenstein) of Poland – continuing her multiple medal career – as for the fact that it contained four world record holders, Wyomia Tyus, Barbara Ferrell and Margaret Bailes (all USA) and Szewinska – Ferrell and Szewinska having tied the existing record of 11.1 in the second round. Tyus, the first male or female to defend an Olympic sprint title successfully, was a clear winner in the final in a world record of 11.08. Szewinska, runner-up in the 200m four years earlier, now set a world record of 22.58 with a following wind exactly on the limit of 2 mph.

In the 400m, the favourite was Lillian Board, 19-year-old blonde darling of the British public. But in one of the major surprises of the Games, Colette Besson from Bordeaux overhauled Board a stride from the finishing line, equalling the Olympic record with 52.03. Board seemed destined for success in Munich, but two years beforehand, she developed cancer and with tragic coincidence died in a Munich clinic shortly after her 22nd birthday.

A further surprise occurred in the 800m when another youthful favourite, Vera Nikolic of Yugoslavia, the 20-year-old world record holder, quit after less than a lap of the semi-final. European champion two years earlier in Budapest, she had carried a daily burden of state expectation, unrelieved even by her coach Alex Petrovic. Her parents and grandparents had been promised state rewards if she won Olympic gold; the mayor of her tiny Serbian town, Cuprija, was promised promotion. The winner was Madeline Manning (USA) in an Olympic record of 2:00.9.

Political overtones touched many events. Czechoslovakia had recently been occupied by the USSR in the 'Prague Spring', President Alexander Dubcek having been overthrown. When

Vera Cáslavská added another four gold and two silver to the three gold and two silver medals which she had won in Tokyo and chose the Mexican Hat Dance as the accompaniment to her final floor exercise, the Mexican public and many others took her to their hearts: not least because Soviets Zinaida Voronina and Natalia Kuchinskaya had been beaten for the individual all-round title, and Larissa Latynina (URS) and Erika Zuchold and Karin Janz of East Germany – which had heavily aided the Prague overthrow – were relegated to the next three places. Cáslavská's four golds equalled those of Kraenzlein (1900), Owens (1936), Blankers-Koen (1948) and Schollander (1964). To cap her triumph, she married her fiancé Josef Odlozil, eighth in the men's 1,500m, in the city's El Zocalo Cathedral with 10,000 admiring supporters in the square outside. She later became president of her NOC and an IOC member.

Domination by the United States in swimming – their 23 gold, 15 silver and 20 bronze medals from a total of a 107 exceeding all other countries combined – rendered the competition almost boring. Michael Wenden, however, brought Australia both freestyle sprint titles, with a world record 52.22 in the 100m and defeating Don Schollander (USA) in the 200m. Roland Matthes (GDR) won both backstroke titles and the local timekeepers abandoned their clipboards in euphoria when 17-year-old Felipe Muñoz triumphed in the 200m breaststroke. Somebody named Mark Spitz won a couple of golds in relays.

A couple of beers cost Sweden the team bronze in the modern pentathlon. With drug testing being operated for the first time, one of their team, Hans-Gunnar Liljenvael, was over the alcohol limit prior to the pistol shooting – the first competitor to be disqualified for 'doping'. The individual medals were won by Sweden, Hungary and the USSR.

In the cycling road time trial, Sweden uniquely took the silver medal with the four Petterson brothers – Erik, Gosta, Sture and Tomas – the only instance of four brothers gaining medals in the same event. The winners were Holland.

George Foreman, climbing his way out of a Houston ghetto after being a teenage alcoholic and delinquent, had reorganised his life sufficiently to win the heavyweight boxing title after only 18 amateur fights. He would later defeat Joe Frazier for the professional title before losing it to Muhammad Ali. Nuria Ortiz of Mexico became the first woman to take part in shooting – finishing 13th in the skeet events.

The balletic Vera Cáslavská (TCH) adds another four gold and two silver to her gymnastics collection. (© Getty Images)

CHAPTER XLIV

Terror

Thomas Bach of Germany, Olympic fencing champion, IOC Vice-President

'The Olympic Games of Munich in 1972 were intended to overthrow barriers, promote understanding, bring together sports and culture – thus meeting the aim of mankind's Games. This dream was shattered with previously unimagined, barbarous brutality on 5 September, leaving the world in shock. The terrorist attack on the athletes of the Israeli team destroyed in one blow all the joyfulness and festival-like atmosphere. It demonstrated to the world the vulnerability of the Olympic philosophy, yet also stressed its value. It was not only Avery Brundage's famous insistence that "the Games must go on" that cemented the will of the public. It was above all the overriding, respectful behaviour of the athletes, officials and spectators in the days following the tragedy that restored the dignity of the Olympic Games. Rarely have the Games touched emotions so strongly as at Munich in 1972. Those Games focused the extremes of human behaviour.

Yet the conception for Munich by that Olympic visionary Willi Daume was fulfilled in every other respect. Germany and Munich presented to the world the friendly festival as promised, in a relaxed and peaceful atmosphere which few had expected the Germans to be able to create. The Western part of the then still-divided Germany took the rare opportunity to show to the world a different country: a country of tolerance, full of heartfelt hospitality. To achieve that, even political barriers were put aside and in the midst of the Cold War the then German Democratic Republic was given the possibility of equal representation.

Willi Daume succeeded not only in providing the organisational framework for those Olympics but also in creating a homogenous work of art. The innovative architecture of the Olympic Park, with its tent-like transparent roof, with its lightness and almost playful elegance, was a pleasant contrast with conventional construction. The architecture smoothly fitted into picturesque scenery, sensitively landscaped, where barren ground had been transformed into a park of dunes and hills, small lakes and romantic ponds. It was there that this contented, serene atmosphere of a true Olympic festival was born. This mood was reflected in the freshness of the visual arrangement of colour, form and design, ranging from the seats of the stands to the flags and the uniforms of the numerous volunteers; everywhere the shining colours of pale blue, green, yellow and ochre delighted the spectator's eye. The visitors let themselves be carried away by this festive mood, thus even extending it. They celebrated the triumphs of athletes from all over the world in fair and identical manner, cheered the winners of the "other" Germany, strolled through the Olympic Park and made contact with athletes from the adjacent Olympic Village and with journalists and guests from all continents. The Olympic Idea had won the people's hearts.'*
(Photograph © IOC/Locatelli)

The Olympiad 1968–72 witnessed mounting controversies amid the declining authority and confounded idealism of the octogenarian Brundage. There was poignancy in what was to befall his cherished organisation, almost as venerated by him as by the founder. So conspicuously successful had the Olympic Games become that increasingly they were a platform for public demonstration of extra-curricular motives. If there had been a foretaste of this with the Black Power demonstration by Tommie Smith and John Carlos, the turmoil of racial–religious conflicts was to reach a horrific climax in Munich with the assassination of Israeli competitors by the Black September branch of the Palestine Liberation Organisation (PLO). This ghastly punctuation of what was the most glorious staging of any Olympics thus far was the bitterest finale for the Chicago multi-millionaire who had devoted such a large part of his life and fortune to championing the universality of the festival of fellowship recreated by de Coubertin.

To compound Brundage's frustration, he and his colleagues had been manoeuvred, prior to the Israeli tragedy, into another political corner, in the months and final days prior to the opening of the Munich Games, by the Organisation of African Unity (OAU), which successfully demanded the exclusion of a Rhodesian team that, on sporting and Charter criteria, was demonstrably eligible. The matter of contention for black Africa was the unilateralist, independent and unrecognised white government of Ian Smith, who had broken from British colonial rule.

Additionally, Brundage's trenchant but outdated views on amateurism led to the farcical disqualification of a single exceptional skier, Karl Schranz of Austria, who was merely one

Willi Daume, former German basketball player and devoted Olympian, organised a brilliant Munich Games intended to charm the world – all in vain. (© IOC/Strahm)

of dozens transgressing the regulations on advertisement-bearing equipment, while Brundage's ongoing antagonism towards any organisational authority by NOCs had engendered a mood of mutual hostility. Within this, furthermore, had come the resignation of Secretary-General Westerhoff, in January 1969, following the move to new offices in Lausanne the previous spring. Brundage was dissatisfied with his work; Westerhoff was overwhelmed by the ever-expanding number of NOCs and the complexity of the Games, for which his supporting staff were inadequate. Westerhoff was succeeded by Monique Berlioux, the Director of Press and Public Relations. She would continue to handle press affairs, thus assuming a double responsibility, not to mention double the salary. A former Olympic swimmer for France, she was a woman of rare industry with a bearing that increasingly came to intimidate some of the less assertive IOC members. She would proceed to overhaul the whole Secretariat, formalising the organisation and acquiring, under the regime of successive, largely absentee, presidents, Brundage and then Lord Killanin, an unprecedented degree of power.

Also on-running at this time, among the IOC's various problems, was the rivalry of the two Chinas: the gargantuan mainland Communist People's Republic and the off-shore, separatist, capitalist haven of Taiwan. The People's Republic was seeking membership of the UN and attempting to restore diplomatic relations worldwide. Its rapport with the United States was clouded by the war in Vietnam but a breach in this stand-off came in the spring of 1971, when the People's Republic sent a table tennis team to the World Championships staged in Nagoya, Japan. Also present was an American team and as a result of this connection the Chinese invited the American team to visit China. Following diplomatic representations, the US table tennis association accepted and the American players were received by Chairman Chou En-lai in person. Henry Kissinger in his memoirs would note: 'The whole

enterprise was vintage Chou En-lai. Like all Chinese moves, it had so many layers of meaning that the brilliantly painted surface was the least significant part.'

This mutual wooing took place against a background confused by Brundage's unilateral nomination, the previous year, of Henry Hsu as an IOC member in Taiwan, forcing the election against unanimous opposition from the Executive Board – another controversy that would be a legacy for Killanin. It was the rational intention of the Executive Board to achieve the return to the fold of mainland China, yet it was impossible to have two NOCs claiming to represent 'China'. A twist in the story came in the autumn of 1971 when the People's Republic was admitted to the UN Security Council, Taiwan thereby being obliged to withdraw from the UN.

In 1971, Brundage described the new Permanent General Assembly of NOCs as 'unnecessary agents'. He saw the PGA as a threat to the authority of the IOC, which was indeed possible, but required more careful analysis than Brundage was either willing or by now emotionally capable of giving to it. While the IOC was a paternal oligarchy, the PGA, under leadership of Giulio Onesti of Italy, was democratically based, though without executive power. At an Executive Board meeting, Brundage even went so far as to recommend that committee members should choose between the IOC and the PGA, and that those who supported the latter should resign from the IOC. Killanin and others protested, asserting that the PGA was necessary. Adetokunbo Ademola of Nigeria commented that many African NOCs felt neglected by the IOC. In spite of Executive Board support for the PGA, Brundage wrote to the three Vice-Presidents of the IOC, stating: 'The PGA must be buried now, and perhaps the three Vice-Presidents will have the courage to report that any IOC member who wishes to participate in PGA activities must first resign from the IOC.' The Vice-Presidents ignored these strictures.

Age and time were running against Brundage, his term of office approaching its end. This conflict was mirrored in the Soviet Union's demand, in 1970, that the Executive Board should be geographically representative. They were assuaged by the election of Konstantin Andrianov (USSR), Juan Antonio Samaranch (Spain), Silvio de Magalhaes Padilha (Brazil) and Prince Tsuyenoshi Takeda (Japan). But the Soviet attempt to make the IOC, NOCs and IFs a tri-lateral body with a strong Communist element, effectively a 'UN of sport', had failed. Some satisfaction for the NOCs was de Beaumont's proposal in 1971 for the founding of an 'Olympic Solidarity Committee', to handle the dispensation of financial benefits, including the NOCs' share of television income. Brundage was in approval of this, with reservations, as ever jealous of the transfer of any power from the IOC. It was intended initially that only IOC members should operate this fund, but provision was made for inclusion of NOC and IF representatives, the fund to begin operation following the Munich Games.

Brundage had been continually tormented by the aspects of amateurism. Prior to the upcoming Winter Games in Sapporo, Marc Hodler, president of international skiing, stated that there was no intention by the FIS to boycott the Games but if, as was mooted by Brundage, a number of skiers were banned as professionals, then the FIS would organise a separate world championship the following year. At the 1971 FIS congress, Austria, France, Italy, Switzerland, West Germany and Yugoslavia had threatened a boycott if Brundage were to fulfil the threat to ban ten skiers who had been compensated for participation at an event in California. Brundage had backed off, merely stating that

'No advertising of any kind is allowed in the Olympic area, either on things or on people.' Immediately prior to the Sapporo Games, however, the Eligibility Commission presented a report recommending 'that considering the activity of Karl Schranz in the field of international Alpine ski competition and the manner in which he has permitted the use of his name and picture in commercial advertising in recent years, he should be declared ineligible to take part in the XIth Olympic Winter Games'. Brundage archly declared: 'Remember, it is not the IOC that disqualifies – competitors disqualify themselves.' Mohamed Mzali, the member for Tunisia, warned, on the other hand: 'If we disqualify Schranz, he will become a national hero in Austria and will be regarded as a martyr.' When the Session voted, 28 members supported the Eligibility Commission's proposal, with 14 against. The Austrian ski federation decided to withdraw their entire team unless the ban were reversed. However, Schranz himself spoke against such action at a press conference and the request was withdrawn. Schranz's appeal for a personal hearing was rejected by Brundage on the grounds that the IOC did not negotiate with individuals. Schranz responded:

> If Mr Brundage had been poor, as I once was and as were many other athletes, I wonder if he wouldn't have a different attitude? If his recommendations were followed, then the Olympics would be a competition only for the rich. No man of ordinary means could ever afford to excel in his sport. This thing of amateur purity is something that dates back to the nineteenth century when amateur sportsmen were regarded as gentlemen and eveyone else was an outcast. The Olympic Games should be a competition of skill and strength and speed – and no more.

So blatant was the professionalism surrounding Karl Schranz, and the mute acceptance of the Austrian and international ski federations, that Brundage was wilfully, and riskily, determined to have him banned. (© IOC/Ruebelt)

Returning home to Vienna from Sapporo, Schranz was greeted by a crowd of 200,000 avid supporters. The US Embassy was besieged with protests. Following the Games, Schranz announced his retirement and was awarded the Austrian Order of Merit. A seething Brundage renewed his demand that the Winter Games be terminated following those scheduled for Denver, Colorado, in 1976. He was warned by Alexandru Siperco of Romania, however, that, were the IOC to take such a step, some other organisation such as UNESCO would almost certainly take over. More alarming still was the view expressed by President Kekkonen of Finland, himself a former athlete, who stated in an interview that it should be the UN and not the IOC who administered the Games.

The winter candidates for 1972, when the decision had been taken in April 1966, had been Banff, in the Canadian Rockies, Salt Lake City, Utah, and Sapporo. The United States had only recently (1960) been hosts at Squaw Valley and Sapporo's chances were doubtful on account of the travelling distance. With Banff strongly opposed by the Canadian Wildlife Association, however, Sapporo was the choice: the ninth largest city in Japan with a population of over a million. The city had first been awarded the Games for 1940, but these had been cancelled on account of the Second World War.

The organisers in Sapporo would outlay more than half a billion dollars on roads, subways and sporting facilities, much of this to handle the needs of 3,000 press, radio and television personnel, who outnumbered competitors by more than two to one. The data-processing centre alone cost over half a million dollars, doubtless to the benefit of the Japanese electronics industry. The Games would be a catalyst for development of the northern island, which has one-fifth of the land area of Japan but at that time only one-twentieth of the population. Accommodating the two Alpine downhill races while preserving the virgin slopes of the 1,220m /4,000 ft Mt Eniwa was a miracle of manipulation by 15,000 men, 850 bulldozers and six tons of explosives, creating two courses serviced by cable cars and a chair-lift, yet all returned to its natural state within weeks of the conclusion of the Games. The bobsleigh course on Mt Teine, together with the slalom and giant slalom courses, likewise was never to be used again.

Following the embarrassing vacillation regarding the legitimacy of South Africa's Olympic status to compete at Mexico City, and the late reversal then of the decision for re-acceptance, the IOC vainly hoped that the South African NOC (SANOC) might, as it were, go away. They were to be disappointed. In the late autumn of 1968, Basil d'Oliveira, a South African-born Cape Coloured player selected for England's cricket tour party for South Africa, was refused entry by Prime Minister Vorster. The tour was cancelled: one of Britain's less equivocal acts in this long-running controversy, undertaken, however, in protection of their own interests. Two summers later, anti-apartheid sympathisers vandalised English cricket grounds, threatening to disrupt a Springbok tour, which was in turn cancelled. Arthur Ashe, the black American tennis player, was refused a visa to play in South Africa, which was then banned from the Davis Cup.

In 1969, the IOC received information that SANOC had used the Olympic Rings to publicise the 'South African Games', an all-white multi-sport event. Brundage suggested that, to be on the safe side, South Africa should be expelled. His colleagues considered this improper, saying that SANOC should be given the opportunity to defend themselves. Therefore SANOC was invited to send a delegate to that year's Session in Warsaw, but there are no records of the presence of such a delegate. Pressure from African NOCs mounted, Brundage stalled. SANOC was scheduled to attend the next Executive Board meeting, but black Africa protested at being required to sit in the same room as SANOC delegates at the proposed meeting of NOCs. As a compromise, SANOC was allowed to make a statement and remain in the room without the right to speak.

Prior to the 1970 Session in Amsterdam, the IOC was intending to offer members an option: expel South Africa, or allow them to remain but not to participate at Munich. However, 19 African NOCs meeting in Cairo voted unanimously that South Africa should be expelled, citing the precedent that many IFs had already taken this step. Brundage, recognising the gravity of the situation, recommended to the Executive Board that the IOC should likewise cede. When asked at the Session whether they approved of 'the withdrawal of recognition' from SANOC, the voting was nonetheless quite close: 35 votes in favour, 28 against, with 3 abstentions. A distraught Reginald Honey asked for time to consider whether he would resign his IOC membership. In an illustration of the inherent decency existing among staunch opponents, who recognised that individuals in rival camps were sometimes trapped in political circumstances beyond their control, Ahmad Touny of Egypt requested Honey to remain. In spite of this decision, the South African door was not finally closed. Brundage and Killanin both believed that some form of contact should continue, in order that SANOC might persist with endeavours to achieve the integrated status for sport. During the Session at Sapporo, some credence was given to the report of Rudolph Opperman, the SANOC delegate, that there was fresh movement towards this.

South Africa was one cross for the IOC to bear. Another was Rhodesia. The increasingly self-confident and highly influential Supreme Council for Sport in Africa (SCSA) wished to impose the same banishment, attempting to raise the issue at Amsterdam. The principle – black integration in former white-administered colonies – was the same, but the detail was markedly different. Rhodesia had competed at the Games of Rome and Tokyo as a British colony, but in 1963 there had been the dissolution of the Federation of Rhodesia and Nyasaland. The country only became a sporting pariah with the Unilateral Declaration of Independence by premier Ian Smith in 1965 and a trade boycott by the UN. It was not until 1969 that black Africa began to make a stand against alleged discrimination within Zimbabwean sport – where, as the Rhodesian NOC asserted, there were mixed teams competing in open competition and the NOC was free of government interference. The Session in Amsterdam found that there were no reasonable grounds on which the Rhodesia NOC could be sanctioned, even though Andrianov of the USSR pedantically made the point that on a political basis the NOC did not now represent a recognised country. In 1971, the SCSA accepted that Rhodesia would participate in Munich, with a subsequent inquiry commission to determine the exact state of domestic sport, notwithstanding that an investigation by IAAF that year had already confirmed that there were no separate or special facilities for whites. It was stipulated that Rhodesia's participation in 1972 would be under the same terms as in 1964: as 'Southern Rhodesia', athletes would travel with British passports and compete under the same colonial flag. The SCSA was wrong-footed by this agreement: Chief Abraham Ordia, their leader, and his colleagues had assumed that Rhodesia would not accept such humiliating conditions.

Just when all seemed calm, a gale blew through the IOC's window. Six days before the Munich opening ceremony, 21 African NOCs drafted a resolution demanding 'the exclusion of

Southern Rhodesia', under threat of their own withdrawal. King Hassan II of Morocco, chairman of the OAU and known to be moderate, nonetheless sent the following message:

> In spite of the wish of 41 African countries to participate in the spirit of good sportsmanship, we feel obliged to state the position of African countries, which envisage withdrawing from the festival of Munich should the decision of the IOC to have Rhodesia participate in these Games be maintained. Moreover, the OAU has already received the assurance of some non-African countries to unite with our continent, should the latter not be present at Munich.

Soviet IOC member Konstantin Andrianov, a central figure in attempts to realign the IOC in a United Nations mould and to expel South Africa and Southern Rhodesia. (© IOC/Strahm)

The IOC was in a cleft stick. Hassan's talk of non-African unity was made in the knowledge of support from the Soviet Union and from black members of the American team. The insistence of SCSA's allies such as Henry Adefope of Nigeria and Andrianov was unrelenting. While there was no regulation within the IOC's Charter under which action could be taken against them, and while a formal decision had been agreed among sports representatives from all continents that 'Rhodesia' might compete, the German organising committee was in understandable panic. The investment in the Games was colossal and the organising committee, led by president Willi Daume, begged the IOC to reconsider the position, never mind that the Rhodesian team, forty-seven men and women including seven blacks, had already arrived in Munich. The OAU focused on the technical excuse that Rhodesia had travelled on Olympic identity cards rather than British passports. Moreover, this tactic was strengthened by the fact that the federal government, a signatory to the UN boycott of Zimbabwe's unilateral government, was being urged by the UN to reject the Rhodesian team. On the other hand, the IOC was divided down the middle, politically if not morally, white versus black, with

IOC members Hugh Weir of Australia and Lance Cross of New Zealand urging their colleagues not to allow the Movement to become a political whipping-boy. Brundage put before the Session in Munich the alternatives: that the members must support either the Rhodesia NOC, their own legitimately affiliated body, or the rest of black Africa; that a vote for Rhodesia would precipitate a mass withdrawal; that a vote for protesting black Africa would be seen as weakness under political pressure; that, in the event of a vote for Rhodesia, the Rhodesians themselves might then voluntarily withdraw in a gesture of goodwill.

The division was as narrow as would be expected. Rhodesia's invitation was withdrawn by thirty-six votes to thirty-one with three abstentions. The Munich Games had been saved, but the IOC had laid itself bare to media attack for ignoring its own statutes. Brundage himself stated:

> Much of the world had judged until now that the IOC was the only international organisation capable of resisting opportunism and political blackmail, and now it has committed suicide . . . this is the first time in my 20 years as IOC President that I have pleaded with the Session to follow my recommendation on an important choice. You have not done that and, therefore, I believe that I should cease to be President.

The election of a new President was already scheduled to take place that week.

Two days later Brundage's successor was chosen, though his own authority, such as it was, would continue, with subsequent acute embarrassment, for the duration of the imminent Games. With some reluctance, Michael Morris, from Dublin, former journalist, film director and company director, who had inherited from his father the hereditary title of Lord Killanin, had agreed to be nominated as a candidate. His only rival was Comte Jean de Beaumont, Paris banker and long-time powerbroker in the IOC, who transparently yearned for the post.

Brundage (right) and President-elect Lord Killanin ponder over the Rhodesian crisis preceding the Munich Games.
(© popperfoto.com)

However, de Beaumont had made enemies and the IOC was disinclined to choose another over-opinionated President, preferring the mild-mannered, if at times indecisive, Killanin. The Communist bloc, perceiving that they would be able to lean upon him, supported Killanin, and on the first ballot he won by 39 votes to 29. Brundage did not vote. 'We need a leader and Michael isn't one,' he is said to have remarked to Daume. Killanin was fundamentally a genial compromiser, friend to all. He had been bequeathed an Olympic Movement at a time of turmoil. Though he was not to know it, the temperature in the kitchen was to continue to rise exponentially. He would endure eight years not just of change, but also of torment.

The Games of Munich were a fresh opportunity for the German nation again to demonstrate its underlying sporting proclivities, evident since the widespread gymnastics societies of the previous century and in its much-criticised, politically motivated staging of the Games in Berlin in 1936 – a Games postponed from 1916. In spite of the devastation of many German cities, in the West as well as the East, generic energy and discipline proved irrepressible in both parts of this divided nation and in 1966 Munich had been elected to host the Games of 1972. Here was the opportunity for the Federal Republic to demonstrate, simultaneously, the recovery of its economy and its capacity to befriend the rest of the world in some kind of unspoken, belated atonement for all the horrors that a previous regime had visited upon civilisation. President Gustav Heinemann proclaimed that Munich's hospitality would be 'a milestone on the road to a new way of life with the aim of realising peaceful co-existence among peoples'.

The Games seemed to all to be an antidote to violence, to the continuing strife that existed for example in Northern Ireland between Catholic and Protestant and in the Middle East between Jew and Arab. How wretchedly this illusion was to be shattered. The Games were poised, indeed, to be triumphant. The total costs of the extravagantly designed new stadia, which were an architectural revolution, and of road and rail development and building construction for the Village, varied in estimate between $650 and $750 million. The Village was within walking distance of many of the competition sites; the transport, the communications, the food, indeed every logistical detail was superbly planned. Admissions totalled nearly four and a half million, filling 90 per cent of seats available. There were crowds of more than 60,000 for preliminary morning sessions of track and field at the first Games in Europe for 12 years and for the first time global television carried live transmission to every corner of the world. There was even a new electronic device for measuring throwing events. Archery and men's handball returned to the programme and with over 4,000 media personnel, the Games received greater coverage than ever. In August 1972, spectators were open-mouthed with awe and appreciation of what the people of Munich had achieved, and the world held its breath in expectation of the next fortnight's deeds as Heidi Schüller, the first woman to do so, took the competitor's oath at the opening ceremony; which included, for the first time, Albania, Dahomey (later Benin), Lesotho, Malawi, North Korea, Upper Volta (later Burkina Faso), Somalia, Swaziland and Togo.

CHAPTER XLV

Sapporo (XI) 1972

Ard Schenk of the Netherlands, Olympic triple speed skating champion

'With the arrival of "open" sport, there was quite a gap between athletes in elite sport, in the way they organised how to deal with the money that was becoming available. With the IOC and the international federations busy negotiating contracts, many of us realised there should be some commercial return to the athletes. Karl Schranz and I knew each other and had discussed this issue. Having won medals in World and European championships, I was one of the favourites in Sapporo, but the Norwegian NOC had written to Avery Brundage, complaining about me and a couple of Norwegian competitors being involved in a soft drink advertisement. The Dutch NOC and I took the attitude that we had not realised there was an infringement and I was allowed to take part. Later, in 1974–5, Karl and I took part in a "Superstars" televised competition in the United States organised by Mark McCormack. Karl reflected: "I possibly became more popular at home when I was expelled than had I won a gold medal."

I really was confident in Sapporo, holding five world records at the time, but I knew I still had to prove myself. Maybe I'd win one event, or none, though I always had the belief that I could win three. Things can go wrong and for the opening 5,000m it was snowing and I was in the first pair. After six pairs, they couldn't clear the ice properly, the surface was rutted and they couldn't water the rink for new ice, so my opening time held up. That's the first, I thought, now for the 1,500m. I hadn't been defeated at this distance for two or three years. Happily it was a good day and there was no wind and I won again, but then fell in the first few strides of the 500m. For the 10,000m, I wanted to go last and our team arranged our ranking groups so that this would happen. Some opponents argued that I ought to be in the first group after winning the 5,000m, but after being third in the recent European Championships I had the right to skate last and this was a big help.

Winning three gold medals was the most important time of my career, yet two weeks later I made a bigger achievement, technically, when winning all four titles in the World Championships in Oslo, plus the all-round title. For the public and the media, however, Sapporo was everything.

The following season, I joined the professional circuit but we were boycotted internationally, barred from rinks, and on one occasion we were racing for a televised competition in the middle of a wood and there were more trees than spectators. I still have my medals somewhere in the garage – these days I'm more concerned with my work in physiotherapy. The federation admitted that they failed us in the transition to the professional era.'*

(Photograph © IOC)

Few contestants enter an Olympic Games with morale to match that of Ard Schenk. Eight years earlier, at 19, he had won the overall Dutch title. Two years later, his feats at the European Championships had caused national celebration and the same year he had set world records at 1,500m and 3,000m. At Grenoble in 1968, he had gained only a silver in 1,500m, but subsequently broke six world records at distances from 1,000m to 10,000m. Expectation was immense for the four events he had entered at Sapporo. When the day arrived for the first, the 5,000m, the elements threatened. It was snowing, which is the worst condition for speed skaters on an open-air rink. Worse still, he was drawn to skate first, allowing him no margin to judge what he had to beat. On the powdered surface at Makomanai Rink, his time of 7:23.61 was way outside his own record. To dim his prospects even further, the snowfall halted and the rink was cleared. But now a wind got up to protect him.

Times declined rather than improved and his arch-rival and colleague Kees Verkerk, skating last, was nearly half a minute slower. Admitting that he did not even know what the Olympic record was he had failed to break, Schenk cheerfully observed that the medal was everything. There were three more awaiting it seemed, but a fall at the start of the 500m sprint eliminated that chance. Undismayed, Schenk went on to set an Olympic record of 2:02.96 in the 1,500m. For the 10,000m, drawn last, he was able to know exactly where he stood. Verkerk had set the standard with an Olympic record of 15:04.70 but with measured judgement over the 25 laps, Schenk improved this by over three seconds, thus becoming the third speed skater to take three Olympic titles.

Even with the contrived removal of Karl Schranz, Austria still had ambitions in the Alpine events but these were to be denied by Italy, Switzerland and, of all 'winter' nations, Spain. The

Ard Schenk of the Netherlands, having closely skirted professionalism investigations prior to imminent open sport, swept to three speed skating gold medals at Sapporo (seen here previously winning silver at Grenoble). (© IOC)

French, too, had hopes for Henri Duvillard in the downhill, but miscalculated on a gamble of making Duvillard one of their lower seeded competitors to gain a later start, hoping that he would thereby enjoy improved conditions on new snow. The snow never arrived and Bernhard Russi of Switzerland, starting fourth, attacked the already crisp piste and his time of 1:51.43 remained unchallenged. The luckless Duvillard, starting 27th, finished 19th on a, by now, scarred course.

In the giant slalom, Erik Håker of Norway had the fastest first run but then fell at the start of the second. Gustavo Thöni of Italy, with unblemished technique on both runs, had a combined time of 3:09.62, more than a second ahead of Edmund Bruggmann of Switzerland, thus becoming the first Italian to win an Alpine gold for 20 years.

French hopes were dashed again in the slalom. Jean-Noël Augert, fifth in the giant slalom, was widely fancied but injured himself in the ribs with his ski-pole. He raced with a pain-killing injection to set the second fastest time on the slalom's first run, only to fade to fifth overall on the second. Thöni and his cousin Roland were technically consistent in claiming silver and bronze places, yet the winner, almost devoid of credentials, was Francisco Fernández Ochoa, a 21-year-old Spaniard from Madrid who had been training with the French team. Ochoa had never previously finished higher than sixth in an international event. His two evenly timed runs for a total of 1:49.27 not only brought the first gold by Spain in a Winter Games but also the country's first victory of any kind since the equestrian team jumping event of 1928.

Under almost as much scrutiny for commercialism as Schranz by the FIS was Annie Famose, the French skier. This may have affected her performance in the women's downhill, in which she finished a disappointing eighth. The lead was taken by the previously unacclaimed Susan Corrock (USA), but she was to be surpassed by an equally unheralded 17 year old, Marie-Thérèse Nadig of Switzerland, who had never won a World Cup race, and by the favourite, Annemarie Pröll of Austria, in second

place. A petulant Pröll declined to attend the medal winners' conference, such was her dejection after having won four of the five major downhill races that season. Furthermore, there had been problems with her coach, Karl Kahr, who had been dismissed as coach to the Austrian women's team for spending too much time with his star individual. It is possible Kahr got the waxing wrong on the most critical race of Pröll's career.

It was to be no better for Pröll in the giant slalom. Starting second, she recorded the fastest time until surpassed by Nadig, tenth out of the gate. Pröll was an example of a favourite unable to cope mentally with the expectation. There is that vital distinction between trying and trying too hard. In the slalom, Pröll was a distant fifth behind Barbara Cochran of Vermont, US, who had been coached by her father to swing the upper body into motion in the starting gate before the legs primed the mechanism. That technique may have been her salvation in winning by two-hundredths of a second from Danièlle Debernard of France. This was America's first Alpine gold medal in 20 years and by the then closest margin in Olympic history.

For the ski jumping, the organisers had constructed a new Olympic 70m hill, with a grandstand for over 24,000 seated spectators. To avoid updrafts, the slope had been dug six metres into the mountainside. It proved to be preparation nationally well-rewarded.

Yukio Kasaya had practised endlessly that winter before winning three consecutive titles in Europe. On the day of the competition, most of Japan halted, even in the streets, to watch Kasaya and his colleagues, Akitsugu Konno and Seiji Aochi, dominate their event. All three were locals from the northern island of Hokkaido and there was a crowd of over six figures. Kasaya proved to be supreme, leading both rounds, his 79 metres on the second equalled by Konno who took the silver medal, with Aochi, who had the second-best first jump, claiming the bronze.

Ondrej Nepela of Czechoslovakia had made steady progress in figure skating since his Olympic debut aged 13 in 1964. Then twenty-second, he had finished eighth four years later. Now, at 21, he was the unanimous choice of nine judges, not withstanding his first fall in competition in four years when attempting a triple toe-loop. The more flamboyant freestyle figure skaters were Americans Ken Shelley and John Petkevich, but they lacked the discipline in the compulsory figures of

Yukio Kasaya (JAP) stops the traffic in the streets as he leaps to fame and gold. (© IOC)

European competitors, such as Nepela, the reigning world champion. Nepela, in fact, gained credit in his error for attempting such a difficult jump. He was to die of Aids in 1989.

The women's title was won by Trixie Schuba of Austria, dominant on compulsories and with unanimous first-place votes in spite of finishing seventh in the free skating. Again there was frustration among North Americans, Karen Magnussen (CAN) and Janet Lynn (USA) finishing second and third.

The Protopopovs had been dethroned from their pairs' pedestal at the 1969 European Championships by Irina Rodnina and Aleksei Ulanov with an exciting programme of elaborate jumps, and the young couple remained undefeated for three years. Rodnina, however, was consistently dismissive off the ice towards her young partner and he in turn had become romantically involved with Lyudmila Smirnova, the partner of Andrei Suraikin, their compatriot rivals. Gossip boiled during the Sapporo contest, but any disharmony within the Soviet team was insufficient to prevent them emphatically taking the first and second places, even if Rodnina did leave the ice in tears. She was duly to change her partner and would remain triumphant over a nine-year period including two subsequent Games. Forgetting emotional conflicts, Rodnina recalls:

> Sapporo was ever so special. The Village was lovely, the competitions were well-organised. Never at a Games did I think about medals, only the ambition to do well, the overall desire just to be there. The best time was 1972, four years later I was with another partner and in 1980, under the cloud of the Afghan conflict, we were under such scrutiny, the press asking nothing but political questions.

The Soviets took the ice hockey title for the third time in a row, in a competition marred by Canada's withdrawal over the amateur–professional debate. The state-employed Soviets clinched the title in a decisive final match in which they defeated Czechoslovakia 5–2. Their equally state-employed cross-country competitors took four titles in each of the men's and women's events, Galina Kulakova gaining three gold medals.

In Sapporo, medals were won by a record 17 countries, 14 of which gained gold.

CHAPTER XLVI

Munich (XX) 1972

Ulrike Meyfarth of West Germany, double Olympic high jump champion

'I enjoyed Munich in a different way to Los Angeles [12 years later], not because of winning for the first time, but because everything was so vivid, so intense, the whole country was so involved. It was home! I was so happy even to participate, having been third in the German championships and getting third place in the team, with Dr Max Danz telling me I should be grateful to him for persuading the selection committee to include me when I was only 16.

At the start of the competition I felt comfortable, with no expectation placed on me. I wasn't afraid, I was looking forward to it, it would just be some fun. My previous best jump a few weeks before had been 1.85m [6 ft ¾ in.] but I thought maybe I could reach 1.90. When my name appeared on the scoreboard for the first time in third place, I was happy. When it became second, then first, I couldn't believe it. The whole atmosphere was like a dream. Life changed, suddenly I was so popular. I even changed my hairstyle one day to try not to be recognised, but I still was. I had to learn to live with this, though it was a shock.

When I had failed on my first attempt at 1.90, the crowd had whistled. That was the first time I became aware of the brutality that the public can show. I thought, 'I'm so young, I'm doing my best, why are you whistling?' Next jump, I cleared and the spectators were happy, but it was a harsh lesson. When Blagoyeva, the Bulgarian, had her third failure at 1.90, the bar shivered a long time before it fell. This made me champion and gave me more impetus for attempting 1.92. When I cleared that, now the public was crying with joy. No one was to know then what was about to happen the next morning, and after the massacre I didn't know what to feel, how could I go on just being happy?

Winning did change my life, though it happened too early for me to gain financial benefit. It was still the so-called amateur era. Yes, some money was available, though nothing like what was to come. Yet 1972 was something unique, that was my story. I did realise that I would have to adjust, that there was another life out there. Later I had a manager, but he was too casual with my money. I was too naive and my husband, who is a lawyer, had to fight him to get the money that was mine.

I'm not sad my time came when it did. As a woman you have other aims – children, a different life – though it's not easy to be popular in your early life and then to lose it, you have to recognise that younger people are unaware of your achievements. When I won again in Los Angeles, that was very satisfying, I was really well prepared and felt I had a chance.'*

(Photograph © IOPP-69)

In the author's view, objectives were triumphantly realised in so many ways at Munich, with some memorable competitions, not least the romantic triumph of a slender German schoolgirl in the high jump, a moment that united the minds and emotions of spectators from a hundred different nations in a common celebration of unique athleticism. Yet on the following day, 5 September, the darkest in Olympic history, a beautiful Olympic festival was pitched into chaos by calculated barbarism, so shocking that for more than 24 hours it riveted the world's attention. As unconfirmed facts filtered through to the watching world hour by hour, the relevance of sport was never more in question.

From its creation in 1948, the state of Israel had been in conflict with Arab states. Refugee Palestinians were spread

A 16-year-old German girl, Ulrike Meyfarth, captures the hearts of an 80,000-strong international audience when equalling the high jump world record. (© DPA)

among neighbouring Arabs, unintegrated and ripe for exploitation. In 1964, the Palestine Liberation Organisation had been formed, effectively helpless in the face of superior Israeli military strength. Radical splinter groups embarked upon international terrorism to publicise their cause.

5 SEPTEMBER, 0400 HRS

Six men, disguised in tracksuits, climb token security wire fence that surrounds Olympic Village. They are to be joined by two colleagues already inside Village; in fact, the leaders, known as Issa and Tony, have respectively secured employment on construction and as cook. They head for Block 31, Connollystrasse, and apartments housing Israel's twenty-eight-strong delegation, seven of whom are absent on this night at other venues.

Terrorists burst through doors, wrestling coach Moshe Weinberg and weightlifter Josef Romano die in hail of bullets. Tuvia Sokolovsky, another wrestling coach, and Gad Tsovari, a weightlifter, both escape, as later do another eight Israelis. A further nine are held hostage.

0500 HRS

Gad Tsovari raises alarm. First ultimatum arrives. Issa drops typewritten message in English demanding that Israel release 236 political prisoners, together with Ulrike Meinhof and Andreas Bader, notorious West German terrorists recently arrested. Ultimatum includes threat to assassinate a further hostage every hour.

By six o'clock Avery Brundage has learned of crisis. Fraulein Graes, police lieutenant from Munich's criminal division, disguised in uniform of Village security service, makes first tentative contact with terrorist leaders.

0700 HRS

Germans set up a crisis committee: Bruno Merk, Bavarian Interior Minister, and his Federal counterpart Hans-Dietrich Genscher, with Manfred Schreiber, Munich Police Commissioner, in operational control. Brundage is co-opted to group.

0800 HRS

Fr. Graes returns to Block 31 to arrange with Issa a meeting with crisis committee, which will include Ahmad Touny, IOC Egyptian member. Germans offer an unlimited ransom, plus exchange of hostages for high-ranking Germans. Offer is rejected. Golda Meir, Israeli Prime Minister, tells Chancellor Willy Brandt: 'No concession to terrorist blackmail.'

1000 HRS

Amid mounting worldwide clamour, Willi Daume, president of organising committee, and Brundage, agree with Schreiber that the day's sports schedule should not be suspended.

1200 HRS

Killanin, first Vice-President, at Kiel for yachting with Herman van Karnebeek, co-Vice-President from Holland, Prince Takeda of Japan, Executive Board member, and Grand Duke of Luxembourg, learns of attack, only for Brundage to say it is unnecessary for him to return to Munich. In quiet fury, Killanin flies back. Maurice Herzog, mountaineer IOC member from France, has enough signatures to call emergency IOC Session.

1500 HRS

Brundage publicly announces the remainder of day's programme cancelled and memorial service at 10.00 a.m. the following day for the two murdered Israelis. Games will resume at 1600 hours.

1600 HRS

Terrorists negotiate to fly to Cairo with hostages, threaten further executions if political prisoners are not released. Deadline is extended to 1900 hours to produce necessary aircraft. Organising committee releases communiqué by Brundage and Daume:

> Olympic peace has been broken by an act of assassination. The civilised world condemns this barbaric crime. With deep respect for the victims and as a sign of sympathy with the hostages not yet released, this afternoon's events are being cancelled . . . a service will take place tomorrow at 10 a.m. in the Olympic stadium in commemoration of the victims . . . demonstrating that the Olympic ideal is stronger than terror and violence.

1700 HRS

Two hostages, André Spitzer and Eliezer Schalfin, paraded at second-floor window to confirm all are still alive.

1900 HRS

Killanin calls emergency Executive Board meeting, which ratifies Brundage's decisions thus far, and following resolution is adopted: 'The Olympic Games are proceeding for the sake of sport and sport only. All official receptions are cancelled, all ceremonies will be kept as simple as possible.'

2000 HRS

Intended police double-cross is that terrorists and hostages are to be flown out of Village by helicopter. Terrorists will then be picked off individually by rifle-men at Fürstenfeldbrück Military Airport south of the city, during transfer from helicopter to plane. Crisis committee believes, inaccurately, there are five terrorists. Five sharp-shooters are detailed to kill the terrorists instantaneously. Ruse cannot succeed otherwise. George Wolf, coordinating police officer, confirms there are only five terrorists. It would be normal to have two marksmen for every target.

2100 HRS

As terrorists and hostages move from Block 31 to waiting helicopters, Bavarian minister Merk is horrified. There are *eight* terrorists. He and Schreiber assume, erroneously, that an adjustment will be made to the number of marksmen at the airport. The emotional detachment among competitors and officials at Village is eerie. 'Don't ask me, I'm in tomorrow's semi-finals,' says one. 'As far as the British are concerned, security here is very good,' states British *chef-de-mission*.

2200 HRS

Brundage and Touny report to Emergency Session on decision to continue Games. At the airport, Wolf, coordinating the intended double-cross, discovers that terrorists outnumber marksmen. No one has bothered to inform him. Helicopters land. Four pilots, two from each, begin to walk clear. Terrorists smell a trap. Issa, their leader, inspects 727 plane. Wolf gives the order to fire. Only three terrorists killed. Others fire Kalashnikovs to extinguish airport floodlights. Silence descends. From this silence arises appalling miscalculation that the terrorists are dead and all hostages still alive: the latter is true, but they are in mortal danger. False rumours ricochet around

Israeli weightlifters Zeev Friedman, David Berger and Josef
Romano, three of the hostages who perished, alongside wrestling
coach Tuvia Sokolovsky, one of two to escape at the moment of
terrorist break-in. (© popperfoto.com)

Munich, simultaneously reaching global news agencies. Daume
receives message and returns to Session, declaring: 'Wir haben
gewonnen' (we have won) – a cruel charade, exposure of which
will not emerge for another four hours.

Agencies chatter fake tale of rescue. In fact, as six armoured
cars arrive close to midnight in a belated attempted overkill, the
surviving terrorists slay the hostages: David Berger (weightlifter),
Mark Slavin (wrestler), Amizur Schapra (athletics coach), Kahat
Shor (shooting coach), and André Spitzer (fencing coach) killed
with fragmentation grenade in one helicopter; Eliezer Schalfin
(wrestler), Zeev Friedman (weightlifter), Josef Gutfreund
(wrestling referee) and Jakov Springer (weightlifting coach) in
second with automatic fire.

2400 HRS
By now, five terrorists have been killed, including Issa, and three
captured in an abysmally planned, grossly misconducted rescue
campaign.

6 SEPTEMBER, 0300 HRS
Manfred Schreiber, security chief, belatedly announces awful
truth, in a 45-minute speech elaborating on entire day's
schedule before finally declaring: 'and all the hostages are dead'.

0800 HRS
Executive Board meets to resolve whether the Games should
continue, already aware that Dutch and several Arab countries
are considering withdrawal. Killanin concurs with Brundage's
instinctive reaction. 'His stubborn determination saved the
Olympic Movement one last time,' Killanin later said. 'My own
feeling coincided with his and was a gut reaction: I was
convinced that to cancel the Games would only bring further
troubles.'

1000 HRS
Memorial service held at the Olympic stadium in front of silent
80,000 crowd, Munich Philharmonic Orchestra plays funeral
march from Beethoven's *Eroica*. Athletes sit on field. No Arab
nation has sent a single representative, nor has the Soviet
Union. As King Constantine, now an IOC member, walks into
the stadium, a figure from the crowd approaches. 'The Games

must not be cancelled,' he says. 'That would be surrender.' It is
Jesse Owens.

The 17 surviving members of the Israeli delegation sit at the
front with 11 eloquently empty seats. Just when sympathy and
understanding should be apparent in Brundage's speech, retiring
President contrives one last insult. Having said 'in this imperfect
world, the greater and more important the Olympic Games
become, the more they are open to commercial, political and
now criminal pressure', he petulantly continues:

> The Games of the 20th Olympiad have been subject to
> *two* [author's italics] savage attacks. We lost the
> Rhodesian battle against naked political blackmail. We
> have only the strength of a great ideal. I'm sure the
> public will agree that we cannot allow a handful of
> terrorists to destroy this nucleus of international
> cooperation and goodwill we have in the Olympic
> Movement. The Games must go on, and we must
> continue our efforts to keep them clean, pure and
> honest and try to extend the sportsmanship of the
> athletic field into other areas.

Every African present, together with Killanin and the majority
of the IOC, stand aghast at Brundage's faux pas in associating
anti-apartheid decision with terrorists.

Retiring President Avery Brundage makes his controversial speech
at the memorial service. (© IOC)

1500 HRS
Another emergency Executive Board meeting rebukes Brundage,
obliging him to release statement of marginal retraction:
'reference to Rhodesia this morning was deliberate . . . intended
to fortify African sports leaders in their efforts to become free
from their political masters . . . there was no intention to tie this
with the criminal terrorist action'.

1700 HRS
Artur Takac hastens to hotel of the African delegations to quell
another political storm. He is greeted by catcalls and whistling,
but together with Chief Abraham Ordia is able to assure them
they can expect more sensitive administration under Killanin.

7 SEPTEMBER, 1400 HRS

Brundage and Killanin meet delegation from the Supreme Council of Sport in Africa, Brundage again expresses regret for his speech.

29 OCTOBER

Ambience of a brilliant Games having been destroyed, Palestinians hijack a Lufthansa flight in Beirut, order it to Munich and demand release of the three terrorists held since the Games. West German authorities consent and terrorists are flown to Tripoli, Libya. Israeli government protests and reprisal planes raid Palestinian bases in Syria and Lebanon.

Although terrorism placed its indelible stamp on the Games in Munich, on a more positive note the Games were also notable for some outstanding competitors and none more so than one who was not outright champion, the diminutive Olga Korbut, a Soviet from Belorussia. The meteoric emergence of this 17-year-old gymnast – aided by saturation television coverage expediently tuned to the subjective sexuality of this women's sport – unfairly obscured the greater brilliance of the all-round individual champion Ludmila Tourischeva, the Russian who was two years Korbut's senior. So elegant, so athletic, so feminine was Tourischeva that she raised still higher the standard that had been established by Cáslavská, yet her rightful acclaim was stolen by the elfin Korbut, who in the overall individual title finished only seventh, Karin Janz (GDR) and Tamara Lazakovitch, another Belorussian, taking silver and bronze. During the overall team programme, Korbut's routine on the

Pert nymph. Olga Korbut, Soviet from Belorussia, transforms the face of gymnastics – and indeed of the Games from thereon. (© DPA)

uneven parallel bars instantaneously projected her into the limelight, with the possibility that she might subsequently win an individual overall medal in her first major international event. However, when she came to the asymetric bars in the overall individual programme, she fell and was out of the race, returning to her seat in tears. The following day, competing in the separate apparatus competitions – a proliferation of medals which the IOC should seriously revise – Korbut was back to her best, taking silver in this and gold in both balance beam and floor exercises. Her pert demeanour, strutting, prancing and winking, had captivated an audience of many millions. She was simultaneously innocent and knowing. Coached by the innovative Reynald Knysch in her idiosyncratic style, she had

Mark Spitz (USA) exploits swimming's proliferation of events on his way to winning seven golds, all in world record times. (© DPA)

only made the Soviet team as a reserve, yet when she returned home her gigantic fan mail required special deliveries. There is little doubt that in the subjective marking to which gymnastics is vulnerable, the judges in Munich had been swayed by the deafening cheering that had accompanied every appearance of the pixie in pigtails who stood less than five feet tall.

The men's event, as with Tourischeva, was all but lost in Korbut's shadow. Japan's six-man team claimed twelve of the eighteen medals on individual apparatus, the team gold by a huge margin and a sweep of the overall individual medals. Sawao Kato retained his Mexico overall title, the third man to achieve this after Alberto Braglia of Italy (1908–12) and Viktor Chukarin of the USSR (1952–6).

As with gymnastics, swimming has a questionable proliferation of events, and Mark Spitz of the United States now took advantage of the situation to harvest seven gold medals: the 100m and 200m freestyle, the 100m and 200m butterfly, and a share in the 4 x 100m, 4 x 200m and 4 x 100m medley relays, a world record being set in every race. Such was the acceleration of fitness and technique in swimming that the pool effervesced as world and Olympic records were broken or equalled 30 and 84 times respectively. The United States was dominant with 17 gold medals from a possible 29, with only 4 other nations – Australia, the GDR, Japan and Sweden – providing champions. Roland Matthes (GDR) and Gunnar Larsson (SWE) each set two world records.

Spitz, 22, from California, had held world records in freestyle and butterfly since he was 16, though by his standard he had under-performed four years earlier in Mexico. Now he had matured. Long hours of toil, including six childhood years in Hawaii, the prejudice against Jewish kids which he had survived in Sacramento, the resolute devotion to the coaching of Sherman Chavoor and George Haines, finally paid dividends. In the perfection of Munich's Schwimhalle, Spitz the loner dominated his sport as comprehensively as Nurmi once did the track, surpassing even the feats of Don Schollander.

In contrast, the 400m freestyle produced controversy. The previous night Rick DeMont, a chronic sufferer of asthma, had woken with a wheeze and taken tablets that contained the banned drug ephedrine. Further doses were taken prior to the final that evening, in which he defeated Brad Cooper of Australia by the tiniest of margins, one-hundredth of a second,

Almost as conspicuous as Spitz. Fifteen-year-old Shane Gould of Australia grabs two gold, a silver and a bronze. (© IOC) (right © Getty Images/Duffy)

in an Olympic record of 4:00.26. Two days later it was declared that his post-race drug test had been positive and he was barred from that evening's final of the 1,500m. This fine athlete was penalised, his medal and his record erased from history, by the simple incompetence of his own officials. Yet the narrowness of his margin of victory emphasised the importance of the possible value of illegal substances.

Shane Gould, an Australian girl just shy of her 16th birthday and as charming and modest as Spitz was often boorish, was almost as conspicuous in her onslaught on women's events. In the previous year she had set freestyle world records at every distance from 100m to 1,500m and now faced twelve races in eight days. Her tally was bronze in the 100m, silver in the 800m, gold in the 200m and 400m. In the 200m she established a substantial lead by halfway over world record holder Shirley Babashoff (USA) and was still way ahead at the finish. The following year, already weary of a swimmer's daily slog, she retired.

An unusual controversy of these Games arose in basketball, in which the United States, having won every Olympic match thus far, were defeated by the Soviet Union in the last three seconds of the final match. This ended a 62-game winning streak for the USA from their victory over Estonia in 1936 to that over Italy in Munich, immediately prior to the 51–50 reverse against their Cold War rivals. At 49–48, with three seconds remaining, Doug Collins of the US was fouled by Zurab Sakandelidze. Silence gripped a rowdy crowd and Collins' two shots plopped decisively into the basket. American celebrations were euphoric. Yet the match was not over. The Soviet coach was asking for a time-out, but this was overlooked by referees Renato Righetto of Brazil and Artenik Arbadjan of Bulgaria and the ball was put into play. Split seconds later, Righetto halted the play again because of alleged confusion at the scorer's table. With the American team busy celebrating what they believed to be victory, the Soviets continued to demand the time-out not granted. The game was ultimately re-started a second time with three seconds still to be played. Modestas Paulauskas threw the ball the length of the court and Belov leapt to tip the ball in and make the score 51–50. The international federation's jury of appeal spent most of the night examining a US protest, including repeated replays of the final three seconds, and it was not until the following afternoon that the result was confirmed. So incensed were the Americans that they refused to collect their silver medals.

Two days before the Israeli massacre, Finland had recovered something of its long-lost place among Olympic mini-gods.

Between 1912 and 1936 their runners had won 20 gold, 19 silver and 9 bronze medals at distances ranging from 1,500m to the marathon. After that, however, they won nothing but bronze in the marathon of 1956. Now they acclaimed a slim 23-year-old policeman, whose running in the northern forests had reduced his resting heartbeat down to the level of Nurmi's, at just over 30.

The inaugural race of Lasse Virén, his heat of the 10,000m, had seemed less than impressive, his time in fourth place of 28:04.4 making him sixth fastest among fifteen qualifiers. The standard was high: the defending champion Temu had been lapped in the first heat and failed to qualify. For the final, there were high expectations surrounding Dave Bedford of Britain, the second-fastest qualifier, a one-pace workaholic whose success was always dependent upon burning off the field with his even-lap early running. Now, Bedford was ahead of world record schedule after 2km and still in the lead at 4km. But the front pack, Virén among them, was still with him. Approaching the halfway mark, Virén's prospects seemed doomed when he collided with Mohamed Gammoudi of Tunisia and fell. Both regained their feet, but though Gammoudi dropped out shortly afterwards, an expressionless Virén quickly hauled his way back into contention and by 6km had passed an ailing Bedford. The leading group now contained Emiel Puttemans of Belgium, the fastest qualifier; Miruts Yifter of Ethiopia, winner of the third heat; Mariano Haro Cisneros (SPA); and Frank Shorter (USA). Virén made his decisive bid with a lap and a half to go, producing a stunning final lap of sub-57. He crossed the line more than a second ahead of Puttemans, for a world record of 27:38.4, a second's improvement on Clarke's record and an unbelievable performance in the light of his fall. Yifter took bronze with Bedford a jaded sixth.

The following day, Virén qualified for the 5,000m final, scheduled for 9 September, the penultimate day of the Games. A leading contender at this distance – besides Gammoudi, the defending champion, Puttemans and Ian Stewart of Britain – was the American extrovert Steve Prefontaine. He had promised fireworks over the last four laps for his many travelling supporters. When he duly made his bid, Virén and Gammoudi stuck with him, Virén taking the lead into the final back straight. Though Gammoudi briefly responded, Virén still had the legs to pull clear for an Olympic record of 13:26.4, a stride or two ahead of Gammoudi, with Stewart stealing the bronze from a fading Prefontaine. Virén thus emulated the long-distance double of Kolehmainen, Zátopek and Kuts. A year later the unfortunate Prefontaine died in a car crash.

For Jim Ryun, Munich offered the chance of redemption in

the 1,500m, in which there would be a re-run of his duel in Mexico City with Kip Keino. Ryun, following interim uncertainties, was again in peak form, but while he had been the victim on the first occasion of oxygen-debt, now he fell foul of a minor administrative stroke of the pen. His qualifying time submitted by USOC was for a mile, not 1,500m, and the longer 'inferior' time, in fact a brilliant 3:52, found him drawn in the same first-round heat as Keino. Involved in an unexpectedly fast race, Ryun was boxed a lap and a half from the finish as Mohammad Younis of Pakistan slowed in front of him and Vitus Aschaba of Uganda accelerated outside him. Ryun tripped on Aschaba's heel, collided with Billy Fordjour of Ghana and fell on the kerb. Though Ryun rose after several seconds, his career effectively ended at that moment.

The final boasted serious quality: Mike Boit, another emerging Kenyan, Rod Dixon of New Zealand, Brendan Foster of Britain and Pekka Vasala of Finland, who had been sick four years earlier. Keino seemed poised to retain his title when leading into the final straight, only to be overtaken by the unpredictable Vasala, who had run a ferocious final two laps. Vasala's 3:36.3, though three seconds outside Ryun's world record, was the sixth fastest of all time.

The versatile Keino had speculatively entered the steeplechase. Taking the obstacles like a succession of high jumps – 'a lot of fun' – he outkicked his colleague Ben Jipcho, to win in an Olympic record of 8:23.6. This most altruistic of men, 28 years later to become an IOC member, was to use his fame and such as was his modest fortune before the era of professionalism to create an orphanage on a farm where he and his wife Phyllis could accommodate at any time up to 40 homeless children. 'My children,' he proudly tells enquiring visitors, as though indeed they were all his own. Growing up in a mud village in the Rift Valley, Keino had been often beaten by a malevolent uncle and it was from this experience that his desire to help other troubled children arose.

Seldom has there been such a victor-in-disguise as there was in the 800m. Dave Wottle from Ohio, perhaps appropriately for someone who had chosen the same occasion for his honeymoon, loped along at the back of the pack. At the US trials, which, being a four-lap man, he entered only as an experiment, he had equalled the world record of 1:44.3, some three seconds faster than he had ever run before.

The versatile Kip Keino (KEN) takes the steeplechase, like most obstacles in his life, in his stride, when leading Tapio Kantanen (FIN), eventual bronze medal winner. (© IOC)

The favourite was Yevgeni Arzhanov (URS), undefeated over the past four years. In the heats, Wottle had been content to qualify with a late rush and in the final he seemed irrelevant when remaining content once again to study the opposition from the back. Mike Boit, the Kenyan who was later to challenge the best, and his colleague Robert Ouko, had set the pace, but into the finishing straight Arzhanov was making his kick for victory. Somewhere behind, Wottle had begun to get serious and 50 yards out realised that not only could he take silver but he might even grab gold. In one of the closest victories of all time, he caught Arzhanov a stride from the line, arms triumphantly aloft, the Ukrainian stumbling as he crossed the line to be defeated by three-hundredths of a second.

Another favourite was defeated in the 400m hurdles. The threat to the defending David Hemery (GBR) was Ralph Mann (USA), and indeed these two seemed untroubled as they led the field after 200 metres. Pursuing them, however, in the unfavoured inside lane – the tighter bends being technically more difficult – was one of the forty-three children of a Ugandan chieftain with eight wives. John Akii-Bua had chased zebras barefoot through the bush as a boy. A trainee at the Kampala police academy, Akii-Bua was now chasing world renown. He had been fourth in the Commonwealth Games two years earlier, had studied everything there was to know about Hemery with the aid of Malcolm Arnold, a British coach in Uganda, and he had Hemery in his sights. By the fifth hurdle, Akii-Bua had drawn level with him, never mind that Hemery had run the first half faster than in Mexico. In breathtaking style, Akii-Bua pulled clear between the eighth and ninth hurdles to win by three strides, astonishing the audience, not to say himself, with a world record 0.30 faster than Hemery's in 47.82; Mann taking silver and Hemery bronze.

Munich's futuristic stadium was the scene of a rare spectacle: the predominantly home audience endlessly cheering for a foreign rival in an emotional duel with their own favourite. Mary Peters was a 33-year-old secretary from terror-torn Belfast. She looked more like a shot putter than an all-round athlete, and indeed that was what she was, yet by will-power as much as talent she had competed in the previous two pentathlon contests, finishing fourth in Tokyo and ninth in Mexico. Here, she was up against the local darling, Heidi Rosendahl, who had won the individual long jump two days earlier, and Burglinde Pollak (GDR), the future world record holder. With her blonde hair, beatific smile and unassuming friendliness, Peters won the hearts of all as the competition moved to its second-day climax.

At the end of the first day, Peters led Pollak by 97 points and Rosendahl by 301. Now came her two worst events, the long jump and 200m. Rosendahl narrowed the gap to 121 with a near-world record long jump of 6.83m (22 ft 5 in.), Pollak to 47 points with 6.21m (20 ft 4 in.). If Rosendahl could equal her 200m best, 23.10, Peters would need hers, 24.20. Rosendahl went like the wind to record 22.96, her best ever, likewise Peters with 24.08. It was enough, by ten points, and a world record of 4,801. As they waited for the result, Peters did not realise she had won the individual until Rosendahl put her arm round her shoulders.

The men's sprinting was notable for an administrative blunder by the Americans. Stan Wright, their coach, misread 1700 hours, on a 24-hour printed schedule, for 7 p.m. Eddie Hart and Ray Robinson, who had both run 9.9 in the US trials, were regarded as the main rivals to Valeri Borzov, the Ukrainian Soviet, who was unbeaten in almost two years. When the second round of the 100m began, the first that Hart, Robinson and their colleague Robert Taylor knew of it was when standing watching ABC television, waiting for the bus to the stadium. Rushing there belatedly by car, only Taylor was in time to run and qualify

Mary Peters (GBR) grits her teeth behind Burglinde Pollak (GDR) in the 200m, her least favourite discipline, to clinch the pentathlon title. (© Getty Images/Duffy)
(right © Getty Images)

for the semi-final. Taylor would come second to Borzov in the short sprint and Borzov comfortably took the 200m ahead of Larry Black (USA) and Pietro Mennea (ITA), to become the first non-North American ever to win the Olympic sprint double and the first competitor to do so since Bobby Morrow in 1956. Borzov subsequently married gymnast Ludmila Tourischeva.

Vince Matthews and Wayne Collett from the US, two black runners who were the first two home in the 400m, massively misread the public mood immediately following the Israeli massacre by staging a nondescript Black Power demonstration on the victory podium. Matthews, the winner, twirled his medal

Vince Matthews and Wayne Collett, Americans finishing first and second in the 400m, scorn their national anthem with a Black Power protest. (© DPA)

round his finger and both of them scorned their national anthem, only to be greeted by a storm of whistles and boos. Collett, a law student, gave the howling crowd a raised-fist Black Power salute as he left the stadium. With neither willing to apologise – 'I'm an athlete, not a politician, I never stand to attention,' Matthews complained – Brundage furiously ordered USOC to have both men banned from Olympic competition for life. This threat was rescinded, but neither athete qualified for the Games again.

The javelin produced drama and joy for the hosts. With Janis Lusis (URS) leading, Klaus Wolfermann, to an accompanying roar, all but threatened spectators with a throw of 90.48m (296 ft 10 in.), a final throw by Lusis getting within two centimetres of that. The pole vault was marred by controversy over the technical eligibility of a new brand of fibreglass pole used by the Americans. The IAAF vacillated, banning it, then approving it, then banning it again two days before the qualifying event, thereby denying Bob Seagren (USA), the defending world record holder, the pole he was currently using. This enabled Wolfgang Nordwig (GDR) to end an American run unbroken since 1896 with an Olympic record. A disgusted Seagren thrust his 'legal' pole into the arms of Adriaan Paulen, IAAF President, at the finish.

The Indian sub-continent's unbroken dominance of hockey since 1928 was ended by Germany, their final with Pakistan disrupted by Pakistan supporters' protests against refereeing. In the dressage, Lorna Johnstone (GBR) set a record as the oldest-ever female competitor in a Games when five days past 70; in the same event Liselott Linsenhoff (FRG) became the first woman to win an individual equestrian event at the age of 45 years and 13 days.

CHAPTER XLVII

Tormented Lord

Richard Pound of Canada, Olympic swimming finalist, IOC member since 1978

'Several factors complicated Montreal's organisation. The lobby to exclude South Africa from the Olympic Movement had finally succeeded at the same IOC Session [1970] that selected Montreal, but that issue was not finished. Second, the terrorist intervention in Munich changed the level of Games security required, to the extent of putting their future at doubt. Third, Montreal's financial plan was dependent on the availability of federal government programmes, but the government of the day was a Quebec-based minority and there was a mood that Expo '67 had exhausted federal funding. Funding was delayed, turning a six-year project into a three-year race for completion. Fourth, labour unions were quick to exploit their bargaining position. Fifth, worldwide inflation with the petroleum crisis of 1973 affected all major budgets by a factor of two or three times the original estimates. Sixth, Mayor Jean Drapeau, seeking a monument to commemorate the Olympics, engaged Roger Taillibert, a French architect whose stadium design was ill-suited to anything except athletics and impractical in relation to extreme Canadian weather conditions with a restricted building 'window'. Seventh, the city mismanaged the construction programme.

It was a foolish decision of Drapeau not to separate the operating and infrastructure budgets. Infrastructure improvement in Montreal was key to the Games' schedule, including a much-needed Metro line extension towards Olympic facilities in a heavily populated area. The facilities, including the Village, were to become civic assets. Commitment to major league baseball [who were to use the stadium after the conclusion of the Games] to have a covered facility was thus much more expensive. Failure to distinguish between the two areas of expenditure allowed the media, lacking judgement, to define the cost of the Games as the sum of infrastructure plus operation, a prejudiced view that remains to this day. Sensible accounting would have divided the costs. The organising committee, despite paying for many capital facilities, including the Village, made a profit well in excess of $100 million, far more per capita than the subsequently much-touted LA Games. The IOC now insists on separation of the budgets to avoid ill-founded conclusions: one of Montreal's Olympic legacies.

The African boycott was another phase in the apartheid impact on the Olympic Movement. Montreal was a further extension of the Rhodesia target four years earlier, aimed at countries maintaining contact with South Africa, an affair badly mismanaged by both sides: by the Africans, who over-reacted with New Zealand, whose NOC had no authority over rugby; and by the IOC, which ignored the Africans until it was too late. The latter was the fault of Killanin and Berlioux. Had Samaranch been present, I am certain there would have been no boycott. Killanin was ineffective both in Montreal and with respect to Moscow.

The sports installations were excellent and the Games were well run. Security was superb and low-key. At the opening ceremony, the crowd was hospitable to the Queen, even though the Province would elect a separatiste *government four months later. The most popular person at the opening ceremony was Jean Drapeau.'**

(Photograph © IOC/Locatelli)

There are divergent views on the presidency of Lord Killanin: whether this decent, dignified, courteous Irishman, by his unruffled equanimity, held the Olympic Movement together during eight years of extreme crisis, or whether, by inaction, he allowed the IOC to slide perilously close to extinction.

His many friends would spring to his defence and few were more socially popular than he. Alain Coupat, an aide in the President's office with Killanin and later Samaranch, defined Killanin's place in the IOC's evolution. 'History should be grateful to him,' Coupat said. 'He was the key element in the change from a totally closed organisation under Brundage to the more open regime of Samaranch. He guided the thinking that led towards modernisation.'

Early comments from Killanin reveal the uncertainty with which he was to govern. 'The IOC has the Olympic Games and

the Olympic Movement well in hand,' he stated reassuringly but complacently during the Congress at Varna, Bulgaria, in 1973 – no doubt intending to convey that the disaster at Munich had been no more than an uncharacteristic blip on the screen. Serene in his approach to life, in spite of his wartime experiences, which included the Normandy landings, he was by nature one who believed that a soft answer turneth away wrath. The violence of war had indeed made him a pacifist and he admitted recoiling from the sight of Mexican armed guards with loaded rifles patrolling the opening ceremony of 1968. He was to discover, however, that gentility was ineffective, that only strength in action commands respect. 'Politics in sport is inevitable, but what I don't like is to be under pressure from political lobbies,' he stated in 1972. 'The decisions of the IOC must be sports decisions. If big powers wish to play power

208

politics, using the Olympic Movement, this must be fought by any means we have. It is essential for the IOC to endeavour to foresee such events and act with strength.'

Foresight was not to prove his forte. Indeed, he tended to hope that problems might go away if action was shelved: as with Madame Berlioux's over-extended authority, which he intended to check but never did, realising he was partially dependent on her knowledge and experience, to the extent of having her accompany him to critical meetings when he should rather have been joined by the senior Vice-President. 'I have the feeling that she was not the best possible Director-General,' he had said, but it would be left to Samaranch to deal with this issue.

The IOC's three-volume history *The International Olympic Committee: 100 Years* went so far as to say of Killanin: 'While he played a crucial role in the survival of the Olympic Movement, and indeed was beset with a myriad of problems during his eight years, Killanin did not take the Movement forward in the way many had expected.'

Courteous, conciliatory Lord Killanin, sixth IOC President, in a happier moment with Mayor Jean Drapeau, initiator of Montreal's troubled stadium, and Roger Rousseau, Games organising president. (© IOC)

The first difficulty he was to encounter was the withdrawal of Denver, in November 1972, as host city for the Winter Games of 1976. There had been an agreement with the IOC that there would be no legal contract: the last time that situation was to exist. From the moment of Denver's election, their ability to deliver had been in doubt, their facilities to be spread over an impractically large area of the Rocky Mountains. The budget at their initial presentation to the IOC, $14 million, had ballooned to $50 million or more, with even the suggestion that the bobsleigh should be shifted to Lake Placid, 2,000 miles away. Grandiose plans had started coming apart as soon as the organising committee returned home after being elected. Had Brundage still been in the IOC chair this could have been the lever for him to terminate 'the poisonous cancer' of what he regarded as 'frosty follies'. Killanin and his colleagues hastened to find an alternative. Meeting in Lausanne early in 1973, the IOC opted for Innsbruck, partially on account of the efficiency of the Winter Games staged there in 1964, and partly no doubt with a sense of guilt for the affronts caused by Brundage's disqualification of Karl Schranz in 1972.

If nothing else, Killanin was progressive on theory. It was his wish that the IOC should no longer be 'the club that it was many years ago': by which he meant a body that under Brundage had actively resented and restricted any self-

determination by its essential partners, the IFs and the NOCs. At the Congress in Varna, a Black Sea resort, the first Congress for 43 years – Brundage did not like them – Killanin sought to repair the partnership with the creation of the Tripartite Commission, in which the three arms had equal representation. This persuaded the IFs and NOCs that their needs were being heard, though they were still without Olympic constitutional power in spite of the separate creation of their own bodies: GAISF (1967) and the NOCs' Permanent General Assembly (PGA) a year later. The IFs, more power-conscious, had the highest proportional attendance at Varna, almost half the 131 NOCs being absent as well as 27 of the 74 IOC members. Nonetheless, the creation of the Tripartite Commission enabled Killanin to resist the 'democratisation' interference by UNESCO, Mocow-led by Soviet Minister for Sport Marat Gramov.

It was at Varna that the word 'amateur' was removed from Rule 26 of the Charter, regarding eligibility, with its impossible definition of pure amateurs being those who observed 'both spiritually and ethically the traditional Olympic ideals'. Killanin, though not believing in a professional Olympics, wanted rules that could be obeyed. 'We obviously have to be more rational about eligibility,' he said, recognising that Rule 26 forced athletes to lie about their status. The new regulation, approved at the Session of 1974 in Vienna, was shortened and liberalised: athletes must adhere to the rules of the IOC and their respective IF; they must not have received any financial material benefit from sport except as permitted in the by-laws. Remuneration for advertising was to be paid to the athletes' NOC or IF, while the duration of training was to be at the discretion of IFs and therefore effectively became a dead issue. Broken-time payment, away from work, was to be permitted, though not to exceed the sum that the competitor would have earned in the same period. If compensation was not paid by the employer it could be paid by the national federation or NOC. While Killanin might have been rationalising the morality of the IOC, the relaxing of eligibility regulations, with the IFs invited to make proposed adjustments to the IOC, inevitably yielded some power to GAISF, providing the platform from which Thomas Keller, president of international rowing and later GAISF, would continue to vainly attempt to challenge the overall authority of the IOC.

Also established at Varna was the new Olympic Solidarity Commission, comprising 20 members and with an initial fund of ten million Swiss francs. The first coordinator was to be Edward Wieczorek under the chairmanship of Herman van Karnebeek of the Netherlands. Included on the Commission were Chief Abraham Ordia of Nigeria and Jean-Claude Ganga of the Congo, prominent African campaigners. Killanin's initiative, however, was only a start. Ten years later Louis Guirandou-N'Daiye, IOC member in the Ivory Coast and head of protocol, would say: 'It was not solidarity at all, just a few gifts to those they knew. There were lots of good words and promises, people were travelling to see what *might* be done, but the money only really arrived with Samaranch. Killanin, being part-time, didn't really have time to think about Olympism around the world.'

A commission of enquiry for Rhodesia was established at Varna, the members being Major de Magalhaes Padilha of Brazil, James Worrall of Canada and Syed Wajid Ali of Pakistan, with a mandate to establish whether the Charter was upheld in that country.

Controversies of the future received only slight attention in 1973. Sports authorities were both ignorant and naive in their response to the emerging evidence of drug taking. Harold Connolly, Olympic hammer champion of 1956, testified to a US Senate committee that in the American team in 1968 there were

Prince Alexandre de Mérode, chairman of the Medical Commission, introduced testing for steroids in 1976.
(© IOC/Locatelli)

athletes who had so many puncture holes from injections it was difficult to find a fresh spot to give themselves a new shot. Connolly admitted to having been personally hooked on steroids for eight years. The following year in Vienna, Prince de Mérode, chairman of the Medical Commission, announced that they were ready to test for steroids in 1976. On the matter of a different kind of drug, gerontocracy, the IOC voted for a further dose, setting the age limit at 72, whereas previously it had been for life.

At the Session of 1974, Moscow and Lake Placid were elected as host cities for the respective Games of 1980. Moscow was opposed by Los Angeles, both of them losing candidates to Montreal for 1976. With most of the West voting for Moscow, however, a stance seen to be politically correct at the height of East–West détente, the decision was near unanimous. Killanin viewed the vote favourably, considering the capitalist world had as much obligation to favour a communist Games as vice-versa. In 1973 he had visited Prime Minister Kosygin at the Kremlin and had been guaranteed that all recognised NOCs would be admitted whether or not the Soviet Union had diplomatic relations with their governments.

Also in 1974, Dr Un Yong Kim, a prime figure in the political and sporting life of South Korea, made a relatively anonymous move that was to have a profound influence for his country in the world of sport. Bidding in Berne, Switzerland, for the world shooting championships of 1978, he undercut Mexico City's offer of ten dollars per head board-and-lodging with a spontaneous gamble: he offered the assembly five dollars a head. Seoul was elected by 62 votes to 40 and by this one snap decision Kim had set in motion a path to hosting the Olympic Games of 1988. 'At that moment,' Kim recalls, 'Seoul had yet to be the stage for any major international championship, though we were due to host the second Asian athletics championships the following year.'

In April 1975, Avery Brundage, now living permanently in Germany, entered a small district hospital in Garmisch with influenza. He failed to recover and on 8 May died at the age of 87. The last three years of what had always been a lonely life had been less than happy. Elizabeth, his wife of 45 years, died in 1971 at their mansion in Santa Barbara, California. On his retirement from the presidency the IOC had made a small office available at the Chateau de Vidy, where Brundage waited in vain for Killanin to ask him for help. Berlioux related that in the past the lonely despot had often invited her to accompany him on long, almost silent walks. In 1973, the 85 year old had married Princess Mariann Charlotte Katherina Stefanie von Reuss, 37-year-old daughter of Heinrich XXXVII of Reuss, a tiny principality long-since submerged within East Germany. Willi Daume was best man, while other close associates of Brundage avoided what they regarded as an embarrassing event. Six-figure bills, accommodating the wishes of the new wife and mother-in-law, started piling up and within two years Brundage's financial adviser informed him he was near-bankrupt. After his death, his loyal, if expensive, new wife took his body home to Chicago for burial.

The same month, the IOC Session at Lausanne considered the report of the Rhodesia enquiry. The commission had found that racial discrimination did exist in private clubs and in some state schools, but that the bias was not evident within the NOC, which insisted on racial equality and upheld the Charter in selection for the Games. The Executive Board was minded to suspend the NOC, though Rule 25 only authorised the withdrawal of recognition and thus de facto expulsion. With Black Africa intent on banishment and choosing to ignore any evidence of the NOC's fairmindedness, and with the IOC membership conscious of the threat of a boycott in Montreal, the vote was a predictable 41–26 for Rhodesia's removal. The IOC was in a situation where anti-racist members were now themselves transparently racist. Jan Staubo of Norway drew attention to the fact that the African petition for Rhodesia's removal was written on a letterhead of the Supreme Council for Sport in Africa, a blatantly political body.

Any concern held by Killanin regarding democratic judgement on Rhodesia's NOC was, however, nothing alongside the crisis by now rampant in the chaotic preparations for Montreal. Standing at the junction of the St Lawrence and Ottawa Rivers, Montreal was founded in 1642, becoming the centre of the North American fur trade under French dominance. The eighteenth-century French–Indian war then allowed Scottish and English merchants to establish an economical and political edge in the cultural centre of what would become the Dominion of Canada in 1867. A Montreal police constable, Etienne Desmarteau, won Canada's first Olympic gold medal in 1904, but the politics of language, nationalism and regionalism, under the bi-lingual pan-Canadianism of Pierre Trudeau's government, made the predominantly French-speaking city – where English speakers comprised only 16 per cent of the population – an inevitably weather-hazardous host city; the more so when the federal government initially decided against financial assistance for the Games. This, moreover, was on the back of an original presentation by Mayor Jean Drapeau with seriously underestimated costs prior to the imminent oil crisis. Buoyed by the success of Expo '67 – itself hugely overspent – his estimate of $300 million was a miscalculation many times under the eventual sum paid by the city and its residents, if infrastructure was included, the latter development central to any successful city bid. A general strike by trade unions in 1972 had meant that three years' preparation time had passed with almost nothing done. Drapeau's choice of Roger Taillibert, with his grandiose

Mayor Drapeau quells anxieties over Montreal's escalating problems. (© IOC)

designs, was serving to exacerbate the crisis, the organising committee unable to cope with the extortionate demands of construction firms and labour unions.

It was fortunate for the part-time President in Dublin that there was in Montreal an expert adviser to the organising committee: Artur Takac, former Technical Director of the IOC, who had resigned in frustration just prior to the end of Brundage's regime in order to accept an invitation from Drapeau to come and mastermind technical details in a city largely ignorant of Olympic affairs. Takac's mind was turned when his close friend Arpad Csanadi, IOC member in Hungary and football expert, had advised: 'You must accept – you will be more valuable both to the organisers and to the Olympic Movement if you are working in Montreal.'

For Killanin, the anxiety at long distance was probably worse than had he been permanently on site. 'I certainly know that my wife believes the coronary I suffered in 1977 was due in part to the increasing burden of problems I had to face during 1975 and 1976,' Killanin wrote in his biographical *My Olympic Years*.

On his side of the Atlantic, Takac found himself working at close quarters with what he describes in his book *Sixty Olympic Years* as almost total ignorance of the Olympic idea and its requirements.

> My concern about this lack of Olympic experience increased as the months passed . . . by March 1973, there was still not a proper strategic plan . . . we [the organising committee] drew on my experience of the European athletics championships in Belgrade in 1962, as well as at the Olympics in Mexico and Munich, to establish a prototype in athletics for which we developed parallel systems for the organisation of all other sports . . . The problems which I saw could be encapsulated as follows: Montreal, Quebec and Canada had to fuse their authority and summon the strength to face the unyielding pressure of the labour unions and the blackmail of construction companies in order to achieve the deadlines . . . they needed to wake up to the traditions of the Olympic Movement . . . we drew up a list of 280 projects and worked out a programme to be adopted by 16 general directors, built around the blueprint from the coordination centre adopted by October 1975.

In addition to outside work being at times impossible in mid-winter, between December 1974 and April 1976 155 working days were lost out of 530 when the workers were on strike, almost 30 per cent of the time available in a crucial period. Though the crisis primarily concerned the completion of the main stadium, the swimming pool and velodrome, all designed by Taillibert, there were further problems with the construction and financing of the Village.

Drapeau conceded, on advice from Takac, that it was not essential for the stadium to have the 50-storey tower that was central to the construction of a sliding roof. This element, for the benefit of baseball, would be completed years later. Victor Goldbloom, Quebec Minister of Communal Affairs, was to prove a catalytic influence when assigned to monitor the realignment of work and report to Quebec and the IOC, the latter already considering possible alternative sites. Killanin's contingency plan was to stage as many events as possible in northern Germany, based around the new stadium in Dusseldorf. Killanin wrote in his memoirs:

> I feel that without Goldbloom, the Games would not have taken place. He set up office in Montreal and was quickly riveted to the belief that Montreal, Quebec and Canada had a responsibility to the competitors around the world to ensure the Games started on time in facilities that would be adequate . . . on 18 November, the Quebec government had passed an Enabling Act to create the Olympic Installations Board under Goldbloom. It was a relief to know that the government was facing the issues.

And now that there would be facilities, who was going to be there? During the Congress at Varna, Prince Gholam Reza Pahlavi, IOC member and president of the Asian Games Federation (AGF), confirmed their decision to admit the People's Republic of China to their next Games in Tehran in 1974. The Asian Games had official IOC patronage, but the People's Republic, of course, was still outside the IOC's own patch. Pahlavi added that he considered the China question should be judged on its merit. International federations increasingly were accepting affiliated national federations from the People's Republic as opposed to Taiwan, still recognised by the IOC under the title 'Republic of China'. The IOC warned the AGF that it risked loss of patronage. So what? By the middle of 1975, the People's Republic had been accepted into nine IFs and had formed its own NOC, notwithstanding that it was unrecognised in Lausanne. The nationalists in Taiwan, although now agreeable to 'two' Chinas, understandably would not accept their own demise. Though the IOC Session of 1975 declined to accept the People's Republic's application for acceptance on condition of simultaneous expulsion of Taiwan, Killanin, always sympathetic to the mainland, ensured that the door was kept open. Meanwhile, Taiwan was busy preparing its team for Montreal. When Montreal was elected in 1970, Prime Minister Trudeau had given the regulation guarantee that all teams would be admitted. In 1972, however, the Canadian government had switched its policy, withdrawing recognition from Taiwan and conferring it upon China. Killanin should have caught wind of likely reaction at the Olympics when, in 1975, Taiwanese boxers and cyclists scheduled for international events in Montreal were denied visas. Subsequently, Spain refused to admit Taiwan to the world judo championships, which were then cancelled.

Killanin claimed in his memoirs, strangely, that 'there was no indication that Taiwan would be excluded, that news did not reach me until the end of May'. He was allegedly surprised to receive, prior to the Executive Board meeting just before the Games, a letter from Mitchell Sharp, Acting Secretary of State for External Affairs, stating that Taiwan would not be admitted so long as they called themselves 'representatives of the Republic of China'. Yet Takac relates in his book that at a meeting in June 1975 with Edward Skerbec, an official in external affairs, Skerbec had quoted from notes of an earlier meeting with Killanin, in April, when it had been stressed that it would be impossible to allow Taiwan into the country under their Olympic title of 'Republic of China'. According to Skerbec's notes, Killanin had said the IOC would intensify its contacts with Taiwan in an attempt to find a compromise. So what had Killanin been doing in the interim? Takac suspects that Killanin was alarmed that if he had earlier raised the issue, the United States NOC, heavily pro-Taiwan in line with Washington, would have threatened its own withdrawal. Killanin presumably persuaded himself to rely on last-minute pressure on Trudeau to uphold the 'guarantee'.

A further complication was that Brundage, while still President, and strongly pro-Taiwan, had unilaterally manipulated Henry Hsu of Taiwan into IOC membership, consolidating Taiwan's status. Trudeau now conceded that Taiwan, some of whose team were already in Canada training for the Games, could take part on the following conditions: that they use their national flag and anthem but not the name 'Republic'. The Taiwanese, themselves politically entrenched even though in a situation morally if not legally unsustainable – being proportionally miniscule and fugitives from the mainland – rejected the compromise and went home. There were no winners because the People's Republic also stayed away, the IOC having refused to expel Taiwan. The Comte de Beaumont recommended cancellation of the Games if Trudeau – committed by the IOC charter to Canada's admission of Taiwan's affiliated NOC – would not relent. With that threat, Trudeau must surely have buckled, but Killanin had no stomach for brinkmanship.

Various observers, such as Richard Esty in his *The Politics of the Olympic Games*, considered the IOC politically naive, though John Lucas, a prominent US historian, suggested that Killanin had been wise to let things take their own turn of events. A consequence of Taiwan's absence was that FIFA, the football federation, felt able to re-admit the People's Republic of China, who had withdrawn in 1958. Whereupon the Communists rejected *that* move on the grounds that FIFA was violating its own constitution by admitting two members from what they, as perversely as the Taiwanese, regarded as one country.

Barely had Killanin cleared the decks of Chinese ninepins than he was swamped by another crisis only days before the opening ceremony: another fire from which the smoke had long been visible. The extent to which Killanin underestimated the issue, both short and long term, is perhaps apparent in his memoirs, in which he devotes a mere *three paragraphs* to an action which, as much or more than any other, threatened to bring tumbling down the edifice to which he himself had given such altruistic devotion. Sixteen African NOCs lodged a last-minute letter stating they had no other peaceful remedy than to request the IOC to bar New Zealand, 'for barefaced support of acts of inhumanity against Africans in South Africa'. Should the IOC not heed this, they reserved their right to reconsider their own participation. At a concurrent meeting in Mauritius of the Organisation of African Unity, there had been demands, however technically irrelevant, for the exclusion of New Zealand from the Games on account of that country's rugby tour of South Africa, completed just before the Games began: seen as

Nigerian Chief Abraham Ordia, president of the Supreme Council for Sport in Africa, and Jean-Claude Ganga, secretary-general, debate the imminent boycott with African colleagues. (© IOC)

support for the apartheid regime and justifying the threat of African withdrawal, never mind rugby not being an Olympic sport and outside NOC jurisdiction.

In Montreal, Jean-Claude Ganga, secretary of the Supreme Council for Sport in Africa, was at the Games' HQ requesting a meeting for leaders of African NOCs. Following this, Ganga confronted Roger Rousseau, president of the Canadian organising committee, suggesting he fly immediately to Mauritius to negotiate with the African politicians. Simultaneously, Ganga saw Lance Cross, IOC member of New Zealand, to seek a joint meeting with Killanin. However, it is known that Berlioux, for whatever reasons, was shielding Killanin from contact with Africans in Montreal: extraordinarily ill-judged of Berlioux if true. Ganga suggested that:

> The boycott by African countries could have been avoided if the Canadian government had been more aware beforehand that it might happen. Yet when Abraham Ordia [president of SCSA] and I confronted IOC members, their general reaction was that 'rugby is not an Olympic sport'. I told Lance Cross that if he would do his bit, actively to speak against the rugby, as a demonstration of the IOC's attitude towards apartheid, I would do what I could with the OAU, to persuade them we should participate in the Games. But the next day Cross failed to show up at our rendezvous. Madame Berlioux knew what I was doing but [nonetheless] I was unable to get to see Killanin. A year later, Trudeau was the first to propose the agreement, reached at Gleneagles, regarding international attitude towards sport in South Africa.

Intransigence by the Africans was understandable, for it was in June 1976 that several hundred youths were killed when the police opened fire on a student protest in Soweto against the imposition of Afrikaans as the teaching language in a number of subjects in secondary schools. Killanin should have been more aware of the threat posed by the SCSA, yet it would be a further 21 years before Killanin's successor called the first-ever meeting between the IOC and African sports leaders. Twenty-seven African countries were absent from Montreal, together with Iraq and Guyana – ten never entering, seventeen withdrawing. This denied the Games some of their most eagerly awaited contests, most of all that between Filbert Bayi of Tanzania, 1,500m world record holder, and John Walker of New Zealand, holder of the mile record, whom Bayi had beaten when setting his own record at the Commonwealth Games two years earlier.

Whatever Killanin might have suffered in emotional stress, he would still enjoy sitting next to the Queen at the opening ceremony; at which, stunningly attired in a pink dress, coat and hat, she received an ovation almost as warm as that for Drapeau. As always when visiting Canada, she spoke in French.

The Montreal Games were praised by all: for the transport, the entertainment centres, the mood of festivity, the congenial restaurants and the efficient venues, though there were fewer tourists than expected despite 3.25 million ticket sales. This was at least partially on account of the cancellation of many events

The reward he did not wish to jeopardise. Lord Killanin sits beside a radiant Queen Elizabeth. (© IOC)

because of the boycott, which saw the departure of 441 competitors. More than 100,000 ticket sales had to be reimbursed. Yet revenue for Montreal was $430 million against operating expenses of $207 million, thereby giving a profit on the administrative, as opposed to construction, operation of $223 million. The investment of $1.2 billion on facilities, widely interpreted abroad as punitive on the taxpayers, was paid from a municipal property tax and by provincial taxes on tobacco etc. over subsequent years – normal budgeting for any city improvements at any Games.

For the time being, though IOC finances were improving with the rise in television rights fees, the position remained one of concern for Killanin, responsible as President for the inter-related functional units of the Olympic Movement comprising 74 IOC members, 13 commissions, 130 NOCs and 26 IFs, with additionally the organising committees of the Winter and Summer Games. The deficit for 1968–71 had been $1.5 million. In six of Killanin's eight years as President annual expenditure would continue to exceed revenue generated, though the margins were narrowing.

Footnotes to his first four years included the abolition of IOC members' annual fee of 300 Swiss francs and rejection of the Executive Board's proposal at the Session in Montreal that a woman could be elected to the IOC even if her country already had one or even two members. Women, and anti-apartheid campaigners, would continue to have to wait.

Anxieties about Montreal had distracted some attention from the Winter Games at Innsbruck, where at short notice the Austrians had staged their second Games for a comparatively moderate $85.6 million, almost half of that spent on transport improvements and a new bridge over the River Inn. Some one and a half million spectators watched the 37-event schedule, with 600 million television viewers around the world. Two of the smallest states, Andorra and San Marino, made their Winter Games debut. Intent on effective security, the Austrians marshalled a force of 5,000 policemen, giving a two-to-one ratio over athletes.

CHAPTER XLVIII

Innsbruck (XII) 1976

Franz Klammer of Austria, Olympic downhill champion

'The topic of sporting debate often tends to centre on the Olympic Games, the goal for all athletes. For me, the emphasis is the same. You can be an ex-this, an ex-that, but you'll always be an Olympic champion, there are so few. The Games stand out from all other events.

A skier's career is often very short, so on the big day you want everything to be right. The pressure on me really was tremendous. The year before, I'd won nine out of ten downhills, including seven consecutively, and this season, after falling at Val d'Isère in the opening race, I'd won the next four or five. Toni Sailer, our triple Alpine champion of 1956, had said to me that this is when the pressure is really on, when you're favourite, when you have just one shot and you have to take it.

By the time I started at Patscherkofel, number 15 out of the gate, the conditions had become very difficult, really rough, but just for my own sake I had to win, to prove I could take the pressure. Here was the difference from all other races. The top of the run was not so difficult, but I made a simple error that left me readjusting the whole way down. I had to do something special and I was having to change the line some of the time. After the intermediate time check, I chose one very high turn, no one else had been up there. I came millimetres close to the safety net and heard a cry; I wondered if I'd caught a spectator with my ski pole, but it was just a shout. I think that was the best move I ever made in racing; I nailed it there. I got the edge you need. It wasn't something worked out with my coach, just instinctive on the spur of the moment.

Even in America, 25 years later, people still remember the man in the yellow suit, even non-skiers. Yellow suit? For that season our team had black-and-gold suits but mine didn't fit me, I couldn't crouch comfortably, so I went back to the previous one.

Emotionally, no other race came close to that. I'd prepared so hard mentally. It wasn't the technique I was striving for. That was already there. It was the courage to go out and take risks. I was very relieved as people had thought I wouldn't be able to take the strain. Now it's history, yet people still remember it.'*
(Photograph © IOC/Locatelli)

Franz Klammer tended mostly to describe himself as a farmer's boy – appropriate for someone strong and stoic. Born on the edge of the Yugoslav/Slovenian border in the little village of Mooswald, such was his early evident talent that he had spent mornings at a special ski school. It was not so much that he was adroit as that he was fearless, seemingly oblivious to danger, yet without being foolhardy. By the age of 18 he was in the national team for the downhill, and within two years, though lacking the all-round technical equipment to be a candidate for the World Cup, which included the slalom and the giant slalom, he had built a formidable record in the Formula 1 event.

In 1976, the perceived insult to Austria and its former favourite son, Karl Schranz, by the late Avery Brundage was still an issue. The whole of Austria expected, indeed demanded, that Klammer should exact a kind of revenge, a posthumous spit in the eye for the former IOC President. Such was the aura that surrounded Klammer, now 22, that it was he who bore the Austrian flag at the opening ceremony. The following day came his moment of destiny at the top of the 3,145m course, which dropped through 870 metres to the finish.

He was by no means without rivals. Bernhard Russi of Switzerland, though beaten by Klammer by half a second in a World Cup downhill at Patscherkofel prior to the Games, was in equally impressive form. Perhaps vitally, Russi was now drawn third in the starting list. On the fresh run he skied superbly and set a time almost ten seconds faster than Klammer's the previous year; though on a course that, admittedly, had been adjusted to produce higher speeds. None of the next 11 racers could match Russi, Herbert Plank of Italy coming closest, just over half a second behind.

Now came Klammer. At the first intermediate time, at 1,000 metres, he was down on both Russi and Plank; still behind at 2,000 metres, by almost a fifth of a second. In his own mind, though unaware of these comparative times, Klammer knew things were desperate. At the so-called Bear's Neck he took the straight line, almost brushing the crowd, to maintain greater momentum. An unofficial timing had him coming out of the turn six miles an hour faster than Russi at 75 mph (120 kph). Whether you were there on the course or watching on television, it was one of the most heart-stopping moments in all of Olympic history, this plummeting figure in yellow seemingly about to fall at every second of a literally hare-brained display that shouted to the world: 'Here I come!' And come he did, a fraction over half a second ahead of Russi in 1:45.73 – the fastest downhill in history thus far, at the greatest average speed yet of 102.828 kph, which would remain unsurpassed for 22 years until Tommy Moe (USA) recorded 103.319 kph in Lillehammer. Given that Klammer had made up the deficit on the final third of the race, this had been a run beyond belief. 'It was perfection, taking the fastest line to the extreme,' Steve Podborski of Canada, a pre-match favourite, recalls. By 0.33 seconds, Russi

There has probably been no braver run, before or since, than Franz Klammer's downhill victory of 1976, in which he defeated the defending champion Bernhard Russi of Switzerland, who offers congratulations. (© IOC) (© IOC/ASL)

had to accept the silver medal. Asked of his plans, Klammer replied: 'My father has the pitchfork waiting, we have to spread the dung for the spring planting.'

As much a favourite for the giant slalom and slalom was Gustavo Thöni of Italy, respectively runner-up and champion from Sapporo and the winner of four previous World Cups. No one thus far had won an Alpine gold medal in consecutive Games, but surely here was the man to do so, even though he had finished an inconspicuous 26th in the downhill. His rivals were the emerging Swede, Ingemar Stenmark, 19, narrowly beaten by Thöni in the last World Cup slalom the previous season; and Piero Gros, World Cup winner of 1974. In the event, Thöni and Stenmark were seen off in the giant slalom by a couple of Swiss, Heini Hemmi and Ernst Good, neither of whom had previously won a World Cup race. Thöni had led on the first run and Stenmark was fastest on the second, but level performances by Hemmi and Good earned them gold and silver respectively. In the slalom, Gros delivered, his second run a second faster than his colleague and admitted hero. Neither, frankly, could initially believe it. Thöni drowned his sorrows by returning to the construction, from his earnings, of a hotel–restaurant. So much for Brundage and amateurism.

No woman Alpinist had emulated the triple sweep of Sailer (AUT, 1956) and Killy (FRA, 1968) but Rosi Mittermaier (FRG) came so close. Though only 25, Mittermaier was known as 'Granny' for her competitive longevity. She had not, however, previously won a downhill, never mind having competed in her tenth World Cup season. This was her third Olympics and at the

perfect moment she found her touch, upstaging Brigitte Totschnig of Austria by half a second; while Marie-Thérèse Nadig, the defending Swiss champion, was bed-ridden with flu. It was Mittermaier's first downhill victory in 100 attempts. One down and two to go.

Four days later her second gold medal came in the slalom, an event at which she was supreme with her classic technique. On a difficult course, on which only 19 of 42 starters completed both courses, Mittermaier lay second to compatriot Pamela Behr on the first run, but clinched the title on the second. Such by now was her prestige among both Austrians and the throng of German followers, that it required a police escort to ease her passage back to her hotel, which was likewise surrounded by a clammering public.

Another two days, the giant slalom. The dream perished when Kathy Kreiner, an 18 year old from Ontario, excelled as the opening skier, never to be surpassed. Off went Mittermaier at number four and at the halfway mark she was ahead, only to lapse on the bottom half of the course and to lose a third gold by twelve-hundredths of a second. Kreiner was almost apologetic. Presented with a bunch of flowers at the finishing line by a despondent yet enthusiastic fan, Mittermaier immediately presented it to Kreiner and together with Danièlle Debernard, the bronze medal winner, lifted Kreiner aloft in triumph: the spirit of Olympism personified.

Success came to John Curry, the British figure skater, only after he rose above a number of obstacles. He saw his first ice show at the age of six, though he then instinctively turned his interest more towards dance and ballet. His father – much like the father in *Billy Elliot*, the Oscar-winning film about a child-boxer-turned-dancer – considered this insufficiently masculine and persuaded him to return to skating. By 16, working part-time as a bank clerk in London, he was training under the

Rosi Mittermaier (FRG), wins her first downhill in 100 attempts (left) and adds the slalom title (right). (© Getty Images/Duffy) (© IOC)

famous coach Arnold Gerschwiler of Switzerland. Already there were antagonists claiming his style was too artistic for convention.

In 1973 came the watershed: sponsorship from an American industrialist, Ed Moser, and the possibility to train at Denver, Colorado, under Carlo Fassi, coach to former Olympic champion Peggy Fleming. In 1975 he was second in the European Championships; in the World Championships, third. By 1976, Curry was ready. He was to bring to axels, lutzes and spins a degree of dexterity never previously seen in an Olympics.

Under-funded, under-estimated, dance-orientated John Curry of Britain rose above logistical obstacles and judging prejudice to reach the top. (© IOC)

So outstanding was his display that seven of the nine judges placed him first, only the Soviet judge putting him second behind Vladimir Kovalev, and the Canadian judge, just as predictably, placing Curry second to Toller Cranston. Had Curry skated last, there is little doubt he would have rated 6.0 (maximum).

Fassi was additionally the trainer of Dorothy Hamill, a 19-year-old American who had been developing under his guidance for five years. She was the reverse of Curry, seeking to bring athleticism to the more feminine women's arena. Her leaps and spins were fluid, dramatic, seemingly achieved without physical wind-up. Though musical, her compulsory figures were comparatively weak and, worse still, she suffered from competition nerves. Runner-up in the two previous World Championships to Christine Errath (GDR) and Dianne de Leeuw (NED), respectively, she was anything but confident. Nonetheless, Fassi's perseverance paid dividends and this time Hamill led on the compulsories and was ideally placed to let rip in the free programme. This she did. The marks were high and the Italian judge awarded a perfect 6.0 for technical merit.

Irina Rodnina and her new skating partner and husband, Alexandr Zaitsev, likewise gained unanimous approval in the pairs, outclassing the two GDR partnerships in second and third place. Rodnina, 26, had lost none of her artistry in making the switch, or from the indignity of being jilted by her former partner. The change, however, did little to improve her social graces, but victory provided a further banner for the Soviet trainer Stanislav Zhuk. Tai Babilonia of America, partnering Randy Gardener in fifth place, was the first black athlete to compete in the Winter Games.

The inaugural ice dance event, controversially accepted as 'sport' following a long campaign for inclusion, was also Soviet dominated. While the lifts and throws characteristic of pairs were excluded by the rules, Lyudmila Pakhomova and Aleksandr Gorschkov, world champions for five of the six previous years, were predictable winners. They were the unanimous choice among the judges, with compatriots Irina Moiseyeva and Andrei Minenkov being runners-up. The disciplined, athletic virtues of the event had become apparent.

It was rational to expect Soviet competitors to dominate speed skating, given their impeccable training centre at Medeo in Central Asia's Pamir Mountains, where glacial water was ideal for sprint training. Yevgeni Kulikov and Valeri Muratov duly ran away with the 500m, Kulikov even setting an Olympic record of 39.17 on Innsbruck's wet track, more than two seconds outside his world record set at Medeo. The bronze narrowly went to Dan Immerfall of America and a mere three-hundredths behind him, in fifth place, came his colleague Peter Müller. Two days later Müller was triumphant in the inaugural 1,000m race with a comfortable margin over Jörn Didriksen (NOR) and Muratov. This was indeed a triumph for a racer from a country that took minor interest in speed skating and possessed few tracks.

Müller's glory was matched in the women's 500m by Sheila Young from Detroit. She had narrowly missed a bronze medal four years earlier and in the interim had won a world title, setting a world record in the process. By the time of Innsbruck, she was regarded as almost unbeatable and indeed proved to be so, setting an Olympic record of 42.76, this being almost two seconds outside her world time. The following day Young took bronze in the 1,000m behind Tatyana Averina (URS), the acknowledged star of the Games who won this and the 3,000m, both in Olympic record times, plus bronze in both 500m and 1,500m.

The debate in Nordic skiing was about whether Finland or the Soviet Union would have the upper hand in women's events, the issue being partially deflected by a disqualification for a positive drug test. Galina Kulakova (URS), 33, would become her country's most decorated Olympic skier, with four gold medals, two silver and two bronze in four Games, 1968–80, but at Innsbruck was declared positive after finishing third in the 5km. Her roommate's nose drops, borrowed on the morning of the race, had contained ephedrine. The IOC deemed this an honest mistake and she was allowed to continue, winning bronze in the 10km and the fourth gold of her career in the 4 x 5km relay. Her colleague, Raisa Smetanina, from the Ural Mountains, was the most successful in these Games with two golds and a silver. She would surpass Kulakova over the course of four Games by winning ten medals. Her silver at Innsbruck came when losing by a second in the 5km to Helena Takalo of Finland.

Bill Koch from Vermont in the US had spent much of his childhood skiing to and from school and by the time he reached these Games, at the age of 20, he was acquiring particular attention for his novel style of skiing, with the points of the blades turned outwards as in skating, rather than conventionally thrust forward in a straight line. In spite of being afflicted by asthma, he took the silver medal in the 30km behind Sergei Savelyev, doughty soldier in the Red Army. Koch's style and persistence also gave him sixth place behind three Soviets, a Finn and a Norwegian in the later discontinued 15km. His silver is the only Nordic skiing medal ever won by an American, at a Games in which the Soviet Union and East Germany won 46 of the 111 medals available.

Long-time specialists did not think too much of the cut-price bobsleigh run constructed by the Austrians at Igls. It was too easy and too slow, the Italians and others sniffed. The fanatical East Germans had other ideas in the nation's headlong sports quest. The previous year they had measured, tested and filmed the bends, then went home and enlisted established athletes to become bob competitors. Meinhard Nehmer, a 35-year-old former javelin thrower, became only the third driver in a Games to win both two- and four-man events. Indeed, the GDR won all but three of the medals available in bob and luge. While Nehmer had a creditable javelin performance of 81.50m (276 ft 4 in.), his crew in the two-man event, Bernhard Germeshausen, was a decathlete who had gained 7,544 points.

How much, retrospectively, should we condemn the competitors of the GDR, honest in their personal effort but collectively guilty of their state's policy regarding drug enhancement? Hans-Georg Aschenbach and Jochen Danneberg took the first two places in the 70m jump. Years later, Aschenbach would admit to having been on a systematic programme of muscle-building steroids; to having been petrified awaiting the drug tests after his victory and the prospect of being exposed as a cheat. 'Nobody can imagine what you go through,' he recalled, 'you even forget that you have won.' Steroids no doubt contributed to Aschenbach's recovery prior to the Games from a crippling knee injury.

CHAPTER XLIX

Montreal (XXI) 1976

Lasse Virén of Finland, unique twice winner of the Olympic 10,000/5,000 double

'*When I was young, busy trying to develop my career as a runner, I never even thought about the Olympic Games. I knew they existed and I was familiar with the names of Paavo Nurmi and Hannes Kolehmainen, but they were somewhere far, far in the past; they never really entered my consciousness. Important for me was the annual match between Finland and Sweden, home or away. I knew some fellows who had competed in that match and to do so myself became my ambition. It was quite a famous match, taking place every alternate year at the Olympic stadium in Helsinki, and almost always sold out for the two days ever since 1925. The Olympic Games, until 1971, was something distant, less important.*

At that time we in Finland were very formal: first you had to run in your area championships, then qualify for the national championships and after that, possibly, for the match against Sweden. We didn't have other big international competitions and, anyhow, I didn't dream about travelling abroad. Until the European Championships of 1971, sport for me was something comfortable. I loved it, making my training runs deep through the forests of Finland. After the championships in 1971, when I was seventh in the 5,000m – and seventeenth in the 10,000m – I suddenly realised that it would be possible to qualify also for the Games.

When I set myself the target to run at the Games in Munich, I also began to realise how much more I had to do, just how important the Games are and would be for me and for my country. I'm always realistic; I tried to keep my feet on the ground, but the Olympic Games were going to be something big, even to be there would be an achievement. To win, that would be even more incredible – and it would be something I could always hold on to. Though records are broken, your medals you can keep . . . the medals and trophies I've won are not on view but in a wardrobe somewhere. When my eldest son, at the age of about six, once opened the door and saw the trophies, he ran to his mother and asked: "Mama, mama, has father been an athlete?"

I doubt whether sport, and running in particular, are the same now as they were in my time. Then, the Olympic Games was the greatest event in the world. Nowadays, they have athletic golden leagues, they have grand prix, they have so many competitions with financial prizes that a medal doesn't mean so much. Back in the 1970s, we didn't have a world championships – other than the Games – and no half-marathon championship, no road relay championship. Today, a championship hardly means anything. All that the athletes ask now is "how much?". The first man to run under four minutes . . . or the first man to pass the million-dollar mark? I don't believe that victory in the Olympic Games is any longer as great as it once was.'*

(Photograph © IOC)

Prior to arriving at Montreal, Lasse Virén was asked why he was attempting to defend his titles when he already had the distinction of his double victory in Munich. It was, he replied, that he wished to stop his countrymen always referring to Nurmi as '*the* Flying Finn', to halt the comparison. In a country with a population of only four and a half million, he had found himself trapped behind an established legend. The question put to him was relevant because his performances since Munich had been mediocre, interrupted by operations for a leg injury and nasal impediment. How could he now possibly handle rivals of the calibre of Carlos Lopez of Portugal, New Zealanders Rod Dixon and Dick Quax, Brendan Foster and Ian Stewart of Britain? It was as though this lonely Finn of few words, a rural policeman, was merely raging at the sky. What was about to happen was a phenomenon.

The absence of the Ethiopians and Kenyans on account of the boycott reduced the depth but not the standard of the 10,000m, for the first eight home would run just as fast as had the first eight in Munich. What was unusual about the tactics was that there were no mid-race breaks, no surges by one runner attempting to open the field. Instead, Lopez set out to burn off the rest by gradually increasing pace in the manner of Dave Bedford, no longer a contender.

Lopez took up the lead after 2km, each kilometre being successively faster: 2:53, 2:50; then 2:49. On and on he drove: 2:49 again, the fifth kilometre in 2:46, with 5km being reached in 14:09.0, half a minute slower than Bedford's schedule for his then existing world record. For all the bravery of Lopez's tactics, some thought this pace disappointing. Lopez continued to lead a patient field of those with faster finishes, his only prospect to lose them. He could not. With just over a lap to go, Virén smoothly accelerated to the front, winning by nearly five seconds to become only the second man in Olympic history to retain this title, following Zátopek. The man from the tiny village of Myrskylä (pop. 2,300), some 70 miles north-east of Helsinki, stood three-quarters of the way towards athletic immortality.

What were his rivals to do about him in the 5,000m? It was a formidable field, yet the others knew not whether to try to kill off his finishing potential early in the race with a fast pace, or to wait and attempt to out-sprint him. There were those present, especially Dixon and Quax, who might have done either, while Foster had set an Olympic record of 13:20.34 in the heats. Compounding all the conjecture was an emerging allegation that Virén's rare plateau of performance was gained by the process of 'blood-doping': whereby a litre or so of blood was removed during training at high altitude, being replaced by natural regeneration, then was injected as a last-minute transfusion to provide additional oxygen-carrying red cells. The process was known to have been explored in Scandinavia but Virén vigorously denied having utilised it; his explanation for peak performances at major events was that these were the only occasions that really counted. Further controversy occurred the day before the 5,000m final when the IOC demanded an explanation for Virén waving his shoes during a celebration lap after the 10,000m. Was this not blatant commercialism, he was asked? No, a blister, he said. The guv'nors tolerantly excused him.

Lasse Virén of Finland, in one of the greatest long-distance finishes of all time, completes the 'double double' in Montreal's 5,000m ahead of Dick Quax (NZL, 291), and Klaus-Peter Hildenbrand (FRG, 420). (© AFP)

With Quax unluckily overtaken by a similar bug from which Foster had suffered in the 10,000m, Virén took it upon himself to share the pace-setting with Foster. A weakened Quax and Klaus-Peter Hildenbrand of West Germany joined them during the fourth kilometre. Virén accelerated with three laps to go, but at the bell barely a couple of strides separated a pack of six. Virén glanced behind him. 'I took in the situation and all its threats,' he said. 'I had put in a couple of 60-second laps and they were all still there. I was the fugitive.' They were still all there as they came off the final bend in one of the most exceptional finishes the author has ever witnessed: a line of five runners fanning out across the track, any one of them the winner. Down that last desperate straight they came, the willowy frame of Virén, stride shortening but rhythm retained and head steady, fractionally holding his advantage as Quax, Dixon and Hildenbrand fought

in his wake for the other two medals in the slim hope that Virén would crack. He would not. Quax, the genial, talkative, talented Kiwi, who recently had been within a whisker of Puttemans' record, was at Virén's shoulder but could not close that arm's length. At the line, Hildenbrand threw himself across to steal the bronze from Dixon, with Foster a fighting fifth. It was a heroic finish to an Olympian climax by the most special of distance runners: now additionally the first to retain the 5,000m title, let alone an extraordinary 'double double'. His time, 13:24.76, was faster than his Olympic record four years previously. 'He mesmerised the race like a rattlesnake,' a rival said at the time.

In 1972, Alberto Juantorena of Cuba failed to survive the semi-final of the 400m. By 1976 he had become formidable not only at this distance but, unusually, also at the two-lap race. In Montreal he was to win both, including a world record at 800m. How an athlete, even one so powerful as Juantorena, could make such an improvement between the age of 22 and 26 is difficult to judge without being privy to his training routines: unusual, one can only say. Such was Juantorena's power, that he seemed able to sustain the anaerobic running that is basic to a one-lap runner far longer than most into a partially aerobic two-lap race. Indeed, he had been persuaded only latterly into competing at 800m, when his coach told him it would increase endurance for the 400m. In the absence of Mike Boit of Kenya on account of the boycott, Rick Wohlhuter, the defending champion, was the favourite, and indeed publicly declared that the inexperienced Juantorena would struggle to make it through three rounds. How wrong could he be? Although a foot operation had caused the Cuban to miss most of the 1975 season, he had recovered to win the Pan-Am Games 400m title and early the following year decided that he would make a double bid in Montreal – something rarely attempted.

For all Wohlhuter's pre-race judgement, Juantorena forged into the lead after the lane-break in the 800m final, quickly responded to a lightweight challenge by Siram Singh of India and then held off a vain challenge from Wohlhuter. With a first lap passed in just over 50 seconds, it was evident a world record was possible. Juantorena never faltered in the run to the line, becoming the first 800m champion from a non-English-speaking country and also beating the world record of Marcello

With his huge physique and stride, Cuban Alberto Juantorena achieved a rare 400/800m double, here outpacing Ivo Van Damme (BEL) and Rick Wohlhuter (USA), to win the latter. (© Getty Images/Duffy)

Fiasconaro of Italy by a fifth of a second in 1:43.50. Ivo Van Damme robbed Wohlhuter of second place. Sadly, however, Van Damme lost his life in a car crash aged 22, in what had been a year of unprecedented acclaim for him, having also taken the silver medal in the 1,500m. Juantorena's triumph was left in question, never mind his record, when within a month Boit twice ran sub-1:44.

Juantorena showed himself anything but weary when it came to his more favoured shorter race. The challenge was likely to come from America, as ever. Fred Newhouse and Herman Frazier led into the back straight and Newhouse looked the winner. Steadily, however, the Americans were overhauled by Juantorena's devouring stride as he judged his pace to perfection. With the line in sight, he moved ahead and his winning time of 44.26, though well outside Lee Evans' world and Olympic record, was the fourth fastest ever and the best by a non-United States competitor. David Jenkins of Britain, subsequently to be convicted and imprisoned for steroid trafficking in America, was with Newhouse at the halfway mark, only to finish seventh.

The biggest loss to the Games through the boycott probably occurred in the 1,500m, in which John Walker of New Zealand and Filbert Bayi of Tanzania were denied a repeat run of their illustrious final in the Commonwealth Games two years earlier at Christchurch, New Zealand. Walker was bent on revenge, but was now likely to have the race to himself, especially with the brilliant Boit also absent. His victory by only a metre was mentally easier than that would suggest.

Spared the challenge of Filbert Bayi (TAN) by the boycott, John Walker (NZL) comfortably wins the 1,500m from Ivo Van Damme (BEL) and Paul-Heinz Wellmann (FRG). (© IOC)

No one seeing Ed Moses during training in the days leading to the 400m hurdles could doubt that here was a champion-to-be. Tall and superbly proportioned, he had refined his technique to be able to maintain 13 strides between the hurdles rather than 15: something that David Hemery and John Akii-Bua, world record breaking champions at each of the two previous Games, had only achieved over the first five hurdles. Moses possessed an even more rhythmic stride pattern than Akii-Bua, now a boycott absentee. Another threat to Moses had been removed by long-term injury to Alan Pascoe, European and Commonwealth champion from Britain two years earlier, whose training was based on a new world record of around 47.5 in Montreal.

The bespectacled African-American had never run the event before March of this year, yet by the time of the US trials was running 48.30, the third fastest time ever. The Games would be

his first international meeting, aged 20. In the final he ran away from everyone to set a world best of 47.64 ahead of colleague Michael Shine and Yevgeni Gavrilenko (URS), with an off-colour Pascoe an exhausted eighth. From August 1977, Moses would sustain an unbeaten span of 107 races over nearly 10 years, with a world record of 47.02 that would stand until 1992.

Another first winner from a non-English-speaking country was Guy Drut of France in the high hurdles. A marvellous all-round performer with near international credentials in all three jumping events, Drut had placed himself under some pressure, first by promising to win the event and second because he had taken an advisory job on sport within the French government at a time when government policy on financing sport was dividing the nation. As a result, he was consistently booed when competing at home.

Seldom do so many fine runners come together as now converged for the steeplechase: Anders Gärderud, Swedish world record holder; Bronislaw Malinowski, European champion from Poland, born of a Scottish mother; Frank Baumgartl of East Germany, former world junior record holder; and Tapio Kantanen of Finland, bronze medal winner in Munich. For Gärderud, mental anxiety was likely to have been acute: he failed in the opening rounds of both 800m and 1,500m in Mexico City and had been unsuccessful in the steeplechase and 5,000m at Munich. Now he set a killing pace, but could not throw off Malinowski or Baumgartl. All three crossed the final water jump within split seconds of each other and sprinted for the last hurdle. Baumgartl, exhausted, tripped and fell, disrupting Malinowski's rhythm as he had to clear both hurdle and prostrate body. A now unchallenged Gärderud improved his own world record to 8:08.0, the seriously injured Baumgartl courageously rising to take the bronze.

It was expected that Nikolai Avilov, defending champion, would have a fascinating decathlon tussle with Guido Kratschmer of West Germany and Bruce Jenner of the United States, who had been tenth in Munich but with annual improvement had become the record holder with 8,538 points. Irresistibly, Jenner ran away with the title, improving his record to 8,634. With personal bests in all of the five first-day events – 100m, long jump, shot, high jump, 400m – he found himself only 17 points behind Avilov and 35 behind Kratschmer. This meant that Jenner, his second-day events being his stonger, was effectively certain of the gold medal, and this remained the case with two events to go. He knew that victory would make him rich and that he would never need to compete again – to the extent that he did not bother to take his vaulting poles home with him.

Under the unwavering US system of trials, neither Steve Williams nor Houston McTear, both injured, were able to qualify for the 100m, never mind that Williams had equalled or broken the world record for this and the 100 yards. LeRoy Walker, long-time team coach, was critical of this rigidity, and for the first time since 1928 the US failed to win a medal. The favourites were Don Quarrie – Jamaica not having joined their boycotting African cousins – and Valeri Borzov, the defending champion, plus Silvio Leonard, the Pan-Am champion of the previous year. With an injured foot, Leonard went out in the second round. Out of the blue appeared Hasely Crawford of Trinidad, who had pulled up injured in the Munich final. Crawford suffered from nerves, but not sufficiently to prevent him overtaking Borzov and then Quarrie in the last 20 metres to win by two-hundredths of a second from Quarrie in 10.06: Trinidad's first Olympic champion in any sport.

In the 200m, Quarrie was even more clearly favourite. This was his third Games, injuries having marred the previous two. A feared rival, James Gilkes of Guyana, the Pan-Am champion, was removed by the boycott, and Pietro Mennea of Italy, though doubting his form, had only entered by public acclaim. Quarrie dominated the race, though his victory in 20.23 over Americans Millard Hampton and Dwayne Evans was achieved with little to spare.

Many sporting sons fail to emerge from the shadow of their famous fathers. Not so Miklos Németh, son of Imre – hammer champion in 1948 and three-times world record holder. By 1967, Miklos had become world number two in the javelin. He then failed to qualify for the final pool in Mexico City, was no better than fifth in three European Championships and finished seventh in the Munich Games. In Montreal, now 29, he fulfilled himself with his first throw, 94.58m (310 ft 4 in.), almost two feet beyond the world record of Klaus Wolfermann, the previous champion, absent through injury. Németh's throw was ten feet beyond his previous personal best, and he and Imre are the only father–son combination to win track and field gold medals.

The marathon field included Virén, attempting to emulate Zátopek's feat in 1952 of winning the three longest distance titles, but the best he could manage was fifth place, just over three minutes behind the winner, Waldemar Cierpinski of the GDR, who had been installed in the Village for more than a month to acclimatise to the time difference. This paid dividends, with an Olympic best of 2:09:55.0.

The Americans and British both suffered from perverse selection principles in this event. The US forced Frank Shorter, the world's number one, to run in the trials a month beforehand, while the British omitted the reigning European and Commonwealth champion Ian Thompson, despite a deluge of criticism for doing so. Shorter finished second, almost a minute behind Cierpinski, with Karel Lismont of Belgium, runner-up in Munich, taking the bronze. Neither Cierpinski nor Lismont had ever beaten Thompson, and on a course free of hills it is probable that the economic Thompson would have had too much pace for the East German. In the now known GDR regime of drug-enhancement, was Cierpinski clean? Shorter expressed his doubts.

Regarding women's events, and writing with hindsight and the knowledge now available of admitted drug use prevalent among coaches and competitors of the former German Democratic Republic, there must be scepticism about the domination in Montreal of the Soviet Union and GDR, who won all but two events in track and field – the GDR nine of the fourteen. The East German superiority was almost as marked and just as suspect in swimming. The only non-Communist winner was Annegret Richter of West Germany, who won the 100m sprint in 11.08, way outside the world record of 10.8 which she shared with Renate Stecher (GDR) who came second. An emerging Evelyn Ashford (USA) finished fifth. The outstanding performance in short distances came from Irena Szewinska (formerly Kirszenstein), who improved her own world record in the 400m to 49.29. She had become the first woman to break 50 seconds in 1974 in only her second race over this distance. She had now won seven medals (three, two and two) in four Games between 1964 and '76.

Bela Karolyi, the Romanian gymnastics coach, discovered Nadia Comaneci when she was five. By the age of eleven, she was national champion and two years later, in 1975, became the youngest ever to win the European title. At fourteen, she burst upon the Games of Montreal, becoming the first gymnast to receive a perfect mark of ten. This was disconcerting for the established might of Soviet gymnastics, within which the rapidly rising Nelli Kim and the established Ludmila Tourischeva, champion at Munich, were vainly trying to come to terms with the favours bestowed upon Olga Korbut, who had

never defeated Tourischeva. Comaneci had achieved that feat in the European Championship and now she was marginally favourite for the Games. Her fearless athleticism captivated television audiences across the world and with first place on the asymmetric bars, for which she received two tens, and the beam, and with third place for floor exercise behind Tourischeva and Kim, she became overall champion. Korbut was a mere fifth. Collecting further maximum scores, Comaneci gained another two gold medals on individual beam and bars. Kim claimed two gold, Tourischeva two silver and a bronze, Korbut a single silver. The only consolation for the Soviets was the team title, held since they first entered the Games in 1952.

Comaneci may have been the perfect gymnast, she may have become more famous than Dracula and been patronised by the despised dictator Nikolae Ceausescu, but the demands of her sporting schedule had repressed her soul. She seldom smiled, never cried and at 15 attempted suicide by drinking bleach. On recovery, she said she was glad about what she had done, because her time in hospital temporarily spared her the rigours of training. She continued for two further Games and then in the winter of 1989 fled across the Hungarian border, wading through mud and ice to begin a new life in America.

If the women's gymnastics brought surprise for the Soviet

Nadia Comaneci of Romania destroys the field, here with a maximum 10.0 on the beam. (© IOC)

Union, the modern pentathlon brought disgrace. Major Boris Onischenko, silver medal winner in Munich where his team had won the gold, was suspended and sent home for cheating. On the second day in the fencing discipline, there had been suspicion when the electric recording system registered a hit against Adrian Parker of Britain. When Jeremy Fox of Britain

Women swimmers of the GDR, with or without chemical additive, were dominant to the dismay of Americans, here relieved by a relay victory for Wendy Boglioli, Kim Peyton, Jill Sterkel and Shirley Babashoff. (© IOC)

was Kornelia Ender with three world records, four including her medley relay. The shock of the GDR's performances in the women's events was, however, greatest for Shirley Babashoff, who had been favoured to win the 100m freestyle but in the event was a distant fifth behind Ender's world record 55.65.

Whether or not the East Germans were the beneficiaries of medical/chemical assistance, their performances in every sport, from luge in winter to swimming, running and most other discplines in summer, were a reflection of detailed attention to sports science and training that amounted to a national industry.

Punctuation of American supremacy in the men's events, in which John Naber took four golds, including two relays, and silver in the 200m freestyle, came when David Wilkie of Britain won the UK's first men's swimming gold since 1908 in the 200m breaststroke with a world record of 2:15.11. The Austrian-born Italian Klaus Dibiasi, competing in his fourth Games, became the first diver to win three consecutive gold medals.

In boxing, the Americans shone once more. Having slumped in Munich, they now produced one of their best teams with five titles by Leo Randolph (flyweight); Howard Davis (lightweight); Sugar Ray Leonard (light-welter); Michael Spinks (middleweight) and his brother Leon (light-heavy). The heavyweight title was successfully defended by Teofilo Stevenson, one of Cuba's three titles.

likewise suffered a hit without being touched, he demanded that Onischenko's foil be examined, whereupon it was discovered that the implement contained a concealed button that enabled the Ukrainian falsely to record a hit. For such an act to be discovered in the modern pentathlon, of all sports, was equivalent to spitting in the Olympic flame. The humiliation for Onischenko was total: a man who had been friend and rival with Fox for more than ten years and whose life had now effectively been extinguished at one stroke. He muttered his apologies to Fox before being hustled to the airport to return home to an existence devoid of every privilege he had gained in a state-orientated society. He had done it, his friends believed, to ensure victory and upon retirement his appointment as chief national coach. As a consequence of the elimination of the Soviet team by this incident, the British team of Parker, Fox and Danny Nightingale spectacularly won the event, their first-ever medal. For Fox it was the climax of his career, aged 34, having missed the individual bronze in Munich. The British lay only fifth after four events, but they claimed victory over the cross-country, thanks primarily to an inspired run over the 4km course by Parker in 12.09.0, the fastest time ever up till then.

In swimming, GDR's women won all but two of thirteen titles, not having won a single gold prior to Montreal. Foremost

Teofilo Stevenson (CUB), successfully defended his heavyweight title, here defeating Johnny Tate (USA) in the semi-final. (© AFP)

CHAPTER L

Cold War, Hot Heads

Lord Killanin of Ireland, sixth President of the IOC, 1972–80

'The problems facing the Games of the XXII Olympiad will be discussed during this Session . . . the Executive Board has already heard the views expressed by the president of the Assembly of NOCs, besides the views of the governments of the United States and Australia. In view of the worldwide publicity surrounding the 1980 Games, I feel it is my duty to recall some important points.

The decision was taken by the IOC in 1974 to allocate these Games to Lake Placid and Moscow. Agreements were signed in accordance with our rules. Judging by world reaction at the time, the decisions were welcomed as a symbol of mutual understanding. Sadly, the current political situation is different, but the agreements of 1974 must be honoured by us all. Unfortunately, since the conception of the modern Games, governments have attempted to make use of them for political purposes. I have never denied or ignored the intrusion of politics, but I believe it to be in all our interests that these intrusions are resisted. We have had to face political problems in Germany and China, racial discrimination in South Africa and Rhodesia. We have always sought to resolve these problems from a sporting point of view, in an effort to bring the peoples of the world together.

. . . We can only pray that leaders of opposing factions can come together to resolve their differences in order to avoid another holocaust. I have continued to attack the chauvinism of certain aspects of the Olympic Games. We have not been helped by those who produce tables of results on a national basis, contrary to our rules which state: "the Games are a contest between individuals and not between countries". Nonetheless, demonstrations of nationalism increase, whether at Olympic ceremonies or on the sports field. The IOC is not infallible and may have also contributed to this, despite its best endeavours. Incidentally, there is sometimes confusion about Olympic ceremonies. Victory ceremonies and medals are the property of the IOC, as are the Games, and not that of the host city.

We live in a world where there are totalitarian regimes of the left and of the right. Are there any countries that can claim fully to respect human rights and not to practise discrimination of some kind? . . . I would implore all those with different opinions and feelings not to use the Olympic Games to divide the world but to unite it. The IOC has called the XIth Olympic Congress in Baden-Baden next year, which will be attended by representatives of the IFs and NOCs, as well as the athletes themselves and governmental and non-governmental sporting bodies . . . Long-term Olympic policy will be debated, including eligibility, commercialisation, politicisation and the size, siting and administration of the Games . . . We sincerely hope these Games will not be used for the furtherance of political aims, or demonstrations of prejudices . . . I now call on Secretary of State Cyrus Vance formally to open the 82nd Session of the International Olympic Committee.' (Address to Session, Lake Placid, February 1980) (Photograph © IOC)

Notwithstanding Killanin's dignified plea for rationality, he and the IOC were about to receive, in blatant breach of protocol at their own function, a straight left to the nose in the form of a blatant political lecture from Vance, flag-bearer for the politically motivated US President Jimmy Carter. In vain, as it turned out, Carter sought to make political capital at election time out of the Soviet Union's recent invasion of Afghanistan.

Killanin himself was a troubled non-political President. The politicians would not leave the IOC alone, such was the attraction of its public platform and the attention it commanded from a global audience. On the positive side, the Session of 1977 in Prague had condemned those countries which had boycotted Montreal but imposed no penalty on

them, and had welcomed the unanimous decision by Commonwealth prime ministers, at a conference in Gleaneagles, Scotland, that there should be no future sporting contact with South Africa. Signatories included Robert Muldoon of New Zealand, which ameliorated African opinion, though British and West Indian rugby players and cricketers remained equivocal in their attitude. A proposal by Canada and others to suspend boycotting countries from the next Games had been resisted, as had the repeated suggestion by Prime Minister Karamanlis of Greece that all Games should be staged in Greece.

The British Olympic Association (BOA) resolved in 1978 that 'no athlete could be deprived of the right to participate in the Olympic Games'. This reflected the attitude of the *Final Report of*

Mayor Tom Bradley (right) of Los Angeles was keen to stage the Games but determined not to spend a dollar doing so. (© IOC/Pi)

the President's Commission on Olympic Sports (IOC, 1977), which deplored 'the actions of governments that deny an athlete the right to take part in international competition'. The BOA's stated principle would be the cornerstone of its resistance 18 months later, when it rejected four letters from Prime Minister Margaret Thatcher requesting them to join Carter's boycott and opposed three similar attempts at persuasion by Foreign Minister Lord Carrington. Sir Denis Follows, chairman of the BOA, obdurately stated: 'We would of course obey any government legislation not to go, but we will not bow to a resolution.'

In 1978, Sarajevo had been elected to host the Winter Games of 1984, and Los Angeles, being the only candidate, to stage the Summer Games. The lack of rivalry to LA was a result of the financial problems suffered by Montreal, and partially because LA had already lost successive bids for 1976 and 1980. It was their turn. Additionally, the Olympic Movement had seldom been at such a low ebb, economically as much as politically, so the IOC was obliged to accept LA's bid. This was done in breach of Charter regulations, the bid being made by a private commercial organisation, the city of LA refusing to commit one dollar to the cost, in spite of Mayor Tom Bradley wishing the city to be closely associated with the event. At the IOC's stipulation, there would be two contracts for the Games: one between the IOC and the organising committee, which would take on the responsibility normally vested in a city; and another between the organising committee and the US Olympic committee. By careful negotiation, the IOC, with its back to the wall, managed to dilute the LA committee's initial arrogance of 'we'll run our Games our way'.

The tide, however, was not all favourable. Indications of the anti-Communist mood in America had come with the refusal of George Meany, a prominent labour leader, to accept honorary membership of the US Olympic committee with its accompanying social cachet. In 1978, his union called for a change of venue from Moscow for the 1980 Games; a view also advocated by the Liberal Party in Britain as a means of protesting against the persecution of Soviet dissidents. A similar position was likewise proposed by Menachem Begin of Israel as a result of Soviet restrictions on Jewish emigration.

Hypocrisy was rampant: American hypersensitivity towards the politics of Communism had not prevented NBC Television signing a network rights deal with Moscow for $87 million.

Vitaly Smirnov, one of two IOC members from the USSR, expressed alarm about a working group set up by the United Nations, under a chairman from Tanzania, to form an international convention on apartheid in sports 'which could be very dangerous to the Olympic Movement, since sportsmen themselves could be boycotted for political reasons'.

Parallel political movements by UNESCO, clandestinely supported by Moscow politicians, manoeuvring for a possible Olympic takeover, were another headache for Killanin. UNESCO camouflaged its actions under the guise of seeking an expansion of school sport as a means of social development. Killanin had partially blocked UNESCO's ambitions, and those of Thomas Keller with GAISF, with the creation of the Tripartite Commission in 1973, and in 1977 agreed to address a UNESCO meeting in Paris at the request of director-general Amadou M'Bow of Senegal. The Tripartite Commission's manifesto had already antagonised UNESCO by 'warning the great mass of sportsmen against certain aspects of interference by governmental and other agencies like UNESCO'. Now Killanin grasped the nettle and welcomed UNESCO's initiative in 'assisting' the development of sport, promising cooperation so long as it was not dictated by political consideration. Meanwhile, Killanin's ambitions to rationalise the eligibility code and amateurism were being given a new twist by FIFA, the football federation. At its congress in 1978, FIFA agreed to exclude from the Moscow tournament European and Latin American players who had taken part in the previous World Cup. This was allegedly to give a better chance to developing countries, yet was also designed to protect the prestige of FIFA's World Cup. Protests to FIFA by Willi Daume, chairman of the Eligibility Commission, were in vain.

Following the controversy at Montreal regarding China/Taiwan, a commission was appointed to visit both countries: Lance Cross (New Zealand), Tony Bridge (Jamaica) and Alexandru Siperco (Romania). Perversely, the latter was refused permission to travel

Henry Hsu, IOC member from Taiwan, perversely brought a law suit against his own private club. (© IOC/Imsand)

to Taipei by his government and Killanin decided to make the journey himself. He was not a wholly passive President: at one stage he even told the members they could find someone else if they did not back him. Because of his long-held affection for China, he was anxious to bring the mainland back into the Olympic fold, an attitude resented by some of his colleagues loyal to Taiwan. He persuaded the Executive Board that this was possible if Taiwan would adjust their name. The Board proposed firstly to confirm the recognition of the NOC in Beijing under the name of 'Chinese Olympic Committee'; secondly to retain the NOC in Taiwan under the name 'Chinese Taipei Olympic Committee', on condition that it adopted a new anthem and flag. Debate at the 1979 Session in Montevideo remained inconclusive. Taiwan, unhappy, threatened legal action. Henry Hsu, their IOC member, himself filed a lawsuit against the body of which he was a member, a seeming contradiction. Courts in both Switzerland and New York heard appeals from Taiwanese athletes wishing to compete at Lake Placid under the 'Republic of China' banner, but attempts to override the IOC's decision failed. When the Taiwan team arrived at Lake Placid with 'Republic' identification cards, they were refused entrance and returned home before the opening ceremony. An untidy situation remained unresolved.

On the Rhodesian front, Premier Ian Smith negotiated with the black majority on law modifications and in 1979 the president of the expelled Rhodesian NOC wrote to the IOC stating that racial discrimination was now prohibited. The IOC felt unable to re-admit the new Zimbabwe/Rhodesia until elections the following February brought to power Robert Mugabe, a leader of the African Peoples' Union. This recognition would be in time for an all-white Zimbabwean women's field hockey team to take part in a boycott-reduced Moscow entry . . . and win the gold medal.

The first bells of alarm concerning Moscow disturbed Killanin's Christmas sojourn in Dublin, when Radio Moscow reported on 28 December 1979 that the Soviet Union had been 'asked' by the government in Kabul to intervene in Afghanistan. How would Jimmy Carter respond? Any action by the UN security council would be vetoed by the USSR. But, wait a minute, the Olympic Games were scheduled for Moscow. There was the chance. Vigorous opposition to the Games would cost nothing. Carter was swift to react, proclaiming the need for the 'free world' to let the Soviets know who held the world's moral conscience.

By mid-January, the House of Representatives had endorsed, by 386–12, their President's demand for boycott, the Senate falling into line by 88–4. This did not legally compel the US Olympic committee to support the proposal, but the promise to do so was swiftly forthcoming. Although prominent Olympians in America such as Edwin Moses might rail against the proposal, an opinion poll revealed that 73 per cent of the population favoured the boycott; including a majority in the media who had been indignant when the Africans walked out four years earlier. Carter sent Muhammad Ali to Africa to convince state leaders of the correctness of his policy, only to find that Ali was persuaded by the Africans that the boycott was ill-advised. They knew from 1976 that boycotts mainly damaged the perpetrators.

Soon Killanin was informed that Lloyd Cutler, counsel to the President, wished to meet him in Dublin. He discovered, upon Cutler's arrival, that the purpose was not to inform but instruct, on behalf of President Carter, that the IOC should either postpone or cancel the Games. Killanin dug in, like the French and Irish rugby packs who were simultaneously playing down the road from his house, telling Cutler that no such interference

was possible on any account; that, irrespective of political activities, the contract with Moscow was legally binding; and reminding him that Olympic Games had continued when the US was at war in Korea and Vietnam.

Arriving at Lake Placid Country Club prior to the Games, Killanin was told by Robert Kane and Don Miller, respective president and executive director of USOC, that they had protested against government interference in their affairs. Frustratingly, USOC's independence of action had been compromised by the Amateur Sports Act (1978), by which they became involuntarily an ad hoc arm of the government. Thereby Kane and Miller were honour bound to support the US government line in discussions with the Executive Board and subsequently at the Session prior to the Games. Cutler was present at Lake Placid, informing Killanin that the Session would be opened not by the head of state but by Cyrus Vance. Killanin reminded Cutler that this would not be the time and

US Foreign Secretary of State Cyrus Vance inexcusably breaches protocol with a political anti-Soviet speech at the Lake Placid Session. (© IOC)

place for political doctrinaire. In vain. The content of Vance's ceremonial speech was not disclosed in advance, as is normal courtesy, but only an hour or so before the event. News agency reports on its essentials reached Killanin first, leaving him much alarmed, for the text was improperly political, in particular quoting from a Soviet document published before the Afghan invasion that claimed the award of the Games to Moscow was a reflection of Soviet political correctness. Nonetheless, Killanin was unduly slow to react prior to the speech. Fat was being ladled onto the American fire as Vance spelled out its President's rooted opposition to the continuation of the Games and his demand for a switch to an alternative site and support for the boycott from all other countries. The Session listened to Vance in silent anger, this unscheduled breach of protocol at a formal function serving only to consolidate determination among IOC members to ignore such dictatorial hectoring.

The Session's debate was vigorous and unanimous and a statement was issued from the 73 members on 12 February under the name of their President. This stated that they were wholly aware of the political situation that precipitated the challenge now confronting them; that the 143 NOCs and the IOC itself were bound by their Charter; that the Games in Moscow must be held as planned; that only NOCs had the right to accept or refuse invitations to the Olympic Games; and that the IOC, unable to resolve political problems, appealed to governments, in particular to those of the superpowers, to meet and resolve their differences. Killanin was of the opinion that the existence of the IOC was now at stake.

To be considered at the same time was the immediate matter of the Lake Placid Games, which had more than enough internal problems of their own. They were, indeed, close to bankruptcy. The organising committee had been in a state of disorganisation almost from the moment of election: short of investment, venues and a Village, as well as being harassed by environmental organisations concerned about preservation of the Adirondack State Park, the effect of a 90-metre ski jump tower, widening of ski trails on Whiteface Mountain, commercialisation in a small town and construction of the Village. To raise funds for the latter, the organising committee obtained backing from the Federal Bureau of Prisons, which would donate $47 million in exchange for subsequent utilisation of the Village for minimum-security detention. The ski jump and hockey rink construction had been delayed by bankruptcy of a steel supplier, the chief fundraiser was charged with nepotism in the awarding of contracts and for the duration of the Games the transportation system proved chronically inadequate. Carter and Vance were, ironically, scared that promotion of the boycott might further damage Lake Placid's event, but the Soviets, with some statesmanship, announced they would not work 'counter to the spirit of the Olympic Movement' by boycotting the Winter Games. The People's Republic of China duly made its reappearance, Cyprus was there for the first time and disgruntled Taiwan again stayed away.

Following the Winter Games, Killanin took the view that the Moscow ball was in the court of the IFs and NOCs, and the national sports associations. It was their responsibility to determine who would not be at Moscow. This attitude of presidential laissez-faire demonstrated Killanin's under-estimation of his own possible influence had he been more actively engaged. He failed fully to understand the power of the US and the swiftness of public reaction. While he correctly gauged there was little he could do to alter the stance of the superpower leaders, a more immediate interventionist policy might have borne fruit from personal meetings with other state leaders who, without his encouragement, might decide their Olympic teams should stay away. Berthold Beitz, head of Krupp industries and IOC member in West Germany, tried to persuade Killanin to go directly to the White House and then Moscow. Carter, eagerly backed by Thatcher, was ignorantly pressing for the creation of an alternative site, wholly unaware – as are, indeed, the majority of the millions who follow the Games, not excluding many journalists – of the countless thousands of hours and personnel and the years of planning that are involved in the staging of any Games. Lord Carrington, likewise ignorant, was despatched to Lausanne to pursue the idea, having already met the BOA and national sports federation leaders in an

attempt to dissuade them from going to Moscow. In the face of this high-level opposition, Sir Denis Follows, chairman of the BOA, resolutely upheld the principle of independence and British participation, never mind that the House of Commons supported Thatcher's ideological blockade of convenience that would not cost a penny in tanks; nor even, let it be said, in lost trade. The hypocrisy of the Moscow boycott was shameful.

Motivated by supposed patriotism, members of USOC voted by more than two to one to support their president, though the figure of 797 against withdrawal was indicative of substantial disapproval, never mind that Vice-President Walter Mondale, addressing USOC, proclaimed: 'History holds its breath, for what is at stake here is no less than the future security of the civilised world.' A tangential risk from the USOC decision was possible reaction from the IOC about the Games scheduled for Los Angeles in four years' time. Killanin, however, reassured Peter Ueberroth, president of the LA organising committee, that the contract remained firm and this resulted in a communication from Carter confirming that the US government would welcome all to the LA Games. Well, they would, wouldn't they? Elsewhere, opinion was oscillating. By one vote, Australia decided to attend, as, narrowly, did Spain, by 20 votes to 13.

Within the result of the latter decision lay a crucial moment for Juan Antonio Samaranch. For the past five years, he had been the first ambassador in Moscow of democratic, post-Franco Spain, and, as one of the candidates to succeed Killanin at the election immediately preceding the Moscow Games, his prospects would have plummeted were Spain to have been absentees. Some of the older members, such as Ashwini Kumar and Lord Exeter – the latter having failed when previously challenging Brundage's re-election – had tried to persuade Killanin to continue, but Killanin had run the distance he had promised and sensed that enough was enough. The other candidates besides Samaranch were James Worrall of Canada, Willi Daume of West Germany and Marc Hodler of Switzerland, the latter also president of international skiing. The genial Worrall had the backing of the Anglo-Saxons. Daume had been at the forefront of policy-making, with his thankless task of attempting to formulate a rational definition of amateurism under the eligibility code. Hodler, popularly regarded as a lawyer of reliability and sensible pragmatism, was a reluctant runner: 'They're pushing me, but I'm not going to campaign for it,' he had said.

Though little known outside the IOC, and though being a protégé of Brundage, Samaranch was unexpectedly identified as the man to provide more of an iron fist than the gentlemanly Killanin. Samaranch said:

> Until Brundage supported my Olympic career I don't think I had any chance of becoming President. I felt I was not on the same level as the IOC, as it then was, either socially or in knowledge of sport. Yet when I arrived, I realised that it was not as special as I had supposed. And we had reached a position in which, had it continued, the IOC could have collapsed. How could it be right, for instance, for competitors to take part in world championships, under the rules of that federation, but then not be eligible for the Olympic Games? When I was elected President, I sensed the IOC *was* prepared to jump into the future.

A decision was reached in the first round of voting at the Session prior to the Games: Samaranch 44, Hodler 21, Worrall 7 and

Daume 5. Daume was damaged by the decision of his own NOC to join the boycott. The subterranean swell of support for Samaranch had been such that Mzali of Tunisia and de Beaumont of France, both against the continuation of these Games, flew into Moscow solely for the vote in loyalty to the 'unknown' Spaniard, before immediately returning home.

As the number of absentees for Moscow mounted, many adjustments of protocol had to be decided. The Antwerp flag, traditionally handed from the mayor of the previous Games to the present incumbent, would now be brought from Montreal by two teenage torchbearers, as Mayor Drapeau was prevented from attending by political pressures. Canada had joined the boycott despite the efforts of Worrall and Richard Pound, current head of the Canadian NOC. NOCs were not required to parade at the opening and closing ceremonies, other than one flag-bearer. It was agreed that NOCs could use their title rather than that of their country and likewise the flag of their NOC, where that existed, or the white flag and rings of the IOC. The same allowances were permitted at the medal ceremonies as for opening and closing with, if wished, the Olympic instead of the national anthem.

In Killanin's view, an effect of the Moscow boycott was to consolidate the support of all NOCs behind the future of the Olympic Movement. A meeting of all branches of the Movement at Lausanne in April served to strengthen the determination of a majority of nations to ignore the American propaganda campaign. Following this gathering, Killanin set about meeting Brezhnev and Carter, though without any optimistic hope of altering Carter's attitude. He saw Brezhnev at the Kremlin on 7 May, accompanied by Berlioux, considering her to be 'the best adviser'. He warned Brezhnev to expect no more than 50 acceptances of the invitation to the Games, the Moscow organising committee having originally hoped for 120. He also requested Brezhnev, who was leaving immediately afterwards to attend the funeral of President Tito of Yugoslavia, to make a statement regarding the quotation being used by American critics from the *Handbook for Party Activists* on the correctness of Soviet foreign policy reflected by the award of the Games. Brezhnev answered that he found nothing wrong with the handbook's statement and Deputy Prime Minister Ignati Novikov, head of the organising committee, stressed that it was an internal document. There would be no public retraction. At this stage, West Germany had yet to withdraw but, although Brezhnev promised to do what he could to improve the atmosphere, there was a marked lack of serious collaboration.

By the time of the Games' opening, the respective acceptance and withdrawal figures would be 81 and 65, substantially better than Killanin's worst forecast. There is no doubt that Novikov and Vitaly Smirnov, one of the Soviet IOC members, were genuinely altruistic in their loyalty to the principles of the Games. Novikov had earlier issued the following statement:

> From the moment when the honour was bestowed upon Moscow to organise the Games, the very fact of staging the Games in the USSR aroused fierce resistance from all those who are against the universal and comprehensive character of the modern Olympic Movement. It is their fault that several political campaigns aimed at undermining the Olympiad were waged during the preparatory years for the Games in Moscow . . . unfortunately the course of events in recent months has arisen from the fact that the US government assumed the right of dictation with regard

to the Olympic Movement and is trying to use sport as a means of political pressure.

A week later Killanin flew to Washington to see Carter. The same day West Germany announced its withdrawal. The manner of the NOC's conference in Düsseldorf was barely constitutional, being conducted in front of live television cameras with the written press also in attendance. Having solidly denounced at the outset the American proposal for a boycott, the German press, under government pressure, had by now conducted a supine volte face. There was no possibility for individual national sports federations to conduct private debate. Even so, the vote divided 59 to 40. This might have been reversed with private discussion.

Facing his second successive boycott, President Killanin meets President Jimmy Carter in a vain effort to thwart an electioneering stunt. (© The White House)

Killanin's conversation with Carter was predictably bland and ineffectual, confirming that any switch of venue or postponement was out of the question and that the Games would proceed, in Killanin's words, 'even if I compete alone against myself'. It was apparent that behind Carter, the man pulling the strings was his adviser Lloyd Cutler, to the extent that Cutler determined who, besides Carter and Killanin, should be present in the Oval Office.

Although Killanin achieved as little in Washington as at the Kremlin, the fences of the IOC were elsewhere being shored up. Steadfast British support had been followed by Italy and France; only Chile in Latin America stayed away and the majority of non-Islamic Africans, conscious of the ineffectiveness of their boycott four years earlier, were now determined to attend. Kenya, Liberia and the Congo were the only south-Sahara nations to join the boycott, as did US-dependent Israel and politically sympathetic Japan.

Regarding the US television coverage by NBC, Cutler had declared – not Carter – that NBC would no longer screen the Games on an exclusive basis, but that all American networks would be permitted to cover the event on a news basis. As a consequence, the American audience saw nothing of the triumphs, which were many and spectacular, that took place in the absence of their competitors.

If he had not tackled the crisis as quickly and vigorously as some of his colleagues might have wished, Killanin remained publicly buoyant and an admirable bearer of the moral flag for which he was responsible. In his memoirs he wrote:

> The boycott, had it succeeded, would have broken the Olympic Movement for good. It did not succeed, but at the same time nobody won and the politicians lost face. Many athletes forfeited their one and only chance of competing in the greatest and most challenging sporting contest in the world. The Games themselves, though brilliantly organised, were fundamentally sad. There were too many absent faces, too many doubts and scruples on the part of those who were there. Certainly I found that Jimmy Carter and his aides were singularly ill-informed on how the Olympic Movement works.

Whatever his disappointments, Killanin left the IOC on a sound financial footing compared with when he took office, thanks to television income. In eight years IOC assets had risen from $2 million to more than $45 million.

Even with a near full attendance, Moscow's administration had there been no boycott would still have been almost on a par with that of Munich eight years earlier, thanks to the efficiency of Gosplan, the state agency which had constructed or reconstructed the facilities in the five cities scheduled for Olympic events: Moscow, the central venue; Tallinn for yachting, on Estonia's Baltic coast; and St Petersburg, Kiev and Minsk for preliminary football matches. All operations had been functional a year beforehand, rehearsed at the 7th Spartakiad, which embraced 10,000 competitors. The Lenin Stadium, built in 1956, had been renovated, including a new Tartan synthetic track, with seating for over 100,000. Swimming, diving, boxing and basketball were staged at the new Palace of Sport; rowing, kayaking and canoeing at the Krylatsko rowing canal built seven years earlier. The Olympic Village for 12,000 competitors and officials was a quarter of an hour from the main stadium, and with absenteeism there was more than usual comfort for all, with food for every palate that would have astonished the majority of Moscow's gastronomically deprived citizens.

With the 73-year-old, near immobile President Leonid Brezhnev conducting the formalities, the opening ceremony was colourful, stunningly precise but a shade militaristic. The final torch runner was triple Olympic triple jump champion

Lost in the crowd. Juan Antonio Samaranch (lower centre), alongside Señora Maria Therese, watches the Moscow opening ceremony beneath an expressionless Lord and Lady Killanin and stone-faced President Leonid Brezhnev. (© IOC)

Viktor Saneyev, who handed the flame to national basketball captain Sergei Belov for ignition of the stadium bowl. Two Soviet cosmonauts appeared on the results television screen to bring greetings from space. Sixteen of the eighty-one teams that marched into the stadium made some form of visual protest, yet the majority of Muscovites smilingly welcomed the Games' visitors, not excluding the babushkas who doubled as surveillance clerks on every floor of every hotel. The only moment of disorganisation that the author encountered was traffic snarl-up on the afternoon of the men's marathon – normal for such occasions. Soviets could afford to smile, I suppose: against reduced opposition they won 80 gold medals, 69 silver and 46 bronze, GDR taking second place with 47–37–42. And Soviet forces remained in Afghanistan. So much for Carter's boycott.

CHAPTER LI

Lake Placid (XIII) 1980

Ingemar Stenmark of Sweden, Olympic double Alpine champion

'An Olympic gold medal is the finest reward you can win as an athlete. I grew up watching the Olympics on television. The most fantastic spectacle I ever saw was Bob Beamon's jump in Mexico. For me to win in Lake Placid was most of all, though, an enormous relief. I had won so many races in the World Cup before the Games and felt so much pressure to do well.

The fact that the giant slalom took place over two days did not make things easier. I was third after the first day, yet I think that was an advantage for me. If I had been in the lead, with that long wait between the races, maybe the pressure would have been too much.

My first run had been bad. I skied too wide and did not attack the way I should have done. I knew I had to take risks on the second run and give everything, to ski really fast. I tried to forget about the first race the day before, disappointing with so many mistakes. But the second course suited me perfectly. I had looked at the upper section and thought to myself that this was where I could gain time. Fifteen minutes before the race I was so nervous that my legs felt wobbly. Then, when I started, I felt nothing of that. It wasn't, however, an ideal run and when I crossed the line I was both frustrated and angry. I didn't think it was fast enough, especially for the upper section, so it was nice to find out that I had won. It had been almost taken for granted that I should but it's always fun when you do it. If I had ended up number two behind Andreas Wenzel of Liechtenstein, it would still have been a good result, but I would have been really, really disappointed.

I knew I had more in store for the second run of the slalom. It had been a disadvantage, because of the snowfall, to start the first run number 13, Phil Mahre of America being the fastest as the first starter. I was especially pleased with the fact that I would start the second run as number two. I was still nervous, even though I didn't need to be, having already won my first gold medal. I should have had a psychological advantage over the others, this time the pressure was on them. In a way, the second gold was more fun. Everyone expected me to win the giant slalom, but this race was more open. To have won two Olympic golds actually felt better than I had expected.

A final reflection: I think Americans and Europeans look upon the Olympics a little differently. In the United States, you are an Olympic champion for ever. In Europe, they view you more as "a former skiing star" . . . If I could start again, I wouldn't have become a slalom skier. I would have gone for a team sport. Then you don't have to be the best all the time to enjoy it and the team can be good even if you have a bad day. You can share everything with others, success as well as failure. I think it's nicer to compete in a team sport.'

(Photograph © IOC)

Conditioned by the surrounding elements of his childhood – the lonely, bitter mountains 700 kilometres north of Stockholm – it was no surprise that Ingemar Stenmark should grow up shy and withdrawn, his few contemporaries being children living close to his grandparents' farm at the tiny village of Tärnaby. 'I skied because I could do it alone,' he said, but in reality there was little other choice in a land where the sun shone for less than an hour on winter days.

Taught by his father until he was 13, his coaching was then passed to Hermann Nogler of Italy, who detected that the boy's single-minded application would one day make him a champion. By 17 he was challenging on the World Cup circuit, nearly upstaging the established Gustavo Thöni in the final race of the season, the latter already having claimed three World Cup titles. By the time Stenmark won the World Cup in 1976 he was supreme, apart from the Olympic title, and in 1979 he established a single-season record of 13 victories, one more than

Killy in 1967. By the time of Lake Placid in 1980, he was standing on a sequence of 14 consecutive giant slalom wins. His consistency was a phenomenon: 86 victories in 270 World Cup events until he retired in 1989 at the age of 33. By comparison, the equally multi-talented Pirmin Zurbriggen of Switzerland won a mere 40 races.

In 1979, Stenmark experienced a bad fall during downhill practice in Italy, suffering serious concussion, but his recovery was complete and in time to prepare for Lake Placid. Because of the nerves to which he has referred, he was too cautious on the first run of the giant slalom and was left lying third behind Wenzel and Bojan Krizaj of Yugoslavia. In style and pace he proved to be unchallengeable on the second run, more than a second faster than the rest for a winning margin ahead of Wenzel of 0.75 seconds, with Hans Enn of Austria taking the bronze.

Phil Mahre of America had also had a bad fall the previous

Ingemar Stenmark, of Sweden, peerless slalom specialist, withdrew from downhill racing following an accident. (© IOC/ASL)

year and had needed a metal plate to repair his left ankle, but he used his early start in the first run of the slalom to good effect and was the leader by more than half a second. That was not sufficient command against a man of Stenmark's quality, however, and for the second time he swept triumphantly through the second run. Mahre's second run was more than half a second off the time he needed for victory, so that Stenmark became one of only four men to win both slalom events at a single Games.

Following his accident, Stenmark had decided against entering the downhill. Here, the Austrian team was so strong, with seven ranked in the world's top twenty, that Franz Klammer, champion four years earlier, did not make the team. Leonhard Stock, who had fractured a collarbone two months previously, was only selected as a reserve, but was promoted into the team after dominating the pre-Games practice runs. Stock had never won a World Cup race, yet within a day of his

Eric Heiden (USA), built like Mr Universe, uniquely won five speed skating titles. (© Getty Images/Duffy)

promotion he out-paced his colleague Peter Wirnsberger by 0.38 to become an Olympic champion. He would not win another downhill for nine years.

For Annemarie Pröll, Lake Placid was to be the climax of a long and notable career. Eight years earlier she had taken two silver medals at Sapporo behind Marie-Thérèse Nadig of Switzerland, though she had regarded that as a failure. By 1979, she had won six out of nine World Cups, twice finishing second, and at Lake Placid none could match her time of 1:37.52, Nadig taking third place behind Wenzel's sister, Hanni. The latter distinguished herself by going on to win both slalom and giant slalom.

Eric Heiden of America set a milestone by winning all five speed skating titles from 500m to 10,000m, with an Olympic record in each, including a world record at 10,000m. Just imagine the 400m track champion also being the winner of the 25-lap event! Skating is so much less physically specialised. Heiden, however, was a sculptor's dream, a definition of male muscularity without any gross excess. He had the look of a Mr Universe and his Scandinavian rivals despaired of beating him.

Irina Rodnina and husband Alex Zaitsev successfully defend their pairs title following the birth of their first child. (© IOC)

'We have no idea how to train to compete with him,' they said, 'we just wait for him to retire.' When he was measured for his uniform for the opening ceremony, in which he was to carry the Stars and Stripes, the only trousers large enough for his 29-inch thighs were those with a 38-inch waist, six inches larger than his own.

The only distance for which he was not now outright favourite was the shortest, 500m, at which he had lost a week earlier in the World Championships. On the day in Lake Placid, paired with world record holder Yevgeni Kulikov of the Soviet Union, Heiden was the steadier coming off the final bend to win by a relatively comfortable 0.34 with his Olympic record 38.03 over a second outside Kulikov's world best. Thereafter, Heiden carried all before him – even in the final of the 10,000m, when he had overslept after watching the previous night's memorable ice hockey confontration with the Soviet Union in which two of his friends were involved. His record of 14:28.13 was almost eight seconds faster than Piet Kleine of Holland in second place. Despite a rushed breakfast, he became the first speed skater to win five gold medals in a single Games.

Heiden belonged to that rare breed: someone embarrassed by

the public acclaim. He soon retired from what he referred to as 'the great whoopee'. Rejecting financial offers in film and TV, he briefly became a professional cyclist before concentrating on a medical career and comparative anonymity.

Undisputed star of figure skating was Irina Rodnina, who, with husband Alex Zaitsev, successfully defended the pairs title, again gaining first-place marks from all nine judges. Two years earlier she had won her tenth consecutive world title, then taken a year off to have a baby. With victory in Lake Placid she had matched the achievement of Sonja Henie: ten world titles and three Olympic gold medals.

Robin Cousins, defending for Britain the title won by John Curry, earned six first-place marks for a victory that some considered should have gone to Jan Hoffmann (GDR). This was Britain's only gold medal in the Games and extended the record of his coach Carlo Fassi, for whom this was a fourth individual winner in three successive Games.

For all the wrong reasons, the most heralded event in upstate New York was the ice hockey final round-robin clash between 'a bunch of college boys', as they were patriotically christened, and the allegedly demonic Soviets. Banners outside the stadium proclaiming 'Boycott Moscow' and 'Get out of Afghanistan' found no echo inside once the match was in motion. Here was a moment at which that strange amalgam of latent American insecurity and brash confidence had reached epidemic proportions. The idea that it could be rationalised on the ice hockey rink was in itself absurd, yet such was the mood promoted in advance – partially in their own self-interest – by media commentators. The final pool consisted of Sweden, Finland, USA and USSR. Part of the fascination was that the bulk of the US team was from the University of Minnesota, as was the coach Herbert Brooks, a stern disciplinarian. They had played 63 preparatory games but three days before the opening of the Olympics had been crushed by the Soviets 10–3. Here was David facing Goliath, the world's best team, professional or amateur. In

National euphoria as the US ice hockey team defeat the Soviets. (© Getty Images)

one of those extraordinary turnarounds that occasionally happen, the US survived endless attacks by the Soviets, their goalkeeper, Jim Craig, making incessant saves. From 2–3 behind with 20 minutes to play, the US scored twice to record an emotional victory that penetrated almost every home in the land. Far from there being bad blood in such an epic match, the Soviet team smilingly congratulated the victors as the cheers raised the roof. It was the stuff of fiction. In their last match against Finland, the US ensured for themselves the gold medal after coming from 2–1 behind to win 4–2. For years afterwards Craig would continue to receive hundreds of congratulatory letters a year.

Raisa Smetanina of the Soviet Union – ten Nordic medals in five Games. (© IOC)

CHAPTER LII

Moscow (XXII) 1980

Sebastian Coe of Great Britain, twice Olympic 1,500m champion

'I was making my first tentative steps as a senior in 1976 while Ovett was being heralded as a favourite for the Games in Montreal. In 1977, he had destroyed a world-class field in the World Cup, including John Walker, the Olympic champion. I wasn't beginning to develop and become rounded as a senior until 1979. I couldn't go to Moscow and just say to myself, well, 1976 and then 1978 – when Steve had beaten me in the European Championships in Prague – simply didn't matter. I was bound to be in awe of his staggering talent. In Moscow, I was almost 24, but I'd been doubting whether I could beat him since I was 18, such was his stature. The 800m defeat in Moscow was, in part, due to this feeling I had about him: this doubt about whether I really could beat him, never mind my world record. It wasn't until 1981 that I acquired a comfortable feeling about confronting him in any race at any distance . . . Losing the 800m in Moscow the way I did was a reflection on my inner self. To come back then in the 1,500m against a guy who had won 42 straight races, as Steve had, demanded going deeper into the well than at any stage in my career.

Sport at the top is mentally complex. When you need an iron will, when the fires are fiercest, the catalyst can often be your own doubts. There is a side of me that has always doubted what I can do and that comes from Angela, my mother, though in some ways she gave me even more than Peter, my father and coach. Yet I had felt vulnerable so often, both she and I at times less sure of my ability than Peter. However, the best performances in life, whatever you do, can stem from a conflict inside you, from a combination of a sense of imminent failure and the need to prove, to yourself and other people, that you're not really afraid at all . . .

Between '80 and '84 there was more than just a change in circumstances. I was a very different person at 27 from what I'd been at 23. For '80, the motivation was purely athletic, to demonstrate as world record holder that I was best at 800m but wondering at the same time whether I could handle the third lap in the 1,500m. I was looking for proof of my ability mentally and physically, and in one I failed, was found wanting on the biggest platform. I'd been asking myself whether I was the complete athlete and I probably wasn't. By Los Angeles I was more rounded, I was together. I didn't have to prove myself athletically; the question was whether I could think myself through a championship. I brought more intellectual rigor to LA.

If the greatest mental stress came in Moscow, the greatest physical strain was in Los Angeles, with seven races in nine days, coming off the back of missing much of the two years beforehand with illness. Climbing back in '84, I had to run the best four rounds I'd done in any championships for the 800m and a day later deal with rivals coming fresh into the 1,500m.

If victory in Moscow in the 1,500m brought sheer relief, in LA it brought momentary rage – having proved the press wrong – and probably gave as much satisfaction. When you are led out from the bowels of the stadium for an Olympic final, you learn a lot about yourself in that half-hour beforehand. Few experiences can compare with that, such intensity, exposed to an audience of millions. That's the competitive element. Yet present also is the camaraderie, the ethos of the Olympics, of being there, and that too is something unique. Together, these experiences put the rest of life into perspective.'*

(Photograph © Getty Images/Powell)

The prelude to one of the most intense rivalries in Olympic history had been building for more than a year. When beaten by Steve Ovett in the European Championships 800m two years earlier, Coe had been running experimentally, testing himself and the field with a supposedly suicidal first lap of around 49.0. He had gained only bronze, but it was a deliberate part of the learning curve upon which he and Peter Coe had worked painstakingly for eight years: having calculated, preposterously some would have said, when Seb was only 15, that he would be ready to break the world record at the time of the Games in Moscow. The problem for father and son was that the potential

arrived a year early, in 1979; creating as Peter would recall 'the most difficult tightrope in training, the frequency with which the stimuli were applied'.

Coe had soared to three world records in 41 days during the summer of '79: a full second off Juantorena's time for the 800m with 1:42.33; a mile in 3:48.95 to emulate Snell's achievement in holding both simultaneously; and the 1,500m in 3:32.03 to shave Bayi's record of 1974. Coe's sudden global fame obliged Ovett, in the weeks prior to Moscow, to enter the same record-breaking mode, which he had previously scorned while concentrating on mere victory, for the benefit of his own morale prior to the Olympic showdown. As Brendan Foster, former Olympic 5,000m record holder reflected: 'You cannot find yourself on the starting line alongside a guy who you know has run seconds faster than you have – not when you're expecting to win.' Ovett's response that year had been to steal the mile record with 3:48.8 within an hour at Oslo of Coe establishing a 1,000m world record of 2:13.4, and to equal Coe's 1,500m time nine days before the 800m heats were scheduled in Moscow. Such was the attention on Coe that the British Amateur Athletic Board decided to stage a press conference upon his arrival to ease demand for interviews. Four hundred journalists were present: the countdown to an inexplicable failure was under way.

Coe had contributed to his own demise by his conviction that the 800m was a race he should not, could not, lose. Looking at the seven other finalists, his estimation was indeed correct, for none was within a second and a half of his best time, and the main concern was not about Ovett but whether two East Germans, Andreas Busse and Detlef Wagenknecht, might run a team race to impede or box him in. New Zealand were among the boycotting nations and former record holder John Walker said: 'If we were all there, with the Americans and West Germans, I think the 1,500m would have been one of the greatest races in history. Though I have enormous respect for Ovett's qualities, I still fancy Coe for both the distances.'

Long before the final, Coe had decided against a run from the front, as in the European Championships. What he produced instead was a disastrous run from the back. 'I've never known pressure like it,' he said. 'I thought people had exaggerated, but they hadn't. There was no comparison . . . I had the worst night's sleep I've ever had, just lying there listening to my own heartbeat.' As the runners set off, Coe looked as if he were running in soft sand, seemingly unaware of what was happening in front of him. Entering the second bend, Ovett characteristically vigorously handed off Wagenknecht, who lost his balance and nearly brought down José Marajo, the Frenchman who was the only runner in the field besides Coe to have bettered 1:44. Coe was still loping along at the back like some stowaway. Around the third bend, David Warren, the third Briton in the race, accelerated to the front – exactly as predicted by Andy Norman, Ovett's prescient manager/guru, who had told his man: 'Warren will probably put in a burst out of bravado and Kirov will go from 280 out, as he always does. Take Kirov, then go, don't slow and wait for someone else's kick. Kirov will come back at you wide and make it difficult for Coe, if he's not then ahead.' Thus it was.

By the time Coe finally woke up, it was too late, for by now he was six strides adrift of Ovett. Never mind Coe's furious final sprint, the gold medal was Ovett's, in a relatively sluggish 1:45.40: the same time that had given him fifth place in Montreal.

Now that the sky had fallen in on Coe, the pressure would be more intense than ever. Were Ovett to do the double, which now seemed inevitable to all but a few of Coe's closest allies, Coe would be condemned for ever as a mere record-breaker, who lacked the moral fibre for the big championship. What he had to find within the space of a few days was not so much form as that fibre.

Several factors, beside the innate ability of his rival, conspired against Ovett in the 1,500m. First, he unnecessarily wished to maintain his unbeaten record, thereby subjecting himself to defeating Jürgen Straub of East Germany in the semi-final, which probably detracted marginally from his reserves for the final, his seventh race in nine days. Second, he admitted subsequently that victory in the 800m, which he had hardly dared to expect, had fractionally reduced his motivation.

The man who was to make the running was Straub. Norman, accurate again, warned Ovett that Straub would go for it from 700 metres out, attempting to burn off the opposition, and that whoever led with 300 remaining would win. This happened, but not in favour of Ovett. Straub and his coach Bernd Diessner, had carefully planned the tactics that they believed gave him a chance of a medal against two undoubtedly faster men: as slow a pace as possible for the first 700 metres, followed by a burn-out all the way from there to the tape. It was to prove a brave and rewarding attempt.

Straub and Coe went straight to the front. It was a pedestrian pace. Straub ran with his head down, locked into his own private world, moving sedately to the 800m mark. It was now that he made the move that would convert the race from a stroll into a scorch: the start of the longest Olympic finishing sprint ever, with the intention of dropping Coe and Ovett. From the amble of the first two laps, 61.6 then 63.3, Straub lifted the third to a searing 54.2. At the bell the order was, strung out in line:

Following a dismal performance over 800m, Sebastian Coe (GBR) rescued his reputation when winning the 1,500m, ahead of Jürgen Straub (GDR, 338), surprise silver medal winner, and Steve Ovett (GBR), left, the 800m champion. (© popperfoto.com)

Straub, Coe, Ovett, Busse (GDR), Fontanella (ITA), Marajo (FRA), with British youngster Steve Cram hanging on in seventh place. Into the final back straight after three laps, Straub released a final assault. Coe had to respond. Into the last bend, he put in his first kick that carried him clear: the split times would show that Coe, even within such a ferocious last 700 metres, was accelerating the whole way from 150 metres to 50 metres out. Coe had won with a last 800 of 1:48.5, the speed with which he had won his first heat in the shorter event. It was the fastest last two laps ever run at that time in a four-lap race. Straub had hung on for silver, with Ovett consigned to the bronze.

Filbert Bayi's decision to opt for the steeplechase was of noble origin. He doubted, with good reason, whether he had the pace to challenge Ovett and Coe in the 1,500m, where his own true strength lay. Desperate to ensure the first Olympic medal for Tanzania, he decided upon the steeplechase, though wholly without experience. To intimidate the field, he led from the start and with 800 metres remaining was 40 metres or more clear of the pursuing Bronislaw Malinowski of Poland, who was biding his time. Malinowski, who at one time said he wished to run for Britain, having a Scottish mother, had finished fourth and

233

second respectively in the two previous Games, and now inexorably began to close on a fading Bayi. With 200 metres remaining, Malinowski moved in front for a comfortable victory, Bayi hanging on to finish second a stride ahead of Eshetu Tura of Ethiopia. Malinowski died a year later in a car crash, aged 30.

Lasse Virén was present again for the long distances, but beyond his best. So too, it might have been supposed, was Miruts Yifter of Ethiopia, said to be 35, who had won the bronze behind Virén in Munich eight years previously. Not a bit of it. In the absence of those baulked by the boycott, the race developed into a contest between three Ethiopians and two Finns. Yifter, Mohammed Kedir and Tolossa Kotu ran as a pack, constantly changing the lead and the pace until only Virén and Kaarlo Maaninka were left in contention after 20 laps. Virén vainly put in a challenge that might have sapped the renowned finishing burst of Yifter, winner of both 5,000m and 10,000m at the previous year's World Cup in Dortmund. Maaninka split Yifter and Kedir by taking the silver medal, with Virén a distant fifth.

Yifter's sprightly sprint for the line suggested that he had much left for the 5,000m, and indeed he had. He had been denied likely medals in 1976 by the African boycott, while his failure to appear for the 5,000m, following his 10,000m bronze in Munich, still remained clouded in contradictory explanations. In Moscow, there was no doubting his presence and, in spite of the addition of a semi-final, he was comfortably poised to strike whenever he chose. After 4km, the 12 finalists had not been separated, and at the bell it was Kedir who led, runners and audience alike awaiting the Yifter kick. At last Yifter struck down the final back straight, catching Eamonn Coghlan, the talented Irishman, off guard. Kedir tripped within the pack and finished last, with Coghlan beaten on the run in by Maaninka for the bronze, Suleiman Nyambui of Tanzania claiming the silver. Yifter had been in no mood to yield his most prized ambition, nor afterwards would he yield his age. 'I don't count the years,' he said and his mother wasn't around to tell us.

One of many events in which the reigning world champion or record holder was an involuntary absentee was the decathlon. Guido Kratschmer of West Germany, beaten by Daley Thompson of Britain two months before the Games – Thompson setting a world record in the process – had regained the record a few weeks later. An epic contest between the two in Moscow was scuppered, though Thompson's performance was

such, a mere 156 points below Kratschmer's new record with a total of 8,522, it would have been hard to match. At 22, Thompson was still short of his prime, as he was subsequently to demonstrate. The son of a Nigerian father and Scottish mother, he was an ebullient personality, bounding in such confidence that he was an intimidating rival at close quarters, where opponents would seldom detect in him any signs of anxiety between throws or jumps. He could appear impervious to challenge.

Predictably, the field events were dominated by the Soviet Union and East Germany, the most surprising winner being Gerd Wessig (GDR) in the high jump, in the absence of joint world record holder Dietmar Mögenburg of West Germany. Wessig had only been selected two weeks prior to the Games, yet at the Lenin Stadium he proceeded to defeat Jacek Wszola of Poland, the defending champion and joint world record holder (2.35m / 7 ft 8½ in.), with a new record of 2.36m – the first man to do so during Olympic competition.

Sara Simeoni of Italy, taking the women's title with an Olympic record of 1.97m (6 ft 5½ in.), gained one of only two women's titles that evaded the Soviet/GDR hegemony, the other being María Colón of Cuba in the javelin. The dominance of Soviet/GDR women was otherwise so consistent as to be tedious: thereby helping to enforce the conviction of Juan Antonio Samaranch, the newly elected President, that 'open' Games, admitting the denigrated professionals of the West, was the only route towards a more geographically, and politically, balanced festival.

Among many innocent sufferers from the boycott, none was more unfortunate than Youssef Nagui Assad of Egypt. In 1968, aged 23, he had missed qualification for Mexico City in the shot put by two centimetres. He qualified for the next three Games, but in Munich his team was withdrawn following the massacre and joined the boycott of both Montreal and Moscow.

The credentials of one of the finest champions, Teofilo Stevenson, remain difficult to gauge. The Cuban heavyweight is the only boxer to have won three consecutive gold medals, 1972–80, in the same weight division, yet as he declined to enter the heat of the professional kitchen, it can never be said for sure whether he might have attained the same prestige as other former Olympic winners such as Ali and Foreman. A continual stream of professional entreaties failed to penetrate Stevenson's ideological guard. 'I will not trade the loyalty of the Cuban

Nobody knew how old was Miruts Yifter of Ethiopia, but everyone discovered how he could run – commanding double long-distance champion. (© popperfoto.com)

How good was Teofilo Stevenson, Cuban three-times champion, here defeating Pyotr Zayev (URS)? He declined to test himself, despite offers, in the professional ring. (© IOC)

people for all the dollars in the world,' Stevenson repeatedly intoned.

Prior to Moscow, Stevenson had been injured, and in a tournament deprived of serious rivals he was never as convincing as he had been in Montreal. Two of his four lethargic bouts went the distance, giving evidence that he was in decline, though as an amateur he still remained strong enough to win the world title six years later at the age of 34. István Levai of Hungary became the first fighter to take him the distance in Olympic competition in the Moscow semi-final.

Women's gymnastics were clouded by the prejudiced attitude of a Soviet judge; though coincidentally there had been the tragic injury shortly before the start to Yelena Mukhina the world champion, who had fractured her spine during practice and was paralysed. In her absence, the way was more open for Nadia Comaneci, the magical Romanian, to defend her title successfully, though as a pubescent 18 year old she was no longer the supreme force she had been. The new eyecatcher was a tiny 15 year old from East Berlin, Maxi Gnauck, who was performing acrobatic miracles which would put a squirrel to shame.

Irrationally overlooked amid attention focused on girl gymnasts, the multi-medalled Alexander Dityatin (URS) was near flawless men's overall champion.

When it came to the final apparatus for the all-round individual title, there was all to play for between Gnauck,

Comaneci and Yelena Davydova (URS). Comaneci required 9.9 to share the gold with Davydova and such a score was eminently possible for a girl accustomed to receiving 10, as she had done in the team event. The aura of tension in the Lenin Sports Palace was such that you could have heard a mouse sneeze. Comaneci's sequence was near flawless, but for nearly half an hour the crowd remained in suspense as the judges argued. Maria Simionescu, the chief judge, from Romania, was refusing to ratify an amalgamated mark of 9.85, pushed downwards on account of 9.8 awarded by the Soviet and Polish judges. Finally the gymnastics federation technical committee decided that the lower mark must stand, Davydova thus being champion, with Comaneci and Gnauck sharing the silver medal.

The previous day's all-round team event had finished Soviet Union–Romania–East Germany, though what the crowd would remember was the beauty of Gnauck's floor exercise and her maximum 10 on the asymmetric bars, which made the rest of us shuffling out of the hall feel like a sack of potatoes.

In 1976, the United States men's swimming team had taken all but one gold medal. Now their team was absent, busy instead participating in their national championships thanks to President Carter, but would probably otherwise have taken half the available 66 medals on the evidence of their domestic performances. The Soviet/GDR axis inevitably held sway, most notably the East German women. Supreme above all was Rica Reinisch, aged 15, three times breaking the world record in the 100m backstroke, and once in the 200m backstroke in an overall haul of four gold medals.

One event where the Americans would not have succeeded was the men's 100m backstroke, in which Bengt Baron of Sweden outpaced the might of East Europe with a time of 56.53, ahead of another Soviet steroid 'positive' Viktor Kuznetsov. Others to punctuate the East European grip upon available glory were Duncan Goodhew of Britain and Michelle Ford of Australia. Goodhew won the 100m breaststroke in 1:03.34 – a time twice bettered in the US championships a week later. Ford's Olympic record 800m freestyle victory in 8:28.90, ahead of two East Germans, was well outside the world record of Kim Linehan in the US nationals two days later.

India won the men's hockey again for the first time in 16 years, while in the inaugural women's event, with five of the six nations due to take part withdrawing because of the boycott, Zimbabwe, a late admission after having been banned in 1972, won the tournament with an ironically all-white team – the only team to avoid defeat.

CHAPTER LIII

Revolutionary

Juan Antonio Samaranch of Spain, IOC President, 1980–2001

'Barely one year ago, [1998] the International Olympic Committee was confronted with one of the most serious crises in its existence. You know all the details. This crisis revealed that our institution was faced with serious problems regarding its composition, organisation and role, as well as some of its procedures, in particular the selection of host cities for the Olympic Games. The errors committed by some members of the IOC and other people alerted world public opinion to this crisis. We were severely criticised and our credibility, even in some cases our integrity, was questioned.

The crisis we are resolving stems from the fact that, since the success of the Olympic Games in Los Angeles in 1984, the organising of the Games has become a source of substantial benefits for host cities not only in public relations but also on an economic level. The amounts we pay to them have been growing increasingly higher, reaching hundreds of millions of dollars.

The IOC is privately funded. It is a fact that bidding for the Olympic Games has become, in many countries, a paramount objective for entire communities – not only the sports community but also the business and civic communities, including the public authorities. In such an environment, the candidate cities have become increasingly aggressive in their quest to host the Games. Each time, the financial stakes are higher. A consequence of these developments is that individuals tend to become more vulnerable. This is no excuse, but a fact. In our society, whenever and wherever money plays a conspicuous role, there is a serious potential risk of human vulnerability.

Our institution was conceived 105 years ago, at a time when such problems and risks did not exist. For many years, the IOC operated without serious flaw. However, we were wrong not to see that our organisation had to adjust itself to a new world, a new environment, a new society, in which money penetrated all aspects of human activities, including sport.

Never has the IOC undertaken so many projects and carried out so much work as during this last year. This would have been impossible without the support, understanding and active participation of the IOC members, the international federations and the national Olympic committees. The crisis has affected each of us not only as leaders but also in our professional and private lives.

We have all been facing harsh criticism, much of which has been unfair. Yet unity has generated the necessary strength to move forward, so that, with the dawn of the new millennium, the credibility and prestige of our Movement can be restored. Any crisis has a positive side. Without the present crisis, the IOC would never have undertaken the fundamental reform programme which has been approved during this historic Session. Thanks to these reforms, the IOC will enter the new millennium stronger, more modern, more democratic, more transparent, more accountable and more responsible.' (Address to the Session, 1999, following constitutional reforms introduced in the wake of the Salt Lake City bidding scandal)
(Photograph © IOC/Strahm)

The presidency of Juan Antonio Samaranch was to encompass a period of development that many of his contemporaries regarded as revolutionary. In the first decade of his administration, Samaranch transformed an elderly, reactionary private club into a progressive, radical sports body: lifting it finally from its long-standing, troubled state of ambivalent amateurism into a professional structure, administratively and competitively, that was simultaneously envied and derided, welcomed and condemned. Here was a President who dealt in the realities of contemporary society. In doing so, he not only made the IOC and the encircling Olympic environment enormously wealthy but, through absence of internal surveillance, also witnessed the organisation plunge into near catastrophe in 1998–9.

With a ringmaster's nerve, and with critics worldwide, even

governments, calling for his resignation, Samaranch steered the IOC back to health prior to his ultimate, twice-deferred retirement, departing in 2001 not long after the staging by Sydney, guided by the IOC's template, of one of the most outstanding of all Games.

During 30 years, Samaranch had stealthily ascended the steps of the Olympic pyramid: beginning as president of roller-hockey in Spain; marshalling the second Mediterranean Games in 1955; becoming an initially inconspicuous figure within the Spanish NOC; favoured by Brundage for election into the IOC in 1966 after heading the Spanish delegation for the Olympic Games of 1960 and 1964. Within two years of his election, he was running, though narrowly defeated, for the Executive Board; was appointed by Brundage as head of protocol; and became

Vice-President, 1974–8, by which time he had also become Spanish Ambassador to Moscow, diplomatic relations with Russia/USSR having been re-opened for the first time since 1917.

Against the expectation of many, after assuming the presidency the quiet Spaniard rapidly emerged as a man of foresight, will-power, subtle negotiating technique and a vision of IOC influence that was inaccurately judged by many to be driven exclusively by personal ambition. Having been assigned, under the dictatorship of General Franco, to assist discreetly in the schooling of Prince Juan Carlos – decreed by Franco to be his successor – Samaranch had worked, like everyone in Spanish public life, within the influence of Franco's regime: a source of regular, often intense foreign criticism when Samaranch came to sporting power. Samaranch responded:

> Spain had evolved under Franco, who in my opinion did three sensible things: to stay out of the Second World War, resisting Hitler, which was not easy; to place the economy in the 1960s under the control of the educated middle class, so that the social evolution in Spain was not the problem it had been in eastern Europe and Latin America, democratic employment laws ensuring we no longer had the rich-and-poor situation that existed prior to the Civil War; and to choose Juan Carlos as his successor. The King represented the unity of Spain, even for the left wing.

His first important decision was the seminal one to base himself in Lausanne. He was offered an office by the Sports University of Madrid, but sensed that to have the control he needed to initiate the revolution, he had to be on hand day by day; not least because of Monique Berlioux, the existing Director-General, who was behaving as though she were the President; and the head of an international federation, Thomas Keller in rowing, who was attempting to prove the IOC was insignificant alongside the continuous activity of the major IFs. Privately, Samaranch had told colleagues he was ready to dispose of Berlioux, but was talked out of it by Alexandru Siperco, IOC member in Romania, who advised him it might be destabilising when facing a difficult Games in LA. 'Living in Lausanne was the best decision I ever took,' Samaranch said. Distant critics might run fantasy stories of the President flying to work daily by helicopter from Geneva; the reality was a relatively frugal hotel existence costing the IOC less than the rental of a small apartment with essential domestic services.

Devoting an hour or more a day to improving his French and English with a tutor, an unpaid President set himself from the outset a string of objectives far broader than any cosmetic surgery. The three fundamentals were unity of the three arms of the Movement, IOC/NOCs/IFs; a secure financial basis; and global universality of Games participants. Intertwined were these subsidiary changes:

- The establishment of continental Olympic associations
- The completion of Killanin's unfulfilled solution to joint IOC membership of China and Taiwan (Killanin's priority had been inclusion of the People's Republic of China – 'the greatest good for the greatest number')
- Relaxation of the eligibility code to admit professionals, in order to counter-balance the superiority of totalitarian state-sponsored amateurs
- Development of commercialisation and marketing to place the IOC, and the Olympic Movement, on a more secure base

- Tighter negotiation, and exploitation, of the potential of television rights fees in order to resist government interference
- The formation, at the Congress in Baden-Baden in 1981, of a Commission for the Olympic Movement, replacing and bringing directly under the Olympic umbrella the former Tripartite Commission
- First-hand acquaintance with 172 NOCs by journeying to visit as many of them as possible
- Broadening of IOC membership, so as to include more athletes, more presidents of IFs and NOCs and, belatedly, women members
- Acceptance by Swiss authorities of IOC opportunity at Vidy having international, independent, untaxed status
- Creation, through donations, of an Olympic Museum in Lausanne on the shore of Lake Geneva
- Resolution of the IOC's 20-year-old cancer involving South Africa
- Transformation of administration in Lausanne, including revision of the authority of the Director

Righting a wrong. The seventh IOC President restores, after an interval of 67 years, the gold medal of Jim Thorpe from 1912, in a presentation to Thorpe's daughter. (© IOC/Pi)

'During Killanin's time, the IOC was sailing gently along, marking time,' Lord Luke, former director of Lloyds Bank International and of Bovril, IOC member in Britain, recalled:

> The Olympic Movement was moving a bit, but not developing. Killanin had a lot of unreasonable problems to distract him. De Beaumont and I had initiated the Finance Commission, realising this was necessary with the arrival of television money. Samaranch proliferated commissions, a big improvement compared with Brundage, who thought he was God, and Killanin, who wasn't awfully good. I liked Samaranch because he was so accessible. I know people will go on about the IOC still being privileged, but I think you want some people who are not necessarily locked in sport, people who live with dignity and have no political ambition.

Keba M'Baye of Senegal, former judge of the international court at The Hague and sometime Vice-President, was equally impressed by Samaranch's policy:

He made members feel responsible and involved in development of the organisation and showed the world that the IOC was socially and politically important as a contributor to peace. I was on the point of resignation in 1980, but after his election Samaranch took me to one side, saying he was relying on me to help change the policy, that there was an important job to do, and I withdrew my resignation. He was an open-minded leader and would change his mind when he felt the majority had another opinion.

A reflection of Samaranch's determination to involve the members – having half an eye on their votes – was the immediate initiation of his bi-lingual *Information Letter*, constituting a progress report sent intermittently to all IOC members, and later introducing a similar letter to NOCs and IFs on subjects concerning them directly.

Arriving for the Congress at Baden-Baden in 1981, in the aftermath of the Moscow boycott, which had left many in a state of sustained anxiety, Samaranch warned the assembled representatives that the dangers were not past. 'The Olympic Movement, during the last few years, has survived storms that would have capsized any other ship,' he said. 'The hostile forces that have tried without success to de-mast it are still there. All athletes, coaches, journalists, officials must remain united if we are to thwart them.' At Baden-Baden, the delegates were rapidly to get a picture of Samaranch as a man on a mission. Many inaugural policies were to emerge in the space of the next few days, which included the annual Session.

While Samaranch recognised that on the issue of Berlioux he would have to bide his time, that of Keller needed swiftly to be resolved. Keller had infuriated Killanin, just prior to the Moscow Games, by sending unilaterally to all members of the Tripartite Commission a letter suggesting that the themes for the next year's Congress should be rearranged on the following basis: Day 1 – IOC debate on years 1973–81; Day 2 – NOC debate on boycott; Day 3 – IFs debate on future of the Olympic Games (!).

Killanin considered this document outrageous, he being chairman of the Tripartite Commission, and duly rebuked Keller. Samaranch knew the time had come to act.

> My first trip from Lausanne as President was to the annual assembly of the General Association of International Sports Federations [GAISF], invited by Keller. He was emphatic that the IOC should deal only with the Olympic Games. I told him that the IOC had some responsibility for the whole of sport. For all his bluff, he was not a particularly strong character.

Together with the threat from Keller, as president of GAISF, Samaranch was likewise concerned, though less so, with the potential power of the Association of National Olympic Committees (ANOC) under the presidency of Mario Vazquez Raña of Mexico, never mind that Raña had helped coordinate Samaranch's election campaign. Samaranch therefore put into effect the ancient policy of divide and rule. Part of Keller's power came from the GAISF's share of revenue from the Olympic Games. He now wanted the finances of the Summer and Winter Games to be amalgamated and then shared among IFs. Samaranch realised the solution was to split the IFs, Summer and Winter, into two groups: ASOIF (Association of Summer Olympic International Federations) and AIOWF (Association of International Olympic Winter Sports Federations), under the respective leadership of Primo Nebiolo of Italy and Marc Hodler

A bid by Thomas Keller, president of the General Association of International Sports Federations, to upstage the IOC was swiftly crushed by Samaranch. (© IOC/Baranyi)

of Switzerland, presidents of athletics and skiing. These two organisations would have the right to deal with the IOC regarding share of Games' revenue, thus leaving the GAISF, and Keller, with reduced influence. Nebiolo, in his own covert move towards personal membership of the IOC, grandly forfeited the 20 per cent share of the IAAF from the total granted to Summer IFs – the remaining 80 per cent having been divided equally among the others – so that now they would all have an equal amount, archery and athletics alike.

In parallel with this development, Samaranch had already established – in collaboration with the Supreme Council for Sport in Africa – the Association of NOCs of Africa (ANOCA), the first assembly of which took place in June 1981 at Lomé, Togo, under the presidency of Anani Matthia, subsequently elected to the IOC in 1983. The Pan-American sports movement, PASO, had been in operation since 1940 – and was now also under the leadership, and financially dependent upon, the wealthy patronage of media multi-millionaire Vazquez Raña. The Olympic Council of Asia (OCA), replacing the Asian Games Federation, would be created in 1982. By such manoeuvres Samaranch was gaining control over existing power bases and simultaneously establishing allegiances with the newly created heads of fresh bodies.

Another move, in 1984, was the creation of ARISF (the Association of IOC Recognised International Sports Federations) under the presidency of Un Yong Kim, by then successor to Keller as president of GAISF. By granting this recognition, the IOC was encouraging collaboration with regard to event schedules, calendar coordination and other matters of mutual interest. 'He had no great sporting achievement, little administrative prominence outside Spain, no one knew his capacity,' Siperco, Romanian intellectual, said of Samaranch. 'At his election, he was given the benefit of the doubt, but once elected there was a huge change in his personality. What worked for him was his charm. He led the Congress outstandingly, holding the three arms of the Movement together. It was the moment he first established himself.'

The perceived possible threat from ANOC concerned, as with GAISF, the distribution of funds. At Baden-Baden, the Solidarity Fund was modified in its composition as the 'Commission for Olympic Solidarity', no longer a joint IOC–NOC Commission, but additionally embracing IFs. Television rights from Lake Placid and Moscow had increased the available fund to $8.5 million. Anselmo Lopez, a Spanish businessman and long-standing friend of Samaranch, became honorary director of a new Solidarity office with a staff of four. Samaranch said:

> ANOC could have been a challenge to the distribution [of funds], but now we were following the true meaning of *solidarity*. Those who needed the money most were Africans. At that time, Africa alone was receiving more than $500,000 a year, but it was going through ANOC to the NOCs, and for this reason channelling the money through continental federations, as we now did, made them strong and avoided many problems.

By 1984, Lopez and his staff would be handling funds of more than $12 million, directly aiding Third World sports development.

Accepted at Baden-Baden was the suggestion for an NOC inspection of potential Olympic candidate cities, an issue that 17 years later would be at the heart of the crisis to which Samaranch referred at the beginning of this chapter. Part of the agenda for the Session that now took place alongside the Congress was the election of the host cities for 1988, and there is no doubt that the report of Don Miller and Dick Palmer, from the respective NOCs of the USA and Britain, helped to determine the IOC's controversial yet imaginative selection of Seoul, South Korea, for the Summer Games. Samaranch admitted himself astonished by the vote, Nagoya of Japan having been the favourite. There was political criticism during and after the Session. The older Japanese IOC member Kiyokawa drew attention to South Korea's $6 billion debt to Japan, while the gymnastics federation president, Titov from the USSR, condemned the country that had no diplomatic relations with more than half the world. The effect of these criticisms, and more particularly the street demonstrations by hundreds of ecological protestors from Japan, plastering lamp-posts around the spa town with banners, was to push the members towards Seoul. The vote was 52–27. The Winter choice was for Calgary. Samaranch, however, was instantly alarmed at the fresh danger facing the IOC with the preference for Seoul.

Other decisions reached at the Session included amendment to eligibility Rule 26, which now stated: 'Each IF is responsible for the wording of the eligibility code relating to its sport', the guideline for which was that a 'competitor's health should not suffer nor should he or she be placed at a social or material disadvantage as a result of preparation for and participation in the Games and other international competitions'. For the moment it remained illegal to be professional, to be involved in advertising other than under IF/NOC/national federation supervision, or to carry advertising material on clothing other than trademarks agreed by the IOC with IFs.

In the evolution of the eligibility rule, the IOC was being more re-active than pro-active. The financial reward for competitors, however illegal in theory, had long been in practice and was rapidly accelerating. Killanin had some while before expressed the view that athletes 'should have some sort of cut'. The IAAF had established in 1981 the principle of Trust Funds. Thereby, monies received could be paid into such funds during the athlete's career but not officially 'cashed' until the athlete had retired. Random cash payments, as alleged grants or awards by equipment companies, were wantonly corrupting any last remnants of the amateur ethic. Samaranch knew that it had become absurd for the IOC to continue to live the lie: the more so when, in 1984, the IAAF would create a Grand Prix of 12 to 15 meetings, comparable to tennis, with hefty financial prizes. Yet anomalies remained. At the Winter Games in Sarajevo, Samaranch would be treading water when asked to explain the moral difference between Carl Lewis freely advertising under the control of his national federation while Ingemar Stenmark of Sweden was excluded from Alpine skiing for similar arrangements. Samaranch passed the question to Hodler, president of skiing – who could not answer it. With eligibility now the responsibility of each IF, some of the heat was off the IOC.

After 87 years, the first two female IOC members were elected: Flor Isava Fonseca (Venezuela) and the Olympic runner Pirjo Häggman (Finland). Many regretted the omission of Nadia Lekarska (Bulgaria), eminent Olympic authority and widow of horseman Kroum Lekarski. The IOC membership of his colleague Vladimir Stoytchev had blocked Nadia's path. Also inaugurated was the Athletes Commission, bringing 12 active competitors inside the corral, Sebastian Coe advocating a life ban for convicted drug offenders.

A third request by Sweden for the award of a boxing silver medal to Ingemar Johansson, denied for 'not fighting' in his 1952 final, was accepted. Other developments were an ultimate

Flor Isava Fonseca (left) of Venezuela and Pirjo Häggman of Finland, belated inaugural women members of the IOC. (© IOC/Riethausen)

agreement between the IOC and, respectively, the People's Republic of China and Taiwan on the recognition of their NOCs. To Samaranch's credit, the IOC was the first international body in any field to embrace the two Chinas within a single organisation. Prior to Samaranch's conclusive intervention, Taiwan's affiliation to IFs had fallen from 18 to 11 as IFs increasingly adopted allegiance with the People's Republic. Concurrently, M'Baye formulated draft statutes for an international arbitration court – ultimately CAS – so that the IOC might keep abreast of litigation issues, real or potential, in which various bodies of the Olympic Movement might be involved, there being previously no such legal centre-point.

It was in Baden-Baden, too, that Samaranch first sounded the introduction of Nebiolo (IAAF) and Vazquez Raña (ANOC) as ex-officio members of the IOC. Constitutionally, it made sense for the leaders of two major branches of the Olympic Movement to hold places on the executive, but he was obliged to back off when it became apparent there was resentment from the floor: less on the basis of the formal position of the two men than on their personalities.

Meanwhile, in Britain, an independent inquiry into sponsorship, under the chairmanship of Denis Howell, Labour MP, former football referee and Minister for Sport in the 1960s, saw fit to make a string of ethical pronouncements:

- Governing bodies negotiating sponsorship linked to television should assess the value to all interested parties.
- The government should refer to the Office of Fair Trading the relation between the International Management Group (Mark McCormack) and UK Sport to establish whether monopoly exists.
- The IOC should involve all NOCs and IFs in a dialogue about the future of the Olympics regarding eligibility and commercialism.
- GAISF must assess the financial involvement of Adidas with FIFA and the IOC.

The findings were something of an insult. The IOC were already knee-deep in analysis of relationships, under the aegis of the Commission of the Olympic Movement, while for GAISF to assess the activities of Adidas was all but laughable, for it was only the benevolence of Horst Dassler that had rescued GAISF itself from financial embarrassment following the formation of the summer and winter federations. The self-righteousness of some observers led to Dassler being branded an ogre bent on manipulating international sport. He was said to have engineered the election of Samaranch and the choice of Seoul as Olympic host city. Of course Dassler was interested in the projection of sportswear and equipment – less than a third of the company's overall output, which was primarily leisurewear – but equally he was a benefactor. He provided sponsorship in kind to numerous African and Eastern European sports bodies, at a substantial loss, as well as the more obvious and expedient promotional provision of footwear and clothing, bearing the familiar three-stripe logo, to prominent athletes. Samaranch knew that the IOC's survival lay in financial independence: that without money they had no strength. It was through commercialisation and collaboration with such men as Dassler that the IOC would be able to generate the wealth that would ensure their survival.

At the Session in New Delhi in 1983, the IOC took charge as sole authority over the marketing of the Games, and its symbols and emblem, at the same time formulating an initial agreement with ISL, a Swiss-based company that would coordinate commercialisation of the Olympic logo in 30 major advertising categories such as petrol, cameras, tobacco, motor cars, electronics and food and drink. ISL was a company owned by Adidas and later jointly with Dentsu of Japan. The project initiated in Delhi rested on Dassler's assurance that he had the personnel to co-opt NOCs in a commercial partnership, this leading to the establishment, post-1984, of The Olympic Programme (TOP). This would specialise in a small number of exclusive contracts for sponsors paying millions of dollars per head for membership, ISL acting on behalf of NOCs worldwide. It was also decided in Delhi that Olympic Solidarity would cover the travel and daily expenses of two competitors and one official for the 1984 Winter Games, and for four athletes and two officials for the Summer Games, for every NOC; and that the eligibility codes of a majority of federations, other than those for ice hockey and football, were approved. Ice hockey was to be a thorn in the Winter Games the following year.

If the IOC still had any doubts about the extent of drug abuse, it should have been removed by the 1983 Pan-American Games in Caracas, Venezuela, where 15 weightlifters tested positive for anabolic steroids. Momentarily the detectors were ahead of the game, now able to identify consumption of steroids retrospectively. Sadly the IOC were to remain insufficiently motivated by the general evidence confronting them and were disinclined to impose pre-emptive discipline. From experimental tests in Cologne in 1981 on unidentified samples taken from competitors at the Moscow Olympics, more than 20 per cent were found positive for excess testosterone. The warning lights were flashing loud and clear. For the inaugural World Track and Field Championsips of 1983, the IAAF strangely decided not to test for testosterone. Why?

Less loud but just as clear were anomalies concerning professionalism in ice hockey at the start of the Winter Games in Sarajevo. Carey Wilson feinted his way past what was left of the crumbling defence of tradition when he scored three times to help Canada inflict a surprise 4–2 defeat on their arch-rivals the United States. This not only caused heart failure within the control room of ABC Television – with its $91.5 million investment in the US market – but also embarrassment for Willi Daume and the IOC as Wilson had played contract professional hockey in Finland. The ice hockey federation (IIHF) excluded from Olympic eligibility professionals in the North American league but not others. As far as they were concerned, professionals in the World Hockey League in Europe were irrelevant. Rick Cunningham of Canada, playing as a naturalised Austrian in their defeat by Finland, had appeared 323 times in WHL matches. Daume and Samaranch were unable to answer media questions on the anomalies.

A year later the situation was eased with the introduction of a low upper age limit, similar to that in football; thereby further opening, in time for the Calgary Games, the admission of full professionals so long as 'he submitted himself to the jurisdiction of both organisations' (i.e. IIHF and NOC of his own country). Samaranch was in mid-stream with his revolution, up to his armpits and still struggling to get to the far bank.

Six years earlier, Sarajevo had been preferred to more likely candidates, becoming the first Communist city to host a Winter Games, the intention being to create a new winter sports centre in central Europe, ignoring the unpredictable weather of the surrounding mountains that divide Bosnia from the sub-Mediterranean climate of Herzegovina.

Sarajevo was a truly multi-cultural town between East and West, with its fascinating narrow alleys dealing in the ancient trades of jewellery, precious metals, leather and cloth. The variable weather, with regular winter fog, made the airport a frustrating destination, but this hitherto tourist-free city of some half a million people, the second largest to stage a Winter Games, did a wonderful job preparing to receive the rest of the world. There was a record attendance of 49 countries, including the first-time appearance of Egypt, Costa Rica, Puerto Rico, Senegal and the Virgin Islands.

Behind the knowledgeable preparation was the hand of Artur Takac, with his unrivalled experience of Olympic requirements. With an initial budget of $160 million, most of the facilities had to be built from scratch, never mind an inflation rate of 50 per cent and $20 billion foreign debt. Such was Yugoslav pride following the death of Tito – what irony in the light of subsequent inter-racial catastrophe for the city and country – that construction projects finished ahead of schedule. Successful foreign marketing, the largest source of income, in addition to the rights fee from ABC Television resulted in the Games having an operational profit. For the first time China and Taiwan, the latter competing under the banner of Chinese Taipei, marched together in an Olympic stadium.

In the city famous for the event that had precipitated the First World War – the assassination of Archduke Ferdinand – the hospitality of the people, modest though their circumstances were, was in the author's experience unrivalled up to that time. Their unsophisticated restaurants and bars cheerfully remained open until the early hours, and the dignity with which the crowds gathered each evening in the town centre for the medal presentations had an enchanting air in the frosty darkness, with not a single impatient motorist horn to be heard. Ominously, however, a former Norwegian cross-country champion, then

A thin smile from the IOC President as Marat Gramov (left), Soviet sports minister, threatens a boycott of the LA Games led by Peter Ueberroth (right). (© IOC)

coaching the Canadian team, inadvertently walked through the wrong door into the Finnish team's dressing-room and witnessed the blood-doping of a silver medal winner, Aki Karvonen, who subsequently admitted the practice – only made illegal the following year – in an interview with America's *Sports Illustrated*.

The possibility of a retaliatory boycott of Los Angeles in the summer by the USSR now began seriously to emerge at the Sarajevo Games, never mind that US–Soviet sporting relations appeared to be positive at the Sarajevo Session. All had seemed optimistic at Baden-Baden in 1981 in the closing report of the Moscow Games by Soviet NOC chairman Ignati Novikov, who had stated: 'We subscribe to the line of the IOC, which deplored the stand of certain NOCs that had refused to participate . . . for reasons counter to the interests of the Olympic Movement.' The Soviets were visibly preparing their team for LA and all seemed well until Konstantin Andrianov, Soviet IOC member, rose at the Session to demand freedom for Soviet participants and press in LA, in the face of predicted restrictions by US authorities. In the interim, President Brezhnev had died, to be succeeded by Andropov at the beginning of *perestroika*. The militant Marat Gramov had replaced Sergei Pavlov as sports minister, and was known as an echo of the Kremlin Central Committee. Besides Andrianov's guarded speech, events took a downward turn when Andropov died in the middle of the Winter Games, being succeeded not by the progressive Mikhail Gorbachev but by Chernenko, from the old guard: a sick man dominated by his foreign minister, Gromyko, who carried an entrenched dislike of the US. The Soviet decision regarding LA, built on a platform of alleged lack of security, would inevitably be made not by the NOC but by the Kremlin. Andrianov's IOC colleague Smirnov recalls:

Bojan Krizaj, Yugoslav skier, takes the athletes' oath at the opening of one of the friendliest of all Games, in politically unstable Sarajevo. (© IOC/Pahud)

> By 1984, we were at liberty to express an opinion, to a degree. My opinion was that we should go. The Central Committee asked Andrianov and me what was our view. I said we ought to go, that if we didn't, we would win nothing, lose the political effect of sporting heroes from among 600 young men and women, right there among ideological rivals. Why sacrifice the athletes? That's interesting, the Committee said, but it's already been decided. I have to admit that in Soviet Russia the

security scare was genuine. Even my mother asked me why I was going.

Samaranch was unsurprised by the change in Soviet attitude. 'Gromyko was a most interesting man, who'd been in the front row for nearly 50 years, there behind Churchill, Roosevelt and Stalin at Yalta in 1945, afterwards Ambassador in Washington and then the UN. Yet it was impossible to get on friendly relations. If Andropov had survived, I think we would have been OK in 1984.'

A confidential Soviet document of 29 April 1984, sent to the Central Committee and signed by Marat Gramov – unearthed by Alex Ratner, experienced Moscow commentator – stated:

> . . . active work on preparing the USSR team for LA being conducted . . . obstructionist position of the Reagan administration . . . meeting on 18 April in LA of 14 anti-Soviet organisations . . . threats of violence and attempts to invite Soviet athletes to defect . . . our principal position aimed at protecting the Olympic Movement . . . bourgeois press of England, West Germany and others not notable for their sympathies with USSR . . . informed IOC that athletes of USSR intend to participate on condition that the Olympic Charter is not violated . . . participation will be hampered if hostile activities not stopped . . . abstention of USSR and developing countries will bring the first 'commercial Games' to economical crash . . . USSR sport committee considers it expedient to go on with active preparation . . . if [security] conditions are not observed [by the US] we shall abstain.

The document had a handwritten comment dated 17 May, noting 'Central Committee decision adopted on 5 May'. Ratner suggested, however, that the decision was not made by the Central Committee but by the Politbureau, the highest political organ, the decisive document then being signed by Central Committee secretary Konstantin Chernenko on the grounds of violation of the Charter and lack of proper security. Ratner confirms the initiator of the boycott as having been Gromyko, supported by Gramov, 'a typical Soviet functionary fulfilling directions received from the top. Security? There were a great number of Soviet officials, referees and journalists in LA, the problem of security didn't exist for them.'

Determined to make every attempt at damage limitation, Samaranch set off on 24 May for Prague and a meeting of the sports ministers and NOCs of 11 socialist countries, seeking an assurance they would not join Big Brother. In vain. Only Romania confirmed it would be in LA, in blatant breach by dictator Ceausescu of political solidarity. Alexandru Siperco recalled:

> It was a huge risk for Romania. I knew Ceausescu from before the Second World War and had some influence to get our Politbureau to agree we should go. Ceausescu balanced independence and evil. He *was* a dictator, but not a killer, there were no concentration camps, but it was a very oppressive regime. His secret service knew everything, it was impossible to organise anything against him, he was a megalomaniac and that is why the revolution, assassinating him, was so spontaneous.

When Ueberroth learned of the boycott, he called HQ in LA the same day and told them immediately to send the appointed 'envoys' to every country that might be in doubt. A part of his policy had been to have for every NOC an envoy with some close connection with that country: in language, culture, business,

whatever, many of the people being of high standing, such as Charles Lee, from the Department of Justice in San Diego, who immediately flew to Beijing to meet the Chinese Minister of Sport. 'We flooded the difficult countries,' Ueberroth said:

> Africa was a key area. We told them that to boycott our Games would have a negative effect on their standing regarding South Africa. The only absentees were Ethiopia and Upper Volta [later Burkina Faso] . . . we could have paid the Third World [to come], all those really needy, but the politicians took over. With Romania, we picked up some of their costs, but theirs wasn't an economic decision. The credit goes to three people who got them there: Samaranch, Siperco and Agnes Mura, our Romanian envoy. She had already built up a relationship with their officials . . .
>
> As far as Reagan was concerned, he would help us reject the Soviet claims that the Games would not be safe. The whole spirit of patriotism that came out of the Games helped Reagan in his re-election . . .
>
> It was an exciting period of Samaranch's life. History will say it was the time at which he saved the Olympic Movement. Calmly, on the surface, he navigated so many crises, public and private, many of which never came to light.

Again in vain, Samaranch travelled to Moscow with Vazquez Raña and Nebiolo, being unable, in spite of his credentials as former Ambassador, to get a meeting with Chernenko. The dominant success for him was the decision to attend by Romania and China, the latter for the first time in 50 years.

'The difference between Samaranch and Killanin,' Richard Pound of Canada observed, 'is that the moment the Soviets withdrew, Samaranch was on his way round the world, not just to see Chernenko and Ronald Reagan, but also many other leaders, in an attempt to hold the Games together. He knew that there were relatively few who would accept the claim of lack of safety if he worked quickly enough.' Besides the USSR, the absentees would be: Afghanistan, Bulgaria, Cuba, Czechoslovakia, Ethiopia, East Germany, Hungary, North Korea, Laos, Mongolia, Poland, Upper Volta, Vietnam, DR Yemen. There would be a record 140 nations present in LA.

The passage of the torch from Greece, and Ueberroth's plan to stage a sponsored run around America, created an unnecessary and hypocritical controversy with Greece, whose NOC protested against alleged 'corruption' of Olympic tradition. There was, however, no mythological derivation of the torch from the mountains of western Greece, the introduction having come at Amsterdam in 1928 on the suggestion of Theodore Lewald, IOC member from Germany, and it was not until 1936 that the ceremony of lighting the torch from the rays of the sun at Olympia was begun. Moreover, the Greeks had themselves been charging the IOC a substantial fee – for LA, $100,000 – for providing the facilities at Olympia. Under the administrative backing of AT&T, the telephone company – sponsorship in kind – Ueberroth raised a sponsored $3,000 per kilometre from every volunteer runner, an inspirational concept in small-town America. From these 4,000 local sponsors, $12 million was donated to YMCA clubs and charities without deduction. The protest of Greek IOC members to the Executive Board indeed looked hollow.

Ueberroth had built from scratch the second largest travel company in America. His administrative ace for the LA Games was to reduce the number of sponsors, thereby creating exclusivity and higher fees – a principle to be steeply developed

Rocket man. Whizz-kid technology greets the world at LA's opening ceremony in the renovated Coliseum.
(© Getty Images/Duffy)

by the IOC. Thereby he raised $470 million, a fraction of what had been spent in Montreal and Moscow. The money had come from television (ABC – $225 million), sponsorship ($115 million), ticketing ($85 million), equipment contributors ($14 million) and trading licences ($13 million). A predicted 10 per cent surplus would be divided, under IOC rules, between USOC, the education department of Southern California and national sports governing bodies. This smooth-tongued American liked to quote Churchill: 'Some see private enterprise as a predatory target to be shot, others as a cow to be milked, few are those who see it as a sturdy horse pulling the wagon.' Economy was effected by using predominantly existing facilities, spreading the Games over 100 miles, from Lake Casitas in the north (rowing), three-day eventing in San Diego County to the south, football at the Pasadena Rose Bowl to the east. The only two new stadia, both sponsored, were for swimming (McDonald's, $3.6 million) and cycling (Southland Food, $3.12 million). The 1932 Coliseum, with its peristyle arched end, was renovated by Atlantic Richfield.

'We've no message, except let's have a nice Games,' was Ueberroth's maxim: so nice, indeed, that the private committee made a profit of a quarter of a billion dollars, on account of which the IOC would revise regulations for future profit distribution. A large lump of LA profit went to the creation of the charitable Amateur Athletics Foundation. An initial 22-person committee grew to 1,700 employees by May 1984 and a paid staff of 12,000 during the Games, aided by 33,000 volunteers (imagine the absurdity of the Carter/Thatcher proposal of shifting the Games in 1980 at three months' notice).

Many had predicted a Games fouled by smog and traffic congestion. Neither materialised. The Games were formally opened by President Reagan, behind bullet-proof glass. The final runner on the torch relay was Gina Hemphill, granddaughter of the legendary Jesse Owens, who had jointly run the first leg on American soil with the grandson, Bill, of the equally legendary Jim Thorpe. She passed the flame to Rafer Johnson, 1960 Olympic decathlon champion, for ignition of the stadium bowl. Ed Moses, who would successfully regain his 400m hurdles title, haltingly took the oath due to failure of the electronic prompt. Though standards were reduced by absentee state-sponsored 'amateurs', nonetheless 13 world records were set or tied in track and field.

A different kind of record was being created in the IOC's corridors of power: the Executive Board was adjusting to an unprecedented daily first meeting at 7.30 a.m. with the LA organising committee, plus one representative each from NOCs, IFs and the Athletes Commission, at which were reviewed written reports from the previous evening on each sport, plus anything untoward such as aspects of security. Walter Tröger, the then Sports Director recollected:

> Those meetings could last two hours and might be followed by an inspection to investigate anything incorrect. The running of the Games was much more difficult now than ever before, with all the aspects relating to sponsors. Previously, these had been neglected. Behind closed doors, Samaranch wanted to be told of *any* deficiency. He intensified the activity of the Executive Board, expanded the staff on the Solidarity Fund, created the Sport-for-All promotion, sport for the disabled, the new Evaluation Commission for bidding cities, the new Museum, the strengthening of the legal department.

A revolution indeed.

Righting a wrong. Gina Hemphill, granddaughter of 'segregated' Jesse Owens, bears the flame at the opening ceremony in LA.
(© DPA)

CHAPTER LIV

Sarajevo (XIV) 1984

Katarina Witt of Germany (formerly GDR), double Olympic figure skating champion

'Setting a meaningful example of peaceful and humane competition to young people and other generations; promoting a contest of strength without destruction: that, for me, has been the inner heart of the Olympic Games over the years. The Olympics demonstrate that peace in conflict, and competition in peace, are possible among men and women. Gestures that go beyond nations and religions, where race plays no role: these are the ideals which still must be striven for, much more than the mere attraction of medals. This ambition is even truer today, when basic values and solidarity between people are increasingly being eroded by a "me first" mentality, by national and individual egotism.

Sport is an astonishing medium. How often do players sit on the sidelines just hoping for the best performance from themselves and perhaps even for a mistake by a fellow player? Yet once the match is over, there is often a genuine, deep, not just superficial reconciliation between those taking part: competition that is within the bounds of sanity, containable rivalry which is still capable of fostering friendship.

One example of this is the friendship I had with Rosalyn Sumners. This began very soon after we had competed so fiercely with one another on the ice, watched by millions in 1984, in Sarajevo and here the word really has its true meaning: competed with one another, and not against one another. I know that members of football teams, when they swap shirts after a game, are often no longer opponents. Some images deceive, but many do not. Cordiality and competition are totally compatible.

There are such pictures from sport which inspire the hope of a new era for humanity. Pictures spread a powerful message. They can speak the language of power. Yet the international power of losers can be found in pictures just as much as of the eternal winners. A single child in Sarajevo with a leg amputated often says more than carefully compiled UN statistics on "children in civil wars". Athletes with different skin colours seen in a brotherly or sisterly embrace are more inspiring than many frantic appeals against racism. Alternatively, a dictator with a friendly smile, a destroyer of the environment presenting impressive economic data, an eternal has-been in a shiny new pin-stripe before the cameras of the media empire over which his rule is absolute: all these too have power within the language of pictures. No, there is nothing so bright and fascinating as a picture that does not require cautious handling. The Olympics, likewise, contain within them dangers, but at the same time immense opportunities for the future of humanity.'*
(Photograph © IOC)

Born in Karl-Marx-Stadt in 1965, Katarina Witt grew up, unsurprisingly, with an affection for the totalitarian, Communist country within which she developed her natural sporting talent. Because that talent made her one of a privileged minority, within a Soviet satellite state that devoted a major part of its national budget to the achievement of international sporting success, it was to be expected that Witt would harbour approval of that social system. Indeed, there are extensive files on her liberal benefits supplied by the Stasi secret police. Yet of all the champions from whom the author requested a reminiscence on their experience of Olympic glory, she is the only one not to have referred primarily to her personal achievement.

She won the first of her eight national titles as a fifteen year old in 1981, and was successively fourteenth, thirteenth and fifth prior to taking the European silver medal in 1982 and winning the first of six successive titles the following year. In Sarajevo, she was up against two world champions: Rosalyn Sumners, the current holder, and Elaine Zayak from 1982. Zayak put herself out of the running with errors in the opening third section of the competition, the compulsories, which were led by Sumners, with Witt in third place.

Witt possessed that special quality of all outstanding figure skaters: her awareness of herself on the ice concerned not so much her feet and her direct connection with a treacherous medium as the poetry in motion of her entire body, thereby creating momentarily the illusion that she was indeed not in touch with the ice at all. In the short programme, Witt now took a slight lead, so that all would depend upon the respective performances by her and Sumners in the free skating.

Nobody can ever be sure about the motivation or technical calculation of judges. Undoubtedly, the youthful Witt was the up-and-coming star, and there had long been an impression of advance collusion in the judging of figure skating. Nevertheless, slight technical errors by Sumners may have tipped the scales against her, so that six of the nine judges awarded Witt first-

Katarina Witt (GDR) calculatedly exploited her sexuality to influence judges and engage the crowd. (© DPA)

double fantasy of the ordinary person: to be successful *and* beautiful.

It would be the gracefulness that would be remembered long after the triumph. Bobby Thompson, an international coach whose American pupils Judy Blumberg and Michael Siebert finished fourth, was astonished by Dean's relatively untrained choreography. 'It is incomprehensible,' Thompson said. 'He is to ice dancing what MacMillan or Ashton are to ballet.' Dean had had advice on choreography from two experts: Gideon Avrahami, a ballet teacher, and Zoltan Nagy, a Hungarian dancer, who showed him how to embrace dancing technique without being effeminate.

So mentally tense was Dean that after a celebration party in the British section of the Village, which continued long after Princess Anne left at 1 a.m., he was awake again after only two hours' sleep. Jayne lay dreaming till late, when she was woken, characteristically in this city, by a chambermaid giving her flowers of personal appreciation. Downstairs, among dozens of telegrams, was one from the Queen: 'Many congratulations on a superb performance which we watched with great pleasure.'

place marks, with only three for Sumners, two judges placing Sumners fourth and fifth respectively. Witt was trained by the formidable Jutta Müller, who had coached her own daughter, Gabrielle Seyfert, to the silver medal in 1968 and had also guided Anett Pötzsch to Olympic victory at Lake Placid.

On the morning of St Valentine's Day, Christopher Dean gave his ice dance partner, Jayne Torvill, an orchid. We could not know of what it spoke, yet it was symbolic of the intensely shared creative brilliance that would win them the Olympic gold medal that evening, with an unprecedented twelve maximum marks from the nine judges, including a clean sweep of 10s for artistic interpretation. As with the greatest exponents of theatrical dance, the romance and tragedy of their 'Bolero' rose above any question of personal affection, which undoubtedly there must have been to have sustained nine years of mutual devotion.

If Torvill and Dean achieved the illusion of being in another world, it was indeed so: a performance instinctive rather than conscious. 'We weren't with the audience last night, we were with each other,' Dean said the following morning, talking in that unassuming way which made the vision of his choreography such an astonishment. They discreetly denied that they were to marry, yet admitted they could not contemplate working without each other, whether performing professionally or teaching.

They had comprehensively defeated their Soviet rivals, Natalya Bestemianova and Andrei Bukin, who four years earlier had finished eighth to the British pair's fifth in Lake Placid. There is no explanation of artistic genius. Millions of television viewers around the world were captivated, not just because Torvill and Dean were physically almost as perfect as kingfishers in flight, but also because the seamless elegance of their movement was Dean's own creation: an unusual achievement for man off a policeman's beat in Nottingham. With his enfolding rosebud of a partner, he touched the

For more than a decade, the artistry of Jayne Torvill and Christopher Dean, policeman–choreographer, entranced a global audience. (© DPA)

With the early demise of America's prospects in the ice hockey tournament, the moguls of the ABC television network were desperate for 'home' achievement. Their male Alpine skiers and a diminutive figure skater provided it. As a healthy child, Scott Hamilton from Ohio had stopped growing at the age of five after contracting a rare disease, and, though cured, he never grew beyond 1.6m (5 ft 3 in.). Initially attempting gymnastics, he began skating at ten, but made no impact until he was nineteen. At Lake Placid, he had finished fifth and in the following three years was world champion. Prior to Sarajevo, he had won 16 consecutive tournament victories, but the expectation of the Games was partially to undermine him. Following the establishment of a huge lead in the compulsories, he performed way below par, being outclassed by the technically superb Brian Orser of Canada. The compulsories, however, proved sufficient to carry Hamilton to victory: the perfect prelude to the inevitable professional contract.

Perverse weather patterns, with erratic wind and snowfall, led to the postponement of the men's downhill three times. No American male skier had ever won the Olympic event, but Bill Johnson, who was far from lacking in self-confidence, remained wholly unfazed by this statistic. 'Just hang around and wait for the victory' was his advice to anyone who bothered to listen. When charged as a teenager with attempted theft of a car, a benign judge had sent Johnson to ski school rather than to prison, which proved to have been perceptive.

Although Johnson arrived at Sarajevo with a patchy record – one victory and a fourth place during the preceding weeks' preparation on the World Cup circuit – the course on Mt Bjelasnica was not difficult, indeed ideal for a skier whose credentials relied on pace rather than technique. There were plenty of Swiss and Austrians out there with credentials much superior – not excluding the still idolised veteran Franz Klammer. However, when Klammer, the third man to start, came in sight on the bottom third of the course, he was already three-tenths of a second behind Pirmin Zurbriggen of Switzerland. For him the dream was over. Then came Mair of Italy, then Catomen of Switzerland. Then Johnson, circus-like in his white-and-pink barber-striped suit that glinted in the sun. His time was one and a half seconds inside Klammer's, half a second better than Zurbriggen. Clearly, he was the man to beat – and nobody could do it. Peter Müller of Switzerland, starting 11th, came within a quarter of a second, the closest. For Swiss and Austrian dignity, the day was a disaster, not to mention for their ski industries. 'A minor catastrophe,' Klammer reflected, though he could return, untroubled, to the hotel he had bought following his gold medal. Johnson reported glibly: 'I motored on the flats.' He had indeed, registering a then record average speed of 104.532 kph down the three-kilometre course.

The best men, it must be said, were absentees from the slalom. Ingemar Stenmark of Sweden, who would have been defending champion, and Marc Girardelli had won six of the seven World Cup races prior to the Games, but neither could take part. Stenmark had been declared a professional, Girardelli was ineligible because he held an Austrian passport but competed under the flag of Luxembourg, such licence prohibited in the Games.

The Mahre twins (USA), while long-standing in competitive respectability, had gone through a poor season, Phil the elder being 62nd and Steve 45th in World Cup rankings. In the giant slalom in Sarajevo, they had just finished eighth and seventeenth respectively. Perhaps the relaxed attitude of the pair worked in their favour, however much their tension-free approach to the slalom irritated their own journalists, who wilfully twisted the knife in two genuine sportsmen representing their country in the manner of de Coubertin's true Olympian. The brothers were not only 2 of the 47 starters out of 101 who completed the course but also managed to take gold and silver. Steve led on the first run by seven-tenths of a second with Phil in third place. A brilliant second run carried Phil into the lead, and immediately he radioed advice that might have given victory to his twin. Disregarding a safe run, however, Steve attacked the course, erred, and came second. To complete Phil's day, he learned that while he was out there playing, his wife Dolly had been

working rather harder at home and had given birth to their second child and first son.

There were few more popular medal winners than Jure Franko, the local skier who won silver in the giant slalom behind Max Julen of Switzerland – in the absence of Stenmark, the holder. A huge crowd duly gathered in the city's main square that evening to acknowledge the performance at the medal ceremony, then quietly made their way home through the snow or to the myriad of small café restaurants that throughout the Games remained open until the early hours of the morning. It had been Yugoslavia's first-ever Winter Games medal.

At 17, Michela Figini of Switzerland became the youngest women's downhill winner. She had recorded her first World Cup victory two weeks earlier and now defeated her more fancied compatriot, Maria Walliser, by five-hundredths of a second. Marja-Liisa Hämäläinen of Finland was numerically the outstanding competitor of the Games, winning all three women's Nordic events at 5km, 10km and 20km, plus a bronze in the relay. She had been skiing since she was five and first competed at six.

Marja-Liisa Hämäläinen dominates all three women's cross-country races, here the 20km. (© DPA)

Vladislav Tretyak, renowned goalkeeper for the Soviet ice hockey team, had rejected a $1 million contract from the Montreal Canadiens to remain true to his national team, not to say Soviet ideology. Tretyak had been around a while: gold medals in '72 and '76, and a silver in '80. In the final against Czechoslovakia, the Soviets were never seriously in trouble, though in a match notable for repeated slashing, holding, tripping and punching – normal for this sport – the Czechs seldom threatened. They did show some dismay when Dusan Pasek was unceremoniously felled from behind with only Tretyak to beat. 'Interference' explained the official result sheet enigmatically.

East Germany dominated the bobsleigh at Mt Trebovic, Wolfgang Hoppe steering both two- and four-man sleds to victory. The most notable competitor on the run, however, was the 53-year-old Carl-Erik Eriksson of Sweden, the first to have competed in six Winter Games. In 1972 he had been sixth in the two-man event; he now finished nineteenth. 'This is for men who have no respect for life,' he said with relish, flexing his walrus moustache. He showed himself to be contemptuous of the modern generation. 'They have small machines now, like Formula 1,' he said. 'In the old days, there would be three or four sleds tipping over every day, but now the competitors are ex-athletes.' A significant aspect of the competition was the relative failure of the new Soviet hammer-head sleds, which achieved only a bronze; and the promise by the international federation president, Klaus Kotter of West Germany, that sleds would be standardised by 1988.

Tomas Gustafson of Sweden won the first of two Olympic 5,000m speed skating titles, being two-hundredths of a second faster than Igor Malkov (URS), but in the 10,000m, in which Gustafson held the world record, the result was reversed with Malkov winning by five-hundredths of a second. In the battle for ski jumping supremacy, Jens Weissflog (GDR) defeated Matti Nykänen of Finland in the 70m event, but the young Finn, with a renowned fragile temperament, won the 90m event by the biggest margin in history. More would be heard of him.

Offers of professional contracts in Canada failed to tempt Vladislav Tretyak (URS), legendary goal-minder in three victorious Olympic tournaments ('72, '76, '84, plus silver '80), to desert his team, or Soviet ideology. (© IOC)

CHAPTER LV

Los Angeles (XXIII) 1984

Carl Lewis of America, who emulated the four gold medals of Jesse Owens

'*Much of the recording of history is dependent on the opinions of those who were involved at the time, not necessarily on the opinions of the critics and historians. History is formed by the people who were there, how they were moved at the time, and I like to feel that is the legacy of the athlete . . . In 1984, I thought of the ups and downs that Jesse Owens experienced in 1936, trying for the same four events, so he was certainly an example because I recognised what he had to go through. He had inspired me as a child to try to do the same, so to emulate him was an honour. Comparisons were made, which was an additional honour because Owens was a legend as well as an athlete.*

My first memorable moment was in 1978, at 17, competing in my age group in the national championships, winning the long jump with my first leap over 7.62m (25 ft) and coming second in the 100m. The second was the following year, when I set the high school national record to make the Pan-American Games, and the third was being at those Games because it gave me experience of competition outside the United States, though I went through a difficult moment of almost being disqualified after a mix-up with the American team officials. Fourth, and foremost, has to be the 1984 Olympic Games, it made all the previous experiences important because they were the stepping stones to the most memorable moments of my life.

The best illustration of performing under stress was without question the Games of '84. I had the whole world staring at me, judging me, focusing on anything you can imagine. People were forecasting I would do this or that, but I was able to hold together under that pressure, despite also having some family problems. In spite of the stress, I was able to win the gold medals I had said I would. My coach, Tom Tellez, demanded perfection. With him there is only one way to run or jump, and that's the right way. End of discussion. Heck, after I won the Olympic 100m in LA and was obviously so delighted, coach T's very first words to me were, "Technically you were bad out of the blocks, you should have broken the world record".

. . . I would like to be remembered as an athlete who took his chances, and never allowed anyone to tell him that what he thought he could do was not possible. I've always believed that if you work hard at whatever you want to do, you can make it. Making it doesn't mean doing "the best", it means doing "the best you can". I want to be remembered as someone who was an innovator in sports, as an athlete and as a black person. I've always felt that I've crossed barriers.' (Courtesy extract from NBC interview video)

(Photograph © Getty Images/Powell)

The first gold medal of the Games was won by Haifeng Xu in shooting, China's first-ever Olympic title, though it is not unfair to say that the sporting world in general and the American audience in particular were not too aware of his success. They were initially eagerly awaiting events in swimming and gymnastics, prior to track and field.

Carl Lewis, the third son of two track coaches, after belated development as a teenager, by the age of 20 in 1981 had become number one in the world for the 100m and long jump. Two years later he took three gold medals at the inaugural World Championships in Helsinki and the inevitable speculation began about whether he would climb onto the pedestal once occupied by Owens. Like Owens, whether running or jumping, he had in full flow an extreme athletic beauty. In the face of speculation that Lewis was involved in the chemical advancement known to embrace many of his rivals it can be said that from his earliest emergence, his muscular profile never

developed the visible characteristics associated with those who resorted to the needle or pill. Throughout his career Lewis would proclaim his own innocence and demonstrably criticise those rivals he suspected as offenders. The revelation in 2003, long after his retirement, that he had tested positive for an insignificant element of ephedrine in 1988 armed the cynical doubters of his clean record, while further diminishing the credibility of an entire sport.

His appearance for the final of the 100m on the second day was the apotheosis of the Games. Some had said, and Lewis himself was aware, that this was the most difficult of the four victories he sought. Yet in the second round he had recorded 10.04, the best at that time at a low-altitude Games. His colleague Sam Graddy had brazenly claimed: 'I'm going to do everything I can to stop Carl from getting four medals – I think my name is written on the gold as much as his.' In the final, Graddy and an unheralded Ben Johnson of Canada were away

Haifeng Xu, China's first gold medal winner, in free pistol shooting. (© DPA)

Two and a half weeks before the US trials, Joan Benoit, a 27 year old from Maine, who had set a world best time the previous year with 2:22:43 in the Boston marathon, had undergone arthroscopic surgery on her right knee. Seventeen days later she ran to qualify for the Games and, in spite of or because of the operation, won the race. Benoit was not new to pain. In 1981 she had needed surgery on both heels. She arrived at the inaugural Olympic event knowing that two Norwegians, Ingrid Kristiansen and Grete Waitz, possessed credentials every bit as impressive as hers: Kristiansen having run the second fastest marathon three months earlier, Waitz being the 1983 world champion. When Benoit, wearing a white peaked cap to protect her from the glare of the sun along the concrete streets of the course, moved into the lead after only three miles, the pack confidently let her go. By the time the Norwegians realised she was not going to fade, she was out of sight. Benoit's winning time of 2:24:52 would have won the gold medal in 13 of the 20 Olympic marathons run by men. Indeed, it was less than two

Modern legend emulates past legend. Carl Lewis on his way to the same four gold medals as Jesse Owens. (© Getty Images/Cannon) (© NOPP/*LA Times*)

fastest, and Graddy was still in the lead with 20 metres to go. With an exceptional finishing burst over the last fifth of the race, Lewis surged clear to win by more than two metres: a huge margin. Graddy took silver and Johnson bronze. One down and three to go.

Two days later came the final of the long jump and the first heats of the 200m. Because of the double demand, it was reasonable that Lewis might not take all six attempts in the long jump. Having cleared 8.54m (28 ft ¼ in.) on his first jump and fouled on his second, he did not bother to take his remaining four jumps and was booed by an ignorant crowd expecting him to go for the world record, still held by Beamon at 8.90. 'Because we got a late start after the hammer throw, it got cold very quickly,' Lewis said, 'and I was a little sore after the second jump so I didn't want to risk any chances unless someone jumped further.' Undeterred, and arrogantly interpreting the boos as a demand for him to be on stage, Lewis proceeded to seal his third gold with as much ease as in the short sprint, setting an Olympic record for the 200m of 19.80, almost six feet, or two metres, ahead of his compatriot, Kirk Baptiste. The time was exceptional, being run into a head wind. World record holder Pietro Mennea, the defending champion running in his fourth consecutive Olympic final, came seventh. Predictably, Lewis was now on an all-time high, and he anchored the one-lap relay team, including Graddy, Ron Brown and Calvin Smith, to victory in a world record of 37.83 – the only world mark in track and field at these Games – his leg on a rolling start being timed at 8.94. For the moment he was the talk of the nation, his parents Bill and Evelyn shared in the adulation, and Joe Douglas, manager of his financial affairs, looked an ever more happy man.

Until the Games of 1960, women were considered, by the condescension of men, to be physically incapable of racing distances even as long as 800 metres. Los Angeles would be remembered for the new dimension in women's running that was released upon a world audience: the 400m hurdles, the 3,000m and the marathon would each provide a significant chapter in the evolution of the Games.

Joan Benoit (USA) overcomes LA's baking sidewalks to win the inaugural women's marathon. (© Getty Images)

minutes slower than Emil Zátopek's time in 1952. She finished 500 metres ahead of Waitz, with Rosa Mota of Portugal, the European champion of 1982, taking the bronze medal. Kristiansen was fourth.

If Benoit's triumph, followed throughout by the 90,000 crowd in the Coliseum on huge video scoreboards, had met with thunderous acclaim on her arrival at the finish, there was stunned dismay at the plight of Gabriele Andersen-Scheiss, a 39-year-old Swiss skiing instructor from Sun Valley, Idaho, who arrived in the stadium 20 minutes after Benoit, as near to the point of collapse as Dorando Pietri of Italy in the London marathon of 1908. Her last lap of the track took over five minutes. Three times she rejected the Samaritan's hand of medical assistants who moved in to help her. Close to delirium, her body distorted, she was conscious enough to wish not to be denied her objective. 'My mind wasn't working too good,' she said, thankfully recovering within a short time. 'I just kept walking and walking by instinct. It was will-power, or something.'

The participation of Zola Budd, a South African, resulted in a double controversy, the second aspect through no fault of her own. South Africa remained expelled from the Olympic Movement but Budd, with British roots, had contrived to evade the contagion of apartheid and run for Britain. Disapproval was widespread. Budd had run an unofficial world record for 5,000m at Stellenbosch, Cape Town, that was seven seconds faster than the personal best of Mary Decker, winner of the 1,500/3,000m double at the previous year's World Championships. With earlier world records at one mile, 5,000m and 10,000m, and winner of the new Grand Prix overall women's title, Decker was the darling of the media, and would now be challenging for 3,000m in her native California. Though having also qualified for the 1,500m, the 26 year old who had missed 1980 through the Carter boycott had decided to run only the longer race.

Although Decker's main rival was expected to be Maricica Puica of Romania, the confrontation with Budd caught the imagination. After four of the seven and a half laps, Budd

overtook Decker to take the lead, moving back onto the *outside* of the inner lane. Decker, with not enough room to retaliate and go by on the inside, maintained a position far too close to the new pace-maker, and 200 metres later Decker's right leg caught Budd's left leg as they entered the home straight with three laps to go. Budd's position on the track as lead runner was established, it was Decker's responsibility not to move so close on the inside. When Budd's leg was caught, Decker stumbled and fell over the kerb on to the infield. There she lay, prostrate, her face contorted by tears of fury. A partisan crowd indignantly booed the unfortunate Budd, who, finishing seventh behind Puica's winning time of 8:35.96, was disqualified but then reinstated upon protest by the British, video recordings revealing the fault to lie exclusively with Decker. Without exception American television and radio commentators had instantly cried 'foul', yet were obliged to retract this view when they paused properly to consider the evidence. The IAAF jury of appeal, overruling the disqualification, rightly referred to Decker's 'aggressive tactics'.

Zola Budd (GBR, No. 151) (third from right) and favourite Mary Decker (USA, No. 372) moments before Decker trips on Budd's heels in the 3,000m, won by Maricica Puica (ROM) behind Decker, with Sly (GBR, No. 175) second. (© Getty Images/Powell)

Little known was Nawal El Moutawakel, who earned Morocco's first Olympic gold medal when winning the 400m hurdles. A student at Iowa State University, she had been backed in her preparations by financial support from King Hassan II. She was aided by the absence of the Soviets and East Germans, but with commendable opportunism took her chance, leading from start to finish to defeat Judi Brown of America: the first Islamic woman to win any Olympic medal.

Evelyn Ashford won the women's 100m in an Olympic record of 10.97, which erased some of the disappointment of missing the Games in Moscow. Now 27, she had been the world's finest sprinter for five years or more, setting a world record of 10.97 in 1983. Her colleague Valerie Brisco-Hooks achieved the rare 200/400m double in the absence of the East Europeans, notably world record holder Jarmila Kratochvilova of Czechoslovakia. In the 400m, Brisco-Hooks turned the table on compatriot Chandra Cheeseborough, who had defeated her in the trials, setting an Olympic record of 48.83. In the 200m, three days later, unthreatened by world record holder Marita

Koch (GDR), Brisco-Hooks set another Olympic record, 21.81, ahead of colleague Florence Griffith and Merlene Ottey (JAM). Brisco-Hooks went on to claim a third gold in the four-lap relay, which saw a further Olympic record of 3:18.29: testimony to the increased strength that many women athletes experience after childbirth.

Ulrike Meyfarth of West Germany had seemingly been consigned to history – a past, 16-year-old, Olympic high jump champion. In 1976 she had been out of sight, in 1980 absent in the boycott, and now she was 28. By clearing 2.02m (6 ft 7½ in.), she not only defeated Sara Simeoni of Italy, the defending champion, but also surpassed Simeoni's Olympic record by five centimetres (two inches) – becoming the oldest winner of this event and the only track and field competitor besides Al Oerter and Irena Szewinska to win gold medals 12 years apart.

The inexorable march of time spares no athletic champion. If the 800m silver medal of Sebastian Coe was a gratifying triumph over two years of adversity, the gold medal of Joachim Cruz of Brazil symbolised the fuel of the Olympic flame: the fire burns in an endlessly renewed era. The loping Cruz, reminiscent of Juantorena, broke the Cuban's Olympic record with his fourth exhibition of supreme pace and judgement in four days. The tale of Cruz, from a nation where track and field ranks nowhere besides soccer, and whose last medal had been Adhemar Ferreira da Silva's triple jump gold in 1956, was extraordinary. A basketball player from a poor family, he was persuaded in 1977, when 15, to run his first-ever race and was so swift that his basketball coach persuaded him to take up the sport. In 1981, he lost to the all-conquering Coe in the World Cup. His father having died that year, he and his coach Luiz Alberto Oliveira both emigrated to America, settling together to study at Oregon University, Eugene.

The satisfaction for Coe was to be gained from the fact that

Joachim Cruz, Brazil's first track champion, awaits the start of the 800m, winning by the largest margin in half a century.
(© IOC/Pahud)

he had been undermined, since losing the European 800m title of 1982 to Hans-Peter Ferner of West Germany – who now failed under the intense competition to reach the final – by a viral infection, toxoplasmosis. So severe was this that in the winter of 1983 it had seemed that he might never compete again. He had not recommenced serious training until the spring, and his selection for the British team had been a matter of lengthy controversy.

In LA, the times of several heats in the first two rounds would have won medals in Munich or Moscow. Five others in the final besides Cruz and Coe were potential champions: Jones and Gray (USA), Konchellah and Koech (Kenya) and Sabia (Italy). The defending champion Steve Ovett had struggled to reach the final with a time in the semi of 1:44.81, his fastest in six years. Suffering from bronchitis, he finished a distant last in the final, collapsed, was taken to hospital, and would unwisely decide to run in the 1,500m.

It was a searing 800m. Cruz and Coe allowed Koech to do the front running, Cruz being at his shoulder at the bell with Coe a stride behind. Down the second back straight Gray and Jones moved level either side of Coe. Cruz made his kick on the peak of the fourth bend, as did Coe, but into the home straight Cruz had more in hand and pulled clear to win by five metres, the largest margin for 56 years. Jones took bronze; he, Konchellah, Sabia and Koech all finishing inside Ovett's winning time in Moscow. Coe's world record of 1:41.73, set in 1981, would survive for another 13 years. Cruz's emotions at the finish were almost too intense for him to speak.

Steve Cram, World, European and Commonwealth champion at 1,500m during the two years of Coe's health problems, had said at the start of the Games that nobody would last seven races in the heat and expected polluted air of LA, the latter, in the event, less a factor. Cruz did not, going down with a chest infection. Steve Scott, American record holder, had the same inkling as Cram: that Coe might be vulnerable in a hard 1,500m, and now went boldly for glory himself. Khalifa of Sudan set a fast first lap of 58 seconds, whereupon Scott shot into the lead, determined to ensure that there would not be just a kickers' finish. His courage served only to assist Coe and condemn his own chances, for Coe was at the peak of his form, sharpened by the four races at 800m. Scott's furious second lap took the field through the 800m in 1:56.8, some eight seconds faster than four years earlier. He was, however, a busted flush, and with a lap and a quarter to go José Abascal of Spain, Coe and Cram all swept by.

Approaching the climax of a fine race there was now the undignified spectacle of Ovett collapsing again, as had always been likely, staggering into the in-field while Abascal grimly clung to his tenuous lead. Into the final bend, Cram, whose injury earlier in the season had disrupted his form, made his kick for the front, only for Coe to do likewise as the pair of them accelerated past Abascal. Coe had the reserve for two further kicks, finishing in 3:32.53 to surpass Keino's 16-year-old Olympic record. With an irate gesture in the direction of the British press, many of whom had flatulently questioned the validity of his place in the team, Coe celebrated the distinction of being the first successfully to defend this elite Olympic title.

One source of debate was whether Carl Lewis or Daley Thompson was the greater champion of these Games; another was whether they were unfair on the public for not attempting respective world records in the long jump and decathlon, which, especially in Thompson's case, were there for the taking. The defence in Thompson's case, perverse though his relative stroll in the ultimate 1,500m event may have been, was that victory was all that mattered; that the world record and accompanying additional prestige could come on another day, commercially useful when the event is relatively rarely competed.

The decathlon was indeed a heroic confrontation between the defending champion and the world record holder, Jürgen Hingsen, the latter never having beaten the former in five meetings. Once more, Thompson would prove superior over two days under intense sunshine, a factor which was partially to undermine Hingsen. In the gap between discus and pole vault on the second day, a relaxing Hingsen fell asleep under the shade of a canopy, only to awake with his head exposed to the sun and suffering from nausea. Two failed vaults and an average 4.50m at his third attempt, alongside a supreme 5.00 by Thompson, left the ailing Hingsen well adrift. Following the javelin, Thompson needed only to run the 1,500m in 4:34.8, against a personal best of 4:20, to claim Hingsen's world record. Instead, he dawdled round in 4:35, thereby failing by one point, with 8,847, to equal Hingsen's record, to the frustration of a 95,000 crowd, which had been well briefed on the relevant statistics.

Daley Thompson (GBR) leaps on his way to retaining his decathlon title, following the collapse of rival Jürgen Hingsen (GER).
(© Getty Images/Duffy)

Edwin Moses went to the line for the 400m hurdles final unbeaten in 104 previous races since 1977. He was not intending to let that record end in the Coliseum, of all places, never mind that he was up against Harald Schmid of West Germany, the only man to have beaten him since 1976, plus his fast-emerging young compatriot, Danny Harris, and Sven Nylander, a consistently outstanding Swede. After a false start, Moses left the field in his wake to win in 47.75. The 18-year-old

Harris, in only his fifth month contesting this event, edged out Schmid for the silver medal: it would be Harris who finally ended Moses's winning streak in its ninth year.

The main interest of the 10,000m would concern, unfortunately, less the winner, Alberto Cova of Italy, than the man who came second, Martti Vainio of Finland, but was subsequently disqualified after failing a drug test. Cova had previously won the European title of 1982 and the World Championships of 1983, each time out-sprinting Werne Schildhauer of East Germany, who was now absent because of the boycott. Cova and Vainio led the field in a slowish race, Cova pulling clear to beat him by a dozen strides in 27:47.54 – well outside the world record of Fernando Mamede, who had dropped out halfway. The drug test on Vainio was to prove positive for anabolic steroids and he was hauled off the track when about to race in the 5,000m final. This was won, all too predictably, by Saïd Aouita, generating a moment of celebration not just in Morocco but throughout North Africa, the more so because he improved Brendan Foster's Olympic record with a time of 13:05.59, sprinting clear of Markus Ryffel of Switzerland over the last half-lap. It was an appropriate payback for the thousands of dollars given by King Hassan II to each Moroccan athlete for preparation and Aouita received the further reward of a villa.

If Mamede had been a severe disappointment to Portugal, Carlos Lopes made amends in the marathon with an Olympic best performance of 2:09:21. Although Lopes had won the silver medal eight years earlier, there were a number of other favourites for this event, not least Alberto Salazar of America and Rob de Castella of Australia, who held the two fastest times, the latter not having lost since 1980, plus Toshihiko Seko of Japan, unbeaten since 1979. In the event, these three were to finish fifteenth, fifth and fourteenth, though the cameras of ABC still focused on Salazar when the leaders were out of sight, providing lamentably prejudiced coverage. One of the leaders, at the halfway stage, was Juma Ikangaa of Tanzania. De Castella was in contention until six miles from the finish, when he lost ground taking brief refreshment. By now Charlie Spedding of Britain, an outsider despite respectable marathon form, was making the pace with only Lopes and John Treacy of Ireland, running in his first marathon, staying in touch. Lopes proved to have the reserves to move clear, never mind that he had been struck by a car while training a fortnight before the race, suffering only minor injury.

The high jump brought simultaneous pride and frustration to Jianhua Zhu of China, holder of the world record at 2.39m (7 ft 10 in.), which he had set two months earlier when defeating Dietmar Mögenburg of West Germany. The German, however, was a man for the big occasion and now cleared every height he attempted until the bar was set at 2.40, at which he failed. The problem for Zhu was that his second attempt at 2.33m (7 ft 7¾ in.) was delayed while medics tended to Steve Ovett, who had just collapsed on the fringe of the high jump area. Zhu decided to pass, then failed at 2.35, so that with Patrik Sjöberg of Sweden clearing 2.33 at this second attempt, Zhu was left with the bronze.

Encouraged by the relentless chauvinism of ABC's presentation, the American public lived in a state of euphoria throughout much of the Games, never more legitimately so than during the gymnastics at Pauley Pavilion, where both their men and women did stirring deeds. Mary Lou Retton, a tiny girl of 16, only 4 ft 9 in. tall and taking size three shoes, became a figure of worldwide attention almost as extreme as that devoted 12 years earlier to Korbut. Such was the crescendo of her sudden fame in winning the women's individual all-round event – the

Mary Lou Retton, 1.45m (4 ft 9 in.) tall, prances to fame, fortune and the all-round gymnastics title, the first medal by an American woman in this sport. (© Getty Images/Powell)

first medal by a US woman in this sport – that she was flooded with endorsement offers from ten different corporations, all worth in excess of six figures. Besides her all-round gold medal, she took silver in the individual vault, bronze for the asymmetric bars and the floor exercise, and silver in the earlier team event, behind Romania and ahead of China in the absence of the otherwise overwhelming favourites from the Soviet Union. For Retton this was her first serious international tournament, yet by the time she had finished competing, together with outstanding colleagues Julianne MacNamara and Kathy Johnson, and male compatriots Peter Vidmar, Bart Conner and Mitchell Gaylord – the American men defeating world champions China – gymnastics was rated ahead of every other sport by the home television audience.

Retton brought to gymnastics a new vein of aggressive muscularity. Her individual duel with Ecaterina Szabo of Romania began with a perfect 10 on the beam for the Romanian, who forged further ahead in her floor exercises, but the lead was cut when Retton achieved 10 with her own floor sequence, which concluded with three different back double somersaults. When Szabo scored 9.90 on the asymmetric bars, all depended on Retton's vault. She needed a 10. Here was the ultimate climax: a long way from her introduction to gymnastics at the age of seven in West Virginia. She flew off the springboard, made a double-twist back somersault and landed perfectly, to a throaty roar from 9,000 spectators. In that instant her fame was sealed. Undismayed, Szabo responded by claiming three gold medals in the individual disciplines.

Maybe it was the pressure of being at the Olympic Games for the first time, but China, men's world champions, fell behind on the first day of the team event, notably Ning Li, their precocious

20 year old, and they never recovered. Certainly all would have been different, in both men's and women's competitions, had the Soviet Union been present, and in their absence the wilful Americans made good. So consistent were Vidmar, Conner, Gaylord, Timothy Daggett, James Hartung and Scott Johnson that America was confident of victory with one rotation remaining. Japan took the bronze, with their leading competitor Koji Gushiken fractionally denying Vidmar the all-round individual title, in which an off-key Ning Li came third.

The swimming pool was the scene of one of the most unexpected results ever. Michael Gross of West Germany, otherwise known as 'The Albatross' on account of his arm-span of 2.2m, (7 ft 2 in.), was expected to win every event he entered. He dominated the 200m freestyle, improving his own world record with 1:47.44, way ahead of American Michael Heath, and was the first West German to win an Olympic swimming title. Gross had already taken the 100m butterfly, also in a world record of 53.08, ahead of American Pablo Morales. Now came the 200m butterfly, where the challenge was expected to come, again, from Morales and from Raphael Vidal of Venezuela. Gross was the world record holder and was leading halfway from his two expected rivals. Seventh at halfway, and two body-lengths behind in fourth place with 50 metres to go, the unheralded Jon Sieben, a 17 year old from Brisbane, blasted through the water not only to take first place in front of Gross and Vidal but also to steal the world record by a hundredth of a second with 1:57.04. Sieben had never previously beaten two minutes.

Greg Louganis was already regarded, at 24, as probably the greatest diver there has ever been. He had not lost on platform or springboard for three years. The child of 15-year-old parents and of Samoan extraction, Louganis had survived a fraught childhood, almost becoming alcoholic as a teenager. Diving provided an outlet to a different world and by 16 he was finishing second in the platform event at Montreal. At Los Angeles he was favourite – and delivered even beyond expectation. For his final dive from the ten-metre platform, with a score thus far of 618, and intending to conclude his second gold medal, he was bent on a total score of 700 or better for ten dives. He chose a reverse three-and-a-half-tuck somersault, the so-called death dive – named in recognition of Sergei Schalibashvili, who died attempting it in international competition. Now Louganis performed to perfection, entered the water with barely a ripple and gained a final score of 710.91, becoming the first man since 1928 to win both springboard and platform. He had earlier won the former by the unprecedented margin of 94 points ahead of Liangde Tan of China.

The emergence of the US as a force in cycling owed something to the development of the solid back wheel, but probably more to the absence of the Soviet Union and East Germans. The US had not produced a cycling medallist since 1912, and now took four gold and a record nine medals in all. Both the individual road races were won by Americans. Connie Carpenter-Phinney ended her 12-year career with a gold medal in the 79.2km race – the first women's cycling event in a Games – while Alexi Grewal won the men's title over 190.2km.

The system of blood-doping was not banned until 1985 and was widely in use in LA – one of the beneficiaries being Steve Hegg, a former US downhill ski champion. He achieved the surprise victory over Rolf Gölz of West Germany in the 4,000m individual pursuit, winning by an exceptional margin of four seconds. Several American cyclists were found to have been blood-doping with other people's blood.

There was a dramatic finish to the modern pentathlon individual event as a result of a change to the final cross-country discipline. The runners began in the order of standing after four

events, with a stagger of one second for each three points of difference. Thereby, the first across the line would be the winner. Daniel Massala of Italy started first, Svante Rasmuson of Sweden eight and a half seconds later, Carlo Massullo of Italy in fifth place a minute and ten seconds after Massala. Rasmuson had caught Massala with 100 metres to go, but fell on a sharp turn and had to settle for second place, with Massullo third. Richard

Phelps of Britain, with a 1:19 stagger, narrowly failed to catch Massullo. The team title went to Italy.

After an absence of 60 years tennis returned to the Games as a demonstration sport with the promise of official status four years later. The singles were duly won by Steffi Graf of West Germany and Milos Mecir of Czechoslovakia.

Teenager Jon Sieben (AUS, right), came from nowhere in the 200m butterfly not only to defeat multi-medalist Michael 'The Albatross' Gross (GER) but also to set a world record. (© IOC/Pi)

CHAPTER LVI

Reality

Walther Tröger of Germany, IOC member, former Sports Director

'*A significant change, during the 21-year presidency of Juan Antonio Samaranch, occurred in his second year of office. The Congress at Baden-Baden decided to abolish the Charter's amateur rule. Chiefly due to the encouragement of his English friends, Baron de Coubertin had formulated the amateur rules, the segregation of "gentlemen" thus becoming established.*

Over the years, unsuccessful attempts were made to define the characteristics of an amateur. Samaranch insisted that a solution be found that would enable top-ranking athletes of any discipline to compete in the Games. A pioneer for the admission of professionals was tennis. Almost 60 years earlier tennis had renounced its Olympic status, but now sought re-admission. A demonstration tournament at the Games of 1984 was intended to serve as the final impetus. I had taken over, within the IOC Programme Commission, reporting to the IOC as Technical Director [title later changed to Sports Director] *prior to the final decision. I was extremely unsure about professionalism. No one knew how athletes under contract to sponsors and promoters, and therefore not independent, would be integrated into the Olympic family and especially into their national team. Following a controversial vote with only a narrow majority, the Programme Commission conceded to the wish of the IOC President, who was plainly in favour of full admission. The further responsibility now rested with the Eligibility Commission, headed by Willi Daume, who initially had also been sceptical. As director of this Committee too, I had also to set standards and formulate the conditions here. These contained two important criteria, upon which the IOC and the international tennis federation soon agreed: competitors were neither to advertise, nor to seek paid employment during the Games. More important, over a given period beyond the duration of the Games, all players were to be integrated within their national federation, their NOC and its tennis team. Thus, in 1988, a restored Olympic tournament took place, with excellent attendance by professional players. In its quality, but most of all in the conduct and appearance of top-ranking players, the tournament vindicated the decision.*

With other sports that had a professional element, the process took a little longer. The international basketball federation was initially reluctant but then switched from categoric rejection to almost unanimous agreement, so that in 1992, the US "Dream Team", representatives of the North American League, was welcomed, winning admiration for its conduct. Ice hockey regulations proved the most difficult. Clashes of dates within the short winter season complicate coordination with the North American Professional League and its clubs, and still do not appear solvable.

The past 20 years show that decisions made have been correct. The growing influence of sponsors, promoters and agents inevitably led to competitors having a share in a significant fount of money. Adhering to the amateur rule would just as inevitably have led to a schism within the Olympic Games. Amendment of the amateur rule has enabled the IOC to retain control of financial transactions and, most importantly of all, the running of the Games.'*

(Photograph © IOC/Locatelli)

With the money flowing into Olympic channels from the Games in Sarajevo and LA, in the autumn of 1984 Samaranch introduced a proposal to give additional aid through Olympic Solidarity to NOCs. For Sarajevo and LA, each NOC had received respectively $5,000 and $5,750 towards expenses for two athletes and one official (Winter) and four athletes and two officials (Summer). This would now be increased to $6,000/$8,000 for three plus one and six plus two respectively for Calgary and Seoul. Up to 1984, NOCs worldwide had been receiving $400,000 for administration and coaching courses; by 1988 this would have risen to $3 million.

In the wake of a third consecutive boycott, an Extraordinary Session was held in December 1984, to consider possible disciplinary or future pre-emptive measures. Predictably, after a flood of views both critical and cautionary, no proposals were put into practice. This was partially on account of the conciliatory attitude of the President, who believed that prevention of boycotts in the future lay more in the creation of improved relations than the threat of stringent regulations. Samaranch had himself revised his view, having advocated suspension of boycotting countries at the Session prior to the LA Games, only to experience his first reverse when vigorously resisted by veteran member Masaji Kiyokawa of Japan and others. He reminded the Session that there was no stipulation in the Charter compelling NOCs to compete, yet that refusal to do so was 'a failure to comply with the fundamental duty of each NOC . . . enabling their athletes to compete against world rivals . . . and that to do so segregated an NOC from other governing bodies'. There were stringent, but rejected, proposals from some: de Beaumont, for instance, proposing the withdrawal of recognition of boycotting countries for the next two Games. The only measure taken was that, in future, invitations to participate would be sent by the IOC rather than the local organising committee.

The Extraordinary Session, however, did little to lessen Samaranch's anxiety about a possible *fourth* consecutive boycott. 'He was now terrified about Seoul,' Richard Pound, long-standing Executive Board member, recalled. 'His first trip after LA was to go to Moscow to test the water and from then on he went to every annual meeting of socialist sports ministers.' Despite the success in LA, Samaranch knew that another serious boycott could again have the IOC fighting for survival. The Democratic People's Republic of (North) Korea presented a two-edged threat: incitement of their ideological allies to stay away and physical obstruction of the Games by clandestine terrorism. South Korea was politically precariously balanced, edging from a US-subsidised military state towards democracy, while living on a 24-hour knife-edge along the demilitarised-zone (DMZ) border with their northern neighbours. Samaranch's key ally in the run-in to Seoul over the coming four years would be Tae Woo Roh, the brains behind the Seoul bid in 1981 and subsequently State President, together with Un Yong Kim. 'Up to the time of the Games in LA, we had no contact with *any* of the Eastern Europeans,' Kim would recall. 'Afterwards, the socialists

Dr Un Yong Kim, the brains behind the Seoul Games and president of GAISF, became a central figure of the Olympic Movement over 20 years. (© IOC/Locatelli)

realised that their athletes had been put at a serious disadvantage and that nothing had been gained politically. Once we guaranteed security, they began to warm. North Korea had demanded a change of site immediately after the election in Baden-Baden, but Samaranch made it clear there would be no alteration.'

In November 1984, Yu Sun Kim, president of North Korea's NOC, informed Samaranch of his country's interest in continuing a debate with South Korea on 'joint-hosting', a concept wholly outside the realms of the Charter and the contracts signed between the IOC and the Seoul organising committee. Despite the fact that Samaranch and Un Yong Kim and his political colleagues in Seoul knew that any scope for joint hosting was out of the question on account of Pyongyang's own internal security policy regarding foreigners, and that Pyongyang's proposals were no more than a politically motivated charade, they agreed to go along with lengthy but empty political negotiation. Three initial meetings had been staged in April/May 1984, at the jointly defended border village of Panmunjom, and a subsequent series of meetings, almost operatic in their conduct, would be staged in Lausanne. Samaranch's principle was that by keeping the door open to the possibility – imagined but unreal – of sharing some events with the North, a perceived concession was being made to the Communist world that would ease the political conscience of the USSR, GDR and the rest, should they decide for expediency to compete in Seoul.

At the 1985 Session in East Berlin – a gesture by the IOC towards the GDR's affiliation – details began to emerge of the North Korean proposals that were to be debated at joint meetings of the two Koreas, staged in Lausanne over the next two years under the supervision of an IOC Commission led by Ashwini Kumar of India, IOC Vice-President, and including Alexandru Siperco, Berthold Beitz of Germany (third Vice-President), Sheikh Fahad of Kuwait (president of the Olympic Council of Asia), and Raymond Gafner, Swiss IOC member and interim administrator following the dismissal, in Berlin, of Monique Berlioux (of which more later).

The North would begin with a list of eight demands, which included joint hosting, a single national team, amalgamated title of 'Korea Olympic Games', joint guarantees to IFs under the Charter and – the most impossible of all – open exchange of travel for all accredited competitors, officials, journalists and tourists. The Wizard of Oz could not have improved on this. The IOC countered with a proposal of two Korean teams marching behind the Olympic flag; the route for marathon and cycling road races to pass through both territories; and preliminary rounds of team sports such as football to be played in the North. The interminable conference-speak would go on and on. Still assembled on the northern side of the DMZ was the largest permanent peacetime armoured force in the history of mankind, a garrison never out of the mind of political leaders in Seoul; especially with the discovery of underground tunnels beneath the border drilled by the North, and the potential damming of the Han River, which with the release of millions of tons of water could create havoc in the 70 miles between Seoul and the border.

Amid the negotiations, South Korea hosted the Asian Games of 1986, doing so with such style, in an already completed new Olympic stadium, that international confidence in this emerging industrial giant of the Far East was freshly enhanced. The prospect of industrial exposure and diplomatic liberalisation were foundation points in Seoul's original quest for the Games. Zhen-liang Hé of China reflected in the late 1980s:

The talks between the two Koreas gave both countries and all NOCs the chance to think more deeply about Olympic ideals. I think it became apparent that the Olympic Movement *can* bring people together, acting as a universal bridge. Although we in China had no relationship with South Korea, we felt obliged to contribute to the success of the Olympic Games and therefore before that to the Asian Games. Our participation in Seoul was an occasion to let our people know better the people of South Korea and vice-versa.

The level of anxiety rose during 1986–7 as bloody political demonstrations in South Korea, fiercely put down by the police, made headline news around the globe. Over-reaction in America, a country with some neurotically nervous civilians, reached a peak. In the *New York Daily News*, an emotive article from Howard Cosell, frontline sports columnist, stated:

> You read it here first . . . William Simon, former head of the United States Olympic committee, told you . . . this reporter told you . . . the Summer Olympics would never be held in Seoul . . . what does it take to make the IOC to respond to threats to the safety of its athletes? A limited nuclear engagement?

In the *New York Post*, Jerry Eisenburg wrote: 'When the time comes when they [the IOC] must comment, they will give you the same self-serving answer as always, "politics, or murder, or genocide, or war has nothing to do with us", and quote de Coubertin's words on the unity of mankind. There is one hell of a gap between that wish and the deed.' Certainly, the pictures of riots from Seoul and elsewhere were disturbing, but there was no doubt that expedient media use of intermittent scuffles gave an exaggerated slant on events.

Throughout the spring and early summer of 1987, North and South stuttered through meetings in Lausanne. Samaranch continued to play a patient tactical game, throwing a succession of lobs as in a five-set tennis doubles match that put the North on the back foot. They were offered women's volleyball, alongside table tennis and archery. Volleyball was the most attractive offer yet made. Slowly, Samaranch was killing them with generosity. An official IOC communiqué stated that both sides had been given until 17 September to accept the latest proposal, this being the date for official invitations to be sent to NOCs. Chin Chung Guk, vice-president of the North's NOC, remained aggressively unappeased, announcing that the proposals were less than the North's demands for eight sports; that the aim of Kim Il Sung, President of North Korea, continued to be an opening and closing ceremony in Pyongyang. Such attempted distortion of the contract for Seoul was out of the question. Samaranch, meanwhile, confirmed his intention to visit Seoul again that November, irrespective of any decision from the North by 17 September. It was his plan to meet the political opposition leaders together with Tae Woo Roh, the South's presidential candidate for the forthcoming election at the end of the year, as a contribution towards stability. Un Yong Kim said:

> There was an element amongst the political opposition to Roh [who was standing as democratic successor to military President Chun Doo Hwan] that supposed the IOC *ought* to have been supporting co-hosting, that the IOC had not been doing enough. Samaranch offered to meet the opposition leaders, Dae Jung Kim, Yung Sam Kim and Jong Pil Kim. After that meeting, they began to

Yu Sun Kim, IOC member from DPR Korea (right), a central figure at the centre of a two-host charade, finds time to smile alongside Samaranch and Chong Ha Kim (South Korea). (© IOC/Riethausen)

understand more about the IOC, about the Charter, and there was no more opposition.

Anxieties were further inflamed when, in November, a Korean Airline plane flying over Burma was destroyed by a bomb implanted by North Korean agents, killing all 115 passengers, while fresh threats emerged from Africa of possible action against the inclusion of tennis players in the Olympic tournament who had participated in the South African championships in Johannesburg. Yet by Christmas 1987, the issue with the North had all but ceased to be a problem.

Part of the vain incentive of North Korea to involve themselves was financial rather than political, so rapidly was the income rising from television and sponsorship. The US rights fee for Seoul had climbed from the $225 million that ABC had paid for Los Angeles to $300 million, painstakingly negotiated with NBC. The deal had been complex. NBC had lost $35 million on Moscow on account of the boycott, and were now doubtful if they could prise back the Summer Games from ABC. The rise for the Winter Games was even more spectacular, and with hindsight hugely out of proportion: from $91.5 million by ABC for Sarajevo to $309 million by ABC for Calgary. This was an undoubted sting by the IOC, negotiated by Richard Pound *before* the viewing figures for Sarajevo had become known. Both ABC and NBC bid $300 million, more than three times what ABC were paying for Sarajevo and indeed more than the figure for LA, but critically now again allied to North American prime time. Pound gave the two stations a quarter of an hour to come up with second sealed bids, in which NBC offered $304 million, and ABC $309 million. While ABC was left to lick its wounds from losses in Calgary, CBS would gain the rights for Albertville 1992 for only $243 million. Outside the United States, rights value was also substantially rising – from $19 million paid by the European Broadcasting Union for Los Angeles to $30 million for Seoul, though this was far too little, EBU protected by Samaranch.

These dealings had taken place under what was erroneously considered by the majority of television experts to be the controlling hand of Monique Berlioux, but Alex Gilady, American-Anglo-Israeli director in Europe for NBC, and their on-site adviser, knew, from close observation of Samaranch, who was really in charge.

Fifteen months after the bidding for Calgary in Sarajevo, negotiations took place for Seoul. The South Koreans, misunderstanding a comment from Barry Frank of Mark McCormack's International Management Group – he having said that Summer rights were usually two and a half times Winter rights – entertained thoughts of a fee in the region of $750 million, this being two and a half times Calgary's $309 million, but such a figure, on Asian time difference, would never have been feasible. Samaranch, conscious that the Calgary fee had 'gone over the top', was concerned that American television should be allowed a profit margin for Seoul. There were many days of anxious telephone calls between Lausanne and Tae Woo Roh, then president of the Seoul organising committee. The Koreans were reluctant to drop below $500 million, but the nervousness of ABC led to NBC gaining the contract at the relatively moderate sum of $300 million – less than ABC's price for Calgary, but of course outside American prime time. To appease the Koreans, NBC offered substantial bonuses in a profit-sharing deal should the market rise to take their revenue beyond $450 million. It never did. The market value in fact was shrinking. When it came to negotiating for 1992, CBS would initially propose that a joint deal should be made for Albertville and Barcelona but this was rejected by the IOC. CBS gained rights for Albertville for $243 million and NBC, with their rivals again getting cold feet, retained the Summer Games in Barcelona at $401 million. In the giddy world of US market values in television and advertising, these have been the fees over a 44-year period:

WINTER GAMES

		US Rights Fee	World Gross
1960	Squaw Valley, USA	CBS $50,000	N/A
1964	Innsbruck, Austria	ABC $597,000	$900,000
1968	Grenoble, France	ABC $2.5m	N/A
1972	Sapporo, Japan	NBC $6.4m	$8.5m
1976	Innsbruck, Austria	ABC $10m	$11.6m
1980	Lake Placid, USA	ABC $15.5m	$21m
1984	Sarajevo, Yugoslavia	ABC $91.5m	$103m
1988	Calgary, Canada	ABC $309m	$325m
1992	Albertville, France	CBS $243m	$292m
1994	Lillehammer, Norway	CBS $300m	$353m
1998	Nagano, Japan	CBS $375m	$513.5m
2002	Salt Lake City, USA	NBC $545m	$738m
2006	Turin, Italy	NBC $613m	$832m
2010	Vancouver, Canada	NBC $820m	N/A

SUMMER GAMES

1960	Rome, Italy	CBS $394,000	N/A
1964	Tokyo, Japan	NBC $1.5m	N/A
1968	Mexico City, Mexico	ABC $4.5m	N/A
1972	Munich, West Germany	ABC $7.5m	$17.8m
1976	Montreal, Canada	ABC $25m	$35m
1980	Moscow, Soviet Union	NBC $87m	$101m
1984	Los Angeles, USA	ABC $225m	$287m
1988	Seoul, South Korea	NBC $300m	$403m
1992	Barcelona, Spain	NBC $401m	$636m
1996	Atlanta, USA	NBC $456m	$892m
2000	Sydney, Australia	NBC $705m	$1,331m
2004	Athens, Greece	NBC $793m	$1,497.5m
2008	Beijing, China	NBC $894m	$1,714.7m
2012		NBC $1,181m	N/A

If Berlioux discerned that power was slipping from her grasp, especially on such matters as television fees, Samaranch's dissatisfaction with the administration was mounting. When

Walther Tröger of West Germany was appointed Sports Director, succeeding the deceased Arpad Csanadi of Hungary, he found that his work was being obstructed by Berlioux. He was one of those to whom Samaranch would talk confidentially in the gardens of Vidy. 'I soon found out,' Tröger recalled, 'that she was efficient and knowledgeable, but was a dictator.' There had been an initial attempt by the Executive Board to question her conduct in 1983, but Samaranch was reluctant to let the matter get in the way of political problems prior to LA and it was decided to tackle the matter at the Session of 1985 in Berlin. Tröger was deputed to raise the difficulties – similar to those experienced by previous sports directors including Artur Takac and Harry Banks – Berlioux believing that all decisions had to be approved by her. When Tröger and then Pound began to say that Berlioux's interference must cease, she lost her nerve, and said she felt unable to continue. She had been tactically backed into a corner. A formidable and cultured woman, a former Olympian, she had created around herself an illusory feeling of confident security, a belief in her own infallibility, a disregard of the fact that she was a paid employee whose influence had grown through the absence, due to their residence in Chicago and Dublin respectively, of successive presidents. She had laid her hand on every appointment, every contract. Letters by IOC members addressed to the President would be answered by her. Such was the severity of her handling of the administrative staff that there had been a turnover of 25 per cent every year. She had boasted to staff that, having been able to control Killanin, once she got Samaranch elected – unsuspectingly supporting his campaign – she would control him too. It was to prove her most serious misjudgement. To quote that ultimate of aristocrats, the Grand Duke of Luxembourg, 'She was a very difficult woman.' She resented Samaranch's increasing delegation of responsibility to other members, particularly the development of commercial

The resignation – or firing – of Director-General Monique Berlioux: (l–r) Berthold Beitz (FRG), Alexandru Siperco (ROM), Alain Coupat (chef de bureau), President Juan Antonio Samaranch, Francoise Garnier (staff), Monique Berlioux, Marie-Thérèse Pansart (staff), Ashwini Kumar (IND), Prince Alexandre de Mérode (BEL). (© IOC/Pi)

marketing by International Sport and Leisure (ISL) based in Lucerne.

Upon her enforced resignation, Berthold Beitz, Keba M'Baye and Prince de Mérode were assigned to arrange settlement terms, which included legal protection for the non-disclosure of IOC affairs: a firm brake on potential memoirs. Ashwini Kumar, Executive Board member since 1981 and Vice-President in 1985,

Samaranch and Horst Dassler sign the contract for TOP I under the watching eye of legal director Howard Stupp.
(© IOC/Riethausen)

recalled: 'There were times she was not even listening to Samaranch and I had said that if a paid employee would not listen to the boss, they must go, yet at that time she was defended by Siperco.' Comte Jean de Beaumont, retired senior IOC member, made the sentient observation: 'You couldn't have two crocodiles in the same pond, and Samaranch didn't want another one behind him.' Her departure was expensive: she was one of the highest paid sports administrators in the world, on a salary in today's terms well in excess of half a million dollars a year.

Changes at Vidy were rapid. Michèle Verdier was promoted to the post of Director of Information, Anne Beddow to Director of NOC Relations, Howard Stupp was appointed Director of Legal Affairs, Michael Payne from ISL as Marketing Director, Jacques Belgrand Director of Finance. Berlioux's role as Director-General was taken over by Raymond Gafner as interim delegate with Francoise Zweifel as Secretary-General, dealing with administrative logistics. From 1989, François Carrard, a Swiss attorney, became Director-General; effectively the chief executive role which Berlioux had assumed for herself, but now with daily reference to an in-house President. When Tröger was elected IOC member in 1989, Gilbert Felli became Sports Director. Pursuing the principle of expansion and delegation, Samaranch now had a harmonious team working together in open communication, with Jean François Pahud as Director of the Olympic Museum project and Anselmo Lopez in charge of the Solidarity Fund. The design of the administrative revolution was finalised that day in Berlin, yet this essential staff, which circumvents the reinvention of the wheel at every Olympic Games, remains largely unknown to the public.

At the Berlin Session, the contract with ISL for the first four years of TOP, the coordinated global sponsorship programme, was signed. Olympic marketing was not new. There had been advertising by Kodak in the official programme at the Inaugural Games of 1896 and the photographic giant would be one of the first to join the TOP initiative. With Ueberroth's structured marketing programme for LA, the first Games so successfully to generate a profit, there was an obvious pattern for Samaranch instantly to seize and improve. LA's programme had been short-term, ignoring the longer-term interests of the Olympic Movement. Sponsors were sold worldwide rights, only to

discover they could not use them without individual approval from the NOCs. In 1984, the IOC's revenue – as opposed to the host city's – was almost wholly derived from the sale of US television rights, creating a vulnerability in what could become a fluctuating market. Samaranch recognised that the Games must not become television dependent and created a New Sources of Finance Commission, initially under the chairmanship of Louis Guirandou-N'Daiye of the Ivory Coast and subsequently of Richard Pound of Canada, who also took over television negotiations. Within four years, 1984–8, thanks to the success of TOP I, the IOC would be able to build up reserves to $5 million, even though it took only 8 per cent of television from worldwide rights itself and 3 per cent from TOP. In the disposal of funds from within the Movement, from 1988 every NOC would receive from TOP alone a flat fee of $10,000 towards administration, plus $300 for every competitor attending Calgary or Seoul. One of the countries perversely refusing to join TOP I was Greece, though they entered thereafter.

There was anxiety about the stability of ISL following the death in 1987 of Horst Dassler, but its success was to continue unabated for a while. Under the direction of Samaranch and Pound, the commercialisation *volume* had been reduced, for there were fewer sponsors, paying substantially more for exclusivity. At the Winter Games of Lake Placid in 1980, there had been some 300 sponsors individually paying small amounts. For TOP I, nine multinational sponsors generated as much money as 35 sponsors did for LA. The Olympic Games remained, and remains, together with the Wimbledon Tennis Championships, the only major sporting event in the world excluding advertising in the stadium: the strongest argument in the defence of the IOC against the challenge of over-commercialisation.

The value to the IOC from sponsors is reciprocal, though the cost to elite sponsors runs into double-figure millions just for the privilege to buy-in. There is then the same cost again, or more, to promote public awareness of identity, the company's involvement with the Games. The exploitation by Visa was classic, American Express having woefully rejected the opportunity of joining TOP when initially invited. Visa's sales volume increased by an astonishing 18 per cent, way beyond the company's projected figure of 12 per cent. IMG, which raised profits of the All England Club at Wimbledon from $70,000 to in excess of $13 million over 20 years, viewed with envy the internal profits now being generated by the IOC in conjunction with ISL, embracing a contract with 159 NOCs worth $95 million for 1984–8 alone.

Another decision at the Berlin Session was the further raising of the retirement age for members from 72 to 75: the sole, if undeclared, purpose being to enable Samaranch to be elected again. Robert Helmick, former president of international swimming, was elected and a year later Anita DeFrantz, in each case preferred to Peter Ueberroth, whose intelligence would have been an asset within Samaranch's revolution. Ueberroth recognised the essential moral stance of the Games and there was an irony in the subsequent forced resignation of Helmick for a conflict of interest in commercial dealing. When Ueberroth was proposed at an Executive Board meeting, the negative view expressed to Samaranch by others was that he was 'too much of a shark'. There was support for DeFrantz, an African-American rowing bronze medal winner in the women's eights in 1976. Samaranch was privately equivocal about Ueberroth.

In 1985 the author accompanied Samaranch on one of his extended trips to visit the outer fringes of the Olympic

Movement: relatively anonymous NOCs and their altruistic officials who fly the flag on the edge of the map, yet whose presence at a Games, however minor, represents the universality that separates the Olympics from all other sporting events. In 11 days, mostly starting at 5.30 in the morning and finishing near midnight – often in circumstances of discomfort and with no personal advantage to Samaranch other than his expanded knowledge of the organisation for the success of which he was responsible – we visited 12 countries: Mauritania, Sierra Leone, Mali, Burkina Faso, Niger, Ghana, Benin, Equatorial Guinea, Chad, Central African Republic, Uganda, Djibouti. We encountered abject poverty among beautiful people, a desperate need for resources, a willingness among children to grasp the smallest sporting opportunity with the generic ambition that is common throughout mankind: whether it was boys wearing unlaced leather shoes in a boarded boxing ring in Chad, or the runners in a half-marathon amid a tropical thunderstorm in decaying Malabo, Fernando Po Island, in the elbow of Africa, left to rot by Spain during years of neglect. Two years later, a similar tour took us through the tiny islands of Micro- and Macro-Melanesia in the Pacific, following which Samaranch wrote in one of his letters to the members: 'Vanuatu, Western and American Samoa, Tonga and the Cook Islands represent no important powers, whether political, economic or sporting. They are nonetheless NOCs like any other . . . they do not merit less than the others, and frequently more, given their enthusiastic efforts to spread our ideals to the youth of their country.' The Cook Islands, with a total area of only 234 square miles, and a population of 15,000, make a larger private per capita contribution to keeping their competitors in the international arena than any country in the world.

In 1986, Samaranch was able to persuade the IOC to change the schedule of the Games, so that Summer and Winter Games would be held in alternate even years. He had been advised by Denis Swanson, head of sport for ABC, that worldwide TV/sponsorship budgets for sport would generate much more from splitting the Games. To adjust to this, there would be Winter Games in 1994, following the double Games of 1992, then succeeded by the Centenary Summer Games of 1996. Samaranch would say later:

> This was one of the best decisions of my presidency. Having two Games in the same year was not easy for some NOCs; finding sponsors for two teams, while negotiating TV rights in the same year was not easy for host cities. There was the impression of a Big Games and a Small Games. With the new move, the Winter Games became much more important. It was vital that we kept the personality of the Winter Games, with only sports on ice or snow.

The election was due in 1986 of the two host cities for 1992 and Samaranch was already becoming concerned at the amounts being spent by candidates and the public criticism of waste – conspicuously by his home city of Barcelona, with their lavish lunches at the mansion of the late Carlos Ferrer, opulent but discreet banker. Samaranch initiated a study on imposing limits on the spending by candidate cities for the hosting of Games in 1994 and 1996, in the light of excesses indulged in by 13 candidates in 1986: (Summer) Amsterdam, Barcelona, Belgrade, Birmingham, Brisbane, Paris; (Winter) Albertville, Anchorage, Berchtesgarten, Cortina, Falun, Lillehammer and Sofia. Already the entertainment of members, as they toured the world inspecting the profusion of offers, had become gross. At the

Session in Lausanne, during which the decisions were to be taken in 1986, the parties were more reminiscent of an impending coronation. A desirable but alarming offshoot of the commercial success of LA was that a formerly unwanted responsibility had now become a coveted luxury for numerous city councils around the world. The IOC was ensnared by its own success, the unprincipled greed of big cities, and the venality of a number of its members, the majority of them open to flattery but naively unthinking rather than wantonly corrupt. The fault, it has to be said, lay as much with the cities, over whom the IOC had no control, as with the members.

In 1986 the bandwagon was truly rolling. The question was whether Paris could counter the attraction of Barcelona, the President's home city. Public and media perception was that Samaranch, his authority now without challenge, had only to snap his fingers to ensure Barcelona's success. The reality was that he attempted, if ineffectually, to remain outside the debate, conscious that if Barcelona won, much of the responsibility for the success of the Games would be loaded onto him; that if they failed, he likewise would be criticised by his own people. Moreover, he was advised privately within the Executive Board that should Barcelona win in the first round, a hornet's nest of criticism would descend upon him for an apparent walkover. Organised tactical voting in the first round resulted in Barcelona's victory being delayed until the third round. The Paris bid, led by the amiable Alain Danet, rather too dramatically glossed over the city's then inadequate facilities, relying on its romantic, cultural reputation. What more could the world want than Paris? On the day, Jacques Chirac made an impassioned speech which nearly swayed the vote, but Barcelona, which had conducted an outstanding lobbying

Pasqual Maragall, socialist mayor of Barcelona, and Juan Antonio Samaranch sign the contract for 1992 following Barcelona's defeat of Paris. (©IOC/Locatelli)

campaign by bankers Leopoldo Rodes and IOC member Ferrer, were the winners by 47–23. For Barcelona, it had been the fourth bid over 60 years.

It was considered by many observers that, had the Winter vote not been taken first, at which the Albertville bid for the region of Savoie – eminently led by local politician Michel Barnier and famed skier Jean-Claude Killy – Paris might have defeated Barcelona. The members, however, were reluctant to vote twice for France in one day. In the event, Albertville, in the sixth round, had double the number of votes of Sofia, the

Bulgarian capital. In the Summer vote, Barcelona had a minority vote overall in the first round, though that was perhaps because of a 'loyalty' tactical vote for Belgrade, on the assumption they would not last till the later rounds. For the Winter, Sofia would have been innovative and preferable to the dispersed regional Games in France. The round by round voting results were:

SUMMER GAMES	I	II	III			
Amsterdam (Netherlands)	5	–	–			
Barcelona (Spain)	29	37	47			
Belgrade (Yugoslavia)	13	11	5			
Birmingham (UK)	8	8	–			
Brisbane (Australia)	11	9	10			
Paris (France)	19	20	23			

WINTER GAMES	I	II	III	IV	V	VI
Albertville (France)	19	26	29	42	–	51
Anchorage (USA)	7	5	–	–	–	–
Berchtesgarten (WG)	6	–	–	–	–	–
Cortina (Italy)	7	6	7	–	–	–
Falun (Sweden)	10	11	11	9	41	9
Lillehammer (Norway)	10	11	9	9	40	–
Sofia (Bulgaria)	25	25	28	24	–	25

The lavish parties given in Lausanne prior to the bidding by most of the cities were not just a waste of taxpayers' money that could have been better spent at home. 'The week was a signal to the IOC that the bidding process risked running out of control,' Kevan Gosper recalled in his autobiographical *An Olympic Life*. 'We'd gone from a period where we were lucky to have Los Angeles running as the only bidder, to having 13 cities vying to be host.' Samaranch was riding a train hurtling along without brakes or signals, though, as he reasoned, 'It is the system I inherited'. It would reach even more dangerous proportions four years later in a contest to host the Centenary Games of 1996. Worldwide public contempt of the system was rapidly mounting.

Much of the public, especially the older generation entrenched in the Olympic concept of true-blue amateurism, and indeed many within the Olympic Movement, were equally sceptical about the growing shift towards professionalism. Yet reality had to be confronted. It was a nonsense that totalitarian states could marshal their teams within a blatantly professional regime, but not the Western or capitalist countries. In 1986, the IAAF had lowered the last barrier by declaring that professionals in sports other than its own were eligible for its competitions, and at Lausanne that year the IOC persuaded IFs to have more sensible rules, specifically regarding track and field events: thereby effectively opening the door to professionals in other sports, whatever they were earning. The previous year, Willi Daume had delivered a key speech at the Session in Berlin, impressing upon the members that the IOC's regulations currently denied justice and equality:

> It has been demanded that the IOC should be exclusively responsible for compiling mandatory eligibility rules for all disciplines in sport. Such demands simply spell intolerance and would mean the end of the Olympic Games. We could never organise the Games against the wishes of the international federations . . . only by this way [adaptation] can we counteract the influence of international agencies and the way in which they make our competitors [financially] dependent. Current conditions are

potentially catastrophic. The Eligibility Rules must be enforceable worldwide. The commercial danger of the Olympics is not whether they are receiving $10 or $50,000 in their normal sporting career. The danger is losing the independence of the IFs to television, promoters and agents.

The IOC thus moved towards the most revolutionary of all its meetings, the Session at Istanbul in 1987, at which it was determined to re-introduce tennis as a full sport, including its millionaire performers. In a four-hour debate that spilled into the afternoon, there were more than 30 speakers. Typically, Samaranch hardly spoke at all. He knew the mood had to come from the floor. Daume, a basketball reserve in the Berlin Olympics, paid tribute to the President who was necessarily transforming the Games. 'An heir to de Coubertin's legacy, Samaranch recognised that the IOC could not afford to abide rigorously by traditions,' Daume said.

> A number of older members were unhappy with this policy, but it was the only way ahead . . . There was no such thing as equal opportunity any longer, except through lies and deception . . . the intention was not to create differing social statuses within existing social orders and ideologies, but to make it possible for the best competitors in the world to take part in the Games . . . In promoting this, Samaranch showed farsightedness.

An influential speaker at Istanbul was Anita DeFrantz, bronze medal oarswoman who appealed to fellow members in the name of competitors aspiring to the highest attainable level in sport; saying that in many sports it was necessary to become a professional to reach the top.

If tennis was the lever that ultimately broke the lock, it was Philippe Chatrier, president of international tennis, who had doggedly trailed Samaranch to convince him of the legitimacy of the re-admission of tennis after 64 years. That the IOC was in tune with the outside world was evident when, at the opening ceremony at Seoul the following year, the Argentine flag was carried by tennis star Gabriella Sabatini. Chatrier had himself been convinced of the need back in 1973, during a Davis Cup tie in Moscow. Did he not realise, Soviet officials asked, that 80 per cent of governments would give no grant to a sport that was not in the Olympic Games?

The tide of change in the Olympic Movement was further evident as countries gathered in Calgary for the Winter Games. Most significant was the influence of the Olympic ethic on the Communist world, which had scorned Los Angeles but was now bracing itself to forego ideological principles and send its teams to Seoul in the summer. Marat Gramov, the Soviet sports minister, a definitive government aparatchik, now found himself having to ride two horses, a foot on each saddle: one political, one sporting. Was the Soviet Union happy with the new state of eligibility? 'Our competitors receive compensation for their participation which does not contradict the Olympic Charter. However, we firmly follow the principle that while involved in sport they should receive some professional qualification.' Did standards decline following the absence from LA? 'There is no doubt that non-participation was reflected in domestic results.' How important was it that the majority of IOC nations intended to be in Seoul? 'There should be as many nations as possible, the Olympic philosophy is to promote cooperation. Now is the time when all countries, irrespective of social systems, believe it is better to find ways of closer understanding. I can tell you firmly that we shall participate.' The era of boycotts was about to be broken. The reason for this was partially the attraction of sharing in the commercial gravy train, yet far more important than that was the irresistible appeal of the Olympic ideal, of being there. There were no medals for absentees.

The main problems of the Games in Calgary, 'Oil City', were not, however, political but meteorological, compounded by the city's wilful insistence on staging some events in the wrong place, contrary to their accepted bid plan. Some $300 million had been invested in preparations. An elaborate campaign had mobilised the population into a gung-ho mood, both sporting and cultural, in this former outpost of the North-West Mounted Police and stopping point on the Canadian Pacific Railway; home, too, of the renowned Calgary Stampede, a rodeo festival. Those calling the tune were Frank King, CEO of the organising committee; Bill Pratt, former manager of the Stampede and organising president; Ralph Klein, egocentric mayor; and the energetic Roger Jackson, president of the Canadian NOC and dean of the PE faculty at the University of Calgary. Determined to avoid the pitfalls of Montreal 12 years earlier, Calgary mobilised its workforce, its funding and volunteers to such a degree that all was ready way in advance. Only the weather was non-collaborative, and that was all too predictable. It had long been said in Calgary that if you do not like the weather, wait five minutes. The renowned Chinook wind could, and did, cause temperature shifts in barely an hour through 30ºC. You never knew whether to wear a polar overcoat or a T-shirt. The luge and bob-run tended to melt, the Mt Allan complex at Nakiska Alpine range required artificial snow machines and additionally was inconveniently windswept, as was the municipally sited ski jump, gravel dust threatening to make this and the bob-run inoperable. Unrivalled, on the other hand, was the Saddledome, a splendid indoor arena for figure skating and ice hockey. The Calgary Games were an unequivocal success, and even if some regretted the money-making expansion over three weekends to further enhance revenue, Canada was happy. The IOC was comforted by a profit of $150 million and a record attendance of 57 countries.

In December 1985, the UN General Assembly had adopted the 'International Convention Against Apartheid in Sport', which was intended to prohibit entry into signatory countries of competitors who had participated in South Africa and those who had acted as hosts to South African teams. Many declined to sign the Convention, including Canada, France, Ireland, Britain and the US. When, in the spring of 1988, there was an indication that Britain might include Zola Budd in their track team – Budd having spent much of the time since 1984 returning to live in her native South Africa and being involved in the promotion of 'illegal races' – the possibility of boycott re-emerged. It was now that Samaranch played an important card, staging in Lausanne a meeting of African sports officials, specifically for the purpose of confirming the IOC's solidarity on anti-apartheid policy in sport. Following this meeting he created the Apartheid and Olympism Commission, mandated to reinforce the anti-apartheid policy. Thus was Black Africa convinced of the IOC's goodwill, the threat of any boycott reduced, and significant steps laid towards South Africa's re-admission within the next three years.

Major-General Henry Adefope of Nigeria, elected IOC member in 1985, with a medical degree from Glasgow University followed by practice as an army doctor before becoming Minister of Foreign Affairs, was a moderate radical.

'The conference in Lausanne was a watershed,' he recollected. 'Everyone who mattered from African sport was there, including the president of the Supreme Council and nine African IOC members. It established that a boycott was not the solution to the problem.' Two years earlier, at the Commonwealth Games of 1986 in Edinburgh, Black Africa had stayed away on account of Prime Minister Thatcher's refusal to impose stricter trade sanctions on South Africa. In the summer of 1988, Budd lost her nerve and returned to the country from which morally she had never departed.

In March 1988, Prince de Mérode, chairman of the Medical Commission, outlined tougher penalties recommended for drug offences – 1: two years' suspension for a first offence, life-time suspension for a second offence (for use of anabolic steroids, stimulants or sedatives of the central nervous system); 2: three months for a first offence, two years for a second; life-time for a third (for use of prohibited substances such as narcotics and amphetamines).

The Medical Commission was alarmed by evidence of a new drug, erythropoietin (EPO), normally used to resist kidney failure but exploited in endurance sports such as cross-country skiing to replace or simplify blood-doping. All detectable traces would disappear within 48 hours of injection. At Calgary, Marty Hall, Canada's cross-country coach, obliquely accused Soviet women cross-country skiers of blood-doping. 'Sport in the world is right now in trouble – and not just in the Olympics,' Hall declared. Indeed, not only was the art of detection lagging behind the biochemical art of cheating but variable attitudes towards discipline were also undermining those who remained honest. The IAAF's reinstatement, for instance, of Martti Vainio of Finland, found positive in LA but allowed to compete in the European Championships of 1986, offended many. In 1987, Sandra Gasser (SUI) was banned for two years by the IAAF for a failed test at the World Championships in Rome, but the IAAF's own system was in a mess, erratic from country to country.

All paled, however, in the face of what happened in Seoul: the failed test of the 100m champion, Ben Johnson of Canada. Not that Johnson was the first in 'dirty' Seoul. Persistent infringements in weightlifting over the previous ten days had already reached the point where there was justification for banning the sport in the future, in the way the Bulgarians had already withdrawn their current team following two positive tests on gold medal winners. The evidence regarding Johnson was particularly significant, for it revealed a sustained period of use of the steroid Stanozolol. Richard Pound, Canadian IOC member, as a lawyer was minded initially to defend Johnson but was warned by Samaranch, during an emergency Executive Board meeting at the time of the initial disclosure by de Mérode of the positive test, to be careful. Pound retrospectively explains: 'I had no alternative, there was no other lawyer around and you should not allow an athlete to be undefended. There was no question of not providing a defence, even if there wasn't much of a defence to offer. I'd do the same again.' The Executive Board was unanimous that suspension must be instantaneous (how could they be otherwise?).

Johnson, whisked out of Seoul by his NOC in the early hours of the morning, lamely protested that a drink could have been 'spiked'. Samaranch, having told the Session prior to the Games that 'doping is death', attempting now to profit from disaster, stated to the world's press: 'The suspension shows the IOC is very serious, that we are winning the battle for a clean Games. I am sorry for Johnson, who is a great athlete, for he is not the only person we have to blame.' More guilty than this Jamaican

Charlie Francis, coach of disgraced Ben Johnson, disqualified sprint champion, admitted to systematic use of steroids among his charges. (© Getty Images)

emigrant of limited intelligence, who had come third in LA, were his coach, Charlie Francis, and doctor, Jamie Astaphan. Francis would later confess that 13 of the male and female athletes he coached had taken steroids.

These Games hung heavy with suspicion of Florence Griffith Joyner, American double sprint champion, never found positive but so conspicuously muscular that her innocence was questioned merely by appearance. Few bothered at the time when Dr Robert Dougal, a Canadian who was a member of a sub-committee of the Medical Commission, revealed that a side-effect of Stanozolol included cancer of the liver. Who cared? Cancer of the Olympics was the theme of the moment. The repercussions were inestimable. Child competitors throughout America began clamouring for Stanozolol. And why not? Johnson was currently driving a $150,000 Ferrari and had been calculated, as champion, to earn $8 million over the next four years. Never had love of money been more the root of evil.

Whatever Samaranch might wish, because of the chemical and procedural limitations of testing, the IOC was losing this particular battle. As Gosper admitted: 'We in the IOC tended to take refuge in arguing that it was the role of the IFs to do more [testing] themselves. I had been surprised that there was so little discussion about the problem on the Executive Board.' Johnson continued for months to protest his innocence, finally admitting under cross-examination his deep involvement in defrauding his sport – and the millions in Canada who had emotionally celebrated his victory over the American foe – during a lengthy enquiry in Toronto chaired by Judge Charles Dubin. At a legal symposium in 1990, Robert Armstrong, QC, counsel to the Dubin enquiry, criticised both IOC and IAAF, alleging lack of reaction to available evidence prior to the Johnson incident. US coaches testified that many competitors on US teams had been on prescribed steroids in 1984.

If Johnson presented the Games, and the IOC, with a nightmare scenario for the future, the celebration of de Coubertin's ideal was otherwise a monumental success: the largest Games in history, in size, technology and publicity, with unparalleled facilities, untold Asian courtesy provoking a mood of universal harmony. As in Calgary, there was a Summer record number of nations: 159. Albania, Cuba and Ethiopia joined North Korea in staying away, and what they missed was a festival that de Coubertin and his colleagues could never have imagined possible. At the closing ceremony, Arabs and Israelis walked around the track side-by-side.

If the South Koreans owed a debt to the IOC for sustaining their opportunity to be hosts to the world in the face of initial Communist scepticism and enduring hostility north of the 38th parallel, they had given, in return, the organisation of the Germans, the manners of the Orient and the financial acumen of the Americans. For a country razed to the ground by civil war 30 years earlier, the accomplishment was sensational. Cultural, economic and political relations with China and Japan – the latter having occupied Korea until 1945 – were re-established, as they were with much of the rest of the world. Within months, for example, a commercial bureau was opened with Hungary and there would soon be a summit meeting in San Francisco between Presidents Gorbachev and Roh. The Games had brought South Korea the invaluable gift of status.

When awarded the Games in 1981, South Korea had no colour television. Seven years later it had become one of the world's ten largest television trading countries. For all their generosity to many competing visitors, they made a profit of half a billion dollars. The torch at the opening ceremony had been carried on to the track by 76-year-old Kee-Chung Sohn, the 1936 marathon champion then obliged to run, during Japanese occupation, as Kitei Son. South Korea could indeed hold its head high for many reasons.

CHAPTER LVII

Calgary (XV) 1988

Vreni Schneider of Switzerland, double Olympic Alpine champion

'*Calgary was my first Olympic Games. I had qualified for an extremely strong Swiss women's team and therefore the mere fact that I was able to participate was itself a major success for me. We lived in Nakiska, very close to Mt Allan where the races were to take place. I felt in better condition day by day, and in the combination downhill section I came in eighth, among the specialists. Unfortunately, I threw away the chance of a medal because I stupidly caught a ski in a gate pole in the slalom section and fell. But my experience during the World Championships at Crans Montana the previous year had taught me to cope with such mishaps and I was able to concentrate fully on the next race, the giant slalom.*

I can still remember every detail. Nervousness woke me at five o'clock and soon I was up and jogging through the forest. Then, after all the preparation of skis and so on, I stood ready at the starting gate, still nervous and tense. On a very hard piste I was only fifth on the first run, but now my nerves were eased. The huge crowd of spectators, wonderful weather and the superb track gave me inspiration. I had a fantastic second run and experienced a flood of emotions because Bianca Fernández-Ochoa, the fastest on the first run, unluckily fell and dropped out, so my dream of a gold medal came true. I could hardly grasp at that moment what this success really meant. I remember vividly the victory ceremony, standing there on the pedestal with wobbly knees in front of a 50,000-strong cheering crowd. Then it was back to Nakiska and the normal training routine, as the slalom was still ahead of us.

Victory in the giant slalom made me feel much more confident for the next race and I was able to make the best time on the first run. Following this, I risked everything on the second, in which I could start as the last racer, and again at the bottom "No. 1" flashed on the scoreboard.

I felt so happy to be a double Olympic champion and was consumed with thoughts of my family. There was sadness that my deceased mother was not there to witness the achievement and I also felt grateful to all those who had helped me to get there. Olympic success enabled me to have a strong inner-confidence. Otherwise, I don't think I changed as a person, though I wanted to train really hard again to confirm as soon as possible that my gold medals were deserved.'*

(Photograph © IOC/Jenny)

Prove it she did. In the following season, Vreni Schneider won a record 14 World Cup races, including all seven slalom, and by 1993 had amassed 41 career victories, the fourth highest-ever total. The favourites for the combined in Calgary – the event had not been staged from between 1952 and 1984 – were Schneider's colleagues Brigitte Oertli and Maria Walliser. Unexpectedly, Anita Wachter of Austria finished as high as third in the downhill section and though Oertli made up ground on the two slalom runs, Wachter, second on the slalom, narrowly held on to her lead.

In the giant slalom, Fernández-Ochoa led on the first run from Christa Kinshofer-Güthlein of Germany, Wachter, and Christine Meier of West Germany, with Schneider in fifth place. Schneider's response was a devastating second run to scatter what remained of the field, only 29 of the 64 starters completing both runs, the steep upper section seeing competitors tumble wholesale. Improving between first run and second was characteristic of Schneider's competitive streak. The event also saw the first black skier to take part in a Games, Seba Johnson of

the Virgin Islands, who was also the youngest competitor at Calgary, aged 14, and finished 28th.

The weather was glorious for the slalom and Schneider skied with matchless style. On the first run Camilla Nilsson of Sweden was close behind her, but fell on the second. Schneider thus joined Hanni Wenzel (1980), Rosi Mittermaier (1976) and Marie-Thérèse Nadig (1972) as double gold medal winner. Mateja Svet maintained Yugoslavia's fine reputation in slalom, taking the silver medal ahead of Kinshofer-Güthlein by three-hundredths of a second.

Marina Kiehl was a German from Munich, daughter of a millionaire with a reputation for being blunt to one and all. When persuaded to show a more agreeable face by her sponsors, her results had declined. Though born with a silver spoon in her mouth, gold had evaded her on the track, as prior to Calgary she had never won a downhill and even her place in the team was unsure. Yet in a helter-skelter performance, all but out of control most of the way down, she now took the title at Nakiska, on a day when gusting winds four times caused the racing briefly to

Vreni Schneider (SUI) scattered the field in slalom and giant slalom. (© Getty Images/Cannon)

Pirmin Zurbriggen (SUI), modest, God-fearing master-skier, fell fractionally short of all-round expectation following triumph in the downhill. (© IOC/Maeder)

be halted. Kiehl finished almost a second in front of Oertli, who took the silver one-hundredth of a second ahead of Canadian Karen Percy. Kiehl had been told by her sorely tried administration that if she finished in the top six of the downhill she could compete in the other speed-event, the super-G, previously never staged. This she did, finishing 12th, victory going to Sigrid Wolf of Austria, ahead of Michela Figini (SUI) and Percy.

The men's downhill course had been designed by the famed Bernhard Russi – beaten by Franz Klammer in 1976 – together with Ken Read of Canada, a former 'Crazy Canuck', who had tested every metre of the course a hundred times. Before the race, the legendary Klammer gave it his critical judgement after making a run. 'Whoever wins is going to have to take risks,' he forecast. 'Yet misjudge one gate at the top and you will lose, because you cannot make it up later. The top of the course may not be as fast as Kitzbühl, but it is much tighter in the turns.' In Ram Alley, near to the top where the snow was foot-packed because no snow-cat could venture there, the pitch was 59 degrees. 'I think it's skiable – just,' said Martin Bell of Britain, who was to distinguish himself by coming eighth, Britain's highest-ever placing.

Thus the scene was set for one of the most testing races, following a day's postponement because of 160 kph winds. Peter Müller of Switzerland was the reigning world champion and his 19 downhill victories ranked him second only behind Klammer. He had taken the silver medal four years earlier. He was as extrovert as Pirmin Zurbriggen, his demure compatriot rival, was shy and understated. Zurbriggen had been world champion in 1985 and was a supremely talented all-round skier, having additionally won the combination in 1985, the giant slalom and super-G in the 1987 World Championships, and being the overall World Cup winner in 1984 and 1987 (subsequently also in 1988 and 1990). He was one of only three men to be World Cup champion at three individual disciplines.

Now Müller was drawn to start No. 1; Zurbriggen No. 14. He had never won a race from No. 1 in his 11-year career. Helicopters blew away loose overnight snow, and there was no better skier on new snow than Müller. His opening time of 2:00.14 was to prove the benchmark: no one subsequently came within a second of it. Until Zurbriggen. Like Klammer 12 years earlier, Zurbriggen had to wait until all his chief rivals had skied. Müller had been near-perfect through the demanding upper section, head and shoulders thrust forward, never a flicker of caution in his frame. On the first third of the course he was a

whole second faster than in his best training run. Yet as Zurbriggen hurtled down the precipice, his line was perfect, with that same marvellous rhythm to his turns that had distinguished Klammer, so that he seemed to accelerate out of the bends. It was a beautiful sight as snowflakes swirled across the mountain side: this orange-clad figure flashing through the pines, heading for destiny. And when he found it, turning to glance at the clicking scoreboard lights as he made an arc in the finishing apron, he was entitled to throw up his skis in delight. He had beaten his great rival by half a second. A religious man, he closed his eyes and cast back his head in gratitude. 'I thanked God that I had won,' he said, 'I couldn't quite understand why it had happened to me.'

There was talk that Zurbriggen might win three races, such was his mastery, to emulate Killy and Sailer, but this was not to be, though for a while in the combined it seemed it might at least be two. He had the fastest run on the downhill section and led by over two seconds after the first run of the slalom, only for fate to strike on the second. He caught a ski tip on the 39th gate, ploughed into the 40th, and was gone. A close friend, Hubert Strolz of Austria, with the best combined time on the slalom runs, was the victor – a welcome end to a losing Austrian sequence in major events.

A cloud had passed over Zurbriggen's sun, for he was to finish fifth in the super-G. Franck Piccard from Albertville – to be hosts of the next Olympic Games – had never previously won a World Cup race, though he had been third behind Zurbriggen in the downhill six days earlier. With the super-G favourites all falling below form, Piccard now claimed France's first Alpine gold medal for 20 years, finishing more than a second faster than Helmut Mayer of Austria.

Zurbriggen did manage to gain bronze in the giant slalom, but was somewhat lost in the shadow of that emerging extrovert, Alberto Tomba from Bologna. The fact that Tomba confined himself to slalom and giant slalom had made it difficult for him to win the overall World Cup title, though he was second in 1988 and 1992. What most distinguished him, however, besides his flamboyant skiing, was his sunny generosity at all times. He never had a bad word to say about anybody and made slightly mocking self-appraisals. 'I was so happy, I had to congratulate myself,' he said after one victory.

There were those who disliked his effusiveness, yet he considered his carefree nature to be basic to his success. Certainly he had never known hardship, brought up in a sixteenth-century family home with landscaped gardens and fountains. Following his triumphs in Calgary, his father would buy him a Ferrari. Prior to the Games, he had won nine of his eighteen races, thanks in part to the wisdom of his coach, former champion Gustavo Thöni, who observed: 'Often I close my eyes when he is undisciplined, yet he succeeds in transmitting his dynamite to his skis.'

On the first run of the giant slalom he destroyed the opposition, being over a second faster than Strolz in second place. A pall was cast over the event between runs when Jörg Oberhammer, the Austrian team's orthopaedic surgeon, fell beneath a course-laying tractor and was killed instantly, witnessed overhead by Zurbriggen in the chair-lift on the way to the start. Martin Hangl, his Swiss colleague, also in the lift, was too overcome to compete.

Carefree Italian superstar Alberto Tomba, a Ferrari on the slopes, with double slalom victory at Calgary. (© IOC/Maeder)

On the second run, Strolz marginally but insufficiently closed on Tomba, whose subsequent victory in the slalom was as stylish but less emphatic. On his first run he took care to avoid error, the leader being world champion Frank Wörndl of Germany, Tomba lying third. Ingemar Stenmark revived his reputation with the fastest second run, though eleventh place on the first restricted him to a final fifth position. Tomba, meanwhile, blasted his way to victory six-hundredths of a second faster than Wörndl overall, the German undermined by misjudging a gate midway.

Confronted by Brian Boitano's majestic free programme in the men's figure skating, the judges seemed not to have noticed: they gave him the gold medal by only the tiniest of margins. A 20,000-strong audience in the imposing Saddledome, at a fever pitch of expectation for Canada's first gold medal from Brian Orser, was left in limp disbelief. They, more understandably, had failed fully to appreciate the sophistication of the United States' first winner at these Games.

Here in competition were three world champions: Alex Fadeyev of the Soviet Union (1985), Boitano (1986) and Orser (1987). Orser had taken the Olympic silver medal behind Scott Hamilton four years earlier. Yet while Orser had come out to skate, a shade histrionically, for the gallery and for a gold medal, Boitano, with unprecedented poise, had skated for himself and for posterity. 'It didn't matter to me whether it was gold, silver or bronze,' he said, uniquely. 'I came to give a performance, the best of my life if possible. I did, and for me, that was it.' For Orser, the medal had mattered so much more than the performance, and therein lay his undoing. The result was in keeping with his reputation: second in 1984, second in three consecutive World Championships, 1984–6. Early in his routine, Orser faulted on a jump, and later downgraded a triple to a double. To the author's unspecialised eye, the difference was as apparent and equally subtle as between silk and satin. Orser, under intense nationalistic expectation, had consulted a psychologist, but to no avail. He had led on the short programme but the free programme saw four judges vote for Orser, three for Boitano and two a tie. The latter two placed Boitano first on technical merit, and this gave him his marginal victory, though morally there was a gulf. 'He was too sophisticated for the judges,' said Sandra Bezic, Boitano's Canadian-Yugoslav choreographer.

Such was now the charismatic appeal of Katarina Witt that she drew the size of pre-competition press conference associated with Sebastian Coe and Carl Lewis. Hundreds were there to hear her say, unaffectedly: 'Every man prefers looking at a well-built woman to someone the shape of a rubber ball. This sport promotes what is feminine. It is possible to be more womanly than in other sports. We can communicate something. And give happiness, and do this better as a woman.' Witt, with the doe-like eyes of Audrey Hepburn, a sensuous mouth and a dazzling smile, intended to make the most of her film-star figure, though there was some resentment that the 20-year-old East German, three-time world champion and now defending her Olympic title, exploited her sexual appeal with the judges. She was an incorrigible flirt once she stepped onto the ice and had been taught by Jutta Müller, her coach, to select beforehand a male face in the audience and to play to him. Witt defended the arbitrary standards of subjective judging. 'We have to try to offer something that is acceptable for the majority,' she said. 'I enjoy the emphasis on artistry and costumes. The dress should enhance the music. When I wear the right costume, I feel much better. Why not?'

She was intent now on achieving a more emotional interpretation of Bizet's *Carmen* to which both she and her main rival, Debra Thomas of America, were to skate their free programme. Thomas had defeated Witt for the world title in 1986, Witt regaining it the next year. They were not exactly friends. 'She dies, I don't,' Thomas said pointedly of their respective interpretations. Witt countered: 'You can skate – or interpret.' Witt cared little for the opening compulsory figures, finishing third on this section behind Kira Ivanova (URS) and Thomas. On the short programme Thomas took the lead, but only fractionally ahead of Witt. In the free programme, Witt's restrained technique, never mind her supreme artistic presentation, left the possibility for her to be surpassed by either Thomas or the diminutive Elizabeth Manley of Canada. Manley rose to the occasion with a performance that, in part due to Thomas's capitulation, earned her the silver medal. Making an early mistake, Thomas, whose five triple jumps if successful could not fail to give her the title, lost confidence, missed further jumps and once needed to maintain balance with a hand on the ice. Thus Witt triumphantly became the first since Henie to retain her title. Thomas, the first black athlete to win a Winter medal – bronze – sank into the arms of her unreproachful coach, Alex McGowan. 'I am sorry, I am sorry,' she repeated, like a child to a parent.

Matti Nykänen predictably made Olympic history by becoming the first ski jumping double gold medal winner. He had won eight of the eleven preceding World Cup events that

Matti Nykänen (FIN) makes history as the first ski jumping double gold winner, predictable given his classic dominance. (© DPA)

earlier, learned on the morning of the final that his sister Jane, weak with leukaemia, was about to die. They communicated by phone and though she could not respond she indicated that she wished him to compete. Before the final that afternoon, Jane's race had ended. Unsurprisingly, her brother fell at the first turn and did so again in the 1,000m four days later, the races being respectively won by Uwe-Jens Mey (GDR), in a world record of 36.45, and Nikolai Gulyayev (URS) in an Olympic record of 1:13.03. Gulyayev had been cleared to compete after allegations that he had been trafficking in steroids with a Norwegian skater proved inconclusive. He and 21 others surpassed the Olympic record of Eric Heiden.

The Soviet Union overtook Canada with its seventh title in ice hockey, the host nation and the United States failing to gain a medal. The Soviets defeated Canada 5–0 and were sure of the gold before their final match against Finland, who stole some of their thunder with a 2–1 victory thanks largely to the goalkeeping of Jukka Tammi. For Finland it was a silver and first medal in hockey, with Sweden taking the bronze.

season. Now 24, he had been world champion at the age of 18 and was defending his 90m title from Sarajevo. He far outclassed all rivals on the 70m hill, finishing ahead of two Czechoslovaks, Pavel Ploc and Jiri Malec. In last place was the myopic Michael Edwards of Britain, sardonically christened 'Eddie the Eagle' for the consistent brevity of his time in the air. His shallow media celebrity was privately resented by superior though unacclaimed members of the British team and was cause for reconsideration of entry qualifications by the IOC.

Competition on the large hill was postponed repeatedly because of dangerous cross-winds but Nykänen supremely defended his crown, which, with victory by Finland in the team event on the large hill, gave him his third gold of the Games. With the onset of fatherhood, he had become less irascible than in former times. His winning jump in the individual large hill competition was the longest in the history of the Games, 118.5m. His 17-point margin on the normal hill was unprecedented in Olympic competition.

A Nordic combined team event (jumping/cross-country relay) was inaugurated at Calgary, the winners being West Germany: Hans-Peter Pohl, Hubert Schwarz and Thomas Müller. Soviet women dominated the four women's Nordic events, taking seven of the nine individual medals and additionally the relay. The 35-year-old Raisa Smetanina, gaining a silver and bronze, raised her total from four Games to a record nine medals.

So innovative was the technology of Calgary's new indoor speed skating arena that the Olympic record was surpassed 16 times in the men's 10km. The world record was broken by the winner, Tomas Gustafson of Sweden, who earlier had successfully defended his 5,000m title. The longer speed skating races are essentially an 'insiders'' occasion for spectators, undramatic despite the speed at which they are going, which is twice as fast as track runners. Only the shorter sprint events, 500m and 1,000m, give a sense of real urgency. In the men's 500m, Dan Jansen from Wisconsin, who had won the world title a week

Despite wind-blown grit on the run, the Swiss No. 1 bobsleigh team take the four-man title. (© DPA)

CHAPTER LVIII

Seoul (XXIV) 1988

Paul Elvstrøm of Denmark, champion Olympic sailor at four successive Games, 1948–60

'*For me, the Olympic Games have always had the highest priority of all the championships in which I have sailed since my first gold medal in 1948. All other regattas were almost practising for the Games and the results were less important. When I was young, gold, silver and bronze medals were only given at the Olympic Games; now medals are awarded at almost any event, which is wrong. It should be at the Olympic Games alone that they can be won. I hope this might be changed one day. To win an Olympic medal is the highest achievement any athlete can attain in sport.*

I had been racing since I was nine. Where I lived was close to the sea, the water was my home. When I was young, I found tactics easy, though it was only as I became older that I really began to understand what I was doing. In 1948, when I was 20 and competing in the Firefly class, I regarded the Games as normal racing, simply because I loved sailing. I was fifth or sixth before the last two races, but was able to win both. The realisation of what it meant to win came later. I began to hear that some people thought I had been lucky and I wanted to prove otherwise. Because I was young and little known, there was resentment, and that was why in 1952 I was defending my reputation. In the event, I was able to do so easily. Subsequently, I became more and more nervous about winning, having the feeling that I had to be perfect, to make no mistakes. Other racing became less important because of this.

Sailing with my daughter Trine was a source of real satisfaction. I would not have come back from retirement without her, going to Los Angeles and then Seoul. Initially, we were not on the Olympic team because the Danish federation did not think we were that good, but we won the European title in the Tornado class in 1983 to prove our point. I was a little sad in Los Angeles that Trine missed a bronze medal, when we finished fourth by less than a point. We would have done it with one place better in one race.

Yacht racing is not a great spectator sport, and it does not get much attention from the press, though events in the Olympic Games are an exception. Winning four gold medals was, therefore, the best way that I have been able to find to promote the sport of dinghy sailing and especially my country Denmark.'*

(Elvstrøm (centre), photograph © IOC/Sturny)

Paul Elvstrøm, born in 1928 in Copenhagen, epitomised sportsmanship at elite level. He won the Firefly/Finn Class four times in successive Games at London/Torbay, Helsinki, Melbourne and Rome/Naples, then competing at Mexico/Acapulco (1968), Munich/Kiel (1972), LA/Long Beach (1984) and Seoul/Pusan (1988), becoming one of only four men to have taken part in eight Games, and also one of four to have competed over a 40-year span. He was a reserve in 1964. When Trine, his daughter, crewed for him in the Tornado class at LA, it was the first time that father and daughter had competed together in a Games. He won thirteen world titles in seven different classes. So successful was the sail manufacturing company which he founded, gaining a global reputation, that the Eligibility Commission, driven by a fanatical Avery Brundage, pedantically scrutinised his entry for Munich/Kiel.

The original accusation that he was 'lucky' arose from his last race at Torbay in 1948. Elvstrøm had failed to finish the first race, but after five races there were three in contention for gold:

Ralph Evans (USA), Paul McLoughlan (CAN) and Richard Sarby (SWE). Elvstrøm was lying eighth but in the sixth race won by a distance to move into third place. Evans needed to finish only third in the final race, but in very strong winds he came fifth, Sarby capsized, Jacobus de Jong (NED) nearly did so, and another first place for Elvstrøm brought him the narrowest victory margin of his four titles.

With Trine at Long Beach in 1984, Elvstrøm's fourth place could hardly have been narrower behind Australia (Chris Cairns and John Anderson), the bronze medal winners. At Pusan they were to finish 15th, father by now being 60. His eighth participation was matched by Durward Knowles of the Bahamas, also over a 40-year span, Knowles having been winning helmsman in the Star class in 1964 at Sagami Bay. Coincidentally, Pusan witnessed an incident characteristic of the inherent sportsmanship in this sport. In near-gale conditions, Larry Lemieux, from Edmonton, Alberta, turned back in his Finn class dinghy – that in itself an extreme exercise in such conditions – to rescue a capsized Singaporean in his 470, then deposited him with a rescue launch before continuing in the race. The course on that day was described, in downhill skiing terms, as being Kitzbühl.

The Olympic Games of 1988 should, more than anything, be remembered as the Games of the African runner: above all, the Kenyan Games. Amid the malignant doubt cast over all champions by Ben Johnson and his advisers, and by weightlifters and others, the Kenyans sustained the Olympic spirit alongside such traditionalists as Elvstrøm. Within a week of the opening ceremony, the athletes' oath taken by Huh Jae, a South Korean basketball player, and Mi-Na Son, a handball player, had been betrayed by others as a lie. We seemingly could believe nothing. While we shuddered at the exposure of the sin that sought to hide its name, the Kenyans assaulted us with the beauty of their running, so that this festival, holding the world's attention, was still worthy of intelligent appreciation. The Kenyans were to win the 800m, 1,500m, 5,000m and the steeplechase, additionally taking bronze in the 10,000m and silver in the marathon and steeplechase.

The tribes of Kalenjin, Kikuyu and Turkana, in the foothills of Mt Elgon and Mt Kenya, lived on the natural medicine of the runner: maize, milk, millet and curdled cow's blood, their exercise chasing their sheep and goat herds and running ten miles to school every day. With almost biblical simplicity, Paul Ereng, who as a boy was a cowherd, came down from the plains to win the 800m. Never having competed at the distance until this year, he came from the back of the field at the final bend, past a host of famous names, defeating not only the defending champion, Joachim Cruz, but also the legendary Saïd Aouita, who had not lost over any distance in three years and had been telling everyone that he regarded himself as unbeatable.

Ereng, 21, from the University of Virginia, Charlottesville, only gained a place on the team because a Nairobi newspaper spotted his results on Reuter's agency tape and the national federation flew him home for the trials. Under the direction of Mike Koskei, the national middle-distance coach, Ereng's colleague Nixon Kiprotich was sacrificed as the front runner, who would draw the sting from Cruz, Aouita, Peter Elliot of Britain and another Brazilian, Jose-Luis Barbosa. At the bell, Barbosa headed Kiprotich in a breathless 49.54, with Ereng lying seventh. Cruz and Elliot led into the final straight only for the

unheralded Ereng to come through on the inside to win by a stride in 1:43.45, with Cruz, Aouita and Elliot in line behind him, and the selfless Kiptrotich eighth. Ereng had run only two big races in the year; and thereby sent a message to both Steve Cram, eliminated in the heats, and Aouita: the damage of over-racing. While wishing to add the 1,500m or 800m title to that of the 5,000m gained in LA, Aouita had pursued so many financial rewards in the interim that he had forgotten what championships required: repetitive stamina. Now he was left with a bronze and would be eliminated in the 1,500m.

Cram also ardently coveted the 1,500m title, missing from his otherwise illustrious career. Overshadowed as a youngster by Coe and Ovett in 1980, he had lost to Coe in LA when world and European champion. This was effectively his last chance, yet he hugely misjudged his own condition, vulnerable from excessive demands, when deciding to go for both middle distances. Injured in Rieti, Italy, a month earlier, he should never have entered the 800m and this critically undermined his effort in the 1,500m, never mind that he confidently held the fastest time of the year, 3:30.95. With Aouita dropping out in the heats, Cruz withdrawing with a cold and current world champion Abdi Bile of Somalia with a stress fracture, the field for the 1,500m was open. The more so with the shameful exclusion of Coe by the British selectors, when he was briefly unwell at the time of the trials, yet elsewhere proved himself still one of the fastest of the year.

Following a predictably idle first two laps, Peter Rono, an outsider from university in Maryland, decided to step up the pace, which had earlier been set by Marcus O'Sullivan of Ireland. At the bell, Rono led from Elliot, Cram and Jens-Peter Herold (GDR). Down the back straight Rono looked at ease and, though repeatedly glancing behind him over the last 200 metres, held off Elliot's vain challenge, with Herold in third place and Cram fourth. The youngest, at 21, to have won the Olympic title, he was as surprised as any by his success. He had run the last 800m in 1:50, with the moderate winning time of 3:35.96. 'It's a dream – my first Olympics and I won,' Rono said.

In the weeks preceding the Games, Koskei had discussed with John Ngugi the idea that he might attempt to run away from the field in the 5,000m. In the previous year's World Championships in Rome, Ngugi had faded because of a knee injury, but two world cross-country titles were proof of his stamina. Was the gamble worth it? After three laps in which to get warm, Ngugi went. Ten yards clear, twenty, thirty: before the others knew it he was all but out of reach. He had covered 800 metres, following the first kilometre, in a burning 2:00, and after 4km it was apparent he was not likely to fade. Domingos Castro of Portugal attempted to close the gap, but in vain, he himself ultimately being overhauled by Dieter Baumann (FRG) and Hansjörg Kunze (GDR) in the last few metres. With his winning time of 13:11.70, Ngugi had given the most audacious example of front running since Filbert Bayi's world record 1,500m against John Walker in 1974.

For the third time in a Games, Kenya took first and second in the steeplechase. Francesco Panetta of Italy, the world champion, attempted to repeat his characteristic front running but, off-form, was overtaken after 2km by Julius Kariuki and Peter Koech, who by turn took the lead. With just over a lap remaining, Kariuki left Koech several strides astern and ended easing up, unaware that the ten-year-old world record of Henry Rono was within his grasp. A tenth of a second outside, his 8:05.51 comfortably beat the 12-year-old Olympic record of Anders Gärderud.

Seldom was there such a favourite as for the women's marathon: Rosa Mota of Portugal, winner of the inaugural

Cowherd to champion. Paul Ereng, 21, Kenyan unknown, defeats the famous, Cruz (BRA) and Aouita (MOR), for the 800m title.
(© Getty Images)

women's marathon at the European Championships of 1982, third in LA in 1984 where she was the first Portugese woman to win any Olympic medal, European champion again in 1986 and world champion in 1987 by an overwhelming seven minutes. Now she had led for much of the race with the outcome reduced to three runners some 5km from the finish. Mota made a break after 36km, leaving Lisa Martin (AUS) and Kathrin Dörre (GDR) to fight for the silver. Martin succeeded.

For two Olympic Games Daley Thompson had justifiably calculated not so much whether he would win the decathlon but by how much. In Seoul, by now aged 30, he knew that it was a question of whether he could steal a medal from a field that was also off-form. He was nursing a previously undisclosed thigh strain, yet his mind was as strong as it had ever been: twice Olympic champion, twice European, once world and three times Commonwealth. His first major defeat had come at the previous year's World Championships. Competition now was unexpectedly further weakened by the disqualification of Jürgen Hingsen, in the first heat of the opening 100m discipline, for three false starts.

The main challenge had always been likely to come from two East Germans, Torsten Voss and Christian Schenk, respectively first and fifth in the previous year's World Championship. The order at the end of the first day was Schenk, Christian Plaziat (FRA), Thompson and Voss. A comparatively weak pole vault score saw Schenk's lead shrink, and a poor javelin throw ended Plaziat's hopes. They went into the final 1,500m with Schenk leading Voss by 62 points and Thompson by 78. Thompson had earned the admiration of all when, in spite of his pole snapping in two places on his first vault, damaging his left hand, he went on to clear 4.90 and retain fourth place, his javelin throw of 64.04 heaving him back to third. When the ultimate race began at 21.20, the competition's second day had been running for 13 hours. With typical guts, Thompson produced a time of 4:45.11 in spite of his thigh injury, but a superb 4:23.20 by Dave Steen of Canada, who had been lying eighth after nine events, denied Thompson the bronze by 22 points. Schenk and Voss were comfortably first and second. It was the end of the road for a notable former champion.

It was also the end of the road, morally and most other ways, for Ben Johnson. In the final of the 100m, he upstaged his world record of the World Championships in Rome, 9.83, with a phenomenal 9.79, thereby ending the speculation on his superiority over Carl Lewis, the defending champion. The first four – he, Lewis, Linford Christie (GBR) and Calvin Smith (USA) – had run under 10.00, Lewis with an American record of 9.92, Christie a European record of 9.97. With an explosive start, Johnson – born in Jamaica and moving with his mother and siblings to Toronto when he was 14 – led from gun to tape, his exaltation being unrestrained. The whole of Canada, so permanently in the shadow of their big-brother neighbour, shared his joy. Only, however, for 48 hours. Glory was overtaken by shame as Johnson's urine test proved positive for the anabolic steroid Stanozolol, and in the middle of the night Carol Anne Letheren, Canadian *chef-de-mission*, came to remove his medal. By dawn Johnson was on the way home. The rest of the world was informed of the then worst scandal in the IOC's history. Samaranch, who had warned in his opening address to the Session before the Games that 'doping is death' – Stanozolol can precipitate cancer of the liver – now expressed optimism. 'The bad news we can transform into good news . . . it shows that we are winning the battle against drugs.' That was to be a false hope. Johnson was the 43rd Olympic competitor to be found guilty, and there were more to come.

Carl Lewis was to be remembered, therefore, for the wrong

Tainted glory. Ben Johnson (CAN) (centre) celebrates defeat of Carl Lewis (USA) (left) and Linford Christie (GBR) (right) before being overtaken by infamy. (© Getty Images)

reasons in 1988: that he won the 100m by default, being upgraded to a better medal together with Christie and Smith, rather than that for the second time in the Games he produced an exceptional performance. He himself had long suspected, and stated, that Johnson was drug assisted with steroids. The irony, revealed only in 2003 as already stated in the introduction, was that Lewis was only competing in Seoul thanks to gross deception on the part of USOC. He and many others benefited from supressed positive tests – in Lewis's case, admittedly, for miniscule amounts of pseudo-ephedrine – during the US trials. Official action was to say that the use of the drug had been 'inadvertent', yet Lewis must have known the rules. A confidential letter of 26 August 1988, addressed to Lewis in Santa Monica from USOC executive director Baaron Pittenger stated that: 'In my review of your appeal in conjunction with our panel of experts, the evidence . . . [will] be treated as a warning rather than a suspension.' By such unashamed manipulation by USOC was one of the most famous reputations in Olympic history protected.

Christie also was given the benefit of the doubt, though formally by the IOC Medical Commission, on a questionable positive test for the stimulant pseudo-ephedrine, on account of consuming ginseng tea. Ironically, when rumours first started to fly that a prominent athlete had tested positive, the BOA, grasping the nettle, had called a press conference to announce that it was their man.

The IAAF retroactively rescinded Johnson's earlier world record, even though his test in Rome had been negative. He now served the standard two-year suspension. Responding in 2003 to the evidence from Dr Exum, Lewis asserted that his herbal intake had given him no advantage. 'There really is no evidence that it [the herbal supplement] does something.' Then why take it, it will be asked? On being told that the Johnson camp was demanding that Lewis should also be stripped of his medal from Seoul, Lewis was duly dismissive. 'Do you expect him to say anything different?' he asked. 'We're talking about Ben Johnson. Let's be realistic.'

Lewis's additive may have been insignificant alongside Johnson's use of steroids, yet knowledge of his previously unrevealed actions will undoubtedly have diminished the admiration previously accorded to him. Much greater damage was done by the revelations of 2003 to the already fragile integrity of USOC.

If Lewis's 100m 'victory' was soured, there was no denying his triumph in retaining the long jump title with a leap well beyond that in LA – 8.72m (28 ft 7¼ in.) – thereby maintaining a winning jumping streak over more than seven years. The final began barely an hour after running in the heats of the 200m, but he was nevertheless in the lead after the first round, extending it in the second and achieving his winning distance in the

Harry 'Butch' Reynolds (USA), extreme favourite for the 400m, surprisingly lost to 19-year-old compatriot Steve Lewis. Before the next Games, Reynolds would also test positive. (© Getty Images)

fourth round: thereby having the best four jumps of the competition and becoming the first to retain this title. Though Lewis was buoyed by this success, he was undoubtedly disappointed to be subsequent runner-up in the 200m final to his compatriot and friend, Joe DeLoach, never mind that he had

competed in three events and in eight races over five days. Tom Tellez, Lewis's coach, was convinced that his determination to compete in all four events, as in Los Angeles, contributed to the defeat; especially the decision to jump all six times in the long jump final, when he slightly strained his ankle on the fifth, believing he could still be under pressure from either of his US rivals, Michael Powell and Larry Myricks, who took silver and bronze. Nonetheless, DeLoach had set an Olympic record of 19.75 to beat Lewis by four-hundredths of a second.

If the 100m saw the end of an ego, the 400m hurdles saw the end of an era. Ed Moses was dethroned as twelve-year master of the event. For nine of those years Andre Phillips had been pursuing Moses, his idol and his inspiration. Moses had maintained his enduring prestige in 1987 by retaining his world title and then defeating home rivals Phillips and Danny Harris in the US trials. Phillips himself was 29, having lost more than 20 times to Moses, now aged 33. This time, however, Phillips led at the start, held off the challenge from Moses at the seventh flight and extended his lead. Moses uncharacteristically faltered and was passed by Amadou Dia Ba of Senegal, who all but caught Phillips. The winning time of 47.19 was an Olympic record and less than a fifth of a second outside Moses' world time. It was Senegal's first Olympic medal

Florence Griffith Joyner, inevitably known as Flo-Jo, would be remembered as much as the Kenyans, the North African Arabs and Johnson, but for reasons of doubt as much as admiration. Aside from her long painted fingernails, her tresses and her leotard, she had much of the physical appearance of a man, and indeed ran the 100m faster than 12 of the men in their second-round heats and all of the men in the decathlon. She completed a sprint double which did nothing to change the minds of the sceptics. Her sudden escalation had begun in the US trials at Indianapolis, when she broke the 100m world record with 10.49 – an improvement of almost three-tenths. She took the Olympic title, all but laughing on the way, with her arms aloft at the line, hair cascading behind her, in a wind-assisted 10.54, way ahead of the veteran Evelyn Ashford. Together with her husband Al Joyner, the triple jump champion in LA, she had consulted Ben Johnson and closely studied his technique. It was in the 200m that suspicion really mounted, when she twice

Florence Griffith Joyner (USA) reveals delight, and exceptional muscularity, in her double sprint triumph. (© DPA)

271

broke the world record: first improving the time of Marita Koch with a semi-final time of 21.56, then bettering it less than two hours later with 21.34. Such a belated rise in form, together with the provocative definition of her muscle development, fuelled suspicions that mounted when she announced her retirement the following year shortly before the imposition of random drug testing.

The queen of 10,000m running for women had for several years been Ingrid Kristiansen of Norway, setting and improving the world record, winning the European and World Championships prior to Seoul. Her first defeat, when unknowingly pregnant, had occurred in Oslo shortly before the Games, beaten by Liz McColgan of Britain, and she had subsequently suffered a miscarriage. Nonetheless she won her heat, McColgan coming first in the other. Lacking a finishing kick, McColgan promised to make a race of it in the final, and this she did, leading for much of the race from halfway. Kristiansen dropped out with a foot injury suffered in the heat. Pursuing McColgan were two Soviets, Olga Bondarenko and Yelena Zhupiyeva. Alone in front with a kilometre to go were McColgan and Bondarenko, the Russian surging to the front down the final back straight to win in an Olympic record of 31:05.21, more than 50 seconds outside Kristiansen's world best.

There are champions . . . and there are heroes. Greg Louganis revealed the qualities of both with a combination of peerless technique and rare courage when retaining his springboard diving title – his third Olympic gold medal. He not only recovered after hitting his head on the board during the preliminaries, qualifying for the final after having stitches in his lacerated scalp, but also audaciously repeated the same technically extrovert dive the following day. 'Louganis showed us that he is made of granite,' the US team manager said. Before the competition the 28-year-old Louganis admitted that he was concerned about the challenge from the Chinese. Twice that year he had been beaten by Liangde Tan, second behind him in

'Showed us that he's made of granite,' said the coach of Greg Louganis (USA), who struck his head on the springboard and needed stitches before becoming the first to win both diving titles in successive Games. (© Getty Images)

LA. Now, on his ninth preliminary dive, Louganis struck the board during a reverse two and a half somersault in the pike position. Though able to haul himself out of the water, he dropped from first to fifth. Reappearing half an hour later after repairs, he smiled in appreciation of the applause and executed to perfection a reverse one and a half somersault with three and a half twists: a remarkable revival.

The following day Tan and Deliang Li were still at his heels. To allay anxiety, Louganis had been through his entire programme in an early morning workout. Only briefly did he lose his lead, to Tan on the fourth round, immediately regaining it. To cap this achievement, Louganis came from behind on his final dive to overtake Xiong Ni of China in the platform diving, thus becoming the first man to win both titles in successive Games.

If the Olympic Games are about sportsmanship as much as about sport, then the modern pentathlon and equestrian three-day event lie at their heart. In no other events are there to be found more graciousness in defeat or modesty in victory. In the space of six hours on the same day there were equal scenes of elation, fulfilment and dignity at the two events. János Martinek of Hungary in the pentathlon and Mark Todd of New Zealand in the three-day event were individual winners instantly acclaimed by their rivals. Both sports are threatened in the long term by cost, measured against the relatively small number of participating nations. Yet de Coubertin rightly believed them to be sports that personified character. As Todd said afterwards, 'Equestrianism belongs to the Games'.

Todd and his little horse Charisma were a rare pair indeed, and Charisma's victory gallop round the stadium with his rider after the individual medal ceremony, ears pricked and head erect, was the clearest indication of a horse's sense of occasion. For Todd it was a double of rare distinction, defending his LA title on the same supreme horse. Only Charles Pahud de Mortanges of the Netherlands, in 1928 and '32, had done the same. The team winners were West Germany.

Across town, Martinek, at 23 the youngest ever to win the title, ran the race of his life in the cross-country, the fifth and final discipline of the pentathlon. With a 29-point deficit on Vakhtang Yagorachvili of the Soviet Union, leader after four days, Martinek had a ten-second gap to close over the 4km course. With the sixth fastest time of the 63 runners, he made it with 18 seconds to spare. Hungary won the team event, the second time they had achieved the double, the first being in 1960, only once equalled, by Italy in 1984. In a tense battle for the bronze, Britain, fifth before the cross-country, got home by a collective eight points, or a fraction under three seconds. First to congratulate the British were the French, beaten into fourth place.

The women's individual all-round gymnastics final was an amalgam of beauty, excellence, prejudice and, ultimately, the absurd. How else could be described the supreme performances of Yelena Chouchounova of the Soviet Union and Daniela Silivas of Romania, and their separation in determining the gold medal for the former by 0.025 of a point, or less than one three-thousandth part of their totals, on the arbitrary opinion of six judges? No logical person can sensibly accept such a refinement of human discretion: to put it another way, the arrogance of the judges is boundless. The virtuosity of the two tiny girls had been astonishing, as had been that of the 15-year-old Svetlana Boguinskaya (URS) in third place. Adrian Goreac, Silivas's coach, was volubly critical of the marking, especially that by Nelli Kim, former Soviet champion, on the final exercise. The inference was that Romania were being penalised for having broken the boycott four years earlier. Silivas, in fact, beat Chouchounova on the day's four exercises by the same tiny margin she lost the gold medal, which was on account of the 0.050 points which the

Yelena Chouchounova (URS), perfection on beam, and Daniela Silivas (ROM) fought a tortuous gymnastics battle with each other and the judges. (© Getty Images/Bruty) (right © Getty Images)

Soviet carried forward from the preliminaries. Of the six judges' marks, top and bottom are discarded with an average taken on the middle four. Kim's persistent low marking pushed into the average the other lowest mark. Unusually depressing, besides the dubious marking, was the blank, programmed look of the medal winners when appearing behind the microphones: conditioned to clichéd replies, seemingly unable to comprehend questions other than the obvious; looking forward to no more, as Boguinskaya admitted, than coaching the next generation of automated geniuses. Silivas had minor compensation when she won three of the separate apparatus events: beam, asymmetric bars and floor exercises.

In the men's gymnastics, the victory of Lou Yun (CHN) in the individual vault was the lone stance against Soviet or Eastern European monopoly, the Soviets winning the team event and the individual all-round with Vladimir Artemov, followed by two compatriots; the bronze remarkably won by Dimitri Bilozertchev, 21, who had recovered from a shattered left leg in a car accident three years earlier.

East Germany was dominant at the Han River regatta, where a particular surprise was the defeat of Peter Kolbe (FRG), five times previously world champion, by the current champion Thomas Lange (GDR) in the single sculls. Lange won by a distance, Kolbe earning his third silver medal at the age of 35 – the same age as Pertti Karppinen of Finland, the winner at the past three Games, who had now finished last in his semi-final. Ronald Florijn and Nicolaas Rienks (NED) won a thrilling double sculls from Switzerland and the Soviets. Steve Redgrave and Andrew Holmes (GBR) comfortably won the coxless pairs from repetitive Romanian rivals Dragus Neagu and Danut Dobre. Attempting the impossible within 24 hours, the British pair were beaten into third place, with Patrick Sweeney, in the coxed pairs. Italians Carmine and Giuseppe Abbagnale, coxed by Giuseppe di Capua, retained their title ahead of the East Germans Mario Streit, Detlev Kirchhoff and René Rensch, who denied the British pair by half a length.

Most conspicuous of all women at the Games was Kristin Otto of East Germany, with her six swimming titles – a record by any woman in any sport at any Games – and she also became the first swimmer with victories at three different strokes at the same Games. Her feat subsequently lost much of its lustre when documentary evidence emerged of the state's systematic use of drugs, which indicted champions such as Otto.

Simultaneously in the men's events, there was the rivalry between Matt Biondi (USA) and Michael Gross (FRG), Biondi emerging triumphant with seven medals – five gold, a silver and bronze. The joy of the swimming tournament, however, was the acclaim for Anthony Nesty of Surinam and Silvia Poll of Costa

Anthony Nesty of Surinam sets four records when defeating celebrated Matt Biondi (USA) at 100m butterfly. (© Getty Images/Duffy)

273

Rica. There was only one 50-metre pool in the whole of Surinam, the former Dutch colony in Latin America. In defeating Biondi in the 100m butterfly, Nesty, Surinam's only competitor at Seoul, set four records: the first black swimming champion of any Games, first South American champion, first Surinam medallist, and an Olympic record of 53.00, one-hundredth ahead of Biondi. Ten metres from the finish, Biondi was still in front, but faltered on his last two strokes.

Poll's success in the women's 200m freestyle was almost equally unique: her silver medal the first in any sport by Costa Rica, and the first by any woman from Central or Latin America. Poll's German-born parents had moved to Costa Rica from Nicaragua when she was a child. With little chance of defeating world record holder Heike Friedrich (GDR), who set an Olympic record of 1:57.65, Poll held off the challenge of Manuela Stellmach (GDR).

Shortly before the opening of the Games the international federation, FINA, decreed that swimmers could now earn money from endorsements and sponsorship. Not that this would have made any difference to the state-sponsored Communist competitors, whose every need was already catered for, but it would aid the preparation of many others – such as Duncan Armstrong, a 20-year-old Australian who gained a startling victory over Gross and Biondi in the 200m freestyle, Gross being the defending champion and world record holder. Armstrong, ranked only 46th in the world, timed his effort late, passing Anders Holmertz (SWE) and Biondi on the final lap, even improving on the world record of Gross – who finished fifth – with 1:47.25.

East Germany's hold on the women's events was consuming: victory in ten of the fifteen events. Swim-conscious Americans had to be content with the deeds of the diminutive 17-year-old Janet Evans, who set records in winning the 400m freestyle (world, 4:03.85) and 800m freestyle (Olympic, 8:20.20) plus a third title in the 400m medley.

Steffi Graf (FRG) turned her Grand Slam year of four major titles into a golden finale when she won the inaugural women's singles on the return of tennis to the programme. She defeated Gabriella Sabatini (ARG), her victim in the US Open final, in straight sets. Milos Mecir (CZE) took the men's title, defeating Tim Mayotte (USA) 3–6, 6–4, 6–2. He had beaten Stefan Edberg (SWE), then current Wimbledon champion, in a five-set semi-final. Competitors were performing for no reward other than the honour, and were sacrificing income available elsewhere.

Nan-Yool Choo achieved fame by winning for the hosts the demonstration sport of taekwondo. A mere 16, she defeated Maria Angela Naranjo of Spain, bigger and stronger but lacking the younger girl's speed and ability to deliver high kicks on the jacket target-area. It was to be a notable Games for South Korean women. Their handball team, handicapped in height and weight, miraculously conjured up a 21–19 victory over the Soviet Union, reigning world champions, to take the gold medal, while Young-Ja Yang and Jung-Hwa Hyun spectacularly beat Zhimin Jiao and Jing Chen (CHN) to win the women's doubles in the augural table tennis tournament. The South Koreans also reached the women's hockey final, but yielded 2–0 to Australia, while in archery, South Korean women took all three medals in the individual event.

The East Germans, revealing new technology in cycling, with reduced-friction frames, furthered the argument for standardised, one-class equipment in all sports. Their four-man team won the 100km road race at a remarkable average of 50.935 kph (31.651 mph). In an extraordinary finish to the women's 82km individual road race, 45 riders simultaneously swept towards the line. Study of the photo-finish revealed Monique Knol, a 24-year-old Dutch school teacher, as the winner from Jutta Niehaus (FRG) and Laima Zilporitee (URS), all in the same time of 2:00:52.

The boxing and weightlifting tournaments were notable for their negative elements: the boxing for appallingly prejudiced judging, the weightlifting for a plethora of positive drug tests that should have seen the exclusion of the sport from future Games. Following two positives, the entire Bulgarian team withdrew. The Soviets won six of the ten events. In boxing's light-middleweight final, Si-Hun Park was given the decision over Roy Jones (USA), who had dominated the fight throughout, even Park admitting he considered he had lost. To compound the controversy the international federation, IABA, subsequently named Jones the best stylist of the tournament. Worse was an earlier incident in which Keith Walker, a New Zealand referee, was jostled by South Korean officials following a disputed decision in which Alex Hristov (BUL) was given the verdict over Jong-Il Byun (KOR) in the bantamweight class, Byun refusing to leave the ring. Five South Korean officials were subsequently suspended indefinitely. Winner of the super-heavyweight class, with a second round technical knock-out over Riddick Bowe (USA) was Lennox Lewis of Canada – subsequently to win the professional world heavyweight title representing Britain.

Defeated South Korean bantamweight Jong-Il Byun refuses to leave the ring following a controversial decision in favour of Alex Hristov (BUL).
(© Getty Images)

Flamboyant Steffi Graf (GER) completes a golden year when adding Olympic victory over Gabriella Sabatini – Argentina flag-bearer in the opening ceremony – to all four Grand Slam titles.
(© IOC/Marquez)

CHAPTER LIX

Excess

Paul Henderson of Canada, former president ISAF (sailing)

'The Session of 2001 in Moscow for me was a painful experience, reinforcing thoughts on how the IOC must improve the bidding-city procedures. The reforms have not worked, indeed have escalated the cost over ten years by making the bids more innovative and even secretive. The Toronto bid for 2008 cost $25 million, almost triple that when bidding for 1996. I suspect Beijing spent three times that. The following are my ideas to curtail what could become a scandal even greater than Salt Lake City, based on experience with two Toronto bids and being the only candidate to provide an in-depth report on the 1990 bid for '96 – then being an IF president and subjected as IOC member since 2000 to the pressures of three subsequent bidding campaigns.

During the bidding for 2008 I witnessed consultants employed to influence the IOC, including two teams from a previously successful candidate. Former IOC employees were hired as bid-city advisers. Evaluation Committee members were offered jobs with winning cities. Former bid officials were paid to advise on how to influence some IOC members. New York and London spin-doctors were hired to position bids positively and to play up errors by other bids. Airport advertising and airline magazine coverage was paid for and some cities had hundreds of supporters in Moscow, all expenses paid. Promotional videos and publications were overpowering. Due to the No-Visit regulations, bid cities attended Regional Games to lobby the IOC. Groupies were paid to sift the Moscow hotel lobbies and feed information back to bid teams.

The awarding of the Games is the highest-profile operation that the IOC performs outside the event itself. The only way to bring it under control is to ensure the system works, is disciplined and leaves policing as a last resort. I feel the new Ethics Commission has been emasculated, when it should be a clandestine body that will jump on cities discreetly rather than conduct public hangings.

I believe that the IOC, or rather the Executive Board, had decided unofficially that Athens and Beijing should get the Games of 2004 and 2008 respectively, and various tactics were employed to help this happen. I think this was improper, and the Evaluation Commission report was too bland. I consider that if there was an official preference for Beijing, this should have been openly stated.

By my calculation, the golden age of sport is probably over. The world is on the brink of severe retrenchment, I believe, and it will be extremely difficult for sport outside the Olympic Games to continue to find the lucrative sponsors they have enjoyed in the last two decades. I consider there should be a continental rotation of Games hosting, thus eliminating bid cities which have no hope and should never even begin a costly campaign, enabling tighter control than exists at present. The rotation should be divided between three regions – Europe, the Americas and the Rest – so that, for example, following Athens and Beijing, the Games of 2012 would be in the Americas. Everybody would know where they stood. The Executive Board should limit the number of proposed cities to no more than three, with the Evaluation Committee doing their work six months prior to the vote and the finalists being announced three months before the Session. No promotion whatsoever should be allowed prior to the last three months.

Perceived obligations to Athens and Beijing have been delivered. The choice of every Games of the rest of the twenty-first century is freely open, no city having a particular right. Jacques, you are the man. You can put your stamp on the IOC by acting decisively.' (From a letter to IOC President Jacques Rogge, July 2001)
(Photograph © IOC/Locatelli)

The hidden, and not so hidden, sinister dangers of the bidding process had become apparent to Paul Henderson, owner of a plumbing business in Toronto, when leading his city's bid to host the Centenary Games. However, Henderson's letter expressing alarm could, indeed should, have been addressed 11 years earlier to Juan Antonio Samaranch. By 1990, Henderson was not the only one who was aware of malpractices. So was Robert Scott, chairman of the first bid by Manchester, and they both expressed their concerns verbally to Samaranch. Also well aware, together with a handful of other international journalists, was the author, expressing these concerns in 1992 in *Olympic Revolution*, an official biography of the then President. Somebody needed to cry halt, but the IOC was riding such a tide of success – financially, and as a result of the widely acclaimed Games of Seoul and then Barcelona – that Samaranch felt disinclined to rock the boat. If a handful of thieves lurked in the shadows, he was prepared to wait until he was provided with real evidence. The implicit testimony from those such as Henderson and Scott served no more than to persuade the Executive Board to instruct Marc Hodler, president of international skiing, to issue restrictive guidelines on bidding practice that were no more effective than requesting schoolchildren not to shout in the playground.

In 1989, at the Session in Puerto Rico, Samaranch was re-elected, for the first time, by acclaim. At this moment, such was the string of achievements of the IOC under his presidency, moving from lame duck to market leader under the all-seeing eye of his progressive planning, together with his subtle manipulation of both events and subordinates, that he stood like Caesar with the world of sport at his feet. The acclaim was to a degree deserved, for his transformation had been perceptive, revolutionary and largely free of criticism thus far. Whatever his detractors might say, he was driven by the cause of promoting the IOC rather than himself. The hours that he worked as an honorary elected official would have exhausted many men of his age within a year, never mind nine. Yet, as with many leaders in positions of sustained authority, he was becoming insulated from some of the attendant dangers. If his status now rivalled that of the IOC's founder, de Coubertin – Merlin the Magician, as Richard Pound called the Spaniard – would likewise tend to become detached from the shop floor. His focus, like de Coubertin's, was always on the horizon, on coordinating the IOC's relationship with international organisations such as the UN, UNESCO, the World Health Organisation, the International Red Cross and others. To those who questioned his involving the IOC in the political sphere, he reminded them that this had been de Coubertin's principle and that it was an objective of the Charter to promote solidarity and understanding.

As the IOC's image mushroomed, many were concerned about allegations of undemocratic practices, administrative as well as financial. Questioned on this, Princess Anne, IOC member from Britain and sometime president of international equestrianism, expressed her anxiety.

> The IOC has dubious methods of coming to a decision, but I don't know that that's corruption. Its host city bid process is one of the areas, and removing possibilities of temptation is a good idea. Equally, I think the democratic process is short-circuited within the IOC by the Executive Board. The democratic process is not seen to function. In many ways, it's hugely unsatisfactory [the IOC's constitution] because it's treated differently by different people.

The temptations of which the Princess spoke were obvious. Fifteen years ago, the staging of an Olympic Games was seen as an exercise in massive risk-management; now, the level of television and sponsorship fees had helped reduce the size of the financial gamble for any successful city, creating a platform for the development not only of multiple sports facilities but also for improvement of basic road, rail, housing and airport infrastructure. This has always been the ambition of any bid city since Tokyo made their Games a commercial promotion of the nation in 1964. It was unsurprising that candidate cities had now become willing to risk millions of dollars on the bidding campaign alone and even more likely than that they should offer material incentives to IOC members. A further

inducememt for cities to enter the race was the decision by Samaranch to allow televising of the voting announcement. This was blatant show business, raising the profile not only of the IOC and the Games but also that of the bid cities, giving them an exposure worldwide that money normally could not buy.

For the 1990 election of the Centenary host, the President and the Executive Board should have been more aware of a particular risk that would provoke damaging publicity. The candidates were Athens, Atlanta, Belgrade, Manchester, Melbourne and Toronto. Without insider-knowledge of the practical capability of each city, global opinion perceived Athens, original home of the modern Games, as being the obvious and honourable choice. If Athens were to be ignored, reaction from the media, much of it as unaware of logistical considerations as its audience, would inevitably be hostile. The preference, in the event, for Atlanta, with a supposed IOC bias for US commercial interests led by Coca-Cola, resulted, therefore, in a vitriolic public reception of the decision. The IOC's lack of public relations was uncomfortably exposed. 'There was no strategic communication or plan to handle either an Atlanta election or, previously, Ben Johnson's suspension in Seoul,' Michael Payne, the IOC's Marketing Director, reflected. 'The knee-jerk reaction by the media over Atlanta was predictable, yet the IOC was able to do little in damage limitation, nor was there any contingency plan when the Johnson story broke at three in the morning.'

There were many misconceptions about the result in Tokyo. For a start, Coca-Cola in Greece was as much a sponsor of the Athens bid as the parent company was in Atlanta. The IOC managed to compound its PR inadequacies by not giving wider publicity to an evaluation report that ranked Athens behind Atlanta, Melbourne and Toronto. On all sides within the Olympic Movement, the informed view was that Athens probably could not cope: a small, traffic-jammed, polluted, under-equipped city with inadequate public transportation, an ancient airport with high security risk, and domestic political uncertainty. The Athens bid team ran a campaign based on history, romance and not a little arrogance, whereas Atlanta, Melbourne and Toronto concentrated on superior logistics, multinationalism, financial security and pervasive hospitality. When the rumour, probably correct, that Samaranch was unofficially supporting Athens started to gather momentum, a senior member of the Executive Board told him he had better stay around until 1996 if they won, in order 'to tidy up the mess'.

By the time everyone arrived in Tokyo, the persuasiveness of Billy Payne, Atlanta's leader, backed by his amiable side-kick, Charlie Battle, plus the internationalism of Andrew Young, former personal aide of human-rights evangelist Martin Luther King, had turned the minds of many IOC members. The voting figures over five rounds revealed that nearly two-thirds of the members preferred *either* of the North American candidates to Athens. For 22 members to have supported Toronto in the fourth round, when Athens and Atlanta had been level in the third, was a clear indication of independence of mind. Yet still the newspapers and television would cry 'fix'.

Three years earlier, the Atlanta committee hardly knew an IOC member from a hall porter, but they had diligently worked the field. While Andrew Young emotionally polled votes in Africa, the Eastern European and Third World members were legitimately attracted by North American prosperity. To avoid the denigration that followed, the IOC should have declared beforehand either that Athens must be the pre-emptive choice or that, under the findings of the Evaluation Committee, they

were logistically ineligible. To have left it open was to be, either way, both right and wrong. The round-by-round voting figures were:

	I	II	III	IV	V
Athens	23	23	26	30	35
Atlanta	19	20	26	34	51
Belgrade	7	–	–	–	–
Manchester	11	5	–	–	–
Melbourne	12	21	16	–	–
Toronto	14	17	18	22	–

Billy Payne, president of the Atlanta bidding committee (seated far right), and Robert Helmick (left), president of USOC, sign the contract as Centenary host city, following the controversial defeat of Athens. (© IOC/Strahm)

Following the furore that surrounded Atlanta's election, the controversy shifted to Birmingham, Britain, for the election at the following year's Session of the Winter Games' host for 1998, for which there were three strong candidates: Nagano of Japan, Östersund of Sweden and Salt Lake City from the Mormon state of Utah. Nagano, though still needing to construct most facilities, offered the chance for expansion of the Olympics in the Orient, in what would be only the second Winter Games in Asia. Östersund was a compact, environmentally attractive bid from an Olympic-orientated nation that had repeatedly attempted and failed to stage a Winter Games. Salt Lake City offered competition facilities, accommodation and transport unrivalled anywhere in the world, yet had the disadvantage of bidding in the wake of disapproval of Atlanta and being potentially a *fifth* North American host in a 20-year span. In the event, Nagano won by four votes ahead of Salt Lake City: a defeat that was to precipitate the scandal that would engulf the IOC seven years later, there having been suspicion, not least among Salt Lake officials, that Nagano's campaigning had exceeded the legitimate boundaries of enticement.

Samaranch was defensive on behalf of Nagano:

> We have to follow the system by which our members take the decision. Other federations, such as FIFA and the IAAF, do it another way, involving only their executive committee or their council . . . It is suggested that we introduce a rotating system, but to do that we would have to change the slogan that the Olympic Movement belongs to the world, that any city should be at liberty to bid.

Samaranch's slogan, it should be added. Nonetheless, in 1991 the IOC issued new guidelines for candidates bidding for the Millennium Games of 2000, the voting scheduled for Monaco, 1993, for which the initial candidates were Beijing, Berlin, Brazilia, Istanbul, Manchester, Milan and Sydney. The guidelines included:

- Air tickets for visiting IOC members to be supplied by the IOC, non-refundable to the individual, and reimbursed by the city to the IOC
- A $200 limit on any gift
- No receptions, cocktail parties or meals to be given beyond normal subsistence during maximum three-day visit
- No boat, restaurant or club to be used for meetings, which must be restricted to a single room
- Prior to the voting day, no exhibitions or demonstrations
- Bid book documents on technical proposals to be on regular A4 format
- City delegations visiting conferences of IOC/IFs/NOCs to be kept to six members or less
- Breach of these regulations to bring disqualification
- No visit by cities to the country of IOC members where a member has already specifically visited that city

This was closing the stable door after the horse had bolted; and anyway the IOC as an honorary body had no surveillance mechanism to enforce its regulations. There are many ways by which material favours to members, volunteered or requested, could be made without breaking the guidelines. At this stage, however, Henderson was already voicing his disquiet: 'There should be no promotion by cities until the list is reduced to four. I would also prohibit IOC members travelling on inspection tours and bringing guests or children, and I would ban *all* gifts.' In contrast to which, Samaranch, ever the subtle politician, was observing:

> You never get what you deserve; you get what you negotiate. The IOC works in strange ways, unpredictable: one plus one is five minus three. In such an institution, you cannot be logical. When I went to Melbourne, the whole city was full of posters, you could feel that the bid was for the people. In Athens there was *nothing*. Atlanta was the most professional group: the essence of what public relations today should be. The key was their timing: they arrived at the peak of their campaign the day before the election, with a personal letter to the IOC members signed by George Bush.

Alongside concerns about the bidding process came another indication of contemporary self-interest and lack of moral sensitivity. In 1991, it was disclosed in *USA Today* that Robert Helmick, president of USOC, Vice-President of the IOC, former president of international swimming and a member of the Executive Board since 1989, had been receiving substantial six-figure fees for legal consultancy: for advising the international amateur golf organisation on possible inclusion in the Olympics and likewise advising Ted Turner's Goodwill Games, even though that event was in potential conflict with the Olympic Games. As none of this conflict of interest had been declared, Helmick was obliged to resign from USOC and, under the pressure of expected expulsion following an IOC investigation, from the IOC itself.

The other major form of corruption in the IOC's disorderly house was, of course, drugs. Samaranch had tried to put a positive spin on the Johnson case by claiming that it proved that the IOC's testing policy was winning the battle. It was a landmark moment but brought no assurance that others with Johnson's urge to capitalise on chemical additives would be henceforth dissuaded. The commission of inquiry set up by the Canadian government under Judge Dubin in the autumn of 1988, prompted by national embarrassment and genuine concern, did the service of raising international awareness. The inquiry revealed widespread cheating and generated a more serious attitude towards the problem from other organisations. It was, therefore, a great pity that the same autumn the IOC chose not to act, at a meeting of the Executive Board coinciding with the Congress of ANOC in Vienna, on the proposal of Vice-President Richard Pound to suspend the weightlifting federation following excessive malpractice in Seoul. Pound was conscious that the Games were being perceived as rotten and that radical discipline was urgently needed. Dr Roger Jackson, chairman of the Canadian NOC, former Olympic oarsman and a practising physiologist, proposed, at the annual summer meeting of the International Olympic Academy, that the national federation of a sport with more than one competitor found positive should itself be suspended from the next Games. He branded national federations as the fourth guilty party in drug abuse, alongside the athlete, the coach and the doctor. A disappointed Pound admitted in Vienna: 'We had a perfect opportunity to take positive action. I'm disappointed and surprised that my colleagues did not accept my recommendation.'

At the Commonwealth Games in Auckland in early 1990, there were further scandals of positive testing in weightlifting, and at an Australian inquiry in Canberra, weightlifters had earlier testified that they were obliged to take steroids or risk losing their scholarships if they failed to attain standards set by the national coach.

Everywhere the evidence was accumulating. The Soviets were jarred into more serious testing when they were eliminated from the track and field World Cup of 1989 as a result of a positive test in the European Cup finals on Alexander Bagach, their shot putter. This meant they forfeited team points and resulted in the GDR – of all people! – replacing the Soviets in second qualifying place for the World Cup in Barcelona. 'The punishment has to be imposed on both the athlete and his coach,' Marat Gramov, Soviet IOC member, said during the 1989 Session in Puerto Rico.

Dr Manfred Donike (second from left),
persistent pursuer of the drug cheats. (© IOC/Maeder)

'Everyone in the Soviet Union, including the press and television, has been highly critical.'

The recourse to drugs had transparent benefits, however. In one year, Bagach had moved from eleventh-ranked in the Soviet Union to fifth-ranked in the world, and the rapid advancement of professionalism in previously amateur sport provided a major incentive for taking performance-enhancing drugs at international level.

Meanwhile, Dr Manfred Donike had theoretically exposed, at the IOC-accredited laboratory in Cologne, the past use of steroids by 50 unnamed competitors who went undetected during the Games in Seoul. Donike's testing produced an endocrine profile over a period, but his methodology had not been validated. Prince de Mérode and his Medical Commission acquired evidence that US cyclists, as far back as the Los Angeles Games, had been blood-doping The trend was rampant and all the time the biochemists of cheating were outflanking their pursuers. At the European Athletics Championships at Split, Yugoslavia, in 1990, Professor Arnold Beckett, researcher at Chelsea College in London, revealed: 'The immediate problem is the replacement of blood-doping by EPO [erythropoietin]. The increasing use of endogenous substances, those already secreted naturally in the body, makes our job exceedingly difficult. How do we determine the "extra" amount present in any athlete? We can measure EPO but where should we set the permitted limit?' Beckett recommended a government mandate that would require manufacturers of EPO to insert an inert 'marker' agent, free of effect on competitors but instantly identifiable. Erythropoietin had just been added to the Medical Commission's list of banned substances and in the spring of 1991 they would approve blood sampling.

There was no unified response to the clearly spiralling problem. The various IFs could not even agree among themselves on uniform suspensions, varying from a matter of months in cycling to four years in athletics and life in weightlifting. The IAAF vacillated more than most, going through a period in the '70s and early '80s in which eighteen-month and then two-year suspensions were sometimes lifted for re-instatement: as was the case with Vainio of Finland, who re-appeared in the European Championships of 1986 at 10,000m after being found positive in LA two years earlier. All the while the federations stood in fear of expensive legal appeals by wealthy competitors such as Butch Reynolds, the 400m world record holder who was suspended for a positive test in the Grand Prix meeting at Monte Carlo in 1991 but subsequently reinstated by his national federation on the grounds of alleged imperfections in procedure. The IAAF was therefore obliged to challenge this appeal against a test conducted by Dr Donike, foremost in his field. Fortunately they won.

An international symposium, ironically under the aegis of the International Athletic Foundation – the charitable arm of the IAAF – and chaired by Robert Armstrong, QC, counsel to the Dubin Inquiry, criticised both the IOC and the IAAF for alleged failure of leadership and lack of reaction to evidence available prior to the Johnson incident. For example, Dr Robert Kerr, of San Gabriel, California, had testified that he had prescribed steroids to 20 US medal winners in LA, while a US Senators' judicial committee had been told by the US women's track coach that almost a quarter of the team were on steroids in 1984, and even more in 1988.

De Mérode and his colleague Dr Arne Ljungqvist of Sweden lamented that they could do nothing without evidence. On the other hand, Gary Roberts of Toulane University, USA, a specialist in American anti-trust laws, suggested to the symposium that IAAF regulations were legally vulnerable. While the international ski federation (FIS), acting on its own behalf, took blood samples in Nordic skiing and the biathlon at the Winter Games in 1992 in Albertville, the IOC Medical Commission stopped short of this in the Barcelona Games. The mud hit the fan when, in February 1992, in a test in South Africa on Katrin Krabbe, the world sprint champion from the former GDR, she and two other athletes were found to have submitted identical urine from an alternative source. She was suspended for four years. As with Reynolds, the IAAF's suspension was lifted by the German domestic federation on the tenuous grounds of security of chain-of-custody of the sample. Krabbe was awarded compensation by the IAAF.

The British, meanwhile, had grown weary of the IAAF dragging its feet. Christine Benning, a middle-distance runner, had withdrawn from the Moscow Games, stating that she had no wish to run against competitors re-instated after previous positive tests. Prior to the Barcelona Games, Willi Daume, chairman of the Eligibility Commission, was proposing that there should be a minimum level of random testing by every NOC in order to be eligible to receive an invitation to the Games.

An example of the perverse resistance that Samaranch would encounter from time to time from the 'floor of the House' concerned Mario Vazquez Raña, variously president of the Mexico NOC, the Pan-American Sports Organisation (PASO) and the Association of NOCs (ANOC), and Primo Nebiolo, variously president of the Italian NOC (CONI), the Italian athletics federation, the World Student Games (FISU) and the IAAF. Samaranch realised in the early 1980s that it was logical for an international, multi-sports body such as the IOC to have on

For 12 years Juan Antonio Samaranch was resisted in his rational wish to enlist as IOC members the essential figures Mario Vazquez Rāna, Mexican leader of NOCs (left), and Primo Nebiolo, president of athletics (right). (© IOC/Locatelli)

board leaders of major arms of the network, such as ANOC and the IAAF. This would be normal practice in any major corporation. Yet when he first attempted to co-opt them, at the time of the Sarajevo Games, he met with resistance. The rank and file objected to the inclusion within their ranks of these two men, less because of their office than their personality. Vazquez Raña was viewed with suspicion on account of his immense wealth from his chain of TV stations and newspapers, and seen as a possible future presidential candidate – though there was no on-record evidence of his privately stated ambition – while

Nebiolo was considered to be a power-hungry former Torino builder. The necessary evolution of the IOC, adjusting to a changing culture, by the turn of the century found the election of ex-officio members from the IFs, NOCs and even the athletes to be a matter of standard practice. In the interim it had cost Samaranch many hours of persuasion and the personal label of having created a Latin Mafia.

The President was determined to get his way, but he had to wait till the Session of 1991 in Birmingham and the retirement of Dr Eduardo Hay, Mexican IOC member, for the vacancy. There was still an undercurrent of opposition. When Vazquez Raña's name as candidate was announced, together with Denis Oswald, president of international rowing from Switzerland, Thomas Bach, fencing gold medallist of West Germany, and Dr Jacques Rogge, three-times Olympic sailor, there was a request from the floor to know whether Vazquez Raña had the support of his own country. Amid confusion, Samaranch called for a show of hands from those opposing him. Six of the seven women members, DeFrantz (USA), Glen-Haig (Great Britain), Häggman (Finland), Letheren (Canada), Princess Nora (Liechtenstein) and Princess Anne (Great Britain) raised their hands, together with Prince Albert (Monaco), Wilson (New Zealand) and Ramirez-Vazquez (Mexico). Flor Isava-Fonseca (Venezuela), the first female member of the Executive Board, abstained, though it was she who coordinated the opposition of the other women. Samaranch then asked for those in favour, and once some 20 hands had risen he announced: 'Right. Elected.' Privately offended, Vazquez Raña remained dignified, suggesting that he had inadvertently contributed to the controversy. 'I'd probably made a mistake two days before,' he said, 'when I was asked who I thought would win the Winter Games vote for 1998 and replied that though I did not have a vote *yet*, there'd been no Asian Games for 20 years and that Nagano deserved it. Some people thought I was intervening on their behalf.'

The election of Nebiolo would take another year. At the Session preceding the Albertville Winter Games, Samaranch was finally granted the right to appoint two discretionary members: an idea first mooted by Killanin, the retiring President, in a letter to Samaranch in 1980. Having been given the nod, Samaranch swiftly nominated Nebiolo and Olaf Poulsen, president of the international skating union (ISU). The terms of the approval granted to Samaranch – there were five abstentions, DeFrantz, Glen-Haig, Häggman, the Princess Royal and Philipp von Schöller of Austria – were that discretionary members' terms of office would end with their relinquishing external office. Nobody objected to Poulsen. Nebiolo's reputation, however, having become president of the IAAF in 1981, had been clouded by the controversy surrounding the bronze medal awarded to an Italian long jumper, Evangelisti, at the World Championships of 1987 in Rome, when his distance had been manipulated by officials controlling the jumping pit. A thread of conspiracy, correct or otherwise, wound its way back to the IAAF president, and he was ousted by his national athletics federation as their president. Indeed, in 1989 there had been a move, never consolidated, to remove him as president of the Association of Summer Olympic International Federations (ASOIF).

While Vazquez Raña's election claimed attention, the arrival on the scene in 1991 of the man who would ultimately become the next President was accompanied by no banners. In 1989 Jacques Rogge had become the first Flemish-speaking president of the Belgium NOC. Three-quarters of the leading competitors are Flemish-speaking in a country that was under Dutch rule in the early nineteenth century. Rogge duly paid tribute to Raoul

Mollet, a sports intellectual who himself would have been elected to the IOC but for there already existing a French-speaking Belgian member, de Mérode. Rogge said:

> Election to the IOC was an honour Mollet deserved. It was he who first developed marketing in the late 1960s. Then there was an NOC budget of $15,000 a year, whereas now we have 50 staff with an annual budget of $10 million. In the 1960s and 1970s, I was a yachting enthusiast, competing in three World Championships and three Olympics, training as an orthopaedic surgeon and playing a bit of rugby. I wasn't thinking about administration and as a competitor was always complaining. Mollett brought me on to the NOC, telling me to sit quiet and learn. It was in '88 that Dick Palmer [secretary of the British NOC] suggested to me that I should stand as president of the European NOCs. What could I and EOC contribute? I'm not a boaster, but the fact is, whether others like it or not, Europe is the leading Olympic continent: in the number of competitors, medals, the range of experts. We don't have continental Games, we don't want them. What we want to do is expand the levels of youth and schools sport, and also to change the attitude of the Solidarity programme. There's enough expertise at the top already, and we felt that Solidarity was helping IFs rather than NOCs. EOC is not there to help train pole vault coaches. We want to reinforce the role of each NOC to become the leading sports body of its country, to be able to speak on behalf of *all* national federations.

When the time eventually arrived at which Rogge succeeded Samaranch in 2001, he would bring to the IOC a sharp awareness of the catholicity of the involvement of NOCs and their strength within the Movement vis-à-vis the IFs. In this he was at one with Vazquez Raña, president of ANOC. As the rotund Mexican said:

> If the day came when we had to reduce the breadth of the empire, that would be the end of the Olympic Games. The IOC would then just have another world championships of international federations. We have to help maintain the participation of the small countries. If the Games were to become dedicated to high society, I wouldn't want to be a part of it.

On the one hand, the need to limit the number of competitors, and indeed the number of events within existing sports and the introduction of new sports, was paramount yet ignored: not least because of the advent of a spate of new nations with the break-up of the Soviet Union and the former Yugoslavia at the end of the 1980s. The inexorable growth of the numbers attending the Games made the burden on any host city extreme, at the same time limiting the number of cities able to consider hosting. As Samaranch said at the conclusion of the Seoul Games: 'We are at the limit. The Olympic bus is full. To take on one more passenger, someone else has to get off.' On the other hand, it was essential to preserve the dream for every sports competitor of achieving the ultimate accolade: of being an Olympic participant.

In the background, Gilbert Felli, the IOC's Technical Director, was working ceaselessly to rationalise the programme in terms of the number of events per sport and the numbers in those events. Shooting, weightlifting and wrestling, for instance, had agreed to reductions for 1992. Others were on fixed quotas, though the

IOC anti-apartheid commission led by Judge Kéba M'Baye meet Nelson Mandela at Nelspruit Airport prior to South Africa's return: (l–r) F. Carrard (Director-General), J.C. Ganga, E. Moses, K. M'Baye, N. Mandela, K. Gosper, H. Adefope, F. Kidane. (© IOC/Locatelli)

pressure on numbers was also mounting with the overdue move towards equal entry for women. Athletics and swimming continued to have the largest numbers, into four figures, yet even rowing, for example, had entries for 1992 of 690, cycling of 470. Much though the IOC would discuss reductions, the overall figure was always climbing with the introduction of new events, especially women's, and new sports: such fringe items as ice dancing, rhythmic gymnastics, synchronised swimming and beach volleyball. Boris Stankovic, the secretary–general of the basketball federation, was one of those appointed to look at adjustments to the programme in a debate during the Centenary Congress of 1994, and he pointed in vain to some of the anomalies. 'If you have team gymnastics events, why not team skating?' he said. 'The problem with multiple sports [modern pentathlon, triathlon] is that they tend to combine sports which are already there on the programme. Provocatively, beach volleyball has more competitors around the world than fencing.'

Short of dictatorship, the problem was insoluble. In the Winter Games, for example, the expensive luge and bobsleigh had member countries that had never taken part in any competition. A succession of chairmen of the Programme Commission, an overweight body, came and went with little happening. Peter Tallberg of Finland, 12 years on the Commission, said with exasperation: 'We've not taken *one* decision. Mostly, things are postponed. I feel that the Commission has no influence. When the skiing federation was allowed to include freestyle, I think they should have been told they could do so only if they eliminated another event.' Freestyle was the face of youth, however, as was mountain-bike cycling, and it was essential for the Games to reflect modern trends and participation.

Following the creation of the Olympic and Apartheid Commission in the Summer of 1988, there followed a series of crucial meetings that would lead towards South Africa's re-admission to the Olympic fold in July 1991, in advance of electoral democracy in that country. This was a triumph for Samaranch and the IOC, but was only possible through the magnanimity of Nelson Mandela and President F.W. de Klerk. The

various meetings in Vienna, Lausanne, Harare, Paris, Kuwait, Johannesburg and Gaborone, Botswana, concluded with a visit to South Africa in March 1990 to negotiate respectively with Prime Minister de Klerk, ANC leader Nelson Mandela and Inkatha Zulu Freedom Party leader Mangosuthu Buthelezi.

The IOC had been motivated throughout by the personal assurances of Mandela, plus its own confidence in the progressive intentions of de Klerk: the latter a politician of uncommon altruism, progressively devising the abolition of his own power. In parallel, the Executive Board was persuading all IFs to liaise with ANOCA and to accept re-admission of new multi-racial South African national federations as and when formally established. The speed at which attitudes towards South Africa were being reversed caught many by surprise.

The political upheaval elsewhere in the years 1989–92 was to cause a multitude of headaches for the IOC. The tumbling of the Berlin Wall, of the Soviet Union and the demise of the conglomeration of Balkan states under the name of Yugoslavia would produce ultimately a flurry of 17 new national states seeking admission to the Olympic Games, with their envied publicity and prestige. The IOC welcomed them, but it became a logistical nightmare for the organising committees in Albertville and Barcelona. The momentum began with the fall of the Berlin Wall on the night of 9 November 1989, the GDR authorities, given no support by Warsaw Pact allies, yielding to public pressure. Within a year there was one less NOC as the two Germanies united. Simultaneously, Croatia and Slovenia became the first Balkans to be recognised independently, as were the three Baltic States, Estonia, Latvia and Lithuania; while Bosnia/Herzegovina was given provisional membership mere days before the opening ceremony in Barcelona, following protracted negotiations by the IOC with the United Nations. Macedonia was unable to compete under its own flag or name due to a dispute with Greece.

Shortly before the Albertville Games, Samaranch flew to Moscow to meet Boris Yeltsin, President of the new Russian Republic. Together they re-structured one of the world's two foremost Olympic nations, achieving last-minute stability for the two Games of 1992. Across the cabinet table within the Kremlin Palace, decorated with freshly picked daffodils, the successor to Mikhail Gorbachev, his eyes deeply bloodshot, agreed with Samaranch to the compromise formation of a unified team embracing nine of the twelve newly independent states of the former USSR, with the shift of administrative power moving directly from the Soviet to the new Russian NOC. As a result of the creation of the unified team, Albertville and Barcelona would not be oversubscribed for beds. The new NOCs would gain recognition on acceptance of the provisional arrangements for 1992, which included use of the Olympic flag and anthem for team and individual medal winners, with the name and flag of the respective republic to be carried on the arm of the competitors' uniform. The three nations of the Caucasus – Georgia, Armenia and Azerbaijan – which over the centuries had produced some of the world's finest intellects and physical accomplishments, collectively contributed 22 competitors to the Confederation of Independent States (CIS) and between them won nine gold, one silver and six bronze medals. Samaranch allowed the $1.5 million owed by Russian television for Games coverage to be deferred, while generous sponsors such as Adidas picked up much of the bill for sending the teams. Intense negotiations by the IOC with the UN Security Council enabled competitors from the remnant Yugoslavia – Serbia/Montenegro – to compete as stateless individuals. None of this massive achievement, in the space of a few months, would have been possible without the IOC's substantial commercial

funding: itself the cause of so much sly criticism. The beneficiaries of this funding in the long run are the world's athletes.

The controversial election of Albertville and Barcelona in 1986 has been described in Chapter LVI. Once elected, Albertville's problems became more acutely focused: the huge spread of the Games over a 650-square-mile area; few venues but plenty of promises from 13 small towns or villages; and extensive debates on environmental protection, the most disastrous example of which was the bobsleigh and luge run at La Plagne, a tiny village, the construction escalating to $37 million. Protection of forest preserves were waived by the government, 35 million cubic feet of earth was removed from various mountainsides to build ski runs and parking lots. Four villages came close to bankruptcy, worst of all Brides-les-Bains, site of the competitors' Village, which had a $10 million deficit. The Games were a logistical horror, with only 18 of the 57 official events taking place at Albertville itself, the Games being a unit only as observed on television. It has to be questioned whether the Games really assisted the 900-year-old community of mountain farmers and cheesemakers, never mind what it did for sportsmen.

A triumph for the French was the opening ceremony on a starlit evening at Albertville's temporary stadium. Elegance, artistry and emotion filled the night air. A shameless attempted intervention by the European Union, to have the Games formally opened by EC President Jacques Delors in exchange for a mere $15 million of tax payers' money, had been properly rejected. Michel Platini, symbol of the spirit of French sport, and Francois-Cyril Grange, an eight-year-old local schoolboy, stood hand-in-hand in silhouette on the lip of the stadium against dark snow-clad peaks in the last of a pink sunset to ignite the Olympic flame.

Barcelona, on the other hand, created a blueprint for what might be achieved in reconstruction of civic facilities, never mind sports venues, by an Olympic city. More than that, it staged what, in the view of this writer, was one of the most spectacular and agreeable of all Games, the involvement of the local population together with visiting spectators continuing in the profusion of cafés and bars long into the night throughout the fortnight and indeed occasionally causing the closure of the Metro system adjacent to the Montjuic main stadium. By moving a stretch of north-bound railway, three miles of city beach were restored for accessibility, a 26-mile ring road was created, and the sewer system was renewed. An $8 billion project by the autonomous region of Catalonia, little different from Montreal's investment, included the commission of 50 works of sculpture for public areas: all this emotionally driven by Mayor Pasqual Maragall and coordinated by organisation president Miguel Abad.

When King Juan Carlos dedicated in 1989 the renovated Olympic Stadium, first built 60 years earlier, he was heckled by the fiercely independent Catalans, but at the opening ceremony three years later, speaking in Catalan as an act of conciliation, he received warm cheers. The ceremony was as emotional as that of the Winter Games six months earlier, the world audience serenaded by Placido Domingo, Jose Carreras and Montserrat Caballe and entertained by Christina Hoyos, the brightest flame in a fire of flamenco dancers. Among a record 169 nations, the Croatian flag-bearer was Wimbledon finalist Goran Ivanisevic, Sweden's was Stefan Edberg. The Cook Islands were headed by their weightlifter Sam Pera, and South Africa by Jan Tau, a black sports instructor born in 1960, the last year in which his country had appeared. Not a man or woman among the 12,000 who took part in the march-past would forget this night. At the climax, Antonio Rebollo, a disabled archer, fired an arrow into the darkness, its ignited tip carrying the cherished Olympic flame to light the bowl.

CHAPTER LX

Albertville (XVI) 1992

Alberto Tomba of Italy, first Alpine skier to retain an Olympic title

'*In terms of importance, the pleasure of being there, the fun, I rate the three Winter Olympic Games in which I won medals all about the same. In a way, Calgary was the best, because it seemed so easy – at that time I was winning so many races. I have to admit that for me it was almost a joke. I was considered the clown of my team and in a way I was playing at skiing. Every race was fun, I was so confident.*

At Albertville, the giant slalom was really difficult. When I won that, I think it was technically my best performance. The slope was tough at the top. I won the first run but was under pressure on the second. At the starting gate, I could hear the sound of 30,000 cheering people waiting at the bottom. Yes, I had been pretending to be confident, saying that these were the "Alberto-ville" Olympics, but inside I wasn't at all sure and now, with conditions difficult, I was genuinely nervous. But from the middle of the second run, down to the finish, I felt great.

At Lillehammer in 1994, where it was really cold, I was lucky when changing the wax on my skis. From 13th on the first run I was fastest on the second, only missing the gold medal by fifteen-hundredths of a second. We all had a great party even though I wasn't the winner. At Nagano four years later, the snow and the weather were really different. I fell in my first race and went home.

I think the Olympics in some ways may be less difficult than World Cup races and World Championships, where the courses tend to be steeper, where you need more strength, where you wake up and know that you have no room in which to feel below par. World Cup events are to a great extent just for sponsors and television stations, but at the Olympics I always felt happy, they're something special. The Olympic Games are like love and they are an inspiration for children.'*
(Photograph © Getty Images/Powell)

Alberto Tomba attracted the adulation associated with Formula One drivers or pop stars. Spectators followed him in their thousands. The number who crossed the Alps to be there at Val d'Isère in 1992 was said to be well into five figures. His aura equalled that of any footballer, even in Italy, and an unusual aspect of his prominence as an Alpine skier was that he came not from a conventional mountain background but from the city of Bologna. The spectators' trip was worth it, for he made history by becoming the first successfully to defend an Alpine title, so tough is the sport physically, so tiny the margins on a treacherous surface. Victory at Albertville in the giant slalom was achieved in the most dramatic manner, snatched with the fastest time of the last of the 15 seeded skiers.

Tomba's career since his double victory in Calgary had been in switchback mode. Fame and riches had blunted his always susceptible self-discipline and his form had slumped until the Italian federation, disturbed that he had won only four races in two years, appointed Gustavo Thöni, the champion of 1972, to be his coach, and also gave him a full-time fitness trainer. In the season approaching the Games, Tomba was back to his peak. Those likely to press him were Kjetil-André Aamodt of Norway and Marc Girardelli of Luxembourg, already winner and runner-up respectively in Albertville's super-G, and Paul Accola (SUI),

current leader of the World Cup. Although Girardelli was surpassed in his total World Cup victories, 36, only by Ingemar Stenmark and Pirmin Zurbriggen, his Olympic credentials thus far were moderate: ninth in the downhill at Calgary.

First of the favourites to ski was Aamodt, setting a fast time, but Tomba, sixth down, surpassed this with his 1:04.57 – a lead which he held by the conclusion of the first run, Girardelli lying in second place. Under his Luxembourg flag of convenience, the Austrian Girardelli then set the challenge with a brilliant second run, meaning that Tomba's reputation was now on the line. He began erratically and the huge crowd stood heart-in-mouth as his split times, flashed on the scoreboard at the finish, showed him to be trailing. On the bottom half of the course, he dramatically closed the gap but had no idea of the result until he saw the response of his wildly celebrating followers. It had been a close-run thing: at the first interval mark on the second run he had been an aggregate twelfth; at the second, sixth. His margin over Girardelli on the first run had been 0.13, on the second 0.19, for a final difference of 0.32 and a time of 2:06.98. Aamodt took the bronze medal with Accola fourth.

Three days later came the slalom at Les Ménuires and again a massive crowd had gathered overnight, defying the ban on private vehicles by arriving hours beforehand. Tomba was

Christian Jagge (NOR), son of an Olympian mother, denies Alberto Tomba a repeat double with victory in the slalom. (© Getty Images/Vandystadt)

aiming for something truly unique: a double defence, unlikely ever to be emulated. Once again he would be placed under immense pressure on his second run, this time by Finn Christian Jagge of Norway, whose mother had competed in the women's slalom at Innsbruck in 1964, finishing seventh. Tomba's form prior to the Games in the slalom had been a little less impressive than in the giant slalom, but now Jagge led him with a supreme first run, more than a second ahead of the second fastest, Michael Tritscher of Austria, and a huge 1.58 ahead of Tomba in sixth place. Tomba rose to the challenge on the second run – the gates coincidentally having been set by Thöni – overhauling all those ahead of him bar Jagge, whose sixth fastest time on the day was just sufficient to retain his overall lead by 0.28. Tomba was one of the first to congratulate him, though he would say later that he and his ski-technician had incorrectly prepared his skis for the course, especially on the first run. He did not dwell on it. 'The silver medal is good, I have no regrets,' he said.

The men's downhill course at Val d'Isère proved to be a test of skiers more than skis. Designed by Bernhard Russi, the Swiss Olympic champion of 1972, it had 25 turns instead of the usual 15 or so, making it an event less for downhill specialists than for all-round skiers. For Patrick Ortlieb, of Austria, in fact. The specialists condemned the course for being closer to a super-G run, the suspicion being that it would assist the 'home' favourite, Franck Piccard (the unsuccessful defending super-G champion). Those most fancied beforehand were Markus Wasmeier (GER), Franz Heinzer (SUI), then current World Cup leader, and the American A.J. Kitt. They would finish fourth, sixth and ninth respectively. Ortlieb himself considered the course not a true downhill, though he had never previously won one.

The drama of the day took some time to arrive. A big man for such a technical course, Ortlieb set the standard as first starter with a time of 1:50.37, the subsequent racers consistently failing to better him. Wasmeier, second starter, held second place, 0.25 behind him. Girardelli and Leonhard Stock of Austria, winner in 1980, both fell. Then Günther Mader overhauled Wasmeier by fifteen-hundredths of a second, to place Austria one and two. Now came a thunder of home supporters' feet on the metal stands as Piccard swept through the opening gate, but on the early section he was only ninth on split time. Gradually he accelerated and by the precipitous Buzzard Bump on the lower gradient he was lying second. Round the ferocious Eagle Turn

and into the final slope he came, but by five-hundredths he had failed to match Ortlieb. From the ovation, you would have supposed he had. 'Technically, it's extremely difficult,' Piccard said. 'Contrary to what some say, the speed at the top is too fast even for super-G skis.'

A cloud over the Games came with the death on the penultimate day of Nicholas Bochatay, a Swiss speed skier. This is potentially the most dangerous event, hurtling downhill at the pace of a Porsche. Bochatay had been a promising junior racer until an injury curtailed his prospects. He carried on with carpentry in the family business and turned his attention to speed skiing, becoming national champion. He had just improved his personal top speed to 210.65 kph. His death occurred in a collision with a course-laying caterpillar tractor while training shortly before the final. The men's demonstration event was won by Mikael Prufer from Savoie with a world record of 229.299 kph (142.470 mph). The sensation as the skiers go past, mid-slope, through the measured 100 metres, is like the sound of a Tornado jet flying low overhead: an approaching rumble mounting to a thundering, screaming hiss.

The women's downhill result at Meribel was as unexpected as the men's. Neither Kerin Lee-Gartner, the Canadian winner, nor Hilary Lindh of America had ever previously won a downhill. Lee-Gartner, fifteenth in her home town of Calgary, had never been higher than third. The course, designed like the men's by Russi, was one of the toughest of anyone's experience, both the longest and the steepest. Nonetheless, Lee-Gartner produced the performance of her life to become the first winner of the event from a non-German-speaking country. 'Four years ago, the dream was just a dream,' she said, 'but this time I knew I had a chance. It is the happiest day since my wedding day.' She was married to Max Gartner, a former Austrian coach. Lindh, from Alaska, never previously better than sixth in a World Cup event, was six-hundredths of a second behind Lee-Gartner's 1:52.55, and a mere three-hundredths ahead of third-placed Veronika Wallinger (AUT).

A smiling Pernilla Wiberg brings Sweden its first women's Alpine medal, when winning the giant slalom. (© Getty Images/Cole)

The women's giant slalom was won by a smiling Swede, Pernilla Wiberg, bringing her country its first-ever women's Alpine medal just when expectation surrounded Schneider of Switzerland, Kronberger and Wachter of Austria and Merle of France. Here was Wiberg, constantly criticised at home, producing, like Lee-Gartner, the race of her life. On the first run

283

she was second behind Maier, Merle half-a-second behind Maier. Schneider, Kronberger and Compagnoni of Italy all failed to complete the run, thinning the field. On the second run, Diann Roffe of America leapt from ninth to second, but Wiberg, with fine consistency in an all but identical time, kept her nose in front, Roffe and Wachter sharing the silver medal.

Frustration for Kronberger was eased by champion form in both slalom and combined events on the last and first day respectively of Alpine competition. She had been overwhelming favourite for the latter, the more so when her colleague and rival Sabine Ginther fell in practice the day before the downhill section. Kronberger won this by such a wide margin that she could afford to be prudent on the slalom section, still finishing way in front of Wachter.

It was steadiness that gave her the slalom title with two level runs three hours apart. Yet if victory was Kronberger's, the *story* was Coberger. Aged 20, Annelise Coberger of New Zealand had been climbing through the World Cup rankings. Now, eighth after the first run, she swept into second place with the fastest time on the second. She was the first competitor from the southern hemisphere to win any medal at a Winter Games. In third place was Bianca Fernández-Ochoa, the first Spanish woman to win either a Winter or Summer medal.

By 1992, ski jumping had become dominated by a new technique, the V-style, in which the skis were splayed rather than held parallel, thereby creating greater lift. Huge G-force is created in the drop and the new style was more dangerous. For Toni Nieminen, however, the technique came naturally and without fear, never mind that he was a mere 16. On the large hill, this year's height increased to 120m, he produced a final jump so huge that it gave Finland the inaugural team gold medal and pushed Austria, the first-round leaders, into second place. An early round of jumping had been terminated because the run was too fast and the starting point had been moved to reduce take-off speed: each kilometre per hour at around 95kph can add ten metres to a jump. Even on a reduced slope, Nieminen in the second round leapt 122 metres, his 245 points overhauling the gap of 30 behind the Austrians. Thus he became the youngest male Winter gold medal winner, at 16 years 259 days, being a day younger than William Fiske, the 1930s bobsleigher. Nieminen subsequently became the youngest individual winner, replacing American figure skater Dick Button from 1948, when claiming the 120m title. He outclassed the field with two massive leaps of 122 and then 123 metres, way beyond Austrians Martin Höllwarth, 17, and Heinz Kuttin. The

Toni Nieminen (FIN) perfects the new V-style jumping technique, surpassing Billy Fiske as the youngest male Winter champion.
(© Getty Images/Vandystadt)

boy-superstar had emerged as replacement for the celebrated Nykänen, yet would fail to make the teams of 1994 or 1998.

Figure skating favourite was clear-cut: Viktor Petrenko from Ukraine (EUN), bronze medal winner four years earlier and runner-up the following two years in the World Championships behind Kurt Browning of Canada, now his strongest rival alongside Petr Barna of the Czech Republic, and Americans Christopher Bowman and Paul Wylie. Nor could Alexei Urmanov and Vyacheslav Zagorodniuk of the Unified Team be discounted. Zagorodniuk in particular, without any affectation of dress and wearing a simple shirt, skated without inhibition, animal-like, while Urmanov displayed the traditional choreography that distinguishes the Russians. Browning was conspicuous for his concentric turns, arched backwards like John Curry; Wylie for his perfect blend between movement and music and his exhilarating jumps. Wylie was one of those who kept his sporting career in perspective while studying at Harvard. Petrenko, with soulful eyes and expressive arms, had both a fawn-like grace and breathtaking athleticism. He led on the short programme, as he usually did, and though he faded towards the end of his long programme, once falling, his string of 5.9s for artistic impression kept him above the erudite Wylie, who took the silver medal ahead of Barna, the latter having recently deposed Petrenko as European champion.

The climax of the ice dance event was the long-awaited duel between former Canadians representing France and a Ukrainian–Russian partnership of the Unified Team. It proved to be the difference between Bernstein and Bach. Isabelle and Paul Duchesnay, sister and brother, bewitched with their interpretation of *West Side Story*, but Marina Klimova and Sergei Ponomarenko had the classic poise with which there could be no argument. The married couple had an inspirational quality in their flowing symmetry which the judges regard above mere show-business novelty. There is a fine line between fun and technical refinement. The two leading pairs provided a dazzling contest, the Canadians causing a stir when Isabelle lifted Paul.

Gustav Weder, a Zurich PE teacher, proved to be the man on form in the two-man bobsleigh, but only at the last gasp, so to speak. By 0.29 and 0.33 respectively, he took the title ahead of the German first and second pairs, driven by Rudolf Lochner and Christoph Langen. Prior to Weder's victory, Switzerland, one of the foremost nations of Winter Sports, had no more than a single bronze medal. The driving of Weder, double world champion in 1990 and runner-up in both events in 1991, arrived as a national face-saver. At the end of the first day's two runs, Weder had been fifth behind Britain, Italy, *Austria II* and *Germany II*. 'I drove from the very worst to the very best in the space of four runs,' he said.

The mountainside echoed to the sound of Austrian cow bells when their four-man team took the title by the closest margin ever in the Olympic tournament. Ingo Appelt and his crew had been tenth in the second run, but their aggregate 3:53.90 over the four runs was two-hundredths faster than *Germany I*, with Weder guiding Switzerland to the bronze medal.

Bonnie Blair of America had set a world record when winning the speed skating 500m in 1988. She lost incentive when her father died later that year but in a determined comeback retained her title in Albertville, though with a time more than a second slower. In doing so she was aided by the coincidental obstruction of Qiaobo Ye of China. Ye had been suspended immediately prior to Calgary for a positive test for steroids, allegedly administered to innocent young competitors by the team doctor, for which she served a 15-month suspension. She had almost quit the sport and now, skating in the second pair against Yelena Tioushniakova (EUN), was momentarily

Bonnie Blair (USA) achieves a speed skating double at 500/1,000m at the expense of Qiaobo Ye (CHN). (© Getty Images/Bruty)

private tragedy, and Uwe-Jens Mey, former East German, the pair having shared repetitive encounters and also the world record. Jansen, however, suffered a mental block and finished fourth, as he had eight years earlier, Mey winning with a relatively slow time.

There was a shock in the men's 10,000m when Johann Olav Koss, the world record holder for whom global fame still lay two years ahead, was defeated by Dutchman Bart Veldkamp. The streets of Albertville rang to the sound of Dutch klaxons. It had been a tough Games for Koss. He had only left hospital the day after the opening ceremony, suffering from gall stones, and had come seventh five days later in the 5,000m, for which he also held the record – won by his colleague Geir Karlstad.

Twelve days before her fortieth birthday, Raisa Smetanina of the Unified Team skied the second lap of the victorious 20km relay team. She thus became the oldest female gold medal winner in any sport at a Winter Games since they began in 1924, extending her collection of medals to ten (four–five–one) and becoming the first woman to win a medal at five consecutive Games. She had been national Nordic champion twenty-one times and seven times world champion. Her ten medals surpassed the nine of Swedish cross-country skier Sixten Jernberg (1956–60).

Vegard Ulvang became the first Norwegian man to win an Olympic cross-country race for 16 years, Norway indeed having a clean sweep in the 30km with Ulvang, Bjørn Daehlie and Terje Langli. Furthermore, the Norwegians were to win all five Nordic events. Ulvang won the 10km even though he fell midway and broke a ski pole, a spectator friend handing him a replacement.

obstructed on the change-over from inside to outside lane. An appeal for a re-run by the Chinese was rejected and Blair, supported by an entourage of family and friends who had crossed the Atlantic, was the winner by eighteen-hundredths of a second. Ye's silver, the first by an Asian woman in the Winter Games, was some compensation.

In the men's 500m, all was set for a showdown between Dan Jansen (USA), whose bid four years ealier had been wrecked by

Ki-Hoon Kim (KOR) leads home Michael McMillen (NZL) 4th, Fred Blackburn (CAN), 2nd and Joon-Ho Lee (KOR), 3rd in the inaugural 1,000m short track. (© Getty Images/Vandystadt/Martin)

Vegard Ulvang (NOR), wins the cross-country 10km after a fall, seen here ahead of Christer Majbäck (SWE), 3rd, and Harri Kirvesniemi (FIN), 6th. (© Getty Images/Cole)

CHAPTER LXI

Barcelona (XXV) 1992

Paraskevi 'Voula' Patoulidou of Greece, Olympic 100m hurdles champion

'*My parents were farmers in Florina, where I was born in 1965, but it was in Germany, where we went to live for four years, that my sporting talent first emerged. Before the Games in Barcelona, there had been lesser successes – silver medallist for the hurdles at the Mediterranean Games in 1991, gold medals for the hurdles and the 100m in the Balkan Games of 1990. Now at last, in Barcelona, I could stop asking myself how it would feel for an athlete to listen to the national anthem of her country inside a crowded stadium with a medal hanging round her neck – not any simple medal, but Olympic gold, all the more rewarding when one's ancestors were those who conceived and set themselves to organise the Olympic Games. While I stood on the podium during the fleeting moments of the award ceremony, tears of liberation filled my eyes.*

For many years I had been tormented, for I had kept locked in my heart two different and mutually exclusive images of my country, Greece. One was Greece as people abroad cared to regard it and the other was Greece as every Greek desired with all his heart for his homeland to be treated. And now there I was – with the strength of my soul, with perseverance and lots of work, I had managed to raise my head and gaze out at the world with pride. Years of repressed experience drove me, at this highest of moments, to an unprecedented burst of emotion. How was I not then to cry out, to the rest of the world, along with all Greeks, with all my strength as I clasped my medal: "For Greece, damn the rest of you."

I could never have known how my life would change. The self-confidence I gained after winning that medal led me down paths I would never have pursued before, such as changing my event and my financial well-being, which I shared not only with my family but also happily with those I knew to be in need. I wrote a book, visited schools, participated in seminars, gave birth to an adorable son and came back to the field of sports competition with my husband Dimitris – who was eighth in weightlifting in the Moscow Games – a loyal supporter by my side. Much of this stemmed from that experience in Barcelona and the awareness that nothing is given away free in life but instead achieved by striving.'*
(Photograph © IOC/Strahm)

The victory of Paraskevi 'Voula' Patoulidou was one of those distinctive moments in sport, aided by mischance befalling another. Patoulidou was the first Greek woman ever to win an Olympic medal in any sport, if we exclude the Interim Games of 1906, and indeed was the first Greek woman even to qualify for a track final. Furthermore, she was the first Greek, man or woman, to win a gold medal in track and field since Konstantin Tsiklitiras in 1912 in the standing long jump. If victory brought her uncontained happiness, it was joy shared by an entire nation, the more so because of its unexpectedness. Victory was supposed to rest between Lyudmila Narozhilenko of Russia, world champion the previous year, and the then runner-up, Gail Devers (USA), who was already champion in Barcelona in the 100m sprint. As it happened, Narozhilenko fell by the wayside in the semi-final, pulling a hamstring, and just when it seemed that Devers was moving untroubled to a second gold medal she struck the final hurdle. Stumbling towards the finishing line, she was passed by four runners separated by only a tenth of a second. Patoulidou was unaware of her victory over LaVonna Martin of America – with defending champion Yordanka

Paraskevi Patoulidou of Greece lunges towards the first gold medal for Greece in 80 years, in the 100m hurdles, ahead of LaVonna Martin (USA), while leader Gail Devers (USA), (right), the favourite, hits the tenth hurdle and stumbles. (© Getty Images/Vandystadt)

Donkova of Bulgaria a further one-hundredth behind in third place – until she saw the video replay on the stadium screen.

Devers could console herself with her earlier title, a hair's-breadth finish requiring a photograph to separate Juliet Cuthbert (JAM) and Irina Privalova (EUN) in second and third place, with pre-race favourites Gwen Torrence (USA) and Merlene Ottey (JAM) further hundredths away. A notable absentee had been Katrin Krabbe, double sprint world champion from the former GDR, suspended during the previous winter following a controversial drug test. During the previous four years, Devers had been suffering headaches and sight problems, and was eliminated in the hurdles semi-finals in Seoul before being diagnosed as suffering from Graves's Disease. For more than two years, during whch she underwent radiation treatment, she was unsure whether she would be able to return to competition.

Though the XXVth Summer Games were a friendly festival that would have delighted the founder, there was, as in Seoul four years earlier, an instance of apparent cheating. Seldom has there been a more blatant example of manipulative tactics than in the climax to the men's 10,000m between Khalid Skah of Morocco and Richard Chelimo of Kenya. The pelting of an Olympic champion with rubbish by the crowd during his lap of honour, his subsequent disqualification for allegedly receiving assistance during the race and then his re-instatement were without parallel. The controversy was that Hammou Boutayeb, compatriot of Skah, had conspicuously assisted his colleague over the final four laps when himself running a lap behind the two leaders. Rule 143/2 of the IAAF defines illegal assistance clearly enough: 'conveying advice, information or help,

including pacing by persons not participating, by runners lapped or about to be lapped . . .'. Whether by design or spontaneously, Boutayeb, having been lapped, was interfering in the race, intermittently setting the pace and arguably even obstructing Chelimo, who initially was awarded the gold medal upon Skah's disqualification. It did not matter whether Skah had or had not sought Boutayeb's assistance – though video evidence suggested he himself was disconcerted by Boutayeb's action – because Boutayeb's intervention inevitably disrupted Chelimo's concentration, physical and mental. Boutayeb deliberately accelerated and then slowed the pace over the final laps, turning a two-man duel into, temporarily, a three-man race. With just over a lap remaining, Boutayeb had received an official warning, Carl Tollemar, chairman of the IAAF technical committee, encroaching on the track to wave him away, and the crowd whistled the Moroccans derisively until Boutayeb abandoned the race. A confused Skah, asked if he was staying on in Barcelona, replied: 'I'll be gone tomorrow . . . legally.' There had been a history of antagonistic racing between Kenya and Morocco over several seasons, of which this race was symptomatic.

Linford Christie of Britain earned acclaim for the style with which he won the 100m at the veteran age of 32. He did so with bravado and self-assurance, though this summit, with its financial rewards running to seven figures, was both unexpected and fortunate. Six years earlier, already middle-aged for a sprinter, Christie had been no more than an average international performer at 200m. He then belatedly converted to the shorter race as his premier distance. In Seoul, Johnson was not the only Jamaican emigrant testing positive, as Christie in third place was also found to have traces of pseudo-ephedrine. He claimed this was the product of drinking excessive amounts of ginseng tea and the quantities found were so slight that the medical commission gave him the benefit of the doubt. Johnson's disqualification promoted Christie to the silver medal behind Carl Lewis.

Now, Lewis had failed to qualify. Though the Olympic year had proved thus far a good season for Christie, the threat was Leroy Burrell of the US, former world record holder. Christie beat him in the heats, then lost to him in the semi-final. For reasons uncertain, Burrell seldom ran with total confidence when Lewis, his club colleague, was not in the race, and now he false-started in the final, losing his focus. Christie, with a poor start, accelerated in each of the first six ten-metre phases, by the end of which he had overhauled Frankie Fredericks of Namibia to take the lead. In second place, Fredericks was the first black African to win a 100m medal.

If a third successive sprint gold was not to be for Lewis, a year younger than Christie, there was no denying him an exceptional third gold in the long jump. Subsequent victory in the sprint relay – his eighth gold medal – meant he had equalled the tally of the 'standing' jumper Ray Ewry at the turn of the century. For ten years or more, the phenomenal Lewis had pursued the world record of Bob Beamon, only to be thwarted in that ambition in 1991 by Mike Powell with 8.95m (29 ft 4½ in.), Lewis himself twice clearing 29 feet. His revenge was to retain his Olympic title for a second time, Powell being confined to the silver medal by three centimetres, or an inch and a quarter. His public relations so often his weakest point, Lewis displeased colleagues and the crowd by taking his victory lap in the middle of a 5,000m semi-final. Powell said graciously: 'He's the best ever. A lot of things are said about him on and away from the track, but I have a tremendous amount of respect for Carl.'

For those wanting records, a notable one came from Kevin Young of the United States. The 400m hurdles mark of 47.02 by

Khalid Skah (MAR), controversial winner, trails Richard Chelimo (KEN), runner-up in the 10,000m. (© Getty Images/Mortimore)

To his and the home crowd's delight, Fermin Cacho wins 1,500m gold for Spain, never mind the slowest time for 36 years. (© Getty Images/Hewitt)

Edwin Moses had stood for almost a decade, seeming as unattainable as Beamon's jump. Prior to the Games, Young had become one of the favourites with repeated dominance over Samuel Matete of Zambia, the reigning world champion, but Young's personal best was a relatively moderate 47.72 achieved some four years back. Now, suddenly, he ran into form, clocking 47.63 in the semi-final, though finishing second to Winthrop Graham of Jamaica by a whisker. Matete, in third place, was disqualified for running out of lane. In a sharp final race, Young destroyed the rest of the field, in spite of clipping the last hurdle, and won by nine-tenths of a second, improving the time of Moses by 0.24 with 46.78. 'I never thought I'd see the day in my generation that someone would bust the record,' said Kriss Akabusi, British bronze winner.

Triumph was almost as sweet for Young-Cho Hwang as it had been for Patoulidou. It had been 56 years to the very day that a Korean won the marathon, but then it had been under an imposed Japanese name during the time of occupation. Now Hwang was nearly half a stadium lap ahead of Koichi Morishita of Japan, having successfully forged his way up the gruelling incline from the city centre to Montjuic Stadium. After a tense mid-race battle with Morishita, Hwang had moved clear of his rival five kilometres from the finish. On the podium, the two men embraced in mutual respect. Stephan Freigang of Germany took the bronze.

The defeats of Noureddine Morceli of Algeria in the 1,500m and Sergei Bubka of Ukraine (EUN) in the pole vault were difficult to accept, for them and for observers. For Fermin

Cacho, winner of the 1,500m, it was the making of his career, never mind that his time, 3:40.12, was the slowest for 36 years. Cacho's own disbelief was such that in his run to the line he looked behind him eight times, becoming the first runner from Spain ever to win a gold medal. Morceli, undefeated over four laps the previous season, when he won the World Championship with ease, was the strongest of favourites until he was set back early in the year by an injury which, prior to the Games, brought an end to his 21-race winning sequence. Nonetheless, the final seemed well within his compass and was invitingly led at a pedestrian pace by Joseph Chesire of Kenya for a dawdling first two laps of 2:06.83, slower than in the women's race. The gold medal should have been in Morceli's palm, but he became boxed in on the final back straight. On the last bend, Cacho overtook Chesire on the inside and surged into a lead of four or five strides. Nobody was able to challenge him as he pounded down the home straight, an ecstatic crowd as astonished as he was. Morceli, trailing home in seventh place, recovered morale to break Saïd Aouita's seven-year-old world record a month later.

More than many, Bubka was disconcerted by the swirling wind and the world champion and record holder departed without any medal. 'My nerves were playing on me,' the emperor of this event strangely admitted. 'Most of us had problems along the run-up from the wind, and I was one of them.' Not so Maksim Tarasov, another member of the Unified Team, who won on fewer attempts than colleague Igor Trandenkov, at the same height of 5.80. Javier Garcia of Spain took the bronze at 5.75, the mark at which Bubka failed. Trandenkov was simultaneously happy and sad. 'My friend and coach, Sergei, failed to achieve what he wanted, but his pupil took the silver,' he said.

Javier Sotomayor became Cuba's first track and field medallist since 1980, though never approaching his high jump world record of 2.44m (8 ft 0 in.): his winning leap of 2.34m (7 ft 8 in.) was the lowest for 16 years. Clearing the same height, Patrik Sjöberg of Sweden took silver, for a second time, on the failure count-back, while three jumpers, Hollis Conway (USA), Tim Forsythe (AUS) and Artur Partyka (POL) tied for the bronze.

The newly reintegrated South Africa had scrambled to assemble a team of sorts and there was celebration when Elana Meyer was second in the women's 10,000m, becoming the first from her politically isolated nation since 1960 to win a track and field medal. The tactics of level-pace attrition that had won Liz

Sporting ideal. Derartu Tulu, Ethiopian winner of the 10,000m, embraces runner-up Elana Meyer of newly re-integrated South Africa. (© Getty Images/Powell)

McColgan of Britain the world title the previous year failed to work a second time: at the halfway stage the pack was still with her and a kilometre later Meyer forged ahead. Derartu Tulu of Ethiopia, not McColgan, moved in pursuit, clinging to Meyer's raised pace and finally making a strike with just over a lap to go, to win by almost six seconds with McColgan a distant fifth. It was symbolic of the Olympic ethos when the first female black African Olympic medal winner, a former shepherd, and a white South African set off hand-in-hand on a lap of mutual triumph. 'It was amazing to get on the track and to know this was for the real South Africa,' Meyer said.

There was equally shared joy at the conclusion of a gruelling women's marathon run in temperatures approaching 30°C (86°F). With a quarter of the race remaining, Valentina Yegorova of Russia had moved into the lead, only to find Yuko Arimori of Japan doggedly clinging to her heels. Together they clawed their way up the intimidating approaching hill to the stadium, Yegorova finding the strength for a final burst that brought her victory by some eight seconds in an expectedly slowish 2:32:41. With the last of their strength the two women hugged in relief and mutual respect.

There was a special kind of defiant self-respect in the stance of Hassiba Boulmerka of Algeria when winning the 1,500m. Her expression was one of pride, awe and satisfaction. Reviled by Muslim fundamentalists in her own country for stripping bare her arms, legs and face in order to run, her victory made her as much a martyr for the free expression of Algerian women as a heroine, having crossed the line a clear winner, despite her ungainly gait, from Ludmila Ragacheva (EUN) and Yunxia Qu (CHN). There she stood, arms and legs spread wide and taut, as though still lunging for victory, and as if to say: 'Here I am, look at me, acknowledge me and accept me.' She tore at her bib number, trying to reveal her country's name on her vest as the cameras converged. She herself was a devout Muslim. This was the first race in which four women beat four minutes.

Defending champion Olga Bryzgina of the Ukraine was defeated in the 400m by the rising French star Marie-José Perec. Born in Guadeloupe, Perec had leapt to the fore when winning the previous year's world title. Bryzgina led into the final straight in Barcelona, only for the girl who doubled as a Paris model to pull away and win by more than a stride in 48.83 – the first sub-49 time to be run for four years. Asked whether she thought she could lower the world record – still held by Marita Koch of the former GDR at 47.60 – Perec said provocatively: 'I think the world record is the race I ran today, to run this race I didn't need any biological preparation.' This veiled accusation of drug assistance brought no comment from Bryzgina, sitting beside her as silver medal winner and one of the five to have previously beaten 49 seconds.

The one-lap hurdles event provided reward for the persistence of Sally Gunnell of Britain, who with commendable steadiness beat the extrovert Sandra Farmer-Patrick of America on the run-in. From their behaviour at the medal interviews it would have been easy to suppose, from their respective modesty and self-acclaim, that the result had been the reverse. Gunnell's inner patience and desire was matched by Ellen van Langen of Holland in the 800m. Langen, who went into the final holding the fastest time of the year, successfully held off the challenge of Lilia Nurutdinova (EUN) and Anna Quirot, the prominent Cuban, whose coach had recently died.

A charming result at the swimming pool was that of Pablo Morales, who at the age of 27 made a belated re-appearance, having won a gold and two silver as a 19 year old in 1984. Then he had been world record holder and favourite for the 100m butterfly, but was swept aside by the formidable Michael Gross

Alexander Popov of the Unified Team (right) achieves the sprint double of 50/100m freestyle, here in the former at the expense of Matt Biondi (USA). (© Getty Images/Vandystadt/Martin)

of West Germany. By the time of Seoul, Morales had regained the record, but failed to qualify in the US trials and retired. To make a comeback after three and a half years was remarkable, though his record was still standing. Morales led from the turn and by three-hundredths got the touch ahead of Rafal Szukala of Poland. Defending champion Anthony Nesty of Surinam was third.

Seldom over the past 32 years had America been shut out of the gold medals in the three men's freestyle 'sprint' events, but now these were dominated by the Unified Team. Alexander Popov took both the 50m and 100m, Yevgeni Sadovyi the 200m and 400m, the latter in a world record 3:45.00. The only medal from these that the Americans could claim was Matt Biondi's silver in the 50m. Now in the twilight of his career, Biondi shared in America's 4 x 100m medley relay for his 11th Olympic medal since 1984.

There was a notable improvement by competitors of the Chinese Republic, particularly the 19-year-old Zhuang Yong, silver medal winner in Seoul, who took the women's 100m freestyle ahead of world record holder Jenny Thompson with an Olympic record of 54.64. Yong was repeatedly forced to deny claims within the swimming community that Chinese training was aided by steroids.

Whatever the deeds in swimming, they were outshone by the magnetism of Mingxia Fu, a tiny 13-year-old girl from Hubei Province in China, who made a diving display of breathtaking daring high on the crown of Montjuic. Already the youngest-ever world champion in the sport, by a massive margin she became the youngest-ever Olympic diving champion. It was not victory so much as a solo exhibition. Barcelona baked like a biscuit as the competition at the open-air pool unfolded against the shimmering, hazy background of Gaudi's Sagrada Familia and the twin towers that formed the entrance to the Olympic Village. The spectacle for the packed crowd, perspiring in the sun, was almost like watching sky-diving. In the preliminaries Fu established a 32-point lead and extended this overnight to 50. The silver medal was taken by Yelena Mirochina, aged 18, from Moscow, with Mary Ellen Clark, a United States veteran at 29, claiming the bronze. The smoothness of Fu's athleticism in the air, especially when viewed in slow motion, had an elegance beyond belief. Not a finger or toe was out of alignment, no sign of muscle as the body twisted and rotated. Some of the bigger girls had shoulders and biceps comparable to the men's, but the

Mingxia Fu, breathtaking 13-year-old from China.
(© Getty Images/Vandystadt)

Chinese had an opalescence of precious stones. Here was one of the most aesthetic sights of the entire Games.

Women's gymnastics is predominantly a competition for gnats: diminutive girl-women who perform dazzling exercises all but impossible for the rest of the human race. In the musical *Chorus Line*, there is the sardonic comment by one of the auditioning dancers, when the producer announces he needs eight girls: 'Do they need any *women*?' In gymnastics, it tends to be the gnats, not the women, who win the medals. In the all-round team competition, Kim Zmeskal, from Houston, Texas, the 1991 individual world champion who barely came up to the bottom rib of Bela Karolyi, her coach, fell off the beam in her first exercise. It was to cost her and her team dearly. Zmeskal, with her sad grey eyes in a child's face, declined to warm up for her second discipline, the floor, talking earnestly to Karolyi. However, she answered disaster with a muscular display, then compensated further on the vault and bars. This was, after all, a team event, with the top thirty-six, including only the best three from one country, proceeding to the individual finals. It was left to another American gnat, Shannon Miller, to counterbalance the team's fortunes with a series in the high nines (out of ten). Yet, for all Miller's leading marks, the USA was able to achieve no better than the bronze behind the Unified Team and Romania, the former serenely led by Svetlana Boguinskaya – a mature giant of five feet (1.83m), aged 19, half-child half-woman. She gave the impression she had already thought about life after the Olympics: in the ex-Soviet Union, you needed to. In the all-round individual she and Zmeskal, respective world champions of 1989 and 1991, were the favourites but Zmeskal was now out of sight and Boguinskaya, from Belorussia, could finish no better than fifth. The title went to a 15-year-old Ukrainian, Tatyana Gutsu, who had also fallen off the beam during the team competition. With only three to advance from the Unified Team, she was out – until officials announced the withdrawal of Roza Galiyeva with a convenient knee injury. Of strikingly similar appearance to Gutsu, Miller distinguished herself by taking the silver medal, hitting a near-perfect vault for a mark of 9.975.

One of the most refined performers, on the same level as Mingxia Fu, was Vitali Scherbo of Belorussia (EUN), with his unique six gold medals in men's gymnastics: team and individual all-round and four in solo apparatus. Like the women, though within a more natural muscular frame, the men

achieve marvels of balance and coordination. It is arguable that Scherbo in 1992 was one of the finest ever exponents of his sport.

Richard Fox of Britain, who had dominated slalom canoeing longer than any competitor at the Games, winning four World Championships and three World Cup series, failed to earn the medal he deserved on the return of the sport for the first time since the Munich Games. 'Someone had to come fourth,' he said philosophically, still sitting in his canoe moments after finishing his second run, which had just failed to dislodge the leaders. The winner was Pierpaolo Ferrazzi of Italy, who commendably jumped in front from 17th place on his first run. Fox, throwing everything into his own first run down the course, with its 25 tortuously positioned gates in an Olympic tournament which came just too late for him at 32, had attempted to frighten the field. Not for nothing was he one of the firmest favourites in any sport. He recorded a time more than two seconds faster than Ferrazzi would at the second attempt, but had clipped the free-hanging poles at three gates for a crippling 15-second penalty. Fox's second, clear run was not quite good enough. Sylvain Curinier (FRA) and Jochen Lettmann (GER) took silver and bronze.

Badminton staged its inaugural Olympic tournament, the respective singles winners being Alan Budi Kusuma of Indonesia – world champion Jianhua Zhao of China having been eliminated in the quarter-final – and compatriot Susi Susanti. The doubles were both won by South Korea. Mixed doubles was excluded, resulting in Myung Hee Chung of South Korea, the best player in either women's or mixed doubles, being an absentee, having discovered too late that she could qualify only for women's doubles. The matter was put right when mixed was included four years later.

There was a stirring result in the subsequently discontinued coxed pairs at the beautiful rowing course at Banyoles. The Abbagnale brothers of Italy, Carmine and Giuseppe, had won seven world and two Olympic championships and were unbeaten since 1986. Jonny and Greg Searle, in contrast, had only become a pair earlier that year, yet it was they who had the fastest times in the heats and semi-finals. Halfway through the final, the Searles trailed the Italians by nearly two lengths and were also astern of Romania. It seemed impossible that the British pair, with their cox Gary Herbert, could haul back the Italians from a greater distance than they had given Romania and Germany in earlier races. They overtook Romania with 300 metres to go, but the Italians, though both now in their 30s, were still a length clear. The Searles, however, produced a devastating finish, five seconds faster than the Italians over the last 500 metres, inching in front with only five strokes to go. 'Everything was going black,' Greg, the stroke, said. 'I did not know what was happening. It was lucky being brothers because we switched on to the same autopilot.' Both had won world junior gold medals as schoolboys. In the coxless pairs Steve Redgrave and Matthew Pinsent successfully defended the title won by Redgrave with Andrew Holmes in Seoul.

In overwhelming heat, many of the world's top professionals fell by the way in the tennis men's singles, including Stefan Edberg, Pete Sampras, Thomas Muster, Michael Chang and Michael Stich. The winner was Marc Rosset of Switzerland, ranked 44th in the world. The women's event was weakened by Monica Seles, Martina Navratilova and Gabriella Sabatini being declared ineligible for refusing to play in the Federation Cup. Steffi Graf, the presumed winner, was beaten in a three-set final by Jennifer Capriati, a teenage American prodigy who had been the youngest semi-finalist in the history of the French and Wimbledon Opens. Capriati was

Magic Johnson, celebrated figure of the celebrated Dream Team.
(© Getty Images/Powell)

now heading for desolate private disintegration from which she would happily recover and return to prominence.

In the table tennis singles the brilliant but often disappointing Jan-Ove Waldner of Sweden was an overwhelming champion, the women's title being won by Yaping Deng of China, a spectacular teenager who had had to contend with lack of height but now defeated Qiao Hong, with whom she had already won the doubles event.

There was never much doubt about the outcome of the men's basketball, the international federation, FIBA, having decided three years earlier to permit the NBA professionals from America to participate. Thus arrived in Barcelona the so-called Dream Team of Magic Johnson, Larry Bird, Michael Jordan, Charles Barclay and the rest. They predictably won as they pleased, following a friendly opening encounter with their ideological rivals from Cuba, eventually defeating Croatia in the final – though the Croats impertinently led 25–23 at one stage and allowed the millionaire Americans their narrowest margin, 117–85. The Unified Team defeated China 76–66 in the women's final.

Sergei Bubka of Ukraine, representing the Unified Team, failed in his defence of the pole vault title – 'problems along the run-up with the wind'. His colleague, and winner, Maksim Tarasov, seemed wind-free. (© IOC)

Susi Susanti of Indonesia smashes her way to the women's singles title, defeating Soo-Hyun Bang on badminton's first Games appearance.
(© Getty Images /Botterill)

CHAPTER LXII

Winter Wonderland

Mario Vazquez Raña of Mexico, IOC Executive Board member, president of ANOC and ODEPA

'As in Olympia of old, the values promoted by sport are an inspiration for youth and a pillar of peace and friendship. The Olympic Movement has the greatest support and participation ever achieved by an international organisation. It has generated faith in human endeavour and has contributed to the development and participation of all countries, making no distinction of sex, race, religion or political beliefs.

It has not been easy to make these principles a reality. In some countries, for various reasons, including incomprehension or lack of strategy, or shortage of material and financial resources, the road has been difficult. Olympism is a part of ethical, aesthetical and moral values. Its consolidation is inherent within education, health and social progress. The Association of National Olympic Committees (ANOC) works together with NOCs to promote Olympic education; to collaborate with governments in programmes guaranteeing sporting activity as a civic right; to support the formation and maintenance of sports facilities; to contribute to the development of athletes; and to guarantee that, even with different levels of development, all countries can participate at the Olympic Games.

The IOC has been receptive to the needs of smaller countries. In coordination with ANOC and the IFs, it has assisted countries' Olympic participation, irrespective of size. The concept of small countries is not confined to population and territorial size, but the level of sports development and of Olympic traditions. A strategy of universality and integration within the Olympic Movement has been effectively applied and we have witnessed what it means to those countries to have their flags and athletes at an Olympic ceremony. If added to that are any outstanding individual performances, it becomes a factor of incalculable strength and motivation. Professionalism and marketing have underlined the breach between the developed and less-developed countries but this must not lead to discrimination or exclusion. Financial resources must be used to address this breach.

In some situations, the concept of Olympism is confined to regional and sub-regional Games that are celebrated every year, where tens of thousands of young athletes participate. ANOC, through its Continental Associations, organises and supports these events, which constitute the antecedents of the Olympic Games. Years of experience devoted to sport, and the progress achieved during recent decades, together with increasing sports consciousness around the world, make me feel optimistic about the future. If we preserve unity, if we adhere to original principles, if we support those who need us most, if competition continues to be the centre of our concern, the Olympic Movement will prevail.'
(Photograph © IOC/Locatelli)

At the 100th Session, at Lausanne in June 1993, there was an attempted collaboration by the IOC with the Association of Summer Olympic International Federations (ASOIF) to launch a double initiative: a unified approach to drug controls and suspensions, among all IFs; and the creation of independence for an International Council of Arbitration in Sport (ICAS), as governing body separate from the IOC, for the Court of Arbitration for Sport (CAS) originally established in 1983. The effective operation of the independent body, ICAS, financed by the Olympic Movement, could limit the extent of damaging litigation in civil courts, such as that brought by Butch Reynolds (USA) and Katrin Krabbe (GER) against the IAAF. The composition of ICAS would be four members from each of the IOC, IFs, NOCs and the competitors – the latter nominated by the Athletes Commission – and four eminent, independent, co-

opted personalities. Any appearance of dependence was to be eliminated in order to secure acceptance of ICAS's decisions by state courts in any country, and their hoped-for reluctance to overthrow such decisions. The Swiss Federal Tribunal (Supreme Court) had already acknowledged this principle. Acceptance of CAS would be an obligatory condition for IF inclusion in the Olympic programme.

The crisis for sport was all too apparent, emphasised in the early 1990s by exceptional performances in swimming and track and field by Chinese women and the subsequent positive tests of many of them; though Arne Ljungqvist, Swedish member of the medical commissions of IOC and IAAF, made the point that with the population size of China, there was the possibility, through extremes of genetic, glandular constitution, of excessive performance that was not classifiable as abnormal:

that China had a greater chance than any other country of producing 'natural freaks'. The Chinese NOC, desperate to earn credibility, not to mention the hosting of a Games, would henceforth pay rigorous attention to domestic testing.

In his report on marketing at the Session of June 1993, Richard Pound revealed that, for the first time, the income from marketing rights exceeded that from US television rights. This was a development Samaranch had been seeking throughout his presidency: avoidance of television dependency and a more evenly balanced spread of income. The IOC had now reached the point at which TOP III (1993–6), up to and including the Centenary Games in Atlanta, would produce a minimum $270 million. This compared with $90 million for TOP I and $175 million for TOP II. The TOP II revenue, together with sponsorship raised by the Barcelona local organising committee, had thus surpassed the NBC rights fee for 1992 of $401 million. One of the newest elite sponsors for TOP III was IBM, which had entered into an eight-year agreement up to 2000, taking in two Summer and two Winter Olympics: the largest ever sponsorship deal by a single company, with a value believed to be in excess of $200 million. Much of that figure would be in kind: the provision of information technology, the results service on which any Games depends, and on account of which IBM's 'entry fee' into TOP III would be less than most of the other members such as Coca-Cola, Kodak, Visa, Matsushita (Panasonic), Zerox, Time-Warner and Bausch and Lomb (Ray-Ban). A hidden cost of any TOP membership, of course, is that, with stadium advertising banned, uniquely in major sport, sponsors have to spend many millions advertising and promoting their exclusive membership – though IBM would enjoy the advantage of its logo being visible in the bottom corner of information screens and television transmissions bearing the results.

The technology challenge to a sponsor such as IBM was immense. For their first Games as sponsor in Lillehammer, there would be 50,000 users of the results/information units distributed throughout the venues, media centres, hotels and competitors' Village. 'If you can handle an Olympics, you can handle anything,' said Paul Wipperfürth, director of IBM's international sports office in Paris. 'If we fail, the Olympics fail.' Other sponsors faced a similar challenge. Kodak, for instance, at

Against the panoramic background of Lake Geneva, President Samaranch addresses the audience at the formal opening of the Olympic Museum, heavily sponsored by oriental multinationals.
(© IOC/Jenny)

an opening ceremony have to handle 500 photographers exposing 30 to 40 rolls of film each and expecting development of these 750,000 frames within two hours of the finish.

If the creation of ICAS and the spectacular development of TOP were milestones, so was the opening in 1993 of the Olympic Museum. Samaranch had pursued this project, too, from the outset, and thanks to the generosity of sponsors from multinational industry, most notably in Japan and South Korea, over $50 million had been donated towards a total cost in excess of $100 million and a dream of de Coubertin was at last fulfilled. Significantly involved was Lausanne city council, donating and administering a sloping parkland site immediately beside Lake Geneva. The Museum would give substance to the philosophy of the Olympic Movement and become the educational and academic home of the Games, as well as a point of fascination for tourist visitors. It was to house shelf-miles of documentary archives, an audio-visual department with thousands of hours of film, a 20,000-volume library and a photographic library eventually exceeding half-a-million pictures. It was to become one of Switzerland's best attended museums and inevitably, if unintentionally, in practical terms it would supersede the International Olympic Academy at Olympia, though the latter would continue to hold its spell for visiting students of antiquity.

A second Session in Monaco in 1993 involved the election of the host city for the Millennium Games of 2000, for which the candidates were Beijing, Berlin, Istanbul, Manchester and Sydney. Following worldwide criticism of the preference for Atlanta rather than Athens for the Centenary Games, the IOC was again under scrutiny. The politically correct view was that Beijing, in the wake of the slaughter of student demonstrators in Tiananmen Square, was an inappropriate host, never mind that it represented a third of the world's population. No comparable fuss had been raised when the Games had been awarded to Moscow – that decision being prior to the Soviet invasion of Afghanistan – but nevertheless politically motivated forces gathered their arguments against China just as they had 65 years earlier against Berlin, even though China was not threatening racial extermination policies and the annexation of foreign lands. Condemnation from the United States House of Representatives was singularly hypocritical, for only the previous year China had been awarded 'most favoured nation status' by the United States in support of commercial interests.

It was already vividly apparent that the twenty-first century would be Pacific-orientated, a factor strongly in the minds of many of the IOC's influential figures, not least Richard Pound, head of marketing. Samaranch's view, not publicly articulated, was that the award of the Games would assist in the social development and democratisation of 'a more open China', as had happened with Moscow and Seoul. Yet the IOC membership was polarised for and against, as with Athens in 1996. The human rights issue and the picture of a lone student standing in front of an armoured tank in Tiananmen Square, one of the most vivid single photographs of the century, was indelibly stamped on the mind.

The chief rival to Beijing was Sydney, Australia's third successive bidding city. The Sydney bid was led by Rod McGeoch, a personable lawyer who maximised every aspect of his country's sporting reputation and the unique geophysical appeal of Sydney with its picturesque harbour and bridge and innovative Opera House, with which the world was almost as familiar as with its own local post office. Who could not want to be in Sydney? However, Kevan Gosper, in his autobiographical

An Olympic Life, relates that he urgently had to head off a plan by advisers to McGeoch to exploit anti-Beijing publicity, a move which could have been dangerously counter-productive. Gosper was a close friend of his fellow Executive Board member Zhenliang Hé, head of the Beijing bid, a scrupulously correct sports leader of moral sensitivity, with whom he had agreed that the bidding should be conducted on a true sports platform.

In the report of the Evaluation Commission, Beijing had been rated behind Sydney, Manchester and Berlin on technical facilities, for so much of Beijing's project remained on the drawing board. Furthermore, a few days before the vote, a member of the Beijing committee at the Session in Monaco damagingly suggested that if Beijing was rejected they might boycott the Games in Atlanta. Frantic denial by Hé during the next 24 hours could not erase the message that had flashed around the world. Though Beijing would lose to Sydney, the fact that it was by a mere two votes helped save face for Beijing. The figures were:

	I	II	III	IV
Sydney	30	30	37	45
Beijing	32	38	40	43
Manchester	11	13	11	–
Berlin	9	9	–	–
Istanbul	7	–	–	–

Thus it could be seen that the division of Manchester's vote after the British city was eliminated swung decisively eight to three in favour of Sydney, which was viewed as a Commonwealth ally. For reasons unknown, David Sibandze of Swaziland – ill-advisedly brought into the IOC by Samaranch as a source of information on South Africa during its exclusion, and later to be forced to resign – disappeared after the second-round vote. By a whisker, the IOC had come to a decision that received widespread acclaim.

Sydney rejoices on its election as Millennium Games host following the narrow defeat of Beijing. (© IOC/Locatelli)

An incident two days prior to the vote in Monaco that surprisingly passed without serious investigation was the donation by John Coates, president of the Australian NOC, of $10,000 each to the NOCs of Kenya and Uganda. This was said to be for sports development in those countries, though it would not have been a far-fetched interpretation to see it as an incentive for the votes of the respective IOC members Charles

Mukora, former coach of Kip Keino, and Major-General Francis Nyangweso, former Olympic boxer. Coates remained free of criticism and was subsequently elected to the IOC (the incident was to be mentioned subsequently in an independent investigation of the Salt Lake City scandal, see Chapter LXVIII). Coincidentally, arising from the scandal, Mukora would be one of those forced to resign.

At the Session preceding the Lillehammer Winter Games, the members debated an Executive Board proposal to reduce the ten candidate cities bidding for the 2002 Winter Games – the decision to be taken the following year in Budapest – to two; this reduction to be by a special commission before putting the final decision to the members. Moreover, the members should only visit the remaining two candidates and travel unaccompanied by wives or family. The majority of speakers from the floor demanded amendment, for a reduction to either three or preferably four cities. Lillehammer, they argued, would never have earned the Games with a pre-selection of two, which would probably have been Sofia and Östersund of Sweden. And, they insisted, honorary officials should be allowed to take wives and husbands. The amendment to four candidates was carried, plus the accompaniment of one guest. In fact, the Executive Board proposal had been a gamble: that if they proposed a short-list of two, they would get approval for four. It was against this resistance from the floor that Samaranch was battling, conscious of the freeloading and first-class travel that some members were exploiting. He himself had long believed that the bidding process should be short-circuited, with the decision taken by the Executive Board, as in football and track and field by FIFA and the IAAF.

If there were any IOC members unaware of the extent to which their Olympic role was under public scrutiny, they would have become conscious of it upon their arrival in Lillehammer, where there was tangible hostility not to the Games but to them. Prominent was criticism on local television by Vegard Ulvang, a national hero as triple gold medal winner in Nordic skiing in 1992, who claimed that Samaranch and the IOC were undemocratic. Walls were daubed with slogans telling the IOC to go home, and even Gerhard Heiberg, Norway's organising chief, was obliged to admit that he had failed to scrutinise the text, prior to publication, of an interview in which he said the IOC was 'unworthy'. Ulvang subsequently met Samaranch to apologise, the President saying that he hoped to meet him again to shake his hand . . . as a 1994 medal winner. So embarrassed were some IOC members by the Norwegian reception that they talked of resignation.

Once the Games were underway, the Norwegians exhibited themselves as the most generous-minded, hospitable and sporting of all peoples in their attitude towards every event and every competitor. Though temperatures were no higher than –15°C during the day when exposed to Arctic winds, the little town at night was, even at –25°C, incandescently beautiful. Set amid dairy farmland beside the beautiful Lake Mjösa, Lillehammer took winter sport back to its roots. It has been said that if the short, intense northern summer is Norway's glory, with its countless spectacular fjords and virgin forests, then winter is Norway's soul. The people embrace winter like a brother, as proof of their character and endurance down the centuries. This is a land where cross-country skiing has been a way of life almost from the Stone Age, a land severe and elegiac, as epitomised by the works of Ibsen, Munch and Grieg. For two-thirds of the year they live close to the razor's edge of winter, yet for these Games thousands of spectators skied across the hills to be present at their festival, hundreds of them camping in the

Stein Gruben, unheralded ski jumper, descends Lillehammer's ski jumping hill bearing the Olympic flame. (© Getty Images/Brunskill)

the world . . . but they can be seen as a means of persuading countries and peoples to use their capabilities in the service of friendly competition, and to aspire beyond the perceived limits of human accomplishment.'

When, against all expectation, Lillehammer had been elected host city in 1988, initial euphoria in the only city in the world with a skier on its coat of arms had swiftly been dampened by the realisation that its frugal budget of $289 million was probably a quarter of that required. Fortunately, the oil-rich national government quickly promised to underwrite the necessary finance, so conscious were the politicians that the Games reflected the country's heritage. The eventual sum would exceed $1 billion, and the creation of some memorable facilities were complicated by rigorous attention to environmental issues, more so than at any previous Olympic venue since Sapporo in 1972. More than 25 per cent of Norway's municipalities adopted the organising committee's 'green' regulations, while the IOC introduced mandatory environmental requirements for future hosts. At adjacent Hamar, the Viking Ship skating hall was created, so called for its roof design resembling an overturned boat, an engineering marvel with wooden roof-beams spanning 100 metres, yet having structural strength greater than that of steel. At Gövik, an ice hockey hall was constructed within a cave blasted into the moutainside, its space-creating design arousing worldwide business interest. Furthermore, the organising committee, led by industrialist Heiberg, worked with national relief agencies to establish the first-ever Olympic humanitarian programme. 'Olympic Aid' created awareness of the plight facing children in Sarajevo, and $4 million was raised, while further programmes were established to build schools in Eritrea. Johann Olav Koss, who was to become one of the outstanding performers of the Games, asked his countrymen to contribute 10 kroner for each Norwegian gold medal won during the Games which, with the IOC offering to match these contributions, raised a further $9 million. Never had an Olympic host city, especially one so small, been so humanitarian-conscious.

Lillehammer further charmed its audience, both live and on television, with an enchanting opening ceremony. Beneath the earth in Norway there exists a secret, mystic people, the *Vette*. They are gentle, shy and peaceful, existing in harmony with nature. They live in the fantasy and the poetry of the Norwegians and offer in part an explanation of the nation's humanity. They are Norway's conscience as well as their secret culture and in the opening ceremony, watched by the world, the Norwegians were saying: 'This is the way we are, we want you to see and share our sensibilities, to understand us and accept us.' In a masque set amid fading, misty mountain light and gently falling snow, its unblemished style devoid of presumption, Norway defied the most hardened cynic not to be moved by an occasion that brought a rotten world in touch with goodness. As the curtain of darkness closed across the surrounding valley, the 67 teams – a record, including 14 first-timers – strode into the stadium, the Bosnians with their symbolic white flag.

fields. They produced a unique ambience of national enthusiasm for their own competitors, yet there was simultaneously equal and spontaneous applause for any medal winner irrespective of nationality. They warmed to Samaranch, too, for his vain plea for a truce and ceasefire within the ravaged former Yugoslavia, where he flew on a dangerous mission to Sarajevo amid the fighting with an IOC donation of food for those embattled in the Olympic city of ten years earlier. As Gro Harlem Brundtland, the Norwegian premier, stated: 'The Games of Lillehammer cannot force peace upon the troubled regions of

CHAPTER LXIII

Lillehammer (XVII) 1994

Johann Olav Koss of Norway, triple Olympic speed skating champion

'*In Norway, skating is a big tradition. We've had great heroes from the early twentieth century and even before. Living amid that tradition, there were heroes in the 1970s when I was very young. I wanted to be one of them when I asked for skates for Christmas. Of course, I was always falling behind in my races, not doing really well, but then I thought, OK, I want to become a world champion at this. I think every boy likes to say that.*

I watched the Olympics as I was growing up and I understood how important they were, especially when Lillehammer was chosen as host. I realised then, six years beforehand, that this would be my target.

In the months prior to the Games my training faltered. It was probably part mental, that I needed to switch off a bit. While this was happening, I was asked to represent Olympic Aid in Eritrea, a tiny nation on the north-east coast of Africa that had recently secured its independence from Ethiopia after decades of civil war. This experience was one of the most significant in my life.

When the time for my three Olympic races arrived, each felt totally different, though they were all intense. For the first, the 5,000m, I was unsure if I could do well. I'd had knee trouble, problems with my skates and poor results in recent months. The longest race, the 10,000m, was my likeliest chance, but I knew I might win nothing. Yet there were 15,000 spectators there at the stadium in Hamar, all going crazy for me to win. Warming up beforehand, I sensed this was when it had to happen, that I had to give my maximum, to have nothing left at the finish, to be totally used. It was a particular, deep gut feeling. When I broke the 5,000m world record, I was so incredibly happy. After this, I knew I could do well in the other two.

For the 1,500m, which came next, success meant more than a gold medal. I'd achieved what I most wanted, a victory. Now I remembered Eritrea, that I was so lucky to have this opportunity compared with the children there, and this gave me a fresh motive, so that when I won I was happy to give my $30,000 reward from my Olympic committee to Olympic Aid, a gift back to the kids who had inspired me.

For the 10,000m, I knew it would be hard and I wanted it to be my best race ever: the climax of my sporting career. When I'd won again, it was such a relief. The future seemed quite simple, just to keep skating in the World Cup and the World Championships. I took a month's rest, intending to start again in May, but suddenly realised I had no goals, that I could no longer fulfil the principle of beating myself. If I couldn't improve, I didn't want to skate any more. The financial donations I had made were so important to me, to give something from my wonderful Olympic experience to those who are unable even to watch.'*

(Photograph © Getty Images/Bruty)

Although Johann Koss may not have equalled the five speed skating gold medals of Eric Heiden of America at Lake Placid in 1980 – with four Olympic records and a world record in the 10,000m – his three world records must be measured against the element of much higher expectation, of more advanced training among more competing nations, and his own decline in form immediately prior to the Games. Heiden, who went on to become a surgeon, had modestly referred to speed skating as 'an obscure sport', but there was nothing obscure as Koss entered the Viking Hall, with its impressive arched wooden roof and expectant crowd, for the opening event. Here was a man who had four times previously improved the world record for 5,000m, but had recently sunk to the point where he finished fourth in the European Championships. Such was his mental transformation, resulting from his African expedition, that he was able to reward his jubilant home crowd by lowering his world record yet again by over half a second to 6:34.96, his colleague Kjell Storelid adding to the frenzy by taking the silver medal some eight seconds behind him. The ambitious Dutch were left with third, fourth and fifth places, Rintje Ritsma taking the bronze.

It was Ritsma who held the world record for the 1,500m, but Koss, with the fastest last two laps of any of the contenders, lowered Ritsma's time by three-tenths to 1:51.29. Ritsma and

Three speed skating races, three records, three bonuses donated to charity: Johann Olav Koss, Norwegian champion and benefactor. (© Getty Images/Bruty)

Falko Zandstra, the latter fourth in the 5,000m, were both faster than Koss with one lap to go, but could not match his final burst. In the 10,000m, Koss and Storelid again gave Norway a one–two, with Koss improving his world record by an astonishing 12.99 seconds. He claimed afterwards that he had been no more than gliding for the first 12 laps, yet he finished almost 20 seconds faster than Storelid and 26 ahead of Bart Veldkamp of Holland, the bronze medal winner. Following the Games, Koss's skates were auctioned on national television, raising further funds for Olympic Aid, and he later returned to Eritrea with tons of sports equipment donated by Norwegian children.

There was initial, seemingly permanent gloom for Dan Jansen, master of sprint skating from Wisconsin, the same state as Heiden. Only two weeks earlier he had lowered his 500m world record in the World Championships to 35.76, no other skater ever having beaten 36 seconds. Now, having done so four times, he has only to stand up to win as he goes to the line with Sean Ireland of Canada, the second pair skating on new ice. Yet nagging at the back of his mind are the past Olympic failures: fourth in 1984 when he was 19, falls in the 500m and 1,000m four years later, then fourth again in 1992. Now, he is heading for a time close to 36-flat as he enters the second bend of the 400m track at around 30 mph. No need to worry: he has done it many thousands of times before. Suddenly, a third of the way into the bend, his left skate, angled underneath him far to the right of the vertical line of his centre of gravity, breaks away, there is a puff of ice splinters, his left hand clutches at the ice. He has lost three-tenths of a second, his time of 36.68 will place him no better than eighth, and Alexander Golubyev, a little-known Russian who was 14th in the World Championships, is the winner. Jansen is left in despair, acknowledging that 'I'll just have to live my life without an Olympic gold medal.' Within five strides, the story of his life has irretrievably been set in stone. The emptiness will always be there.

There is, however, still the 1,000m to come: not his favoured event, yet nonetheless an opportunity to grasp at a straw, the chance for dignity. At 28, this will be his last Olympic race, though in three previous attempts he has never finished better than 16th. A man of unassuming demeanour, he still wishes to make some mark as private commemoration for the sister who had died of leukaemia on the morning of the 500m final in 1988. It is to be a sensational event with a rare conclusion. Also competing is Igor Zhelezovsky of Belorussia, whose Olympic

history is almost as chequered as Jansen's. He has been six times world sprint champion, but has nothing more than an Olympic bronze from the 1,000m in 1988. He is two years older than Jansen: for him, too, it is the last chance. Zhelezovsky is drawn first-out, alongside Sergei Klevchenya, who has taken silver in the 500m. He and Zhelezovsky set times which Jansen cannot expect to match. After two more pairs have raced, it is Jansen's turn. He is nervous, yet inexplicably something inside him clicks as he leaps into the race alongside Junichi Inoue of Japan. At the 600 mark, unbelievably, Jansen is on world record schedule. On the second last bend, his inner skate comes within a fraction of catching a lane marker, his left hand touches the ice, he is perilously close to a fall. To a man, the crowd's pulse beats with him and amid the clamour he crosses the line in 1:12.43: a world record, three-tenths faster than Zhelezovsky. As he sees the time flash on to the screen, he clasps his hands to his head and keeps them there as he coasts around the track, momentarily alone among thousands. When he walks out to the medal presentation, he has less the look of a victor than of a hostage unexpectedly released. He looks down at his medal almost disbelievingly, knowing that the man standing next to him is the acknowledged master at this distance. Then he sets off on a touching finale, lapping the track hand-in-hand with Kristin and Haakon, the Games' mascots. Halfway down the finishing straight, his eight-month-old daughter, Jane, named after his sister, is passed into his arms and gracefully the four of them circle the rink in time to Strauss's 'Skater's Waltz'.

A less complicated distinction was gained by Bonnie Blair of the United States when winning her third consecutive Olympic 500m one month short of her 30th birthday. She had a comparatively comfortable margin ahead of Canadian Susan Auch. Though marginally outside her world record, with 39.25,

Following years of disappointment, Dan Jansen (USA) cradles baby daughter Jane, named after his deceased sister, during a 1,000m lap of honour. (© Getty Images)

a few weeks later she became the first woman to break 39 seconds. Subsequently she retained her 1,000m title, the oldest competitor in the field. While 0.60 separated the other top seven finishers, Blair's winning margin was a withering 2.62 seconds. In the 1,500m she would take fourth place behind Emese Hunyady who, born in Budapest, represented Hungary in the 1984 Olympics but the following year defected to Austria, for which this was the first speed skating medal.

A story bordering on fiction disproportionately consumed the bulk of media attention worldwide. On 6 January, Nancy Kerrigan, darling of figure skating in the United States, who had finished third in Albertville and was now favourite, had been attacked after a practice session in Detroit – clubbed across the knee with a baton. The attacker was Shane Stant, a nephew of Derek Smith, who in turn was a friend of Shaun Eckardt, a childhood colleague of Jeff Gillooly, husband of Tonya Harding, Kerrigan's arch rival. The background to this planned assault, designed to eliminate Kerrigan from the Games, and the complicity of Harding, had gripped the American public for six weeks. The coincidental consequence of the crime was to produce record viewing figures for CBS television.

Tonya Harding (USA) encounters the grief, in the figures event, intended for her arch-rival. (© Getty Images/Cole)

Harding was an unfortunate antithesis of the world in which she was attempting to make her fame and fortune: cigarette-smoking, pool-playing toughie with scarlet finger nails and ambition as sharp as her skate blades. Her early life was one of deprivation, both financial and emotional, her temperamentally unstable mother walking out when Harding was 15. Though the mother had stitched her outfits and worked night shifts as a waitress to pay for her daughter's training, she had also beaten and insulted her for inferior performances. In a spell living with her father, Tonya gained physical strength from chopping logs, which aided her outstanding jumping technique, and learned how to strip the engine of a pick-up truck. No wonder she was

hard as iron. Her father also deserted her and unsurprisingly she entered a fraught teenage marriage with Gillooly, who continued her life of abuse. Twice she obtained restraining orders and filed for divorce, but kept returning to him.

At the 1992 Games, Harding had been fourth and the following season the gap behind Kerrigan widened. Her resentment of Kerrigan mounted, the contrast between their lives accentuating the disparity: Kerrigan having a loving family and increasingly earning the attention of commercial sponsors. Harding's comparative hardship gained the sympathy of baseball-owner George Steinbrenner, who contributed $20,000 to her training expenses. Some of this would go to fund the attack on Kerrigan.

In late December 1993, Gillooly, Eckardt, Smith and Stant met to plan the attack, for which Gillooly promised to pay. Fortunately for Kerrigan, Stant's blow left her only with severe bruising and swelling. Stant escaped in a getaway car. Within days, Harding was interrogated, Gillooly and Eckardt were arrested. The scandal was public.

Without confirmed evidence of Harding's involvement, the United States Olympic committee could not suspend her from Olympic competition, under threat of legal action. For the public, Disney's Snow White and the Wicked Witch had been brought to life. Amid the frenzied speculation, it tended to be overlooked that there was a range of rival candidates for the gold medal as good as if not superior to Kerrigan, and certainly in a class above Harding: Oksana Baiul of Ukraine, the 16-year-old world champion; Surya Bonaly of France, the runner-up; Chen Lu of China, who had taken third place; Yuka Sato of Japan, fourth. USOC, under legal pressure, prevaricated over Harding's inclusion before predictably selecting her. 'It would be risky to deny Harding the natural process of law,' observed Richard Pound of Canada, QC and member of the IOC's Executive Board.

Following the thuggery offstage, it was a relief when the competitors finally reached the ice. The technical programme went as expected, with the difference that Kerrigan not only showed no sign of after-effects from the assault but also performed with such élan that she was marked in first place above Baiul and Bonaly. Harding was out of contention in tenth place, making surprising technical errors on jumps. Could Kerrigan's flowing lines and flawless jumping out-distance the fragrant Baiul in the free programme?

Harding presents a broken bootlace to the judges, entitling her, in vain, to a re-start. She finished eighth. (© Getty Images/Brunskill)

Further controversy was to mark the finale. During the intervening practice day, Baiul and Tanja Szewczenko of Germany collided, Baiul needing stitches on her right shin. When the moment came for Harding's turn the following day, she initially failed to appear, arriving on the rink only just in time to avoid disqualification. After less than a minute she halted at the judges' desk in tears, requesting time to adjust her right boot, on which a lace had broken. She was granted a re-skate, but her performance was to be irrelevant.

The woman who was destined to make millions, Kerrigan, came second. The girl who, in a sense, had nothing, Baiul, was triumphant. Sometimes, life produces the right result for the wrong reasons. This doe-eyed girl of childlike innocence, aged 16, her legs so frail she appeared incapable of triple jumps, her shoulders so narrow that you doubted whether she could generate the power, had the favour of five of the nine judges, three of them, puzzlingly, for technique rather than presentation. For many among the packed stadium, the magic lay with her elf-like interpretation. Yet her mother and grandmother were dead, and she had never known her father. When she stood on the victory rostrum and the yellow-and-blue flag was raised, her sad face, with hollow eyes and cherry-red mouth, seemed on the point of disintegration from a mixture of joy and the tribulations of her young life. She had triumphed in spite of her coach having emigrated to Canada, only the protective attention of her fellow Ukrainian, Viktor Petrenko, the men's champion of 1992, giving her financial support, while Galina Zmievskaya, Petrenko's coach, had given her refuge. From such bleak circumstances had arisen a world and Olympic champion.

While Kerrigan was a skater doing figures, Baiul was a theatrical whole, something of subtle complexion with our uncertainty as to what she would do next. The applause, however, was not as prolonged as for Kerrigan and when the technical marks were unpromising Baiul had collapsed in dismay on the shoulder of a friend, leaving the rink grief-stricken and seemingly unaware of the fractional superiority she gained from the five judges on presentation. So Kerrigan went off to her fortune, Harding to three years' probation, 500 hours of community service and a $100,000 fine, being also stripped of her national title and banned for life by her national skating association, the latter later rescinded. Another marriage was followed by another divorce. Baiul duly emigrated to take advantage of the commercial benefits available in America.

There was further dispute in the ice dance event, though more conventionally this involved the judging. Jayne Torvill and Christopher Dean, the champions of 1984 in Sarajevo, were by now permitted to return to the sport as professionals. At the immediately preceding European Championships in Copenhagen, they had won a desperately close contest over two Russian pairs. The British pair believed the judges were prejudiced against them as professionals and this belief was vindicated by the outcome in Lillehammer, even though, following the compulsory dances and the original dance sections, the latter of which they won with their rumba, they went into the third-section free dance leading both Russian pairs: Yevgeny Platov and Oksana Grischuk, Aleksandr Zhulin and Maia Usova. An aside to the contest was that Grischuk had earlier had an affair with Zhulin, an alliance terminated when Usova had challenged her in a bar in America and punched her on the nose.

The free dance programme was complicated by what was technically allowed under new regulations. Grischuk and Platov were thought to have included illegal moves, while it had been considered that Torvill and Dean, following Copenhagen, would

Nancy Kerrigan, darling of America, survived the assault on her knee but not the artistry of waif-like Oksana Baiul of Ukraine. (© Getty Images/Brunskill)

need to introduce new elements to meet the judges' demands. Grischuk and Platov unashamedly went for the sexiest, most spectacular programme of the three, she in a provocative dress, for their presentation of 'Rock around the Clock'. Usova and Zhulin were inhibited by the new ban on classical music, as were Torvill and Dean. The British pair introduced a back-somersault by Torvill over Dean's shoulder which, though hugely enjoyed by the crowd, met with disapproval from the judges and lower technical marks, including 5.6 from the German judge and five 5.7s, compared with the 5.8s and 5.9s for both Russian pairs. The result, even though the British judge's 6.0 for artistic impression matched that of the Russian for Grischuk and Platov, was that Torvill and Dean gained only the bronze, with Usova and Zhulin taking silver.

The majority of the crowd at the Hammar Stadium awarded the judges a tin medal for insensitivity. It was evident to specialists that Grischuk and Platov had broken the rules repeatedly and Usova refused to attend the medal-winners' conference. The IOC President protested to the International Skating Union – 'in the same kind of uncertain position as boxing was after the 1988 Games in Seoul, the sport must reconsider its judging process so that it can be seen to be properly in control' – that its credibility was under serious threat. Torvill and Dean meanwhile rued the investment of £100,000 in their Olympic comeback. More rewardingly, a television audience of 23 million in Britain alone had been reminded of their matchless grace. 'We should have gone with our emotions and been more daring,' Dean said. 'We like to think that the audience tonight were our judges. For ourselves, we won.' Under subsequent pressure, the International Skating

Union admitted the British pair should have won the silver medal, even possibly the gold.

The men's figures title was won by the 20-year-old Alexei Urmanov from St Petersburg, whose confident technical display to highlights from Rossini, looking like some Romanov prince in his white silk shirt, was too much for established stars Elvis Stojko, Viktor Petrenko, Kurt Browning and Brian Boitano, two of them former champions. The more famous names made technical errors on the short programme, leaving themselves too far adrift of Urmanov, who was steady and fault-free. Though the others raised their level for the free programme, he could not be displaced; Philippe Candeloro might have done so had he not fallen moments before the end of his routine. The 21-year-old Frenchman had the crowd both laughing and applauding: it was as though he did not care what the judges thought.

There was keen home disappointment at the outcome of the Alpine blue riband event, the men's downhill. For almost four minutes Kjetil-André Aamodt, the home boy, stood waiting in the starting gate, gazing down the Kvitfjell course and contemplating the hundred-odd seconds that would maybe fashion the rest of his life. No Scandinavian had ever won the men's downhill, one of all sports' fiercest test of nerves. Victory now, and Aamodt would become a legend fit to stand alongside Sonja Henie. And Koss. But Cary Mullen of Canada, starting immediately before him, had fallen, and stewards had to check the course. The young Norwegian all-rounder waited and waited, a coat slung around his shoulders by a trainer, while others busily massaged his thighs in the vicious temperature of –20°C, which was freezing photographers' fingers to their cameras at the top of the 2,900-metre course. Expectation down below among a crowd of more than 30,000 was at fever pitch. Marc Girardelli of Luxembourg, first down the run, had set the target time, 1:45.75. Aamodt knew what he had to beat.

It was not an intimidating course, but highly technical, requiring the racer to carry his speed through the turns. It would favour the fast men, if they made no mistakes. On the fearsome left–right early turns, Aamodt was perfect, his times on this section bettered by none. But on the negative camber of the Elk Traverse, almost halfway down, he nearly lost the edge on his left ski. In those split seconds, glory evaporated. Hurtling down the mountainside like some crazed ball-bearing, the sight of Aamodt thrilled a watching nation. A huge roar greeted his finish: faster than Girardelli by 0.34.

Disillusionment, however, was close at hand. Next down was Tommy Moe from Alaska. They said he was a knuckle-head, a wild boy who would never get his act together to fulfil his talents. Twice as a teenager he had been put on probation by the US federation for smoking marijuana. His father had taken him north from Montana to work on a building site in an attempt to knock some sense into him. As yet, young Moe had never even won a World Cup race. When he first encountered Kvitfjell in practice, he thought it suited him. Who was going to come second, he asked himself? By the second interval time, however, he was only fourth fastest on the day, but thereafter began to find the perfect line. A minute down the course, he was ahead, and nobody would be able to surpass him. Not Edward Podivinsky of Canada, who would take the bronze, or Patrick Ortlieb, the Austrian defending champion. The crowd sighed as his time flashed on the screen and so did Aamodt, who was to hold on to second place. The crowd contented itself with the reflection that Moe's grandfather was a villager from near Oslo. Like the only other American to win an Olympic downhill, Bill Johnson in 1984, Moe never again won a major race.

Few stories if any were better than Alberto Tomba's. Having three gold medals and one silver from the two previous Games, the Italian had failed to retain for a second time his giant slalom title – spectacularly first won in Calgary – and now it was a question of whether he could win any medal in the slalom, having previously gained successive gold and silver. He had been in sharp form prior to Lillehammer, with four firsts, a second and a third in eight races. Now, first down the course on the first run, he had a no better than average time, some two seconds slower than Thomas Stangassinger of Austria, the leader. It was a margin seemingly impossible to close even for Tomba, renowned for powerful second runs like that which gained his silver at Albertville. Worse for him, here was one of the most difficult courses, 27 starters failing to finish or disqualified on the first run for missing one of the 68 gates. With Aamodt and Peter Roth of Germany less than a second behind Stangassinger, Tomba's hopes were slim. He was also in an uncertain mood. The view from within the Italian camp was that he had difficulty deciding whether he should be happy or sad at his likely final Games.

Alberto Tomba's finest medal? The Italian maestro surpassed himself when finishing second to Thomas Stangassinger of Austria in the slalom. (© Getty Images/Bruty)

On the second run, he was fourth starter and unleashed a ferocious run on a piste now alarmingly icy at the top. With a formidable time of 59.33, he had closed more than a second on Stangassinger. Could anyone match him? One by one they failed. Roth straddled a pole at the second gate and was out. Aamodt missed the gate completely. By the time it came to Stangassinger, Tomba was already guaranteed of at least the silver, Thomas Sykora of Austria, another threat, having lost a ski at the fourth gate. With his big lead to cushion him, Stangassinger skied a cautious course and managed to cross the line a mere 0.15 in front on aggregate. 'It was one of the most testing courses I ever met,' the winner said. 'So icy at the top and such tricky turns at the bottom.' Tomba revealed that he had switched skis between runs, risking the ice at the top with less of an edge, so as to be faster on the lower slopes. 'The second run was really tough, particularly because there was no sun and you couldn't see the line,' he said. 'There was a lot of stress.' Nonetheless he smiled when Stangassinger crossed the line as winner: Tomba, more than anyone, knew how well he had skied to come second.

It was frustrating all-round for Aamodt, who had won gold and bronze respectively at Albertville in the super-G and giant slalom. In Lillehammer's super-G he took the bronze behind a relaxed Markus Wasmeier of Germany and Moe. Wasmeier, with a creased, smiling face much like that of Steve McQueen, sported the attitude that 'if you want to win too much, there's little chance of fun, and less of winning'. His super-G victory, by a mere 0.08 from Moe, was his first since the giant slalom in the World Championship of 1985. Always the realist, he had abandoned any hope in the downhill after the first half-minute, telling himself to forget it and think about the super-G. 'It's the hardest of disciplines, the super-G,' he said, 'finding the right line, learning the course.' He had never skied better than now. Moe's silver made him the first American ever to win two Alpine medals in the same Games. Neither Aamodt nor Girardelli could get close to the front two. 'I found myself yawning at the starting gate – a good sign, meaning I'm relaxed,' Moe said.

To his own surprise, Wasmeier proceeded to take the giant slalom title on a day when Tomba, Aamodt and Girardelli all failed to find their touch. 'A double champion? I can't believe it,' he said, with his usual sincerity. Prior to the start, a sunny morning had been distinguished by the sight of Queen Sonja sweeping down the slopes in traditional home-spun woollen attire with a group of ladies from the Kjerringsleppet Club.

For the women's super-G at Kvitfjell, everyone was thinking of Ulrike Maier, not least her friend Diann Roffe. This was the first time that the Austrian women's team had raced since Maier's death during the downhill at Garmisch two weeks earlier. 'I thought about her in the morning, just as I had the night before,' 26-year-old Roffe said, after achieving her first-ever gold medal in the final season of a nine-year career that had begun with a precocious giant slalom victory in the World Championships of 1985. Her technique had come to her aid on a day when Katja Seizinger, the German World Cup leader, had lost an edge after 30 seconds and Deborah Compagnoni, the defending champion, had finished 17th. While the press waited for post-medal interviews, they were entertained by a local guitarist and his teenage daughter, symptomatic of the Norwegians' cosy approach to these Games. Quite unaware of the poignancy, their first song was Dylan's 'Knocking on Heaven's Door'. A few experience-hardened men had to turn away.

Vreni Schneider had been the doyenne of slalom racing ever since her double including the giant slalom title in 1988. Prior to Lillehammer's slalom, her major rival, Pernilla Wiberg of Sweden, had beaten her into second place in the combined, while Schneider had gained bronze in the giant slalom behind Compagnoni of Italy. The slalom was her forte, yet there was to be a surprise on the first run. First out of the gate, Schneider recorded 59.68, but this was improved by Wiberg, with 59.05, and then Katja Koren of Slovenia with 59.00. Could Schneider answer the challenge? Emphatically so. She went at the second run with such a vengeance that she had three-tenths of a second to spare over the 68 gates, ahead of Elfriede Eder of Austria, with the 18-year-old Koren in third place and Wiberg fourth. Thus Schneider and not Wiberg became the first woman to win three Olympic Alpine gold medals and the highest medal winner with five, alongside Aamodt, whose tally included only one gold.

There was no finer hero of the Games than Vladimir Smirnov. The reception he received when winning the gruelling 50km cross-country left one of the most lasting impressions of an exceptional two weeks. This bear of a man from Kazakhstan, winner of two silver medals and one bronze in 1988, who had subsequently moved to Sweden when offered sponsorship, had become through his reputation a brother to Norwegians. He was almost a minute and a half ahead of Mika Myllylä of Finland, who had a furious finishing sprint into the stadium to beat Sture Sivertsen of Norway for the silver medal. Smirnov's face later in the evening, receiving his medal at the ceremony beside

Big bear Vladimir Smirnov (KAZ) earned the critical admiration of Norwegians with his 50km cross-country victory.
(both © Getty Images)

Haakon's Hall, was a picture of defiant triumph. And how the crowd loved him. 'The perfect ending to a great Olympics,' said Gro Harlem Brundtland, the Prime Minister.

The 10km classical had been as much or more of a delight for the huge crowd that gathered at the top of the hill above the town for every Nordic event. While one of their favourite sons failed, another triumphed. Vegard Ulvang, who had won three titles at Albertville, could only finish seventh, but the winner was Bjørn Daehlie, by an 18-second margin. Norwegian joy was restrained in the 4 x 10km relay when, in front of a crowd of 120,000, Silvio Fauner, anchor skier of Italy, inched ahead of Daehlie by half a second – thereby denying Daehlie his third gold medal of the Games. Here was a heartstopper. Italy trailed Norway and Finland by almost ten seconds at the first change-over, but, by the second, Albarello of Italy, Ulvang of Norway and Kirvesniemi of Finland were neck and neck. It was on this leg that Ulvang accused Albarello of breaking the ski-pole of Kirvesniemi with a deliberate blow when overtaking. On the third leg, Giorgio Vanzetta of Italy, Thomas Alsgaard and Jari Räsänen of Finland pulled clear. Fauner, Daehlie and Jari Isometsä of Finland were together on the final leg for three kilometres until the Finn fell away. Fauner clung to Daehlie, who had claimed beforehand he would be too fast for the Italian. Poetic justice was on hand.

The women's Nordic events were predominantly a duel between Lyubov Yegorova of Russia and Manuela Di Centa of Italy. At home, Yegorova was known as 'the Steel Lady', her sport less flatteringly as 'a sport for horses'. In their most ferocious conflict, the 30km classical, the 31-year-old Di Centa – who had already ended her sequence of 23 World Championship and Olympic races without a gold medal in the opening 15km freestyle – now won with a 16-second margin over Marit Wold of Norway, with Yegorova back in fifth place. By the time of this race, Yegorova, from the Siberian city of Tomsk, had already won three gold and one silver. For Di Centa, this was her fifth medal of the Games, following a gold, two silver and a bronze. Marja-Liisa Kirvesniemi, winner of the bronze, was a 38-year-old mother of two, who, when single, had won three gold medals in 1984 under the name of Hämäläinen. You would see few healthier-looking women than the three medal winners, Di Centa of such character that when blood-doping was still a

Manuela Di Centa, who had previously quit the Italian team in protest against blood-doping, flings herself across the line to win the 30km classical and is helped to her feet by bronze winner Marja-Liisa Kirvesniemi (FIN). (© Getty Images)

known practice, she refused to contemplate such biochemical exploitation and temporarily quit the team. Few would forget the frenzy of Di Centa's last desperate surge down into the stadium's finishing straight, applauded by spectators whose own favourites she was surpassing, finally to fling herself across the line and collapse in a heap like some butchered animal.

The large hill of the ski jump witnessed a rare comeback. Espen Bredesen of Norway seemed to have the title in hand after a huge first-round leap of 135.5m, an Olympic record, for a combined distance/style mark of 144.4. This was more than ten marks ahead of German Jens Weissflog, the Olympic champion of 1984 for the normal hill. In the second round, Weissflog himself leapt 133m, 11 metres farther than Bredesen's second attempt. The sporting Norwegians warmly cheered the 29-year-old German. For what had seemed an age, Weissflog, with his skis splayed V-shaped and his pale tangerine suit glinting against the clear blue sky, had hung bird-like in the air. When the marks appeared on the screen, he danced around like a teenager. His had been the longest span between Olympic titles in the history of the Games.

In the team jumping event, Japan had a secure lead. Their last jumper, Masahiko Harada, with 122 metres on his first jump, needed only some 105 on his second to take the gold, but managed just 97.5, the shortest of the day, conceding victory to Germany. His failure, and that inflicted on his colleagues, would haunt him for the next four years.

Jens Weissflog (GER), former East German, hangs like a bird before clearing 133 metres to secure ski jumping's large hill – ten years after winning the normal hill at Sarajevo. (© Getty Images)

A technical delay at the start, in -20°C, possibly cost young Kjetil-André Aamodt, the home boy, Scandinavia's first downhill gold – defeated by four-hundredths by Tommy Moe (USA). (© IOC/Maeder)

CHAPTER LXIV

Centenary

Professor Arne Ljungqvist of Sweden, Olympic high jumper, IOC member and chairman of the Medical Commission

'Some widely used assertions such as "all top athletes are doped" and "no Olympic medal can be won without doping" have created a misleading atmosphere about the illegal exploitation of drugs in sport. This has proved really difficult to eliminate from the public mind, in spite of the fact that none of these statements is supported by statistical analysis. A further false statement suggests that there are magic substances capable of masking the use of drugs while being themselves undetectable. This is also untrue. It would be highly surprising indeed if the drug users and their entourage were more scientifically advanced than all those professional scientists in accredited laboratories and various research centres around the world who are working against performance-enhancing drugs in sport.

The fact is that there are analytical methods available to expose all possible masking agents and illegally used substances. The problem is how to interpret the analytical data, particularly those related to endogenous substances secreted naturally within the body. Do they prove an exogenous intake, or could they be the result of an endogenous over-production? That is where the problem lies, since we cannot tolerate possibly inaccurate positive results. This has created the illusion that magic and non-detectable drug substances exist. Were this really the case, then we would not have exposed world-famous front-line athletes who were drugged with amphetamines, cocaine, anabolic steroids and other common doping substances.

The most widely fostered misapprehension, in my opinion, is that those who exploit illegal drugs are always and inevitably a step ahead of those who are attempting to fight against the problem. This is not surprising, since it used to be true in the early days of testing. When the IOC launched the campaign against doping in the late 1960s, illegal practices had existed for decades. There was a large gap to close. The strategy for doing so contained several elements, one being the imposition of doping controls. Yet a vital element was missing, namely the necessary funding for research. As new substances and methods come into use, adequate analytical methods need to be developed and that costs money and effort. Nevertheless, the gap became increasingly narrow once the campaign was underway.

With the creation of the World Anti-Doping Association (WADA) in 1999, an international fund for the support of research on various aspects of doping finally became available. Sports authorities are, therefore, in a better position than ever before to be pro-active rather than re-active. This is even more important at a time when gene therapy, or rather gene transfer technique, has been identified as an area for potential misuse in elite sport. The Human Genome Organisation project (HUGO), which was created with the aim of identifying human genes, was completed much more quickly than expected. The next step is to clarify the functional roles of the genes and how they interact. Once this is fully understood, gene transfer could theoretically be misused for the purpose of enhancing body strength and endurance. The erythropoietin (EPO) gene has, in fact, already been identified and used experimentally to promote the endogenous production of EPO. In the future, the intake of EPO may, therefore, become obsolete as a doping method and replaced by the administration of the EPO gene. Sport must have methods for the detection of gene transfer available as soon as possible, since gene transfer is already beginning to be applied as a theraputic measure in human beings. Misuse in sport is around the corner, if not already here. Detection of misuse is therefore a high-priority research item for WADA.'*

(Photograph © IOC/Imsand)

As the Olympic Games approached their centenary in Atlanta, 1996, the IOC's position was more than ever anomalous: riding on the crest of the most successful of all Winter Games, yet never more in danger of foundering inadvertently on the evils of drug abuse by competitors – a problem which was itself a by-product of the rampant new wealth that was threatening the IOC's own integrity, never mind that their jurisdiction extended only to two weeks every other year. Sadly, attempted internal legislation against IOC corruption by a minority was equally ineffective.

'It's clear you don't have to be one of the major countries to host a financially successful Games,' Richard Pound, head of IOC finances, observed after Lillehammer had created record winter revenues of $525 million, including the $300 million US television rights fee from CBS. Unprecedented worldwide accumulated television viewing of ten billion had left the IOC, and Samaranch in particular, in euphoric mood, yet barely were the Games over than Samaranch was voicing anxiety about where the Games and the IOC were respectively heading. Of particular concern was the size and structure of both the Games and the IOC, the former with too many events and too many sports, the latter with an imbalance of its membership; there then being, for instance, twenty-eight NOC presidents among the membership and only seven from the IFs. Samaranch declared:

> The IOC cannot be an organisation of NOCs, we have to find a way to have a minimum of ten to fifteen IF presidents. I know the problem, but I don't have a solution. It would be a disaster to be reduced to having a fight with the IFs. I know that in the future things must be changed if we are to sustain our importance in sport and society.

His wish, privately, was that the Executive Board should take all major decisions, including the choice of Olympic host city, but he knew it was impossible to get such change past the members; to persuade them to vote for their own extinction. What he did not know was that the IOC, amid its collective plutocratic self-satisfaction, was to encounter a scandal that would force upon it the changes it was currently reluctant even to consider.

For the moment, the preoccupation was with the Centenary Congress, a lavish event designed to mark the foundation of the IOC by Pierre de Coubertin at the Sorbonne in 1894. Yet so provocatively, almost obscenely expensive was the Congress that the IOC was openly inviting further criticism to be directed at its seemingly uncontrolled excesses. At one stage the Congress was to have been in Tokyo but was then switched to Paris, original home of the Movement, bringing together more than 1,000 delegates from its three arms. The cost of $16 million invited public scorn, though, admittedly, only $6 million came from the IOC's own budget, the rest being paid by the city of Paris, the French government and by sponsors.

The schedule of speeches and issues for debate over four days had been studiously planned by Raoul Mollet, Alexandru Siperco, the veteran Romanian, and Boris Stankovic, secretary-general of basketball. Diligently though they prepared and honourable though the attention of speakers was to the many issues, the nature of the Congress – as at the previous two, post-war, at Varna in 1973 and Baden-Baden in 1981 – was too academic, too far removed from the priorities that needed resolving. In consequence, this huge gathering was a brontosaurus that gave birth to a beetle. Informed suspicion is that Samaranch, while knowing he was obliged to stage the

Raoul Mollet of Belgium, *eminence grise* of the Olympic Movement and a coordinator of the IOC Centenary Congress in Paris, 1994. (© IOC/Baranyi)

Congress, did not want to grant it administrative authority and deliberately sought to keep it dull.

Although under Theme 1, Item 3, there was debate on Olympic sports that had lost public interest and no longer met technical requirements, on the introduction of new eligible sports that had earned prestige, on the reduction of events so that sports were not merely repeating their world championships, and on selection of participants through Continental Games' 'eliminators', barely a single significant new idea emerged; and, as with most Congresses, no worthy resolution was passed beyond acceptance of a new medical code. Many tongues were loosed but brains mostly remained conspicuously in neutral. The most progressive step was the accelerated introduction of athletes on to the administrative front. Harald Schmid, former European 400m hurdles record holder, and Dr Jacques Rogge also drew attention to the need for all organised sport to come to terms with competitors' agents if their commercial intervention was not to become even more damagingly disruptive.

As one left the Congress, it was with the feeling that nothing had been achieved that could not have been better done by the IOC President and the Vice-Presidents sitting informally together round a table for one morning. In *The Times* of London the author wrote: 'The Olympic sports world, gathered here in Paris to celebrate the centenary of Pierre de Coubertin's foundation of the IOC, is in a mood of mutual celebration. It dangerously overlooks the fact that sport has never been faced with greater threat from drug abuse, commercial preoccupation and public scepticism.'

How easy it was to believe that all was well, that the sun would never set, as tributes flowed from the high and mighty. In 1994, Boutros Boutros-Ghali, Secretary-General of the UN, stated: 'In the International Olympic Committee, the United Nations has a precious ally in its action in the service of peace and bringing peoples together.' True indeed. As a non-governmental organisation, the IOC had ever-mounting respect. Three months after the Centenary Congress, the 49th Session of the UN General Assembly adopted a resolution entitled: 'Building a peaceful and better world through sport and the Olympic ideal', with 95 co-author member states. The UN re-affirmed, at its 50th session the following year, sympathetic support for the Olympic Truce. It was on this occasion that Samaranch, by invitation, became the first representative of an NGO without status within the UN to address the 185-member assembly. Other speakers included former Olympic champions Guy Drut (France), Lia Manoliu (Romania) and Bart Connor (USA).

A further, unfortunate error was made that year, however, at the IOC's own Session in Budapest. With encouragement from some of his senior colleagues, notably Judge Keba M'Baye on the Executive Board and Primo Nebiolo and Mario Vazquez Raña, Samaranch agreed on two things: to allow himself to be available once again for re-election in 1997, for a third time and for a fourth term – for which it was little secret that he yearned – and crucially to extend the retirement age from 75 to 80. The IOC was already under fire for being an alleged gerontocracy and this latest change was duly condemned by critics. Samaranch, unusually, had strategically misread the situation. His perception was that the only circumstance in which his re-election beyond the existing retirement age of 75 – which he passed in 1995 – would be acceptable was if it came *within* the regulations. A Charter amendment therefore would be needed.

Frank Joklik (left), president Tom Welch and Dave Johnson, successful bidders for Salt Lake City to host the Winter Games of 2002 – a future Everest of problems. (© IOC/Locatelli)

The reality was probably the reverse: that the acceptable circumstance would be for him to be an *exception*, re-elected at the specific request of the members and leaving the retirement age as it was. In an extended muddle, the Executive Board offered the members at the Session a series of alternatives and ultimately the age was set at 80. 'It was a mistake,' Samaranch would say afterwards, 'and it was my mistake. Many members said that they wished me again to be available, but I didn't want an exception to be made for *me*.' Nonetheless, the deed was done and the clouds around him darkened.

It was at this Session that Salt Lake City was elected as Winter Games host for 2002, runaway victors in the first round, with 54 votes ahead of Östersund (14), Sion (14) and Quebec (7). Wholly correctly, they were the popular and ideal choice, but the ramifications of alleged improper behaviour by the bidding

officials and also by a minority of unscrupulous IOC members were subsequently almost to overthrow de Coubertin's sporting monument; notwithstanding that at this Session the nine prospective bid cities had been reduced to four on the findings of the Evaluation Commission, thereby reducing the IOC's provocative travel bonanza.

Samaranch's years were mounting and so was the IOC's income. During the IAAF World Championships at Gothenburg in 1995, the IOC had been able to announce a contract with NBC for the rights for both Sydney 2000 and Salt Lake City 2002 of $1.25 billion. This staggering joint bid had come about on account of NBC and its partner General Electric wishing to head off any possible rival bidding from the giant corporations emerging from recent mergers: ABC with Walt Disney and CBS with Westinghouse. Dick Ebersol, head of NBC Sport, flew by private jet to put the proposal to Samaranch, present in Gothenburg, Samaranch instantly requesting him to return to Montreal to do the deal with Richard Pound, the division being $705 million for Sydney, and $545 million for Salt Lake, way above the $456m that NBC had paid for Atlanta. Buoyed by the success of this contract, NBC signed a further deal in December 1995 for the rights for 2004 (Summer), 2006 (Winter) and 2008 (Summer) for $2.3 billion. This, even before the host cities had been determined. Thus the IOC was assured of income for the next 12 years, and a month later, in January 1996, announced yet another coup with the European Broadcasting Union: a $1.441 billion contract also up to 2008. This maintained Samaranch's philosophy that, irrespective of price, the coverage should reach the widest possible audience. Rupert Murdoch's News Corporation had bid some 50 per cent more, but the EBU deal ensured coverage in less affluent Eastern Europe, while the 12-year deal would breed confidence among TOP sponsors. The fee included $443 million for the Summer Games 2008 of unknown destination, more than had been paid by US television for any Summer Games until Atlanta ($456 million). With all this money flowing into the Olympic financial pool, the Executive Board agreed in March 1996 to an additional $32 million to be given to ASOIF, the summer sports body, as compensation for the non-involvement of IFs in TOP revenue, a major share of this going to the IAAF, which, unsurprisingly, as the IOC's largest sports grouping, was pressing for a greater share of the latest spoils.

Amid this glow of sporting wealth, how would Atlanta, perceived as having been granted the Games because of its commercial clout, handle the ambience of the Centenary event, with its historic overtones? Though the Georgia hosts produced some outstanding sports facilities, there were many disappointing glitches, resulting in the Centenary Games being a festival of mixed emotions. It had been a fine ambition by Billy Payne, organising chairman, and his colleagues to put the southern city, reduced to ashes by General Sherman during the Civil War, on the Olympic map. By now a thriving metropolis of three million, Atlanta was an expanding industrial hub, though it harboured, like many American big cities, areas of substantial racial inequality. Part of the strength of Atlanta's bid had been the presence of Andrew Young and the influence on African voters of his reputation in civil rights history. Once theory moved into practice, difficulties began to emerge, even though the organisers were insistent on a politically correct attitude, with minority- and female-owned companies receiving more than 40 per cent of all contracts. This policy undoubtedly assisted the development programme of the state's under-privileged, including one aimed at predominantly black Clark

University, providing up to 1,200 students with the technical training needed for jobs available within the broadcasting network. Other policies were less successful.

Given the size of Atlanta's task – nearly 11,000 competitors in the Olympic Village with a further 7,000 personnel involved in team management from 197 countries, together with the attendance of television networks covering 214 countries – problems were to be expected, though not in two particular instances. Artur Takac, former Technical Director with the IOC, being asked to advise on the new main stadium which was planned subsequently to be given over to baseball, discovered a number of unsatisfactory details of construction that needed urgent adjustment, including the closing of an open end of the stadium. Of even more concern was a failure of the vast IBM communications and information system. Two months before the Games, at the last meeting between the Atlanta organising committee (ACOG) and the IOC's Coordination Commission, François Carrard, the IOC's Director-General, requested a test of the IBM system. Unnecessary, ACOG replied overconfidently. Was this not the world's most technologically advanced nation? Within 24 hours of the Games opening, ACOG was floundering in communications chaos. There was further disorganisation, for both some competitors and media, in transportation, many volunteer drivers failing to arrive or, as they were from other towns in Georgia, being unfamiliar with the routes, some even turning back off the freeway to the departure point because they had got lost. Worst of all, the sidewalks of downtown Atlanta were so crowded with huckster souvenir stalls of the cheapest variety that visiting spectators, often obliged to walk in the roadway, felt unnecessarily harassed.

Thus an often brilliant Games under the experienced management of individual IFs was undermined by local logistical incompetence. In addition there was the usual chauvinism of US broadcasting, which so relentlessly focused on every American competitor that the Games were made to seem like a competition between the United States and the rest of the world rather than an integrated international event.

The media continued to hound Samaranch. The *New York Times* affected not to understand the term 'Olympic Movement' and was seemingly immune to the sociological traditions that are the basis of the Olympic spirit. In a television interview, Frank Deford, a front-line commentator, tricked Samaranch about the meaning when talking in English: for Samaranch a foreign language. Samaranch was further criticised for alleging that the Olympics was more important than religion, when in fact he was suggesting that, around the globe, the Games had more followers than the Christian faith.

In spite of these blips the Centenary message of the Games still shone through loud and clear. In the final two days of the torch run, tens of thousands lined the streets of Atlanta, as they had for three months across America, just for a glimpse of the flame as it passed by, families picnicking beside the road. There may have been crass decisions within the organisation, yet the vision of Payne and Young, whose Christian and social convictions had brought the Games to Atlanta, would imperceptibly alter the city for all time. Awaiting the start of the opening ceremony, I met Herb McKenley of Jamaica, the 400m runner-up in 1948. His hero, still, was Emil Zátopek. 'His will-power was a reflection of the trials of all our lives,' McKenley observed.

The opening ceremony reflected the lives of two men whose careers reached around the globe, whose personalities spoke the same message in different ways: Martin Luther King and Muhammad Ali, prophet and pugilist, each so articulate and so courageous in their pursuit of the emancipation of the African-American, that they once more touched eveyone's emotions. We heard the voice of Dr King, son of a Baptist minister, born in Atlanta in 1939, non-violent human rights leader and Nobel Peace Prize winner. With Coretta, his widow, sitting among us serene in primrose dress, many were reduced to tears by the inspiring words of his speech from the 1963 march on Washington. 'I have a dream' filled the stadium air. On to the centre stage came the heroes of yesteryear: Dawn Fraser, Bob Beamon, Mark Spitz, Nadia Comaneci, Carl Lewis and others, including, at a spry 97, Leon Stukelj, Yugoslavian gymnast from 1924, the oldest living Olympic champion.

To signify the fires of competition for the next 16 days' competition, the flame must be lit. For three months it has wound its way across the United States, and now the last carriers complete the journey: Al Oerter, four times discus champion, yet never once the favourite; on to Evander Holyfield, son of Atlanta, and heavyweight bronze medal winner in 1984; to Voula Patoulidou, Greek hurdles champion from Barcelona; then Janet Evans, darling of American swimming, who climbs a ramp to the lip of the stadium. There, in silhouette against a violet sky, stands Ali, light-heavyweight champion of 1960, the most known, the most admired figure of a century of sport, for whom the heart aches in his present state of physical disablement. Still defiant and erect, he lights the priming fuse which flies up a wire to ignite the cauldron. The spirit of human endeavour, Ali's spirit, is alight in a city whose history has been shaped by civil war and civil rights.

Two flames of the twentieth century. A universally acclaimed Muhammad Ali about to light the pedestal flame of the Centenary Games. (© Getty Images/Cooper)

In his closing comments, Samaranch spoke of 'an exceptional Games', which was true, even if ambitious Payne and his colleagues had craved an acclaim of the greatest yet. The Games had survived a random terrorist attack in Centennial Park – part of Payne's gift to the city – where sadly Alice Hawthorne, from Albany, Georgia, was killed. Twenty-four years after the infinitely worse horror of Munich, Olympic competitors, mentally and physically isolated within their culture by the necessity of competitive focus, remained unchanged. Sympathetic, yes. Concerned, little. We should not complain. We, the public, have demanded of our athletes this exclusive concentration, for we too readily condemn them when they fail. We expect them to endure, and survive, their own exposed hardships, loneliness, social and long-term career deprivation. We should not be surprised if, with the immaturity of youth, they are immune to the catastrophe of others. For Olympic competitors in Atlanta, as in Munich, this was just another day: winning or losing. We, the public, have become cynical towards terrorism, which is part of our strength. If we became frightened, then the terrorists would win. In a sensitive column in the *Atlanta Journal-Constitution*, Colin Campbell wrote: 'It would be a sad illumination if Atlanta's moment in the sun provided an unexpected glimpse of a vulnerable superpower, an empire that sometimes resembles the Third World, a country that in some ways lags behind Europe.' It was a glimpse that would be given horrendous reality on 11 September 2001.

As Campbell wrote, Atlanta was notable for its rich and poor, for second-rate public schools, for weak and visionless politicians, for the private exploitation of public trusts, for lack of health care, for crime and fear, whole classes locked in poverty, and, looming over everything, the money and power of huge corporations, edging out governments, religion and culture. Nonetheless, Atlanta had triumphed. There had been a record eight and a half million live spectators, three million more than ever before, more than Los Angeles and Barcelona combined. There had been new emerging countries. Kazakhstan won more gold medals than Britain. Adjusting the medal tables to take account of per capita GDP in every country, the top five states which did the most with the least were all Communist or ex-Communist states with low general standards of living: China, Cuba, Ethiopia, Russia and the Ukraine. It had been proved once again that there is no identifiable, cost-calculable equation for the triumph of the Olympic spirit.

In 1992, decathlon world champion Dan O'Brien failed to qualify in the US trials, recording no clearance in the pole vault, but he would convincingly redeem himself when gaining the Centenary title. (© Getty Images/Powell)

CHAPTER LXV

Atlanta (XXVI) 1996

Josiah Thugwane of South Africa, Olympic marathon champion

'One afternoon in 1988, a group of runners passed the house where I was working as a gardener. I followed them in my casual clothes and working shoes and soon caught up with them. They were from the athletic team of the local mine and invited me to join them each day for training. Soon I entered a few local road races, winning one or two, and because of this I was selected to represent the province at the national championships. Five years later I won the national marathon in Capetown, but then had to stop running to attend my tribe's initiation school to obtain manhood, a prerequisite for marriage. In 1995, I started running again, did quite well in the national half-marathon and was selected for the World Championships, where I finished fifth. I won again in the humid Honolulu race and after that the national title in 1996, which meant that I was selected for Atlanta.

Two weeks later, I was shot through the chin in a car hijacking incident, the scar's still there, but I was able to recover in time for the Olympics. After I'd won in Atlanta, many people at home were jealous and I received death threats, so the mine company where I worked contributed 150,000 rand to help me buy a house in Middleburg, with four bedrooms. This was really something. I no longer had to fetch water and light candles at night.

Early in 1997, I was hijacked again in my car and received some nasty injuries, but was still able to recover in time for the London Marathon where I came third in my best time yet. This silenced the suggestion that my win in Atlanta was a flash in the pan. When I came home from London, Jacques Malan, my coach and manager, arranged for me to have an English teacher, Welcome Mabuza. He taught me to read and write in Zulu and to start speaking some English. Now I could read Zulu magazines and not just look at the pictures.

Winning the Olympic Games eliminated the poverty I had known all my life, but much more important, it gave me the opportunity to learn to read and write, the education I'd been denied and which I will now be able to give my children. In November 1997, I received the State President's gold medal for sport from Mr Mandela. I knew that if I was hijacked on the way home from the function the thieves could steal my medal, but what they could not steal was my new education and all that Welcome, my teacher, had taught me.'*
(Photograph © Getty Images/Powell)

Josiah Thugwane's climb to fame is a moving tale in the Olympic annals. Born 15 April 1971, in Bethal, Uphumalanga, he was only six when his parents divorced and left him in the care of a penniless grandmother. Unable to go to school, he started work as a farm herd and his early sport, as for so many urchins, was barefoot soccer. When his running ability became apparent, he was employed as a kitchen cleaner by a coal mine intent on utilising his talent in their team. He could still only communicate in the dialect of his Ndebele tribe. His first serious success in a half-marathon earned him 50 rand and he was able to build a shack for his family at Mzinoni Township east of Johannesburg. Despite his various victories, he went to the line in Atlanta ranked only 41st in the world, the shortest runner in a field of 123 at 1.58m (5 ft 2 in.). Because of the humidity, there was still a close pack of leading runners at the halfway mark, but over the next 10km Luis dos Santos of Brazil began to stretch the pace. Unable to sustain this, he was passed by Thugwane and

then Bong-Ju Lee of South Korea, Eric Wainaina of Kenya keeping them within range. Approaching the stadium, Thugwane accelerated into a two- or three-second lead, the two behind him refusing to concede. The three were circling the stadium track at the same time. Thugwane held on to win by three seconds from Lee with Wainaina a further five seconds away. Steve Moneghetti of Australia, a pre-race favourite, was two minutes adrift in seventh place. Abdul Baser Wasigi, from Kabul, Afghanistan, who had a previous personal best time of just over two and a half hours, was injured immediately prior to the race but, determined to take part, crossed the line 111th and last, nearly an hour and a half after the rest of the field, in the slowest-ever Olympic time of 4:24:17. Finishing 107th was Islam Djugum of Bosnia, a survivor of the war with Yugoslavia who had continued training throughout the fighting.

Hardly better known than Thugwane in his ascent of the Olympic pedestal was Jefferson Perez of Ecuador. An outsider

Josiah Thugwane, former kitchen-cleaner, puts poverty, illiteracy and Bong-Ju Lee (KOR) behind him in bringing integrated South Africa its first gold medal by winning the marathon.
(© Getty Images/Prior)

with few credentials, having been 33rd in the previous year's World Championships, he metaphorically came from nowhere to win the 20km walk, the first-ever medal of any colour for his country, where his glory shot him to fame. His victory brought his country's traffic to a standstill, a congratulatory fax from the State President and the promise by his home city of Cuenca to name a stadium after him. And all for a man with an accidental first name, brought up in poverty and formerly a middle-distance runner. He was called Jefferson because the registry office clerk could not spell the one presented by his brother and suggested one she could. He had prepared by varying his training on the beach and at altitude, possible in Ecuador because of the proximity of mountains to the sea, and when his moment came he walked faster than ever before, his time of 1:20:07 only ten seconds off the Olympic record set in 1988. So weak he had to be assisted off the track, Perez said: 'When I took the lead, I felt so tired . . . I was half-asleep. It felt like a dream, but I thought I must go for it, even if I die.' Such is the motivation of the Olympics.

Yet another unheralded distance winner was Fatuma Roba, a farmer's daughter from Ethiopia who in the women's marathon upstaged the three favourites – defending champion Yegorova of Russia and the 1992 runner-up Arimori, together with world champion Manuela Machado of Portugal – by a convincing two-minute margin. With early morning rain showers that ended just before the race, the women had a cooler run than the men would have. For a long while the leader was Uta Pippig, multi-Boston winner, but, hard-pressed by Roba and the favourites,

she dropped out after 37km, the point at which Roba began to move away from the rest. Improving her own time by over three minutes, she was the first African woman to win the event.

Track and field experts considered the 200/400m double by Michael Johnson truly exceptional, the first by a man. It included his blistering world record in the shorter race. Yet for the author – resisting the widely held prejudice that sought to condemn Lewis without reservation, on account of the retrospective exposure in 2003 of a minor positive test in the US trials of 1988 – the fourth consecutive long jump title by Carl Lewis will have the most enduring acclaim. Records are broken: Lewis's longevity is more rare.

Johnson longed to be seen as unique. True, he was a special runner. His misfortune was that his 400m victory should come on the same night that Lewis extended his unique saga in front of a transfixed crowd of 82,000. He had failed to make the team in the 100m and had gained a place in the long jump during the US trials only by an inch, ahead of Mike Conley. Mike Powell, world champion of 1991 and 1993 during a run of 34 straight victories, won the trials, was favourite for Atlanta and was lying second after the first three jumps, behind leader Emmanuel Bangue of France, with three more jumps to follow. In third place after two jumps was Lewis. On his third attempt, he cleared 8.50m (27 ft 10 in.), his longest sea-level jump since beating Powell in Barcelona. Tension mounted over the remaining jumps but only James Beckford of Jamaica was able to improve, climbing to second place on his sixth jump, while Powell injured himself on his fifth. Thus Lewis entered that elite club which Steve Redgrave, the British oarsman, had joined two days previously: a gold medal in four consecutive Games, another being Al Oerter in the discus. Oerter was there to embrace Lewis at the post-medal press conference. Lewis also emulated the three Olympians who had won nine golds: Paavo Nurmi in long-distance running, Mark Spitz in swimming and Larissa Latynina in gymnastics. Aladár Gerevich (HUN), however, won six consecutive gold medals in fencing.

Few, certainly, deserved Olympic reward more than Johnson, with his unbroken sequence of 54 victories since 1989, including the past two World Championships, a dominance interrupted only by food poisoning in 1992. This 400m victory was regarded as inevitable even by his rivals. Only defeat would be news. Come the day, his performance was the most impressive in this event in the century: an Olympic record with

Michael Johnson (USA), supreme American quarter-miler, is vainly chased by Roger Black (GBR), silver, and Alvin Harrison (USA), fourth. (© Getty Images)

a ten-metre margin over Roger Black of Britain, as noble in his way as the winner. Aged 30, Black had been around almost as long as Carl Lewis. He had ten gold medals from major championships, four individual and six relay, but nothing previously from an Olympics. His succession of injuries read like a medical reference book: foot injury, out of the 1987 World Championships after winning the 1986 European title; following injury, absent from the Seoul Games; an ankle operation, 1989; retaining European title, 1990; hip operation following semi-final defeat, Barcelona, 1992; virus infection prior to European silver, 1994; cartilage operation in 1995 after finishing seventh in the World Championships. For 24 hours after crossing the line ahead of Davis Kamoga of Uganda, Black did not stop smiling. Probably not even when asleep. 'A silver behind Johnson,' he said, repeatedly, 'is like a gold ahead of anyone else. I ran, for me, the perfect race.' He too had epitomised the Olympic spirit.

Johnson remained haunted by the spectre of Lewis's fame. Brought up by a father who was a perfectionist, the son's grail was the double, which he had achieved in the previous year's World Championships. Immediately prior to the Games, Frankie Fredericks of Namibia had ended Johnson's unbeaten sequence in the 200m, never mind Johnson's world record of 19.66 in the US trials when breaking the 17-year-old record of Pietro Mennea at altitude. The Atlanta schedule initially had the 200m semi-final the same day as the final of the 400m, but special dispensation by the IAAF allowed a day of rest before the opening round of the 200m. Coincidence continued to plague him. Lewis stole some of his thunder from the 400m and now, shortly prior to the 200m final, Marie-José Pérec completed the identical women's double. In his pursuit of glory, Johnson was momentarily inspired, lowering his own record by a further 0.34 seconds. With his strange upright stance, the Texan covered the first 100 metres in 10.12 round the curve, then ran the second 100, with a rolling start, in 9.20. Thus the average for the two halves was 9.66 – compared with the world record of Donovan Bailey from Canada in the 100m a few days earlier of 9.84. It was the biggest slice off the world record since Eddie Tolan's 21.12 at the Los Angeles Games in 1932, a record that had lasted for 20 years. Fredericks and Ato Boldon of Trinidad claimed the minor medals.

There was an inelegant prelude to Bailey's record in the 100m. The eliminations had seen some fast times: Fredericks with 9.93 in the heats, then 9.94 in the first semi-final, and 9.93 by Boldon in the second. There were then three false starts in the final, the first by Boldon, the second by Linford Christie, then Christie again, earning disqualification. Aged 36, already a grandfather, the defending champion reacted poorly, the more so as captain of the British team. He refused to go, arguing with officials, the other starters disconcerted as they limbered up during the delay until Christie was confronted by the track referee. Naively, Christie thought that he could manipulate the situation and be reinstated. His reaction time now, 0.086, confirmed justification for recording a false start, anticipation of the gun being triggered at 0.10. Michael Marsh of the USA, who finished fifth, commented: 'I very rarely think or say that somebody has acted immaturely, but Linford did.' Some thought that Christie deliberately false started so as not to be embarrassed by finishing outside the medals, the probability of which was apparent both in his semi-final and in the World Championships the previous year, when he fell, claiming an injured hamstring which not everybody believed.

Bailey, a third successive Jamaican emigrant to win the title, following Ben Johnson and Christie, had become world champion in 1995, but had not had an impressive season, and

Defending sprint champion Linford Christie (GBR), disqualified for false starts, strolls off stage with ill grace, the race won by Donovan Bailey (CAN) with a world record 9.84.
(© Getty Images/Hewitt)

when the seven got away at the fourth attempt, he was at the back. Coincidentally, 'Bent' Ben, making his return, had failed to survive the semi-finals. By 60 metres, Fredericks was leading Boldon, yet Bailey recorded in the last phase of the race an exceptional 27 mph (12.1 mps) and zipped past them for his record of 9.84 – one-hundredth faster than Leroy Burrell. Dennis Mitchell of America was without a medal in spite of beating 10.0. The cloud over Christie was not to disappear: having been given the benefit of the doubt for a positive test in 1988, he was found positive for nandrolone at a subsequent meeting in Germany.

Nurmi, Lovelock, Elliott, Snell, Keino, Walker, Coe: the illustrious cavalcade of Olympic champions in the 1,500m was incomplete without one of history's finest runners, Noureddine Morceli of Algeria: three times world champion, world record holder at four distances, with the then four fastest 1,500m times ever run. Victory was an anticlimax for all but him, an echo of the Decker–Budd controversy in 1984 but without the false accusations. With just over a lap to go, Hicham El Guerrouj, the fast-rising young Moroccan, intent on shadowing Morceli stride for stride, closed in too sharply as they approached the bell. He spiked Morceli's heel and fell in a heap, nearly bringing down with him the three immediately behind: Fermin Cacho, the defending champion, Stephen Kipkorir of Kenya and the veteran Abdi Bile of Somalia. Morceli half stumbled, quickly recovered his balance, and with half a glance over his shoulder at the carnage behind him, sped into a five-yard lead. The others dodged or hurdled the fallen Moroccan, but the natural rhythm and drama of the race had fallen apart. Though Morceli now won with ease in 3:35.78, maybe he was fortunate: El Guerrouj, second fastest of the year behind him, was capable of victory. Instead, he finished last, the silver and bronze going to Cacho and Kipkorir. Bile, now 33, a survivor of the Somalian civil war in which 20 members of his family had died, and world champion nine years earlier, faded to finish sixth. It had required a different kind of spirit for him to be there at all.

It is said that Haile Gebrselassie of Ethiopia ran with a strangely bent left arm as a legacy of carrying school books for the ten kilometres he ran every day to and from home. The exercise had done his legs and lungs no harm: twice world champion at 10,000m and world record holder. Now he set an Olympic record of 27:07.34 in a tight finish with his Kenyan rival Paul Tergat, the world cross-country champion.

Gebrselassie had been tangling with Kenyans since he was a junior and there was little love lost. Kenyans Paul Koech and Josphat Machuka led after halfway, then with 2km remaining Tergat made a break, dropping everyone but Gebrselassie. At the bell, the Ethiopian drove to the front, moved six strides clear and resisted Tergat's late retaliation as they pushed for the line. The winner had run the second 5,000 in 13:11.4, a time that would have won every Olympic 5,000m final bar those of 1984 (Aouita) and that in Atlanta. The latter was won by Venuste Niyongabo of Burundi in 13:07.96, world record holder Gebrselassie having decided to withdraw after his 10,000m victory, which had left his feet bleeding.

At the age of 36, Johnny Gray of the US was running in his fourth Olympic 800m final: seventh in '84, fifth in '88, third in '92. He knew he must start fast to burn off the finishing kicks of the others, but all that he achieved was to set up one of the finest 800m and the first in which four men ran under 1:43. His first lap of 49.7 made the race, but he was spent and finished seventh. Vebjörn Rodal of Norway, bronze winner of the previous year's World Championship, made his move from the back with 300 metres to go, followed by Hezekiel Sepeng of South Africa, who had run barefoot at school until a benevolent white school governor had sponsored him four years before. There, too, were Fred Onyancha of Kenya and Norberto Tellez of Cuba, but the three of them could not close on Rodal, the first Norwegian to win a track gold medal. Sepeng became the first black South African medal winner in any sport ahead of Thugwane, yet all might have been different but for the absence of Wilson Kipketer, the world champion who had twice beaten Rodal but, having emigrated to Denmark, found himself denied citizenship due to a seven-year residence regulation. Refused release by Kenya, he in turn refused to run for them. He defeated Rodal a further three times that season and the following year lowered Coe's 16-year-old world record to 1:41.11.

Jonathan Edwards of Britain arrived at the Games with a succession of 21 victories, including the first two leaps in the triple jump at the previous year's World Championship to exceed 18 metres: first 18.19m (59 ft 7 in.), followed by the first over 60 ft (18.29m). Kenny Harrison of America was the unknown factor, having been world champion in 1991, missing the Olympic team in 1992 and only qualifying for Atlanta on the strength of an indoor performance. With little competition in the last year, Harrison nonetheless recorded a huge jump of 17.99m (59 ft ¼ in.) in the first round of the final. Edwards, with four faults in the final series, could get no closer than 17.88m (58 ft 8 in.) in the fourth round, Harrison then adding another four inches to his best (18.09m). Edwards' fifth attempt was beyond 59 feet, but his take-off had been a toe-nail beyond the board. Harrison relaxed between jumps watching Gail Devers, his girlfriend, run in the 100m semi-finals. 'I couldn't get my act together,' Edwards said, 'and I didn't get any rhythm until the fifth round. That jump might have been about 18.20, but I'm thrilled to bits to have silver. I could have come away with nothing.'

The previous Games had been an embarrassment for Dan O'Brien, not to say his sponsors, Reebok, when he failed to qualify for the decathlon with no clearance in the pole vault at the US trials, never mind that he was world champion. Casting off this setback – and financial loss – he had proceeded to break Daley Thompson's eight-year-old world record a month after the Barcelona Games, went on to retain the next two world titles and was overwhelming favourite in Atlanta. Now there was no blip, and even though his pole vault of 5.00m was moderate, he was under no pressure for the ultimate 1,500m, having a clear margin over Frank Busemann of Germany of more than 100 points, 67 points short of his world record. It was the

Noureddine Morceli of Algeria completes a cavalcade of triumphs with 1,500m victory, challenger Hicham El Guerrouj of Morocco having fallen in a collision which Morceli survived. (© Getty Images/Hewitt)

culmination of a rags to riches story. Born like Thompson of mixed parents, O'Brien had been brought up in foster homes, survived early alcoholism and had been rescued when Visa sponsored a decathlon development programme.

Junxia Wang, a defector from 'Ma's Army', the group of Chinese women under the direction of Junren Ma, the noted coach, failed in her bid for a double victory. Having won the inaugural 5,000m in 14:59.88 ahead of Pauline Konga of Kenya, she was then beaten into second place in the 10,000m by co-favourite Fernanda Ribeiro of Portugal. Wang was world record holder for the longer race and unbeaten over 13 starts. One and a half laps from the finish she overtook Ribeiro to take a six-stride lead. Ribeiro responded with a late sprint 50 metres out to pass Wang and set an Olympic record of 31:01.63, with defending champion Derartu Tulu of Ethiopia in fourth place behind her compatriot Gete Wami.

Gail Devers, American defending champion for the women's 100m, was under threat from her compatriot Gwen Torrence and Merlene Ottey of Jamaica, the latter a veteran with four Olympic and five world bronze medals to her credit. Remarkably, at the age of 36, Ottey made her strongest bid yet for a gold, sharing the same time of 10.94 with Devers. Torrence, having defeated Devers in the US trials, was a breath away on 10.96, all three having crossed the line as one and then awaited the official decision. Ottey's torso seemed to have won it, but Devers got the photo verdict with her head-and-neck dip at the line. Necks count. The Jamaican team lodged a vain protest, Devers becoming the first consecutive winner since Tyus in 1964–8. An 81,000 crowd had been rooting for Torrence, their home girl.

As in Barcelona, Devers was to fail in her more favoured event, the sprint hurdles, which was won by Ludmila Engquist, a Soviet emigrant who had first competed in Seoul. Engquist was banned for four years in 1993 for use of steroids – allegedly fed to her by her husband in revenge for her divorce proceedings.

She then married her manager Johan Engquist and moved to Sweden, and seemed likely to miss Atlanta through still being officially stateless. The Russian NOC released her registration two weeks before the Games and by one-hundredth of a second she took the gold medal ahead of Slovenian Brigita Bukovec.

Gymnastics saw two men make their comebacks to the arena. For one, the oldest living Olympic champion of any sport, it had been a 60-year break, for the other, arguably the greatest gymnast in history, only a matter of months. The emotional circumstances were very different for Leon Stukelj and Vitali Scherbo. Stukelj was last at an Olympic Games in Berlin, where, at the age of 38, representing the Kingdom of Yugoslavia, he won a silver medal on the rings to add to golds from Paris and Amsterdam. He had been the first to accomplish the exercise of holding the rings, upside-down, with the arms extended horizontally. Stukelj was in Atlanta, by invitation, to honour the Games' centenary and to present the medals on the first evening of gymnastics. Scherbo, from Belorussia, had won six gold medals in 1992, representing the Unified Team. The following February he and his wife, Irina, emigrated to Pennsylvania, wanting their unborn child to be an American citizen and to have the security and freedom unavailable in the liberated Soviet state. In December 1995, Irina had hovered close to death, her car having hit a lamp-post and left her with severed spleen, broken pelvis and seven broken ribs. Gymnastics had suddenly become unimportant to Scherbo. He had cared for her 24 hours a day. In the process, he consoled himself with vodka, put on weight and ceased training. When she recovered, Irina had begged him to return to the gym, to revive the dream of another Games, to stay in touch, so that maybe he might represent America in Sydney. So here he was with his Belorussia colleagues, bidding for the team title. Though Scherbo had the

Diminutive gymnast Kerri Strug (USA) memorably put her team before herself when handicapped by injury. (© popperfoto.com)

second highest individual total behind Alexei Nemov of Russia, they failed by a fraction to beat Ukraine for the bronze medal, Russia winning ahead of China. Scherbo had defied gravity in the floor exercise, never mind that in the past three years he had had operations on shoulder, arm and knee. When he leapt, he hung in the air like Baryshnikov on the ballet stage.

When Stukelj, a mere 1.57m (5 ft 2 in.), presented the medals, he was dwarfed by the winning Russians, though the reception he received from a 31,000 crowd at the Georgia Dome was almost as loud as for them. Here was a man who had been friend of Nurmi, Weissmuller and Owens.

There was further frustration for Scherbo in the individual event. In Barcelona, he had won six gold medals. Now he was grumbling round by round not only about his own scores but also about those, unfairly low he considered, for Nemov in his duel with Xiaoshuang Li of China, the ultimate winner. Scherbo, with his bronze medal, wore a look that could kill. Asked what his wife would think of his bronze, he replied tartly: 'She expected the gold. We don't know the colour of other medals.'

A minor revelation came with the gold medal of Ioannis Melissanidis for the individual floor exercise title, the first Greek victory by a man in any current event since Spyridon Louis a century ago. The son of a Salonica busdriver, Melissanidis had earned a World Championship silver medal in 1994.

For the bulk of the female television viewing audience of the United States, women's gymnastics was the focal point of any Summer Games, so it was a rare emotional moment when the American girls won the country's first gold medal. There had been many heroes in American women's sport – Babe Didrikson, Helen Wills, Maureen Connolly, Wilma Rudolph, Mary Decker, Mary-Lou Retton – it is doubtful, however, whether such deep affection has been earned in a single evening as by this team of youngsters who denied Russia the prize. Sport can contrive a

Vitali Scherbo from Belorussia, defending individual gymnastics champion, but undermined by his wife's horrific road accident, could now finish only third behind Xiaoshuang Li (CHN) and Alexei Nemov (RUS). (© Getty Images/Bruty)

rare climax, and never more so than now, the title seemingly resting on the final vault of Kerri Strug, an 18-year-old daughter of a Houston surgeon. The problem was that Strug could barely run, let alone leap a vaulting horse, having sprained her ankle when landing on her first jump. The Russians, simultaneously engaged on the floor exercise, had made errors to give the US a slight edge. Now came Strug's second jump. 'I could feel the gold medal slipping away,' she admitted later.

Women's gymnastics is condemned for putting dangerous stress on the physical development of girls and the minimum age limit was to be raised for the next Games. None of this was in Strug's mind as she went down the run once more, gathering her body for a one-and-a-half-turn twist. Miraculously, she landed cleanly, then sank to her knees in intense pain. The jump improved her score. The gold was won. America cheered. Bela Karolyi, the coach, gathered Strug in his arms. Ironically, her dedication was unnecessary: the US margin was just sufficient to have won without her second jump.

Following the euphoria came the anticlimax . . . if you were American. Lilia Podkopayeva was only 17, but said to be the breadwinner for three generations of her Ukrainian family. Her grandmother, who had introduced her to gymnastics at the age of five, had recently died. She came to Atlanta as world champion and disconcertingly discovered that the audience had no interest in her, only in her US rivals Shannon Miller and Dominique Dawes. Yet the home favourites, lying third and first respectively after two exercise rotations, disappeared from

In the modern pentathlon, Eduard Zenovka (RUS) suffered disaster in his second consecutive Games, stumbling yards from the finish of the cross-country to finish second.
(© Getty Images/Mortimore)

contention with muffed floor routines, the 'veterans' of 19 each leaving the mat in tears. When it came to the final apparatus, Podkopayeva's other rivals also fell away: Huilan Mo, the tiny Chinese, on the floor, her compatriot Dina Kochetkova on the vault. Though pressed by Romanians Gina Gogean and Simona Amanar with outstanding vaulting, Podkopayeva's immaculate floor display, including a rare double-front somersault with a half-twist which earned her a mark of 9.887, assured her of the title. 'Without my grandmother's help, I would not be here today,' she said, clutching her medal.

Money could not buy the publicity given to the modern pentathlon by the unfortunate Eduard Zenovka of Russia. In one of the most dramatic moments of the Games alongside Strug's vault, he stumbled and fell within eight strides of a gold medal. NBC television was running live for this million-dollar tumble. At the conclusion of four disciplines, Zenovka was in sixth place. With the staggered start for the four-lap cross-country, he was 45 seconds behind the team leader Cesare Toraldo of Italy. Fifteen seconds behind was Alex Parygin of Kazakhstan, then János Martinek of Hungary. By the last lap, Zenovka had overhauled them all when entering the stadium two strides ahead of Parygin. In Barcelona, he had taken the bronze after falling three times from his horse, and now the gold was in his grasp. Approaching the line, he glanced over his shoulder. In that instant, Parygin passed him on the other side. Trying in vain to accelerate, Zenovka fell but staggered to his feet to rescue second place, with Martinek third.

Mingxia Fu, now an elderly 17, retained her platform title in diving, Annika Walter of Germany and Mary Ellen Clark of the US taking silver and bronze. Though now aged 33, Clark thus retained the position she gained in Barcelona, becoming America's oldest diving medal winner. 'A year ago I wasn't even wearing a bathing suit,' Clark related, having undergone psychotherapy to overcome the vertigo that for nearly a year had prevented her from stepping on a diving board. Fu also won the springboard title ahead of Irina Laschko of Russia, to become the first woman in 36 years to win both diving events.

Alexander Popov of Russia successfully defended his 100m freestyle swimming title, but so close was his struggle with American Gary Hall Jr, a matter of inches in the touch, that he had to look at the scoreboard to see who was the winner. The margin was seven-hundredths of a second, allowing him to become the first since Weissmuller to win consecutive titles in this event. Their comparative times were 58.6 and 48.74. Popov was unbeaten in major competition for five years and he also became the first to retain both 100m and 50m titles, his victory in the latter achieved with fractionally more ease against Hall: a margin of thirteen-hundredths.

Fred Deburghgraeve of Belgium had taken up swimming to ease his asthma. In the 100m breaststroke, he not only set a world record in the heats but also became his country's first winner of a gold medal in swimming.

The Chinese women swimmers had dominated the World Championships two years earlier, winning 12 of the 16 gold medals, thereby arousing the suspicion of drug use. This was substantiated when seven of their swimmers, including two of the champions, tested positive at the Asian games the following year. Alarmed by this, the Chinese NOC worked hard to eliminate cheating, possibly with some success because on the first day of the Games three of their entries failed to reach their respective finals, though one who did, Jingyi Le, set an Olympic record in the 100m freestyle with 54.50. Two Chinese ranked first and second in the world, Yan Chen and Yanyan Wu, failed to make even the consolation final of the 400m medley, unexpectedly won by Michelle Smith of Ireland. Western

Michelle Smith gained acclaim for herself and Ireland amid widespread suspicion of malpractice. (© Getty Images/Hewitt) (right © Getty Images/Bruty)

coaches were quick to attribute the new trend to stricter testing, but the emergence of Smith from relative obscurity was a major controversy, arousing intense speculation. No swimmer from Ireland, which did not have a regulation-sized pool, had ever won an Olympic medal, no Irish woman – other than Northern Ireland's Mary Peters – had won a medal in any sport and Smith had been relatively anonymous in the Games of 1988 and 1992. Yet here she was in Atlanta, at the age of 26, winning three gold medals and a bronze.

During the Barcelona Games, Smith had met and subsequently married Erik de Bruin, a Dutch discus thrower, who the following year tested positive for excessive testosterone and traces of gonadatropin. The IAAF overruled a Dutch appeal. Subsequently and provocatively, de Bruin admitted that 'some people are not going to make it without extra help'. Throughout 1995 the international swimming federation had difficulty tracing Smith for random testing. In her first event in Atlanta, the 400m medley, she had improved her personal best over three years to an aggregate of more than 17 seconds, comfortably winning the event. Included also in the 400m freestyle, after a disputed late entry, her victory in 4:07.25 was the fastest in two years, defeating the defending champion, Dagmar Hase of Germany.

The shock for the United States, and indeed others, was the failure in the preliminaries of Janet Evans, one of their finest ever swimmers, eliminated in ninth position from the final because of Smith's inclusion. Two days later, Smith won her third gold in the 200m medley, followed by bronze in the 200m butterfly. A hero at home, Smith was everywhere else pilloried in the media. When randomly tested in January 1998, after some evasion, her sample was found to contain dangerously excessive amounts of alcohol, the international federation concluding the sample had been manipulated, with alcohol used as a masking agent. She was suspended for four years, her appeal denied by CAS. The fracas marred the Atlanta Games, though it could not detract from other fine performances, such as that of Penny Heyns of South Africa in

winning her country's first gold medal in 44 years in the 200m breaststroke. She was white: only a fifth of South Africa's team was black. Some considered a springbok tattoo on her shoulder, insignia of the former apartheid regime, to be offensive, but it did not bother Deputy State President Thabo Mbeki, who shed tears when 'God Bless Africa' was played for the first time at an Olympic Games.

Blyth Tait of New Zealand praised his mount, Ready Teddy – 'the biggest heart of any horse I've ever ridden' – when winning the prestigious three-day event. With compatriot Sally Clark having a clear show-jumping round, Tait needed the same to take the title, achieving it in spite of clipping one rail that stayed firm.

Andre Agassi (USA) defeated Sergi Bruguera of Spain in straight sets to take the tennis title, fortunate not to be expelled for obscenities in his quarter-final against Wayne Ferreira of South Africa.

Andre Agassi (USA), flanked by Sergi Bruguera (ESP), runner-up, and Leander Paes (IND) third, protested his patriotism in the face of earlier Davis Cup withdrawals. (© Getty Images/Prior)

Leander Paes gained India's first medal of any kind since their men's hockey team won in Moscow 16 years earlier, and the first individual medal since a wrestling bronze in 1952, when defeating Fernando Meligeni of Brazil for third place in the men's tennis singles.

Miguel Induráin of Spain, having failed in his bid to win a sixth consecutive Tour de France, gained some compensation when winning the individual time trial over 52.2km in 1:04:05 from compatriot Abraham Olano and Chris Boardman (GBR). In the first road race opened to professionals, the winner had been Pascal Richard of Switzerland, who won only by the length of his bicycle in a desperate finish with Rolf Sörensen of Denmark.

Jeannie Longo-Ciprelli, an organic vegetable grower from Grenoble, rode a bicycle to market for housekeeping. She rode rather more venomously when racing: the most decorated female competitor on the road, with five world titles and two in individual pursuit. This was her last chance for Olympic gold and under a burning sun she took it with 25 seconds to spare.

Spain were surprise finalists in men's field hockey, defeating Germany, Pakistan and Australia to reach the final in which they lost to the Netherlands 3–1. The United States won the inaugural women's soccer tournament against China, watched by a crowd of 76,000 in the little town of Athens, the then largest crowd ever for a women's game. Steve Redgrave and Matthew Pinsent of Britain made history when winning the coxless pairs, thereby Redgrave winning his fourth consecutive gold medal to emulate Paul Elvstrøm of Denmark in Finn-class yachting and discus thrower Al Oerter of America. Carl Lewis would join them before the Games were over. Though Redgrave would say he was retiring after 16 years at the top this was to prove, exceptionally, not to be so.

The imperial Haile Gebrselassie of Ethiopia snatches 10,000m gold by three strides from entrenched Kenyan rival Paul Tergat, in an Olympic record of 27:07.34 – the second 5,000 of 13:11.4 having been fast enough to have won every previous Olympic 5,000m bar 1984.
(© Getty Images)

CHAPTER LXVI

Athens' Reprieve

Nikos Filaretos of Greece, IOC member, 1981–2007

'*At long last! After 108 years, the Olympic Games are finally returning to their native land, to the city where they were revived back in 1896, having been suspended for many centuries. Greece and its people passionately wanted to celebrate in Athens in 1996, the centenary of the revival of the Olympic Games, but we were accused of arrogance when some of us expressed the view that we had a right to hold them. We are, of course, too small a country to claim any automatic granting of hosting these Games of 2004. Yet we were absolutely right about 1996. A brief examination of the contribution of Greece to the Olympic Movement for the past hundred years reveals that: thanks to the persistence of Demetrius Vikelas of Greece, elected first President of the IOC, the realisation of the dream of the visionary Pierre de Coubertin became possible; thanks to George Averoff of Greece and the 920,000 sovereigns he offered – in essence making him the first IOC sponsor – the reconstruction of the Panathenaikon Stadium, where the first modern Games were celebrated, was made possible; thanks to the persistence of the Greek people, and under the pretext of celebration of the tenth anniversary of their revival, the Games of the Interim Olympiad were organised in 1906, bringing the spirit of the Games back on the right track, following the traumatic experience in Paris and St Louis respectively of the Games of 1900 and 1904. Greece, with its flag and national anthem, has taken part in every Olympic Games so far; our country has offered the Olympic Movement the educational and pedagogical institution of the International Olympic Academy, where more than 60,000 students, teachers, NOC officials, sports journalists and others have been educated during the past 40 years. For its running and maintenance, the Greek government spends some $2 million annually.*

Nevertheless, the IOC did not honour Greece with the award of hosting the Centenary Games. In my opinion, the IOC should have entrusted Athens with their organisation honoris causa *and without any voting procedure. For the Games of 2004 we are fully aware of our responsibilities. We are not going to have luxurious Games, though I hope that the red carpet will be laid for the athletes, for they alone are protagonists of the Games. What will determine the level of success of the Athens Games will be a return to simplicity and the true Olympic spirit, which is currently in jeopardy.*

The modern Games have had a very positive influence on the youth of five continents every four years. On the other hand, the evolution of the Games has taken the wrong, even if unavoidable course towards full commercialisation, a consequence of which is widespread doping. During the Cold War, sport as well as art became a powerful tool of propaganda. The East tried exploitation through doping experimentation, while the West reacted the other way, with the exploitation of money as incentive. Elite competitors need money, and you cannot expect them to train for six hours a day and not provide the means to live or a pension post-performance. Elite sport can be sustained, but only so long as sponsors can be controlled and remain at the service of sport, not vice-versa. Undoubtedly they will try to turn the tables.'*

(Photograph © IOC/Imsand)

The snowball of cities wishing to attach themselves to the publicity machine created by the host bidding process had gathered eleven names which the IOC's Selection College of fourteen, headed by Marc Hodler, would reduce to a shortlist of five in March 1997, for consideration by the IOC members at the Session in Lausanne in September that year. The eleven were: Athens, still bearing its wounded pride from seven years earlier, Buenos Aires, Cape Town, Istanbul, Lille, Rio de Janeiro, Rome, St Petersburg, San Juan, Seville and Stockholm. The expectation was that Athens and Rome, with their historic origins, would be the frontrunners; that Cape Town would be selected for political correctness if nothing else; that Buenos Aires would likewise represent Latin America; and that Stockholm, representing the traditional excellence of Swedish sport, would make a third European city in the final five. And so it would prove to be. Rationality required the reduction, but for many it was a shame to see, in particular Istanbul and St Petersburg, the latter with its thousands of historic monuments including 250 museums, fall by the wayside. The Goodwill Games of 1994 had demonstrated just how attractive an Olympics could be in this city of crowded church spires nestling on the Baltic shore. Elimination was a particular personal blow to Sinan Erdem, dignified IOC member of Turkey and bid leader who died in 2003, and Alex Kozlovsky, Russian NOC vice-president and exhaustive campaigner for the nobility of the city that survived Hitler's 900-day siege and would have been flag-bearer of the new Russia. Of the 111 voting members, 46 were European, 21 from Africa and the same number from the Americas, 18 from Asia and 5 from Oceania.

The author should declare an interest, having worked as a consultant to Stockholm for three months between a switch in journalistic employment. The acceptance of a personal approach by Stockholm was on account of not only a long-standing belief in Swedish administrative competence but also a conviction that the Scandinavian summer climate and the compact nature of the proposed waterfront site would provide a perfect ambience.

There was no denying the emotional pull of Athens, however, and of a lingering sense of debt on the part of IOC members following their previous rejection. The choice of Athens would also ameliorate worldwide opinion of a critically beleaguered IOC. While the 1990 bid for the Centenary Games had perversely managed to antagonise the voters, leaving aside all its logistical shortcomings, the new bid was led with theatrical brio by Gianna Angelopoulos-Daskalaki, a former politician, and her husband Theodore Angelopoulos, the pair of them multimillionaires who uninhibitedly stretched some of the IOC's entertainment guidelines. Wanton flattery characterised the Athens' campaign, with IOC members being invited to plant a tree that would commemorate their names and possibly help them overlook the fact that it was difficult to breathe in Athens in mid-summer, or that transportation was a crisis unlikely to disappear over the next seven years.

Among the other candidates, Buenos Aires was expected to be the first to fall in the voting rounds, though South America had never been an Olympic host. This was the city's fifth bid, and the Evaluation Commission reported favourably on Argentina's blueprint in spite of a recent, seriously disorganised Pan-Am Games at Mar del Plata. African ambassadors in the US were mandated by Thabo Mbeki, South Africa's Deputy President, to give their public support to Cape Town's bid, yet in the event not all of Africa's 21 members voted for the Cape in the first round, in spite of lobbying by continental leaders such as Lamine Diack, vice-president of the IAAF. For Africa it would also be a first Olympic Games and as Sam Ramsamy, South African IOC member, claimed: 'It is not only what the Games can do for Cape Town, South Africa and Africa but also what a Games in Africa can do for the Olympic Movement. Cape Town provides the most magnificent setting.'

The bid was not without controversy. Its leader Chris Ball was accused by Mario Pescante, president of the Italian NOC and chairman of the Rome bid, of deliberate misrepresentation. Ball was quoted in a Reuters interview as accusing Rome of a defamatory campaign aimed at undermining Cape Town on account of its crime rate. Ball, in return correspondence, claimed he had been misrepresented, though the text of the interview did not suggest that. Irrespective of this spat, widespread emotional support for Cape Town was undermined by recognition of its commercial and contemporary social limitations.

Rome itself was embroiled in the Nebiolo factor: would his involvement be a positive or negative influence? The controversial aura that tended to surround him could hardly help the bid, yet the appeal to IOC members of two weeks in the Eternal City was not be underestimated. The affinity between Rome and ancient culture is almost as strong as that of Greece; the fact that Rome already possessed a majority of the necessary sporting structures made it a prime candidate.

None of the virtues of the other candidates, however, could compare with the athletic preference for Stockholm by a majority of both competitors and those whose job it is to run a Games, that is the IFs and NOCs. More than 70 per cent of IFs, in a poll conducted by a British agency, considered Stockholm had the edge on climate, environmental sensitivity, the proximity of the Village to venues and an unrivalled transport system. Among NOCs, 34 per cent gave a clear preference for Stockholm compared with the 14 per cent for Rome and only 7 per cent for Athens. Olof Stenhammar, the Swedish bid leader, promised that Stockholm would do for the Summer Games what Lillehammer had for the Winter. Sadly for Stockholm, however, credibility was undermined in the weeks immediately prior to the voting by isolated incidences of terrorism that could not be attributed to identified opponents of the bid, approval of the Games in Stockholm having in fact risen to 60 per cent of the population.

Voting preference on the day for Athens was emphatic, Rome being defeated in the fourth round by a majority of 25. One hundred and one years after Greece had staged the first modern Games, the IOC granted them the chance to do so for a second time. Whether or not the voters had already made up their minds, they had been assaulted by the passionate plea of Angelopolous-Daskalaki. A keynote of her theme was criticism of the Athens bid for the 1996 Games, admitting mistakes and simultaneously not over-emphasising any historic 'right' to be hosts. The shock was Stockholm's elimination in the second round, IOC members seemingly immune to the interests of competitors. The Buenos Aires vote was split evenly in the second round between Athens, Cape Town and Rome, while the failed vote for Stockholm then divided two to one in favour of Athens rather than Rome. Eliminated Cape Town's vote swung heavily to Athens. Pescante, Primo Nebiolo and the others from Rome were left licking their wounds as they looked at the outcome:

	I	II	III	IV
Athens	32	38	52	66
Buenos Aires	16 (44)	–	–	–
Cape Town	16 (62)	22	20	–
Rome	23	28	35	41
Stockholm	20	19	–	–

Speculation now focused on who might become the head of the Athens organising committee and it became evident that Prime

Gianna Angelopoulos-Daskalaki rises in celebration after leading Athens to belated success when bidding for a return of the Games to their homeland in 2004. (© IOC/Locatelli)

Minister Kostas Simitis did not wish to have the post assigned to the demonstrative lady who had just won the bid. The Greeks requested a delay for the first official report they were supposed to deliver to the Executive Board, under the direction of Kostas Bakouris, who had been appointed general manager of the organising committee of which Stratis Stratigis was chairman. With Simitis being chairman of the 'National Council', a quasi-supervisory board for the Games, Angelopoulos-Daskalaki was excluded from the 15-member executive. It was not long, though, before Bakouris would be quoted in Greek newspapers as stating that all Olympic projects were 'beset with problems' as the organising committee slid into crisis inside the first year of operation. The re-involvement of Angelopoulos-Daskalaki became more likely by the week, even though Jacques Rogge, as chairman of the Coordination Commission, diplomatically attempted to show no sign of sea-sickness as the waves mounted.

Having salved their conscience, the IOC, and its President in particular, had to ensure that the Athens venture did not collapse. Samaranch had once more put his name forward for re-election for a third renewal of his term for four years at the Lausanne Session, and though he would now definitely retire in 2001, it would be his duty to ensure that his successor did not inherit a crumbling temple. Also elected at the Lausanne Session was Anita DeFrantz as the Executive Board's first woman Vice-President, to serve alongside de Mérode, M'Baye and Hé.

Anita DeFrantz, bronze medal oarswoman for the USA in 1976, becomes the Executive Board's first woman Vice-President.
(© IOC/Locatelli)

If Samaranch already had in mind that Rogge was his preferred candidate as successor, he was certainly ensuring that the Belgian had a good schooling, appointing him chairman of the Coordination Commissions for both Sydney and Athens. While there were already anxieties about Athens, there were also concerns, though less extreme, about Sydney, when by 1997 the organising committee had lost its third leading executive with the forced resignation of Dr Mal Hemmerling. He had succeeded John Iliffe, who in turn had followed Gary Pemberton. Michael Knight, so-called 'Olympics Minister' of New South Wales and president of the organising committee, having dismissed Hemmerling now appointed civil servant Sandy Holway, former chief of staff under ex-Prime Minister Bob Hawke. IOC Director-General Carrard played down the significance of Hemmerling's departure, never mind internal problems over sponsors, communications and alleged politicisation of the organising committee under the New South Wales Labour government.

Over in Salt Lake City public opinion was still vibrating from the departure of Tom Welch, president of the organising committee of the 2002 Winter Games, his resignation enforced by an acrimonious split with his wife Alma, a particularly sensitive issue in the Mormon State, the more so because there was the possibility of police charges of assault against Welch. In the event, no charges were preferred in an undisputed divorce. The local *Desert News* reported that barely half the population was now in favour of the Games and only 36 per cent were confident that there would not be a deficit at taxpayers' expense. Welch would continue as a consultant for the organising committee, Frank Joklik succeeding him as president.

Despite the best efforts of the Executive Board – a body of honorary officials meeting too infrequently given the extent of their responsibilities – there was in the late 1990s an uncomfortable feeling of skeletons lurking in different cupboards. Most worrying was that of doping control. The Medical Commission was a body of men of integrity but their reputation had been undermined in some countries by lack of vigilance or outright evasiveness. In an interview with *Süddeutsche Zeitung* of Munich, Professor Arne Ljungqvist revealed his concerns about alleged undeclared positive tests from Atlanta in the official report from the Games. Ljungqvist admitted that in 1997 the Medical Commission still did not have the final report from Atlanta, yet were aware that Don Catlin from the Atlanta laboratory had discovered some additional positive tests. Ljungqvist stated: 'If something is found we must be notified.' The ambivalence in the American attitude towards the conducting of rigorous testing and declaration of results was a story that would run and run, yet this seemingly wilful neglect of IOC policy applied to many of the IFs within the Olympic framework. Three years after the Centenary Congress, 19 IFs, including the IAAF, had still not accepted the full range of regulations agreed upon at the Congress: a syndrome referred to by Thomas Bach, German IOC member, as 'a falsely understood autonomy'.

There was no misunderstanding on the part of the Chinese. Conscious of damage to China's image by positive tests on their swimmers and supposed malpractice among many of their track and field performers, the Chinese NOC, in conjunction with its sports ministry, had realised that its formal attitude must alter. Random domestic testing and suspensions became standard practice and the so-called 'Ma's Army' of women runners under the exclusive direction of China's most famed coach quickly disintegrated, as China strategically aligned itself in order to make a fresh bid for hosting the Games in 2008. Continuing its new spirit of broadmindedness, China even agreed to the continued independent membership of the IOC for Hong Kong, though under the title 'Hong Kong, China', and using the Chinese national anthem.

A reflection of the possible tragic consequence of performance-enhancing drugs would come in 1998 with the premature death of Florence Griffith Joyner, known to all as Flo-Jo when she had stormed to success with three gold medals in the Seoul Games ten years before. The exceptional advance in Flo-Jo's performances between 1987 and 1988 inevitably led to suspicion that she had resorted to the same kind of chemical assistance as Ben Johnson, the Canadian sprinter found positive at the same Games. Although it had never been proven that Flo-Jo had taken drugs, the coincidence of such athletic improvement at the age of 28 had been too dramatic for any normally acquired advance at that age. Philip Hersh of the

Chicago Tribune reported Bob Kersee, her brother-in-law and former coach, as asserting: 'It has never been proven by anyone that Florence had ever used anything illegal to improve her performance.' She had, however, fed speculation on her ability suddenly to win the short sprints by retiring less than five months after the Games, when she could have been earning substantial five-figure sums for any race in which she chose to compete. She died of an apparent heart seizure, her collapse discovered by her husband Al Joyner, the 1984 Olympic triple jump champion. Medical evidence could not categorically relate her death to possible doping abuse.

At the Session prior to the Nagano Winter Games in early 1998, Jacques Rogge was elected to the Executive Board, decisively preferred by the members to Olegario Vazquez Raña, president of international shooting. This was an essential personal development for Rogge if he were to be in position three and a half years later to challenge as a successor to Samaranch. A further two women were also elected as IOC members: Nawal El Moutawakel of Morocco, 400m hurdles champion in 1984, succeeding the late Mohamed Benjelloun, and multiple Olympic medallist Irena Szewinska-Kirszenstein of Poland in place of the retired Wlodzimeirz Reczek.

Nagano, a winter resort with a population approaching a million some 150 kilometres north-west of Tokyo, had lost the contest with Sapporo to be Winter host in 1972, but had surprisingly on the one hand, but predictably on the other, outbid Salt Lake City in 1991. The IOC would have been most unlikely to vote for two US cities in consecutive years. A Nagano budget for the Games approaching $6 billion would include the cost of a bullet-train track from Tokyo. Preparations were marred by revelations of corruption over construction contracts and other Games-related incentives. It was significant that records of the city's entertainment and other costs in the bid procedure were destroyed. Nonetheless, part of the incentive in the election of Nagano was the establishment of the first major winter sports centre of the highest standard in eastern Asia and there would be 72 participant nations compared with the 67 at Lillehammer four years earlier.

Somehow, the Games survived the downturn in the Japanese economy, in spite of concessions to environmental issues such as switching the biathlon course in order to protect the nesting of gosshawks, and a compromise on a higher start to the downhill, demanded by the international ski federation, in order to preserve protected parkland. There would be an abundance of technology, especially regarding security, with iris eye-scanners screening biathletes when gaining access to their rifles. Seiko's equipment included 100-frame-per-second cameras on the landing slope of the ski jumping to measure the distance previously judged by eye.

Not all opening ceremonies have a message. Nagano's message was unmistakable: an appeal for global peace and the sanctity of the next generation. President Samaranch renewed the call for an Olympic Truce in the light of an imminent threat of armed attack on Iraqi chemical warfare targets. The ceremony was both international and wholly Japanese. The three-centuries-old bell of the Zenkoji Temple, dating back 1,300 years, brought the sound of ancient purification, and the folk festival of Onbashra, held every seven years, representing the home of residing gods, made the new Minami Stadium a sacred area. The children of Nagano sang Andrew Lloyd Webber's pleading ballad, 'When Children Rule the World'. So easily the naive virtue of youth can be cynically dismissed, yet to almost every adult in the world the most precious gift in life is another life, that of a child. And how hugely they are so often betrayed.

Midori Ito of Japan, figures silver medal winner six years earlier, ignites the stadium bowl at Nagano's opening ceremony. (© Getty Images/Bello)

First to enter the stadium with the flame, surrounded by another swarm of children, was Chris Moon, a former British Army sapper who had lost one leg and hand when training others to defuse landmines in Mozambique. Moon worked for HALO, the anti-mine charity to which the Japanese are substantial donors. The cauldron was ultimately lit by Midori Ito, the only home skater to have won a medal, silver, in figure skating. The ceremony closed to a technically remarkable rendering of the fourth movement of Beethoven's *Choral Symphony*. Seiji Ozawa, the conductor, besides assembling some of the foremost young operatic singers from around the world, was able simultaneously to embrace, by electronic magic, choirs from the five continents, in Berlin, Beijing, Cape Point (South Africa), New York and Sydney. Such was the efficient management of the Games, in the face of persistently malevolent weather, that Sydney 2000 would have to be on alert to maintain the level of excellence in successive IOC festivals.

Despite the organisational success, scepticism regarding the Olympic Games remained rampant, most of all regarding perceived inefficiency in the anti-doping problem, a Danish opinion poll conducted in six European countries revealing that 50 per cent believed the majority of professional athletes used performance-enhancing substances; though it can be argued that there is no equivalence between many Olympic sports and the majority of professional spectator events, often uncaring about drug use. Everywhere, IOC members found themselves harangued by the media, largely on no more than hearsay, as being, in the terminology of even some of the more responsible press outlets, a bunch of sleaze-bags. However, the world was about to discover just who the guilty minority were. It may be relevant that, during interviews by the author conducted at the Nagano Games with more than 30 IOC members – none of them, coincidentally, being those subsequently punished for having seriously abused their post, though three were ensnared in lesser controversies – the author found nothing but altruistic concern for the Olympic Movement, fear and optimism equally expressed. The following is a synopsis of some of the views:

JEAN-CLAUDE KILLY (FRANCE), OLYMPIC ALPINE CHAMPION: 'The Games must be preserved so that thousands will have the experience in the future and that millions will dream about it and may be the better for it. The Games can improve someone's life, help them out of the ghetto, and this is what we're here for.'

RAYMOND GAFNER (SWITZERLAND), IOC MEMBER: 'The Games as conceived by de Coubertin can bring the answer to some of the problems of humanity in an awful world. The next decade will be decisive, and at the moment the future seems full of danger. What we need are leaders who know and love sport and are willing to give a third of their time to the Olympic Games. They can be men of money, but should not be looking to the Games to make money for themselves.'

BERTHOLD BEITZ (GERMANY), HEAD OF KRUPP INDUSTRIES SINCE 1957: 'Under Samaranch, the IOC has become an umbrella for the whole of world sport. There is no way to halt its development in the attempt to keep the Games special, there will be no retreat from professionalism and the problem is that the IOC is a mixture of some who are clever and many who have no idea of real organisation.'

KEBA M'BAYE (SENEGAL), JUDGE AT THE INTERNATIONAL COURT OF JUSTICE: 'In my mind, it was at first unthinkable to commercialise the Olympic Rings, yet I now realise I was being middle-aged in this view. We must realise it is not possible to live outside the epoch within which we exist, commercialisation was unavoidable. Do we lose the moral message, the interest of the public, the enthusiasm of young participants, unless we embrace subsidy? It is the closing ceremony which is primarily the message, the symbol of the Games, the friendship between people on the final day.'

RICHARD POUND (CANADA), OLYMPIAN SWIMMER: 'As the Games become bigger and more important they're like a microcosm of the world, a model for the world, therefore it is bad when there are problems in the Games because this means disillusionment for the world. If you compare the Games to other sport, the difference is that the public cares so much more.'

ALEXANDRU SIPERCO (ROMANIA), ACADEMIC, IOC GURU: 'People ask for something to believe in. What brings youth to our stadiums is not money. In sport, you *give* something. Sport was a metaphor for an honourable life, that was the gift that England gave to the world. Now, chivalry has gone, chivalry and profit don't mix.'

HRH PRINCESS ANNE (GREAT BRITAIN), OLYMPIC EQUESTRIAN: 'Maybe we should go back to basics and focus on individual elite sports [rather than team sports]. The IOC nowadays misses people like Reggie Alexander of Kenya, people not afraid to make points of order at Sessions. The chance is there, but people won't take it. The IOC must be clearer on rules and not just apply them when convenient. Continental rotation in host city bidding is an essential. Regarding ceremonies, to a professional they're a waste of time. To an amateur, they're so much a part of it.'

ANITA DEFRANTZ (USA), OLYMPIC OARSWOMAN: 'The challenge is to manage the success. Samaranch was willing to anger the members and go with the marketing programme. I don't

Alexandru Siperco, one of those expressing wisdom on the future of the IOC in February 1998, prior to a near catastrophic scandal. (© IOC/Strahm)

think the sponsors do manipulate the Games, only the extent of their own exposure.'

FRANÇOIS CARRARD (SWITZERLAND), IOC DIRECTOR-GENERAL, ATTORNEY: 'Samaranch raised the IOC to a status it never had before. With the financial development of society over the last 20 years, the IOC was lucky to catch the train, otherwise we might have lost the race for survival. Yet we are still stuck with twentieth-century concepts, big stadiums that become white elephants and such like. The future will be dependent on the new President.'

PRINCE ALEXANDRE DE MÉRODE (BELGIUM), CHAIRMAN, MEDICAL COMMISSION: 'There is a tendency in life to ignore the welfare of the individual. No one is interested if a trade union leader or the first violinist is taking medication to enhance their performance. We are the only activity in society with this preoccupation, but without it we lose everything. We are dependent on leaders. There is a need for government to measure what is the cost of drug-related work-absence and to become more involved in the anti-doping campaign.'

THOMAS BACH (GERMANY), OLYMPIC FENCING CHAMPION, EXECUTIVE BOARD VICE-PRESIDENT: 'The derivation of the Games is mythological, connected with culture, history, simply an idea. That myth can be lost in a generation, yet the Olympics, vitally, have a message beyond sport. The more we can hold on to the myth, the easier it will be to hold on to the competitors.'

VITALY SMIRNOV (RUSSIA), EXECUTIVE BOARD VICE-PRESIDENT: 'I'm not sure the basketball Dream Team was a good innovation, unsure of their presence every Games, unsure of their control. Competitively, we have had too many losses compared with gains, ours is no longer an equal competition.

This is serious, the weak part of Samaranch's regime. When we have people ignoring the IOC Charter, we are the losers. Competitors *must* be in the Village – that was one of the genius inventions and Atlanta absenteeism was a disaster.'

HM KING CONSTANTINE (GREECE), OLYMPIC SAILING CHAMPION, HONORARY IOC MEMBER: 'Rome in 1960 was the last cosy Games, though just as competitive as today. There was a period of decline under President Killanin, with Monique Berlioux in control, but we've grown now to a point where intimacy is missing. Nobody can say whether the present juggernaut can survive. The biggest threat is complacency and we must be very careful who is selected to succeed Samaranch. The next few years are the most crucial for the IOC, and for my country, the hosts of 2004.'

RAOUL MOLLET (BELGIUM), MODERN PENTATHLON OLYMPIAN, FORMER PRESIDENT OF THE BELGIAN NOC AND INTERNATIONAL MILITARY SPORTS COUNCIL: 'The battle for universality has been achieved – and everyone wants to be there because of the money. The IOC membership of way over 100 is too many, the maximum should be 60. Samaranch has achieved unity after previous attempts to break up the IOC by Indonesia and the Soviet Union. There are still not enough women involved. If you look at Scandinavia, women are the teachers. The rise of agents is killing off volunteers, on whom sport lives.'

PHILIPP VON SCHÖLLER (AUSTRIA), HONORARY IOC MEMBER: 'The IOC needs a phase of consolidation, it's becoming too much a matter of show business.'

FRANCISCO ELIZALDE (PHILIPPINES), BUSINESSMAN/FINANCIER: 'Everything must be open to reform and revision. We are a very disparate group, some members even boast about not reading bid books or evaluation reports. The IOC should keep its emphasis on sport, not on peripheral issues of peace, environment, children. Don't let us be candidates for the Nobel Peace Prize. If it comes, it comes. Our strength is through sport, we're not the UN.'

ZHEN-LIANG HÉ (CHINA), EXECUTIVE BOARD MEMBER: 'The IOC must alter its composition, become a fully representative world body. At present, more than half the members are still from Europe. We must not allow commercialisation to deprive sport of its moral soul. There is commercialisation as a development process and commercialisation as corruption. We must not dig our own grave. Society recycles itself, historically. The mainstream may one day find a more moral objective.'

PAUL HENDERSON (CANADA), PRESIDENT, INTERNATIONAL SAILING: 'The 10,000 competitors at the Games must be elite. I believe it is a mistake to be broad-based [in quality], the scope for that should be regional games. The Olympic Games should become even more elite.'

DR UN YONG KIM (SOUTH KOREA), EXECUTIVE BOARD VICE-PRESIDENT: 'The Olympic Games are supreme, are special, and even children recognise this – that is why we must do everything to protect the Games for the future. However,

Dr Un Yong Kim (KOR), seen here (right) consulting with Thomas Bach (GER): 'We must do everything to protect the Games for the future.' (© IOC/Locatelli)

ideals or commercialisation, which is the leader? Are we going too fast, are the Games merely part of entertainment, are we becoming just brokers and businessmen? Sport cannot solve the problems in our lives, but the spirit of Olympic ideals does inspire.'

KEVAN GOSPER (AUSTRALIA), OLYMPIC TRACK SILVER MEDAL WINNER, EXECUTIVE BOARD VICE-PRESIDENT: 'Sport mirrors society, but what places it above some of the weaknesses elsewhere is a code of behaviour, of fair play, the experience of winning and losing. Sport's no different for anyone from any walk of life, there will be cycles when the bad seems to get the upper hand. At present in the Western world there is an attitude that the tougher elements of training are not worth the effort, and if parents also start to feel this way there could be a long-term decline, if sport is not seen as an alternative to delinquency, joblessness and drugs.'

JACQUES ROGGE (BELGIUM), OLYMPIC YACHTSMAN: 'Should we not make the Games less expensive, and achieve a larger net surplus? The strains within the Olympic Movement are mainly financial. We need to review the [lower] capacity venues, the programme, the number of events, the overhead costs, especially that of technology. We should trim on all fronts. The added value of the Games of *all* sports together is irreplaceable. Under the next President there will have to be more collective management, more delegation to the Executive Board. He will have to have a *team*, the IOC will have to get leaner on core activities. And on drugs, the belief of competitors at the Olympic Games is dependent on the assurance that it will be fair.'

CHAPTER LXVII

Nagano (XVIII) 1998

Masahiko Harada of Japan, Olympic ski jumping team champion

'It was four years after the failure of my jump in Lillehammer in 1994. The day of the team event at the Nagano Olympics was the occasion when I could finally make amends for my earlier flop. A blizzard had been blowing but now this had stopped and I was standing on the platform awaiting my second jump. On my first I had failed to build up the necessary speed. This was my last chance to succeed. I kept urging myself, thinking: "This is at home, here in Japan. I simply cannot afford to fail this time. It must be a big jump, even if it means ending up with a compound fracture." Motivated by the cheering of a huge crowd, urging me on, I succeeded in making a jump of 137m. We had captured the gold medal and my emotion was one of untold happiness. I could not express my feelings in words and I burst into tears.

Looking back on the four long and difficult years between Lillehammer and Nagano, I realise now that in 1994 I simply did not understand myself sufficiently. I lacked confidence in my ability and at that time I was making one jump after another without continuity, without having acquired the technique necessary for sustained success. It would be wrong to talk in terms of failing. In truth, I believe now that I just did not possess the ability at that time to win the gold medal. I still think of Noriaki Kasai and Jinya Nishikata, my colleagues in Lillehammer who were now not on the team in 1998. When I think of their feelings, it's very tough on me. I eventually did get a gold medal, but the experience of four years ago is still in my mind, the disappointment I caused then for them.

The year after Lillehammer, I was in too much of a hurry to restore my reputation. I lost my way and my form reached an all-time low. What rescued me from this slump was the encouragement of my wife, my friends and the staff of the national committee. Chance meetings with a number of other people who encouraged me helped me to grow in stature and my jumping ability returned. I captured the World Championship in 1997 and then won four events in the World Cup before the Games in Nagano. The complete recovery at this time led to my success in the Games. It also taught me that, providing a strong will to win eventually does still exist, it is possible to get over a major setback, make amends for previous failure. The Olympics have also taught me that the pain that accompanies a setback is not necessarily in vain, if viewed in the context of life's long journey. There can be no success without failure. Yet I still considered I had a lot to do to perfect my technique and achieve big jumps on a more regular basis. I could not call it a day with victory at Nagano.'*

(Photograph © Getty Images/Bello)

For the first day of ski jumping there was a crowd of more than 33,000 at the Hakuba Stadium. The unquestioned favourite for the normal hill was Masahiko Harada, winner of four World Cup events already that season. There was even a hope that Japan, with three prominent jumpers, might repeat its clean sweep of medals at Sapporo in 1972. The triumph, sadly for the host nation, was not to materialise. For the second successive Games, Harada, seemingly, could not handle the pressure. The consolation was a silver medal by Kazuyoshi Funaki. The winner was from that home of ski jumping – Finland.

Jani Soininen came from the same town as Matti Nykänen, former quadruple gold medal winner. He had been joint favourite with Harada and now proved the more consistent. Harada led on the first jump, with Soininen second, but on the second round, run in reverse order, Funaki, having been in fourth place behind Andreas Wiidhölz of Austria, became the

fifth in the competition to clear 90m and moved into the lead, with only Soininen and Harada remaining. Then came a delay because of gusting winds, and when the all-clear was given, a solid 89m carried Soininen ahead of Funaki. With a miserable 84.5, Harada slumped to fifth. He denied being affected by the expectation of his country, throwing up a smokescreen that he was 'very happy just to be jumping in an Olympics staged in Japan'. Whatever way he viewed the outcome, it was an echo of Lillehammer and an anticlimax for millions of his countrymen glued to their television sets. The large hill lay ahead.

An even bigger crowd was present and the climax of the event left them in near silence – not because Harada had failed but because he had jumped so far on his second leap that he had landed beyond the capacity of the electronic measuring system, requiring his jump to be measured manually while the remaining competitors continued. With the jumping completed, his score had still not appeared on the board. In the first round, Funaki, the favourite following his acclaimed recent victories in Germany and Austria, had placed only fourth behind Wiidhölz, Takanobu Okabe of Japan and Soininen. Harada was lying sixth on 120m. Harada's second jump exceeded imagination, as though divinity had touched him. As he landed there were shouts of relief and joy from the unrestrained admirers for whom the 29 year old was a national hero on account of his unassuming nature, regardless of his disaster in the team event four years earlier. But how far had he jumped? While everybody waited, Funaki also had a big jump, 132.5m, with such style that he received a mark of a perfect 20 from all five judges to go into the lead. At last Harada's figures appeared: a massive 136m. Had he landed with his feet extended one in front of the other, as required, rather than together, the gold medal would have been his. Instead he took bronze behind Soininen, yet such was his own relief that he could say: 'I will hold on to this memory as long as I live.' Now for the crucial team event.

It was the kind of day to make you resent taking the dog out: wind down the collar, driving snow clogging your eyelashes, the chill pinching your spine. Not a day on which you would wish to be inching your way onto a narrow seat at the top of a precipice, wearing skis and looking down at a 40,000 crowd waiting to judge whether you are a man. Okabe, Hiroya Saito, Harada and Funaki met, and passed, the test of their morale, of their manhood, among the nation of samurai warriors. In doing so, they ignited celebrations equivalent to those of a country winning the World Cup in football. In a manner touching to foreign observers, the Japanese shed their emotional conservatism and their moment of national fulfilment was the climax of the Games. If his individual bronze medal had absolved Harada from some of his sense of guilt, now to win the title most prized by his countrymen would be the ultimate sanctification.

Not that it was easy, for after the first round the Japanese quartet were lying in fourth place. Indeed, Harada's career had been a story of mixed joy and despair. Becoming the first Japanese to win a World Championship in 1993, he had then been haunted by the shadow of 1994; then was dropped from the World Championship team the following year but, with an automatic qualification as defending champion, finished 53rd. This slump had been followed by revival in 1997, with gold on the large hill and silver for both normal hill and team event. National anxiety now intensified when a snowstorm caused the start to be delayed by half an hour. Okabe and Saito established a substantial early lead for Japan, but then came disaster again for Harada. With the fog so thick that he was now invisible from the landing area, he achieved the fifth lowest score of any of the 48 jumpers, so that, although Funaki jumped well, Japan dropped to fourth place behind Germany, Austria and Norway. Japanese officials lodged a protest, wishing the round to be annulled because conditions were so bad, but they were overruled. Redemption, however, was at hand. On the first jump of the second round, Okabe recorded a massive 137m, an Olympic record which lifted Japan back into second place. Saito followed with 124m to sustain the lead. Now came Harada. Matching the moment, a blur in the blizzard, he soared from the ramp to reach another heart-stopping 137m. 'I did it, I did it,' he sobbed, as the microphones relentlessly closed in, the thunder of the crowd drowning the questions.

The outcome rested with Funaki. 'Before the jump, I truly sympathised with Harada,' the 22 year old said later. 'I was overwhelmed, overburdened.' Nonetheless undeterred, his 125m was sufficient. The stadium erupted in a frenzy of horns

Winner Kazuyoshi Funaki and Masahiko Harada, third, raise their arms at the moment of redemption, in front of a vast home crowd for ski jumping on the large hill. (© Getty Images/Bello)

and waving flags. The victory gave Japan their fourth gold medal in Nagano – more than in all previous Winter Games combined – and made Funaki the most successful male competitor thus far, with two gold and a silver. Germany took the silver, Austria the bronze.

Expectation in Austria for Hermann Maier was as intense as that in Japan for Harada. After being discarded as a teenage racer and becoming a bricklayer, Maier had made an astonishing return in his mid-20s, winning the European and World Cup and arriving in Nagano as leading contender in three of the five Alpine events, including the downhill, although in this his compatriot Andreas Schifferer was ranked ahead of him. There had been extended controversy over the site and length of the run between the organising committee and the FIS, on account of the top of the course being in a protected national park. This was resolved only two months beforehand; and then the race was postponed three times over five days because of bad weather, with a further 50-minute delay on the day because of wind.

The crucial phase of an icy run would prove to be Gate 7. Jean Luc Cretier of France, who had never won a World Cup race and now at 31 was at the end of his career, was taking part in his fourth Games. Third man out of the gate, he treated the course with caution and his time of 1:50.11, though not exceptional, set a high standard in the conditions. Next out was Maier, for whom caution was a foreign language. At Gate 7, a tight left turn with the ground simultaneously falling away to the right, and requiring the racer to have firm edge control, Maier hit it flat out. As he belatedly searched for a double inside edge, it was to discover that there was no ground there. He was airborne, sideways, at over 100 kph, his skis rotating skywards. Hurtling upside down towards the double safety netting, he landed on his head, bounced twice, his momentum carrying him through both nettings, and came to rest in soft snow, miraculously uninjured. He walked back up the gradient with bruising and a

Hermann Maier of Austria captured mid-air prior to a horrific fall in the downhill, from which he was miraculously uninjured, going on to win the super-G. (© Getty Images/Powell) (© Getty Images/Botterill)

headache and had to withdraw from the combined downhill later in the day. The same gate eliminated others. Lasse Kjus of Norway and Hannes Trinkl of Austria moved into second and third place behind Cretier. Wretchedly out of luck was Brian Stemmle, a member of the Canadian team for twelve years and survivor of a horrifying crash at Kitzbühl nine years earlier. Approaching the bottom of the run, he was nearly four-tenths inside Cretier's time but caught a rut and veered off course into that private anguish which would never leave him.

Maier, however, was to rise and shake his fists at the gods. In the super-G, seemingly mentally unimpaired, he won by more than half a second from Didier Cuche (SUI) and Hans Knauss (AUT), the two having identical times and sharing the silver. 'It's unbelievable that he came back from a crash like that,' Knauss said. When Maier went to inspect the super-G course, the same impression of driven will-power was left with the American Tommy Moe. 'He looks crazy-eyed, like a barbarian,' Moe said. Though Maier blamed the Austrian coach for not advising him that Gate 7 of the downhill had been changed from the training runs, he admitted to a degree of caution in the super-G.

His redeeming gold, three days later, in the super-G was something of a bonus for the Austrian federation, which in the 1990s had invested more than three million dollars in the search for international success, from which Maier had largely been excluded. As he stood on the victory rostrum, it was a far cry from the days at his mountain home town of Flachau, south of Salzburg, where he used to ask to be a fore-runner, one of those pre-race test skiers who clear the course for the serious men. In the giant slalom he had been fastest on both runs and on the second 'I was charging like always, I had to ski on the limit, I did not expect to win . . . I'm not a great hero, I'm just happy.'

The slalom was to provide an anonymous exit for the legendary Alberto Tomba in his fourth Games. Two seconds adrift on the first run and sore from a fall in the giant slalom, he quietly withdrew and watched the conclusion from the sanctuary of his hotel room. Thomas Sykora of Austria, the World Cup champion, led on the first run, faltered on the second and finished in third place behind Hans Petter Buraas and Ole Christian Furuseth, both of Norway.

Victory tears are a common enough Olympic occurrence, yet seldom more justified than for Hiroyasu Shimizu, whose father and coach, Hitoshi, had died from stomach cancer seven years earlier. At 1.62m (5 ft 3½ in.), Shimizu was the shortest of all competitors in men's speed skating and when he won the 500m, for Japan's first gold medal of the Games, he was dwarfed on the medal podium by Jeremy Wotherspoon and Kevin Overland, the Canadians who took respective silver and bronze. Here was a champion – and world record holder – admired not just by an ecstatic audience but by his peers. 'He has the best technique,' Overland said. 'He gets everything out of each stride, that's why he wins gold medals and sets records' – on this occasion an Olympic record in both the first and second races, on the first occasion when the event was staged over two legs.

'My father in heaven is the first person I would like to tell that I've achieved my dream,' Shimizu said in his shy, almost diffident manner. His mother Sueko was there to watch him, a diminutive woman unable to see the finish when the crowd rose in front of her. Only her diligence had made possible Shimizu's triumph. When her husband died, she had worked on road construction sites as a tarmac paver to support her four children. In return for her dedication, Shimizu intended to use his $15,000 bonus from the Japan NOC as a down-payment on a house for her. He said that he thought he could improve on his world record 'when I get better at the clap-skates'. The new hinged skates were in use at Nagano for the first time, the toe-end hinge allowing the skate a fraction longer on the ice on each stride to give additional thrust.

Indeed, in the opening event, the men's 5,000m, all three medal winners had broken the world record, the winning time of 6:22.20 by Gianni Romme of Holland being more than 12 seconds faster than that set by Johann Olav Koss four years earlier. Romme had watched first Bart Veldkamp break the record – Veldkamp having switched nationality from Holland to Belgium to ensure qualification – and then Rintje Ritsma, his compatriot, before going out and skating more than six seconds faster. Romme repeated his victory with another world record in the 10,000m, with his compatriots, Bob de Jong and Ritsma, making it a clean sweep. Veldkamp, champion at Albertville six years earlier, beat the pre-Olympic world record of Koss, yet failed to gain a medal. Dutch domination was further bolstered by Ids Postma and Jan Bos taking first and second in the 1,000m, Postma improving Dan Jansen's world record in Lillehammer.

There can be universal satisfaction, in the name of a level playing field, when favourites fail. The United States ice hockey squad, boasting six NHL players with 50 goals each to their credit plus 17 other supposed NHL stars, had been greeted as

His mother worked as a road-paver to help diminutive Hiroyasu Shimizu (JPN) fulfil his potential as Olympic speed skating champion at 500m, defeating Canadians Jeremy Wotherspoon (silver, left) and Kevin Overland. (© Getty Images/Doug Pensinger) (© Getty Images/Brunskill)

another Dream Team; the more so following a World Cup final victory over Canada in 1996. Yet they opened with a 4–2 loss to Sweden, defending champions, and had to pack their bags after a 4–1 quarter-final defeat by the Czech Republic: the fifth consecutive Games in which the US had failed to win a medal. Hero for the Czechs was goal-minder Dominic Hasek. The Americans outshot the Czechs 39–20, only to be defied by Hasek's 38 saves. In the final, the Czechs claimed their third major scalp, defeating Russia 1–0 . . . with Hasek yet again outstanding, deflecting 20 Russian shots.

Michelle Kwan (USA) first came to the notice of a wider public when winning the Goodwill Games at St Petersburg in 1994 as a precocious teenager. In Nagano she was part of a fascinating group of six in the final pool for the free programme: two Americans and a Chinese, two Russians and a French woman, all of them artists. From among them would emerge the youngest individual champion, Tara Lipinski, aged 15 years and 255 days, younger by 60 days than Sonja Henie in 1928. Win or lose, Lipinski intended to enjoy her Games: she arrived early, to be sure of marching in the opening ceremony.

Kwan, her compatriot and closest rival, and a relative adult at 17, had led Lipinski on the short programme. First onto the rink for the free programme, Kwan flowed like a raindrop on glass to the background of Willam Alwyn's 'Orchestration for Harp and Strings'. The judges gave her a unanimous 5.9 for presentation, but her technical merit marks left a loophole for Lipinski. Irina Slutskaya from Moscow, with polished-apple smile, was the first to have performed a triple-salchow-triple-loop, but the warmth of her balalaika folk tunes could not improve her fifth position. Chen Lu of China, competing in her third Games, presented petal-like elegance and climbed, temporarily, from fourth to second. Surya Bonaly, out of the reckoning, entertained the crowd but did nothing for her marking with acrobatic but illegal back somersaults. Next came Lipinski, a powder-blue crystal. She wowed the judges with triples a few metres from their desks and bubbled across the ice like champagne escaping from the bottle.

The men's figures event, as you would expect, was less a matter of artistry than technique, and the lingering debate was whether a stomach injury to Elvis Stojko of Canada, three times world champion, undermined his attempt to emulate Ilya Kulik, a 20-year-old Russian. Stojko was a marvellously aggressive

Tara Lipinski (USA), younger than Sonja Henie 70 years earlier, steals a march on fancied compatriot Michelle Kwan in the figures. (© Getty Images/Botterill)

skater but his injury during the Canadian championships a month earlier inhibited him to a degree that made it difficult to challenge the flawless Kulik. When Stojko landed a triple towards the end of his programme, he was clearly in pain and appeared wearing trainers for the medal ceremony. He had missed many days of training: his silver was a medal for courage. Kulik's had been an exhilarating display. Having led on the short programme, he skated to Gershwin's 'Rhapsody in Blue' with a display of confidence rare for one his age.

The ambivalent morality of some sports was furtively present in the Nordic men's 30km cross-country. Mika Myllylä won Finland's first cross-country medal for 34 years by the substantial margin of one and a half minutes over Erling Jeune of Norway. Fancied entries such as Bjørn Daehlie and the defending champion Thomas Alsgaard, and Vladimir Smirnov of Kazakhstan, were all outside the top ten, Alsgaard failing to finish. Three years later, Myllylä would test positive following Finland's relay victory in the World Championships staged at Lahti in Finland, one of six who were caught. He duly expressed

Elegance of the Musketeers from Philippe Candeloro (FRA) attracted the public more than the judges in men's figures, leaving him with bronze. (© Getty Images/Brunskill)

public penitence but what difference does an apology make?

Women's Alpine events were dogged by the same delays as the men's. Katja Seizinger had won most of the season's downhills and now became, after a two-day delay, the first female skier successfully to defend her Olympic title. Soft snow and freezing ice were known to be her favourite menu for breakfast, but her margin over Pernilla Wiberg of Sweden was only 0.29 on a hard and rutted course. Wiberg had twice suffered injuries during the current season, so silver was more than she might have expected. Two hours later she again followed Seizinger home on the same course to take the downhill leading positions in the combined event; but the following day, in the event's second stage, Wiberg, a slalom specialist, missed a gate close to the finishing line, silver and bronze being won respectively by Germans Martina Ertl and Hilde Gerg. Seizinger thus became the second woman, following Vreni Schneider from Switzerland, to win three Olympic Alpine gold medals.

In women's speed skating it seemed that Tomomi Okazaki of Japan might emulate Shimizu when lying third on the first run of the 500m. She temporarily climbed a place when repeating her time, 38.55, on the second run – but only for as long as it took Catriona LeMay-Doan to improve her Olympic record of 38.39 on the first run with 38.21 on the second. LeMay-Doan had been the outstanding favourite after a series of world record runs at the end of 1997. Susan Auch of Canada was expected to be her main rival – and indeed was, retaining the silver medal that she won in Lillehammer ahead of Okazaki. Marianne Timmer of Holland knocked three seconds off her previous best to astonish herself as much or more than the crowd by winning

the 1,500m in 1:57.58, three-tenths inside the time of LeMay-Doan, who strangely finished 13th, two days after her earlier gold.

Nowhere have women been more impressive in their emulation of men than in the biathlon, that cruel combination of insane cross-country muscularity and attempted immobile calm with the rifle. Ekaterina Dafovska gained Bulgaria's first-ever gold medal in a Winter Games when she took the women's 15km title, the country's only previous medal being Ivan Lebanov's bronze for 30km classical in 1980. Dafovska at 22 was something of a novice, ranked only 51st in the World Cup. On the final circuit, she missed only one of 20 shooting targets in spite of a steady snowfall.

With victories in the men's 30km biathlon relay together with the four-man bobsleigh, the German team moved into an unassailable Games lead of 12 gold medals, with only one day remaining. Nor could their overall total of 29 medals be overtaken. Here was a satisfying reward for the German NOC's sports-aid programme, with a fund of $18 million aimed at a broad base of 3,500 competitors, not merely at the elite.

It was no surprise that gold and silver medals in the inaugural women's Olympic ice hockey tournament respectively went to the United States and Canada, countries boasting four-fifths of the world's registered players. Meeting in the final round-robin game, Canada led 4–1 only for the Americans to unleash fresh impetus and accelerate to a 7–4 victory.

The inaugural event of snowboarding was won by a Canadian, Ross Rebagliati from Whistler, his giant slalom victory heavy with emotion as he dedicated it to Geoff Leidal, a

Katja Seizinger (GER) became the first woman to successfully defend her downhill title. (© Getty Images/Brunskill)

colleague who had died the previous month in an avalanche. Rebagliati's slightly anarchic image was substantiated when he now tested positive for marijuana and disqualification by the IOC's Executive Board followed. After an appeal by the Canadian NOC, this decision was overturned by the Court for Arbitration in Sport (CAS), on the grounds that there was no legality for the suspension, there being no agreement concerning the use of this substance between the IOC and the FIS.

CHAPTER LXVIII

Laws and Ethics

Keba M'Baye of Senegal, judge, International Court of Justice, IOC Vice-President 1998–2002

'The idea of creating a court for sport was born soon after Juan Antonio Samaranch was elected President. At the Congress at Baden-Baden in 1981, Samaranch mentioned his intention to create "a kind of Hague Court for Sport", referring to the International Court of Justice, and he asked me to give some thought to this. Initially, I imagined it to be a short-lived idea. Realising he was serious, I set to work, and the Court of Arbitration for Sport (CAS) was founded in 1983. This was a veritable revolution, for we were then in the era of federal organisations which, jealously guarding their autonomy, were disinclined to allow a court, even a state one, to interfere with their jurisdiction. Within a few years, the CAS became accepted and respected internationally not only by sports organisations but also by state courts, which prefer to stand down in its favour within fields where its competence is accepted by the parties involved. The CAS was the first body to set rules, and particularly legal norms, to govern the running of the IOC, and in fact its first decisions consisted in reversing sanctions imposed by the IOC's Executive Board. This was indeed a revolution. The work of the CAS – which later became independently governed by the International Council of Arbitration for Sport (ICAS) – is both jurisprudential and educational.

In the administration of a legal person such as the IOC – and the same applies to natural persons – it is not enough merely to remain within the boundaries of law. While it is true that we live today in a Promethean world, where morality looks like an old tool stored away with the spinning wheels and oil lamps, the general view is increasingly that everyone is required to go beyond that which is merely legal: that, above the law, there are moral principles to be respected even in acts authorised by law.

In the IOC, full awareness of such a requirement abruptly arrived with the Salt Lake City scandal. With this American city's candidature to host the Olympic Games in 2002, it became apparent that there had been abuses, particularly concerning breaches of the rules of conduct that the IOC had previously set for itself and its members. Contrary to what some people repeat mechanically, and at times with a certain amount of bad faith, this hardly constituted corruption. Indeed, corruption has a legal meaning to which the acts that gave rise to the title of Salt Lake City scandal do not correspond. Corruption strictly requires proof of a promise duly fulfilled. Now there are unwritten rules like those which Antigone followed in Sophocles' tragedy, and which must now govern the conduct of both legal and natural persons. Thus it was that the IOC established its Ethics Commission, to complement the work of the ICAS.

Composed of eight personalities, five chosen from outside the Olympic Movement, this Commission closely monitors the conduct of every "Olympic party", be it the IOC itself, its members, the cities bidding to host the Olympic Games, the organising committees of those Games, the national Olympic committees concerned and even the candidature committees. The surveillance role of the Ethics Commission is broadening; its authority is growing stronger. Of course, the difficulties that this Commission faces are commensurate with the ambitions that the IOC has set itself, yet little by little these two new bodies in the world of international sport, ICAS and Ethics Commission, are making an impact in setting rules on the conduct of members of the Olympic Movement. There is no need of soothsaying powers to predict that the synergy of the work by these two institutions will inevitably result in the constituents of the Olympic Movement: an obligation to show scrupulous respect for both the law and for ethics, which basically means fair play.'*

(Photograph © IOC/Locatelli)

In 1991, half an hour after Nagano of Japan had narrowly defeated Salt Lake City, the favourites, for the right to host the Winter Games of 1998, the author was standing in Salt Lake's small hospitality suite at the conference hotel in Birmingham, Britain, when a Nagano representative came to make a gesture of commiseration. With a steely gaze, Alma Welch, wife of Tom Welch, president of Salt Lake's bid, replied: 'We just ran out of money.' In those six words partially lay the origins of the worst scandal in the IOC's history. While Welch and his assistant Dave Johnson had reached the point of meeting expenses from their personal credit cards through lack of funding, they were aware of allegations that Nagano had indulged in vote inducement. If that was the name of the game, Welch determined that Salt Lake would radically adjust their campaign programme when bidding for 2002. This included creating long-term, vote-influencing relationships with IOC members, with other influential individuals in the so-called Olympic family, and within USOC. It was a campaign that would amount to expenditure of millions of dollars, and in that it was little different from many other bid campaigns, albeit that Salt Lake would encounter devastating repercussions from the revelation of details.

For the next seven and a half years the waters over which Juan Antonio Samaranch ruled remained relatively calm, even if there was mounting external criticism of the lavish 'entertainment' of bidding cities, expected as of right by a minority of IOC members in the election campaigns of 1993, 1995 and 1997, which saw the respective selection of Sydney, Salt Lake and Athens. The Executive Board made continuing and ineffectual attempts to limit the extravagance, but these 'rules' were wantonly ignored by some on both sides. The gravy train was gathering steam rather than slowing.

In 1993, when Samaranch opened the new Olympic Museum in the presence of the King and Queen of Spain and the president of the Swiss federation, and when he presided over the Centenary Congress of 1994 in Paris and the Centenary Games in Atlanta, he must truly have felt he rivalled Pierre de Coubertin as architect of one of the world's foremost international organisations. Indeed, did not the IOC itself now contain no fewer than 29 former Olympic competitors, a reflection of the democracy of Samaranch's reign? For Samaranch himself subsequently to be accused during the Salt Lake City scandal of receiving the gift of an expensive shotgun, even though all such formal gifts were sent straight to the IOC's storeroom, was something of a red herring. Nor was there any doubt that the majority of IOC members, though enjoying first-class travel in the exercise of their responsibilities, were not bribable. If there were some rotten apples in the barrel, that was normal in any organisation, an unseen liability that could be handled, Samaranch erroneously supposed. It would have been advisable, with hindsight, to have initiated an independent inquiry by at least 1990.

On 24 November 1998, the first rumblings were felt of what was rapidly to become a mega sporting earthquake. A Utah television station, KTVX, reported that the Salt Lake organising committee had been paying the university fees and accommodation for Sonia Essomba, daughter of the late Cameroon member of the IOC. This initially minor revelation was on a par with the Watergate break-in. The ramifications were to prove similarly far-reaching. It swiftly became apparent that this was only one detail in Salt Lake's systematic programme of vote enticement. Within a few weeks the scandal was the lead story on television and in newspapers around the globe, as the extent of scholarships for relatives of IOC members, allegedly worth some half a million dollars, were

revealed alongside other inducements. Samaranch instantly requested that the IOC's juridical commission investigate and at an Executive Board meeting in Lausanne on 11 December, Richard Pound was delegated to chair an ad hoc commission to investigate the variety of allegations of malpractice by IOC members, and of other bid cities besides Salt Lake.

If the IOC was belatedly getting to grips, through *force majeure*, with internal immorality, any hope of containing the scandal was blown apart during the Executive Board's lunch-break the same day. Marc Hodler, IOC member for 35 years, octogenarian Swiss lawyer and long-time president of international skiing, unilaterally decided to take the lid off the IOC's can of worms, giving an unscheduled press conference to the attendant bevy of news agencies and international correspondents. Hodler claimed that 5 to 7 per cent of the members were involved in voting malpractice and alleged that bid cities involved included Atlanta, Sydney and Nagano. Significantly, however, when requested by Pound's new commission to provide details, all Hodler could reply was that

An off-the-cuff, free-speaking interview by Marc Hodler, octogenarian Swiss lawyer and IOC member, and former president of international skiing, accelerated a mounting IOC scandal. (© IOC/Locatelli)

everything was hearsay. For a lawyer to make such unquantified, unspecific allegations was unwise, but it was meat and drink to the media. By the turn of the year, further revelations were tumbling onto news desks by the day. Alfredo Lamont, an official of USOC, resigned over allegations that he had provided information to Salt Lake on Latin American IOC members. It had already been reported that Jean-Claude Ganga of the Congo had made a $60,000 profit on a land deal arranged by Salt Lake, and on 9 January, Frank Joklik, CEO of the Salt Lake Organising Committee (SLOC), and his senior vice-president, Dave Johnson, both resigned.

On 19 January, Pirjo Häggman of Finland, one of the first two women elected to the IOC in 1981, became the first to resign because she felt her position was no longer tenable (of which more later). This was followed by the resignation of Bashir Mohamed Attarabulsi of Libya, on account of his son having attended Brigham Young University in Salt Lake City at a cost to SLOC of thousands of dollars. Simultaneously, a host of investigative committees were being established. SLOC formed its own Board of Ethics inquiry and USOC set up a panel to examine the IOC's administration – some impertinence! – under the title Special Bid Oversight Commission, headed by George Mitchell, former US Senator from Maine. The FBI began an inquiry into SLOC, regarding possible violation of federal laws under the Foreign Corrupt Practices Act. Amid all this action, Samaranch called for an Extraordinary Session in Lausanne on 17–18 March, simultaneously stating that he did not intend to resign in spite of worldwide media calls for him to do so. Prior to this Session, the Mitchell Commission, as the aggressive USOC inquiry became known, published a fifty-page document of findings including seven pages of recommendations.

In Australia, the Sheridan Report – under the aegis of Tom Sheridan, former Australian Auditor General – was reviewing the Sydney bid and drawing critical conclusions about the bid committee's employment of two professional groupies, whose global responsibility was to lobby on Sydney's behalf. Also under scrutiny was the questionable action by John Coates, president of the Australian NOC, who had made substantial gifts 'for coaching developments' to the IOC members of Kenya and Uganda – Charles Mukora and Major-General Francis Nyangweso respectively – 48 hours before Sydney's two-vote victory over Beijing in 1993.

On 23 January, the Executive Board heard the early findings of the Pound Ad Hoc Commission, as a result of which six IOC members were suspended, pending a vote on this at the Extraordinary Session. The six were Augustin Arroyo (Equador), Fantini Santander (Chile), Zein El Abdin Abdel Gadir (Sudan), Jean-Claude Ganga (Congo), Lamine Keita (Mali) and Seuili Paul Wallwork (Western Samoa). Two further members, Charles Mukora and David Sibandze (Swaziland) had resigned and

investigation continued into the status of three others: Louis Guirandou-N'Daiye (Ivory Coast), Un Yong Kim (South Korea) and Vitaly Smirnov (Russia). Samaranch widened the investigation by sending letters of inquiry to all bidding cities back to 1990, but the horses had long since bolted.

The following month, SLOC's Board of Ethics issued its report, which gave substantiation to the Executive Board's suspensions and, like the Mitchell Commission, made a range of recommendations for revising the activities of the IOC and its bidding process, and on financial transparency. All the while the media was thriving on rumour, to the extent that the *International Herald Tribune*, under its headline 'The Journalism that Doesn't Bother to Check its Facts', was moved to pronounce: 'America is moving toward a journalism of assertion rather than verification . . . We have seen the new, impatient culture of journalism at work. It is not a culture dedicated to establishing whether a story is true. It disregards verification and focuses on some secondary controversy to talk about the story.' The same was true in most countries, not least in Britain, where much of the spicy dish was a mixture of hearsay and speculation. It was argued in the *Daily Telegraph* that the Swiss government should 'close down' the IOC. And replace it with what? The saner voices of Pound and Jacques Rogge of Belgium, a member of Pound's inquiry panel, counted for little among the gossipmongers. Pound, in order, it is believed, that there should be no back-tracking by the Executive Board, deliberately leaked the early inquiry findings to the *Wall Street Journal*.

It was widely and inaccurately reported in much of the press that the impending expulsions would be the first in the IOC's history, when in fact there had been 11 previous instances of a

Expulsion of IOC members, 1999 (clockwise): Augustin Arroyo (Equador) (© IOC/Imsand); Zein El Abdin Abdel Gadir (Sudan) (© IOC); Jean-Claude Ganga (Congo) (© IOC/Locatelli); Lamine Keita (Mali) (© IOC/Imsand); Fantini Santander (Chile) (© IOC/Locatelli); Seuili Paul Wallwork (Western Samoa) (© IOC/Imsand); Rene Essomba (Cameroon) (guilty but deceased). (© IOC/Imsand)

member's forced departure, though only that of Robert Helmick in 1991 had been as a result of financial misdemeanour. Five of them were technical, for breach of regulations in failing to attend Sessions.

Investigative journalism half a century ago not being what it is today, there had been little comment regarding the vested interest of three IOC Presidents in promoting the Berlin Games. Pierre de Coubertin gave his blessing, the Hitler government having nominated him for the Nobel Peace Prize, which in the event went to Karl von Ossietzky, the German anti-fascist who died in Dachau concentration camp. Henri de Baillet-Latour, then in office, would have profited from the merger of the Banque de la Société Générale de Belgique, of which his family was founder and major shareholder, with Deutsche Bank. Avery Brundage, who would become President in 1952, had a written agreement to build a new German Embassy in Washington, a project scuppered by the Second World War.

The full list of those implicated in the Salt Lake scandal is as follows:

> *Expelled*: Arroyo, aged 75 (Ecuador, elected 1968); Santander, 72 (Chile, 1992); Gadir, 58 (Sudan, 1990) (previously member 1983–7, expelled for absence while a political prisoner in Sudan); Ganga, 64 (Congo, 1986), president of African NOCs (ANOCA); Keita, 65 (Mali, 1977); Wallwork, 57 (W. Samoa, 1987). A seventh proven offender, Rene Essomba (Cameroon, 1978) predeceased the inquiry.
> *Resigned*: Attarabulsi, 61 (Libya, 1977); Häggman, 47 (Finland, 1981), Olympic 400m runner 1972/76/80; Mukora, 64 (Kenya, 1990); Sibandze, 76 (Swaziland, 1984).
> *Severe Warning*: Smirnov, 63 (Russia, 1971) president of Moscow 1980 organising committee; Kim, 67 (South Korea, 1986) president of GAISF.
> *Warning*: Coles, 68 (Australia, 1982); Geesink, 64 (Holland, 1987), Olympic judo champion 1964; Guirandou-N'Daiye, 75 (Ivory Coast, 1969), former head of IOC protocol.

Several of the 16 involved were relatively innocent. Pirjo Häggman resigned 'even though I have not broken my Olympic Oath nor violated IOC rules, but because I've lost my ability to function as a constructive IOC member'. The accusation was that her former husband had taken a modest job, for which he was qualified and which had been advertised, as forestry management adviser to the Ontario Ministry of National Resources at the time of Toronto's bid in 1990 for the Centenary Games and Paul Henderson, leader of the Toronto bid (and later IOC member) provided temporary accommodation while the Häggmans were looking for a house. As Henderson said: 'It was a gesture taken for granted by friends.' Anton Geesink was warned for accepting $5,000 from the Salt Lake Committee for his 'Friends of Anton Geesink' foundation, a professional consultancy which had earned previous criticism in Holland.

The case against Dr Un Yong Kim, mastermind of the Seoul Games and a senior figure involved in the investigation, was oblique. David Simmons, an American businessman, pleaded guilty to a tax charge, stating that he had employed John Kim, son of Un Yong, allegedly to help him obtain permanent, green card, resident work-status. John Kim's salary was said to have been paid by SLOC. In a defamation lawsuit, a Seoul civil court found against Simmons, who refused to appear, and fined him $18,000. The case took a fresh twist in June 2003 when John Kim was arrested in Bulgaria and held on a US warrant requesting

extradition in connection with the green card affair: an unusual three-nation triangle. Ultimately the charge was withdrawn.

The worst excesses were those surrounding Ganga, evidence suggesting that over several years he profited from SLOC in various ways, including medical treatment for himself and his mother-in-law, to the extent of over $300,000. Ganga had exploited his front-line position as one of the prime negotiators of the anti-apartheid movement.

It was unfortunate for the IOC that its intended creation of a new World Anti-Doping Agency (WADA), planned in the summer of 1998 following exposure of widespread drug abuse in the Tour de France and scheduled to stage a launching conference in February the following year, should have been clouded by the simultaneous crisis. Government representatives invited to attend the February conference, instead of offering support for a project of serious significance even to those not involved in sport, preferred to try to tell the IOC how to reorganise its administration. The intention with WADA was to create an overseeing independent body similar to ICAS with CAS. Foremost amongst the critics was Barry McCaffrey, director of the White House Drug Agency appointed by US President Bill Clinton. Coming from America, where the battle against drug abuse was transparently failing, McCaffrey's criticisms were ill-received and caused Richard Pound, chief architect of WADA, to write to him regarding his allegation that WADA, as proposed, was neither independent or accountable. 'With the greatest respect, your view is plainly wrong,' wrote Pound, in trenchant, characteristic terms.

In a circular to IOC members, Samaranch had outlined six key points in the programme of WADA, which initially was to be funded by $25 million from the IOC:

1. Tests outside competition in agreement with IFs
2. Harmonisation of standards and technical levels of testing laboratories
3. Harmonisation of disciplinary measures
4. Promotion, coordination and financing of research
5. Educational programmes
6. Intensification of promotion of ethical principles

As Pound wrote to McCaffrey:

> An international concensus would be that much easier to achieve if the leading sports nations had strong domestic policies. The US is clearly one such nation. It could contribute a great deal in this regard were its own policies clear, unequivocal and fully implemented in its own territory . . . There is an enormous disconnection between your views expressed in relation to the Olympic Movement and those that prevail in professional sport in your country.

Subsequently, McCaffrey executed a total about-turn, pronouncing Pound to be the right man to coordinate the project, 'a huge pay-off for the Olympic Movement'.

At the time of WADA's launch in Lausanne, few gossip-hungry journalists, eager to see Samaranch placed in the tumbrel, had any time to listen to Jacques Rogge or Denis Oswald, president of international rowing, explaining in detail the need in positive tests for variable penalties between sports, never mind that Oswald's own sport, rowing, recommends a life ban; between competitors of different ages; and between those who were victims of an NOC entourage of medics and those who were wilfully and individually responsible for their own use of drugs. Ambitious hopes for WADA's efficiency came against a background of a Berlin regional court bringing charges against Manfred Ewald and Dr Manfred Höpner, respective former heads of GDR sport and GDR sport medicine, for involvement in systematic doping within the GDR. They were accused of being accessories to bodily injury on 142 counts.

To return to the Salt Lake City scandal, had Hodler not launched into his unilateral press conference the previous December, would the Executive Board have had the resolution to put into effect the same extreme penalty of expulsions, and the consequent ethical restructuring of the organisation? François Carrard, then Director-General, is open-minded. 'I think probably so, but it's not possible to be categoric.' Either way, Richard Pound was emphatic when addressing the Extraordinary Session in March as chairman of the Ad Hoc Commission:

> We have received explanations from all individuals involved, met those who requested interviews and reviewed all records and documents. Today, we presented our findings to the Executive Board and received their unanimous support for our recommendations. I do want to reiterate, in the strongest terms, that the decisions taken today represent a beginning, not an end, to this process. I can assure you that the IOC will use this pivotal episode as an opportunity for renewal and reform on an ongoing basis . . . None of the situations the Commission has examined, regarding the individuals proposed for expulsion, was the result of accidental or inadvertent conduct. In each case it was conscious and knowing, and the actions were a serious and irreparable breach of the IOC oath of membership and caused damage to the IOC . . . Let me also say that this is not an issue of geography, culture or race. It is a matter of individual conduct in an organisation that places the highest importance on its members' personal integrity.

The six members previously mentioned were duly expelled by a majority vote.

The Pound report responded to some of the critics' suggestions – as, say, in editorials of *The Times* of London and the *New York Times* – that the IOC had fostered a culture of corruption. First, the report stated, the IOC had set guidelines concerning gifts from bid cities in 1988, immediately following the first of the incentive-stained elections in 1986; second, the first inquiry into evidence of impropriety had been initiated by the IOC prior to any other investigation; and third, the IOC was prepared to take decisive action to prevent any repetition. The recommendations of the Pound report included radical changes to the host city selection process, limitation on travel to bid cities by IOC members and the creation of a permanent Ethics Commission.

This latter was immediately formed on 18 March, consisting of eight members, five of whom were independent of the IOC: Howard Baker, former White House chief of staff and former leader of the Senate; Javier Perez de Cuellar, former UN Secretary-General; Robert Badinter, former president of the French Constitution Court; Kurt Fürgler, former president of the Swiss Confederation; Charmaine Crooks of Canada, five-time Olympian. These five, together with three IOC members, Judge Keba M'Baye, as chairman, Kevan Gosper (Australia) and Chiharu Igaya (Japan), were swiftly to produce a code of ethics under seven headings: Dignity, Integrity, Resources, Candidatures, Relation with States, Confidentiality and Implementation. Another of the

Inaugural meeting of the new IOC Ethics Commission, May 1999: Standing (l to r) Howard Baker (USA), Javier Perez de Cuellar (PER), Kurt Furgler (SUI), Robert Badinter (FRA). Seated (l to r) Kevan Gosper (IOC/AUS), Charmaine Crooks (IOC/CAN), Keba M'Baye (IOC/SEN), Chiharu Igaya (IOC/JPN). (© IOC/Locatelli).

first responsibilities of this commission was to continue the investigation of the various members who were to receive a warning, though the impetus of this perceptibly slowed.

In spite of the swiftness of the investigation and findings of the Pound commission and the creation of the Ethics Commission, the media continued to call for Samaranch's head. Weathering the charge that he must take the blame for the corruption among the predominantly uninfluential minority of members of his organisation, Samaranch called for a vote of confidence at the Extraordinary Session.

Media criticism now centred on the fact that many of the members who would vote owed their position on the IOC in the first place to his influence. Against this tirade of protest, however, was the rationale that he was the only individual with the personality to push through radical reforms in the shortest possible time. Any change of leadership at this moment could have been disastrous, with a new incumbent unsure of his mandate or support. Additionally, the vultures of the sport/leisure industry were waiting in the wings for any sign of weakness that they might exploit, with the potential to entice willing IFs to create a new multi-sports commercial venture. Such an enterprise was quite possible.

There were, however, stabilising forces at work. Henri Serandour, French NOC president, asserted: 'I am not one of those who want the captain to leave the ship in the midst of the wildest storm. His job is to steer it back into calmer waters.' Samaranch wisely insisted on a secret ballot and the outcome was a predictable landslide, the President gaining 86 of the 90 votes.

In addition to the expulsions and the formation of the Ethics Commission, a radical step at the Extraordinary 108th Session was the creation of the 'IOC 2000 Commission', with a mandate to prepare and propose, at a further Extraordinary Session in December, those recommendations considered appropriate for a realigned IOC structure, its rules and procedures. The Commission was to be composed of 80 members, 36 of them from outside the IOC, including Henry Kissinger, Giovanni Agnelli, Peter Ueberroth, Boutros Boutros-Ghali, and Olympic historian John MacAloon. Twenty-six members of Commission 2000 were athletes who had participated in an Olympic Games,

President Samaranch elicited the opinions of Henry Kissinger among members of the emergency 'IOC 2000 Commission', created to recommend revised IOC structure and procedure. (© IOC/Locatelli)

44 were IOC members: 12 of these current or past IF presidents, 24 current or past NOC presidents. Three working groups were created to study specific areas:

● Composition, structure and organisation of the IOC (Coordinator: Franco Carraro, IOC member from Italy, assisted by Gilbert Felli, IOC Director of Sports)
● Role of the IOC (Coordinator: Thomas Bach, IOC member from Germany, Executive Board member, assisted by Pere Miro, IOC Director of NOC Relations)
● Designation of Olympic host cities (Coordinator: Anita DeFrantz, IOC Vice-President from America, assisted by Thierry Sprunger, IOC Director of Coordination)

Not least of the IOC's anxieties throughout the crisis was the attitude of their leading sponsors with TOP. Michael Payne, Director of Marketing, flew back and forth to the United States

Michael Payne, IOC Director of Marketing: 'We didn't know whether the institution would survive.' (© IOC/Locatelli)

and Japan to try to quell unease among the multinational industries who are the backbone of the IOC's commercial wealth. With equal urgency they were being reassured and held in reign by Pound. Payne admits:

> There was a period when we didn't know whether the institution would survive. The attention focused on us in Lausanne was brutal. The fact that Samaranch remained as President was, I believe, fundamental to our survival. We would not have been able to push through the changes that were made if he'd not been there to fire the shots. No one else could have done it. We might have been able to find a short-term fix, but not to make the radical changes.

One of the first to press the action button was David D'Alessandro, president of TOP sponsor John Hancock, an insurance company, who was calling for Samaranch's resignation. He wanted the problem solved instantly, including a change of IOC President. It was explained to him that the IOC was not a corporate body, able to dismiss its President with a fat pay-off, but had to work within its existing constitution. 'By the end of '99, even D'Alessandro realised that Samaranch's focus and ability to push through major issues was the key to the future, that it would have been impossible for a new President to achieve this,' Payne reflects.

> Thankfully, TOP structure was not undermined, all the sponsors remained on board, except for IBM [with whom the IOC split after the conclusion of the contract at Sydney, switching to Sema]. At the time, the crisis had a serious impact on sponsors' activation, just as companies were selling their self-promotion programmes. Dick [Pound] and I put in a tremendous amount of time reassuring them, convincing them that the IOC was determined to use the crisis as a catalyst.

Fresh fuel was heaped on the fire at the normally scheduled annual Session at Seoul in June. Phil Coles of Australia, former Olympic canoeist and subsequently secretary-general of the Australian NOC, had been censured in March for excessive travel favours from SLOC and a claim by his former wife of jewellery gifts worth $6,000 from a contract involved with the failed bid of Athens for the Centenary Games. Now, with Sydney battling to raise its financial budget for the following year, came the embarrassing revelation of a dossier written by Coles' current partner, Patricia Rosenbrock, for use by bid cities, outlining the alleged weaknesses and appropriate favours to be exploited with individual IOC members. Michael Knight, head of the Sydney organising committee, wanted the removal of Coles – a member of the organising committee as IOC member of his country – because his presence was undermining local confidence. Senior IOC figures urged that Coles should be expelled, but he was prevailed upon to resign from the Sydney committee, thereby retaining by a whisker his IOC membership. His popularity in Sydney remained undimmed.

The main decision of the June Session was to elect the Winter Games host for 2006. Temporary voting regulations were imposed, including the banning of visits and the introduction of a so-called 'Selection College', by which the six candidate cities would be reduced to two prior to voting by the members. There was immediate criticism that Sion of Switzerland held an advantage. The city had been a candidate against Salt Lake City for 2002 – when it received 14 votes – and thereby had already been visited by a number of IOC members. Sion representatives countered with the accusation that Giovanni Agnelli, owner of Fiat and a key figure in the Turin bid, was a member of Commission 2000.

In the preliminary ranking of an Evaluation Commission, Sion ranked first, closely followed by Helsinki and then Turin, with Klagenfurt (Austria) a distant fourth ahead of Poprad Tatry (Slovakia) and Zakopane (Poland). Predictably, Sion and Turin were the choice of the Selection College, but the vote by the members produced a crushing rejection for the Swiss: Turin 53, Sion 36. This was undoubtedly a backlash against the whistle-blowing Hodler. The majority of IOC members were embarrassed and angry at the deluge of defamation that now surrounded anyone connected with the IOC.

A month after Turin's election, Tom Welch and Dave Johnson, original leaders of Salt Lake City's bid committee, were indicted on federal fraud and other charges. A central issue, under American law, would be whether or not information on improper expenditure was exclusive to them, or whether others on the bid committee were equally aware. Lawyers for Welch and Johnson insisted that many others were party to the attempts to improperly acquire votes. In July 2001, four counts on the charges were dismissed by Judge Sam in the US District Court of Utah, the remainder dismissed in December. The government prosecution office appealed against the dismissal and in April 2003, three judges of the 10th US Circuit Court of Appeals reinstated the fifteen felony charges against the two leaders. The embarrassment for a number of other Salt Lake committee members, who could be drawn into the web, is that Gordon Hall, a former judge on Utah's Supreme Court and a member of the SLOC's Ethics Commission, is certain that many were aware of the inducements. 'It was perfectly obvious,' Hall said. 'It wasn't hidden, limos were there, helicopters were there, someone was paying for all that. It's not correct to put all the blame on Welch and Johnson.'

Johnson remained optimistic that his conduct together with Welch would be exonerated by the trial, expected to be concluded before the end of 2003 and an event which he welcomed. 'The executive committee of the Salt Lake City Bid Committee had authorised those actions designed to influence the vote of IOC members,' Johnson said. 'There was broad knowledge of the multiple visits, with the inclusion of children, of the financial contributions to NOCs and so on. We feel we have good evidence that every host city campaign saw bid cities offering such facilities including medical care. I am confident we can prove that there wasn't any bribery, that we didn't do anything that hadn't happened in other bids.' Legal defence costs were being met by insurance paid by the organising committee of the Salt Lake City Winter Games.

Elsewhere, Mohamed 'Bob' Hasan, Indonesian IOC member, was sentenced to six years in jail by the Jakarta High Court for forestry frauds running into millions of dollars: an IOC member the choice of whom had done Samaranch no credit. Hasan's expulsion by the IOC was suspended later in 2002 pending his appeal against the conviction in Jakarta.

The autumn of 1999 brought the unexpected death of Primo Nebiolo, one of sport's foremost leaders, a man who had done much to transform the image of the IAAF, if not always with sensitivity. There had been no doubting Nebiolo's passion for his sport. He was succeeded by senior vice-president Lamine Diack of Senegal, who, paying tribute, was speaking with more realism than he may have intended when saying: 'There is no Pope any more, no dictator any more.' Not only would Diack, his position confirmed at the next IAAF Congress, bring a less autocratic leadership, but there would also be a change within the body of Summer IFs, the ASOIF, when Denis Oswald was

elected to succeed Nebiolo as its president. Oswald's tribute likewise stated that Nebiolo's singular style of leadership was tolerated, 'which would not have been accepted with anyone else'. Nebiolo had died shortly before a planned meeting with Samaranch at which he had intended to make further financial demands on behalf of ASOIF.

The second Extraordinary Session of the year, an historic occasion, was on 11–12 December in Lausanne. Writing in *Olympic Review*, Samaranch reflected that the worldwide media criticism, unprecedented in its severity, had indirectly proved the IOC's importance in contemporary society. 'The acerbic criticism to which we have been subjected did not undermine the great majority of IOC members,' Samaranch asserted. 'I am convinced this is the first and last time we will have to deal with such cases . . . They cannot overshadow the gigantic edifice built over more than a century.' The Session agreed to implement all 50 of the recommendations made by Commission 2000, the most important being:

- Age limit reduced to 70 for IOC members
- Eight-year term for most members (renewable by re-election)
- Eight-year term for the President with option of re-election for one further term of four years
- Creation of four categories of IOC members – (a) 15 active athletes (having competed within the past four years), (b) 15 IF presidents, (c) 15 presidents of NOCs or continental associations, (d) 70 members to be elected individually; the total to be 115
- Elimination of visits to bid cities
- Revision of host city selection process
- Sessions to be opened to the media via closed-circuit TV
- Enlarging the Executive Board to 15
- Greater all-round transparency of decisions and Olympic finances

This 110th Session was itself in part open, for the first time, to the media. The recommendations introduced would require extensive adjustments to the Charter, and their introduction

Gathered for the IOCs most crucial Session in 105 years, Lausanne, December 1999: (l–r) former Olympic champions and IOC members Guy Drut (FRA), Charmaine Crooks (CAN), Sergei Bubka (UKR) and Valery Borzov (UKR). (© IOC/Locatelli)

within 12 months of the outbreak of the crisis was remarkable. Samaranch, together with Richard Pound and Keba M'Baye, could be satisfied that the IOC had been hauled back from the brink, even if there were continuing occasional thunderclaps of disapproval from the independent committees of inquiry. Back in April 1999, the US Senate Commerce Committee had held a hearing to focus on the Salt Lake City bid and the IOC's actions, to prevent a recurrence. Anita DeFrantz and James Easton, the two IOC members from America, both testified. Both were mercilessly grilled and gave equivocal responses. The government's Sub-Committee on Oversight and Investigation, inquiring into the Atlanta bid for 1996, assigned the investigation to an Atlanta law firm headed by Griffin Bell, former US Attorney-General. The 'Bell' report released in September 1999 listed various gifts beyond the IOC guideline limit of $200, but stated: 'This is not a corrupt system but is subject to abuse.' Andrew Young, co-chairman of the Atlanta bid committee, had offered two scholarships to IOC members, both of which had been declined. Other excessive gifts were noted, but not of a dimension that required further discipline by the IOC. In October 1999, the 'oversight' sub-committee held a hearing to debate the Bell Report, and again DeFrantz and Easton testified, as did IOC Director-General François Carrard and Dr Henry Kissinger.

Shortly after the second Extraordinary Session, Samaranch, reassured that his ship was once again stable, felt willing to appear before a US Congressional panel in Washington. Despite his assurance that the 50 reforms just adopted would be swiftly implemented, the reception he received was hostile. Republican Joe Barton (Texas) reiterated his call for Samaranch to resign, to which the President responded by confirming that all reforms would be in place before the Sydney Games the following year. Republican Fred Upton (Michigan), chairman of the Congressional panel, expressed doubts that the alleged IOC 'culture of corruption' would be so simply resolved by new written rules. He was right to believe that the IOC, sadly but unavoidably, would henceforth need an element of watchdog supervision in their administration. It would take time before the IOC and the watching world could certain that the reforms were effective. George Mitchell of the USOC investigation committee stated:

> Our Commission made 50 recommendations to the IOC under three categories: financial transparency, host city selection and IOC accountability. The actions taken by the IOC last weekend represent progress in all three categories . . . in one important respect, the matter which sparked the scandal – visits to bidding cities – the ban adopted by the IOC goes even further than we recommended.

IOC action, led by Commission 2000, had indeed been positive. The Olympic Movement was evidently not the uniform fount of evil that its foremost critics had claimed: 'sport dressed up in cosy, phoney virtue . . . An infected, untreated toe becoming a case of galloping gangrene,' according to the sophism of *The Times* of London. However, Hein Verbruggen of Holland, president of international cycling, agreed that 'the Olympic image is the major asset of Olympism and drastic measures are required to restore that image'. Amid the crisis, Don Porter of America, president of international softball, secretary-general of GAISF, executive member of ASOIF and vice-chairman of USOC international relations, had been moved to write:

With a US Senate hearing scheduled, here comes government again playing overseer to the world, yet not really knowing what is going on . . . At the recent world conference on doping, the USA and others tried to lay blame on the IOC [for inaction] when in fact those political appointees came with stained hands. The US presence and position during the conference were reprehensible, especially considering that country's own house was not in order. In the midst of all the hullabaloo about the conduct of the IOC one senses a general conclusion: a lynch-mob mentality among certain US politicians and others. This is a classic rush to judgement without considering the side-effects that it could have on the United States; the fact that there is growing resentment towards the US on the part of the international sports community . . . Regardless of the past wrongs the IOC may have committed, it is making positive efforts to right them. The US should be helping rather than trying intimidation tactics . . . Many of the allegations of wrong-doing are based on facts and circumstances that are insignificant in comparison to the numerous overt acts by governments and businesses that rarely draw the attention of the media . . . We never hear about the good things the IOC and Samaranch have done – the humanitarian aid and financial support that the IOC has provided for many countries is something you do not read or hear about.

As another IF president observed, 'The total incentive involved at Salt Lake, a million dollars, is peanuts compared with the slush funds in multinational business deals.'

And Dr Kissinger stated:

> We outside members of Commission 2000 did not consider it our task to sit in judgement on matters that have occurred in recent years that have been the subject of much controversy. We thought it was our duty to enable the Olympic Movement, which has been brought this far by the dedication and the hard work of the various Olympic committees over the decades, and by the overwhelming majority of IOC members, to continue to function in a modern period.

It was unfortunate for Kevan Gosper, IOC Vice-President, that he should feel obliged to resign early in 2000 from the Ethics Commission for which he had himself been such a powerful advocate. The Australian press and others raised the matter of the cost of a holiday visit taken by Gosper and his family in Salt Lake City at a time when he was travelling between official Executive Board functions elsewhere. The family's expenses had been reimbursed to the SLOC, but such was the hue and cry of the media, especially in America and Australia, that Gosper felt obliged to withdraw. He was to suffer further crucifixion in print, unfairly, prior to the Sydney Games, for having allowed his young daughter to be invited to run in the torch relay from Olympia. The cry was 'cronyism', yet never previously has the matter of the participant runners in Greece been a story of concern. Once Gosper had accepted the invitation from Greek IOC member Lambis Nikolaou, and Nikolaou had passed the name to the local council at Olympia, the order of running was totally out of their hands. The fact that Gosper's daughter was given the second stage, rather than another Australian-Greek girl, turned the Australian press into a frenzy of accusations of nepotism. Anyone reading the correspondence from the Greeks regarding the issue would find the press reaction implausibly excessive.

Celebrating the future. Newly elected IOC members gather on stage at Sydney's closing ceremony: (l –r) Charmaine Crooks (CAN), Sergei Bubka (UKR), Robert Ctvrtlik (USA), Manuel Estiarte (ESP), Michael Knight (president of organising committee), Juan Antonio Samaranch, John Coates (AUS), Jan Zelezny (CZE), Alexander Popov (RUS), Susie O'Neill (AUS). (© IOC/Locatelli)

Australia, a noble country of small population far-removed from the beaten track for much of the twentieth century, was indeed paranoiac about the way it might be perceived internationally and therefore hyper-sensitive to any action that might be alleged to be incorrect. There would be many agonies as the famous city of Sydney, well-known even to those who had never been there, edged towards its appointment with history, once Rod McGeoch's bidding committee had defeated Beijing with a lunge at the line at Monte Carlo in 1993. A major incentive had been the offer, costing $24 million, to provide free travel for athletes, coaches and officials, plus a further $8 million to cover the transport of sporting equipment. There may have been the ticket scams that overtake many host cities, yet Sydney, with the unrivalled hospitality from its tens of thousands of volunteers, was to provide a unique setting for the re-establishment of the reputation of both the IOC and the Olympic Games. Sydney, in almost every way, was, in a word, good: for the athletes, for the spectators, for the presentation of events, for generating that ambience of fun, of shared experience, of optimism, of involvement in something so honestly worthwhile, that a debt of gratitude was owed to every Australian who worked to make

this possible. It helped, of course, that Australia is politically and strategically one of the safest, most secure countries in the world and above all that their people know how to make the most of life. Sydney's contribution, a turning point in Olympic history, will come to be seen, sociologically, as the most significant Games since Stockholm in 1912.

The beleaguered Samaranch was himself touched by some of the magic of the occasion. A year after his worldwide denunciation, he had, by that wilful streak that was central to his nature, lifted the organisation for which he was responsible, and indeed himself, back onto a platform of respectability. Even his most trenchant denigrators had been touched by his dedication when making the round trip from Sydney to Barcelona and back again at the beginning of the Games for the funeral of his wife Maria Therese, the most gracious consort any man could wish for. If Samaranch had been an inspired but at times flawed innovator, in spite of all his nerve now held firm and at the closing ceremony he offered Australia its favourite chant. 'Aussie, Aussie, Aussie,' he called from the dais and back came the fulsome response, 'Oi, Oi, Oi.' The Australian public was beginning to appreciate him for helping them to do, for the Olympic Games, what he now signalled without reservation. 'These are my last Games as President of the IOC,' he said. 'They could not have been better. I am proud to proclaim that you have presented to the world the best Olympic Games ever.'

Maria Therese Samaranch, elegant and dutiful wife of the seventh President. (©IOC/Locatelli)

CHAPTER LXIX

Sydney (XXVII) 2000

Sir Steve Redgrave of Britain, gold medal oarsman in five successive Games, 1984–2000

'*The Olympic Games are the ultimate challenge. Richard Burnell, himself a gold-medal winner in 1948, said to me after the first time I won in 1984: "You're world champion for one year, you're Olympic champion for life." That sums it up. It's the event that means the most, one day every four years, so different from a world championship. Some oarsmen may not even go to every world championship, saving their big effort for the Olympics. There are fewer Olympic champions, making it a more exclusive club.*

My first three Games had all been well organised, special in their own right for their different cultures: Los Angeles, South Korea and Spain. In 1996, however, although the hosts in Atlanta boasted about it being "the home of hospitality", they failed to achieve that atmosphere – I felt something was missing. Also, the pressure and build-up for those Games was incredibly intense, particularly as we were carrying the public expectation of being favourites. When we pulled it off, I initially felt I could call it a day. However, after a few hours, the disappointment of the surrounding elements of the Games made it seem worth doing once more and Sydney, with its sporting culture, would be different again. I kept it quiet, even from my family, for a couple of months, but because of the venue I wanted to be part of those Games. There was a special challenge with Australia, Sydney's a fantastic place and I love the Australians. It would be a unique climax. I know I said after Atlanta that anyone had the right to shoot me if I stepped in a boat again, but on the pontoon you're able to escape from some of the media pressure. The emotions I expressed at the time in Atlanta were not a true representation of my feelings.

In the build-up to Sydney there were questions over my fitness. I wanted to have a realistic chance, and gradually I felt that I really did – that if I went through the usual training process, if I struggled to hold my form, I could be confident that when we got to the Games I could do it. The physical build-up to Sydney was not too oppressive, even though I had my problem with diabetes, and this time, once it was over and when we got home, the response of the public was amazing.

If you ask which medal was the best, which was unique, it must be the first in LA. You have the dream as a kid of standing on the podium, being a champion. I had this dream even before I knew what rowing was, watching the Games at Munich when I was ten and realising it was something special. I began rowing at 14 and a year later someone was saying, "You're capable of being a champion" – I thought to myself: "I want to be an Olympic champion."

It was a particular thrill to carry the British flag twice at the Opening Ceremony, in Barcelona and Atlanta; no one else has done that. But besides all this, what I have gained from the Olympics is the friendship with Matt [Matthew Pinsent], and that's something much more important than rowing. After 11 years as a partnership, there's a special bond between us.'*
(Photograph © Getty Images)

When Jürgen Grobler, the former East German rowing coach, joined the Leander Club in 1991, he was aware that Steve Redgrave's future might be less glorious than his past: that following gold medals in 1984, in the coxed four, and 1988, in the coxless pairs – plus, remarkably, bronze in the coxed pairs – it was expecting a lot for Redgrave to continue victorious.

Grobler himself was experienced in producing Olympic champions. Since 1972 he had not failed to secure a gold medal for one of his crews, but one of his first coaching decisions at the Leander Club caused consternation among many rowing experts at the time. Matthew Pinsent had been introduced as Redgrave's partner following the retirement of

Andrew Holmes, and Grobler proceeded to switch Pinsent, Old Etonian son of a clergyman and twice winner of the Oxford–Cambridge Boat Race, to stroke, putting Redgrave in the 'back' of the boat. Would Redgrave, the dyslexic son of a carpenter/builder from Marlow on the River Thames, accept this seeming relegation?

Like lions in their prime, the new pairing roared to triumph in the coxless pairs in 1992, then repeated this success in 1996. Having threatened retirement, Redgrave could not resist one further attempt at an Olympic crown, and for Sydney the pair revised their target and were joined in a coxless four by Tim Foster and James Cracknell, both of whom rapidly adapted to the mood of invincibility. It was an unprecedented ambition in an endurance sport for a man who would be 38 by the time of the race.

Following their victory in the World Cup in 1997, the four would remain undefeated until their last pre-Olympic race, the World Cup final at Lucerne, Switzerland, six weeks prior to the Games. There they finished fourth behind Italy, New Zealand and Australia, all of whom they had consistently beaten during the previous three years. Suddenly doubts hovered over Redgrave. Had his ailments – debilitating colitis and, latterly, insulin-dependent diabetes – made him the weak link in the crew? Did he still deserve his place? Grobler, however, was quick to identify the cause of the sudden crisis: over-training and a drop in glycogen levels. They needed a break. The worst aspect of the defeat was that rivals would no longer be intimidated.

By the time they reached the final in Sydney, their own doubts and decline had been put behind them and they were back at a peak, once more able to sustain Pinsent's attacking sprints of 45 strokes to the minute. 'We had the passion again that had been lacking in recent races,' Redgrave said. But what a desperate climax was to ensue.

As expected, the British boat made an explosive start and with 1,500 metres to go seemed to be on cruise control with a lead of a full second, but then the Italians and Australians began to close the gap. Redgrave, who controlled race strategy from the No. 3 seat, called for a push. It had been intended to delay this until the last 250 metres, but now the danger was already looming. 'It got very painful,' Pinsent said. 'When you dig deep after going flat out for five minutes, it's going to hurt.' Foster, an experienced oarsman sitting behind him, had not quite realised what would be required over the last 500 metres. 'They told me if we won, it wouldn't hurt,' he said. 'They lied.' With Italy squeezing ever closer, Redgrave and his colleagues held on to win by 0.4 seconds. With 13 World and Olympic titles, Redgrave had become one of the greatest Olympians of all time, ancient or modern.

Cathy Freeman surges to victory in the 400m, then sits to gather her composure while the record crowd raises the roof.
(© Getty Images/Powell) (© Getty Images/Hewitt)

Steve Redgrave (2nd from right) slumps exhausted, moments after achieving his historic fifth gold medal in five consecutive Games. His colleagues in Britain's coxless four are Matthew Pinsent (stroke), arms aloft, Tim Foster and James Cracknell.
(© Getty Images/Kinnaird)

'He's become an icon of rowing,' said James Stewart, from the third-placed Australian crew. 'To win one gold is a dream come true, but five, that's almost beyond imagination.' As the British

crew's heads drooped towards their knees in their state of exhaustion, Pinsent, precariously balanced, clambered past Foster to throw his arms round Redgrave in a gesture that was more one of admiration than triumph. More than anyone, he knew the sacrifices and resolution that Redgrave had made to reach this unique moment of fame.

Pinsent's embrace captured something of the timelessness of the Olympic ethic, yet the profound emotional link that had been established between these two very different men was something that neither of them has ever been able fully to express: a bond beyond conventional words.

At the medals ceremony Redgrave was presented, additionally, with a commemorative pin by the IOC President: 'I was there to congratulate him because he is in the golden book of the history of the Olympic Games,' Samaranch said. It was a victory that cloaked the waters of Penrith Lakes outside Sydney in unrestrained awe. It left even rivals lost for words of admiration and none begrudged him his position on Mount Olympus. On the morning of the race, Redgrave had been approached by an unknown New Zealander who wished him luck, saying: 'I really hope you win.' And then, after a pause: 'There's only one problem – you're rowing against my son.'

The minute, or rather less, that it took Cathy Freeman to win the women's 400m was the longest minute in 200 years of Australian history, enacted in front of a (paying) crowd of 102,254 – the largest ever at a Games – and the watching millions worldwide. The country's 100th Olympic gold medal was the first for an individual indigenous Aborigine, and neither the home audience nor the lone athlete were wholly sure at the moment of triumph precisely what this meant to them. Some of the socio-political significances have been discussed earlier, but at the moment she became Olympic champion Freeman continued to exhibit the same self-contained composure that during the preceding days and weeks had enabled her to reach this point. Instead of immediately cavorting in celebration and self-acclaim, she sat down on the track in her hooded, enveloping green bodysuit and for another whole minute or more remained there, privately contemplating who she was and what she had just done. She has a tattoo on her arm that reads 'Cos I'm Free'. Now she truly was, and she wished to savour it. 'Sport is this great arena for drama, it's a reflection of life,' she would say later. 'Sometimes favourites don't win. My Olympic dream came true when I crossed that line. It was just relief, I was totally overwhelmed because I could feel the crowd all around and all over me. I just felt everyone's happiness and joy, so I had to sit down and make myself feel normal and get comfortable.' It was a unique response to a unique moment.

This symbol of the Aboriginal people had waited more than a decade for the ultimate opportunity to express so gloriously the identity of her oppressed race. She had first waved simultaneously – to the disapproval of the then team manager – the flags of Australia and the Aborigines at the Commonwealth Games in 1994. She had twice been world champion, in 1997 and 1999, while at the Atlanta Games she had finished second to the successful defending champion Marie-José Pérec of France, but none of these occasions could compare with the victory in Sydney.

Pérec, in a fit of nerves, had fled home from Sydney because she felt unequal to the pressure. She had paraded a range of excuses, claiming she was harassed throughout her time in Sydney and even alleged that she had been threatened by a stranger in her hotel room. Video surveillance cameras recorded no presence of such a stranger, however, and all the evidence pointed towards psychological breakdown. Pérec's career had wavered since 1996. She had withdrawn from the following year's world championship, then suffered the Epstein Barr viral condition in 1998, raced only occasionally in 1999 and had cancelled appearances at five meetings at short notice in the current season. Introspective and a loner, she had lost sympathy among colleagues and French officials. Philippe Lamblin, president of the French Athletics Association, said of her disappearance: 'The whole of France is penalised by this decision. The most suitable phrase to use in this tale is that she left like a thief.' An irony of her conduct was that she had sought coaching from Wolfgang Meier, the former East German coach whose wife, Marita Koch, held the world record which Pérec had publicly labelled as being drug assisted.

Pérec's absence raised the expectations placed upon Freeman in a small nation that can be intimidatingly intimate. Freeman proved herself equal to the occasion, though there would be athletically superior achievements at those Games. Her winning time of 49.11 was indeed inferior to the 48.63 she had recorded behind Pérec's Olympic record of 48.25 four years earlier.

The noise when Freeman appeared for the start of the final was like a squadron of jets at take-off. 'I was pretty nervous, but there was a voice in my head saying, "Just do what you know." All I was conscious of was my lane,' she would recall. Fortunately she had recovered from a bout of laryngitis, possibly brought on during the Opening Ceremony but stemmed by a course of antibiotics. The race tactics discussed with her coach Peter Fortune were simple: fast out, relax down the back straight and into the start of the second bend, attack coming out of the bend.

The 100m was the first gold in Marion Jones's 'Drive for Five', a feat that would prove beyond this supreme but corrupted sprinter. (© Getty Images/Powell)

According to plan, she was smoothly into that elegant long stride down the back straight, though inside in lanes four and three Lorraine Graham of Jamaica and Katherine Merry of Britain were making ground, while Donna Fraser of Britain in lane two was even-pace with Freeman. Round the second bend, Graham and Merry were marginally ahead. Now Freeman's nerve had to hold. Now she must attack, if the strength was still there. The finishing kick took effect, she pulled clear, the cascade of noise within the stadium mounting with every stride. She was three metres clear at the line, with Graham taking silver and Merry bronze. 'A lovely race, a lovely last 50,' her coach would say.

While Freeman sat down to think, Australia overflowed as much with relief as with joy. When she had composed herself, Freeman collected the two flags – those of her people and her country – and lapped the stadium as if on a magic carpet. Receiving her medal, she sang the national anthem with the biggest accompanying choir ever assembled in Australia and then took her bouquet of flowers to her mother, Cecilia. Such was the inferno of emotion welling in the stadium that the subsequent victory of Michael Johnson in the men's 400m was reduced almost to an addendum. The soul of Australia had momentarily been condensed into the figure of this one Aborigine: until this moment, a lesser Australian. 'When we walked into new places, we were totally intimidated because we felt that, being black, we had no right to be there,' Freeman had said in her autobiography. 'It's weird, but we felt bad about being black.'

Seventeen years earlier, when she was aged ten, her stepfather Bruce Barber had told her she would one day run in the Olympics, that she was 'a stone that needed to be polished'.

Aged seventeen, Freeman's talent had been identified by a sports reporter on the *Melbourne Herald Sun*. 'When she raced, you could see the tiger in her,' said Nick Bideau, who was to become her manager. When the moment came to race as the adopted child of an entire nation, she was equal to it.

Another female sprinter who attracted a great deal of attention at Sydney was the American Marion Jones, who made an unsuccessful bid to win five gold medals in a single Games while burdened by the revelation of the positive drug test of her husband C.J. Hunter. Jones was one of the foremost competitors in any sport at Sydney and she commanded sustained attention for her virtues as much as for her marital embarrassment. Her much-publicised ambition, the 'Drive for Five', had amplified media curiosity even before the emergence of her husband's guilt. It would be seven years before her own guilt was finally exposed (as related in the Introduction).

Though she did not achieve her primary goal, Jones confirmed her exceptional qualities by winning five individual medals, three gold and two bronze, and rode the storm of the allegations with feigned dignity and a firm demeanour, repeatedly asserting that she herself was 'clean'. She duly won the 100m by the widest margin ever seen in this event in any Games, 0.37 seconds ahead of Ekatarini Thanou of Greece in 10.75 in a slight headwind on a cold evening. Tanya Lawrence of Jamaica thwarted her veteran compatriot Merlene Ottey, gaining the bronze by one-hundredth of a second. Though Jones's time was well outside the questionable world record Griffith Joyner had set 12 years earlier, her face was tear-stained with pride as she went on her lap of honour carrying the Stars and Stripes plus the flag of Belize, where her mother had been born.

It was said that if Freeman ran with the whole nation on her back, Jones ran the 200m with her rhino-built husband on hers. 'He has my full support,' the supposedly loyal wife doggedly declared, though the smiles that had followed the 100m victory were now gone as she and C.J. staged a defiant press conference prior to the longer sprint, which was as much to protect her interests as his.

The couple had originally met in the weight-training room at the University of North Carolina and C.J., seven years older, said the last thing he wanted to do was to hurt her: in the circumstances, a forlorn declaration. Hurt she was, and would remain, though in the stadium her equilibrium was to continue seemingly unaffected, even during the parallel demands of qualifying for the finals of both 200m and long jump. She won the long sprint with easy assurance, never troubled by Pauline Davis-Thompson of the Bahamas or Susanthika Jayasinghe of Sri Lanka, who took the lesser medals. From the gun, there was never a doubt about her victory, even though all eight runners recorded their best time of the year.

For Cathy Freeman, the 200m was an anti-climactic evening in which she finished seventh, having narrowly qualified from the semi-final. For Davis-Thompson, aged 34, this was her fifth Games and her first individual medal, and she chose the press conference to issue a warning to Jones regarding the sprint relay. 'We [Bahamas] are only a small country of a quarter of a million people, so small you can hardly find us on the map . . . we had three women in the final of the 100m, and I'm telling you, we are going to give you one hell of a race.'

Jones's ambition, tarnished though it might have been, was fine while it lasted; yet not only with hindsight was the long jump probably an event too far. At the world championships in Seville the previous year, she had collapsed with a back injury during the 200m semi-final, the possibility being that the exertions of the long jump had undermined her. Her lack of technique for this event was palpable: she had only her speed, and in Sydney her speed was not enough. Moreover it did nothing for her popularity: some viewed Jones as an opportunist jumper on a medal hunt. Several of her rivals made no secret of their delight that the title should be taken by Heike Drechsler, the former East German who won her second Olympic crown eight years after her first in Barcelona – the first athlete ever to win this event twice. She had been 18 and a member of the GDR team when she took the silver medal in 1988, and had been breaking records when Jones was a toddler. 'I'm glad this was won by a real long jumper,' Susen Tiedtke of Germany remarked to Jackie Edwards of the Bahamas.

The US qualified for the finals of both relays, the fourth and fifth legs of Jones's 'Drive'. However, Davis-Thompson's warning was fulfilled in the sprint relay when the Bahamas claimed first place ahead of Jamaica, with the USA pushed into third place, handicapped by the absence of Inger Miller and Gail Devers, who were both injured. Thus Jones on the anchor leg was 'relegated' to her second bronze. Ottey's anchor leg for Jamaica brought her an eighth Olympic medal, more than any other female athlete, though none of hers were gold.

There was added corrupt fortune for Jones in the four-lap relay, where she ran a powerful third leg to give Colander Richardson a lead into the final lap, Jamaica holding off Russia for the silver. Jones had run as fast as Freeman in the individual event, thus ending her Olympic crusade on a high note. 'You can't break her,' said her coach, Trevor Graham.

Several great deeds in track and field were inadvertently placed in relative shade by the attention focused on Freeman, and one of these came in the men's 10,000m, which was a classic encounter. Haile Gebrselassie of Ethiopia had been unbeaten for seven years, a period which had included the breaking of eleven world records, and was now defending his Atlanta title. His inspiration as a boy had been listening to radio commentaries of his countryman Miruts Yifter, and now in the hills above Addis Ababa he had acquired a stature superior even to his famous forebear. Confronting him was his long-time Kenyan rival Paul Tergat, runner-up in Atlanta, and the plot was further thickened by the presence of Tergat's colleagues, Patrick Ivuti and John Korir, and Gebrselassie's teammate, Assefa Mezegebu.

It was not until seven laps out that Tergat took the initiative, immediately tracked by the champion. Temporarily, Ivuti and then Korir took up the challenge. An original pack of thirteen had been cut to six: the Kenyans, Ethiopians and Said Berioui of Morocco. By the bell, Mezegebu had joined Gebrselassie at the front, running wide so that any Kenyan bidder would have to move into the third lane. Into the straight Tergat did just that, but Gebrselassie held him stride for stride amid a pandemonium of noise until finding the strength for a final lunge that gave him victory by nine-hundredths of a second. His time of 27:18.20 was the fastest of the season and he now stood alongside Olympian masters Nurmi, Zátopek, Kuts and Virén.

The two middle-distance events witnessed the shock defeat of world record holders considered worthy of Olympic honour even by their rivals. Having fallen in the multiple 1,500m collision of the 1996 final and finished last, Hicham El Guerrouj had been unbeaten in the subsequent four years. His stature was as lofty as that of Jim Ryun 30 years earlier, but he too was to be ambushed. For much of the four years he had been stalked by Noah Ngeny, another young Kenyan from the Rift Valley. At 19, Ngeny had paced El Guerrouj to his world record of 3:26.00. Two years later, he had himself lowered Sebastian Coe's long-unchallenged 1,000m record and had

Noah Ngeny (KEN) finally nails his illustrious rival Hicham El Guerrouj (MAR). (© Getty Images/Barbour)

been at El Guerrouj's heels during the 1999 world championship victory. El Guerrouj's weakness was his strange lack of self-esteem, an anxiety that he might not win a slower race, the haunting sound of Ngeny's footsteps always close behind him. He permanently carried a picture of his fall in Atlanta to help drive him in his relentless preparation for Sydney, but come the day he crucially misjudged the race, underestimating Ngeny's growing menace. For the first lap Youssef Baba, El Guerrouj's compatriot, made the pace, then the favourite took over, unwisely easing the pace of the second lap but at the bell seemingly poised to win the coveted title. As they entered the final turn, El Guerrouj glanced up at the huge television screen to see the image of his trailing nemesis. With 80 metres remaining, Ngeny accelerated, passed the Moroccan 18 metres out and erased Coe's Olympic record of 3:32.53 by almost half a second (3:32.07). El Guerrouj was left a sobbing, temporarily broken man, garnering no comfort from his silver medal. Bernard Lagat of Kenya had taken the bronze.

Another error of judgement was made in the 800m by Wilson Kipketer, the naturalised Dane from Kenya and world record holder who had been ineligible for Atlanta. He too made the error of holding back, in spite of the previous year's warning in the world championship when he only snatched victory by a whisker from Hezekiel Sepeng of South Africa. Following Atlanta, Kipketer had suffered an attack of malaria and at 29 this was effectively his last chance for the Olympic title, yet his miscalculation was on a par with Coe's at Moscow in 1980. The title instead went to Nils Schumann of Germany in the slowest time since Coe lost to Steve Ovett, 1:45.08.

Poor Michael Johnson. Though he completed a unique defence of his 400m title, the aura of acclaim for this exceptional runner was muted on account of his achievement occurring on the same evening as Freeman's moonshot. With

the conditions cool, his time of 43.84, though well ahead of compatriot Alvin Harrison, was nowhere near the sub-43 for which he yearned. He would have to remain content with his world record of 43.18, nine victories in five world championships and five Olympic titles.

Anything but predictable was the 200m triumph of Kostas Kenteris: the first Greek man to win a running event since Spyridon Louis in 1896 and the first white sprinter to become champion since Italy's Pietro Mennea in 1980 (in the absence of America). At 27, his credentials were unexceptional. He had been eliminated in the quarter-finals of the world championships in 1999, had competed only once outside Greece in the current season and had beaten no one of account. Until shifting his focus the previous year, he had been a moderate 400m runner, ranking a mere 55th at 200m. There were those who questioned his sudden improvement at such an age: suspicions over this result only heightened by his ban in 2004 (see Chapter LXXII).

Jonathan Edwards was more of a veteran at 34 than Johnson, with three Olympics behind him and no better than a silver medal in 1996. The career of this son of a church minister had started late and he had first reached the podium at the 1993 world championship triple jump in third place, with his memorable world record coming two years later. From somewhere he now produced a winning leap of 17.71m (58 ft 1¼ in.), half a metre short of his record and less than his second-place distance in Atlanta, but enough to overcome Yoel Garcia of Cuba.

Women's track and field events regularly provide some of the most human stories of the Games and this time tragedy struck for Glory Alozie of Nigeria. Hyginus Anugo, her fiancé, had missed selection for the four-lap relay but had travelled from Nigeria's training base in Adelaide to arrange private accommodation in Sydney. Three weeks before Alozie's high hurdles final, having just left evening prayers at a college hall of residence, he stepped into the road, was run down and died. The pair were from the same village, had trained together and were to be married the following year. At the time of the accident Alozie was competing in Japan and the news was withheld from her – she was told only that he was injured – until she returned to Sydney. So distraught that she had to be force-fed; she was only persuaded to compete in honour of her fiancé's memory. Such was her fortitude that she missed the gold medal by only three-hundredths of a second, the winner being Olga Shishigina of Kazakhstan in 12.65. Alozie had led until the tenth flight. She had yet to return home with Anugo's body for the funeral. 'I'm grateful to God for giving me the strength to see this through,' she said.

For Irina Privalova, Sydney was the moment to end a 15-year career as runner-up in major championships. Married at 18, mother at 19, divorced at 20, she now became an Olympic champion at 32 when winning the 400m hurdles. In 1992 she had been third in the 100m behind Gail Devers, was the winner of the World Cup 400m two years later and then runner-up in the 200m at the 1995 world championships. She had switched to hurdles only the previous season, recognising she was no match for Freeman and Pérec. The final in Sydney was only her seventh race over the distance and she led all the way to defeat the defending champion Deon Hemmings of Jamaica by nearly half a second.

A Russian immigrant, Tatiana Grigorieva, made the pole vault memorable, though it suffered somewhat from its simultaneous scheduling with Freeman on the track. The glamorous Grigorieva cleared 4.55m (14 ft 11¼ in.) at the first attempt, world champion Stacy Dragila of America making it only on her second. Dragila, however, then flew over 4.60m

Tatiana Grigorieva, Russian–Australian, combines glamour with muscle in claiming silver medal in the augural women's pole vault.
(© Getty Images/Pretty)

Diminutive Andreea Raducan (ROM) wows them all in the floor exercise, and celebrates a gymnastics all-round title prior to traumatic disqualification.
(© Getty Images/Botterill)
(© Getty Images/Shaw)

(15 ft 1¼ in.) at her first attempt, at which height Grigorieva failed; though no doubt appearing semi-naked upside down in public will have done no harm to her modelling career.

Maria Mutola of Mozambique had been bidding for Olympic fame since she was a teenager and at 27 this was her fourth attempt. Finally she did it, winning the 800m by a comfortable margin from Stephanie Graf of Austria, with the 30-year-old Kelly Holmes of Britain, having overcome repeated setbacks, taking the bronze. Mutola, once a footballer, had failed to survive the heats as a 15 year old in Seoul, finished fifth in Barcelona and third in Atlanta. Holmes had been a medal winner at 800m and 1,500m in the world championships five years earlier, only to suffer a subsequent string of injuries. Mutola's gold doubled her country's Olympic tally: her bronze had been their first medal.

Derartu Tulu of Ethiopia recaptured the 10,000m title she had won eight years earlier with an Olympic record of 30:17.49, five seconds ahead of compatriot Gete Wami, who had finished third in the 5,000m. The bronze medal here went to Fernanda Ribeiro of Portugal but the agony of the race belonged to Paula Radcliffe of Britain, who, conscious of her lack of finishing pace, had led for all but two laps of the twenty-five in the attempt to burn off her rivals, only to be left flagging over the last 400 metres. Knowledgeable viewers sensed the probable outcome, making the viewing of the race like awaiting an execution. There was no answer to Tulu's final lap of sixty seconds, and though the other two medal winners were five seconds or so behind, they were still four seconds faster than Radcliffe, who was brave enough to say of Tulu: 'To run something like that at the end of the race was just superb. I didn't get a medal – that's life.'

A notable aspect of track and field was the USA's decline, with just ten victories, only six of which were by men. The total of twenty medals was the lowest by an American team since 1936. Russia were equally modest, with three individual gold medals compared with six in the previous year's world championships. Decline was visible elsewhere, with one silver medal for Italy and none at all for France for the first time in 64 years.

Most sports at any Games have their distress stories. Women's gymnastics at Sydney had two of the worst, though the context of failure was contrastingly different. Svetlana Khorkina of Russia, the most accomplished gymnast in the field with a regal presence and a string of titles, for whom defeat was not in the dictionary, twice blundered to forego the team title for her country and any prospect of the individual all-round title for herself. Andreea Raducan, a 16-year-old Romanian of regulation diminutive stature at 1.47m (4 ft 10 in.) compared with Khorkina's lofty 1.65m (5 ft 5 in.), secured through her own brilliance the rewards seemingly awaiting the woman among the gathering of gnats, only then to have the individual gold wrenched from her grasp when found guilty yet personally innocent of a drug offence. The immovable – and correct – decision of the IOC, upheld by CAS, aroused fury in Romania, sympathy throughout the watching world and a warning, if such were still needed, to every competitor of an unforgiving principle in testing.

Khorkina's fall from the asymmetric bars cost Russia the team gold, handing the title to Romania by 0.205 of a point – in the absurd mathematics of an arbitrarily judged sport – with China taking the bronze. Then, to compound Khorkina's dismay, she was the victim of an administrative foul-up, technicians failing to adjust the springboard for the vault between the men's events the previous night and the women's, so that Khorkina, always in search of perfection, instead landed knees-down on the mat. Belated protest was irrelevant, and with her concentration frayed she then erred again on the asymmetric bars. Raducan dramatically exploited her rival's lapse with a wonderful performance in the floor exercise, her colleagues Simona Amanar and Maria Olaru gaining silver and bronze behind her. It was a clean sweep that recalled the dominance of Russia 40 years earlier in Rome, but the celebration with team leader Nadia Comaneci and by those back home was to be shortlived.

An innocuous Nurofen pill, administered to Raducan by the Romanian team doctor two hours before the event to counteract breathing difficulties, carried the banned substance pseudoephedrine. The drug was unlikely to have assisted her performance in any way, and the Romanian NOC, under the direction of its chairman Ion Tiriac, mounted an emotional and legal defence of their tiny heroine, but on appeal against IOC discipline the CAS verdict remained resolute:

> A strict liability test must be applied, the consequence being automatic disqualification as a matter of law and in fairness to all other athletes . . . factors such as the athlete's age, weight, medical condition, reliance on the team's doctor are irrelevant. The panel is aware of the impact of its decision on a fine young elite athlete . . . but the code must be enforced.

Amanar and Olaru were, reluctantly, promoted to gold and silver, Xuan Li of China from fourth place to bronze, while Dr Loacham Oana, the Romanian medic, was banned for four years. 'I am not going to quit,' said a dignified, defiant Raducan at a tearful press conference. 'I want to prove that I can do better, that I am the person I really am. I'm not a cheat. I have nothing to be ashamed of.' Because of the timing of the dosage before the individual competition, the prior team result was unaffected.

Having three times taken the silver medal since their re-entry to the arena in 1984, China's men were finally victorious in gymnastics, despite competing without Yufu Lu, their number one, who had injured his neck in training. Alexei Nemov, twice world champion, who topped the individual rankings, secured bronze for Russia, the defending champions, with his supreme performance on parallel bars; the silver went to the Ukraine. Nemov went on to take the individual all-round title as well as gold and two bronze medals for the respective separate apparatus finals of horizontal bar, pommel horse and parallel bars.

Euphoric frenzy surrounded much of the men's swimming on account of the teenage home hero, Ian Thorpe, who was prematurely being spoken of in the same terms as Tiger Woods in golf. It was perhaps going too far for Don Talbot, Australian head coach, to claim that Thorpe was 'the greatest swimmer of the century': unless, of course, he was talking of the twenty-first century, and even that would be open to debate. Pieter van den

Dutch courage. Pieter van den Hoogenband (NED) and Ian Thorpe (AUS) reflect on the Dutchman's unexpected 200m freestyle victory. (both © Getty Images/Bello)

Hoogenband of Holland not only defeated Thorpe in the 200m freestyle but also took the 100m, beating the esteemed Alex Popov of Russia in the process, and claimed bronze in the 50m freestyle.

The launchpad of Thorpe's glory was a special night on which he initially and predictably won the 400m freestyle, in world record time and almost without challenge ahead of Massimiliano Rosolino of Italy, and then anchored Australia to victory in the 4 x 100m relay, an event which the USA had never lost since it was introduced in 1964. The climax of the latter all but lifted the roof at the Olympic pool. The 100m was not Thorpe's speciality and on the final leg he was up against the formidable sprinter Gary Hall of America. Hall led down the first length and was still in front 15 metres out. Finally Thorpe's size-17 feet, plus immense determination, took effect and he touched first by nineteen-hundredths of a second. Victory was no more than poetic justice, for Hall had boasted that the Americans would 'smash the Australians like a guitar'. Australia gambled on opening with Michael Klim, their fastest man, and he swam his leg in 48.18, three-hundredths of a second inside the world record. Thorpe and Hall launched themselves on the final leg almost level and at the turn Hall was almost half a second in front. It was character as much as quality that the young Australian revealed in overhauling him. The defending US team had swum over a second inside the old world record, yet were still beaten by Australia's 3:13.67. 'Those last 20 metres were just a blur,' said the heroic Thorpe.

It was a resounding anti-climax, therefore, when van den Hoogenband inflicted defeat in the individual 200m freestyle. This was not on the planned Australian schedule, and the Dutchman doubled the domestic pain by first stealing Thorpe's 200m world record in the semi-final, then repeating it in the final to win by almost half a second. Thorpe's error was to overspend his strength during the first three lengths; it was his first defeat in two years at either 200m or 400m. 'I know I gave it my best shot,' Thorpe said. 'This is the Olympic Games and I'm privileged to be swimming here. It's an opportunity that so few people have. A great athlete beat me.' It should not have been a complete surprise, for van den Hoogenband had won six gold medals in the previous year's European championships. When he now beat Alexander Popov in the 100m, to deny the Russian the chance of three consecutive Games' doubles of 50m and 100m titles, some of the post-race questioning turned nasty. Was he clean? 'I have to provide a sample every day, sometimes two times a day,' he responded. 'It's impossible to be taking drugs.' Hall, who took the bronze behind Popov, countered the suspicions. 'You can't accuse someone of taking drugs just because they swim fast,' he said. The previous year Hall himself had tested positive for marijuana, had suffered depression and allegedly even threatened suicide.

Lenny Krayzelburg had already been included among the world's 50 most handsome men by *People* magazine before becoming the first man since 1984 to win both Olympic backstroke titles, three times breaking the Olympic record for the 200m. Hollywood, it seemed, now awaited a new Weissmuller. Eleven years earlier Krayzelburg's parents had emigrated from Odessa, Ukraine, to give their family a better life in the United States. As he collected his respective medals, his tearful mother Yelena was watching, dressed from head to toe in patriotic red, white and blue. She remembered all too well the days when there was no bread to eat in Odessa and the mood of anti-Semitism that had prevailed. It was his father Oleg who had kept Lenny on track for the Games, when as a boy he was tempted by the soft life of the States. Yet though Krayzelburg held his hand on his heart as the Stars and Stripes were played, he admitted to not feeling wholly American. 'I don't want to,' he said. 'It's important to remember where I came from, what my heritage is.'

Star of the women's events was Inge de Bruijn of the Netherlands, with three gold medals in the 50m and 100m freestyle and then the 100m butterfly. In the 100m freestyle, she had the biggest winning margin since Kristin Otto of the GDR in 1988. With two world records into the bargain, de Bruijn also aroused speculation concerning drugs, to which she responded: 'It hurts a little, but now I am on top of the world and there is nothing that can change that.' Susie O'Neill, home favourite and winner of the 200m freestyle, had been unbeaten for six years in the 200m butterfly. She was, however, denied a glowing end to a distinguished career by American Misty Hyman – named on a slightly rainy morning in Arizona – who led her from start to finish to win by 0.7 of a second with an Olympic record of 2:05.88.

Rounding up events in the pool were diving and water polo. Mingxia Fu of China had retired at 18. In Atlanta she had retained the diving platform title and won the springboard – three gold medals before she could legally drink in an Australian

The two Koreas join hands for the opening ceremony. (© IOC)

bar. She then quit diving for Qinghua University in Beijing to study economics, but made a comeback 'just for fun' to retain the springboard title, her fourth, to rank alongside Greg Louganis and Pat McCormick. Additionally, she won silver as half of a pair in the inaugural synchronised diving discipline. It was Fu who once said austerely to some questioner: 'The only exercise I don't like is the one I can't do.'

There is nothing a Hungarian likes better, beyond the more normal mortal pleasures, than beating Russia at water polo. They did it in 1956 at Melbourne, weeks after the Soviet crushing of the Budapest revolt, and they did it again now with a 13–6 rout in which Tibor Benedek scored four goals.

In Barcelona, America's 'Dream Team' of Michael Jordan, Magic Johnson and the rest – the first professional all-stars to grace the Olympics – had charmed the public. In Sydney, however, this had become the 'Mean Team', charming no one as they moved edgily to a final victory over France by 85–75, following an equally uncertain semi-final over Lithuania. Shaquille O'Neal and other leading players from the NBA had stayed at home, and what was effectively a B-team brought only B-class sportsmanship to Sydney, with the vain introspection of men such as Vince Carter and Kevin Garnett.

Since 1972 Cuba have won more gold medals in boxing – 27 – than any other nation in the same period. In Sydney, Guillermo Rigondeaux (bantamweight), Mario Kindelan (lightweight), Jorge Gutierrez (middleweight) and Félix Savón (heavyweight) continued the trend. Only Gutierrez had a close fight. For Savón it was his third consecutive title, matching the record of his countryman Teofilo Stevenson, though Savón was in his usual sombre mood before, during and after his notable achievement, defeating southpaw Sultanahmed Ibzagimov of Russia by a 21–14 margin. Savón was once offered a contract by that dubious impresario Don King but preferred to retain the questionable benefits of a favoured amateur in Cuba. To accept King's enticement would have necessarily entailed defection.

343

Start and finish. Simon Whitfield (CAN) with arms raised at the finish of the inaugural men's triathlon. (both © Getty Images/Pretty)

Stephanie Cook (GBR) completes cross-country run to take the first women's modern pentathlon title. (© Getty Images/Fortser)

No sport was more suited to the ambience of Sydney than the inaugural Olympic triathlon competitions. And few favourites were more established than Simon Lessing of Britain, four times men's world champion. In the cruel tradition that haunts some red-hot favourites, however, he was to finish a minute behind the winner, Simon Whitfield of Canada, whose quality as a runner carried him to victory over the third discipline, cross-country, following the draining demands of the first two. He overhauled Stephan Vuckovic of Germany in the finishing straight, with Jan Rehula of the Czech Republic taking the bronze. A luckless Lessing finished ninth in a sport where mental calculation during the different challenges of a 1.5km swim in open water, a 40km cycle ride and a 10km cross-country run are ever conflicting during almost two hours of sustained endurance. Lessing had emerged second as he left the water, only to lose his rhythm during the cycle ride. Yet, if he had forfeited his previously unrivalled status, the credibility of this splendid modern sport was emphatically established.

So too was the inaugural modern pentathlon for women, as Stephanie Cook of Britain surged to triumph. Having put her medical career on hold temporarily to be a full-time competitor, she had been lying fourteenth after three events and eighth after four. Now came her strongest discipline, the 3km cross-country. Starting 49 seconds behind Emily de Riel of America, in the staggered system that makes the first home the overall winner, she had moved to the front with 400 metres remaining. Her

biggest influence, she said, was Eric Liddell, the Scottish sprinter whose place in history was secured for all time by the film *Chariots of Fire*. Dimitri Svatkowsky of Russia coming from fifth place on the cross-country section was the men's winner.

It is argued that the provision of a random pool of unknown horses – a perplexity for the individual competitor that is part of modern pentathlon's appeal – could prove a deterrent against the continuation of the sport. In conventional equestrianism, also a sport for a minority of nations, riders bring their own mount at vast expense, though not on this occasion for the Australians, who won their third successive victory in the three-day event; it was a third gold for 47-year-old Andrew Hoy, who thus joined Dawn Fraser at the top of his country's list of all-time winners.

Alex Karelin, Russian Greco-Roman wrestler, suffers his first defeat in 13 years at the hands at Rulon Gardner (USA). (© Getty Images/Strickland)

A defeat as unpredictable as that of Lessing was Alex Karelin's in the super-heavyweight category of Greco-Roman wrestling. The Russian was unbeaten in 13 years and bidding for his fourth Olympic title; a man of such formidable strength that he once carried a large refrigerator, unaided, up eight flights of stairs at his Siberian home when the elevator was out of action. His downfall came in the meeting with Rulon Gardner, youngest of nine children of a Mormon family, whose great-great-grandfather had sired forty-nine children with eleven wives. Almost as huge as Karelin, for much of his early life Gardner had been mocked, called 'Fatso' at school. His training on a Utah farm, carrying new-born calves on his shoulders in mid-winter, gave him the upper-body strength now to halt the Siberian bear, a vice-like grip and a single penalty-point margin against Karelin bringing Gardner victory in front of an astonished audience that included Vladimir Putin.

Twelve years after his first gold medal – the cycling team pursuit in Seoul – at the age of 34, Vyacheslav Yekimov of Russia surprised the field to win the time-trial, for which the more famous Lance Armstrong (USA), already twice Tour de France champion, and Jan Ullrich (GER), once the winner, were the commanding favourites. During the current season Yekimov had been subsidiary to Armstrong on the professional US Postal Team, but now the American was relegated to third place behind Ullrich. However, the latter was champion in the road race event, ahead of his Deutsche Telekom teammates Alex Vinokourov from Kazakhstan and Jens Voigt. There were allegations that the Telekom team had breached Olympic ethics by riding tactically as a group. And why not, some would say. The women's road race went to Leontien Zijlaard of the Netherlands, who distinguished herself by winning three titles during the Games.

Unfamiliar scribes denigrate beach volleyball as an excuse to present scantily dressed women to the television audience. Ignored is the considerable fitness required to leap endlessly in soft sand, while the tactics of the game are comparable if not superior to doubles play in tennis. Never mind the bikini gear, there was wild celebration at Bondi when Kerri Pottharst and Nathalie Cook defeated the world's number one pair from Brazil, Adriana Behar and Shelda Bede, by 12–11, 12–10, after being 7–3 down in the first set. In the conventional game, Cuba's women won their third successive gold medal, defeating Russia 3–2, while Yugoslavia's men defeated Russia 3–0, having lost to them 3–1 in the qualifying round-robin.

Norway's women were surprise winners of the football title against a United States team that had regarded victory as a formality, while Cameroon completed a double when adding the men's title, in the defeat of Spain, to that in the African Nations Cup.

Amid the political overtones of the baseball final, the United States defeated Cuba 4–0, having introduced professionals for the first time, yet having lost to Cuba 6–1 during a preliminary match. Asian rivalry was decided in South Korea's favour when defeating Japan 3–1 for the bronze medal.

New generations of Aborigine spirits emerge from the deserts during *Awakening*, a masque in Sydney's opening ceremony, while a congregation of desert women chant 'Inma Kungkarankalpa', the Dance of the Seven Emu Sisters. (© Getty Images/Squire)

CHAPTER LXX

China-Bound

Zhen-liang Hé of China, IOC Vice-President, 1989–93

'At the IOC's 112th Session at Moscow in July 2001, Beijing was elected as host city of the XXIXth Olympic Summer Games of 2008, out-distancing Toronto, the runner-up, by a record 34 votes. In spite of some disapproving noises during Beijing's bidding process, the majority of the IOC members strongly approved, through their vote, the honouring of Beijing with the privilege of hosting the Games. Why?

I think the reason is simple: most of the members were convinced that the time had come to grant the Games to the most populous nation in the world. The staging of the Games in China will not only constitute an excellent opportunity to bring the ambience and spirit of the Games directly to 1.3 billion Chinese people, but also to demonstrate the valuable role which the Olympic Movement plays in promoting, through the Games, the development of the host country and even the whole world economically, culturally and socially.

Indeed, the 2008 Olympic Games will serve as a catalyst for furthering reform and the liberalisation process in China. Coupled with the far-reaching impact of China's access to the World Trade Organisation, China's economy will become more closely linked internationally. Obviously, this effect will go beyond the confines of the region: it will be a milestone in world development. The Olympic Games of 1964 in Tokyo marked the take-off of the Japanese economy and brought about a change in the world economic map. The Games of 1988 in Seoul signalled that the economy of South Korea had entered the global arena. The Games of 2008 in Beijing will inevitably assist the progress of all societies and provide a more beneficial environment for China's social emancipation.

The promotion that the Games will bring to sports in China will be comprehensive. At Sydney, Chinese athletes made an outstanding achievement, gaining 59 medals, including 28 gold. The Beijing Games will unquestionably promote elite sports in China. Yet more important, it will enhance the perception of sport amongst Chinese people, promote sport throughout the nation at grass-roots level and bring healthy sporting activity into the lives of many ordinary people. It is coincidental that the sports industry of China will also gain lift-off from this basement. As was stated in the report of the IOC's Evaluation Commission, the Beijing Games will leave a unique legacy to China and to sport.'*
(Photograph © IOC/Locatelli)

At the 112th Session in Moscow the future direction of the IOC was critically determined by voting on two issues: first, whether the world's largest nation should be awarded the Games in the face of political opposition; second, three days later, who should succeed Juan Antonio Samaranch as President. An unfortunate complication of the two decisions being scheduled for the same Session was that the outcome of the first could have some bearing on the second. The five bidding cities were Beijing, Istanbul, Paris, Osaka and Toronto. The five presidential candidates were, alphabetically, Anita DeFrantz (USA), Dr Un Yong Kim (South Korea), Richard Pound (Canada), Dr Jacques Rogge (Belgium) and Pal Schmidt (Hungary). On the second issue, Rogge, Pound and Kim were viewed as favourites. Yet, human nature being what it is, the members might resist voting twice on the same day for the same continent and on that theory the election of Toronto could damage the prospects of Pound, that of Paris could harm Rogge and that of Beijing could affect Kim.

The credentials of Beijing were identical to what they had been eight years earlier when the city had narrowly lost to Sydney: immense potential, sporting and economic, which could not be continuously ignored, and the powerful if unofficial support then and now again by Samaranch, Pound and others. Moreover, the Olympic Games are not the games of the 'free world', but the Games of the world. If the Chinese are eligible to participate, by definition they are eligible to play host. Right-wing opposition in the US was now muted when the Bush administration decided not to take a high-profile position, Secretary of State Colin Powell observing that, if elected, Beijing would get 'seven years of supervision by the international community'.

Paris was possibly the last potential site for a romantic, city-centre Games, based adjacent to the new Stade de France, a ten-minute metro ride from the Champs-Elysées. The bid was not helped by unwisely deciding to play the human rights card against Beijing. Toronto's bid was superior to that defeated by Atlanta for the Centenary Games but was undermined by a racist gaffe by Mayor Mel Lastman that incensed African and much Asian support. In a petty piece of ethics-mongering in the rampant post-Salt Lake mood of correctness, Charmaine Crooks, Canadian Olympian and member of the Ethics Commission, was forced to resign because of her natural support for Toronto. And under the new Code of Practice, no IOC member from the country of a bidding city was permitted to vote while that city was still in contention.

In the event, the decision was quick and clear-cut in favour of Beijing, with Paris plunged into self-recrimination when pushed into fourth place by Istanbul in the first round. The voting figures round by round were:

	I	II
Beijing	44	56
Istanbul	17	9
Osaka	6	–
Paris	15	18
Toronto	20	22

The outcome met with general international approval, most predictably from the financial press. 'For Beijing, winning its Olympic bid is the beginning, not the end, of its quest for normalcy,' stated the *Wall Street Journal*. 'Most comparisons made by critics have been with the 1936 Games in Nazi

ABOVE: A decisive vote in favour of Beijing, at their second attempt, to host the Games of 2008.
BELOW: Zhen-liang Hé being congratulated by Juan Antonio Samaranch. (both © IOC/Locatelli)

Germany or with the 1980 Games in Communist Moscow. The more immediate parallel may be with the 1988 Games in Seoul . . . Plainly, the South Koreans in the 1980s, like the Chinese today, hoped that winning the Olympics would help to mitigate their pariah status.' The *Financial Times* of Britain editorialised: 'The IOC took the right decision . . . even if the balance between [Beijing] reformists and conservatives remains fluid. Intelligent engagement can influence the balance towards reform.'

There were early illustrations of the significance of the vote. While the IOC would provide a billion dollars from television rights and sponsorship for the Beijing organising committee, TOP sponsors such as Coca-Cola, Kodak, Schlumberger-Sema and Swatch quickly renewed their contracts. Beijing gave promises to embody the concept of a 'Green, Cultural and Scientific Olympics', with massive investment in communication technology throughout the country and the creation of a national lottery from which $121 million, out of an income of $340 million, would go to the Games project, for which gross investment, including structural city development, would be $22 billion. Samaranch, the imminently retiring President, observed: 'The IOC did the world a favour. This will change China.'

There were unsatisfactory overtones to the presidential election on account of hyper-sensitive 'conduct' directions issued by the Ethics Commission three and a half months beforehand that were overheated in the pursuit of correctness. For a start, they could not be consistent in application on account of the differing official hats worn by the five candidates, which could enable them, in conducting other legitimate ex-officio responsibilities, to bypass some of the Ethics Commission's intended limitations. One of the most perverse of these was Instruction 1, Item 6, prohibiting members saying in any form who they were supporting: a literal ban on conversation. As a consequence of this, Kevan Gosper, for example, found himself reprimanded, in a personal letter from Keba M'Baye, chairman of the Commission, for having said to the Associated Press that he supported Pound. In the long term, ethics attitudes were going to need revision if the Commission was not to appear like an arm of the KGB or the McCarthyism of the 1950s.

There was a major blunder when the manifesto of Richard Pound, permitted by the regulations, improperly appeared on the IOC's website. If the manifesto was legitimate, surely everyone was entitled to know what it contained? There was also the rumour, which Pound quickly denied, that his campaign was being bankrolled by the Royal Bank of Canada – this was part of the mood of mistrust that began to surround the approach to the election. The attitude of the retiring President involved endless speculation. Did he support Kim, his right-hand man in the creation of a brilliant Games in Seoul; or Pound, mastermind in the acquisition of billions of dollars in sponsorship; or Rogge, whom he had appointed Coordination Commission chairman for both Sydney 2000 and Athens 2004? Indications were that Samaranch was clandestinely lobbying for Rogge. The clear outsiders were DeFrantz, president of the US Amateur Athletic Foundation, and Schmidt, Hungarian Ambassador in Spain, the former complaining that, based in America, she was inhibited by the Ethics regulations from communicating with potential supporters in Europe, Africa and Asia.

The main limitation for Pound, Montreal QC and the sharpest intellect within the Olympic Movement, was his forthright, sometimes insensitive manner towards lesser IOC colleagues, who felt intimidated by his intellectual grasp and the administrative power granted to him over a 20-year period by

Richard Pound, Montreal QC, regarded by many as the brightest brain in the IOC, yet leaving some uncomfortably in awe. (© IOC/Locatelli)

Samaranch. That power, controversially, had included chairing the Ad Hoc Commission investigating Salt Lake improprieties. Had that been a calculated poisoned chalice? It was always going to be a long shot for a North American to gain enough votes and the author claims no special foresight in having predicted in London's *Sunday Telegraph* that, in the first round, Pound would garner 20 votes to Rogge's 45: accurate to the extent that Rogge gained 46.

The most contentious issue of the run-in was Dr Kim's repetition, in an interview 48 hours beforehand, of his manifesto statement that IOC members should receive financial assistance for running an office within their own country for promotion of IOC interests; which, indeed, is their duty. Putting a figure of $50,000 a year on this principle – in total a minor item for the IOC – Kim was construed as having offered a bribe to voters. Clearly the timing of his comments was unfortunate and the consequence was a public reprimand prior to the vote. It was alleged that this reprimand had been precipitated by a letter to the Ethics Commission from Crown Prince Willem, the Netherlands' new member. Subsequently Prince Willem stated that he had never named an individual candidate, that he was surprised at the Commission's immediate action regarding Dr Kim and that he, Prince Willem, indeed approved of financial compensation to members 'to limit further possibilities of other illegal and unethical funding'. At the time, informed sources were suggesting that potential voting support for Kim was sufficient to press Rogge harder than was expected. However, the formal reprimand, in conjunction with lingering memories of the Salt Lake affair involving Kim's son, John, was sufficient to impede any threat he might have posed. 'Whether members should be financially supported is an ongoing issue within the Executive Board,' Rogge would later say, but Kim's timing was not good. Yet I believe this played no role in the outcome of the vote. Insiders, not least Rogge himself, knew that the likely percentages would be 60–20–20, which, in the event, they were:

	DeFrantz	Kim	Pound	Rogge	Schmidt
I	9	21	20	46	11
II	–	23	22	59	6

Pound and Kim were both dismayed, not to say offended, not just by the result but also the margin. Kim quit the conference

hall for his hotel room and was not seen again prior to returning home. Both men detected the hand of the retiring President at work – a right which they did not constitutionally oppose. Pound, indignant, gave Rogge an immediate letter of resignation from all his positions in the IOC, including chairman of the Marketing Commission. He later reflected: 'The new President had to be able to found a new team with his own people, so I think it would be normal to resign in these circumstances. I didn't want him to feel uncomfortable. And such resignations are fair play and good corporate practice in the business world.' Kim said:

> I didn't mind losing but felt there were elements that were less than fair. My contention is that IOC members should uphold the authority of the organisation but need financial assistance in order properly to do so. Whatever I have done [such as achieving the joint march of Korean teams in Sydney], I have always allowed Samaranch to carry the flower of the achievement. At one time we had been the closest of friends.

An ironic aspect of any in-house antagonism towards Kim is that he had been a substantial personal benefactor of the Olympic Movement. In 2001 and 2002 he had made donations of $100,000 to the International Olympafrica Foundation. Anita DeFrantz was succinct in her analysis of her poor showing. 'I lost because I was American and because I was a woman,' she said.

Anita DeFrantz (USA), the IOC's foremost woman member and presidential candidate in 2001: 'I lost because I was American and because I was a woman.' (© IOC/Locatelli)

The Session was required to hold a number of elections, including those of new members. The acceptance of Els van Breda Vriesman of Holland (president of hockey), Randhir Singh of India (NOC member), Timothy Fok of Hong Kong, China (NOC member), John Coates of Australia (NOC member) and Issa Hayatou of Cameroon (individual member) were voted through almost as a matter of course, though some disapproval of Coates was registered. However, the retiring President also sought for his son, Juan Antonio Samaranch Jr, to be elected as an individual member from Spain. Though the son had done valuable work for the modern pentathlon union, his father's closest friends advised him there would inevitably be accusations of nepotism. In spite of this, father insisted and son was elected, though with a number of counter-votes and

Dr Jacques Rogge, always the favourite, is roundly congratulated as he becomes the eighth IOC President. (© IOC/Locatelli)

objectives as the new President, Rogge cited: support for women's sports participation and management; continued protection of the environment; support for the International Olympic Academy and the Olympic Museum; humanitarian actions built around the practice of sport; creation of an International Olympic Truce Foundation, backed by governments; less expensive Games; less expensive Sessions and Commission meetings; a more balanced IOC membership across the continents; more interactive Sessions in the debate between Executive Board and members; and a review of the role of members as ambassadors within their own country.

The continental balancing of members would indeed be difficult. The underlying strength of Rogge's successful election campaign had been the efficiency of the backing from the European majority led by Mario Pescante of Italy. Rogge, as an Olympian, transparently wished to embrace all factors in open government, to introduce change from the all-powerful government of Samaranch. But as the *International Herald Tribune* observed: 'To be inclusive without projecting weakness will be Rogge's challenge.'

The inclusivity began with the decision, in spite of Pound's abrupt resignations, to retain the Canadian as chairman of WADA. Yet scarcely had Rogge demonstrated his valuation of Pound's involvement than Pound wrote a precipitate letter, regarding the election, to all the IOC's leading sponsors. However factually correct, it was a provocative action. Pound's frank letter – in fact leaked by the sponsors themselves – stated that: the IOC was not as committed to the reform process as he had hoped; the new President reflected the personal choice of Samaranch (though he, Pound, had no objection to the new man); the person who finished second (Kim) had received severe warnings for improper conduct in the Salt Lake affair; the other person who also received a serious warning ran, unopposed, for the position of Vice-President (Vitaly Smirnov); the person most identified

abstentions. In resistance to a fifth IOC member from Switzerland, the proposal for Adolph Ogi, former president of the Swiss Federation, failed.

The size of the task confronting the new President only time would measure. In the post-scandal environment, he was the ideal palliative: orthopaedic surgeon, former Olympic yachtsman, with some commercial background from his involvement in the development of Belgian NOC finances, yet free of any politico-social labels or private agendas that might be difficult baggage. Though he might say in his acceptance speech 'from Juan Antonio Samaranch, I learned the politics of sport', just how much he understood of politics of the geographic forces of self-interest, which endlessly tore at the heart of the Olympic community, was yet to be discovered. At the end of his eight-year term he would be eligible for re-election if he wished, a year after Beijing 2008. The responsibility for the tranquil running of those Games, not to mention Athens 2004, would have tested his diplomacy and tact to the limit. His presidency of European NOCs (EOC) had suggested he was equal to the demands. It would be a tough agenda: enforcing, and possibly adjusting, the IOC's structural and ethical reforms; containing and even reducing the size and cost of the Games; and ensuring the democracy and transparency of all the functions within the Olympic Movement, which attract a wholly disproportionate element of media attention on account of the exceptional contemporary status of the Games.

It was relevant that, like his predecessor, he too would be supported by his wife: Anne Rogge, also a doctor, a woman of poise and tranquillity like the late Maria Therese Samaranch, albeit that she had been a student demonstrator at the Sorbonne during 1968. He would, like Samaranch, base himself at Lausanne, an essential for the IOC's unpaid CEO. In listing his

Active President. Jacques Rogge, four-time Olympian, shows his style on the water. (© IOC)

with solving the Salt Lake misdemeanours, for funding the Olympic Movement over 20 years and for leading the fight against doping [i.e. Pound] had fared worst in the election; lastly, that the first- and second-place candidates in the election had campaigned on the premise that the Games were over-commercialised, which he, Pound, regarded as unsupportive of the ideals of the Olympic Movement, the Olympic Games being less visibly commercialised than any other major sport. The tone of the letter shocked some of Pound's IOC colleagues, and there was further controversy in September when it was revealed that, throughout his time as head of marketing and the Finance Commission, he, or rather his Montreal law firm, had been receiving, in lieu of his hundreds of hours' work in the interests of the IOC, an annual fee believed to be in excess of $200,000. In fact, his altruism towards the IOC had lost Pound money: the $200,000 was not included in the total from which his firm paid bonuses, while Pound himself was penalised in his salary for his absences. By sharp comparison, the president of one IF personally made several million dollars from negotiating his sport's television contract. Besides Samaranch, the Finance Commission knew of Pound's payment from the IOC's 'consulting account': a fee wholly proper, in recognition and compensation for Pound's time and expertise, but a payment that should have been more openly declared, the more so since Pound was regularly voicing the importance of the *honorary* work of his colleagues.

Rogge remained undemonstrative in the light of these revelations, but by December had taken the decision to appoint Gerhard Heiberg, Norwegian head of the Lillehammer organising committee seven years earlier, as chairman of the Marketing Commission; this was believed to be after Jean-Claude Killy had rejected the post. Pound's reservations were met by the new President not with resentment but with polite compliments for past services; though, as Pound would caustically observe, having run the programme for over 17 years he was 'not once subsequently asked for comment or advice'. With his departure, the IOC decided expensively to buy out full control of the Meridien Agency, thereby ill-advisedly, in Pound's opinion, removing the buffer between themselves and their sponsors.

In early 2000, Samaranch, prompted by a report from Rogge as chairman of the Coordination Commission, had issued a sharp warning to the Athens organising committee on lack of progress, particularly on the absence of important decisions, never mind that the committee, ATHOC, had been revitalised by the re-appointment as chairman of the successful bidding leader Gianna Angelopoulos-Daskalaki. A year later there was still anxiety, with warnings that essential construction projects were suffering repeated delays. Denis Oswald of Switzerland, who had replaced Rogge as Coordination Chairman, gave ATHOC a deadline of 21 November to produce a construction timetable and expressed surprise that some projects had even been cancelled, including a linking road between the Olympic Village and the main sports complex. On receipt of the deadline, Angelopoulos-Daskalaki held an emergency meeting with Greek premier Kostas Simitis, amid reports that she was on the point of resignation. Although Simitis had appointed her the previous year following the IOC's warning, relations remained unstable between her and the socialist government.

Another major complaint of Oswald's was the continuing lack of hotel space, the majority of available rooms being scheduled for the Olympic family. Further anxiety was a row between town officials of Marathon and ATHOC, on the decision to switch the canoe and kayak centre from the Marathon beachfront to the site of the old international airport south of the city. Following his complaints, Oswald was able to report to the IOC Session in Salt Lake that there was fresh acceleration in the Athens preparation; though no one familiar with the city would be convinced that all was well until the Games were actually over.

Prior to the Salt Lake Session of 2002, Rogge, at the time of his first official meeting with Sepp Blatter, president of FIFA, in 2001, announced a call for an Olympic Truce during the Winter Games. Both Rogge and Blatter affirmed that the two major sporting events of the following year, the Winter Games and the Korea/Japan World Cup, would be unaffected by security and political concerns in the wake of the terrorism of 11 September 2001.

However, on the occasion of presiding over his first Session the following February, Rogge encountered the first rumblings of discontent. He had spoken at its opening of a priority being the implementation of reforms adopted at the 110th Session in 1999. Yet when the new Conflict of Interest Rules, drawn up by the Ethics Commission, were presented to the members, there was concerted resistance from the floor, the complaint being that they went too far and would make the legitimate activities of many members impossible, quite apart from complexities of enforcement. Craig Reedie of Britain led the opposition and was supported by Tay Wilson of New Zealand and others. '[The Ethics draft] goes much further than some members want it to go. I am wondering if we're creating a huge amount of work and the Ethics Commission will be snowed under,' Wilson said. 'I'm disappointed that we have so little confidence in ourselves that we need an Ethics Commission to tell us how to act.' As another member complained: 'The rules are so badly drafted, it means that if I have shares in Coca-Cola and Coke is the sponsor of the Games then I am in a position of conflict of interest. That is ridiculous.' Richard Pound, while claiming the rules were a sound start, stressed there were problems for members who were also representatives of IFs and NOCs. Among the complaints was the banning of visits to bid cities, the focal point of the scandal that the IOC had only recently survived. Conscious of the emotional temperature of the Session, Rogge deferred further debate to an Extraordinary Session to be staged in November 2002 in Mexico. 'The Executive will fine-tune these rules,' a conciliatory Rogge promised. The Session additionally discussed the possibility of moving some Summer disciplines, such as boxing, gymnastics, judo and weightlifting, to the Winter Games schedule and the trimming of events from some over-endowed sports such as swimming.

As proof that relations were no longer strained between Rogge and Pound, the Canadian had accepted the post of chairman of the 'Olympic Studies Commission', responsible for streamlining the financial structure and logistics of a Games' 16-day schedule. In aligning his forces in the various commissions, Rogge had appointed – besides Heiberg in Marketing – Hein Verbruggen of Holland, president of international cycling, as chairman of the Beijing Coordination Committee; Oswald and Killy as respective Coordination chairmen for Athens 2004 and Turin 2006; Richard Carrión, Puerto Rican banker, as chairman of the Finance Commission; Thomas Bach as chairman of both Juridical and Sport-and-Law Commissions, in succession to the retiring Judge M'Baye; and Mario Vazquez Raña as provisional chairman of the Solidarity Commission (a Charter alteration would be required to remove that post from the IOC President). Prince de Mérode, Dr Kim, Anita DeFrantz and Kevan Gosper continued in their roles as respective heads of the Medical, Television, Women's and Press Commissions.

The resignation as athletes' member by Olympic javelin champion Jan Zelezny, for the reason that IOC responsibilities interfered with competition, required approval of his replacement, Matthew Pinsent of Britain, long-time winning partner of oarsman Sir Steve Redgrave. New athlete members elected were Pernilla Wiberg (Sweden), Jari Kurri (Finland) and Adne Sondral (Norway). New members also elected were HRH Prince Abdul Aziz of Saudi Arabia (NOC), Kikis Lazarides of Cyprus (NOC), Yong Sung Park of South Korea (IFs), Patrick Chamunda of Zambia (individual), Sheikh Tamim Al-Thani of Qatar (NOC), Sandra Baldwin of America (NOC), Kai Holm of Denmark (individual), Francois Narmon of Belgium (NOC) and Youssoupha Ndiaye of Senegal (individual). This brought the total current membership to 131.

suspensions. With the CAS ruling seen as perverse, it was proposed to alter the Charter the following November. There was controversy between the IOC and SLOC over the wish for US competitors to parade the Ground Zero flag from 11 September, an issue mishandled by Games chief Mitt Romney and subsequently resolved with the IOC, as Director-General Carrard said, 'as a gesture of respect to the victims and heroes'.

The Salt Lake City Games were to cost $1.9 billion, which together with state transportation improvements would raise the total to $3 billion. Television, sponsorship and ticket sales would be sufficient to cover the operational costs. The whole exercise, in the words of Dick Ebersol, chief sports executive of NBC, 'is the equivalent of putting on seven Super Bowls'. Pushing up the cost was the additional $55 million added to the security budget following 11 September: 15,000 additional law enforcement and military personnel spread over 900 square miles, including 22 weapons and medical specialists from the Weapons of Mass Destruction Civil Support Team from Buckley airforce base, trained to respond to biological, chemical or nuclear attacks. Yet Romney, his self-confidence at times abrasive, would be able to boast a Games profit of $56 million, with a donation of $10 million handed to USOC. In the face of terrorist potential, the support of sponsors had remained strong. Corporate America made possible the profit, the scandal of 1999 and the catastrophe of 2001 if anything adding a commercial determination to continue investment in the Games. It was well rewarded. For a month, Campbell's soup sold like water in the desert. David D'Allessandro, chairman of TOP sponsor John Hancock, who had even removed the Olympic rings from the company's stationery in the wake of the scandal, was sufficiently impressed by the Games' success to extend the contract up to Beijing 2008, at a cost of $50 million, in the light of the IOC's reforms. The Russian team, which had become dependent directly after the collapse of Communism on Western sponsorship, was now funded predominantly by home sponsorship, notably RusAl, the world's second-largest aluminium producer.

Mitt Romney, head of the organising committee, had the innovative idea of inviting eight living legends to carry the flag at the Opening Ceremony, representing the five continents and the three pillars of the Olympic Movement, sport culture and environment: Jean-Claude Killy for sport, Steven Spielberg for culture and Jean-Michel Cousteau for environment; astronaut John Glenn representing Americas; Lech Walesa, Nobel Laureate, Europe; Archbishop Desmond Tutu, Nobel Laureate, Africa; Kazuyoshi Funaki, 1998 ski jump champion, Asia; and Cathy Freeman, who had lit the Sydney flame, Oceania. At the conclusion of his first Games as President, Rogge proclaimed the event 'outstanding, the best I have seen'. NBC's opening ceremony ratings had surpassed those for the Summer Games in Sydney and of CBS's for the previous Winter Games in Nagano.

On the downside was the fact that yet again every foreigner was either embarrassed or irritated by the rampant American media chauvinism. George W. Bush breached protocol when declaring the Games open 'on behalf of a proud, determined and grateful nation'. In the space of five months the American people seemed wholly to have forgotten what they had temporarily begun to acknowledge on 11 September: that while the immense achievements of the nation over two centuries are regarded with admiration and not a little envy, there are many who find US triumphalism unacceptable.

Tay Wilson of New Zealand: 'I'm disappointed that we have so little confidence in ourselves that we need an Ethics Commission to tell us how to act.' (© IOC/Imsand)

Jim Easton (USA) was elected fourth Vice-President, defeating Paul Henderson of Canada by a 52–32 vote.

Eight cities declared themselves candidates for the Winter Games of 2010: Andorra; Berne, Switzerland; Harbin, China; Jaca, Spain; Pyeongchang, South Korea; Salzburg, Austria; Sarajevo, Bosnia-Herzegovina, previously host in 1984; and Vancouver, Canada. These eight applicants would be trimmed by the Executive Board, the final selection by the members to be in Prague in July 2003.

When Samaranch retired at the Moscow Session, there had been widespread supposition that he might be a permanent shadow at Rogge's shoulder, having been granted the status of Honorary Life President, with continuing secretarial and accommodation facilities in Lausanne and the post of president of the Museum. On a visit to the Salt Lake Session prior to the Winter Games to pay his respects to former colleagues – the only Session or Executive Board meeting he had visited since retiring – the 81-year-old Samaranch related that he had been so ill the previous July he thought he was close to death. He had now recovered his health and again assured members that he would not intervene in Rogge's authority: 'I think I was not a bad President. Now I have to try to be an excellent ex-President – which means no intervening.' Pound cryptically observed that 'there's nothing so past as a past President'.

There was a minor reverse for Rogge when the CAS had rejected, prior to the opening of the Games, the Executive Board's decision to ban Latvian bobsledder Sandis Prusis for a positive test. The bobsleigh federation had imposed a three-month retroactive ban but this was overruled by the Executive Board for being contrary to the intention of testing by timing the ban so that Prusis could compete. CAS ruled that the IOC had contravened their own Charter, which allowed IFs autonomy on

CHAPTER LXXI

Salt Lake City (XIX) 2002

Janica Kostelic of Croatia, unique winner of four Olympic Alpine medals in one Games

'I'd competed in all five Alpine events at Nagano at the age of 16, my best position being eighth in the combined. The following season I had my first World Cup victory, on my 17th birthday, though I don't remember much about it, and came seventh in the combined in the World Championships. In most events I knew I was lacking power. The next season I won a couple of World Cup slaloms, but then crashed and injured my knee at St Moritz in December '99 – my first serious injury, and a bad one. I just thought, "That's normal." I was soon back in action, though I was having quite a lot of pain. Two months after my 19th birthday I won the overall World Cup title, but at the end of that season I needed three operations on my knee and I guess some of the problem is still there.

Growing up in skiing has been so much a family thing: training with my brother Ivica, being coached by my father, my mum always being there on the sideline. I have no emotional difficulty having my dad, Ante, as my coach. I like him as a coach because he's my father, because he knows me better than anyone. My father doesn't argue with me or my opinions, but he's always right!

The victory I enjoyed most at Salt Lake was the combined because that started the sequence. If I hadn't won that, I probably wouldn't have won the others, it gave me confidence. In recent World Cup events I'd not skied well and had been injured. When I then came second in the super-G, I'd never expected it, not even any medal, so I was really surprised. This meant I was under no pressure now for the slalom – I already had two medals and could just go out and enjoy the race. The last of the four, the giant slalom, was really fun. I wasn't specially thinking of a fourth medal and anyway someone will beat that record at another Games, it's not a big deal.

There were thousands waiting at the airport when I got home to Zagreb, giving me a welcome I could never have dreamed of. I hope I still have lots more races, maybe another two Olympics. They are the biggest challenge of all, always. As a kid I felt that. A World Championships is never so special a place, it's just one of a World Cup series.'*

(Photograph © IOC/De Marichard)

Janica Kostelic's story is particularly unusual. Her spectacular emergence was achieved against a background of family hardship, of two recoveries from injury while still a teenager and current loss of form. The reception she received on returning home surpassed that for the national football team when they brought back the bronze medal from the 1998 World Cup. There was the extraordinary sight during the giant slalom, the last of her four events at Snowbasin, Salt Lake City, of her coming down the slope like a ballerina and wearing almost the whole way the broadest of smiles. We see so many equipment-promotion smiles in the finishing pan, but this was the spontaneous smile of joy. It was easy to understand. During her formative years, amid the disintegration of the former Yugoslavia, she and her brother and father, touring the race circuit, had often slept under canvas or crammed into the car when the weather was too cold. 'It's true, we had no money,' she recalls, 'but when you're a kid, you don't really bother about it. Things are a lot better now.'

Skiing with the initials I-V-I-C-A painted on the nails of her left hand, her opening victory in the combined was Croatia's first

medal at a Winter Games, upstaging Ivica who was among the favourites for the men's slalom. She beat Renate Götschl of Austria and Martina Ertl of Germany into second and third place. Throughout her young career, Kostelic had been in the top ten for the super-G and had been fourth in her last competition prior to Salt Lake. The victory of Daniela Ceccarelli of Italy was almost as much a surprise as Kostelic's silver medal. 'Impossible!' the Italian had thought to herself as she came to a halt and saw her name at the top of the leader board. With several medal contenders still to race, she felt sure someone would beat her. Even when she saw the time, 1:13.59, she momentarily thought she was only ninth, until realising that was her start number! 'So I called my husband at home, but I couldn't understand anything he was saying, he was crying so much. So I guessed I had won.' She had indeed, by five-hundredths of a second from Kostelic. Regarded as a downhill specialist, Ceccarelli had been depressed by her twentieth place in that event, went out to enjoy the super-G, and relaxation brought its reward. Her colleague Karen Putzer took the bronze medal, two-tenths behind Kostelic. The previous season, Kostelic had won eight consecutive World Cup slaloms en route to the

Rare technique, unique achievement. Janica Kostelic, Croatian superstar, overjoyed with her third gold and fourth medal from the giant slalom, celebrates with Anja Pärson (SWE), second, and Sonja Nef (SUI). (© Getty Images/Powell) (© Getty Images/Jacobsohn)

overall title. Champions in any sport are made in the mind as much as the body and when she beat Laure Pequegnot of France for her second gold medal, the Frenchwoman observed: 'She is very strong in her head.' Racing in near white-out conditions, Pequegnot, the then current World Cup slalom leader, was two-tenths behind Kostelic on the first run, with Anja Pärson of Sweden lying fourth. Pärson's second run, in worsening conditions, lifted her to third place and then Pequegnot laid down the challenge for Kostelic with an aggressive second run. The father at the finish radioed to the daughter up the mountain that her lead was in jeopardy. On the toughest course the competitors had seen all season, Kostelic was equal to the moment. It was maybe her finest performance of the Games, having had no respectable result in slalom throughout December and January.

So tough was the course that 30 out of 70 starters failed to finish either first or second run, some considering the course unfairly difficult. Kostelic thus joined four other women, Rosi Mittermaier (Germany '76), Hanni Wenzel (Liechtenstein '80), Vreni Schneider (Switzerland '88) and Katja Seizinger (Germany '98), to have won three medals in the same Games, but the youngster dismissed all talk of history – 'Not something I think about, I'm too busy skiing.'

The giant slalom, her fourth event for a third gold, was

memorable. Never previously having been on a podium for this event, she annihilated the opposition to take her place alongside legends of the past, winning by a huge margin of 1.32 seconds. She had taken a half-second lead on the morning run and could have skied conservatively on the second. Instead, she nearly tripled her margin, in spite of an early error. Going for an even faster time, she nearly lost her right ski edge but dropped further onto her left hip and just made the next gate. Her rhythm was perfect and her skis seemed never to lose touch with the ground, with an uncanny link between thigh and foot. And all the while that radiant smile. 'I wonder if she's human,' Pärson, this time silver medal winner, said. 'She's so mentally tough, nothing bothers her.' Sonja Nef of Switzerland, top-ranked in slalom, took the bronze medal. No longer was there the need for Kostelic to rummage for a Croatian flag from the car boot, as had happened at a World Cup race in Salt Lake four years earlier.

The eminence of the youthful Kostelic was matched by the 30-something Norwegian, Kjetil-André Aamodt, dominant in Alpine for a decade. Winning first the combined, he followed this with a second gold medal in the men's super-G, having first won this event at Albertville in 1992, thus collecting his seventh Alpine medal in all: a men's record. His seventeen medals from Olympics and World Championships had been gathered across all disciplines; and he now joined the three other men to have won three golds: Sailer, Killy and Alberto Tomba of Italy. No other skier, male or female, has won more than five Alpine medals.

On what was described as the most unforgiving super-G course any of the racers had encountered, Aamodt's colleague Lasse Kjus was one of the victims at the Rendezvous face, a 74-degree drop that the racers came to blind at 60 mph (100 kph), making it nearly impossible for those moving at full speed to hold on to the turn. One of those who only just survived this obstacle was Stephan Eberhalter of Austria, who recovered from an uncontrolled slide to take second place, with fellow Austrian Andreas Schifferer taking the bronze. It was an anxious wait for Aamodt, who saw one rival after another being faster down the course only to falter in that final phase of the race.

'Our sport has gangrene,' Sophie Moniotte, a recently retired French ice dancer, told Newsweek magazine. 'In most sports doping is the problem. With figure skating, it's deals and manipulation.' Never was this more evident than with the opening figure skating event, the pairs, in which Yelena Berezhnaya and Anton Sikharulidze of Russia were judged to have defeated Jamie Salé and David Pelletier of Canada. When the verdict was announced, the Canadians having drawn a warm response from a crowd of nearly 11,000, there was a storm of booing and Salé collapsed in tears. In the controversy that would drag on for several days, embracing not only the International Skating Union (ISU) and the IOC but also even President Putin of Russia, there were no clear-cut answers – then, or to the present day. While NBC commentator Scott Hamilton, men's figures champion of 1984, whipped up the furore by describing the result as disgraceful, other experts declared the Russians, skating first of the two pairs, to have won legitimately. Sikharulidze told Tass, the Russian news agency: 'Honestly speaking, we should have a skate-off.' Adding to the controversy, the Canadian pair, romantically as well as sportingly linked, alleged that after winning the previous year's World Championship they had received half a dozen answerphone messages saying they had not deserved to win – 'and would not do so at the Olympics'. The significance of the latter took harsher shape when, on the day following the event, Marie-Reine Le Gougne, the French judge, emotionally broke down at the post-competition briefing of judges. She claimed to have been put under pressure prior to the event, allegedly by the president of her own federation, to vote for the Russians as part of a supposed deal whereby the Russian judge would reciprocally support the French ice dance pair. Le Gougne insisted she had in fact voted by conscience, considering the Russians the deserving pair.

Receiving the evidence of the judges' post-mortem, the ISU knew they must investigate. The IOC, however, sensed the need for an urgent resolution. Hyper-sensitive to scandal in this of all cities, they did not wish an 'unfair' decision in the arena involving possible judging malpractice to further stain the Olympics' good name. A quick fix was required; the easiest, considered acceptable to all parties, was the sharing of first place with a second set of gold medals. Ottavio Cinquanta, president of the ISU, meanwhile revealed receipt of letters implicating Russian and French federations in improper collaboration. Among continuing official comments, President Rogge stated: 'I don't think this [second pair of gold medals] has created damage to the Olympic Movement because it was resolved quickly . . .' At the same time, Le Gougne was continuing to insist she had resisted the 'deal', claiming in an interview with French sports daily *L'Équipe* that she had made no pact. Against this, Jon Jackson, San Francisco attorney and ISU judge, alleged that Le Gougne had confronted him and Sally Stapleford, British chairwoman of the ISU technical

Vladimir Putin, having himself been savaged at home for a politically strategic alliance with the White House, saw an opportunity for counter-propaganda and asserted that the Salt Lake Games were a failure under the administrative bias and commercialism of the IOC. The Russian Liberal Democratic Party called for the team to be flown home, while Russian Aluminium, RusAl, pledged to bring legal action for loss of publicity. The emotional temperature rose even further when Larissa Lazutina, Russia's nine-time Olympic Nordic medallist, was disqualified immediately prior to the women's 20km relay because of an abnormal blood-test count in a pre-race test. There was no time to replace her in a race won by Germany and the Russian NOC joined ranks with Putin, saying they might boycott the Summer Games in Athens. After placatory intervention by Vitaly Smirnov, Russian IOC Vice-President, all parties cooled down and the withdrawal threat was forgotten. Rogge wrote a conciliatory letter to Putin, the Canadians received their gold medals, while Lazutina was allowed to retain the two silver medals won prior to the positive test. John Lucas, retired Olympic historian of Penn State University, said of Rogge: 'He's moving rapidly and making decisions as quickly as he can, recognising that speed is important in this modern age.'

Figure skating judging, always controversial, sank to a new low with the assertion by Marie-Reine Le Gougne of France that she was coerced to vote for the Russian pairs contenders.
(© AP/Bukajlo)

Jamie Salé and David Pelletier (CAN) show the style that, with IOC intervention, earned them duplicate pairs gold medals alongside the Russians. (© Getty Images/Prior) (© Getty Images/Brunskill)

committee, admitting to a deal with her federation. To the spice of the scandal was added the undercurrent of former Cold War conspiracies: the five judges who gave the gold medal to Russia were those of China, Poland, Ukraine, Russia . . . and France.

Mihir Bose of London's *Daily Telegraph* suggested that the CAS had issued an injunction preventing Le Gougne from leaving the US and requiring her fellow judges to appear before them. This was hardly a development the IOC would wish, hence the urgency for a solution. Richard Pound, notwithstanding his Canadian nationality, had urged Rogge to act. 'It's our brand they're destroying,' he said of the ISU, himself telling Cinquanta, 'You've fouled up our festival, sort it out now, this is a contrived situation, not a random error.' Following the CAS injunction, the Canadian NOC itself lodged an application with ICAS for an investigation, in order to put further pressure on the ISU.

How alarming for the future was the IOC's action? 'I see no dangerous precedent,' Rogge said at the time. 'If a judging error is made in good faith we would never seek to alter things. The result is the result. We can only act when an IF tells us there has been categoric manipulation. The ISU told us so.' Rogge was duly supported by his Executive Board colleagues, Kevan Gosper and Thomas Bach, anxious to be seen backing a new President. 'Our responsibility is to encourage IFs to protect athletes' interests,' Gosper said. 'I think this was the right thing to do. Our action was to hasten the ISU's decision.' Bach's view was that the IOC could ride with their decision so long as they were consistent. 'You cannot suspend a coach and at the same time say the result is effective,' Bach said. 'Discipline was down to the IF, the pressure from us was for speed, that something must be done before the ice dance competition in the interests of public confidence in judging.'

Inevitably, for all Rogge's confidence, questions immediately began to arise about past injustices: the US boxer Roy Jones being denied the clearest of gold medals against a South Korean in 1988 through subjective judging; Shirley Babashoff, supreme US swimmer, overpowered by GDR competitors training within an admitted systematic drugs regime. One of the worst aspects of the controversy was its shameless exploitation by NBC in the interest of their own ratings, creating and sustaining a news story partially built on political rather than sporting antagonism. On the other hand, Sikharulidze found a capitalist lining to the clouds. 'They made a free advertisement for us,' he admitted. 'We're getting invited to shows, to joint appearances with the Canadians. Our exhibition programme is sold out.'

Yet in the final analysis, Rogge would admit, a year later in an interview with George Vecsey of the *New York Times*, that the rush to award duplicate gold medals had been wrong. He had wanted to make it right for the athletes, he said. 'I should have been more proactive, should have consulted the Russians. I admit my errors.'

Amid the hue and cry, Cinquanta, himself having risen from the ranks of speed skating, but wishing to appear a president ahead of the action, announced a plan for radical revision of the judging process. Not before time. Judging had been prejudiced, nationalistic and suspected of deals as long as anyone could remember. Richard Pound, heading a new commission with a brief to revise the entire Olympic programme, promised that there would be a careful examination of all arbitrarily judged sports at Athens and Turin, the next Summer and Winter Games. Cinquanta's proposals came up for examination at the ISU's congress the following June, to be further studied in time for introduction for Turin 2006.

Some are born to greatness, others view it perennially from close range but never succeed in touching it. Sadly for Michelle Kwan, she was stranded among the latter. She had been upstaged at the Nagano Games by 15-year-old compatriot Tara Lipinski. Salt Lake was to be her moment of truth on home soil. The showdown was expected to be between the elf-like Asian-American and the sultry Irina Slutzkaya of Russia, who had come second to Kwan in three World Championships but shown repeatedly superior form over the past few seasons: Kwan the artist; Slutzkaya the technician. All seemed well for Kwan when she led after the short programme and compulsories, being marked substantially ahead of Slutzkaya for presentation while only fractionally behind on technical requirements. Kwan's father, Danny, who had accompanied her since she split from her long-time coach Frank Carroll four months before the Games, had told her to enjoy herself and that was what she seemed to be doing. She still needed to win the free programme and there was an assurance about her that seemed strong, suggesting her teenage colleagues Sasha Cohen and Sarah Hughes would have to wait their time, never mind how high the 17-year-old Cohen might jump and spin. If there was a flaw in Kwan, it was the wish for public love. Slutzkaya had no such illusions. 'You feel here a war on ice,' she said, prior to the free programme. Slutzkaya determined the outcome, but not in her own interest.

Touching something of the originality and uninhibited *joie de vivre* of Sonja Henie long ago, the bubbling 16-year-old Hughes, youngest of 27 competitors, soared from fourth place to surpass her three rivals. For the moment, she restored the face of figure skating, which with Alpine skiing is the premier sport of most Winter Games. Hughes herself had no idea that she might win, yet flawlessly completed the most difficult programme of the competition, including seven triple jumps involving two triple-combinations. With Kwan, Slutzkaya and Cohen all making errors, the door for her had opened. It was extraordinary. How can you be, at 16, a technically supreme Olympic champion yet emotionally as ordinary as apple pie? At the recent US trials she had been only third, as in the World Championships the previous

year. It was no more than a matter of months since Kwan had been her idol. Her appealing Doris Day simplicity was predicted to make her $10 million in endorsements.

It would long be argued whether Kwan's decision to dispense with Carroll, her coach since she was 11, aided her failure. The key to the free programme, however, was the pair of marks from the Finnish judge. From the other eight judges, Hughes and Slutzkaya each had four first-rank places. The Finnish judge crucially marked Hughes 5.7 for technique and 5.8 for presentation, with Slutzkaya the reverse. The 5.8 for presentation thus gave Hughes Finland's first-place vote, while Slutzkaya's overall second pushed Kwan into third-place bronze. There had been anxiety rather than assurance in Kwan's face, whereas Hughes carried the same expression of uninhibited joy as Kostelic.

Timothy Goebel of the United States became the first skater in one programme to land three quadruple jumps in the men's figure skating and this helped him to take third place behind the favourites Alexei Yagudin and Evgeni Plushenko, the Russian pair. There was no doubting Yagudin's supremacy in his intense rivalry with his compatriot. Yagudin scored a uniform 5.9 on technical merit, with four 6.0s for artistic impression. Never previously had anyone scored more than two. Plushenko had marred his chances with a heavy fall in the short programme.

In another triumph of medicine over misfortune Christine Witty from Wisconsin not only won the women's 1,000m speed skating event but did so with a world record of 1:13.83. She had not expected even to be first in her pair, in which she was drawn against two-time Olympic 500m champion Catriona LeMay-Doan. A month earlier, in Norway, Witty had been diagnosed as suffering from the debilitating virus, mononucleosis. From thereon she had been obliged to cut her training to alternate days. Ambition for the Games had been limited to a bronze medal at best. Weakened by the virus throughout the season, Witty had failed to make the podium in any World Cup event. 'On the last lap, I didn't feel any pain,' Witty said, 'and when I saw the 1:13 at the finish it really

Michelle Kwan was favourite but 16-year-old Sarah Hughes blew away her American colleague – and her former heroine – with an enrapturing free programme. (© Getty Images/Pensinger)

shocked me. I was shaking with disbelief. It had been an effortless race and I felt like I was floating the whole way.'

A world record for overt public emotion was surpassed when Jim Shea Jr won the restored skeleton event – hitherto staged only twice at St Moritz – carrying a photograph of his recently deceased Olympic champion grandfather in his racing helmet. Jack Shea had won two gold medals in speed skating at Lake Placid in 1932. His son Jim had been an Olympic skier, so Jim junior was a third-generation Olympian. A month before the Games, 91-year-old Jack had died in a motor accident. The mood of unrestrained emotion was magnified by Shea's victory over the world champion Martin Rettl of Austria being by five-hundredths of a second at the end of 15 twisting curves. Announcement of victory was drowned by the chanting of 'U-S-A', the Sheas becoming the second family to have two gold medal winners following Bill Christian and his son Dave, members of the ice hockey teams of 1960 and 1980.

Chauvinism also rocketed to fever pitch in men's short track speed skating in which Apolo Anton Ohno from Seattle was involved in two bizarre races. Quite apart from the American press inflicting jaw-cracking jokes about his name on their readers for more than a week, there were moments when it was made to seem that Ohno *was* the Olympics. In the 1,000m final of this so-often controversial sport, there was a four-man pile-up 50 metres from the finish. The only man left standing was Steven Bradbury of Australia in last place. Barely able to believe his own fortune, he glided through the carnage to win the gold medal, Ohno scrambling across the line for second place with Mathieu Turcotte of Canada third. The other two in the fall were Hyun-Soo Ahn of South Korea and Jiajun Li of China. Ohno needed six stitches in a thigh wound. A flood of boos greeted the outcome, which was allowed to stand by Australian referee Jim Hewish. Bradbury was all but dumbfounded. 'I don't think I'll take the medal for the minute-and-a-half race I won,' he said, 'I'll take it for the ten years of hard slog I've put into this sport.' He had been a member of the 1994 5,000m relay bronze medal winning team, the same year in which he needed 111 stitches in a skating accident, while two years earlier he had suffered a broken neck and spent six weeks wearing a brace.

Ohno was taken to the medal ceremony in a wheelchair but his Games were far from over. Pushing on the final bend for first place in the 1,500m, shoulder to shoulder with South Korean Dong-Sung Kim, Ohno histrionically threw up his arms as though impeded. At the line, Kim was the winner and he picked

James and Jim Shea Jr, father and son Olympians, carry the flame prior to Jim Jr winning the first skeleton race for 54 years. (© Getty Images/Jacobsohn) (© Getty Images/Hewitt)

up a Korean flag and went on a victory lap. Again the crowd was booing. After a short delay there was an announcement that Kim was disqualified. Kim threw down his flag in anger, Ohno was promoted to first place with Jia Jun Li of China second and Marc Gagnon of Canada third. 'He made a move across me and that was it,' Ohno said. Views varied. Bradbury thought Kim was innocent, others including the referee that Ohno was impeded. The South Korean skating federation filed a protest with the ISU and the IOC and threatened not to march in the closing ceremony. Ohno was attempting to go by on the inside, indicating that Kim was harshly penalised for 'squeezing' his rival on the last bend. Contested results can be good publicity – but not too often in one Games.

The inaugural women's bobsleigh competition was notable for a 28-year-old African-American making an unusual transfer from Summer to Winter Games. Vonetta Flowers from Alabama had failed to qualify for the long jump at Sydney 2000 and now, as brake-man of the *USA II* sled driven by Jill Bakken, earned a gold medal. Following the long jump failure, Flowers' husband had read an advertisement for trials for the US bobsleigh team. Never having seen the sport except on television, she knew nothing of the G-forces that shrink your spine, but was about to find out.

In bobsleigh, the driver not the coach chooses the brake-man. Bakken had replaced her friend Shauna Rohbock with Flowers after a push-off test. Likewise Jean Racine, driver of *USA I*, had replaced her friend and brake-man Jen Davidson with Gea Johnson. A few days before the Salt Lake racing, Racine tried to lure Flowers from Bakken. Flowers rejected the approach. From this domestic subterfuge Bakken/Flowers emerged as champions ahead of *Germany I* and *Germany II*, the Racine/Johnson partnership being undermined by Johnson's hamstring injury. Flowers' transfer from sun to snow made her an overnight folk hero, while most Americans considered that Racine's disloyalty to Davidson had brought her deserved failure.

To unrestrained scenes of celebration, Canada won both ice hockey titles, defeating the USA; the women gaining revenge for a title unexpectedly surrendered four years earlier in the inaugural competition. The USA's big hitters, Cammi Granato and Karyn Bye, failed to deliver in the women's final, Canada winning 3–2 to end an eight-game losing streak to the Americans.

Vonetta Flowers, African-American, switched from being failed Olympic long-jump candidate to bobsleigh brake-man to help driver Jill Bakken to take the first women's bobsleigh title. (© Getty Images/Munday) (© Getty Images/Hewitt)

CHAPTER LXXII

Going Home

Dr Jacques Rogge of Belgium, eighth President of the IOC

'I am wholly optimistic about the future of the Olympic Games. With the desire of successive generations of young people either to participate or to watch, the dream of the Games remains. So long as the International Olympic Committee retains the two-week focus, continues the policy of the Games being hosted in a single city and the characteristic of having an Olympic Village, retains the protocol of medal presentations and opening and closing ceremonies, the dream is still out there. The ceremonies are an essential feature, something that for the competitors is sacred. I detect this when speaking to them, sensing that they long for the atmosphere of the Village; that even the elite would participate without any consideration of the financial rewards that are now available in the professional era. It is still a goal, an achievement, and the ceremonies are part of the whole. Though we in the IOC are looking at means of cost reduction, it would never be a part of any economy to curtail ceremonies or deny competitors the opportunity to be present at the opening and closing of the Games. The ceremonies are the base of the Olympic experience.

What helps to distinguish the Games is that we have no advertising in the stadia, that the Games are televised to the whole world, 220 countries, by terrestrial networks free of charge; that the welfare of the athletes is our priority, that we look after them but offer no prize money. This puts huge expectation on the shoulders of the IOC, alongside the IFs and NOCs, the organising committees, all the broadcasters and media sponsors. These are the stakeholders with the duty to keep alive the dream.

I believe the Games are more professionally organised than 30 years ago, that the Village is far more comfortable than when there were six to an apartment in Mexico and Montreal, that the transport and security, the media coverage, the quality of venues have all advanced. The rarity of occurrence – once every four years – the unity of competition in many sports at the same time and place, that is what competitors want.

Yet it is also our duty continually to try to make sport an ever more appealing product. Young people today, particularly in developed countries, no longer think automatically about sport, there is the attraction of so many other cultural products, especially electronic games, which together with motorised transport to and from school turn youngsters into couch potatoes. The future will not necessarily be easy, and not only on the cultural front. There are dangers in the political, financial and moral fields. World peace is threatened. In the event of a major conflict, we might conceivably have to cancel a Games. This happened in 1916, 1940 and 1944, but the Games survived. We could have financial difficulties if we do not reduce our costs and raise our reserves so as to withstand the possibility of a cancellation. We could face a moral crisis if we do not reduce the dangers from the drugs issue.

We can never totally eliminate drugs, but there has to be a continuing reduction. You cannot rule out criminality from normal society, it's human nature, but we have an obligation to do the maximum we can. I believe our control is increasing and we are giving every support to WADA. In the eighteen Winter Games from Chamonix to Nagano, there were only five positive tests, whereas in Salt Lake City alone there were seven, which demonstrates that surveillance is becoming more thorough. Yet doping has itself become more professional. Competitors are counselled by a devious network of scientists and doctors who supply them. WADA's task is immense.

Transparency among competitors is no less important than transparency and democracy within the IOC. The many reforms introduced in 1999 have been effective, ethical issues have been formalised, and the Code of Conduct was accepted at the Extraordinary Session at Mexico City in December 2002. The reforms have changed our organisation, giving a new strength to the IOC. World leaders, economists, industrialists, the media, public opinion have all taken a fresh look at the IOC, have re-assessed us. Yet we have to fight every second of every day to uphold our credibility, our prestige, to be accountable and acceptable to society. President Samaranch began that when initiating the reforms following the crisis of Salt Lake City. Some people complain that the Ethics Commission is too pedantic, but, as with pregnancy, you cannot be partially ethical. You either are or you are not.

Our economies are already well under way, both within the IOC administration and the operation of the Games. We have achieved a substantial annual reduction for the past two years within the IOC, with many rationalisations such as introducing more streamlined integration between the IOC and the Olympic Museum. My objective is to consolidate within my eight-year term what President Samaranch built over twenty-one years. We need a financial reserve sufficient to survive any crisis. When I was elected in 2001, it was $110m, today it is $145m; what we need is $200m. Regarding the Games, where possible we hope to downsize venues and the cost and availability of luxury technologies. Why, for instance, should the screen at the main stadium for track and field be able to zap to fencing and sailing, a facility that costs a fortune? We must shave the number of accreditations, which rose from 130,000 at Barcelona '92 to 195,000 at Atlanta '96 for the same number of events.

Although the IOC members postponed, for the time being, the proposed removal of three sports from the programme – baseball, modern pentathlon and softball – at the Extraordinary Session at Mexico City, I am glad they have accepted the principle proposed by the Executive Board of periodic reassessment of the programme, on the basis of recognised, approved criteria. I was not surprised by the resistance to change, for it was the first time since 1936 that there was a recommendation for deletion from the programme. Yet, for the first time since 1948 there has been no growth to the programme, for we had to halt the constant inflation of events. At the same time, we cannot eternally say that "If you're in the programme, you stay." We will review the situation again after Athens '04. It is significant that some sports have effected important changes in presentation and economy: for instance equestrianism, reducing the size of the venue for the three-day event by 75 per cent, and baseball and softball agreeing to share the same venue. We must continually try to find a balance between traditional sports, such as fencing, wrestling and modern pentathlon, and what the youth of today is doing, with, for instance, the introduction of windsurfing, snowboarding and triathlon. What is essential for any included sport is that it should require hard training but also, in the contemporary world, that it should appeal to public interest.

There is continual discussion as to whether the election of host cities should be on the basis of continental rotation. My hope would be that this would be a voluntary rather than mandatory factor. If mandatory, and the only two candidates available are weak, you would be obliged to accept one of them. My recommendation would be to try to persuade the IOC electorate that, where you have equal candidates, you go for the continent not recently selected. That is what prevailed in the choice between Paris, Toronto and Beijing for 2008, but this is an area of individual decision.

People ask whether I have felt under pressure from comparison with a previously powerful President. It is something I have never really thought about, though I warmly acknowledge his achievements. He started at a time when the IOC was without money or international influence. Changes in the external world gave him the opportunity for imaginative expansion through the mediums of television and sponsorship and the change to professionalism. I will have a shorter time in office than he had. He could preside almost alone on many issues, but now the members want to participate more in a new environment of transparency. We also now have circumstances of a shrinking economy and more intense requirements in security. While the presidency of the IOC is not easy, I do not consider it daunting. There are far more difficult issues in life than running the IOC. The essentials are to preserve the assets created by President Samaranch; the financial independence that ensures the success of the Games; the redistribution of 93 per cent of our income throughout the Olympic Movement; the continuation of the campaign for the inclusion of more women in all fields; the protection of the environment; and the enhancement of the Museum. I shall do my best.'* (From interview with the author in 2003)

(Photograph © IOC/Locatelli)

The eighth President of the IOC, multiple linguist in Flemish, French, English, German and Spanish, has a particular affinity with competitors. His first of three Games as a Belgian yachtsman was at Acapulco, Mexico, in 1968, in a luxurious beachfront hotel, moving after competition to a room with five other competitors in the Village of Mexico City. He played rugby for Belgium ten times as an open-side flanker (the back row of the scrummage) and was five times Belgium's *chef-de-mission*, or team leader. He identified instantly with the competitors and their problems, being, for example, sensitive to the conflict in interest in any Games Village between those who have finished and wish to celebrate, and those still preparing for events ahead. He is equally conscious of the volatility of the all-important image of the Games, the factor which intoxicates the would-be sponsors who pick up the bill, and is aware of critics such as Marian Salzman, a US media analyst who forgivably told the *Washington Post* after Sydney that American viewers were losing interest because most of the sports contested in the Games were wholly foreign to the regular viewer and that 'the Games are over'. Like Samaranch, Rogge is alert to the image-thermometer of each sport.

In a world of ever-mounting political correctness, there are so many issues to which the IOC President must be sensitive. High on the list is the perceived notion that competitors should figure prominently in the administration: through the Athletes Commission and, increasingly since the reforms of 1999, as IOC members. To some extent this latest move was inevitably

Sergei Bubka of Ukraine, pole vault champion in 1988, became the first chairman of the Athletes Commission to be elected by his peers. (© Getty Images)

cosmetic, because, however intelligent the athletes, they are inexperienced regarding most of the complexities of running a Games and have little first-hand knowledge of the criteria or the candidates when it comes to elections. Nevertheless, Rogge introduced the appointment of the chairman of the Athletes Commission by election among the athletes themselves, rather than by the President; the first such chairman, succeeding yachtsman Peter Tallberg of Finland, being Sergei Bubka of the Ukraine, world record pole vaulter, with a 12–5 margin over Robert Ctvrtlik, American volleyball player. Of the nineteen Commission members, twelve are elected by Games participants and seven by the President. Twelve of the Commission are IOC members. A contemporary IOC President must attempt to be all things to all people. Whereas Samaranch, who would scrupulously listen to every viewpoint, was essentially, and occasionally brutally, concerned with maintenance of the objective even if at the expense of others' vested interests, Rogge professes to be dedicated to open government.

At the Centenary Congress of 1994 in Paris, he had notably spoken of the need on the one hand for NOCs to be more efficient in giving competitors necessary support, but on the other hand queried whether the NOCs were losing their authority over competitors, the mutual trust between the two being dissolved because of competitors becoming surrounded by managers, sponsors, accountants and equipment suppliers. It has been his concern in this area that has made him dogmatic about the responsibilities of the Ethics Commission, ensuring the absence of any possible conflict of interest. He considered it wholly correct, for example, that Charmaine Crooks, Canadian athlete and member of both the IOC and the Ethics Commission, should resign from the latter if she wished to represent the host-city bid by Toronto in 2001: one or the other. At the same time, he has been party to maintaining the scope for Executive Board members to be eligible for re-election two years rather than four after compulsory retirement – as either ordinary member or as vice-president – in the interest of maintaining continuity of knowledge and experience, with the additional adjustment that an ordinary Executive Board member, when failing after four years to be elected as a vice-president, may be re-elected as an ordinary member for a further four-year term.

Nonetheless, both President and Executive Board encountered some headwinds in 2002. Discovering during the Session preceding the Salt Lake City Winter Games that there was opposition to the reform that bars members from visiting bid cities, and a possible revision of the programme by the removal of lesser sports, an Extraordinary Session was called for the following November. Prior to this, it became apparent from an Executive Board meeting, in rather clumsy fashion, that the Programme Commission, under the chairmanship of Franco Carraro of Italy, was proposing the elimination of baseball, modern pentathlon and softball. This provoked a considerable hue and cry, and not just among the threatened sports. Part of the anxiety, mostly unreasonable, was that the initiative stemmed from Gilbert Felli, the then IOC Staff Director of Sports, Olympic Games Coordination and Relations with IFs: a specialist who has worked tirelessly to rationalise an overcrowded schedule of events which are likewise competitor-inflated. Rogge's authority would be tested at the Session in Mexico City in the autumn.

Adroitly stage-managing the debate – in the manner of Samaranch – on confirmation of the ban on visiting, with a succession of key supportive speakers from the floor, Rogge gained resounding approval. Yet, if this was an important victory, the following day there was a serious knockback. All but one of more than thirty speakers, in a debate that bypassed

lunch and ran well into the afternoon, opposed the elimination of the three sports: some on a matter of principle, some demanding a clearer definition of criteria for the inclusion or exclusion of any sport. Calling for a brief coffee break and discussion with the Executive Board, the President swiftly acknowledged the opposition, postponing the proposals for further review following the Athens Games of 2004.

Rogge was content that the principle of continual review of the programme had been acknowledged. In the search for open government, he had been happy to put the proposals to the test and withdraw temporarily in the face of opposition. Samaranch would have known the outcome beforehand and avoided reversal by withdrawal of the debate. Rogge had said in advance: 'If support is not sufficient, then we'll wait until another time.' Klaus Schormann, president of modern pentathlon, had impressively defended the continuation of a traditional sport devised by de Coubertin, a sport that for many epitomises the soul of the Olympics. Without the Olympic stage, modern pentathlon would die. The biggest loser of the debate, in the event, was Carraro, the Commission chairman, perceived to be out of touch with realities. On Rogge's personal kite-flying – the introduction to the Games of golf and rugby – there was, for the

Prince Albert of Monaco, Olympic bobsleigh enthusiast, modern pentathlon advocate. (© IOC/Strahm)

time being, no serious debate. Meanwhile, the equestrian federation, its inclusion threatened by logistical expense, had agreed drastically to reduce by three-quarters the open-country area required for its three-day event.

The scale of Rogge's partial revision of an IOC administration changed beyond recognition by Samaranch over 20 years had gradually become apparent. A policy analysis, prior to likely alterations, was taking place on three fronts. In addition to that on the programme, for the moment shunted into a siding, there were the major undertakings of a management audit, under the scrutiny of new Finance and Administration Director, Thierry Sprunger, and Richard Pound's all-embracing Games Study (or Review) Commission. Sprunger, a suddenly emerging force within the staff at Lausanne, had been manoeuvred by Rogge into the vacancy created by the dismantling into different departments of the office of retired Secretary-General Francoise Zweifel. Sprunger's brief included four sections: an audit of the management of day-to-day IOC administration; of Games management; of marketing streamlining; and the partnership between the IOC and the Olympic Museum. Foremost among the recommendations regarding the internal administration was refinement of its information and knowledge assets as a leverage factor in new contractual terms with host cities: abolition of the reinvention of the wheel every four years. On Games management, recommendations were for realignment and greater power for the Coordination Commission in its terms of reference with host organising committees. On marketing operations, the IOC should take total control, under the chairman of the Marketing Commission, Gerhard Heiberg of Norway, relieving in-house marketing partner Meridian of its former authority from 2004. And fourth, there should be closer integration of the headquarters of the IOC and the Museum.

The realignment of marketing and the demise of Meridian was anything but a seamless operation, involving extensive internal controversy. Meridian Management had been founded in 1996 by former staff members of ISL. The IOC held a 25 per cent interest but 50 per cent of the voting rights. Rogge and Heiberg had come to believe that the administrators were extracting a disproportionate profit share, but the takeover, ultimately effected in 2004, also led eventually to the departure of Marketing Director Michael Payne, who had been responsible for negotiating broadcasting and media rights alongside Dick Pound. The exemplary Heiberg found himself treading water in certain areas with which he was not wholly familiar, to the dismay of some TOP sponsors. Unrelated to these difficulties would be the signing, in March 2004, of Lenovo, the Chinese computer giant, as part of the TOP team, while Xerox, an IOC partner since 1964 and a TOP sponsor since 1994, had withdrawn from the programme the previous autumn.

Included in Rogge's reorganisation had been the appointment of Gilbert Felli as Olympic Games Executive Director, his role as IOC Sports Director being taken by Kelly Fairweather, former director of the South African Hockey Association, who had played a leading role in creating the Transfer of Knowledge Programme, schemed to simplify the

From a sixth place in the 100m freestyle in Rome, 1960, Richard Pound has always gone headlong for IOC objectives. (Photograph courtesy of Robert Dubeau/McGill University)

administrative passage from one Games to the next. There was also an adjustment of revenue distribution policy for Athens '04 onwards, allocating 49 per cent to the Organising Committee and 51 per cent to the Olympic family. Additionally, from 2010 onwards, there would no longer be a guarantee of any percentage, merely a sum allocated to the Organising Committee, index-linked in line with the previous Games, with further upturn in revenue diverted to NOCs and IFs.

It was decided, as a financial tactic, that the US network television negotiations for 2010 and 2012 would take place prior to the Prague Session in July 2003, meaning that broadcasters would be bidding blind, not even knowing on which continent each Games would be staged. If one network wanted to lock up the rights in advance, they would need to lodge a bid beyond the scope of rivals. Moreover, it was made clear to ABC, CBS, Fox, NBC and the rest that, in conjunction with their bids, they would as usual have to sign a binding broadcast agreement in advance, to avoid lengthy subsequent negotiations and concessions by the IOC on the small print. On 5 June, the networks arrived in Lausanne and, following respective presentations, placed their bids in a sealed box. In their presentation, NBC outlined a new proposal for the promotion of the Olympic brand – a several hundred-million-dollar commitment over and above any rights fee. When Richard Carrión, co-negotiator with Rogge, opened the bids, it became apparent that NBC had left their rivals trailing: not only a $2.001 billion offer for the two Games, neither yet determined, but also a huge increase in Games coverage of up to 3,000 hours, in multiple languages. Part of every deal on US rights requires approval by USOC, represented in Lausanne by Jim Sherr, USOC's new executive director. USOC attempted to stall, hoping for a higher figure, but given the agreement that USOC receives 12.75 per cent of US broadcast rights, in this instance $250 million, their representatives came to the table after obtuse posturing that extended the signing by NBC until the early hours of the morning. CBS had withdrawn beforehand, and ABC and Fox returned home duly chastened.

The Games Study (Review) Commission had coincidentally further established the conviction of the new President that Richard Pound, one of those defeated in the presidential election, remained a crucial member of the IOC. The study involved hundreds of hours of work for a commission including 12 IOC members: besides Pound, Reuben Acosta (Mexico, president volleyball IF), John Coates (Australia NOC), Robert Ctvrtlik (US, volleyball), Lamine Diack (Senegal, president IAAF), Sinan Erdem (Turkey NOC), Bruno Grandi (Italy, president gymnastics IF),

Lamine Diack of Senegal, harmonising president of IAAF. (© IOC/Locatelli)

Gerhard Heiberg of Norway (right with Samaranch), Lillehammer Winter Games organiser and key figure in the maintenance of IOC marketing funds. (© IOC/Strahm)

Patrick Hickey (Ireland NOC), Gian-Franco Kasper (Switzerland, president skiing IF), Mustapha Larfaoui (Algeria, president swimming IF), Randhir Singh (India, secretary-general Olympic Council of Asia), Ching-Kuo Wu (Taiwan NOC). The essence of their preliminary recommendations in 2002 was: to reduce accepted finance inflation levels of Games' service facilities, which should be limited to 'reasonable' standard and carry acceptable risk levels for the sake of economy; to minimise cost and maximise use of competition, non-competition and training venues, with reduction/efficiency usage in terms of hours/space/services; guidelines and containment/decrease of accredited personnel; clearer definition of IOC/host organising committee relationship in pursuit of refined work practices; and all such changes in relation to the Charter to be reviewed by the Juridical Commission.

Pound's refinements would be fundamental for the long-term survival of the Olympic Games. As Rogge pointed out, while technology at Seoul '88 accounted for 8 per cent of the budget, by Sydney '00 this had risen to 28 per cent. 'We have to reduce expectations,' he said, 'to cut back, to consolidate, rather than let the beast grow forever, untamed. We don't any more want to have Olympic stadiums with 125,000 seats, because that leaves white elephants.' Rogge's oft-repeated mantra is that the Games must never exceed the figures of Sydney: 28 sports, 272 events, 10,651 competitors. Yet the Rogge–Pound axis on the policy of economic reductions was challenged by Paul Henderson, Rogge's former Canadian sailing rival and at that time president of the ISF. 'By Pound's calculation, each athlete attending a Games costs the organising committee $30,000,' Henderson said. 'Therefore you could, say, add another 500 athletes, a cost of $15m, which is only 0.05 per cent of the budget. Every Games is riddled with crisis management. Real economy would come with cuts in construction costs: definite dates for completion of new venues within the first three years rather than the last three, with appropriate penalties.' Henderson perhaps overlooked that additional athletes would 'ratchet up' the whole administration, activating Village accommodation, security etc. at an earlier date, the logisitical cost of the Games running at $10 million per day. Therefore another 500 athletes could cost $70 million.

Rogge's alliance with Pound in the search for economies made sound sense, for the commercial bounty of recent years was unlikely to last for ever. Economies are best designed while the Olympic image continues to ride high and its marketable value continues at a peak. This peak is currently sustained by the Olympic rings remaining, according to Sponsorship Research International, the most recognised symbol in the world (78 per cent), ahead of Shell (72 per cent), McDonald's (66 per cent) and Mercedes (61 per cent). 'Take away sponsorship and commercialism from sport today,' Pound asks, 'and what is left? A large, sophisticated, finely tuned engine developed over a period of 100 years – with no fuel.' The supply of fuel was still out there in plenty, if it could be harvested. In 2002, the dream goal of Phil Knight, founder and chairman of leading Olympic sponsor Nike, was accomplished – the passing of the worldwide earnings mark, pre-tax, of $10 billion for the company. Gerhard Heiberg, succeeding Pound as chairman of the Marketing Commission, indeed found himself in an extraordinary position: an honorary executive controlling one of the biggest incomes of any organisation in the world and one that is non-profit orientated.

Yoshihiro Yasui, chairman of former sponsor Brother Industries of Japan, spoke for all sponsors of the Olympic Games when he stated: 'Among the IOC's contributions to the Olympic Movement, the most remarkable is that, while maintaining the long-established traditions and prestige of the Games, it has brought such success to it on a commercial basis.' This growth in broadcast and marketing revenue had enabled the IOC to increase significantly the financial support to NOCs, IFs and organising committees. Over 93 per cent of all income was being distributed throughout sectors of the Movement (later reduced below 90 per cent). Long-term contracts allow the IOC to provide the majority of an organising committee's budget up front; over the 24 years since 1980 this has risen ten-fold for the Summer Games and thirty-fold for the Winter Games. In the same period, Olympic Solidarity, established in 1971 and funded by a share of the Olympic broadcast revenue, has increased fifteen-fold, while the IOC's contribution is the largest single source of revenue to the majority of IFs.

Over the past 20 years, the IOC has concluded broadcast and international sponsorship agreements worth more than $12 billion. The IOC directly provides funding to all 200 NOCs and provides travel and accommodation grants for all participant athletes at a Games.

The growth in broadcast coverage over 20 years had been exceptional: an audience penetration of 3.7 billion viewers in 220 countries, with more than 36 million cumulative viewing hours for the Summer Games and 20 million hours for the Winter Games, all based on free-to-air broadcasting channels with availability for all. The IOC achieved this growth through direct negotiation, without agency or third-party commission. Gross broadcast revenue from 1984 to 2008 exceeded $9.925 billion, growing more than fifteen-fold from $101 million for Moscow '80 to $1.715 billion for Beijing '08. Winter broadcast revenue increased forty-fold, 1980–2006, from $21 million to $83.2 million.

Olympic broadcast rights fees outside the United States also grew substantially, 1980–2008, thereby reducing the Olympic Movement's dependency on US broadcast revenue alone.

As previously mentioned in Chapter LXI, the creation of The Olympic Programme (TOP) in 1985 provided funding not only to all NOCs but also essential value-in-kind sponsorship in technology resources for organising committees, plus a global promotional platform for the Olympic image across 220 countries. Critically, TOP reached a different market threshold that enabled the IOC not to squeeze upwards the broadcast rights fees. TOP I and TOP II, modest by comparison in their early achievements, successively demonstrated the concept and provided an incentive for other sponsors. The IOC remained loyal to existing clients, renewing sponsorship contracts wherever possible, though that with IBM, one of the largest for TOP III, was unsustainable because of its complexity and a serious communications failure at Atlanta '96. By now, however, sponsors understood how to activate a publicity programme among their own clients, beyond mere use of the Games' rings logo.

The division of the income deriving from a Games for the IFs, allocated according to an internal formula devised by the Association of Summer Olympic International Federations (ASOIF) is a matter of regular thorny debate, seldom more so than at a meeting in Colorado Springs in December 2002. Anxious to get in on the act were the newly affiliated triathlon and taekwondo federations. ASOIF chairman Denis Oswald gamely attempted to achieve conciliation between big and small, telling his colleagues that 'we have to agree on compromise figures if we do not want a solution to be imposed from the outside'. Hogging the greater share – originally agreed because it then had no independent world championship – was the IAAF. An eventual new formula was reached, with the coding of the IFs into five different categories, as follows: group A – athletics, $26.3 million; group B – basketball, cycling, football, gymnastics, swimming, tennis, volleyball, $12.1 million each; group C – handball, hockey, equestrianism, rowing, $7.6 million each; group D – 16 sports, $6.2 million each; group E – taekwondo, triathlon, $5.4 million each.

Funding of Olympic Solidarity, and its multitude of programmes for the benefit of NOCs, comes from a share of broadcast rights. This is Solidarity's only source of income. The quadrennial plan, 2001–04, had a budget totalling $209.5 million, more than seven times higher than for its first four-year plan, 1985–88. Thus far it had organised more than 10,000 activities worldwide. Including a share of TOP revenue of $95 million for the quadrennium Salt Lake–Athens, the gross donation from the IOC to NOCs would be $304.5 million. This was no less than fair; by Rogge's reckoning the NOCs themselves contribute $150 million to the staging of the Games, divided between the sending of their teams and preparing them at qualifying events. How far times have changed from the days when President Brundage resisted any collective organisation of NOCs.

The rise to administrative prominence by Pound and then Heiberg might not have happened to the same degree had Samaranch, nearly 20 years ago, been able to enlist Peter Ueberroth as an IOC member. The management and commercial mastermind of the Los Angeles Games of 1984, this most financially aware 'co-opted' official up to that time would have been an invaluable adviser on future development, even a potential presidential successor. Rank-and-file members, however, disapproved, considering Ueberroth, as they did Horst Dassler, as being too clever for his own good. Too clever for their good, more likely. Yet the IFs and the NOCs were only too happy to accept all the financial advantages that flowed from Ueberroth and Dassler, and which helped to create the financial high ground which the Olympic Movement would enjoy.

The rejection of Ueberroth was said to have amounted to one of Samaranch's defeats. These were not many, and there is the suspicion that he himself feared Ueberroth's potential power. He had built around himself an aura of unrivalled influence and kudos, a sports official who mixed as easily with state presidents, kings and dictators as he did – though few witnessed this – with unheralded competitors, unknown secretaries and chairmen of the least conspicuous NOCs, his door never closed to anyone. Some critics mocked him for his assumed international statesman status, yet his widely respected role as quasi-diplomat could effectively pull together politicians from China, South Africa, the Koreas and elsewhere. After riding a tide of external criticism for much of his 21-year presidency, accused by sparsely informed media of creating a Louis XIVth-style court in Lausanne – where he ate a frugal lunch alongside his staff in the canteen – he had no doubts about his own capabilities. Questioned in 1993 about the African boycott of 1976, he said: 'The African teams left two days before the inauguration of the Games . . . I believe that if there had been an opportunity [to talk] it might have been possible to solve the problem. I can tell you that never, never had I been responsible at that time would the African teams have left. Never!'

Although inadvertently, by being unable to unearth the malpractices of a minority – known to some others such as leaders of bidding host cities – Samaranch may have allowed the IOC to drift into its crisis of 1999, the rehabilitation through reforms that he effected within 12 months was a prime example of crisis management, and he was thus able to achieve the preservation of the organisation which he had sought to lift to global prominence. When keeping the Seoul Games on the rails during the seven years from the city's election in 1981, he made fifteen trips to South Korea. As Pound aptly observed, 'He circled the wagons.' Some members, including Pound and Thomas Bach of Germany, recognised Samaranch's misjudgement in the election of particular IOC members, especially from the developing world, in the interest of universality. Pound considered that he should have removed from Marc Hodler the control of regulations on visiting bid cities, entrusting this to a vigorous younger man. Yet when Samaranch's public credibility was at its lowest ebb during 1999, and he was metaphorically shielded in his Lausanne bunker, the television companies and sponsors crucially held firm, thanks to the almost daily chorus from Payne and Pound promising impending consitutional reform – thus fortifying the platform for recovery.

Contrary to speculation at the time of his retirement in 2001 – having been granted as Life President a continuing office and secretarial facilities in Lausanne – Samaranch was for six months distant from the action, being seriously unwell and making only occasional courtesy calls and visits. Reflecting on his time, there was plenty he would have wished different. He admitted:

> We had very bad public relations, always defending ourselves, not knowing how to sell the positive side, all that we had done regarding sports politics with China–Taiwan, North and South Korea, Yugoslavia's disintegration, the re-admission of South Africa. My main regret is not having been able to convince some members to respect the Charter. Maybe I was at fault not to get the approval of the Session to ban visits, though I had tried within the Executive Board. Yet thanks to the crisis, it opened the way for reforms that otherwise would never have been agreed.
>
> I was criticised from the start in some journals: that I allegedly lived in a palace, travelled daily by helicopter; and there were exaggerations about my past in Spain. Yet people should judge where the IOC was in 1980 and then in 2001. At Sydney, women competitors amounted to 42 per cent, though there's still the problem of their minority in administration. My dream from the start was to make the IOC inclusive of all branches of the Movement. We now have, besides thirteen women members, a fourth arm, alongside IFs and NOCs – the active athletes, though ironically without the crisis of '99 it would likewise not have been possible to convince the members to make this step. I tried to say that within the Executive Board there must be places for IFs, NOCs and athletes. Finally, it is done.

Work on the continuing campaign against drugs was anything but done, though the year 2002 witnessed the death of two men at the opposite ends of the medical spectrum: Manfred Ewald and Alexandre, Prince de Mérode. Ewald had been president of the GDR gymnastics and sport federation and of the NOC, as such effectively controlling the entire sports machine of the Soviet satellite, notwithstanding the irony that his greatest ambition had been to defeat the Soviet masters in the medal haul of the LA Games, which in the event were boycotted. It had been Ewald who directed official government policy in the drive to use sporting success for political prestige in 'occupied' Germany and in exploiting performance-enhancing drugs – as later testified by many unwitting competitors who had undergone a controlled programme of scientific diet, often at the cost of severe damage to their health. In 2000, Ewald and his biochemical associate Dr Manfred Höppner had been tried on 142 cases of inflicting bodily harm, Ewald, his own health now deteriorating at the age of 74, being given a suspended sentence. In a career devoted to sports administration, he had been *chef-de-mission* of the combined German team at Tokyo '64, becoming president of the new GDR NOC in 1973, leading his nation of under 12 million to second place in the Summer medals table of 1976, 1980 and 1988 and first place at Sarajevo '84.

De Mérode, as chairman of the IOC Medical Commission, had been dedicated to halting this cynical march, though he was continually criticised for the Commission's evident failure to abolish rampant malpractice, whether operated by perverted medics and coaches or voluntarily exercised by competitors. He had been chairman from 1967 to his death at the age of 68, following long illness, and was twice IOC Vice-President: an aristocrat of ancient lineage and unfailing courtesy, he was too often ensnared by the scientific complexities that his Commission endlessly sought to penetrate. His approach to the problem was intellectually moral, believing among other things that competitors should be protected from themselves by regulations on over-training, just as there are forms of time-limitation in other work employment. There was none who was better informed in the area of academic, ethical argument.

The relevance of the Medical Commission would inevitably decline with a fully operational and effective World Anti-Doping Agency (WADA). A move towards this took a substantial step forward with WADA's first international conference in early March 2003 in Copenhagen. Four years earlier, the inaugural launch in February 1999 had been clouded by events of the then-emerging Salt Lake City scandal, the media hijacking the WADA news event in their hungry pursuit of the guilty in vote bribery. Now the footlights shone gratifyingly upon on a unified campaign. Richard Pound, president of WADA, called it 'an extraordinary consensus'. Jacques Rogge, IOC President, said that the confrontation with drugs, threatening the Games' very existence, had entered a new era. WADA's carefully drafted World Anti-Doping Code, following unprecedented consultation among all Olympic stakeholders, received acceptance and the signature – following many, and one or two continuing, debates on detail – of all IFs. And, most significantly, by the autumn of 2003, 63 governments had already signed on, with 27 others pledged to do so subsequently. Without this collaboration at civic and legal, not to say financial, level the impact of the code would be far less stringent.

A standardisation of testing and penalties was fundamental to WADA's success, and though the cycling and football federations, for instance, would continue to debate the suitability of a basic two-year ban for positive tests on performance-enhancing substances, the conference represented the biggest breakthrough in 40 years against the factor that not

Paula Radcliffe (GBR), seen here leading the 10,000m in Sydney, only to finish fourth, courageously demonstrated the following year against drug cheats. (© IOC/King)

merely tarnished the image of all of sport but also threatened its future through loss of public confidence. As Pound observed: 'There were very few leaders in the campaign before 1999 but now we have a concerted front, including the athletes.' Sergei Bubka, Ukrainian pole vault champion, and Australian swimmer Susie O'Neill, from the IOC's Athletes' Commission, were there in Copenhagen to bolster the drive to eliminate cheats. In his opening address, Pound had emphasised four objectives: acceptance of the Code as the global basis for the fight against drugs; the assurance by all stakeholders – governments, IFs, athletes, and all involved organisations – that they would take steps to adopt the Code domestically; full acceptance of the Code in time for the Olympic Games of 2004 in Athens; and intensification and harmonisation of the Code at all levels. Speaking of concern among some about the nature and duration of penalties, Pound said:

> There is an overwhelming consensus that the first infraction of a serious nature requires a serious sanction and the norm is viewed as two years. There may be special circumstances that could lead to a lesser sanction, and the Code recognises this fact . . . [all matters should be] referred to independent legal experts . . . some are concerned that it may take governments longer than the sports movement fully to adopt and implement the Code and to formalise the financing for their share of WADA budgets . . . even if governments were never to act we would have our own duty to proceed. What is important is that there are twice as many governments present at this conference as there were in Lausanne four years ago, committed to the fight.

Rogge had left no doubt about the IOC's attitude when stating: 'There should be no place in the Games for IFs and NOCs who refuse to implement the Code. Likewise, no hosting of the Games should be awarded to a country whose government has neglected or refused to implement the Code and I urge all IFs and NOCs to apply the same philosophy.' WADA was at a crossroads, Rogge said. So long as the Code was in operation by the Athens Games and governments were pulling their weight, and providing WADA's funding could be rationalised and WADA's strategy was complementary to existing policies of governments and sports organisations, then the future was bright. 'If not, WADA will become irrelevant.'

Pound's comment was that much more significant in the light of the exposure in April 2003 of wanton abuse, long suspected, of testing procedures by USOC stretching back to 1988 and the already mentioned suppression of positive tests on Carl Lewis and others. WADA had to be absolute in its actions. When, a few weeks after the Copenhagen conference it became apparent that Denise Lewis of Britain, heptathlon champion of 2000, had elected to train with the discredited former East German coach Dr Ekkart Arbeit, who was banned in both Australia and South Africa for his known involvement in drug programmes, Pound was typically forthright: 'My philosophy is that if there is anyone at any level of coaching who condones or administers drug taking, we should get him or her out of the sport. We have not been as diligent as we should have been where coaches are concerned. The new anti-doping policy we are formulating and which will be in place not later than the Olympic Games in Athens will redress that issue.'

WADA's rigour would be compromised by the equivocation among leading sports administrators, notably in track and field in both America and Britain, and in cycling, especially regarding the Tour de France, when confronting issues of association with guilty parties as opposed to personal positive tests: as in the case of Denise Lewis and Dr Arbeit. It was small consolation that in January 2004 President George W. Bush incorporated a message against drug use in sport into his State of the Union Address – the first time that the issue had been emphasised at that level of US administration – against the background of lack of commitment by USOC and the US Track and Field governing body (USATF). While in late 2003 USOC had provided the IOC with a 50-page dossier on 24 American athletes who had tested positive between 1998 and 2002, and confirmed that Jerome Young, gold medal winner in Sydney in the 4 x 400m relay had indeed tested positive for nandrolone the previous year (USATF having continually refused to name Young), the Americans were slow to come to terms with the evidence in the prosecution of Victor Conte and his Bay Area Laboratory Co-operative (BALCO). This included the testimony of Kelli White, the American sprinter victorious in the 2003 World Championships, who admitted in an interview with USA Today that she had been involved with BALCO on an extensive drug programme, through which she eventually tested positive, losing her titles. She hated herself for it, admitting: 'It was just so obvious something was going on, especially to people in the track world. I felt that to do this, I had to become someone totally different than I was. I had to compromise my integrity. I knew it was so wrong.' More than 40 athletes were subpoenaed in the BALCO trial, while Dr Brian Goldman, a psychiatrist who had worked with Conte for many years, testified to prescribing Modafinil for White.

In Britain, there was depressing complacency. Frank Dick, former head coach of British athletics, dismissed criticism of the acceptance of Arbeit within the national programme as 'just a bit of history', never mind that he was barred in Australia and South Africa. David Moorcroft, former world record breaker and head of UK Athletics, made little meaningful comment, and the same could be said of UK Sport's chief executive Richard Callicott. Elsewhere, there was profuse condemnation. John Anderson, renowned coach for 40 years, stated: 'I'm dismayed that the leaders of our sport and government have not made a clear and unequivocal statement that they deplore the employment of anyone who has been so central to the promotion and use of prohibited substances.' Dame Mary Peters, pentathlon heroine of 1972, said: 'It would be a tragedy if her [Lewis] continued success was damaged by this association',

while Tom McNab, prominent track and rugby coach described it as 'putting Al Capone in charge of law enforcement'.

Tension also grew between Dick Pound and Hein Verbruggen, Dutch president of international cycling, on account of WADA's report on doping test practice during the Tour de France. Verbruggen claimed the report was filled with errors and objected to WADA's allegation that tests for the banned endurance hormone EPO showed anomalies – indications of possible use of the drug but no proof – even though there was only one confirmed test. WADA's instincts and Verbruggen's objections would be put into perspective by continuing revelations of abuse in subsequent Tours.

Controversially, Pound voiced the possibility of random surveillance by third parties within the sporting arena, saying: 'Anyone can call me or our doping control staff at any time and say, "Here's what's going on, these are the substances, we've heard this, that or the other" . . . if we're happy about the credibility of the intelligence, then we use it to develop targeted tests.' Such a proposal for clandestine Big Brother disclosures did not go down well with the athletes. Bubka and O'Neill opposed athletes becoming informants. Also disputed was the question of whether recreational drugs should be drawn into the spectrum of banned substances, with many believing this would only add confusion. Dr Andrew Pipe, chairman of the Canadian Centre for Ethics in Sport and a WADA scrutineer of banned substances, admitted that the future would be complex. 'Doping practices are changing and sophisticated, and the resources needed for counteraction are enormous.'

With the host city election for 2012 now on the horizon, due to take place at the Singapore Session in 2005, attention was turning to the leading likely bidders, including New York, Paris and London. There were clear difficulties for New York and London, given their countries' involvement in the war in Iraq, and early anxieties in New York were aroused when Dick Pound suggested that they should be disqualified as a candidate if the US government failed to contribute to WADA fees, this reinforced when Jacques Rogge was quoted as saying: 'If they want to bid for the Games, they have to keep to agreements.' The then acting USOC president Bill Martin immediately contacted Rogge to say that the government would be paying the $800,000 due to WADA.

The affairs of the US Olympic Committee had degenerated into near chaos. There had been the all-too-brief presidency of Sandra Baldwin, who had been succeeded by Marty Mankamyer, primarily a figure from football, and the administrative confusion was brought to a head by allegations of erratic financial dealing by chief executive Lloyd Ward in connection with the Pan-American Games in the Dominican Republic. Ward was criticised on all fronts, with USOC summoned to explain themselves to senators in Washington. Under continuing pressure from USOC, Ward resigned, though no charges were brought. Subsequently, Senator John McCain, Republican chairman of the Commerce Committee, had stated: 'We need to have a new organisation in place to prepare for the upcoming Olympics.' This would require changes in legislation regarding the Amateur Sports Act (1978), which revised USOC's charter.

Not only was USOC's disarray likely to leave IOC members anything but impressed, but disaffection also lingered from the Salt Lake City scandal. Even though an American bid city had been equally responsible for vote-incentive malpractice, the most stringent invective and condemnation of the IOC had come from US politicians. Additionally, Mitt Romney, summoned from the east coast as emergency president of a wobbling Games organising committee, had magnified American scorn for the IOC proprietors who made the Games possible: condescending in manner, offensive in downgrading IOC hotel facilities and security, cheeseparing on ceremonial details. 'We cut all that stuff to the bone,' a self-satisfied Romney said, while emerging from the Games with a surplus approaching $56 million. American disregard for the IOC had left its mark, the nadir having been the summons for the then President Samaranch to appear in 1999 before the US Congress, at which point the man to become his successor had remarked: 'The spittle of the toad does not reach the stars' – a proverb from the seventeenth-century French author Jean de la Fontaine. There would be IOC members who would vote for anybody but America, never mind the massive financial input from the world's most powerful economy – the more so when President Bush declined the invitation to meet IOC members following the opening ceremony at the Salt Lake City Games. There was, too, the fact that North America had staged three Games – Calgary '88 and Salt Lake City '02, both Winter, and Atlanta '96, Summer – in the past 12 years. And the USATF was in disarray. The subsequent appointment of Peter Ueberroth as USOC president would haul the organisation back on track.

The voting at the 2003 Session in Prague for the Winter Games host city for 2010 was as unpredictable as any in memory: not in the choice of Vancouver, but in the tiny margin of three votes by which it defeated the little-known Korean resort of Pyeongchang in the second round, 56–53. Salzburg, regarded by many as favourite, was eliminated in the first round with 16 votes, Pyeongchang, inexplicably, failing by only six votes to be outright winner on the first count: Pyeongchang 51, Vancouver 40, Salzburg 16.

There was, as is so often the case with the IOC, more to it than met the eye. Many Europeans with a vested interest in a European election for 2012 in the shape of Paris, Madrid or London, were keen to avoid a European vote this time: a built-in handicap for Salzburg, whose presentation on the day inappropriately dwelt on Austria's musical rather than sporting heritage. The choice of Vancouver would unquestionably be helpful to any of the Europeans bidding for 2012, and damaging to the prospects for New York, but the slender margin over Pyeongchang raised many question marks.

The most serious of these concerned the activities, prior to and during the Session in Prague, of Samsung, the TOP sponsor from Korea. Their heavy-handed presence and hustling approach to NOCs and individual IOC members should have provoked the Executive Board into further reconsideration of the conditions and regulations regarding elections. A common private opinion in Prague, it seems, was that had Pyeongchang won, there would have been an inquiry into their bid procedures, never mind that the facilities and potential for another major winter resort for competition in Asia were excellent. The feeling was that Samsung carried more weight in Prague than did the Prime Minister of Korea when addressing the Session as part of Pyeongchang's presentation.

Many at the Session were disconcerted in other ways, not least in the continuing prohibition on visiting bid cities and thereby the unavoidable dependence on information regarding the cities from the Evaluation Commission's official report. The Commission headed by Gerhard Heiberg had provoked many pages of corrections from the cities, to the extent that members tended to disregard the report and rely on presentations. At the same time, Koreans back home attempted to place blame for defeat – notwithstanding that the number of their votes had been way beyond expectation – on the decision of Un Yong Kim to run for re-election for a vacant vice-presidency seat: thereby, arguably, dividing support for South Korea among those supposedly unwilling to vote twice for the Asian peninsula on the same day.

That theory is effectively discounted by the 53 votes but was likely to give Kim a difficult time at home. What his election clearly did demonstrate was the continued depth of backing for the candidate who came second in the presidential election two years previously – an anti-European vote. After some vacillation, Heiberg had also run for the vice-presidency seat, from the supposedly strong platform of chairman of the Marketing Commission, but lost to Kim 55–44, though Heiberg did gain one of the two vacant seats on the Executive Board, together with Alpha Ibrahim Diallo from Guinea.

There was concern at the Session that governments were dragging their feet in the advance payment of subscriptions to WADA, due each December prior to the following year's budget. With the IOC scheduled to match governmental increments, there was therefore double the shortfall, threatening WADA's investment in software and research. Dick Pound, president of WADA, said: 'This is not a lack of willingness, I suspect, but of organisation. We still expect the funds to come in.' The IOC itself was by no means under-funded. Having built reserves of $150 million following Salt Lake '02, it was expected to add a further $50 million in the wake of the recent deal with NBC on US TV broadcasting rights for 2010 ($820 million) and 2012 ($1.18 billion).

Coincidentally, from the time of the Prague Session, François Carrard would be succeeded as Director-General by Urs Lacotte, a colonel from the Swiss Army and recently director of armament planning with the Swiss Ministry of Defence. Prior to military service he had worked with the Swiss Sports Confederation and had been technical delegate of the national ski federation. Less happy was the situation of Mohamad Hasan, IOC member from Indonesia, whose suspended expulsion pending appeal, while imprisoned for financial fraud, seemed likely to be put into effect.

Although London had announced its bid for 2012, with official backing from the then Prime Minister Tony Blair, the British Olympic Association found itself by 2004 in some controversy over the selection, in conjunction with government departments, of its bid leader, Barbara Cassani. Her credentials were impressive, having wielded powerful positions in the airline industry, but it was considered unfortunate that she had an American background and American accent. World opinion of Britain as an ally of the US in the war with Iraq was itself a possible negative voting factor for 2012: already apparent in some elections of officers among IFs. To be led by an American voice was possibly less than tactful, as was Cassani's early suggestion to involve, in some PR function, the less-than-articulate England football captain David Beckham. That notion brought a swift rebuff, applicable to all bidding cities, from President Rogge when he said, following a meeting with Blair at 10 Downing Street: 'Stick to the fundamentals; bidding is about substance and not appearance. We are not impressed with big names . . . he [Beckham] will not add a single vote.' Seeming disarray came for London with the sudden resignation of Cassani in the spring of 2004, her replacement being deputy chairman Sebastian Coe, former double Olympic champion at 1,500m. P.Y. Gerbeau, the Frenchman formerly in charge of the controversial Millennium Dome, simultaneously resigned as ambassador for the bid in reaction to what some believed clandestinely amounted to Cassani's dismissal, internal administration of the bid being in grave disorder. Cassani was regarded by many insiders as bossy and volatile, undermining coherence, and there had been a further resignation by Jane Willacy, a campaign project manager. Gerbeau called for greater involvement by Tony Blair, making adverse comparison with the frontline involvement in Paris of Jacques Chirac. Pessimism in London had been accentuated by the report of an IOC working party heavily critical of London's transport situation, even though on 31 May London had been included in the shortlist of five candidates, together with Madrid, Moscow, New York and Paris. Those cities rejected were Havana, Istanbul, Leipzig and Rio de Janeiro.

Comfort in Athens in 2004, with the return of the Games to its homeland, was becoming a matter of speculation, and not just that concerning the temperature. Ioannis Spanudakis, the organising committee's managing director, was on record as stating the year before: 'Thank God we didn't get it in 1996. We would never have been able to do it.' But then adding: 'We now have a team of people that can deliver and it should be fantastic.' Optimism had not always been that forceful. Gianna Angelopoulos-Daskalaki, the dynamic woman whose compelling words had convinced IOC members in the election of 1997, had all but resigned from the organising committee, ATHOC, during a characteristic Greek administrative squall, only for Prime Minister Kostas Simitis to plead with her to return and get the train back on the rails. The IOC, alarmed by the sight of three years' inaction since election, had threatened to take the Games elsewhere. Continue she did, though by the time of a visit of the Coordination Commission late in 2001, IOC anxieties had been little eased. The woman who partially modelled herself on Margaret Thatcher's maxim, borrowed from Churchill – 'never give in' – was the voice of national social conscience, having the verbal punching power of a Muhammad Ali. She compelled the government, construction management, the transport ministry, the consortium of hotels, the directors of Greek cultural heritage, to mount the equivalent of a D-Day landing, which transformed this historic city as never before – not just for the brief period of the Games but also for the benefit of inhabitants for years afterwards. The Games provided Greece with a peacetime ultimatum that their politicians have been needing for the past hundred years or more. In meeting it head-on, the nation spent around $7 billion.

This Games visionary, approaching her 50th year, invaluably possessed a clear understanding of the psychology of her compatriots: contradictorily and simultaneously ardent nationalists and wilful individualists. She had previously organised a seminar at Harvard entitled: 'The Greek paradox – promise versus performance'. Her singular objective, which many with experience of Greek affairs regarded as an impossibility, was to persuade fellow Greeks to unite and work as a team. Her confidence remained impenetrable:

> When leading the bid for 2004, and remembering how my country had responded with dismay and criticism to the award of the Centenary Games to Atlanta, I knew what was important. Besides what benefits the Games might bring to Greece was what we, the Greeks, could give to the Games. We had to re-focus on Olympic values. We decided we wanted to touch the world with our ancient tradition, yet we didn't want to show only ancient values, but the modern Greece. We have the heritage, but we want that to work in proving that our country has values for today and tomorrow.
>
> We believe that for the Games there is no place like home, returning here where the Games began in 776 BC, a homecoming for world sport and the chance to rediscover ancient virtues, the values of competition, friendship and peace. It is, too, an opportunity for

Greece to become international at a number of meaningful levels, the continuation of a proud nation that gave many things to civilisation, ideas that were born here.

> The legacy to our people will be huge – in lifting the economy, in upgrading transportation. We can see this transforming before our eyes. The Games will bequeath low-income housing. Athens will be almost a different city, with its expansion of technical expertise and managerial skills among the workforce. It will create 65,000 permanent jobs in a country already growing within the European Union. Our celebration of the return to the site of the inaugural Games will bolster a mood of Greek confidence as our nation enters the twenty-first century and our public is eager to show the world what we can organise.

Gianna Angelopoulos-Daskalaki, talismanic Athens leader: 'Continuation of a proud nation that gave many things to civilisation.' (© IOC/Locatelli)

In this civic revolution, there would be the benefit of a new airport, the raising of the capacity of public transport by 50 per cent on a typical day, the construction of more than 200 kilometres of ring-road, highways and suburban light-rail connections, the opening of an ecological park, marine leisure centre, open-air theatre and aquarium, the devising of pedestrian routes that would unite the archaeological sites of Acropolis, Agora, Roman Forum and new Acropolis Museum. Thousands would be accommodated on cruise liners in Piraeus Bay.

Undoubtedly, the Olympic Games bring some benefits to most of us. R. Stephen Rubin, president of the World Federation of Sporting Goods Industry, has said: 'The IOC, under President Samaranch, has used sport as a means of making a more inclusive world. Sport and the resulting media attention has, by far, the most influential effect on the youth of the world, and the IOC has used the Olympic Games to bring hope and a sense of belonging to many of its inhabitants.' The contemporary situation is indeed a far cry from the exclusive regime of sport as organised by the amateur gentleman-only clubs and associations of Britain in the late nineteenth century. The incorporation of the amateur rule and the exclusion of workers was allowed by de Coubertin for complex reasons of administration at that time, whereas his liberal attitude abhorred the distinction: 'It seemed to me as childish to make all this [the affiliation of sport and its dogmas as a quasi-religious activity] depend on whether an athlete had received a five-franc coin, as automatically to consider the parish verger an unbeliever because he receives a salary for looking after the church.' He regarded the IOC's rule, which would blight much of the next century, as a form of social protection and relic of the class system. Willi Daume, German visionary, would observe, on the acceptance of professionalism in 1987: 'This rejection of class concepts constitutes a tremendous success for the Olympic peace movement far greater than any success in sport.'

What we must hope continue to be bred within Olympic competition are the qualities described by Homer, even if his writing mostly concerned aristocratic warriors, those privileged individuals called *agatho* in Greek, trained for war and therefore brave, and including *aristos*, the high-born. The characteristics of *agathos* and *aristos* were defined as *arete*, the qualities inherent in a warrior: strength, skill, bravery and heroism, or, in a single word, excellence, personified by Achilles and Odysseus. Pursuit of *arete* stands higher than victory. This attitude must apply as much to administrators as to competitors, which is the author's reason for attempting to write this parallel history of the IOC and the Games. Though educated at school and university exclusively within an amateur ethic in the mid-twentieth century, the author never viewed professionalism with disdain, only as a mark of attempted excellence. The author has met or watched thousands of honourable professionals, and occasionally some pretty rotten, unethical amateurs. What matters most about the Olympic Games is the spirit in which they are conducted, the honour of the participants, winners and losers. The Greeks had far more to help try to uphold, in their second staging of the Games, than a reliable timetable and efficient transport.

In the event, to their considerable credit, they managed to do so, with Games that were immensely courteous and friendly, safe from violent intervention in spite of all the preceding fears and, at the last gasp, pleasingly efficient. At the Session preceding the Games, Gunilla Lindberg, 57, former secretary of the Swedish NOC and now of ANOC, was elected Vice-President, the unfavoured Franco Carraro having wisely withdrawn following his controversial involvement in rescheduling within the Programme Commission. Lindberg thus became only the second woman Vice-President, following Anita DeFrantz (USA), also being only the third woman to have reached the EB. Some unrest within IOC ranks was reflected in the fact that in the re-election to the Board of four members – ANOC president Mario Vazquez Raña, athletes' representative Sergei Bubka, ASOIF president Denis Oswald and ISF president Ottavio Cinquanta – they were returned without unanimous votes. Richard Carrión and Nawal El Moutawakel, hurdles champion of 1984, were elected to the Board as new members. Following the provocative BBC programme *Panorama*, containing allegations of voting corruption, Ivan Slavkov, IOC member of Bulgaria, was suspended from all rights, while in association with the same programme, Goran Takac, Gabor Komyathy, Mahmood El Farnawani and Muttaleb Ahmad were declared personae non grata within the Olympic Movement. Mohamad Hasan of Indonesia was expelled as a member for his prior domestic financial impropriety.

The matter of Un Yong Kim, IOC Vice-President from South Korea, hung in the balance. Widely accused in Korea of having damaged the bid by Pyeongchang as Winter hosts for 2010 by himself campaigning, and succeeding, for election to the EB as Vice-President, Kim had lodged law suits for libel damages against several high-ranking political and sporting officials, including

Man-Lip Choi, actions as yet unconcluded. However, the accusations against him, driven by what appeared to be political intrigue and having a sense of vengeance, had led to formal investigation on corruption charges including embezzlement, with $5.4 million in cash and jewellery being seized from Kim's office and home. Amid the controversy, Kim resigned as parliamentary member of the Democratic Millennium opposition and also as president of the World Taekwondo Federation, which he had founded. Officially charged in early 2004, his case was immediately referred to the IOC's Ethics Commission, which made unanimous recommendation to the EB for his suspension. Simultaneously, he was confined to hospital in mid-January in a condition that should have precluded his imprisonment pending conviction. The indictment accused him of bribery in connection with the selection of competitors for taekwondo competitions, though the selection process was far removed from his jurisdiction; of financial 'assistance' to North Korea, notwithstanding that north–south sporting cooperation was already in operation since Sydney 2000; of 'embezzlement', for salaries and expenses officially paid to formally employed taekwondo secretaries; and of 'entertainment', including accommodation and meals for foreign IOC members on official visits to Korea. Kim had been duly convicted in May with imprisonment for two and a half years by a court priding itself on a 99 per cent conviction rate – the presiding judge alleged not to have pronounced an acquittal in two decades – and accepting as a matter of principle that allegations offered by the prosecution were necessarily true: in other words, conviction by assumption of guilt, without documentary substantiation, Kim being denied proper defence procedure. His fellow Korean IOC members, Kun-Hee Lee, under serious financial investigation in 2008, and Yong-Sung Park, himself subsequently convicted of fraud, did not give evidence in Kim's defence in court, simply petitioning instead for leniency. Rule 25.2.1.1 of the IOC Charter, paragraph 4, states that suspension is discretionary not mandatory. With Kim gravely ill, and in danger of losing his sight, the IOC's trenchant zero-tolerance stance was in contrast, in the eyes of his many friends among IOC members, to the relative leniency extended towards other erring IOC members such as Guy Drut of France. Kim awaited, without optimism, an appeal to the Supreme Court, but meanwhile he was notified that his presidency of GAISF was terminated under the statutes on account of his resignation from the taekwondo federation.

A jolt as ground-shaking and as damaging in terms of public relations as the Ben Johnson affair of 1988 engulfed Greece and the IOC on the day of the opening ceremony: an ironic occurrence given Rogge's words in his speech days earlier at the opening of the IOC Session, when he had said: 'News recently has been marked by a growing number of positive doping cases. Paradoxically, this is an encouraging sign that the fight against doping is gaining ground and that it is becoming increasingly hard to cheat.' There was nothing encouraging, however, about the embarrassment and shame into which the host nation was plunged when two of the projected home stars of the forthcoming fortnight failed to show for a scheduled doping test, alleging that they had crashed on a motorcycle loaned by their coach, being unavoidably detained in hospital. The Athens police could find no evidence or witnesses to the alleged crash, nor the random car said to have ferried them to hospital, while their injuries were slight and contradictory to the circumstances. The Greek track federation requested postponement of an IOC inquiry over the weekend, while the Hellenic Olympic Committee suspended them without withdrawing them from the Games, against the wishes of the HOC's president Lambis Nikolaou, defeated in a vote 5–1. The two athletes vainly requested to be allowed to give drug tests while in hospital. 'They hoped to be tested in hospital, believing this to be in their favour,' Arne Ljungqvist, chairman of the IOC Medical Commission said. 'I don't know what their strategy was, but we did not fall for it . . . You can fix things there so you don't get a positive result.' With the media worldwide feasting on the latest scandal, not least the Greek press demanding 'the truth', Kenteris and Thanou, conscious that the IOC remained adamant on several missed tests being equivalent to a positive, decided after three days to surrender their accreditations, thereby circumventing a direct ban from the Games by the IOC. It was truly a Greek tragedy of a dimension undeserved by a little country with an historic past which had put so much toil and heart into a project that, truthfully, was financially excessive. (At the time of writing, January 2008, Thanou and Kenteris were due to go on trial in June 2008 on charges of perjury.)

From supremacy to ridicule for Kostas Kenteris: triumphant in Sydney, hounded out in Athens.
(© IOC/Locatelli) (© Getty Images/Bicanski)

They had deserved better than this at the beginning of their celebrations, on the return to the front line of the event they had founded those thousands of years before and last formerly staged in 1896. They had gambled $7 billion or more on the project. Over a century before, 14 nations had been represented here in Athens: now, for the XXVIIIth Olympiad, there were a record 201. From 43 events in 1896, the total had grown to 301, including the newest: women's wrestling. From 245 athletes, all male, the total had climbed to 10,625, of these 4,329 female. 'The citizens of Greece have proved the doomsayers wrong,' pronounced Peter Ueberroth, USOC president. 'Once again, the Olympic family has learned the lesson from Greece.' In recognition of their heritage, the Greeks decided to take one event, the shot put, to the original Olympia site, with little harmful damage despite the protests of archaeologists, and to stage, on the imaginative recommendation of James Easton, president of the International Archery Federation, the competition for that elegant sport in the gracious marble Panathinaiko Stadium of the inaugural modern Games. The Koreans, North and South, would march side by side, as in

Sydney, and if there were a record 24 drug violations, surprisingly none of them American, Dick Pound's stance was being upheld: 'If we catch you, you're gone. If we can't catch you now, we'll get you later and you're gone.' His confidence in effectiveness would be both supported and dented, however, by an internal memorandum within the IAAF following the Games, titled 'After Athens: Improving the Athletics Anti-Doping Campaign', which declared: 'The doping-related incidents in Athens and earlier this year are evidence that neither national federations nor the IAAF itself are doing enough to ensure fair competition and a positive reputation for athletics. There are weaknesses in our rules, our policies, and the enforcement of our rules.' The document alleged absence of out-of-competition testing in many nations and questioned the allowance of three no-shows before declaring an offence.

The only political blip of the fortnight came with anti-American protests when Bush's government planned to send Secretary of State Colin Powell as an official visitor to the closing ceremony, against the background of an election campaign utilising the Olympic rings, the government refusing to withdraw the use in spite of protests by USOC, and with the IOC remaining strangely silent, Rogge announcing: 'We have no reason to intervene on something that is purely a domestic American issue.' Nonetheless, Powell's appearance was cancelled. At the closing ceremony, Costas Karamanlis managed to thank Hellenic people for the success of the Games while avoiding mention of the woman without whom they would probably never have staged them, Gianna Angelopoulos-Daskalaki. 'A new chapter has begun for our society,' he proclaimed.

It was short of being a new society in South Africa, though, with IOC member Sam Ramsamy lamenting 'too many athletes from privileged areas', with only 21 out of a team of 106 being non-white. 'It's an indictment of all of us in South African sport that we are not accelerating development,' Ramsamy said. And there would be no more sport for Eleni Ioannou, 20-year-old member of the Greek judo squad who died in hospital 17 days after sustaining multiple injuries when she jumped from the balcony of the apartment of her fiancé following a romantic rift.

Perhaps *The Times* of London put these Games, indeed all Games, into perspective, when its editorial observed:

> It takes but a quick appreciation of the risks of rotary as opposed to in-line shot-putting to remember what the Olympics is: a parade of largely unknown people straining every fibre of their beings in unfamiliar costumes, against excruciating odds, for their honour and our fascination. Up close, the Olympics can look laughable (we are only now approaching the nose-clip phase in the aquatics centre), but, taken as a whole, it is one of the most impressive and important things our species does.

A shade patronising, it might be said. For thousands of competitors, the Olympics continue to provide their particular Everest, at different levels, occasionally conquered but always educational, in life and, if they are fortunate, providing life-long friendships.

CHAPTER LXXIII

Athens (XXVIII) 2004

Hicham El Guerrouj of Morocco, Olympic 1,500m and 5,000m champion

'*When I was a boy of 13, I began to have the dream of winning in the Olympic Games. By the time I reached the age of 16 and had won the Moroccan cross-country, I realised I could perhaps one day be an Olympic champion. The feeling was there that I had the endurance in me to do it. For my generation, the legend, the inspiration, was Saïd Aouita. We didn't know too much about Sebastian Coe, the renowned double champion, but I did begin watching videos of him in the late '90s. At 29, sadly I was still dreaming, having failed in the 1,500m in two consecutive Games, at Atlanta and then Sydney.*

When I fell in Atlanta with a lap to go, I was devastated. Slowly, however, I began to accept that this was not a defeat, and my regime altered: all strategy, training, philosophy, changed in almost every way, to the point where the Atlanta result was reduced in my mind to some small passing moment in my career. When you are at the top, such things can happen, so you have to remain determined, strong; you have to acknowledge that misfortune is possible. This made me work harder, pushing myself to my limits. This further developed my running, but more devastation was to follow when I lost in Sydney.

I had kept a photo of that fall in Atlanta above my bed for four years, but I felt depressed whenever I looked at it and after Sydney I removed it. I realised that if you somehow mentally surrender to a picture, the same may happen again.

With that Sydney defeat, the young Kenyan [Ngeny] had been finishing second behind me for such a long time that in a way I was happy for him when he won, though that disappeared with the realisation that I must again change many things. All except one: my supporting entourage – my coach, those helping me, they had to remain the same, especially when there was a lot of outside pressure for me to change them, too. But the fact was that for the 1,500m final in Sydney I was very strong physically, following arduous training, but I arrived at the Games both physically and mentally tired.

From then on, I gained in maturity. I didn't accept what the critics said, and everyone close to me knew I still had the ambition to become Olympic champion. The desire, the need, grew ever stronger. I knew I could not let my career end with the world title in Paris in 2003, my fourth, or I'd be unhappy for the rest of my life.

When did I decide to attempt both 1,500m and 5,000m in Athens? It was before the championships in Paris. I discussed the possibility with Lamine Diack [president of the IAAF], and he said that it was also possible to adjust the Athens programme to let me run in both races. It was my last chance for the Olympic 1,500m and a unique possibility for the double. I won the 1,500m in Paris and came second in the 5,000m, mainly because I made an error, attacking too early two laps out.

By the time I arrived in Athens, my experience, the history of all that had gone before, made me incredibly strong. I was at an absolute peak. When mind and body are synchronised, you're in good shape, and I was eager to race. Taking a shower after a heat, I wanted the next day to be now, for tomorrow to be today. It was the exact opposite of my feeling in Sydney, when I just didn't want to run and was crying two hours before leaving my room.

After I won the 1,500m in Athens, I was so happy; I was wondering if I could win a 10,000m as well as the 5,000m. Entering the stadium was like stepping onto a theatre stage; I felt so confident, though I have to admit that winning the 5,000m was not the same feeling as the 1,500m. I think it was something like it must have been for Seb Coe: for him, to win the 800m had been so important.

I think I changed the way the 1,500m is run. Previously, it had been down to who ran the fastest over the last 300 metres. Starting in 1996, there was a revolution: it became a race of rhythm at a very high level, and that's why I was able to run 37 times under 3:30. I like to feel that my career showed that a young Moroccan who works hard can do what others can do, and this was part of my mission. Twenty years ago, young Moroccans didn't have the right to dream; there were a lot of problems in our society, and they would have laughed at me if I'd spoken about my dreams. Now the Moroccan mentality has changed.'*

(Photograph © IOC/Mifune)

To describe a competitor as 'the greatest Olympian' would be subjective and misleading, but there is no question that Hicham El Guerrouj placed himself among the pantheon of legends with his emulation of Paavo Nurmi, 80 years earlier, by becoming the second to achieve the 1,500m and 5,000m double. The previous summer, Sebastian Coe, a performer with the status to make such a statement, had described El Guerrouj as 'arguably the best middle-distance runner we have ever seen', and that was even before the Moroccan had recorded his fourth successive world title at 1,500m. After his phenomenal deed in Athens, it was speculated what El Guerrouj might now achieve at 10,000m, yet illness and injury would force his unexpected retirement in May 2006. It was, perhaps, appropriate to quit at the top, and El Guerrouj was able to admit: 'For the first time in ten years, I was now able to spend time with my family. I'd thought a lot about the future and was not so much focused on athletics.'

It had been a fabulous career, winning 84 of his 89 races between 1996 and 2004, dominating the mile and the metric mile and still holding world records, indoor and outdoor, at both distances. His landmarks were well documented: third at 5,000m in the World Junior Championships in 1992; sudden emergence at 1,500m two years later with 3:33.61 at senior level; first world indoor title in 1995 at 1,500; more than a second clipped off Morceli's world mark the following year with a 3:26.0; first of four consecutive world titles at 1,500m in 1997, in which year he set indoor records for the mile and 1,500m; established, and still standing, one mile and 2,000m records (3:43.13/4:44.79) in 1999. On retirement, he would reflect on the self-discipline that distinguishes every great middle-distance runner and which contemporary aspirants find so unappealing: 'I train hard. Twice a day. Between 25 and 30 kilometres a day. I like to suffer when I train. If I train and I am not suffering, I am not training well.' Non-political by nature, he nonetheless intended to become involved politically at some stage 'to help the people of Morocco'.

When El Guerrouj came to the line for the final of the 1,500m in Athens, worldwide expectation, and judgement, of any competitor has seldom been more intense, not to mention that the entire population of Morocco were praying for him as though he were a brother. Suspended somewhere in his consciousness, even though he had lost only five races in eight years and run seven of the ten fastest times ever, was that haunting question from a Moroccan journalist following his failure in Sydney, prior to which he had won 28 consecutive finals: 'How do you explain your shame to 30 million Moroccans?' At the age of 30, here was his final chance to answer.

His mood will not have been aided by a false start, rarely seen at this distance, and he spent the first lap tracking his feared rival, Bernard Lagat of Kenya, bronze winner in Sydney who had just defeated him two weeks earlier in Zurich. Two laps out, El Guerrouj hit the front, yet seemed a sitting target for the Kenyan. With Lagat attacking off the final bend, 60 yards out, and drawing level, it seemed as though disaster was once more about to strike this exemplary runner, someone who commendably had never dodged a rival in his race schedule, as some others had done. What had he in hand to deflect a third perceived humiliation in what after all is only a foot race? What he had was courage, and as the pair strove for the line, with El Guerrouj's friends and admirers barely daring to watch, he held his stride, defied fate, refused to surrender to Lagat and crossed the line for his ultimate reward with a margin of twelve-hundredths of a second in 3:34.18. Lagat's was the same margin behind him as when finishing third in Sydney, yet times in an

Olympic final are all but irrelevant. It was the closest margin since John Walker's victory over Ivo Van Damme in 1976, the bronze going to Rui Silva of Portugal. With El Guerrouj on his knees in thanksgiving, kissing the track, Lagat dropped down to congratulate his friend, reflecting later: 'I had nothing left. I came on strong, and today he was stronger.' Having discarded the mantle of American Jim Ryun as the greatest runner never to win this title, El Guerrouj went on his lap of honour, pausing only for a jig of unbridled joy to the loudspeakers' 'Zorba's Dance' and to take a mobile phone call of congratulation from Mohammed VI, King of Morocco. Afterwards, he would identify the source of his strength as Hiba, his daughter born two months earlier, whom he had seen only three times.

El Guerrouj signals 'two' – the 1,500/5,000m double emulating the legendary Nurmi in 1924. (© IOC/Kishimoto)

And now, improbably, for the 5,000m. When Nurmi had last achieved the double, in 1924, the gap between his two finals had been only two hours, Finnish officials persuading the French hosts to widen that from half an hour. El Guerrouj had 24 hours between his 1,500m victory and a 5,000m semi-final, but whatever his ambition it was widely believed that he would not have the endurance to match Kenenisa Bekele, the 21-year-old Ethiopian who had already won the 10,000m with a devastating sprint over the last lap. Bekele himself was chasing an historic double, achieved six times by five athletes: Hannes Kolehmainen (1912), Emile Zátopek (1952), Vladimir Kuts (1956), Lasse Virén (1972 and 1976) and Miruts Yifter, another Ethiopian (1980). The odds against El Guerrouj now joining this elite group were further lengthened by the fact that this would be only his seventh race at this distance, and besides Bekele he would also be up against the current world champion, Eliud Kipchoge of Kenya, who had beaten them both in the previous summer's final. In the event, with no one prepared to set the stern early pace that might have drained the capacity of El Guerrouj for a late strike, the Moroccan ran a tactically perfect race, conveniently for him then dependent on basic speed over the last 100 metres. Bekele had set an early pedestrian lead, others took over in turn, and El Guerrouj coasted comfortably in seventh place. A kick by Bekele, with seven of the twelve and a half laps remaining, failed to establish a gap, and Kipchoge moved to the front three and a half laps out, the two passing the bell together but with El Guerrouj in attendance. As they came into the final straight, he still possessed sufficient acceleration to whip past them both, exhilaratingly crossing the line in an admittedly slowish 13:14.39, with two-tenths of a second to spare over Bekele. Pointedly, he raised two fingers to the cameras in celebration of his historic double. He reflected later: 'Nurmi is a legend. My grandfather was watching him, and now I have two gold medals like him. Four years ago in Sydney I cried like a child, now I'm as happy as a child.'

Mounting his pedestal, El Guerrouj joined another legend, Haile Gebrselassie, the foremost distance runner of his generation who had said farewell to the Games at the age of 31 with fifth place in the 10,000m in the wake of his successive victories at Atlanta and Sydney. The honour had remained in Ethiopia, claimed by his young compatriot Bekele, with another, Sileshi Sihine, taking silver ahead of Zersenay Tadesse, who became Eritrea's first-ever Olympic medallist. In a defining example of sportsmanship, Bekele and Sihine, training partners of Gebrselassie, had eased the pace mid-race to help their compatriot stay near the front, but once they became aware of his fading stride they soared away after nine kilometres to take the prizes, Bekele's second-last lap of 53.02 giving him an Olympic record of 27:05.10. Gebrselassie had been undermined by Achilles problems, and though he had moved to the front after two kilometres, he was unable to sustain his effort. Several others, including Disi of Rwanda, Tanzanians Yuda and Joseph, Mosop of Kenya and Kiprop of Uganda, led at some stage, but none could challenge the young Ethiopians. The nation's strength at this distance was repeated in the women's long-distance events, with Meseret Defar winning the 5,000m ahead of Isabella Ochichi (KEN) and compatriot Tirunesh Dibaba, while Ejegayehu Dibaba and Derartu Tulu, the latter the winner in Sydney, took silver and bronze in the 10,000m behind Huina Xing (CHN).

Greece having been elected Olympic hosts primarily in recognition of their sporting history rather than contemporary commercial power or international sporting prowess, it was appropriate that these Games should return, if only briefly, to their original ancient home. Shortly after sunrise on the fifth day, the gates to the site of Olympia opened to an audience from the modern world, from the USA to Russia, from Europe to the Far East, for the staging of the men's and women's shot put competitions: a return after 1,611 years, even if not for an historic event such as the javelin or discus. Administratively, the shot put was convenient, a relatively quick competition needing a small arena of no more than 30 metres. It would cause the least disruption to the sense of antiquity and proprietorial archaeologists' dignity. So there, against a backdrop of olive groves, alongside the low stretch of marble that, with its parallel grooves, used to give the ancient sprinters a toehold on the starting line, modern Olympians took to the stage first occupied 2,780 years ago. Now, at the peak of the afternoon finals, there were a mere 20,000 spectators rather than the 40,000 of long ago, with dress strictly conventional, never mind the stifling heat. 'You wouldn't want us to throw naked,' said the American John Godina to a group of reporters. Another sharp contrast, of which modern founder Pierre de Coubertin would not have approved, was the presence of women – as competitors. The stadium's most dramatic link to ancient time was the remnant of a marble tunnel through which competitors passed on their way to the dirt throwing circle.

By coincidence, the day that the Greeks sought an echo of their glorious past was the day that their two most prominent athletes, sprinters Kostas Kenteris and Ekaterini Thanou, were obliged to surrender their competitors' passes in the wake of

their missed drug tests. Sadly, Olympia was also to produce an echo of the present with the subsequent expulsion of the women's event winner, Irina Korzhanenko, who tested positive for steroids. The Russian had the distinction of being both the first modern winner at Olympia and simultaneously testing positive, as did Olga Shchukina, who finished last. 'This tarnishes what was intended to be a symbolic event,' lamented Arne Ljungqvist, chairman of the IOC's Medical Commission. Korzhanenko's shame was scarcely unprecedented. She had been banned from participation in the 2000 Games after testing positive and being stripped of her silver medal in the World Championships of 1999. Thus the title instead went to Yumileidi Cumba of Cuba, ahead of Nadine Kleinert (GER) and Svetlana Krivelyova (RUS). The men's title on this historic day was suitably climactic. Yuriy Bilonog of Ukraine and American Adam Nelson tied with the longest throws of 21.16m (69 ft 5 in.), produced by Nelson in the first round and Bilonog in the sixth and final, Bilonog prevailing on account of the best second throw (69 ft 4 in.). Nelson might have won with his sixth throw, which was his fifth consecutive foul, conceding it was illegal after a view of the re-run. Joachim Olsen (DEN) took the bronze.

With the reputation of track and field, indeed of the whole Games, tarnished by drug offences among sprinters and the heavy throwers, the honour and credibility of the sport has increasingly become dependent on long-distance competitors, especially those at the summit of endurance, the marathon. In the intense heat of Athens, both men's and women's races were conspicuous for controversial dramas, each concluding at the inaugural but now modernised Panathinaiko Stadium. On the final night of the Games, Vanderlei de Lima of Brazil was unexpectedly leading the men's race by almost half a minute at the 36km/22-mile mark when an intruder leapt from the crowd and thrust him off the road into a group of spectators. Immediately arrested by police, Cornelius Horan, 57, a defrocked Irish priest, had previously intervened at the British F1 motor event the previous year, running onto the track in front of drivers. An unhappy de Lima, quickly recovering to re-enter the race, though having lost at least 30 metres of his lead, inevitably had his mental and physical rhythm impaired. His pursuers admittedly had been shortening his lead, and some seven minutes after his assault he was overtaken by Stefano Baldini of Italy with three kilometres remaining. De Lima, twice Pan-American champion who had finished 47th in the 1996 Olympic race, had at one stage led by almost a minute and a half. So convincing was Baldini's form in the latter stages, covering the last 10 kilometres in under 29 minutes, that de Lima's prospects would have been under severe challenge even without his misfortune. Baldini reached the finish of this most punishing of events in 2:10:55, 34 seconds ahead of the unexpected silver medal winner, Mebrahtom Keflezighi of America. A magnanimous de Lima declined to criticise security. 'I think this was an isolated incident,' he said. 'I was afraid, I didn't know what he had with him, and I lost my rhythm. If you stop in the middle of a marathon, it's really difficult to get your rhythm back.' As consolation, he was awarded the Pierre de Coubertin medal for exceptional sportsmanship, though the subsequent appeal by Brazil for him to be granted the victor's gold medal was dismissed by both the IAAF and then the Court of Arbitration for Sport. Baldini became only the second Italian to win the marathon title, while Keflezighi's silver was the first for the US since Frank Shorter's in 1976. Jon Brown (GBR) finished fourth for the second consecutive Olympics, but an unhappy Paul Tergat, world record holder, faded over the final two kilometres to finish tenth.

371

Vanderlei de Lima of Brazil, awarded the Pierre de Coubertin medal for exceptional sportsmanship. (© IOC/Sugimoto)

The women's marathon was a revelation for at least one distraught competitor, Paula Radcliffe of Britain, who learned that, whatever her own illustrious prior achievements, whatever the expectation of her performance at home and indeed by some of her rivals, there were other great competitors out there: from the Far East, from Africa, from America. The outcome proved a triumph for Mizuki Noguchi of Japan, a country where marathon running has become almost addictive in the years since 1997, when Athens hosted the World Championships and the women's winner was Horimi Suzuki, followed by the Sydney Olympics, where the winner was Naoko Takahashi. Instead of Radcliffe, setter of world best times and winner of all three marathons that she had run, sustaining a pace that would break the others, it was Noguchi's performance over the sustained climb between 25km and 30km that was to prove critical. By the time she reached 30km, after running the previous five kilometres in under seventeen minutes, she had established a near half-minute lead on Elfenesh Alemu of Ethiopia and slightly more over Radcliffe. Circumstances provided an unholy challenge to the runners, with temperatures around 38°C in the shade. After a little more than a third of the race, the lead group from an entry of ninety-three was reduced to ten: three Japanese, two Romanians, two Kenyans, Alemu, Olivera Jevtic (SCG) and Radcliffe. This group shortly became seven, by the halfway stage in 1:14:02. Way back was Deena Kastor of America, wisely preserving herself for a strong finish. At 32km, the summit of the long climb, both Radcliffe and then Alemu were overtaken by Catherine Ndereba of Kenya. Dreams of even a medal for Radcliffe – whose luckless syndrome at previous championships had been to be overtaken in the later stages of races which she had led – had now evaporated, and at the 36km mark she collapsed in tears. Ndereba's pursuit of Noguchi, second behind her in the previous year's World Championship, could not draw her closer than twelve seconds, while Kastor, with a final five kilometres in under sixteen and a half minutes, brought the first American medal since Joan Benoit won the inaugural event twenty years before. Not only did the tiny Noguchi, a mere 40 kg and 1.5 m tall, renew Japanese triumph, but compatriots Reiko Tosa and Naoko Sakamoto finished fifth and seventh respectively. Radcliffe's tears in failure were compounded by a sense back home that she should have kept going, no matter where she finished, though she would always be remembered for her courage at the World Championships of 2001 when unfurling a banner in the face of drug abusers: 'EPO Cheats Out'.

If Noguchi was a dramatic part of the prominent presence of women at the Athens Games, and Radcliffe too in the manner that she would least wish, there were many others strengthening the profile of the gender which de Coubertin had deemed unacceptable. Not least Françoise Mbango Etone. In only the third Olympic staging of the women's triple jump, the girl from Cameroon not only set the best mark of 15.30 but did so twice to defeat the favourite, Hrysopiyi Devetzi of Greece, by five centimetres, with Tatyana Lebedeva in third place. It was a supreme moment for Mbango Etone, 28 yet still shy and without a sense of presence in her moment of glory as her country's first track and field gold medal winner. To help her celebrate, his voice loud and clear in rendering the national anthem as their flag was raised, was the better-known Roger Milla, renowned for his deeds in football's World Cup of 1990. It took time for Mbango Etone to realise the full significance of what she had done, but she was then able to dance in a mutual celebration with Devetzi, generous in her congratulations.

Even newer to the programme, and an event by now surrounded in glamorous anticipation, is the women's pole vault, first staged at Sydney and won by American Stacy Dragila ahead of Russian/Australian show-woman Tatiana Grigorieva. Now there was fresh drama, Dragila having failed to qualify for the final and Grigorieva having retired: a long-running Russian rivalry between Yelena Isinbayeva and Svetlana Feofanova, from Volgograd and Moscow respectively. The two were less than the best of friends, Isinbayeva, the younger by two years at twenty-two, from a materially comfortable background, Feofanova contrastingly the child of a single mother whose life had been at full stretch to sustain her family. Both had originally been gymnasts, and rivalry intensified with their conversion to the bar of ever-ascending height. Feofanova had seemingly possessed the Olympic pedigree, winning both outdoor and indoor world titles the previous year, yet Isinbayeva had set the tone for a stirring climax when improving both those marks prior to Athens, the pair exchanging the outdoor title twice more before the Games. It would be an enthralling competition, with more than 20,000 people staying late into the night to witness the outcome. With Feofanova stalling at 4.75m, the glory was Isinbayeva's, with yet another world record at 4.91m, Anna Rogowska of Poland taking the bronze. In the men's event, Tim Mack of America set a new Olympic record of 5.95 at his third attempt at the height to deny his compatriot Toby Stevenson, he in turn shading the reigning world champion Giuseppe Gibilisco of Italy.

Queen of all the women, it might be said, was that blonde Swede with a charismatic talent the sincerity of which defies the belief of cynics: Carolina Kluft. Competitors just aren't like that in the twenty-first century, the cynics assert. Yet Kluft truly is a throwback to the era of Chariots of Fire and beyond, who competes for the improbable satisfaction of friendliness and fun. With her Olympic heptathlon title added to those of world and European, she was acclaimed not just by spectators – 70,000 at the Olympic stadium – but almost every other front-line athlete. With her winning points total of 6,952, the 7,000 barrier now beckoned. There is something awesomely courageous in Kluft's approach to her sport: an apparent crisis, say, in one of the seven events generates not anxiety but exhilaration. Her sense of attack at all times is captivating for the audience. In Athens, she was driven towards excellence in the final discipline, the 800m, by Kelly Sotherton, a relatively inexperienced Briton who set off at a burning pace in search of the silver medal. She was defied by Austra Skujyte of Lithuania, a 25 year old gaining the first women's Olympic track medal for her country. Kluft had all but secured the title with her prior javelin throw of 48.89m, her season's best.

Carolina Kluft, Swedish heroine, captivates the audience with her sense of attack. (© IOC/Kishimoto)

If Kluft's triumph was to a degree predictable, then the double gold by Kelly Holmes, veteran British middle-distance runner, verged on fantasy land. At the age of 34, and having previously considered retirement several times when repetitively frustrated by injury, now in the space of six days Holmes soared to unimagined glory, achieving the 800/1,500m double that had eluded all but a handful of great runners of the past, women or men. Albert Hill (GBR) had achieved it in 1920, Peter Snell (NZL) in 1964, Tatyana Kazankina (SOV) in 1976 and Svetlana Masterkova (RUS) in 1996. The nadir of Holmes' career had arrived seven years before in the same stadium, when, having just established at home a UK record for 1,500m, she arrived as favourite for the World Championships only to be floored by an Achilles injury. It was not an exaggeration to say that her career had been badly advised, Coe himself stating several years previously that she was 'a Rolls-Royce athlete receiving back-street servicing'. Lottery funding resolved that, and her Athens torch was ignited when, with characteristic will-power, she drove herself past the defending 800m champion Maria Mutola of Mozambique three metres from the line. This was a title Holmes had believed unlikely, but she recorded her season's best of 1:53.38. The unfortunate Mutola, defeated only once in the previous 38 races, herself set a season's best of 1:56.51, but in that final surge to the tape she was overtaken also by Hasna Benhassi of Morocco and Jolanda Ceplak of Slovenia, both recording 1:56.43, Ceplak shaded by inches. At one stage, Holmes had not even planned to run this event, never mind her extensive training alongside Mutola, but sound current

form persuaded her otherwise. In a fast early pace, she had remained patiently at the back. As Mutola made her move on the second back straight, Holmes went with her, passing the front runners. Stronger now than when she had finished fourth in 1996 and then third in Sydney, Holmes forged through in lane three to seal success, unaware that she had won until watching the re-run on the video screen.

To follow this with victory in the 1,500m was, as they say, beyond belief. Coe attributed the feat to her mental discipline: 'It would have been easy to spend the day off between the semi-final and final [of the 1,500m] looking at what she had already done rather than looking ahead to the battle still to be fought.' Holmes ran with calm tactical sense, generating a devastating finish over the last 120 metres, improving her own national record set in 1997 by 0.17, with 3:57.90. Seven of the first eight also recorded personal bests, the first six inside four minutes. On the final bend, Tatyana Tomashova (RUS) and Maria Cioncan of Romania jostled, Holmes steering clear of them on the bend in lane three to drive for the line. The other two recovered their balance to take silver and bronze.

Kelly Holmes of Britain, as surprised as anyone when adding 1,500m victory to 800m: a combination of mental discipline and tactical sense that outpaced Tatyana Tomashova of Russia. (© IOC/Kishimoto)

China, bent on enhancing its credentials as Olympic hosts for 2008, was already enjoying a surge in the medal tally when Xiang Liu, 21 year old from Shanghai, became the first Chinese man to win a track gold and more particularly the first to take a medal in a sprint: the 110m hurdles. That was barely a surprise, for he already held the world record with 12.91, and now equalled it with the yawning margin of 0.27 seconds ahead of Terrence Trammell of America, with the defending champion Anier Garcia of Cuba a fraction further behind for the bronze. 'This will be a great encouragement and very influential for developing sports in the future,' Xiao Tian, secretary-general of China's sports federation, said. 'Track and field is the mother of other sports, the most basic.' Liu himself was demonstrative in his view: 'I hope the result will change people's minds – that an Asian nation, in terms of the hurdles or the sprints, lags behind the Europeans and Americans.' His perfected technique, indeed, had enabled him to extend his lead hurdle by hurdle. He had begun his career as a high jumper, being 1.88m tall (6 ft 2 in.), and now he gave a flawless performance at his preferred event. It made him confident for the prospect four years hence. 'I'll be 25 then, and that age will be optimum for any athlete. I will not miss that opportunity,' he asserted.

World record holder Xiang Liu's yawning margin as he takes China's first-ever men's track gold medal ahead of Wignall (JAM) 4th and Doucoure (FRA) 8th. (© IOC/Kishimoto)

Unprecedented improvement by any athlete in their mid-20s always generates surprise and, indeed, demand for a degree of explanation. How has this been achieved against a background of conventional training? When Fani Halkia gladdened 70,000 Greek hearts, not to mention a few million others following on television, by winning the women's 400m hurdles with a time improved by four seconds in the space of a single season, the feat was bound to provoke speculation. She was the most unexpected Olympic champion since, it must be said, her shamed compatriot Kenteris, winner of the 200m in 2000. Her previous best time, having converted to the track from the high jump, was 56.40 seconds. In her semi-final, Halkia ran 52.77 to break the Olympic record of 52.82 – set by Deon Hemmings of Jamaica in 1996 – and then took the final in that time ahead of Ionela Tirlea-Manolache (ROM) and Tetiana Tereshchuk-Antipova (UKR). Her seven competitions that year had produced five national records. She attributed her dramatic improvement to an injury-free winter of training for the first time in six years, under the guidance of former sprinter Yorgas Panayiotopoulos. He had previously been coached by Christos Tzekos, the same man who had guided Kenteris and Thanou.

There was less surprise about the victory of Felix Sanchez in the men's event, the twenty-seven-year-old Dominican having won the last two world titles as well as the Golden League (2002), the inaugural IAAF world final (2003), and having topped the rankings for 158 weeks – a dominance almost on a par with Edwin Moses, including forty-two consecutive victories. He remained consistent to the last, claiming his title with a season's best of 47.63, comfortably ahead of Danny McFarlane (JAM) and Naman Keita (FRA).

The supreme Michael Johnson was missing, and missed, after his two successive Olympic 400m titles, but up stepped Jeremy Wariner from Waco, Texas, the same city where Johnson had been primed in the one-lap race. The twenty-year-old American did not emulate Johnson's two sub-44 victories – a mark surpassed every time since 1984 – clocking 44 precisely, his eighth sub-45 of the season, yet brought to nineteen the number of American victories in the twenty-six Olympic editions of this event. It is not being racist to observe that he was the first white man to win it in a non-boycotted Games since Mike Larrabee of America in 1964 – a feature viewed with common sense by Otis Harris and Derrick Brew, the two African-Americans who took the medals behind him. 'Race has nothing to do with it,' Harris said. 'When people break down stereotypes, that's what the sport should be about.' Harris's time of 44.16 was a personal best, with an American medal clean sweep repeating that of 1988. The race was significant also in that seven of the eight runners bettered 45.

The standard over two laps, however, has temporarily declined, and the 800m title went to Yuriy Borzakovskiy, a 23-year-old Russian, with a moderate time of 1:44.45, his late kick easing him ahead of South African Mbulaeni Mulaudzi, the world indoor champion. His season shortened by injury and illness, Mulaudzi managed to hold off Wilson Kipketer, the adopted Dane and three-time world champion, whose Olympic ambition was once more scuppered. He paid the price of the slow race, then being vulnerable to Borzakovskiy's pace over the final 200. Kipketer's former compatriots Ezekiel Kemboi, Brimin Kipruto and Paul Koech gave Kenya a sweep in the 3,000m steeplechase, a repeat of Kenya's feat in 1992. Kemboi's 8:05.81 was only a fraction off the Olympic record.

Roman Sebrle of the Czech Republic earned eminence as outstanding all-round male athlete with victory in the decathlon, exceeding Daley Thompson's 20-year-old record of 8,847 points with 8,893, the fifth-highest score ever, having been the first man to surpass 9,000 points for his world record three years earlier. He had begun indifferently in the 100m, slowly climbing towards fulfilment, though it was not until the penultimate event, the javelin, that he gained the lead. American Bryan Clay took silver with 8,820, the highest total ever to fail to win. Dmitriy Karpov (RUS), who had earlier led the competition, faded over the second day for bronze.

Who now believes in sprinters? What once used to be a blue riband of events, the heritage from Jesse Owens and later Wilma Rudolph defamed by Ben Johnson and a host of Americans and others, has become so discredited ever since 1988 by repetitive drug scandals emanating from every quarter of the sprinting world that nobody, least of all the Olympic viewing public, has serious expectation of clean champions. Such a mood had been reinforced by the shabby incidents immediately preceding the Games involving two Greek sprinters (see Chapter LXXII). Now, the men's 100m proved to be, in terms of times, collectively the fastest ever, with the first five running under ten seconds. Four had done so in 1996, and now the winner was Justin Gatlin, one of the less flamboyant of American sprinters, whose winning time of 9.85 was exceeded in the Olympics only by Canadian Donovan Bailey's 9.84 in 1996. One-hundredth of a second behind was Francis Obikwelu of Portugal, with Maurice Greene, world record holder and Olympic winner in 2000, taking bronze, a further hundredth behind. Obikwelu's silver – eclipsing the European record – would deny the US a sweep of medals in all three sprints. The 9.89 performance of Shawn Crawford, the third American in fourth place, would have won all but two previous Olympic titles. He had led at sixty metres, but was fractionally passed by three on the razor-close run-in. Crawford would gain some consolation by taking the 200m title, the stadium having long been a sell-out in the expectation of witnessing Kenteris successfully defend his Sydney title. When the runners duly appeared without him, heckling by the crowd and chants of 'Hellas!' delayed the start by five minutes. Crawford was comfortably ahead of Bernard Williams, with Gatlin taking bronze, and Frankie Fredericks (NAM), twice previously silver medallist, finishing fourth. Yet glory, such as it now was, would be tarnished once more when Gatlin, self-proclaimed as clean, would fail a subsequent test and further lower his sport into the pit of shame.

Justin Gatlin (USA) takes 100m gold in a race in which the first five ran in under ten seconds. Gatlin later tested positive but appealed. (© IOC/Nagaya)

The women's 100m went to Yuliya Nesterenko of Belarus, three-hundredths ahead of American Lauryn Williams, with Veronica Campbell of Jamaica a further hundredth back. Williams, world junior champion, had led until 70 metres. Nesterenko's subsequent press conference witnessed the now regular veiled questions about drugs, enquiring how she might have improved so much over the past year. Campbell, who preceded Williams as junior champion, won the 200m with a

personal best of 22.05, followed home by an 18-year-old American, Allyson Felix, whose 22.18 set a new junior world record. Campbell would conclude a rewarding Games by gaining the sprint relay together with Sherone Simpson, Tayna Lawrence and Aleen Bailey – thanks in part to encouragement from Jamaican legend Merlene Ottey, Olympic heroine of eight medals and thirteen final appearances.

Veronica Campbell of Jamaica completes anchor leg in Jamaica's sprint relay gold. (© IOC/Kishimoto)

For Marion Jones, shadowed throughout her career by the spectre of drugs, the Games were to prove a depressing anti-climax. Having won both sprints in Sydney, she had failed to make the team now in either event, and though she did so with her best leap for six years in the long jump, that event was to bring further dejection with fifth place behind three medal-winning Russians and an Australian. Ultimately, there would be total discredit for her, for track and field, and for Olympic credibility, with her exposure and confession in October 2007 of long-standing drug abuse dating back seven years (as described in the Introduction).

With or without the drug ramifications, Jones within her own country was a figure of far less Olympic impact than the girls, for that is what they are, from gymnastics: the sport that is the focus of so much American attention at the summer event. This was the year when interest could not have been higher, with Carly Patterson, a 16 year old from Plano, Texas, becoming the first American woman since Mary Lou Retton in 1984 to win the all-round title, and only the third to win any all-round medal, following Shannon Miller with silver in 1992. Patterson did so within 24 hours of Paul Hamm winning the men's title in circumstances that were to prove, through no fault of his, highly disagreeable. Moreover she did so, sparkling in her red leotard, at the expense of the perceived darling of the sport, Svetlana Khorkina, a relative veteran at 25 and still pursuing the one title to have eluded her in an illustrious career. More than that, Khorkina's reputation far exceeded any gymnastics apparatus. Besides having been a centrefold attraction in Russian *Playboy*, she enjoyed multiple careers in acting, modelling and appearing in yoghurt commercials. With no dissension from her, she was accompanied at most tournaments by banners proclaiming 'Queen Khorkina'. Her self-belief knew no bounds, but in young Patterson she was to encounter a character of no less self-assurance. For Khorkina, this was to have been her apotheosis following the misfortune four years earlier when, again being the all-round favourite, the vaulting horse had been five centimetres out of position. Stumbling in that event, she had ploughed the next, finally to finish eleventh. Triple world and European all-round champion, and twice taking Olympic gold on the uneven bars, she was entitled to feel superior, and after the opening vault in Athens she marginally led her young American rival and went on to record the highest score of the night on the asymmetric bars. Yet on the balance beam, Khorkina lacked technical difficulty, and Patterson moved ahead. Now the gold was to be won or lost on the floor. Khorkina's performance combined every element of her interpretative art. It was not enough. One flawless performance was met by another, Patterson's tumbling routine surpassing even the queen of the sport. It was a revolutionary turnaround after Patterson and her colleagues had under-performed in the team competition, conceding the title to Romania while remaining narrowly ahead of the Russians, Khorkina and all. For Khorkina it was not the last setback of the Games. Bidding for a third consecutive title on the uneven bars, she lost her grip on the upper bar, failed to complete a swing, hung for a moment and then dropped to the mat. Finishing the routine, she received a proportionally low mark and flounced from the arena, finishing a lame eighth with her title going to Emilie Lepennec of France. Posterity will probably judge Patterson as superior even to Retton, for in 1984 the Soviet bloc was absent from Los Angeles.

'Queen Khorkina' of Russia, superstar in the floor exercise but less so on the beam, fell short of apotheosis.
(both photos © IOC/Kishimoto)

The unfortunate Hamm was subjected to a grim aftermath to his victory while a disputed judging decision raged between respective national Olympic committees. Having dropped from first to twelfth when he stumbled from his landing on the vault, he nonetheless clinched victory with his 9.837 points in his concluding routine on the horizontal bars. Admittedly, his achievement was aided by a fall from the horizontal bars by Wei Yang of China, runner-up in both Sydney and then the world championships of 2003. His error would plunge him to seventh.

The final rotation (each on different apparatus) began with Tae Young Yang of Korea leading his compatriot Dae Eun Kim by 0.138 of a point, both Hamm and his colleague Brett McClure being within range. With Kim receiving 9.650 for his floor exercise and Yang only 9.457 on the high bar, the gold seemed Kim's, only for Hamm, the reigning world champion, to snatch the title with his stunning display on the horizontal bars. This was not to be the end of the story. The following day, the gymnastics federation acknowledged an error by one of the judges, giving Tae Young Yang 9.9 start value for his parallel bars routine when it should have been 10. Given that difference, Yang would have won with Hamm second and Kim third. The federation suspended the judges but said they could not alter the result, Bruno Grandi, the president, stating: 'I don't have the possibility, our rules don't allow it.' With both the South Korean and US Olympic committees mounting vigorous counter-protests, Grandi then made an unprecedented, and singularly ill-advised, request to the USOC: that Hamm should relinquish his medal and present it to Yang. Grandi stated that both the International Federation and the IOC 'would highly appreciate the magnitude of this gesture'. The IOC promptly disowned any such stance, USOC was furious and the luckless Hamm was left in a fog: 'I felt really horrible that no one was defending me: not USA gymnastics, not the FIG [the federation] who caused the whole thing, nobody.' He rightly declined to relinquish his medal. USOC officials discussed with their Korean counterparts the seeking of a second gold medal for Yang in the light of double gold medals having been awarded following the skating controversy at Salt Lake City. Bob Colarossi, president of USA gymnastics, attempted to diffuse the situation with the opinion that while judges got things right more often than not there would always be the chance of error: 'There's the judges' view on the floor that has to be respected. You have to stand by the decisions that are made on the field of play; you absolutely have to. If you don't, the competition will never end, and you open everything up to speculation.' In the event, Jacques Rogge, IOC President, stated that there would be no duplicate medals, and an aggrieved Hamm duly held on to his gold. It was only fair to say that Tae Young Yang must have felt even more sore, but that sadly is the nature of sport: the penalty erroneously awarded by a referee in football remains a penalty the following morning.

With changes in the regulations for the team event following Sydney, teams still having six members but only three performing on each apparatus, Japan revived memories of a glorious past when out-pointing favourites China and the US to win the title for the first time in twenty-eight years. Consistent performances enabled Japan – represented by Takehiro Kashima, Hisashi Mizutori, Daisuke Nakano, Hiroyuki Tomita, Naoya Tsukahara and Isao Yoneda – to overhaul the USA, early leaders. Romania, floundering on the horizontal bars, were left with bronze while China, defending champions, erred in their floor exercises to finish fifth. Five times previously successful, Japan last won in 1976 when the inimitable Mitsuo Tsukahara was on the team. It was his son Naoya who now paraded the trophy.

Gymnastic dispute was not confined to Hamm. In the competition for individual horizontal bars, the Russian Olympic Committee protested against low marks for Alexei Nemov, while the Bulgarians were incensed by perceived prejudice against Jordan Jovtchev on the men's rings. Bulgarian sensitivity was no doubt heightened by the intense local support for Dimosthenis Tampakos, the Greek who took the title ahead of Jovtchev, with Yuri Chechi of Italy taking the bronze. Nadia Comaneci, famed Romanian, observed that while the judging process should be re-evaluated, judges' errors in Athens should not affect medal standings.

Home celebration for Dimosthenis Tampakos of Greece, rings champion. (© IOC/Sugimoto)

In the steepling rivalry between the two prime figures in the swimming arena, Ian Thorpe of Australia may have proved himself the king of freestyle, but Michael Phelps, a younger American, having lost to Thorpe in the 200m freestyle, had proved himself to be one of the most versatile medal winners in swimming history. It would be inappropriate to suggest which of them was the greater: what they had done was to provide competitive entertainment at a unique level that enthralled the crowds and enhanced their personal reputations both as swimmers and people. Phelps had swum seventeen races, beaten only twice, and had set one world and three Olympic records – his bid to emulate Mark Spitz's record of seven golds just falling shy of the $1-million bonus that was on offer from sponsors. It was not insignificant that Phelps' progress, under the direction of his coach Bob Bowman, had traced the career path of Thorpe, Bowman having studied the Australian's progress from the age of 15 when he had precociously broken the 400m world record.

Australian Ian Thorpe triumphant in the 200m freestyle 'battle of the giants' with Michael Phelps of America. (© IOC/Kishimoto)

Besides this spectacular rivalry, the swimming gala was otherwise notable for several features: Japan enjoyed its most successful Games for nearly seventy years, finishing third behind the US and Australia with three gold medals, two from Kosuke Kitajima in the breaststroke and eight medals in total; Kirsty Coventry from Zimbabwe, which had never won a swimming medal, came away with one of each colour; South Africa set a 4 x 100m world record; Poland won its first-ever gold through Otylia Jedrzejczak in the 200m butterfly; and Laure Manaudou, only 17, won the women's 400m, France's first title since Jean Boiteux won that men's freestyle event in 1952.

Overall, gold was won by 11 different nations, 19 nations gaining a medal of some hue. An expansion of the sport is clearly evident from the unaccustomed success of such countries as Argentina, Croatia, and Trinidad and Tobago.

Women's 100m backstroke (l to r): Kirsty Coventry (ZIM) 2nd, Natalie Coughlin (USA) 1st, and Laure Manaudou (FRA) 3rd – one of Coventry's three medals, Zimbabwe never previously having won any. (© IOC/Mifune)

Expectation prior to the men's 200m freestyle was bursting the seams of debate, with Thorpe first seeking revenge for his defeat by Pieter van den Hoogenband of Holland in Sydney and, second, trying to resist the menacing challenge of the 19-year-old Phelps, the kid from Baltimore whose 2.01m (6 ft 7 in.) arm-span makes him so formidable at butterfly. Nonetheless, freestyle was Thorpe's speciality, and he had already retained his 2000 title at 400m, a fraction ahead of Phelps' compatriot Grant Hackett, the last man to have beaten him over that distance seven years earlier. The evidence of a close race made some wonder whether Thorpe was now in danger from the young pretender. On the night it was van den Hoogenband, the oldest man in the race, who led at the first turn. For three lengths, Thorpe stayed at the Dutchman's shoulder, with Phelps increasingly building his challenge. As they came out of the third and final turn, Thorpe attacked, and his surge brought him an Olympic record of 1:44.71 with a massive half-second advantage over the Dutchman, Phelps taking the bronze. In that moment, Spitz's record was safe. Phelps, commendably, was undismayed. 'How can I be disappointed?' he asked, having only begun competing in this event a year ago. 'I swam in a field with the two fastest 200m freestylers of all time, and I was right there with them. It's a lot more emotionally draining than anything I've done before, and it takes a lot out of you, race by race, particularly at night. When those guys are going so fast, it makes it real exciting, but it's tough.' Here was magnanimity. Phelps did not even have to swim the 200m, did not have to accept the challenge, yet he did. 'One of the things I've wanted to do is to race Thorpe in a freestyle event before either one of us is done.' There rides the spirit of sport.

Phelps' odyssey proceeded as he established his pile of medals in butterfly and medleys, exhibiting a fine resilience when holding off much fresher opposition in the 200m butterfly and setting an Olympic record – as in the 100m butterfly – with 1:54.04, the second-fastest in history, at the expense of Takashi Yamamoto (JPN) and Stephen Parry (GBR). An hour later, he was leading the US quartet in ending Australia's six-year domination of the 200m freestyle relay. His 100m butterfly record, beating Ian Crocker of the United States by four-hundredths, brought his tally at that point to seven medals including five gold in seven days.

377

Michael Phelps (USA) sweeps to 100m butterfly title, his fifth gold among seven medals. (© IOC)

It was in the 200m medley, Phelps' fourth gold, another Olympic record, ahead of American Ryan Lochte, that George Bovell became Trinidad's first swimming medallist with the bronze. The 200m breaststroke victory of Kitajima, with an Olympic record of 2:09.44, was temporarily in doubt with the accusation, by America, that he had been involved, in his previous 100m breaststroke victory, in the use of an illegal dolphin-kick at the start of the race. Aaron Peirsol, who had won the 100m backstroke for America, had made the accusation, but now, following a pause after the announcement, the disqualification was in fact for Jim Piper of Australia in lane eight. Brendan Hansen (USA), the world record holder, had taken the bronze, with Kitajima the first Japanese ever to win two Olympic golds, Daniel Gyurta of Hungary having claimed silver. Peirsol was himself involved in dispute in the 200m backstroke, three judges submitting an indecipherable reason for his disqualification that made it unclear whether it was for a dolphin-kick or some other offence. The disqualification was dismissed, as were the three judges. In the freestyle short sprints, the 50m title was retained by Gary Hall (USA), joint winner in 2000, while van den Hoogenband, then the bronze winner at that distance, successfully defended his title in the 100m, a fraction ahead of South African Roland Schoeman, with Thorpe in third place, despite his best time ever at the shorter distance. This brought Thorpe's total of medals to nine, breaking a tie with two other Australian swimmers, Susie O'Neill and Dawn Fraser.

Yana Klochkova of Ukraine joined an elite band when winning the 200m individual medley, adding that to the 400m for a double in consecutive Games – the same feat as Alexander Popov of Russia in the freestyle sprints in 1992/96. A name for the future, indeed for now, was the 17-year-old Laure Manaudou of France, who stylishly added a 100m backstroke bronze to her 400m freestyle gold.

While the Games may rightly focus on winners, there are the other thousands who create a unique ambience, none more so than Bryan Nickson, a 14-year-old Malaysian who only missed a place in the men's 10m platform diving semi-final by four points. He had carried his nation's flag at the opening ceremony and would finish 19th out of 33 divers in the preliminary competition, with 18 to qualify. Standing only 1.37m (4 ft 6 in.), he admitted disappointment but insisted: 'I'm happy. It's a dream to be at the Olympic Games.' He had qualified to compete with his performance at the China Open, only his third international event. He had been named after Bryan Robson, the Manchester United and England captain.

Jingjing Guo of China, nine years older than Nickson, was perfection itself when taking the women's 3m springboard title ahead of her 19-year-old compatriot Minxia Wu. What a prospect there was for their projected duel at home four years later, Wu by then having matured. With unusual honesty, Wu admitted: 'At the moment beforehand, I feel on the edge and sometimes even scared, but I repeatedly picture the motion in my head, feel more confident, and leap.' Bo Peng and Jia Hu won the respective 3m and 10m men's titles to bring China three of the main diving awards.

It is regularly said that football does not need the Olympics but certainly the Games would be poorer without football, even allowing for the age restriction imposed by FIFA, with no more than three players permitted over the age of twenty-three. While the 'news' story of the tournament was the progress of Iraq to the bronze medal play-off, which they lost by a solitary goal to Italy, Argentina's gold, with a 41,000 attendance, was distinguished by the emerging Carlos Tevez, at 20 the outstanding player of the tournament and subsequently headed for fame and controversy in the English Premiership. It was appropriate he should score the lone goal against Paraguay, confirming his role as the top scorer with eight. It came after 18 minutes when his speed deceived the defence, including goalkeeper Diego Barreto, as he intercepted a cross from the right by Mauro Rosales. Argentina's emphasis on attack and the absence of tactical cynicism made the final a delight. The influential presence of their left-back Heinze, a Manchester United absentee summer signing from Paris Saint-Germain, had not pleased Sir Alex Ferguson. Alberto Gilardino's winning goal for Italy ended the dream of Iraq, who had astonished the football world by surviving thus far, defeating Costa Rica and then a Portuguese team including Cristiano Ronaldo of Manchester United. No longer was the Iraqi team fearful of defeat and subsequent torture when returning home, as had been the fate those who played under the regime of Uday Hussein, son of Saddam. More than half of the Iraqi competitors at the Games were footballers, and all of the team's qualifying matches had been played away from Iraq. Italy's players wore black armbands for the third-place match in honour of Enzo Baldoni, their journalist killed in Iraq by kidnappers.

Future star: Carlos Tevez inspired Argentina's victory en route to prominence with Manchester United via West Ham. (© IOC/Tanaka)

Mia Hamm, Julie Foudy, Joy Fawcett, Kristine Lilly and Brandi Chastain, five pioneers who had helped win football's first Women's World Cup in 1991 and the first Olympic gold medal in 1996, were there to triumph in an extra-time victory against Brazil, the winner coming in the 112th minute from Abby Wambach. The Americans were outplayed for almost the entire two hours, Brazil failing to capitalise on their superiority. Brazilian women had been scorned in the development of their game: now their skills were coming to fruition and defeat was a matter of lack of application rather than talent.

Triathlon has rapidly become one of the most eagerly awaited sports on the programme, and there could not have been more drama than in the climax of the women's race. Loretta Harrop of Australia led the charge coming out of the water phase, was still there at the front at the conclusion of the cycle ride and seemed to have gold in her grasp as she ran towards the finishing line at Vouliagmeni's upper-crust resort. Yet over the last 200 metres, Kate Allen, another Australian now controversially representing Austria, swept past to deny Harrop. Having met and married an Austrian triathlete, Marcel Diechtler, Allen, an all-rounder, belatedly began to specialise at triathlon. Though Harrop had an 18-second lead at the end of the cycling leg, Allen steadily overhauled her and many others over the 10km run, having been placed no better than 28th as she changed her cycle shoes. As Harrop sadly faded on the run-in, Allen's winning margin was more than six seconds, while American Susan Williams, recovering from a crash on her cycle, gained the bronze. So severe was the heat that six of the fifty starters failed to finish.

In the men's race, in which New Zealanders Hamish Carter and Bevan Docherty were first and second ahead of the Swiss Sven Riederer, Marc Jenkins of Britain set an example for the likes of Paula Radcliffe. On the fourth of five laps of the cycle section, his wheel broken, he picked up his bike and ran with it, uphill, for almost two kilometres. By the time he had changed his wheel at the next pit stop, he was close to being lapped. Last by almost two minutes at the end of the run, he received a standing ovation but was unconsoled: 'Last? I don't want to be a romantic hero for coming last.'

Nobody much likes to win in the committee room rather than on the field, but this was the unappealing lot of Leslie Law, winner of the equestrian individual three-day event. Indeed, by the time it was confirmed that he had won, and not the unfortunate Bettina Hoy of Germany, Law was riding in a novice trials at home in Solihull. The decision had been taken by the Council of Arbitration for Sport, overriding the appeal committee of FEI, the equestrian governing body, which itself had overturned the initial suspension by the competition's three-man jury; that indeed headed by Christoph Hess, a German, which had imposed penalty points against Hoy for prematurely riding through the starting clock, which was then incorrectly returned to zero before she started technically a second time. Law thus became Britain's first winner since Richard Meade 32 years before, while Kimberly Severson of America rose one place to take silver and Pippa Funnell of Britain was promoted to bronze. The error also cost Germany the team gold, which went to France, ahead of Britain and America, with Germany demoted to fourth place. It is fair to say that Hoy's misfortune depressed everyone in the tournament, for it was acknowledged that she was a rightful champion yet had made the fundamental pony-club error of triggering the start mechanism during her warm-up, which, when improperly corrected, allowed her to believe she had more time in hand than was technically accurate. The equestrian world is probably the most regimentally moral of the entire Games, and though Law could console himself that the

victory was technically correct, he will have been aware how fortunate he was. The British Olympic lawyer who argued their case to the CAS admitted: 'I would be worried if everyone thinks they can decide medals in a court. They should still be decided on the field of play, but the rules of the Games must be followed even if they lead to unhappy decisions.' Anky van Grunsven, iconic in her native Holland, earned her second successive gold on Salinero in dressage.

Cycling reluctantly stands alongside track and field and weightlifting as a sport wretchedly degraded by doping scandals. The Australian team arrived in Greece against a troubled background of allegations and suspensions. In spite of these upheavals, the team enjoyed unparalleled success, with six gold medals, enabling Australia to leapfrog the USA and Italy to become the third most successful nation in Games' history, behind only Britain and France. A resonant series in Athens concluded with Ryan Bayley winning the keirin track event, never losing a round and defeating among others the British world champion Jamie Staff. Bayley, from Perth, had earlier won the track sprint, Australia's first ever, in the deciding ride comfortably outpacing an over-confident Theo Bos (NED), who took silver ahead of Rene Wolff (GER). Unimpeded by any lack of self-confidence, Bailey asserted that any scandal was non-existent: 'We've trained every day to be here, we believe we've done a good job.' Paolo Bettini of Italy, in a desperate sprint finish to the road race, defeated Sergio Paulinho of Portugal by a second, with Axel Merckx of Belgium, son of the legendary Eddy, taking the bronze eight seconds back. In the unrelenting heat of 40°C, almost half the field failed to finish. Sarah Ulmer of New Zealand set a world record in the 3km pursuit by two seconds, with 3:24.537, adding to her world title at the expense of Australian Katie Mactier. Leontien Zijlaard van Moorsel (NED) gained bronze, following gold in the road time trial, and retired from the Olympic scene as the most successful rider in history with four gold, one silver and one bronze. And with fine style, the 38-year-old Lori-Ann Münzer of Canada, the oldest woman competing at the velodrome, overhauled Tamila Abassova of Russia in the second race of the track sprint to earn Canada its first gold in cycling.

Its future in the programme constantly under threat, modern pentathlon, having reduced its five-sport schedule to a single day in the interests of both economy and drama for the audience, justified its continuation with two fine competitions. Andrei Moiseev of Russia had sufficient time at the end of his concluding run, ahead of Andrejus Zadneprovskis of Lithuania, to grab a flag from a spectator before crossing the line. He had begun the cross-country with an 11-second lead. Libor Capalini of the Czech Republic took bronze. World champion Gabor Balogh of Hungary slumped to eighth when faltering in both shooting and swimming. There were nearly 5,000 spectators in the sold-out stadium. His compatriot Zsuzsanna Vörös took the women's title, followed home by Jelena Rublevska (LAT) and Georgina Harland (GBR). Harland might well have challenged the winner but for her shooting, in which she finished 30th out of 32 competitors. Samantha Harvey, an American competing for Brazil and finishing 25th, spoke for all in the sport when she told the *International Herald Tribune*:

> The ancient pentathlon involved different sports to ours, but the idea remains being able to balance combat sports with individual sports, strength sports with endurance sports. It's an ancient idea, and we're in danger of losing that spirit in the Olympics. I love commercial sports, they're important, but there has to be a preserve for others, sustaining the spirit of all nations and all sports coming together, big and small.

Honour was elusive for weightlifting in Athens, hardly a new occurrence for the sport as doping pariah, now with seven positives in the first few days. A depressed Tamás Aján, president of the international federation, lamented: 'I'm smiling at the presence of 79 countries but crying because of the drug taking. For 30 years our federation has been the leader in the fight.' No less than 30 per cent of the federation's annual budget is spent on drug testing, uniquely all competitors being tested prior to the Games. Five of the positives in Athens came from the federation's own pre-Games analysis. Given the primitive, strength-orientated nature of the sport, it is unsurprising that it should be so vulnerable to strength-enhancing chemistry, yet who could fail to admire the massive Iranian Hossein Reza Zadeh, champion at the heavyweight category, when lifting an incredible 472.5 kilos in two lifts, which is about the weight of four well-built men. In recognition of Reza Zadeh's status, Mohammad Khatami, Iranian president, gifted him a house in Teheran, while a bank was named after him. When he releases the weights after a lift, there is a clap of thunder as they strike the floor. It is fair to say that weightlifting, as basic as running and boxing, will always be there whatever the repetitive transgressions.

De Coubertin would have shuddered, after 108 years, as women's wrestling made its entry with four freestyle events, the respective winners being Irini Merlini (UKR), Saori Yoshida (JPN), Kaori Icho (JPN) and Xu Wang (CHN). It may be difficult for some men, and even some women, to witness women grappling with each other, distorting each other's features and contorted in poses that might have caused arrest not so long ago, but Icho also had her sister Chiharu at it, taking silver in the 48kg category. Patricia Miranda, American bronze medal winner, whose parents were political refugees from Brazil, intended to study for a law degree at Yale.

Racket sports, which as yet do not include joint-devouring squash on the programme, regularly provide some of the best entertainment in the entire Games, and for the time being it is Asia which tends to dominate. China secured both doubles titles in table tennis and the women's singles through Yining Zhang. The men's singles saw the most intense final between Seung Min Ryu of South Korea and Hao Wang of China, the Korean bearing an expression throughout that suggested abdominal surgery without an anaesthetic but demonishly getting the better of his opponent in a brilliant encounter. The veteran Jan-Ove Waldner of Sweden, winner in 1992 after finishing eighth when favourite four years earlier, was by now thirty-nine and competing in his fifth Games, and in what could be regarded as a young player's sport did astonishingly well to finish fourth.

To confirm that veterans are by no means excluded, Ning Zhang of China, who had left home at 12 to become a full-time player and was now making it to her first Olympics at the age of 29, claimed the women's badminton title with her defeat of Mia Audina of the Netherlands. Zhang's career had been blighted when losing to Audina, 14 at the time, in the Uber Cup in 1994. 'It was strange to see each other ten years later in the Olympic final,' Audina said. 'I think it was just who had the best day, and today she did.' The men's title went to Taufik Hidayat of Indonesia, defeating Seung Mo Shon of South Korea.

It is widely argued that tennis and the Olympics do not need each other, and the possible truth of that was emphasised in Athens by the absence of many of the top players, including Kim Clijsters, Serena Williams, Lindsay Davenport and Wimbledon champion Maria Sharapova among the women, Sharapova failing to qualify because the entry cut-off preceded her Wimbledon victory that year. Justine Henin-Hardenne, the Belgian champion of France, defeated Amelie Mauresmo of France in the final while Nicolás Massú of Chile beat Mardy Fish of America in the men's final. 'The value of tennis to the Games is a bit similar to that of football,' argues Francisco Ricci Bitti, Italian president of the international federation. 'They need us more than we need them, yet it is a fact that many of our players such as Roger Federer are anxious to play because the circumstances are so different – representing your country, as in the Davis Cup or Federation Cup, rather than yourself and enjoying the unique experience of being among so many other sports.'

Ground-stroke queen Justine Henin-Hardenne's technique was supreme on court. (© IOC/Tanaka)

Seung Min Ryu, victor in a table tennis final that touched the heights. (© IOC/Sugimoto)

The Olympic Games of 2004, following seven years of fluctuating anxiety since the city's selection in 1997, ultimately proved visually rich and a likely long-term benefit to the Greek capital, with its infrastructure investment in road, rail and airport, not withstanding the white-elephant legacy of some facilities for minor sports. The financial analysis would reveal, contrary to initial reports, an upturn in civic benefits. The most notable sporting statistic was the high profile of the Chinese team, with 63 medals, 32 of them gold. 'They have a great sports machine that we're just seeing coming to the fore,' said Jim Scherr, CEO of USOC. 'Their team is going to be really impressive in Beijing.' The US had extended its medal reign to three consecutive Summer Olympics, winning 102 medals overall with 36 gold, Russia tallying 92. Notable in particular was that four-fifths of the Chinese competitors were making their debut in Athens and would be likely to be in their prime four years later. By contrast, Russia had slipped in the gold medal tally to third behind China. Much of the former Soviet system had come to a halt, including the use of training facilities in such former satellite countries as Kazakhstan and Armenia. Anatoly Kolesov, head of the Russian delegation, admitted that sports infrastructure had declined. 'That belonged to the past.' The incentives of tax-free bonuses, $50,000 for gold, $20,000 for silver and $10,000 for bronze, less than the lavish benefits in Soviet times, would not alone sustain Russian sporting momentum, though it was likely that with the upturn of Russia's huge mineral and fuel resources, expenditure on sports investment would substantially increase before 2008 – especially in the light of Sochi's unexpected election in 2007 as Winter Games host for 2014. China, too, would be extending its huge government investment in sport: $100 million in 2004, this to be augmented over the next four years, including the employment of many foreign coaches in sports less familiar to Chinese competitors, such as tennis and track and field.

Athens closing ceremony. (© IOC/Abe)

CHAPTER LXXIV

London's Late Run

Ser Miang Ng of Singapore, IOC Executive Board member

'With 60 per cent of the world's population, Asia represents the next great frontier for the Olympic movement and the promotion of Olympic ideals and values. Rapid and sustainable economic growth in Asian countries will be the impetus not just for greater emphasis on active participation in sports but also for heightening the passion for Olympic success that will boost national pride and celebrate the human spirit.

The diverse and unique culture of Asia will definitely add depth and strength to the fabric of the Olympic movement. The twenty-first century will witness Asia playing a prominent role in the Olympic family and contributing to the universality of the movement.

Asian nations have already demonstrated their exceptional capability and outstanding hospitality in playing host to the Olympic Movement. Tokyo (1964) and Seoul (1988) hosted the Summer Olympic Games whilst Sapporo and Nagano were hosts for the 1972 and 1998 Winter Games respectively. The much-anticipated Beijing Games in 2008 will no doubt be a most spectacular Games that will leave a long-lasting legacy not just for China but for Asia and the rest of the world. The success of these Games and the impact on the host country's economy, as well as the enhancement of national prestige, will attract even more Asian cities to vie for the privilege and honour of hosting future Olympic Games.

The ambition to be involved with the Olympic Movement extends to the smaller nations in Asia as well. Kuwait built a multi-million-dollar complex which, when it was completed in 2007, was capable of housing the headquarters of the Olympic Council of Asia and the Asian Olympic Academy. Qatar demonstrated their commitment to the Olympic movement with the construction of world-class sports facilities that hosted more than 10,000 athletes during the 2006 Asian Games at Doha. The city-state of Singapore received a "Perfect Six" from President Jacques Rogge for organising the 117th IOC Session in 2005 and is embarking on a multi-million-dollar Sports Hub to fulfil its aspirations as a sporting nation.

Since Japan won the first Olympic medals for Asia in Antwerp in 1920, Asian athletes have improved by leaps and bounds at the Olympic Games. Asian countries won 71 medals or 11 per cent of the total at the Los Angeles Games in 1984; in Athens 2004, Asia accounted for 285 or 31 per cent of the medals. From a solitary bronze medal in the Calgary Winter Games (1988), Asia won 44 in Nagano (1998) and more recently 23 in Turin. With more and more of Asia's athletes registering world-class performances, the twenty-first century is poised to be a golden age for Asian athletes. China is widely expected to top the medal tally in Beijing 2008 and will continue to challenge the dominance of the US thereafter. No doubt other Asian countries will also be battling to improve their Olympic successes. The highly successful Asian Games will continue to play a useful role of bonding Asian countries and as a stepping stone to the Olympic Games.

More Asians now hold leadership positions in the Olympic Movement: such positions have included the Vice-Presidency and Executive Board membership of the IOC; chairmanship of various IOC commissions; and presidency, vice-presidency and board membership of international sports federations. The Asian sports leaders bring different perspectives to these international sports organisations and make them truly world bodies. More qualified and capable Asians are indeed coming forward to offer their services. I see in the next 100 years an increase in the number of Asian IOC members and active Asian athletes becoming IOC members. It is likely that the first active Asian athlete will be elected as an IOC member in Beijing at the 2008 Games. This will be a reflection of the growing importance of Asia in the Olympic Movement as well as the abilities and recognition accorded to Asia's sports leaders. Who knows, an Asian might even emerge to take the helm of the IOC in time to come. The Olympic Movement in Asia is, indeed, growing faster, higher and stronger in the twenty-first century.'*

(Photograph © IOC/Goh)

Ser Miang Ng's optimism is well placed, yet within the Movement there still exist the habitual tensions, some of these as worrying as ever, if not indeed alarming. Causing widespread concern, not confined merely within the ranks of the IOC, were issues relating to the World Anti-Doping Agency, the Ethics Commission and the sports programme. All lay at the heart of the health of the Games, not to say their credibility. For the first, the policy of zero tolerance – in the definition of the President as distinct as the defining line between being and not being pregnant – was acceptable within WADA for anyone who properly recognised the dangers of public cynicism that could engulf the Games, but on the parallel ethics level there was debate on inconsistency in actions regarding errant behaviour of different individuals.

Were it not for a century of famous Olympic deeds that so outshone any background of squabbles and controversies – political, financial and moral – events of the past ten years could have laid low any administration not cushioned by such an historic legacy. Drugs continued to circle the organisation like an ever-present thunderstorm, haunting the whole world of sport in the autumn of 2004. Kenteris and Thanou were suspended by the IAAF after consultation with WADA – the long-term disciplinary threat to competitors coming not from action by the IOC within a Games but from a subsequent decision by the relevant IF. Next, a howitzer was fired in December through all sport with revelations by Victor Conte, founder of the San Francisco-based Bay Area Laboratories Co-operative (BALCO), one of four men charged with drugs distribution. In an interview with ABC Television, Conte made accusations not only against renowned track and field names such as Marion Jones and Tim Montgomery but also household figures of American domestic sports, baseball and football. His was a strange act considering he was due to plead innocent at his trial, but, in conjunction with grand jury testimony by American sports stars of being programmed on steroids, the American public, previously immune to the dirty side of Olympic sport, was suddenly aware of the fouling of its own nest. During the previous 15 years, major league baseball had not suspended a single player. Among his reported evidence, duplicated in ESPN's *The Magazine*, Conte alleged:

> The whole system is rotten. I have too much information to go quietly. They want to expose the rotten side of sports? Bring it on. People have asked me if I feel guilty about what I did, am I ashamed? The answer is no. I got to a point where I realised elite sport is about doing what you have to do to win. I've seen athletes being forced to decide whether to use or not use, and it's much more painful for them to entertain the idea of giving up their dream than to use steroids.

President Rogge responded by stating, during a meeting of European Olympic Committees in Dubrovnik, Croatia: 'I hope the truth will emerge. We want to know what happened and the more we know the better.'

Never mind these intimidating facts, WADA itself and chairman Dick Pound continued to encounter opposition, notably regarding the intended comprehensive two-year ban for positive tests, whatever the sport. Leading the objections were Denis Oswald – with his multiple roles as president of rowing, EB member, president of ASOIF and now lapsed chairman of the Athens Coordination Commission – and Hein Verbruggen, then president of cycling. While they felt the uniformity of the ban was inoperable, they also considered WADA's fundamental stance to be provocative: in Verbruggen's words, 'positioning itself as a

Clouded glory: Marion Jones and Ekatarini Thanou (GRE), on the podium with 100m bronze winner Tanya Lawrence (JAM), cast long shadows across the Olympic Movement.
(© Allsport/Powell)

police watchdog instead of an aid agency'. Further criticism came in Rogge's home country, Belgium, from 11 prominent sports officials, among them Robert van der Walle, sometime Olympic team chief, and track promoter Wilf Meert. In the face of this, Pound was not one to wilt, and he continued his pressure on FIFA to increase its inadequate initial six-month penalty and urged that WADA rules be upheld in its Olympic football tournament in 2008. To outsiders, the protesters' case seemed lightweight in view of overwhelming evidence, a view emphasised by Professor Helmut Diegel, German vice-president of the IAAF, who asserted: 'We should sue the athletes. When four or five are caught during Olympic competitions, the sport suffers considerable economic damage for which no one is held accountable.' Some IFs were doing their best. FINA, governing body of swimming, had been able to announce that of 437 tests during the World Championships, on 237 competitors from 42 countries immediately prior to and during competition, all were negative.

Meanwhile, a beleaguered Dr Tamás Aján, Hungarian president of the international weightlifting federation and IOC member, found himself ousted as secretary-general of his NOC, supposedly for having given adverse evidence on the expulsion of three Hungarian lifters during the Athens Games. Aján claimed to have resigned on account of his multiple other responsibilities, including being a delegate on the WADA board.

Tamás Aján from Hungary, beleaguered president of weightlifting, meets President Putin, IOC Session 2001. (© IOC/Locatelli)

Fluctuations in discipline severity by the Ethics Commission, originally viewed as flag-bearer of the new, sanitised IOC, were such that some had begun to view ethics as the 29th Olympic sport, to the point where it was felt that the most needed assessment was of the Ethics Commission's own guidelines under the chairmanship of Keba M'Baye of Senegal. Intermittent malpractice in a leviathan body such as the Olympic Movement should surprise nobody. Proportion is everything, but inconsistent strictures were unsettling. Marc Hodler, veteran IOC member and past president of the ski federation for 47 years, who had been given the thankless task 20 years earlier by President Samaranch of attempting to bring to heel the excesses of self-serving members – with predictable lack of success – now implied that there were 'too many moralising formalists sitting on the Ethics Commission, and the IOC President is passing too much on to them'. Hodler believed that the Commission's function should be exact, concise and consistent, dealing with factual issues rather than dwelling on ideological theories that were too often inoperable. Long ago he had recommended then President Lord Killanin, on information supplied by host city bid committees, to act against corrupt individuals, but the IOC was forestalled by the risk of excessive libel suits at a time when they were cash-strapped. Now, the past was repeatedly creeping out of the woodwork. Yoshiaki Tsutsumi, granted distinguished election as IOC Member of Honour – on account of donations towards creation of the Olympic Museum – was once rated the world's richest man when head of the Seibu Railway Company, with a conglomerate of businesses in the hotel and entertainment industries. Now he was obliged to resign from the IOC when charged with financial irregularities – a sinister echo of rumours surrounding the successful bid by Nagano for the 1998 Winter Games, behind which he was the motivating force.

Ethics Commission inconsistency was apparent in its action, or inaction, regarding members' publicly expressed opinions on election candidates. In 2001, Kevan Gosper had been censured for announcing he supported Dick Pound's candidacy for the IOC presidency, yet apparently it was now permissible for Zaiqing Yu, Chinese member of the EB, to inform *Le Parisien* that he was in favour of the Paris bid for the Games of 2012. Meanwhile, Nawal El Moutawakel, Moroccan chairperson of the Evaluation Commission for 2012, was conspicuously absent from the Laureus Sports Awards in Portugal, supposedly on grounds that it would be inadvisable for her to be seen in the company of Sebastian Coe, newly president of London's bidding committee, the two of them having been track champions in 1984. Avoidance of friends was becoming reminiscent of the Stasi era. On the other hand the IOC, and the Ethics Commission, seemingly saw nothing wrong in being represented at a general assembly of the United Nations – in the autumn of 2005, for its adoption of the Olympic Truce resolution – by Frenchman Guy Drut, who accompanied fellow members Alpha Ibrahim Diallo of Guinea and Tommy Sithole, director of international cooperation. Drut had been on probation for over a year and been fined for financial malpractice. Not long after his UN visit, the Ethics Commission postponed action against him pending further inquiry, though he was temporarily barred from a member's functional rights. Equally confusing was the stalling of any action against Korean member Yong-Sung Park, regarding which, on the recommendation of the Ethics Commission, the EB remained uncommitted. No judicial decision had yet been taken in Korea regarding Park, president of world judo and former chairman of the Doosan Group, who was alleged to have embezzled company funds of $32 million in conjunction with his three brothers. He had resigned both from Doosan and as chairman of

the Korean Chamber of Commerce – but not from his Olympic posts. Here was rank inconsistency. Had not Dr Un Yong Kim been suspended instantly the previous year even before charges were filed against him in South Korea? Three months later the EB did provisionally suspend Park, who had avoided confronting his colleagues at the time of the Session preceding the Turin Games by staying at home. Concurrently, Park wrote to colleagues within the judo family claiming he was to appeal.

 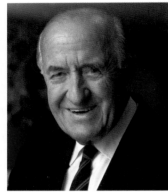

LEFT: Paquerette Girard Zappelli, French lawyer and influential, co-opted special representative on the Ethics Commission. Variable strictures were confusing some IOC members. (© IOC)

RIGHT: Swiss Veteran Marc Hodler, previously appointed by Samaranch to quell financial abuse, accused the Ethics Commission of having 'too many moral formalists'. (© IOC)

These were discrediting times for Koreans. Wary of the controversy raised by Samsung's energetic but improper support of Pyeongchang prior to the election for the Winter Games of 2010 at Prague in 2003, Gerhard Heiberg, chairman of the Marketing Commission, addressed a letter to TOP sponsors outlining rules of conduct by which seven bidding cities were bound prior to the election of the 2014 Winter Games host city at Guatemala City in 2007. The TOP partners were to refrain 'from any kind of support or promotion of a 2014 applicant', though the IOC was prepared to assist partners 'in exploring how their knowledge and expertise could be of assistance'. Also missing from the Session in Turin was Korea's third member, Kun-Hee Lee, whose excuse was a broken leg following a five-month absence in the United States, where he had undergone surgery for lung cancer. He was implicated in controversial fund dealings within the Samsung group, itself a member of the IOC's TOP sponsorship programme. All these incidents were seen to be increasingly harmful for the renewed Winter bid by Pyeongchang for 2014. Unhelpful to Paris, in addition to the affair of Drut, was the suspended sentence and five-figure fine imposed on Henri Serandour, president of their NOC, for 'inappropriate' employment practices in connection with a communications company.

A fresh Winter bid by Sofia, Bulgaria, after two earlier failed attempts, was already foundering before the IOC membership of Ivan Slavkov was terminated at the Session of 2005 in Singapore. He had appeared in a controversial BBC *Panorama* documentary prior to the Athens Games, in which he had seemed to be available for soliciting colleagues' votes at elections, for example, for the host of 2012. Slavkov claimed he was playing along in an attempt to expose what he thought was a real attempt at extortion. When it came to that Session in 2005, Slavkov, variously president of both his NOC and national football federation, chose not to seek sympathy when protesting his innocence, though 12 colleagues did vote against the motion for his expulsion. It was an undistinguished end to the Olympic career of Bulgaria's leading television entrepreneur who, in the 1980s, had put Sofia on the map with imaginative Winter bids. Yet, at home, as the son-in-law of former communist dictator Todor Zhivkov – whose daughter, his wife Lyudmilla, a popular politician as minister for art, had died following an unexplained car accident – Slavkov had always walked the social highwire. Expulsion cost him his NOC presidency and in the autumn he was voted out of his football post with the election of former national goalkeeper Borislav Mikhailov. In conjunction with Slavkov's expulsion, a number of individuals connected with the *Panorama* programme were declared personae non gratae, barred from Olympic accreditation in any form, including Goran Takac: publisher for the IOC for many years of the official Games Report, promotional agent for a number of bidding cities and son of respected former IOC technical director Artur Takac – who died mysteriously in his 80s when supposedly skiing, the body not found for many months, then suddenly discovered and swiftly cremated.

Ivan Slavkov, jovial member from Bulgaria, unwisely allowed himself to be trapped in a BBC *Panorama* 'sting' and was expelled. (© IOC)

Languishing in seriously declining ill-health in jail was Un Yong Kim, now seventy-three, his appeal against conviction in the high court in June 2004 rejected in September in less than five minutes, though the sentence was reduced by six months to two years, meaning that he could be freed, if still alive, shortly prior to the Turin Games. Final appeal was due to be heard in the Supreme Court. The only chance for the IOC to expel him prior to his liberation would occur at the Singapore Session, assuming his appeal was rejected. The IOC's stance remained unflinching. Though Rogge visited Korea in the autumn of 2004 for a meeting with Kun-Hee Lee, chief executive of Samsung – himself subsequently to be in deep water – the President, neither on technical nor administrative grounds, had any cause to visit Kim, notwithstanding that the latter had still been denied any access to lawyers though briefly granted hospital attention for

his failing eyesight. Although the Supreme Court predictably upheld the initial verdict, the risk for the EB, in recommending Kim's expulsion, was that it might fall short of reaching the Session's necessary two-thirds majority. In his election as Vice-President in 2003 – admittedly a tactically unwise move in juxtaposition to Pyenogchang's host city bid – he had gained 55 votes, and many of those supporters were still out there and waiting to demonstrate loyalty towards a man who had done so much for Olympic sport, for Korean sport and for global development of taekwondo. Following the Supreme Court's verdict, Rogge wrote to Kim informing him of the EB's unanimous decision, prior to any formal nod, to propose his expulsion – though reminding him that he could avert such a possible outcome should he opt to resign. That, of course, would be preferable for the EB, bypassing the potential embarrassment of the motion failing. Kim had a couple of months within which to notify whether he would attend in Singapore to put his case: impossible while he remained in prison. Kim's daughter Helen, a lawyer who had trained and worked in London, wrote unavailingly to Keba M'Baye, chairman of the Ethics Commission, reminding them of Charter Rule 16.3.8.2 – that her father had the right to be informed of the charges against him by the IOC and the right to be represented at the Session. She further advised the IOC that the United Nations Human Rights Commission, in its report of April 2005, had specifically cited the injustice suffered by Dr Kim, as a consequence of South Korean lack of jurisprudence, and that his alleged offences in the IOC's eyes differed little from other offenders who had not been or would not be expelled. Such letters to the EB and individuals were deemed by the IOC to be inapplicable and, however emotionally and adroitly legally worded, were probably counter-productive. Anxiety for the EB was well founded: messages of support sent to Kim by colleagues included Julio Maglione (Uruguay), Chang Ung (PR Korea), Sam Ramsamy (South Africa), Alex Gilady (Israel), Antun Vrdoljak (Croatia), Nat Indrapana (Thailand), Phil Coles and Kevan Gosper (Australia), Ivan Dibos (Peru), Ser Miang Ng (Singapore), Shagdarjav Magvan (Mongolia), Mohamed Mzali (Tunisia), Tamás Aján (Hungary), Tay Wilson (New Zealand), Vitaly Smirnov (Russia), Timothy Fok (Hong Kong), Zhenliang He (China), Shun-ichiro Okano (Japan), Walther Tröger (Germany), Syed Ali (Pakistan), Francis Nyangweso (Uganda), Mustapha Larfaoui (Algeria), Francisco Elizalde (Philippines), Juan Antonio Samaranch Jr (Spain), Fernando Bello (Portugal) and Sheikh Ahmad (Kuwait).

In the event, Kim did resign, surrounded by rumour, and was released on parole – but was he pushed or was it voluntary? There was coincidence in the formal visit, shortly beforehand, of President Rogge to the Blue House, Korean government headquarters, with speculation that political leverage may have been exerted, though Rogge emphatically assured the author there were no negotiations between him and the Blue House. There was the oddity, however, that Kim's letter of resignation, dated 9 May, took 11 days to travel from Seoul to Lausanne, those friends who met him in intervening days detecting no indication of an impending announcement. Additionally, an article scheduled for the subsequent July issue of *Joon Ang Monthly*, a current affairs magazine, supposedly casting light on Blue House involvement, was suddenly withdrawn. The authors alleged that editor and publisher Jin-Yong Kim deleted the article following a meeting with a government official on 16 June, after which he and his chief executive resigned. According to Un Yong Kim, he was interviewed three times in prison by government officials, signing three different documents agreeing to resign on condition of being granted parole.

Kim's friends were dismayed at the continuing absence of a pardon. In late 2007, Kim stated: 'I do not believe that a resignation obtained under physical pressure while in prison in ill-health has any legal validity.' A relieved Rogge, attending the centenary celebration in 2005 of the British Olympic Association in London, had commented: 'It's always good not to have to vote on the exclusion of a colleague, though I still believe that the Session would have taken the right decision had we had to vote.' An ironic aftermath was that, in the late autumn of 2005, the EB approved the principle of a $5,000 annual expense allowance to IOC members: a reduced sum compared with the principle proposed by Kim at the time of his abortive presidential campaign in 2001 and for which he had been censured. The enduring gulf between the now-resigned Vice-President and some of his former colleagues was evident in the spring of 2006 when, at two social functions in Seoul during the annual Sport Accord meetings, Kim tactically withdrew, on receipt of clandestine advice, rather than provoke formal confrontation with Rogge, instead holding his own dinner among those sympathetic to him. The fall of this Asian sports leader would remain one of the IOC's enigmas.

The world which Kim had inescapably relinquished would continue with its many upheavals, negotiations and deals, publicised and unpublicised. Heading towards the Session in Singapore, the IFs, under their umbrella body ASOIF, were on one hand seeking early confirmation of the revenue they would be due from the Athens Games income, while on the other doing a collective political foxtrot under the impending prospect of a programme revision, some sensing they were as vulnerable to exclusion as Dr Kim. Rogge had confirmed to Denis Oswald, ASOIF president, prior to the Games that gross revenue for the IFs should be some $250 million, from which the most prominent sport, track and field, would receive $25.2 million and the least favoured, taekwondo and triathlon, $6.07 million each. The federations were collectively irritated by the IOC holding them responsible for indemnity insurance costs for Athens, but distribution would be unchanged from Sydney 2000, that is:

Group A:	Athletics	$25.2 million
Group B:	Basketball, Cycling, Football, Gymnastics, Swimming, Tennis, Volleyball	$12.2 million
Group C:	Equestrian, Handball, Hockey, Rowing	$8.1 million
Group D:	Archery, Badminton, Baseball, Boxing, Canoeing, Fencing, Judo, Modern Pentathlon, Shooting, Softball, Table Tennis, Weightlifting, Wrestling, Yachting	$6.7 million
Group E:	Taekwondo, Triathlon	$6.07 million

Such lingering unrest as there was among individual federations – including resentment of Rogge's decision to include NOCs within a working group to discuss ways of ensuring a more visible presence for IFs at Olympic venues, IFs being the only non-commercial Olympic partner without identification, NOCs already possessing this through their uniforms – were overridden by a sweet-talking letter of acceptance of the financial gradings from Oswald to Rogge. In his many roles, Swiss lawyer Oswald was so often the compromiser, searching

for communal equilibrium, even when that quality was absent elsewhere – such as in the triathlon federation. Canadian president Les McDonald affected indignation when challenged for office by Professor Sarah Springman of Britain, former champion, prominent academic and leader in development of women's sport. McDonald protested in vain that Springman's candidacy was being backed by IOC member Craig Reedie, though that was no less than Reedie's right as chairman of BOA. Nonetheless, McDonald would successfully defend his post at the meeting in his home town of Vancouver by 40 votes to 33.

The Winter Games host city for 2010 would be glad that the International Skating Union, self-motivated but under severe pressure from the IOC following the controversies of Salt Lake City 2002, was now introducing a fundamentally revised scoring system – replacement for the archaic, arbitrary and subjective maximum 6.0 system – in time for the Turin Games. The system had been successfully tested at the European Championships in Lyon, but skating president Ottavio Cinquanta claimed that there were improvements still to be made in the points-based scoring that would measure jumps, spins and footwork as much as artistic impression.

Fear among IFs of programme evaluation scheduled for Singapore was real. The principle had been under discussion for more than a decade, and though they collectively resisted a wish to call off the debate, Oswald's letter to Rogge, acknowledging that a vote for the retention of each individual sport would be taken, requested that the figures should remain confidential, to avoid the destabilising effect of public comparisons. The IOC had presented to the IFs a catalogue of 29 criteria for retention from members' observations during the Athens Games. From this the Programme Commission would assemble a final catalogue to be submitted to the EB, prior to the Singapore evaluation, though this would avoid applying strict rankings – and thereby, of course, leave the issue indecipherably fudged. Alert to the imminent threat, UIPM, the modern pentathlon federation, devised a tightened schedule of their sport, where all five events took place within a single day at a single venue, making it spectator- and television-friendly.

Klaus Schormann from Germany, president of threatened modern pentathlon – seen here at the 2004 Olympic Art and Sport contest – steered a shrewd protective strategy. (© IOC/Locatelli)

Rogge, sensitive to the tensions running among the twenty-eight sports to be reviewed, and among the five recognised federations – golf, karate, roller sports, rugby sevens and squash – to be considered for admission, stated: 'The review does not mean that we are obliged to modify the programme. Rather, it will allow each member to express themselves on the future of the Games by voting for the programme he or she considers the best for the IOC and the Olympic Movement.' While it was unrealistic even to contemplate whether or not, say, track and field should continue to hold its place on the programme – a prospect that would have roused the late Primo Nebiolo to volcanic levels – his successor Lamine Diack reacted with unruffled equanimity.

It was not the first time a ballot was to be held on the programme. In 1961, determining the programme for 1964 in Tokyo, President Brundage decreed that 15 was to be the minimum number and 22 the maximum. Baron Frenckell of Finland proposed this be reduced to 20. Only six sports had been free of any vote for elimination – athletics, gymnastics, rowing, swimming, weightlifting and wrestling – while archery and handball, with twenty-six and twenty-eight negative votes respectively, had been removed. It is interesting that, at that time, the next two least popular sports among members were football and modern pentathlon, with sixteen and fifteen negatives. Four years later, in the ballot for the programme for Mexico City, only athletics, boxing and swimming were free of negative votes; judo was removed following its inaugural appearance in Tokyo, while volleyball stayed only because water polo was designated an event within swimming. By the twenty-first century, however, the financial significance of exclusion from the Olympic arena was so overriding it was no surprise that emotions should be as volatile as a political election in Haiti or Azerbaijan.

The outcome was stalemate and, to a degree, regressive: frustrating for the President, a relief for modern pentathlon, which survived, while at least temporary disaster for baseball and softball, which were voted out, with no new sport gaining entry. Behaviour from the floor was at times rowdy, the President was heckled, and many considered that the IOC had gone into reverse gear instead of seeking imaginative development. By a complicated procedural process, two of the proposed new sports were voted to be eligible for inclusion in 2012, but neither secured the necessary two-thirds majority: the voting for squash 63–39, for karate 63–38. Squash was deemed past its peak of popularity, while karate would merely be adding another martial art, even if many regarded it as preferable to taekwondo. Above all, the outcome was a harrowing blow for the United States, with the loss of two sports in which it was a major practitioner. 'The US has become a wallflower at the Olympic party,' observed Phil Hersh in the *Chicago Tribune*. He attributed the problem partially to instability within USOC over many years that had weakened its relationship with the Olympic world. Former IOC vice-president Anita DeFranz stated: 'It does feel like it [the decision] is painfully directed at the US. I am unhappy that a women's sport like softball has been dropped.' It was the first time since polo in 1936 that a sport had been removed other than, temporarily, judo. Golf's cause had been undermined by the Programme Commission's warning that 'there is no certainty the top professionals would take part'. Rugby, though enthusiastically supported by its former player, the President, would have been welcomed by London. It had last been staged in the Games, 15-a-side, in 1924. The author is surprised that no one has ever seriously considered or promoted a revival of tug-of-war or the introduction of water-skiing: one formerly contested in six Olympics and an ideal

sport for television, technologically undemanding, inexpensive in staging, visually dramatic and arousing national fervour as a team sport, the other trendy, youthful, visually thrilling, the motor-boat irrelevant to performance skills, serving a dozen or more competitors as a 'horizontal hill' and uniformly supplied by the IOC.

The belated election of Peter Ueberroth as president of USOC in 2004, long overdue amid the turmoil of the world's most powerful NOC, though widely welcomed abroad had not come in sufficient time to help protect the positions of baseball and softball, nor for him to have sufficiently influential impact on the bid being mounted by New York as host city for 2012. Only time would tell – following an era in which USOC had experienced a succession of internal scandals and oft-replaced chairmen/women and chief executives – whether Ueberroth, mastermind of the Los Angeles Games 20 years earlier, could restore American authority in the Olympic arena, where it now stood without a single leading figure in any IF or commission bar James Easton, then president of archery. Ueberroth's arrival was the result of reforms insisted upon by government, among which a previous committee of 125 had been reduced to an 11-member board of directors. Ueberroth replaced Bill Martin, the acting president since February 2003, who had guided USOC through its obligatory reorganisation.

Peter Ueberroth (left), newly elected president of a chaotic US Olympic Committee, arrived too late to help Don Porter, ageing president of softball, prevent its exclusion from the programme. (both photos © IOC)

If USOC had been overdue for reform, there was less satisfactory evidence of the IOC's dedication to increasing women's involvement in all levels of administration, though there were shifts here and there. In Bulgaria, following the IOC expulsion of Slavkov, his NOC post was taken by Stefka Kostadinova, 1996 Olympic winner and several-time world high jump champion – the first woman to attain this position and voted in ahead of Svetla Otsetova, Olympic rowing champion of 1976. At the same time, Zambia became the second NOC in the world to elect women both as president and secretary-general, there now being nine women NOC presidents and fourteen female secretaries-general. Miriam Moyo, previously secretary-general, succeeded Patrick Chamunda as president, while Hazel Kennedy, recently elected to the executive of the African Hockey Federation, became secretary. At this time, Africa was the leading continent in the appointment of female NOC officials, followed by Europe and the Americas. It was noted with hindsight, however, that Belgium sent not a single female athlete to the Winter Games in Salt Lake City, rousing the ire of the International League for Women's Rights, though Belgium was one of 22 countries to have sent all-male teams to Salt Lake. If liberalisation might not be moving sufficiently swiftly for women activists, in the author's view development was spectacular at participation level with, for instance, pole vault and wrestling now included in the Games. For the moment, women's boxing remained excluded, the EB rejecting an application from AIBA, the boxing federation. Kelly Fairweather, IOC Sports Director, said the decision had been taken 'on a technical basis, but we look forward to seeing progress in women's boxing over the next few years'.

If IFs were obsessed all too expectedly with the art of self-preservation on the programme rather than what might be good for the Games, they were also ill at ease with their lack of influence within the Executive Board and the IOC membership as a whole. This mood was increased by elections in Singapore, where Lambis Nikolaou (Greece) and Chiharu Igaya (Japan) became Vice-Presidents, neither of them powerful voices in any IF-orientated debate, notwithstanding Igaya's background long ago as an Alpine medal winner and his interest in triathlon. Nikolaou was NOC-based, and this increasing trend disturbed those with the day-to-day responsibility of maintaining the profile of sport globally. Nikolaou had joined another NOC-based Vice-President, Gunilla Lindberg (Sweden), while among the rest of the then EB Mario Vazquez Raña (Mexico), the president of ANOC; Toni Khoury (Lebanon); Ibrahim Diallo (Guinea); Zaiqing Yu (China); Richard Carrión (Puerto Rico); and Ser Miang Ng (Singapore), also elected to the Board in his home city, all shared a background in their respective NOCs. Among the rest of the IOC membership, no fewer than 22 were presidents of their NOC. Here was the ever-present power rivalry within the triangle of IOC, IFs and NOCs, and it would continue to fuel the many problems that confront any IOC president.

In the summer of 2004, the IOC was able to negotiate broadcasting rights for 2010/2012 with the European Broadcasting Union (EBU) that, for percentage increase, more than matched the US deal with NBC. That had been over 30 per cent, but the EBU deal, covering 51 countries excluding Italy, represented a 40 per cent increase. Though well short of the $2 billion paid by NBC for Turin/Beijing, it was a significant rise on past negotiations. Italy was excluded on account of the power of Silvio Berlusconi, Prime Minister, controller of the state-owned station RAI and other commercial channels. The Italian withdrawal coincided with mounting concern over preparations by Turin's organising committee, especially in mountain venues.

The success of the EBU negotiations had occurred in spite of the departure at the end of August 2004 of Michael Payne, Director of Olympic Global Broadcast and New Media Rights. Following the IOC's annexation of Meridian Management, drawing in-house the control of sponsorship, Payne's position had become vulnerable, and when the time came for renewal of his contract, never mind his influence in the 2010/2012 deal, he was offered a controversial salary reduction: an incentive it was easy to decline in favour of joining Formula 1 as special adviser to president Bernie Ecclestone. Whether Payne, artfully building his own little empire within the IOC commercial conglomerate following his days with ISL, had been over-rewarded was one thing; the IOC would be losing accumulated experience and wisdom that was difficult to replace, though there would be compensation in the subsequent return to the Marketing

Commission of Dick Pound, making advice available to its chairman Gerhard Heiberg. Pound's chairmanship of WADA was due to expire in November 2007.

Dominating attention between the Games of Athens and Turin was the campaign by bidding host cities for the summer of 2012, the election scheduled for the Singapore Session in 2005. Paris, bidding again following defeat by Beijing in 2001, inevitably was the favourite, though an array of powerful rivals was there to challenge: London, Madrid, Moscow and New York, not forgetting lesser candidates such as Leipzig. Paris's platform was thought to be enhanced by the staging in 2003 of the Athletics World Championships at their modern Stade de France, though later-emerging evidence would reveal that the IAAF had been less than happy with much of the French administration. Also, financial scandal involving Guy Drut was a nettle that the French campaign would have to grasp.

Financial scandal involving Guy Drut, 1976 Olympic champion from France, was an embarrassment to Paris's host city bid. (© IOC/Locatelli)

In London, Barbara Cassani, a 43-year-old Princetown graduate and prominent businesswoman chosen to lead the bid, found herself becoming waterlogged in rising criticism, never mind her respected record in the management of low-price airline Go, the sale of which earned her millions of pounds. By the early spring of 2004, she was to be replaced by her deputy Sebastian Coe, who was left in no doubt about the enormity of the task ahead. At every turn he would be reminded of past British incompetence in venue construction, notably at Wembley, and having had to concede the athletics championships to France when unable to create a new stadium in east London. On the other hand, statistics that would encourage Coe – and any other city caring to listen – came from analysis of sixteen world and European sporting events staged in Britain over six years: for every £1 of National Lottery funding invested there was a return of more than £7 in economic impact.

Conscious of the hovering surveillance of the Ethics Commission, Feliciano Mayoral, secretary-general of ANOC, resigned from that office so as to be seen uncompromised in his role as chief executive of the Madrid bid. Leipzig, key venue for football's World Cup of 2006, had their Olympic candidacy dented when Denis Oswald declared that a city with only half a million of a population was too small: what hope Helsinki ever again? As rivalry began to mount among the big guns, Rogge, addressing the European Olympic Committees in Dubrovnik, asserted: 'They should stop looking at what others are doing, stop bickering and accusing each other. I'm not happy about the atmosphere.'

In the new regime of purity and transparency, IOC members being banned from visiting bid cities, the function of the Evaluation Commission had become more important, yet there was unease at the appointment as chair of Nawal El Moutawakel, personable Moroccan and, in 1984, first African female track champion. Although ethically impeccable on every count, some questioned her capacity to make the Commission's report meaningful for those unable to go and see for themselves. Alongside this was the suspicion that the structure of the report would be guided by Gilbert Felli, the unelected Olympic Games Executive Director, an influential hand among an otherwise honorary committee that included IOC members Els van Breda Vriesman (Holland), Paul Henderson (Canada), Mustapha Larfaoui (Algeria), José Luis Marco (Argentina), Ser Miang Ng (Singapore) and Sam Ramsamy (South Africa).

True to expectation, El Moutawakel would be politely complimentary to each of the five leading cities – once the also-rans Havana, Istanbul, Leipzig and Rio had been eliminated by the EB – on the Commission's tour of the candidate sites. During the preparation of the subsequent report, a leak by Agence France Presse correspondent Erskine McCullough claimed to reveal pluses and minuses indicated against different candidates. McCullough, as ever, was well informed, though Jacqueline Barrett, director of candidate city relations in Felli's office, was instructed to send a letter throughout the Movement stating the story should not be given any credibility. When the report came to be published, without a ranking list – contrary to the recommendation of Dick Pound when saying, 'You have to be allowed to find out what the Commission has decided even if you don't agree with the assessment' – Paris rated highly, as did Madrid, while London found its transport system heavily criticised. The report stated: 'Rail public transport is often obsolete and considerable investments must be made to upgrade the existing system in terms of capacity and safety. Urban expressways and main arterial road facilities lack the capacity to provide reasonable travel times and speed' and further voiced the opinion that London had overestimated the impact of the Channel Tunnel link between Stratford and King's Cross stations in east London. Frankly, any resident commuter in the UK capital could have told them as much in half a minute. If the report made anything markedly clear, it was that New York had a problem in its plan for creating a new stadium and that Moscow was, as they say, off the pace. Although Michael Bloomberg, New York's Mayor, was confident regarding a stadium, a choice between two sites was yet to be secured, and there was vigorous opposition among community leaders and citizens. This did not prevent Ueberroth being subjectively upbeat, telling the *New York Times* that 'our Olympic bid is superb in every area'. He claimed the technical plan met IOC requirements on venues, transportation and housing, that the Village view across the East River was unrivalled and that the Games would 'add to the quality of life for future generations of New Yorkers'. In the *Los Angeles Times*, Alan Abrahamson suggested that New York was capable of generating more revenue than any of the rival cities – some $3 billion, he suggested, or 15 per cent more than others. The report was seen, and not just by cynics, as suspiciously favourable towards Paris. It did not, however, integrate any cost-of-living factor. Had it done so, Madrid would have ranked first: the only city where a visitor

would be able to exist at tolerable everyday rates. In a study by Mercer Human Resources Consultancy, London was the most expensive city in Europe followed by Moscow, with New York and Paris ranked 11th and 12th, Madrid a mere 45th. Alberto Jofre, Madrid's CEO, further complained that the report had done less than justice to the compact nature of the Spanish bid, travel times between Village accommodation and competition surpassing that of the other cities: 83 per cent of competitors able to reach 93 per cent of venues within five minutes.

Michael Bloomberg, Mayor of New York (above), and Jean-Claude Killy (below left) and Bertrand Delanoë, Mayor of Paris, appeal in vain to members during presentations at Singapore.
(© IOC and © IOC/Romeu)

The scene in Singapore was the usual bees' nest of activity, thousands of workers clamouring around the handful of interview-worthy queens. Forecasts ran at a rate faster than anyone could count or compare. Paris was still unquestionably favourite, but in recent weeks and even days the field was thought to have narrowed, London and Madrid to have each closed in, while no one could be sure of the extent of the clandestine impact of honorary Life President Samaranch on behalf of the Spanish.

There is a general view of bid city presentations prior to the decision that while they do little towards winning votes they can sometimes hamper them. It is true that a single-handed superwoman performance in 1997 in Lausanne had secured the vote for Athens, but now there was speculation whether Paris would be able to ride the tide supposedly running in its favour. In the event, several factors hugely influenced the outcome: a magnetic speech by Sebastian Coe, expressing how much a Games in London could assist the very being of the IOC as much as London itself, backed by the engaging presence of then Prime Minister Tony Blair – who privately met numerous IOC members to impress upon them the extent of government support – alongside a lacklustre display by Paris and President Jacques Chirac, which strangely underplayed a hand seeming to hold many trumps. In Coe, London possessed a born winner, as twice demonstrated on the track, yet here at Singapore was a performance more based in inspiration and ideology than technical talent.

To deal first with the figures. Excluded from the voting round by round until their own nation was eliminated from the competition – beside the President, who does not vote – were Killy and Serandour of France; DeFrantz, Easton and Ctvrtlik of America; Smirnov, Tarpischev and Popov of Russia; Princess Royal, Reedie and Craven of Britain; L'Infanta Dona Pilar de Bourbon and Samaranch Jr of Spain. In the first round, Moscow, predictably, was first to fall, and in the second, no less predictably, troubled New York. Now came the vital third round. London led with 39, Madrid eliminated only two votes behind Paris's 33, and in the final round London, to the unrestrained astonishment of the watching world, was declared to have beaten Paris by four votes, 54–50

First round:	London 22, Paris 21, Madrid 20, New York 19, Moscow 15
Second round:	London 27, Paris 25, Madrid 32, New York 16.
Third round:	London 39, Paris 33, Madrid 31.
Fourth round:	London 54, Paris 50.

How did it happen? Let Coe explain how he came to make a speech that was to help sway a largely unemotional, occasionally prejudiced, commercially focused, geopolitically orientated audience:

> Having the Games in your own country with the opportunity to reach young people, not just for seventeen days of competition but the seven years in the build-up, with all the things you can meld onto it and the broader issues beyond simply sport, gives a golden opportunity. It's something I've spent most of my working life trying to do something about [in Britain], and I suppose this is the biggest vehicle I can imagine for making those changes, not just domestically but internationally as well.

Craig Reedie, chairman of the British Olympic Association, and Sebastian Coe congratulated on London's victory by Jacques Rogge. (© IOC/Romeu)

So concentrated was he on what he intended to say that he avoided listening to the other presentations but spent the time in his hotel room listening to jazz. He knew what he had to do, which was to remind the IOC, at a time when the ravages of a commercial, computerised world were eroding children's physical joys and horizons, that London's bid was about youth and hope, a regeneration of priorities – the idea that the 30th modern Olympiad could inspire a great city, a nation and maybe the wider world to regard sport afresh. So he said to them:

> Let us show the world what you can do for us – and what we can do for you . . . choose London today and you send a clear message to the youth of the world – that the Olympic Games are for them. Some might say your decision is between five similar bids, but that would undervalue the opportunity before us. In the past, you have made bold decisions that have taken the Movement forward in powerful and exciting ways. It's now a decision about which city will help us show a new generation that, in a world of many distractions, Olympic sport matters in the twenty-first century.

Prior to his address, Coe had handwritten some 40 letters to members outlining his dream, and in conjunction with Blair's battery-charged charm, even prosaic IOC members were moved to consider carefully their duty. It had become apparent, in the final hours before the vote, that Coe and his team had not come to Singapore to give them the conventional 40-minute travel documentary. It might not have been crucial but was certainly significant window-dressing that part of London's presentation team included over 30 multi-ethnic schoolchildren led by 15-year-old Amber Charles, an aspiring basketball player. The outcome was not, in that conventional cliché, beyond the wildest dreams, because the possibility had grown increasingly. From talking to members in the preceding days, the author, while conscious of the serious threat of Madrid being a possible runner-up, became attuned to conceivable victory: even going so far as to suggest, during that intolerable hour while everyone waited for the one word to drop from the President's lips, that London could even have won by six votes.

Discussing afterwards a result which left the French and their supporters grief-stricken, the emotion among IOC members, albeit that the margin of approval of Coe's message was so achingly close, was widely apparent. 'His letter was everything,' Willi Kaltschmitt, member for Guatemala, said. 'It was so human and from the heart. It set the tone of his speech.' Mario Pescante of Italy, believed to have helped coordinate Rogge's election, was likewise emphatic. 'Seb's presentation was not so much on London as on sport,' he said. 'Usually presentations do not matter that much, people already know their mind, but with Seb, here was something different.' (Paris was scathing in its suspicion that Pescante might have defected to London under pressure from Berlusconi, confidant of Blair.) Anton Geesink, the Dutchman who stunned the host nation in judo's first appearance in 1964, was fulsome: 'Coe explained the British effort for sport. He knows sport, he is sport.' The emotion in Coe's speech caught Nat Indrapana of Thailand: 'He wasn't being arrogant, just very sincere, wanting to look after kids. We all have kids, and we understood. This message was one of humanity and responsibility.'

Could the French have avoided this apocalypse? Every loser in life can ease discomfort by recourse to excuse, real or imaginary. Certainly the French would voice their excuses, though the more objective among their supporters would acknowledge the power and originality of Coe's message. Nonetheless, for a nation that likes to believe itself the trustee of all that is precious from the founder of the modern Games, it was humiliating to have been defeated for the third time in 20 years. Their bid committee had gone out of their way to avoid any semblance of arrogance, yet in an abstract way this was still present: their presentation team an assembly of white middle-aged men in suits without the presence of a single woman or non-white. Moreover, the brief appearance of President Chirac, lending Paris's case little more than bland politik-speak, was hardly worth his journey. Jean-François Lamour, Minister for Sport, was pragmatic enough to admit: 'There is a problem between us and the Olympic world. I'm not at this moment able to say what it is, but we need to understand what was missing for us. We must have some more time.' Alain Danet, veteran of French sports administration and Member of Honour – who was to die a few months later – gave the view that France's vote against the European Constitution had offended many Eastern Europeans, while Henri Serandour, NOC president, conceded: 'London had a sporting project with a political framework, whereas Paris was pursuing a political project with a sporting disguise.' Bertrand Delanoë, Mayor of Paris, was forthright in his condemnation of London's tactics:

> I don't understand the result, and I've met many IOC members who tell me they don't understand it. I want to follow the rules of fair play and to congratulate London and Londoners. I have warm relations with Ken Livingstone, their Mayor. I am not so affectionate towards the promoters of the London candidature, because I am not sure that they have taken part in this competition with exactly the same methods, the same kind of spirit. The day before, when I was going up to my hotel room to sleep, there were people coming down from successive meetings with Tony Blair. I don't understand that. I had believed it was necessary to have the best dossier, the best kind of spirit, and I believe that a large majority of the IOC thought that of Paris. We lost by observing the rules of fair play.

To which Jean-Paul Huchon, president of Paris Regional Council, added: 'The English lobbying went to the limits of the acceptable.' Yet there can be little doubt that the French, along with all candidates, had lobbied IOC members assiduously and systematically over many months, and in the absence of permitted visiting, there was no regulation against Tony Blair meeting whomever he wished. Armand de Rendinger, formerly an adviser to Albertville's Winter Games in 1992, subsequently published a book *Jeux Perdus* (*Lost Games*), in which he suggested that the Paris bid had been riven by two political camps, socialists and Gaullists. That de Rendinger could claim 65 IOC members had promised hand-on-heart that they would vote for Paris indicates both naivety within the Olympic arena – where several hundred votes are regularly promised by a hundred people – and the invalid claim by Delanoë that the French had not lobbied. Though it might not have been conclusive within a margin of four votes, Chirac's gauche comment the preceding week may have jeopardised two votes from Finland when in conversation with Chancellor Gerhard Schroeder and President Putin. 'You can't trust people who cook as badly as that [the British], after Finland it is the country with the worst food,' quoted *Libération*.

President Chirac's gaffe about the quality of British and Finnish cooking may have cost Paris two Finnish votes. (© IOC/Goh)

Failure by New York was a surprise to few other than themselves, every bid campaign existing on the momentum of optimism. The *New York Times* reflected objectively:

> The city's bid was always a dark horse at best . . . it is easy to come up with reasons why New York did so poorly. Organisers never really managed to communicate their excitement to the public. Insisting that the main stadium could be built only as part of a plan to move the Jets to the west side of Manhattan was a huge mistake.

In conversation with Phil Hersh of the *Chicago Tribune*, Bob Ctvrtlik, US IOC member, said:

> We had a solid Olympic bid and didn't get support. We are a proponent of women in sports, and one of the largest sports involving women was voted off the programme, while baseball is our national pastime. For a long time the US was able to rely on being so strong from a sponsorship standpoint, but we haven't had continuity with international relations.

Jim Easton, another American member of the IOC, emphasised: 'We would be better served if we had more people in the top positions of federations, of continental associations and of the IOC.' Hersh posed the problem that US financial support for the Olympics was diminishing. The leading sponsors of TOP now came from seven countries, making the IOC less dependent on US money, alongside worldwide hostility to the international politics of George W. Bush.

An enigma of the contest was the thirty-one third-round votes gained by Madrid in what was seen as a late surge, denied a place in the final round only by two votes behind Paris. The circumstances aroused speculation at the time – Samaranch Sr's influence? – and were brought to a head a few months later when it was alleged in an interview with BBC News by Alex Gilady, Israeli member and former vice-president of NBC, that one vote had gone the wrong way in the third round: to Paris instead of Madrid, which, if given the other way, would have forced a tie and a run-off. With London supporters considering Paris was the main danger, their votes in the decider would have swung to Madrid, and in a Madrid–London final, the probability was that Paris votes would then have supported Madrid, which would have become the winner. Lodged at the centre of the controversy was Lambis Nikolaou of Greece, initially believed to be the one to have misplaced his vote. In fact, with 104 electronically recorded boxes allocated, only 103 votes were cast: Nikolaou failed to record his vote. So even had he voted (erroneously?) for Madrid, they would still have been defeated by a margin of one. The story provoked an irritated response from the President, while Alejandro Blanco, head of the Spanish NOC, conceded: 'Talking about this now is very difficult because we're dealing with a hypothesis and we can't change what actually happened. There is little sense going over it six months later.' With slightly exaggerated bravado, Craig Reedie, former chairman of BOA, asserted: 'London won the Games hands-down. If you're looking for reasons for London's win, I suspect you should look at the quality of the bidding, of the lobbying and above all of the presentation.' A postscript to the election was that at the IOC's debriefing, Reedie and Keith Mills, London's vice-chairman, successfully pressed for alterations governing city conduct: that this should no longer be governed by the Ethics Commission but should be, like any sports competition, the responsibility of the NOC Relations Department, in other words under the guidance of Gilbert Felli rather than the Ethics Commission's special representative Paquerette Girard Zappelli.

Lambis Nikolaou, member from Greece, was involved in a post-voting debate which, it was incorrectly alleged, could have given Madrid victory over London. (© IOC/Goh)

The rampant euphoria that flowed across Britain was appallingly dissolved the following day by terrorist bomb attacks in London, with mass casualties on underground lines and buses. Britain's mood of joy was frozen in its tracks, but, as it had under wartime assault from Germany, amid the carnage the population grimly returned to its daily schedules, Londoners proving to Al Qaeda and its followers, echoing the long UK struggle with the IRA, that, as *The Times* observed: 'You failed again'. The Labour government Home Secretary Charles Clarke, subsequently replaced in office, was appointed chair of an Olympic security committee for 2012 with a budget of $350 million, way below expenditure of the multi-national security screen for Athens but based on long-standing expertise within the British police force in handling such threats.

Meanwhile, adding to his many other hats, Denis Oswald was appointed chairman of the Coordination Commission for 2012, and he welcomed the simultaneous appointment of Lord Coe as leader of the local organising committee, Keith Mills

continuing as his right-hand man. Overseeing the infrastructure projects for venues, London created an Olympic Delivery Authority, Paul Deighton the chief executive. By early 2006, however, there would be modifications of the London project – the affliction of every Games' host city – with a worrying escalation of the overall government budget: public analysis of which, as always, took no account of the difference between Games administration costs for 16 days and government/city overload, exploiting the emotional momentum of the Games for creating new civic infrastructures of rail, road and housing. The IOC should address this perennial adverse publicity.

When the IOC reassembled eight months after Singapore, for its Session prior to the Turin Winter Games, Copenhagen was voted host for the Congress of 2009, the 13th such gathering of all arms of the Olympic Movement: a decision boldly made in the face of violent controversy in the Danish capital. There had been domestic uproar, echoed worldwide, over domestic cartoons about Prophet Muhammad. There was poignancy that Copenhagen was chosen, with political neutrality, in preference to Cairo by 59–40, ignoring protests by the Muslim world. Other candidates for the Congress had been Athens, Taipei, Pusan, Riga and Singapore. Unexpected was the withdrawal of Mexico City; an indication that Mario Vazquez Raña might be losing some of his influence at home, where he was said to be in political opposition to the state President and to Sports Minister Nelson Vargas, who were supposedly hesitant to commit the necessary budget. Addressing the Session, Danish IOC member Kai Holm, said:

> We deeply regret that these cartoons are seen as defamatory by cultures different from our own. Personally, I would never myself have chosen to show religious symbols in that way. The situation is one that all of us in Danish sport deeply regret, one that reminds us how important it is to separate sport from politics.

Elected to the IOC as Athletes Commission representatives were Beckie Scott, Canadian cross-country skier, and Saku Koivu, hockey professional from Finland, over 78 per cent of athletes present at Turin taking part in the vote.

Eight eminent women bear the flag at Turin's opening ceremony: (clockwise from far right) Susan Sarandon (USA), Nawal El Moutawakel (MAR), Isabel Allende (CHI), Sophia Loren (ITA), Wangari Muta Maathai (KEN), Manuela di Centa (ITA), Maria Mutola (MOZ), Somaly Mam (CAM). (© IOC/Kishimoto)

The torch arrives with celebrated cross-country skier Stefania Belmondo. (© IOC/Kishimoto)

The journey towards Turin, since its election in preference to Sion of Switzerland in 1999 – a backlash action against the involvement of Swiss veteran Marc Hodler in the Salt Lake City scandal as whistleblower – had been vexatious, the completion of facilities regularly open to doubt. Yet for Turin, as for many host cities, the event was more than a matter of staging some sports. It was an attempted regeneration of a declining industrial city, for so long heavily dependent on the Fiat motor organisation but which over recent years had lost some 300,000 inhabitants, a quarter of the population, as they drifted elsewhere. Former seat of Dukes of Savoy, it had once been the capital of the Kingdom of Sardinia and for three centuries a jewel of baroque architecture. Now, it was to be hoped, the city might find fresh momentum, not least with the birth of its first

subway line at a cost of $500 million. Local politicians dreamed of establishing cleaner modern technology and an attraction to tourists that might leave them no longer in the shadow of more fashionable Milan. The Games were going to cost $3.5 billion, the government subsiding the greater part of this, though the city expected to lose $50 million on the Games project. As compensation, it was hoped to create 2,000 permanent new housing units; an upgrading of the airport; a second exhibition centre for the city once the speed skating venue was no longer required; and a new convention centre able to accommodate 15,000, from the ice-hockey arena. Much of this was to be fulfilled, but in the management of the Games, expectations fell short, especially at the mountain venues, while much of cosmopolitan Turin found it difficult to generate the city's slogan: 'Passion lives here'. Turin had earned the Games with active support from legendary Fiat patron Gianni Agnelli, but he was some while dead, and domestic bickering between the right-wing government of Silvio Berlusconi and Turin's labour-orientated local council had created enduring friction. Some thought that Berlusconi had paid little attention to preparations, and he did not attend the opening ceremony. One of the consequences of inadequate organisation was the reduction in visiting supporters on account of transport difficulties. For instance, whereas 10,000 Norwegians would normally attend cross-country competitions within Europe, at Turin there were only two-thirds of that number present. Frequent alarms at lack of progress had led to the removal a year beforehand of CEO Paolo Rota and deputy Marcello Pochettino.

It was Italy's most decorated Winter Olympian, cross-country skier Stefania Belmondo, who would ignite the Olympic flame: a fountain of white fireworks that raced around the stadium, climbed the 60-metre Olympic torch and burst into glory at the apex. For the first time, the Olympic flag was carried into the stadium by eight eminent women from all walks of life: Nobel Peace Prize winner Wangari Muta Maathai of Kenya; Chilean author Isabel Allende; Cambodian human rights activist Somaly Mam; Italian film icon Sophia Loren; American actress and activist Susan Sarandon; and three Olympic champions, Nawal El Moutawakel of Morocco, Manuela di Centa of Italy and Maria Mutola of Mozambique.

Turin opening ceremony masque, Hellenic period of Alexander the Great's Macedonian conquest of Greece, 336 BC. (© IOC/Kishimoto)

CHAPTER LXXV

Turin (XX) 2006

Evgeni Plushenko of Russia, Olympic figure skating champion

'My Olympic triumph in Turin was a long-awaited goal; I had been working towards it for many years. I'd hoped to win gold in Salt Lake City, but failed to control my emotions and came only second. Even so, at 19, it was a rewarding result, and I became one of the youngest skaters to win an Olympic medal at that age. So I didn't see that previous silver as defeat, just another fine result that I was proud of, and like any sportsman I continued to dream of gold.

The next four years were spent preparing for Turin. I suffered a serious injury, needing surgery, and had a long recovery, during which I concentrated on getting back into shape and studying new programmes. At present, men's solo skating is a fast-developing sport with many strong skaters from different countries, but years of preparation have taught me not to dwell on one's rivals. First of all a skater, and generally any sportsman, should compete only with himself. Each time you go out on the ice, you should try to push yourself and improve on previous performances. This is what allowed me to achieve such a high score in both the short programme and the free skate in Turin, even though I was facing strong opponents. The judges gave me 258.33 points, a 27-point lead over my nearest rival. A real victory! Over the other competitors, over myself, over my emotions, as well as bringing another gold medal to the Russian team.

I was thrilled to see so many Russian supporters in Turin. There were Russian flags everywhere, and I could hear the cheering. "We are with you, Zhenya", "We will win, Zhenya", "Go Russia". I don't think I ever had such serious support at any international competition before, and it was very important to me during the Olympics. The feeling that so many people believe in you and are wishing you luck gives you tremendous strength. I'm so appreciative of my fans, and I believe that without the support we receive from them, figure skating would not have reached its present standards.

I'm also very grateful to my coach, Alexei Nikolaevich Mishin, who has been with me since I was a small child and trained me since I first moved to St Petersburg. It was he who taught me everything I can do today and who invested so much effort in me. It's true that being a coach is an uncertain occupation, yet it demands complete commitment. I'm happy to have had such a wise and talented person as Alexei Nikolaevich, and I'm sure he will produce more talented youngsters who will not only reach my level but surpass me. Figure skating does not stand still: every year sees more complicated jumps, spins, footwork. It's been said that Alexei Nikolaevich is a second father to me, but of course I have my own father, Viktor, whom I love, and he has supported me my whole life. He has been another coach through years of training, competitions, seminars and travelling: everything.

I'm not going to give up competitive sport for the professional exhibition world. The euphoria of victory is important to every sportsman, and I will try to bring more medals to Russia. Already I'm planning for the next Games in Vancouver. First, I have to look at my fitness, and there is some surgery that I've postponed because of preparing for competitions. So, in 2006–07 I decided not to compete. But after that I aim to be a two-time Olympic champion. With fresh energy, new programmes and the audience's applause, I will be sincerely happy if at least a small part of my dream comes true.

Can an American break the Russian winning streak and capture the gold at Vancouver 2010? Maybe, though Russian men continue to dominate because we have a powerful tradition and also because of our excellent coaches. It's hard to explain why we regularly win. Perhaps it's because inside we're different, as if we have a fire that will either consume us or work for us. We like to work, and we have a need to win.'*

(Photograph © IOC)

So technically gifted was Evgeni Plushenko, so superior to the rest of the field by the time of the Turin Games, that the American Johnny Weir felt able to say beforehand, and without resentment of an exceptional rival: 'The rest of us are competing for silver.' In the event, Weir would disappointment himself and his many supporters by finishing only fifth, but his forecast was all too true: Plushenko was in a class of his own, technically out of reach, though the fact that he could weave quadruple jumps in his programme was not to remain exclusive in the seasons immediately following, as others began to close the gap. His had been an exceptional career beginning at the age of four, and when the ice rink closed in his home city of Volgagrad when he was eleven he was sent to St Petersberg to train under Mishin, and his development was rapid. By 15, he had won the world junior title and finished third in the senior event in the same year. With Mishin also being the coach of another rising star, Alexei Yagudin, a fierce rivalry developed and continued over the coming years. In the Olympics at Salt Lake City, Yagudin took the crown with the highest free-skate marks under the old system of 6.0 maximum, with Plushenko second. Yagudin then retired, and Plushenko now became all but unchallengeable, being the first to perform the quadruple toe loop–triple toe loop–double loop jump combination and being the youngest male skater to receive a perfect six, doing so seventy times before the judging system was altered.

Technical perfection, leaving the rest competing for silver. (© IOC)

In Turin, the three-time world champion lived up to expectation. In the short programme, he was so flawless that he led the field by a stunning ten points ahead of Weir on 90.66, with the previous year's world champion Stéphane Lambiel of Switzerland close behind. Plushenko's score was the highest ever under the new scoring system. Weir was overawed by his rival. 'It's wild. I didn't think anyone could get past 80, and to see a score of 90 is incredible.' Plushenko had successfully landed his combination of quadruple toe loop and triple loop, and was effectively already out of reach bar accident, though nursing the anxiety of several injuries suffered during 2005. In the free skating programme, his performance was again exalted. Some said he played safe within the new marking system, yet once again he was a joy to watch, this exceptional athlete who brought to the ice rink the touch of ballet. With Weir faltering, Lambiel secured the silver, Jeffrey Buttle of Canada earning

bronze. Plushenko had taken his place in history, yet was fortunate when avoiding serious injury in a car crash on his way to the airport the following day. Operations already scheduled were temporarily to remove him from competition, but by late in 2007 there were indications that this emerald performer might be defending his title in Vancouver.

Debate on the new scoring system was extensive. The International Skating Union was satisfied with the innovative computer-based scheme that made the judges anonymous, the votes of nine of the twelve judges being selected randomly and with each technical move scored separately, allowance made for levels of difficulty and the quality of the competitors' execution. Some, such as Robin Cousins, of Britain, champion at Lake Placid in 1980, suggested that creativity was being repressed by the emphasis on technical skills, but general opinion was that the system had gone a long way in eliminating the controversies that had been a regrettable part of the figure skating scene for so long, culminating four years before with the allegations of corruption surrounding Marie-Reine Le Gougne of France. To some extent, Le Gougne had dug her own grave with admissions of political intrigue among judges that had long been rampant, and she duly became the sacrificial lamb. Another casualty of the revolution had been Sally Stapleford, former chairwoman of the ISU technical committee, who was embraced in a political row following Salt Lake City and voted out of office.

If Plushenko's victory was, in its way, confirmation of the obvious, there was simultaneous surprise and dismay at the outcome of the women's title. Plushenko's compatriot Irina Slutskaya, seven-time European champion and twice world champion, seemed predestined to complete a Russian clean sweep of figures events, the pairs and ice dancing trophies being already annexed by Russians. But for the 27-year-old supposed queen of the ice, her silver medal at Salt Lake City was to be followed not by gold but bronze as she fluffed her free programme. Lying second after the short programme, she was now overtaken by Sasha Cohen of America, gold being claimed by the elegant, almost statuesque Shizuka Arakawa, who earned Japan its first-ever figure skating title. Arakawa gave that rare, distinctive impression that she was skating for herself; she was alone on the ice in a mental sense. Perhaps she held that capacity as the holder of a university degree, or maybe it was her age: at twenty-four the oldest champion in the four most recent Games succeeding Sarah Hughes (USA), sixteen, Tara Lipinski (USA), fifteen, and Oksana Baiul (Ukraine), sixteen. Yet, if Arakawa was a picture of composure, she was defying a past history of gaffes in her free programme. Indeed, she had been close to retirement two years earlier after becoming world champion. What dismay for Slutskaya, reigning world champion and on the short programme closely shadowing Cohen, the leader, who had finished fourth at Salt Lake City, with Arakawa a fraction behind Slutskaya in third place. Arakawa would claim that she had felt destiny calling when Luciano Pavarotti sang from the opera *Turandot* during the opening ceremony, her own music for her free programme being from Puccini's *Violin Fantasy on Turandot*. She was to give a spellbinding performance, even if the programme did not include the triple–triple combinations of previous winners. Working with a Russian coach, Nikolai Morozov, Arakawa had studied the judging system, identifying spins and spirals as the key to victory. Neither Cohen nor Slutskaya could match her. A strong element of American interest had surrounded Emily Hughes, seventeen, controversial replacement for the once-fancied Michelle Kwan, runner-up in 1998, third in 2002, holder of five world championships, now undermined by injury. The young replacement finished a creditable seventh.

Shizuka Arakawa of Japan, 'alone on the ice in a mental sense'.
(© Getty Images/Bello)

Dan Zhang limps off the ice after grotesque fall, she and Hao
returning to secure silver medal (© IOC/Nagaya)

The pros and cons of the judging system were plunged into debate by the pairs silver medal won by Dan Zhang and Hao Zhang after a four-minute interruption of their final programme following a horrendous fall. With their performance having run little more than half a minute, Hao launched his partner into the air but Dan, mistiming her spin, fell heavily to the ice, grotesquely twisting one knee. As she doubled over in pain, the music halted and the pair left the ice. With some confusion and delay they were permitted the statutory two minutes in which to recover and resume. When they did, it was widely supposed their chance of a medal behind world champions and favourites Tatiana Totmianina and Maxim Marinin had evaporated. Yet not only did they retain second place but their final score was a personal best. The explanation was that the throw-spin at the moment of the fall was only one of nineteen elements in their programme, the majority of the other eighteen techniques being performed as well or better than any of their rivals, the Russians apart. For the fall, they lost only one point and were assured of the silver. No doubt protests at a delay fully four minutes in total might have been louder had not the bronze position and fourth place been occupied by the other two Chinese pairs, Xue Shen/Hongbo Zhao and Qing Pang/Jian Tong. Nonetheless, it was a stupendously brave continuation by the 20-year-old Dan, equivalent to that of American gymnast Kerri Strug in 1996. 'I thought it was the end,' she admitted later. 'You cannot imagine how painful it was. It challenges the power of a human being.' She admitted she was responsible for the fall, having let go of Hao's hand too early in the risky throw-quadruple salchow. The event made front-page news back home, the pair previously having lived in the shadow of the bronze-medal winners. Despite the controversy of the fall delay, the ISU confirmed that the referee had acted correctly.

The circumstances inevitably diminished full appreciation of a glittering performance by Totmianina and Marinin. More ominous controversy surrounded the sixth-placed German pair, Aliona Savchenko and Robin Szolkowy, and their coach Ingo Steuer. It was alleged that Steuer, a former East German, had been an informer with the Stasi secret police, and in an investigation by the German Olympic Committee into all 162 of their coaches and officials, Steuer was one of three suspended. Savchenko, however, herself a Ukrainian who had partnered Szolkowy possibly as a ticket to a new life, demanded Steuer's reinstatement if she were to compete. Appeals were heard, Steuer travelled to Turin, but the political pressures proved too great and the pair seriously underperformed. 'It has all been too much for us,' lamented Savchenko.

Following Plushenko and the pairs victory, Tatiana Navka and Roman Kostomarov gave Russia their third figures victory in the ice dance event, even though they were not at their peak. This was still sufficient, however, to ease them ahead of Americans Tanith Belbin and Benjamin Agosto, with Ukrainians Elena Grushina and Ruslan Goncharov winning bronze. The gold–silver–bronze placings were a repetition of the previous year's world championship. Canadian-born Belbin had watched the Salt Lake City Games on television, not yet being a US citizen, her passport being granted in December 2005 in time for eligibility for Turin. The competition was notable for a picture that circled the world: Barbara Fusar-Poli's expression of mute fury when dropped by Italian partner Maurizio Margaglio when the pair were well placed for a medal but thereafter slid to sixth place.

There are few prime events of a Winter Games regularly less predictable than the Alpine men's downhill. Turin's was true to form, with Frenchman Antoine Deneriaz, number 30 in the field, sweeping down the mountain at Sestriere to overhaul Austrian pre-race favourite Michael Walchhofer to win by seven-tenths of a second. A little over a year earlier, Deneriaz had been lying on a stretcher beside the downhill in Chamonix with a torn cruciate ligament, but he had vowed there and then that he would still do something in the Olympic Games. And he did, never mind not having been placed higher than seventh during the season and not having won a World Cup event for three years. On a marvellously sunny day, Deneriaz emulated the surprise win of compatriot Jean Luc Cretier eight years earlier. Though he had excelled down the icy course, he could barely believe his fortune. 'When I saw my time, I thought it was incredible,' he said, 'but the course was the type that suits me best, because you can go flat out all the way, and I had been feeling that I was in top form.' He had been fastest in the final training run, and though Walchhofer's earlier run on the day for a while looked safe, Deneriaz successfully passed him. Bruno Kernen of Switzerland took bronze, while the fancied and much self-publicised Bode Miller of America, who had been out drinking the previous evening, blew his chances when finishing fifth. He had previously been warned by his National Association for admission of drinking prior to races. The much medalled Norwegian Kjetil-André Aamodt had missed the bronze by six-hundredths, while Austrian Hermann Maier, he of the memorable Nagano crash, finished sixth. Fritz Strobl, Austria's defending champion, could finish only eighth. If victory brought euphoria for the huge French contingent, the medal ceremony was less joyful, taking place not in the centre of Turin at the Piazza Castello, scene of nightly medal celebrations, but in front of half-empty stands when most of the spectators had already departed: a sad contradiction of the Games' motto, 'La passione vive qui' (passion lives here).

to take the title ahead of Ivica Kostelic, the too-often injured brother of famed Croatian Janica. As well as Miller having ploughed his chance, Ben Raich, the Austrian favourite, likewise skied off course to leave the way open for Ligety, who had been placed no better than 32nd after the downhill section. Rainer Schoenfelder of Austria was third. Four years earlier, Ligety had been a seventeen-year-old forerunner at Salt Lake City. Aamodt, having hurt a knee in the prime downhill event, had withdrawn to preserve himself for subsequent races.

It proved to have been a wise decision. In the super-G, Aamodt won his fourth medal in the event, his third gold and his eighth medal Olympic medal at the grand old age of 34 – the oldest and most be-medalled Olympic Alpine skier. Defending his title from Salt Lake City, he produced a textbook run. 'I'd been skiing on the children's slopes after my knee injury and wasn't sure how it would go today,' he said. 'When I kicked out of the start, I felt a little pain, and maybe I was faster, because if you feel you are at a disadvantage you tend to take more risks.' Hermann Maier returned to the medal rostrum, eight years after his double gold in Nagano, with silver, bronze going to Ambrosi Hoffmann of Switzerland. There was more dismay for Miller, who again blew out. If nothing else, he demonstrated an element of his rare technique when remaining upright on one ski at 100 kph after hitting a gate head-on. For the controversial American, it was a Games of collision with either bars or gates. Aamodt would not be giving his latest medal to his father, the previous seven having been stolen two days after being briefly loaned to him.

Antoine Deneriaz of France conquers an icy course, not having enjoyed a World Cup win in three years. (© IOC)

Kjetil-André Aamodt of Norway, oldest and most be-medalled Alpine Olympian, takes super-G gold (above), while Bode Miller, boastful American, contemplates profound anti-climax. (© IOC and © IOC/Gallmann)

Bode Miller's winter of discontent continued in his next event, the combined slalom/downhill, when, having established what seemed a useful lead on the downhill section he straddled a gate in the first of two slalom runs. Compensation for America came from Ted Ligety, who blended the two fastest slalom runs

The men's slalom, as is the way of sport, was one of those occasions of disaster and triumph: the former for Giorgio Rocca of Italy, hitherto the most accomplished slalom skier of the season with a sequence of five straight World Cup victories but now making an elementary mistake halfway down his first run when crossing his skis like a novice and disappearing out of contention; the latter for Benjamin Raich, leading a national sweep alongside Reinfried Herbst and Rainer Schoenfelder to give Austria another three Alpine medals: only the fifth time in Olympic Alpine history for a national triple. It was a triumph that would only marginally offset the scandal of an Italian police drug investigation of the private residence of their Nordic squad. Raich's victory lifted him from no better than consistent status behind the event's leading personalities: now it was calmness and composure that carried him to the top. His crowning moment made it a double, for the 27 year old had already claimed the giant slalom title, ahead of Joel Chenal of France and Maier, a victory that had rendered the little-known Raich almost speechless. No higher than fifth after the opening leg, he secured the gold with a flawless second run. Repetition in the slalom made him the first since Alberto Tomba in Calgary to claim both titles, and though home crowds mourned the failure of Rocca, the unassuming Raich, dogged by the adjacent doping scandal, could hardly claim to embrace Tomba-like prestige. Protesting his own innocence, he insisted: 'They could test me day and night, though it's annoying when you have to inform them where you're going to eat in the evening. I'm hardly likely to beat it to Africa overnight.' Miller's misery had continued with sixth place in the giant slalom.

The first since Alberto Tomba to achieve the giant slalom/slalom double, Benjamin Raich of Austria holds his line. (© IOC)

Emulating Raich was compatriot Michaela Dorfmeister, with her own double in downhill and super-G. She was, at 32, the oldest female Alpine skier of the Games, and held off Martina Schild of Switzerland and Swedish star Anja Pärson to win her first brace in three appearances at a Winter Games. She had lost by one-hundredth of a second to American Picabo Street at Nagano's super-G, and finished ninth (in the downhill), fourth, fifth and sixth in four events in 2002. 'It was that elusive medal which kept me skiing,' she admitted after the downhill, for which she was favourite following a dominant World Cup season, and she duly became the first Austrian woman champion since Pröll in 1980. Schild, second, was granddaughter of Hedy Schlunegger, winner of the inaugural event at St Moritz in 1948. An error late on the course cost Pärson a better medal. When Dorfmeister completed her double

in the super-G, with a narrow margin ahead of Janica Kostelic, she was euphoric enough to be able to ignore a fluffed national anthem at the presentation. Pärson, a relatively youthful twenty-four and 'just a little girl from the same little village from which Ingemar Stenmark also comes, but less famous', as she demurely put it, had long aimed to be a five-event contender at Turin, and her bronze, with another in the combined behind the versatile Kostelic and Marlies Schild of Austria, was crowned with gold in the slalom. She had defied a knee injury, so heavily strapped that her foot temporarily went numb during the race – her doctor, having given a painkilling injection, saying, 'If it's too painful at the first jump, quit!' Her pinnacle brought Sweden's first Alpine gold medal for 12 years, but in the micro-margins of the sport she had fractions to spare over Nicole Hosp and Marlies Schild, with Kostelic, fighting off illness, there again though in fourth place. Kostelic would be obliged to withdraw from the giant slalom, won in a blizzard by American Julia Mancuso, with Pärson sixth.

There can be no particular reason why speed skaters should hold a position of moral altruism superior to other sportsmen, but Joey Cheek chose to follow in the path of Johann Olav Koss of Norway when donating his $25,000 bonus from winning speed skating's 500m title to the charity Right to Play, an African organisation founded by Koss with his earnings from three gold medals in 1994. Cheek had been inspired as a boy when watching Koss and wished his donation to go towards help for deprived children in Darfur, Sudan. It was the spectacle of Koss in Lillehammer that persuaded Cheek to switch from in-line skating to speed skating, notwithstanding his home being in North Carolina with a marked absence of ice, which led to a move to Canada at the age of 16. Cheek was doubtless motivated also by his mother, who worked in her spare time assisting homeless and abused children. Not that Cheek's title was particularly a surprise: he was already world champion, and his combined time from two runs gave him a margin of 0.65 seconds – the widest in the three Games in which the 500m had been determined by two races instead of one – over Dmitriy Dorofeyev of Russia, with Korean Kang Seok Lee in third place.

There was silver, too, for Cheek in the 1,000m, in which Shani Davis became the first African-American to win an individual gold medal in a Winter Games. It had been a difficult passage for the boy from the south side of Chicago, mocked by his peers when appearing after practice in skating tights: a boy with ambitions in a sport almost exclusively as white as the ice. Nor had it helped his image within the US team when he earlier, and justifiably, withdrew in Turin from the relay event to concentrate on his own speciality. Maybe he was pressed by his ever-critical mother Cherie, said to drive him as unsparingly in his 20s as when he was a teenager. 'You have to ride it out,' Davis reflected later on his many difficulties, 'because eventually, if you've worked hard enough, you'll get a chance to do something great.' And that came with his two and a half laps in the 1,000m, his uniform a symbolic charcoal shade, where he secured a handsome margin over Cheek and Erben Wennemars of the Netherlands. Chad Hedrick, one of Davis's least supportive colleagues, who had questioned 'What is right and wrong?' over the relay decision, finished sixth. He began his own ultimately vain quest for five medals and the emulation of Eric Heiden in 1980, with victory in the 5,000m. The twenty-eight-year-old Texan had, like Cheek, been an in-line skater until three years previously. His time of 6:14.68 was a fraction outside the Olympic record but way ahead of Sven Kramer (NED), the man who had robbed him of the world record two months earlier. It was typical of the huge, enthusiastic band of Dutch supporters that in their disappointment they should give Hedrick a standing ovation on his lap of honour.

Davis finished seventh, while Enrico Fabris of Italy, bronze winner, was to drive the home crowd wild with excitement with his victory in the 1,500m, edging out Davis, former world record holder, by sixteen-hundredths, with Hedrick in third place. Hedrick's odyssey would include a silver in the 10,000m; there was no traditional handshake between him and Davis on the 1,500m podium. The success of Fabris was exceptional in a country where there are fewer than 100 elite skaters, compared with 14,000 in the Netherlands among some 170,000 affiliated to Dutch clubs. Additionally leading Italy to victory in the relay, frontrunners from start to finish, Fabris's bonuses would, including a bronze in the 5,000m, push his annual income as a policeman from $15,000 to $300,000.

Star of the women's events, indeed arguably the most spectacular woman performer of the entire Games, was Cindy Klassen of Canada with five medals: two bronze (3,000m, 5,000m), two silver (1,000m, relay) and gold (1,500m), the most medals of any athlete in Turin. Hers was a brave story. More than two years earlier she had been close to death when a fall during training and collision with a rival's blade severed 12 tendons and an artery in her arm, leaving her unconscious. On recovery, rather than dwell in self-pity, she had engaged in charity work in Mexico. Such is Dutch fanaticism in the sport that during her time in hospital, many of the goodwill messages had Dutch postmarks. 'They're such knowledgeable fans, we're really fortunate to have them here,' Klassen said on winning the 1,500m, followed home by colleague Kristina Groves and Dutch girl Ireen Wust. It was Wust who took the 3,000m title, Svetlana Zhurova of Russia, world sprint champion, the 500m, and Clara Hughes of Canada the 5,000m, the latter notable for the fact that she had won two bronze medals in cycling at Atlanta in 1996.

Short track speed skating witnessed overwhelming dominance by South Korea at the expense of the other leading nations, China, Canada and the United States, with Hyun-Soo Ahn and Sun-Yu Jin winning three golds each in the respective men's and women's events out of a total of ten Korean medals in all. A moment of revenge of a kind for a controversial loss in 2002 came with Ahn's victory in the 1,500m. Apolo Anton Ohno had become the most reviled American in Korea when winning the event in Salt Lake City, gaining the gold medal on the disqualification of Dong-Sung Kim, who had allegedly blocked him. Now there was the expectation of a showdown between Ahn, four-time world champion, and Ohno, but the latter fell in the semi-final, Ahn claiming gold by the habitual split seconds from compatriot Ho-Suk Lee, with Jia Jun Li of China in third place. Korean self-respect was further restored when Ahn took gold in the 1,000m, in Olympic record time of 1:26.739, with Ohno third, though these positions were reversed in the 500m, won by Ohno with François-Louis Tremblay of Canada splitting the pair. China, which will no doubt be busting guts in Beijing to overhaul South Korea in this sport, had some reward when Meng Wang earned gold, silver and bronze respectively in the 500m, 1,000m and 1,500m.

Hyun-Soo Ahn of South Korea gains revenge for controversial defeat at Salt Lake, he and compatriot Ho-Suk Lee completing a 1–2 double at 1,000m and 1,500m. (© IOC)

Giorgio Di Centa on the final day enabled Italy to feel good about their own Games, which had not always been the case throughout the fortnight. With an impressive finish over the final stretch, he won the Nordic men's cross-country 50km event with the sort of time that marathon runners similarly endure: 2:06:11.8. One of those he surpassed was Eugeni Dementiev of Russia, previously winner of the 30km pursuit event on the opening day of the cross-country programme, and Mikhail Botwinov of Austria, the latter medal overshadowed by the controversy of the investigation of Austria's Nordic team by the police and IOC. The Russian-born Botwinov had been himself involved with Austrian coach Walter Mayer four years earlier at the Salt Lake City Games, where he won silver in the 30km event. Subsequently Mayer was banned, and his unscheduled visit to the current Austrian team ignited the newest scandal. Botwinov, a former Russian competing in 1992 and 1994 before switching nationality, had never been directly implicated in a doping case, and his untarnished medal was Austria's first in cross-country in Turin.

Cindy Klassen of Canada earns woman-of-the-Games badge with five speed-skating medals following life-threatening injury. (© IOC)

Reviving Italian pride on last day of the Games, Giorgio Di Centa drives to victory in Nordic 50km. (© Getty Images/AFP)

Di Centa's margin, four-tenths of a second, was the narrowest in the Olympic event's history. Brother of former Olympic champion Manuela, who had won five medals in 1994, Di Centa was the first competitor from outside Scandinavia or the former Soviet Union to win this event at the Games. He had earlier helped Italy take the relay prize. 'Usually someone overruns me,' he said, 'but today I didn't hear the noise of skis behind me, and with the finish line closer and closer I realised my legs were still powerful.'

In the Nordic combined team event, Austria won for the first time in the Olympics when Jens Gaiser squandered Germany's chance on the last leg. Germany had led on the jumping phase and had extended their lead to 47 seconds midway through the 4 x 5km cross-country section. Felix Gottwald then halved this deficit for Austria on the third leg, and Mario Stecher swept past the faltering Gaiser to give Austria victory by 17 seconds. Finland, defending champions, took the bronze. Gottwald's decisive contribution was mirrored in his victory in the individual sprint event ahead of Magnus Moan of Norway and Georg Hettich of Germany. The same three medal winners had taken the prizes in the individual combined, but there it was Hettich, with a gigantic leap of 104 metres on his second jump, who led at the halfway stage, convincingly maintaining control in the cross-country, Gottwald finishing second and Moan third. Kristina Smigun of Estonia achieved a notable double in women's cross-country with 15km pursuit and 10km classical victories. Driven by the belief that millions back home were

willing her onwards in the 15km, Smigun won by two seconds from Katerina Neumannova of the Czech Republic. She had restricted her competition this season to concentrate on training for the Olympics, and her fitness told during wet conditions as rain fell on overnight snow. Her father Anatoli had taken part in the 1976 Olympics a year before she was born. Marit Bjorgen of Norway, who took silver behind Smigun in the 10km individual, was World Cup leader and favourite but dropped out of the 15km pursuit with an upset stomach. The field was also devoid of 2002 relay winner Evi Sachenbacher-Stehle of Germany, one of those suspended the previous week for undue levels of haemoglobin, while defending champion Beckie Scott of Canada finished sixth. Chandra Crawford, a 22 year old from Canmore, Alberta, took the women's sprint to raise Canadian expectations for Vancouver 2010.

Thomas Morgenstern and Andreas Kofler added to Austria's divided emotions at these Games by claiming first and second place on the large hill jump and then combining with Martin Koch and Andreas Widhölzl to clinch the team event. The competition was a wretched experience for Janne Ahonen of Finland, widely considered the foremost in his sport yet failing once more in the Olympics, as did Andreas Kuttel of Switzerland, also fancied for a medal. Morgenstern, 19, was a protégé still living on expectation rather than ultimate fulfilment, having notched up his first World Cup victory at the age of 16. Now, unexpectedly, came the realisation. Second after the first jump at Pragelato's big hill, he relaxed: so often the key to peak performance. The power of youth took hold of him, the wind which had blemished Ahonen's jumps instead gave him lift, and his second jump of 140 metres was a mere 50 centimetres short of the hill record and enabled him to squeeze past Kofler.

Aged 19, Thomas Morgenstern of Austria brings the power of youth to the big hill. (© Getty Images/Simon)

The creation of an Olympic star can be a dramatic revelation, but likewise so can be their demise with the rise of another. Thus it was with Ole Einar Björndalen of Norway and Michael Greis of Germany. Björndalen, with four gold medals at Salt Lake City and one from Nagano, intended to tilt at all five biathlon events but had to settle for taking second and third place respectively in the 20km and 15km events behind Greis. Björndalen's downfall in the 20km was to miss two targets with his rifle, but for which he would probably have retained his title. His disappointment protected the reputation of Bjørn Daehlie, his compatriot who held the Winter Games record of eight gold medals. Björndalen, already 32, promised that he would continue in 2012. 'Maybe I can do one, maybe two more

Olympics. I think I can come near Daehlie's record. It would be difficult but I will try.' Björndalen is a better shot than Daehlie, and his prowess in biathlon has raised the sport's profile even higher in his home country. In the 15km mass start, he and Thomasz Sikora of Poland led at the fourth and last shooting stage, but each would miss the target, and this permitted Greis, with five bullseyes, to leap the pair and grab the title. It was ironic that Björndalen, such an accomplished shot, should now be prone to error, as he also was in the 10km sprint, won by Sven Fischer of Germany, who skied and shot without flaw at the age of 34. At the finish, Fischer remained prostrate for a while in the winning arena, not through exhaustion but the pleasure of self-reflection. 'When you become Olympic champion when young, you do not fully appreciate what you have achieved,' he said. Unsurprisingly, Germany won the team relay ahead of Russia and France, with favourites Norway in dispirited fifth place despite an aggressive final leg by Björndalen. Shooting at a stationary target when your lungs are burning and searching for breath is no easy matter, and it was missed shots by rivals that enabled Russian Svetlana Ishmouratova to gain victory in the women's 15km. Her colleague Olga Pyleva came second, only to be disqualified for a positive drug test, the silver medal passing to Martina Glagow of Germany with a third Russian, Albina Akhatova, taking bronze, the Russians also regaining the team title they last held in 1994.

Victory in all three bobsleigh events helped consolidate Germany's standing as the Games' leading medal winners for the second time, though some suspicion surrounded the two-man gold by André Lange and Kevin Kuske. The coaches of six nations, including the USA, Canada and France considered whether to launch a protest after the final runs. Doubts concerned a technology barred by the international federation (FIBT) on the treatment of the steel runners, making them harder and faster. The start times of the two German teams were slower than their rivals', yet they appeared to pick up undue acceleration during the subsequent helter-skelter, but in the end no action was taken. The international bobsleigh federation FIBT said the runners passed pre-training inspection. There was, however, no doubting the technique of the winning German pair when successfully defending the title won by compatriots Langen and Zimmermann four years earlier – not withstanding that Kuske nearly missed his leap onto the bob when pushing at the start of the second run. Kuske and Lange had been in the winning four-man crew at Salt Lake City and successfully defended that too, though with different additional crew in Rene Hoppe and Martin Putze. Canada and Russia took respective silver and Switzerland both bronze places, while Sandra Kiriasis and Anja Schneiderheinze brought Germany the two-woman title: Kiriasis a powerful red-headed courageous pilot at speeds of 130 kph with the reported ambition of being an F1 driver.

André Lange and Kevin Kuske (GER) win controversial gold in two-man bob. (© IOC/Nagaya)

Ole Einar Björndalen (above), supreme Norwegian aiming at five biathlon events, faltered through missed targets, opening the way for Michael Greis of Germany (far right).
(© IOC/Strahm and © IOC/Locatelli)

Germany was still to the fore in luge with their three women contenders, Sylke Otto, Sylke Kraushaar and Tatjana Hüfner, claiming the respective medals. Otto and Kraushaar had won gold and bronze four years earlier, the veteran Otto, now 36, having first competed in 1992. The men's singles title was taken by defending title-holder Armin Zöggeler of Italy, a German-speaking resident of the Tyrol whose victory was overshadowed by the failure of Georg Hackl of Germany, winner or runner-up of the past five Olympic events. Now he had to make do with an undignified seventh place, the other medals taken by Albert Demtschenko (RUS) and Martins Rubenis (LAT). Maya Pedersen, a Swiss woman married to a Norwegian, who had finished fifth in skeleton's inauguration in 2002, now took the title with two brilliant runs. She enjoyed a huge margin of 1.23 seconds over Shelley Rudman (GBR), who had moved from novice to the medal podium in barely three years. Mellisa Hollingsworth-Richards (CAN) won bronze, Diana Sartor (GER) taking fourth place for the second time running. Canada claimed three of the top four places in the men's race, Duff Gibson and Jeff Pain earning gold and silver, with Gregor Staehli (SUI) denying Paul Boehm the clean sweep.

Finland, successive bronze medal winners in ice hockey at Lillehammer and Nagano, seemed to be heading for triumph when unbeaten in seven games in Turin, playing at an unaccustomed peak, only to fall in the final to their ardent rivals from Sweden. Winners in 1994, the Swedes have always been there or thereabouts, another six times having been on the Olympic podium. Now there was deadlock at 2–2 in the third period until Niklas Lidstrom struck the winner. Lidstrom starred for Detroit Red Wings in the NHL, as did the Swedes' two other scorers, Niklas Kronwall and Henrik Zetterberg. The Czech Republic ousted Russia in the bronze medal play-off, Alex Ovechkin, 20-year-old Russian with Washington Capitals, being regarded by no less than Wayne Gretzky as the most exciting player in the tournament – which, for Gretzky-coached Canada, the favourites and holders, proved to be a sore disappointment in seventh place. There was some atonement when their women's team defeated Sweden for the other title.

Henrik Sedin of Sweden jousts with Scott Gomez of America under the eye of referee Dan Marouelli (CAN) en route to gold against arch-rivals Finland. (© IOC/Juilliart)

Curling, continuing to make its mark as an Olympic sport, saw Canada run to an easy 10–4 victory over Finland, Russ Howard at 50 becoming the oldest Olympic champion of all time. Finland has struggled to establish curling in competition against 100,000 ice-hockey players, though apparently one in five of the country's five million population tuned into the final. America won a see-saw bronze-medal match against Britain 8–6. Sweden's women, world and European champions, defeated Switzerland 7–6 with an extra end in the final, Anette Norberg placing the crucial winning stone. Canada took bronze.

The Swiss brothers Schoch, Philipp and Simon, won gold and silver in snowboard's parallel giant slalom, Philipp successfully defending his Salt Lake City title ahead of Simon, a year older and World Cup leader at the time. The pair became the third set of brothers to have earned gold and silver in the same Winter Games event. American Shaun White, still short of his 20th birthday and having overcome a heart defect as a boy, had narrowly missed qualification for 2002 but now won the half-pipe, wearing the title, in this extrovert sport, of the Flying Tomato. He had a comfortable margin over compatriot Daniel Kass and Markku Koski of Finland. The USA also took the top prizes in the women's half-pipe with Hannah Teter and Gretchen Bleiler, ahead of Kjersti Buaas of Norway, American girls placing four in the top six in this American-dominated sport. Sadly proving that disaster can

project your name way beyond imminent victory, however, Lindsey Jacobellis was heading for gold in the snowboard cross, 50 metres ahead of her nearest rival, when she unaccountably, and detractors would say foolishly, grabbed one-handed at her board at the last innocuous jump. Losing her balance, she crashed on her backside, and before she could recover Tanja Frieden of Switzerland had swept past for the title. Dominique Maltais of Canada took bronze. If snowboard is a fun sport, any element of that had evaporated for the tearful Jacobellis.

Shaun White, 18, better known as the 'Flying Tomato', struts his stuff in the half-pipe. (© IOC/Nagaya)

Xiaopeng Han of China, aerialist extraordinaire with a catalogue of tricks on skis to rival White on his snowboard, became the first Chinese to win a freestyle skiing event, under the direction of coach Dustin Wilson. Is there no limit to international collaboration in the world of extrovert sport? His compatriot Nina Li took silver in the women's aerials behind Evelyne Leu of Switzerland, while Jennifer Heil of Canada took gold in the moguls.

On a point of principle that Jacques Rogge had privately established, irrespective of venue, in his address at the closing ceremony he declined to say that these had been the best Games ever – and well he might, for there had been innumerable blips in administration in the mountains and a lack of passion for many events in the city. It could merely be said that the people of Turin had done their best on the day with characteristic heartfelt enthusiasm. 'Magnificent,' as stated by Rogge, was perhaps a generous wee exaggeration. On the other hand, that certainly

Jennifer Heil of Canada puts on the style in sunlit moguls. (© IOC/Kishimoto)

could be said of Germany's 29 medals (11–12–6), ahead of USA's 25 (9–9–7), with Austria's 23 (9–7–7) surprisingly ahead of Russia's 22 (8–6–8), an indication of the former giants' at least temporarily declining powers. For all Austria's success, the saga of the night-time police raids and testers at their Nordic quarters outside the Village, though without positive results, cast a shadow over the fortnight and would come back to haunt the bid by Salzburg as candidate hosts for the Winter Games of 2014 at the following summer's vote. In fact, during 16 days of competition and 1,162 urine and blood tests, only one athlete had failed: Olga Pyleva in biathlon. Twelve biathlon and cross-country skiers who recorded high levels of haemoglobin had received five-day suspensions, none testing positive for banned substances.

Despite the Austrian furore, and the ongoing blight of medical corruption in sport, Turin's Games had shown a marked improvement on the Summer event in Athens two years earlier, where there had been twenty-six positive violations. Yes, there had been some empty seats, but the Italian hosts were more than satisfied with sales that made the event more than respectable. Whether television coverage, especially in America, had lived up to NBC's expectations was less clear. Certainly viewing figures were down on Salt Lake City – predictable when that had been on home territory – but there was evidence that US viewers, in the absence of American success in the first week, were switching their remote control knobs to Fox Channel's *American Idol*, with the show's host Simon Cowell observing: 'The US and the UK are in the same boat this year – we're not interested in Swiss people winning things.' NBC was going to be needing to do its sums carefully for the future.

Turin closing ceremony. (© IOC/Kishimoto)

CHAPTER LXXVI

Beijing Centre Stage

Dick Ebersol, chairman of NBC Sports and Olympics

'As the Olympic Movement marches further into the twenty-first century, the Games of 2008 in Beijing a landmark in an increasingly Pacific-orientated world, the importance of revision of the programme is an ongoing issue for us at NBC. Considering for a moment the Winter Games, the work done by the IOC over the last 15 years in making the event more contemporary has been hugely successful. A number of new sports included, such as snowboarding, short-track and freestyle skiing, have developed a following among young people, and that's the key to the ongoing strength of the Winter Games. The IOC has been on top of the evolution, and part of the success has been due to the flexibility of the international federations. The Winter Games are in good shape.

There are, however, some concerns about the Summer Games. They've added BMX biking, and I would have loved to see skateboarding included by the time of London 2012. That's a great recreational sport throughout the world, including South America and Japan, but the issues with the Summer Games are that much more complex. The programme is bigger, more developed, there are so many new sports pressing for inclusion, and this causes concern for the federations already there. They're worried about whether the arrival of new sports might put them in danger of being eliminated. At present, baseball and softball are out, and nothing new has been added, possibly because a third of IOC members are federation-connected and concerned for their own future. So movement is a bit slow on the Summer front, and this will become increasingly important to NBC. I do feel that President Rogge and Gilbert Felli, the Olympic Games' Director at Lausanne headquarters, have an understanding of the importance of this issue. The members are clearly split: some sports are bulletproof and are not going to fall away, but I believe in certain instances this may be necessary with others. For example, modern pentathlon, which ably lobbied for its survival, is a sport that touches so few people around the world.

At the same time, while the IOC must modernise and ensure that the Games are relevant, they have a responsibility to ensure that any new sport is not just a temporary craze, like the hula-hoop. Once a sport is in practice on all continents, has legitimate world championships, with 40 or 50 countries having an established following among youth, I would like to see it come up for the vote with a real chance. My fear for the Summer Games is that the alarm of some federations will prevent them voting for anything new. This reduces confidence that the IOC will shift. I think the leadership is willing, but the way the votes are lined up there must be doubt. There was a push a few years ago before the Athens Games for waterskiing, which the Greeks were anxious to include, and I recall a long talk with President Samaranch, who said that he did not think any sport involving motors should be involved. Then there's ballroom dancing, with huge followings in the UK, America and Asia, though I'm not sure where the line should be drawn between sport and hobby entertainment. I wouldn't put my foot down that dancing is sport – it's a fetish area. Some people argue against the inclusion of synchronised diving and rhythmic gymnastics, though I consider them a legitimate addition. In Athens, we had some of the best audience figures when two young Greek boys won the men's diving.

At NBC, we're trying to broaden the viewing potential of all sports, but we are equally committed to maintaining free-to-air transmission. With apologies to some of my corporate partners, I wouldn't want to be involved if Olympic coverage did not remain that way. The Games belong to the world, and if they go down the pay-per-view route, they're no longer the Olympics. One day, somebody I work for may hate that I said that, but it's from the heart. If you take the paid route, you begin denying access to young people. The legacy of each Games is the dreams of those youngsters who have been watching, every two years – a point illustrated by Sebastian Coe, relating his own experience as a young boy, when addressing the IOC prior to the vote for the Games of 2012. I received hundreds of letters after every Olympics from parents talking about their children having broadened their vision of the world. That makes NBC's legacy so important, and I want to see that continue. There is no evidence of pay-per-view television doing anything but diminishing your audience by 90 per cent. Once you make the viewers pay, then immediately certain sports that the public won't "buy" will not be seen again.

Starting with Athens in 2004, NBC adopted a philosophy of coverage as a more complete package. With the availability of cable, coverage suddenly expanded to 1,200 hours over seventeen days on six channels – more than the combined coverage of the previous five Games at Los Angeles, Seoul, Barcelona, Atlanta and Sydney. We expect to announce coverage for Beijing of 2,000 hours. One of the ways we'll get there is with 800 hours of video streaming of nine or ten sports, so that those who normally don't see much of such sports are able on the Internet to watch the entire competition. We'll still hold the big sports – swimming, gymnastics and track and field – for the main network.

Undoubtedly the identification of NBC with the Olympics has become much stronger since there has been a Games, Winter or Summer, every two years. We signed three deals: two with the IOC in 1995, from 2000 to 2008, and a further deal in 2003, for 2010/2012. So, NBC having had every Games from 2000 to 2012 gives us the cachet of being the Olympic channel. It's not something you go to the bank on in non-Olympic years, but it reminds people why you're important. Yes, we have had some hiccups. There was low-level interest in the US about the Sydney Games, but those Games were hurt by the long time delay. The second reason was that, with the most important sports for US viewers being swimming, gymnastics and track and field, there was only one US gymnastics medal, won on the last day, and that hurt a lot. Yet four years later in Athens there was surprising viewer success, one of the reasons being that the gymnastics team won nine gold medals, including both men's and women's individual titles and silver in both teams. At the Winter Games in Turin, the US had some outstanding results, but a key factor in audience figures was that the momentum did not come till the Games were half over. Our hockey team fared poorly, but it's not team sports that have the overall impact: it's figure skating in Winter and gymnastics and track and field in Summer. Our partnership with the IOC, our commitment to the Games remains absolute.'

(Photograph © IOC)

That partnership and commitment by NBC could not be more relevant at a time when the youth of the world is drifting away not just from the Olympic concept but in general from participation in sport. Aware of this problem since the day he took office in 2001, Jacques Rogge had in mind the creation of a Youth Olympic Games, an idea resisted by his predecessor Samaranch, only to be partially realised with a European Olympic Youth Festival. Undeterred, Rogge pressed ahead and consulted the EB in April 2007, securing agreement to place a proposal before the Session in Guatemala in July. Pockets of resistance remained – Walter Tröger, IOC member from Germany, wondered whether Rogge was inadvertently further encouraging gigantism, while Dick Pound questioned whether such games would drag a single child couch-potato out of his or her chair – but in the Session's debate few voices were raised in opposition. Pound's conviction is that youth expansion should primarily be directed at obese children outside sport, rather than overload already financially stretched IFs and NOCs. The President's intention was that the Youth Games should essentially allow exposure to the Olympic experience rather than encourage strife in pursuit of achievement: that events would be chosen to safeguard physical and mental development among competitors between the ages of 14 and 18. Summer and Winter Games would alternate every four years in an opposite cycle to the existing Olympic Games, the first edition to be summer sports in 2010, the year of Vancouver's Winter Games. Numbers are expected to range from 1,000 to 3,000 for Winter and Summer respectively. The Youth Games will be an educational experiment, instilling Olympic values and emphasising the importance of a healthy lifestyle, social and physical, alongside competition. Rogge intends that there should be neither flags nor national anthems, thereby encouraging brotherhood, de Coubertin's basic philosophy. Applicant candidate host cities were to be scrutinised in the autumn of 2007 prior to naming the shortlist with a postal vote election in February 2008. Eleven cities initially were nominated by their NOCs – Algiers, Athens, Bangkok, Belgrade, Debrecen (Hungary), Guatemala, Kuala Lumpur, Moscow, Poznan (Poland), Singapore and Turin – subsequently narrowed to five: Athens, Bangkok, Moscow, Singapore and Turin: finally Moscow or Singapore.

Although Jacques Rogge can appear debonair, behind the scenes he is often treading water amid a sea of difficulties: the lot of every President. It is no help to suggest leaving the kitchen if it gets too hot. For Rogge, and the Olympic Movement, the drugs issue is an ongoing challenge. By a weird twist of circumstances, it was feared before the Turin Winter Games that the severity of Italian anti-drug laws would find the police randomly raiding the Village and imprisoning suspects. Some might say that was no bad prospect, given the extent of abuse. In the event, a police raid outside the Village, on the residence of Austria's Nordic team (see Chapter LXXV) was predictably damaging to Olympic credibility, following the Greek sprinters episode two years earlier. Events from Turin would resonate for another five months.

The first sortie in control testing had come with the temporary suspension of several competitors, prior to the Opening Ceremony, on account of abnormally high red blood cell counts. Because haemoglobin count is variable, competitors are subjected to a further test five days later, and this is no more than a health check. In the Turin instance, the subsequent tests were negative and none were banned. The scandal that would rock the Games was yet to emerge.

After receiving a tip-off through WADA that Walter Mayer – a coach banned from the Olympics following a blood-doping revelation at Salt Lake City in 2002 – was consorting with the Austrian team, the IOC notified the Italian police, who raided the private accommodation of their cross-country and biathlon teams, discovering a plethora of suspect medical equipment and blood samples. The Austrian management initially protested at improper interruption of their athletes' preparations – their quarters looked as though they had been hit by a whirlwind – and initial urine tests were all negative. But offences had been committed; moreover, Mayer's picture existed on an official team postcard. Dick Pound, WADA president, was quoted as saying: 'It's provocation, the guy has been banned till 2010 and they're saying, "He's still here and we love him." Pound added that it was not necessary to have a positive analysis for there to be a doping infraction: for example, the possession of medical equipment used for doping would also be grounds for action by the authorities. Meanwhile, Mayer fled to Austria, crashed into a police roadblock, was arrested and admitted to a psychiatric unit. The Austrian ski federation subsequently cleared him of involvement in doping at Turin.

Professor Arne Ljungqvist, Swedish chairman of the Medical Commission, accompanied by communications director Giselle Davies, holds aloft incriminating evidence: an Austrian team postcard including banned coach Mayer. (© IOC)

It was humiliation for the Austrian team, which by ironic coincidence had that day moved into second place in the medals table, claiming their eighth gold through Felix Gottwald in the Nordic combined sprint: wisely staying in the Village, he was not involved in the testing raid, his preferred tincture being a small daily dose of schnapps. It was five days before the negative tests were announced, but complexities in Italian law, and the relationship between the IOC, the Turin organising committee and the police, meant that investigations concerning materials seized at the Pragelato Nordic area – some 100 syringes, unlabelled medicine bottles, boxes of prescription drugs and a blood transfusion machine that some speculated could be used to inject oxygen-enhanced blood prior to competition to improve endurance – would continue, in a country where guilt is a criminal offence, possibly leading to six months' imprisonment. Belatedly, the Austrians affirmed that they had severed all links with Mayer, but this would not dissolve reverberations singularly unhelpful to Salzburg's bid for 2014, never mind that the vote was still 16 months away.

The IOC established an investigation commission composed of Thomas Bach (Germany), Denis Oswald (Switzerland) and Sergei Bubka (Ukraine). In April, they recommended that the EB declare permanently ineligible for all future Olympic Games six athletes: Roland Diethart, Johannes Eder, Jürgen Pinter and Martin Tauber from cross-country, Wolfgang Perner and Wolfgang Rottmann from biathlon. Simultaneously, the EB barred the Austrian NOC from receiving or applying for grants or subsidies from the IOC to the tune of $1 million. Part of the nightmare for the IOC and all IFs in the attempt, often unavailing, to keep sport drug-free is the threat of legal action by the accused. There was even the possibility that Mayer's lawyer might subpoena Jacques Rogge and Dick Pound in his subsequent attempted prosecution – later withdrawn – alleging their defamation of him.

The relentless pursuit of wealth by unscrupulous competitors was a reflection of human nature and never-ending. The cause was marred by the procrastination of governments to approve and sign the UNESCO International Convention. Former role models such as Edwin Moses, Olympic hurdles champion of 1976 and 1984, could plead all they liked that drug taking was not the unavoidable elixir for success, but in the ongoing battle

the EB debated new measures with the IAAF prior to the 11th World Championships in Osaka in 2007. These aimed to reinforce the already existing zero-tolerance policy, in conjunction with a 90 per cent increase in testing at Beijing in 2008 compared with Sydney 2000: some 4,500 tests. New measures included:

- Exclusion from the Olympics for a drug violation during the previous four years which led to a sanction of more than six months.
- Automatic suspension after a positive A sample.
- Reduced penalties for guilty athletes agreeing to provide information on suppliers and persons in the doping chain.
- The imposition of financial penalties.

It was horrific for the image of the Olympics that track and field, historically its number one sport, continued to be among the worst offending of all sports globally, alongside cycling, baseball and weightlifting. It was about to receive another body blow with the confirmation, as related in the Introduction, of Marion Jones's long-suspected abuses. Concurrently with the championships in Osaka, Trevor Graham, the US coach who had helped guide her, Tim Montgomery and Justin Gatlin to international eminence, was scheduled for trial in San Francisco, accused of making false statements to federal agents when supposedly aiding the government's official investigation of doping within the USA, but at the time of writing the trial is still pending. It was Graham who had helped uncover the Bay Area Laboratory Co-operative (BALCO) abuse that led to a number of criminal convictions and more than a dozen bans for athletes. Simultaneously, Justin Gatlin, Athens 100m champion who had borne a moral banner claiming to be drug-free was then suspended for eight years, this later halved on appeal. At the time of writing (February 2008), he had launched another appeal, hoping to clear himself in time to compete in Beijing.

The aura of track and field doping criminality was becoming comparable to that of the prison parole system: guilty but liberal leniency. Dave Collins, performance director of UK Athletics, the national governing body, had controversially appeared to be negotiating for Linford Christie, Olympic champion of 1992 subsequently revealed positive for the steroid nandrolone, to become mentor for the upcoming generation of British sprinters but later said that his role would be continuing as coach. What an example! Luciano Barra, former council member of the European Athletic Association, was a voice crying in the wilderness when issuing a document prior to the European Championships of 2006, proclaiming:

> So long as athletes are the only ones hit by punishment we will not solve the problem. Is it credible that an athlete aged between 20 and 25 does everything by himself . . . there are many coaches and doctors still around who were directly responsible for their competitors' doping cases but have not been punished. They are even officially accredited to attend IAAF events.

Barra's plea coincided with the revelation, exactly two years prior to Beijing's opening ceremony, of mass doping of teenage students at Anshan Athletics School in the Northern Province of Liaoning, the school caught off-guard by a surprise visit by the NOC's anti-doping commission. So much for China's optimism that their team for the home Games would be uniformly drug-free.

No less worrying than track and field, and perhaps even worse, was cycling. At times there even seemed to be active resistance by officialdom within the sport to exhaustive testing, in spite of continuing adverse evidence. Such was the IOC's concern that in May 2007 a disciplinary commission was appointed, chaired by Denis Oswald together with Sergei Bubka and Gunilla Lindberg, to examine revelations concerning the Telekom cycling team and possible violations at previous Games – their inquiries as yet unconcluded. The commission would also investigate the activities of associated physicians from Freiburg University in Germany. Hostilities between WADA and UCI, the international federation, were longstanding, particularly between Pound and cycling's one-time president. 'Pound has created an environment where people believe every athlete is doped,' claimed Verbruggen. The truth was that the public had good reason for suspecting so. Negative news had been continuous. The previous year more than 50 riders in the Tour had been implicated by investigations in Spain. WADA statistics revealed 480 positive tests for cyclists in 2005, almost 100 ahead of baseball, 150 more than football and track and field. In spite of widespread guilt in the sport, Lance Armstrong, the seven-time winner of the Tour who won a libel case (for allegations of cheating) against the British newspaper *The Sunday Times*, denounced Pound, calling for his resignation, a stance supported by the National Hockey League in the light of Pound's criticism of that sport. He had asserted that up to a third of NHL players were using illegal substances and that the NHL's testing programme was in question. A similar contretemps existed between him and major league baseball.

Pat McQuaid, having become president of UCI, announced in 2006 a survey of the professional structure of the sport 'to try to define the cause of this illness' following a positive test on Floyd Landis, that year's Tour winner. McQuaid promised a revision of rules for the 2008 season. 'The time for easy excuses or for forgiveness is past, it's all-out war against doping,' he was quoted as saying by Reuters. Landis, denying the apparent proof against him, impugned the French anti-doping laboratory at Châtenay-Malabry, one of WADA's 33 worldwide accredited laboratories. According to WADA guidelines, any urine sample with a hormone ratio of testosterone to epitestosterone of greater than 4:1 is suspect. Normal is about 1:1. Landis's on the Tour's seventeenth stage was 11:1. His appeal against suspension was to be heard in 2008.

Sport's credibility was threatened at every turn. At Helsinki airport, figures indicated an alarming rise in drug substances discovered by customs control – a crime in Finland – some of the passengers being known sports personnel and suspected of conducting a profitable trade in performance-enhancing additives.

While Pound encountered perplexing evasion in his determination to establish, through WADA, honourable levels of drug-free performance, the world of ethics likewise continued to witness manipulative episodes. IOC member Yong-Sung Park, having received a three-year jail term, suspended for five years, for million-dollar embezzlement when chairman of Korean industrial giant Doosan, earned amnesty from state president Moo-Hyun Roh in the spring of 2007, doubtless in recognition of his importance to Pyeongchang's renewed bid as Olympic host. The ruse would prove to be in vain, as described later, but for the time being enabled Park to continue in his function with the IOC and also as president of international judo, though he was suspended from the right to be a member of any IOC commission for five years. The pardon was granted immediately prior to the site inspection of Pyeongchang by the IOC's Evaluation Commission, Park thus

being able to front the bid, seemingly immune to the indignity of his suspension. In spite of public pressure from officials within Korean sport, no such pardon was granted to Un Yong Kim. In the cynical arena of international politics, following Pyeongchang's second failure in July (to be related) Park would quit both his IOC and judo posts.

Discredited Yong-Sung Park of South Korea resigns in early 2007 following a suspended three-year jail sentence for domestic embezzlement. (© IOC)

International Judge Keba M'Baye having died in January, his place as chairman of the Ethics Commission was filled by compatriot Youssoupha Ndiaye, former Senegal Minister of Sport and former Secretary-General of their Supreme Court. Chiharu Igaya of Japan, having resigned from his Ethics position due to conflict of interest as a member of Tokyo's bidding committee for 2016, was replaced on the Commission by Craig Reedie, past chairman of the British Olympic Association.

Meanwhile, the sponsorship and television-network deals that fund Olympic existence continued their merry way. McDonald's extended their TOP sponsorship till 2012, joining Coca-Cola, Atos Origin (formerly Schlumberger), General Electric, John Hancock, Kodak, Swatch and Visa as the IOC's core backers – leaving aside any question of McDonald's dietary contribution to obese youth. Samsung, conveniently overlooking the troubled background of their chairman, IOC member Kun-Hee Lee, renewed their TOP membership until 2016, as did Panasonic of Japan, the two companies securing global marketing rights for another four Games, Winter and Summer. The idea was floated by Sochi, the Black Sea resort bidding for the Winter Games of 2014, that Russian energy giant Gazpron was an imminent TOP candidate, though this would conflict with the policy's definition of sponsors being of international, as opposed to national, category. All sponsorship programmes, including TOP, had reached an astonishing $866 million for the Olympiad 2005–08. While competitive performance and ethical administrative behavioural trends were too often downward, commercial activity continued to climb. An enhanced free-to-air television deal was signed with TV Record, a privately owned Brazilian channel, for 2010/2012 with a significant increase for coverage of Vancouver and London compared with that for Beijing. ASOIF, the summer conglomerate of federations, rubbed its hands at the prospect of a substantial increase from Beijing compared with Athens.

Such deals, especially with American television, have their price. As with the Games of 1988 in Seoul, NBC twisted the arms of the IOC and Beijing into adjusting the competition schedule for swimming and gymnastics finals, switching to the morning. There were howls of protest both from IFs and from some rival television stations in Europe, allied to EBU, and in the Asia-Pacific region, now confronted with inconvenient air times. Attempting to ease itself out of an embarrassing fait accompli, the IOC released a formal statement:

> . . . after a thorough consultation process, the IOC Executive Board has approved a final version of the competition schedule which sees a spread of events throughout the day . . . there can never be a perfect one-size-fits-all solution which suits every stakeholder equally, but the IOC decision has endeavoured to find the best balance for the Olympic Movement as a whole. Key in this decision was ensuring that the physiology of the athletes was not affected, and therefore their needs were thoroughly discussed with the IOC Athletes Commission . . . [the] decision is not without precedent.

The IOC's statement was justified: with adequate sleep/diet/training/time-zone preparation, an athlete can adapt to compete anywhere any time.

If cash, at least for the time being, continued to pour into IOC coffers, debate continued to swirl around the seemingly insoluble problem of how it should be spent: in other words, what should be the programme? The controversy having rumbled along ever since the indecisive Extraordinary Session of 2002 in Mexico City, the 2007 Session in Guatemala City did at least make minimal progress – without any change to the programme. The voting process was simplified, arguably making it easier to admit new sports. The IOC reported that adjustment of the Charter would specify:

> The number of core sports has been increased from 15 to 25 from the Summer Games of 2020 onwards. For the 2016 Games of the Olympiad, the 26 core sports from London 2012 will be proposed. The maximum number of sports included in the programme remains capped at 28. In the future, the Session will cast a bloc vote for 25 core Summer sports, proposed by the EB. These . . . will require a simple majority to be included in the Olympic programme. If no majority is reached to vote for the core, additional rounds of votes by the Session, determined by the President, will be implemented. The President complimented this new system for 'providing a better flexibility to change the Olympic programme through the introduction of up to three new sports'. Seven core sports will be included in the programme for the Olympic Winter Games [with the same procedure as for the Summer Sports]. Today, the Session applied the bloc vote for the first time and voted for the seven core sports to be in the 2014 Winter Games, of which Sochi was elected as host city two days ago.

Within this formula, core sports would continue to adapt their individual schedules in the attempt to ensure their survival. Ice hockey, though unlikely to melt away, had revised its men's tournament for Vancouver 2010 by seeding its twelve-team event, as in Turin, into three groups of four instead of two groups of six. While baseball clung to the hope that a spectacular tournament in Beijing would enhance the possibility of a subsequent return to the programme – having been voted out in 2005 – there were policy disputes within the international federation (IBAF) between newly elected American president Harvey Schiller and some leading figures of national federations in Central America on readmission tactics. The Boxing Federation (AIBA) remained enmeshed in administrative knots in spite of the belated removal of Anwar Chowdhry of Pakistan as president – a man who had schemed his own survival for many years amid endless controversies. His successor, by 83 votes to 79, was Ching-Kuo Wu from Chinese Taipei. Wu was left handling internal tensions between Muslim supporters of Chowdhry, while the planned switching of the World Championships, from Moscow to Chicago in November 2007, raised spurious ethical question marks on account of Chicago being a host candidate for 2016. Wu, stretched in a dozen different directions, promised to write a book on his experiences within this hell's kitchen.

Ching-Kuo Wu from Chinese Taipei, president of boxing, keeps smiling amid administrative turmoil. (© IOC)

In the unofficial but essential sport of female inclusivity, progress was being made, even if with insufficient rapidity either in participation or administration, the former being the stronger. From providing 15 per cent of competitors at Munich '72, with 1,059 women, there would be 45 per cent at Beijing, with more than 4,700. On the administrative front, with a short-term goal of 20 per cent women, by 2007 this had been achieved by only 30 per cent of NOCs and 32 per cent of IFs. Dick Pound, a strong advocate, suggested financial incentives for administrative bodies by withholding grants from those that were slow moving. Yet what about the IOC itself? With the election of Princess Haya bint Al-Hussein (UAE) and Rita Subowo, Indonesia's first woman NOC president, as members at the Guatemala Session, the female count rose to 16, way below 20 per cent among the 115. Women were swift to utilise every means for competitive inclusion. Denied a place for ski jumping in the Vancouver programme, Canadian women jumpers lodged complaint with the Canadian Human Rights Commission, pointing to the fact that the government's Heritage department had donated many millions towards Vancouver infrastructure, including the ski jump facility. Meanwhile, in the IOC's Women and Sport awards, the 2007 World Trophy went to Portia Simpson Miller, first female Jamaican Prime Minister, for her work in promoting women and girls in sports. Other awards were: Africa – Fridah Bilha Shiroya, first female executive of Kenya NOC; Americas – Jackie Joyner-Kersee, creator of a youth foundation in St Louis, Illinois; Asia – Naila Shatara-Kharroub, initiator of PE at 50 girls' schools in Bethlehem and Jericho, Palestine; Europe – Ilse Bechthold, lecturer in PE at Frankfurt University, Germany; Oceania – Veitu Apana Diro, founder of the national netball federation and NOC vice-president, Papua New Guinea. At a different ceremony, Canadian Ljiljana Ljubisic, blind world and paralympic champion, received the Juan Antonio Samaranch Disabled Award as five-time Paralympic Games competitor with discus gold medal in 1992 and world records in discus and shot in 1996.

IOC award ceremony for Women and Sport 2007: N. Shatara-Kharroub (PLE), Fridah Bilha Shiroya (KEN), J. Joyner-Kersee (USA), P. Simpson Miller (JAM), Jacques Rogge, Anita DeFrantz (USA) and Ilse Bechthold (GER). (© IOC/Tobler)

Besides the two new women members of the IOC, also elected at Guatemala in an ex-officio capacity were Patrick Baumann, secretary-general of international basketball, and Princess Haya, president of international equestrianism. Subuwo and Andrés Botero, president of Columbian NOC and international water skiing, were voted in as ordinary members. Gerhard Heiberg, Chairman of the Marketing Commission, was re-elected to the EB, securing more votes than Juan Antonio Samaranch Jr (Spain), swimming president Mustapha Larfaoui (Algeria) and Anita DeFrantz (USA). 'We [America] are still out of favour,' lamented DeFrantz, the most powerful of all NOCs now being without representation on the EB. (Coincidentally, USOC had enlisted the former right-hand-man of Primo Nebiolo and subsequent director of ASOIF, Robert Fasulo, as director of international relations to mastermind Chicago's bid for 2016.)

In the IOC's 'transparency' trend, the cumbersome innovation of re-electing members after eight years in office, an impractical idea when introduced in the Charter, resulted in those twenty-seven members seeking re-election being voted in en bloc in what was transparently a pointless exercise. Concurrently, the election of Montenegro and Tuvalu brought the number of NOCs to 205. Any idea of Australia shifting ground to become adopted Asians, competing in future Asian Games, had been blocked by OCA president Sheikh Ahmad – himself re-elected for a fifth period of office – on the grounds that such a move by Australia would harm the rest of Oceania sport.

Enhancing the development of international sport within their region was the incentive, or perhaps the camouflage, surrounding the host city bids by Pyeongchang of Korea and Sochi of Russia for the Winter Games of 2014. Pyeongchang, riven with internal political controversy after narrowly losing to Vancouver, were relying heavily, and misguidedly, in their renewed bid on the momentum from 2003 still being with them approaching the vote in 2007 in Guatemala City. They were wrong. Their presumption in itself had a negative effect; the victimisation and imprisonment of Un Yong Kim as a scapegoat had left a scar on the campaign, and the controversy surrounding their two other members, Park and Lee, weakly disciplined by the IOC, earned no likely favours. Nor, from conversation among members, did the plea by President Moo-Hyun Roh that the award of the Games would 'bring peace to the divided peninsula'. So Pyeongchang's massive delegation headed for Central America on a wave of false optimism, believing they had left no stone unturned. One IOC member alone had endured three visits from the Korean ambassador of a neighbouring country hoping to enlist his vote. The Koreans, perhaps unwittingly, had been further damaged by the insensitive parallel and successful bids of Daegu and Incheon respectively to host the World Athletics Championships of 2011 and the Asian Games of 2014. International officialdom considered Korea already over-rewarded, and additionally there was the knowledge that China had their eye on the Winter Games of 2018: their supporters would not want an Asian Winter Olympics four years earlier.

Kun-Hee Lee's financial misdemeanours when chairman of sponsors Samsung damaged Pyeongchang's host city bid. (© IOC)

Sochi, glittering Black Sea resort and Russians' favourite summer haunt, was riding a difficult ticket: they could build indoor ice facilities by the sea, but their mountain resort was virtually virgin territory requiring development from scratch, existing only on the drawing board. Up stepped President Putin, and suddenly it seemed that the Russians, who unquestionably deserved a Winter Games for the first time in the light of their overwhelming past achievements during 50 years, could create anything they promised. And they promised a lot. Whether or not Sochi's bidding campaign remained within the boundaries of the Ethics Commission's somewhat nebulous regulations – an area of uncertainty for any city – was one thing: that they had as little administrative experience as they had existing mountain facilities was another. Nevertheless, money was no obstacle in their self-promotion, to the extent that many members became alarmed that the election process was becoming submerged in politics and finance. The Evaluation Commission, headed by Chiharu Igaya of Japan and officially 'steered' by Gilbert Felli, did its conventional investigation of the three candidates, including Salzburg. Igaya had been skiing locally with both Putin and Roh, pardonable wooing within the bragging that is standard for every bid. When Igaya questioned the extensive construction required at Sochi within a seven-year limit, Dmitry Chernyshenko, bid chairman, boasted that the Krasnaya Polyana mountain site was 'a blank canvas ready for a painter to create a masterpiece'. The Commission, perhaps neglectfully, took little note of the potential terrorist threat to Sochi from neighbouring Dagestan and Georgia's breakaway region of Abkhazia, with their Muslim elements. The aggressive Jama'at Sharia organisation went as far as issuing a warning that jihad would exist until the clearance of Russian occupation of the North Caucasus.

Alfred Gusenbauer, Austrian Chancellor, exchanges greetings with President Putin prior to the vote in Guatemala (above), where Salzburg's presentation led by IOC member Leo Wallner (below) met largely deaf ears. (both photos © IOC/Juilliart)

Igaya, needless to say, was as complimentary at the time of his visit to Salzburg as to rival candidates. The Austrian city, heavily outplayed in the 2003 voting, had won a domestic battle against Innsbruck for renewing its bid, but there had been uncertainty about the extent of state and city approval, and huge tensions within the NOC. Ultimately the dazzling array of established sports facilities, beckoning accommodation of 100,000 rooms within a 50-mile radius in an arena familiar to thousands of holidaymakers, and international transport access almost without equal, plus historic Salzburg's fame as a cultural centre with exemplary theatres, concert halls, museums and hotels, made the city an obvious favourite, a potential auditorium-replica of lauded Lillehammer: except that the nation had staged the Games twice before at Innsbruck.

The Commission's published report, without specifically stating as much, indicated support for Pyeongchang, some supposed through the influence of Felli, though anyone who had experienced football's World Cup in 2002 or visited Pyeongchang would know that the ambience and social life in Korea would be very low-key adjoining the venues. Grapevine indication during weeks prior to the Session increasingly indicated anxiety among those more conservative IOC members about the overriding commercial element surrounding Sochi and Pyeongchang. Numerous IFs had done deals, for instance, with Samsung, whose backing had helped persuade the IAAF to elect Daegu for 2011 in preference to Brisbane. Samsung, Korea's foremost electronics company, was sponsoring the European Olympic Committee's anti-obesity campaign and also a sports aid programme in Africa – which would have 14 votes in Guatemala. In parallel, FISA, the rowing federation, had signed up with OJSC, Russia's dairy-product conglomeration.

Though it was way beyond the influence of the Ethics Commission, China's sports ministry had publicly declared its support for Sochi – with a calculated influence on maybe a dozen votes – while Fausto Bertinotti, Italian parliament Speaker, had told counterpart Boris Gryzlov, of the Russo-Italy interparliamentary commission, that 'Italy will support Sochi', never mind that he had little if any direct influence on Italy's five votes. All this political and sponsorship intervention caused Craig Reedie, recently elected member of the Ethics Commission, to state: 'The IOC must reassess the rules of conduct, and essentially before the election for the Summer Games of 2016, when there will be big hitters out there such as Chicago, Tokyo and Madrid.'

Evgeni Plushenko (centre) celebrates Sochi's victory. (© IOC/Juilliart)

Guatemala City, often plagued by gun crime, was safe enough during the Session, with a massive police presence which could not detract from the distinctive grace, charm and collaboration of the historic Mayan people, in the author's experience almost without equal worldwide. Instead of bullets, the Session was riddled with ethical abuse of the system. Sponsorship advertisement swamped the streets and television coverage – the latter worldwide – while the Russians had erected, at exorbitant air-transport cost, an ice-skating rink in a sub-tropical climate beside the IOC's hotel . . . from which IOC members were in effect barred by regulation. For security, Putin had purchased, for two days' use, a private house. The overkill was almost on a par with a US presidential election.

The presentation of the bids to the Session had no particular distinction. Pyeongchang dwelt on peace and harmony, Putin, speaking unexpected and fluent English, talked of the dreams of millions of Russians, while the most important message, for some, came from Heinz Schaden, mayor of Salzburg, when he promised: 'What we offer is: no surprises. An Olympic brand that will rock the world, a spirit of welcome like no other.' At media question time, the Russians did not really want to discuss the domestic assassination of journalists, their killers still at large, or the internal suppression of freedom of expression.

And so to the vote. Whether or not they were undermined by their drug scandal from Turin, Salzburg, the perceived sporting favourite, was eliminated in the first round with 25 votes, behind Pyeongchang, 36 and Sochi, 34. The clandestine influence of Honorary Life President Samaranch was alleged by some to have been at work, as will be related. In the play-off, Sochi leapfrogged the distraught Koreans to win 51–47. That there are private agreements in these matters was evident to the author an hour before the declaration, when João Havelange, veteran member from Brazil, was emphatic that Sochi would have won.

Samaranch, in uncertain health, had not been expected to attend but unexpectedly arrived the afternoon prior to the vote. It is widely believed that he was returning favours for the support by the former Soviet Union during Samaranch's campaign for election as IOC President in 1980, when he had enlisted the backing of the Soviet bloc while in residence in Moscow as Spanish ambassador. The unconfirmable assumption is that he helped swing the sufficient six votes away from Salzburg, to ensure Sochi's first-round survival: six votes the other way and Sochi would have been out, 29–30. In the instant that Sochi's victory was declared by Rogge, Dmitry Chernyshenko, campaign leader, and Vitaly Smirnov sped across stage fulsomely to embrace Samaranch.

Thus a majority of the IOC, trustees of Olympic ideals, had preferred Russia's wealth rather than Salzburg's potential packed-house festival. The second-preference votes of Austria's supporters provided Sochi with their springboard, Pyeongchang thereby suffering the same fate as in 2003 after initially leading. Yet 50 per cent of the projects embraced in Sochi's bid were subject to question marks, and the IOC was persuaded only by Putin's guarantee in a bid with a Games' budget of $1.5 billion behind a regional development programme of £12 billion. And the latter was the real reason for the bid: a Black Sea resort expansion for which the Games were a focus that could be exploited. The IOC had thereby committed itself to a worrying precedent in opting for political power and money, though there was some justification in the vote since Russia, with the end of the Soviet Empire, had lost its former winter sports centres in Central Asia. Gian-Franco Kasper, president of international skiing, forecast: 'With this trend, it will become difficult if not impossible for Scandinavian and smaller alpine cities, dependent on taxpayer funding, to compete with richer nations.' Rogge defended Sochi's election on the grounds of its total support by the Russian Federation, while bid leader Chernyshenko disarmingly claimed that the decision would 'assist Russia as a developing world democracy'. Reuters reported that in Moscow the election was seen as proof of 'the country's return to global prominence following a post-Soviet slump'. It could be said that Putin had outperformed Tony Blair, two years earlier, in achieving an election for a venue that at the time did not exist. Television analysis reported that half the adult Russian population watched the announcement from Guatemala, while land values in Sochi's Krasnodar Territory immediately rocketed, European investors seizing on thousands of investment sites, never mind that regional development would require a huge slice of the government's projected budget, $3 billion, to be spent on the provision of the electricity supply. Within two months of the vote, a consortium of businesses meeting in Sochi signed collective development contracts worth $22 billion, a figure dwarfing regional redevelopment in east London on the back of the 2012 Games. In a sympathetic gesture, Putin was said to have invited Korean businesses to become involved in Sochi's Olympic constructions. The unenvied post of chairman of the IOC's Coordination Commission for 2014 fell to Jean-Claude Killy, who was already aware that problems lay ahead in the Russians' promise to construct a two-track rail line and four-lane motor expressway to the mountain region: a project calculated, prior to the vote but undisclosed, by the German construction and tunnelling engineering company Strabag to be next-to-impossible within the seven-year time scale.

The silence that engulfed Pyeongchang representatives and their host of supporters after the announcement was stunning to behold, but they largely had only themselves to blame. Self-analysis would continue for months, and cynics debated who would this time become the scapegoat. The first stones to be cast came from the Democratic Labour Party in the local Gangwon Province, who were critical of the bid committee's accounts regarding a $51 million budget for two bids over the past eight years. Yet Jin-Sun Kim, province governor, announced the probability of a third bid for 2018. A deflecting smokescreen? Were a Chinese city to bid, Pyeongchang could count itself likely to suffer a third defeat. In the debriefing of 2007, one objective official suggested: 'Four years ago, we lost because Un Yong Kim was there, this time we lost because he was not there.'

Not that varying constructions costs and administrative wobbles within an organising committee were anything but the norm for an upcoming Olympic Games. So it was with Vancouver. Within two years of election, in 2003, labour problems and escalating costs were causing a headache for John Furlong, CEO of the organising committee – who had led the successful bid – with the realisation that the $470 million was going to fall short in the creation of obligatory venues. Colin Hanson, Minister for Economic Development, assured everyone all would be well and that the British Columbia provincial government would be able to meet demand. As Dick Pound was quoted as saying to the *Vancouver Sun*: 'There is hardly a venue that hasn't changed from when it was first proposed . . . compendiums of fiction.' The cost of venues for speed skating, bobsleigh and Nordic skiing had all risen by 20 per cent or more, and reserve finance had to be called upon for development of competitor accommodation at the Whistler alpine centre. Beds for the vast Olympic family, including sponsor guests, was another headache for a Games generating huge interest, to the extent that, even before sales began, unofficial agencies were advertising tickets for the opening and closing ceremonies at inflated prices approaching $2,000: proof that the Olympics truly continue to be the champagne of sport.

Ditto the scene in London. Two years after election, the imaginative project for expansion and redevelopment in the nineteenth-century Victorian area of Stratford, east London, was drowning in adverse publicity from uniformly ignorant media sources wholly unfamiliar with the administrative base of bidding for, constructing and organising a Games in conjunction with government backing. As already observed, the media fail to distinguish between operational cost of a Games and government/city exploitation of the event to accelerate civic facilities in local transport and housing. *The Observer* screeched that the bill had risen to $9 billion, whereas the specific budget of LOCOG, the organising committee, remained at their bid level of under $3 billion. Nonetheless, the IOC was becoming embarrassed by adverse criticism, and on a visit to London early in 2007 Denis Oswald, chairman of the IOC's Coordination Commission, and Gilbert Felli, Olympic Executive Director, were moved to assert that the IOC was satisfied and confident in the preparations, never mind that public figures from the House of Lords, the upper house of Parliament, were denouncing a waste of public money comparable to that of the ill-fated Millennium Dome. Subsequently, the Olympic Delivery Authority, the body formed to supervise construction of facilities, was obliged to admit that rising construction costs since estimates were calculated in 2004 could push the Games' operational budget above $5 billion. Tessa Jowell, Minister for Culture and Sport, continued to be hounded over government uncertainty on the contribution from public money, including diversion of Lottery Fund sums from other causes to enable the fulfilment of civic development beyond the sporting boundary. A further, briefly passing cloudburst of hostility arrived with the publication of the logo for London 2012, dismissed, from cabinet rank to the lowliest public bar, as 'puerile'. Admittedly incomprehensible at first sight to the uninitiated, it achieved such public attention in the first couple of weeks that its PR function had been amply fulfilled almost before the outcry had subsided. As one agency observed: 'The logo achieved more in a week than we've been able to manage in 40 years.' In a show of support, the IOC President stated: 'It takes a little mental effort to read the numbers [2012], which I think is a good thing. It appealed to me, but I can understand why some don't like it . . . People will get used to it, and I'm sure it will not be a hot topic by the time of the opening ceremony in 2012.' And he added: 'The reports I am receiving on progress in London show that in the initial period of two years they are ahead of every host city we have had in the past, and that includes Beijing.' Sebastian Coe, well versed in adverse publicity as well as praise, as competitor, administrator or politician, kept his head down and got on with the job.

Whatever the difficulties encountered during the past two Games at Turin and Athens respectively, and by Vancouver and London in their energetic preparations, there was certainly no shortage of ambitious would-be successors, backed in the main by the rising tide of Asian and Middle Eastern wealth. London might come to realise they had mounted the Olympic stage,

Presentation of the London 2012 logo, derided at home, accepted without demur at the IOC Guatemala Session. (© IOC/Juilliart)

for a unique third time, not a moment too soon as the financial competition escalated: demonstrably so with the election of Sochi after intense economic rivalry with Pyeongchang. Equally conspicuous had been the performance of Doha of Qatar when staging the 15th Asian Games in late 2006. The event, with its sumptuously extravagant opening ceremony and high quality of facilities during two weeks of competition, was an exceptional demonstration of the oil wealth of the Gulf and sent the clearest message to the IOC: wake up to the twenty-first-century reality of Asia, adjust to the forces of the Gulf's oil, of China's and India's population power, of Asian sports culture, or surrender your century-long European-based authority and relevance. Here was a blatant dress rehearsal for becoming an Olympic host candidate, with the fulsome support of OCA president Sheik Ahmad, which had cost $4 billion and inevitably widened the gap between those nations now able to contemplate an Olympic bid and smaller traditional sporting countries lacking such governmental power. So spectacular was Doha's opening ceremony that Chen Weiya, senior member of Beijing's ceremony planners for 2008, admitted: 'There's a lot to learn from this, and we will make a thorough scan of their technical devices. This was better than Athens. Doha has shown its best to the world.' Liu Qi, president of Beijing's Olympic committee, forecast: 'The quality of our opening ceremony will be a decisive indication of whether China can host a special high-level Games.' It matters not to the rulers of Qatar that the population is under a million, the majority of these migrant workers: whatever Qatar wants, Qatar imports, and that includes people, even spectators, were they exceptionally to be elected Olympic hosts. In a disorientated, economically controlled world, almost anything is possible, and Sheik Ahmad declared at the OCA Congress in Kuwait that Qatar was eminently capable of staging an Olympics.

Extravagant scenes (above) from Doha's Asian Games opening ceremony in 2006. (photos © IOC/Juilliart)

Sheikh Tamin bin Hamas bin Khalifa Al-Thani, son of the Emir, and head of the Qatar Equestrian Federation, arrives with the flame. (photo © IOC/Juilliart)

So it was no surprise that Doha should be among seven cities in 2007 entering their names for the campaign for 2016, alongside Baku (Azerbaijan), Chicago, Madrid, Prague, Rio de Janeiro and Tokyo. This list was scheduled to be reduced to a shortlist of four by June 2008, and it was intriguing to speculate whether Doha might lead to the exclusion of one of the favourites – Chicago, Madrid, Rio and Tokyo – or even be included as an auxiliary fifth candidate. The final vote would be taken at the 121st Session at Copenhagen in 2009. Slightly left on the sidelines, at least for the time being, were frustrated NOC officials of India, their country's economy growing almost as rapidly as that of China, their population set to surpass China's by 2020. The Indians had been thrown into internal confusion when outvoted as bidding host for the 2014 Asian Games by the shameless financial promises on offer from Incheon of South Korea. New Delhi had been outright favourites in a rivalry that, ironically, would indirectly do measurable damage to Korea's almost simultaneous Olympic bid by Pyeongchang. Suresh Kalmadi, India's NOC president, said: 'Had our government committed more money, we could have got the Asian Games, but with such an attitude by Mani Shankar Aiyar, our Minister

for Sport, we cannot think of holding any Games in the future. We have missed a big opportunity to make Delhi a global city.' If Chicago were confident of making a better show for 2016 than had New York for 2012, the Windy City's bid, dependent as it essentially would be on private funding, might encounter problems, never mind the creation of World Sport Chicago, a foundation designed to promote youth and sport and attract global events to the city.

At the last EB meeting of 2007, besides the disciplinary action regarding Marion Jones (see Introduction), Lord Condon, chairman of the Anti-Corruption Security Unit at the International Cricket Council, was invited to address the members on the risks involved in illegal betting, Rogge being concerned that the IOC should have a clear understanding of the risks and necessary protective action.

The prestige and lasting reputation of Jacques Rogge as President would to an extent depend on the success of the Beijing Games, particularly if he intended to run for election for a further four years in 2009 under the newly established Charter regulations. His had not been an easy reign, confronted by many problems: the nature of the job. Despite his almost obligatory expression of satisfaction with the Games in Athens and then Turin, it being the duty of a president to be upbeat, there are IOC members who sensed that on both occasions something had been missing. Robert Ctvrtlik of America, forthright former volleyball star, observed: 'That special quality was absent, I felt, something that we have to try to re-establish.' If Rogge intends to continue, he will need fulsome support from the floor at the Session in Copenhagen, though it has never been known for a standing president to be opposed. In either 2009 or 2013, who might succeed him? There is by no means a broad choice of candidates. The time has passed for Richard Pound to run again, and the two most likely contenders are Thomas Bach, Olympic fencing champion in 1976, and German lawyer, and Richard Carrión, Puerto Rican banker. Neither would oppose Rogge but the problem for Bach is that by 2013, by which time he would be 60, it might be too late, though Samaranch was elected at the same age in 1980. For Carrión to gain serious consideration, coming from Central America, he would need the vigorous backing of a campaign including support from

Asia. Though there have been no overt indications, Rogge's delegation of Bach to lead important commissions has suggested the German would have his backing.

ABOVE: Thomas Bach from Germany (centre), thought to be favoured by Jacques Rogge (left), debates issues together with Sergei Bubka (UKR). (© IOC/Lopez)
BELOW: Bach's rival Richard Carrión reminisces with disabled award-winning discus thrower Ljiljana Ljubisic. (© IOC/Juilliart)

As momentum gathered towards a Games hosted by an ancient, talented, often enigmatic Asian race in 2008, a provocative thorn was the question of human rights in China, more specifically that nation's attitude towards Tibet and, drawing increasing attention, towards Sudan and the crisis in Darfur. The equation put forward in moral debate, by those arguing in favour of China's inclusion within the Olympic family, was that exposure to the world as hosts would inevitably loosen and improve their restrictive conventions in civil freedoms, a benefit that had occurred within the Soviet Union at the time of the 1980 Games in Moscow. Admitting the rest of the world to your house cannot but be educational. Widespread calls around the world, many of them cosmetic lip-service to 'good causes', for a boycott of the Games were as empty-headed and devoid of influential effect as had been the boycotts of 1976, 1980 and 1984, the political world not even having had to change gear as the Games proceeded in Montreal, Moscow and Los Angeles with the achievement of nothing more than a damaged sporting event, the only punitive targets being athletes, while commercial and other scheduled cultural contracts continued unaffected. Sport is an easily available tool for political gesture without the firing of bullets. Celebrities such as Mia Farrow and Steven Spielberg – the latter resigning as Ceremony Consultant in early 2008 – might protest about China's stance in Darfur, Tibet and Myanmar (Burma), but as Rogge stressed: 'Would any cause, be it Darfur, be it human rights, be aided by a boycott? On the contrary, the Games will open up China, being under the scrutiny of 25,000 media representatives. We will witness changes in Chinese society.' Formal organisations such as Amnesty International, the International Federation for Human Rights, the World Organisation Against Torture, would continue to publish their protests. It had been particularly insensitive that Beijing should have selected as one of its Olympic mascots the Tibetan antelope, an endangered species following the slaughter of thousands by the Chinese People's Liberation Army during the invasion. Further international hostility arose with regard to the planned torch relay through Tibet, though some argued that this would bring valuable attention to the occupied region. The Dalai Lama, on the other hand, alleged continuing repression. Amnesty International called in particular for the abolition of China's death penalty, calculated to number 3,400 executions out of a total of 3,800 worldwide, from figures published in 2003, the Chinese total estimated to be probably substantially higher.

A disturbing revelation of human rights conditions in China occurred in the autumn of 2007 with the broadcast of *Unreported World* by Channel 4 in the UK. Aidan Hartley's film crew gained unique access to one of what are known as China's 'black jails', where poor Chinese from the provinces, seeking the assistance of state officials in grievances over appropriation of farm land or housing – a legal right in China – and known as petitioners, are branded troublemakers by the authorities, thrown into prison and left there indefinitely in a 'cleansing' project. Hartley's crew found starving figures, many old, some handicapped, existing in appalling conditions, some of them attempting to clear their name after jail sentences as counter-revolutionaries during Mao's reign of terror but now stranded without either aid or trial.

All too predictably there was an ongoing political wrangle between the governments of China and Olympic-titled Chinese Taipei over whether the torch relay should pass through Taiwan, for those uninvolved an argument as shallow as Tweedledum versus Tweedledee, given that both NOCs are co-members of the Olympic family. It might be supposed, as Australian Kevan Gosper, vice-president of the IOC's Coordination Commission for Beijing, suggested, that Taiwan 'should be gracious about being included in the relay'. The Taiwanese, unrecognised by the UN, ought to be grateful for their exposure in the Olympic footlights. Simultaneous with this debate was that between the two Koreas on the prospect of a joint team, an advance on marching together in the opening ceremony at Sydney and again at Athens, though South Korea were insisting on selection by ability rather than by equal numbers.

If foreign opinion was suggesting that an influx of tens of thousands of visitors would open Chinese eyes to the ways of the rest of the world, there were admittedly parallel concerns about police and security checks, surveillance of foreign guests and freedom of normal movement, such security admittedly necessary for Beijing's own protection against possible terrorism. How effective Chinese surveillance would be introspectively in the matter of drugs control among their own team – inevitably the largest of the Games – was another matter. Jian Zhao, head of their testing commission, had announced a programme of up to 10,000 tests in the year prior to the Games, while Tu Mingde, an NOC official known internationally from his involvement in China's host bidding since the early '90s, promised that 'China's doping problems are a thing of the past, these will be a clean Games, at least for Chinese athletes'. Random evidence suggested that his optimism might be inflated.

Whatever the eventual scenario, be it in the celebration of outstanding performances, the heralding of a broadening relationship between China and the world in which it is an increasingly significant nation, or the success or failure to reduce and detect the cheats of all nationalities, the realisation that sport offers all peoples the scope for mutual understanding and benevolence that is, perplexingly, as basic to human nature as physical violence, the Olympic Games of 2008 promise to be one of the historic landmarks of our times.

2008 torch-run inauguration: Games' Coordination leader Hein Verbruggen (NED) and Zhili Chen, organising committee first vice-president. (© IOC/Juilliart)

415

APPENDIX A

IOC Members 1894–2007

With acknowledgement to compiler Wolf Lyberg of Sweden (ISOH)

NO.	NAME	NATION	MANDATE	BORN	DIED	STATUS
1.	DE COUBERTIN, Pierre	FRA	1894–1925	01.01.1863	02.09.1937	
2.	CALLOT, Felix Ernest	FRA	1894–1912	15.05.1840	29.12.1912	
3.	VIKELAS, Demetrius	GRE	1894–1897	06.06.1835	20.07.1908	
4.	DE BUTOVSKI, Alexei	RUS	1894–1900	09.06.1838	25.02.1917	
5.	BALCK, Viktor G.	SWE	1894–1921	25.04.1844	31.05.1928	
6.	SLOANE, William	USA	1894–1925	12.11.1850	11.09.1928	
7.	GUTH-JARKOVSKI, Jiri	TCH	1894–1943	23.01.1861	08.01.1943	
8.	KEMENY, Ferenc	HUN	1894–1907	17.07.1860	21.11.1944	
9.	Lord AMPTHILL	GBR	1894–1898	04.10.1869	07.09.1935	
10.	HERBERT, Charles	GBR	1894–1906	19.01.1846	17.02.1924	
11.	ZUBIAUR, José Benjamin	ARG	1894–1907	31.03.1856	06.09.1921	
12.	CUFF, Leonard A.	NZL	1894–1905	28.03.1866	09.10.1954	
13.	LUCCHESI PALLI, Mario A.	ITA	1894–1895	31.12.1860	16.10.1922	
14.	DE BROUSIES, Maxime	BEL	1894–1900	18.08.1865	11.05.1942	
15.	D'ANDRIA CARAFA, Riccardo	ITA	1894–1898	18.02.1859	19.10.1920	
16.	GEBHARDT, Willibald	GER	1895–1909	17.01.1861	30.04.1921	
17.	DE COURCY-LAFFAN, Robert	GBR	1897–1927	18.01.1853	16.01.1927	
18.	MERCATI, Alexandre	GRE	1897–1925	09.10.1874	05.04.1947	
19.	BRUNETTA D'USSEAUX, Eugenio	ITA	1897–1919	13.12.1857	08.01.1919	
20.	VAN TUYLL, F.W. Christiaan	NED	1898–1924	27.03.1851	13.02.1924	
21.	DE TALLEYRAND, Archambaud	FRA	1899–1902	25.03.1845	18.04.1918	
22.	HOLBECK, Niels V.	DEN	1899–1906	22.09.1857	12.11.1937	
23.	BIBESCO, Georges	ROM	1899–1902	14.03.1834	07.02.1902	
24.	DE BLONAY, Godefroy	SUI	1899–1937	25.07.1869	14.02.1937	
25.	STANTON, Theodore	USA	1900–1904	10.02.1851	01.03.1925	
26.	WHITNEY, Caspar	USA	1900–1904	02.09.1864	18.01.1929	
27.	HEBRARD DE VILLENEUVE, Henri	FRA	1900–1911	10.09.1848	22.03.1925	
28.	BELIOSSELSKI, Sergei	RUS	1900–1908	13.07.1867	27.04.1951	
29.	DE RIBEAUPIERRE, Georges	RUS	1900–1913	15.08.1854	23.07.1934	
30.	VON ROSEN, Clarence	SWE	1901–1948	12.05.1867	19.08.1955	
31.	DE SALEM-HORSTMAR, Edouard	GER	1901–1905	22.08.1841	23.12.1923	
32.	REYNTIENS, Guy	BEL	1901–1902	26.08.1813	13.10.1913	
33.	VINCENT, Howard	GBR	1901–1908	31.05.1849	07.04.1908	
34.	DE BEISTEGUI, Miguel	MEX	1901–1931	16.12.1861	06.11.1931	
35.	DE MEJORADA, Gonzalo	ESP	1902–1921	18.08.1861	05.06.1921	
36.	DE WARTENSLEBEN, Cesar	GER	1903–1913	17.07.1872	03.02.1930	
37.	DE BAILLET-LATOUR, Henri	BEL	1903–1942	01.03.1876	07.01.1942	
38.	HYDE, James	USA	1903–1908	06.06.1876	26.07.1959	
39.	DE CANDAMO, Carlos	PER	1903–1922	– 1840	–	
40.	BERTIER DE SAUVIGNY, Albert	FRA	1904–1920	– 1861	05.05.1948	
41.	VON DER ASSEBURG, Egbert	GER	1905–1909	01.01.1847	31.03.1909	
42.	COOMBES, Richard	AUS	1905–1932	17.03.1858	15.04.1935	
43.	DE SOLMS BRAUNFELS, Alex	AUT	1905–1909	04.11.1855	03.06.1926	
44.	AGNELL, Heinrik	NOR	1905–1907	22.08.1861	26.01.1922	
45.	TZOKOV, Dimitri	BUL	1906–1912	27.02.1864	– 1926	
46.	GRUT, Torben	DEN	1906–1912	23.08.1865	29.08.1952	
47.	Lord DESBOROUGH	GBR	1906–1913	30.10.1855	11.01.1945	

NO.	NAME	NATION	MANDATE	BORN	DIED	STATUS
48.	DE LANCASTRE, Antonio	POR	1906–1912	20.08.1881	30.10.1940	
49.	QUINTANO JR, Manuel	ARG	1907–1910	– 1867	09.03.1920	E
50.	ANDRASSY, Geza	HUN	1907–1938	22.07.1856	29.08.1938	
51.	HEFTEY, Thomas	NOR	1907–1908	10.04.1860	19.09.1921	
52.	ARMOUR, Allison Vincent	USA	1908–1919	18.03.1868	06.03.1941	
53.	VON WILLEBRAND, Reinhold	FIN	1908–1920	23.02.1858	06.05.1935	
54.	BORGHESE, Scipion	ITA	1908–1909	11.01.1871	15.03.1927	
55.	GAUTIER VIGNAL, Albert	MON	1908–1940	26.05.1854	18.10.1940	
56.	SVERRE, Johan T.	NOR	1908–1927	07.10.1867	06.06.1934	
57.	PLAGINO, Georges A.	ROM	1908–1949	16.11.1876	03.05.1949	
58.	TROUBETSKI, Simon	RUS	1908–1910	23.07.1861	08.02.1923	
59.	SIRRI BEY TARCAN, Selim	TUR	1908–1930	25.03.1874	02.03.1957	
60.	VON VENNINGEN, Karl	GER	1909–1914	15.01.1866	25.10.1914	
61.	COOK, Theodore Andrew	GBR	1909–1915	28.03.1867	16.09.1928	
62.	DE MUSZA, Jules	HUN	1909–1946	27.07.1862	23.02.1946	
63.	BRUNIALTI, Attilio	ITA	1909–1913	02.04.1849	02.12.1920	
64.	KANO, Jigoro	JPN	1909–1938	18.10.1860	04.05.1938	
65.	SIERSTORPFF, Adalbert	GER	1910–1919	30.09.1856	27.05.1922	
66.	BOLANAKI, Angelo	EGY/GRE	1910–1963	17.09.1877	26.07.1963	
67.	PESCATORE, Maurice	LUX	1910–1929	06.03.1870	30.04.1929	
68.	UROUSSOV, Léon	RUS	1910–1933	31.12.1877	08.01.1933	
69.	DE WINDISCH-GRÄTZ, Othon	AUT	1911–1919	07.10.1873	27.12.1952	
70.	HANBURY-WILLIAMS, John	CAN	1911–1920	19.10.1859	19.10.1946	
71.	WENDELL, Evert Jansen	USA	1911–1917	05.12.1860	27.08.1917	
72.	BALIFF, Abel	FRA	1911–1913	14.12.1845	03.12.1934	
73.	DE COLLOREDO-MANSFELD, Rudolf	AUT	1911–1919	16.08.1876	21.03.1948	
74.	GARCIA, Oscar N.	CHI	1911–1919	–	–	
75.	PENHA GARCIA, José	POR	1912–1940	02.06.1879	27.05.1940	
76.	DJUKIC, Svetomir V.	SER	1912–1948	29.05.1882	19.10.1960	
77.	HANSEN, Fritz	DEN	1912–1921	30.01.1855	11.11.1921	
78.	DE RIO BRANCO, Raul	BRA	1913–1938	20.02.1873	– 1938	
79.	STANCHOV, Dimitri	BUL	1913–1929	09.05.1863	25.03.1940	
80.	FARRAR, Sydney	RSA	1913–1919	18.11.1856	12.09.1917	
81.	GLANDAZ, Albert	FRA	1913–1944	–	11.03.1944	
82.	Duke of SOMERSET	GBR	1913–1920	22.07.1846	22.10.1923	
83.	DUPERRON, Georges	RUS	1913–1915	– 1877	23.07.1934	
84.	DE LAVELEY, Edouard	BEL	1913–1938	22.10.1854	25.11.1938	
85.	VON ARNIM-MUSKAU, Arnold	GER	1914–1919	31.03.1875	31.05.1931	
86.	MONTU, Carlo	ITA	1914–1939	10.01.1869	20.10.1949	
87.	DE POLIGNAC, Melchior	FRA	1914–1950	27.09.1880	18.12.1950	
88.	DE MATHEU, P.J.	CAM	1919–1941	16.05.1875	30.08.1940	
89.	DORN Y DE ALSUA, Enrique	ECU	1919–1929	–	–	
90.	SUMTER WEEKS, Bartow	USA	1919–1922	25.04.1861	03.02.1922	
91.	GUGLIELMI, Giorgio	ITA	1919–1930	17.04.1879	21.04.1945	
92.	SILVA VILDOSOLA, Carlo	CHI	1920–1922	– 1870	22.12.1939	
93.	KROGIUS, Ernst	FIN	1920–1948	06.06.1865	21.09.1955	
94.	DE CLARY, Justinien	FRA	1920–1933	20.11.1860	14.06.1933	
95.	TATA, Dorabji J.	IND	1920–1930	18.11.1859	03.06.1932	
96.	MARRYATT, Arthur	NZL	1920–1925	01.10.1871	23.11.1949	
97.	NOURSE, Henry	RSA	1920–1942	23.04.1857	06.10.1942	
98.	BUCAR, Franjo	YUG	1920–1946	25.11.1866	26.12.1946	
99.	EDSTRÖM, J. Sigfrid	SWE	1920–1952	21.11.1870	18.03.1964	
100.	KENTISH, Reginald John	GBR	1921–1933	29.12.1876	05.07.1956	
101.	MERRICK, James	CAN	1921–1946	14.05.1871	08.04.1946	
102.	ECHEVARRIETA, Horacio	ESP	1921–1923	15.09.1870	20.05.1963	
103.	ENAMI KHOI, Nizzamoddin	IRI	1921–1923	05.06.1891	30.04.1969	
104.	GHIGLIANI, Francisco	URU	1921–1936	07.06.1882	10.11.1936	
105.	LUBOMIRSKI, Etienne	POL	1921–1923	28.05.1895	18.08.1934	
106.	ALVEAR, Marcelo T.	ARG	1922–1932	04.10.1868	23.03.1942	
107.	WANG, Chen-ting	CHN	1922–1957	25.07.1882	21.05.1961	
108.	NYHOLM, Ivar	DEN	1922–1931	02.06.1864	21.04.1953	
109.	GUELL Y LOPEZ, Guillermo	ESP	1922–1954	02.06.1888	02.08.1954	
110.	GARLAND, William May	USA	1922–1948	31.03.1866	26.09.1948	
111.	SHERRILL, Charles H.	USA	1922–1936	13.04.1867	25.06.1936	
112.	KEAN, John Joseph	IRL	1922–1951	10.06.1870	01.04.1956	
113.	CADOGAN, Gerald Oakley	GBR	1923–1929	28.05.1869	04.10.1933	
114.	LUBOMIRSKI, Casimir	POL	1923–1930	16.07.1869	15.12.1930	
115.	ALDAO, Riccardo Camillo	ARG	1923–1949	24.04.1863	12.07.1958	
116.	GUINLE, Arnaldo	BRA	1923–1961	02.03.1884	26.08.1963	
117.	FERREIRA SANTOS, Joaquim	BRA	1923–1962	17.03.1892	14.12.1962	
118.	MATTE GORMAZ, J.	CHI	1923–1938	11.04.1876	–	La

NO.	NAME	NATION	MANDATE	BORN	DIED	STATUS
119.	FRANCA Y ALVAREZ, Porfirio	CUB	1923–1937	22.07.1879	03.05.1950	
120.	DE GUADELOUPE, Carlos	MEX	1923–1924	29.07.1874	07.06.1950	
121.	BENAVIDES, Alfredo	PER	1923–1957	30.08.1880	02.08.1967	
122.	LEWALD, Theodore	GER	1924–1938	18.08.1860	15.08.1947	
123.	RUPERTI, Oscar	GER	1924–1929	16.04.1877	19.12.1958	
124.	TAYLOR, James	AUS	1924–1944	01.12.1871	27.06.1944	
125.	HAUDEK, Martin	AUT	1924–1928	27.11.1880	09.03.1931	
126.	Duke of ALBA	ESP	1924–1927	17.10.1878	24.09.1953	
127.	SCHARROO, Peter W.	NED	1924–1957	16.09.1883	19.08.1963	
128.	KISHI, Seichi	JPN	1924–1933	04.07.1867	29.10.1933	
129.	GOMEZ DE PARADA, Jorge	MEX	1924–1927	25.04.1885	–	
130.	KHAN MOMTAZO, Samad	PER/IRI	1924–1927	05.06.1891	30.04.1969	
131.	KINLEY, David	USA	1925–1927	02.08.1861	03.12.1944	
132.	Baron SCHIMMELPENNINCK VAN DER OYENED		1925–1943	06.04.1880	30.04.1943	
133.	BONACOSSA, Alberto	ITA	1925–1953	24.08.1883	30.01.1953	
134.	FIRTH, Joseph Pentland	NZL	1925–1928	25.03.1859	13.04.1931	
135.	VON MECKLENBURG, Adolf	GER	1926–1956	10.10.1873	05.08.1969	
136.	AVEROV, Georges	GRE	1926–1930	– 1867	05.05.1930	
137.	DIKMANIS, Janis	LAT	1926–1946	10.06.1882	07.06.1960	
138.	Lord ROCHDALE	GBR	1927–1933	09.06.1866	24.03.1945	
139.	JAHNCKE, Ernest Lee	USA	1927–1936	13.10.1877	16.11.1960	E
140.	FEARNLEY, Thomas	NOR	1927–1950	16.01.1880	12.01.1961	
141.	FALCO Y ESCANDON, Manuel	ESP	1928–1930	02.09.1892	28.07.1975	
142.	SAENZ, Moises	MEX	1928–1933	13.02.1888	24.10.1941	
143.	SCHMIDT, Theodor	AUT	1928–1939	03.08.1891	18.10.1973	F
144.	McLAREN BROWN, George	CAN	1928–1939	29.10.1865	28.06.1939	
145.	AKEL, Friedrek	EST	1928–1932	05.09.1871	02.07.1941	
146.	Lord FREYBERG	NZL	1928–1930	21.03.1889	04.07.1963	
147.	MATUSZEWSKI, Ignacy	POL	1928–1939	10.09.1891	03.08.1946	
148.	RITTER VON HALT, Karl	GER	1929–1964	02.06.1891	05.08.1964	
149.	TCHAPRATCHIKOV, Stephan	BUL	1929–1944	15.04.1874	06.09.1944	
150.	EWING, Alfredo	CHI	1929–1933	–	–	La
151.	Lord ABERDARE	GBR	1929–1957	02.08.1885	04.10.1957	
152.	POLITIS, Nicolas	GRE	1930–1933	– 1872	05.03.1942	
153.	TURATI, Augusto	ITA	1930–1931	– 1888	07.09.1955	
154.	SAMI PASHA, Kremalettin	TUR	1930–1933	– 1884	15.04.1934	
155.	Comte DE VALLELANO	ESP	1931–1950	03.08.1886	06.09.1964	La
156.	WRAY, Cecil James	NZL	1931–1934	13.03.1868	08.10.1955	
157.	ROUPPERT, Stanislas	POL	1931–1945	15.04.1887	13.08.1945	
158.	BUSTOS MORON, Horacio	ARG	1932–1952	10.09.1885	19.03.1952	
159.	Prince AXEL	DEN	1932–1958	12.08.1888	14.07.1964	
160.	SONDHI, Guru Dutt	IND	1932–1966	10.12.1890	19.11.1966	
161.	THAON DI REVEL, Paolo	ITA	1932–1964	02.05.1888	31.05.1973	
162.	LUXTON, Harold	AUS	1933–1951	12.09.1910	24.10.1957	
163.	Marquis of EXETER	GBR	1933–1981	09.02.1905	22.10.1981	
164.	CURTIS BENNETT, Noel	GBR	1933–1950	14.05.1882	02.12.1950	
165.	SUGIMURA, Jotaro	JPN	1933–1936	10.09.1884	14.03.1939	
166.	ATABINEN, Rechid Saffet	TUR	1933–1950	– 1884	– 1965	La
167.	PIETRI, Francois	FRA	1934–1966	10.08.1882	18.08.1966	
168.	PORRITT, Arthur	NZL	1934–1967	10.08.1900	01.01.1994	
169.	TAHER PASHA, Mohamed	EGY	1934–1968	– 1897	27.01.1970	
170.	SOYESHIMA, Michimasa	JPN	1934–1948	14.10.1871	15.10.1948	
171.	MARTE RODOLFO GOMEZ, Segura	MEX	1934–1973	04.07.1896	15.12.1973	
172.	BRUNDAGE, Avery	USA	1936–1972	28.09.1887	08.05.1975	
173.	Archduke FRANZ-JOSEF III	LIE	1936–1980	16.08.1906	13.11.1989	
174.	PUKH, Joakim	EST	1936–1942	25.05.1888	13.05.1942	
175.	TOKUGAWA, Yesato	JPN	1936–1939	11.07.1863	05.06.1940	
176.	VARGAS, Jorge B.	PHI	1936–1980	24.08.1890	22.02.1980	
177.	COUDERT, Frederic René	USA	1937–1948	11.02.1871	01.04.1955	
178.	GUISAN, Henri	SUI	1937–1939	21.10.1874	07.04.1960	
179.	SERRATOSA CIBILS, Joaquim	URU	1937–1956	05.09.1884	22.05.1958	
180.	VON REICHENAU, Walther	GER	1938–1942	08.10.1884	17.01.1942	
181.	MOENCK, Miguel A.	CUB	1938–1969	18.09.1890	31.08.1969	
182.	PRADO Jr, Antonio	BRA	1938–1955	05.04.1880	17.11.1955	
183.	RANGELL, Johan Wilhelm	FIN	1938–1967	25.10.1894	12.03.1982	
184.	DE TRANNOY, Gaston	BEL	1939–1957	18.10.1880	22.12.1960	
185.	KONG, Xiang-xi	CHN	1939–1955	11.09.1889	05.08.1967	
186.	VACCARO, Giorgio	ITA	1939–1950	12.10.1892	25.09.1983	La
187.	NAGAI, Matsuzo	JPN	1939–1950	05.03.1877	19.04.1957	
188.	TAKAISHI, Shingoro	JPN	1939–1967	22.09.1878	25.02.1967	

NO.	NAME	NATION	MANDATE	BORN	DIED	STATUS
189.	LINDBERGH, A.V.	RSA	1939–1939	25.11.1872	12.11.1939	
190.	HORTHY Jr, Miklos	HUN	1939–1948	14.02.1907	11.05.1993	La
191.	WEIR, Hugh Richard	AUS	1946–1975	21.07.1894	06.03.1975	
192.	SEELDRAYERS, Rodolphe W.	BEL	1946–1955	11.12.1876	07.10.1955	
193.	PATTESON, John Coleridge	CAN	1946–1954	05.12.1896	12.01.1954	
194.	GRUSS, Josef	TCH	1946–1965	08.07.1884	21.05.1968	
195.	MASSARD, Armand Emile	FRA	1946–1971	01.12.1884	08.04.1971	
196.	PAHUD DE MORTANGES, Charles	NED	1946–1964	13.04.1896	07.04.1971	
197.	WAAGE, Benedikt G.	ISL	1946–1966	14.06.1889	08.11.1966	
198.	Archduke JEAN	LUX	1946–1998	05.01.1921		
199.	PONTES, José Joaquim	POR	1946–1956	22.04.1879	23.09.1961	
200.	DOWSETT, Sydney Charles	RSA	1946–1951	15.04.1880	05.07.1951	
201.	HONEY, Reginald	RSA	1946–1982	04.12.1886	24.03.1982	
202.	MAYER, Albert	SUI	1946–1968	19.07.1890	06.12.1968	
203.	KETSEAS, Ioannis	GRE	1946–1965	16.09.1887	06.04.1965	
204.	MAUTNER-MARKHOF, Manfred	AUT	1947–1969	17.09.1903	04.08.1981	
205.	DAWES, Sidney	CAN	1947–1967	05.12.1888	03.03.1968	
206.	SHOU, Yi-tung	CHN	1947–1958	04.10.1895	13.06.1978	
207.	SINGH, Bhalendra	IND	1947–1992	09.08.1919	16.04.1992	
208.	EKELUND, Bo	SWE	1948–1965	26.07.1894	01.04.1983	
209.	LOTH, Jerzy	POL	1948–1961	04.08.1880	30.09.1967	
210.	BLOUDEK, Stanko	YUG	1948–1959	11.02.1890	26.11.1959	
211.	MEZÖ, Ferenc	HUN	1948–1961	13.03.1885	21.11.1961	
212.	BARBOZA BAEZA, Enrique	CHI	1948–1950	05.11.1882	09.08.1976	La
213.	GARLAND, John Jewett	USA	1948–1968	20.04.1902	30.11.1968	
214.	VON FRENCKELL, Eric	FIN	1948–1976	18.11.1887	13.09.1977	
215.	IDIGORAS FUENTES, Miguel	GUA	1948–1950	17.10.1895	06.10.1952	La
216.	DITLEV SIMONSEN Jr, Olaf	NOR	1948–1966	02.01.1897	19.02.1978	
217.	Prince RAINIER III	MON	1949–1950	31.05.1923		
218.	JAFFER, Ahmed E.H.	PAK	1949–1956	27.12.1881	–	
219.	AZUMA, Ryotaro	JPN	1950–1969	16.01.1893	15.04.1983	
220.	BROOKS PARKER, James	USA	1950–1951	25.12.1889	30.11.1951	
221.	Prince PIERRE	MON	1950–1964	24.10.1895	10.11.1964	
222.	Lord LUKE	GBR	1951–1988	07.06.1905	27.05.1996	
223.	Comte DE BEAUMONT, Jean	FRA	1951–1990	13.01.1904	18.06.2002	
224.	DE STEFANI, Giorgio	ITA	1951–1992	24.02.1904	22.10.1992	
225.	ANDRIANOV, Konstantin	URS	1951–1988	16.02.1910	18.01.1988	
226.	LUXTON, Lewis	AUS	1951–1974	12.09.1910	09.11.1985	
227.	STOYTCHEV, Vladimir	BUL	1952–1987	07.04.1892	26.04.1990	
228.	Lord KILLANIN	IRL	1952–1980	30.07.1914	25.04.1996	
229.	GEMAYEL, Gabriel	LIB	1952–1987	24.03.1907	09.11.1987	
230.	DE CLARK FLORES, José	MEX	1952–1971	28.11.1908	17.04.1971	
231.	ROMANOV, Aleksei	URS	1952–1971	16.10.1904	03.11.1979	
232.	ALBERDI, Enrique	ARG	1952–1959	15.10.1910	06.11.1959	
233.	GERLEIN COMELIN, Julio	COL	1952–1986	07.09.1902	18.19.1986	
234.	DE YBARRA Y MAC MAHON, P.	ESP	1952–1985	28.04.1913	20.12.1993	
235.	ROBY, Douglas Ferguson	USA	1952–1985	24.03.1898	31.03.1992	
236.	SOSA, Augustin	PAN	1952–1967	15.04.1905	04.03.1990	
237.	DYRSSEN, Gustaf	SWE	1952–1970	24.11.1891	13.05.1975	
238.	BUSTAMANTE, Julio	VEN	1952–1968	17.08.1903	20.06.1968	
239.	RIVERA BASCUR, Alejandro	CHI	1955–1984	28.08.1901	08.03.1985	
240.	ERLER, Suat	TUR	1955–1984	16.08.1910	02.07.1984	
241.	LEE, Ki Pong	KOR	1955–1960	20.12.1896	18.04.1960	
242.	REZA PAHLAVI, Golam	IRI	1955–1980	15.05.1923		
243.	SIPERCO, Alexandru	ROM	1955–1998	05.11.1920	26.10.1998	
244.	DAUME, Willi	GER	1956–1991	24.05.1913	20.05.1996	
245.	FERREIRA PIRES, Saul	POR	1957–1962	23.04.1906	06.05.1978	E
246.	ALBERT of LIÈGE	BEL	1958–1964	06.06.1934		
247.	DIBOS, Eduardo	PER	1958–1982	28.01.1897	05.06.1987	
248.	WAJID ALI, Syed	PAK	1959–1996	20.12.1911		HM
249.	VIND, Ivar	DEN	1959–1977	05.01.1921	11.02.1977	
250.	ALEXANDER, Reginald S.	KEN	1960–1989	14.11.1914	31.03.1990	
251.	BAKRAC, Boris	YUG	1960–1987	25.03.1912	29.11.1989	
252.	NEGRI, Mario Luis José	ARG	1960–1974	14.04.1889	30.03.1977	
253.	TOUNY, Ahmad Eldemerdash	EGY	1960–1992	10.08.1907	10.09.1997	
254.	RECZEK, Wlodzimierz	POL	1960–1996	24.02.1911		
255.	BENJELLOUN, Mohamed	MAR	1961–1997	25.01.1912	20.09.1997	
256.	ADEMOLA, Adetokunbo	NGR	1963–1985	01.02.1906	29.01.1993	
257.	PEREIRA CASTRO, Raul	POR	1963–1989	11.06.1905	02.01.1991	
258.	HAVELANGE, João Marie	BRA	1963–	11.05.1916		L
259.	HODLER, Marc	SUI	1963–	26.10.1918		L

NO.	NAME	NATION	MANDATE	BORN	DIED	STATUS
260.	INCIARTE, Alfredo	URU	1963–1975	26.01.1900	29.12.1975	
261.	King CONSTANTINE	GRE	1963–1974	02.06.1920		HM
262.	CSANADI, Arpad	HUN	1964–1983	23.02.1923	07.03.1983	
263.	Peince Alexandre DE MÉRODE	BEL	1964–2002	24.05.1934	20.11.2002	
264.	DE MAGALHAES PADILHA, S.	BRA	1964–1994	05.06.1909	28.08.2002	
265.	ONESTI, Giulio	ITA	1964–1981	04.01.1912	11.12.1981	
266.	VAN KARNEBEEK, Herman	NED	1964–1977	11.11.1903	13.07.1989	
267.	LEE, Sang Beck	KOR	1964–1966	05.08.1903	14.04.1966	
268.	BARRY, Amadou	SEN	1965–1969	15.11.1904	22.03.1969	
269.	ERICSSON, Gunnar	SWE	1965–1996	29.06.1919		HM
270.	KROUTIL, Frantisek	TCH	1965–1981	23.06.1907	08.02.1987	
271.	LAPPAS, Pyrros	GRE	1965–1980	11.01.1900	14.06.1981	
272.	MZALI, Mohamed	TUN	1965–	23.12.1925		L
273.	VON OPEL, Georg	GER	1966–1971	18.05.1912	14.08.1971	
274.	SAMARANCH, Juan Antonio	ESP	1966–2001	17.07.1920		HLP
275.	SCHÖBEL, Heinz	GDR	1966–1980	14.10.1913	26.04.1980	
276.	Prince Georg of HANOVER	IOA	1966–1971	18.03.1915	08.01.2006	
277.	STAUBO, Jan	NOR	1967–2002	28.09.1920	15.06.2003	
278.	CHANG, Key Young	KOR	1967–1977	02.05.1916	11.04.1977	
279.	HONKAJUURI, Paavo	FIN	1967–1981	26.11.1914	2001	
280.	TAKEDA, Tsuyenoshi	JPN	1967–1981	04.03.1909	11.05.1992	
281.	WORRALL, James	CAN	1967–1989	23.06.1914		HM
282.	ARROYO, Agustin Carlos	ECU	1968–1999	22.07.1923		E
283.	BERACASA, José	VEN	1968–1981	11.01.1908	28.08.1986	
284.	HALIM, Abdel Mohamed	SUD	1968–1982	10.04.1910		
285.	HAMENGKU BUWONO IX	INA	1968–1976	12.04.1912	02.10.1988	
286.	RAKOTOBE, René	MAD	1968–1971	08.07.1918	25.07.1971	
287.	CROSS, Cecil Lancelot	NZL	1969–1987	12.11.1912	13.05.1989	
288.	GAFNER, Raymond	SWI	1969–1990	17.12.1915	26.11.2002	
289.	GUIRANDOU-N'DAIYE, Louis	CIV	1969–1999	04.02.1923	08.06.1999	
290.	KIYOKAWA, Masaji	JPN	1969–1988	11.02.1913	12.04.1999	
291.	DE LEON, Virgilio	PAN	1969–1994	07.02.1919	17.03.1998	
292.	NEMETSCHKE, Rudolf	AUT	1969–1976	09.05.1902	05.06.1980	
293.	HERZOG, Maurice	FRA	1970–1994	15.01.1919		HM
294.	HSU, Henry	TPE	1970–1987	06.12.1912		HM
295.	THOFELT, Sven	SWE	1970–1976	19.05.1904	01.02.1993	
296.	CHARUSATHIARA, Prabhas	THA	1971–1974	25.12.1912	– 1997	
297.	SMIRNOV, Vitaly	RUS	1971–	14.02.1935		2008 80
298.	TESSEMA, Ydnekatchew	ETH	1971–1987	11.09.1921	19.08.1987	
299.	BEITZ, Berthold	GER	1972–1988	26.09.1913		HM
300.	RAMIREZ-VAZQUEZ, Pedro	MEX	1972–1995	16.04.1919		HM
301.	BRIDGE, Anthony	JAM	1973–2000	04.02.1921	13.12.2000	
302.	GONZALEZ-GUERRA, Manuel	CUB	1973–1992	25.04.1917	20.04.1997	
303.	KUMAR, Ashwini	IND	1973–2000	27.12.1920		HM
304.	M'BAYE, Keba	SEN	1973–2000	05.08.1924	11.01.2007	
305.	CHULLASAPYA, Da Wee	THA	1974–1989	08.08.1914	06.02.1996	
306.	HAY, Eduardo	MEX	1974–1991	19.02.1915	05.01.2005	
307.	McKENZIE, David	AUS	1974–1981	15.07.1936	10.08.1981	
308.	ROOSEVELT, Julian K.	USA	1974–1986	14.11.1924	27.03.1986	
309.	ZERGUINI, Mohamed	ALG	1974–2001	23.04.1922	21.06.2001	
310.	PETRALIAS, Epaminondas	GRE	1975–1977	25.08.1908	24.11.1977	
311.	CARLGREN, Matts	SWE	1976–1992	24.09.1917	23.09.1999	
312.	O'FLANAGAN, Kevin Patrick	IRL	1976–1995	10.06.1919	26.05.2006	
313.	TALLBERG, Peter	FIN	1976–	15.07.1937		2009 80
314.	VALLARINO VERACIERTO, J.	URU	1976–2000	14.02.1920	30.10.2001	
315.	ATTARABULSI, Bashir	LBA	1977–1999	27.09.1937		R
316.	GOSPER, Kevan Richard	AUS	1977–	19.12.1933		2007 80
317.	HOLST-SORENSEN, Niels	DEN	1977–2002	19.12.1922		HM
318.	KEITA, Lamine	MLI	1977–1999	08.08.1933		E
319.	KERDEL, Cornelis	NED	1977–1986	19.03.1915	08.11.1986	
320.	KIM, Taik Soo	KOR	1977–1983	10.09.1926	17.07.1983	
321.	MAGVAN, Shagdarjav	MGL	1977–2007	20.08.1927		
322.	PEPER, Guillermo	ARG	1977–1988	27.06.1913	23.07.1999	
323.	RIECKEHOFF, German	PUR	1977–1990	05.02.1915	02.09.1997	
324.	VON SCHÖLLER, Philipp	AUT	1977–2001	23.08.1921		HM
325.	SUPRAYOGI, Dadang	THA	1977–1989	12.04.1914	13.09.1998	
326.	ESSOMBA, Rene	CMR	1978–1999	06.04.1932	31.08.1999	
327.	HAMZAH BIN ABU SAMAH, Datuk Seri	MAL	1978–	05.01.1924		2004 80
328.	KIM, Yu Sun	PRK	1978–1994	02.02.1932	10.08.1994	
329.	NISSIOTIS, Nikolaos	GRE	1978–1986	21.05.1925	18.08.1986	
330.	POUND, Richard W.	CAN	1978–	22.03.1942		2009 80

NO.	NAME	NATION	MANDATE	BORN	DIED	STATUS
331.	CERNUSAK, Vladimir	TCH/SVK	1981–2002	25.11.1921		
332.	FILARETOS, Nikos	GRE	1981–2007	26.03.1925	28.03.2007	
333.	HÄGGMAN, Pirjo	FIN	1981–1999	08.06.1951		R
334.	HÉ, Zhen-liang	CHN	1981–	29.12.1929		2007 80
335.	HEINZE, Günther	GDR	1981–1991	26.07.1923		HM
336.	ISAVA FONSECA, Flor	VEN	1981–2001	20.05.1921		HM
337.	Sheikh FAHAD AL SABAH	KUW	1981–1991	10.06.1945	03.08.1991	
338.	CARRARO, Franco	ITA	1982–	06.12.1939		2009 80
339.	COLES, Phillip Walter	AUS	1982–	20.07.1931		2008 80
340.	DIBOS, Ivan	PER	1982–	18.01.1939		2009 80
341.	GLEN-HAIG, Mary Alison	GBR	1982–1994	12.07.1918		HM
342.	IGAYA, Chiharu	JPN	1982–	20.05.1931		2009 80
343.	FAHD ABDUL AZIZ, Faisal	KSA	1983–1999	07.07.1946	21.08.1999	
344.	GADIR, Zein El Abdin Abdel	SUD	1983–1999	07.05.1940		E
345.	MATTHIA, Anani	TOG	1983–2007	08.03.1927		
346.	MUNOZ PENA, Roque Napoleon	DOM	1983–	13.01.1928		2008 80
347.	SCHMITT, Pal	HUN	1983–	13.05.1942		2009 80
348.	ATAKOL, Turgut	TUR	1983–1988	10.10.1915	10.04.1988	
349.	Princess NORA	LIE	1984–	31.10.1950		2009 80
350.	PARK, Chong Kyu	KOR	1984–1985	28.05.1930	03.12.1985	
351.	SIBANDZE, David	SWZ	1984–1999	20.02.1932		R
352.	ADEFOPE, Henry Olufemi	NGR	1985–2006	15.03.1926		
353.	ELIZALDE, Francisco	PHI	1985–	10.10.1932		2009 80
354.	FERRER, Carlos	ESP	1985–1998	22.03.1931	18.10.1998	
355.	HELMICK, Robert	USA	1985–1991	05.03.1937		R
356.	Prince ALBERT	MON	1985–	14.03.1958		2007 80
357.	KIM, Un Yong	KOR	1986–2005	19.03.1931		
358.	NIKOLAOU, Lambis W.	GRE	1986–	23.11.1935		2008 80
359.	DEFRANTZ, Anita	USA	1986–	04.10.1952		2008 80
360.	GANGA, Jean-Claude	CGO	1986–1999	28.02.1934		E
361.	SLAVKOV, Ivan Borissov	BUL	1987–2005	11.05.1940		
362.	GEESINK, Anthonius	NED	1987–	06.04.1934		2009 80
363.	FILIPOVIC, Slobodan	YUG	1987–1995	10.07.1939	14.06.1995	
364.	WALLWORK, Seuili Paul	SAM	1987–1999	15.01.1942		E
365.	Princess ANNE	GBR	1988–	15.08.1950		2008 80
366.	CARRASQUILLA, Fidel M.	COL	1988–2005	07.07.1925		
367.	WILSON, Edward (Tay)	NZL	1988–2005	03.02.1925		
368.	WU, Ching-Kuo	TPE	1988–	18.10.1946		2007 80
369.	RUHEE, Rampaul	MRI	1988–2007	12.10.1927		
370.	GRAMOV, Marat	URS	1988–1991	27.11.1927		R
371.	ERDEM, Sinan	TUR	1988–	08.05.1927	24.07.2003	
372.	KLATSCHMITT LUJAN, Willi	GUA	1988–	13.08.1939		2007 80
373.	NYANGWESO, Francis Were	UGA	1988–	29.09.1939		2009 80
374.	STANKOVIC, Borislav	YUG	1988–2005	09.07.1925		
375.	LIMA-BELLO, Fernando	POR	1989–	27.11.1931		2007 80
376.	TRÖGER, Walther	GER	1989–	04.02.1929		2007 80
377.	CHATRIER, Philippe	FRA	1989–1995	02.02.1928	23.06.2000	
378.	LETHEREN, Carol Anne	CAN	1990–2001	27.07.1942	01.02.2001	
379.	OKANO, Shunichiro	JPN	1990–	28.08.1931		2009 80
380.	CARRION, Richard L.	PUR	1990–	26.11.1952		2008 80
381.	INDRAPANA, Nat	THA	1990–	06.03.1939		2008 80
382.	MUKORA, Charles Nderitu	KEN	1990–1999	18.10.1934		R
383.	RODRIGUEZ, Antonion	ARG	1990–2006	17.03.1926		
384.	OSWALD, Denis	SUI	1991–	09.05.1947		2008 80
385.	ROGGE, Jacques	BEL	1991–	02.05.1942		2007 80
386.	VAZQUEZ RAÑA, Mario	MEX	1991–	07.06.1932		2008 80
387.	BACH, Thomas	GER	1991–	29.12.1953		2008 80
388.	NEBIOLO, Primo	ITA	1992–1999	14.07.1923	17.11.1999	
389.	POULSEN, Olaf	NOR	1992–1994	27.07.1920		EO/La
390.	SANTANDER, Fantini Sergio	CHI	1992–1999	05.05.1926		E
391.	Sheikh AHMAD AL-FAHAD AL-SABAH	KUW	1992–	12.08.1961		2009 80
392.	EASTON, James L.	USA	1994–	26.07.1935		2007 80
393.	REEDIE, Craig	GBR	1994–	06.05.1941		2009 80
394.	HASAN, Mohamed	INA	1994–2004	24.02.1931		
395.	PESCANTE, Mario	ITA	1994–	07.07.1938		2008 80
396.	HEIBERG, Gerhard	NOR	1994–	20.04.1939		2008 80
397.	LJUNGQVIST, Arne	SWE	1994–	23.04.1931		2007 80
398.	SEALY, Austin Llewellyn	BAR	1994–	17.09.1939		2009 80
399.	MITCHELL, Robin	FIJ	1994–	10.03.1946		2008 80
400.	DIALLO, Alpha Ibrahim	GUI	1994–	12.06.1932		2007 80
401.	GILADY, Alex	ISR	1994–	09.12.1942		2008 80

NO.	NAME	NATION	MANDATE	BORN	DIED	STATUS
402.	TARPISCHEV, Shamil	RUS	1994–	07.03.1948		2009 80
403.	BORZOV, Valeriy	UKR	1994–	20.10.1949		2007 80
404.	FASEL, René	SUI	1995–	06.02.1950		2007 80 ‡‡
405.	KILLY, Jean-Claude	FRA	1995–	30.08.1943		2008 80
406.	RAMSAMY, Sam	RSA	1995–	27.01.1938		2008 80
407.	GONZALEZ LOPEZ, Reynaldo	CUB	1995–	14.09.1948		2007 80
408.	VAZQUEZ RAÑA, Olegario	MEX	1995–	10.12.1935		2008 80
409.	VRDOLJAK, Antun	CRO	1995–	04.06.1931		2007 80
410.	HICKEY, Patrick	IRL	1995–	17.06.1945		2007 80
411.	KHOURY, Toni	LEB	1995–	26.09.1935		2008 80
412.	LARFAOUI, Mustapha	ALG	1995–	27.11.1932		2008 80 ‡‡
413.	TITOV, Jury	RUS	1995–1996	27.11.1935		EO/La
414.	ALI, Syed Shahid	PAK	1996–	29.12.1946		2007 80
415.	CHANG, Ung	PRK	1996–	05.07.1938		2008 80
416.	LINDBERG, Gunilla	SWE	1996–	06.05.1947		2007 80
417.	MAGLIONE, Julio César	URU	1996–	14.11.1935		2008 80
418.	LU, Shengrong	CHN	1996–2001	27.11.1940		EO/La
419.	CÁSLÁVSKA, Vera	CZE	1966–2001	03.05.1942		Rt
420.	LEE, Kun Hee	KOR	1996–2007	09.01.1942		R
421.	SITHOLE, Tomas Amos Ganda	ZIM	1996–	26.08.1948		2008 80
422.	VERBRUGGEN, Hein	NED	1996–2006	21.06.1941		‡R
423.	CINQUANTA, Ottavio	ITA	1996–	15.08.1938		2007 80 ‡‡
424.	BORBON, Doña Pilar de	ESP	1996–2006	30.07.1936		HM
425.	DRUT, Guy	FRA	1996–	06.12.1950		2008 80
426.	SZEWINSKA, Irena	POL	1998–	24.05.1946		2007 80
427.	KOSS, Johan	NOR	1988–2002	29.10.1948		R
428.	Grand-Duc HENRI	LUX	1998–	16.04.1955		2007 80
429.	SABET, Mounir	EGY	1998–	29.10.1936		2009 80
430.	EL MOUTAWAKEL, Nawal	MAR	1998–	15.04.1962		2007 80
431.	SANCHEZ RIVAS, Melitón	PAN	1998–	08.11.1934		2007 80
432.	SMIRNOV, Vladimir	KAZ	1998–2002	07.03.1964		R
433.	WALLNER, Leo	AUT	1998–	04.11.1934		2009 80
434.	Prince of ORANGE	NED	1998–	27.04.1967		2007 80
435.	NG, Ser Miang	SIN	1998–	06.04.1949		2009 80
436.	MOUDALLAL, Samih	SYR	1998–	20.09.1939		2008 80
437.	BLATTER, Joseph	SUI	1999–	10.03.1936		2006 70 ‡‡
438.	DIACK, Lamine	SEN	1999–	07.06.1933		2003 70 ‡‡
439.	BAAR, Roland	GER	1999–	12.04.1965		2004 70 †
440.	BOULMERKA, Hassiba	ALG	1999–2000	10.07.1968		R
441.	BUBKA, Sergei	UKR	1999–	04.12.1963		2008 70 †
442.	CROOKS, Charmaine	CAN	1999–	08.08.1962		2004 70 †
443.	CVRTLIK, Robert	USA	1999–	07.08.1963		2008 70 †
444.	DI CENTA, Manuela	ITA	1999–	31.01.1963		2010 70 †
445.	HYBL, William	USA	1999–2000	16.07.1942		EO/La
446.	POPOV, Alexander	RUS	1999–	16.11.1971		2008 70 †
447.	ZELEZNY, Jan	CZE	1999–2002	10.01.1966		R
448.	ACOSTA, Reuben	MEX	2000–	04.04.1934		2004 70 ‡
449.	AJAN, Tamas	HUN	2000–	12.01.1939		2008 70 ‡
450.	GOYENECHE, Alfredo	ESP	2000–2002	13.12.1938	16.03.2002	
451.	GRANDI, Bruno	ITA	2000–2004	09.05.1934		‡
452.	HASHEMI TABA, Seyed Mostafa	IRI	2000–	22.05.1946		2008 70 ††
453.	HENDERSON, Paul	CAN	2000–	17.11.1934		2004 70 ‡
454.	KASPER, Gian-Franco	SUI	2000–	24.01.1944		2008 70 ‡
455.	KEINO, Kipchoge	KEN	2000–	07.01.1940		2008 70 ††
456.	NUZMAN, Carlos Arthur	BRA	2000–	17.03.1942		2008 70 ††
457.	PALENFO, Lassana	CIV	2000–	25.11.1941		2008 70 ††
458.	SERANDOUR, Henri	FRA	2000–	15.04.1937		2007 70 ††
459.	STEADWARD, Robert	USA	2000–2001	26.05.1946		EO/La
460.	YU, Zaiqing	CHN	2000–	26.04.1951		2008 70 ††
461.	O'NEILL, Susie	AUS	2000–2005	02.08.1973		R
462.	ESTIARTE, Manuel	ESP	2000–	26.10.1961		2004 70 †
463.	FOK, Timothy Tsun Ting	HKG	2001–	14.02.1946		2009 70 ††
464.	SINGH, Randhir	IND	2001–	18.10.1946		2009 70 ††
465.	COATES, John Dowling	AUS	2001–	07.05.1950		2009 70 ††
466.	HAYATOU, Issa	CMR	2001–	09.08.1946		2009 70
467.	SAMARANCH Jr, Juan Antonio	ESP	2001–	01.11.1959		2009 70
468.	VAN BREDA VRIESMAN, Els	NED	2001–	18.03.1941		2009 70 ‡
469.	Prince ABDUL AZIZ	KSA	2002–	01.04.1978		2010 70 ††
470.	LAZARIDES, Kikis	CYP	2002–2005	15.03.1935		HM
471.	PARK, Yong Sung	KOR	2002–2007	11.09.1940		R
472.	CHAMUNDA, Patrick	ZAM	2002–	22.07.1945		2010 70

NO.	NAME	NATION	MANDATE	BORN	DIED	STATUS	
473.	Sheikh AL-THANI	QAT	2002–	03.06.1980		2010 70	††
474.	BALDWIN, Sandra	USA	2002–2002	07.09.1939		R	
475.	HOLM, Kai	DEN	2002–	01.12.1938		2010 70	
476.	NARMON, Francois	BEL	2002–2004	26.01.1934			
477.	NDIAYE, Youssoupha	SEN	2002–	09.05.1938		2010 70	
478.	PINSENT, Matthew	GBR	2002–2004	10.10.1970			
479.	WIBERG, Pernilla	SWE	2002–	15.10.1970		2010 70	†
480.	KURRI, Jari	FIN	2002–2004	18.05.1960			
481.	SONDRAL, Adne	NOR	2002–2004	10.05.1971			
482.	CRAVEN, Philip	GBR	2003–	04.07.1950			†
483.	FREDERICKS, Frank	NAM	2004–	02.10.1960		2012	†
484.	ZELEZNY, Jan	CZE	2004–	16.06.1966		2012	†
485.	EL GUERROUJ, Hicham	MAR	2004–	14.09.1974		2012	†
486.	ELWANI, Rania	EGY	2004–	14.10.1977		2012	†
487.	KENDALL, Barbara	NZL	2005–	30.08.1967		2008	†
488.	RICCI BITTI, Francesco	ITA	2006–	15.01.1942		2014	‡
489.	Prince TUNKU IMRAN	MAS	2006–	21.03.1948		2014	‡
490.	HOEVERTSZ, Nicole	ARU	2006–	30.05.1964		2014	‡
491.	ALLEN, Beatrice	GAM	2006–	08.08.1950		2014	‡
492.	SCOTT, Rebecca	CAN	2006–	08.01.1974		2014	†
493.	KOIVU, Saku	FIN	2006–	23.11.1974		2014	†
494.	BOTERO PHILLIPSBOURNE, Andre	COL	2007–	23.12.1945		2015	
495.	BAUMANN, Patrick	SUI	2007–	05.08.1967		2015	‡
496.	Princess, HAYA BINT AL HUSSEIN	UAE	2007–	03.05.1974		2015	‡
497.	SUBOWO, Rita	INA	2007–	27.07.1948		2015	‡

NOTES

Where – is marked in the list, this indicates that the information has not been available to Wolf Lyberg or the author

L	= life member
80	= member until aged 80, subject to re-election every eight years
70	= member until aged 70, subject to re-election every eight years
†	= elected as the result of a candidature as an active athlete
††	= elected as the result of a candidature linked to a function of an NOC or association of NOCs
‡	= elected as the result of a candidature linked to a function of an IF or association of IFs
‡‡	= elected 'ex-officio' before 12 December 1999 on the basis of their function (IF)
F	= Jewish fugitive/wartime exile in USA
EO/La	= Ex-officio/Lapsed
E	= Expelled
La	= Lapsed
HM	= Honorary Member
HLP	= Honorary Life President
R	= Resigned
Rt	= Retired

Olympic Games Results

d.n.a. – data not available

n.t.a – no time available

Korea = South Korea

* Asian names carry family names last as far as is known

The following tables have been compiled by an independent statistician

ARCHERY

Double Fita Round – Men
(Maximum possible score 2880 points)

	GOLD	SILVER	BRONZE
1972	John Williams(USA) 2528pts	Gunnar Jarvil(SWE) 2481pts	Kyösti Lassonen(FIN) 2467pts
1976	Darrell Pace(USA) 2571pts	Hiroshi Michinaga(JPN) 2502pts	Giancarlo Ferrrari(ITA) 2495pts
1980	Tomi Poikolainen(FIN) 2455pts	Boris Isachenko(URS) 2452pts	Giancarlo Ferrari(ITA) 2449pts
1984	Darrell Pace(USA) 2616pts	Richard McKinney(USA) 2564pts	Hiroshi Yamamoto(JPN) 2563pts
1988	Jay Barrs(USA) 338 pts (2605)	Sung-Soo Park(KOR) 336pts (2614)	Vladimir Yecheyev(URS) 335pts (2600)
1992(1)	Sebastien Flute(FRA)	Jae-Hun Chung(KOR)	Simon Terry(GBR)
1996	Justin Huish(USA)	Magnus Petersson(SWE)	Kyun-Moon Oh(KOR)
2000	Simon Fairweather(AUS)	Victor Wonderle(USA)	Wietse Van Alten(NED)
2004	Marco Galiazzo(ITA)	Hiroshi Yamamoto(JPN)	Tim Cuddihy(AUS

1896–1968 Event not held

(1) 1992 onwards, points no longer comparable

Team – Men

	GOLD	SILVER	BRONZE
1988	KOREA	UNITED STATES	GREAT BRITAIN
1992	SPAIN	FINLAND	GREAT BRITAIN
1996	UNITED STATES	KOREA	ITALY
2000	KOREA	ITALY	USA
2004	KOREA	CHINESE TAIPEI	UKRAINE

1896–1984 Event not held

Double Fita Round – Women

	GOLD	SILVER	BRONZE
1972	Doreen Wilber(USA) 2424pts	Irena Szydlowska(POL) 2407pts	Emma Gapchenko(URS) 2403pts
1976	Luann Ryon(USA) 2499pts	Valentina Kovpan(URS) 2460pts	Zebeniso Rustamova(URS) 2407pts
1980	Keto Losaberidze(URS) 2491pts	Natalya Butuzova(URS) 2477pts	Päivi Meriluoto(FIN) 2449pts
1984	Hyang-Soon Seo(KOR) 2568pts	Lingjuan Li(CHN) 2559pts	Jin-Ho Kim(KOR) 2555pts
1988	Soo-Nyung Kim(KOR) 344pts (2683)	Hee-Kyung Wang(KOR) 332pts (2612)	Young-Sook Yung(KOR) 327pts (2603)
1992	Youn-Jeong Cho(KOR)	Soo-Nyung Kim(KOR)	Natalia Valeyeva(EUN)
1996	Kyung-Wook Kim(KOR)	Ying He(CHN)	Olena Sadovnycha(UKR)
2000	Mi-Yin Yun(KOR)	Nam-Soon Kim(KOR)	Soo-Njung Kim(KOR)
2004	Sung-Hyun Park(KOR)	Sung-Jin Lee(KOR)	Alison Williamson(GBR)

1896–1968 Event not held

Team – Women

	GOLD	SILVER	BRONZE
1988	KOREA	INDONESIA	UNITED STATES
1992	KOREA	CHINA	UNIFIED TEAM
1996	KOREA	GERMANY	POLAND
2000	KOREA	UKRAINE	GERMANY
2004	KOREA	CHINA	CHINESE TAIPEI

1896–1984 Event not held

ARCHERY – DISCONTINUED EVENTS

	GOLD	SILVER	BRONZE
Au cordon doré–50m – Men			
1900	Henri Hérouin(FRA)	Hubert van Innis(BEL)	Emile Fisseux(FRA)
Au cordon doré–33m – Men			
1900	Hubert van Innis(BEL)	Victor Thibaud(FRA)	Charles Petit(FRA)
Au chapelet–50m – Men			
1900	Eugène Mougin(FRA)	Henri Helle(FRA)	Emile Mercier(FRA)
Au chapelet–33m – Men			
1900	Hubert van Innis(BEL)	Victor Thibaud(FRA)	Charles Petit(FRA)
Sur la perche à la herse – Men			
1900	Emmanuel Foulon(FRA)	Pierre Serrurier(FRA) Emile Druart Jr(BEL)	–
Sur la perche à la pyramide – Men			
1900	Emile Grumiaux(FRA)	Auguste Serrurier(FRA)	Louis Glineaux(BEL)
Double York Round – Men			
1904	Phillip Bryant(USA)	Robert Williams(USA)	William Thompson(USA)
Double American Round			
1904	Phillip Bryant(USA)	Robert Williams(USA)	William Thompson(USA)
Team Round – Men			
1904	Potomac Archers(USA)	Cincinnati Archery Club(USA)	Boston AA(USA)
Double National Round – Women			
1904	Lida Howell(USA)	Jessie Pollack(USA)	Emma Cooke(USA)
Double Columbia Round – Women			
1904	Lida Howell(USA)	Emma Cooke(USA)	Jessie Pollack(USA)
York Round – Men			
1908	William Dod(GBR)	Reginald Brooks-King(GBR)	Henry Richardson(USA)
Continental Style – Men			
1908	Eugène Grisot(FRA)	Louis Vernet(FRA)	Gustave Cabaret(FRA)
National Round – Women			
1908	Queenie Newall(GBR)	Charlotte Dod(GBR)	Beatrice Hill-Lowe(GBR)
Fixed bird target–small birds–individual			
1920	Edmond van Moer(BEL)	Louis van der Perck(BEL)	Joseph Hermans(BEL)
Fixed bird target–small birds–team			
1920	BELGIUM	–	–
Fixed bird target–large birds–individual			
1920	Edouard Cloetens(BEL)	Louis van der Perck(BEL)	Firmin Flamand(BEL)
Fixed bird target–large birds–team			
1920	BELGIUM	–	–
Moving bird target–28m–individual			
1920	Hubert van Innis(BEL)	Léone Quentin(FRA)	–

Moving bird target–team

1920	NETHERLANDS	BELGIUM	FRANCE

Moving bird target–33m–individual

1920	Hubert van Innis(BEL)	Julien Brulé(FRA)	–

Moving bird target–33m–team

1920	BELGIUM	FRANCE	–

Moving bird target–50m–individual

1920	Julien Brulé(FRA)	Hubert van Innis(BEL)	–

Moving bird target–50m–team

1920	BELGIUM	FRANCE	–

ATHLETICS

100m – Men

	GOLD	SILVER	BRONZE
1896	Thomas Burke(USA) 12.0	Fritz Hofmann(GER) 12.2	Alajos Szokolyi(HUN) 12.6
1900	Frank Jarvis(USA) 11.0	Walter Tewksbury(USA) 11.1	Stanley Rowley(AUS) 11.2
1904	Archie Hahn(USA) 11.0	Nathaniel Cartmell(USA) 11.2	William Hogenson(USA) 11.2
1906	Archie Hahn(USA) 11.2	Fay Moulton(USA) 11.3	Nigel Barker(AUS) 11.3
1908	Reginald Walker(RSA) 10.8	James Rector(USA) 10.9	Robert Kerr(CAN) 11.0
1912	Ralph Craig(USA) 10.8	Alvah Meyer(USA) 10.9	Donald Lippincott(USA) 10.9
1920	Charles Paddock(USA) 10.8	Morris Kirksey(USA) 10.8	Harry Edward(GBR) 11.0
1924	Harold Abrahams(GBR) 10.6	Jackson Scholz(USA) 10.7	Arthur Porritt(NZL) 10.8
1928	Percy Williams(CAN) 10.8	Jack London(GBR) 10.9	Georg Lammers(GER) 10.9
1932	Eddie Tolan(USA) 10.3(10.38)	Ralph Metcalfe(USA) 10.3(10.38)	Arthur Jonath(GER) 10.4(10.50)
1936	Jesse Owens(USA) 10.3	Ralph Metcalfe(USA) 10.4	Martinus Osendarp(NED) 10.5
1948	Harrison Dillard(USA) 10.3	Norwood Ewell(USA) 10.4	Lloyd LaBeach(PAN) 10.4
1952	Lindy Remigino(USA) 10.4(10.79)	Herb McKenley(JAM) 10.4(10.80)	Emmanuel McDonald Bailey(GBR) 10.4(10.83)
1956	Bobby Joe Morrow(USA) 10.5(10.62)	Thane Baker(USA) 10.5(10.77)	Hector Hogan(AUS) 10.6(10.77)
1960	Armin Hary(GER) 10.2(10.32)	David Sime(USA) 10.2(10.35)	Peter Radford(GBR) 10.3(10.42)
1964	Bob Hayes(USA) 10.0(10.06)	Enrique Figuerola(CUB) 10.2(10.25)	Harry Jerome(CAN) 10.2(10.27)
1968	James Hines(USA) 9.9(9.95)	Lennox Miller(JAM) 10.0(10.04)	Charles Greene(USA) 10.0(10.07)
1972	Valeri Borzov(URS) 10.14	Robert Taylor(USA) 10.24	Lennox Miller(JAM) 10.33
1976	Hasely Crawford(TRI) 10.06	Don Quarrie(JAM) 10.08	Valeri Borzov(URS) 10.14
1980	Allan Wells(GBR) 10.25	Silvio Leonard(CUB) 10.25	Petar Petrov(BUL) 10.39
1984	Carl Lewis(USA) 9.99	Sam Graddy(USA) 10.19	Ben Johnson(CAN) 10.22
1988	Carl Lewis(USA) 9.92 (1)	Linford Christie(GBR) 9.97	Calvin Smith(USA) 9.99
1992	Linford Christie(GBR) 9.96	Frankie Fredericks(NAM) 10.02	Dennis Mitchell(USA) 10.04
1996	Donovan Bailey(CAN) 9.84	Frankie Fredericks(NAM) 9.89	Ato Boldon(TRI) 9.90
2000	Maurice Greene(USA) 9.87	Ato Boldon(TRI) 9.99	Obadele Thompson(BAR) 10.04
2004	Justin Gatlin(USA) 9.85	Francis Obikwelu(POR) 9.86	Maurice Greene(USA) 9.87

(1) Ben Johnson(CAN) won in 9.79 but was later disqualified

200m – Men

	GOLD	SILVER	BRONZE
1900	Walter Tewksbury(USA) 22.2	Norman Pritchard(GBR) 22.8	Stanley Rowley(AUS) 22.9
1904	Archie Hahn(USA) 21.6	Nathaniel Cartmell(USA) 21.9	William Hogenson(USA) d.n.a.
1908	Robert Kerr(CAN) 22.6	Robert Cloughen(USA) 22.6	Nathaniel Cartmell(USA) 22.7
1912	Ralph Craig(USA) 21.7	Donald Lippincott(USA) 22.1	Willie Applegarth(GBR) 22.0
1920	Allen Woodring(USA) 22.0	Charles Paddock(USA) 22.1	Harry Edward(GBR) 22.2
1924	Jackson Scholz(USA) 21.6	Charles Paddock(USA) 21.7	Eric Liddell(GBR) 21.9
1928	Percy Williams(CAN) 21.8	Walter Rangeley(GBR) 21.9	Helmut Kornig(GER) 21.9
1932	Eddie Tolan(USA) 21.2(21.12)	George Simpson(USA) 21.4	Ralph Metcalfe(USA) 21.5
1936	Jesse Owens(USA) 20.7	Mack Robinson(USA) 21.1	Martinus Osendarp(NED) 21.3
1948	Mel Patton(USA) 21.1	Norwood Ewell(USA) 21.1	Lloyd LaBeach(PAN) 21.2
1952	Andrew Stanfield(USA) 20.7(20.81)	Thane Baker(USA) 20.8(20.97)	James Gathers(USA) 20.8(21.08)
1956	Bobby Joe Morrow(USA) 20.6(20.75)	Andrew Stanfield(USA) 20.7(20.97)	Thane Baker(USA) 20.9(21.05)
1960	Livio Berruti(ITA) 20.5(20.62)	Lester Carney(USA) 20.6(20.69)	Abdoulaye Seye(FRA) 20.7(20.83)
1964	Henry Carr(USA) 20.3(20.36)	Paul Drayton(USA) 20.5(20.58)	Edwin Roberts(TRI) 20.6(20.63)
1968	Tommie Smith(USA) 19.8(19.83)	Peter Norman(AUS) 20.0(20.06)	John Carlos(USA) 20.0(20.10)
1972	Valeri Borzov(URS) 20.00	Larry Black(USA) 20.19	Pietro Mennea(ITA) 20.30
1976	Don Quarrie(JAM) 20.23	Millard Hampton(USA) 20.29	Dwayne Evans(USA) 20.43
1980	Pietro Mennea(ITA) 20.19	Allan Wells(GBR) 20.21	Don Quarrie(JAM) 20.29
1984	Carl Lewis(USA) 19.80	Kirk Baptiste(USA) 19.96	Thomas Jefferson(USA) 20.26
1988	Joe DeLoach(USA) 19.75	Carl Lewis(USA) 1979	Robson da Silva(BRA) 20.04
1992	Mike Marsh(USA) 20.01	Frankie Fredericks(NAM) 20.13	Michael Bates(USA) 20.38
1996	Michael Johnson(USA) 19.32	Frankie Fredericks(NAM) 19.68	Ato Boldon(TRI) 19.80

2000	Konstantinos Kenteris(GRE) 20.09		Darren Campbell(GBR) 20.14		Ato Boldon(TRI) 20.20	
2004	Shawn Crawford(USA) 19.79		Bernard Williams(USA) 20.01		Justin Gatlin(USA) 20.03	

1896, 1906 Event not held

400m – Men

	GOLD	SILVER	BRONZE
1896	Thomas Burke(USA) 54.2	Herbert Jamison(USA) 55.2	Fritz Hofmann(GER) 55.6
1900	Maxey Long(USA) 49.4	William HJolland(USA) 49.6	Ernst Schultz(DEN) 15m
1904	Harry Hillman(USA) 49.2	Frank Waller(USA) 49.9	Herman Groman(USA) 50.0
1906	Paul Pilgrim(USA) 53.2	Wyndham Halswelle(GBR) 53.8	Nigel Barker(AUS) 54.1
1908	Wyndham Halswelle(GBR) 50.0 (1)		
1912	Charles Reidpath(USA) 48.2	Hanns Braun(GER) 48.3	Edward Lingberg(USA 48.4
1920	Bevil Rudd(RSA) 49.6	Guy Butler(GBR) 49.9	Nils Engdahl(SWE) 50.0
1924	Eric Liddell(GBR) 47.6	Horatio Fitch(USA) 48.4	Guy Butler(GBR) 48.6
1928	Ray Barbuti(USA) 47.8	James Ball(CAN) 48.0	Joachim Büchner(GER) 48.2
1932	William Carr(USA) 46.2(46.28)	Ben Eastman(USA) 46.4(46.50)	Alexander Wilson(CAN) 47.4
1936	Archie Williams(USA) 46.5(46.66)	Godfrey Brown(GBR) 46.7(46.68)	James LuValle(USA) 46.8(46.84)
1948	Arthur Wint(JAM) 46.2	Herb McKenley(JAM) 46.4	Mal Whitfield(USA) 46.6
1952	George Rhoden(JAM) 45.9(46.09)	Herb McKenley(JAM) 45.9(46.20)	Ollie Matson(USA) 46.8(46.94)
1956	Charles Jenkins(USA) 46.7(46.85)	Karl-Friedrich Haas(GER) 46.8(47.12)	Voitto Hellsten(FIN) 47.0(47.15)
			Ardalion Ignatyev(URS) 47.0(47.15)
1960	Otis Davis(USA) 44.9(45.07)	Carl Kaufmann(GER) 44.9(45.08)	Mal Spence(RSA) 45.5(45.60)
1964	Mike Larrabee(USA) 45.1(45.15)	Wendell Mottley(TRI) 45.2(45.24)	Andrzej Badenski(POL) 45.6(45.64)
1968	Lee Evans(USA) 43.8(43.86)	Lareence James(USA) 43.9(43.97)	Ron Freeman(USA) 44.4(44.41)
1972	Vince Matthews(USA) 44.66	Wayne Collett(USA) 44.80	Julius Sang(KEN) 44.92
1976	Alberto Juantorena(CUB) 44.26	Fred Newhouse(USA) 44.40	Herman Frazier(USA) 44.95
1980	Viktor Markin(URS) 44.60	Rick Mitchell(AUS) 44.84	Frank Schaffer(GDR) 44.87
1984	Alonzo Babers(USA) 44.27	Gabriel Tiacoh(CIV) 44.54	Antonio McKay(USA) 44.71
1988	Steve Lewis(USA) 43.87	Butch Reynolds(USA) 43.93	Danny Everett(USA) 44.09
1992	Quincy Watts(USA) 43.50	Steve Lewis(USA) 44.21	Samson Kitur(KEN) 44.24
1996	Michael Johnson(USA) 43.49	Roger Black(GBR) 44.41	Davis Kamoga(UGA) 44.53
2000	Michael Johnson(USA) 43.84	Alvin Harrison(USA) 44.40	Greg Haughton(JAM) 44.70
2004	Jeremy Wariner(USA) 44.00	Otis Harris(USA) 44.16	Derrick Brew(USA) 44.42

(1) Halswelle 'walked over' for the title

800m – Men

	GOLD	SILVER	BRONZE
1896	Edwin Flack(AUS) 2:11.0	Nándor Dáni(HUN) 2:11.8	Dimitrios Golemis(GRE) 2:28.0
1900	Alfred Tysoe(GBR) 2:01.2	John Cregan(USA) 2:03.0	David Hall(USA) d.n.a.
1904	James Lightbody(USA) 1:56.0	Howard Valentine(USA) 1:56.3	Emil Breitkreutz(USA) 1:56.4
1906	Paul Pilgrim(USA) 2:01.5	James Lightbody(USA) 2:01.6	Wyndham Halswelle(GBR) 2:03.0
1908	Mel Sheppard(USA) 1:52.8	Emilio Lunghi(ITA) 1:54.2	Hanns Braun(GER) 1:55.2
1912	James Meredith(USA) 1:51.9	Mel Sheppard(USA) 1:52.0	Ira Davenport(USA) 1:52.0
1920	Albert Hill(GBR) 1:53.4	Earl Eby(USA) 1:53.6	Bevil Rudd(RSA) 1:54.0
1924	Douglas Lowe(GBR) 1:52.4	Paul Martin(SUI) 1:52.6	Schuyler Enck(USA) 1:53.0
1928	Douglas Lowe(GBR) 1:51.8	Erik Bylehn(SWE) 1:52.8	Hermann Engelhardt(GER) 1:53.2
1932	Thomas Hampson(GBR) 1:49.7	Alexander Wilson(CAN) 1:49.9	Phil Edwards(CAN) 1:51.5
1936	John Woodruff(USA) 1:52.9	Mario Lanzi(ITA) 1:53.3	PhilEdwards(CAN) 1:53.6
1948	Mal Whitfield(USA) 1:49.2	Arthur Wint(JAM) 1:49.5	Marcel Hansenne(FRA) 1:49.8
1952	Mal Whitfield(USA) 1:49.2	Arthur Wint(JAM) 1:49.4	Heinz Ulzheimer(GER) 1:49.7
1956	Tom Courtney(USA) 1:47.7	Derek Johnson(GBR) 1:47.8	Audun Boysen(NOR) 1:48.1
1960	Peter Snell(NZL) 1:46.3	Roger Moens(BEL) 1:46.5	George Kerr(BWI) 1:47.1 (1)
1964	Peter Snell(NZL) 1:45.1	Bill Crothers(CAN) 1:45.6	Wilson Kiprugut(KEN) 1:45.9
1968	Ralph Doubell(AUS) 1:44.3	Wilson Kiprugut(KEN) 1:44.5	Tom Farrell(USA) 1:45.4
1972	Dave Wottle(USA) 1:45.9	Yevgeni Arzhanov(URS) 1:45.9	Mike Boit(KEN) 1:46.0
1976	Alberto Juantorena(CUB) 1:43.5	Ivo Van Damme(BEL) 1:43.9	Richard Wohlhuter(USA) 1:44.1
1980	Steve Ovett(GBR) 1:45.4	Sebastian Coe(GBR) 1:45.9	Nikolai Kirov(URS) 1:46.0
1984	Joachim Cruz(BRA) 1:43.00	Sebastian Coe(GBR) 1:43.64	Earl Jones(USA) 1:43.83
1988	Paul Ereng(KEN) 1:43.45	Joachim Cruz(BRA) 1:43.90	Saïd Aouita(MAR) 1:44.06
1992	William Tanui(KEN) 1:43.66	Nixon Kiprotich(KEN) 1:43.70	Johnny Gray(USA) 1:43.97
1996	Vebjörn Rodal(NOR) 1:42.58	Hezekiel Sepeng(RSA) 1:42.74	Fred Onyancha(KEN) 1:42.79
2000	Nils Schumann(GER) 1:45.08	Wilson Kipketer(DEN) 1:45.14	Aissa Said-Guerni(ALG) 1:45.16
2004	Yuriy Borzakovskiy(RUS) 1:44.45	Mbulaeni Mulaudzi(RSA) 1:44.61	Wilson Kipketer(DEN) 1:44.65

(1) Kerr was member of a combined Antilles team

1,500m – Men

	GOLD	SILVER	BRONZE
1896	Edwin Flack(AUS) 4:33.2	Arthur Blake(USA) 4:34.0	Albin Lermusiaux(FRA) 4:36.0
1900	Charles Bennett(GBR) 4:06.2	Henri Deloge(FRA) 4:06.6	John Bray(USA) 4:07.2
1904	James Lightbody(USA) 4:05.4	William Verner(USA) 4:06.8	Lacey Hearn(USA) d.n.a.
1906	James Lightbody(USA) 4:12.0	John McGough(GBR) 4:12.6	Kristian Hellström(SWE) 4:13.4
1908	Mel Sheppard(USA) 4:03.4	Harold Wilson(GBR) 4:03.6	Norman Hallows(GBR) 4:04.0

1912	Arnold Strode-Jackson(GBR) 3:56.8	Abel Kiviat(USA) 3:56.9	Norman Taber(USA) 3:56.9
1920	Albert Hill(GBR) 4:01.8	Philip Baker(GBR) 4:02.4	Lawrence Shields(USA) 4:03.1
1924	Paavo Nurmi(FIN) 3:53.6	Willy Schärer(SUI) 3:55.0	Henry Stallard(GBR) 3:55.6
1928	Harri Larva(FIN) 3:53.2	Jules Ladoumègue(FRA) 3:53.8	Eino Purje(FIN) 3:56.4
1932	Luigi Beccali(ITA) 3:51.2	John Cornes(GBR) 3:52.6	Phil Edwards(CAN) 3:52.8
1936	Jack Lovelock(NZL) 3:47.8	Glenn Cunningham(USA) 3:48.4	Luigi Beccali(ITA) 3:49.2
1948	Henry Eriksson(SWE) 3:49.8	Lennart Strand(SWE) 3:50.4	Willem Slijkhuis(NED) 3:50.4
1952	Josef Barthel(LUX) 3:45.1	Bob McMillen(USA) 3:45.2	Werner Lueg(GER) 3:45.4
1956	Ron Delany(IRL) 3:41.2	Klaus Richtzenhain(GER) 3:42.0	John Landy(AUS) 3:42.0
1960	Herb Elliott(AUS) 3:35.6	Michel Jazy(FRA) 3:38.4	István Rószavölgyi(HUN) 3:39.2
1964	Peter Snell(NZL) 3:38.1	Josef Odlozil(TCH) 3:39.6	John Davies(NZL) 3:39.6
1968	Kipchoge Keino(KEN) 3:34.9	Jim Ryun(USA) 3:37.8	Bodo Tümmler(FRG) 3:39.0
1972	Pekka Vasala(FIN) 3:36.3	Kipchoge Keino(KEN) 3:36.8	Rod Dixon(NZL) 3:37.5
1976	John Walker(NZL) 3:39.2	Ivo Van Damme(BEL) 3:39.3	Paul-Heinz Wellmann(FRG) 3:39.3
1980	Sebastian Coe(GBR) 3:38.4	Jürgen Straub(GDR) 3:38.8	Steve Ovett(GBR) 3:39.0
1984	Sebastian Coe(GBR) 3:32.53	Steve Cram(GBR) 3:33.40	José Abascal(ESP) 3:34.30
1988	Peter Rono(KEN) 3:35.96	Peter Elliott(GBR) 3:36.15	Jens-Peter Herold(GDR) 3:36.21
1992	Fermin Cacho(ESP) 3:40.12	Rachid El Basir(MAR) 3:40.62	Mohamed Suleiman(QAT) 3:40.69
1996	Noureddine Morceli(ALG) 3:35.78	Fermin Cacho(ESP) 3:36.40	Stephen Kipkorir(KEN) 3:36.72
2000	Noah Ngeny(KEN) 3:32.07	Hicham El Guerrouj(MAR) 3:32.32	Bernard Lagat(KEN) 3:32.44
2004	Hicham El Guerrouj(MAR) 3:34.18	Bernard Lagat(KEN) 3:34.30	Rui Silva(POR) 3:34.68

5,000m – Men

	GOLD	SILVER	BRONZE
1912	Hannes Kolehmainen(FIN) 14:36.6	Jean Bouin(FRA) 14:36.7	George Hutson(GBR) 15:07.6
1920	Joseph Guillemot(FRA) 14:55.6	Paavo Nurmi(FIN) 15:00.0	Erik Backman(SWE) 15:13.0
1924	Paavo Nurmi(FIN) 14:31.2	Ville Ritola(FIN) 14:31.4	Edvin Wide(SWE) 15:01.8
1928	Ville Ritola(FIN) 14:38.0	Paavo Nurmi(FIN) 14:40.0	Edvin Wide(SWE) 14:41.2
1932	Lauri Lehtinen(FIN) 14:30.0	Ralph Hill(USA) 14:30.0	Lauri Virtanen(FIN) 14:44.0
1936	Gunnar Höckert(FIN) 14:22.2	Lauri Lehtinen(FIN) 14:25.8	Henry Jonsson(SWE) 14:29.0
1948	Gaston Rieff(BEL) 14:17.6	Emil Zátopek(TCH) 14:17.8	Willem Slijkhuis(NED) 14:26.8
1952	Emil Zátopek(TCH) 14:06.6	Alain Mimoun(FRA) 14:07.4	Herbert Schade(GER) 14:08.6
1956	Vladimir Kuts(URS) 13:39.6	Gordon Pirie(GBR) 13:50.6	Derek Ibbotson(GBR) 13:54.4
1960	Murray Halberg(NZL) 13:43.4	Hans Grodotzki(GDR) 13:44.6	Kazimierz Zimny(POL) 13:44.8
1964	Bob Schul(USA) 13:48.8	Harald Norpoth(GER) 13:49.6	Bill Dellinger(USA) 13:49.8
1968	Mohamed Gammoudi(TUN) 14:05.0	Kipchoge Keino(KEN) 14:05.2	Naftali Temu(KEN) 14:06.4
1972	Lasse Virén(FIN) 13:26.4	Mohamed Gammoudi(TUN) 13:27.4	Ian Stewart(GBR) 13:27.6
1976	Lasse Virén(FIN) 13:24.8	Dick Quax(NZL) 13:25.2	Klaus-Peter Hildenbrand(FRG) 13:35.4
1980	Miruts Yifter(ETH) 13:21.0	Suleiman Nyambui(TAN) 13:21.6	Kaarlo Maaninka(FIN) 13:22.0
1984	Saïd Aouita(MAR) 13:05.59	Markus Ryffel(SUI) 13:07.54	Antonio Leitao(POR) 13:09.20
1988	John Ngugi(KEN) 13:11.70	Dieter Baumann(FRG) 13:15.52	Hansjörg Kunze(GDR) 13:15.73
1992	Dieter Baumann(GER) 13:12.52	Paul Bitok(KEN) 13:12.71	Fita Bayissa(ETH) 13:13.03
1996	Venuste Niyongabo(BDI) 13:07.96	Paul Bitok(KEN) 13:08.16	Khalid Boulami(MAR) 13:08.37
2000	Million Wolde(ETH) 13:35.49	Ali Said-Sief(ALG) 13:36.20	Brahim Lahlafi(MAR) 13:36.47
2004	Hicham El Guerrouj(MAR) 13:14.39	Kenenisa Bekele(ETH) 13:14.59	Eliud Kipchoge(KEN) 13:15.10

1896–1908 Event not held

10,000m – Men

	GOLD	SILVER	BRONZE
1906(1)	Henry Hawtrey(GBR) 26:11.8	John Svanberg(SWE) 26:19.4	Edward Dahl(SWE) 26:26.2
1908(1)	Emil Voigt(GBR) 25:11.2	Edward Owen(GBR) 25:24.0	John Svanberg(SWE) 25:37.2
1912	Hannes Kolehmainen(FIN) 31:20.8	Louis Tewanima(USA) 32:06.6	Albin Stenroos(FIN) 32:21.8
1920	Paavo Nurmi(FIN) 31:45.8	Joseph Guillemot(FRA) 31:47.2	James Wilson(GBR) 31:50.8
1924	Ville Ritola(FIN) 30:23.2	Edvin Wide(SWE) 30:55.2	Eero Berg(FIN) 31:43.0
1928	Paavo Nurmi(FIN) 30:18.8	Ville Ritola(FIN) 30:19.4	Edvin Wide(SWE) 31:00.8
1932	Janusz Kusocinski(POL) 30:11.4	Volmari Iso-Hollo(FIN) 30:12.6	Lauri Virtannen(FIN) 30:35.0
1936	Ilmari Salminen(FIN) 30:15.4	Arvo Askola(FIN) 30:15.6	Volmari Iso-Hollo(FIN) 30:20.2
1948	Emil Zátopek(TCH) 29:59.6	Alain Mimoun(FRA) 30:47.4	Bertil Albertsson(SWE) 30:53.6
1952	Emil Zátopek(TCH) 29:17.0	Alain Mimoun(FRA) 29:32.8	Alexander Anufriyev(URS) 29:48.2
1956	Vladimir Kuts(URS) 28:45.6	József Kovács(HUN) 28:52.4	Allan Lawrence(AUS) 28:53.6
1960	Pyotr Bolotnikov(URS) 28:32.2	Hans Grodotzki(GDR) 28:37.0	David Power(AUS) 28:38.2
1964	Billy Mills(USA) 28:24.4	Mohamed Gammoudi(TUN) 28:24.8	Ron Clarke(AUS) 28:25.8
1968	Naftali Temu(KEN) 29:27.4	Mamo Wolde(ETH) 29:28.0	Mohamed Gammoudi(TUN) 29:34.2
1972	Lasse Virén(FIN) 27:38.4	Emiel Puttemans(BEL) 27:39.6	Miruts Yifter(ETH) 27:41.0
1976	Lasse Virén(FIN) 27:44.4	Carlos Lopes(POR) 27:45.2	Brendan Foster(GBR) 27:54.9
1980	Miruts Yifter(ETH) 27:42.7	Kaarlo Maaninka(FIN) 27:44.3	Mohammed Kedir(ETH) 27:44.7
1984	Alberto Cova(ITA) 27:47.54	Mike McLeod(GBR) 28:06.22	Mike Musyoki(KEN) 28:06.46
1988	Brahim Boutayeb(MAR) 27:21.46	Salvatore Antibo(ITA) 27:23.55	Kipkemboi Kimeli(KEN) 27:25.16
1992	Khalid Skah(MAR) 27:46.70	Richard Chelimo(KEN) 27:47.72	Adiis Abebe(ETH) 28:00.07
1996	Haile Gebrselassie(ETH) 27:07.34	Paul Tergat(KEN) 27:08.17	Salah Hissou(MAR) 27:24.67
2000	Haile Gebrselassie(ETH) 27:18.20	Paul Tergat(KEN) 27:18.29	Assefa Mezegebu(ETH) 27:19.75
2004	Kenenisa Bekele(ETH) 27:05.10s	Sileshi Sihine(ETH) 27:09.39	Zersenay Tadesse(ERI) 27:22.57

1896–1904 Event not held

(1) Distance was 5 miles (8046m)

Marathon – Men

(Marathon standardised from 1924 at the 1908 distance of 26 miles, 385 yards (42,195m). In 1896 and 1904 – 40,000m, 1900 – 40,260m, 1906 – 41,860m, 1912 – 40,200m, 1920 – 42,750m)

	GOLD	SILVER	BRONZE
1896	Spyridon Louis(GRE) 2h 58:50	Charilaos Vasilakos(GRE) 3h 06:03	Gyula Kellner(HUN) 3h 09:35
1900	Michel Theato(FRA) 2h 59:45 (1)	Emile Champion(FRA) 3h 04:17	Ernst Fast(SWE) 3h 36:14
1904	Thomas Hicks(USA) 3h 28:35	Albert Coray(FRA) 3h 34:52 (2)	Arthur Newton(USA) 3h 47:33
1906	William Sherring(CAN) 2h 51:23.6	John Svanberg(SWE) 2h 58:20.8	William Frank(USA) 3h 00:46.8
1908	John Hayes(USA) 2h 55:18.4 (3)	Charles Hefferon(RSA) 2:56:06.0	Joseph Forshaw(USA) 2h 57:10.4
1912	Kenneth McArthur(RSA) 2h 36:54.8	Christian Gitsham(RSA) 2h 37:52.0	Gaston Strobino(USA) 2h 38:42.4
1920	Hannes Kolehmainen(FIN) 2h 32:35.8	Jüri Lossman(EST) 2h 32:48.6	Valerio Arri(ITA) 2h 36:32.8
1924	Albin Stenroos(FIN) 2h 41:22.6	Romeo Bertini(ITA) 2h 47:19.6	Clarence DeMar(USA) 2h 48:14.0
1928	Mohamed El Ouafi(FRA) 2h 32:57	Miguel Plaza Reyes(CHI) 2h 33:23	Martti Marttelin(FIN) 2h 35:02
1932	Juan Carlos Zabala(ARG) 2h 31:36	Sam Ferris(GBR) 2h 31:55	Armas Toivonen(FIN) 2h 32:12
1936	Kee-Chung Sohn (JPN) 2h 29:19.2 (4)	Ernest Harper(GBR) 2h 31:23.2	Seong-Yong Nam (JPN) 2h 31:42:0 (4)
1948	Delfo Cabrera(ARG) 3h 34:51.6	Tom Richards(GBR) 2h 35:07.6	Etienne Gailly(BEL) 2h 35:33.6
1952	Emil Zátopek(TCH) 2h 23:03.2	Reinaldo Gorno(ARG) 2h 25:35.0	Gustav Jansson(SWE) 2h 26:07.0
1956	Alain Mimoun(FRA) 2h 25:00	Franjo Mihalic(YUG) 2h 26:32	Veikko Karvonen(FIN) 2h 27:47
1960	Abebe Bikila(ETH) 2h 15:16.2	Rhadi Ben Abdesselem(MAR) 2h 15:41.6	Barry Magee(NZL) 2h 17:18.2
1964	Abebe Bikila(ETH) 2h 12:11.2	Basil Heatley(GBR) 2h 16:19.2	Kokichi Tsuburaya(JPN) 2h 16:22.8
1968	Mamo Wolde(ETH) 2h 20:26.4	Kenji Kimihara(JPN) 2h 23:31.0	Michael Ryan(NZL) 2h 23:45.0
1972	Frank Shorter(USA) 2h 12:19.8	Karel Lismont(BEL) 2h 14:31.8	Mamo Wolde(ETH) 2h 15:08.4
1976	Waldemar Cierpinski(GDR) 2h 09:55.0	Frank Shorter(USA) 2h 10:45.8	Karel Lismont(BEL) 2h 11:12.6
1980	Waldemar Cierpinski(GDR) 2h 11:03	Gerard Nijboer(NED) 2h 11:20	Satymkul Dzhumanazarov(URS) 2h 11:35
1984	Carlos Lopes(POR) 2h 09:21	John Treacy(IRL) 2h 09:56	Charles Spedding(GBR) 2h 09:58
1988	Gelindo Bordin(ITA) 2h 10:32	Douglas Wakiihuri(KEN) 2h 10:47	Ahmed Saleh(DJI) 2h 10:59
1992	Young-Cho Hwang(KOR) 2h 13:23	Koichi Morishita(JPN) 2h 13:45	Stephan Freigang(GER) 2h 14:00
1996	Josiah Thugwane(RSA) 2h 12:36	Bong-Ju Lee(KOR) 2h 12:39	Eric Wainaina(KEN) 2h 12:44
2000	Gezahegne Abera(ETH) 2h 10:11	Eric Wainaina(KEN) 2h 10:31	Tesfaye Tola(ETH) 2h 11:10
2004	Stefano Baldini(ITA) 2h:10:55	Mebrahtom Keflezighi(USA)2h:11:29	Vanderlei de Lima(BRA) 2h:12:11

(1) Born in Luxembourg

(2) US resident

(3) Dorando Pietri(ITA) was first but was disqualified due to assistance

(4) In 1936 they were called Kitei Son and Shoryu Nan respectively – actually both were Korean

3,000m Steeplechase – Men

(Prior to 1920 distances were: 1900 – 2,500m and 4,000m, 1904 – 2,590m, 1908 – 3,200m)

	GOLD	SILVER	BRONZE
1900	George Orton(CAN) 7:34.4	Sidney Robinson(GBR) 7:38.0	Jacques Chastanié(FRA) 7:41.0
1900	John Rimmer(GBR) 12:58.4	Charles Bennett(GBR) 12:58.6	Sidney Robinson(GBR) 12:58.8
1904	James Lightbody(USA) 7:39.6	John Daly(GBR) 7:40.6	Arthur Newton(USA) 25m
1908	Arthur Russell(GBR) 10:47.8	Archie Robertson(GBR) 10:48.4	John Eisele(USA) 11:00.8
1920	Percy Hodge(GBR) 10:00.4	Patrick Flynn(USA) 100m	Ernesto Ambrosini(ITA) 50m
1924	Ville Ritola(FIN) 9:33.6	Elias Katz(FIN) 9:44.0	Paul Bontemps(FRA) 9:45.2
1928	Toivo Loukola(FIN) 9:21.8	Paavo Nurmi(FIN) 9:31.2	Ove Andersen(FIN) 9:35.6
1932(1)	Volmari Iso-Hollo(FIN) 10:33.4	Tom Evenson(GBR) 10:46.0	Joseph McCluskey(USA) 10:46.2
1936	Volmari Iso-Hollo(FIN) 9:03.8	Kaarlo Tuominen(FIN) 9:06.8	Alfred Dompert(GER) 9:07.2
1948	Tore Sjöstrand(SWE) 9:04.6	Erik Elmsäter(SWE) 9:08.2	Göte Hagström(SWE) 9:11.8
1952	Horace Ashenfelter(USA) 8:45.4	Vladimir Kazantsev(URS) 8:51.6	John Disley(GBR) 8:51.8
1956	Chris Brasher(GBR) 8:41.2	Sándor Rozsnói(HUN) 8:43.6	Ernst Larsen(NOR) 8:44.0
1960	Zdzslaw Krzyszkowiak(POL) 8:34.2	Nikolai Sokolov(URS) 8:36.4	Semyon Rzhischin(URS) 8:42.2
1964	Gaston Roelants(BEL) 8:30.8	Maurice Herriott(GBR) 8:32.4	Ivan Belyayev(URS) 8:33.8
1968	Amos Biwott(KEN) 8:51.0	Benjamin Kogo(KEN) 8:51.6	George Young(USA) 8:51.8
1972	Kipchoge Keino(KEN) 8:23.6	Benjamin Jipcho(KEN) 8:24.6	Tapio Kantanen(FIN) 8:24.8
1976	Anders Gärderud(SWE) 8:08.0	Bronislaw Malinowski(POL) 8:09.1	Frank Baumgartl(GDR) 8:10.4
1980	Bronislaw Malinowski(POL) 8:09.7	Filbert Bayi(TAN) 8:12.5	Eshetu Tura(ETH) 8:13.6
1984	Julius Korir(KEN) 8:11.80	Joseph Mahmoud(FRA) 8:13.31	Brian Diemer(USA) 8:14.06
1988	Julius Kariuki(KEN) 8:05.51	Peter Koech(KEN) 8:06.79	Mark Rowland(GBR) 8:07.96
1992	Matthew Birir(KEN) 8:08.84	Patrick Sang(KEN) 8:09.55	William Mutwol(KEN) 8:10.74
1996	Joseph Keter(KEN) 8:07.12	Moses Kiptanui(KEN) 8:08.33	Alessandro Lambruschini(ITA) 8:11.28
2000	Reuben Kosgei(KEN) 8:21.43	Wilson Boit Kipketer(KEN) 8:21.77	Ali Ezzine(MAR) 8:22.15
2004	Ezekiel Kemboi(KEN) 8:05.81	Brimin Kipruto (KEN) 8:06.11	Paul Koech(KEN) 8:06.64

1896,1906,1912 Event not held

(1) Finalists ran 3,460m due to error. Iso-Hollo clocked 9:14.6 in his heat

110m Hurdles – Men

	GOLD	SILVER	BRONZE
1896	Thomas Curtis(USA) 17.6	Grantley Goulding(GBR) 18.0	– (1)
1900	Alvin Kraenzlein(USA) 15.4	John McLean(USA) 15.5	Fred Moloney(USA) 15.6
1904	Frederick Schule(USA) 16.0	Thadeus Shideler(USA) 16.3	Lesley Ashburner(USA) 16.4

1906	Robert Leavitt(USA) 16.2	Alfred Healey(GBR) 16.2	Vincent Duncker(GER) 16.3 (2)
1908	Forrest Smithson(USA) 15.0	John Garrels(USA) 15.7	Arthur Shaw(USA) 15.8
1912	Frederick Kelly(USA) 15.1	James Wendell(USA) 15.2	Martin Hawkins(USA) 15.3
1920	Earl Thomson(CAN) 14.8	Harold Barron(USA) 15.1	Frederick Murray(USA) 15.2
1924	Daniel Kinsey(USA) 15.0	Sydney Atkinson(RSA) 15.0	Sten Pettersson(SWE) 15.4
1928	Sydney Atkinson(RSA) 14.8	Stephen Anderson(USA)	John Collier(USA) 15.0
1932	George Saling(USA) 14.6(14.57)	Percy Beard(USA) 14.7	Don Finlay(GBR) 14.8
1936	Forrest Towns(USA) 14.2	Don Finlay(GBR) 14.4	Fred Pollard(USA) 14.4
1948	William Porter(USA) 13.9	Clyde Scott(USA) 14.1	Craig Dixon(USA) 14.1
1952	Harrison Dillard(USA) 13.7(13.91)	Jack Davis(USA) 13.7(14.00)	Art Barnard(USA) 14.1(14.40)
1956	Lee Calhoun(USA) 13.5(13.70)	Jack Davis(USA) 13.5(13.73)	Joel Shankle(USA) 14.1(14.25)
1960	Lee Calhoun(USA) 13.8(13.98)	Willie May(USA) 13.8(13.99)	Hayes Jones(USA) 14.0(14.17)
1964	Hayes Jones(USA) 13.6(13.67)	Blaine Lindgren(USA) 13.7(13.74)	Anatoli Mikhailov(URS) 13.7(13.78)
1968	Willie Davenport(USA) 13.3(13.33)	Ervin Hall(USA) 13.4(13.42)	Eddy Ottoz(ITA) 13.4(13.46)
1972	Rod Milburn(USA) 13.24	Guy Drut(FRA) 13.34	Tom Hill(USA) 13.48
1976	Guy Drut(FRA) 13.30	Alejandro Casanas(CUB) 13.33	Willie Davenport(USA) 13.38
1980	Thomas Munkelt(GDR) 13.39	Alejandro Casanas(CUB) 13.40	Alexander Puchkov(URS) 13.44
1984	Roger Kingdom(USA) 13.20	Greg Foster(USA) 13.23	Arto Bryggare(FIN) 13.40
1988	Roger Kingdom(USA) 12.98	Colin Jackson(GBR) 13.28	Tonie Campbell(USA) 13.38
1992	Mark McKoy(CAN) 13.12	Tony Dees(USA) 13.24	Jack Pierce(USA) 13.26
1996	Allen Johnson(USA) 12.95	Mark Crear(USA) 13.09	Florian Schwarthoff(GER) 13.17
2000	Anier Garcia(CUB) 13.00	Terrence Trammell(USA) 13.16	Mark Crear(USA) 13.22
2004	Liu Xiang(CHN) 12.91	Terrence Trammell(USA) 13.18	Anier Garcia(CUB) 13.20

(1) Only two finalists
(2) Duncker is often, incorrectly, shown as South African

400m Hurdles – Men

	GOLD	SILVER	BRONZE
1900	Walter Tewksbury(USA) 57.6	Henri Tauzin(FRA) 58.3	George Orton(CAN) d.n.a.
1904(1)	Harry Hillman(USA) 53.0	Frank Waller(USA) 53.2	George Poage(USA) d.n.a.
1908	Charles Bacon(USA) 55.0	Harry Hillman(USA) 55.3	Leonard Tremeer(GBR) 57.0
1920	Frank Loomis(USA) 54.0	John Norton(USA) 54.3	August Desch(USA) 54.5
1924	Morgan Taylor(USA) 52.6	Erik Vilén(FIN) 53.8	Ivan Riley(USA) 54.2
1928	Lord Burghley(GBR) 53.4	Frank Cuhel(USA) 53.6	Morgan Taylor(USA) 53.6
1932	Bob Tisdall(IRL) 51.7(51.67)	Glenn Hardin(USA) 51.9(51.85)	Morgan Taylor(USA) 52.0(51.96)
1936	Glenn Hardin(USA) 52.4	John Loaring(CAN) 52.7	Miguel White(PHI) 52.8
1948	Roy Cochran(USA) 51.1	Duncan White(SRI) 51.8	Rune Larsson(SWE) 52.2
1952	Charlie Moore(USA) 50.8(51.06)	Yuri Liyuyev(URS) 51.3(51.51)	John Holland(NZL) 52.2(52.26)
1956	Glenn Davis(USA) 50.1(50.29)	Eddie Southern(USA) 50.8(50.94)	Josh Culbreath(USA) 51.6(51.74)
1960	Glenn Davis(USA) 49.3(49.51)	Cliff Cushman(USA) 49.6(49.77)	Dick Howard(USA) 49.7(49.90)
1964	Rex Cawley(USA) 49.6	John Cooper(GBR) 50.1	Salvatore Morale(ITA) 50.1
1968	David Hemery(GBR) 48.1(48.12)	Gerhard Hennige(FRG) 49.0(49.02)	John Sherwood(GBR) 49.0(49.03)
1972	John Akii-Bua(UGA) 47.82	Ralph Mann(USA) 48.51	David Hemery(GBR) 48.52
1976	Edwin Moses(USA) 47.64	Mike Shine(USA) 48.69	Yevgeni Gavrilenko(URS) 49.45
1980	Volker Beck(GDR) 48.70	Vasili Arkhipenko(URS) 48.86	Gary Oakes(GBR) 49.11
1984	Edwin Moses(USA) 47.75	Danny Harris(USA) 48.13	Harald Schmid(FRG) 48.19
1988	Andre Phillips(USA) 47.19	Amadou Dia Ba(SEN) 47.23	Edwin Moses(USA) 47.56
1992	Kevin Young(USA) 46.78	Winthrop Graham(JAM) 47.66	Kriss Akabusi(GBR) 47.82
1996	Derrick Adkins(USA) 47.54	Samuel Matete(ZAM) 47.78	Calvin Davis(USA) 47.96
2000	Angelo Taylor(USA) 47.50	Hadi Al-Somaily(KSA) 47.53	Llewellyn Herbert(RSA) 47.81
2004	Felix Sanchez(DOM) 47.63s	Danny McFarlane(JAM) 48.11	Naman Keita(FRA) 48.26

1896,1906,1912 Event not held
(1) Height of hurdles only 76.2cm (2 ft 6 in.)

4 x 100m Relay – Men

	GOLD	SILVER	BRONZE
1912	GREAT BRITAIN 42.4	SWEDEN 42.6	– (1)
1920	UNITED STATES 42.2	FRANCE 42.6	SWEDEN 42.9
1924	UNITED STATES 41.0	GREAT BRITAIN 41.2	NETHERLANDS 41.8
1928	UNITED STATES 41.0	GERMANY 41.2	GREAT BRITAIN 41.8
1932	UNITED STATES 40.0(40.10)	GERMANY 40.9	ITALY 41.2
1936	UNITED STATES 39.8	ITALY 41.1	GERMANY 41.2
1948	UNITED STATES 40.6	GREAT BRITAIN 41.3	ITALY 41.5
1952	UNITED STATES 40.1(40.26)	SOVIET UNION 40.3(40.58)	HUNGARY 40.5(40.83)
1956	UNITED STATES 39.5(39.60)	SOVIET UNION 39.8(39.92)	GERMANY 40.3(40.34)
1960	GERMANY 39.5(39.66) (2)	SOVIET UNION 40.1(40.24)	GREAT BRITAIN 40.2(40.32)
1964	UNITED STATES 39.0(39.06)	POLAND 39.3(39.36)	FRANCE 39.3(39.36)
1968	UNITED STATES 38.2(38.24)	CUBA 38.3(38.40)	FRANCE 38.4(38.43)
1972	UNITED STATES 38.19	SOVIET UNION 38.50	FRG 38.79
1976	UNITED STATES 38.33	GDR 38.66	SOVIET UNION 38.78
1980	SOVIET UNION 38.26	POLAND 38.33	FRANCE 38.53
1984	UNITED STATES 37.83	JAMAICA 38.62	CANADA 38.70

1988	SOVIET UNION 38.19	GREAT BRITAIN 38.28	FRANCE 38.40
1992	UNITED STATES 37.40	NIGERIA 37.98	CUBA 38.00
1996	CANADA 37.69	UNITED STATES 38.05	BRAZIL 38.41
2000	UNITED STATES 37.61	BRAZIL 37.90	CUBA 38.04
2004	.GREAT BRITAIN 38.07	UNITED STATES 38.08	NIGERIA 38.23

1896–1908 Event not held
(1) Germany won silver medal but was disqualified
(2) United States won (39.60) but was disqualified

4 x 400m Relay – Men

	GOLD	SILVER	BRONZE
1908(1)	UNITED STATES 3:29.4	GERMANY 3:32.4	HUNGARY 3:32.5
1912	UNITED STATES 3:16.6	FRANCE 3:20.7	GREAT BRITAIN 3:23.2
1920	GREAT BRITAIN 3:22.2	SOUTH AFRICA 3:24.2	FRANCE 3:24.8
1924	UNITED STATES 3:16.0	SWEDEN 3:17.0	GREAT BRITAIN 3:17.4
1928	UNITED STATES 3:14.2	GERMANY 3:14.8	CANADA 3:15.4
1932	UNITED STATES 3:08.2(3:08.14)	GREAT BRITAIN 3:11.2	CANADA 3:12.8
1936	GREAT BRITAIN 3:09.0	UNITED STATES 3:11.0	GERMANY 3:11.8
1948	UNITED STATES 3:10.4	FRANCE 3:14.8	SWEDEN 3:16.3
1952	JAMAICA 3:03.9(3:04.04)	UNITED STATES 3:04.0(3:04.21)	GERMANY 3:06.6 (3:06.78)
1956	UNITED STATES 3:04.8(3:04.81)	AUSTRALIA 3:06.2(3:06.19)	GREAT BRITAIN 3:07.2(3:07.19)
1960	UNITED STATES 3:02.2(3:02.37)	GERMANY 3:02.7(3:02.84)	ANTILLES 3:04.0(3:04.13)
1964	UNITED STATES 3:00.7	GREAT BRITAIN 3:01.6	TRINIDAD & TOBAGO 3:01.7
1968	UNITED STATES 2:56.1(2:56.16)	KENYA 2:59.6(2:59.64)	FRG 3:00.5(3:00.57)
1972	KENYA 2:59.83	GREAT BRITAIN 3:00.46	FRANCE 3:00.65
1976	UNITED STATES 2:58.65	POLAND 3:01.43	FRG 3:01.98
1980	SOVIET UNION 3:01.08	GDR 3:01.26	ITALY 3:04.3
1984	UNITED STATES 2:57.91	GREAT BRITAIN 2:59.13	NIGERIA 2:59.32
1988	UNITED STATES 2:56.16	JAMAICA 3:00.30	FRG 3:00.56
1992	UNITED STATES 2:55.74	CUBA 2:59.51	GREAT BRITAIN 2:59.73
1996	UNITED STATES 2:55.99	GREAT BRITAIN 2:56.60	JAMAICA 2:59.42
2000	UNITED STATES 2:56.35	NIGERIA 2:58.68	JAMAICA 2:58.78
2004	UNITED STATES 2:55.91	AUSTRALIA 3:00.60	NIGERIA 3:00.90

1896–1906 Event not held
(1) Medley relay comprising 200m, 200m, 400m, 800m

20,000m Road Walk – Men

	GOLD	SILVER	BRONZE
1956	Leonid Spirin(URS) 1h 31.27.4	Antonas Mikenas(URS) 1h 32:03.0	Bruno Junk(URS) 1h 32:12.0
1960	Vladimir Golubichni(URS) 1h 34:07.2	Noel Freeman(AUS) 1h 34:16.4	Stan Vickers(GBR) 1h 34:56.4
1964	Ken Matthews(GBR) 1h 29:34.0	Dieter Lindner(GER) 1h 31:13.2	Vladimir Golubichni(URS) 1h 31:59.4
1968	Vladimir Golubichni(URS) 1h 33:58.4	José Pedraza(MEX) 1h 34:00.0	Nikolai Smaga(URS) 1h 34:03.4
1972	Peter Frenkel(GDR) 1h 26:42.4	Vladimir Golubichni(URS) 1h 26:55.2	Hans Reimann(GDR) 1h 27:16.6
1976	Daniel Batista(MEX) 1h 24:40.6	Hans Reimann(GDR) 1h 25:13.8	Peter Frenkel(GDR) 1h:25:29.4
1980	Maurizio Damilano(ITA) 1h 23:35.5	Pyotr Pochenchuk(URS) 1h 24:45.4	Roland Wieser(GDR) 1h 25:58.2
1984	Ernesto Canto(MEX) 1h 23:13	Raul Gonzalez(MEX) 1h 23:20	Maurizio Damilano(ITA) 1h 23:26
1988	Jozef Pribilinec(TCH) 1h 19:57	Ronald Weigel(GDR) 1h 20:00	Maurizio Damilano(ITA) 1h 20:14
1992	Daniel Plaza(ESP) 1:21:45	Guillaume Leblanc(CAN) 1h 22:25	Giovanni de Benedictus(ITA) 1h 23:11
1996	Jefferson Perez(ECU) 1h 20:07	Ilya Markov(RUS) 1h 20:16	Bernardo Segura(MEX) 1h 20:23
2000	Robert Korzeniowski(POL) 1:18:59	Noe Hernandez(MEX) 1:19:03	Valdimir Andreyev(RUS) 1:19:27
2004	Ivano Brugnetti(ITA) 1h:19:40	Francisco Fernandez(ESP)1h:19:45	Nathan Deakes(AUS) 1h:20:02

1896–1952 Event not held

50,000m Road Walk – Men

	GOLD	SILVER	BRONZE
1932	Thomas Green(GBR) 4h 50:10	Janis Dalinsh(LAT) 4h 57:20	Ugo Frigerio(ITA) 4h 59:06
1936	Harold Whitlock(GBR) 4h 30:41.1	Arthur Schwab(SUI) 4h 32:09.2	Adalberts Bubenko(LAT) 4h 32:42.2
1948	John Ljunggren(SWE) 4h 41:52	Gaston Godel(SUI) 4h 48:17	Tebbs Lloyd Johnson(GBR) 4h 48:31
1952	Giuseppe Dordoni(ITA) 4h 28:07.8	Josef Dolezal(TCH) 4h 30:17.8	Antal Tóka(HUN) 4h 31:27.2
1956	Norman Read(NZL) 4h 30:42.8	Yevgeni Maskinov(URS) 4h 32:57.0	John Ljunggren(SWE) 4h 35:02.0
1960	Don Thompson(GBR) 4h 25:30.0	John Ljunggren(SWE) 4h 25:47.0	Abdon Pamich(ITA) 4h 27:55.4
1964	Abdon Pamich(ITA) 4h 11:12.4	Paul Nihill(GBR) 4h 11:31.2	Ingvar Pettersson(SWE) 4h 14:17.4
1968	Christoph Höhne(GDR) 4h 20:13.6	Antal Kiss(HUN) 4h 30:17.0	Larry Young(USA) 4h 31:55.4
1972	Bernd Kannenberg(FRG) 3h 56:11.6	Venjamin Soldatenko(URS) 3h 58:24.0	Larry Young(USA) 4h 00:46.0
1980	Hartwig Gauder(GDR) 2h 49:24	Jorge Llopart(ESP) 3h 51:25	Yevgeni Ivchenko(URS) 3h 56:32
1984	Raul Gonzalez(MEX) 3h 47:26	Bo Gustafsson(SWE) 3h 53:19	Sandro Bellucci(ITA) 3h 53:45
1988	Vyacheslav Ivanenko(URS) 3h 38:29	Ronald Weigel(GDR) 3h 38:56	Hartwig Gauder(GDR) 3h 39:45
1992	Andrei Perlov(EUN) 3h 50:13	Carlos Mercenario(MEX) 3h 52:09	Ronald Weigel(GER) 3h 53:45
1996	Robert Korzeniowski(POL) 3h 43:30	Mikhail Shchennikov(RUS) 3h 43:46	Valentin Massana(ITA) 3h 44:19
2000	Robert Korzeniowski(POL) 3h 42:21	Aigars Fadejevs(LAT) 3h 43:40	Joel Sanchez(MEX) 3h 44:35
2004	Robert Korzeniowski(POL) 3h:38.46	Denis Nizhegorodov(RUS) 3h:42:50	Alexey Voyevodin(RUS) 3h:43:34

1896–1928,1976 Event not held

High Jump – Men

	GOLD	SILVER	BRONZE
1896	Ellery Clark(USA) 1.81m	James Connolly(USA) 1.65m	–
		Robert Garrett(USA) 1.65m	
1900	Irving Baxter(USA) 1.90m	Patrick Leahy(GBR) 1.78m	Lajos Gönczy(HUN) 1.75m
1904	Samuel Jones(USA) 1.80m	Garrett Serviss(USA) 1.77m	Paul Weinstein(GER) 1.77m
1906	Con Leahy(GBR) 1.77m	Lajos Gönczy(HUN) 1.75m	Herbert Kerrigan(USA) 1.72m
			Themistoklis Diakidis(GRE) 1.72m
1908	Harry Porter(USA) 1.905m	Con Leahy(GBR) 1.88m	–
		István Somodi(HUN) 1.88m	
		Georges André(FRA) 1.88m	
1912	Alma Richards(USA) 1.93m	Hans Liesche(GER) 1.91m	George Horine(USA) 1.89m
1920	Richmond Landon(USA) 1.94m	Harold Muller(USA) 1.90m	Bo Ekelund(SWE) 1.90m
1924	Harold Osborn(USA) 1.98m	Leroy Brown(USA) 1.95m	Pierre Lewden(FRA) 1.92m
1928	Robert King(USA) 1.94m	Ben Hedges(USA) 1.91m	Claude Ménard(FRA) 1.91m
1932	Duncan MacNaughton(CAN) 1.97m	Robert Van Osdel(USA) 1.97m	Simeon Toribio(PHI) 1.97m
1936	Cornelius Johnson(USA) 2.03m	David Albritton(USA) 2.00m	Delos Thurber(USA) 2.00m
1948	John Winter(AUS) 1.98m	Björn Paulsen(NOR) 1.95m	George Stanich(USA) 1.95m
1952	Walt Davis(USA) 2.04m	Ken Wiesner(USA) 2.01m	Jose Telles da Conceicao(BRA) 1.98m
1956	Charlie Dumas(USA) 2.12m	Chilla Porter(AUS) 2.10m	Igor Kashkarov(URS) 2.08m
1960	Robert Shavlakadze(URS) 2.16m	Valeri Brumel(URS) 2.16m	John Thomas(USA) 2.14m
1964	Valeri Brumel(URS) 2.18m	John Thomas(USA) 2.18m	John Rambo(USA) 2.16m
1968	Dick Fosbury(USA) 2.24m	Ed Caruthers(USA) 2.22m	Valentin Gavrilov(URS) 2.20m
1972	Jüri Tarmak(URS) 2.23m	Stefan Junge(GDR) 2.21m	Dwight Stones(USA) 2.21m
1976	Jacek Wszola(POL) 2.25m	Greg Joy(CAN) 2.23m	Dwight Stones(USA) 2.21m
1980	Gerd Wessig(GDR) 2.36m	Jacek Wszola(POL) 2.31m	Jörg Freimuth(GDR) 2.31m
1984	Dietmar Mögenburg(FRG) 2.35m	Patrik Sjöberg(SWE) 2.33m	Jianhua Zhu(CHN) 2.31m
1988	Gennadi Avdeyenko(URS) 2.38m	Hollis Conway(USA) 2.36m	Rudolf Povarnitsin(URS) 2.36m
			Patrik Sjöberg(SWE) 2.36m
1992	Javier Sotomayor(CUB) 2.34m	Patrik Sjöberg(SWE) 2.34m	Hollis Conway(USA) 2.34m
			Tim Forsythe(AUS) 2.34m
			Artur Partyka(POL) 2.34m
1996	Charles Austin(USA) 2.39m	Artur Partyka(POL) 2.37m	Steve Smith(GBR) 2.35m
2000	Sergei Klyugin(RUS) 2.35m	Javier Sotomayor(CUB) 2.32m	Abderahmane Haddad(ALG) 2.32m
2004	Stefan Strand(SWE) 2.36m	Matt Hemingway(USA) 2.34m	Jarislav Baba(CZE) 2.34m

Pole Vault – Men

	GOLD	SILVER	BRONZE
1896	William Hoyt(USA) 3.30m	Albert Tyler(USA) 3.20m	Ioannis Theodoropoulos(GRE) 2.60m
			Vasilios Xydas(GRE) 2.60m
			Evangelos Damaskos(GRE) 2.60m
1900	Irving Baxter(USA) 3.30m	Meredith Colkett(USA) 3.25m	Carl-Albert Andersen(NOR) 3.20m
1904	Charles Dvorak(USA) 3.50m	LeRoy Samse(USA) 3.43m	Louis Wilkins(USA) 3.43m
1906	Fernand Gonder(FRA) 3.50m	Bruno Söderstrom(SWE) 3.40m	Edward Glover(USA) 3.35m
1908	Edward Cooke(USA) 3.70m	–	Edward Archibald(CAN) 3.58m
	Alfred Gilbert(USA) 3.70m		Bruno Söderstrom(SWE) 3.58m
			Charles Jacobs(USA) 3.58m
1912	Harry Babcock(USA) 3.95m	Frank Nelson(USA) 3.85m	Bertil Uggla(SWE) 3.80m
		Marcus Wright(USA) 3.85m	William Hapenny(CAN) 3.80m
			Frank Murphy(USA) 3.80m
1920	Frank Foss(USA) 4.09m	Henry Petersen(DEN) 3.70m	Edwin Meyers(USA) 3.60m
1924	Lee Barnes(USA) 3.95m	Glenn Graham(USA) 3.95m	James Brooker(USA) 3.90m
1928	Sabin Carr(USA) 4.20m	William Droegemuller(USA) 4.10m	Charles McGinnis(USA) 3.95m
1932	William Miller(USA) 4.31m	Shuhei Nishida(JPN) 4.30m	George Jefferson(USA) 4.20m
1936	Earle Meadows(USA) 4.35m	Shuhei Nishida(JPN) 4.25m	Sueo Oe(JPN) 4.25m
1948	Guinn Smith(USA) 4.30m	Erkki Kataja(FIN) 4.20m	Bob Richards(USA) 4.20m
1952	Bob Richards(USA) 4.55m	Don Laz(USA) 4.50m	Ragnar Lundberg(SWE) 4.20m
1956	Bob Richards(USA) 4.56m	Bob Gutowski(USA) 4.53m	Georgios Roubanis(GRE) 4.50m
1960	Don Bragg(USA) 4.70m	Ron Morris(USA) 4.60m	Eeles Landstrom(FIN) 4.55m
1964	Fred Hansen(USA) 5.10m	Wolfgang Reinhardt(GER) 5.05m	Klaus Lehnertz(GER) 5.00m
1968	Bob Seagren(USA) 5.40m	Claus Schiprowski(FRG) 5.40m	Wolfgang Nordwig(GDR) 5.40m
1972	Wolfgang Nordwig(GDR) 5.50m	Bob Seagren(USA) 5.40m	Jan Johnson(USA) 5.35m
1976	Tadeusz Slusarski(POL) 5.50m	Antti Kalliomaki(FIN) 5.50m	David Roberts(USA) 5.50m
1980	Wladislaw Kozakiewicz(POL) 5.78m	Tadeusz Slusarski(POL) 5.65m	–
		Konstantin Volkov(URS) 5.65m	
1984	Pierre Quinon(FRA) 5.75m	Mike Tully(USA) 5.65m	Earl Bell(USA) 5.60m
			Thierry Vigneron(FRA) 5.60m
1988	Sergei Bubka(URS) 5.90m	Rodion Gataullin(URS) 5.85m	Grigori Yegorov(URS) 5.80m
1992	Maksim Tarasov(EUN) 5.80m	Igor Trandenkov(EUN) 5.80m	Javier Garcia(CUB) 5.75m
1996	Jean Galfione(FRA) 5.92m	Igor Trandenkov(RUS) 5.92m	Andrei Tivontchik(GER) 5.92m
2000	Nick Hysong(USA) 5.90m	Lawrence Johnson(USA) 5.90m	Maksim Tarasov(RUS) 5.90m
2004	Timothy Mack(USA) 5.95	Toby Stevenson(USA) 5.90m	Giuseppe Gibilisco(ITA) 5.85m

Long Jump – Men

	GOLD	SILVER	BRONZE
1896	Ellery Clark(USA) 6.35m	Robert Garrett(USA) 6.18m	James Connolly(USA) 6.11m
1900	Alvin Kraenzlein(USA) 7.18m	Myer Prinstein(USA) 7.17m	Patrick Leahy(GBR) 6.95m
1904	Myer Prinstein(USA) 7.34m	Daniel Frank(USA) 6.89m	Robert Stangland(USA) 6.88m
1906	Myer Prinstein(USA) 7.20m	Peter O'Connor(GBR) 7.02m	Hugo Friend(USA) 6.96m
1908	Francis Irons(USA) 7.48m	Daniel Kelly(USA) 7.09m	Calvin Bricker(CAN) 7.08m
1912	Albert Guttersson(USA) 7.60m	Calvin Bricker(CAN) 7.21m	Georg Aberg(SWE) 7.18m
1920	William Pettersson(SWE) 7.15m	Carl Johnson(USA) 7.09m	Erik Abrahamsson(SWE) 7.08m
1924	William DeHart Hubbard(USA) 7.44m	Ed Gourdin(USA) 7.27m	Sverre Hansen(NOR) 7.26m
1928	Edward Hamm(USA) 7.73m	Silvio Cator(HAI) 7.58m	Alfred Bates(USA) 7.40m
1932	Ed Gordon(USA) 7.63m	Lambert Redd(USA) 7.60m	Chuhei Nambu(JPN) 7.44m
1936	Jesse Owens(USA) 8.06m	Lutz Long(GER) 7.87m	Naoto Tajima(JPN) 7.74m
1948	Willie Steele(USA) 7.82m	Theodore Bruce(AUS) 7.55m	Herbert Douglas 7.54m
1952	Jerome Biffle(USA) 7.57m	Meredith Gourdine(USA) 7.53m	Odön Földessy(HUN) 7.30m
1956	Greg Bell(USA) 7.83m	John Bennett(USA) 7.68m	Jorma Valkama(FIN) 7.48m
1960	Ralph Boston(USA) 8.12m	Irvin Roberson(USA) 8.11m	Igor Ter-Ovanesian(URS) 8.04m
1964	Lynn Davies(GBR) 8.07m	Ralph Boston(USA) 8.03m	Igor Ter-Ovanseian(URS) 7.99m
1968	Bob Beamon(USA) 8.90m	Klaus Beer(GDR) 8.19m	Ralph Boston(USA) 8.16m
1972	Randy Williams(USA) 8.24m	Hans Baumgartner(FRG) 8.18m	Arnie Robinson(USA) 8.03m
1976	Arnie Robinson(USA) 8.35m	Randy Williams(USA) 8.11m	Frank Wartenberg(GDR) 8.02m
1980	Lutz Dombrowski(GDR) 8.54m	Frank Paschek(GDR) 8.21m	Valeri Podluzhni(URS) 8.18m
1984	Carl Lewis(USA) 8.54m	Gary Honey(AUS) 8.24m	Giovanni Evangelisti(ITA) 8.24m
1988	Carl Lewis(USA) 8.72m	Mike Powell(USA) 8.49m	Larry Myricks(USA) 8.27m
1992	Carl Lewis(USA) 8.67m	Mike Powell(USA) 8.64m	Joe Greene(USA) 8.34m
1996	Carl Lewis(USA) 8.50m	James Beckford(JAM) 8.29m	Joe Greene(USA) 8.24m
2000	Ivan Pedroso(CUB) 8.55m	Jai Taurima(AUS) 8.49m	Roman Shchurenko(UKR) 8.31m
2004	Dwight Phillips(USA) 8.59m	John Moffitt(USA) 8.47m	Joan Lino Martinez(ESP 8.32m

Triple Jump – Men

(Formerly known as the Hop, Step and Jump)

	GOLD	SILVER	BRONZE
1896	James Connolly(USA) 13.71m	Alexandre Tuffere(FRA) 12.70m	Ioannis Persakis(GRE) 12.52m
1900	Myer Prinstein(USA) 14.47m	James Connolly(USA) 13.97m	Lewis Sheldon(USA) 13.64m
1904	Myer Prinstein(USA) 14.35m	Frederick Englehardt(USA) 13.90m	Robert Stangland(USA) 13.36m
1906	Peter O'Connor(GBR) 14.07m	Con Leahy(GBR) 13.98m	Thomas Cronan(USA) 13.70m
1908	Tim Ahearne(GBR) 14.92m	Garfield McDonald(CAN) 14.76m	Edvard Larsen(NOR) 14.39m
1912	Gustaf Lindblom(SWE) 14.76m	Georg Aberg(SWE) 14.51m	Erik Amlöf(SWE) 14.17m
1920	Vilho Tuulos(FIN) 14.50m	Folke Jansson(SWE) 14.48m	Erik Amlöf(SWE) 14.27m
1924	Anthony Winter(AUS) 15.52m	Luis Brunetto(ARG) 15.42m	Vilho Tuulos(FIN) 15.37m
1928	Mikio Oda(JPN) 15.21m	Levi Casey(USA) 15.17m	Vilho Tuulos(FIN) 15.11m
1932	Chuhei Nambu(JPN) 15.72m	Erik Svensson(SWE) 15.32m	Kenichi Oshima(JPN) 15.12m
1936	Naoto Tajima(JPN) 16.00m	Masao Harada(JPN) 15.66m	John Metcalfe(AUS) 15.50m
1948	Arne Ahman(SWE) 15.40m	George Avery(AUS) 15.36m	Ruhi Sarialp(TUR) 15.02m
1952	Adhemar Ferreira da Silva(BRA) 16.22m	Leonid Shcherbakov(URS) 15.98m	Arnoldo Devonish(VEN) 15.52m
1956	Adhemar Ferreira da Silva(BRA) 16.35m	Vilhjalmur Einarsson(ISL) 16.26m	Vitold Kreyer(URS) 16.02m
1960	Jozef Schmidt(POL) 16.81m	Vladimir Goryayev(URS) 16.63m	Vitold Kreyer(URS) 16.43m
1964	Jozef Schmidt(POL) 16.85m	Oleg Fedoseyev(URS) 16.58m	Viktor Kravchenko(URS) 16.57m
1968	Viktor Saneyev(URS) 17.39m	Nelson Prudencio(BRA) 17.27m	Giuseppe Gentile(ITA) 17.22m
1972	Viktor Saneyev(URS) 17.35m	Jörg Drehmel(GDR) 17.31m	Nelson Prudencio(BRA) 17.05m
1976	Viktor Saneyev(URS) 17.29m	James Butts(USA) 17.18m	Joao de Oliveira(BRA) 16.90m
1980	Jaak Uudmae(URS) 17.35m	Viktor Saneyev(URS) 17.24m	Joao de Oliveira(BRA) 17.22m
1984	Al Joyner(USA) 17.26m	Mike Conley(USA) 17.18m	Keith Connor(GBR) 16.87m
1988	Khristo Markov(BUL) 17.61m	Igor Lapshin(URS) 17.52m	Alexander Kovalenko(URS) 17.42m
1992	Mike Conley(USA) 18.17m	Charles Simkins(USA) 17.60m	Frank Rutherford(BAH) 17.36m
1996	Kenny Harrison(USA) 18.09m	Jonathan Edwards(GBR) 17.88m	Yoelbi Quesada(CUB) 17.44m
2000	Jonathan Edwards(GBR) 17.71m	Yoel Garcia(CUB) 17.47m	Denis Kapustin(RUS) 17.46m
2004	Christian Olsson(SWE) 17.79m	Marian Oprea(ROM) 17.55m	Danila Burkenya(RUS) 17.48m

Shot Put – Men

(1896–1904 performed from 2.13m square)

	GOLD	SILVER	BRONZE
1896	Robert Garrett(USA) 11.22m	Miltiades Gouskos(GRE) 11.15m	Georgios Papasideris(GRE) 10.36m
1900	Richard Sheldon(USA) 14.10m	Josiah McCracken(USA) 12.85m	Robert Garrett(USA) 12.37m
1904	Ralph Rose(USA) 14.81m	Wesley Coe(USA) 14.40m	Leon Feuerbach(USA) 13.37m
1906	Martin Sheridan(USA) 12.32m	Mihály Dávid(HUN) 11.83m	Eric Lemming(SWE) 11.26m
1908	Ralph Rose(USA) 14.21m	Dennis Horgan(GBR) 13.61m	John Garrels(USA) 13.18m
1912	Patrick McDonald(USA) 15.34m	Ralph Rose(USA) 15.25m	Lawrence Whitney(USA) 13.93m
1920	Ville Pörhöla(FIN) 14.81m	Elmer Niklander(FIN) 14.155m	Harry Liversedge(USA) 14.15m
1924	Clarence Houser(USA) 14.99m	Glenn Hartranft(USA) 14.89m	Ralph Hills(USA) 14.64m
1928	John Kuck(USA) 15.87m	Herman Brix(USA) 15.75m	Emil Hirschfield(GER) 15.72m
1932	Lero Sexton(USA) 16.00m	Harlow Rothert(USA) 15.67m	Frantisek Douda(TCH) 15.60m
1936	Hans Woellke(GER) 16.20	Sulo Bärlund(FIN) 16.12m	Gerhard Stöck(GER) 15.66m

1948	Wilbur Thompson(USA) 17.12m	Jim Delaney(USA) 16.68m	Jim Fuchs(USA) 16.42m
1952	Parry O'Brien(USA) 17.41m	Darrow Hooper(USA) 17.39m	Jim Fuchs(USA) 17.06m
1956	Parry O'Brien(USA) 18.57m	Bill Nieder(USA) 18.18m	Jiri Skobla(TCH) 17.65m
1960	Bill Nieder(USA) 19.68m	Parry O'Brien(USA) 19.11m	Dallas Long(USA) 19.01m
1964	Dallas Long(USA) 20.33m	Randy Matson(USA) 20.20m	Vilmos Varju(HUN) 19.39m
1968	Randy Matson(USA) 20.54m	George Woods(USA) 20.12m	Eduard Gushchin(URS) 20.09m
1972	Wladyslaw Komar(POL) 21.18m	George Woods(USA) 21.17m	Hartmut Briesenick(GDR) 21.14m
1976	Udo Beyer(GDR) 21.05m	Yevgeni Mironov(URS) 21.03m	Alexander Baryshnikov(URS) 21.00m
1980	Volodomir Kiselyev(URS) 21.25m	Alexander Baryshnikov(URS) 21.08m	Udo Beyer(GDR) 21.06m
1984	Alessandro Andrei(ITA) 21.26m	Michael Carter(USA) 21.09m	Dave Laut(USA) 20.97m
1988	Ulf Timmermann(GDR) 22.47m	Randy Barnes(USA) 22.39m	Werner Günthör(SUI) 21.99m
1992	Mike Stulce(USA) 21.70m	James Doehring(USA) 20.96m	Vyacheslav Lykho(EUN) 20.94m
1996	Randy Barnes(USA) 21.62m	John Godina(USA) 20.79m	Alexander Bagach(UKR) 20.75m
2000	Arsi Harju(FIN) 21.29m	Adam Nelson(USA) 21.21m	John Godina(USA) 21.20m
2004	Yuriy Bilonog(UKR) 21.16m	Adam Nelson(USA) 21.16m	Joachim Olsen(DEN) 21.07m

Discus – Men
(1896–1900 from 2.50m circle)

	GOLD	SILVER	BRONZE
1896	Robert Garrett(USA) 29.15m	Panoyotis Paraskevopoulos(GRE) 28.95m	Sotirios Versis(GRE) 28.78m
1900	Rudolf Bauer(HUN) 36.04m	Frantisek Janda-Suk(BOH) 35.25m	Richard Sheldon(USA) 34.60m
1904(1)	Martin Sheridan(USA) 39.28m	Ralph Rose(USA) 39.28m	Nicolaos Georgantas(GRE) 37.68m
1906	Martin Sheridan(USA) 41.46m	Nicolaos Georgantas(GRE) 38.06m	Werner Järvinen(FIN) 36.82m
1908	Martin Sheridan(USA) 40.89m	Merritt Griffin(USA) 40.70m	Marquis Horr(USA) 39.44m
1912	Armas Taipale(FIN) 45.21m	Richard Byrd(USA) 42.32m	James Duncan(USA) 42.28m
1920	Elmer Niklander(FIN) 44.68m	Armas Taipale(FIN) 44.19m	Augustus Pope(USA) 42.13m
1924	Clarence Houser(USA) 46.15m	Vilho Niittymaa(FIN) 44.95m	Thomas Lieb(USA) 44.83m
1928	Clarence Houser(USA) 47.32m	Antero Kivi(FIN) 47.23m	James Corson(USA) 47.10m
1932	John Anderson(USA) 49.49m	Henri Laborde(USA) 48.47m	Paul Winter(FRA) 47.85m
1936	Ken Carpenter(USA) 50.48m	Gordon Dunn(USA) 49.36m	Giorgio Oberweger(ITA) 49.23m
1948	Adolfo Consolini(ITA) 52.78m	Giuseppe Tosi(ITA) 51.78m	Fortune Gordien(USA) 50.77m
1952	Sim Iness(USA) 55.03m	Adolfo Consolini(ITA) 53.78m	James Dillion(USA) 52.38m
1956	Al Oerter(USA) 56.36m	Fortune Gordien(USA) 54.81m	Des Koch(USA) 54.40m
1960	Al Oerter(USA) 59.18m	Rink Babka(USA) 58.02m	Dick Cochran(USA) 57.16m
1964	Al Oerter(USA) 61.00m	Ludvik Danek(TCH) 60.52m	Dave Weill(USA) 59.49m
1968	Al Oerter(USA) 64.78m	Lothar Milde(GDR) 63.08m	Ludvik Danek(TCH) 62.92m
1972	Ludvik Danek(TCH) 64.40m	Jay Silvester(USA) 63.50m	Ricky Bruch(SWE) 63.40m
1976	Mac Wilkins(USA) 67.50m	Wolfgang Schmidt(GDR) 66.22m	John Powell(USA) 65.70m
1980	Viktor Rashchupkin(URS) 66.64m	Imrich Bugár(TCH) 66.38	Luis Delis(CUB) 66.32m
1984	Rolf Danneberg(FRG) 66.60m	Mac Wilkins(USA) 66.30m	John Powell(USA) 65.46m
1988	Jürgen Schult(GDR) 68.82m	Romas Ubartas(URS) 67.48m	Rolf Danneberg(FRG) 67.38m
1992	Romas Ubartas(LTU) 65.12m	Jürgen Schult(GER) 64.94m	Roberto Moya(CUB) 64.12m
1996	Lars Riedel(GER) 69.40m	Vladimir Dubrovchik(BLR) 66.60m	Vasili Kaptyukh(BLR) 65.80m
2000	Virgiljus Alekna(LAT) 69.30m	Lars Riedel(GER) 68.50m	Frantz Kruger(RSA) 68.19m
2004(2)	Virgilijus Alekna(LTU) 69.89m	Zoltán Kövágó(HUN) 67.94m	Alexander Tammert(EST) 66.66m

(1) Title decided by a throw-off
(2) Robert Fazekas (HUN) threw 70.93m but was disqualified

Hammer – Men
(In 1900 from 2.74m circle)

	GOLD	SILVER	BRONZE
1900	John Flanagan(USA) 49.73m	Truxton Hare(USA) 49.13m	Josiah McCracken(USA) 42.46m
1904	John Flanagan(USA) 51.23m	John De Witt(USA) 50.26m	Ralph Rose(USA) 45.73m
1908	John Flanagan(USA) 51.92m	Matt McGrath(USA) 51.18m	Con Walsh(CAN) 48.50m
1912	Matt McGrath(USA) 54.74m	Duncan Gillis(CAN) 48.39m	Clarence Childs(USA) 48.17m
1920	Patrick Ryan(USA) 52.87m	Carl Lind(SWE) 48.43m	Basil Bennett(USA) 48.25m
1924	Fred Tootell(USA) 53.29m	Matt McGrath(USA) 50.84m	Malcolm Nokes(GBR) 48.87m
1928	Patrick O'Callaghan(IRL) 51.39m	Ossian Skjöld(SWE) 51.29m	Edmund Black(USA) 49.03m
1932	Patrick O'Callaghan(IRL) 53.92m	Ville Pörhöla(FIN) 52.27m	Peter Zaremba(USA) 50.33m
1936	Karl Hein(GER) 56.49m	Erwin Blask(GER) 55.04m	Fred Warngard(SWE) 54.83m
1948	Imre Németh(HUN) 56.07m	Ivan Gubijan(YUG) 54.27m	Bob Bennett(USA) 53.73m
1952	József Csermák(HUN) 60.34m	Karl Storch(GER) 58.86m	Imre Németh(HUN) 57.74m
1956	Harold Connolly(USA) 63.19m	Mikhail Krivonosov(URS) 63.03m	Anatoli Samotsvetov(URS) 62.56m
1960	Vasili Rudenkov(URS) 67.10m	Gyula Zsivótzky(HUN) 65.79m	Tadeusz Rut(POL) 65.64m
1964	Romuald Klim(URS) 69.74m	Gyula Zsivótzky(HUN) 69.09m	Uwe Beyer(GER) 68.09m
1968	Gyula Zsivótzky(HUN) 73.36m	Romuald Klim(URS) 73.28m	Lázár Lovász(HUN) 69.78m
1972	Anatoli Bondarchuk(URS) 75.50m	Jochen Sachse(GDR) 74.96m	Vasili Khmelevski(URS) 74.04m
1976	Yuri Sedykh(URS) 77.52m	Alexei Spriridonov(URS) 76.08m	Anatoli Bondarchuk(URS) 75.48m
1980	Yuri Sedykh(URS) 81.80m	Sergei Litvinov(URS) 80.64m	Juri Tamm(URS) 78.96m
1984	Juha Tiainen(FIN) 78.08m	Karl-Hans Riehm(FRG) 77.98m	Klaus Ploghaus(FRG) 76.68m
1988	Sergei Litvinov(URS) 84.80m	Yuri Sedykh(URS) 83.76m	Juri Tamm(URS) 81.16m
1992	Andrei Abduvalyev(EUN) 82.54m	Igor Astapkovich(EUN) 81.96m	Igor Nikulin(EUN) 81.38m

1996	Balázs Kiss(HUN) 81.24m	Lance Deal(USA) 81.12m	Alexander Krykun(UKR) 80.02m
2000	Szymon Ziolkowski(POL) 80.02m	Nicola Vizzoni(ITA) 79.64m	Igor Astapkovich(BLR) 79.17m
2004(1)	Koji Mirofushi(JPN) 82.91m	Ivan Tikhon(BLR) 79.81m	Esref Apak(TUR) 79.51m

1896,1906 Event not held
(1) Adrian Annus (HUN) threw 83.19m but was disqualified

Javelin – Men

	GOLD	SILVER	BRONZE
1906	Eric Lemming(SWE) 53.90m	Knut Lindberg(SWE) 45.17m	Bruno Söderström(SWE) 44.92m
1908	Eric Lemming(SWE) 54.82m	Arne Halse(NOR) 50.57m	Otto Nilsson(SWE) 47.09m
1912	Eric Lemming(SWE) 60.64m	Juho Saaristo(FIN) 58.66m	Mór Kóczán(HUN) 55.50m
1920	Jonni Myyrä(FIN) 65.78m	Urho Peltonen(FIN) 63.50m	Pekka Johansson(FIN) 63.09m
1924	Jonni Myyrä(FIN) 62.96m	Gunnar Lindström9SWE0 60.92m	Eugene Oberst(USA) 58.35m
1928	Erik Lundkvist(SWE) 66.60m	Béla Szepes(HUN) 65.26m	Olva Sunde(NOR) 63.97m
1932	Matti Järvinen(FIN) 72.71m	Matti Sippala(FIN) 69.79m	Eino Penttila(FIN) 68.69m
1936	Gerhard Stöck(GER) 71.84m	Yrjö Nikkanen(FIN) 70.77m	Kalervo Toivonen(FIN) 70.72m
1948	Tapio Rautavaara(FIN) 69.77m	Steve Seymour(USA) 67.56m	József Várszegi(HUN) 67.03m
1952	Cyrus Young(USA) 73.78m	Bill Miller(USA) 72.46m	Toivo Hyytiäinen(FIN) 71.89m
1956	Egil Danielsen(NOR) 85.71m	Janusz Sidlo(POL) 79.98m	Viktor Tsibulenko(URS) 79.50m
1960	Viktor Tsibulenko(URS) 84.64m	Walter Krüger(GER) 79.36m	Gergely Kulcsár(HUN) 78.57m
1964	Pauli Nevala(FIN) 82.66m	Gergely Kulcsár(HUN) 82.32m	Janis Lusis(URS) 80.57m
1968	Janis Lusis(URS) 90.10m	Jorma Kinnunen(FIN) 88.58m	Gergely Kulcsár(HUN) 87.06m
1972	Klaus Wolfermann(FRG) 90.48m	Janis Lusis(URS) 90.46m	Bill Schmidt(USA) 84.42m
1976	Miklos Németh(HUN) 94.58m	Hannu Siitonen(FIN) 87.92m	Gheorghe Megelea(ROM) 87.16m
1980	Dainis Kula(URS) 91.20m	Alexander Makarov(URS) 89.64m	Wolfgang Hanisch(GDR) 86.72m
1984	Arto Härkonen(FIN) 86.76m	David Ottley(GBR) 85.74m	Kenth Eldebrink(SWE) 83.72m
1988	Tapio Korjus(FIN) 84.28m	Jan Zelezny(TCH) 84.12m	Seppo Räty(FIN) 83.26m
1992(1)	Jan Zelezny(TCH) 89.66m	Seppo Räty(FIN) 86.60m	Steve Backley(GBR) 83.38m
1996	Jan Zelezny(CZE) 88.16m	Steve Backley(GBR) 87.44m	Seppo Räty(FIN) 86.98m
2000	Jan Zelezny(CZE) 90.17m	Steve Backley(GBR) 89.85m	Sergei Makarov(RUS) 88.67m
2004	Andreas Thorkildsen(NOR) 86.50m	Vadims Vasilevski(RUS) 84.95m	Sergei Makarov(RUS) 84.84m

1896–1904 Event not held
(1) New specification javelin introduced

Decathlon – Men

(Comprises 100m, long jump, shot put, high jump, 400m, 110m hurdles, discus, pole vault, javelin, 1,500m). Scores 1912–80 have been recalculated on the 1984 tables. Note that on a number of occasions the original medal order would have been different if these tables had been operating. In 1912 Jim Thorpe (USA) finished first, 6,564 pts, but was disqualified as a professional. He was reinstated posthumously in 1982, but as joint first.

	GOLD	SILVER	BRONZE
1904(1)	Thomas Kiely(GBR) 6036pts	Adam Gunn(USA) 5907pts	Truxton Hare(USA) 5813pts
1912	Hugo Wieslander(SWE) 5966pts	Charles Lomberg(SWE) 5722pts	Gösta Holmer(SWE) 5768pts
1920	Helge Lövland(NOR) 5803pts	Brutus Hamilton(USA) 5739pts	Bertil Ohlsson(SWE) 5640pts
1924	Harold Osborn(USA) 6476pts	Emerson Norton(USA) 6117pts	Alexander Klumberg(EST) 6057pts
1928	Paavo Yrjölä(FIN) 6587pts	Akilles Järvinen(FIN) 6645pts	Ken Doherty(USA) 6428pts
1932	Jim Bausch(USA) 6736pts	Akilles Järvinen(FIN) 6879pts	Wolrad Eberle(GER) 6661pts
1936	Glenn Morris(USA) 7254pts	Robert Clark(USA) 7063pts	Jack Parker(USA) 6760pts
1948	Bob Mathias(USA) 6628pts	Ignace Heinrich(FRA) 6559pts	Floyd Simmons(USA) 6531pts
1952	Bob Mathias(USA) 7592pts	Milt Campbell(USA) 6995pts	Floyd Simmons(USA) 6945pts
1956	Milt Campbell(USA) 7614pts	Rafer Johnson(USA) 7457pts	Vasili Kuznetsov(URS) 7337pts
1960	Rafer Johnson(USA) 7926pts	Chuan-Kwang Yang(TPE) 7839pts	Vasili Kuznetsov(URS) 7557pts
1964	Willi Holdorf(GER) 7794pts	Rein Aun(URS) 7744pts	Hans-Joachim Walde(GER) 7735pts
1968	Bill Toomey(USA) 8144pts	Hans-Joachim Walde(FRG) 8094pts	Kurt Bendlin(FRG) 8071pts
1972	Nikolai Avilov(URS) 8466pts	Leonid Litvinenko(URS) 7970pts	Ryszard Katus(POL) 7936pts
1976	Bruce Jenner(USA) 8634pts	Guido Kratschmer(FRG) 8407pts	Nikolai Avilov(URS) 8378pts
1980	Daley Thompson(GBR) 8522pts	Yuri Kutsenko(URS) 8369pts	Sergei Zhelanov(URS) 8135pts
1984	Daley Thompson(GBR) 8847pts	Jürgen Hingsen(FRG) 8695pts	Siegfried Wentz(FRG) 8416pts
1988	Christian Schenk(GDR) 8488pts	Torsten Voss(GDR) 8399pts	Dave Steen(CAN) 8328pts
1992	Robert Zmelik(TCH) 8611pts	Antonio Penalver(CUB) 8412pts	Dave Johnson(USA) 8309pts
1996	Dan O'Brien(USA) 8824pts	Frank Busemann(GER) 8706pts	Tomas Dvorak(CZE) 8664pts
2000	Erki Nool(EST) 8641pts	Roman Sebrle(CZE) 8606pts	Chris Huffins(USA) 8595pts
2004	Roman Sebrle(CZE) 8893pts	Bryan Clay(USA) 8820	Dmitriy Karpov(KAZ) 8725

1896–1900,1906–08 Event not held
(1) Consisted of 100yd, 1 mile, 120yd hurdles, 880yd walk, high jump, long jump, pole vault, shot put, hammer and 56lb weight

100m – Women

	GOLD	SILVER	BRONZE
1928	Elizabeth Robinson(USA) 12.2	Fanny Rosenfeld(CAN) 12.3	Ethel Smith(CAN) 12.3
1932	Stanislawa Walasiewicz(POL) 11.9	Hilda Strike(Can) 11.9	Wilhelmina von Bremen(USA) 12.0
1936	Helen Stephens(USA) 11.5	Stanislawa Walasiewicz(POL) 11.7	Kathe Krauss(GER) 11.9
1948	Fanny Blankers-Koen(NED) 11.9	Dorothy Manley(GBR) 12.2	Shirley Strickland(AUS) 12.2
1952	Marjorie Jackson(AUS) 11.5(11.67)	Daphne Hasenjager(RSA) 11.8(12.05)	Shirley Strickland(AUS) 11.9(12.12)
1956	Betty Cuthbert(AUS) 11.5(11.82)	Christa Stubnick(GER) 11.7(11.92)	Marlene Matthews(AUS) 11.7(11.94)

1960	Wilma Rudolph(USA) 11.0(11.18)	Dorothy Hyman(GBR) 11.3(11.43)	Giuseppina Leone(ITA) 11.3(11.48)
1964	Wyomia Tyus(USA) 11.4(11.49)	Edith Maguire(USA) 11.6(11.62)	Ewa Klobukowska(POL) 11.6(11.64)
1968	Wyomia Tyus(USA) 11.0(11.08)	Barbara Ferrell(USA) 11.1(11.15)	Irena Szewinska(POL) 11.1(11.19)
1972	Renate Stecher(GDR) 11.07	Raelene Boyle(AUS) 11.23	Silvia Chivas(CUB) 11.24
1976	Annegret Richter(FRG) 11.08	Renate Stecher(GDR) 11.13	Inge Helten(FRG) 11.17
1980	Ludmila Kondratyeva(URS) 11.06	Marlies Göhr(GDR) 11.07	Ingrid Auerswald(GDR) 11.14
1984	Evelyn Ashford(USA) 10.97	Alice Brown(USA) 11.13	Merlene Ottey(JAM) 11.16
1988	Florence Griffith-Joyner(USA) 10.54	Evelyn Ashford(USA) 10.83	Heike Drechsler(GDR) 10.85
1992	Gail Devers(USA) 10.82	Juliet Cuthbert(JAM) 10.83	Irina Privalova(EUN) 10.84
1996	Gail Devers(USA) 10.94	Merlene Ottey(JAM) 10.94	Gwen Torrence(USA 10.96
2000	Marion Jones(USA) 10.75	Ekaterini Thanou(GRE) 11.12	Tanya Lawrence(JAM) 11.18
2004	Yuliya Nesterenko(BLR) 10.93	Lauryn Williams(USA) 10.96	Veronica Campbell(JAM) 10.97

1896–1924 Event not held

200m – Women

	GOLD	SILVER	BRONZE
1948	Fanny Blankers-Koen(NED) 24.4	Audrey Williamson(GBR) 25.1	Audrey Patterson(USA) 25.2
1952	Marjorie Jackson(AUS) 23.7(23.89)	Bertha Brouwer(NED) 24.2(24.25)	Nadyezda Khnykina(URS) 24.2(24.37)
1956	Betty Cuthbert(AUS) 23.4(23.55)	Christa Stubnick(GER) 23.7(23.89)	Marlene Matthews(AUS) 23.8(24.10)
1960	Wilma Rudolph(USA) 24.0(24.13)	Jutta Heine(GER) 24.4(24.58)	Dorothy Hyman(GBR) 24.7(24.82)
1964	Edith Maguire(USA) 23.0(23.05)	Irena Kirszenstein(POL) 23.1(23.13)	Marilyn Black(AUS) 23.1(23.18)
1968	Irena Szewinska(POL) 22.5(22.58)	Raelene Boyle(AUS) 22.7(22.74)	Jennifer Lamy(AUS) 22.8(22.88)
1972	Renate Stecher(GDR) 22.40	Raelene Boyle(AUS) 22.45	Irena Szewinska(POL) 22.74
1976	Bärbel Eckert(GDR) 22.37	Annegret Richter(FRG) 22.39	Renate Stecher(GDR) 22.47
1980	Bärbel Wöckel(GDR) 22.03	Natalya Bochina(URS) 22.19	Merlene Ottey(JAM) 22.20
1984	Valerie Brisco-Hooks(USA) 21.81	Florence Griffith(USA) 22.04	Merlene Ottey(JAM) 22.09
1988	Florence Giffith Joyner(USA) 21.34	Grace Jackson(JAM) 21.72	Heike Drechsler(GDR) 21.95
1992	Gwen Torrence(USA) 21.81	Juliet Cuthbert(JAM) 22.02	Merlene Ottey(JAM) 22.09
1996	Marie-José Pérec(FRA) 22.12	Merlene Ottey(JAM) 22.24	Mary Onyali(NGR) 22.38
2000	Marion Jones(USA) 21.84	Pauline Davis-Thompson(BAH) 22.27	Susanthika Jayasinghe(SRI) 22.28
2004	Veronica Campbell(JAM) 22.05	Allyson Felix(USA) 22.18	Debbie Ferguson(BAH) 22.30

1896–36 Event not held

400m – Women

	GOLD	SILVER	BRONZE
1964	Betty Cuthbert(AUS) 52.0(52.01)	Ann Packer(GBR) 52.2(52.20)	Judith Amoore(AUS) 53.4
1968	Colette Besson(FRA) 52.0(52.03)	Lillian Board(GBR) 52.1(52.12)	Natalya Burda(URS) 52.2(52.25)
1972	Monika Zehrt(GDR) 51.08	Rita Wilden(FRG) 51.21	Kathy Hammond(USA) 51.64
1976	Irena Szewinska(POL) 49.29	Christina Brehmer(GDR) 50.51	Ellen Streidt(GDR) 50.55
1980	Marita Koch(GDR) 48.88	Jarmila Kratochvilová(TCH) 49.46	Christina Lathan(GDR) 49.66
1984	Valerie Brisco-Hooks(USA) 48.83	Chandra Cheeseborough(USA) 49.05	Kathy Cook(GBR) 49.43
1988	Olga Bryzgina(URS) 48.65	Petra Müller(GDR) 49.45	Olga Nazarova(URS) 49.90
1992	Marie-José Pérec(FRA) 48.83	Olga Bryzgina(EUN) 49.05	Ximena Restrepo(COL) 49.64
1996	Marie-José Pérec(FRA) 48.25	Cathy Freeman(AUS) 48.63	Falilat Ogunkoya(NGR) 49.10
2000	Cathy Freeman(AUS) 49.11	Lorraine Graham(JAM) 49.58	Katharine Merry(GBR) 49.72
2004	Tonique Williams(BAH) 49.41s	Ana Guevara(MEX) 49.56	Natalya Antyukh(RUS) 49.89

1896–1960 Event not held

800m – Women

	GOLD	SILVER	BRONZE
1928	Lina Radke(GER) 2:16.8	Hitomi Kinue (JPN) 2:17.6	Inga Gentzel(SWE) 2:17.8
1960	Ludmila Shevtsova(URS) 2:04.3	Branda Jones(AUS) 2:04.4	Ursula Donath(GER) 2:05.6
1964	Ann Packer(GBR) 2:01.1	Maryvonne Dupureur(FRA)	Marise Chamberlain(NZL) 2:02.8
1968	Madeline Manning(USA) 2:00.9	Ilona Silai(ROM) 2:02.5	Maria Gommers(NED) 2:02.6
1972	Hildegard Falck(FRG) 1:58.6	Niole Sabaite(URS) 1:58.7	Gunhild Hoffmeister(GDR) 1:59.2
1976	Tatyana Kazankina(URS) 1:54.9	Nikolina Shtereva(BUL) 1:55.4	Elfi Zinn(GDR) 1:55.6
1980	Nadyezda Olizarenko(URS) 1:53.5	Olga Mineyeva(URS) 1:54.9	Tatyana Providokhina(URS) 1:55.5
1984	Doina Melinte(ROM) 1:57.60	Kim Gallagher(USA) 1:58.63	Fita Lovin(ROM) 1:58.83
1988	Sigrun Wodars(GSR) 1:56.10	Christine Wachtel(GDR) 1:56.64	Kim Gallagher(USA) 1:56.91
1992	Ellen van Langen(NED) 1:55.54	Lilia Nurutdinova(EUN) 1:55.99	Ana Quirot(CUB) 1:56.80
1996	Svetlana Masterkova(RUS) 1:57.73	Ana Quirot(CUB) 1:58.11	Maria Mutola(MOZ) 1:58.71
2000	Maria Mutola(MOZ) 1:56.15	Stephanie Graf(AUT) 1:56.64	Kelly Holmes(GBR) 1:56.80
2004	Kelly Holmes(GBR) 1:56.38	Hasna Benhassi(MAR) 1:56.43	Jolanda Ceplak(SLO) 1:56.43

1896–1924, 1932–56 Event not held

1,500m – Women

	GOLD	SILVER	BRONZE
1972	Ludmila Bragina(URS) 4:01.4	Gunhild Hoffmeister(GDR) 4:02.8	Paola Cacchi-Pigni(ITA) 4:02.9
1976	Tatyana Kazankina(URS) 4:05.5	Gunhild Hoffmeister(GDR) 4:06.0	Ulrike Klapezynski(GDR) 4:06.1
1980	Tatyana Kazankina(URS) 3:56.6	Christiane Wartenberg(GDR) 3:57.8	Nadyezda Olizarenko(URS) 3:59.6
1984	Gariella Dorio(ITA) 4:03.25	Doina Melinte(ROM) 4:03.76	Maricica Puica(ROM) 4:04.15
1988	Paula Ivan(ROM) 3:53.96	Laima Baikauskaite(URS) 4:00.24	Tatyana Samolenko(URS) 4:00.30

1992	Hassiba Boulmerka(ALG) 3:55.30	Ludmila Ragacheva(EUN) 3:56.91	Yunxia Qu(CHN) 3:57.08
1996	Svetlana Masterkova(RUS) 4:00.83	Gabriela Szabo(ROM) 4:01.54	Theresia Kiesl(AUT) 4:03.02
2000	Nouria Merah-Benida(ALG) 4:05.10	Violeta Szekely(ROM) 4:05.15	Gabriela Szabo(ROM) 4:05.27
2004	Kelly Holmes(GBR) 3:57.90s	Tatyana Tomashova(RUS) 3:58.12	Maria Cioncan(ROM) 3:58.39

1896–1968 Event not held

3,000m – Women

(Replaced by 5,000m in 1996)

	GOLD	SILVER	BRONZE
1984	Maricica Puica(ROM) 8:35.96	Wendy Sly(GBR) 8:39.47	Lynn Williams(CAN) 8:42.14
1988	Tatyana Samolenko(URS) 8:26.53	Paula Ivan(ROM) 8:27.15	Yvonne Murray(GBR) 8:29.02
1992	Yelena Romanova(EUN) 8:46.04	Tatyana Dorovskikh(EUN) 8:46.85	Angela Chalmers(CAN) 8:47.22

1896–1980 Event not held

5,000m – Women

	GOLD	SILVER	BRONZE
1996	Junxia Wang(CHN) 14:59.88	Pauline Konga(KEN) 15:03.49	Roberta Brunet(ITA) 15:07.52
2000	Gabriela Szabo(ROM) 14:40.79	Sonia O'Sullivan(IRL) 14:41.02	Gete Wami(ETH) 14:42.23
2004	Meseret Defar(ETH) 14:45.65	Isabella Ochichi(KEN) 14:48.19	Tirunesh Dibaba(ETH) 14:51.83

1896–1992 Event not held

10,000m – Women

	GOLD	SILVER	BRONZE
1988	Olga Bondarenko(URS) 31:05.21	Liz McColgan(GBR) 31:08.44	Yelena Zhupiyeva(URS) 31:19.82
1992	Derartu Tulu(ETH) 31:06.02	Elana Meyer(RSA) 31:11.75	Lynn Jennings(USA) 31:19.89
1996	Fernanda Ribeiro(POR) 31:01.63	Junxia Wang(CHN) 31:02.58	Gete Wami(ETH) 31:06.65
2000	Derartu Tulu(ETH) 30:17.49	Gete Wami(ETH) 30:22.48	Fernanda Ribeiro(POR) 30:22.88
2004	Xing Huina(CHN) 30:24.36	Ejagayehu Dibaba(ETH) 30:24.98	Derartu Tulu(ETH) 30:26.42

1896–1984 Event not held

Marathon – Women

	GOLD	SILVER	BRONZE
1984	Joan Benoit(USA) 2h 24:52	Grete Waitz(NOR) 2h 26:18	Rosa Mota(POR) 2h 26:57
1988	Rosa Mota(POR) 2h 25:40	Lisa Martin(AUS) 2h 25:53	Kathrin Dörre(GDR) 2h 26:21
1992	Valentina Yegorova(EUN) 2h 32:41	Yuko Arimori(JPN) 2h 32:49	Lorraine Moller(NZL) 2h 33:59
1996	Fatuma Roba(ETH) 2h 26:05	Valentina Yegorova(RUS) 2h 28:05	Yuko Arimori(JPN) 2h 28:39
2000	Naoko Takahashi(JPN) 2:23:14	Lidia Simon(ROM) 2:23:22	Joyce Chepchumba(KEN) 2:24:45
2004	Mizuki Noguchi(JPN) 2h:26:20	Catherine Ndereba(KEN) 2h:26:32	Deena Kastor(USA) 2h:27:20

1928–80 Event not held

100m Hurdles – Women

(Held over 80m hurdles 1932–68)

	GOLD	SILVER	BRONZE
1932	Mildred Didrikson(USA) 11.7	Evelyne Hall(USA) 11.7	Marjorie Clark(RSA) 11.8
1936	Trebisonda Valla(ITA) 11.7(11.75)	Anny Steuer(GER) 11.7(11.81)	Elizabeth Taylor(CAN) 11.7(11.81)
1948	Fanny Blankers-Koen(NED) 11.2	Maureen Gardner(GBR) 11.2	Shirley Strickland(AUS) 11.4
1952	Shirley de la Hunty(AUS) 10.8(11.01)	Maria Golubichnaya(URS) 11.1(11.24)	Maria Sander(GER) 11.1(11.38)
1956	Shirley de la Hunty(AUS) 10.7(10.96)	Gisela Köhler(GER) 10.9(11.12)	Norma Thrower(AUS) 11.0(11.25)
1960	Irina Press(URS) 10.8(10.93)	Carol Quinton(GBR) 10.9(10.99)	Gisela Birkemeyer(GER) 11.0(11.13)
1964	Karin Balzer(GER) 10.5(10.54)	Teresa Ciepla(POL) 10.5(10.55)	Pam Kilborn(AUS) 10.5(10.56)
1968	Maureen Caird(AUS) 10.3(10.39)	Pam Kilborn(AUS) 10.4(10.46)	Chi Cheng(TPE) 10.4(10.51)
1972	Annelie Ehrhardt(GDR) 12.59	Valeria Bufanu(ROM) 12.84	Karin Balzer(GDR) 12.90
1976	Johanna Schaller(GDR) 12.77	Tatyana Anisimova(URS) 12.78	Natalya Lebedyeva(URS) 12.80
1980	Vera Komisova(URS) 12.56	Johanna Klier(GDR) 12.63	Lucyna Langer(POL) 12.65
1984	Benita Fitzgerald-Brown(USA) 12.84	Shirley Strong(GBR) 12.88	Kim Turner(USA) 13.06
			Michele Chardonnet(FRA) 13.06
1988	Yordanka Donkova(BUL) 12.38	Gloria Siebert(GDR) 12.61	Claudia Zackiewicz(FRG) 12.75
1992	Paraskevi Patoulidou(GRE) 12.64	LaVonna Martin(USA) 12.69	Yordanka Donkova(BUL) 12.70
1996	Ludmila Engquist(SWE) 12.58	Brigita Bukovec(SLO) 12.59	Patricia Girard-Leno(FRA) 12.65
2000	Olga Shishigina(KAZ) 12.65	Glory Alozie(NGR) 12.68	Melissa Morrison(USA) 12.76
2004	Joanna Hayes(USA) 12.37	Olena Krasovska(UKR) 12.45	Melissa Morrison(USA) 12.56

1896–1928 Event not held

400m Hurdles – Women

	GOLD	SILVER	BRONZE
1984	Nawal El Moutawakel(MAR) 54.61	Judi Brown(USA) 55.20	Cristina Cojocaru(ROM) 55.41
1988	Debbie Flintoff-King(AUS) 53.17	Tatyana Ledovskaya(URS) 53.18	Ellen Fiedler(GDR) 53.63
1992	Sally Gunnell(GBR) 53.23	Sandra Farmer-Patrick(USA) 53.69	Janeene Vickers(USA) 54.31
1996	Deon Hemmings(JAM) 52.82	Kim Batten(USA) 53.08	Tonja Buford-Bailey(USA) 53.22
2000	Irina Privalova(RUS) 53.02	Deon Hemmings(JAM) 53.45	Nezha Bidouane(MAR) 53.57
2004	Fani Halkia(GRE) 52.82s	Ionela Tirlea Manolache(ROM)53.38	Tetiana Tereshchuk-Antipova(UKR)53.44

1896–1980 Event not held

4 x 100m Relay – Women

	GOLD	SILVER	BRONZE
1928	CANADA 48.4	UNITED STATES 48.8	GERMANY 49.2
1932	UNITED STATES 47.0(46.86)	CANADA 47.0	GREAT BRITAIN 47.6
1936	UNITED STATES 46.9	GREAT BRITAIN 47.6	CANADA 47.8
1948	NETHERLANDS 47.5	AUSTRALIA 47.6	CANADA 47.8
1952	UNITED STATES 45.9(46.14)	GERMANY 45.9(46.18)	GREAT BRITAIN 46.2(46.41)
1956	AUSTRALIA 44.5(44.65)	GREAT BRITAIN 44.7(44.70)	UNITED STATES 44.9(45.04)
1960	UNITED STATES 44.5(44.72)	GERMANY 44.8(45.00)	POLAND 45.0(45.19)
1964	POLAND 43.6(43.69)	UNITED STATES 43.9(43.92)	GREAT BRITAIN 44.0(44.09)
1968	UNITED STATES 42.8(42.88)	CUBA 43.3(43.36)	SOVIET UNION 43.4(43.41)
1972	FRG 42.81	GDR 42.95	CUBA 43.36
1976	GDR 42.55	FRG 42.59	SOVIET UNION 43.09
1980	GDR 41.60	SOVIET UNION 42.10	GREAT BRITAIN 42.43
1984	UNITED STATES 41.65	CANADA 42.77	GREAT BRITAIN 43.11
1988	UNITED STATES 41.98	GDR 42.09	SOVIET UNION 42.75
1992	UNITED STATES 42.11	UNIFIED TEAM 42.16	NIGERIA 42.81
1996	UNITED STATES 41.95	BAHAMAS 42.14	JAMAICA 42.24
2000	BAHAMAS 41.95	JAMAICA 42.13	UNITED STATES 42.20
2004	JAMAICA 41.73	RUSSIA 42.27	FRANCE 42.54

1896–1924 Event not held

4 x 400m Relay – Women

	GOLD	SILVER	BRONZE
1972	GDR 3:22.95	UNITED STATES 3:25.15	FRG 3:26.51
1976	GDR 3:19.23	UNITED STATES 3:22.81	SOVIET UNION 3:24.24
1980	SOVIET UNION 3:20.12	GDR 3:20.35	GREAT BRITAIN 3:27.5
1984	UNITED STATES 3:18.29	CANADA 3:21.21	FRG 3:22.98
1988	SOVIET UNION 3:15.17	UNITED STATES 3:15.51	GDR 3:18.29
1992	UNIFIED TEAM 3:20.20	UNITED STATES 3:20.92	GREAT BRITAIN 3:24.23
1996	UNITED STATES 3:20.91	NIGERIA 3:21.04	GERMANY 3:21.14
2000	UNITED STATES 3:22.62	JAMAICA 3:23.25	RUSSIA 3:23.44
2004	UNITED STATES 3:19.01	RUSSIA 3:20.16	JAMAICA 3:22.00

1896–1968 Event not held

10,000m Walk – Women

(Replaced by a 20,000m walk in 2000)

	GOLD	SILVER	BRONZE
1992	Yueling Chen(CHN) 44:32	Yelena Nikoleyeva(EUN) 44:33	Chunxiu Li(CHN) 44:41
1996	Yelena Nikolayeva(RUS) 41:49	Elisabetta Perrone(ITA) 42:12	Yan Wang(CHN) 42:19

1896–1988 Event not held

20,000m Walk – Women

	GOLD	SILVER	BRONZE
2000	Liping Wang(CHN) 1:29:05	Kjersti Plätzer(NOR) 1:29:33	Maria Vasco(ESP) 1:30:23
2004	Athanasia Tsouméléka(GRE)1h:29:12	Olimpiada Ivanova(RUS)1h:29:16	Jane Saville(AUS)1h:29:25

1896–1996 Event not held

High Jump – Women

	GOLD	SILVER	BRONZE
1928	Ether Catherwood(CAN) 1.59m	Carolina Gisolf(NED) 1.56m	Mildred Wiley(USA) 1.56m
1932	Jean Shiley(USA) 1.657m (1)	Mildred Didrikson(USA) 1.657m (1)	Eva Dawes(CAN) 1.60m
1936	Ibolya Csák(HUN) 1.60m	Dorothy Odam(GBR) 1.60m	Elfriede Kaun(GER) 1.60m
1948	Alice Coachman(USA) 1.68m	Dorothy Tyler(GBR) 1.68m	Micheline Ostermeyer(FRA) 1.61m
1952	Esther Brand(RSA) 1.67m	Sheila Lerwill(GBR) 1.65m	Alexandra Chudina(URS) 1.63m
1956	Mildred McDaniel(USA) 1.76m	Thelma Hopkins(GBR) 1.67m Maria Pisaryeva(URS) 1.67m	–
1960	Iolanda Balas(ROM) 1.85m	Jaroslawa Józwiakowska(POL) 1.71m Dorothy Shirley(GBR) 1.71m	–
1964	Iolanda Balas(ROM) 1.90m	Michelle Brown(AUS) 1.80m	Tasia Chenchik(URS) 1.78m
1968	Miloslava Rezková(TCH) 1.82m	Antonina Okorokova(URS) 1.80m	Valentina Kozyr(URS) 1.80m
1972	Ulrike Meyfarth(FRG) 1.92m	Yordanka Bloyeva(BUL) 1.88m	Ilona Gusenbauer(AUT) 1.88m
1976	Rosemarie Ackermann(GDR) 1.93m	Sara Simeoni(ITA) 1.91m	Yordanka Blagoyeva(BUL) 1.91m
1980	Sara Simeoni(ITA) 1.97m	Urszula Kielan(POL) 1.94m	Jutta Kirst(GDR) 1.94m
1984	Ulrike Meyfarth(FRG) 2.02m	Sara Simeoni(ITA) 2.00m	Joni Huntley(USA) 1.97m
1988	Louise Ritter(USA) 2.03m	Stefka Kostadinova(BUL) 2.01m	Tamara Bykova(URS) 1.99m
1992	Heike Henkel(GER) 2.02m	Galina Astafei(ROM) 2.00m	Ioamnet Quintero(CUB) 1.97m
1996	Stefka Kostadinova(BUL) 2.05m	Niki Bakogianni(GRE) 2.03m	Inga Babakova(UKR) 2.01m
2000	Yelena Yelesina(RUS) 2.01m	Hestrie Cloete(RSA) 2.01m	Oana Pantelimon(ROM) 1.99m Kajsa Bergqvist(SWE) 1.99m
2004	Yelena Slesarenko(RUS) 2.06m	Hestrie Cloete(RSA) 2.02m	Viktoriya Styopina(UKR) 2.02m

1896–1924 Event not held
(1) Sometimes given as 1.66m

Pole Vault – Women

	GOLD	SILVER	BRONZE
2000	Stacy Dragila(USA) 4.60m	Tatiana Grigorieva(AUS) 4.55m	Vala Flosadottir(ISL) 4.50m
2004	Yelena Isinbayeva(RUS) 4.91m	Svetlana Feofanova(RUS) 4.75m	Anna Rogowska(POL) 4.70m

1896–1996 Event not held

Long Jump –Women

	GOLD	SILVER	BRONZE
1948	Olga Gyarmati(HUN) 5.69m	Noëmi Simonetta de Portela(ARG) 5.60m	Ann-Britt Leyman(SWE) 5.57m
1952	Yvette Williams(NZL) 6.24m	Alexandra Chudina(URS) 6.14m	Shirley Cawley(GBR) 5.92m
1956	Elzbieta Krzesinska(POL) 6.35m	Willye White(USA) 6.09m	Nadyezda Dvalishvili(URS) 6.07m
1960	Vera Krepkina(URS) 6.37m	Elzbieta Krzesinska(POL) 6.27m	Hildrun Claus(GER) 6.21m
1964	Mary Rand(GBR) 6.76m	Irena Kirszenstein(POL) 6.27m	Tatyana Schelkanova(URS) 6.42m
1968	Niorica Viscopoleanu(ROM) 6.82m	Sheila Sherwood(GBR) 6.68m	Tatyana Talysheva(URS) 6.66m
1972	Heidemarie Rosendahl(FRG) 6.78m	Diana Yorgova(BUL) 6.77m	Eva Suranová(TCH) 6.67m
1976	Angela Voigt(GDR) 6.72m	Kathy McMillan(USA) 6.66m	Lidia Alfeyeva(URS) 6.60m
1980	Tatyana Kolpakova(URS) 7.06m	Brigitte Wujak(GDR) 7.04m	Tatyana Skatchko(URS) 7.01m
1984	Anisoara Stanciu(ROM) 6.96m	Vali Ionescu(ROM) 6.81m	Susan Hearnshaw(GBR) 6.80m
1988	Jackie Joyner-Kersee(USA) 7.40m	Heike Drechsler(GDR) 7.22m	Galina Chistiakova(URS) 7.11m
1992	Heike Drechsler(GDR) 7.14m	Inessa Kravets(EUN) 7.12m	Jackie Joyner-Kersee(USA) 7.07m
1996	Chioma Ajunwa(NGR) 7.12m	Fiona May(ITA) 7.02m	Jackie Joyner-Kersee(USA) 7.00m
2000	Heike Drechsler(GER) 6.99m	Fiona May(ITA) 6.92m	Marion Jones(USA) 6.92m
2004	Tatyana Lebedeva(RUS) 7.07m	Irina Simagina(RUS) 7.05m	Tatyana Kotova(RUS) 7.05m

1896–1936 Event not held

Triple Jump – Women

	GOLD	SILVER	BRONZE
1996	Inessa Kravets(UKR) 15.33m	Inna Lasovskaya(RUS) 14.98m	Sarka Kasparkova(CZE) 14.98m
2000	Tereza Marinova(BUL) 15.20m	Tatyana Lebedeva(RUS) 15.00m	Olena Govorova(UKR) 14.96m
2004	Françoise Mbango Etone(CMR)15.30m	Hrysopiyi Devetzi(GRE) 15.25m	Tatyana Lebedeva(RUS) 15.14m

1896–1992 Event not held

Shot Put – Women

	GOLD	SILVER	BRONZE
1948	Micheline Ostermeyer(FRA) 13.75m	Amelia Piccinini(ITA) 13.09m	Ina Schäffer(AUT) 13.08m
1952	Galina Zybina(URS) 15.28m	Marianne Werner(GER) 14.57m	Klavdia Tochonova(URS) 14.50m
1956	Tamara Tyshkevich(URS) 16.59m	Galina Zybina(URS) 15.53m	Marianne Werner(GER) 15.61m
1960	Tamara Press(URS) 17.32m	Johanna Lüttge(GER) 16.61m	Earlene Brown(USA) 16.42m
1964	Tamara Press(URS) 18.14m	Renate Garisch(GDR) 17.61m	Galina Zybina(URS) 16.42m
1968	Margitta Gummel(GDR) 19.61m	Marita Lange(GDR) 18.78m	Nadyezda Chizhova(URS) 18.19m
1972	Nadyezda Chizhova(URS) 21.03m	Margitta Gummel(GDR) 20.22m	Ivanka Khristova(BUL) 19.35m
1976	Ivanka Khristova(BUL) 21.16m	Nadyezda Chizhova(URS) 20.96m	Helena Fibingerová(TCH) 20.67m
1980	Ilona Slupianek(GDR) 22.41m	Svetlana Krachevskaya(URS) 21.42m	Margitta Pufe(GDR) 21.20m
1984	Claudia Losch(FRG) 20.48m	Mihaela Loghin(ROM) 20.47m	Gael Martin(AUS) 19.19m
1988	Natalya Lisovskaya(URS) 22.24m	Kathrin Neimke(GDR) 21.07m	Meisu Li(CHN) 21.06m
1992	Svetlana Krivelyova(EUN) 21.06m	Zhihong Huang(CHN) 20.47m	Kathrin Neimke(GER) 19.78m
1996	Astrid Kumbernuss(GER) 20.56m	Xinmei Sui(CHN) 19.88m	Irina Khudorozhkina(RUS) 19.35m
2000	Yanina Korolchik(BLR) 20.56m	Larisa Peleshenko(RUS) 19.92m	Astrid Kumbernuss(GER) 19.62m
2004(1)	Yumileidi Cumba(CUB) 19.59m	Nadine Kleinert(GER) 19.55m	Svetlana Krivelyova(RUS) 19.49m

1896–1936 Event not held

(1) Irina Korzhanenko (RUS) threw 21.06m but was disqualified

Discus – Women

	GOLD	SILVER	BRONZE
1928	Helena Konopacka(POL) 39.62m	Lilian Copeland(USA) 37.08m	Ruth Svedberg(SWE) 35.92m
1932	Lilian Copeland(USA) 40.58m	Ruth Osburn(USA) 40.11m	Jadwiga Wajsówna(POL) 38.73m
1936	Gisela Mauermayer(GER) 47.63m	Jadwiga Wajsówna(POL) 46.22m	Paula Mollenhauer(GER) 39.80m
1948	Micheleine Ostermeyer(FRA) 41.92m	Edera Gentile(ITA) 41.17m	Jacqueline Mazéas(FRA) 40.47m
1952	Nina Romashkova(URS) 51.42m	Elizaveta Bagryantseva(URS) 47.08m	Nina Dumbadze(URS) 46.29m
1956	Olga Fikotová(TCH) 53.69m	Irina Beglyakova(URS) 52.54m	Nina Ponomaryeva(URS) 52.02m
1960	Nina Ponomaryeva(URS) 55.10m	Tamara Press(URS) 52.59m	Lia Manoliu(ROM) 52.36m
1964	Tamara Press(URS) 57.27m	Ingrid Lotz(GER) 57.21m	Lia Manoliu(ROM) 56.97m
1968	Lia Manoliu(ROM) 58.28m	Liesel Westerman(FRG) 57.76m	Jolán Kleiber(HUN) 54.90m
1972	Faina Melnik(URS) 66.62m	Argentina Menis(ROM) 65.06m	Vasilka Stoyeva(BUL) 64.34m
1976	Evelin Sclaak(GDR) 69.00m	Maria Vergova(BUL) 67.30m	Gabriele Hinzmann(GDR) 66.84m
1980	Evelin Jahl(GDR) 69.96m	Maria Petkova(BUL) 67.90m	Tatyana Lesovaya(URS) 67.40m
1984	Ria Stalman(NED) 65.36m	Leslie Deniz(USA) 64.86m	Florenta Craciunescu(ROM) 63.64m
1988	Martina Hellmann(GDR) 72.30m	Diane Gansky(GDR) 71.88m	Tsvetanka Khristova(BUL) 69.74m
1992	Maritza Marten(CUB) 70.06m	Tsvetanka Khristova(BUL) 67.78m	Daniela Costian(AUS) 66.24m
1996	Ilke Wyludda(GER) 69.66m	Natalya Sadova(RUS) 66.48m	Elya Zvereva(BLR) 65.64m
2000	Ellina Zvereva(BLR) 68.40m	Anastasia Kelesidou(GRE) 65.31m	Irina Yatchenko(BLR) 65.20m

| 2004 | Natalya Sadova(RUS) 67.02m | Anastasia Kelesidou(GRE) 66.68m | Irina Yatchenko(BLR) 66.17m |

1896–1924 Event not held

Hammer – Women

	GOLD	SILVER	BRONZE
2000	Kamila Skolimowska(POL)	Olga Kuzenkova(RUS)	Kirsten Muenchow(GER)
2004	Olga Kuzenkova(RUS) 75.02m	Yipsi Moreno(CUB) 73.6m	Yunaika Crawford(CUB)73.16m

1896–1996 Event not held

Javelin – Women

	GOLD	SILVER	BRONZE
1932	Mildred Didrikson(USA) 43.68m	Ellen Braumüller(GER) 43.49m	Tilly Fleischer(GER) 43.40m
1936	Tilly Fleischer(GER) 45.18m	Louise Krüger(GER) 43.29m	Marja Kwasniewska(POL) 41.80m
1948	Herma Bauma(AUT) 45.57m	Kaisa Parviainen(FIN) 43.79m	Lily Carlstedt(DEN) 42.08m
1952	Dana Zátopková(TCH) 50.47m	Alexandra Chudina(URS) 50.01m	Yelena Gorchkova(URS) 49.76m
1956	Inese Jaunzeme(URS) 53.86m	Marlene Ahrens(CHI) 50.38m	Nadyezda Konyayeva(URS) 50.28m
1960	Elvira Ozolina(URS) 55.98m	Dana Zátopková(TCH) 53.78m	Birute Kalediene(URS) 53.45m
1964	Mihaela Penes(ROM) 60.64m	Márta Rudas(HUN) 58.27m	Yelena Gorchkova(URS) 57.07m
1968	Angéla Németh(HUN) 60.36m	Mihaela Penes(ROM) 59.92m	Eva Janko(AUT) 58.04m
1972	Ruth Fuchs(GDR) 63.88m	Jacqueline Todten(GDR) 62.54m	Kathy Schmidt(USA) 59.94m
1976	Ruth Fuchs(GDR) 65.94m	Marion Becker(FRG) 64.70m	Kathy Schmidt(USA) 63.96m
1980	María Colón(CUB) 68.40m	Saida Gunba(URS) 67.76m	Ute Hommola(GDR) 66.56m
1984	Tessa Sanderson(GBR) 69.56m	Tiina Lillak(FIN) 69.00m	Fatima Whitbread(GBR) 67.14m
1988	Petra Felke(GDR) 74.68m	Fatima Whitbread(GBR) 70.32m	Beate Koch(GDR) 67.30m
1992	Silke Renk(GER) 68.34m	Natalya Shikolenko(EUN) 68.26m	Karen Forkel(GER) 66.86m
1996	Heli Rantanen(FIN) 67.94m	Louise McPaul(AUS) 65.54m	Trine Hattestad(NOR) 64.68m
2000(1)	Trine Hattestad(NOR) 68.91m	Miréla Tzelili(GRE) 67.51m	Osleidys Menendez(CUB) 66.18m
2004	Osleidys Menendez(CUB) 71.53m	Steffi Nerius(GER) 65.82m	Mirela Manjani(GRE) 64.29m

1896–1928 Event not held
(1) Specification of implement changed in 1999

Pentathlon – Women

	GOLD	SILVER	BRONZE

(Consisted of 100m hurdles, shot, high jump, long jump, 200m from 1964–76. In 1980, 200m replaced by 800m. In 1984 event replaced by Heptathlon)

	GOLD	SILVER	BRONZE
1964	Irina Press(URS) 5246pts	Mary Rand(GBR) 5035pts	Galina Bystrova(URS) 4956pts
1968	Ingrid Becker(FRG) 5098pts	Liese Prokop(AUT) 4966pts	Annamaria Tóth(HUN) 4959pts
1972(1)	Mary Peters(GBR) 4801pts	Heidemarie Rosendahl(FRG) 4791pts	Burglinde Pollak(GDR) 4768pts
1976	Siegrun Siegl(GDR) 4745pts	Chrstine Laser(GDR) 4745pts	Burglinde Pollak(GDR) 4740pts
1980	Nadyezda Tkachenko(URS) 5083pts	Olga Rukavishnikova(URS) 4937pts	Olga Kuragina(URS) 4875pts

1896–1960, 1984–2004 Event not held
(1) New scoring tables in 1971

Heptathlon – Women

(Consists of 100m hurdles, high jump, shot, 200m on first day; long jump, javelin and 800m on second day. Replaced Pentathlon in 1984)

	GOLD	SILVER	BRONZE
1984(1)	Glynis Nunn(AUS) 6387pts	Jackie Joyner(USA) 6363pts	Sabine Everts(FRG) 6388pts
1988	Jackie Joyner-Kersee(USA) 7291pts	Sabine John(GDR) 6897pts	Anke Behmer(GDR) 6858pts
1992	Jackie Joyner-Kersee(USA) 7044pts	Irina Belova(EUN) 6845pts	Sabine Braun(GER) 6649pts
1996	Ghada Shouaa(SYR) 6780pts	Natasha Sazanovich(BLR) 6563pts	Denise Lewis(GBR) 6489pts
2000	Denise Lewis(GBR) 6584pts	Yelena Prokhorova(RUS) 6531pts	Natalya Sazanovich(BLR) 6527pts
2004	Carolina Kluft(SWE) 6952pts	Austra Skujyte(LTU) 6435ts	Kelly Sotherton(GBR) 6424pts

1896–1980 Event not held
(1) Recalculated on current tables

ATHLETICS – DISCONTINUED EVENTS

	GOLD	SILVER	BRONZE

60m – Men

	GOLD	SILVER	BRONZE
1900	Alvin Kraenzlein(USA) 7.0	Walter Tewsbury(USA) 7.1	Stanley Rowley(AUS) 7.2
1904	Archie Hahn(USA) 7.0	William Hogenson(USA) 7.2	Fay Moulton(USA) 7.2

3,000m Team Race – Men

	GOLD	SILVER	BRONZE
1912	UNITED STATES 9pts	SWEDEN 13pts	GREAT BRITAIN 23pts
1920	UNITED STATES 10pts	GREAT BRITAIN 20pts	SWEDEN 24pts
1924	FINLAND 8pts	GREAT BRITAIN 14pts	UNITED STATES 25pts

3 mile Team Race – Men

	GOLD	SILVER	BRONZE
1908	GREAT BRITAIN 6 pts	UNITED STATES 19pts	FRANCE 32pts

5,000m Team Race – Men
1900   GREAT BRITAIN 26pts   FRANCE 29pts   –

4 mile Team Race – Men
1904   UNITED STATES 27pts   UNITED STATES 28pts   –

Individual Cross-Country – Men
1912(1)   Hannes Kolehmainen(FIN) 45:11.6   Hjalmar Andersson(SWE) 45:44.8   John Eke(SWE) 46:37.6
1920(2)   Paavo Nurmi(FIN) 27:15.0   Erick Backman(SWE) 27:27.6   Heikki Liimatainen(FIN 27:37.4
1924(3)   Paavo Nurmi(FIN) 32:54.8   Ville Ritola(FIN) 34:19.4   Earle Johnson(USA) 35:21.0
(1) 12,000m
(2) 8,000m
(3) 10,000m

Team Cross-Country – Men
1912   SWEDEN 10pts   FINLAND 11pts   GREAT BRITAIN 49pts
1920   FINLAND 10pts   GREAT BRITAIN 21pts   SWEDEN 23pts
1924   FINLAND 11pts   UNITED STATES 14pts   FRANCE 20pts

200m Hurdles – Men
1900   Alvin Kraenzlein(USA) 25.4   Norman Pritchard(GBR) 26.6   Walter Tewksbury(USA) n.t.a.
1904   Harry Hillman(USA) 24.6   Frank Castleman(USA) 24.9   George Poage(USA) n.t.a.

1,500m Walk – Men
1906   George Bonhag(USA) 7:12.6   Donald Linden(CAN) 7:19.8   Konstantin Spetsiosis(GRE) 7:22.0

3,000m Walk – Men
1906   György Szantics(HUN) 15:13.2   Hermann Müller(GER) 15:20.0   Georgios Saridakis(GRE) 15:33.0
1920   Ugo Frigerio(ITA) 13:14.2   George Parker(AUS) n.t.a.   Richard Remer(USA) n.t.a.

3,500m Walk – Men
1908   George Larner(GBR) 14:55.0   Ernest Webb(GBR) 15:07.4   Harry Kerr(NZL) 15:43.4

10,000m Walk – Men
1912   George Goulding(CAN) 46:28.4   Ernest Webb(GBR) 46:50.4   Fernando Altimani(ITA) 47:37.6
1920   Ugo Frigerio(ITA) 48:06.2   Joseph Pearman(USA) n.t.a.   Charles Gunn(GBR) n.t.a.
1924   Ugo Frigerio(ITA) 47:49.0   Gordon Goodwin(GBR) 200m   Cecil McMaster(RSA) 300m
1948   John Mikaelsson(SWE) 45:13.2   Ingemar Johansson(SWE) 45:43.8   Fritz Schwab(SUI) 46:00.2
1952   John Mikaelsson(SWE) 45:02.8   Fritz Schwab(SUI) 45:41.0   Bruno Junk(URS) 45:41.2
1928–36 Event not held

10 mile Walk – Men
1908   George Larner(GBR) 1h 15:57.4   Ernest Webb(GBR) 1h 17:31.0   Edward Spencer(GBR) 1h 21:20.2

Standing High Jump
1900   Ray Ewry(USA) 1.655m   Irving Baxter(USA) 1.525m   Lewis Sheldon(USA) 1.50m
1904   Ray Ewry(USA) 1.50m (1)   James Stadler(USA) 1.45m   Lawson Robertson(USA) 1.45m
1906   Ray Ewry(USA) 1.565m   Martin Sheridan(USA) 1.40m   –
                                                    Léon Dupont(BEL) 1.40m
                                                    Lawson Robertson(USA) 1.40m
1908   Ray Ewry(USA) 1.575m   Konstantin Tsiklitiras(GRE) 1.55m
                                                    John Biller(USA) 1.55m
1912   Platt Adams(USA) 1.63m   Benjamin Adams(USA) 1.60m   Konstantin Tsiklitiras(GRE) 1.55m
(1) Some reports suggest height was 1.60m

Standing Long Jump – Men
1900   Ray Ewry(USA) 3.21m   Irving Baxter(USA) 3.135m   Emile Torchebeouf(FRA) 3.03m
1904   Ray Ewry(USA) 3.476m   Charles King(USA) 3.28m   John Biller(USA) 3.26m
1906   Ray Ewry(USA) 3.30m   Martin Sheridan(USA) 3.095m   Lawson Robertson(USA) 3.05m
1908   Ray Ewry(USA) 3.335m   Konstantin Tsiklitiras(GRE) 3.23m   Martin Sheridan(USA) 3.225m
1912   Konstantin Tsiklitiras(GRE) 3.37m   Platt Adams(USA) 3.36m   Benjamin Adams(USA) 3.28m

Standing Triple Jump – Men
1900   Ray Ewry(USA) 10.58m   Irving Baxter(USA) 9.95m   Robert Garrett(USA) 9.50m
1904   Ray Ewry(USA) 10.55m   Charles King(USA) 10.16m   James Stadler(USA) 9.53m

Stone Put (6.40kg) – Men
1906   Nicolaos Georgantas(GRE) 19.925m   Martin Sheridan(USA) 19.035m   Michel Dorizas(GRE) 18.585m

Shot (Both Hands) – Men
(Aggregate of throws with right and left hands)
1912   Ralph Rose(USA) 27.70m   Patrick McDonald(USA) 27.53m   Elmer Niklander(FIN) 27.14m

Discus (Both Hands) – Men
(Aggregate of throws with right and left hands)
1912   Armas Taipale(FIN) 82.86m   Elmer Niklander(FIN) 77.96m   Emil Magnusson(SWE) 77.37m

Discus (Greek Style) – Men
1906   Werner Järvinen(FIN) 35.17m   Nicolaos Georgantas(GRE) 32.80m   István Mudin(HUN) 31.91m
1908   Martin Sheridan(USA) 38.00m   Marquis Horr(USA) 37.325m   Werner Järvinen(FIN) 36.48m

Javelin (Both Hands) – Men
(Aggregate of throws with right and left hands)
1912   Juho Saaristo(FIN) 109.42m   Väinö Siikamiemi(FIN) 101.13m   Urho Peltonen(FIN) 100.24m

Javelin (Free Style) – Men
1908   Eric Lemming(SWE) 54.445m   Michel Dorizas(GRE) 51.36m   Arne Halse(NOR) 49.73m

56-Pound (25.4kg) Weight Throw – Men
1904   Étienne Desmateau(CAN) 10.465m   John Flanagan(USA) 10.16m   James Mitchell(USA) 10.135m
1920   Patrick McDonald(USA) 11.265m   Patrick Ryan(USA) 10.965m   Carl Lind(SWE) 10.25m

Pentathlon – Men
1906(1)   Hjalmar Mellander(SWE) 24pts   István Mudin(HUN) 25pts   Eric Lemming(SWE) 29pts
1912(2)   Ferdinand Bie(NOR) 16pts (3)   James Donahue(USA) 24pts   Frank Lukeman(CAN) 24pts
1920(2)   Eero Lehtonen(FIN) 14pts   Everett Bradley(USA) 24pts   Hugo Lahtinen(FIN) 26pts
1924(2)   Eero Lehtonen(FIN) 14pt   Elemér Somfay(HUN) 16pts   Robert LeGendre(USA) 18pts

(1) Consisted of standing long jump, discus (Greek style), javelin, one-lap (192m) race, Greco-Roman wrestling
(2) Consisted of long jump, javelin, 200m, discus, 1500m
(3) Jim Thorpe (USA) finished first with 7 pts but was subsequently disqualified. He was reinstated posthumously in 1982, but only as joint first

BADMINTON

Singles – Men

	GOLD	SILVER	BRONZE
1992	Alan Budi Kusuma(INA)	Ardy Wiranata(INA)	Thomas Stuer-Lauridsen(DEN)
			Hermawan Susanto(INA)
1996	Poul-Erik Høyer-Larsen(DEN)	Jiong Dong(CHN)	Rashid Sidek(MAS)
2000	Xinopeng Ji(CHN)	Hendrawan(INA)	Xuanze Xia(CHN)
2004	Taufik Hidayat(INA)	Seung Mo Shon(KOR)	Soni Dwi Kuncoro(INA)

1896–1988 Event not held

Doubles – Men

	GOLD	SILVER	BRONZE
1992	KOREA	INDONESIA	MALAYSIA
			CHINA
1996	INDONESIA	MALAYSIA	INDONESIA
2000	INDONESIA	KOREA	KOREA
2004	KOREA	KOREA	INDONESIA

1896–1988 Event not held

Mixed Doubles

	GOLD	SILVER	BRONZE
1996	KOREA	KOREA	CHINA
2000	CHINA	INDONESIA	GREAT BRITAIN
2004	CHINA	GREAT BRITAIN	DENMARK

1896–1992 Event not held

Singles – Women

	GOLD	SILVER	BRONZE
1992	Susi Susanti(INA)	Soo-Hyun Bang(KOR)	Hua Huang(CHN)
			Jiuhong Tang(CHN)
1996	Soo-Hyun Bang(KOR)	Mia Audina(INA)	Susi Susanti(INA)
2000	Zhuchao Gong(CHN)	Camilla Marti(DEN)	Zhaoying Ye(CHN)
2004	Ning Zhang(CHN)	Mia Audina(NED)	Mi Zhou(CHN)

Doubles – Women

	GOLD	SILVER	BRONZE
1992	KOREA	CHINA	KOREA
			CHINA
1996	CHINA	KOREA	CHINA
2000	CHINA	CHINA	CHINA
2004	CHINA	CHINA	KOREA

1896–1988 Event not held

BASEBALL

	GOLD	SILVER	BRONZE
1992	CUBA	TAIWAN	JAPAN
1996	CUBA	JAPAN	UNITED STATES
2000	UNITED STATES	CUBA	KOREA
2004	CUBA	AUSTRALIA	JAPAN

1896–1988 Event not held

BASKETBALL

Men

	GOLD	SILVER	BRONZE
1936	UNITED STATES	CANADA	MEXICO
1948	UNITED STATES	FRANCE	BRAZIL
1952	UNITED STATES	SOVIET UNION	URUGUAY
1956	UNITED STATES	SOVIET UNION	URUGUAY
1960	UNITED STATES	SOVIET UNION	BRAZIL
1964	UNITED STATES	SOVIET UNION	BRAZIL
1968	UNITED STATES	YUGOSLAVIA	SOVIET UNION
1972	SOVIET UNION	UNITED STATES	CUBA
1976	UNITED STATES	YUGOSLAVIA	SOVIET UNION
1980	YUGOSLAVIA	ITALY	SOVIET UNION
1984	UNITED STATES	SPAIN	YUGOSLAVIA
1988	SOVIET UNION	YUGOSLAVIA	UNITED STATES
1992	UNITED STATES	CROATIA	LITHUANIA
1996	UNITED STATES	YUGOSLAVIA	LITHUANIA
2000	UNITED STATES	FRANCE	LITHUANIA
2004	ARGENTINA	ITALY	UNITED STATES

1896–1932 Event not held

Women

	GOLD	SILVER	BRONZE
1976	SOVIET UNION	UNITED STATES	BULGARIA
1980	SOVIET UNION	BULGARIA	YUGOSLAVIA
1984	UNITED STATES	KOREA	CHINA
1988	UNITED STATES	YUGOSLAVIA	SOVIET UNION
1992	UNIFIED TEAM	CHINA	USA
1996	UNITED STATES	BRAZIL	AUSTRALIA
2000	UNITED STATES	AUSTRALIA	BRAZIL
2004	UNITED STATES	AUSTRALIA	RUSSIA

1896–1972 Event not held

BEACH VOLLEYBALL

Doubles – Men

	GOLD	SILVER	BRONZE
1996	UNITED STATES	UNITED STATES	CANADA
2000	UNITED STATES	BRAZIL	GERMANY
2004	BRAZIL	SPAIN	SWITZERLAND

1896–1992 Event not held

Doubles – Women

	GOLD	SILVER	BRONZE
1996	BRAZIL	BRAZIL	AUSTRALIA
2000	AUSTRALIA	BRAZIL	BRAZIL
2004	USA	BRAZIL	USA

1896–1992 Event not held

BOXING

Light-Flyweight
(Weight up to 48kg/105.8lb)

	GOLD	SILVER	BRONZE
1968	Francisco Rodriguez(VEN)	Yong-Ju Jee(KOR)	Harlan Marbley(USA)
			Hubert Skrzypczak(POL)

1972	György Gedo(HUN)	U Gil Kim(PRK)	Ralph Evans(GBR)
			Enrique Rodriguez(ESP)
1976	Jorge Hernandez(CUB)	Byong Uk Li(PRK)	Payao Pooltarat(THA)
			Orlando Maladonado(PUR)
1980	Shamil Sabirov(URS)	Hipolito Ramos(CUB)	Byong Uk Li(PRK)
			Ismail Moustafov(BUL)
1984	Paul Gonzales(USA)	Saltore Todisco(ITA)	Keith Mwila(ZAM)
			Jose Bolivar(VEN)
1988	Ivailo Hristov(CUB)	Michael Carabajal(USA)	Robert Isaszegi(HUN)
			Leopoldo Serantes(PHI)
1992	Rogelio Marcelo(CUB)	Daniel Bojinov(BUL)	Roel Velasco(PHI)
			Jan Quast(GER)
1996	Daniel Petrov(BUL)	Mansueto Velsco(PHI)	Oleg Kuryukhin(UKR)
			Rafael Lozano(ESP)
2000	Brahim Asloum(FRA)	Rafel Lozano Munoz(CUB)	Un Chol Kim(KOR)
			Maikro Romero(CUB)
2004	Yan Varela Bhartelemy(CUB)	Atagün Yalçinkaya(TUR)	Sergei Kazakov(RUS)
			Shiming Zou(CHN)

1896–1964 Event not held

Flyweight
(From 1948 the weight limit has been 51kg/112.5lb. In 1904 it was 47.6kg/105lb. From 1920 to 1936 it was 50.8kg/112lb)

	GOLD	SILVER	BRONZE
1904	George Finnegan(USA)	Miles Burke(USA)	– (1)
1920	Frank Di Gennara(USA)	Anders Petersen(DEN)	William Cuthbertson(GBR)
1924	Fidel LaBarba(USA)	James McKenzie(GBR)	Raymond Fee(USA)
1928	Antal Kocsis(HUN)	Armand Appel(FRA)	Carlo Cavagnogli(ITA)
1932	István Enekes(HUN)	Francisco Cabanas(MEX)	Louis Salica(USA)
1936	Willi Kaiser(GER)	Gavino Matta(ITA)	Louis Lauria(USA)
1948	Pascual Perez(ARG)	Spartaco Bandinelli(ITA)	Soo-Ann Han(KOR)
1952	Nathan Brooks(USA)	Edgar Basel(GER)	Anatoli Bulakov(URS)
			William Toweel(RSA)
1956	Terence Spinks(GBR)	Mircea Dobrescu(ROM)	John Caldwell(IRL)
			René Libeer(FRA)
1960	Gyula Török(HUN)	Sergei Sivko(URS)	Kyoshi Tanabe(JPN)
			Abdelmoneim Elguindi(EGY)
1964	Fernando Atzori(ITA)	Artur Olech(POL)	Robert Carmody(USA)
			Stanislav Sorokin(URS)
1968	Ricardo Delagdo(MEX)	Artur Olech(POL)	Servilio Oliveira(BRA)
			Leo Rwabwogo(UGA)
1972	Gheorghi Kostadinov(BUL)	Leo Rwabwogo(UGA)	Leszek Blazynski(POL)
			Douglas Rodriguez(CUB)
1976	Leo Randolph(USA)	Ramón Duvalon(CUB)	Leszek Blazynski(POL)
			David Torsyan(URS)
1980	Petar Lessov(BUL)	Viktor Miroschnicheko(URS)	Hugh Russel(IRL)
			Janos Varadi(HUN)
1984	Steve McCrory(USA)	Redzep Redzepovski(YUG)	Eyup Can(TUR)
			Ibrahim Bilali(KEN)
1988	Kwang-Sun Kim(KOR)	Andreas Tew(GDR)	Mario González(MEX)
			Timofey Skriabin(URS)
1992	Chol-Su Choi(PRK)	Rául González(CUB)	Timothy Austin(USA)
			István Kovács(HUN)
1996	Maikro Romero(CUB)	Bulat Dzumadilov(KAZ)	Albert Pakeyev(RUS)
			Zoltan Lunka(GER)
2000	Wijan Ponlid(THA)	Bulat Dzumalidov(KAZ)	Jerome Thomas(USA)
			Vladimir Sidorenko(UKR)
2004	Yuriorkis Gamboa Toledano(CUB)	Jerôme Thomas(FRA)	Rustamhodza Rahimov(GER)
			Fuad Aslanov(AZE

1896–1900, 1906–12 Event not held
(1) No third place

Bantamweight
(From 1948 the weight limit has been 54kg/119lb. In 1904 it was 52.16kg/115lb and in 1908 it was 52.62kg/116lb. From 1920 to 1936 it was 53.52kg/118lb)

	GOLD	SILVER	BRONZE
1904	Oliver Kirk(USA)	George Finnegan(USA)	– (1)
1908	Henry Thomas(GBR)	John Condon(GBR)	William Webb(GBR)
1920	Clarence Walker(RSA)	Christopher Graham(CAN)	James McKenzie(GBR)
1924	William Smith(RSA)	Salvadore Tripoli(USA)	Jean Ces(FRA)
1928	Vittorio Tamagnini(ITA)	John Daley(USA)	Harry Issacs(RSA)
1932	Horace Gwynne(CAN)	Hans Ziglarski(GER)	José Villanueva(PHI)
1936	Ulderico Sergo(ITA)	Jack Wilson(USA)	Fidel Ortiz(MEX)
1948	Tibor Csik(HUN)	Giovanni Zuddas(ITA)	Juan Venegas(PUR)

	GOLD	SILVER	BRONZE
1952	Pentti Hämäläinen(FIN)	John McNally(IRL)	Gennadi Garbuzov(URS)
1956	Wolfgang Behrendt(GER)	Chun-Song Soon(KOR)	Joon-Ho Kang(KOR) Frederick Gilroy(IRL)
1960	Oleg Grigoriev(URS)	Primo Zamparini(ITA)	Claudio Barrientos(CHI) Brunoh Bendig(POL)
1964	Takao Sakurai(JPN)	Shin Cho Chung(KOR)	Oliver Taylor(AUS) Juan Fabila Mendoza(MEX)
1968	Valeri Sokolov(URS)	Eridadi Mukwanga(UGA)	Washington Rodriguez(URU) Eiji Morioka(JPN)
1972	Orlando Martinez(CUB)	Alfonso Zamora(MEX)	Kyou-Chull Chang(KOR) George Turpin(GBR)
1976	Yong Jo Gu(PRK)	Charles Mooney(USA)	Ricardo Carreras(USA) Patrick Cowdell(GBR)
1980	Juan Hernandez(CUB)	Bernando Pinango(VEN)	Viktor Rybakov(URS) Dumitru Cipere(ROM)
1984	Maurizio Stecca(ITA)	Hector Lopez(MEX)	Michael Anthony Parris(GUY) Dale Walters(CAN)
1988	Kennedy McKinney(USA)	Alexandar Hristov(BUL)	Pedro Nolasco(DOM) Jorge Julio Rocha(COL)
1992	Joel Casamayor(CUB)	Wayne McCullough(IRL)	Phajol Moolsan(THA) Gwang-Sik Li(PRK)
1996	István Kovács(HUN)	Arnoldo Mesa(CUB)	Mohamed Achik(MAR) Raimkul Malakhbekov(RUS)
2000	Guillermo Rigondeaux(CUB)	Raimkul Malakhbekov(RUS)	Khadpo Vichairachanun(THA) Sergei Danilchenko(UKR)
2004	Guillermo Rigondeaux Ortiz(CUB)	Worapoj Petchkoom(THA)	Clarence Vinson(USA) Bahodirjon Soltonov(UZB) Aghasi Mammadov(AZE)

1896–1900, 1906, 1912 Event not held
(1) No third place

Featherweight

(From 1952 the weight limit has been 57kg/126lb. In 1904 it was 56.70kg. From 1908 to 1936 it was 57.15kg/126lb. In 1948 it was 58kg/128lb)

	GOLD	SILVER	BRONZE
1904	Oliver Kirk(USA)	Frank Haller(USA)	Fred Gilmore(USA)
1908	Richard Gunn(GBR)	Charles Morris(GBR)	Hugh Roddin(GBR)
1920	Paul Fritsch(FRA)	Jean Gachet(FRA)	Edoardo Garzena(ITA)
1924	Jackie Fields(USA)	Joseph Salas(USA)	Pedro Quartucci(ARG)
1928	Lambertus van Klaveren(NED)	Victor Peralta(ARG)	Harold Devine(USA)
1932	Carmelo Robeldo(ARG)	Josef Schleinkofer(GER)	Carl Carlsson(SWE)
1936	Oscar Casanovas(ARG)	Charles Cattterall(RSA)	Josef Miner(GER)
1948	Ernesto Foremnti(ITA)	Denis Shepherd(RSA)	Alexei Antkiewicz(POL)
1952	Jan Zachara(TCH)	Sergio Caprari(ITA)	Joseph Ventaja(FRA) Leonard Leisching(RSA)
1956	Vladimir Safronov(URS)	Thomas Nicholls(GBR)	Henryk Niedzwiedzki(POL) Pentti Hämäläinen(FIN)
1960	Francesco Musso(ITA)	Jerzy Adamski(POL)	William Meyers(RSA) Jorma Limmonen(FIN)
1964	Stanislav Stepashkin(URS)	Anthony Villaneuva(PHI)	Charles Brown(USA) Heinz Schultz(GER)
1968	Antonio Roldan(MEX)	Albert Robinson(USA)	Philip Waruinge(KEN) Ivan Michailov(BUL)
1972	Boris Kuznetsov(URS)	Philip Waruinge(KEN)	Clemente Rojas(COL) András Botos(HUN)
1976	Angel Herrera(CUB)	Richard Nowakowski(GDR)	Juan Peredes(MEX) Leszek Kosedowski(POL)
1980	Rudi Fink(GDR)	Adolfo Horta(CUB)	Viktor Rybakov(URS) Krzysztof Kosedowski(POL)
1984	Meldrick Taylor(USA)	Peter Konyegwachie(NGR)	Turgut Aykac(TUR) Omar Peraza(VEN)
1988	Giovanni Parisi(ITA)	Daniel Dumitrescu(ROM)	Jae-Hyuk Lee(KOR) Abdelhak Achik(MAR)
1992	Andreas Tew(GER)	Faustino Reyes Lopez(ESP)	Hocine Soltani(ALG) Ramazi Paliani(EUN)
1996	Somluck Kamsing(THA)	Serafim Todorov(BUL)	Pablo Chacon(ARG) Floyd Mayweather(USA)
2000	Beksat Sattarkhanov(KAZ)	Ricardo Suarez(USA)	Tahar Tamsamani(MAR) Kamil Dzamalutdinov(RUS)
2004	Alexei Tichtchenko(RUS)	Song-Guk Kim(PRK)	Vitali Tajbert(GER) Seok-Hwan Jo(KOR)

1896–1900, 1906, 1912 Event not held

Lightweight

(From 1952 the weight has been 60kg/132lb. In 1904 and from 1920 to 1936 it was 61.24kg/135lb. In 1908 it was 63.50kg/140lb. In 1948 it was 62kg/136.5lb)

	GOLD	SILVER	BRONZE
1904	Harry Springer(USA)	James Eagan(USA)	Russell Van Horn(USA)
1908	Frederick Grace(GBR)	Frederick Spiller(GBR)	Harry Johnson(GBR)
1920	Samuel Mosberg(RSA)	Gotfried Johansen(DEN)	Clarence Newton(CAN)
1924	Hans Nielsen(DEN)	Alfredo Coppello(ARG)	Frederick Boylstein(USA)
1928	Carlo Orlandi(ITA)	Stephen Halaiko(USA)	Gunnar Berggren(SWE)
1932	Lawrence Stevens(RSA)	Thure Ahlqvist(SWE)	Nathan Bor(RSA)
1936	Imre Harangi(HUN)	Nikolai Stepulov(EST)	Erik Agren(SWE)
1948	Gerald Dreyer(USA)	Joseph Vissers(BEL)	Svend Wad(DEN)
1952	Aureliano Bolognesi(ITA)	Alexei Antkiewicz(POL)	Gheorge Fiat(ROM)
			Erkki Pakkanen(FIN)
1956	Richard McTaggart(GBR)	Harry Kurschat(GER)	Anthony Byren(IRL)
			Anatoli Lagetko(URS)
1960	Kazimierz Pazdzior(POL)	Sandro Lopopoli(ITA)	Richard McTaggart(GBR)
			Abel Laudonio(ARG)
1964	Józef Grudzien(POL)	Velikton Barannikov(URS)	Ronald A. Harris(USA)
			James McCourt(IRL)
1968	Ronald W. Harris(USA)	Józef Grudzien(POL)	Calistrat Cutov(ROM)
			Zvonimir Vujin(YUG)
1972	Jan Szczepanksi(POL)	László Orban(HUN)	Samuel Mbugna(KEN)
			Alfonso Perez(COL)
1976	Howard Davis(USA)	Simion Cutov(ROM)	Ace Rusevski(YUG)
			Vasiliy Solomin(URS)
1980	Angel Herrara(CUB)	Viktor Demianenko(URS)	Kazimierz Adach(POL)
			Richard Nowakowski(GDR)
1984	Pernell Whitaker(USA)	Luis Ortiz(PUR)	Martin Mbanga(CMR)
			Chi-Sung Chun(KOR)
1988	Andreas Zülow(GDR)	George Cramme(SWE)	Nerguy Enkhbat(MGL)
			Romallis Ellis(USA)
1992	Oscar de la Hoya(CUB)	Marco Rudolph(USA)	Namjil Bayarsaikhan(MGL)
			Sung-Sik Hong(KOR)
1996	Hocine Soltani(ALG)	Tontcho Tonchev(BUL)	Terrance Cauthen(USA)
			Leonard Doroftei(ROM)
2000	Mario Kindelan(CUB)	Andrei Kotelnyk(UKR)	Alexander Maletin(RUS)
			Christian Bejarano Benitez(MEX)
2004	Mario Kindelan(CUB)	Amir Khan(GBR)	Serik Yeleuov(KAZ)
			Murat Khrachev(RUS)

1896–1900, 1906, 1912 Event not held

Light-Welterweight

(Weight up to 63.5kg/140lb)

	GOLD	SILVER	BRONZE
1952	Charles Adkins(USA)	Viktor Mednov(URS)	Errki Mallenius(FIN)
			Bruno Visintin(ITA)
1956	Vladimir Yengibarvan(URS)	Franco Nenci(ITA)	Henry Loubscher(RSA)
			Constantin Dumitrescu(ROM)
1960	Bohumil Nemecek(TCH)	Clement Quartey(GHA)	Quincy Daniels(USA)
			Marian Kasprzyk(POL)
1964	Jerzy Kulej(POL)	Yevgeni Frolov(URS)	Eddie Blay(GHA)
			Habib Galhia(TUN)
1968	Jerzy Kulej(POL)	Enrique Regueiforos(CUB)	Arto Nilsson(FIN)
			James Wallington(USA)
1972	Ray Seales(USA)	Anghel Anghelov(BUL)	Zvonimir Vujin(YUG)
			Issaka Daborg(NGR)
1976	Ray Leonard(USA)	Andres Aldama(CUB)	Vladimir Kolev(BUL)
			Kazimierz Szczerba(POL)
1980	Patrizio Oliva(ITA)	Serik Konakbeyev(URS)	Jose Aguilar(CUB)
			Anthony Willis(GBR)
1984	Jerry Page(USA)	Dhawee Umponmana(THA)	Mircea Fuger(ROM)
			Mirko Puzovic(YUG)
1988	Vycheslav Janovski(URS)	Grahame Cheney(AUS)	Lars Myrberg(SWE)
			Reiner Gies(FRG)
1992	Hector Vinent(CUB)	Marc Leduc(CAN)	Jyri Kjall(FIN)
			Leonard Doroftei(ROM)
1996	Hector Vinent(CUB)	Oktay Urkal(GER)	Bolat Niyazymbetov(KAZ)
			Fathi Missaoui(TUN)
2000	Mahamadkadis Abdullayev(UZB)	Ricardo Williams(USA)	Diogenes Luna Martinez(CUB)
			Mohamed Allalou(ALG)
2004	Manus Boonjumnong(THA)	Yudel Johnson Cedeno(CUB)	Boris Georgiev(BUL)
			Ionut Gheorghe(ROM)

1896–1948 Event not held

Welterweight

(From 1948 the weight limit has been 67kg/148lb. In 1904 it was 65.27kg/147.5lb. From 1920 to 1936 it was 66.68kg/147lb)

	GOLD	SILVER	BRONZE
1904	Albert Young(USA)	Harry Springer(USA)	Joseph Lydon(USA)
			James Eagan(USA)
1920	Albert Schneider(CAN)	Alexander Ireland(GBR)	Frederick Colberg(USA)
1924	Jean Delarge(BEL)	Héctor Mendez(ARG)	Douglas Lewis(CAN)
1928	Edward Morgan(NZL)	Raul Landini(ARG)	Raymond Smillie(CAN)
1932	Edward Flynn(USA)	Erich Campe(GER)	Bruno Ahlberg(FIN)
1936	Sten Suvio(FIN)	MIchael Murach(GER)	Gerhard Petersen(DEN)
1948	Julius Torma(TCH)	Horace Herring(USA)	Alessandro D'Ottavio(ITA)
1952	Zygmunt Chycla(POL)	Sergei Schtsherbakov(URS)	Victor Jörgensen(DEN)
			Günther Heidemann(GER)
1956	Nicholae Lince(ROM)	Frederick Tiedt(IRL)	Kevin Hogarth(AUS)
			Nicholas Gargano(GBR)
1960	Giovanni Benvenutti(ITA)	Yuriy Radonyak(URS)	Leszek Drogosz(POL)
			James Lloyd(GBR)
1964	Marian Kasprzyk(POL)	Ritschardas Tamulis(URS)	Pertti Perhonen(FIN)
			Silvano Bertini(ITA)
1968	Manfred Wolfe(GDR)	Joseph Bessala(CMR)	Vladimir Musalinov(URS)
			Mario Guillot(ITA)
1972	Emilio Corea(CUB)	Janos Kajdi(HUN)	Dick Murunga(KEN)
			Jesse Valdez(USA)
1976	Jochen Bachfeld(GDR)	Pedro Gamarro(VEN)	Reinhard Skricek(FRG)
			Victor Zilberman(ROM)
1980	Andrew Aldama(CUB)	John Mugabi(UGA)	Karl-Heinz Krüger(GDR)
			Kazimierz Szczerba(POL)
1984	Mark Breland(USA)	Young-Su An(KOR)	Joni Nyman(FIN)
			Luciano Bruno(ITA)
1988	Robert Wanglia(KEN)	Laurent Boudouani(FRA)	Jan Dydak(POL)
			Kenneth Gould(USA)
1992	Michael Carruth(IRL)	Juan Hernandez(CUB)	Akrom Chenglai(THA)
			Anibal Acevedo(PUR)
1996	Oleg Saitov(RUS)	Juan Hernandez(CUB)	Marian Simion(ROM)
			Daniel Santos(PUR)
2000	Oleg Saitov(RUS)	Sergei Dotsenko(UKR)	Dorel Simion(ROM)
			Vitali Grusac(MDA)
2004	Bakhtiyar Artayev(KAZ)	Lorenzo Aragon Armenteros(CUB)	Jung-Joo Kim(KOR)
			Oleg Saitov(RUS)

1896–1900, 1906–12 Event not held

Light-Middleweight

(Weight up to 71kg/157lb)

	GOLD	SILVER	BRONZE
1952	László Papp(HUN)	Theunis van Schalkwyk(RSA)	Boris Tishin(URS)
			Eladio Herrera(ARG)
1956	László Papp(HUN)	José Torres(USA)	John McCormack(GBR)
			Zbigniew Pietrzkowski(POL)
1960	Wilbert McClure(USA)	Carmelo Bossi(ITA)	Boris Lagutin(URS)
			William Fisher(GBR)
1964	Boris Lagutin(URS)	Josef Gonzales(FRA)	Nohim Maivegun(NGR)
			Jozef Grzsiak(POL)
1968	Boris Lagutin(URS)	Rolondo Garbey(CUB)	John Baldwin(USA)
			Günther Meier(FRG)
1972	Dieter Kottysch(FRG)	Wieslaw Rudkowski(POL)	Alan Minter(GBR)
			Peter Tiepold(GDR)
1976	Jerzy Rybicki(POL)	Tadiji Kacar(YUG)	Rolando Garbey(CUB)
			Viktor Savchenko(URS)
1980	Armando Martinez(CUB)	Alexander Koshkin(URS)	Jan Franck(TCH)
			Detlef Kastner(GDR)
1984	Frank Tate(USA)	Shawn O'Sullivan(CAN)	Manfred Zielonka(FRG)
			Christophe Tiozzo(FRA)
1988	Si-Hun Park(KOR)	Roy Jones(USA)	Richard Woodhall(GBR)
			Raymond Downey(CAN)
1992	Juan Carlos Lemus(CUB)	Orhan Delibas(NED)	György Mizsei(HUN)
			Robin Reid(GBR)
1996	David Reid(USA)	Alfredo Duvergel(CUB)	Karim Tulaganov(UZB)
			Ezmouhan Ibzaimov(KAZ)
2000	Jermachan Ibraimov(KAZ)	Marian Simion(ROM)	Pornchai Thongburan(THA)
			Jermain Taylor(USA)

1896–1948, 2004 Event not held

Middleweight

(From 1952 the weight has been 75kg/165lb. From 1904 to 1908 it was 71.68kg/158lb. From 1920 to 1936 it was 72.57kg/160lb. In 1948 it was 73kg/161lb)

	GOLD	SILVER	BRONZE
1904	Charles Mayer(USA)	Benjamin Spradley(USA)	– (1)
1908	John Douglas(GBR)	Reginald Baker(AUS/NZL)	William Philo(GBR)
1920	Harry Mallin(GBR)	Georges Prud'homme(CAN)	Moe Herscovich(CAN)
1924	Harry Mallin(GBR)	John Elliott(GBR)	Joseph Beecken(BEL)
1928	Piero Toscani(ITA)	Jan Hermandek(TCH)	Léonard Steyaert(BEL)
1932	Carmen Barth(USA)	Amado Azar(ARG)	Ernest Pierce(RSA)
1936	Jean Despeaux(FRA)	Henry Tiller(NOR)	Raúl Villareal(ARG)
1948	László Papp(HUN)	John Wright(GBR)	Ivano Fontana(ITA)
1952	Floyd Patterson(USA)	Vasile Tita(ROM)	Boris Nikolov(URS)
			Stig Sjolin(SWE)
1956	Gennadi Schatkov(URS)	Ramon Tapia(CHI)	Gilbert Chapron(FRA)
			Victor Zalazar(ARG)
1960	Edward Crook(USA)	Tadeusz Walasek(POL)	Ion Monea(ROM)
			Yevgeni Feofanov(URS)
1964	Valeri Popenchenko(URS)	Emil Schultz(GER)	Franco Valle(ITA)
			Tadeusz Walasek(POL)
1968	Christopher Finnegan(GBR)	Alexei Kisselyov(URS)	Agustin Zaragoza(MEX)
			Alfred Jones(USA)
1972	Vyatcheslav Lemechev(URS)	Reima Virtanen(FIN)	Prince Armartey(GHA)
			Marvin Johnston(USA)
1976	Michael Spinks(USA)	Rufat Riskiev(URS)	Alec Nastac(ROM)
			Luis Martinez(CUB)
1980	Jose Gomez(CUB)	Viktor Savchenko(URS)	Jerzy Rybicki(POL)
			Valentin Silaghi(ROM)
1984	Joop-Sup Shin(KOR)	Virgil Hill(USA)	Mohammed Zaoui(ALG)
			Aristides Gonzales(PUR)
1988	Henry Maske(GDR)	Egerton Marcus(CAN)	Chris Sande(KEN)
			Hussain Shaw Syed(PAK)
1992	Ariel Hernandez(CUB)	Chris Byrd(USA)	Chris Johnson(CAN)
			Seung-Bae Lee(KOR)
1996	Ariel Hernandez(CUB)	Malik Beyleroglu(TUR)	Mohamed Bahari(ALG)
			Roshii Wells(USA)
2000	Jorge Gutierrez(CUB)	Gaidarbek Gaidarbekov(RUS)	Vugar Alekperov(AZE)
			Zsolt Erdei(HUN)
2004	Gaydarbek Gaydarbekov(RUS)	Gennadi Golovkin(KAZ)	Andre Dirrell(USA)

1896–1900, 1906, 1912 Event not held
(1) No third place

Light-Heavyweight

(From 1952 the weight limit has been 81kg/178.5lb. From 1920 to 1936 it was 79.38kg/175lb. In 1948 it was 80kg/186.25lb)

	GOLD	SILVER	BRONZE
1920	Edward Eagan(USA)	Sverre Sörsdal(NOR)	Harold Franks(GBR)
1924	Harry Mitchell(GBR)	Thyge Petersen(DEN)	Sverre Sörsdal(NOR)
1928	Victor Avendano(ARG)	Ernst Pistulla(GER)	Karel Miljon(NED)
1932	David Carstens(RSA)	Gino Rossi(ITA)	Peter Jörgensen(DEN)
1936	Roger Michelot(FRA)	Richard Vogt(GER)	Francisco Risiglione(ARG)
1948	George Hunter(RSA)	Donald Scott(GBR)	Maurio Cla(ARG)
1952	Norvel Lee(USA)	Antonio Pacenza(ARG)	Anotoli Perov(URS)
			Harri Siljander(FIN)
1956	James Boyd(USA)	Gheorghe Negrea(ROM)	Carlos Lucas(CHI)
			Romualdas Murauskas(URS)
1960	Cassius Clay(USA)	Zbigniew Pietrzykowski(POL)	Anthony Madigan(AUS)
			Giulio Saraudi(ITA)
1964	Cosimo Pinto(ITA)	Alexei Kisselyov(URS)	Alexander Nikolov(BUL)
			Zbigniew Pietrzykowski(POL)
1968	Dan Poznyak(URS)	Ion Monea(ROM)	Georgy Stankov(BUL)
			Stanislav Gragan(POL)
1972	Mate Petlov(YUG)	Gilberto Carrillo(CUB)	Issac Ikhouria(NGR)
			Janusz Gortat(POL)
1976	Leon Spinks(USA)	Sixto Soria(CUB)	Costica Danifoiu(ROM)
			Janusz Gortat(POL)
1980	Slobodan Kacar(YUG)	Pavel Skrzecz(POL)	Herbert Bauch(GDR)
			Ricardo Rojas(CUB)
1984	Anton Josipovic(YUG)	Kevin Barry(NZL)	Mustapha Moussa(ALG)
			Evander Holyfield(USA)
1988	Andrew Maynard(USA)	Nourmagomed Chanavazov(URS)	Damir Skaro(YUG)
			Henryk Petrich(POL)
1992	Torsten May(GER)	Rostislav Zaoulitchyni(EUN)	Wojciech Bartnik(POL)
			Zoltan Beres(HUN)

1996	Vasili Jirov(KAZ)	Seung-Bae Lee(KOR)	Antonio Tarver(USA)
2000	Alexander Lebziak(RUS)	Rudolf Kraj(CZE)	Thomas Ulrich(GER)
			Andrei Fedtchuk(UKR)
2004	Andre Ward(USA)	Magomed Aripgadjiev(BLR)	Sergei Mikhailov(UZB)
			Utkirbek Haydarov(UZB)
			Ahmed Ismail(EGY)

1896–1912 Event not held

Heavyweight

(From 1984 the weight limit has been 91kg/200.5lb. From 1904 to 1908 it was over 71.67kg/158lb. From 1920 to 1936 it was over 79.38kg/175lb. In 1948 it was over 80kg/176.25lb. From 1952 to 1980 it was over 81kg/178.25lb)

	GOLD	SILVER	BRONZE
1904	Samuel Berger(USA)	Charles Mayer(USA)	William Michaels(USA)
1908	Albert OldmanGBR)	Sydney Evans(GBR)	Frederick Parks(GBR)
1920	Ronald Lawton(GBR)	Sören Petersen(DEN)	Xavier Eluère(FRA)
1924	Otto von Porat(NOR)	Sören Petersen(DEN)	Alfredo Porzio(ARG)
1928	Arturo Rodriguez Jurado(ARG)	Nils Ramm(SWE)	Jacob Michaelsen(DEN)
1932	Santiago Lovell(ARG)	Luigi Rovati(ITA)	Frederick Feary(USA)
1936	Herbert Runge(GER)	Guillermo Lovell(ARG)	Erling Nilsen(NOR)
1948	Rafael Iglesias(ARG)	Gunnar Nilsson(SWE)	John Arthur(RSA)
1952	Hayes Edward Sanders(USA)	Ingemar Johansson(SWE) (1)	Andries Nieman(RSA)
			Ilkka Koski(FIN)
1956	Peter Rademacher(USA)	Lev Mukhin(URS)	Daniel Bekker(RSA)
			Giacomo Ros(ITA)
1960	Franco de Piccoli(ITA)	Daniel Bekker(RSA)	Josef Nemec(TCH)
			Günther Siegmund(GER)
1964	Joe Frazier(USA)	Hans Huber(GER)	Guiseppe Ros(ITA)
			Vadim Yemeynaov(URS)
1968	George Foreman(USA)	Ionas Tschepulis(URS)	Giorgio Bambini(ITA)
			Joaquim Rocha(MEX)
1972	Teofilo Stevenson(CUB)	Ion Alexe(ROM)	Peter Hussing(FRG)
			Hasse Thomsen(SWE)
1976	Teofilo Stevenson(CUB)	Mircea Simon(ROM)	Johnny Tate(USA)
			Clarence Hill(BER)
1980	Teofilo Stevenson(CUB)	Pyotr Zayev(URS)	Jürgen Fanghanel(GDR)
			István Levai(HUN)
1984	Henry Tillman(USA)	Willie Dewitt(CAN)	Angelo Musone(ITA)
			Arnold Vanderlijde(NED)
1988	Ray Mercer(USA)	Hyun-Man Baik(KOR)	Andrzej Golota(POL)
			Arnold Vanderlidje(NED)
1992	Félix Savón(CUB)	David Izonretei(NGR)	David Tua(NZL)
			Arnold Vanderlijde(NED)
1996	Félix Savón(CUB)	David Defiagbon(CAN)	Nate Jones(USA)
			Luan Krasniqui(GER)
2000	Félix Savón(CUB)	Sultanahmed Ibzagimov(RUS)	Vladimir Tchantouria(GEO)
			Sebastian Kober(GER)
2004	Odlanier Solis Fonte(CUB)	Viktor Zuyev(BLR)	Naser El Shami(SYR)
			Mohamed El Sayed(EGY)

1896–1900, 1906, 1912 Event not held
(1) Originally Johansson was disqualified and no medal awarded, but he was reinstated in 1982

Super-Heavyweight

(From 1984 the class has been for those over 91kg/200.5lb)

	GOLD	SILVER	BRONZE
1984	Tyrell Biggs(USA)	Francesco Damiani(ITA)	Robert Wells(GBR)
			Salihu Azis(YUG)
1988	Lennox Lewis(CAN)	Riddick Bowe(USA)	Alexander Mirochnitchenko(URS)
			Jasz Zarenkiewicz(POL)
1992	Roberto Balado(CUB)	Richard Igbineghu(NGR)	Brian Nielsen(DEN)
			Svilen Roussinov(BUL)
1996	Vladimir Klichko(UKR)	Paea Wolfgram(TGA)	Alexei Lezin(RUS)
			Duncan Dokwari(NGR)
2000	Audley Harrison(GBR)	Muchtarchan Dildabekov(KAZ)	Rustam Saidov(UZB)
			Paolo Vidoz(ITA)
2004	Alexander Povyetkin(RUS)	Mohamed Aly(EGY)	Roberto Cammarelle(ITA)
			Michel Lopez Nunez(CUB)

1896–1980 Event not held

CANOEING

500m Kayak Singles (K1) – Men

	GOLD	SILVER	BRONZE
1976	Vasile Diba(ROM) 1:46.41	Zoltán Szytanity(HUN) 1:46.95	Rüdiger Helm(GDR) 1:48.30
1980	Vladimir Parfenovich(URS) 1:43.43	John Sumegi(AUS) 1:44.12	Vasile Diba(ROM) 1:44.90
1984	Ian Ferguson(NZL) 1:47.84	Lars-Erik Möberg(SWE) 1:48.18	Bernard Bregeon(FRA) 1:48.41
1988	Zsolt Gyulay(HUN) 1:44.82	Andreas Stähle(GDR) 1:46.38	Paul McDonald(NZL) 1:46.46
1992	MIkko Kolehmainen(FIN) 1:40.34	Zsolt Gyulay(HUN) 1:40.64	Knut Holmann(NOR) 1:40.71
1996	Antonio Rossi(ITA) 1:37.42	Knut Holmann(NOR) 1:38.33	Piotr Markiewicz(POL) 1:38.61
2000	Knut Holmann(NOR) 1:57.847	Petar Markov(BUL) 1:58.393	Michael Kolganov(ISR) 1:59.563
2004	Adam van Koeverden(CAN)1:37.919	Nathan Baggaley(AUS) 1:38.467	Ian Wynne(GBR) 1:38.547

1896–1972 Event not held

1,000m Kayak Singles (K1) – Men

	GOLD	SILVER	BRONZE
1936	Gregor Hradetsky(AUT) 4:22.9	Helmut Cämmerer(GER) 4:25.6	Jacob Kraaier(NED) 4:35.1
1948	Gert Fredriksson(SWE) 4:33.2	Johann Kobberup(DEN) 4:39.9	Henri Eberhardt(FRA) 4:41.4
1952	Gert Fredriksson(SWE) 4:07.9	Thorvald Strömberg(FIN) 4:09.7	Louis Gantois(FRA) 4:20.1
1956	Gert Fredriksson(SWE) 4:12.8	Igor Pissaryev(URS) 4:15.3	Lajos Kiss(HUN) 4:16.2
1960	Erik Hansen(DEN) 3:53.00	Imre Szöllösi(HUN) 3:54.02	Gert Fredriksson(SWE) 3:55.89
1964	Rolf Peterson(SWE) 3:57.13	Mihály Hesz(HUN) 3:57.28	Aurel Vernescu(ROM) 4:00.77
1968	Mihály Hesz(HUN) 4:02.63	Alexander Shaparenko(URS) 4:03.58	Erik Hansen(DEN) 4:04.39
1972	Aleksandr Shaparenko(URS) 3:48.06	Rolf Peterson(SWE) 3:48.35	Géza Csapó(HUN) 3:49.38
1976	Rüdiger Helm(GDR) 3:48.20	Géza Csapó(HUN) 3:48.84	Vasile Diba(ROM) 3:49.65
1980	Rüdiger Helm(GDR) 3:48.77	Alain Lebas(FRA) 3:50.20	Ion Birladeanu(ROM) 3:50.49
1984	Alan Thompson(NZL) 3:45.73	Milan Janic(YUG) 3:46.88	Greg Barton(USA) 3:47.38
1988	Greg Barton(USA) 3:55.27	Grant Davies(AUS) 3:55.28	Andre Wohliebe(GDR) 3:55.55
1992	Clint Robinson(AUS) 3:37.26	Knut Holmann(NOR) 3:37.50	Greg Barton(USA) 3:37.93
1996	Knut Holmann(NOR) 3:25.78	Beniamino Bonomi(ITA) 3:27.07	Clint Robinson(AUS) 3:29.71
2000	Knut Holmann(NOR) 3:33.269	Petar Markov(BUL) 3:34.649	Tim Brabants(GBR) 3:35.057
2004	Eirik Larsen(NOR) 3:25.897	Ben Fouhy(NZL) 3:27.413	Adam van Koeverden(CAN) 3:28.218

1896–1932 Event not held

10,000m Kayak Singles (K1) – Men

	GOLD	SILVER	BRONZE
1936	Ernst Krebs(GER) 46:01.6	Fritz Landertinger(AUT) 46:14.7	Ernest Riedel(USA) 47:23.9
1948	Gert Fredriksson(SWE) 50:47.7	Kurt Wires(FIN) 51:18.2	Ejvind Skabo(NOR) 51:35.4
1952	Thorvald Strömberg(FIN) 47:22.8	Gert Fredriksson(SWE) 47:34.1	MIchel Scheuer(GER) 47:54.5
1956	Gert Fredriksson(SWE) 47:43.4	Ferenc Hatlaczky(HUN) 47:53.3	Michel Scheuer(GER) 48.00.3

1896–1932, 1960–2004 Event not held

500m Kayak Pairs (K2) – Men

	GOLD	SILVER	BRONZE
1976	GDR 1:35.87	SOVIET UNION 1:36.81	ROMANIA 1:37.43
1980	SOVIET UNION 1:32.38	SPAIN 1:33.65	GDR 1:34.00
1984	NEW ZEALAND 1:34.21	SWEDEN 1:35.26	CANADA 1:35.41
1988	NEW ZEALAND 1:33.98	SOVIET UNION 1:34.15	HUNGARY 1:34.32
1992	GERMANY 1:28.27	POLAND 1:29.84	ITALY 1:30.00
1996	GERMANY 1:28.69	ITALY 1:28.72	AUSTRALIA 1:29.40
2000	HUNGARY 1:47.055	AUSTRALIA 1:47.895	GERMANY 1:48.771
2004	GERMANY 1:27.040	AUSTRALIA 1:27.920	BELARUS 1:27.996

1896–1972 Event not held

1,000m Kayak Pairs (K2) – Men

	GOLD	SILVER	BRONZE
1936	AUSTRIA 4:03.8	GERMANY 4:08.9	NETHERLANDS 4:12.2
1948	SWEDEN 4:07.3	DENMARK 4:07.5	FINLAND 4:08.7
1952	FINLAND 3:51.1	SWEDEN 3:51.1	AUSTRIA 3:51.4
1956	GERMANY 3:49.6	SOVIET UNION 3:51.4	AUSTRIA 3:55.8
1960	SWEDEN 3:34.7	HUNGARY 3:34.91	POLAND 3:37.34
1964	SWEDEN 3:38.4	NETHERLANDS 3:39.30	GERMANY 3:40.69
1968	SOVIET UNION 3:37.54	HUNGARY 3:38.44	AUSTRIA 3:40.71
1972	SOVIET UNION 3:31.23	HUNGARY 3:32.00	POLAND 3:38.33
1976	SOVIET UNION 3:29.01	GDR 3:29.33	HUNGARY 3:30.56
1980	SOVIET UNION 3:26.72	HUNGARY 3:28.49	SPAIN 3:28.66
1984	CANADA 3:24.22	FRANCE 3:25.97	AUSTRALIA 3:26.80
1988	UNITED STATES 3:32.42	NEW ZEALAND 3:32.71	AUSTRALIA 3:33.76
1992	GERMANY 3:16.10	SWEDEN 3:17.70	POLAND 3:18.86
1996	ITALY 3:09.19	GERMANY 3:10.51	BULGARIA 3:11.20
2000	ITALY 3:14.461	SWEDEN 3:16.075	HUNGARY 3:16.357
2004	SWEDEN 3:18.420	ITALY 3:19.484	NORWAY 3:19.528

1896–1932 Event not held

10,000m Kayak Pairs (K2) – Men

	GOLD	SILVER	BRONZE
1936	GERMANY 41:45.0	AUSTRIA 42:05.4	SWEDEN 43:06.1
1948	SWEDEN 46:09.4	NORWAY 46:44.8	FINLAND 46:48.2
1952	FINLAND 44:21.3	SWEDEN 44:21.7	HUNGARY 44:26.6
1956	HUNGARY 43:37.0	GERMANY 43:40.6	AUSTRALIA 43:43.2

1896–1932, 1960–2004 Event not held

1,000m Kayak Fours (K4) – Men

	GOLD	SILVER	BRONZE
1964	SOVIET UNION 3:14.67	GERMANY 3:15.39	ROMANIA 3:15.51
1968	NORWAY 3:14.38	ROMANIA 3:14.81	HUNGARY 3:15.10
1972	SOVIET UNION 3:14.38	ROMANIA 3:15.07	NORWAY 3:15.27
1976	SOVIET UNION 3:08.69	SPAIN 3:08.95	GDR 3:10.76
1980	GDR 3:13.76	ROMANIA 3:15.35	BULGARIA 3:15.46
1984	NEW ZEALAND 3:02.28	SWEDEN 3:02.81	FRANCE 3:03.94
1988	HUNGARY 3:00.20	SOVIET UNION 3:01.40	GDR 3:02.37
1992	GERMANY 2:54.18	HUNGARY 2:54.82	AUSTRALIA 2:56.97
1996	GERMANY 2:51.52	HUNGARY 2:53.18	RUSSIA 2:55.99
2000	HUNGARY 2:55.188	GERMANY 2:55.704	POLAND 2:57.192
2004	HUNGARY 2:56.919	GERMANY 2:58.659	SLOVAKIA 2:59.314

1896–1960 Event not held

500m Canadian Singles (C1) – Men

	GOLD	SILVER	BRONZE
1976	Alexander Rogov(URS) 1:59.23	John Wood(CAN) 1:59.58	Matija Ljubek(YUG) 1:59.60
1980	Sergei Postrekhin(URS) 1:53.37	Lubomir Lubenov(BUL) 1:53.49	Olaf Heukrodt(GDR) 1:54.38
1984	Larry Cain(CAN) 1:57.01	Henning Jakobsen(DEN) 1:58.45	Costica Olaru(ROM) 1:59.86
1988	Olaf Heukrodt(GDR) 1:56.42	Mikhail Slivinski(URS) 1:57.26	Martin Marinov(BUL) 1:57.27
1992	Nikolai Boukhalov(BUL) 1:51.15	Mikhail Slivinski(EUN) 1:51.40	Olaf Heukrodt(GER) 1:53.00
1996	Martin Doktor(CZE) 1:49.93	Slavomir Knazovicky(SLO) 1:50.51	Imre Pulai(ITA) 1:50.75
2000	György Kolonics(HUN) 2:24.813	Maksim Opalev(RUS) 2:25.809	Andreas Dittmer(GER) 2:27.591
2004	Andreas Dittmer(GER) 1:46.383	David Cal(ESP) 1:46.723	Maxim Opalyev(RUS) 1:47.767

1896–1972 Event not held

1,000m Canadian Singles (C1) – Men

	GOLD	SILVER	BRONZE
1936	Francis Amyot(CAN) 5:32..1	Bohuslav Karlik(TCH) 5:36.9	Erich Koschik(GER) 5:39.0
1948	Josef Holocek(TCH) 5:42.0	Douglas Bennet(CAN) 5:53.3	Robert Boutigny(FRA) 5:55.9
1952	Josef Holocek(TCH) 4:56.3	János Parti(HUN) 5:03.6	Olavi Ojanpera(FIN) 5:08.5
1956	Leon Rotman(ROM) 5:05.3	István Hernek(HUN) 5:06.2	Gennadi Bukharin(URS) 5:12.7
1960	János Parti(HUN) 4:33.93	Alexsandr Silayev(URS) 4:34.41	Leon Rotman(ROM) 4:35.87
1964	Jürgen Eschert(GER) 4:35.14	Andrei Igorov(ROM) 4:37.89	Yevgeni Penyayev(URS) 4:38.31
1968	Tlbor Tatai(HUN) 4:36.14	Detlef Lewe(FRG) 4:38.31	Vitali Galkov(URS) 4:40.42
1972	Ivan Patzaichin(ROM) 4:08.94	Tamas Wichmann(HUN) 4:12.42	Detlef Lewe(FRG) 4:13.36
1976	Matija Ljubek(YUG) 4:09.51	Vassili Urchenko(URS) 4:12.57	Tamas Wichmann(HUN) 4:14.11
1980	Lubomir Lubenov(BUL) 4:12.38	Sergei Postrekhin(URS) 4:13.53	Eckhard Leue(GDR) 4:15.02
1984	Ulrich Eicke(FRG) 4:06.32	Larry Cain(CAN) 4:08.67	Henning Jakobsen(DEN) 4:09.51
1988	Ivans Klementjevs(URS) 4:12.78	Jörg Schmidt(GDR) 4:15.83	Nikolai Boukhalov(BUL) 4:18.94
1992	Nikolai Boukhalov(BUL) 4:05.92	Ivans Klementjevs(LAT) 4:06.60	Gyorgy Zala(HUN) 4:07.35
1996	Martin Doktor(CZE) 3:54.41	Ivans Klementjevs(LAT) 3:54.95	Gyorgy Zala(HUN) 3:56.36
2000	Andreas Dittmer(GER) 3:54.379	Ledys Frank Balceiro(CUB) 3:56.071	Steve Giles(CAN) 3:56.437
2004	David Cal(ESP) 3:46.201	Andreas Dittmer(GER) 3:46.721	Attila Vajda(HUN) 3:49.025

1896–1932 Event not held

10,000m Canadian Singles (C1) – Men

	GOLD	SILVER	BRONZE
1948	Frantisek Capek(TCH) 62:05.2	Frank Havens(USA) 62:40.4	Norman Lane(CAN) 64:35.3
1952	Frank Havens(USA) 57:41.1	Gabór Novák(HUN) 57:49.2	Alfréd Jindra(TCH) 57:33.1
1956	Leon Rotman(ROM) 56:41.0	János Parti(HUN) 57:11.0	Gennadi Bukharin(URS) 57:14.5

1896–1936, 1960–2004 Event not held

500m Canadian Pairs (C2) – Men

	GOLD	SILVER	BRONZE
1976	SOVIET UNION 1:45.81	POLAND 1:47.77	HUNGARY 1:47.35
1980	HUNGARY 1:43.39	ROMANIA 1:44.12	BULGARIA 1:44.83
1984	YUGOSLAVIA 1:43.67	ROMANIA 1:45.68	SPAIN 1:47.71
1988	SOVIET UNION 1:41.77	POLAND 1:43.61	FRANCE 1:43.81
1992	UNIFIED TEAM 1:41.54	GERMANY 1:41.68	BULGARIA 1:41.94
1996	HUNGARY 1:40.42	MOLDOVA 1:40.45	ROMANIA 1:41.33
2000	HUNGARY 1:51.284	POLAND 1:51.536	ROMANIA 1:54.260
2004	CHINA 1:40.278	CUBA 1:40.350	RUSSIA 1:40.442

1896–1972 Event not held

1,000m Canadian Pairs (C2) – Men

	GOLD	SILVER	BRONZE
1936	CZECHOSLOVAKIA 4:50.1	AUSTRIA 4:53.8	CANADA 4:56.7
1948	CZECHOSLOVAKIA 5:07.1	UNITED STATES 5:08.2	FRANCE 5:15.2
1952	DENMARK 4:38.3	CZECHOSLOVAKIA 4:42.9	GERMANY 4:48.3
1956	ROMANIA 4:47.4	SOVIET UNION 4:48.6	HUNGARY 4:54.3
1960	SOVIET UNION 4:17.94	ITALY 4:20.77	HUNGARY 4:20.89
1964	SOVIET UNION 4:04.64	FRANCE 4:06.52	DENMARK 4:07.48
1968	ROMANIA 4:07.18	HUNGARY 4:08.77	SOVIET UNION 4:11.30
1972	SOVIET UNION 3:52.60	ROMANIA 3:52.63	BULGARIA 3:58.10
1976	SOVIET UNION 3:52.76	ROMANIA 3:54.28	HUNGARY 3:55.66
1980	ROMANIA 3:47.65	GDR 3:49.93	SOVIET UNION 3:51.28
1984	ROMANIA 3:40.60	YUGOSLAVIA 3:41.56	FRANCE 3:48.01
1988	SOVIET UNION 3:48.36	GDR 3:51.44	POLAND 3:54.33
1992	GERMANY 3:37.42	DENMARK 3:39.26	FRANCE 3:39.51
1996	GERMANY 3:31.87	ROMANIA 3:32.99	HUNGARY 3:32.51
2000	ROMANIA 3:37.355	CUBA 3:38.753	GERMANY 3:41.129
2004	GERMANY 3:41.802	RUSSIA 3:42.990	HUNGARY 3:43.106

1896–1932 Event not held

10,000m Canadian Pairs (C2) – Men

	GOLD	SILVER	BRONZE
1936	CZECHOSLOVAKIA 50.33.5	CANADA 51:15.8	AUSTRIA 51:28.0
1948	UNITED STATES 55:55.4	CZECHOSLOVAKIA 57:38.5	FRANCE 58:00.8
1952	FRANCE 54:08.3	CANADA 54:09.9	GERMANY 54:28.1
1956	SOVIET UNION 54:02.4	FRANCE 54:48.3	HUNGARY 55:15.6

1896–1932, 1960–2004 Event not held

4 x 500m Kayak Singles (K1) Relay – Men

	GOLD	SILVER	BRONZE
1960	GERMANY 7:39.43	HUNGARY 7:44.02	DENMARK 7:46.09

1896–1956, 1964–2004 Event not held

10,000m Folding Kayak Singles (K1) – Men

	GOLD	SILVER	BRONZE
1936	Gregor Hradetzky(AUT) 50:01.2	Henri Eberhardt(FRA) 50:04.2	Xaver Hörmann(GER) 50:06.5

1896–1932, 1948–2004 Event not held

10,000m Folding Kayak Pairs (K2) – Men

	GOLD	SILVER	BRONZE
1936	SWEDEN 45:48.9	GERMANY 45:49.2	NETHERLANDS 46:12.4

1896–1932, 1948–2004 Event not held

Slalom Racing – Kayak Singles (K1) – Men

	GOLD	SILVER	BRONZE
1972	Siegbert Horn(GDR) 268.56pts	Norbert Sattler(AUT) 270.76pts	Harald Gimpel(GDR) 277.95pts
1992	Pierpaolo Ferrazzi(ITA) 106.89pts	Sylvain Curinier(FRA) 107.06pts	Jochen Lettmann(GER) 108.52pts
1996	Oliver Fix(GER) 141.22pts	Andraz Vehovar(SLO) 141.65pts	Thomas Becker(GER) 142.79pts
2000	Thomas Schmidt(GER) 217.25pts	Paul Radcliffe(GBR) 223.71pts	Pierpaolo Ferrazzi(ITA) 225.03pts
2004	Benoit Peschier(FRA)187.96pts	Campbell Walsh(GBR) 190.17pts	Fabien Lefevre(FRA) 190.99pts

1896–1968, 1976–88 Event not held

Slalom Racing – Canadian Singles (C1) – Men

	GOLD	SILVER	BRONZE
1972	Reinhard Eiben(GDR) 315.84pts	Reinhold Kauder(FRG) 327.89pts	Jamie McEwan(USA) 335.95pts
1992	Lukas Pollert(CZE) 113.69pts	Gareth Marriott(GBR) 116.48pts	Jacky Avril(FRA) 117.18pts
1996	Michel Martikan(SLK) 151.03pts	Lukas Pollert(CZE) 151.17pts	Patrice Estanguet(FRA) 152.84pts
2000	Tony Estanguet(FRA) 231.87pts	Michal Martikan(SVK) 233.76pts	Juraj Mincik(SVK) 234.22pts
2004	Tony Estanguet(FRA)189.16pts	Michal Martikan(SVK) 189.28pts	Stefan Pfannmöller(GER) 191.56pts

1896–1968, 1976–88 Event not held

Slalom Racing – Canadian Pairs (C2) – Men

	GOLD	SILVER	BRONZE
1972	GDR 310.68	FRG 311.90	FRANCE 315.10
1992	UNITED STATES 122.41pts	CZECHOSLOVAKIA 124.25pts	FRANCE 124.38pts
1996	FRANCE 158.82pts	CZECH REPUBLIC 160.16pts	GERMANY 163.72pts
2000	SLOVAKIA 237.74pts	POLAND 243.81pts	CZECH REPUBLIC 249.45pts
2004	SLOVAKIA 207.16pts	GERMANY 210.98pts	CZECH REPUBLIC 212.86pts

1896–1968, 1976–88 Event not held

500m Kayak Singles (K1) – Women

	GOLD	SILVER	BRONZE
1948	Karen Hoff(DEN) 2:31.9	Alide Van de Anker-Doedans(NED) 2:32.8	Fritzi Schwingl(AUT) 2:32.9
1952	Slyvi Saimo(FIN) 2:18.4	Gertrude Liebhart(AUT) 2:18.8	Nina Savina(URS) 2:21.6
1956	Yelisaveta Demntyeva(URS) 2:18.9	Therese Zenz(GDR) 2:19.6	Tove Söby(DEN) 2:22.3
1960	Antonina Seredina(URS) 2:08.8	Therese Zenz(GDR) 2:08.22	Daniele Walkowiak(POL) 2:10.46
1964	Ludmila Khvedosyuk(URS) 2:12.87	Hilde Lauer(ROM) 2:15.35	Marcia Jones(USA) 2:15.68
1968	Ludmila Pinyeva(URS) 2:11.09	Renate Breuer(FRG) 2:12.71	Viorica Dumitru(ROM) 2:13.22
1972	Yulia Ryabchinskaya(URS) 2:03.17	Mieke Jaapies(NED) 2:04.03	Anna Pfeffer(HUN) 2:05.50
1976	Carola Zirzow(GDR) 2:01.05	Tatyana Korshunova(URS) 2:03.07	Klara Rajnai(HUN) 2:05.01
1980	Birgit Fischer(GDR) 1:57.96	Vanya Gheva(BUL) 1:59.48	Antonina Melnikova(URS) 1:59.66
1984	Agneta Andersson(SWE) 1:58.72	Barbara Schuttpelz(FRG)	Annemiek Derckx(NED) 2:00.11
1988	Vania Guecheva(BUL) 1:55.19	Birgit Schmidt(GDR) 1:55.31	Izabella Dylewska(POL) 1:57.38
1992	Birgit Schmidt(GER) 1:51.60	Rita Koban(HUN) 1:51.96	Izabella Dylewska(POL) 1:52.36
1996	Rita Koban(HUN) 1:47.65	Caroline Brunet(CAN) 1:47.89	Josefa Idem(ITA) 1:48.73
2000	Josefa Idem Guerrini(ITA) 2:13.848	Caroline Brunet(CAN) 2:14.646	Katrin Borchert(AUS) 2:25.138
2004	Natasa Janics(HUN) 1:47.741	Josefa Idem(ITA) 1:49.729	Caroline Brunet(CAN) 1:50.601

1896–1936 Event not held

500m Kayak Pairs (K2) – Women

	GOLD	SILVER	BRONZE
1960	SOVIET UNION 1:54.76	GERMANY 1:56.66	HUNGARY 1:58.22
1964	GERMANY 1:56.95	UNITED STATES 1:59.16	ROMANIA 2:00.25
1968	FRG 1:56.44	HUNGARY 1:58.60	SOVIET UNION 1:58.61
1972	SOVIET UNION 1:53.50	GDR 1:54.30	ROMANIA 1:55.01
1976	SOVIET UNION 1:51.15	HUNGARY 1:51.69	GDR 1:51.81
1980	GDR 1:43.88	SOVIET UNION 1:46.91	HUNGARY 1:47.95
1984	SWEDEN 1:45.25	CANADA 1:47.13	FRG 1:47.32
1988	GDR 1:43.46	BULGARIA 1:44.06	NETHERLANDS 1:46.00
1992	GERMANY 1:40.29	SWEDEN 1:40.41	HUNGARY 1:40.81
1996	SWEDEN 1:39.32	GERMANY 1:39.68	AUSTRALIA 1:40.64
2000	GERMANY 1:56.996	HUNGARY 1:58.580	POLAND 1:58.787
2004	HUNGARY 1:38.101	GERMANY 1:39.533	POLAND 1:40.077

1896–1956 Event not held

500m Kayak Fours (K4) – Women

	GOLD	SILVER	BRONZE
1984	ROMANIA 1:38.34	SWEDEN 1:38.87	CANADA 1:39.40
1988	GDR 1:40.78	HUNGARY 1:41.88	BULGARIA 1:42.63
1992	HUNGARY 1:38.32	GERMANY 1:38.47	SWEDEN 1:39.79
1996	GERMANY 1:31.07	SWITZERLAND 1:32.70	SWEDEN 1:32.91
2000	GERMANY 1:34.532	HUNGARY 1:34.946	ROMANIA 1:37.010
2004	GERMANY 1:34.340	HUNGARY 1:34.536	UKRAINE 1:36.192

1896–1980 Event not held

Slalom Racing – Kayak Singles (K1) – Women

	GOLD	SILVER	BRONZE
1972	Angelika Bahmann(GDR) 364.50pts	Gisela Grothaus(FRG) 398.1pts	Magdelena Wunderlich(FRG) 400.50pts
1992	Elisabeth Micheler(GER) 126.41pts	Danielle Woodward(AUS) 128.27pts	Diana Chladek(USA) 131.75pts
1996	Stepanka Hilgertova(CZE) 169.49pts	Dana Chladek(USA) 169.49pts	Myriam Fox-Jerusalmi(FRA) 171.00pts
2000	Stepanka Hilgertova(CZE) 247.04pts	Brigitte Guibal(FRA) 251.88pts	Anne-Lise Bardet(FRA) 254.77pts
2004	Elena Kaliska(SVK) 210.03pts	2. Rebecca Giddens(USA) 214.62pts	3. Helen Reeves(GBR) 218.77pts

1896–1968, 1976–88 Event not held

CYCLING

1,000m Time Trial – Men

	GOLD	SILVER	BRONZE
1896(1)	Paul Masson(FRA) 24.0	Stamatios Nikolpoulos(GRE) 25.4	Adolf Schmal(AUT) 26.6
1906(1)	Francesco Verri(ITA) 22.8	Herbert Crowther(GBR) 22.8	Menjou(FRA) 23.2
1928	Willy Falck-Hansen(DEN) 1:14.4	Gerard Bosch van Drakestein(NED) 1:15.2	Edgar Gray(AUS) 1:15.6
1932	Edgar Gray(AUS) 1:13.0	Jacobus van Egmond(NED) 1:13.3	Charles Rampelberg(FRA) 1:13.4
1936	Arie van Vliet(NED) 1:12.0	Pierre Georget(FRA) 1:12.8	Rudolf Karsch(GER) 1:13.2
1948	Jacques Dupont(FRA) 1:13.5	Pierre Nihant(BEL) 1:14.5	Thomas Godwin(GBR) 1:15.0
1952	Russell Mockridge(AUS) 1:11.1	Marino Morettini(ITA) 1:12.7	Raymond Robinson(RSA) 1:13.0
1956	Leandro Faggin(ITA) 1:09.8	Ladislav Foucek(TCH) 1:11.4	J. Alfred Swift(RSA) 1:11.6
1960	Sante Gaiardoni(ITA) 1:07.27	Dieter Giessler(GER) 1:08.75	Rotislav Vargshkin(URS) 1:08.86
1964	Patrick Sercu(BEL) 1:09.59	Giovanni Pettonella(ITA) 1:10.09	Pierre Trentin(FRA) 1:10.42
1968	Pierre Trentin(FRA) 1:03.91	Niels-Christian Fredborg(DEN) 1:04.61	Janusz Kierkowski(POL) 1:04.63

1972	Niels-Christian Fredborg(DEN) 1:06.44	Daniel Clark(AUS) 1:06.87	Jürgen Schütze(GDR) 1:07.02
1976	Klaus-Jürgen Grunke(GDR) 1:05.93	Michel Vaarten(BEL) 1:07.52	Niels-Christian Fredborg(DEN) 1:07.62
1980	Lothar Thomas(GDR) 1:02.955	Alexander Pantilov(URS) 1:04.845	David Weller(JAM) 1:05.241
1984	Fredy Schmidke(FRG) 1:06.10	Curtis Harnett(CAN) 1:06.44	Fabrice Colas(FRA) 1:06.65
1988	Alexander Kiritchenko(URS) 1:04.499	Martin Vinnicombe(AUS) 1:04.784	Robert Lechner(FRG) 1:05.114
1992	Jose Manuel Moreno(ESP) 1:03.342	Shane Kelly(AUS) 1:04.288	Erin Hartwell(USA) 1:04.753
1996	Florian Rousseau(FRA) 1:02.712	Erin Hartwell(USA) 1:02.940	Takandu Jumonji(JPN) 1:02.261
2000	Jason Queally(GBR) 1:01.689	Stefan Nimke(GER) 1:02.487	Shane Kelly(AUS) 1:02.818
2004	Chris Hoy(GBR) 1:00.711	Arnaud Tournant(FRA) 1:00.896	Stefan Nimke(GER) 1:01.186

1900–04, 1908–24 Event not held
(1) Distance was 333.33m

1,000m Sprint – Men

	GOLD	SILVER	BRONZE
1896(1)	Paul Masson(FRA) 4:56.0	Stamatios Nikopoulos(GRE)	Léon Flemeng(FRA)
1900(1)	Georges Taillandier(FRA) 2:52.0	Fernand Sanz(FRA)	John Lake(USA)
1906	Francesco Verri(ITA) 1:42.2	Herbert Bouffler(GBR)	Eugène Debougnie(BEL)
1908(2)			
1920	Maurice Peeters(NED) 1:38.3	Horace Johnson(GBR)	Harry Ryan(GBR)
1924(3)	Lucien Michard(FRA) 12.8	Jacob Meijer(NED)	Jean Cugnot(FRA)
1928	René Beaufrand(FRA) 13.2	Antoine Mazairac(NED)	Willy Falck-Hansen(DEN)
1932	Jacobus van Egmond(NED) 12.6	Louis Chaillot(FRA)	Bruno Pellizzari(ITA)
1936	Toni Merkens(GER) 11.8	Arie van Vliet(NED)	Louis Chaillot(FRA)
1948	Mario Ghella(ITA) 12.0	Reginald Harris(GBR)	Axel Schandorff(DEN)
1952	Enzo Sacchi(ITA) 12.0	Lionel Cox(AUS)	Werner Potzernheim(GER)
1956	Michel Rousseau(FRA) 11.4	Guglielmo Presenti(ITA)	Richard Ploog(AUS)
1960	Sante Gaiardoni(ITA) 11.1	Leo Sterckz(BEL)	Valentino Gasparella(ITA)
1964	Giovanni Petternella(ITA) 13.69	Sergio Bianchetto(ITA)	Daniel Morelon(FRA)
1968	Daniel Morelon(FRA) 10.68	Giordano Turrini(ITA)	Pierre Trentin(FRA)
1972	Daniel Morelon(FRA) 11.25	John Nicholson(AUS)	Omar Pchakadze(URS)
1976	Anton Tkac(TCH) 10.78	Daniel Morelon(FRA)	Hans-Jürgen Geschke(GDR)
1980	Lutz Hesslich(GDR) 11.40	Yave Cahard(FRA)	Sergey Kopylov(URS)
1984	Mark Gorski(USA) 10.49	Nelson Vails(USA)	Tsutomu Sakamoto(JPN)
1988	Lutz Hesslich(GDR)	Nikolai Kovche(URS)	Gary Neiwand(AUS)
1992	Jens Fiedler(GER)	Gary Neiwand(AUS)	Curtis Harnett(CAN)
1996	Jens Fiedler(GER)	Marthy Nothstein(USA)	Curtis Harnett(CAN)
2000	Marty Nothstein(USA)	Florian Rousseau(FRA)	Jens Fiedler(GER)
2004	Ryan Bayley(AUS)	Theo Bos(NED)	Rene Wolff(GER)

1904,1912 Event not held
(1) Distance was 2,000m. Taillander's last 200m in 1900 was 13.0 sec.
(2) The event was held during the 1908 Games, but was declared void due to riders exceeding the time limit
(3) From 1924 times only taken over final 200m

4,000m Individual Pursuit – Men
(Third places are decided in a separate race, thus times can be faster than those in first or second positions)

	GOLD	SILVER	BRONZE
1964	Jiri Daler(TCH) 5:04.75	Giorgio Utsi(ITA) 5:05.96	Preben Isaksson(DEN) 5:01.90
1968	Daniel Rebillard(FRA) 4:41.71	Mogens Frey Jensen(DEN) 4:42.43	Xaver Kurmann(SUI) 4:39.42
1972	Knut Knudsen(NOR) 4:45.74	Xaver Kurmann(SUI) 4:51.96	Hans Lutz(FRG) 4:50.80
1976	Gregor Braun(FRG) 4:47.61	Herman Ponsteen(NED) 4:49.72	Thomas Huschke(GDR) 4:52.71
1980	Robert Dilli-Bundi(SUI) 4:35.66	Alain Bondue(FRA) 4:42.96	Hans-Henrik Orsted(DEN) 4:36.54
1984	Steve Hegg(USA) 4:39.35	Rolf Gölz(FRG) 4:43.82	Leonard Nitz(USA) 4:44.03
1988	Gintaoutas Umaras(URS) 4:32.00	Dean Woods(AUS) 4:35.00	Bernd Dittert(GDR) 4:34.17
1992	Chris Boardman(GBR) (1)	Jens Lehmann(GER) –	Gary Anderson(NZL) 4:31.061
1996	Andrea Collinelli(ITA) 4:20.893	Philippe Ermenault(FRA) 4:22.714	Brad McGee(AUS) 4:26.121
2000	Robert Bartko(GER) 4:18.515	Jens Lehmann(GER) 4:23.824	Brad McGee(AUS) 4:19.250
2004	Bradley Wiggins(GBR) 4:16.304	Brad McGee(AUS) 4:20.436	Sergi Escobar(ESP) 4:17.947

1896–1960 Event not held
(1) Lapped opponent

4,000m Team Pursuit – Men
(Third places are decided in a separate race, thus times can be faster than those in first or second positions)

	GOLD	SILVER	BRONZE
1908(1)	GREAT BRITAIN 2:18.6	GERMANY 2:28.6	CANADA 2:29.6
1920	ITALY 5:14.2 (2)	GREAT BRITAIN 5:13.8	SOUTH AFRICA 5:17.8
1924	ITALY 5:15.0	POLAND n.t.a.	BELGIUM n.t.a.
1928	ITALY 5:01.8	NETHERLANDS 5:06.2	GREAT BRITAIN n.t.a.
1932	ITALY 4:53.0	FRANCE 4:55.7	GREAT BRITAIN 4:56.0
1936	FRANCE 4:45.0	ITALY 4:51.0	GREAT BRITAIN 4:52.6
1948	FRANCE 4:57.8	ITALY 5:36.7	GREAT BRITAIN 4:55.8
1952	ITALY 4:46.1	SOUTH AFRICA 4:53.6	GREAT BRITAIN 4:51.5

1956	ITALY 4:37.4	FRANCE 4:39.4	GREAT BRITAIN 4:42.2
1960	ITALY 4:30.90	GERMANY 4:35.78	SOVIET UNION 4:34.05
1964	GERMANY 4:35.67	ITALY 4:35.74	NETHERLANDS 4:38.99
1968	DENMARK 4:22.44	FRG 4:18.94 (3)	ITALY 4:18.35
1972	FRG 4:22.14	GDR 4:25.25	GREAT BRITAIN 4:23.78
1976	FRG 4:21.06	SOVIET UNION 4:27.15	GREAT BRITAIN 4:22.41
1980	SOVIET UNION 4:15.70	GDR 4:19.67	CZECHOSLOVAKIA n.t.a. (4)
1984	AUSTRALIA 4:25.99	UNITED STATES 4:29.85	FRG 4:25.60
1988	SOVIET UNION 4:13.31	GDR 4:14.09	AUSTRALIA 4:16.02
1992	GERMANY 4:08.791	AUSTRALIA 4:10.218	DENMARK 4:15.860
1996	FRANCE 4:05.930	RUSSIA 4:07.730	AUSTRALIA 4:07.570
2000	GERMANY 3:59.710	UKRAINE 4:04.520	GREAT BRITAIN 4:01.979
2004	AUSTRALIA 3:58.233	GREAT BRITAIN 4:01.760	SPAIN 4:05.523

1896–1906, 1912 Event not held
(1) Distance was 1810.5m
(2) Great Britain won but were relegated for alleged interference
(3) Federal Republic of Germany (FRG) won but disqualified for illegal assistance. However, after the Games the International Cycling Federation awarded them the silver medal
(4) Italy disqualified in third place

2,000m Tandem – Men

	GOLD	SILVER	BRONZE
1906	GREAT BRITAIN 2:57.0	GERMANY 2:57.2	GERMANY n.t.a.
1908	FRANCE 3:07.8	GREAT BRITAIN n.t.a.	GREAT BRITAIN n.t.a.
1920	GREAT BRITAIN 2:94.4	SOUTH AFRICA n.t.a.	NETHERLANDS n.t.a.
1924(1)	FRANCE 12.6	DENMARK	NETHERLANDS
1928	NETHERLANDS 11.8	GREAT BRITAIN	GERMANY
1932	FRANCE 12.0	GREAT BRITAIN	DENMARK
1936	GERMANY 11.8	NETHERLANDS	FRANCE
1948	ITALY 11.3	GREAT BRITAIN	FRANCE
1952	AUSTRALIA 11.0	SOUTH AFRICA	ITALY
1956	AUSTRALIA 10.8	CZECHOSLOVAKIA	ITALY
1960	ITALY 10.7	GERMANY	SOVIET UNION
1964	ITALY 10.75	SOVIET UNION	GERMANY
1968	FRANCE 9.83	NETHERLANDS	BELGIUM
1972	SOVIET UNION	GDR	POLAND

1896–1904, 1912, 1976–2004 Event not held
(1) From 1924 times only taken over last 200m

Individual Points Race – Men

	GOLD	SILVER	BRONZE
1984	Roger Ilegems(BEL) 37pts	Uwe Messerschmidt(FRG) 15pts	Jose Youshimatz(MEX) 29pts
1988	Dan Frost(DEN) 38pts	Leo Peelen(NED) 26pts	Marat Ganeyev(URS) 46pts
1992	Giovanni Lombardi(ITA) 44pts	Leon van Bon(NED) 43pts	Cedric Mathy(BEL) 41pts
1996	Silvio Martinello(ITA) 37pts	Brian Walton(CAN) 29pts	Stuart O'Grady(AUS) 25pts
2000	Juan Llaneras(ESP) 14pts	Milton Wynants(URU) 18pts	Alexai Markov(RUS) 16pts
2004	Mikhail Ignatyev(RUS) 93pts	Joan Llaneras(ESP) 82pts	Guido Fulst(GER) 79pts

1896–1980 Event not held

Olympic Sprint – Men

	GOLD	SILVER	BRONZE
2000	FRANCE 44.233	GREAT BRITAIN 44.680	AUSTRALIA 45.161
2004	GERMANY 43.980	JAPAN 44:246	FRANCE 44.359

1896–1996 Event not held

Keirin – Men

	GOLD	SILVER	BRONZE
2000	Florian Rousseau(FRA)	Gary Niewand(AUS)	Jens Fiedler(GER)
2004	Ryan Bayley(AUS)	Jose Escuredo(ESP)	Shane Kelly(AUS)

1896–1996 Event not held

Madison – Men

	GOLD	SILVER	BRONZE
2000	AUSTRALIA 26pts	BELGIUM 22pts	ITALY 15pts
2004	AUSTRALIA 22pts	SWITZERLAND 15pts	GREAT BRITAIN 12pts

1896–1996 Event not held

Team Road Race – Men

(Consisting of the combined times of the best three – best four 1912–20 – riders from each country in the individual race. In 1956 based on placings. In 1960 replaced by Road Team Time Trial)

	GOLD	SILVER	BRONZE
1912	SWEDEN 44h 35:33.6	GREAT BRITAIN 44h 44:39.2	UNITED STATES 44h 47:55.5
1920	FRANCE 19h 16:43.2	SWEDEN 19h 23:10.0	BELGIUM 19h 28:44.4

1924	FRANCE 19h 30:14.0	BELGIUM 19h 46:55.4	SWEDEN 19h 59:41.6
1928	DENMARK 15h 09:14.0	GREAT BRITAIN 15h 14:49.0	SWEDEN 15h 27:49.0
1932	ITALY 7h 27:15.2	DENMARK 7h 38:50.2	SWEDEN 7h 39:12.6
1936	FRANCE 7h 39:16.2	SWITZERLAND 7h 39:20.4	BELGIUM 7h 39:21.0
1948	BELGIUM 15h 58:17.4	GREAT BRITAIN 16h 03:31.6	FRANCE 16h 08:19.4
1952	BELGIUM 15h 20:46.6	ITALY 15h 33:27.3	FRANCE 15h 38:58.1
1956	FRANCE 22pts	GREAT BRITAIN 23pts	GERMANY 27pts

1896–1908, 1960–2004 Event not held

Road Team Time Trial – Men
(Over 100km except in 1964 – 108.89km, 1968 – 102km, 1980 – 101km)

	GOLD	SILVER	BRONZE
1960	ITALY 2h 14:33.53	GERMANY 2h 16:56.31	SOVIET UNION 2h 18:41.67
1964	NETHERLANDS 2h 26:31.19	ITALY 2h 26:55.39	SWEDEN 2h 27:11.52
1968	NETHERLANDS 2h 07:49.06	SWEDEN 2h 09:26.60	ITALY 2h 10:18.74
1972	SOVIET UNION 2h 11:17.8	POLAND 2h 11:47.5	– (1)
1976	SOVIET UNION 2h 08:53.0	POLAND 2h 09:13.0	DENMARK 2h 12:20.0
1980	SOVIET UNION 2h 01:21.7	GDR 2h 02:53.2	CZECHOSLOVAKIA 2h 02:53.9
1984	ITALY 1h 58:28.0	SWITZERLAND 2h 02:38.0	UNITED STATES 2h 02:46.0
1988	GDR 1h 57:47.7	POLAND 1h 57:54.2	SWEDEN 1h 59:47.3
1992	GERMANY 2h 01:39	ITALY 2h 02:39	FRANCE 2h 05:25

1896–1954, 1996–2004 Event not held

(1) Netherlands finished in third place but their bronze medal was withdrawn following a drugs test

Road Individual Time Trial – Men
(Distance: 52km in 1996; 46.8km in 2000)

	GOLD	SILVER	BRONZE
1996	Miguel Induráin(ESP) 1h 04:05	Abraham Olano(ESP) 1h 04:17	Chris Boardman(GBR) 1h 04:36
2000	Vyacheslav Yekimov(RUS) 57:40	Jan Ullrich(GER) 57:48	Lance Armstrong(USA) 58:14
2004	Tyler Hamilton(USA) 57:31.74s	Vyacheslav Ekimov(RUS) 57:50.58	Bobby Julich(USA) 57.58.19

1896–1992 Event not held

Individual Road Race – Men

	GOLD	SILVER	BRONZE
1896	Aristidis Konstantinidis(GRE) 3h 22:31.0	August Goedrich(GER) 3h 42:18.0	F. Battel(GBR) d.n.a.
1906	Fernand Vast(FRA) 2h 41:28.0	Maurice Bardonneau(FRA) 2hr 41:28:4	Edmund Lugnet(FRA) 2h 41:28.6
1912	Rudolph Lewis(RSA) 10h 42:39.0	Frederick Grubb(GBR) 10h 51:24.2	Carl Schutte(USA) 10h 52:38.8
1920	Harry Stenqvist(SWE) 4h 40:01.8	Henry Kaltenbrun(RSA) 4h 41:26.6	Fernand Canteloube(FRA) 4h 42:54.4
1924	Armand Blanchonnet(FRA) 6h 20:48.0	Henry Hoevenaers(BEL) 6h 30:27.0	René Hamel(FRA) 6h 40:51.6
1928	Henry Hansen(DEN) 4h 47:18.0	Frank Southall(GBR) 4h 56:06.0	Gösta Carlsson(SWE) 5h 00:17.0
1932	Attilio Pavesi(ITA) 2h 28:05.6	Guglielmo Segato(ITA) 2h 29:21.4	Bernhard Britz(SWE) 2h 29:45.2
1936	Robert Charpentier(FRA) 2h 33:05.0	Guy Lapébie(FRA) 2h 33:05.2	Ernst Nievergeit(SUI) 2h 33:05.8
1948	José Bevaert(FRA) 5h 18:12.6	Gerardus Voorting(NED) 5h 18:16.2	Lode Wouters(BEL) 5h 18:16.2
1952	André Noyelle(BEL) 5h 06:03.4	Robert Grondelaers(BEL) 5h 06:51.2	Edi Ziegler(GER) 5h 07:47.5
1956	Ercole Baldini(ITA) 5h 21:17.0	Arnaud Gevre(FRA) 5h 23:16.0	Alan Jackson(GBR) 5h 23:16.0
1960	Viktor Kapitonov(URS) 4h 20:37.0	Livio Trapé(ITA) 4h 20:37.0	Willy van den Berghen(BEL) 4h 20:57.0
1964	Mario Zanin(ITA) 4h 39:51.63	Kjell Rodian(DEN) 4h 39:51.65	Walter Godefroot(BEL) 4h 39:51.74
1968	Pierfranco Vianelli(ITA) 4h 41:25.24	Leif Mortensen(DEN) 4h 42:49.71	Gösta Pettersson(SWE) 4h 43:15.24
1972	Hennie Kuiper(NED) 4h 14:37.0	Kevin Sefton(AUS) 4h 15:04.0	– (1)
1976	Bernt Johansson(SWE) 4h 46:52.0	Giuseppe Martinelli(ITA) 4h 47:23.0	Mieczyslaw Nowicki(POL) 4h 47:23.0
1980	Sergey Sukhoruchenkov(URS) 4h 48:28.9	Czeslaw Lang(POL) 4h 51:26.9	Yuri Barinov(URS) 4h 51:26.9
1984	Alexi Grewal(USA) 4h 59:57.0	Steve Bauer(CAN) 4h 32:25.0	Dag Otto Lauritzen(NOR) 5h 00:18.0
1988	Olaf Ludwig(GDR) 4h 32:22.0	Bernd Gröne(FRG) 4h 32:25.0	Christian Henn(FRG) 4h 32:46.0
1992	Fabio Casartelli(ITA) 4h 35:21	Hendrik Dekker(NED) 4h 35:22	Dainis Ozols(LAT) 4h 35:24
1996	Pascal Richard(SUI) 4h 53:56	Rolf Sörensen(DEN) 4h 53:56	Max Sciandri(GBR) 4h 53:58
2000	Jan Ullrich(GER) 5h 29:08	Alexander Vinokourov(KAZ) 5h 29:17	Jens Voigt(GER) 5h 29:20
2004	Paolo Bettini(ITA) 5h 41:44	Sergio Paulinho(POR) 5h 41:45	Axel Merckx(BEL) 5h 41:52

1900–1904, 1908 Event not held

Held over the following distances: 1896 – 87km; 1906 – 84km; 1912 – 329km; 1920 – 175km; 1924 – 188km; 1928 – 168km; 1932 and 1936 – 100km; 1948 – 194.63km; 1952 – 190.4km; 1956 – 187.73km; 1960 – 175.38km; 1968 – 196.2km; 1972 – 182.4km; 1976 – 175km; 1980 – 189km; 1984 – 190km; 1988 – 196.8km; 1992 – 194km; 1996 – 221km; 2000 – 239.4km

(1) Jaime Huelano (ESP) third but medal withdrawn after a drug test

Mountain Bike – Men

	GOLD	SILVER	BRONZE
1996	Bart Brentjens(NED) 2h 17:38	Thomas Frischknecht(SUI) 2h 20:14	Miguel Martinez(FRA) 2h 20:26
2000	Miguel Martinez(FRA) 2h 09:02.50	Filip Meirhoeghe(BEL) 2h 10:05.51	Christoph Sauser(SUI) 2h 11:21.40
2004	Julien Absalon(FRA) 2h:15:02	Jose Hermida(ESP)2h:16:02	Bart Brentjens(NED) 2h:17:05

1896–1992 Event not held

Sprint – Women

	GOLD	SILVER	BRONZE
1988	Erika Salumäe(URS)	Christa Röthenburger-Luding(GDR)	Connie Young(USA)
1992	Erika Salumäe(EST)	Annett Neumann(GER)	Ingrid Haringa(NED)
1996	Felicia Ballanger(FRA)	Michelle Ferris(AUS)	Ingrid Haringa(NED)
2000	Felicia Ballanger(FRA)	Oksana Grichina(RUS)	Irina Janovich(UKR)
2004	Lori-Ann Münzer(CAN)	Tamila Abassova(RUS)	Anna Meares(AUS)

1896–1984 Event not held

3,000m Individual Pursuit – Women

	GOLD	SILVER	BRONZE
1992	Petra Rossner(GER) 3:41.753	Kathryn Watt(AUS) 3:43.438	Rebecca Twigg(USA) 3:52.429
1996	Antonella Bellutti(ITA) 3:33.595	Marion Clignet(FRA) 3:38.571	Judith Arnt(GER) 3:38.744
2000	Leontien Zijlaard(NED) 3:33.360	Marion Clignet(FRA) 3:38.751	Yvonne McGregor(GBR) 3:38.850
2004	Sarah Ulmer(NZL) 3:24.537s	Katie Mactier(AUS) 3:27.650s	Leontien Zijlaard van Moorsel(NED) 3:27.037

1896–1988 Event not held

500m Time Trial – Women

	GOLD	SILVER	BRONZE
2000	Felicia Ballanger(FRA) 34.140	Michelle Ferris(AUS) 34.696	Cuihua Jiang(CHN) 34.768
2004	Anna Meares(AUS) 33.952	Yonghua Jiang (CHN) 34.112	Natalia Tsylinskaya(BLR) 34.167

1896–1996 Event not held

Individual Road Race – Women

(Distance: 79.2km in 1984; 82km in 1988; 81km in 1992; 104km in1996; 119.7km in 2000)

	GOLD	SILVER	BRONZE
1984	Connie Carpenter-Phinney(USA) 2h 11:14.0	Rebecca Twigg(USA) 2h 11:14.0	Sandra Schumacher(FRG) 2h 11:14.0
1988	Monique Knol(NED) 2h 00.52	Jutta Niehaus(FRG) close	Laima Zilporitee(URS) close
1992	Kathryn Watt(AUS) 2h 04:02	Jeannie Longo-Ciprelli(FRA) 2h 05:02	Monique Knol(NED) 2h 05:03
1996	Jeannie Longo-Ciprelli(FRA) 2h 36:13	Imelda Chiappa(USA) 2h 36.38	Clara Hughes(CAN) 2h 36.44
2000	Leontien Zijlaard(NED) 3:06:31	Hanka Kupfgernagel(GER) 3:06:31	Diana Ziliute(LTU) 3:06:31
2004	Sara Carrigan(AUS) 3h 24:24	Judith Arndt(GER) 3h 24:31	Olga Slyusareva(RUS) 3h 25:03

1896–1980,1996 Event not held

Road Individual Time Trial – Women

(Distance: 26km in 1996; 31.2km in 2000)

	GOLD	SILVER	BRONZE
1996	Zulfiya Zabirova(RUS) 36:40	Jeannie Longo-Ciprelli(FRA) 37:00	Clara Hughes(CAN) 37:13
2000	Leontien Zijlaard(NED) 42:00	Mari Holden(USA) 42:37	Jeannie Longo-Ciprelli(FRA) 42:52
2004	Leontien Zijlaard (NED)31:11.53 van Moorsel	Deidre Demet-Barry(USA)31:35.62	Karin Thuerig(SUI) 31:54.89

1896–1992 Event not held

Points Race – Women

	GOLD	SILVER	BRONZE
1996	Nathalie Lancien(FRA) 24pts	Ingrid Haringa(NED) 23pts	Lucy Tyler-Sharman(UAS) 17pts
2000	Antonella Bellutti(ITA) 19pts	Leontien Zijlaard(NED) 16pts	Olga Slyussaryeva(RUS) 15pts
2004(1)	Olga Slyusareva(RUS) 20pts	Belem Mendez(MEX) 14pts	Maria Luisa Williams (COL) 12pts

1896–1992 Event not held

(1) Maria Luisa Calle Williams (COL) finished third with 12tsp, was initially disqualified, but later reinstated

Mountain Bike – Women

	GOLD	SILVER	BRONZE
1996	Paola Pezzo(ITA) 1h 50:51	Alison Sydor(CAN) 1h 51:58	Susan DiMattei(USA) 1h 52:36
2000	Paola Pezzo(ITA) 1h 49:24.38	Barbara Blatter(SUI) 1h 49:51.42	Margarita Fulliana(ESP) 1h 49:57.39
2004	Gunn-Rita Dahle(NOR) 1h:56:51	Marie Helene Premont(CAN) 1h:57.50	Sabine Spitz(GER) 1h:59.21

1896–1992 Event not held

CYCLING – DISCONTINUED EVENTS

	GOLD	SILVER	BRONZE

440 yards Track (402.34m) – Men

1904	Marcus Hurley(USA) 31.8	Burton Downing(USA)	Edward Billingham(USA)

0.33 mile Track (536.45m) – Men

1904	Marcus Hurley(USA) 43.8	Burton Downing(USA)	Edward Billingham(USA)

660 yards Track (603.5m) – Men

1908	Victor Johnson(GBR) 51.2	Emile Demangel(FRA) close	Karl Neumer(GER) 1 length

880 yards Track (804.67m) – Men
1904	Marcus Hurley(USA) 1:09.0	Edward Billingham(USA)	Burton Downing(USA)

1 mile Track (1609.34m) – Men
1904	Marcus Hurley(USA) 2:41.4	Burton Downing(USA)	Edward Billingham(USA)

2 miles Track (3218.6m) – Men
1904	Burton Downing(USA) 4:57.8	Oscar Goerke(USA)	Marcus Hurley(USA)

5,000m Track – Men
1906	Francesco Verri(ITA) 8:35.0	Herbert Crowther(GBR)	Fernand Vast(FRA)
1908	Benjamin Jones(GBR) 8:36.2	Maurice Schilles(FRA)	Andre Auffray(FRA)

5 mile Track (8046.57m) – Men
1904	Charles Schlee(USA) 13:08.2	George Wiley(USA)	Arthur Andrews(USA)

10,000m Track – Men
1896	Paul Masson(FRA) 17:54.2	Léon Flameng(FRA)	Adolf Schmal(AUT)

20,000m Track – Men
1906	William Pett(GBR) 29:00.0	Maurice Bardonneau(FRA) 29:30.0	Fernand Vast(FRA) 29:32.0
1908	Clarence Kingsbury(GBR) 34:13.6	Benjamin Jones(GBR)	Joseph Werbrouck(BEL)

25 miles Track (40.225m) – Men
1904	Burton Downing(USA) 1h 10:55.4	Arthur Andrews(USA)	George Wiley(USA)

50,000m Track – Men
1920	Henry George(BEL) 1h 16:43.2	Cyril Alden(GBR) (1)	Petrus Ikelaar(NED)
1924	Jacobus Willems(NED) 1:18:24	Cyril Alden(GBR)	Frederick Wyld(GBR)

(1) Most eyewitnesses considered that Ikelaar finished second

100km Track – Men
1896	Leon Flameng(FRA) 3h 08:19.2	Georgios Kolettis(GRE) 6 laps	– (1)
1908	Charles Bartlett(GBR) 2h 41:48.6	Charles Denny(GBR)	Octave Lapize(FRA)

(1) Only two riders finished

12 hours Track – Men
1896	Adolf Schmal(AUT) 314.997km	Frank Keeping(GBR) 314.664km	Georgios Paraskevopoulous(GRE)

EQUESTRIAN

Grand Prix (Jumping)

	GOLD	SILVER	BRONZE
1900	Aimé Haegeman(BEL) Benton II	Georges van der Poële(BEL) Windsor Squire	Louis de Champsavin(FRA) Terpsichore
1912	Jean Cariou(FRA) 186pts Mignon	Rabod von Kröcher(GER) 186 Dohna	Emanuel de Blomaert de Sove(BEL) 185 Clonmore
1920	Tommaso Lequio(ITA) 2 flts Trebecco	Alessandro Valerio(ITA) 3 Cento	Gustaf Lewenhaupt(SWE) 4 Mon Coeur
1924	Alphonse Gemuseus(SUI) 3 flts Lucette	Tommaso Lequio(ITA) 8.75 Trebecco	Adam Krolikiewicz(POL) 10 Picador
1928	Frantisek Ventura(TCH) 0 flts Eliot	Pierre Bertrand de Balanda(FRA) 2 Papillon	Charles Kuhn(SUI) 4 Pepita
1932	Takeichi Nishi(JPN) 8pts Uranus	Harry Chamberlain(USA) 12 Show Girl	Clarence von Rosen Jr(SWE) 16 Empire
1936	Kurt Hasse(GER) 4 flts Tora	Henri Rang(ROM) 4 Delius	József von Platthy(HUN) 8 Sellö
1948	Humbeto Mariles Cortés(MEX) 6.25 flts Arete	Rubén Uriza(MEX) 8 Harvey	Jean d'Orgeix(FRA) 8 Sucre de Pomme
1952	Pierre Jonquères d'Oriola(FRA) 0 flts Ali Baba	Oscar Cristi(CHI) 4 Bambi	Fritz Thiedemann(GER) 8 Meteor
1956	Hans Günter Winkler(GER) 4 flts Halla	Raimondo d'Inzeo(ITA) 8 Merano	Piero d'Inzeo(ITA) 11 Uruguay
1960	Raimondo d'Inzeo(ITA) 4 flts Halla	Piero d'Inzeo(ITA) 16 The Rock	David Broome(GBR) 23 Sunslave
1964	Pierre Jonquères d'Oriola(FRA) 9 flts Lutteur	Hermann Schriddle(GER) 12.75 Dozent	Peter Robeson(GBR) 16 Firecrest
1968	William Steinkraus(USA) 4 flts Snowbound	Marian Coakes(GBR) 8 Stroller	David Broome(GBR) 12 Mister Softee
1972	Graziano Mancinelli(ITA) 8 flts Ambassador	Ann Moore(GBR) 8 Psalm	Neal Shapiro(USA) 8 Sloopy

1976	Alwin Schockemöhle(FRG)	Michael Vaillancourt(CAN)	François Mathy(BEL)
	0 flts Warwick Rex	12 Branch County	12 Gai Luron
1980	Jan Kowalcyzk(POL)	Nikolai Korolkov(URS)	Joaquim Perez Heras(MEX)
	8 flts Artemor	9.50 Espadron	12 Alymony
1984	Joe Fargis(USA)	Conrad Homfeld(USA)	Heidi Robbiani(SUI)
	4 flts Touch of Class	4 Abdullah	8 Jessica V
1988	Pierre Durand(FRA)	Greg Best(USA)	Karsten Huck(FRG)
	1.25 flts Jappeloup	4 Gem Twist	4 Nepomuk 8
1992	Ludger Beerbaum(GER)	Piet Raymakers(NED)	Norman Dello Joio(USA)
	0 flts Classic Touch	0.25 Ratina Z	4.75 Irish
1996	Ulrich Kirchkoff(GER)	Willi Melliger(SUI)	Alexandra Ledermann(FRA)
	1 flt Jus de Pommes	4.00 Calvaro	4.00 Rochet M
2000	Jeroen Dubbeldam(NED)	Albert Voorn(NED)	Khaled al Eid(KSA)
	0 flts Sjiem	4 Lando	4.00 Khashim al Aan
2004(1)	1.Rodrigo Pessoa(BRA) on	2.Chris Kappler(USA) on	Marco Kutscher(GER) onr
	8pts Baloubet du Rouet	8pts Royal Kaliber	9pts Montender

1896, 1904–08 Event not held

(1) Cian O'Connor(IRL) on Waterford Crystal placed first with 4pts but was disqualified

Grand Prix (Jumping) Team

	GOLD	SILVER	BRONZE
1912	SWEDEN 25pts	FRANCE 32pts	GERMANY 40pts
1920	SWEDEN 14pts	BELGIUM 16.25pts	ITALY 18.75pts
1924	SWEDEN 42.25pts	SWITZERLAND 50pts	PORTUGAL 53pts
1928	SPAIN 4pts	POLAND 8pts	SWEDEN 10pts
1932(1)	–	–	–
1936	GERMANY 44pts	NETHERLANDS 51.5	PORTUGAL 56pts
1948	MEXICO 34.25pts	SPAIN 56.50pts	GREAT BRITAIN 67pts
1952	GREAT BRITAIN 40.75pts	CHILE 45.75pts	UNITED STATES 52.25pts
1956	GERMANY 40pts	ITALY 66pts	GREAT BRITAIN 69pts
1960	GERMANY 46.50pts	UNITED STATES 66pts	ITALY 80.50pts
1964	GERMANY 68.50pts	FRANCE 77.75pts	ITALY 88.50pts
1968	CANADA 102.75pts	FRANCE 110.50pts	FRG 117.25pts
1972	FRG 32pts	UNITED STATES 32.25pts	ITALY 48pts
1976	FRANCE 40pts	FRG 44pts	BELGIUM 63pts
1980	SOVIET UNION 16pts	POLAND 32pts	MEXICO 39.25pts
1984	UNITED STATES 12pts	GREAT BRITAIN 36.75pts	FRG 39.25pts
1988	FRG 17.25pts	UNITED STATES 20.50pts	FRANCE 27.50pts
1992	NETHERLANDS 12.00pts	AUSTRIA 16.75pts	FRANCE 24.75pts
1996	GERMANY 1.75pts	UNITED STATES 12.00pts	BRAZIL 17.25pts
2000	GERMANY 15pts	SWITZERLAND 16pts	BRAZIL 24pts
2004(2)	UNITED STATES 20pts	SWEDEN 20pts	GERMANY 8pts

1896–1908 Event not held

(1) No team had three competitors finish the course

(2) Germany placed first with 8pts, but one of their horses was disqualified and the team relegated to third

Grand Prix (Dressage)

	GOLD	SILVER	BRONZE
1912	Carl Bonde(SWE) 15pts	Gustaf-Adolf Boltenstern Sr(SWE) 21pts	Hans von Blixen-Finecke(SWE) 32pts
	Emperor	Neptun	Maggie
1920	Janne Lundblad(SWE) 27.9375pts	Bertil Sandström(SWE) 26.3125pts	Hans von Rosen(SWE) 25.1250pts (1)
	Uno	Sabel	Running Sister
1924	Ernst Linder(SWE) 276.4pts	Bertil Sandström(SWE) 275.8pts	Xavier Lesage(FRA) 265.8pts
	Piccolomini	Sabel	Plumard
1928	Carl von Langen(GER) 237.42pts	Charles Marion(FRA) 231.00pts	Ragnar Olsson(SWE) 229.78pts
	Draüfgänger	Linon	Günstling
1932	Xavier Lesage(FRA) 1031.25pts	Charles Marion(FRA) 916.25pts	Hiram Tuttle(USA) 901.50pts
	Taine	Linon	Olympic
1936	Heinz Pollay(GER) 1760pts	Friedrich Gerhard(GER) 1745.4pts	Alois Podhajsky(AUT) 1721.5pts
	Kronos	Absinth	Nero
1948	Hans Moser(SUI) 492.5pts	André Jousseaume(FRA) 480.0pts	Gustaf-Adolf Boltenstern Jr(SWE) 477.5pts
	Hummer	Harpagon	Trumpf
1952	Henri St Cyr(SWE) 561pts	Lis Hartel(DEN) 541.5pts	André Jousseauame(FRA) 541.0pts
	Master Rufus	Jubilee	Harpagon
1956	Henri St Cyr(SWE) 860pts	Lis Hartel(DEN) 850pts	Liselott Linsenhoff(GER) 832pts
	Juli	Jubilee	Adular
1960	Sergei Filatov(URS) 2144pts	Gustav Fischer(SUI) 2087pts	Josef Neckermann(GER) 2082 pts
	Absent	Wald	Asbach
1964	Henri Chammartin(SUI) 1504pts	Harry Boldt(GER) 1503pts	Sergei Filatov(URS) 1486pts
	Woermann	Remus	Absent
1968	Ivan Kizimov(URS) 1572pts	Josef Neckermann(FRG) 1546pts	Reiner Klimke(FRG) 1527pts
	Ikhov	Mariano	Dux
1972	Liselott Linsenhoff(FRG) 1229pts	Yelena Petuchkova(URS) 1185pts	Josef Neckermann(FRG) 2082pts
	Piaff	Pepel	Venetia

	GOLD	SILVER	BRONZE
1976	Christine Stückelberger(SUI) 1486 Granat	Harry Boldt(FRG) 1435pts Woycek	Reiner Klimke(FRG) 1395pts Mehmed
1980	Elisabeth Theuer(AUT) 1370pts Mon Cherie	Yuri Kovshov(URS) 1300pts Igrok	Viktor Ugyumov(URS) 1234pts Shkval
1984	Reiner Klimke(FRG) 1504pts Ahlerich	Anne Grethe Jensen(DEN) 1442pts Martzog	Otto Hofer(SUI) 1364pts Limandus
1988	Nicole Uphoff(FRG) 1521pts Rembrandt	Margit Otto Crepin(FRA) 1462pts Corlandus	Christine Stückelberger(SUI) 1417pts Gauguin De Lully
1992	Nicole Uphoff(FRG) 1626pts Rembrandt	Isabell Werth(GER) 1551pts Gigolo	Klaus Balkenhol(GER) 1515pts Goldstern
1996	Isabel Werth(GER) 235.09pts Gigolo	Anky van Grunsven(NED) 233.02pts Bonfire	Sven Rothenberger(NED) 224.94pts Weyden
2000	Anky van Grunsven(NED) 239.18pts Bonfire	Isabell Werth(GER) 234.19pts Gigolo	Ulla Salzgeber(GER) 230.57pts Rusty
2004	Anky van Grunsven(NED) 79.278pts Salinero	Ulla Salzgeber(GER) 78.833pts Rusty	Beatriz Ferrer-Salat(ESP) 76.667pts Beauvalais

1896–1908 Event not held
(1) Gustaf-Adolf Boltenstern Sr (SWE) was third (26.1875pts) but later disqualified

Grand Prix (Dressage Team)

	GOLD	SILVER	BRONZE
1928	GERMANY 669.72pts	SWEDEN 650.86pts	NETHERLANDS 642.96pts
1932	FRANCE 2828.75pts	SWEDEN 2678pts	UNITED STATES 2576.75pts
1936	GERMANY 5074pts	FRANCE 4846pts	SWEDEN 4660.5pts
1948	FRANCE 1269pts (1)	UNITED STATES 1256pts	PORTUGAL 1182pts
1952	SWEDEN 1597.5pts	SWITZERLAND 1759pts	GERMANY 1501pts
1956	SWEDEN 2475pts	GERMANY 2346pts	SWITZERLAND 2346pts
1964	GERMANY 2558pts	SWITZERLAND 2526pts	SOVIET UNION 2311pts
1968	FRG 2699pts	SOVIET UNION 2657pts	SWITZERLAND 2547pts
1972	SOVIET UNION 5095pts	FRG 5083pts	SWEDEN 4849pts
1976	FRG 5155pts	SWITZERLAND 4684pts	UNITED STATES 4670pts
1980	SOVIET UNION 4383pts	BULGARIA 3580pts	ROMANIA 3346pts
1984	FRG 4955pts	SWITZERLAND 4673pts	SWEDEN 4630pts
1988	FRG 4302pts	SWITZERLAND 4164pts	CANADA 3969pts
1992	GERMANY 5224pts	NETHERLANDS 4742pts	UNITED STATES 4643pts
1996	GERMANY 5553pts	NETHERLANDS 5437pts	UNITED STATES 5309pts
2000	GERMANY 5632pts	NETHERLANDS 5579pts	UNITED STATES 5166pts
2004	GERMANY 74.653pts	SPAIN 72.917pts	UNITED STATES 71.500pts

1896–1924, 1960 Event not held
(1) Sweden won with 1366pts but were disqualified a year later

Three-Day Event

	GOLD	SILVER	BRONZE
1912	Axel Nordlander(SWE) 46.59pts Lady Artist	Friedrich von Rochow(GER) 46.42pts Idealist	Jean Cariou(FRA) 46.32pts Cocotte
1920	Helmer Mörner(SWE) 1775pts Germania	Age Lundström(SWE) 1738.75pts Yrsa	Ettore Caffaratti(ITA) 1733.75pts Traditore
1924	Adolf van de Voort van Zijp(NED) 1976pts Silver Piece	Fröde Kirkebjerg(DEN) 1853.5pts Meteor	Sloan Doak(USA) 1845.5pts Pathfinder
1928	Charles Pahud de Mortanges(NED) 1969.82pts Marcroix	Gerard de Kruyff(NED) 1967.26pts Va-t-en	Bruno Neumann(GER) 1944.42pts Ilja
1932	Charles Pahud de Mortanges(NED) 1813.83pts Marcroix	Earl Thomson(USA) 1811pts Jenny Camp	Clarence von Rosen Jr(SWE) 1809.42pts Sunnyside Maid
1936	Ludwig Stubbendorff(GER) 37.7 Nurmi	Earl Thomson(USA) 99.9pts Jenny Camp	Hans Mathiesen Lunding(DEN) 102.2pts Jason
1948	Bernard Chevallier(FRA) +4pts Aiglonne	Frank Henry(USA) -21 Swing Low	Robert Selfelt(SWE) -25 Claque
1952	Hans von Blixen-Finecke(SWE) 28.33 flts Jubal	Guy Lefrant(FRA) 54.50pts Verdun	Wilhelf Büsing(GER) 55.50pts Hubertus
1956	Petrus Kasenman(SWE) 66.53 flts Illuster	August Lütke-Westhues(GER) 84.87pts Trux van Kamax	Frank Weldon(GBR) 85.48pts Kilbarry
1960	Lawrence Morgan(AUS) +7.15pts Salad Days	Neale Lavis(AUS) -16.50 Mirrabooka	Anton Bühler(SUI) -51.21pts Gay Spark
1964	Mauro Checcoli(ITA) 64.40pts Surbean	Carlos Moratorio(ARG) 56.40pts Chalan	Fritz Ligges(GER) 49.20pts Donkosak
1968	Jean-Jaques Guyon(FRA) 38.86pts Pitou	Derek Allhusen(GBR) 41.61pts Lochinvar	Michael Page(USA) 52.31pts Faster
1972	Richard Meade(GBR) 57.73pts Laurieston	Alessa Argenton(ITA) 43.33pts Woodland	Jan Jonsson(SWE) 39.67pts Sarajevo

1976	Edmund Coffin(USA) 114.99pts Bally-Cor	Michael Plumb(USA) 125.85pts Better & Better	Karl Schultz(FRG) 129.45pts Madrigal
1980	Federico Roman(ITA) 108.60pts Rossinan	Aleksandr Blinov(URS) 120.80pts Galzun	Yuriy Salinikov(URS) 151.60pts Pintset
1984	Mark Todd(NZL) 51.60pts Charisma	Karen Stives(USA) 54.20pts Ben Arthur	Virginia Holgate(GBR) 56.80pts Priceless
1988	Mark Todd(NZL) 42.60pts Charisma	Ian Stark(GBR) 52.80pts Sir Wattie	Virginia Leng(GBR) 62.00pts Master Craftsman
1992	Matthew Ryan(AUS) 70pts Kibah Tic Toc	Herbert Blocker(GER) 81.30pts Feine Dame	Blyth Tait(NZL) 87.60pts Messiah
1996	Blyth Tait(NZL) 56.80pts Ready Teddy	Sally Clark(NZL) 60.40pts Squirrel Hill	Kerry Millikin(USA) 73.70pts Out & About
2000	David O'Connor(USA) 34.00pts Custom Made	Andrew Hoy(AUS) 39.80pts Swizzle	Mark Todd(NZL) 42.00pts Eyespy II
2004(1)	Leslie Law(GBR) 44.40tps Shear L'Eau	Kim Severson(USA) 45.20pts Winsome Adante	Pippa Funnell(GBR) 46.60pts Primmore's Pride

1896–1908 Event not held
(1) Bettina Hoy(GER) on Ringwood Cockatoo originally placed first with 41.60pts but was relegated to ninth with 55.60pts

Three-Day Event Team

	GOLD	SILVER	BRONZE
1912	SWEDEN 139.06pts	GERMANY 138.48pts	UNITED STATES 137.33pts
1920	SWEDEN 5057pts	ITALY 4375pts	BELGIUM 4560pts
1924	NETHERLANDS 5297.5pts	SWEDEN 4743.5pts	ITALY 4512.5pts
1928	NETHERLANDS 5865.68pts	NORWAY 5395.68pts	POLAND 5067.92pts
1932	UNITED STATES 5038.08pts	NETHERLANDS 4689.08pts	– (1)
1936	GERMANY 676.75pts	POLAND 991.70pts	GREAT BRITAIN 9195.90pts
1948	UNITED STATES 161.50pts	SWEDEN 165.00pts	MEXICO 305.25pts
1952	SWEDEN 221.49pts	GERMANY 2£5.49pts	UNITED STATES 587.16pts
1956	GREAT BRITAIN 355.48pts	GERMANY 475.61pts	CANADA 572.72pts
1960	AUSTRALIA 128.18pts	SWITZERLAND 386.02pts	FRANCE 515.71pts
1964	ITALY 85.80pts	UNITED STATES 65.86pts	GERMANY 56.73pts
1968	GREAT BRITAIN 175.93pts	UNITED STATES 245.87pts	AUSTRALIA 331.26pts
1972	GREAT BRITAIN 95.53pts	UNITED STATES 10.81pts	FRG -18.00pts
1976	UNITED STATES 441.00pts	FRG 584.60pts	AUSTRALIA 599.54pts
1980	SOVIET UNION 457.00pts	ITALY 656.20pts	MEXICO 1172.85pts
1984	UNITED STATES 186.00pts	GREAT BRITAIN 189.20pts	FRG 234.00pts
1988	FRG 225.95pts	GREAT BRITAIN 256.80pts	NEW ZEALAND 271.20pts
1992	AUSTRALIA 288.60pts	NEW ZEALAND 290.80pts	GERMANY 300.30pts
1996	AUSTRALIA 203.85pts	UNITED STATES 261.10pts	NEW ZEALAND 268.55pts
2000	AUSTRALIA 146.80pts	GREAT BRITAIN 161.00pts	UNITED STATES 175.80pts
2004	FRANCE 140.40pts	GREAT BRITAIN 143.00pts	UNITED STATES 145.60pts

1896–1908 Event not held
(1) Only two teams finished

EQUESTRIAN – DISCONTINUED EVENTS

	GOLD	SILVER	BRONZE
Equestrian High Jump			
1900	Dominique Gardére(FRA) 1.85m Canéla Gian Giorgio Trissino(ITA) 1.85m Oreste	–	André Moreaux(FRA) 1.70 Ludlow
Equestrian Long Jump			
1900	Constant van Langhendonck(BEL) 6.10m Extra Dry	Federico Caprilli(ITA) 5.70m Oreste	de Bellegarde(FRA) 5.30m Tolla
Figure Riding			
(Only open to soldiers below the rank of NCO)			
1920	Bouckaert(BEL) 30,500pts	Field(FRA) 29,500	Finet(BEL) 29.000
Figure Riding – Teams			
1920	BELGIUM 87,500	FRANCE 81,083	SWEDEN 59,416

FENCING

Individual Foil – Men

(Champions are assessed on wins (2pts) and draws (1pt), thus winners do not always have the most wins)

	GOLD	SILVER	BRONZE
1896	Emile Gravelotte(FRA) 4 wins	Henri Callott(FRA) 3	Perikles Mavromichalis-Pierrakos(GRE) 2
1900	Emile Cost(FRA) 6 wins	Henri Masson(FRA) 5	Jacques Boulenger(FRA) 4
1904	Ramón Fonst(CUB) 3 wins	Albertson Van Zo Post(USA) 2	Charles Tatham(USA) 1
1906	Georges Dillon-Kavanagh(FRA) d.n.a.	Gustav Casmir(GER) d.n.a.	Pierre d'Hugues(FRA) d.n.a.
1912	Nedo Nadi(ITA) 7 wins	Pietro Speciale(ITA) 5	Richard Verderber(AUT) 4
1920	Nedo Nadi(ITA) 10 wins	Philippe Cattiau(FRA) 9	Roger Ducret(FRA) 9
1924	Roger Ducret(FRA) 6 wins	Philippe Cattiau(FRA) 5	Maurice van Damme(BEL) 4
1928	Lucien Gaudin(FRA) 9 wins	Ermin Casmir(GER) 9	Giulio Gaudini(ITA) 9
1932	Gustavo Marzi(ITA) 9 wins	Joseph Lewis(USA) 6	Giulio Bocchino(ITA) 4
1936	Giulio Gaudini(ITA) 7 wins	Edouard Gardère(FRA) 6	Lajos Maszlay(HUN) 4
1948	Jehan Buhan(FRA) 7 wins	Christian d'Oriola(FRA) 5	Lajos Maszlay(HUN) 4
1952	Christian d'Oriola(FRA) 8 wins	Edouard Gardère(FRA) 6	Manlio di Rosa(ITA) 5
1956	Christian d'Oriola(FRA) 6 wins	Giancarlo Bergamini(ITA) 5	Antonio Spallino(ITA) 5
1960	Viktor Zhdanovich(URS) 7 wins	Yuriy Sissikin(URS) 4	Albert Axelrod(USA) 3
1964	Egon Franke(POL) 3 wins	Jean-Claude Magnan(FRA) 2	Daniel Revenu(FRA) 1
1968	Ion Drimba(ROM) 4 wins	Jenö Kamuti(HUN) 3	Daniel Revenu(FRA) 3
1972	Witold Woyda(POL) 5 wins	Jenö Kamuti(HUN) 4	Christian Nöel(FRA) 2
1976	Fabio Dal Zotto(ITA) 4 wins	Alexander Romankov(URS) 4	Bernard Talvard(FRA) 3
1980	Vladimir Smirnov(URS) 5 wins	Paskal Jolyot(FRA) 5	Alexander Romankov(URS) 5
1984	Mauro Numa(ITA)	Matthias Behr(FRG)	Stefano Cerioni(ITA)
1988	Stefano Cerioni(ITA)	Udo Wagner(GDR)	Alexander Romankov(URS)
1992	Phillipe Omnes(FRA)	Sergei Goloubiski(EUN)	Elvis Gregory(CUB)
1996	Alessandro Puccini(ITA)	Lionel Plumenail(FRA)	Franck Boidin(FRA)
2000	Young-Ho Kim(KOR)	Ralf Bissdorf(GER)	Dimitri Chevchenko(RUS)
2004	Brice Guyart(FRA)	Salvatore Sanzo(ITA)	Andrea Cassara(ITA)

Individual Épée – Men

	GOLD	SILVER	BRONZE
1900	Ramón Fonst(CUB)	Louis Perrée(FRA)	Léon Sée(FRA)
1904	Ramón Fonst(CUB)	Charles Tatham(USA)	Albertson Van Zo Post(USA)
1906	Georges de la Falaise(FRA)	Georges Dillon-Kavanagh(FRA)	Alexander van Blijenburgh(NED)
1908	Gaston Alibert(FRA) 5 wins	Alexandre Lippmann(FRA) 4	Eugène Olivier(FRA) 4
1912	Paul Anspach(BEL) 6 wins	Ivan Osiier(DEN) 5	Philippe Le Hardy de Beaulieu(BEL) 4
1920	Armand Massard(FRA) 9 wins	Alexandre Lippmann(FRA) 7	Gustave Buchard(FRA) 6
1924	Charles Delporte(BEL) 8 wins	Roger Ducret(FRA) 7	Nils Hellsten(SWE) 7
1928	Lucien Gaudin(FRA) 8 wins	Georges Buchard(FRA) 7	George Calman(USA) 6
1932	Giancarlo Cornaggia-Medici(ITA) 8	Georges Buchard(FRA) 7	Carlo Agostini(ITA) 7
1936	Franco Riccardi(ITA) 5 wins	Saverio Ragno(ITA) 6	Giancarlo Cornaggia-Medici(ITA) 6
1948	Luigi Cantone(ITA) 7 wins	Oswald Zappelli(SUI) 5	Edoardo Mangiarotti(ITA) 5
1952	Edoardo Mangiarotti(ITA) 7 wins	Dario Mangiarotti(ITA) 6	Oswald Zappelli(SUI) 6
1956	Carlo Pavesi(ITA) 5 wins	Giuseppe Delfino(ITA) 5	Edoardo Mangiarotti(ITA) 5
1960	Giuseppe Delfino(ITA) 5 wins	Allan Jay(GBR) 5	Bruno Khabarov(URS) 4
1964	Grigori Kriss(URS) 2 wins	William Hoskyns(GBR) 2	Guram Kostava(URS) 1
1968	Gyözö Kulcsár(HUN) 4 wins	Grigori Kriss(URS) 4	Gianluigi Saccaro(ITA) 4
1972	Csaba Fenyvesi(HUN) 4 wins	Jacques la Degaillerie(FRA) 3	Gyözö Kulcsár(HUN) 3
1976	Alexander Pusch(FRG) 3 wins	Jürgen Hehn(FRG)	Gyözö Kulcsár(HUN) 3
1980	Johan Harmenberg(SWE) 4 wins	Ernö Kolczonay(HUN) 3	Philippe Riboud(FRA) 3
1984	Philippe Boisse(FRA)	Björne Väggö(SWE)	Philippe Riboud(FRA)
1988	Arnd Schitt(FRG)	Philippe Riboud(FRA)	Andrei Chouvalov(URS)
1992	Eric Srecki(FRA)	Pavel Kolobkov(EUN)	Jean-Michel Henry(FRA)
1996	Alexander Beketov(RUS)	Ivan Trevejo Perez(CUB)	Geza Imre(HUN)
2000	Pavel Kolobkov(RUS)	Hugues Obry(FRA)	Sang-Ki Lee(KOR)
2004	Marcel Fischer(SUI)	Lei Wang(CHN)	Pavel Kolobkov(RUS)

1896 Event not held

Individual Sabre – Men

	GOLD	SILVER	BRONZE
1896	Jean Georgiadis(GRE) 4 wins	Telemachos Karakalos(GRE) 3	Holger Nielsen(DEN) 2
1900	Georges de la Falaise(FRA) d.n.a.	Léon Thiébault(FRA) d.n.a.	Siegfried Flesch(AUT) d.n.a.
1904	Manuel Diaz(CUB) 4 wins	William Grebe(USA) 3	Albertson Van Zo Post(USA)
1906	Jean Georgiadis(GRE) d.n.a.	Gustav Casmir(GER) d.n.a.	Federico Cesarano(ITA) d.n.a.
1908	Jeno Fuchs(HUN) 6 wins	Béla Zulavsky(HUN) 6	Vilem Goppold von Lobsdorf(BOH) 4
1912	Jeno Fuchs(HUN) 6 wins	Béla Békéssy(HUN) 5	Ervin Mészaros(HUN) 5
1920	Nedo Nadi(ITA) 11 wins	Aldo Nadi(ITA) 9	Adrianus E.W. de Jong(NED) 7
1924	Sándor Posta(HUN) 5 wins	Roger Ducret(FRA) 5	János Garai(HUN) 5
1928	Odön Tersztyansky(HUN) 9 wins	Attila Petschauer(HUN) 9	Bino Bini(ITA) 8
1932	György Piller(HUN) 8 wins	Giulio Gaudini(ITA) 7	Endre Kabos(HUN) 5

	GOLD	SILVER	BRONZE
1936	Endre Kabos(HUN) 7 wins	Gustavo Marzi(ITA) 6	Aladár Gerevich(HUN) 6
1948	Aladár Gerevich(HUN) 7 wins	Vincenzo Pinton(ITA) 5	Pál Kovács(HUN) 5
1952	Pál Kovács(HUN) 8 wins	Aladár Gerevich(HUN) 7	Tibor Berczelly(HUN) 5
1956	Rudolf Kárpáti(HUN) 6 wins	Jerzy Pawlowski(POL) 5	Lev Kuznyetsov(URS) 4
1960	Rudolf Kárpáti(HUN) 5 wins	Zoltán Horvath(HUN) 4	Wladimiro Calarese(ITA) 4
1964	Tibor Pézsa(HUN) 2 wins	Claude Arabo(FRA) 2	Umar Mavlikhanov(URS) 1
1968	Jerzy Pawlowski(POL) 4 wins	Mark Rakita(URS) 4	Tribor Pézsa(HUN) 3
1972	Viktor Sidiak(URS) 4 wins	Peter Maroth(HUN) 3	Vladimir Nazilimov(URS) 3
1976	Viktor Krovopouskov(URS) 5 wins	Vladimir Nazlimov(URS) 4	Viktor Sidiak(URS) 3
1980	Viktor Krovopouskov(URS) 5 wins	Mikhail Burtsev(URS) 4	Imre Gedovari(HUN) 3
1984	Jean François Lamour(FRA)	Marco Marin(ITA)	Peter Westbrook(USA)
1988	Jean François Lamour(FRA)	Janusz Olech(POL)	Giovanni Scalzo(ITA)
1992	Bence Szabo(HUN)	Marco Marin(ITA)	Jean François Lamour(FRA)
1996	Sergei Podnyakov(RUS)	Stanislav Sharikov(RUS)	Damien Touya(FRA)
2000	Mihai Covaliu(ROM)	Mathieu Gourdain(FRA)	Wiradech Kothny(GER)
2004	Aldo Montano(ITA)	Zsolt Nemcsik(HUN)	Vladislav Tretiak(UKR)

Team Foil – Men

	GOLD	SILVER	BRONZE
1904	CUBA/USA	UNITED STATES	– (1)
1920	ITALY	FRANCE	UNITED STATES
1924	FRANCE	BELGIUM	HUNGARY
1928	ITALY	FRANCE	ARGENTINA
1932	FRANCE	ITALY	UNITED STATES
1936	ITALY	FRANCE	GERMANY
1948	FRANCE	ITALY	BELGIUM
1952	FRANCE	ITALY	HUNGARY
1956	ITALY	FRANCE	GERMANY
1960	SOVIET UNION	ITALY	GERMANY
1964	SOVIET UNION	POLAND	FRANCE
1968	FRANCE	SOVIET UNION	POLAND
1972	POLAND	SOVIET UNION	FRANCE
1976	FRG	ITALY	FRANCE
1980	FRANCE	SOVIET UNION	POLAND
1984	ITALY	FRG	FRANCE
1988	SOVIET UNION	FRG	HUNGARY
1992	GERMANY	CUBA	POLAND
1996	RUSSIA	POLAND	CUBA
2000	FRANCE	CHINA	ITALY
2004	ITALY	CHINA	RUSSIA

1896–1900, 1906–12 Event not held
(1) Only three teams entered

Team Épée – Men

	GOLD	SILVER	BRONZE
1906	FRANCE	GREAT BRITAIN	BELGIUM
1908	FRANCE	GREAT BRITAIN	BELGIUM
1912	BELGIUM	GREAT BRITAIN	NETHERLANDS
1920	ITALY	BELGIUM	FRANCE
1924	FRANCE	BELGIUM	ITALY
1928	ITALY	FRANCE	PORTUGAL
1932	FRANCE	ITALY	UNITED STATES
1936	ITALY	SWEDEN	FRANCE
1948	FRANCE	ITALY	SWEDEN
1952	ITALY	SWEDEN	SWITZERLAND
1956	ITALY	HUNGARY	FRANCE
1960	ITALY	GREAT BRITAIN	SOVIET UNION
1964	HUNGARY	ITALY	FRANCE
1968	HUNGARY	SOVIET UNION	POLAND
1972	HUNGARY	SWITZERLAND	SOVIET UNION
1976	SWEDEN	FRG	SWITZERLAND
1980	FRANCE	POLAND	SOVIET UNION
1984	FRG	FRANCE	ITALY
1988	FRANCE	FRG	SOVIET UNION
1992	GERMANY	HUNGARY	UNIFIED TEAM
1996	ITALY	RUSSIA	FRANCE
2000	ITALY	FRANCE	CUBA
2004	FRANCE	HUNGARY	GERMANY

1896–1904 Event not held

Team Sabre – Men

	GOLD	SILVER	BRONZE
1906	GERMANY	GREECE	NETHERLANDS
1908	HUNGARY	ITALY	BOHEMIA
1912	HUNGARY	AUSTRIA	NETHERLANDS
1920	ITALY	FRANCE	NETHERLANDS
1924	ITALY	HUNGARY	NETHERLANDS
1928	HUNGARY	ITALY	POLAND
1932	HUNGARY	ITALY	POLAND
1936	HUNGARY	ITALY	GERMANY
1948	HUNGARY	ITALY	UNITED STATES
1952	HUNGARY	ITALY	FRANCE
1956	HUNGARY	POLAND	SOVIET UNION
1960	HUNGARY	POLAND	ITALY
1964	SOVIET UNION	ITALY	POLAND
1968	SOVIET UNION	ITALY	HUNGARY
1972	ITALY	SOVIET UNION	HUNGARY
1976	SOVIET UNION	ITALY	ROMANIA
1980	SOVIET UNION	ITALY	HUNGARY
1984	ITALY	FRANCE	ROMANIA
1988	HUNGARY	SOVIET UNION	ITALY
1992	UNIFIED TEAM	HUNGARY	FRANCE
1996	RUSSIA	HUNGARY	ITALY
2000	RUSSIA	FRANCE	GERMANY
2004	FRANCE	ITALY	RUSSIA

1896–1904 Event not held

Individual Foil – Women

	GOLD	SILVER	BRONZE
1924	Ellen Osiier(DEN) 5 wins	Gladys Davis(GBR) 4	Grete Heckscher(DEN) 3
1928	Helène Mayer(GER) 7 wins	Muriel Freeman(GBR) 6	Olga Oelkers(GER) 4
1932	Ellen Müller-Preiss(AUT) 9 wins	Heather Guinness(GBR) 8	Erna Bogen(HUN) 7
1936	Ilona Elek(HUN) 6 wins	Helène Mayer(GER) 5	Ellen Müller-Preiss(AUT) 5
1948	Ilona Elek(HUN) 6 wins	Karen Lachmann(DEN) 5	Ellen Müller-Preiss(AUT) 5
1952	Irene Camber(ITA) 5 wins	Ilona Elek(HUN) 5	Karen Lachmann(DEN) 4
1956	Gillian Sheen(GBR) 6 wins	Olga Orban(ROM) 6	Renée Garilhe(FRA) 5
1960	Heidi Schmid(GER) 6 wins	Valentina Rastvorova(URS) 5	Maria Vicol(ROM) 4
1964	Ildikó Ujlaki-Rejtö(HUN) 2 wins	Helga Mees(GER) 2	Antonella Ragno(ITA) 2
1968	Elena Noivkova(URS) 4 wins	Pilar Roldan(EMX) 3	Ildikó Ujlaki-Rejtö(HUN) 3
1972	Antonella Ragno-Lonzi(ITA) 4 wins	Ildikó Bóbis(HUN) 3	Galina Gorokhova(URS)
1976	Ildikó Schwarczenberger(HUN) 4 wins	Maria Collino(ITA) 4	Elena Novikova-Belova(URS) 3
1980	Pascale Trinquet(FRA) 4 wins	Magda Maros(HUN) 3	Barbara Wysoczanska(POL) 3
1984	Jujie Luan(CHN)	Cornelia Hanisch(FRG)	Dorina Vaccaroni(ITA)
1988	Anja Fichtel(FRG)	Sabine Bau(FRG)	Zita Funkenhauser(FRG)
1992	Giovanna Trillini(ITA)	Huifeng Wang(CHN)	Tatyana Sadovskaya(EUN)
1996	Laura Badea(ROM)	Valentin Vezzali(ITA)	Giovanna Trillini(ITA)
2000	Valentina Vezzali(ITA)	Rita König(GER)	Giovanna Trillini(ITA)
2004	Valentina Vezzali(ITA)	Giovanna Trillini(ITA)	Sylwia Gruchala(POL)

1896–1920 Event not held

Individual Épée – Women

	GOLD	SILVER	BRONZE
1996	Laura Flessel(FRA)	Valerie Bartlois(FRA)	Györgyi Horvathné-Szalay(HUN)
2000	Timea Nagy(HUN)	Gianni Hablützel-Bürki(SUI)	Laura Flessel-Colovic(FRA)
2004	Timea Nagy(HUN)	Laura Flessel-Colovic(FRA)	Maureen Nisima(FRA)

1896–1992 Event not held

Individual Sabre – Women

2004	Mariel Zagunis(USA)	Xue Tan(CHN)	Sada Jacobson(USA)

1896–2000 Event not held

Team Foil – Women

	GOLD	SILVER	BRONZE
1960	SOVIET UNION	HUNGARY	ITALY
1964	HUNGARY	SOVIET UNION	GERMANY
1968	SOVIET UNION	HUNGARY	ROMANIA
1972	SOVIET UNION	HUNGARY	ROMANIA
1976	SOVIET UNION	FRANCE	HUNGARY
1980	FRANCE	SOVIET UNION	HUNGARY
1984	FRG	ROMANIA	FRANCE
1988	FRG	ITALY	HUNGARY
1992	ITALY	GERMANY	ROMANIA

| 1996 | ITALY | ROMANIA | GERMANY |
| 2000 | ITALY | POLAND | GERMANY |

1896–1956, 2004 Event not held

Team Épée – Women

	GOLD	SILVER	BRONZE
1996	FRANCE	ITALY	RUSSIA
2000	RUSSIA	SWITZERLAND	CHINA
2004	RUSSIA	GERMANY	FRANCE

1896–1992 Event not held

FENCING – DISCONTINUED EVENTS

	GOLD	SILVER	BRONZE

Foil for Fencing Masters

| 1896 | Léon Pyrgos(GRE) | Jean Perronnet(FRA) | – |
| 1900 | Lucien Mérignac(FRA) | Alphonse Kirchhoffer(FRA) | Jean-Baptiste Mimiague(FRA) |

Épée for Fencing Masters

| 1900 | Albert Ayat(FRA) | Emile Bougnol(FRA) | Henri Laurent(FRA) |
| 1906 | Cyrille Verbrugge(BEL) | Carlo Gandini(ITA) | Ioannis Raissis(GRE) |

Épée for Amateurs and Fencing Masters

| 1900 | Albert Ayat(FRA) | Ramón Fonst(CUB) | Léon Sée(FRA) |

Sabre for Fencing Masters

| 1900 | Antonio Conte(ITA) | Italo Santelli(ITA) | Milan Neralic(AUT) |
| 1906 | Cyrille Verburgge(BEL) | Ioannis Raissis(GRE) | – |

Three-Cornered Sabre

| 1906 | Gustav Casmir(GER) | George van Rossem(NED) | Péter Tóth(HNU) |

Single Sticks

| 1904 | Albertson Van Zo Post(USA) | William Grebe(USA) | William O'Connor(USA) |

1896–1992 Event not held

FOOTBALL

Men

	GOLD	SILVER	BRONZE
1900	GREAT BRITAIN	FRANCE	BELGIUM
1904	CANADA	UNITED STATES	UNITED STATES
1906	DENMARK	GREECE	GREECE
1908	GREAT BRITAIN	DENMARK	NETHERLANDS
1912	GREAT BRITAIN	DENMARK	NETHERLANDS
1920	BELGIUM	SPAIN	NETHERLANDS
1924	URUGUAY	SWITZERLAND	SWEDEN
1928	URUGUAY	ARGENTINA	ITALY
1936	ITALY	AUSTRIA	NORWAY
1948	SWEDEN	YUGOSLAVIA	DENMARK
1952	HUNGARY	YUGOSLAVIA	DENMARK
1956	SOVIET UNION	YUGOSLAVIA	BULGARIA
1960	YUGOSLAVIA	DENMARK	HUNGARY
1964	HUNGARY	CZECHOSLOVAKIA	GERMANY
1968	HUNGARY	BULGARIA	JAPAN
1972	POLAND	HUNGARY	GDR (1)
			SOVIET UNION (1)
1976	GDR	POLAND	SOVIET UNION
1980	CZECHOSLOVAKIA	GDR	SOVIET UNION
1984	FRANCE	BRAZIL	YUGOSLAVIA
1988	SOVIET UNION	BRAZIL	FRG
1992	SPAIN	POLAND	GHANA
1996	NIGERIA	ARGENTINA	BRAZIL
2000	CAMEROON	SPAIN	CHILE
2004	ARGENTINA	PARAGUAY	ITALY

1896 Event not held, 1932 FIFA withdrew
(1) Tie after extra time

Women

	GOLD	SILVER	BRONZE
1996	UNITED STATES	CHINA	NORWAY
2000	NORWAY	UNITED STATES	GERMANY
2004	UNITED STATES	BRAZIL	GERMANY

1896–1992 Event not held

GYMNASTICS

Team – Men

	GOLD	SILVER	BRONZE
1904	USA/AUSTRIA 374.43pts(1)	UNITED STATES 356.37(2)	UNITED STATES 349.69
1906	NORWAY 19.00pts	DENMARK 18.00	ITALY 16.71
1908	SWEDEN 438pts	NORWAY 425	FINLAND 405
1912	ITALY 265.75pts	HUNGARY 227.25	GREAT BRITAIN 184.50
1920	ITALY 359.855pts	BELGIUM 346.745	FRANCE 340.100
1924	ITALY 839.058pts	FRANCE 820.528	SWITZERLAND 816.661
1928	SWITZERLAND 1718.652pts	CZECHOSLOVAKIA 1712.250	YUGOSLAVIA 1648.750
1932	ITALY 541.850pts	UNITED STATES 522.275	FINLAND 509.995
1936	GERMANY 657.430pts	SWITZERLAND 654.802	FINLAND 638.468
1948	FINLAND 1358.3pts	SWITZERLAND 1356.7	HUNGARY 1330.35
1952	SOVIET UNION 575.4pts	SWITZERLAND 567.5	FINLAND 564.2
1956	SOVIET UNION 568.25	JAPAN 566.40	FINLAND 555.95
1960	JAPAN 575.20pts	SOVIET UNION 572.70	ITALY 559.05
1964	JAPAN 577.95pts	SOVIET UNION 575.45	GERMANY 565.10
1968	JAPAN 575.90pts	SOVIET UNION 571.10	GDR 557.15
1972	JAPAN 571.25pts	SOVIET UNION 564.05	GDR 559.70
1976	JAPAN 576.85pts	SOVIET UNION 576.45	GDR 654.65
1980	SOVIET UNION 589.60pts	GDR 581.15	HUNGARY 575.00
1984	UNITED STATES 591.40pts	CHINA 590.80	JAPAN 586.70
1988	SOVIET UNION 593.350pts	GDR 588.450	JAPAN 585.600
1992	UNIFIED TEAM 585.450pts	CHINA 580.375	JAPAN 578.250
1996	RUSSIA 576.778pts	CHINA 575.539	UKRAINE 571.541
2000	CHINA 231.919pts	UKRAINE 230.306	RUSSIA 230.019
2004	JAPAN 173.821pts	UNITED STATES 172.933pts	ROMANIA 172.384pts

1896–1900 Event not held
(1) Composite team
(2) Countries allowed multiple entries at this time

Individual Combined Exercises – Men

	GOLD	SILVER	BRONZE
1900	Gustave Sandras(FRA) 302pts	Noël Bas(FRA) 295pts	Lucien Démanet(FRA) 293pts
1904	Julius Lenhart(AUT) 69.80pts	Wilhelm Weber(GER) 69.10pts	Adolf Spinnler(SUI) 67.99pts
1906(1)	Pierre Paysse(FRA) 97pts	Alberto Braglia(ITA) 95pts	Georges Charmoille(FRA) 94pts
1906(1)	Pierre Paysse(FRA) 116pts	Alberto Paglia(ITA) 115pts	Georges Charmoille(FRA) 113pts
1908	Alberto Braglia(ITA) 317.0pts	S Walter Tysal(GBR) 312.0pts	Louis Ségura(FRA) 297.0pts
1912	Alberto Braglia(ITA) 135.0pts	Louis Ségura(FRA) 132.5pts	Adolfo Tunesi(ITA) 131.5pts
1920	Giorgio Zampori(ITA) 88.35pts	Marco Torres(FRA) 87.62pts	Jean Gounot(FRA) 87.45pts
1924	Leon Stukelj(YUG) 110.340pts	Robert Prazák(TCH) 110.323pts	Bedrich Supcik(TCH) 106.930pts
1928	Georges Miez(SUI) 247.500pts	Herman Hänggi(SUI) 246.625pts	Leon Stukelj(YUG) 244.875pts
1932	Romeo Neri(ITA) 140.625pts	István Pelle(HUN) 134.925pts	Heikki Savolainen(FIN) 134.575pts
1936	Alfred Schwarzmann(GER) 113.100pts	Eugen Mack(SUI) 112.334pts	Konrad Frey(GER) 111.532pts
1948	Veikko Huhtanen(FIN) 229.7pts	Walter Lehmann(SUI) 229.0pts	Paavo Aaltonen(FIN) 228.8pts
1952	Viktor Chukarin(URS) 115.70pts	Grant Shaginyan(URS) 114.95pts	Josef Stalder(SUI) 114.75pts
1956	Viktor Chukarin(URS) 114.25pts	Takashi Ono(JPN) 114.20pts	Yuri Titov(URS) 113.80pts
1960	Boris Shakhlin(URS) 115.95pts	Takashi Ono(JPN) 115.90pts	Yuri Titov(URS) 115.60pts
1964	Yukio Endo(JPN) 115.95pts	Shuji Tsurumi(JPN) 115.40pts Viktor Lisitsky(URS) 115.40pts	–
1968	Sawao Kato(JPN) 115.90pts	Mikhail Voronin(URS) 115.85pts	Akinori Nakayama(JPN) 115.65pts
1972	Sawao Kato(JPN) 114.650pts	Eizo Kenmotsu(JPN) 114.575pts	Akinori Nakayama(JPN) 114.325pts
1976	Nikolai Andrianov(URS) 116.650pts	Sawao Kato(JPN) 115.650pts	Mitsuo Tsukahara(JPN) 115.375pts
1980	Alexander Dityatin(URS) 118.650pts	Nikolai Andrianov(URS) 118.225pts	Stoyan Deltchev(BUL) 118.000pts
1984	Koji Gushiken(JPN) 118.700pts	Peter Vidmar(USA) 118.675pts	Ning Li(CHN) 118.575pts
1988	Vladimir Artemov(URS) 119.125pts	Valeriy Lyukhine(URS) 119.025pts	Dimitri Bilozertchev(URS) 118.975pts
1992	Vitali Scherbo(EUN) 59.025pts	Grigori Mistyutin(EUN) 58.925pts	Valeri Belenki(EUN) 58.625pts
1996	Xiaoshuang Li(CHN) 58.423pts	Alexei Nemov(RUS) 58.374pts	Vitali Scherbo(BLR) 58.197pts
2000	Alexei Nemov(RUS) 58.474pts	Wei Yang(CHN) 58.361pts	Alexander Beresch(UKR) 58.212pts
2004	Paul Hamm(USA) 57.823pts	Dae Eun Kim (KOR) 57.811pts	Tae Young Yang(KOR) 57.774pts

1896 Event not held
(1) There were two competitions in 1906, of five events and six respectively

Floor Exercises – Men

	GOLD	SILVER	BRONZE
1932	István Pelle(HUN) 9.60pts	Georges Miez(SUI) 9.47pts	Mario Lertora(ITA) 9.23pts
1936	Georges Miez(SUI) 18.666pts	Josef Walter(SUI) 18.5pts	Konrad Frey(GER) 18.466pts
			Eugen Mack(SUI) 18.466pts
1948	Ferenc Pataki(HUN) 38.7pts	János Mogyorosi-Klencs(HUN) 38.4pts	Zdenek Ruzicka(TCH) 38.1pts
1952	William Thoresson(SWE) 19.25pts	Tadao Uesako(JPN) 19.15pts	–
		Jerzy Jokiel(POL) 19.15pts	
1956	Valentin Muratov(URS) 19.20pts	Nobuyuki Aihara(JPN) 19.10pts	–
		Viktor Chukharin(URS) 19.10pts	
1960	Nobuyuki Aihara(JPN) 19.450pts	Yuri Titov(JPN) 19.325pts	Franco Menichelli(ITA) 19.275pts
1964	Franco Menichelli(ITA) 19.45pts	Viktor Lisitsky(URS) 19.35pts	–
		Yukio Endo(JPN) 19.35pts	
1968	Sawao Kato(JPN) 19.475pts	Akinori Nakayama(JPN) 19.400pts	Takeshi Kato(JPN) 19.275pts
1972	Nikolai Andrianov(URS) 19.175pts	Akinori Nakayama(JPN) 19.125pts	Shigeru Kasamatsu(JPN) 19.025pts
1976	Nikolai Andrianov(URS) 19.450pts	Vladimir Marchenko(URS) 19.425pts	Peter Kormann(USA) 19.300pts
1980	Roland Brückner(GDR) 19.750pts	Nikolay Andrianov(URS) 19.725pts	Aleksandr Dityatin(URS) 19.700pts
1984	Ning Li(CHN) 19.925pts	Lou Yun(CHN) 19.775pts	Koji Sotomura(JPN) 19.700pts
			Philippe Vatuone(FRA) 19.700pts
1988	Sergei Kharikov(URS) 19.925pts	Vladimir Artemov(URS) 19.900pts	Lou Yun(CHN) 19.850pts
			Yukio Iketani(JPN) 19.850pts
1992	Xiaoshuang Li(CHN) 9.925pts	Grigori Misyutin(EUN) 9.787pts	–
		Yukio Iketani(JPN) 9.787pts	
1996	Ioannis Melissanidis(GRE) 9.950pts	Xiaoshuang Li(CHN) 9.837pts	Alexei Nemov(RUS) 9.800pts
2000	Igor Vihrovs(LAT) 9.812pts	Alexei Nemov(RUS) 9.800pts	Jordan Jovtchev(BUL) 9.787pts
2004	Kyle Shewfelt(CAN) 9.787pts	Marian Dragulescu(ROM) 9.787pts	Jordan Jovtchev(BUL) 9.775pts

1896–1928 Event not held

Parallel Bars – Men

	GOLD	SILVER	BRONZE
1896	Alfred Flatow(GER) d.n.a.	Jules Zutter(SUI) d.n.a.	Hermann Weingärtner(GER) d.n.a.
1904	George Eyser(USA) 44pts	Anton Heida(USA) 43pts	John Duha(USA) 40pts
1924	August Güttinger(SUI) 21.63pts	Robert Prazák(TCH) 21.61pts	Giorgio Zampori(ITA) 21.45pts
1928	Ladislav Vácha(TCH) 18.83pts	Josip Primozic(YUG) 18.50pts	Hermann Hänaggi(SUI) 18.08pts
1932	Romeo Neri(ITA) 18.97pts	István Pelle(HUN) 18.60pts	Heikki Savolainen(FIN) 18.27pts
1936	Konrad Frey(GER) 19.067pts	Michael Reusch(SUI) 109.034pts	Alfred Schwarzmann(GER) 18.967pts
1948	Michael Reusch(SUI) 39.5pts	Veikkö Huhtanen(FIN) 39.3pts	Christian Kipfer(SUI) 39.1pts
			Josef Stalder(SUI) 39.1pts
1952	Hans Eugster(SUI) 19.65pts	Viktor Chukarin(URS) 19.60pts	Josef Stalder(SUI) 19.50pts
1956	Viktor Chukarin(URS) 19.20pts	Masami Kubota(JPN) 19.15pts	Takashi Ono(JPN) 19.10pts
			Masao Takemoto(JPN) 19.10pts
1960	Boris Shakhlin(URS) 19.40pts	Giovanni Carminucci(ITA) 19.375pts	Takashi Ono(JPN) 19.350pts
1964	Yukio Endo(JPN) 19.675pts	Shuji Tsurumi(JPN) 19.450pts	Franco Menichelli(ITA) 19.350pts
1968	Akinori Nakayama(JPN) 19.475pts	Mikhail Voronin(URS) 19.425pts	Vladimir Klimenko(URS) 19.225pts
1972	Sawao Kato(JPN) 19.475pts	Shigeru Kasamatsu(JPN) 19.375pts	Eizo Kenmotsu(JPN) 19.25pts
1976	Sawao Kato(JPN) 19.675pts	Nikolai Andrianov(URS) 19.500pts	Mitsuo Tsukahara(JPN) 19.475pts
1980	Alexander Tkachev(URS) 19.775pts	Alexander Dityatin(URS) 19.750pts	Roland Brückner(GDR) 19.650pts
1984	Bart Conner(USA) 19.950pts	Nobuyuki Kajitani(JPN) 19.925pts	Mitchell Gaylord(USA) 19.850pts
1988	Vladimir Artemov(URS) 19.925pts	Valeriy Lyukhine(URS) 19.900pts	Sven Tippelt(GDR) 19.750pts
1992	Vitali Scherbo(EUN) 9.900pts	Jing Li(CHN) 9.812pts	Linyao Guo(CHN) 9.800pts
			Igor Korobchinkski(EUN) 9.800pts
			Masayuki Matsunaga(JPN) 9.800pts
1996	Rustam Sharipov(UKR) 9.837pts	Jair Lynch(USA) 9.825pts	Vitali Scherbo(BLR) 9.800pts
2000	Xiaopeng Li(CHN) 9.825pts	Joo-Hyung Lee(CHN) 9.812pts	Alexei Nemov(RUS) 9.800pts
2004	Valeri Goncharov(UKR) 9.787pts	Hiroyuki Tomita(JPN) 9.775pts	Xiaopeng Li(CHN) 9.762pts

1900, 1906–20 Event not held

Pommel Horse – Men

	GOLD	SILVER	BRONZE
1896	Jules Zutter(SUI) d.n.a.	Hermann Weingärtner(GER) d.n.a.	Gyula Kakas(HUN) d.n.a.
1904	Anton Heida(USA) 42pts	George Eyser(USA) 33pts	William Merz(USA) 29pts
1924	Josef Wilhelm(SUI) 21.23pts	Jean Gutweiniger(SUI) 21.13pts	Antoine Rebetez(SUI) 20.73pts
1928	Hermann Hänggi(SUI) 19.75pts	Georges Miez(SUI) 19.25pts	Heikki Savolainen(FIN) 18.83pts
1932	István Pelle(HUN) 19.07pts	Omero Bonoli(ITA) 18.87pts	Frank Haubold(USA) 18.57pts
1936	Konrad Frey(GER) 19.333pts	Eugen Mack(SUI) 19.167pts	Albert Bachmann(SUI) 19.067pts
1948	Paavo Aaltonen(FIN) 38.7pts	Luigi Zanetti(ITA) 38.3pts	Guido Figone(ITA) 38.2pts
	Veikkö Huhtanen(FIN) 38.7pts		
	Heikki Savolainen(FIN) 38.7pts		
1952	Viktor Chukarin(URS) 19.50pts	Yevgeni Korolkov(URS) 19.40pts	–
		Grant Shaginyan(URS) 19.40pts	
1956	Boris Shakhlin(URS) 19.25pts	Takashi Ono(JPN) 19.20pts	Viktor Chukarin(URS) 19.10pts
1960	Eugen Ekman(FIN) 19.375pts	–	Shuji Tsurumi(JPN) 19.150pts
	Boris Shakhlin(URS) 19.375pts		

467

1964	Miroslav Cerar(YUG) 19.525pts	Shuji Tsurumi(JPN) 19.325pts	Yuri Tsapenko(URS) 19.200pts
1968	Miroslav Cerar(YUG) 19.325pts	Olli Laiho(FIN) 19.225pts	Mikhail Voronin(URS) 19.200pts
1972	Viktor Klimenko(URS) 19.125pts	Sawao Kato(JPN) 19.00pts	Eizo Kenmotsu(JPN) 18.950pts
1976	Zoltän Magyar(HUN) 19.700pts	Eizo Kenmotsu(JPN) 19.575pts	Nikolai Andrianov(URS) 19.525pts
1980	Zoltän Magyar(HUN) 19.925pts	Alexander Dityatin(URS) 19.800pts	Michael Nikolay(GDR) 19.775pts
1984	Ning Li(CHN) 19.950pts Peter Vidmar(USA) 19.950pts	–	Timothy Daggert(USA) 19.825pts
1988	Lubomir Gueraskov(BUL) 19.950pts Zsolt Borkai(HUN) 19.950pts Dimitri Bilozertchev(URS) 19.950pts	–	–
1992	Vitali Scherbo(EUN) 9.925pts Gil-Su Pae(PRK) 9.925pts	–	Andreas Wecker(GER) 9.887pts
1996	Lin Donghua(SUI) 9.875pts	Marius Urzica(ROM) 9.825pts	Alexei Nemov(RUS) 9.787pts
2000	Marius Urzica(ROM) 9.862	Eric Poujade(FRA) 9.825pts	Alexei Nemov(RUS) 9.800pts
2004	Haibin Teng (CHN) 9.837pts	Marius Daniel Urzica(ROM) 9.825pts	Takehiro Kashima(JPN) 9.787pts

1900, 1906–20 Event not held

Rings – Men

	GOLD	SILVER	BRONZE
1896	Ioannis Mitropoulos(GRE) d.n.a.	Hermann Weingärtner(GER) d.n.a.	Petros Persakis(GRE) d.n.a.
1904	Herman Glass(USA) 45pts	William Merz(USA) 35pts	Emil Voight(USA) 32pts
1924	Franco Martino(ITA) 21.553pts	Robert Prazák(TCH) 21.483pts	Ladislav Vácha(TCH) 21.430pts
1928	Leon Skutelj(YUG) 19.25pts	Ladislav Vácha(TCH) 19.17pts	Emanuel Löffler(TCH) 18.83pts
1932	George Gulack(USA) 18.97pts	William Denton(USA) 18.60pts	Giovanni Lattuada(ITA) 18.50pts
1936	Alois Hudec(TCH) 19.433pts	Leon Skutelj(YUG) 18.867pts	Matthias Volz(GER) 18.667pts
1948	Karl Frei(SUI) 39.60pts	Michael Reusch(SUI) 39.10pts	Zdenek Ruzicka(TCH) 38.30pts
1952	Grant Shaginyan(URS) 19.75pts	Viktor Chakarin(URS) 19.55pts	Hans Eugster(SUI) 19.40pts Dimitri Leonkin(URS) 19.40pts
1956	Albert Azaryan(URS) 19.35pts	Valentin Muratov(URS) 19.15pts	Masao Takemoto(JPN) 19.10pts Masami Kubota(JPN) 19.10pts
1960	Albert Azaryan(URS) 19.475pts	Boris Shakhlin(URS) 19.500pts	Velik Kapsazov(BUL) 19.425pts Takashi Ono(JPN) 19.425pts
1964	Takuji Hayata(JPN) 19.475pts	Franco Menichelli(ITA) 19.425pts	Boris Shakhlin(URS) 19.400pts
1968	Akinori Nakayama(JPN) 19.450pts	Mikhail Voronin(URS) 19.325pts	Sawao Kato(JPN) 19.225pts
1972	Akinori Nakayama(JPN) 19.350pts	Mikhail Voronin(URS) 19.325pts	Mitsuo Tsukahara(JPN) 19.225pts
1976	Nikolai Andrianov(URS) 19.875pts	Alexander Dityatin(URS) 19.550pts	Danut Grecu(ROM) 19.500pts
1980	Alexander Dityatin(URS) 19.875pts	Alexander Tkachev(URS) 19.725pts	Jiri Tabak(TCH) 19.600pts
1984	Koji Gushiken(JPN) 19.850pts Ning Li(CHN) 19.850pts	–	Mitchell Gaylord(USA) 19.825pts
1988	Holger Behrendt(GDR) 19.925pts Dmitri Bilozerchev(URS) 19.925pts	–	Sven Tippelt(GDR)pts
1992	Vitali Scherbo(EUN) 9.937pts	Jing Li(CHN) 9.875pts	Xiaoshuang Li(CHN) 9.862pts Andreas Wecker(GER) 9.862pts
1996	Yuri Chechi(ITA) 9.887pts	Szilveszter Csollany(HUN) 9.812pts Dan Burnica(ROM) 9.812pts	–
2000	Szilveszter Csollany(HUN) 9.850pts	Dimosthenis Tampakos(GRE) 9.762pts	Jordan Jovtchev(BUL) 9.737pts
2004	Dimosthenis Tampakos(GRE) 9.862pts	Jordan Jovtchev(BUL) 9.850pts	Yuri Chechi(ITA) 9.812pts

1900, 1906–20 Event not held

Horizontal Bar – Men

	GOLD	SILVER	BRONZE
1896	Hermann Weingärtner(GER) d.n.a.	Alfred Flatow(GER) d.n.a.	d.n.a
1904	Anton Heida(USA) 40pts Edward Henning(USA) 40pts	–	George Eyser(USA) 39pts
1924	Leon Stukelj(YUG) 19.730pts	Jean Gutweniger(SUI) 19.236pts	André Higelin(FRA) 19.163pts
1928	Georges Miez(SUI) 19.17pts	Romeo Neri(ITA) 19.00pts	Eugen Mack(SUI) 18.92 pts
1932	Dallas Bixler(USA) 18.33pts	Heikki Savolainen(FIN) 18.07pts	Einari Teräsvirta(FIN) 18.07pts
1936	Aleksanteri Sarvaala(FIN) 19.367pts	Konrad Frey(GER) 19.267pts	Alfred Schwarzmann(GER) 19.233pts
1948	Josef Stalder(SUI) 39.7pts	Walter Lehmann(SUI) 39.4pts	Veikkö Huhtanen(FIN) 39.2pts
1952	Jack Günthard(SUI) 19.55pts	Josef Stalder(SUI) 19.50pts Alfred Schwarzmann(GER) 19.50pts	–
1956	Takashi Ono(JPN) 19.60pts	Yuri Titov(URS) 19.40pts	Masao Takemoto(JPN) 19.30pts
1960	Takashi Ono(JPN) 19.60pts	Masao Takemoto(JPN) 19.525pts	Boris Shakhlin(URS) 19.475pts
1964	Boris Shakhlin(URS) 19.625pts	Yuri Titov(URS) 19.55pts	Miroslav Cerar(YUG) 19.50pts
1968	Mikhail Voronin(URS) 19.550pts Akinori Nakayama(JPN) 19.550pts	–	Eizo Kenmotsu(JPN) 19.375pts
1972	Mitsuo Tsukahara(JPN) 19.725pts	Sawao Kato(JPN) 19.525pts	Shigeru Kasamatsu(JPN) 19.450pts
1976	Mitsuo Tsukahara(JPN) 19.675pts	Eizo Kenmotsu(JPN) 19.500pts	Eberhard Gienger(FRG) 19.475pts Henry Boërio(FRA) 19.475pts
1980	Stoyan Deltchev(BUL) 19.825pts	Alexander Dityatin(URS) 19.750pts	Nikolai Andrianov(URS) 19.675pts
1984	Shinje Morisue(JPN) 20.00pts	Fei Tong(CHN) 19.955pts	Koji Gushiken(JPN) 19.950pts
1988	Vladimir Artemov(URS) 10.900pts Valeri Lyukhine(URS) 19.900pts	–	Holger Behrendt(GDR) 19.800pts Marius Germann(ROM) 19.800

1992	Trent Dimas(USA) 9.875ptspts	Andreas Wecker(GER) 9.837pts	
		Grigori Misyutin(EUN) 9.837pts	
1996	Alexei Nemov(RUS) 9.787pts	Hong-Chul Yeo(KOR) 9.756pts	Vitali Scherbo(BLR) 9.724pts
2000	Alexei Nemov(RUS) 9.787pts	Benjamin Varonian(FRA) 9.787pts	Joo-Hyung Lee(CHN) 9.775pts
2004	Igor Cassina(ITA) 9.812pts	Paul Hamm(USA) 9.812pts	Isao Yoneda(JPN) 9.787pts

1900, 1906–20 Event not held

Horse Vault – Men

	GOLD	SILVER	BRONZE
1896	Carl Schuhmann(GER) d.n.a.	Jules Zutter(SUI)	d.n.a.
1904	Anton Heida(USA) 36pts	–	William Merz(USA) 31pts
	George Eyser(USA) 36pts		
1924	Frank Kriz(USA) 9.98pts	Jan Koutny(TCH) 9.97pts	Bohumil Morkovsky(TCH) 9.93pts
1928	Eugen Mack(SUI) 9.58pts	Emanuel Lóffler(TCH) 9.50pts	Stane Derganc(YUG) 9.46pts
1932	Savino Guglielmetti(ITA) 18.03pts	Alfred Jochim(USA) 17.77pts	Edward Carmichael(USA) 17.53pts
1936	Alfred Schwarzmann(GER) 19.200pts	Eugen Mack(SUI) 18.967pts	Matthias Volz(GER) 18.467pts
1948	Paavo Aaltonen(FIN) 39.10pts	Olavi Rove(FIN) 39.00pts	János Mogyorosi-Klencs(HUN) 38.50pts
			Ferenc Pataki(HUN) 38.50pts
			Leos Sotornik(TCH) 38.50pts
1952	Viktor Chukarin(URS) 19.20pts	Masao Takemoto(JPN) 19.15pts	Tadao Uesako(JPN) 19.10 pts
			Takashi Ono(JPN) 19.10pts
1956	Helmuth Bantz(GER) 18.85pts	–	Yuri Titov(URS) 18.75pts
	Valentin Muratov(URS) 18.85pts		
1960	Takashi Ono(JPN) 19.350pts	–	Vladimir Portnoi(URS) 19.225pts
	Boris Shakhlin(URS) 19.350pts		
1964	Haruhiro Yamashita(JPN) 19.600pts	Viktor Lisitsky(URS) 19.325pts	Hannu Rantakari(FIN) 19.300pts
1968	Mikhail Voronin(URS) 19.000pts	Yukio Endo(JPN) 18.950pts	Sergei Diomidov(URS) 18.925pts
1972	Klaus Koste(GDR) 18.850pts	Viktor Klimenko(URS) 18.825pts	Nikolai Andrianov(URS) 18.800pts
1976	Nikolai Andrianov(URS) 19.450pts	Mitsuo Tsukahara(JPN) 19.375pts	Hiroshi Kajiyama(JPN) 19.275pts
1980	Nikolai Andrianov(URS) 19.825pts	Alexander Dityatin(URS) 19.800pts	Roland Brückner(GDR) 19.775pts
1984	Lou Yun(CHN) 19.950pts	Ning Li(CHN) 19.825pts	–
		Koji Gushiken(JPN) 19.825pts	
		Mitchell Gaylord(USA) 19.825pts	
		Shinje Morisue(JPN) 19.825pts	
1988	Lou Yun(CHN) 19.875pts	Sylvio Kroll(GDR) 19.862pts	Jong-Hoon Park(KOR) 19.775pts
1992	Vitali Scherbo(EUN) 9.856pts	Grigori Misyutin(EUN) 9.781pts	Ok-Youl Yoo(KOR) 9.762pts
1996	Andreas Wecker(GER) 9.850pts	Krasimir Dounev(BUL) 9.825pts	Vitali Shcherbo(BLR) 9.800pts
			Bin Fan(CHN) 9.800pts
			Alexei Nemov(RUS) 9.800pts
2000	Gevasio Deferr(ESP) 9.712pts	Alexei Bondarenko(RUS) 9.587pts	Leszek Blanik(POL) 9.475pts
2004	Gervasio Deferr(ESP) 9.737pts	Evgeni Sapronenko(LAT) 9.706pts	Marian Dragulescu(ROM) 9.612pts

1900, 1906–1920 Event not held

Trampolining – Men

	GOLD	SILVER	BRONZE
2000	*Alexander Moskalenko(RUS) 41.70pts*	Ji Wallace(AUS) 39.30pts	Mathieu Turgeon(CAN) 39.10pts
2004	Yuri Nikitin(UKR) 41.50	Alexander Moskalenko(RUS) 41.20	Henrik Stehlik(GER) 40.80pts

1896–1996 Event not held

Team – Women

	GOLD	SILVER	BRONZE
1928	NETHERLANDS 316.75pts	ITALY 289.00pts	GREAT BRITAIN 258.25pts
1936	GERMANY 506.50pts	CZECHOSLOVAKIA 503.60pts	HUNGARY 499.00pts
1948	CZECHOSLOVAKIA 445.45pts	HUNGARY 440.55pts	UNITED STATES 422.63pts
1952	SOVIET UNION 527.03pts	HUNGARY 520.96pts	CZECHOSLOVAKIA 503.32pts
1956	SOVIET UNION 444.80pts	HUNGARY 443.50pts	ROMANIA 438.20pts
1960	SOVIET UNION 382.320pts	CZECHOSLOVAKIA 373.323pts	ROMANIA 372.053pts
1964	SOVIET UNION 380.890pts	CZECHOSLOVAKIA 379.989pts	JAPAN 377.889pts
1968	SOVIET UNION 382.85pts	CZECHOSLOVAKIA 382.20pts	GDR 379.10pts
1972	SOVIET UNION 380.50pts	GDR 376.55pts	HUNGARY 368.25pts
1976	SOVIET UNION 390.35pts	ROMANIA 387.15pts	GDR 385.10pts
1980	SOVIET UNION 394.90pts	ROMANIA 393.50pts	GDR 392.55pts
1984	ROMANIA 392.20pts	UNITED STATES 391.20pts	CHINA 388.60pts
1988	SOVIET UNION 395.475pts	ROMANIA 394.125pts	GDR 390.875pts
1992	UNIFIED TEAM 395.666pts	ROMANIA 395.079pts	UNITED STATES 394.704pts
1996	UNITED STATES 389.225pts	RUSSIA 388.40pts	ROMANIA 388.246pts
2000	ROMANIA 154.608pts	RUSSIA 154.403pts	CHINA 154.008pts
2004	ROMANIA 114.283pts	UNITED STATES 113.584pts	RUSSIA 113.235pts

1896–1924, 1932 Event not held

Individual Combined Exercises – Women

	GOLD	SILVER	BRONZE
1952	Maria Gorokhovskaya(URS) 76.78pts	Nina Bocharova(URS) 75.94pts	Margit Korondi(HUN) 75.82pts
1956	Larissa Latynina(URS) 74.933pts	Agnes Keleti(HUN) 74.633pts	Sofia Muratova(URS) 74.466pts
1960	Larissa Latynina(URS) 77.031pts	Sofia Muratova(URS) 76.696pts	Polina Astakhova(URS) 76.164pts
1964	Vera Cáslavská(TCH) 77.564pts	Larissa Laytnina(URS) 76.998pts	Polina Astakhova(URS) 76.965pts
1968	Vera Cáslavská(TCH) 78.25pts	Zinaida Voronina(URS) 76.85pts	Natalia Kuchinskaya(URS) 76.75pts
1972	Ludmila Tourischeva(URS) 77.025pts	Karin Janz(GDR) 76.875pts	Tamara Lazakovitch(URS) 76.850pts
1976	Nadia Comaneci(ROM) 79.275pts	Nelli Kim(URS) 78.675pts	Ludmila Tourischeva(URS) 78.625pts
1980	Yelena Davydova(URS) 79.150pts	Maxi Gnauck(GDR) 79.075pts Nadia Comaneci(ROM) 79.075pts	–
1984	Mary Lou Retton(USA) 79.175pts	Ecaterina Szabo(ROM) 79.125pts	Simona Pauca(ROM) 78.675pts
1988	Yelena Chouchounova(URS) 79.662pts	Daniela Silivas(ROM) 79.637pts	Svetlana Boguinskaya(URS) 79.40pts
1992	Tatyana Gutsu(EUN) 39.737pts	Shannon Miller(USA) 39.725pts	Lavinia Milosovici(ROM) 39.687pts
1996	Lilia Podkopayeva(UKR) 39.255pts	Gina Gogean(ROM) 39.075pts	Lavinia Milosovici(ROM) 39.067pts Simona Amanar(ROM) 39.067pts
2000	Simona Amanar(ROM) 38.642pts	Maria Olaru(ROM) 38.581pts	Xuan Li(CHN) 38.418pts
2004	Carly Patterson(USA) 38.387pts	Svetlana Khorkina(RUS) 38.211pts	Nan Zhang (CHN) 38.049pts

1896–1948 Event not held

Assymmetrical Bars – Women

	GOLD	SILVER	BRONZE
1952	Margit Korondi(HUN) 19.40pts	Maria Gorokhovskaya(URS) 19.26pts	Agnes Keleti(HUN) 19.16pts
1956	Agnes Keleti(HUN) 18.966pts	Larissa Latynina(URS) 18.833pts	Sofia Muratova(URS) 18.800pts
1960	Polina Astakhova(URS) 19.616pts	Larissa Latynina(URS) 19.416pts	Tamara Lyukhina(URS) 19.399pts
1964	Polina Astakhova(URS) 19.332pts	Katalin Makray(HUN) 19.216pts	Larissa Latynina(URS) 19.199pts
1968	Vera Cáslavská(TCH) 19.650pts	Karin Janz(GDR) 19.500pts	Zinaida Voronina(URS) 19.425pts
1972	Karin Janz(GDR) 19.675pts	Olga Korbut(URS) 19.450pts Erika Zuchold(GDR) 19.450	–
1976	Nadia Comaneci(ROM) 20.00pts	Teodora Ungureanu(ROM) 19.800pts	Marta Egervari(HUN) 19.775pts
1980	Maxi Gnauck(GDR) 19.875pts	Emila Eberle(ROM) 19.850pts	Steffi Kräker(GDR) 19.775pts Melita Rühn(ROM) 19.775pts Maria Filatova(URS) 19.775pts
1984	Yanhong Ma(CHN) 19.950pts Julianne McNamara(USA) 19.950pts	–	Mary Lou Retton(USA) 19.800pts
1988	Daniela Silivas(ROM) 20.00pts	Dagmar Kersten(GDR) 19.987pts	Yelena Chouchounova(URS) 19.962pts
1992	Lu Li(CHN) 10.00pts	Tatyana Gutsu(EUN) 9.975pts	Shannon Miller(USA) 9.962pts
1996	Svetlana Khorkina(RUS) 9.850pts	Wengji Bi(CHN) 9.837pts Amy Chow(USA) 9.837pts	–
2000	Svetlana Khorkina(RUS) 9.862pts	Jie Ling(CHN) 9.837pts	Yun Yang(CHN) 9.787pts
2004	Emilie Lepennec(FRA) 9.687pts	Terin Humphrey(USA) 9.662pts	Courtney Kupets(USA) 9.637pts

1896–1948 Event not held

Balance Beam – Women

	GOLD	SILVER	BRONZE
1952	Nina Bocharova(URS) 19.22pts	Maria Gorokhovskaya(URS) 19.13pts	Margit Korondi(HUN) 19.02pts
1956	Agnes Keleti(HUN) 18.80pts	Eva Bosáková(TCH) 18.63pts Tamara Manina(URS) 18.63pts	–
1960	Eva Bosáková(TCH) 19.283pts	Larissa Latynina(URS) 19.233pts	Sofia Muratova(URS) 19.232pts
1964	Vera Cáslavská(TCH) 19.449pts	Tamara Manina(URS) 19.399pts	Larissa Latynina(URS) 19.382pts
1968	Natalya Kuchinskaya(URS) 19.650pts	Vera Cáslavská(TCH) 19.575pts	Larissa Petrik(URS) 19.250pts
1972	Olga Korbut(URS) 19.575pts	Tamara Lazokovitch(URS) 19.375pts	Karin Janz(GDR) 18.975pts
1976	Nadia Comaneci(ROM) 19.950pts	Olga Korbut(URS) 19.725pts	Teodora Ungureanu(ROM) 19.700pts
1980	Nadia Comaneci(ROM) 19.800pts	Yelena Davydova(URS) 19.750pts	Natalya Shaposhnikova(URS) 19.725pts
1984	Simona Pauca(ROM) 19.800pts Ecaterina Szabo(ROM) 19.800pts	–	Kathy Johnson(USA) 19.650pts
1988	Daniela Silivas(ROM) 19.924pts	Yelena Chouchounova(URS) 19.875pts	Gabriela Potorac(ROM) 19.837pts Phoebe Mills(USA) 19.837pts
1992	Tayana Lyssenko(EUN) 9.975pts	Lu Li(CHN) 9.912pts Shannon Miller(USA) 9.912pts	–
1996	Shannon Miller(USA) 9.862pts	Lilia Podkopayeva(UKR) 9.825pts	Gina Gogean(ROM) 9.787pts
2000	Xuan Liu(CHN) 9.825pts	Yekaterina Lobaznyuk(RUS) 9.787pts	Yelena Produnova(RUS) 9.775pts
2004	Catalina Ponor(ROM) 9.787pts	Carly Patterson(USA) 9.775pts	Alexandra Eremia(ROM) 9.700pts

1896–1948 Event not held

Floor Exercises – Women

	GOLD	SILVER	BRONZE
1952	Agnes Keleti(HUN) 19.36pts	Maria Gorokhovskaya(URS) 19.20pts	Margit Korondi(HUN) 19.00pts
1956	Larissa Altynina(URS) 18.733pts Agnes Keleti(HUN) 18.733pts	–	Elena Leustean(ROM) 18.70pts
1960	Larissa Latynina(URS) 19.583pts	Polina Astakhova(URS) 19.532pts	Tamara Lyukhina(URS) 19.449pts
1964	Larissa Latynina(URS) 19.599pts	Polina Astakhova(URS) 19.500pts	Anikó Jánosi(HUN) 19.300pts

1968	Larissa Petrik(URS) 19.675pts	–	Natalya Kuchinskaya(URS) 19.650pts
	Vera Cáslavská(TCH) 19.675pts		
1972	Olga Korbut(URS) 19.575pts	Ludmila Tourischeva(URS) 19.550pts	Tamara Lazakovitch(URS) 19.450pts
1976	Nelli Kim(URS) 19.850pts	Ludmila Tourischeva(URS) 19.825pts	Nadia Comaneci(ROM) 19.750pts
1980	Nelli Kim(URS) 19.875pts	–	Natalya Shaposhnikova(URS) 19.825pts
	Nadia Comaneci(ROM) 19.875pts		Maxi Gnauck(GDR) 19.825pts
1984	Ecaterina Szabo(ROM) 19.975pts	Julianne McNamara(USA) 19.950pts	Mary Lou Retton(USA) 19.775pts
1988	Daniela Silivas(ROM) 19.937pts	Svetlana Boguinskaya(URS) 19.887pts	Diana Doudeva(BUL) 19.850pts
1992	Lavinia Milosovici(ROM) 10.00pts	Henrietta Onodi(HUN) 9.950pts	Tatyana Gutsu(EUN) 9.912pts
			Christina Bontas(ROM) 9.912pts
			Shannon Miller(USA) 9.912pts
1996	Lilia Podkopayeva(UKR) 9.887pts	Simona Amanar(ROM) 9.850pts	Dominique Dawes(USA) 9.837pts
2000	Yelena Zamolodtchikova(RUS) 9.850pts	Svetlana Khorkina(RUS) 9.812pts	Simona Amanar(ROM) 9.712pts
2004	Catalina Ponor(ROM) 9.750pts	Nicoleta Sofronie(ROM) 9.562pts	Patricia Moreno(ESP) 9.487pts

1896–1948 Event not held

Horse Vault – Women

	GOLD	SILVER	BRONZE
1952	Yelena Kalinchuk(URS) 19.20pts	Maria Gorokhovskaya(URS) 19.19pts	Galina Minaitscheva(URS) 19.16pts
1956	Larissa Latynina(URS) 18.833pts	Tamara Manina(URS) 18.800pts	Ann-Sofi Colling(SWE) 18.733pts
			Olga Tass(HUN) 18.733pts
1960	Margarita Nikolayeva(URS) 19.316pts	Sofia Muratova(URS) 19.049pts	Larissa Latynina(URS) 19.016pts
1964	Vera Cáslavská(TCH) 19.483pts	Larissa Latynina(URS) 19.283pts	–
		Birgit Radochla(GER) 19.283pts	
1968	Vera Cáslavská(TCH) 19.775pts	Erika Zuchold(GDR) 19.625pts	Zinaida Voronina(URS) 19.500pts
1972	Karin Janz(GDR) 19.525pts	Erika Zuchold(GDR) 19.275pts	Ludmila Tourischeva(URS) 19.250pts
1976	Nelli Kim(URS) 19.800pts	Ludmila Tourischeva(URS) 19.650pts	–
		Carola Dombeck(GDR) 19.650pts	
1980	Natalya Shaposhnikova(URS) 19.725pts	Steffi Kräker(GDR) 19.675pts	Melita Rühn(ROM) 19.650pts
1984	Ecaterina Szabo(ROM) 19.875pts	Mary Lou Retton(USA) 19.850pts	Lavinia Agache(ROM) 19.750pts
1988	Svetlana Boguinskaya(URS) 19.905pts	Gabriela Potorac(ROM) 19.830pts	Daniela Silivas(ROM) 19.818pts
1992	Lavinia Milosovici(ROM) 9.925pts	–	Tatyana Lyssenko(EUN) 9.912pts
	Henrietta Onodi(HUN) 9.925pts		
1996	Simona Amanar(ROM) 9.825pts	Huilan Mo(CHN) 9.768pts	Gina Gogean(ROM) 9.750pts
2000	Yelena Zamolodtchikova(RUS) 9.731pts	Andreea Raducan(ROM) 9.693pts	Yekaterina Lobaznyuk(RUS) 9.674pts
2004	Monica Rosu(ROM) 9.656pts	Annia Hatch(USA) 9.481pts	Anna Pavlova(RUS) 9.475pts

1896–1948 Event not held

Modern Rhythmic – Women

	GOLD	SILVER	BRONZE
1984	Lori Fung(CAN) 57.950pts	Doina Staiculescu(ROM) 57.900pts	Regina Weber(FRG) 57.700pts
1988	Marina Lobatch(URS) 60.00pts	Adriana Dounavska(BUL) 59.950pts	Alexandra Timochenko(URS) 59.875pts
1992	Aleksandra Timoschenko(EUN) 59.037pts	Carolina Garcia(ESP) 58.100pts	Oksana Skaldina(EUN) 57.912pts
1996	Yekaterina Serebryanskaya(UKR) 39.683pts	Yanina Batyrchina(RUS) 39.382pts	Yelena Vitrichenko(UKR) 39.331pts
2000	Yulia Barsukova(RUS) 39.632pts	Yulia Raskina(BLR) 39.548pts	Alina Kabayeva(RUS) 39.466pts
2004	Alina Kabayeva(RUS) 108.400pts	2. Irina Tchachina(RUS) 107.325	3. Anna Bessonova(UKR) 106.700pts

1896–1980 Event not held

Rhythmic Team – Women

	GOLD	SILVER	BRONZE
1996	SPAIN 38.933pts	BULGARIA 38.866pts	RUSSIA 38.365pts
2000	RUSSIA 39.500pts	BELARUS 39.500pts	GREECE 39.283pts
2004	RUSSIA 51.100pts	ITALY 49.450pts	BULGARIA 48.600pts

1896–1992 Event not held

Trampolining – Women

	GOLD	SILVER	BRONZE
2000	Irina Karavayeva(RUS) 38.90pts	Oxana Tsyhuleva(RUS) 37.70pts	Karen Cockburn(CAN) 37.40pts
2004	Anna Dogonadze(GER) 39.60pts	Karen Cockburn(CAN) 39.20pts	Shanshan Huang(CHN) 39.00pts

1896–1996 Event not held

GYMNASTICS – DISCONTINUED EVENTS

	GOLD	SILVER	BRONZE
Parallel Bars – Men's Teams			
1896	GERMANY	GREECE	GREECE

Horizontal Bars – Men's Teams
1896   GERMANY(1)
(1) Walkover

Rope Climbing – Men
1896	Nicolaos Andriakopoulos(GRE) 23.4sec	Thomas Xenakis(GRE)	– (1)
1904	George Eyser(USA) 7.0sec	Charles Krause(USA) 7.8	Emil Voigt(USA) 9.8
1906	Georgios Aliprantis(GRE) 11.4sec	Béla Erödy(HUN) 13.8	Konstantinos Kozantis(GRE) 13.8
1924	Bedrich Supchik(TCH) 7.2sec	Albert Séguin(FRA)	August Güttinger(SUI) 7.8
			Ladislav Vácha(TCH) 7.8
1932	Raymond Bass(USA) 6.7sec	William Galbraith(USA) 6.8	Thomas Connelly(USA) 7.0

(1) Fritz Hofmann(GER) did not finish

Club Swinging – Men
1904	Edward Hennig(USA) 13pts	Emil Voigt(USA) 9pts	Ralph Wilson(USA) 5pts
1932	George Roth(USA) 8.97pts	Philip Erenberg(USA) 8.90pts	William Kuhlmeier(USA) 8.63pts

Tumbling – Men
1932	Rowland Wolfe(USA) 18.90pts	Edward Gross(USA) 18.67pts	William Herrmann(USA) 19.37pts

Nine-Event Competition – Men
1094	Adolf Spinnler(SUI) 43.49pts	Julius Lenhart(AUT) 43.00pts	Wilhelm Weber(GER) 41.60 pts

Triathlon – Men
(Comprised 100 yards, long jump and shot put)
1904	Max Emmerich(USA) 35.70pts	John Grieb(USA) 34.00pts	William Merz(USA) 33.90pts

Four-Event Competition – Men
1904	Anton Heida(USA) 161pts	George Eyser(USA) 152pts	William Merz(USA) 135pts

Sidehorse Vault – Men
1924	Albert Séguin(FRA) 10.00pts	Jean Gounot(FRA) 9.93pts	–
		François Gangloff(FRA) 9.93pts	

Swedish System – Men's Teams
1912	SWEDEN 937.46pts	DENMARK 898.84pts	NORWAY 857.21pts
1920	SWEDEN 1364pts	DENMARK 1325pts	BELGIUM 1094pts

Free System – Men's Teams
1912	NORWAY 114.25pts	FINLAND 109.25pts	DENMARK 106.25pts
19209(1)	DENMARK 51.35pts	NORWAY 48.55pts	–

(1) Only two teams competed.

Portable Apparatus – Women's Teams
1952	SWEDEN 74.20pts	SOVIET UNION 73.00pts	HUNGARY 71.60pts
1956	HUNGARY 75.20pts	SWEDEN 74.20pts	POLAND 74.00pts

HANDBALL

Men
	GOLD	SILVER	BRONZE
1936(1)	GERMANY	AUSTRIA	SWITZERLAND
1972	YUGOSLAVIA	CZECHOSLOVAKIA	ROMANIA
1976	SOVIET UNION	ROMANIA	POLAND
1980	GDR	SOVIET UNION	ROMANIA
1984	YUGOSLAVIA	FRG	ROMANIA
1988	SOVIET UNION	KOREA	YUGOSLAVIA
1992	UNIFIED TEAM	SWEDEN	FRANCE
1996	CROATIA	SWEDEN	SPAIN
2000	RUSSIA	SWEDEN	SPAIN
2004	CROATIA	GERMANY	RUSSIA

1896–1932, 1948–68 Event not held
(1) Played outdoors

Women
	GOLD	SILVER	BRONZE
1976	SOVIET UNION	GDR	HUNGARY
1980	SOVIET UNION	YUGOSLAVIA	GDR
1984	YUGOSLAVIA	KOREA	CHINA
1988	KOREA	NORWAY	SOVIET UNION

1992	KOREA	NORWAY	UNIFIED TEAM
1996	DENMARK	KOREA	HUNGARY
2000	DENMARK	HUNGARY	NORWAY
2004	DENMARK	KOREA	UKRAINE

1896–1972 Event not held

HOCKEY

Men

	GOLD	SILVER	BRONZE
1908(1)	ENGLAND	IRELAND	SCOTLAND(2)
			WALES(2)
1920	ENGLAND (3)	DENMARK	BELGIUM
1928	INDIA	NETHERLANDS	GERMANY
1932	INDIA	JAPAN	UNITED STATES
1936	INDIA	GERMANY	NETHERLANDS
1948	INDIA	GREAT BRITAIN	NETHERLANDS
1952	INDIA	NETHERLANDS	GREAT BRITAIN
1956	INDIA	PAKISTAN	GERMANY
1960	PAKISTAN	INDIA	SPAIN
1964	INDIA	PAKISTAN	AUSTRALIA
1968	PAKISTAN	AUSTRALIA	INDIA
1972	FRG	PAKISTAN	INDIA
1976	NEW ZEALAND	AUSTRALIA	PAKISTAN
1980	INDIA	SPAIN	SOVIET UNION
1984	PAKISTAN	FRG	GREAT BRITAIN
1988	GREAT BRITAIN	FRG	NETHERLANDS
1992	GERMANY	AUSTRALIA	PAKISTAN
1996	NETHERLANDS	SPAIN	AUSTRALIA
2000	NETHERLANDS	KOREA	AUSTRALIA
2004	AUSTRALIA	NETHERLANDS	GERMANY

1896–1906, 1912, 1924 Event not held
(1) Four teams from Great Britain entered
(2) Tie for third place
(3) The England team represented Great Britain

Women

	GOLD	SILVER	BRONZE
1980	ZIMBABWE	CZECHOSLOVAKIA	SOVIET UNION
1984	NETHERLANDS	FRG	UNITED STATES
1988	AUSTRALIA	KOREA	NETHERLANDS
1992	SPAIN	GERMANY	GREAT BRITAIN
1996	AUSTRALIA	KOREA	NETHERLANDS
2000	AUSTRALIA	ARGENTINA	NETHERLANDS
2004	GERMANY	NETHERLANDS	ARGENTINA

1896–1976 Event not held

JUDO

Open Category – Men
(No weight limit)

	GOLD	SILVER	BRONZE
1964	Antonius Geesink(NED)	Akio Kaminaga(JPN)	Theodore Boronovskis(AUS)
			Klaus Glahn(GER)
1972	Willem Ruska(NED)	Vitali Kuznetsov(URS)	Jean-Claude Brondani(FRA)
			Angelo Parisi(GBR)
1976	Haruki Uemura(JPN)	Keith Remfry(GBR)	Shota Chochoshvili(URS)
			Jeaki Cho(KOR)
1980	Dietmar Lorenz(GDR)	Angelo Parisi(FRA)	András Ozsvar(HUN)
			Arthur Mapp(GBR)
1984	Yasuhiro Yamashita(JPN)	Mohamed Rashwan(EGY)	Mihai Cioc(ROM)
			Arthur Schnabel(FRG)

1896–1960, 1968, 1988–2004 Event not held

Over 100kg – Men
(Over 95kg 1980–96)

	GOLD	SILVER	BRONZE
1980	Angelo Parisi(FRA)	Dimitar Zaprianov(BUL)	Vladimir Kocman(CZE)
			Radomir Kovacevic(YUG)

1984	Hitoshi Saito(JPN)	Angelo Parisi(FRA)	Yong-Chul Cho(KOR)
			Mark Berger(CAN)
1988	Hitoshi Saito(JPN)	Henry Stöhr(GDR)	Yong-Chul Cho(KOR)
			Grigori Veritchev(URS)
1992	David Khakhaliashvili(EUN)	Naoya Ogawa(JPN)	David Douillet(FRA)
			Imre Csösz(HUN)
1996	David Douillet(FRA)	Ernesto Perez(ESP)	Harry van Barneveld(BEL)
			Frank Moeller(GER)
2000	David Douillet(FRA)	Shinichi Shinohara(JPN)	Indrek Pertelson(EST)
			Tamerlan Timenov(RUS)
2004	Keiji Suzuki(JPN)	Tamerlan Tmenov(RUS)	Dennis van der Geest(NED)
			Indrek Pertelson(EST)

1896–1976 Event not held

Up to 100kg – Men
(Up to 95kg 1980–96)

	GOLD	SILVER	BRONZE
1980	Robert Van de Walle(BEL)	Tengiz Khubuluri(URS)	Dietmar Lorenz(GDR)
			Henk Numan(NED)
1984	Hyoung-Zoo Ha(KOR)	Douglas Vieira(BRA)	Bjarni Fridriksson(ISL)
			Gunther Neureuther(FRG)
1988	Aurelio Miguel(BRA)	Marc Meiling(FRG)	Robert Van de Walle(BEL)
			Dennis Stewart(GBR)
1992	Antal Kovacs(HUN)	Ray Stevens(GBR)	Dmitri Sergeyev(EUN)
			Theo Meijer(NED)
1996	Pawel Nastula(POL)	Min-Soo Kim(KOR)	Stephane Traineau(FRA)
			Miguel Fernandez(BRA)
2000	Kosei Inoue(JPN)	Nicolas Gill(CAN)	Stephane Traineau(FRA)
			Yuri Stepkin(RUS)
2004	Igor Makarov(BLR)	Sung-Ho Jang(KOR)	Michael Jurack(GER)
			Ariel Zeevi(ISR)

1896–1976 Event not held

Up to 90kg – Men
(Up to 86kg 1980–96)

	GOLD	SILVER	BRONZE
1980	Jürg Röthlisberger(SUI)	Issac Azcuy Oliva(CUB)	Detlef Ultsich(GDR)
			Alexander Yatskevitch(URS)
1984	Peter Seisenbacher(AUT)	Robert Berland(USA)	Seiki Nose(JPN)
			Walter Carmona(BRA)
1988	PeterSeisenbacher(AUT)	Vladimir Chestakov(URS)	Ben Spijkers(NED)
			Akinobu Osako(JPN)
1992	Waldemar Legien(POL)	Pascal Tayot(FRA)	Hirotaki Okada(JPN)
			Nicolas Gill(CAN)
1996	Ki-Young Jeon(KOR)	Armen Bagdasarov(UZB)	Marko Spittka(GER)
			Mark Huizinga(NED)
2000	Mark Huizinga(NED)	Carlos Hohorato(BRA)	Frederick Demontfaucon(FRA)
			Ruslan Mashurenko(UKR)
2004	Zurab Zviadauri(GEO)	Hiroshi Izumi(JPN)	Mark Huizinga(NED)
			Khasanbi Tayov(RUS)

1896–1976 Event not held

Up to 81kg – Men
(Up to 78kg 1980–96)

	GOLD	SILVER	BRONZE
1980	Shota Khabeleri(URS)	Juan Ferrer La Hera(CUB)	Harald Heinke(GDR)
			Bernard Tchoullouyan(FRA)
1984	Frank Weineke(FRG)	Neil Adams(GBR)	Michel Nowak(FRA)
			Mirces Fratica(ROM)
1988	Waldemar Legien(POL)	Frank Wieneke(FRG)	Torsten Brechot(GDR)
			Bachir Varayev(URS)
1992	Hidehiko Yoshida(JPN)	Jason Morris(USA)	Byung-Joo Kim(KOR)
			Betrand Damaisin(FRA)
1996	Djamel Bouras(FRA)	Toshihiko Koga(JPN)	Soso Liparteliani(GEO)
			In-Chul Cho(KOR)
2000	Makoto Takimoto(JPN)	In-Chul Cho(PRK)	Nuno Delgado(POR)
			Alexei Badolin(EST)
2004	Ilias Iliadis(GRE)	Roman Gontyuk(UKR)	Dmitri Nossov(RUS)
			Flavio Canto(BRA)

1896–1976 Event not held

Up to 73kg – Men
(Up to 71kg 1980–96)

	GOLD	SILVER	BRONZE
1980	Ezio Gamba(ITA)	Neil Adams(GBR)	Karl-Heinz Lehmann(GDR) Ravdan Davaadalai(MGL)
1984	Byeong-Keun Ahn(KOR)	Ezio Gamba(ITA)	Luis Onmura(BRA) Kerrith Brown(GBR)
1988	Marc Alexandre(FRA)	Sven Loll(GDR)	Michael Swain(USA) Guergui Tenadze(URS)
1992	Toshihiko Koga(JPN)	Bertalan Hajtós(HUN)	Hoon Chung(KOR) Shay Smadga(ISR)
1996	Kenzo Nakamura(JPN)	Dae-Sung Kwak(KOR)	James Pedro(USA) Christophe Gagliano(FRA)
2000	Giuseppe Madaloni(ITA)	Tiago Camilo(BRA)	Vsevolods Zelonijs(LAT) Anatoli Laryukov(BLR)
2004	Won-Hee Lee (KOR)	Vitaly Makarov(RUS)	Leandro Guilheiro(BRA) James Pedro(USA)

1896–1976 Event not held

Up to 66kg – Men
(Up to 65kg 1980–96)

	GOLD	SILVER	BRONZE
1980	Nikolai Solodukhin(URS)	Tsendying Damdin(MGL)	Ilian Nedkov(BUL) Janusz Pawlowski(POL)
1984	Yoshiyuki Matsuoka(JPN)	Jung-Oh Hwang(KOR)	Josef Reiter(AUT) Marc Alexandre(FRA)
1988	Kyeung-Keun Lee(KOR)	Janusz Pawlowski(POL)	Bruno Carabeta(FRA) Yosuke Yamamoto(JPN)
1992	Rogerio Sampaio(BRA)	Jozsef Csák(HUN)	Udo Quellmalz(GER) Israel Hernandez(CUB)
1996	Udo Quellmalz(GER)	Yukimasa Nakamura(JPN)	Israel Plana Hernandez(CUB) Henrique Guimares(BRA)
2000	Husein Ozkan(TUR)	Larbi Benboudaoud(FRA)	Girolamo Giovinazzo(ITA) Georgi Vazagashvili(GEO)
2004	.Masato Uchishiba(JPN)	Jozef Krnac(SVK)	Georgi Georgiev(BUL) Yordanis Arencibia(CUB)

1896–1976 Event not held

Up to 60kg – Men

	GOLD	SILVER	BRONZE
1980	Thierry Rey(FRA)	Rafael Carbonell(CUB)	Tibor Kinces(HUN) Aramby Emizh(URS)
1984	Shinji Hosokawa(JPN)	Jae-Yup Kim(KOR)	Edward Liddie(USA) Neil Eckersley(GBR)
1988	Jae-Yup Kim(KOR)	Kevin Asano(USA)	Shinji Hosokawa(JPN) Amiran Totikachvili(URS)
1992	Nazim Gousseinov(EUN)	Hyun Yoon(KOR)	Tadamori Koshino(JPN) Richard Trautmann(GER)
1996	Tadahiro Nomura(JPN)	Girolamo Giovanazzo(ITA)	Doripalam Narmandakh(MGL) Richard Trautmann(GER)
2000	Tadahiro Nomura(JPN)	Bu-Kyung Jung(KOR)	Ajdin Smagulov(KGZ) Manolo Poulot(CUB)
2004	Tadahiro Nomura(JPN)	Nestor Khergiani(GEO)	Min-Ho Choi(KOR) Khashbaatar Tsagaanbaatar(MGL)

1896–1976 Event not held

Up to 48kg – Women

	GOLD	SILVER	BRONZE
1992	Cecile Nowak(FRA)	Ryoko Tamura(JPN)	Hulya Senyurt(TUR) Amarilis Savon(CUB)
1996	Kye Sun(PRK)	Ryoko Tamura(JPN)	Amarilis Savon(CUB) Yolanda Soler(ESP)
2000	Ryoko Tamura(JPN)	Lyubov Bruletova(RUS)	Ann Simons(BEL) Anna-Maria Gradante(GER)
2004	Ryoko Tani(JPN)	Frederique Jussinet(FRA)	Julia Matijass(GER) Feng Gao(CHN)

1896–1988 Event not held

Up to 52kg – Women

	GOLD	SILVER	BRONZE
1992	Almudena Munoz(ESP)	Noriko Mizuguchi(JPN)	Zhongyun Li(CHN) Sharon Rendle(GBR)

1996	Marie-Claire Restoux(FRA)	Sook-Hee Hyun(KOR)	Legna Verdecia(CUB)
2000	Legna Verdecia(CUB)	Noriko Narazaki(JPN)	Noriko Sugawara(JPN)
			Hui Kye Sun(KOR)
2004	Dongmei Xian(CHN)	Yuki Yokosawa(JPN)	Yuxiang Liu(CHN)
			Ilse Heylen(BEL)
			Amarylis Savon(CUB)

1896–1988 Event not held

Up to 57kg – Women
(Up to 56kg 1992–96)

	GOLD	SILVER	BRONZE
1992	Miriam Blasco(ESP)	Nicola Fairbrother(GBR)	Chiyori Tateno(JPN)
			Driulis Gonzalez(CUB)
1996	Driulis Gonzalez(CUB)	Sae-Yong Jung(KOR)	Isabel Fernandez(ESP)
			Chuang Liu(CHN)
2000	Isabel Fernandez(ESP)	Driulis Gonzalez(CUB)	Maria Pekli(AUS)
			Kie Kusakobe(JPN)
2004	Yvonne Bönisch(GER)	Sun-Hui Kye (PRK)	Deborah Gravenstijn(NED)
			Yurisleidy Lupetey(CUB)

1896–1988 Event not held

Up to 63kg – Women
(Up to 61kg 1992–96)

1992	Catherine Fleury(FRA)	Yael Arad(ISR)	Di Zhang(CHN)
			Yelena Petrova(EUN)
1996	Yuko Emoto(JPN)	Gella Van De Caveye(BEL)	Jenny Gal(NED)
			Sung-Sook Jung(KOR)
2000	Severine Vandenhende(FRA)	Shu-Jung Li(CHN)	Gella Vandecaveye(BEL)
			Sung Sook Jung(KOR)
2004	Ayumi Tanimoto(JPN)	Claudia Heill(AUT)	Driulys Gonzalez(CUB)
			Urska Zolnir(SLO)

1896–1988 Event not held

Up to 70kg – Women
(Up to 66kg 1992–96)

1992	Odalis Reve(CUB)	Emanuela Pierantozzi(ITA)	Kate Howey(GBR)
			Heidi Rakels(BEL)
1996	Mia-Sun Cho(KOR)	Aneta Szczepanska(POL)	Claudia Zwiers(NED)
			Xianbo Wang(CHN)
2000	Sibelis Veranes(CUB)	Kate Howey(GBR)	Yelena Scapia(ITA)
			Mia-Sun Cho(KOR)
2004	Masae Ueno(JPN)	Edith Bosch(NED)	Dongya Qin(CHN)
			.Annett Böhm(GER)

1896–1988 Event not held

Up to 78kg – Women
(Up to 72kg 1992–96)

	GOLD	SILVER	BRONZE
1992	Mi-Jung Kim(KOR)	Yoko Tanabe(JPN)	Laetitia Meignan(FRA)
			Irene de Kok(NED)
1996	Ulla Werbrouck(HUN)	Yoko Tanabe(JPN)	Ylenia Scapin(ITA)
			Diadenis Luna(CUB)
2000	Lin Tang(CHN)	Celine Lebrun(FRA)	Emanuela Pierantozzi(ITA)
			Simona Richter(ROM)
2004	Noriko Anno(JPN)	Xia Liu(CHN)	Lucia Morico(ITA)
			Yurisel Laborde(CUB)

1896–1988 Event not held

Over 78kg – Women
(Over 72kg 1992–96)

	GOLD	SILVER	BRONZE
1992	Xiaoyan Zhuang(CHN)	Estela Rodriguez(CUB)	Yoko Sakuae(JPN)
			Natalia Lupino(FRA)
1996	Fu-Ming Sun(CHN)	Estela Rodriguez(CUB)	Johanna Hagn(GER)
			Christine Cicot(FRA)
2000	Hua Yuan(CHN)	Dayma Beltran(CUB)	Seon-Young Kim(KOR)
			Mayumi Yamashita(JPN)
2004	Maki Tsukada(JPN)	Dayma Beltran(CUB)	Fuming Sun(CHN)
			Tea Donguzashvili(RUS)

1896–1988 Event not held

JUDO – PREVIOUS WINNERS (CATEGORIES CHANGED IN 1980)

Over 93kg – Men

	GOLD	SILVER	BRONZE
1964	Isao Inokuma(JPN)	A. Douglas Rogers(CAN)	Parnaoz Chikviladze(URS)
			Anzor Kiknadze(URS)
1972	Willem Ruska(NED)	Klaus Glahn(FRG)	Givi Onashvili(URS)
			Motoki Nishimura(JPN)
1976	Sergei Novrikov(URS)	Gunther Neureuther(FRG)	Sumio Endo(JPN)
			Allen Coage(USA)

1968 Event not held

80kg to 93kg – Men

	GOLD	SILVER	BRONZE
1972	Shoto Chochoshvili(URS)	David Starbrook(GBR)	Chiaki Ishii(BRA)
			Paul Barth(FRG)
1976	Kazuhiro Ninomiya(JPN)	Ramaz Harshiladze(URS)	David Starbrook(GBR)
			Jürg Röthlisberger(SUI)

1964–68 Event not held

70kg to 80kg – Men

	GOLD	SILVER	BRONZE
1964	Isao Okano(JPN)	Wolfgang Hofmann(GER)	James Bergman(USA)
			Eui Tae Kim(KOR)
1972	Shinobu Sekine(JPN)	Seung-Lip Oh(KOR)	Brian Jacks(GBR)
			Jean-Paul Coche(FRA)
1976	Isamu Sonoda(JPN)	Valeri Dvoinikov(URS)	Slavko Obadov(URS)
			Young-Chul Park(KOR)

1968 Event not held

63kg to 70kg – Men

	GOLD	SILVER	BRONZE
1972	Toyojazu Nomura(JPN)	Anton Zajkowski(POL)	Dietmar Hötger(GDR)
			Anatoli Novikov(URS)
1976	Vladimir Nevzorov(URS)	Koji Kuramoto(JPN)	Partrick Vial(FRA)
			Marian Talaj(POL)

1964–68 Event not held

Up to 63kg – Men

	GOLD	SILVER	BRONZE
1964	Takehide Nakatani(JPN)	Eric Hänni(SUI)	Oleg Stepanov(URS)
			Aron Bogulubov(URS)
1972	Takao Kawaguchi(JPN)	– (1)	Yong Ik Kim(PRK)
			Jean Jacques Mounier(FRA)
1976	Hector Rodriguez(CUB)	Eun-Kyung Chang(KOR)	Felice Mariani(ITA)
			Jozsef Tuncsik(HUN)

1968 Event not held
(1) Bakhaavaa Buidaa (MGL) disqualified after positive drug test

MODERN PENTATHLON

Individual – Men

	GOLD	SILVER	BRONZE
1912	Gösta Lilliehöök(SWE) 27	Gösta Asbrink(SWE) 28pts	Georg de Laval(SWE) 30pts
1920	Gustaf Dyrssen(SWE) 18	Erik de Laval(SWE) 23pts	Gösta Rüno(SWE) 27pts
1924	Bo Lindman(SWE) 18	Gustaf Dyrssen(SWE) 39.5pts	Bertil Uggla(SWE) 45pts
1928	Sven Thofelt(SWE) 47	Bo Lindman(SWE) 50pts	Helmuth Kahl(GER) 52pts
1932	Johan Gabriel Oxenstierna(SWE) 32	Bo Lindman(SWE) 35.5pts	Richard Mayo(USA) 38.5pts
1936	Gotthard Handrick(SWE) 31.5	Charles Leonard(USA) 39.5pts	Silvano Abba(ITA) 45.5pts
1948	Willie Grut(SWE) 16	George Moore(USA) 47pts	Gösta Gärdin(SWE) 49pts
1952	Lars Hall(SWE) 32	Gábor Benedek(HUN) 39pts	István Szondi(HUN) 41pts
1956	Lars Hall(SWE) 4843pts	Olavi Nannonen(FIN) 4774.5pts	Väinö Korhonen(FIN) 4750pts
1960	Ferenc Németh(HUN) 5024pts	Imre Nagy(HUN) 4988pts	Robert Beck(USA) 4981pts
1964	Ferenc Török(HUN) 5116pts	Igor Novikov(URS) 5067pts	Albert Mokeyev(URS) 5039pts
1968	Björn Ferm(SWE) 4964pts	András Balczó(HUN) 4953pts	Pavel Lednev(URS) 4795pts
1972	András Balczó(HUN) 5412pts	Boris Onischenko(URS) 5335pts	Pavel Lednev(URS) 5328pts
1976	Janusz Pyciak-Peciak(POL) 5520pts	Pavel Lednev(URS) 5485pts	Jan Bartu(TCH) 5466pts
1980	Anatoli Starostin(URS) 5568pts	Tamás Szombathelyi(HUN) 5502pts	Pavel Lednev(URS) 5282pts
1984	Daniel Massala(ITA) 5469pts	Svante Rasmuson(SWE) 5456pts	Carlo Massullo(ITA) 5406pts
1988	János Martinek(HUN) 5404pts	Carlo Massullo(ITA) 5379pts	Vakhtang Yagorachvili(URS) 5367pts

1992	Arkadiusz Skrzypaszek(POL) 5559pts	Attila Mizsér(HUN) 5446pts	Eduard Zenovka(EUN) 5361pts
1996	Alexander Parygin(KZK) 5551pts	Eduard Zenovka(RUS) 5530pts	János Martinek(HUN) 5501pts
2000	Dimitri Svatkowsky(RUS) 5376pts	Gabor Balogh(HUN) 5353pts	Pavel Dovgal(BLR) 5338pts
2004	Andrei Moiseyev(RUS) 5480pts	Andrejus Zadneprovskis(LTU) 5428pts	Libor Capalini(CZE) 5392pts

1896–1908 Event not held

Team – Men

	GOLD	SILVER	BRONZE
1952	HUNGARY 116	SWEDEN 182	FINLAND 213
1956	SOVIET UNION 13 690.5	UNITED STATES 13 482	FINLAND 13 185.5
1960	HUNGARY 14 863	SOVIET UNION 14 309	UNITED STATES 14 192
1964	SOVIET UNION 14 961	UNITED STATES 14 189	HUNGARY 14 173
1968	HUNGARY 14 325	SOVIET UNION 14 248	FRANCE 13 289
1972	SOVIET UNION 15 968	HUNGARY 15 348	FINLAND 14 812
1976	GREAT BRITAIN 15 559	CZECHOSLOVAKIA 15 451	HUNGARY 15 395
1980	SOVIET UNION 16 126	HUNGARY 15 912	SWEDEN 15 845
1984	ITALY 16 060	UNITED STATES 15 568	FRANCE 15 565
1988	HUNGARY 15 886	ITALY 15 571	GREAT BRITAIN 15 276
1992	POLAND 16 018	UNIFIED TEAM 15 924	ITALY 15 760

1896–1948,1996–2004 Event not held

Women

	GOLD	SILVER	BRONZE
2000	Stephanie Cook(GBR) 5318pts	Emily de Riel(USA) 5310pts	Kate Allenby(GBR) 5273pts
2004	Zsuzsanna Vörös(HUN) 5448pts	Jelena Rublevska(LAT) 5380pts	Georgina Harland(GBR) 5344pts

1896–1996 Event not held

ROWING

Single Sculls – Men

	GOLD	SILVER	BRONZE
1900	Henri Barrelet(FRA) 7:35.6	André Gaudin(FRA) 7:41.6	St George Ashe(GBR) 8:15.6
1904	Frank Greer(USA) 10:08.5	James Juvenal(USA) 2 lengths	Constance Titus(USA) 1 length
1906	Gaston Delaplane(FRA) 5:53.4	Joseph Larran(FRA) 6:07.2	(1)
1908	Harry Blackstaffe(GBR) 9:26.0	Alexander McCulloch(GBR) 1 length	Bernhard von Gaza(GER) d.n.a.
			Károly Levitsky(HUN) d.n.a.
1912	William Kinnear(GBR) 7:47.6	Potydore Veirman(BEL) 1 length	Everard Butter(CAN) d.n.a.
			Mikhail Kusik(RUS) d.n.a.
1920	John Kelly(USA) 7:35.0	Jack Beresford(GBR) 7:36.0	Clarence Hadfield d'Arcy(NZL) 7:48.0
1924	Jack Beresford(GBR) 7:49.2	William Garrett-Gilmore(USA) 7:54.0	Josef Schneider(SUI) 8:01.1
1928	Henry Pearce(AUS) 7:11.0	Kenneth Myers(USA) 7:20.8	David Collett(GBR) 7:19.8
1932	Henry Pearce(AUS) 7:44.4	William Miller(USA) 7:45.2	Guillermo Douglas(URU) 8:13.6
1936	Gustav Schäfer(GER) 8:21.5	Josef Hasenöhri(AUT) 8:25.8	Daniel Barrow(USA) 8:28.0
1948	Mervyn Wood(AUS) 7:24.4	Eduardo Risso(URU) 7:38.2	Romolo Catasta(ITA) 7:51.4
1952	Yuri Tyukalov(URS) 8:12.8	Mervyn Wood(AUS) 8:14.5	Teodor Kocerka(POL) 8:19.4
1956	Vyacheslav Ivanov(URS) 8:02.5	Stuart Mackenzie(AUS) 8:07.0	John Kelly(USA) 8:11.8
1960	Vyacheslav Ivanov(URS) 7:13.96	Achim Hill(GER) 7:20.21	Teodor Kocerka(POL) 7:21.26
1964	Vyacheslav Ivanov(URS) 8:22.51	Achim Hill(GER) 8:26.34	Gottfried Kottmann(SUI) 8:29.68
1968	Henri Jan Wienese(NED) 7:47.80	Jochen Meissner(FRG) 7:52.00	Alberto Demiddi(ARG) 7:57.19
1972	Yuri Malishev(URS) 7:10.12	Alberto Demiddi(ARG) 7:11.53	Wolfgang Güldenpfennig(GDR) 7:14.45
1976	Pertti Karpinnen(FIN) 7:29.03	Peter Kolbe(FRG) 7:31.67	Joachim Dreifke(GDR) 7:38.03
1980	Pertti Karpinnen(FIN) 7:09.61	Vasili Yakusha(URS) 7:11.66	Peter Kersten(GDR) 7:14.88
1984	Pertti Karpinnen(FIN) 7:00.24	Peter Kolbe(FRG) 7:02.19	Robert Mills(CAN) 7:10.38
1988	Thomas Lange(GDR) 6:49.86	Peter Kolbe(FRG) 6:54.77	Eric Verdonk(NZL) 6:58.86
1992	Thomas Lange(GER) 6:51.40	Vaclav Chalupa(CZE) 6:52.93	Kajetan Broniewski(POL) 6:56.82
1996	Xeno Mueller(SUI) 6:44.85	Derek Porter(CAN) 6:47.45	Thomas Lange(GER) 6:47.72
2000	Bo Waddell(NZL) 6:48.90	Xeno Müller(SUI) 6:50.55	Marcus Hacker(GER) 6:50.83
2004	Olaf Tufte(NOR) 6:49.30	Jüri Jaanson(EST) 6:51.42	Ivo Yanakiev(BUL) 6:52.80

1896 Event not held
(1) Only two competitors

Double Sculls – Men

	GOLD	SILVER	BRONZE
1904	UNITED STATES 10:03.2	UNITED STATES d.n.a.	UNITED STATES d.n.a.
1920	UNITED STATES 7:09.0	ITALY 7:19.0	FRANCE 7:21.0
1924	UNITED STATES 7:45.0	FRANCE 7:54.8	SWITZERLAND d.n.a.
1928	UNITED STATES 6:41.4	CANADA 6:51.0	AUSTRIA 6:48.8
1932	UNITED STATES 7:17.4	GERMANY 7:22.8	CANADA 7:27.6
1936	GREAT BRITAIN 7:20.8	GERMANY 7:26.2	POLAND 7:36.2
1948	GREAT BRITAIN 6:51.3	DENMARK 6:55.3	URUGUAY 7:12.4

1952	ARGENTINA 7:32.2	SOVIET UNION 7:38.3	URUGUAY 7:43.7
1956	SOVIET UNION 7:10.66	UNITED STATES 7:13.16	AUSTRALIA 7:37.4
1960	CZECHOSLOVAKIA 6:47.50	SOVIET UNION 6:50.49	SWITZERLAND 6:50.59
1964	SOVIET UNION 7:10.66	UNITED STATES 7:13.16	CZECHOSLOVAKIA 7:14.23
1968	SOVIET UNION 6:51.82	NETHERLANDS 6:52.80	UNITED STATES 6:54.21
1972	SOVIET UNION 7:01.77	NORWAY 7:02.58	GDR 7:05.55
1976	NORWAY 7:13.20	GREAT BRITAIN 7:15.26	GDR 7:17.45
1980	GDR 6:24.33	YUGOSLAVIA 6:26.34	CZECHOSLOVAKIA 6:29.07
1984	UNITED STATES 6:36.87	BELGIUM 6:38.19	YUGOSLAVIA 6:39.59
1988	NETHERLANDS 6:21.13	SWITZERLAND 6:22.59	SOVIET UNION 6:22.87
1992	AUSTRALIA 6:17.32	AUSTRIA 6:18.42	NETHERLANDS 6:22.82
1996	ITALY 6:16.98	NORWAY 6:18.42	FRANCE 6:19.85
2000	SLOVENIA 6:16.63	NORWAY 6:17.98	ITALY 6:20.49
2004	FRANCE 6:29.00	SLOVENIA 6:31.72	ITALY 6:32.93

1896–1900, 1906–12 Event not held

Coxless Quadruple Sculls – Men

	GOLD	SILVER	BRONZE
1976	GDR 6:18.65	SOVIET UNION 6:19.89	CZECHOSLOVAKIA 6:21.77
1980	GDR 5:49.81	SOVIET UNION 5:51.47	BULGARIA 5:52.38
1984	FRG 5:57.55	AUSTRALIA 5:57.98	CANADA 5:59.07
1988	ITALY 5:53.37	NORWAY 5:55.08	GDR 5:56.13
1992	GERMANY 5:45.17	NORWAY 5:47.09	ITALY 5:47.33
1996	GERMANY 5:56.93	UNITED STATES 5:59.10	AUSTRALIA 6:01.65
2000	ITALY 5:45.56	NETHERLANDS 5:47.91	GERMANY 5:48.64
2004	RUSSIA 5:56.85	CZECH REPUBLIC 5:57.43	UKRAINE 5:58.87

1896–1972 Event not held

Coxless Pairs – Men

	GOLD	SILVER	BRONZE
1904	UNITED STATES 10:57.0	UNITED STATES d.n.a.	UNITED STATES d.n.a.
1908	GREAT BRITAIN 9:43.0	GREAT BRITAIN 2.5 lengths	CANADA d.n.a.
			GERMANY d.n.a
			– (1)
1924	NETHERLANDS 8:19.4	FRANCE 8:21.6	UNITED STATES 7:20.4
1928	GERMANY 7:06.4	GREAT BRITAIN 7:08.08	POLAND 8:08.2
1932	GREAT BRITAIN 8:00.0	NEW ZEALAND 8:02.4	ARGENTINA 8:23.0
1936	GERMANY 8:16.1	DENMARK 8:19.2	ITALY 7:31.5
1948	GREAT BRITAIN 7:21.11	SWITZERLAND 7:23.9	SWITZERLAND 8:32.7
1952	UNITED STATES 8:20.7	BELGIUM:23.5	AUSTRIA 8:11.8
1956	UNITED STATES 7:55.4	SOVIET UNION 8:03.9	FINLAND 7:03.80
1960	SOVIET UNION 7:02.01	AUSTRIA 7:03.69	GERMANY 7:38.63
1964	CANADA 7:32.94	NETHERLANDS 7:33.40	DENMARK 7:31.84
1968	GDR 7:26.56	UNITED STATES 7:26.71	NETHERLANDS 6:58.70
1972	GDR 6:53.16	SWITZERLAND 6:57.06	FRG 7:30.03
1976	GDR 7:23.31	UNITED STATES 7:26.73	GREAT BRITAIN 6:51.47
1980	GDR 6:48.01	SOVIET UNION 6:50.50	NORWAY 6:51.81
1984	ROMANIA 6:45.39	SPAIN 6:48.47	YUGOSLAVIA 6:41.01
1988	GREAT BRITAIN 6:36.84	ROMANIA 6:38.06	SLOVENIA 6:33.43
1992	GREAT BRITAIN 6:27.72	GERMANY 6:32.68	FRANCE 6:22.15
1996	GREAT BRITAIN 6:20.09	AUSTRALIA 6:21.02	AUSTRALIA 6:34.26
2000	FRANCE 6:32.97	UNITED STATES 6:33.80	SOUTH AFRICA 6:33.40
2004	AUSTRALIA 6:30.76	CROATIA 6:32.64	

1896–1900, 1912–20 Event not held
(1) Only two teams

Coxed Pairs – Men

	GOLD	SILVER	BRONZE
1900	NETHERLANDS 7:34.2	FRANCE I 7:34.4	FRANCE II 7:57.2
1906(1)	ITALY I 4:23.0	ITALY II 4:30.0	FRANCE d.n.a.
1906(2)	ITALY 7:32.4	BELGIUM 8:03.0	FRANCE 8:08.6
1920	ITALY 7:56.0	FRANCE 7:57.0	SWITZERLAND d.n.a.
1924	SWITZERLAND 8:39.0	ITALY 8:39.1	UNITED STATES 3m
1928	SWITZERLAND 7:42.6	FRANCE 7:48.4	BELGIUM 7:59.4
1932	UNITED STATES 8:25.8	POLAND 8:31.2	FRANCE 8:41.2
1936	GERMANY 8:36.9	ITALY 8:49.7	FRANCE 8:54.0
1948	DENMARK 8:00.5	ITALY 8:12.2	HUNGARY 8:25.2
1952	FRANCE 8:28.6	GERMANY 8:32.1	DENMARK 8:34.9
1956	UNITED STATES 8:26.1	GERMANY 8:29.2	SOVIET UNION 8:31.0
1960	GERMANY 7:29.14	SOVIET UNION 7:30.17	UNITED STATES 7:34.58
1964	UNITED STATES 8:21.23	FRANCE 8:23.15	NETHERLANDS 8:23.42
1968	ITALY 8:04.81	NETHERLANDS 8:06.80	DENMARK 8:08.07
1972	GDR 7:17.25	CZECHOSLOVAKIA 7:19.57	ROMANIA 7:21.36
1976	GDR 7:58.99	SOVIET UNION 8:01.82	CZECHOLSLOVAKIA 8:03.28
1980	GDR 7:02.54	SOVIET UNION 7:03.35	YUGOSLAVIA 7:04.92
1984	ITALY 7:05.99	ROMANIA 7:11.21	UNITED STATES 7:12.81

	GOLD	SILVER	BRONZE
1988	ITALY 6:58.79	GDR 7.00.63	GREAT BRITAIN 7:01.95
1992	GREAT BRITAIN 6:49.83	ITALY 6:50.98	ROMANIA 6:51.58

1896, 1904, 1908–12,1996–2004 Event not held
(1) Distance 1,000m
(2) Distance 1,600m

Coxless Fours – Men

	GOLD	SILVER	BRONZE
1904	UNITED STATES 9:05.8	UNITED STATES d.n.a.	UNITED STATES d.n.a.
1908	GREAT BRITAIN 8:34.0	GREAT BRITAIN 1.5 lengths	NETHERLANDS d.n.a.
			CANADA d.n.a.
1924	GREAT BRITAIN 7:08.6	CANADA 7:18.0	SWITZERLAND 2 lengths
1928	GREAT BRITAIN 6:36.0	UNITED STATES 6:37.0	ITALY 6:31.6
1932	GREAT BRITAIN 6:58.2	GERMANY 7:03.0	ITALY 7:04.0
1936	GERMANY 7:01.8	GREAT BRITAIN 7:06.5	SWITZERLAND 7:10.6
1948	ITALY 6:39.0	DENMARK 6:43.5	UNITED STATES 6:47.7
1952	YUGOSLAVIA 7:16.0	FRANCE 7:18.4	FINLAND 7:23.3
1956	CANADA 7:08.8	UNITED STATES 7:18.4	FRANCE 7:20.9
1960	UNITED STATES 6:26.26	ITALY 6:28.78	SOVIET UNION 6:29.62
1964	DENMARK 6:59.30	GREAT BRITAIN 7:00.47	UNITED STATES 7:01.37
1968	GDR 6:39.18	HUNGARY 6:41.64	ITALY 6:44.01
1972	GDR 6:24.27	NEW ZEALAND 6:25.64	FRG 6:28.41
1976	GDR 6:37.42	NORWAY 6:41.22	SOVIET UNION 6:42.52
1980	GDR 6:08.17	SOVIET UNION 6:11.81	GREAT BRITAIN 6:16.58
1984	NEW ZEALAND 6:03.48	UNITED STATES 6:06.10	DENMARK 6:07.72
1988	GDR 6:03.11	UNITED STATES 6:05.53	FRG 6:06.22
1992	AUSTRALIA 5:55.04	USA 5:56.68	SLOVENIA 5:58.24
1996	AUSTRALIA 6:06.37	FRANCE 6:07.03	GREAT BRITAIN 6:07.28
2000	GREAT BRITAIN 5:56.24	ITALY 5:56.62	AUSTRALIA 5:57.61
2004	GREAT BRITAIN 6:06.98	CANADA 6:07.06	ITALY 6:10.41

1896–1900, 1906, 1912–20 Event not held

Coxed Fours – Men

	GOLD	SILVER	BRONZE
1900(1)	GERMANY 5:59.0	NETHERLANDS 6:33.0	GERMANY 6:35.0
1900(1)	FRANCE 7:11.0	FRANCE 7:18.0	GERMANY 7:18.2
1906	ITALY 8:13.0	FRANCE d.n.a.	FRANCE d.n.a.
1912	GERMANY 6:59.4	GREAT BRITAIN 2 lengths	NORWAY d.n.a.
			DENMARK d.n.a.
1920	SWITZERLAND 6:54.0	UNITED STATES 6:58.0	NORWAY 7:02.0
1924	SWITZERLAND 7:18.4	FRANCE 7:21.6	UNITED STATES 1 length
1928	ITALY 6:47.8	SWITZERLAND 7:03.4	POLAND 7:12.8
1932	GERMANY 7:19.0	ITALY 7:19.2	POLAND 7:26.8
1936	GERMANY 7:16.2	SWITZERLAND 7:24.3	FRANCE 7:33.3
1948	UNITED STATES 6:50.3	SWITZERLAND 6:53.3	DENMARK 6:58.6
1952	CZECHOSLOVAKIA 7:33.4	SWITZERLAND 7:36.5	UNITED STATES 7:37.0
1956	ITALY 7:19.4	SWEDEN 7:22.4	FINLAND 7:30.9
1960	GERMANY 6:39.12	FRANCE 6:41.62	ITALY 6:43.72
1964	GERMANY 7:00.44	ITALY 7:02.84	NETHERLANDS 7:06.46
1968	NEW ZEALAND 6:45.62	GDR 6:48.20	SWITZERLAND 6:49.04
1972	FRG 6:31.85	GDR 6:33.30	CZECHOSLOVAKIA 6:35.64
1976	SOVIET UNION 6:40.22	GDR 6:42.70	FRG 6:46.96
1980	GDR 6:14.51	SOVIET UNION 6:19.05	POLAND 6:22.52
1984	GREAT BRITAIN 6:18.64	UNITED STATES 6:20.28	NEW ZEALAND 6:23.68
1988	GDR 6:10.74	ROMANIA 6:13.58	NEW ZEALAND 6:15.78
1992	ROMANIA 5:59.37	GERMANY 6:00.34	POLAND 6:03.27

1896, 1904, 1908, 1996–2004 Event not held
(1) Two finals in 1900

Eights – Men

	GOLD	SILVER	BRONZE
1900	UNITED STATES 6:09.8	BELGIUM 6:13.8	NETHERLANDS 6:23.0
1904	UNITED STATES 7:50.0	CANADA d.n.a.	–
1908	GREAT BRITAIN I 7:52.0	BELGIUM 2 lengths	GREAT BRITAIN d.n.a.
			CANADA d.n.a.
1912	GREAT BRITAIN I 6:15.0	GREAT BRITAIN II 6:19.0	GERMANY d.n.a.
1920	UNITED STATES 6:02.6	GREAT BRITAIN 6:05.0	NORWAY 6:36.0
1924	UNITED STATES 6:33.4	CANADA 6:49.0	ITALY 0.75 length
1928	UNITED STATES 6:03.2	GREAT BRITAIN 6:05.6	CANADA 6:03.8
1932	UNITED STATES 6:37.6	ITALY 6:37.8	CANADA 6:40.4
1936	UNITED STATES 6:25.4	ITALY 6:26.0	GERMANY 6:26.4
1948	UNITED STATES 5:56.7	GREAT BRITAIN 6:06.9	NORWAY 6:10.3
1952	UNITED STATES 6:25.9	SOVIET UNION 6:31.2	AUSTRALIA 6:33.1

1956	UNITED STATES 6:35.2	CANADA 6:37.1	AUSTRALIA 6:39.2
1960	GERMANY 5:57.18	CANADA 6:01.52	CZECHOSLOVAKIA 6:04.84
1964	UNITED STATES 6:18.23	GERMANY 6:23.9	CZECHOSLOVAKIA 6:25.11
1968	FRG 6:07.00	AUSTRALIA 6:07.98	SOVIET UNION 6:09.11
1972	NEW ZEALAND 6:08.94	UNITED STATES 6:11.61	GDR 6:11.67
1976	GDR 5:58.29	GREAT BRITAIN 6:00.82	NEW ZEALAND 6:03.51
1980	GDR 5:49.05	GREAT BRITAIN 5:51.92	SOVIET UNION 5:52.66
1984	CANADA 5:41.32	UNITED STATES 5:41.74	AUSTRALIA 5:42.40
1988	FRG 5:46.05	SOVIET UNION 5:48.01	UNITED STATES 5:48.26
1992	CANADA 5:29.53	ROMANIA 5:29.67	GERMANY 5:31.00
1996	NETHERLANDS 5:42.74	GERMANY 5:44.58	RUSSIA 5:45.77
2000	GREAT BRITAIN 5:33.08	AUSTRALIA 5:33.88	CROATIA 5:34.85
2004	UNITED STATES 5:42.48	NETHERLANDS 5:43.75	AUSTRALIA 5:45.38

1896, 1906 Event not held

Lightweight Double Sculls – Men

	GOLD	SILVER	BRONZE
1996	SWITZERLAND 6:23.27	NETHERLANDS 6:26.48	AUSTRALIA 6:26.69
2000	POLAND 6:21.75	ITALY 6:34.47	FRANCE 6:24.85
2004	POLAND 6:20.93	FRANCE 6:21.46	GREECE 6:23.23

1896–1992 Event not held

Lightweight Coxless Fours – Men

	GOLD	SILVER	BRONZE
1996	DENMARK 6:09.58	CANADA 6:10.13	UNITED STATES 6:12.29
2000	FRANCE 6:01.68	AUSTRALIA 6:02.09	DENMARK 6:03.51
2004	DENMARK 6:01.39	AUSTRALIA 6:02.79	ITALY 6:03.74

1896–1992 Event not held

Singles Sculls – Women

	GOLD	SILVER	BRONZE
1976	Christine Scheiblich(GDR) 4:05.56	Joan Lind(USA) 4:06.21	Elena Antonova(URS) 4:10.24
1980	Sandra Toma(ROM) 3:40.69	Antonina Makhina(URS) 3:41.65	Martina Schröter(GDR) 3:43.54
1984	Valeria Racila(ROM) 3:40.68	Charlotte Geer(USA) 3:43.89	Ann Haesebrouck(BEL) 3:45.72
1988	Jutta Behred8nt(GDR) 7:47.19	Anne Marden(USA) 7:50.28	Magdalene Gueorguivea(BUL) 7:53.65
1992	Elisabeta Lipa(ROM) 7:25.54	Annelies Bredael(BEL) 7:26.64	Silken Laumann(CAN) 7:28.85
1996	Ekaterina Khodotovich(BLR) 7:32.21	Silken Laumann(CAN) 7:35.15	Trine Hansen(DEN) 7:37.20
2000	Ekaterina Khodotovich-Karsten(BLR) 7:28.14	Rumyana Neykova(BUL) 7:28.15	Katrin Rutschow-Stomporowski(GER) 7:28.99
2004	Katrin Rutschow-Stomporowski(GER) 7:18.12	Ekaterina Karsten(BLR) 7:22.04	Rumyana Neykova(BUL) 7:23.10

1896–1972 Event not held

Double Sculls – Women

	GOLD	SILVER	BRONZE
1976	BULGARIA 3:44.36	GDR 3:47.86	SOVIET UNION 3:49.93
1980	SOVIET UNION 3:16.27	GDR 3:17.63	ROMANIA 3:18.91
1984	ROMANIA 3:26.75	NETHERLANDS 3:29.13	CANADA 3:29.82
1988	GDR 7:00.48	ROMANIA 7:04.36	BULGARIA 7:06.03
1992	GERMANY 6:49.00	ROMANIA 6:51.47	CHINA 6:55.16
1996	CANADA 6:56.84	CHINA 6:58.35	NETHERLANDS 6:58.72
2000	GERMANY 6:55.44	NETHERLANDS 7:00.36	LITHUANIA 7:01.71
2004	NEW ZEALAND 7:01.79	GERMANY 7:02.78	GREAT BRITAIN 7:07.58

1896–1972 Event not held

Coxed Quadruple Sculls – Women

	GOLD	SILVER	BRONZE
1976	GDR 3:29.99	SOVIET UNION 3:32.49	ROMANIA 3:32.76
1980	GDR 3:15.32	SOVIET UNION 3:15.73	BULGARIA 3:16.10
1984	ROMANIA 3:14.11	UNITED STATES 3:15.57	DENMARK 3:16.02
1988(1)	GDR 6:21.06	SOVIET UNION 6:23.47	ROMANIA 6:23.81
1992	GERMANY 6:20.18	ROMANIA 6:24.34	UNIFIED TEAM 6:25.07
1996	GERMANY 6:27.44	UKRAINE 6:30.36	CANADA 6:30.38
2000	GERMANY 6:19.58	GREAT BRITAIN 6:21.64	RUSSIA 6:21.65
2004(2)	GERMANY 6:29.29	GREAT BRITAIN 6:31.26	AUSTRALIA 6:34.73

1896–1972 Event not held
(1) Not coxed
(2) Ukraine finished third in 6:34.31 but were disqualified

Coxless Pairs – Women

	GOLD	SILVER	BRONZE
1976	BULGARIA 4:01.22	GDR 4:01.64	FRG 4:02.35

1980	GDR 3:30.49	POLAND 3:30.95	BULGARIA 3:32.39
1984	ROMANIA 3:32.60	CANADA 3:36.06	FRG 3:40.50
1988	ROMANIA 7:28.13	BULGARIA 7:31.95	NEW ZEALAND 7:35.68
1992	CANADA 7:06.22	GERMANY 7:07.96	USA 7:08.11
1996	AUSTRALIA 7:01.39	UNITED STATES 7:01.78	FRANCE 7:03.82
2000	ROMANIA 7:11.00	AUSTRALIA 7:12.56	UNITED STATES 7:13.00
2004	ROMANIA 7:06.55	GREAT BRITAIN 7:08.66	BELARUS 7:09.86

1896–1972 Event not held

Coxed Fours – Women

	GOLD	SILVER	BRONZE
1976	GDR 3:45.08	BULGARIA 3:38.24	SOVIET UNION 3:49.38
1980	GDR 3:19.27	BULGARIA 3:20.75	SOVIET UNION 3:20.92
1984	ROMANIA 3:19.30	CANADA 3:21.55	AUSTRALIA 3:23.29
1988	GDR 6:56.00	CHINA 6:58.78	ROMANIA 7:01.13

1896–1972, 1992–2004 Event not held

Coxless Fours – Women

	GOLD	SILVER	BRONZE
1992	CANADA 6:30.85	USA 6:31.86	GERMANY 6:32.34

1896–1988, 1996–2004 Event not held

Eights – Women

	GOLD	SILVER	BRONZE
1976	GDR 3:33.32	SOVIET UNION 3:36.17	UNITED STATES 3:38.68
1980	GDR 3:03.32	SOVIET UNION 3:04.29	ROMANIA 3:05.63
1984	UNITED STATES 2:59.80	ROMANIA 3:00.87	NETHERLANDS 3:02.92
1988	GDR 6:15.17	ROMANIA 6:17.44	CHINA 6:21.83
1992	CANADA 6:02.62	ROMANIA 6:06.26	GERMANY 6:07.80
1996	ROMANIA 6:19.73	CANADA 6:24.05	BELARUS 6:24.44
2000	ROMANIA 6:06.44	NETHERLANDS 6:09.39	CANADA 6:11.58
2004	ROMANIA 6:17.70	UNITED STATES 6:19.56	NETHERLANDS 6:19.85

1896–1972 Event not held

Lightweight Double Sculls – Women

	GOLD	SILVER	BRONZE
1996	ROMANIA 7:12.78	UNITED STATES 7:14.65	AUSTRALIA 7:16.56
2000	ROMANIA 7:02.64	GERMANY 7:02.95	UNITED STATES 7:06.37
2004	ROMANIA 6:56.05	GERMANY 6:57.33	NETHERLANDS 6:58.54

1896–1992 Event not held

ROWING – DISCONTINUED EVENTS

	GOLD	SILVER	BRONZE

Naval Rowing Boats (200m) – Men
1906	ITALY 10:45.0	GREECE d.n.a.	GREECE d.n.a.

Coxed 16-Man Naval Rowing Boats (3,000m) – Men
1906	GREECE 16:35.0	GREECE 17:09.5	ITALY d.n.a.

Coxed Fours (Inriggers) – Men
1912	DENMARK 7:47.0	SWEDEN 1 length	NORWAY d.n.a.

SAILING

Olympic Monotype – Men

	GOLD	SILVER	BRONZE
1920(1)	NETHERLANDS (Franciscus Hin) (Johannes Hin)	NETHERLANDS (Arnoud van der Biesen) (Petrus Beukers)	–
1924(2)	Léon Huybrechts(BEL)	Henrik Robert(NOR)	Hans Dittmar(FIN)
1928(3)	Sven Thorell(SWE)	Henrik Robert(NOR)	Bertil Broman(FIN)
1932(4)	Jacques Lebrun(FRA)	Adriaan Maas(NED)	Santiago Cansino(ESP)
1936(5)	Daniel Kagchelland(NED)	Werner Krogmann(GER)	Peter Scott(GBR)
1948(6)	Paul Elvström(DEN)	Ralph Evans(USA)	Jacobus de Jong(NED)
1952(7)	Paul Elvström(DEN)	Charles Currey(GBR)	Rickard Sarby(SWE)
1956	Paul Elvström(DEN)	André Nelis(BEL)	John Marvin(USA)
1960	Paul Elvström(DEN)	Aleksandr Chuchelov(URS)	André Nelis(BEL)

1964	Willi Kuhweide(GER)	Peter Barrett(USA)	Henning Wird(DEN)
1968	Valentin Mankin(URS)	Hubert Raudaschl(AUT)	Fabio Albarelli(ITA)
1972	Serge Maury(FRA)	Ilias Hatzipavlis(GRE)	Viktor Potapov(URS)
1976	Jochen Schümann(GDR)	Andrei Balashov(URS)	John Bertrand(AUS)
1980	Esko Rechardt(FIN)	Wolfgang Mayrhofer(AUT)	Andrei Balashov(URS)
1984	Russell Coutts(NZL)	John Bertrand(AUS)	Terry Neilson(CAN)
1988	José Luis Doreste(ESP)	Peter Holmberg(ISV)	John Cutler(NZL)
1992	José Maria van der Ploeg(ESP)	Brian Ledbetter(USA)	Craig Monk(NZL)
1996	Mateusz Kuznierewicz(POL)	Sebastian Godefroid(BEL)	Roy Heiner(NED)
2000	Iain Percy(GBR)	Luca Devoti(ITA)	Fredrik Lööf(SWE)
2004	Ben Ainslie(GBR)	Rafael Trujillo(ESP)	Mateusz Kusznierewicz(POL)

1896–1912 Event not held
(1) 12-foot dinghy (two-man), no third place
(2) Meulan class, 12-foot dinghy
(3) International 12-foot class
(4) Snowbird class
(5) International Olympia class
(6) Firefly class
(7) 1952–2004 Finn class

Sailboard Class – Men

	GOLD	SILVER	BRONZE
1984(1)	Steve Van Den Berg(NED)	Randall Steele(USA)	Bruce Kendall(NZL)
1988(2)	Bruce Kendall(NZL)	Jan Boersma(AHO)	Michael Gebhardt(USA)
1992(2)	Franck David(FRA)	Michael Gebhardt(USA)	Lars Kleppich(AUS)
1996(3)	Nikolas Kaklamanakis(GRE)	Carlos Espiñola(ARG)	Gal Fridman(ISR)
2000(3)	Christoph Sieber(AUT)	Carlos Espiñola(ESP)	Aaron McIntosh(NZL)
2004(3)	Gal Fridman(ISR)	Nikolaos Kaklamanakis(GRE)	Nick Dempsey(GBR)

1896–1980 Event not held
(1) Windglider
(2) Lechner
(3) Mistral

International Soling – Men

	GOLD	SILVER	BRONZE
1972	UNITED STATES	SWEDEN	CANADA
1976	DENMARK	UNITED STATES	GDR
1980	DENMARK	SOVIET UNION	GREECE
1984	UNITED STATES	BRAZIL	CANADA
1988	GDR	UNITED STATES	DENMARK
1992	DENMARK	UNITED STATES	GREAT BRITAIN
1996	GERMANY	RUSSIA	UNITED STATES
2000	DENMARK	GERMANY	NORWAY

1896–1968, 2004 Event not held

International 470 – Men

	GOLD	SILVER	BRONZE
1976	FRG	SPAIN	AUSTRALIA
1980	BRAZIL	GDR	FINLAND
1984	SPAIN	UNITED STATES	FRANCE
1988	FRANCE	SOVIET UNION	UNITED STATES
1992	SPAIN	UNITED STATES	ESTONIA
1996	UKRAINE	GREAT BRITAIN	PORTUGAL
2000	AUSTRALIA	UNITED STATES	ARGENTINA
2004	UNITED STATE	GREAT BRITAIN	JAPAN

1896–1972 Event not held

International Tornado – Men

	GOLD	SILVER	BRONZE
1976	GREAT BRITAIN	UNITED STATES	FRG
1980	BRAZIL	DENMARK	SWEDEN
1984	NEW ZEALAND	UNITED STATES	AUSTRALIA
1988	FRANCE	NEW ZEALAND	BRAZIL
1992	FRANCE	UNITED STATES	AUSTRALIA
1996	SPAIN	AUSTRALIA	BRAZIL
2000	AUSTRIA	AUSTRALIA	GERMANY
2004	AUSTRIA	UNITED STATES	ARGENTINA

1896–1972 Event not held

International Star – Men

	GOLD	SILVER	BRONZE
1932	UNITED STATES	GREAT BRITAIN	SWEDEN

1936	GERMANY	SWEDEN	NETHERLANDS
1948	UNITED STATES	CUBA	NETHERLANDS
1952	ITALY	UNITED STATES	PORTUGAL
1956	UNITED STATES	ITALY	BAHAMAS
1960	SOVIET UNION	PORTUGAL	UNITED STATES
1964	BAHAMAS	UNITED STATES	SWEDEN
1968	UNITED STATES	NORWAY	ITALY
1972	AUSTRALIA	SWEDEN	FRG
1980	SOVIET UNION	AUSTRIA	ITALY
1984	UNITED STATES	FRG	ITALY
1988	GREAT BRITAIN	UNITED STATES	BRAZIL
1992	UNITED STATES	NEW ZEALAND	CANADA
1996	BRAZIL	SWEDEN	AUSTRALIA
2000	UNITED STATES	GREAT BRITAIN	BRAZIL
2004	BRAZIL	CANADA	FRANCE

1896–1928, 1976 Event not held

Flying Dutchman – Men

	GOLD	SILVER	BRONZE
1956(1)	NEW ZEALAND	AUSTRALIA	GREAT BRITAIN
1960	NORWAY	DENMARK	GERMANY
1964	NEW ZEALAND	GREAT BRITAIN	UNITED STATES
1968	GREAT BRITAIN	FRG	BRAZIL
1972	GREAT BRITAIN	FRANCE	FRG
1976	FRG	GREAT BRITAIN	BRAZIL
1980	SPAIN	IRELAND	HUNGARY
1984	UNITED STATES	CANADA	GREAT BRITAIN
1988	DENMARK	NORWAY	CANADA
1992	SPAIN	UNITED STATES	DENMARK

1896–1952,1996–2004 Event not held
(1) Sharpie class

Laser – Men

	GOLD	SILVER	BRONZE
1996	Robert Scheidt(BRA)	Ben Ainslie(GBR)	Per Moberg(NOR)
2000	Ben Ainslie(GBR)	Robert Scheidt(BRA)	Michael Blackburn(AUS)
2004	Robert Scheidt(BRA)	Andreas Geritzer(AUT)	Vasilij Zbogar(SLO)

1896–1992 Event not held

49er – Men

	GOLD	SILVER	BRONZE
2000	FINLAND	GREAT BRITAIN	UNITED STATES
2004	SPAIN	UKRAINE	GREAT BRITAIN

1896–1996 Event not held

Sailboard Class – Women

	GOLD	SILVER	BRONZE
1992(1)	Barbara Kendall(NZL)	Xiaodong Zhang(CHN)	Dorien de Vries(NED)
1996(2)	Lai-Shan Lee(HKG)	Barbara Kendall(NZL)	Alessandra Sensini(ITA)
2000(2)	Alessandra Sensini(ITA)	Amelie Lux(GER)	Barbara Kendall(NZL)
2004(2)	Faustine Merret(FRA)	Jian Yin(CHN)	Alessandra Sensini(ITA)

1896–1988 Event not held
(1) Lechner
(2) Mistral

International 470 – Women

	GOLD	SILVER	BRONZE
1988	UNITED STATES	SWEDEN	SOVIET UNION
1992	SPAIN	NEW ZEALAND	UNITED STATES
1996	SPAIN	JAPAN	UKRAINE
2000	AUSTRALIA	UNITED STATES	UKRAINE
2004	GREECE	SPAIN	SWEDEN

1896–1984 Event not held

Europe Class – Women

	GOLD	SILVER	BRONZE
1992	Linda Andersen(NOR)	Natalia Dufresne(ESP)	Julia Trotman(USA)
1996	Kristine Roug(DEN)	Margriet Matthijsse(NED)	Courtney Becker-Dey(USA)
2000	Shirley Robertson(GBR)	Margriet Matthijsse(NED)	Sereña Amato(ARG)
2004	Siren Sundby(NOR)	Lenka Smidova(CZE)	Signe Livbjerg(DEN)

1896–1988 Event not held

Yngling – Women

	GOLD	SILVER	BRONZE
2004	GREAT BRITAIN	UKRAINE	DENMARK

1896–2000 Event not held

SAILING – DISCONTINUED EVENTS

	GOLD	SILVER	BRONZE

Swallow

	GOLD	SILVER	BRONZE
1948	GREAT BRITAIN	PORTUGAL	UNITED STATES

International Tempest

1972	SOVIET UNION	GREAT BRITAIN	UNITED STATES
1976	SWEDEN	SOVIET UNION	UNITED STATES

Dragon

1948	NORWAY	SWEDEN	DENMARK
1952	NORWAY	SWEDEN	GERMANY
1956	SWEDEN	DENMARK	GREAT BRITAIN
1960	GREECE	ARGENTINA	ITALY
1964	DENMARK	GERMANY	UNITED STATES
1968	UNITED STATES	DENMARK	GDR
1972	AUSTRALIA	GDR	UNITED STATES

30 Square Metres

1920	SWEDEN	–	–

40 Square Metres

1920	SWEDEN	–	–

5.5 Metres

1952	UNITED STATES	NORWAY	SWEDEN
1956	SWEDEN	GREAT BRITAIN	AUSTRALIA
1960	UNITED STATES	DENMARK	SWITZERLAND
1964	AUSTRALIA	SWEDEN	UNITED STATES
1968	SWEDEN	SWITZERLAND	GREAT BRITAIN

6 Metres

1908	GREAT BRITAIN	BELGIUM	FRANCE
1912	FRANCE	DENMARK	SWEDEN
1920	NORWAY	BELGIUM	–
1924	NORWAY	DENMARK	NETHERLANDS
1928	NORWAY	DENMARK	ESTONIA
1932	SWEDEN	UNITED STATES	CANADA
1936	GREAT BRITAIN	NORWAY	SWEDEN
1948	UNITED STATES	ARGENTINA	SWEDEN
1952	UNITED STATES	NORWAY	FINLAND

6 Metres (1907 Rating)

1920	BELGIUM	NORWAY	NORWAY

6.5 Metres

1920	NETHERLANDS	FRANCE	–

7. Metres

1908	GREAT BRITAIN	–	–
1920	GREAT BRITAIN	–	–

1912 Event not held

8 Metres

1908	GREAT BRITAIN	SWEDEN	GREAT BRITAIN
1912	NORWAY	SWEDEN	FINLAND
1920	NORWAY	NORWAY	BELGIUM
1924	NORWAY	GREAT BRITAIN	FRANCE
1928	FRANCE	NETHERLANDS	SWEDEN
1932	UNITED STATES	CANADA	–
1936	ITALY	NORWAY	GERMANY

8 Metres (1907 Rating)

1920	NORWAY	NORWAY	–

10 Metres

1912	SWEDEN	FINLAND	RUSSIA

10 Metres (1907 Rating)

1920	NORWAY	–	–

10 Metres (1919 Rating)

1920	NORWAY	–	–

12 Metres

1908	GREAT BRITAIN	GREAT BRITAIN	–
1912	NORWAY	SWEDEN	FINLAND

12 Metres (1907 Rating)

1920	NORWAY	–	–

12 Metres (1919 Rating)

1920	NORWAY	–	–

0.5 Ton Class

1900	FRANCE	FRANCE	FRANCE

0.5–1 Ton Class

1900	FRANCE	GREAT BRITAIN	FRANCE

1–2 Ton Class

1900	SWITZERLAND	FRANCE	FRANCE

2–3 Ton Class

1900	GREAT BRITAIN	FRANCE	FRANCE

3–10 Ton Class

1900	FRANCE	NETHERLANDS	FRANCE
			GREAT BRITAIN

10–20 Ton Class

1900	FRANCE	FRANCE	GREAT BRITAIN

Open Class

1900	GREAT BRITAIN	GERMANY	FRANCE

Over 20 Ton Class

1900	GREAT BRITAIN	GREAT BRITAIN	UNITED STATES

SHOOTING

Free Pistol (50m) – Men

	GOLD	SILVER	BRONZE
1896	Sumner Paine(USA) 442	Holger Nielsen(DEN) 280	Nikolaos Morakis(GRE) d.n.a.
1900	Karl Röderer(SUI) 503	Achille Paroche(FRA) 466	Konrad Stäheli(SUI) 453
1906	Georgios Orphanidis(GRE) 221	Jean Fouconnier(FRA) 219	Aristides Rangavis(GRE) 218
1912	Alfred Lane(USA) 499	Peter Dolfen(USA) 474	Charles Stewart(GBR) 470
1920	Karl Frederick(USA) 496	Afranio da Costa(BRA) 489	Alfred Lane(USA) 481
1936	Torsten Ullmann(SWE) 559	Erich Krempel(GER) 544	Charles des Jammonières(FRA) 540
1948	Edwin Vazquez Cam(PER) 545	Rudolf Schnyder(SUI) 539	Torsten Ullmann(SWE) 539
1952	Huelet Benner(USA) 553	Angel Léon de Gozalo(ESP) 550	Ambrus Balogh(HUN) 549
1956	Pentti Linnosvuo(FIN) 556	Makhmud Oumarov((URS) 556	Offutt PInion(USA) 551
1960	Alexei Gushkin(URS) 560	Makhmud Oumarov(URS) 552	Yoshihisa Yoshikawa(JPN) 552
1964	Väinö Markkanen(FIN) 560	Franklin Green(USA) 557	Yoshihisa Yoshikawa(JPN) 554
1968	Grigori Kossykh(URS) 562	Heinz Mertel(FRG) 562	Harald Vollmar(GDR) 560
1972	Ragnar Skanakar(SWE) 567	Dan Iuga(ROM) 562	Rudolf Dollinger(AUT) 560
1976	Uwe Potteck(GDR) 573	Harald Vollmar(GDR) 567	Rudolf Dollinger(AUT) 560
1980	Alexander Melentyev(URS) 581	Harald Vollmar(GDR) 568	Lubcho Diakov(BUL) 565
1984	Haifeng Xu(CHN) 566	Ragnar Skanaker(SWE) 565	Yifu Wang(CHN) 564
1988	Sorin Babii(ROM) (566+94) 660	Ragnar Skanaker(SWE) (564+93) 657	Igor Bassinki(URS) (570+87) 657
1992	Konstantin Loukachik(EUN) 658	Yifu Wang(CHN) 657	Ragnar Skanaker(SWE) 657
1996	Boris Kokoryev(RUS) 666.4	Igor Basinski(BLR) 692.1	Roberto Di Donna(ITA) 661.8
2000	Tanyu Kiryakov(BUL) 666.0	Igor Basinski(BLR) 663.3	Martin Tenk(CZE) 662.5
2004	Mikhail Nestruyev(RUS) 663.3	Jong-Oh Jin(PRK) 661.5	3. Jong-Su Kim (PRK) 657.7

1904, 1908, 1924–32 Event not held

Rapid-Fire Pistol – Men

	GOLD	SILVER	BRONZE
1896	Jean Phrangoudis(GRE) 344	Georgios Orphanidis(GRE)	Holger Nielsen(DEN) d.n.a.
1900	Maurice Larrouy(FRA) 58	Léon Moreaux(FRA) 57	Eugene Balme(FRA) 57
1906	Maurice Lecoq(FRA) 250	Léon Moreaux(FRA) 149	Aristides Rangavis(GRE) 245
1908	Paul van Asbroeck(BEL) 490	Réginald Storms(BEL) 487	James Gorman(USA) 485
1912	Alfred Lane(USA) 287	Paul Palén(SWE) 286	Johan von Holst(SWE) 283
1920	Guilherme Paraense(BRA) 274	Raymond Bracken(USA) 272	Fritz Zulauf(SUI) 269
1924	Paul Bailey(USA) 18	Vilhelm Carlberg(SWE) 18	Lennart Hannelius(FIN) 18
1932	Renzo Morigi(ITA) 36	Heinz Hax(GER) 36	Domenico Matteucci(ITA) 36
1936	Cornelius van Oyen(GER) 36	Heinz Hax(GER) 35	Torsten Ullmann(SWE) 34
1948	Károly Takács(HUN) 580	Carlos Diaz Sáenz Valiente(ARG) 571	Sven Lundqvuist(SWE) 569
1952	Károly Takács(HUN) 579	Szilárd Kun(HUN) 578	Gheorghe Lichiardopol(ROM) 578
1956	Stefan Petrescu(ROM) 587	Evgeniy Shcherkasov(URS) 585	Gheorghe Lichiardopol(ROM) 581
1960	William McMillan(USA) 587	Penttii Linnosvuo(FIN) 587	Aleksandr Zabelin(URS) 587
1964	Penttii Linnosvuo(FIN) 592	Ion Tripsa(ROM) 591	Lubomir Nacovsky(TCH) 590
1968	Jozef Zapedzki(POL) 593	Marcel Rosca(ROM) 591	Renart Suleimanov(URS) 591
1972	Jozef Zapedzki(POL) 593	Ladislav Faita(TCH) 594	Victor Torshin(URS) 593
1976	Norbert Klaar(GDR) 597	Jürgen Wiefel(GDR) 596	Roberto Ferraris(ITA) 595
1980	Corneliu Ion(ROM) 596	Jürgen Wiefel(GDR) 596	Gerhard Petrisch(AUT) 596
1984	Takeo Kamachi(JPN) 595	Corneliu Ion(ROM) 593	Rauno Bies(FIN) 591
1988	Afanasi Kouzmine(URS) (598+100) 698	Ralf Schumann(GDR) (597+99) 696	Zoltán Kovács(HUN) (594+99) 693
1992	Ralf Schumann(GER) 885	Afanasijs Kuzmins(LAT) 882	Vladimir Vokhmianine(EUN) 882
1996	Ralf Schumann(GER) 698.0	Emil Milev(BUL) 692.1	Vladimir Vokhmianine(KAZ) 691.5
2000	Sergei Aliferenko(RUS) 687.6	Michel Ansermet(SUI) 686.1	Iulian Raicea(ROM) 684.6
2004	Ralf Schumann(GER) 694.9	Sergei Poliakov(RUS) 692.7	3. Sergei Alifirenko(RUS) 692.3

1904, 1928 Event not held

Small-Bore Rifle (Prone) – Men

	GOLD	SILVER	BRONZE
1908(1)	Arthur Carnell(GBR) 387	Harry Humby(GBR) 386	George Barnes(GBR) 385
1912(1)	Frederick Hird(USA) 194	William Milne(GBR) 193	Harry Burt(GBR) 192
1920(2)	Lawrence Nuesslein(USA) 391	Arthur Rothrock(USA) 386	Dennis Fenton(USA) 385
1924	Pierre Coquelin de Lisle(FRA) 398	Marcus Dinwiddie(USA) 396	Josias Hartmann(SUI) 394
1932	Bertil Rönnmark(SWE) 294	Gustavo Huet(MEX) 294	Zoltán Hradetsky-Soos(HUN) 293
1936	Willy Rögeberg(NOR) 300	Ralph Berzsenyi(HUN) 296	Wladyslaw Karás(POL) 296
1948	Arthur Cook(USA) 599	Walter Tomsen(USA) 599	Jonas Jonsson(SWE) 597
1952	Josif Sarbu(ROM) 400	Boris Andreyev(URS) 400	Arthur Jackson(USA) 399
1956	Gerald Ouellette(CAN) 600 (3)	Vasiliy Borrisov(URS) 599	Gilmour Boa(CAN) 598
1960	Peter Kohnke(GER) 590	James Hill(USA) 589	Enrico Pelliccione(VEN) 587
1964	László Hammerl(HUN) 597	Lonas Wigger(USA) 597	Tommy Pool(USA) 596
1968	Jan Kurka(TCH) 598	László Hammerl(HUN) 598	Ian Ballinger(NZL) 597
1972	Ho Jun Li(PRK) 599	Victor Auer(USA) 598	Nicolae Rotaru(ROM) 595
1976	Karlheinz Smieszek(FRG) 599	Ulrich Lind(FRG) 597	Gennadi Luschikov(URS) 595
1980	Karoly Varga(HUN) 599	Hellfried Helifort(GDR) 599	Petar Zapianov(BUL) 598
1984	Edward Etzel(USA) 599	Michel Bury(FRA) 596	Michael Sullivan(GBR) 596
1988	Miroslav Varga(TCH) (600+103.9) 703.9	Young-Chul Cha(KOR) (598+104.8) 702.8	Attila Zahonyi(HUN) (597+104.9) 701.9
1992	Eun-Chul Lee(KOR) 702.5	Harald Stenvaag(NOR) 701.4	Stefan Pletikosic(IOP) 701.1
1996	Christian Klees(GER) 704.8	Sergei Belyayev(KAZ) 703.3	Jozef Gobci(SLO) 701.9
2000	Jonas Edman(SWE) 701.3	Torben Grimmel(DEN) 700.4	Sergei Martinyov(BLR) 700.3
2004	Matthew Emmons(USA) 703.3	Christian Lusch(GER) 702.2	Sergei Martynov(BLR) 701.6

1896–1906, 1928 Event not held
(1) 1908/1912 any position
(2) 1920 standing position
(3) Short range – record not accepted

Small-Bore Rifle (Three Positions: Prone, Kneeling, Standing) – Men

	GOLD	SILVER	BRONZE
1952	Erling Kongshaug(NOR) 1164	Viho Ylönen(FIN) 1164	Boris Andreyev(URS) 1163
1956	Anatoliy Bogdanov(URS) 1172	Otakar Horinek(TCH) 1172	Nils Sundberg(SWE) 1167
1960	Viktor Shamburkin(URS) 1149	Marat Niyasov(URS) 1145	Klaus Zähringer(GER) 1139
1964	Lones Wigger(USA) 1164	Velitchko Khristov(BUL) 1152	László Hammerl(HUN) 1151
1968	Bernd Klingner(FRG) 1157	John Writer(USA) 1156	Vitali Parkhimovich(URS) 1154
1972	John Writer(USA) 1166	Lanny Bassham(USA) 1157	Werner Lippoldt(GDR) 1153
1976	Lanny Bassham(USA) 1162	Margaret Murdock(USA) 1162	Werner Seibold(FRG) 1160
1980	Viktor Vlasov(URS) 1173	Bernd Hartstein(GDR) 1166	Sven Johansson(SWE) 1185
1984	Malcolm Cooper(GBR) 1173	Daniel Kipkow(SUI) 1163	Alister Allan(GBR) 1162
1988	Malcolm Cooper(GBR) (1180+99.3) 1279	Alister Allan(GBR) (1181+94.6) 1275.6	Kirill Ivanov(URS) (1173+102) 1275.0
1992	Gratchia Petikiane(EUN) 1267.4	Robert Foth(USA) 1266.6	Ryohei Koba(JPN) 1265.9
1996	Jean-Pierre Amat(FRA) 1273.9	Sergei Belyayev(KAZ) 1272.3	Wolfram Waibel(AUT) 1269.6

2000	Rajmond Debevec(SLO) 1275.1	Juha Hirvi(FIN) 1270.5	Harald Stenvaag(NOR) 1268.6
2004	Zhanbo Jia(CHN) 1264.5	Michael Anti(USA) 1263.1	Christian Planer(AUS) 1262.8

1896–1948 Event not held

Running Game Target – Men

	GOLD	SILVER	BRONZE
1900	Louis Debray(FRA) 20	Pierre Nivet(FRA) 20	Comte de Lambert(FRA) 19
1972	Lakov Zhelezniak(URS) 569	Hanspeter Bellingrodt(COL) 565	John Kynoch(GBR) 562
1976	Alexander Gazov(URS) 579	Alexander Kedyarov(URS) 576	Jerzy Gresziewicz(POL) 571
1980	Igor Sokolov(URS) 589	Thomas Pfeffer(GDR) 589	Alexander Gasov(URS) 587
1984	Yuwei Li(CHN) 587	Helmut Bellingrodt(COL) 584	Shiping Huang(CHN) 581
1988	Tor Heiestad(NOR) (591+98) 689	Shiping Huang(CHN) (589+98) 686	Gennadi Avramenko(URS) (591+95) 685

1896, 1904–68,1992–2004 Event not held

10m Running Target – Men

	GOLD	SILVER	BRONZE
1992	Michael Jakosits(GER) 673	Anatoli Asrabayev(EUN) 672	Lubos Racansky(TCH) 670
1996	Ling Yang(CHN) 685.8	Jun Xiao(CHN) 679.8	Miroslav Janus(CZE) 678.4
2000	Ling Yang(CHN) 681.1	Oleg Moldovan(MDA) 681.0	Zhiyuan Niu(CHN) 677.4
2004	Manfred Kurzer(GER) 682.4	Oleksandr Blinov(RUS) 678.0	Dmitri Lykin(RUS) 677.1

1896–1988 Event not held

Olympic Trap Shooting – Men

	GOLD	SILVER	BRONZE
1900	Roger de Barbarin(FRA) 17	René Guyot(FRA) 17	Justinien de Clary(FRA) 17
1906(1)	Gerald Merlin(GBR) 24	Ioannis Peridis(GRE) 23	Sidney Merlin(GBR) 21
1908(2)	Sidney Merlin(GBR) 15	Anastasios Metaxas(GRE) 13	Gerald Merlin(GBR) 12
1908	Walter Ewing(CAN) 72	George Beattie(CAN) 60	Alexander Maunder(GBR) 57 Anastasios Metaxas(GRE) 57
1912	James Graham(USA) 96	Alfred Goeldel-Bronikowen(GER) 94	Harry Blau(URS) 91
1920	Marke Arie(USA) 95	Frank Troeh(USA) 93	Frank Wright(USA) 87
1924	Gyula Halasy(HUN) 98	Konrad Huber(FIN) 98	Frank Hughes(USA) 97
1952	George Généreux(CAN) 192	Knut Holmqvist(SWE) 191	Hans Lijedahl(SWE) 191
1956	Galliano Rossini(ITA) 195	Adam Smelczynski(POL) 190	Alessandro Ciceri(ITA) 188
1960	Ion Dumitrescu(ROM) 192	Galliano Rossini(ITA) 191	Sergei Kalinin(URS) 190
1964	Ennio Mattarelli(ITA) 198	Pavel Senichev(URS) 194	William Morris(USA) 194
1968	Robert Braithwaite(GBR) 198	Thomas Garrigus(USA) 196	Kurt Czekalla(GDR) 196
1972	Angelo Scalzone(ITA) 199	Michel Carrega(FRA) 198	Silvano Basnagi(ITA) 195
1976	Don Haldeman(USA) 190	Armando Marques(POR) 189	Ulbaldesco Baldi(ITA) 189
1980	Luciano Giovanetti(ITA) 198	Rustam Yambulatov(URS) 196	Jörg Damme(GDR) 196
1984	Luciano Giovanetti(ITA) 192	Francisco Boza(PER) 192	Daniel Carlisle(USA) 192
1988	Dmitri Monakov(URS) (197+25) 222	Miloslav Bednarik(TCH) (197+25) 222	Frans Peeters(BEL) (195+24) 219
1992	Petr Hrdilicka(CZE) 219	Kazumi Watanabe(JPN) 219	Marco Venturini(ITA) 218
1996	Michael Diamond(AUS) 149	Josh Lakatos(USA) 147.0	Lance Bade(USA) 147.0
2000	Michael Diamond(AUS) 147	Ian Peel(GBR) 142	Giovanni Pellielo(ITA) 140
2004	Aleksei Alipov(RUS) 149	Giovanni Pellielo(ITA) 146	Adam Vella(AUS) 145

1896, 1904, 1928–48 Event not held
(1) Single shot
(2) Double shot

Double Trap – Men

	GOLD	SILVER	BRONZE
1996	Russell Mark(AUS) 189.0	Albano Pera(ITA) 183.0	Bang Zhang(CHN) 183.0
2000	Richard Faulds(GBR) 187	Russell Mark(AUS) 187	Fehaid Al Deehani(KUW) 186
2004	Sheikh Ahmed Al-Maktoum(UAE) 189	Rajyardrahan Rathore(IND) 179	3. Zheng W ang(CHN) 178

1896–1992 Event not held

Skeet Shooting – Men

	GOLD	SILVER	BRONZE
1968	Yevgeni Petrov(URS) 198	Romano Garagnani(ITA) 198	Konrad Wirnhier(FRG) 198
1972	Konrad Wirnhier(FRG) 195	Yevgeni Petrov(URS) 195	Michael Buchheim(GDR) 195
1976	Josef Panacek(TCH) 198	Eric Swinkels(NED) 198	Wieslaw Gawlikowski(POL) 196
1980	Hans Kjeld Rasmussen(DEN) 196	Lars-Goran Carlsson(SWE) 196	Roberto Garcia(CUB) 196
1984	Matthew Dryke(USA) 198	Ole Rasmussen(DEN) 196	Luca Scribiani Rossi(ITA) 196
1988	Axel Wegner(GDR) (198+24) 222	Alfonso de Iruarrizaga(CHI) (198+23) 221	Jorge Guardiola(ESP) (196+24) 220
1992	Shan Zhang(CHN) 233	Juan Jorge Giha(PER) 222	Bruno Rosetti(ITA) 222
1996	Ennio Falco(ITA) 149.0	Miroslav Rzeprkowski(POL) 148.0	Andrea Benelli(ITA) 147.0
2000	Mykola Milchev(UKR) 150	Petr Malek(CZE) 148	James Graves(USA) 147
2004	Andrea Benelli(ITA) 149	Marko Kemppainen(FIN) 149	Juan Miguel Rodriguez(CUB) 147

1896–1964 Event not held

Air Pistol – Men

	GOLD	SILVER	BRONZE
1988	Taniou Kiriakov(BUL) (585+102.9) 687.9	Erich Buljung(USA) (590+97.9) 687.9	Haifeng Xu(CHN) (584+100.5) 684.5
1992	Yifu Wang(CHN) 684.8	Sergei Pyzhano(EUN) 684.1	Sorin Babii(ROM) 684.1
1996	Roberto di Donna(ITA) 684.2	Yifu Wang(CHN) 684.1	Taniu Kiryakov(BUL) 683.8
2000	Franck Dumoulin(FRA) 688.9	Yifu Wang(CHN) 686.9	Igor Basinski(BLR) 682.7
2004	Yifu Wang(CHN) 690.0	Mikhail Nestruyev(RUS) 689.8	3. Vladimir Isakov(RUS)684.3

1896–1984 Event not held

Air Rifle – Men

	GOLD	SILVER	BRONZE
1984	Philippe Herberle(FRA) 589	Andreas Kronthaler(AUT) 587	Barry Dagger(GBR) 587
1988	Goran Maksimovic(YUG) (594+101.6) 695.6	Nicolas Berhtelot(FRA) (593+101.2) 694.2	Johann Riederer(FRG) (592+102) 694.0
1992	Yuri Fedkine(EUN) 695.3	Franck Badiou(FRA) 691.9	Johann Riederer(GER) 691.7
1996	Artem Khadzhibekov(RUS) 695.7	Wolfram Waibel(AUT) 695.2	Jean-Pierre Amat(FRA) 693.1
2000	Yalin Cai(CHN) 696.4	Artem Khadzhibekov(RUS) 695.1	Yevgeni Aleinikov(RUS) 693.8
2004	Qinan Zhu(CHN) 702.7	Jie Li(CHN) 701.3	Jozef Gönci(SVK) 697.4

1896–1980 Event not held

Sport Pistol – Women

	GOLD	SILVER	BRONZE
1984	Linda Thom(CAN) 585	Ruby Fox(USA) 585	Patricia Dench(AUS) 583
1988	Nino Saloukvadze(URS) (591+99) 690	Tomoko Hasegawa(JPN) (587+99) 686	Jasna Sekaric(YUG) (591+95) 686
1992	Marina Logvinenko(EUN) 684	Duihong Li(CHN) 680	Dorzhsuren Munkhbayar(MGL) 679
1996	Duihong Liu(CHN) 687.9	Diana Yorgova(BUL) 684.8	Marina Logvinenko(RUS) 684.2
2000	Maria Grozdeva(BUL) 690.3	Kuna Tao(CHN) 689.8	Lolita Yevglevskaya(BLR) 686.0
2004	Maria Grozdeva(BUL) 688.2	Lenka Hykova(CZE) 687.8	3. Irada Ashumova(AZE) 687.3

1896–1980 Event not held

Small-Bore Rifle – Three Positions – Women

	GOLD	SILVER	BRONZE
1984	Xiaoxuan Wu(CHN) 581	Ulrike Holmer(FRG) 578	Wanda Jewell(USA) 578
1988	Silvia Sperber(FRG) (590+95.6) 685.6	Vessela Letcheva(BUL) (583+100.2) 683.2	Valentina Tcherkasova(URS) (586+95.4) 681.4
1992	Launi Melli(USA) 684.3	Nonka Matova(BUL) 682.7	Malgorzata Ksiazkiewicz(POL) 681.5
1996	Alexandra Ivosev(YUG) 686.1	Irina Gerasimenok(POL) 680.1	Renata Mauer(POL) 679.8
2000	Renata Mauer-Rozanska(POL) 684.6	Tatyana Goldobina(RUS) 680.9	Maria Feklistova(RUS) 679.9
2004	Lyubov Galkina(RUS) 688.4	Valentina Turisini(ITA) 685.9	3. Chengyi Wang(CHN) 685.4

1896–1980 Event not held

Air Pistol – Women

	GOLD	SILVER	BRONZE
1988	Jasna Sekaric(YUG) (389+100.5) 489.5	Nino Saloukvadze(URS) (390+97.9) 487.9	Marina Dobrantcheva(URS) (385+100.2) 485.2
1992	Marina Logvinenko(EUN) 486.4	Jasna Sekaric(IOP) 486.4	Maria Grozdeva(BUL) 481.6
1996	Olga Klochneva(RUS) 490.1	Marina Logvinenko(RUS) 488.5	Maria Grozdeva(BUL) 488.5
2000	Luna Tao(CHN) 488.2	Jasna Sekaric(YUG) 486.5	Annemarie Forder(AUS) 484.0
2004	Olena Kostevych(UKR) 483.3	Jasna Sekaric(SCG) 483.3	Maria Grozdeva(BUL) 482.3

1896–1984 Event not held

Air Rifle – Women

	GOLD	SILVER	BRONZE
1984	Pat Spurgin(USA) 393	Edith Gufler(ITA) 391	Xianxuan Wu(CHN) 389
1988	Irina Chilova(URS) (395+103.5) 498.5	Silvia Sperber(FRG) (393+104.5) 497.5	Anna Maloukhina(URS) (394+101.8) 495.8
1992	Kab-Soon Yeo(KOR) 498.2	Vesela Letcheva(BUL) 495.3	Aranka Binder(IOP) 495.1
1996	Renata Mauer(POL) 497.6	Petra Horneber(GER) 497.4	Alexandra Ivosev(YUG) 497.2
2000	Nancy Johnson(USA) 497.7	Cho-Hyun Kang(KOR) 497.5	Jing Gao(CHN) 497.2
2004	Du Li(CHN) 502.0	Lyubov Galkina(RUS) 501.5	Katerina Kurkova(CZE)501.1

1896–1980 Event not held

Trap – Women

	GOLD	SILVER	BRONZE
2000	Daina Gudzineviciute(LTU) 93	Delphine Racinet(FRA) 92	E. Gao(CHN) 90
2004	Suzanne Balogh(AUS) 88	Maria Quintanal(ESP) 84	Bo-Na Lee(KOR) 83

1896–1996 Event not held

Double Trap – Women

	GOLD	SILVER	BRONZE
1996	Kim Rhode(USA) 141	Susanne Keirmayer(GER) 139	Deserie Huddleston(AUS) 139
2000	Pia Hensen(SWE) 148	Deborah Gelisto(ITA) 144	Kim Rhode(USA) 139
2004	Kimberly Rhode(USA) 146	Bo-Na Lee(KOR) 145	E Gao(CHN) 142

1896–1992 Event not held

Skeet – Women

	GOLD	SILVER	BRONZE
2000	Zemfira Meftakhetdinova(AZE) 98	Svetlana Demina(RUS) 95	Diana Igaly(HUN) 90
2004	Diana Igaly(HUN) 97	Ning Wei(CHN) 93	Zemfira Meftakhetdinova(AZE) 93

1896–1996 Event not held

SHOOTING – DISCONTINUED EVENTS

	GOLD	SILVER	BRONZE

Free Rifle (Three Positions) – Men

1896	Georgios Orphanidis(GRE) 1583	Jean Phrangoudis(GRE) 1312	Viggo Jensen(DEN) 1305
1906	Gudbrand Skatteboe(NOR) 977	Konrad Stäheli(SUI) 943	Jean Reich(SUI) 933
1908	Albert Helgerud(NOR) 909	Harry Simon(USA) 887	Ole Saether(NOR) 883
1912	Paul Colas(FRA) 987	Lars Madsen(DEN) 981	Niels Larsen(DEN) 962
1920	Morris Fisher(USA) 997	Niels Larsen(DEN) 985	Östen Östensen(NOR) 980
1924	Morris Fisher(USA) 95	Carl Osrubn(USA) 95	Niels Larsen(DEN) 93
1948	Emil Grunig(SUI) 1120	Pauli Janhonen(FIN) 1114	Willy Rögeberg(NOR) 1112
1952	Anatoliy Bogdanov(URS) 1123	Robert Bürchler(SUI) 1120	Lev Vainschtein(URS) 1109
1956	Vasili Borissov(URS) 1138	Allan Erdman(URS) 1137	Vilho Ylönen(FIN) 1128
1960	Hubert Hammerer(AUT) 1129	Hans Spillmann(SUI) 1127	Vasili Borissov(URS) 1127
1964	Gary Anderson(USA) 1153	Shota Kveliashvili(URS) 1151	Martin Gunnarsson(USA) 1136
1968	Gary Anderson(USA) 1157	Vladimir Kornev(URS) 1151	Kurt Müller(SUI) 1148
1972	Lones Wigger(USA) 1155	Boris Melnik(URS) 1155	Lajos Papp(HUN) 1149

1900–04, 1928–36 Event not held

Free Rifle – Men

1896(1)	Pantelis Karasevdas(GRE) 2320	Paulas Pavlidis(GRE) 1978	Nicolaos Tricoupes(GRE) 1718
1906(2)	Marcel de Stadelhofen(SUI) 243	Konrad Stäheli(SUI) 238	Léon Moreaux(FRA) 234
1906(3)	Gudbrand Skatteboe(NOR) 339	Louis Richardet(SUI) 332	Konrad Stäheli(SUI) 328
1906(4)	Konrad Stäheli(SUI) 340	Louis Richardet(SUI) 338	Jean Reich(SUI) 320
1906(5)	Gudbrand Skatteboe(NOR) 324	Julius Braathe(NOR) 310	Albert Helgerud(NOR) 305
1908(6)	Jerry Millner(GBR) 98	Kellogg Casey(USA) 93	Maurice Blood(GBR) 92

1900–04 Event not held
(1) Distance 200m
(2) Any position (300m)
(3) Prone (300m)
(4) Kneeling (300m)
(5) Standing (300m)
(6) Distance 1,000 yards

Free Rifle (Team) – Men

1906	SWITZERLAND 4596	NORWAY 4534	FRANCE 4511
1908	NORWAY 5055	SWEDEN 4711	FRANCE 4652
1912	SWEDEN 5655	NORWAY 5605	DENMARK 5529
1920	UNITED STATES 4876	NORWAY 4741	SWITZERLAND 4698
1924	UNITED STATES 676	FRANCE 646	HAITI 646

1896–1904 Event not held

Military Rifle – Men

1900(1)	Emil Kellenberger(SUI) 930	Anders Nielsen(DEN) 921	Ole Östmo(NOR) 917
1900(2)	Lars Madsen(DEN) 305	Ole Östmo(NOR) 299	Charles du Verger(BEL) 298
1900(3)	Konrad Stäheli(SUI) 324	Emil Kellenberger(SUI) 314 Anders Nielsen(DEN) 314	–
1900(4)	Achille Paroche(FRA) 332	Anders Nielsen(DEN) 330	Ole Östmo(NOR) 329
1906(5)	Léon Moreaux(FRA) 187	Louis Richardet(SUI) 187	Jean Reich(SUI) 183
1906(6)	Louis Richardet(SUI) 238	Jean Reich(SUI) 234	Raoul de Boigne(FRA) 232
1912(1)	Sándor Prokopp(HUN) 97	Carl Osburn(USA) 96	Embret Skogen(NOR) 95
1912(7)	Paul Colas(FRA) 94	Carl Osburn(USA) 94	Joseph Jackson(USA) 93
1920(4)	Otto Olsen(NOR) 60	Léon Johnson(FRA) 59	Fritz Kuchen(SUI) 59
1920(2)	Carl Osburn(USA) 56	Lars Madsen(DEN) 55	Lawrence Nuesslein(USA) 54
1920(8)	Hugo Johansson(SWE) 58	Mauritz Eriksson(SWE) 56	Lloyd Spooner(USA) 56

1908 Event not held
Footnotes – see below next event

Military Rifle (Team) – Men

1900	SWITZERLAND 4399	NORWAY 4290	FRANCE 4278
1908	UNITED STATES 2531	GREAT BRITAIN 2497	CANADA 2439
1912	UNITED STATES 1687	GREAT BRITAIN 1602	SWEDEN 1570
1920(2)	DENMARK 266	UNITED STATES 255	SWEDEN 255
1920(4)	UNITED STATES 289	FRANCE 283	FINLAND 281

| 1920(8) | UNITED STATES 287 | SOUTH AFRICA 287 | SWEDEN 287 |
| 1920(9) | UNITED STATES 573 | NORWAY 565 | SWITZERLAND 563 |

1896, 1904 Event not held
(1) Three positions (300m)
(2) Standing (300m)
(3) Kneeling (300m)
(4) Prone (300m)
(5) Standing or kneeling (200m)
(6) Standing or kneeling (300m)
(7) Any position (600m)
(8) Prone (600m)
(9) Prone (300m and 600m)

Small Bore Rifle – Men

1908(1)	John Fleming(GBR) 24	M.K. Matthews(GBR) 24	W.B. Marsden(GBR) 24
1908(2)	William Styles(GBR) 45	H.I. Hawkins(GBR) 45	Edward Amoore(GBR) 45
1912(2)	Wilhelm Carlberg(SWE) 242	Johan von Holst(SWE) 233	Gustaf Ericsson(SWE) 231

(1) Moving target
(2) Disappearing target

Small Bore Rifle (Team) – Men

1908	GREAT BRITAIN 771	SWEDEN 737	FRANCE 710
1912(1)	SWEDEN 925	GREAT BRITAIN 917	UNITED STATES 881
1912(2)	GREAT BRITAIN 762	SWEDEN 748	UNITED STATES 744
1920	UNITED STATES 1899	SWEDEN 1873	NORWAY 1866

(1) Distance 25m
(2) Distance 50m

Live Pigeon Shooting – Men

| 1900 | Léon de Lunden(BEL) 21 | Maurice Faure(FRA) 20 | Donald MacIntosh(AUS) 18 |
| | | | Crittenden Robinson(USA) 18 |

Clay Pigeons (Team) – Men

1908	GREAT BRITAIN 407	CANADA 405	GREAT BRITAIN 372
1912	UNITED STATES 532	GREAT BRITAIN 511	GERMANY 510
1920	UNITED STATES 547	BELGIUM 503	SWEDEN 500
1924	UNITED STATES 363	CANADA 360	FINLAND 360

Running Deer Shooting – Men

1908(1)	Oscar Swahn(SWE) 25	Ted Ranken(GBR) 24	Alexander Rogers(GBR) 24
1908(2)	Walter Winans(USA) 46	Ted Ranken(GBR) 46	Oscar Swahn(SWE) 38
1912(1)	Alfred Swahn(SWE) 41	Ake Lundeberg(SWE) 41	Nestori Toivonen(FIN) 41
1912(2)	Ake Lundeberg(SWE) 79	Edvard Benedicks(SWE) 74	Oscar Swahn(SWE) 72
1920(1)	Otto Olsen(NOR) 43	Alfred Swahn(SWE) 41	Harald Natwig(NOR) 41
1920(2)	Ole Lilloe-Olsen(NOR) 82	Fredrik Landelius(SWE) 77	Einar Liberg(NOR) 71
1924(1)	John Boles(USA) 40	Cyril Mackworth-Praed(GBR) 39	Otto Olsen(NOR) 39
1924(2)	Ole Lilloe-Olsen(NOR) 76	Cyril Mackworth-Praed(GBR) 72	Alfred Swahn(SWE) 72

(1) Single shot
(2) Double shot

Running Deer Shooting (Team) – Men

1908	SWEDEN 86	GREAT BRITAIN 85	– (1)
1912	SWEDEN 151	UNITED STATES 132	FINLAND 123
1920(2)	NORWAY 178	FINLAND 159	UNITED STATES 158
1920(3)	NORWAY 343	SWEDEN 336	FINLAND 284
1924(2)	NORWAY 160	SWEDEN 154	UNITED STATES 158
1924(3)	GREAT BRITAIN 263	NORWAY 262	SWEDEN 250

(1) Only two teams
(2) Single shot
(3) Double shot

Running Deer Shooting (Single & Double Shot) – Men

| 1952 | John Larsen(NOR) 413 | Per Olof Sköldberg(SWE) 409 | Tauno Mäki(FIN) 407 |
| 1956 | Vitali Romanenko(URS) 441 | Per Olof Sköldberg(SWE) 432 | Vladimir Sevrugin(URS) 429 |

Military Revolver – Men

1896	John Paine(USA) 442	Sumner Paine(USA) 380	Nikolaos Morakis(GRE) 205
1906	Louis Richardet(SUI) 253	Alexandros Theophilakis(GRE) 250	Georgios Skotadis(GRE) 240
1906(1)	Jean Fouconnier(FRA) 219	Raoul de Boigne(FRA) 219	Hermann Martin(FRA) 215

1900–04 Event not held
(1) Model 1873

Duelling Pistol – Men

1906(1)	Léon Moreaux(FRA) 242	Cesare Liverziani(ITA) 233	Maurice Lecoq(FRA) 231
1906(2)	Konstantinos Skarlatos(GRE) 133	Johann von Holst(SWE) 115	Wilhelm Carlberg(SWE) 115

1896–1904 Event not held
(1) Distance 20m
(2) Distance 25m

Team Event – Men

1900	SWITZERLAND 2271	FRANCE 2203	NETHERLANDS 1876
1908	UNITED STATES 1914	BELGIUM 1863	GREAT BRITAIN 1817
1912(1)	UNITED STATES 1916	SWEDEN 1849	GREAT BRITAIN 1804
1912(2)	SWEDEN 1145	RUSSIA d.n.a.	GREAT BRITAIN d.n.a.
1920(1)	UNITED STATES 2372	SWEDEN 2289	BRAZIL 2264
1920(2)	UNITED STATES 1310	GREECE 1285	SWITZERLAND 1270

1904–06 Event not held
(1) Distance 50m
(2) Distance 30m

SOFTBALL

Women

	GOLD	SILVER	BRONZE
1996	UNITED STATES	CHINA	AUSTRALIA
2000	UNITED STATES	JAPAN	AUSTRALIA
2004	UNITED STATES	AUSTRALIA	JAPAN

1896–1992 Event not held

SWIMMING

50m Freestyle – Men

	GOLD	SILVER	BRONZE
1904(1)	Zóltán Halmay(HUN) 28.0	Scott Leary(USA) 28.6	Charles Daniels(USA) n.t.a.
1988	Matt Biondi(USA) 22.14	Thomas Jager(USA) 22.36	Gennadi Prigoda(URS) 22.71
1992	Alexander Popov(EUN) 21.91	Matt Biondi(USA) 22.09	Tom Jager(USA) 22.30
1996	Alexander Popov(RUS) 22.13	Gary Hall Jr(USA) 22.26	Fernando Scherer(BRA) 22.29
2000	Anthony Ervin(USA) 21.98	–	Pieter van den Hoogenband(NED) 22.03
	Gary Hall Jr(USA) 21.98		
2004	Gary Hall Jr(USA) 21.93	Duje Draganja(CRO) 21.94	Roland Schoeman(RSA) 22.02

1896–1900, 1906–84 Event not held
(1) Distance 50 yards

100m Freestyle – Men

	GOLD	SILVER	BRONZE
1896(1)	Alfréd Hajós(HUN) 1:22.2	Efstathios Chorophas(GRE) 1:23.0	Otto Herschmann(AUT) d.n.a.
1904(2)	Zóltán Halmay(HUN) 1:02.8	Charles Daniels(USA) d.n.a.	Scott Leary(USA) d.n.a.
1906	Charles Daniels(USA) 1:13.4	Zóltán Halmay(HUN) 1:14.2	Cecil Healy(AUS) d.n.a.
1908	Charles Daniels(USA) 1:05.6	Zóltán Halmay(HUN) 1:06.2	Harald Julin(SWE) 1:08.0
1912	Duke Kahanamoku(USA) 1:03.4	Cecil Healy(AUS) 1:04.6	Kenneth Huszagh(USA) 1:05.6
1920	Duke Kahanamoku(USA) 1:01.4	Pua Kealoha(USA) 1:02.2	William Harris(USA) 1:03.0
1924	Johnny Weissmuller(USA) 59.0	Duke Kahanamoku(USA) 1:01.4	Sam Kahanamoku(USA) 1:01.8
1928	Johnny Weissmuller(USA) 58.6	István Bárány(HUN) 59.8	Katsuo Takaishi(JPN) 1:00.0
1932	Yasuji Miyazaki(JPN) 58.2	Tatsugo Kawaishi(JPN) 58.6	Albert Schwartz(USA) 58.8
1936	Ferenc Csik(HUN) 57.6	Masanori Yusa(JPN) 57.9	Shigeo Arai(JPN) 58.0
1948	Walter Ris(USA) 57.3	Alan Ford(USA) 57.8	Géza Kádas(HUN) 58.1
1952	Clarke Scholes(USA) 57.4	Hiroshi Suzuki(JPN) 57.4	Göran Larsson(SWE) 58.2
1956	Jon Hendricks(AUS) 55.4	John Devitt(AUS) 55.8	Gary Chapman(AUS) 56.7
1960	John Devitt(AUS) 55.2(55.16)	Lance Larson(USA) 55.2(55.10) (3)	Manuel dos Santos(BRA) 55.4
1964	Don Schollander(USA) 53.4	Bobbie McGregor(GBR) 53.5	Hans-Joachim Klein(GER) 54.0
1968	Mike Wenden(AUS) 52.2	Ken Walsh(USA) 52.8	Mark Spitz(USA) 53.0
1972	Mark Spitz(USA) 51.22	Jerry Heidenreich(USA) 51.65	Vladimir Bure(URS) 51.77
1976	Jim Montgomery(USA) 49.99	Jack Babashoff(USA) 50.81	Peter Nocke(FRG) 51.31
1980	Jörg Woithe(GDR) 50.40	Per Holmertz(SWE) 50.91	Per Johansson(SWE) 51.29
1984	Ambrose Gaines(USA) 49.80	Mark Stockwell(AUS) 50.24	Per Johansson(SWE) 50.31
1988	Matt Biondi(USA) 48.63	Chris Jacobs(USA) 49.08	Stephan Caron(FRA) 49.62
1992	Alexander Popov(EUN) 49.02	Gustavo Borges(BRA) 49.43	Stephan Caron(FRA) 49.50
1996	Alexander Popov(RUS) 48.74s	Gary Hall Jr(USA) 48.81s	Gustavo Borges(BRA) 49.02s
2000	Pieter van den Hoogenband(NED) 48.30	Alexander Popov(RUS) 48.69	Gary Hall Jr(USA) 48.73
2004	Pieter van den Hoogenband(NED) 48.17	Roland Schoeman(RSA) 48.23	Ian Thorpe(AUS) 48.56

1900 Event not held

(1) Experts disagree about the second and third placings
(2) Distance 100 yards
(3) Original manual time of 55.1 for Larson was revised by judges (automatic times were unofficial)

200m Freestyle – Men

	GOLD	SILVER	BRONZE
1900	Frederick Lane(AUS) 2:25.2	Zóltán Halmay(HUN) 2:31.4	Karl Ruberi(AUT) 2:32.0
1904(1)	Charles Daniels(USA) 2:44.2	Francis Gailey(USA) 2:46.0	Emil Rausch(GER) 2:56.0
1968	Mike Wenden(AUS) 1:55.2	Don Schollander(USA) 1:55.8	John Nelson(USA) 1:58.1
1972	Mark Spitz(USA) 1:52.78	Steven Genter(USA) 1:53.73	Werner Lampe(FRG) 1:53.99
1976	Bruce Furniss(USA) 1:50.29	John Naber(USA) 1:50.50	Jim Montgomery(USA) 1:50.58
1980	Sergei Kopliakov(URS) 1:49.81	Andrei Krylov(URS) 1:50.76	Graeme Brewer(AUS) 1:51.60
1984	Michael Gross(FRG) 1:47.44	Michael Heath(USA) 1:49.10	Thomas Fahrner(FRG) 1:49.69
1988	Duncan Armstrong(AUS) 1:47.25	Anders Holmertz(SWE) 1:47.89	Matt Biondi(USA) 1:47.99
1992	Yevgeni Sadovyi(EUN) 1:46.70	Anders Holmertz(SWE) 1:46.86	Antti Kasvio(FIN) 1:47.63
1996	Danyon Loader(NZL) 1:47.63	Gustavo Borges(BRA) 1:48.08	Daniel Kowalski(AUS) 1:48.25
2000	Pieter van den Hoogenband(NED) 1:45.35	Ian Thorpe(AUS) 1:45.83	Massimiliano Rosolino(ITA) 1:46.65
2004	Ian Thorpe(AUS) 1:44.71	Pieter van den Hoogenband(NED) 1:45.23	Michael Phelps(USA)1:45.32

1896, 1906–64 Event not held
(1) Distance 220 yards

400m Freestyle – Men

	GOLD	SILVER	BRONZE
1896(1)	Paul Neuman(AUT) 8:12.6	Antonios Pepanos(GRE) d.n.a.	Efstathios Choraphas(GRE) d.n.a.
1904(2)	Charles Daniels(USA) 6:16.2	Francis Gailey(USA) 6:22.0	Otto Wahle(AUT) 6:39.0
1906	Otto Scheff(AUT) 6:23.8	Henry Taylor(GBR) 6:24.4	John Jarvis(GBR) 6:27.2
1908	Henry Taylor(GBR) 5:36.8	Frank Beaurepaire(AUS) 5:44.2	Otto Scheff(AUT) 5:46.0
1912	George Hodgson(CAN) 5:24.4	John Hatfield(GBR) 5:25.8	Harold Hardwick(AUS) 5:31.2
1920	Norman Ross(USA) 5:26.8	Ludy Langer(USA) 5:29.2	George Vernot(CAN) 5:29.8
1924	Johnny Weismuller(USA) 5:04.2	Arne Borg(SWE) 5:05.6	Andrew Charlton(AUS) 5:06.6
1928	Alberto Zorilla(ARG) 5:01.6	Andrew Charlton(AUS) 5:03.6	Arne Borg(SWE) 5:04.6
1932	Buster Crabbe(USA) 4:48.4	Jean Taris(FRA) 4:48.5	Tautomu Oyokota(JPN) 4:52.3
1936	Jack Medica(USA) 4:44.5	Shumpei Uto(JPN) 4:45.6	Shozo Makino(JPN) 4:48.1
1948	William Smith(USA) 4:41.0	James McLane(USA) 4:43.4	John Marshall(AUS) 4:47.7
1952	Jean Boiteux(FRA) 4:30.7	Ford Konno(USA) 4:31.3	Per-Olof Ostrand(SWE) 4:35.2
1956	Murray Rose(AUS) 4:27.3	Tsuyoshi Yamanaka(JPN) 4:30.4	Goerge Breen(USA) 4:32.5
1960	Murray Rose(AUS) 4:18.3	Tsuyoshi Yamanaka(JPN) 4:21.4	John Konrads(AUS) 4:21.8
1964	Don Schollander(USA) 4:12.2	Frank Wiegand(GER) 4:14.9	Allan Wood(AUS) 4:15.1
1968	Mike Burton(USA) 4:09.0	Ralph Hutton(CAN) 4:11.7	Allan Mosconi(FRA) 4:13.3
1972	Brad Cooper(AUS) 4:00.27	Steven Genter(USA) 4:01.94	Tom McBeen(USA) 4:02.64
1976	Brian Goodell(USA) 3:51.93	TIm Shaw(USA) 3:52.54	Vladimir Raskatov(URS) 3:55.76
1980	Vladimir Salnikov(URS) 3:51.31	Andrei Krylov(URS) 3:53.24	Ivar Stukolkin(URS) 3:55.76
1984	George DiCarlo(USA) 3:51.23	John Mykkanen(USA) 3:51.49	Justin Lemberg(AUS) 3:51.79
1988	Uwe Dassler(GDR) 3:46.95	Duncan Armstrong(AUS) 3:47.15	Artur Wojdat(POL) 3:47.34
1992	Yevgeni Sadovyi(EUN) 3:45.00	Kieren Perkins(AUS) 3:45.16	Anders Holmertz(SWE) 3:46.77
1996	Danyon Loader(NZL) 3:47.97	Paul Palmer(GBR) 3:49.00	Daniel Kowalski(AUS) 3:48.39
2000	Ian Thorpe(AUS) 3:40.59	Massimiliano Rosolino(ITA) 3:43.40	Klete Keller(USA) 3:47.00
2004	Ian Thorpe(AUS) 3m 43.10	Grant Hackett(AUS)3m 43.36	Klete Keller(USA)3m 44.11

1900 Event not held
(1) Distance 500m
(2) Distance 440 yards

1,500m Freestyle – Men

	GOLD	SILVER	BRONZE
1896(1)	Alfréd Hajós(HUN) 18:22.2	Jean Andreou(GRE) 21:03.4	Efstathios Choraphas(GRE) d.n.a.
1900(2)	John Jarvis(GBR) 13:40.2	Otto Wahle(AUT) 14:53.6	Zóltán Halmay(HUN) 15:16.4
1904(3)	Emil Rausch(GER) 27:18.2	Géza Kiss(HUN) 28:28.2	Francis Gailey(USA) 28:54.0
1906(3)	Henry Taylor(GBR) 28:28.0	John Jarvis(GBR) 30:31.0	Otto Scheff(AUT) 30.59.0
1908	Henry Taylor(GBR) 22:48.4	Sydney Battersby(GBR) 22:51.2	Frank Beaurepaire(AUS) 22:56.2
1912	George Hodgson(CAN) 22:00.0	John Hatfield(GBR) 22:39.0	Harold Hardwick(AUS) 23:15.4
1920	Norman Ross(USA) 22:23.2	George Vernot(CAN) 22:36.4	Frank Beaurepaire(AUS) 23:04.0
1924	Andrew Charlton(AUS) 20:06.6	Arne Borg(SWE) 20:41.4	Frank Beaurepaire(AUS) 21:48.4
1928	Arne Borg(SWE) 19:51.8	Andrew Charlton(AUS) 20:02.6	Buster Crabbe(USA) 20:28.8
1932	Kusuo Kitamura(JPN) 19:12.4	Shozo Makino(JPN) 19:14.1	James Christy(USA) 19:39.5
1936	Noboru Terada(JPN) 19:13.7	Jack Medica(USA) 19:34.0	Shumpei Uto(JPN) 19:34.5
1948	James McLane(USA) 19:18.5	John Marshall(AUS) 19:31.3	György Mitro(HUN) 19:43.2
1952	Ford Konno(USA) 18:30.0	Shiro Hasizune(JPN) 18:41.4	Tetsuo Okamoto(JPN) 18:51.3
1956	Murray Rose(AUS) 17:58.9	Tsuyoshi Yamanaka(JPN) 18:00.3	George Breen(USA) 18:08.2
1960	John Konrads(AUS) 17:19.6	Murray Rose(AUS) 17:21.7	George Breen(USA) 17:30.6
1964	Bob Windle(USA) 17:01.7	John Nelson(USA) 17:03.0	Allan Wood(AUS) 17:07.7
1968	Mike Burton(USA) 16:38.9	John Kinsella(USA) 16:57.3	Greg Brough(AUS) 17:04.7

1972	Mike Burton(USA) 15:52.58	Graham Windeatt(AUS) 15:58.48	Doug Northway(USA) 16:09.25
1976	Brian Goodell(USA) 15:02.40	Bobby Hackett(USA) 15:03.91	Steve Holland(AUS) 15:04.66
1980	Vladimir Salnikov(URS) 14:58.27	Alexander Chaev(URS) 15:14.30	Max Metzker(AUS) 15:14.49
1984	Michael O'Brien(USA) 15:05.20	George DiCarlo(USA) 15:10.59	Stefan Pfeiffer(FRG) 15:12.11
1988	Vladimir Salnikov(URS) 15:00.40	Stevan Pfeiffer(FRG) 15:02.69	Uwe Dassler(GDR) 15:06.15
1992	Kieren Perkins(AUS) 14:43.48	Glen Housman(AUS) 14:55.29	Jörg Hoffmann(GER) 15:02.29
1996	Kieren Perkins(AUS) 14:56.40	Daniel Kowalski(AUS) 15:02.43	Graeme Smith(GBR) 15:02.48
2000	Grant Hackett(AUS) 14:48.33	Kieren Perkins(AUS) 14:53.59	Chris Thompson(USA) 14:56.81
2004	Grant Hackett(AUS) 14:43.40	Larsen Jensen(USA) 14:45.29	David Davies(GBR) 14:45.95

(1) Distance 1,200m
(2) Distance 1,000m
(3) Distance 1 mile

100m Breaststroke – Men

	GOLD	SILVER	BRONZE
1968	Don McKenzie(USA) 1:07.7	Vladimir Kossinky(URS) 1:08.0	Nikolai Pankin(URS) 1:08.0
1972	Nobutaka Taguchi(JPN) 1:04.94	Tom Bruce(USA) 1:05.43	John Hencken(USA) 1:05.61
1976	John Hencken(USA) 1:03.11	David Wilkie(GBR) 1:03.43	Arvidas Iuozaytis(URS) 1:04.23
1980	Duncan Goodhew(GBR) 1:03.34	Arsen Miskarov(URS) 1:03.92	Peter Evans(AUS) 1:03.96
1984	Steve Lundquist(USA) 1:01.65	Victor Davis(CAN) 1:01.99	Peter Evans(AUS) 1:02.97
1988	Adrian Moorhouse(GBR) 1:02.04	Karoly Guttler(HUN) 1:02.05	Dmitri Volkov(URS) 1:02.20
1992	Nelson Dreibel(USA) 1:01.50	Norbert Rósza(HUN) 1:01.68	Phil Rogers(AUS) 1:01.76
1996	Frederik Deburghgraeve(BEL) 1:00.65	Jeremy Linn(USA) 1:00.77	Mark Warnecke(GER) 1:01.33
2000	Domenico Fioravanti(ITA) 60.46	Ed Moses(USA) 60.73	Roman Sludnov(RUS) 60.91
2004	Kosuke Kitajima(JPN) 1:00.08	Brendan Hansen(USA) 1:00.25	Hugues Duboscq(FRA) 1:00.88

1896–1964 Event not held

200m Breaststroke – Men

	GOLD	SILVER	BRONZE
1908	Frederick Holman(GBR) 3:09.2	William Robinson(GBR) 3:12.8	Pontus Hansson(SWE) 3:14.6
1912	Walter Bathe(GER) 3:01.8	Wilhelm Lützow(GER) 3:05.2	Kurt Malisch(GER) 3:08.0
1920	Häken Malmroth(SWE) 3:04.4	Thor Henning(SWE) 3:09.2	Arvo Aaltonen(FIN) 3:12.2
1924	Robert Shelton(USA) 2:56.5	Joseph de Combe(BEL) 2:59.2	William Kirschbaum(USA) 3:01.0
1928	Yoshiyuki Tsuruta(JPN) 2:48.8	Erich Rademacher(GER) 2:50.6	Teofilo Ylidefonzo(PHI) 2:56.4
1932	Yoshiyuki Tsuruta(JPN) 2:45.4	Reizo Koike(JPN) 2:46.4	Teofilo Ylidefonzo(PHI) 2:47.1
1936	Tetsuo Hamuro(JPN) 2:42.5	Erwin Sietas(GER) 2:42.9	Reizo Koike(JPN) 2:44.2
1948	Joseph Verdeur(USA) 2:39.3 (1)	Keith Carter(USA) 2:40.2	Robert Sohl(USA) 2:43.9
1952	John Davies(AUS) 2:34.4 (1)	Bowen Stassforth(USA) 2:34.7	Herbert Klein(GER) 2:35.9
1956	Masaru Furukawa(JPN) 2:34.7 (2)	Masihiro Yoshimura(JPN) 2:36.7	Charis Yunitschev(URS) 2:36.8
1960	William Mulliken(USA) 2:37.4	Yoshihiko Osaki(JPN) 2:38.0	Weiger Mensonides(NED) 2:39.7
1964	Ian O'Brien(AUS) 2:27.8	Georgi Prokopenko(URS) 2:28.2	Chester Jastremski(USA) 2:29.6
1968	Felipe Munoz(MEX) 2:28.7	Vladimir Kossinsky(URS) 2:29.2	Brian Job(USA) 2:29.9
1972	John Hencken(USA) 2:21.55	David Wilkie(GBR) 2:23.67	Nobutaka Taguchi(JPN) 2:23.88
1976	David Wilkie(GBR) 2:15.11	John Hencken(USA) 2:17.26	Rick Colella(USA) 2:19.20
1980	Robertas Shulpa(URS) 2;15.85	Alban Vermes(HUN) 2:16.93	Arsen Miskarov(URS) 2:17.28
1984	Victor Davis(CAN) 2:13.34	Glenn Beringen(AUS) 2:15.79	Etienne Dagon(SUI) 2:17.41
1988	József Szabó(HUN) 2:13.52	Nick Gillingham(GBR) 2:14.12	Sergio Lopez(ESP) 2:15.21
1992	Mike Barrowman(USA) 2:10.16	Norbert Rózsa(HUN) 2:11.23	Nick Gillingham(GBR) 2:11.29
1996	Norbert Rózsa(HUN) 2:12.57	Károly Guttler(HUN) 2:13.03	Alexei Korneyev(RUS) 2:13.17
2000	Domenico Fioravanti(ITA) 2:10.87	Terence Parkin(RSA) 2:12.50	Davide Rummolo(ITA) 2:12.73
2004	Kosuke Kitajima(JPN) 2:09.44	Daniel Gyurta(HUN) 2:10.80	Brendan Hansen(USA) 2:10.87

1896–1906 Event not held
(1) Used butterfly stroke
(2) Used underwater technique

100m Backstroke – Men

	GOLD	SILVER	BRONZE
1904(1)	Walter Brack(GER) 1:16.8	Georg Hoffmann(GER) 1:18.0	Georg Zacharias(GER) 1:19.6
1908	Arno Bieberstein(GER) 1:24.6	Ludvig Dam(DEN) 1:26.6	Herbert Haresnape(GBR) 1:27.0
1912	Harry Hebner(USA) 1:21.2	Otto Fahr(GER) 1:22.4	Paul Kellner(GER) 1:24.0
1920	Warren Kealoha(USA) 1:15.2	Ray Kegeris(USA) 1:16.2	Gérard Blitz(BEL) 1:19.0
1924	Warren Kealoha(USA) 1:13.2	Paul Wyatt(USA) 1:15.4	Károly Bartha(HUN) 1:17.8
1928	George Kojac(USA) 1:08.2	Walter Laufer(USA) 1:10.0	Paul Wyatt(USA) 1:12.0
1932	Masaji Kiyokawa(JPN) 1:08.6	Toshio Irie(JPN) 1:09.8	Kentaro Kawatsu(JPN) 1:10.0
1936	Adolf Kiefer(USA) 1:05.9	Albert Van de Weghe(USA) 1:07.7	Masaji Kiyokawa(JPN) 1:08.4
1948	Allen Stack(USA) 1:06.4	Robert Cowell(USA) 1:06.5	Georges Vallerey(FRA) 1:07.8
1952	Yoshinobu Oyakawa(JPN) 1:05.4	Gilbert Bozon(FRA) 1:06.2	Jack Taylor(USA) 1:06.4
1956	David Thiele(AUS) 1:02.2	John Monckton(AUS) 1:03.2	Frank McKinney(USA) 1:04.5
1960	David Thiele(AUS) 1:01.9	Frank McKinney(USA) 1:02.1	Robert Bennett(USA) 1:02.3
1968	Roland Matthes(GDR) 58.7	Charles Hickox(USA) 1:00.2	Ronnie Mills(USA) 1:00.5
1972	Roland Matthes(GDR) 56.58	Mike Stamm(USA) 57.70	John Murphy(USA) 58.35
1976	John Naber(USA) 55.49	Peter Rocca(USA) 56.34	Roland Matthes(GDR) 57.22

1980	Bengt Baron(SWE) 56.53	Viktor Kuznetsov(URS) 56.99	Vladimir Dolgov(URS) 57.63
1984	Richard Carey(USA) 55.79	David Wilson(USA) 56.35	Mike West(CAN) 56.49
1988	Daichi Suzuki(JPN) 55.05	David Berkoff(USA) 55.18	Igor Polianski(URS) 55.20
1992	Mark Tewksbury(CAN) 53.98	Jeff Rouse(USA) 54.04	David Berkoff(USA) 54.78
1996	Jeff Rouse(USA) 54.10	Rodolfo Cabrera(CUB) 54.98	Neisser Bent(CUB) 55.02
2000	Lenny Krayzelburg(USA) 53.72	Matt Welsh(AUS) 54.07	Stev Theloke(GER) 54.82
2004	Aaron Peirsol(USA) 54.06	Markus Rogan(AUT) 54.35	Tomomi Morita(JPN) 54.36

1896–1900, 1906, 1964 Event not held
(1) Distance 100 yards

200m Backstroke – Men

	GOLD	SILVER	BRONZE
1900	Ernst Hoppenberg(GER) 2:47.0	Karl Ruberl(AUT) 2:56.0	Johannes Drost(NED) 3:01.0
1964	Jed Graef(USA) 2:10.3	Gary Dilley(USA) 2:10.5	Robert Bennett(USA) 2:13.1
1968	Roland Matthes(GDR) 2:09.6	Mitchell Ivey(USA) 2:10.6	Jack Horsley(USA) 2:10.9
1972	Roland Matthes(GDR) 2:02.82	Mike Stamm(USA) 2:04.09	Mitchell Ivey(USA) 2:04.33
1976	John Naber(USA) 1:59.19	Peter Rocca(USA) 2:00.55	Don Harrigan(USA) 2:01.35
1980	Sándor Wladár(HUN) 2:01.93	Zóltán Verraszto(HUN) 2:02.40	Mark Kerry(AUS) 2:03.14
1984	Richard Carey(USA) 2:00.23	Frederic Delcourt(FRA) 2:01.75	Cameron Henning(CAN) 2:02.37
1988	Igor Polianski(URS) 1:59.37	Frank Baltrausch(GDR) 1:59.50	Paul Kingsman(NZL) 2:00.48
1992	Martin Lopez-Zubero(ESP) 1:58.47	Vladimir Selkov(EUN) 1:58.87	Stefano Battistelli(ITA) 1:59.40
1996	Brad Bridgewater(USA) 1:58.54	Tripp Schwenk(USA) 1:58.99	Emanuele Meris(ITA) 1:59.18
2000	Lenny Krayzelburg(USA) 1:56.76	Aaron Piersol(USA) 1:57.35	Matt Welsh(AUS) 1:57.59
2004	Aaron Peirsol(USA) 1:54.95	Markus Rogan(AUT) 1:57.35	Razvan Florea(ROM) 1:57.56

1896, 1904–60 Event not held

100m Butterfly – Men

	GOLD	SILVER	BRONZE
1968	Doug Russell(USA) 55.9	Mark Spitz(USA) 56.4	Ross Wales(USA) 57.2
1972	Mark Spitz(USA) 54.27	Bruce Robertson(CAN) 55.56	Jerry Heidenreich(USA) 55.74
1976	Matt Vogel(USA) 54.35	Joe Bottom(USA) 54.50	Gary Hall(USA) 54.65
1980	Pär Arvidson(SWE) 54.92	Roger Pyttel(GDR) 54.94	David Lopez(ESP) 55.13
1984	Michael Gross(FRG) 53.08	Pablo Morales(USA) 53.23	Glenn Buchanan(AUS) 53.85
1988	Anthony Nesty(SUR) 53.00	Matt Biondi(USA) 53.01	Andy Jameson(GBR) 53.30
1992	Pablo Morales(USA) 53.32	Rafal Szukala(POL) 53.35	Anthony Nesty(SUR) 53.41
1996	Denis Pankratov(RUS) 52.27	Scott Miller(AUS) 52.53	Vladislav Kulikov(RUS) 52.13
2000	Lars Frölander(SWE) 52.00	Michael Klim(AUS) 52.18	Geoff Huegill(AUS) 52.22
2004	Michael Phelps(USA) 51.25	Ian Crocker(USA) 51.29	Andriy Serdinov(UKR) 51.36

1896–1964 Event not held

200m Butterfly – Men

	GOLD	SILVER	BRONZE
1956	William Yorzyk(USA) 2:19.3	Takashi Ishimoto(JPN) 2:23.8	György Tumpek(HUN) 2:23.9
1960	Mike Troy(USA) 2:12.8	Neville Hayes(AUS) 2:14.6	David Gillanders(USA) 2:15.3
1964	Kevin Berry(AUS) 2:06.6	Carl Robie(USA) 2:07.5	Fred Schmidt(USA) 2:09.3
1968	Carl Robie(USA) 2:08.7	Martyn Woodroffe(GBR) 2:09.0	John Ferris(USA) 2:09.3
1972	Mark Spitz(USA) 2:00.70	Gary Hall(USA) 2:02.86	Robin Backhaus(USA) 2:03.23
1976	Mike Bruner(USA) 1:59.23	Steven Gregg(USA) 1:59.54	William Forrester(USA) 1:59.96
1980	Sergey Fesenko(URS) 1:59.76	Phil Hubble(GBR) 2:01.20	Roger Pyttel(GDR) 2:01.39
1984	Jon Sieben(AUS) 1:57.04	Michael Gross(FRG) 1:57.40	Rafael Castro(VEN) 1:57.51
1988	Michael Gross(FRG) 1:56.94	Benny Nielsen(DEN) 1:58.24	Anthony Mosse(NZL) 1:58.28
1992	Mel Stewart(USA) 1:56.26	Danyon Loader(NZL) 1:57.93	Franck Esposito(FRA) 1:58.51
1996	Denis Pankratov(RUS) 1:56.51	Matt Malchow(USA) 1:57.44	Scott Miller(AUS) 1:57.48
2000	Tom Malchow(USA) 1:55.35	Denys Sylantyev(UKR) 1:55.76	Justin Norris(AUS) 1:56.17
2004	Michael Phelps(USA) 1:54.04	Takashi Yamamoto(JPN) 1:54.56	Stephen Parry(GBR) 1:55.52

1896–1952 Event not held

200m Individual Medley – Men

	GOLD	SILVER	BRONZE
1968	Charles Hickox(USA) 2:12.0	Greg Buckingham(USA) 2:13.0	John Ferris(USA) 2:13.3
1972	Gunnar Larsson(SWE) 2:07.17	Tim McKee(USA) 2:08.37	Steve Furniss(USA) 2:08.45
1984	Alex Baumann(CAN) 2:01.42	Pablos Morales(USA) 2:03.05	Neil Cochran(GBR) 2:04.38
1988	Tamás Darnyi(HUN) 2:00.17	Patrick Kühl(GDR) 2:01.61	Vadim Yarochtchouk(URS) 2:02.40
1992	Tamás Darnyi(HUN) 2:00.76	Gregory Burgess(USA) 2:00.97	Attila Czene(HUN) 2:01.00
1996	Attila Czene(HUN) 1:59.91	Jani Sievinen(FIN) 2:00.13	Curtis Myden(CAN) 2:01.13
2000	Massimiliano Rosolino(ITA) 1:58.98	Tom Dolan(USA) 1:59.77	Tom Wilkens(USA) 2:00.87
2004	Michael Phelps(USA) 1:57.14	Ryan Lochte(USA) 1:58.78	George Bovell(TRI) 1:58.80

1896–1964, 1976–1980 Event not held

400m Individual Medley – Men

	GOLD	SILVER	BRONZE
1964	Richard Roth(USA) 4:45.4	Roy Saari(USA) 4:47.1	Gerhard Hetz(GER) 4:51.0
1968	Charles Hickox(USA) 4:48.4	Gary Hall(USA) 4:48.7	Michael Holthaus(GER) 4:51.4
1972	Gunnar Larsson(SWE) 4:31.98	Tim McKee(USA) 4:31.98	András Hargitay(HUN) 4:32.70

1976	Rod Strachan(USA) 4:23.68	Tim McKee(USA) 4:24.62	Andrei Smirnov(URS) 4:26.90
1980	Alexander Sidorenko(URS) 4:22.89	Sergei Fesenko(URS) 4:23.43	Zóltán Verraszto(HUN) 4:24.24
1984	Alex Baumann(CAN) 4:17.41	Ricardo Prado(BRA) 4:18.45	Robert Woodhouse(AUS) 4:20.50
1988	Tamás Darnyi(HUN) 4:14.75	David Wharton(USA) 4:17.36	Stefano Battistelli(ITA) 4:18.01
1992	Tamás Darnyi(HUN) 4:14.23	Erik Namesnik(USA) 4:15.57	Luca Sacchi(ITA) 4:16.34
1996	Tom Dolan(USA) 4:14.90	Eric Namesnik(USA) 4:15.25	Curtis Myden(CAN) 4:16.28
2000	Tom Dolan(USA) 4:11.76	Erik Vendt(USA) 4:14.23	Curtis Myden(CAN) 4:15.33
2004	Michael Phelps(USA) 4m 08.26	Erik Vendt(USA) 4m 11.81	Laszlo Cseh(HUN) 4m 12.15

1896–1960 Event not held

4 x 100m Freestyle Relay – Men

	GOLD	SILVER	BRONZE
1964	UNITED STATES 3:33.2	GERMANY 3:37.2	AUSTRALIA 3:39.1
1968	UNITED STATES 3:31.7	SOVIET UNION 3:34.2	AUSTRALIA 3:34.7
1972	UNITED STATES 3:26.42	SOVIET UNION 3:29.72	GDR 3:32.42
1984	UNITED STATES 3:19.03	AUSTRALIA 3:19.68	SWEDEN 3:22.69
1988	UNITED STATES 3:16.53	SOVIET UNION 3:18.33	GDR 3:19.82
1992	UNITED STATES 3:16.74	UNIFIED TEAM 3:17.56	GERMANY 3:17.90
1996	UNITED STATES 3:15.41	RUSSIA 3:17.06	GERMANY 3:17.20
2000	AUSTRALIA 3:13.67	UNITED STATES 3:13.86	BRAZIL 3:17.40
2004	SOUTH AFRICA 3:13 .17	NETHERLANDS 3:14.36	UNITED STATES 3:14.62

1896–1960, 1976–80 Event not held

4 x 200m Freestyle Relay – Men

	GOLD	SILVER	BRONZE
1906(1)	HUNGARY 16:52.4	GERMANY 17:16.2	GREAT BRITAIN n.t.a.
1908	GREAT BRITAIN 10:55.6	HUNGARY 10:59.0	UNITED STATES 11:02.8
1912	AUSTRALASIA 10:11.6 (2)	UNITED STATES 10:20.2	GREAT BRITAIN 10:28.2
1920	UNITED STATES 10:04.4	AUSTRALIA 10:25.4	GREAT BRITAIN 10:37.2
1924	UNITED STATES 9:53.4	AUSTRALIA 10:02.2	SWEDEN 10:06.8
1928	UNITED STATES 9:36.2	JAPAN 9:41.4	CANADA 9:47.8
1932	JAPAN 8:58.4	UNITED STATES 9:10.5	HUNGARY 9:31.4
1936	JAPAN 8:51.5	UNITED STATES 9:03.0	HUNGARY 9:12.3
1948	UNITED STATES 8:46.0	HUNGARY 8:48.4	FRANCE 9:08.0
1952	UNITED STATES 8:31.1	JAPAN 8:33.5	FRANCE 8:45.9
1956	AUSTRALIA 8:23.6	UNITED STATES 8:31.5	SOVIET UNION 8:34.7
1960	UNITED STATES 8:10.2	JAPAN 8:13.2	AUSTRALIA 8:13.8
1964	UNITED STATES 7:52.1	GERMANY 7:59.3	JAPAN 8:03.8
1968	UNITED STATES 7:35.78	AUSTRALIA 7:53.7	SOVIET UNION 8:01.6
1972	UNITED STATES 7:35.78	FRG 7:41.69	SOVIET UNION 7:45.76
1976	UNITED STATES 7:23.22	SOVIET UNION 7:27.97	GREAT BRITAIN 7:32.11
1980	SOVIET UNION 7:23.50	GDR 7:28.60	BRAZIL 7:29.30
1984	UNITED STATES 7:15.69	FRG 7:16.73	GREAT BRITAIN 7:24.78
1988	UNITED STATES 7:12.51	GDR 7:13.68	FRG 7:14.35
1992	UNIFIED TEAM 7:11.95	SWEDEN 7:15.31	UNITED STATES 7:16.23
1996	UNITED STATES 7:14.84	SWEDEN 7:17.56	GERMANY 7:17.71
2000	AUSTRALIA 7:07.05	UNITED STATES 7:12.64	NETHERLANDS 7:12.70
2004	UNITED STATES 7.07.33	AUSTRALIA 7:07.46	ITALY 7:11.83

1896–1904 Event not held
(1) Distance 4 x 250m
(2) Team consisted of three Australians and a New Zealander

4 x 100m Medley Relay – Men

	GOLD	SILVER	BRONZE
1960	UNITED STATES 4:05.4	AUSTRALIA 4:12.0	JAPAN 4:12.2
1964	UNITED STATES 3:38.5	GERMANY 4:01.6	AUSTRALIA 4:02.3
1968	UNITED STATES 3:54.9	GDR 3:57.5	SOVIET UNION 4:00.7
1972	UNITED STATES 3:48.16	GDR 3:52.12	CANADA 3:52.26
1976	UNITED STATES 3:42.22	CANADA 3:43.23	FRG 3:47.29
1980	AUSTRALIA 3:45.70	SOVIET UNION 3:45.92	GREAT BRITAIN 3:47.71
1984	UNITED STATES 3:39.30	CANADA 3:43.23	AUSTRALIA 3:43.25
1988	UNITED STATES 3:36.93	CANADA 3:39.28	SOVIET UNION 3:39.96
1992	UNITED STATES 3:36.93	UNIFIED TEAM 3:38.56	CANADA 3:39.96
1996	UNITED STATES 3:34.84	RUSSIA 3:37.55	AUSTRALIA 3:39.56
2000	UNITED STATES 3:33.73	AUSTRALIA 3:35.27	GERMANY 3:35.88
2004	UNITED STATES 3:30.68	GERMANY 3:33.62	JAPAN 3:35.22

1896–1956 Event not held

DIVING

Springboard Diving – Men

	GOLD	SILVER	BRONZE
1908	Albert Turner(GER) 85.5	Kurt Behrens(GER) 85.3	George Giadzik(USA) 80.8
			Gottlob Walz(GER) 80.8
1912	Paul Günther(GER) 79.23	Hans Luber(GER) 76.78	Kurt Behrens(GER) 73.73
1920	Louis Kuehn(USA) 675.4	Clarence Pinkston(USA) 655.3	Louis Balbach(USA) 649.5
1924	Albert White(USA) 696.4	Pete Desjardins(USA) 693.2	Clarence Pinkston(USA) 653
1928	Pete Desjardins(USA) 185.04	Michael Galitzen(USA) 174.06	Farid Simaika(EGY) 172.46
1932	Michael Galitzen(USA) 161.38	Harold Smith(USA) 158.54	Richard Degener(USA) 151.82
1936	Richard Degener(USA) 163.57	Marshall Wayne(USA) 159.56	Al Greene(USA) 146.29
1948	Bruce Harlan(USA) 163.64	Miller Anderson(USA) 157.29	Samuel Lee(USA) 145.52
1952	David Browning(USA) 205.29	Miller Anderson(USA) 199.84	Robert Clotworthy(USA) 184.92
1956	Robert Clotworthy(USA) 159.56	Donald Harper(USA) 156.23	Joaquin Capilla Pérez(MEX) 162.30
1960	Gary Tobian(USA) 170.00	Samuel Hall(USA) 167.08	Juan Botella(MEX) 162.30
1964	Kenneth Sitzberger(USA) 159.90	Francis Gorman(USA) 157.63	Larry Andreasen(USA) 143.77
1968	Bernard Wrightson(USA) 170.15	Klaus Dibiasi(ITA) 159.74	James Henry(USA) 158.09
1972	Vladimir Vasin(URS) 594.09	F. Giorgio Cagnotto(ITA) 591.63	Craig Lincoln(USA) 577.29
1976	Philip Boggs(USA) 619.05	F. Giorgio Cagnotto(ITA) 570.48	Alexander Kosenkov(URS) 567.24
1980	Alexander Portnov(URS) 905.025	Carlos Giron(MEX) 892.140	F. Giorgio Cagnotto(ITA) 871.500
1984	Greg Louganis(USA) 754.41	Liangde Tan(CHN) 662.31	Ronald Merriott(USA) 661.32
1988	Greg Louganis(USA) 730.80	Liangde Tan(CHN) 704.88	Deliang Li(CHN) 665.28
1992	Mark Lenzi(USA) 676.530	Liangde Tan(CHN) 645.570	Dmitri Sautin(EUN) 627.780
1996	Xiong Ni(CHN) 701.46	Zhoucheng Yu(CHN) 690.93	Mark Lenzi(USA) 686.49
2000	Xiong Ni(CHN) 708.72	Fernando Platas(MEX) 708.42	Dmitri Sautin(RUS) 703.20
2004	Bo Peng(CHN) 787.38	Alexandre Despatie(CAN) 755.97	Dmitri Sautin(RUS) 753.27

1896–1906 Event not held

Synchronised Springboard – Men

	GOLD	SILVER	BRONZE
2000	CHINA 365.58	RUSSIA 329.97	AUSTRALIA 322.86
2004	GREECE 353.34	GERMANY 350.01	AUSTRALIA 349.59

1896–1996 Event not held

Platform Diving – Men

	GOLD	SILVER	BRONZE
1904(1)	George Shelton(USA) 12.66	Georg Hoffmann(GER) 11.66	Frank Kehoe(USA) 11.33
			Alfred Braunschweiger(GER) 11.33
1906	Gottlob Walz(GER) 156.00	Georg Hoffmann(GER) 150.20	Otto Satzinger(AUT) 147.40
1908	Hajalmar Johansson(SWE) 83.75	Karl Malmström(SWE) 78.73	Arvid Spangberg(SWE) 74.00
1912	Erik Adlerz(SWE) 73.94	Albert Zürner(GER) 72.60	Gustaf Blomgren(SWE) 69.56
1920	Clarence Pinkston(USA) 100.67	Erik Adlerz(SWE) 99.08	Haig Prieste(USA) 93.73
1924	Albert White(USA) 97.46	David Fall(USA) 97.30	Clarence Pinkston(USA) 94.60
1928	Pete Desjardins(USA) 98.74	Farid Simaika(EGY) 99.58	Michael Galitzen(USA) 92.34
1932	Harold Smith(USA) 124.80	Michael Galitzen(USA) 124.28	Frank Kurtz(USA) 121.98
1936	Marshall Wayne(USA) 113.58	Elbert Root(USA) 110.60	Hermann Stork(GER) 110.31
1948	Samuel Lee(USA) 130.05	Bruce Harlan(USA) 122.30	Joaquin Capilla Pérez(MEX) 113.52
1952	Samuel Lee(USA) 156.28	Joaquin Capilla Pérez(MEX) 145.21	Günther Haase(GER) 141.31
1956	Joaquin Capilla Pérez(MEX) 152.44	Gary Tobian(USA) 152.41	Richard Connor(USA) 149.79
1960	Robert Webster(USA) 165.56	Gary Tobian(USA) 165.25	Brian Phelps(GBR) 157.13
1964	Robert Webster(USA) 148.58	Klaus Dibiasi(ITA) 147.54	Thomas Gompf(USA) 153.93
1968	Klaus Dibiasi(ITA) 164.18	Alvaro Gaxiola(MEX) 154.49	Edwin Young(USA) 153.93
1972	Klaus Dibiasi(ITA) 504.12	Richard Rydze(USA) 480.75	F. Giorgio Cagnotto(ITA) 475.83
1976	Klaus Dibiasi(ITA) 600.51	Greg Louganis(USA) 576.99	Vladimir Aleynik(URS) 548.61
1980	Falk Hoffmann(GDR) 835.650	Vladimir Aleynik(URS) 819.705	David Ambartsumyan(URS) 817.440
1984	Greg Louganis(USA) 710.91	Bruce Kimball(USA) 643.50	Kongzheng Li(CHN) 638.28
1988	Greg Louganis(USA) 638.61	Xiong Ni(CHN) 637.47	Jesus Mena(MEX) 594.39
1992	Shunwei Sun(CHN) 677.310	Scott Donie(USA) 633.6	Xiong Ni(CHN) 600.150
1996	Dmitri Sautin(RUS) 692.34	Jan Hempel(GER) 663.27	Hailiang Xiao(CHN) 658.20
2000	Liang Tian(CHN) 724.53	Jia Hu(CHN) 713.55	Dmitri Sautin(RUS) 679.26
2004	Jia Hu(CHN) 748.08	Mathew Helm(AUS) 730.56	Liang Tian (CHN) 729.66

1896–1900 Event not held
(1) Combined springboard/platform

Synchronized Platform – Men

	GOLD	SILVER	BRONZE
2000	RUSSIA 365.04	CHINA 358.74	GERMANY 338.88
2004	CHINA 383.88	GREAT BRITAIN 371.52	AUSTRALIA 366.84

1896–1996 Event not held

SWIMMING

50m Freestyle – Women

	GOLD	SILVER	BRONZE
1988	Kristin Otto(GDR) 25.49	Wenyi Yang(CHN) 25.64	Katrin Meissner(GDR) 25.71
			Jill Sterkel(USA) 25.71
1992	Wenyi Yang(CHN) 24.79	Zhuang Yong(CHN) 25.08	Angel Martino(USA) 25.23
1996	Amy van Dyken(USA) 24.87	Jingyi Le(CHN) 24.90	Sandra Volker(GER) 25.14
2000	Inge de Bruijn(NED) 24.32	Therese Alshammar(SWE) 24.51	Dara Torres(USA) 24.63
2004	Inge de Bruijn(NED) 24.58	Malia Matella(FRA) 24.89	Lisbeth Lenton(AUS) 24.91

1896–1984 Event not held

100m Freestyle – Women

	GOLD	SILVER	BRONZE
1912	Fanny Durack(AUS) 1:22.2	Wilhelmina Wylie(AUS) 1:25.4	Jennie Fletcher(GBR) 1:27.0
1920	Etheda Bleibtrey(USA) 1:13.6	Irene Guest(USA) 1:17.0	Frances Schroth(USA) 1:17.2
1924	Ethel Lackie(USA) 1:12.4	Mariechen Wehselau(USA) 1:12.8	Gertrude Ederle(USA) 1:14.2
1928	Albina Osipowich(USA) 1:11.0	Eleanor Garatti(USA) 1:11.4	Joyce Cooper(GBR) 1:13.6
1932	Helene Madison(USA) 1:06.8	Willemijntje den Ouden(NED) 1:07.8	Eleanor Garatti-Saville(USA) 1:08.2
1936	Henrika Mastenbroek(NED) 1:05.9	Jeanette Campbell(ARG) 1:06.4	Gisela Arendt(GER) 1:06.6
1948	Greta Andersen(DEN) 1:06.3	Ann Curtis(USA) 1:06.5	Marie-Louise Vaessen(NED) 1:07.6
1952	Katalin Szöke(HUN) 1:06.8	Johanna Termeulen(NED) 1:07.0	Judit Temes(HUN) 1:07.1
1956	Dawn Fraser(AUS) 1:02.0	Lorraine Crapp(AUS) 1:02.3	Faith Leech(AUS) 1:05.1
1960	Dawn Fraser(AUS) 1:01.2	Christine von Saltza(USA) 1:02.8	Natalie Steward(GBR) 1:03.1
1964	Dawn Fraser(AUS) 59.5	Sharon Stouder(USA) 59.9	Kathleen Ellis(USA) 1:00.8
1968	Jan Henne(USA) 1:00.0	Susan Pedersen(USA) 1:00.3	Linda Gustavson(USA) 1:00.3
1972	Sandra Neilson(USA) 58.59	Shirley Babashoff(USA) 59.02	Shane Gould(AUS) 59.06
1976	Kornelia Ender(GDR) 55.65	Petra Priemer(GDR) 56.49	Enith Brigitha(NED) 56.65
1980	Barbara Krause(GDR) 54.79	Caren Metschuck(GDR) 55.16	Ines Diers(GDR) 55.65
1984	Carrie Steinsiefer(USA) 55.92	–	Annemarie Verstappen(NED) 56.08
	Nancy Hogshead(USA) 55.92		
1988	Kristin Otto(GDR) 54.93	Zhuang Yong(CHN) 55.47	Catherine Plewinski(FRA) 55.49
1992	Zhuang Yong(CHN) 54.64	Jenny Thompson(USA) 54.84	Franziska van Almsick(GER) 54.94
1996	Jingyi Le(CHN) 54.50	Sandra Volker(GER) 54.88	Angel Martino(USA) 54.93
2000	Inge de Bruijn(NED) 53.83	Therese Alshammar(SWE) 54.33	Jenny Thompson(USA) 54.43
			Dara Torres(USA) 54.43
2004	Jodie Henry(AUS) 53.84	Inge de Bruijn(NED) 54.16	Natalie Coughlin(USA) 54.40

1896–1908 Event not held

200m Freestyle – Women

	GOLD	SILVER	BRONZE
1968	Debbie Meyer(USA) 2:10.5	Jan Henne(USA) 2:11.0	Jane Barkman(USA) 2:11.2
1972	Shane Gould(AUS) 2:03.56	Shirley Babashoff(USA) 2:04.33	Keena Rothhammer(USA) 2:04.92
1976	Kornelia Ender(GDR) 1:59.26	Shirley Babashoff(USA) 2:01.22	Enith Brigitha(NED) 2:01.40
1980	Barbara Krause(GDR) 1:58.33	Ines Diers(GDR) 1:59.64	Carmela Schmidt(GDR) 2:01.44
1984	Mary Wayte(USA) 1:59.23	Cynthia Woodhead(USA) 1:59.50	Annemarie Verstappen(NED) 1:59.69
1988	Heike Friedrich(GDR) 1:57.65	Silvia Poll(CRC) 1:58.67	Manuela Stellmach(GDR) 1:59.01
1992	Nicole Haislett(USA) 1:57.90	Franziska van Almsick(GER) 1:58.00	Kirsten Kielgass(GER) 1:59.67
1996	Claudia Poll(CRC) 1:58.16	Franziska van Almsick(GER) 1:58.57	Dagmar Hase(GER) 1:59.56
2000	Susie O'Neill(AUS) 1:58.24	Martina Moravcova(SVK) 1:58.32	Claudia Poll(CRC) 1:58.81
2004	Camelia Potec(ROM) 1:58.03	Federica Pellegrini(ITA) 1:58.22	Solenne Figues(FRA) 1:58.45

1896–1964 Event not held

400m Freestyle – Women

	GOLD	SILVER	BRONZE
1920(1)	Etheda Bleibtrey(USA) 4:34.0	Margaret Woodbridge(USA) 4:42.8	Frances Schroth(USA) 4:52.0
1924	Martha Norelius(USA) 6:02.2	Helen Wainwright(USA) 6:03.8	Gertrude Ederle(USA) 6:04.8
1928	Martha Norelius(USA) 5:42.8	Marie Braun(NED) 5:57.8	Jospehine McKim(USA) 6:00.2
1932	Helene Madison(USA) 5:28.5	Lenore Kight(USA) 5:28.6	Jennie Maakal(RSA) 5:47.3
1936	Henrika Mastenbroek(NED) 5:26.4	Ragnhild Hveger(DEN) 5:27.5	Lenore Kight-Wingard(USA) 5:29.0
1948	Ann Curtis(USA) 5:17.8	Karen Harup(DEN) 5:21.2	Cathy Gibson(GBR) 5:22.5
1952	Valeria Gyenge(HUN) 5:12.1	Eva Novak(HUN) 5:13.7	Evelyn Kawamoto(USA) 5:14.6
1956	Lorraine Crapp(AUS) 4:54.6	Dawn Fraser(AUS) 5:02.5	Sylvia Ruuska(USA) 5:07.1
1960	Christine von Saltza(USA) 4:50.6	Jane Cederquist(SWE) 4:53.9	Catharina Lagerberg(NED) 4:56.9
1964	Virginia Duenkel(USA) 4:43.3	Marilyn Ramenofsky(USA) 4:44.6	Terri Stickles(USA) 4:47.2
1968	Debbie Meyer(USA) 4:31.8	Linda Gustavson(USA) 4:35.5	Karen Moras(AUS) 4:37.0
1972	Shane Gould(AUS) 4:19.04	Novella Calligaris(ITA) 4:22.44	Gudrun Wegner(GDR) 4:23.11
1976	Petra Thuemer(GDR) 4:09.89	Shirley Babashoff(USA) 4:10.46	Shannon Smith(CAN) 4:14.60
1980	Ines Diers(GDR) 4:08.76	Petra Schneider(GDR) 4:09.16	Carmela Schmidt(GDR) 4:10.86
1984	Tiffany Cohen(USA) 4:07.10	Sarah Hardcastle(GBR) 4:10.27	June Croft(GBR) 4:11.49
1988	Janet Evans(USA) 4:03.85	Heike Friedrich(GDR) 4:05.94	Anke Möhring(GDR) 4:06.62
1992	Dagmar Hase(GER) 4:07.18	Janet Evans(USA) 4:07.37	Hayley Lewis(AUS) 4:11.22
1996	Michelle Smith(IRL) 4:07.25	Dagmar Hase(GER) 4:08.30	Kirsten Vlieghuis(NED) 4:08.70
2000	Brooke Bennett(USA) 4:05.80	Diana Munz(USA) 4:07.07	Claudia Poll(CRC) 4:07.83

2004   Laure Manaudou(FRA) 4:05.34   Otylia Jedrzejczak(POL) 4:05.84   Kaitlin Sandeno(USA) 4:06.19
1896–1912 Event not held
(1) Distance 300m

800m Freestyle – Women

	GOLD	SILVER	BRONZE
1968	Debbie Meyer(USA) 9:24.0	Pamela Kruse(USA) 9:35.7	Maria Ramirez(MEX) 9:38.5
1972	Keena Rothhammer(USA) 8:53.68	Shane Gould(AUS) 8:56.39	Novella Calligaris(ITA) 8:57.46
1976	Petra Thuemer(GDR) 8:37.14	Shirley Babashoff(USA) 8:37.59	Wendy Weinberg(USA) 8:42.60
1980	Michelle Ford(AUS) 8:28.9	Ines Diers(GDR) 8:32.55	Heike Dähne(GDR) 8:33.48
1984	Tiffany Cohen(USA) 8:24.95	Michele Richardson(USA) 8:30.73	Sarah Hardcastle(GBR) 8:32.60
1988	Janet Evans(USA) 8:20.20	Astrid Strauss(GDR) 8:22.09	Julie McDonald(AUS) 8:22.93
1992	Janet Evans(USA) 8:25.52	Hayley Lewis(AUS) 8:30.34	Jana Henke(GER) 8:30.99
1996	Brooke Bennett(USA) 8:27.89	Dagmar Hase(GER) 8:29.91	Kirsten Vlieghuis(NED) 8:30.84
2000	Brooke Bennett(USA) 8:19.67	Jana Klochkova(UKR) 8:22.66	Kaitlin Sandeno(USA) 8:24.29
2004	Ai Shibata(JPN) 8:24.54	Laure Manaudou(FRA) 8:24.96	Diana Munz(USA) 8:26.61

1896–1964 Event not held

100m Breaststroke – Women

	GOLD	SILVER	BRONZE
1968	Djurdjica Bjedov(YUG) 1:15.8	Galina Prozumenschchikova(URS) 1:15.9 (1)	Sharon Wichman(USA) 1:16.1
1972	Catherine Carr(USA) 1:13.58	Galina Stepanova(URS) 1:14.99	Beverley Whitfield(AUS) 1:15.73
1976	Hannelore Anke(GDR) 1:11.16	Lubov Rusanova(URS) 1:13.04	Marina Kosheveya(URS) 1:13.30
1980	Ute Geweniger(GDR) 1:10.22	Elvira Vasilkova(URS) 1:10.41	Susanne Nielsson(DEN) 1:11.16
1984	Petra Van Staveren(NED) 1:09.88	Anne Ottenbrite(CAN) 1:10.69	Catherine Poirot(FRA) 1:10.70
1988	Tania Dangalakova(BUL) 1:07.95	Antoaneta Frankeva(BUL) 1:08.74	Silke Hörner(GDR) 1:08.83
1992	Yelena Rudkovskaya(EUN) 1:08.00	Anita Nall(USA) 1:08.17	Samantha Riley(AUS) 1:09.25
1996	Penny Heyns(RSA) 1:07.73	Amanda Beard(USA) 1:08.09	Samantha Riley(AUS) 1:09.18
2000	Megan Quann(USA) 1:07.05	Leisel Jones(AUS) 1:07.49	Penny Heyns(RSA) 1:07.55
2004	Xuejuan Luo(CHN) 1:06.64	Brooke Hanson(AUS) 1:07.15	Leisel Jones(AUS) 1:07.16

1896–1964 Event not held
(1) Later Stepanova

200m Breaststroke – Women

	GOLD	SILVER	BRONZE
1924	Lucy Morton(GBR) 3:33.2	Agnes Geraghty(USA) 3:34.0	Gladys Carson(GBR) 3:35.4
1928	Hilde Schrader(GER) 3:12.6	Mietje Baron(NED) 3:15.2	Lotte Mühe(GER) 3:17.6
1932	Claire Dennis(AUS) 3:06.3	Hideko Maehata(JPN) 3:06.4	Else Jacobsen(DEN) 3:07.1
1936	Hideko Maehata(JPN) 3:03.6	Martha Genenger(GER) 3:04.2	Inge Sörensen(DEN) 3:07.8
1948	Petronella van Vliet(NED) 2:57.2	Nancy Lyons(AUS) 2:57.7	Eva Novák(HUN) 3:00.2
1952	Eva Székely(HUN) 2:51.7 (1)	Eva Novák(HUN) 2:54.4	Helen Gordon(GBR) 2:57.6
1956	Ursula Happe(GER) 2:53.1 (2)	Eva Székely(HUN) 2:54.8	Eva-Maria ten Elsen(GER) 2:55.1
1960	Anita Lonsbrough(GBR) 2:49.5	Wiltrud Urselmann(GER) 2:50.0	Barbara Göbel(GER) 2:53.6
1964	Galina Prozumenschchikova(URS) 2:46.4	Claudia Kolb(USA) 2:47.6	Svetlana Babanina(URS) 2:48.6
1968	Sharon Wichman(USA) 2:44.4	Djurdjica Bjedov(YUG) 2:46.4	Galina Prozumenschchikova(URS) 2:47.0
1972	Beverley Whitfield(AUS) 2:41.7	Dana Schoenfield(USA) 2:42.05	Galina Stepanova(URS) 2:42.36
1976	Marina Kosheveya(URS) 2:33.35	Marina Yurchenia(URS) 2:36.08	Lubov Rusanova(URS) 2:36.22
1980	Lina Kachushite(URS) 2:29.54	Svetlana Varganova(URS) 2:29.61	Yulia Bogdanova(URS) 2:32.39
1984	Anne Ottenbrite(CAN) 2:30.38	Susan Rapp(USA) 2:31.15	Ingrid Lempereur(BEL) 2:31.40
1988	Silke Hörner(GDR) 2:26.71	Xiaomin Huang(CHN) 2:27.49	Antoaneta Frankeva(BUL) 2:28.34
1992	Kyoko Iwasaki(JPN) 2:26.65	Lin Li(CHN) 2:26.85	Anita Nall(USA) 2:26.88
1996	Penny Heyns(RSA) 2:25.41	Amanda Beard(USA) 2:25.75	Agnes Kovacs(HUN) 2:26.57
2000	Agnes Kovacs(HUN) 2:24.35	Kristy Kowal(USA) 2:24.56	Amanda Beard(USA) 2:25.35
2004	Amanda Beard(USA) 2:23.37	Leisel Jones(AUS) 2:23.60	Anne Poleska(POL) 2:25.82

1896–1920 Event not held
(1) Used butterfly stroke
(2) Used underwater technique

100m Backstroke – Women

	GOLD	SILVER	BRONZE
1924	Sybil Bauer(USA) 1:23.2	Phyllis Harding(GBR) 1:27.4	Aileen Riggin(USA) 1:28.2
1928	Marie Braun(NED) 1:22.0	Ellen King(GBR) 1:22.2	Joyce Cooper(GBR) 1:22.8
1932	Eleanor Holm(USA) 1:19.4	Philomena Mealing(AUS) 1:21.3	Valerie Davies(GBR) 1:22.5
1936	Dina Senff(NED) 1:18.9	Hendrika Mastenbroek(NED) 1:19.2	Alice Bridges(USA) 1:19.4
1948	Karen Harup(DEN) 1:14.4	Suzanne Zimmermann(USA) 1:16.0	Judy Davies(AUS) 1:16.7
1952	Joan Harrison(RSA) 1:14.3	Geertje Wielema(NED) 1:14.5	Jean Stewart(NZL) 1:15.8
1956	Judy Grinham(GBR) 1:12.9	Carin Cone(USA) 1:12.9	Margaret Edwards(GBR) 1:13.1
1960	Lynn Burke(USA) 1:09.3	Natalie Steward(GBR) 1:10.8	Satoko Tanaka(JPN) 1:11.4
1964	Cathy Ferguson(USA) 1:07.7	Cristine Caron(FRA) 1:07.9	Virginia Duenkel(USA) 1:08.0
1968	Kaye Hall(USA) 1:06.2	Elaine Tanner(CAN) 1:06.7	Jane Swaggerty(USA) 1:08.1
1972	Melissa Belote(USA) 1:05.78	Andrea Gyarmati(HUN) 1:06.26	Susie Atwood(USA) 1:06.34

1976	Ulrike Richter(GDR) 1:01.83	Birgit Treiber(GDR) 1:03.41	Nancy Garapick(CAN) 1:03.71
1980	Rica Reinisch(GDR) 1:00.86	Ina Kleber(GDR) 1:02.07	Petra Reidel(GDR) 1:02.64
1984	Theresa Andrews(USA) 1:02.55	Betsy Mitchell(USA) 1:02.63	Jolanda De Rover(NED) 1:02.91
1988	Kristin Otto(GDR) 1:00.89	Krisztina Egerszegi(HUN) 1:01.56	Cornelia Sirch(GDR) 1:01.57
1992	Krysztina Egerszegi(HUN) 1:00.68	Tunde Szabo(HUN) 1:01.14	Lea Loveless(USA) 1:01.43
1996	Beth Botsford(USA) 1:01.19	Whitney Hedgepeth(USA) 1:01.47	Marianne Kriel(RSA) 1:02.12
2000	Diana Mocanu(ROM) 1:00.21	Mai Nakamura(JPN) 1:00.55	Nina Zhivanevskaya(ESP) 1:00.89
2004	Natalie Coughlin(USA) 1:00.37	Kirsty Coventry(ZIM) 1:00.50	Laure Manaudou(FRA) 1:00.88

1896–1920 Event not held

200m Backstroke – Women

	GOLD	SILVER	BRONZE
1968	Lillian Watson(USA) 2:24.8	Elaine Tanner(CAN) 2:27.4	Kaye Hall(USA) 2:28.9
1972	Melissa Belote(USA) 2:19.19	Susie Atwood(USA) 2:20.38	Donna Marie Gurr(CAN) 2:23.22
1976	Ulrike Richter(GDR) 2:13.43	Birgit Treiber(GDR) 2:14.97	Nancy Garapick(CAN) 2:15.60
1980	Rica Reinisch(GDR) 2:11.77	Cornelia Polit(GDR) 2:13.75	Birgit Treiber(GDR) 2:14.14
1984	Jolanda De Rover(NED) 2:12.38	Amy White(USA) 2:13.04	Aneta Patrascoiu(ROM) 2:13.29
1988	Krysztina Egerszegi(HUN) 2:09.29	Kathrin Zimmermann(GDR) 2:10.61	Cornelia Sirch(GDR) 2:11.45
1992	Krysztina Egerszegi(HUN) 2:07.06	Dagmar Hase(GER) 2:09.46	Nicole Stevenson(AUS) 2:10.20
1996	Krysztina Eegrszegi(HUN) 2:07.83	Whitney Hedgepeth(USA) 2:11.98	Cathleen Rund(GER) 2:12.06
2000	Diana Mocanu(ROM) 2:08.16	Roxana Maracineanu(FRA) 2:10.25	Miki Nakao(JPN) 2:11.05
2004	Kirsty Coventry(ZIM) 2:09.19	Stanislava Komarova(RUS)2:09.72	Reiko Nakamura(JPN) 2:09.88
			3. Antje Buschschulte(GER) 2:09.88

1896–1964 Event not held

100m Butterfly – Women

	GOLD	SILVER	BRONZE
1956	Shelley Mann(USA) 1:11.0	Nancy Ramey(USA) 1:11.9	Mary Sears(USA) 1:14.4
1960	Carolyn Schuler(USA) 1:09.5	Marianne Heemskerk(NED) 1:10.4	Janice Andrew(AUS) 1:12.2
1964	Sharon Stouder(USA) 1:04.7	Ada Kok(NED) 1:05.6	Kathleen Ellis(USA) 1:06.0
1968	Lynette McClements(AUS) 1:05.5	Ellie Daniel(USA) 1:05.8	Susan Shields(USA) 1:06.2
1972	Mayumi Aoki(JPN) 1:03.34	Roswitha Beier(GDR) 1:03.61	Andrea Gyarmati(HUN) 1:03.73
1976	Kornelia Ender(GDR) 1:00.13	Andrea Pollack(GDR) 1:00.98	Wendy Bognoli(USA) 1:01.17
1980	Caren Metschuck(GDR) 1:00.42	Andrea Pollack(GDR) 1:00.90	Christiane Knacke(GDR) 1:01.44
1984	Mary Meagher(USA) 59.26	Jenna Johnson(USA) 1:00.19	Karin Seick(FRG) 1:00.36
1988	Kristin Otto(GDR) 59.00	Birte Weigang(GDR) 59.45	Qian Hong(CHN) 59.52
1992	Qian Hong(CHN) 58.62	Chrissy Ahmann-Leighton(USA) 58.74	Catherine Plewinski(FRA) 59.01
1996	Amy van Dyken(USA) 59.1	Limin Liu(CHN) 59.14	Angel Martino(USA) 59.23
2000	Inge de Bruijn(NED) 56.61	Martina Moravcova(SVK) 57.97	Dara Torres(USA) 58.20
2004	Petria Thomas(AUS) 57.72	Otylia Jedrzejczak(POL) 57.84	Inge de Bruijn(NED) 57.99

1896–1952 Event not held

200m Butterfly – Women

	GOLD	SILVER	BRONZE
1968	Ada Kok(NED) 2:24.7	Helga Lindner(GDR) 2:24.8	Ellie Daniel(USA) 2:25.9
1972	Karen Moe(USA) 2:15.57	Lynn Colella(USA) 2:16.34	Ellie Daniel(USA) 2:26.74
1976	Andrea Pollack(GDR) 2:11.41	Ulrike Tauber(GDR) 2:12.45	Rosemarie Gabriel(GDR) 2:12.86
1980	Ines Geissler(GDR) 2:10.44	Sybille Schönrock(GDR) 2:10.45	Michelle Ford(AUS) 2:11.66
1984	Mary Meagher(USA) 2:06.90	Karen Phillips(AUS) 2:10.56	Ina Beyermann(FRG) 2:11.91
1988	Kahleen Nord(GDR) 2:09.51	Birte Weigang(GDR) 2:09.91	Mary Meagher(USA) 2:10.80
1992	Summer Sanders(USA) 2:08.67	Xiaohong Wang(CHN) 2:09.01	Susan O'Neil(AUS) 2:09.03
1996	Susan O'Neil(AUS) 2:07.76	Petria Thomas(AUS) 2:09.82	Michelle Smith(IRL) 2:09.91
2000	Misty Hyman(USA) 2:05.88	Susie O'Neill(AUS) 2:06.58	Petria Thomas(AUS) 2:07.12
2004	Otylia Jedrzejczak(POL) 2:06.05	Petria Thomas(AUS) 2:06.36	Yuko Nakanishi(JPN) 2:08.04

1896–1964 Event not held

200m Individual Medley – Women

	GOLD	SILVER	BRONZE
1968	Claudia Kolb(USA) 2:24.7	Susan Pedersen(USA) 2:28.8	Jan Henne(USA) 2:31.4
1972	Shane Gould(AUS) 2:23.07	Kornelia Ender(GDR) 2:23.59	Lynn Vidali(USA) 2:24.06
1984	Tracy Caulkins(USA) 2:12.64	Nancy Hogshead(USA) 2:15.17	Michele Pearson(AUS) 2:15.92
1988	Daniela Hunger(GDR) 2:12.59	Yelena Dendeberova(URS) 2:13.31	Noemi Ildiko Lung(ROM) 2:14.85
1992	Lin Li(CHN) 2:11.65	Summer Sanders(USA) 2:11.91	Daniela Hunger(GDR) 2:13.62
1996	Michelle Smith(IRL) 2:13.93	Marianne Limpert(CAN) 2:14.35	Lin Li(CHN) 2:14.74
2000	Jana Klochkova(UKR) 2:10.68	Beatrice Caslaru(ROM) 2:12.57	Cristina Teuscher(USA) 2:13.32
2004	Yana Klochkova(UKR) 2:11.14	Amanda Beard(USA) 2:11.70	Kirsty Coventry(ZIM) 2:12.72

1896–1964, 1976–1980 Event not held

400m Individual Medley – Women

	GOLD	SILVER	BRONZE
1964	Donna De Varona(USA) 5:18.7	Sharon Finneran(USA) 5:24.1	Martha Randall(USA) 5:24.1
1968	Claudia Kolb(USA) 5:08.5	Lynn Vidali(USA) 5:22.2	Sabine Steinbach(GDR) 5:25.3
1972	Gail Neall(AUS) 5:02.97	Leslie Cliff(CAN) 5:03.57	Novella Calligaris(ITA) 5:03.99

1976	Ulrike Tauber(GDR) 4:42.77	Cheryl Gibson(CAN) 4:48.10	Becky Smith(CAN) 4:50.48
1980	Petra Schneider(GDR) 4:36.29	Sharron Davies(GBR) 4:46.83	Agnieszka Czopek(POL) 4:48.17
1984	Tracy Caulkins(USA) 4:39.24	Suzanne Landells(AUS) 4:48.30	Petra Zindler(FRG) 4:48.57
1988	Janet Evans(USA) 4:37.76	Noemi Ildiko Lung(ROM) 4:39.46	Daniela Hunger(GDR) 4:39.76
1992	Krysztina Egerszegi(HUN) 4:36.54	Lin Li(CHN) 4:36.73	Summer Sanders(USA) 4:37.58
1996	Michelle Smith(IRL) 4:39.18	Allison Wagner(USA) 4:42.03	Krysztina Egerszegi(HUN) 4:42.53
2000	Jana Klochkova(UKR) 4:33.59	Yasuko Tajima(JPN) 4:35.96	Beatrice Caslaru(ROM) 4:37.18
2004	Yana Klochkova(UKR) 4:34.83	Kaitlin Sandeno(USA) 4:34.95	Georgina Bardach(ARG)4:37.51

1896–1960 Event not held

4 x 100m Freestyle Relay – Women

	GOLD	SILVER	BRONZE
1912	GREAT BRITAIN 5:52.8	GERMANY 6:04.6	AUSTRIA 6:17.0
1920	UNITED STATES 5:11.6	GREAT BRITAIN 5:40.8	SWEDEN 5:43.6
1924	UNITED STATES 4:58.8	GREAT BRITAIN 5:17.0	SWEDEN 5:35.6
1928	UNITED STATES 4:47.6	GREAT BRITAIN 5:02.8	SOUTH AFRICA 5:13.4
1932	UNITED STATES 4:38.0	NETHERLANDS 4:47.5	GREAT BRITAIN 4:52.4
1936	NETHERLANDS 4:36.0	GERMANY 4:36.8	UNITED STATES 4:40.2
1948	UNITED STATES 4:29.2	DENMARK 4:29.6	NETHERLANDS 4:31.6
1952	HUNGARY 4:24.4	NETHERLANDS 4:29.0	UNITED STATES 4:30.1
1956	AUSTRALIA 4:17.1	UNITED STATES 4:19.2	SOUTH AFRICA 4:25.7
1960	UNITED STATES 4:08.9	AUSTRALIA 4:11.3	GERMANY 4:19.7
1964	UNITED STATES 4:03.8	AUSTRALIA 4:06.9	NETHERLANDS 4:12.0
1968	UNITED STATES 4:02.5	GDR 4:05.7	CANADA 4:07.2
1972	UNITED STATES 3:55.19	GDR 3:55.55	FRG 3:57.93
1976	UNITED STATES 3:44.82	GDR 3:45.50	CANADA 3:48.81
1980	GDR 3:42.71	SWEDEN 3:48.93	NETHERLANDS 3:49.51
1984	UNITED STATES 3:43.43	NETHERLANDS 3:44.40	FRG 3:45.56
1988	GDR 3:40.63	NETHERLANDS 3:43.39	UNITED STATES 3:44.25
1992	UNITED STATES 3:39.46	CHINA 3:40.12	GERMANY 3:41.60
1996	UNITED STATES 3:39.29	CHINA 3:40.48	GERMANY 3:41.48
2000	UNITED STATES 3:36.61	NETHERLANDS 3:39.83	SWEDEN 3:40.30
2004	AUSTRALIA 3:35.94	UNITED STATES 3:36.39	NETHERLANDS 3:37.59

1896–1908 Event not held

4 x 200m Freestyle Relay – Women

	GOLD	SILVER	BRONZE
1996	UNITED STATES 7:59.87	GERMANY 8:01.55	AUSTRALIA 8:05.47
2000	UNITED STATES 7:57.80	AUSTRALIA 7:58.52	GERMANY 7:58.64
2004	UNITED STATES 7:53.42	CHINA 7:55.97	GERMANY 7:57.35

1896–1992 Event not held

4 x 100m Medley Relay – Women

	GOLD	SILVER	BRONZE
1960	UNITED STATES 4:41.1	AUSTRALIA 4:45.9	GERMANY 4:47.6
1964	UNITED STATES 4:33.9	NETHERLANDS 4:37.0	SOVIET UNION 4:39.2
1968	UNITED STATES 4:28.3	AUSTRALIA 4:30.0	FRG 4:36.4
1972	UNITED STATES 4:20.75	GDR 4:24.91	FRG 4:26.46
1976	GDR 4:06.95	UNITED STATES 4:14.55	CANADA 4:15.22
1980	GDR 4:06.67	GREAT BRITAIN 4:12.24	SOVIET UNION 4:13.61
1984	UNITED STATES 4:08.34	FRG 4:11.97	CANADA 4:12.98
1988	GDR 4:03.74	UNITED STATES 4:07.90	CANADA 4:10.49
1992	UNITED STATES 4:02.54	GERMANY 4:05.19	UNIFIED TEAM 4:06.44
1996	UNITED STATES 4:02.88	AUSTRALIA 4:05.08	CHINA 4:07.34
2000	UNITED STATES 3:58.30	AUSTRALIA 4:01.59	JAPAN 4:04.16
2004	AUSTRALIA 3:57.32	UNITED STATES 3:59.12	GERMANY 4:00.72

1896–1956 Event not held

DIVING

Springboard Diving – Women

	GOLD	SILVER	BRONZE
1920	Aileen Riggin(USA) 539.9	Helen Wainwright(USA) 534.8	Thelma Payne(USA) 534.1
1924	Elizabeth Becker(USA) 474.5	Aileen Riggin(USA) 460.4	Caroline Fletcher(USA) 434.4
1928	Helen Meany(USA) 78.62	Dorothy Poynton(USA) 75.62	Georgia Coleman(USA) 73.78
1932	Georgia Coleman(USA) 87.52	Katherine Rawls(USA) 82.56	Jane Fauntz(USA) 82.12
1936	Majorie Gestring(USA) 89.27	Katherine Rawls(USA) 88.35	Dorothy Poynton-Hill(USA) 82.36
1948	Victoria Draves(USA) 108.74	Zoe Ann Olsen(USA) 108.23	Patricia Elsener(USA) 101.30
1952	Patricia McCormick(USA) 147.30	Madeleine MoreauFRA) 139.34	Zoe Ann Jensen(USA) 127.57
1956	Patricia McCormick(USA) 142.36	Jeanne Stunyo(USA) 125.89	Irene MacDonald(CAN) 121.40
1960	Ingrid Krämer(GER) 155.81	Paula Myers-Pope(USA) 141.24	Elizabeth Ferris(GBR) 139.09

1964	Ingrid Krämer-Engel(GER) 145.00	Jeanne Collier(USA) 138.36	Mary Willard(USA) 138.18
1968	Sue Gossick(USA) 150.77	Tamara Pogozheva(URS) 145.30	Keala O'Sullivan(USA) 145.23
1972	Micki King(USA) 450.03	Ulrika Knape(SWE) 434.19	Marina Janicke(GDR) 430.92
1976	Jennifer Chandler(USA) 506.19	Christa Kohler(GDR) 469.41	Cynthia McIngvale(USA) 466.83
1980	Irina Kalinina(URS) 725.910	Martina Proeber(GDR) 698.895	Karin Guthke(GDR) 685.245
1984	Sylvie Bernier(CAN) 530.70	Kelly McCormick(USA) 527.46	Christina Seufert(USA) 517.62
1988	Min Gao(CHN) 580.23	Qing Li(CHN) 534.33	Kelly Anne McCormick(USA) 533.19
1992	Min Gao(CHN) 572.400	Irina Laschko(EUN) 514.140	Brita Baldus(GER) 503.070
1996	Mingxia Fu(CHN) 547.68	Irina Laschko(RUS) 512.19	Annie Pelletier(CAN) 509.64
2000	Mingxia Fu(CHN) 609.42	Jungjing Guo(CHN) 597.81	Dörte Lindner(GER) 574.35
2004	Jingjing Guo(CHN) 633.15	Minxia Wu(CHN) 612.00	Yulia Pakhalina(RUS) 610.62

1896–1912 Event not held

Synchronized Springboard – Women

	GOLD	SILVER	BRONZE
2000	RUSSIA 332.64	CHINA 321.60	UKRAINE 290.34
2004	CHINA 352.14	RUSSIA 340.92	CANADA 327.78

1896–1996 Event not held

Platform Diving – Women

	GOLD	SILVER	BRONZE
1912	Greta Johnson(SWE) 39.9	Lisa Regnell(SWE) 36.0	Isabelle White(GBR) 34.0
1920	Stefani Fryland-Clausen(DEN) 34.6	Eileen Armstrong(GBR) 33.3	Eva Ollivier(SWE) 33.3
1924	Caroline Smith(USA) 10.5	Elizabeth Becker(UsA) 11.0	Hjördis Töpel(SWE) 15.5
1928	Elizabeth Pinkston(USA) 31.6	Georgia Coleman(USA) 30.6	Lala Sjöqvist(SWE) 29.2
1932	Dorothy Poynton(USA) 40.26	Georgia Coleman(USA) 35.56	Marion Roper(USA) 35.22
1936	Dorothy Poynton-Hill(USA) 33.93	Velma Dunn(USA) 33.63	Käthe Köhler(GER) 33.43
1948	Victoria Draves(USA) 68.87	Patricia Elsener(USA) 66.28	Birte Christoffersen(DEN) 66.04
1952	Patricia McCormick(USA) 79.37	Paula Myers(USA) 71.63	Juno Irwin(USA) 70.49
1956	Patricia McCormick(USA) 84.85	Juno Irwin(USA) 81.64	Paula Myers(USA) 81.58
1960	Ingrid Krämer(GER) 91.28	Paula Myers-Pope(USA) 88.94	Ninel Krutova(URS) 86.99
1964	Lesley Bush(USA) 99.80	Ingrid Krämer-Engel(GER) 98.45	Galina Alekseyeva(URS) 97.60
1968	Milena Duchkova(TCH) 109.59	Natalia Lobanova(URS) 105.14	Ann Peterson(USA) 101.11
1972	Ulrika Knape(SWE) 390.00	Milena Duchkova(TCH) 370.92	Marina Janicke(GDR) 360.54
1976	Elena Vaytsekhovskaya(URS) 406.59	Ulrika Knape(SWE) 402.60	Deborah Wilson(USA) 401.07
1980	Martina Jäschke(GDR) 596.250	Servard Emirzyan(URS) 576.465	Liana Tsotadze(URS) 575.925
1984	Jihong Zhou(CHN) 435.51	Michele Mitchell(USA) 431.19	Wendy Wyland(USA) 422.07
1988	Yanmei Xu(CHN) 445.20	Michele Mitchell(USA) 436.95	Wendy Williams(USA) 400.44
1992	Mingxia Fu(CHN) 461.430	Yelena Mirochina(EUN) 411.630	Mary Ellen Clark(USA) 401.910
1996	Mingxia Fu(CHN) 521.58	Annika Walter(GER) 429.22	Mary Ellen Clark(USA) 472.95
2000	Laura Wilkinson(USA) 543.75	Na Li(CHN) 542.01	Anne Montminy(CAN) 540.15
2004	Chantelle Newbery(AUS) 590.31	Lishi Lao(CHN) 576.30	Loudy Tourky(AUS) 561.66

1896–1908 Event not held

Synchronized Platform – Women

	GOLD	SILVER	BRONZE
2000	CHINA 345.12	CANADA 312.03	AUSTRALIA 301.50
2004	CHINA 336.90	RUSSIA 330.84	AUSTRALIA 309.30

1896–1996 Event not held

Synchronised Swimming Solo – Women

	GOLD	SILVER	BRONZE
1984	Tracie Ruiz(USA) 198.467	Carolyn Waldo(CAN) 195.300	Miwako Motoyoshi(JPN) 187.050
1988	Carolyn Waldo(CAN) 200.150	Tracie Ruiz-Conforto(USA) 197.633	Miwako Motoyoshi(JPN) 191.850
1992	Kristen Babb-Sprague(USA) 191.848	Fumiko Okuno(JPN) 187.056	Sylvia Frechette(CAN) d.n.a.

1896–1980, 1996–2004 Event not held

Synchronised Duet – Women

	GOLD	SILVER	BRONZE
1984	UNITED STATES 195.584	CANADA 194.234	JAPAN 187.992
1988	CANADA 197.717	UNITED STATES 197.284	JAPAN 190.159
1992	UNITED STATES 192.175	CANADA 189.394	JAPAN 186.868
1996	UNITED STATES 99.720	CANADA 98.367	JAPAN 97.753
2000	RUSSIA 99.580	JAPAN 98.650	FRANCE 97.437
2004	RUSSIA 99.334	JAPAN 98.417	UNITED STATES 96.918

1896–1980 Event not held

Synchronised Swimming Team – Women

	GOLD	SILVER	BRONZE
2000	RUSSIA 99.146	JAPAN 98.860	CANADA 97.357
2004	RUSSIA 99.501	JAPAN 98.501	UNITED STATES 97.418

1896–1996 Event not held

SWIMMING – DISCONTINUED EVENTS

	GOLD	SILVER	BRONZE
100m Freestyle (Sailors) – Men			
1896	Ioannis Maloknis(GRE) 2:20.4	Spiridon Khasapis(GRE) n.t.a.	Dimitrios Drivas(GRE) n.t.a.
200m Obstacle Event – Men			
1900	Frederick Lane(AUS) 2:38.4	Otto Wahle(AUT) 2:40.0	Peter Kemp(GBR) 2:47.4
400m Breaststroke – Men			
1904	Georg Zacharias(GER) 7:23.6	Walter Brack(GER) 20m	Jamison Hardy(USA) d.n.a.
1912	Walter Bathe(GER) 6:29.6	Thor Henning(SWE) 6:35.6	Percy Courtman(GBR) 6:36.4
1920	Hakan Malmroth(SWE) 6:31.8	Thor Henning(SWE) 6:45.2	Arvo Aaltonen(FIN) 6:48.0
880 Yards Freestyle – Men			
1904	Emil Rausch(GER) 13:11.4	Francis Gailey(USA) 13:23.4	Géza Kiss(HUN) n.t.a.
4,000m Freestyle – Men			
1900	John Jarvis(GBR) 58:24.0	Zoltán Halmay(HUN) 1:08:55.4	Louis Martin(FRA) 1:13.08.4
Underwater Swimming – Men			
1900	Charles de Vendeville(FRA) 188.4	André Six(FRA) 185.4	Peder Lykkeberg(DEN) 147.0
Plunge for Distance – Men			
1904	Paul Dickey(USA) 19.05m	Edgar Adams(USA) 17.53m	Leo Goodwin(USA) 17.37m
200m Team Swimming – Men			
1900	GERMANY 32pts	FRANCE 51	FRANCE 61
4 x 50 Yards Relay – Men			
1904	UNITED STATES (New York AC) 2:04.6	UNITED STATES(Chicago AC) n.t.a.	United States (Missouri AC) n.t.a.
Plain High Diving – Men			
1912	Erik Adlerz(SWE) 40.0	Hjalmar Johansson(SWE) 39.3	John Jansson(SWE) 39.1
1920	Arvid Wallmann(SWE) 183.5	Nils Skoglund(SWE) 183.0	John Jansson(SWE) 175.0
1924	Richmond Eve(AUS) 160.0	John Jansson(SWE) 157.0	Harold Clarke(GBR) 158.0

WATER POLO

Men

	GOLD	SILVER	BRONZE
1900(1)	GREAT BRITAIN	BELGIUM	FRANCE
1904(1)	UNITED STATES	UNITED STATES	UNITED STATES
1908	GREAT BRITAIN	BELGIUM	SWEDEN
1912	GREAT BRITAIN	SWEDEN	BELGIUM
1920	GREAT BRITAIN	BELGIUM	SWEDEN
1924	FRANCE	BELGIUM	UNITED STATES
1928	GERMANY	HUNGARY	FRANCE
1932	HUNGARY	GERMANY	UNITED STATES
1936	HUNGARY	GERMANY	BELGIUM
1948	ITALY	HUNGARY	NETHERLANDS
1952	HUNGARY	YUGOSLAVIA	ITALY
1956	HUNGARY	YUGOSLAVIA	SOVIET UNION
1960	ITALY	SOVIET UNION	HUNGARY
1964	HUNGARY	YUGOSLAVIA	SOVIET UNION
1968	YUGOSLAVIA	SOVIET UNION	HUNGARY
1972	SOVIET UNION	HUNGARY	UNITED STATES
1976	HUNGARY	ITALY	NETHERLANDS
1980	SOVIET UNION	YUGOSLAVIA	HUNGARY
1984	YUGOSLAVIA	UNITED STATES	FRG
1988	YUGOSLAVIA	UNITED STATES	SOVIET UNION
1992	ITALY	SPAIN	UNIFIED TEAM
1996	SPAIN	CROATIA	ITALY
2000	HUNGARY	RUSSIA	YUGOSLAVIA
2004	HUNGARY	SERBIA/MONTENEGRO	RUSSIA

1896, 1906 Event not held
(1) Clubs represented their countries

Women

	GOLD	SILVER	BRONZE
2000	AUSTRALIA	UNITED STATES	RUSSIA
2004	ITALY	GREECE	UNITED STATES

1896–1996 Event not held

TABLE TENNIS

Singles – Men

	GOLD	SILVER	BRONZE
1988	Nam-Kyu Yoo(KOR)	Ki-Taik Kim(KOR)	Erik Lindh(SWE)
1992	Jan-Ove Waldner(SWE)	Jean-Philippe Gatien(FRA)	Wenge Ma(CHN) (1)
			Taek-Soo Kim(KOR) (1)
1996	Guoliang Liu(CHN)	Wang Tao(CHN)	Jörg Rosskoff(GER)
2000	Linghui Kong(CHN)	Jan-Ove Waldner(SWE)	Guoliang Liu(CHN)
2004	.Seung-Min Ryu(KOR)	Hao Wang(CHN)	Liqin Wang(CHN)

1896–1984 Event not held
(1) No play-off, two bronze medals awarded

Doubles – Men

	GOLD	SILVER	BRONZE
1988	CHINA	YUGOSLAVIA	KOREA
1992	CHINA	GERMANY	KOREA (1)
			PRK (1)
1996	CHINA	CHINA	KOREA
2000	CHINA	CHINA	FRANCE
2004	CHINA	HONG KONG	DENMARK

1896–1984 Event not held
(1) No play-off, two bronze medals awarded

Singles – Women

	GOLD	SILVER	BRONZE
1988	Chen Jing(CHN)	Huifen Li(CHN)	Jiao Zhimin(CHN)
1992	Yaping Deng(CHN)	Qiao Hong(CHN)	Jung-Hwa Hyung(KOR) (1)
			Bun-Hui Li(PRK) (1)
1996	Yaping Deng(CHN)	Jing Li(TPE)	Qiao Hong(CHN)
2000	Nan Wang(CHN)	Ju Li(CHN)	Jing Li(TPE)
2004	Yining Zhang(CHN)	Hyang-Mi Kim(PRK)	Kyung-Ah Kim(KOR)

1896–1984 Event not held
(1) No play-off, two bronze medals awarded

Doubles – Women

	GOLD	SILVER	BRONZE
1988	KOREA	CHINA	YUGOSLAVIA
1992	CHINA	CHINA	KOREA (1)
			PRK (1)
1996	CHINA	CHINA	KOREA
2000	CHINA	CHINA	KOREA
2004	CHINA	KOREA	CHINA

1896–1984 Event not held
(1) No play-off, two bronze medals awarded

TAEKWONDO

Up to 58kg – Men

	GOLD	SILVER	BRONZE
2000	Michail Mouroutsos(GRE)	Gabriel Esparza(ESP)	Chih-Hsiung Huang(TPE)
2004	Mu Yen Chu(TPE)	Oscar Salazar Blanco(MEX)	Tamer Bayoumi(EGY)

1896–1996 Event not held

Up to 68kg – Men

	GOLD	SILVER	BRONZE
2000	Steven Lopez(USA)	Joon-Sik Sin(KOR)	Hadi Saeibonehkohal(IRI)
2004	Hadi Saei Bonehkohal(IRI)	Chih Hsiung Huang (TPE)	Myeong-Seob Song (KOR)

1896–1996 Event not held

Up to 80kg – Men
	GOLD	SILVER	BRONZE
2000	Angel Fuentes(CUB)	Faissal Ebnoutalib(GER)	Victor Garibay(MEX)
2004	Steven Lopez(USA)	Bahri Tanrikulu(TUR)	Yossef Karami(IRI)

1896–1996 Event not held

Over 80kg – Men
	GOLD	SILVER	BRONZE
2000	Kyong-Hun Kim(KOR)	Daniel Trenton(AUS)	Pascal Gentil(FRA)
2004	Dae Sung Moon(KOR)	Alexandros Nikolaidis(GRE)	Pascal Gentil(FRA)

1896–1996 Event not held

Up to 49kg – Women
	GOLD	SILVER	BRONZE
2000	Lauren Burns(AUS)	Urbia Rodriguez(CUB)	Shu-Ju Chi(TPE)
2004	.Shih Hsin Chen(TPE)	Yanelis Labrada Diaz(CUB)	Yaowapa Boorapolchai(THA)

1896–1996 Event not held

Up to 57kg – Women
	GOLD	SILVER	BRONZE
2000	Jae-Eun Jung(KOR)	Hieu Ngan Tran(VIE)	Hamide Bikcin(TUR)
2004	Ji Won Jang(KOR)	Nia Abdallah(USA)	Iridia Salazar Blanco(MEX)

1896–1996 Event not held

Up to 67kg – Women
	GOLD	SILVER	BRONZE
2000	Sun-Hee Lee(CHN)	Trude Gundersen(NOR)	Yoriko Okamoto(JPN)
2004	Wei Luo(CHN)	Elisavet Mystakidou(GRE)	Kyung Sun Hwang(KOR)

1896–1996 Event not held

Over 67kg – Women
	GOLD	SILVER	BRONZE
2000	Zhong Chen(CHN)	Natalya Ivanova(RUS)	Dominique Bosshart(CAN)
2004	Zhong Chen(CHN)	Myriam Bavarel(FRA)	Adriana Carmona(VEN)

1896–1996 Event not held

TENNIS

Singles – Men
	GOLD	SILVER	BRONZE
1896	John Boland(GBR)	Dionysios Kasdaglis(GRE)	Momcilló Tapavica(HUN)
			Konstantinos Paspatis(GRE)
1900	Hugh Doherty(GBR)	Harold Mahoney(GBR)	Reginald Doherty(GBR)
			Arthur Norris(GBR)
1904	Beals Wright(USA)	Robert LeRoy(USA)	Edgar Leonard(USA)
			Alphonzo Bell(USA)
1906	Max Décugis(FRA)	Maurice Germot(FRA)	Zdenek Zemla(BOH)
1908	Josiah Ritchie(GBR)	Otto Froitzheim(GER)	Wilberforce Eves(GBR)
1908	Wentworth Gore(GBR)	George Caridia(GBR)	Josiah Ritchie(GBR)
1912	Charles Winslow(RSA)	Harold Kitson(RSA)	Oscar Kreuzer(GER)
1912	André Gobert(FRA)	Charles Dixon(GBR)	Anthony Wilding(NZL)
1920	Louis Raymond(RSA)	Ichiya Kumagae(JPN)	Charles Winslow(GBR)
1924	Vincent Reynolds(USA)	Henri Cochet(FRA)	Umberto De Morpurgo(ITA)
1988	Miloslav Mecir(TCH)	Tim Mayotte(USA)	Stefan Edberg(SWE)
			Brad Gilbert(USA)
1992	Marc Rosset(SUI)	Jordi Arrese(ESP)	Goran Ivanisevic(CRO)
			Andrei Cherkasov(EUN)
1996	Andre Agassi(USA)	Sergi Bruguera(ESP)	Leander Paes(IND)
2000	Yevgeni Kafelnikov(RUS)	Thomas Haas(GER)	Arnaud di Pasquale(FRA)
2004	Nicolás Massú(CHI)	Mardy Fish(USA)	Fernando Gonzalez(CHI)

1928–84 Event not held

Doubles – Men
	GOLD	SILVER	BRONZE
1896	GBR/GERMANY	GREECE	GREAT BRITAIN/AUSTRALIA
1900	GREAT BRITAIN	USA/FRANCE	FRANCE
			GREAT BRITAIN
1904	UNITED STATES	UNITED STATES	UNITED STATES
			UNITED STATES
1906	FRANCE	GREECE	BOHEMIA

1908	GREAT BRITAIN	GREAT BRITAIN	GREAT BRITAIN
1908	GREAT BRITAIN	GREAT BRITAIN	SWEDEN
1912	SOUTH AFRICA	AUSTRIA	FRANCE
1912	FRANCE	SWEDEN	GREAT BRITAIN
1920	GREAT BRITAIN	JAPAN	FRANCE
1924	UNITED STATES	FRANCE	FRANCE
1988	UNITED STATES	SPAIN	CZECHOSLOVAKIA
			SWEDEN
1992	GERMANY	SOUTH AFRICA	CROATIA
			ARGENTINA
1996	AUSTRALIA	GREAT BRITAIN	GERMANY
2000	CANADA	AUSTRALIA	SPAIN
2004	CHILE	GERMANY	CROATIA

1928–84 Event not held

Mixed Doubles

	GOLD	SILVER	BRONZE
1900	GREAT BRITAIN	FRANCE/GBR	BOHEMIA/GBR
			UNITED STATES/GBR
1906	FRANCE	GREECE	GREECE
1912	GERMANY	SWEDEN	FRANCE
1912	GREAT BRITAIN	GREAT BRITAIN	SWEDEN
1920	FRANCE	GREAT BRITAIN	CZECHOSLOVAKIA
1924	UNITED STATES	UNITED STATES	NETHERLANDS

1896, 1904, 1908, 1928–2004 Event not held

Singles – Women

	GOLD	SILVER	BRONZE
1900	Charlotte Cooper(GBR)	Hélène Prévost(FRA)	Marion Jones(USA)
			Hedwiga Rosenbaumova(BOH)
1906	Esmee Simiriotou(GRE)	Sophia Marinou(GRE)	Euphrosine Paspati(GRE)
1908	Dorothea Chambers(GBR)	Dorothy Boothby(GBR)	Joan Winch(GBR)
1908(1)	Gwen Eastlake-Smith(GBR)	Angela Greene(GBR)	Märtha Adlerstrahle(SWE)
1912	Marguerite Broquedis(FRA)	Dora Köring(GER)	Molla Bjurstedt(NOR)
1912(1)	Ethel Hannam(GBR)	Thora Castenschoid(DEN)	Mabel Parton(GBR)
1920	Suzanne Lenglen(FRA)	Dorothy Holman(GBR)	Kitty McKane(GBR)
1924	Helen Wills(USA)	Julie Vlasto(FRA)	Kitty McKane(GBR)
1988	Steffi Graf(FRG)	Gabriela Sabatini(ARG)	Zina Garrison(USA)
			Manuela Maleyeva(BUL)
1992	Jennifer Capriati(USA)	Steffi Graf(GER)	Mary-Jo Fernandez(USA)
			Arantxa Sanchez-Vicario(ESP)
1996	Lindsay Davenport(USA)	Arantxa Sanchez-Vicario(ESP)	Jana Novotna(CZE)
2000	Venus Williams(USA)	Yelena Dementyeva(RUS)	Monica Seles(USA)
2004	Justine Henin-Hardenne(BEL)	Amelie Mauresmo(FRA)	Alicia Molik(AUS)

1896, 1904, 1928–84 Event not held

(1) Indoor tournament

Doubles – Women

	GOLD	SILVER	BRONZE
1920	GREAT BRITAIN	GREAT BRITAIN	FRANCE
1924	UNITED STATES	GREAT BRITAIN	GREAT BRITAIN
1988	UNITED STATES	CZECHOSLOVAKIA	AUSTRALIA
			FRG
1992	UNITED STATES	SPAIN	AUSTRALIA
			UNIFIED TEAM
1996	UNITED STATES	CZECH REPUBLIC	SPAIN
2000	UNITED STATES	NETHERLANDS	BELGIUM
2004	CHINA	SPAIN	ARGENTINA

1896–1912, 1928–84 Event not held

TRIATHLON

Men

	GOLD	SILVER	BRONZE
2000	Simon Whitfield(CAN) 1h 48:24.02	Stephan Vuckovic(GER) 1h 48:37.58	Jan Rehula(CZE) 1h 48:46.64
2004	Hamish Carter(NZL) 1h:51:07.73	Bevan Docherty(NZL) 1h:51:15.60	Sven Riederer(SUI) 1h:51:33.26

1896–1996 Event not held

Women

	GOLD	SILVER	BRONZE
2000	Brigitte McMahon(SUI) 2h 00:40.52	Michelle Jones(AUS) 2h 00:42.55	Magali Messmer(SUI) 2h 01:08.83
2004	Kate Allen(AUT) 2h:04:43.45	Loretta Harrop(AUS) 2h:04:50.17	Susan Williams(USA) 2h:05:08.92

1896–1996 Event not held

VOLLEYBALL

Men

	GOLD	SILVER	BRONZE
1964	SOVIET UNION	CZECHOSLOVAKIA	JAPAN
1968	SOVIET UNION	JAPAN	CZECHOSLOVAKIA
1972	JAPAN	GDR	SOVIET UNION
1976	POLAND	SOVIET UNION	CUBA
1980	SOVIET UNION	BULGARIA	ROMANIA
1984	UNITED STATES	BRAZIL	ITALY
1988	UNITED STATES	SOVIET UNION	ARGENTINA
1992	BRAZIL	NETHERLANDS	USA
1996	NETHERLANDS	ITALY	YUGOSLAVIA
2000	YUGOSLAVIA	RUSSIA	ITALY
2004	BRAZIL	ITALY	RUSSIA

1896–1960 Event not held

Women

	GOLD	SILVER	BRONZE
1964	JAPAN	SOVIET UNION	POLAND
1968	SOVIET UNION	JAPAN	POLAND
1972	SOVIET UNION	JAPAN	PRK
1976	JAPAN	SOVIET UNION	KOREA
1980	SOVIET UNION	GDR	BULGARIA
1984	CHINA	UNITED STATES	JAPAN
1988	SOVIET UNION	PERU	CHINA
1992	CUBA	UNIFIED TEAM	USA
1996	CUBA	CHINA	BRAZIL
2000	CUBA	RUSSIA	BRAZIL
2004	CHINA	RUSSIA	CUBA

1896–1960 Event not held

WEIGHTLIFTING
(Since 1976 there have been only two lifts, snatch and jerk)

Up to 52kg 1972–92; up to 54kg 1996; up to 56kg 2000 – Men

	GOLD	SILVER	BRONZE
1972	Zygmunt Smalcerz(POL) 337.5kg	Lajos Szücs(HUN) 330kg	Sándor Holczreitzer(HUN) 327.5kg
1976	Alexander Voronin(URS) 242.5kg	György Köszegi(HUN) 237.5kg	Mohammad Nassiri(IRI) 235kg
1980	Kanybek Osmonoliev(URS) 245kg	Bong Chol Ho(PRK) 245kg	Gyond Si Han(PRK) 245kg
1984	Guoqiang Zeng(CHN) 235kg	Peishujn Zhou(CHN) 235kg	Kazushito Manabe(JPN) 232.5kg
1988	Sevdalin Marinov(BUL) 270kg	Byung-Kwan Chun(KOR) 260kg	Zhuogiang He(CHN) 257.5kg
1992	Ivan Ivanov(BUL) 265kg	Qisheng Lin(CHN) 262.5kg	Traian Ciharean(ROM) 252.5kg
1996	Halil Mutlu(TUR) 287.5kg	Xiangsen Zhang(CHN) 280.0kg	Sevdalin Minchev(BUL) 277.5kg
2000	Halil Mutlu(TUR) 305kg	Wenxiang Wu(CHN) 287.5kg	Xiangxiang Zheng(CHN) 287.5kg
2004	Halil Mutlu(TUR) 295.0kg	Meijin Wu(CHN) 287.5kg	Sedat Artuc(TUR) 280.0kg

1896–1968 Event not held

Up to 56kg 1948–92; up to 59kg 1996; up to 62kg 2000 – Men

	GOLD	SILVER	BRONZE
1948	Joseph de Pietro(USA) 307.5kg	Julian Creus(GBR) 297.5kg	Richard Tom(GBR) 295kg
1952	Ivan Udolov(URS) 315kg	Mahmoud Namdjou(IRI) 307.5kg	Ali Mirzai(IRN) 300kg
1956	Charles Vinci(USA) 342.5kg	VladimirStogov(URS) 337.5kg	Mahmoud Namdjou(IRI) 332.5kg
1960	Charles Vinci(USA) 345kg	Yoshinobu Miyake(JPN) 337.5kg	Esmail Khan(IRI) 330kg
1964	Alexei Vakhonin(URS) 357.5kg	Imre Földi(HUN) 355kg	Shiro Ichinoseki(JPN) 347.5kg
1968	Mohammed Nassiri(IRI) 367.5kg	Imre Földi(HUN) 367.5kg	Henryk Trebicki(POL) 357.5kg
1972	Imre Földi(HUN) 377.5kg	Mohammed Nassiri(IRI) 370kg	Gennadi Chetin(URS) 367.5kg
1976	Norair Nurikyan(BUL) 262.5kg	Grzegorz Cziura(POL) 252.5kg	Kenkichi Ando(JPN) 250kg
1980	Daniel Nunez(CUB) 275kg	Yurik Sarkasian(URS) 270kg	Tadeusz Demboncyzk(POL) 265kg
1984	Shude Wu(CHN) 267.5kg	Runming Lai(CHN) 265kg	Masahiro Kotaka(JPN) 252.5kg
1988(1)	Oksen Mirzoyan(URS) 292.5kg	Yingqiang He(CHN) 287.5kg	Shoubin Liu(CHN) 267.5kg
1992	Byung-Kwan Chun(KOR) 287.5kg	Shoubin Liu(CHN) 277.5kg	Jianming Luo(CHN) 277.5kg

1996	Ningsheng Tang(CHN) 307.5kg	Leonidas Sabanis(GRE) 305.0kg	Nikolay Pechalov(BUL) 302.5kg
2000	Nikolay Pechalov(BUL) 325kg	Leonidas Sabanis(GRE) 317.5kg	Gennadi Oleschuk(BLR) 317.5kg
2004(2)	Zhiyong Shi(CHN) 325.0kg	Maosheng Le(CHN) 312.5kg	Israel José Rubio(VEN) 295.0kg

1896–1936 Event not held
(1) Mitko Grablev (BUL) finished first but was disqualified
(2) Leonidas Sampanis (GRE) finished third with 312.5kg but was disqualified

Up to 60kg 1920–92; up to 64kg 1996; up to 69kg 2000 – Men

	GOLD	SILVER	BRONZE
1920	Frans de Haes(BEL) 220kg	Alfred Schmidt(EST) 212.5kg	Eugène Ryther(SUI) 210kg
1924(1)	Pierino Gabetti(ITA) 402.5kg	Andreas Stadler(AUT) 385kg	Arthur Reinmann(SUI) 382.5kg
1928	Franz Andrysek(AUT) 287.5kg	Pierino Gabetti(ITA) 282.5kg	Hans Wölpert(GER) 282.5kg
1932	Raymond Suvigny(FRA) 287.5kg	Hans Wölpert(GER) 282.5kg	Anthony Terlazzo(USA) 280kg
1936	Anthony Terlazzo(USA) 312.5kg	Saleh Mohammed Soliman(EGY) 305kg	Ibrahim Shams(EGY) 300kg
1948	Mahmoud Fayad(EGY) 332.5kg	Rodney Wilkes(TRI) 317.5kg	Jaffar Salmassi(IRI) 312.5kg
1952	Rafael Chimishkyan(URS) 337.5kg	Nikolai Saksonov(URS) 332.5kg	Rodney Wilkes(TRI) 332.5kg
1956	Isaac Berger(USA) 352.5kg	Yevgeni Minayev(URS) 342.5kg	Marian Zielinski(POL) 335kg
1960	Yevgeni Minayev(URS) 372.5kg	Isaac Berger(USA) 362.5kg	Sebastiano Mannironi(ITA) 352.5kg
1964	Yoshinobu Miyake(JPN) 397.5kg	Isaac Berger(USA) 382.5kg	Mieczyslaw Nowak(POL) 377.5kg
1968	Yoshinobu Miyake(JPN) 392.5kg	Dito Shanidze(URS) 387.5kg	Yoshiyuki Miyake(JPN) 385kg
1972	Norair Nurikyan(BUL) 402.5kg	Dito Shanidze(URS) 400kg	Janos Benedek(HUN) 390kg
1976	Nikolai Kolesnikov(URS) 285kg	Georgi Todorov(BUL) 280kg	Kuzumasa Hirai(JPN) 275kg
1980	Viktor Mazin(URS) 290kg	Stefan Dimitrov(BUL) 287.5kg	Marek Seweryn(POL) 282.5kg
1984	Weiqiang Chen(CHN) 282.5kg	Gelu Radu(ROM) 280kg	Wen-Yee Tsai(TPE) 272.5kg
1988	Naim Suleymanoglu(TUR) 342.5kg	Stefan Topourov(BUL) 312.5kg	Huanming Ye(CHN) 287.5kg
1992	Naim Suleymanoglu(TUR) 320kg	Nikolai Peshalov(BUL) 305kg	Yingqiang He(CHN) 295kg
1996	Naim Suleymanoglu(TUR) 357.5kg	Valerios Leonidis(GRE) 332.5kg	Jiangang Xiao(CHN) 322.5kg
2000	Galabin Boyevski(BUL) 357.5kg	Georgi Markov(BUL) 352.5kg	Sergei Lavrenov(BLR) 340kg
2004	Guozheng Zhang(CHN) 347.5kg	Bae-Young Lee(KOR) 342.5kg	Nikolay Pechalov(CRO) 337.5kg

1896–1912 Event not held
(1) Total of five lifts

Up to 67.5kg 1920–92; up to 70kg 1996 – Men

	GOLD	SILVER	BRONZE
1920	Alfred Neuland(EST) 257.5kg	Louis Williquet(BEL) 240kg	Florimond Rooms(BEL) 230kg
1924(1)	Edmond Décottignies(FRA) 440kg	Anton Zwerina(AUT) 427.5kg	Bohumil Durdis(TCH) 425kg
1928(2)	Kurt Helbig(GER) 322.5kg Hans Haas(AUT) 322.5kg	–	Fernand Arnout(FRA) 302.5kg
1932	René Duverger(FRA) 325kg	Hans Haas(AUT) 307.5kg	Gastone Pierini(ITA) 302.5kg
1936(2)	Anwar Mohammed Mesbah(EGY) 342.5kg Robert Fein(AUT) 342.5kg	–	Karl Jensen(GER) 327.5kg
1948	Ibrahim Shams(EGY) 360kg	Attia Hamouda(EGY) 360kg	James Halliday(GBR) 340kg
1952	Tommy Kono(USA) 362.5kg	Yevgeni Lopatin(URS) 350kg	Verne Barberis(AUS) 350kg
1956	Igor Rybak(URS) 380kg	Ravil Khabutdinov(URS) 372.5kg	Chang-Hee Kim(KOR) 370kg
1960	Viktor Bushuyev(URS) 397.5kg	Howe-Liang Tan(SIN) 380kg	Abdul Wahid Aziz(IRQ) 380kg
1964	Waldemar Baszanowksi(POL) 432.5kg	Vladimir Kaplunov(URS) 432.5kg	Marian Zielinski(POL) 420kg
1968	Waldemar Baszanowski(POL) 437.5kg	Parviz Jalayer(IRI) 422.5kg	Marian Zielinski(POL) 420kg
1972	Mukharbi Kirzhinov(URS) 460kg	Mladen Koutchev(BUL) 450kg	Zbigniew Kaczmarek(POL) 437.5kg
1976(3)	Pyotr Korol(URS) 305kg	Daniel Senet(FRA) 300kg	Kazimierz Czarnecki(POL) 295kg
1980	Yanko Rusev(BUL) 342.5kg	Joachim Kunz(GDR) 335kg	Mintcho Pachov(BUL) 325kg
1984	Jingyuan Yao(CHN) 320kg	Andrei Socaci(ROM) 312.5kg	Journi Gronman(FIN) 312.5kg
1988	Joachim Kunz(GDR) 340kg	Israil Militossian(URS) 337.5kg	Jinhe Li(CHN) 325kg
1992	Israil Militossian(EUN) 337.5kg	Yoto Yotov(BUL) 327.5kg	Andreas Behm(GER) 320kg
1996	Xugang Zhan(CHN) 357.5kg	Myong-Nam Kim(PRK) 345.0kg	Attila Feri(HUN) 340.0kg

1896–1912, 2000, 2004 Event not held
(1) Total of five lifts
(2) Tie-breaker rule not yet introduced
(3) Zbigniev Kaczmarek (POL) finished first but was disqualified

Up to 75kg 1920–92; up to 76kg 1996; up to 77kg 2000 – Men

	GOLD	SILVER	BRONZE
1920	Henri Gance(FRA) 245kg	Pietro Bianchi(ITA) 237.5kg	Albert Pettersson(SWE) 237.5kg
1924(1)	Carlo Galimberti(ITA) 492.5kg	Alfred Neuland(EST) 455kg	Jaan Kikas(EST) 450kg
1928	Roger Francois(FRA) 335kg	Carlo Galimberti(ITA) 332.5kg	August Scheffer(NED) 327.5kg
1932	Rudolf Ismayr(GER) 345kg	Carlo Galimberti(ITA) 340kg	Karl Hipfinger(AUT) 337.5kg
1936	Khadr El Thouni(EGY) 387.5kg	Rudolf Ismayr(GER) 352.5kg	Adolf Wagner(GER) 352.5kg
1948	Frank Spellman(USA) 390kg	Peter George(USA) 412.5kg	Sung-Jip Kim(KOR) 380kg
1952	Peter George(USA) 400kg	Gérard Gratton(CAN) 390kg	Sung-Jip Kim(KOR) 382.5kg
1956	Fyodor Bogdanovski(URS) 420kg	Peter George(USA) 412.5kg	Ermanno Pignatti(ITA) 382.5kg
1960	Aleksandr Kurinov(URS) 437.5kg	Tommy Kono(USA) 427.5kg	Gyözö Veres(HUN) 405kg
1964	Hans Zdrazila(TCH) 445kg	Viktor Kurentsov(URS) 440kg	Masashi Ouchi(JPN) 437.5kg
1968	Viktor Kurentsov(URS) 475kg	Masashi Ouchi(JPN) 455kg	Károly Bakos(HUN) 440kg

1972	Yordan Bikov(BUL) 485kg	Mohamed Trabulsi(LIB) 472.5kg	Anselmo Silvino(ITA) 470kg
1976	Yordan Bikov(BUL) 335kg	Vartan Militosyan(URS) 330kg	Peter Wenzel(GDR) 327.5kg
1980	Asen Zlatev(BUL) 360kg	Aleksandr Pervy(URS) 357.5kg	Nedeltcho Kolev(BUL) 345kg
1984	Karl-Heinz Radschinsky(FRG) 340kg	Jaques Demers(CAN) 335kg	Dragomir Cioroslan(ROM) 332.5kg
1988	Borislav Guidikov(BUL) 375kg	Ingo Steinhöfel(GDR) 360kg	Alexander Varbanov(BUL) 357.5kg
1992	Fedor Kassapu(EUN) 357.5kg	Pablo Lara(CUB) 357.5kg	Myong-Nam Kim(PRK) 352.5kg
1996	Pablo Lara(CUB) 367.5kg	Yoto Yotov(BUL) 360.0kg	Chol-Ho Jon(PRK) 357.5kg
2000	Xugang Zhan(CHN) 367.5kg	Viktor Mitrou(GRE) 367.5kg	Arsen Melikyan(ARM) 365kg
2004	Taner Sagir(TUR) 375.0kg	Sergei Filimunov(KAZ) 372.5kg	Oleg Perepetchenov(RUS) 365.0kg

1896–1912 Event not held
(1) Total of five lifts

Up to 82.5kg 1920–92; up to 83kg 1996; up to 85kg 2000 – Men

	GOLD	SILVER	BRONZE
1920	Ernest Cadine(FRA) 290kg	Fritz Hünenberger(SUI) 275kg	Erik Pettersson(SWE) 272.5kg
1924(1)	Charles Rigoulot(FRA) 502.5kg	Fritz Hünenberger(SUI) 490kg	Leopold Friedrich(AUT) 490kg
1928	Said Nosseir(EGY) 355kg	Louis Hostin(FRA) 352.5kg	Johannes Verheijen(NED) 337.5kg
1932	Louis Hostin(FRA) 372.5kg	Svend Olsen(DEN) 360kg	Henry Duey(USA) 330kg
1936	Louis Hostin(FRA) 372.5kg	Eugen Deutsch(GER) 365kg	Ibrahim Wasif(EGY) 360kg
1948	Stanley Stanczyk(USA) 417.5kg	Harold Sakata(USA) 380kg	Gösta Magnussen(SWE) 375kg
1952	Trofim Lomakin(URS) 417.5kg	Stanley Stanczyk(USA) 415kg	Arkadi Vorobyev(URS) 407.5kg
1956	Tommy Kono(USA) 447.5kg	Vassili Stepanov(URS) 427.5kg	James George(USA) 417.5kg
1960	Ireneusz Palinski(POL) 442.5kg	James George(USA) 430kg	Jan Bochenek(POL) 420kg
1964	Rudolf Plukfelder(URS) 475kg	Géza Tóth(HUN) 467.5kg	Gyözö Veres(HUN) 467.5kg
1968	Boris Selitsky(URS) 485kg	Vladimir Belyayev(URS) 485kg	Norbert Ozimek(POL) 472.5kg
1972	Leif Jenssen(NOR) 507.5kg	Norbert Ozimek(POL) 497.5kg	György Horváth(HUN) 495kg
1976	Valeriy Shary(URS) 365kg	Trendachil Stoichev(BUL) 360kg (2)	Peter Baczako(HUN) 345kg
1980	Yurik Vardanyan(URS) 400kg	Blagoi Blagoyev(BUL) 372.5kg	Dusan Poliacik(TCH) 367.5kg
1984	Petre Becheru(ROM) 355kg	Robert Kabbas(AUS) 342.5kg	Ryoji Isaoka(JPN) 340kg
1988	Israil Arsamokov(URS) 377.5kg	István Messzi(HUN) 370kg	Hyung-Kun Lee(KOR) 367.5kg
1992	Pyrros Dimas(GRE) 370kg	Krzysztof Siemion(POL) 370kg	– (3)
1996	Pyrros Dimas(GRE) 392.5kg	Marc Huster(GER) 382.5kg	Andrzej Cofalik(POL) 372.5kg
2000	Pyrros Dimas(GRE) 390kg	Marc Huster(GER) 390kg	George Asinidze(GEO) 390kg
2004	Georgi Asanidze(GEO) 382.5kg	Andrei Rybakov(BLR) 380.0kg	Pyrros Dimas(GRE) 377.5kg

1896–1912 Event not held
(1) Total of five lifts
(2) Blagoi Blagoyev (BUL) finished second but was disqualified
(3) Ibraghim Samadov (EUN) finished third but was disqualified, no bronze awarded

Up to 90kg 1952–92; up to 91kg 1996; up to 94kg 2000 – Men

	GOLD	SILVER	BRONZE
1952	Norbert Schemansky(USA) 445kg	Grigori Nowak(URS) 410kg	Lennox Kilgour(TRI) 402.5kg
1956	Arkadi Vorobyev(URS) 462.5kg	David Sheppard(USA) 442.5kg	Jean Debuf(FRA) 425kg
1960	Arkadi Vorobyev(URS) 472.5kg	Trofim Lomakin(URS) 457.5kg	Louis Martin(GBR) 445kg
1964	Vladimir Golovanov(URS) 487.5kg	Louis Martin(GBR) 475kg	Ireneusz Palinski(POL) 467.5kg
1968	Kaarlo Kanganiemi(FIN) 517.5kg	Jan Talts(URS) 507.5kg	Marek Golab(POL) 495kg
1972	Andon Nikolov(BUL) 525kg	Atanas Chopov(BUL) 517.5kg	Hans Bettembourg(SWE) 512.5kg
1976	David Rigert(URS) 382.5kg	Lee James(USA) 362.5kg	Atanas Chopov(BUL) 360kg
1980	Péter Baczakó(HUN) 377.5kg	Rumen Alexandrov(BUL) 375kg	Frank Mantek(GDR) 375kg
1984	Nicu Vlad(ROM) 392.5kg	Dumitru Petre(ROM) 360kg	David Mercer(GBR) 352.5kg
1988	Anatoli Khrapati(URS) 412.5kg	Nail Moukhamediarov(URS) 400kg	Slawomir Zawada(POL) 400kg
1992	Kakhi Kakhiashvili(EUN) 412.5kg	Sergei Syrtsov(EUN) 412.5kg	Serguisz Wolczaniecki(POL) 392.5kg
1996	Alexei Petrov(RUS) 402.5kg	Leonidas Kokas(GRE) 390.0kg	Oliver Caruso(GER) 390.0kg
2000	Akakios Kakiavilis(GRE) 405kg (1)	Szymon Kolecki(POL) 405kg	Alexei Petrov(RUS) 402.5kg
2004	Milen Dobrev(BUL) 407.5kg	Khadjimourad Akayev(RUS) 405.0kg	Eduard Tjukin(RUS) 397.5kg

1896–1948 Event not held
(1) Same person as 1992 champion

Up to 100kg 1980–92; up to 99kg 1996 – Men

	GOLD	SILVER	BRONZE
1980	Ota Zaremba(TCH) 395kg	Igor Nikitin(URS) 392.5kg	Alberto Blanco(CUB) 385kg
1984	Rolf Milser(FRG) 385kg	Vasile Gropa(ROM) 382.5kg	Pekka Niemi(FIN) 367.5kg
1988	Pavel Kuznetsov(URS) 425kg	Nicu Vlad(ROM) 402.5kg (1)	Peter Immesberger(FRG) 367.5kg
1992	Viktor Tregubov(EUN) 410kg	Timur Taimazov(EUN) 402.5kg	Waldemar Malak(POL) 400kg
1996	Akakios Kakiavilis(GRE) 420.0kg (2)	Anatoli Khrapati(KAZ) 410.0kg	Denis Gotfrid(UKR) 402.5kg

(1) Andor Szanyi (HUN) finished second but was disqualified
(2) See previous weight class
1896–1976, 2000, 2004 Event not held

Over 82.5kg 1920–48; over 90kg 1952–68; up to 110kg 1972–92; up to 108kg 1996; up to 105kg 2000 – Men

	GOLD	SILVER	BRONZE
1896(1)	Launceston Eliot(GBR) 71kg	Viggo Jensen(DEN) 57.2kg	Alexandros Nikolopoulos(GRE) 57.2kg
1896(2)	Viggo Jensen(DEN) 111.5kg	Launceston Eliot(GBR) 111.5kg	Sotirios Versis(GRE) 90kg
1904(3)	Oscar Osthoff(USA) 48pts	Frederick Winters(USA) 45pts	Frank Kungler(USA) 10pts
1904(2)	Perikles Kaklousis(GRE) 111.5kg	Oscar Osthoff(USA) 84.36kg	Frank Kungler(USA) 79.83kg
1906(1)	Josef Steinbach(AUT) 76.55kg	Tullio Camilotti(ITA) 73.75kg	Heinrich Schneidereit(GER) 70.75kg
1906(2)	Dimitrios Tofalos(GRE) 142.5kg	Josef Steinbach(AUT) 136.5kg	Alexandre Maspoli(FRA) 129.5kg
			Heinrich Rondl(GER) 129.5kg
			Heinrich Schneidereit(GER) 129.5kg
1920	Filippo Bottino(ITA) 270kg	Joseph Alzin(LUX) 225kg	Louis Bernot(FRA) 250kg
1924(4)	Giuseppe Tonani(ITA) 517.5kg	Franz Aigner(AUT) 515kg	Harald Tammer(EST) 497.5kg
1928	Josef Strassberger(GER) 372.5kg	Arnold Luhaäär(EST) 360kg	Jaroslav Skobla(TCH) 375.5kg
1932	Jaroslav Skobla(TCH) 380kg	Václav Psenicka(TCH) 377.5kg	Josef Strassberger(GER) 377.5kg
1936	Josef Manger(GER) 410kg	Václav Psenicka(TCH) 402.5kg	Arnold Luhaäär(EST) 400kg
1948	John Davis(USA) 452.2kg	Norbert Schemansky(USA) 425kg	Abraham Charité(NED) 412.5kg
1952	John Davis(USA) 460kg	James Bradford(USA) 437.5kg	Humberto Selvetti(ARG) 432.5kg
1956	Paul Anderson(USA) 500kg	Humberto Selvetti(ARG) 500kg	Alberto Pigaiani(ITA) 452.5kg
1960	Yuriy Vlasov(URS) 537.5k	James Bradford(USA) 512.5kg	Norbert Schemansky(USA) 500kg
1964	Leonid Zhabotinsky(URS) 572.5kg	Yuri Vlasov(URS) 570kg	Norbert Schemansky(USA) 537.5kg
1968	Leonid Zhabotinsky(URS) 572.5kg	Serge Reding(BEL) 555kg	Joseph Dube(USA) 555kg
1972	Jan Talts(URS) 580kg	Alexandre Kraitchev(BUL) 562.5kg	Stefan Grützner(GDR) 555kg
1976	Yuri Zaitsev(URS) 385kg (5)	Krastio Semerdiev(BUL) 385kg	Tadeusz Rutkowski(POL) 377.5kg
1980	Leonid Taranenko(URS) 422.5kg	Valentin Christov(BUL) 385kg	György Szalai(HUN) 390kg
1984	Norberto Oberburger(ITA) 390kg	Stefan Tasnadi(ROM) 380kg	Guy Carlton(USA) 377.5kg
1988	Yuriy Zakharevich(URS) 455kg	József Jacsó(HUN) 427.5kg	Ronny Weller(GDR) 425kg
1992	Ronny Weller(GER) 432.5kg	Artur Akoyev(EUN) 430kg	Stefan Botev(BUL) 417.5kg
1996	Timur Taimazov(UKR) 430.0kg	Sergei Syrtsov(RUS) 420.0kg	Nicu Vlad(ROM) 420.0kg
2000	Hossain Tavakoli(IRI) 425kg	Alan Tsagayev(BUL) 422.5kg	Said Saif Asaad(QAT) 420kg
2004(6)	Dmitri Berestov(RUS) 425.0kg	Igor Razoronov(UKR) 420.0kg	Gleb Pisarevski(RUS) 415.0kg

1900, 1908–1912 Event not held
(1) One-hand lift
(2) Two-hand lift
(3) Dumbell lift
(4) Total of five lifts
(5) Valentin Christov (BUL) finished first but was disqualified
(6) Ferenc Gyurkovics (HUN) finished second with 420.0kg but was disqualified

Over 110kg 1972–92; over 108kg 1996; over 105kg 2000 – Men

	GOLD	SILVER	BRONZE
1972	Vasili Alexeyev(URS) 640kg	Rudolf Mang(FRG) 610kg	Gerd Bonk(GDR) 572.5kg
1976	Vasili Alexeyev(URS) 440kg	Gerd Bonk(GDR) 405kg	Helmut Losch(GDR) 387.5kg
1980	Sultan Rakhmanov(URS) 440kg	Jürgen Heuser(GDR) 410kg	Tadeusz Rutkowski(POL) 407.5kg
1984	Dinko Lukin(AUS) 412.5kg	Mario Martinez(USA) 410kg	Manfred Nerlinger(FRG) 397.5kg
1988	Alexander Kurlovich(URS) 462.5kg	Manfred Nerlinger(FRG) 430kg	Martin Zawieja(FRG) 415kg
1992	Alexander Kurlovich(EUN) 450kg	Leonid Taranenko(EUN) 425kg	Manfred Nerlinger(GER) 412.5kg
1996	Andrei Chemerkin(RUS) 457.5kg	Ronny Weller(GER) 455.0kg	Stefan Botev(AUS) 455.0kg
2000	Hossein Reza Zadeh(IRI) 472.5kg	Ronny Weller(GER) 467.5kg	Andrei Chemerkin(RUS) 462.5kg (1)
2004	Hossein Reza Zadeh(IRI)472.5kg	Viktors Scerbatihs(LAT)455.0kg	Velichko Cholakov(BUL) 447.5kg

1896–1968 Event not held
(1) Askot Danielyan (ARM) finished third but was disqualified

Up to 48kg – Women

	GOLD	SILVER	BRONZE
2000	Tara Nott(USA) 185kg	Raema Lisa Rumbewas(INA) 185kg	Sri Indriyani(INA) 182.5kg
2004	Nurcan Taylan(TUR) 210.0kg	Zhuo Li(CHN) 205.0kg	Aree Wiratthaworn(THA) 200.0kg

1896–1996 Event not held

Up to 53kg – Women

	GOLD	SILVER	BRONZE
2000	Xia Yang(CHN) 225kg	Feng-Ying Li(TPE) 212.5kg	Winarni Binti Slamet(INA) 202.5kg
2004	Udomporn Polsak(THA)222.5kg	Raema Lisa Rumbewas(INA)210.0kg	Mabel Mosquera(COL)197.5kg

1896–1996 Event not held

Up to 58kg – Women

	GOLD	SILVER	BRONZE
2000	Soraya Jiminez(MEX) 222.5kg	Song Hui Ri(PRK) 220kg	Khassaraporn Suta(INA) 210kg
2004	Yanqing Chen(CHN) 237.5kg	Song Hui Ri(PRK) 232.5kg	Wandee Kameaim(THA) 230.0kg

1896–1996 Event not held

Up to 63kg – Women

	GOLD	SILVER	BRONZE
2000	Xiaomin Chen(CHN) 242.5kg	Valentina Popova(RUS) 235kg	Ioanna Chatziioannou(GRE) 222.5kg
2004	Natalya Skakun(UKR) 242.5kg	Hanna Batsyushka(BLR) 242.5kg	Tatsiana Stukalava(BLR) 222.5kg

1896–1996 Event not held

Up to 69kg – Women

	GOLD	SILVER	BRONZE
2000	Weining Lin(CHN) 242.5kg	Erzsabet Markus(HUN) 242.5kg	Karnam Malleswari(IND) 240kg
2004	Chunhong Liu(CHN) 275.0kg	Eszter Krutzler(HUN) 262.5kg	Zarema Kasayeva(RUS) 262.5kg

1896–1996 Event not held

Up to 75kg –Women

	GOLD	SILVER	BRONZE
2000	Maria Urrutia(CUB) 245kg	Ruth Ogbeifo(NGR) 245kg	Yi-Hang Kuo(TPE) 245kg
2004	Pawina Thongsuk(THA) 272.5kg	Natalia Zabolotnaya(RUS) 272.5kg	Valentina Popova(RUS) 265.0kg

1896–1996 Event not held

Over 75kg – Women

	GOLD	SILVER	BRONZE
2000	Meiyuan Ding(CHN) 300kg	Agata Wrobel(POL) 295kg	Cheryl Haworth(USA) 270kg
2004	Gonghong Tang(CHN) 305.0kg	Mi Ran Jang(KOR) 302.5kg	Ageta Wrobel(POL) 290.0kg

1896–1996 Event not held

WRESTLING

Freestyle up to 48kg – Men

	GOLD	SILVER	BRONZE
1904	Robert Curry(USA)	John Heim(USA)	Gustav Thiefenthaler(USA)
1972	Roman Dmitriev(URS)	Ognian Nikolov(BUL)	Ebrahim Javadpour(IRI)
1976	Khassan Issaev(BUL)	Roman Dmitriev(URS)	Akira Kudo(JPN)
1980	Claudio Pollio(ITA)	Se Hong Jang(PRK)	Sergei Kornilayev(URS)
1984	Robert Weaver(USA)	Takashi Irie(JPN)	Gab-Do Son(KOR)
1988	Takashi Kobaysahi(JPN)	Ivan Tozorov(BUL)	Sergei Karemtchakov(URS)
1992	Il Kim(PRK)	Jong-Shin Kim(KOR)	Vougar Oroudzhov(EUN)
1996	Il Kim(PRK)	Armen Mkrchyan(ARM)	Alexis Vila(CUB)

1896–1900, 1906–68, 2000, 2004 Event not held

Freestyle up to 115lb (52.16kg) 1904; up to 52kg 1948–96; up to 54kg 2000 – Men

	GOLD	SILVER	BRONZE
1904	George Mehnert(USA)	Gustave Bauer(USA)	William Nelson(USA)
1948	Lennart Viitala(FIN)	Halit Balamir(TUR)	Thure Johansson(SWE)
1952	Hasan Gemici(TUR)	Yushu Kitano(JPN)	Mahmoud Mollaghessemi(IRI)
1956	Mirian Tslkalamanidze(URS)	Mohamad-Ali Khojastenpour(IRI)	Hüseyin Akbas(TUR)
1960	Ahmet Bilek(TUR)	Masayuki Matsubara(JPN)	Mohamad Saifpour Saidabadi(IRI)
1964	Yoshikatsu Yoshida(JPN)	Chang-Sun Chang(KOR)	Said Aliaakbar Haydari(IRI)
1968	Shigeo Nakata(JPN)	Richard Sanders(USA)	Surenjav Sukhbaatar(MGL)
1972	Kiyomi Kato(JPN)	Arsen Alakhverdyev(URS)	Hyong Kim Gwong(PRK)
1976	Yuji Takada(JPN)	Alexander Ivanov(URS)	Hae-Sup Jeon(KOR)
1980	Anatoli Beloglazov(URS)	Wladyslaw Stecyk(POL)	Nermedin Selimov(BUL)
1984	Saban Trstena(YUG)	Jong-Kyu Kim(KOR)	Yuji Takada(JPN)
1988	Mitsuru Sato(JPN)	Saban Trstena(YUG)	Vladimir Togouzov(URS)
1992	Hak-Son Li(PRK)	Larry Lee Jones(USA)	Valentin Jordanov(BUL)
1996	Valentin Jordanov(BUL)	Namik Abdullayev(AZE)	Maulen Mamirov(KZK)
2000	Namik Abdullayev(AZE)	Samuel Henson(USA)	Amiran Karntanov(GRE)

1896–1900, 1906–36, 2004 Event not held

Freestyle up to 125lb (56.7kg) 1904; up to 119lb (54kg) 1908; up to 56kg 1924–36; up to 57kg 1948–96; up to 58kg 2000 – Men

	GOLD	SILVER	BRONZE
1904	Isidor Niflot(USA)	August Wester(USA)	Zenon Strebler(USA)
1908	George Mehnert(USA)	William Press(GBR)	Aubert Coté(CAN)
1924	Kustaa Pihlajamaki(FIN)	Kaarlo Mäkinen(FIN)	Bryant Hines(USA)
1928	Kaarlo Mäkinen(FIN)	Edmond Spapen(BEL)	James Trifunov(CAN)
1932	Robert Pearce(USA)	Odön Zombori(HUN)	Aatos Jaskari(FIN)
1936	Odön Zombori(HUN)	Ross Flood(USA)	Johannes Herbert(GER)
1948	Nasuk Akar(TUR)	Gerald Leeman(USA)	Charles Kouyov(FRA)
1952	Shohachi Ishii(JPN)	Rashid Mamedbekov(URS)	Kha-Shaba Jadav(IND)
1956	Mustafa Dagistanli(TUR)	Mohamad Yaghoubi(IRI)	Mikhail Chakhov(URS)
1960	Terrence McCann(USA)	Nejdet Zalev(BUL)	Tadeusz Trojanowski(POL)
1964	Yojiro Uetake(JPN)	Hüseyin Akbas(TUR)	Aidyn Ibragimov(URS)

1968	Yojiro Uetake(JPN)	Donald Behm(USA)	Abutaleb Gorgori(IRI)
1972	Hideaki Yanagide(JPN)	Richard Sanders(USA)	László Klinga(HUN)
1976	Vladimir Yumin(URS)	Hans-Dieter Brüchert(GDR)	Masao Arai(JPN)
1980	Sergei Beloglazov(URS)	Ho Pyong Li(PRK)	Dugarsuren Ouinbold(MGL)
1984	Hideyaki Tomiyama(JPN)	Barry Davis(USA)	Eui-Kon Kim(KOR)
1988	Sergei Beloglazov(URS)	Askari Mohammadian(IRI)	Kyung-Sun No(KOR)
1992	Alejandro Puerto Diaz(CUB)	Sergei Smal(EUN)	Yong-Sik Kim(PRK)
1996	Kendall Cross(USA)	Giga Sissaouri(CAN)	Yong-Sam Ri(PRK)
2000	Alireza Dabir(IRI)	Yevgeni Buslovich(UKR)	Terry Brands(USA)
2004	Mavlet Batirov(RUS)	Stephen Abas(USA)	Chikara Tanabe(JPN)

1896–1900, 1906, 1912–20 Event not held

Freestyle up to 135lb (61.24kg) 1904; up to 133lb (60.3kg) 1908; up to 60kg 1920; up to 61kg 1924–36; up to 63kg 1948–68; up to 62kg 1972–96; up to 63kg 2000

	GOLD	SILVER	BRONZE
1904	Benjamin Bradshaw(USA)	Theodore McLear(USA)	Charles Clapper(USA)
1908	George Dole(USA)	James Slim(GBR)	William McKie(GBR)
1920	Charles Ackerly(USA)	Samuel Gerson(USA)	P.W. Bernard(GBR)
1924	Robin Reed(USA)	Chester Newton(USA)	Katsutoshi Naito(JPN)
1928	Allie Morrison(USA)	Kustaa Pihlajamäki(FIN)	Hans Minder(SUI)
1932	Hermanni Pihlajamäki(FIN)	Edgar Nemir(USA)	Einar Karlsson(SWE)
1936	Kustaa Pihlajamäki(FIN)	Francis Millard(USA)	Gösta Jönsson(SWE)
1948	Gazanfer Bilge(TUR)	Ivar Sjölin(SWE)	Adolf Müller(SUI)
1952	Bayram Sit(TUR)	Nasser Givétchi(IRI)	Josiah Henson(USA)
1956	Shozo Sasahara(JPN)	Joseph Mewis(BEL)	Erkki Penttilä(FIN)
1960	Mustafa Dagistanli(TUR)	Stantcho Ivanov(BUL)	Vladimir Rubashbili(URS)
1964	Osamu Watanabe(JPN)	Stantcho Ivanov(BUL)	Nodar Khokhashvili(URS)
1968	Masaaki Kaneko(JPN)	Enyu Todorov(BUL)	Shamseddin Seyed-Abbassi(IRI)
1972	Zagalav Abdulbekov(URS)	Vehbi Akdag(TUR)	Ivan Krastev(BUL)
1976	Jung-Mo Yang(KOR)	Zeveg Oidov(MGL)	Gene Davis(USA)
1980	Magomedgasan Abushev(URS)	Mikho Doukov(BUL)	Georges Hadiioannidis(GRE)
1984	Randy Lewis(USA)	Kosei Akaishi(JPN)	Jeung-Keun Lee(KOR)
1988	John Smith(USA)	Stepan Sarkissian(URS)	Simeon Chterev(BUL)
1992	John Smith(USA)	Askari Mohammadian(IRI)	Lazaro Reinoso(CUB)
1996	Thomas Brands(USA)	Jae-Sung Jang(KOR)	Elbrus Tedeyev(UKR)
2000	Murad Oumakhanov(RUS)	Serafim Barzakov(BUL)	Jae-Sung Jang(KOR)
2004	Yandro Miguel Quintana(CUB)	Masoud Jokar(IRI)	Kenji Inoue(JPN)

1896–1900, 1906, 1912 Event not held

Freestyle up to 145lb (65.77kg) 1904; up to 146lb (66.6kg) 1908; up to 67.5kg 1920; up to 66kg 1924–36; up to 67kg 1948–60; up to 70kg 1964–68; up to 68kg 1972–96; up to 69kg 2000 – Men

	GOLD	SILVER	BRONZE
1904	Otton Roehm(USA)	Rudolph Tesing(USA)	Albert Zirkel(USA)
1908	George de Relwyskow(GBR)	William Wood(GBR)	Albert Gingell(GBR)
1920	Kalle Anttila(FIN)	Gottfried Svensson(SWE)	Peter Wright(GBR)
1924	Russell Vis(USA)	Volmart Wickström(FIN)	Arvo Haavisto(FIN)
1928	Osvald Käpp(EST)	Charles Pacome(FRA)	Eino Leino(FIN)
1932	Charles Pacome(FRA)	Károly Kápáti(HUN)	Gustaf Klarén(SWE)
1936	Károly Kápáti(HUN)	Wolfgang Ehrl(GER)	Hermanni Pihlajamäki(FIN)
1948	Celál Atik(TUR)	Gösta Frandfors(SWE)	Hermanni Pihilajamäki(FIN)
1952	Olle Anderberg(SWE)	Thomas Evans(USA)	Djahanbakte Tovfighe(IRI)
1956	Emamali Habibi(IRI)	Shigeru Kasahara(JPN)	Alimberg Bestayev(URS)
1960	Shelby Wilson(USA)	Viktor Sinyavskiy(URS)	Enyu Dimov(BUL) (1)
1964	Enyu Valtschev(BUL) (1)	Klaus-Jürgen Rost(GER)	Iwao Horiuchi(JPN)
1968	Abdollah Movahed Ardabili(IRI)	Enyu Valtschev(BUL)	Sereeter Danzandarjaa(MGL)
1972	Dan Gable(USA)	Kikuo Wada(JPN)	Ruslan Ashuraliev(URS)
1976	Pavel Pinigin(URS)	Lloyd Keaser(USA)	Yasaburo Sagawara(JPN)
1980	Saipulla Absaidov(URS)	Ivan Yankov(BUL)	Saban Sejdi(YUG)
1984	In-Tak You(KOR)	Andrew Rein(USA)	Jukka Rauhala(FIN)
1988	Arsen Fadzayev(URS)	Jang-Soon Park(KOR)	Nate Carr(USA)
1992	Arsen Fadzayev(EUN)	Valentin Getzov(BUL)	Kosei Akaishi(JPN)
1996	Vadim Bogiyev(RUS)	Townsend Saunders(USA)	Zaza Zazirov(UKR)
2000	Daniel Igali(CAN)	Arsen Gitinov(RUS)	Lincoln McIlravy(USA)
2004	Elbrus Tedeyev(UKR)	Jamill Kelly(USA)	Makhach Murtazaliev(RUS)

1896–1900, 1906, 1912 Event not held
(1) Valtschev was Dimov in 1960.

Freestyle up to 158lb (71.67kg) 1904; up to 72kg 1924–36; up to 73kg 1948–60; up to 74kg 1972–96; up to 76kg 2000 – Men

	GOLD	SILVER	BRONZE
1904	Charles Erikson(USA)	William Beckmann(USA)	Jerry Winholtz(USA)
1924	Hermann Gehri(SUI)	Eino Leino(FIN)	Otto Müller(SUI)
1928	Arvo Haavisto(FIN)	Lloyd Appleton(USA)	Maurice Letchford(CAN)

1932	Jack van Bebber(USA)	Daniel MacDonald(CAN)	Eino Leino(FIN)
1936	Frank Lewis(USA)	Ture Andersson(SWE)	Joseph Schleimer(CAN)
1948	Yasar Dogu(TUR)	Richard Garrard(AUS)	Leland Merrill(USA)
1952	William Smith(USA)	Per Berlin(SWE)	Abdullah Modjtabavi(IRI)
1956	Mitsuo Ikeda(JPN)	Ibrahim Zengin(TUR)	Vakhtang Balavadze(URS)
1960	Douglas Blubaugh(USA)	Ismail Ogan(TUR)	Mohammed Bashir(PAK)
1964	Ismail Ogan(TUR)	Guliko Sagaradze(URS)	Mohamad-Ali Sanatkaran(IRI)
1968	Mahmut Atalay(TUR)	Daniel Robin(FRA)	Dagvasuren Purev(MGL)
1972	Wayne Wells(USA)	Jan Karlsson(SWE)	Adolf Seger(FRG)
1976	Jiichiro Date(JPN)	Mansour Barzegar(IRI)	Stanley Dziedzic(USA)
1980	Valentin Raitchev(URS)	Jamtsying Davaajav(MGL)	Dan Karabin(TCH)
1984	David Schultz(USA)	Martin Knosp(FRG)	Saban Sejdi(YUG)
1988	Kenneth Monday(USA)	Adlan Varayev(URS)	Rakhmad Sofiadi(BUL)
1992	Jang-Soon Park(KOR)	Kenneth Monday(USA)	Amir Khadem(IRI)
1996	Buvaisa Saityev(RUS)	Jang-Soon Park(KOR)	Taykuo Ota(JPN)
2000	Brandon Slay(USA) (1)	Eui Jae Moon(KOR)	Adem Bereket(TUR)
2004	Buvaisa Saityev(RUS)	Gennadi Laliyev(KAZ)	Ivan Fundora(CUB)

1896–1900, 1908–20 Event not held
(1) Alexander Leipold (GER) won title but was disqualified

Freestyle up to 161lb (73kg) 1908; up to 75kg 1920; up to 79kg 1924–60; up to 87kg 1964–68; up to 82kg 1972–96; up to 85kg 2000 – Men

	GOLD	SILVER	BRONZE
1908	Stanley Bacon(GBR)	George de Relwyskow(GBR)	Frederick Beck(GBR)
1920	Eino Reino(FIN)	Väinö Penttala(FIN)	Charles Johnson(USA)
1924	Fritz Hagmann(SUI)	Pierre Ollivier(BEL)	Vilho Pekkala(FIN)
1928	Ernst Kyburz(SUI)	Donald Stockton(CAN)	Samuel Rabin(GBR)
1932	Ivar Johansson(SWE)	Kyösti Luukko(FIN)	József Tunyogi(HUN)
1936	Emile Poilvé(FRA)	Richard Voliva(USA)	Ahmet Kirecci(TUR)
1948	Glen Brand(USA)	Adil Candemir(TUR)	Erik Lindén(SWE)
1952	David Tsimakuridze(URS)	Gholam Reza Takhti(IRI)	György Gurics(HUN)
1956	Nikola Stantchev(BUL)	Daniel Hodge(USA)	Georgi Skhirtladze(URS)
1960	Hasan Güngör(TUR)	Georgi Skhirtladze(URS)	Hans Antonsson(SWE)
1964	Prodan Gardshev(BUL)	Hasan Güngör(TUR)	Daniel Brand(USA)
1968	Boris Mikhailovich Gurevich(URS)	Munkbat Jigjid(MGL)	Prodan Gradshev(BUL)
1972	Leven Tediashvili(URS)	John Peterson(USA)	Vasile Jorga(ROM)
1976	Joh Peterson(USA)	Viktor Novoshilev(URS)	Adolf Seger(FRG)
1980	Ismail Abilov(BUL)	Magomedhan Aratsilov(URS)	István Kovács(HUN)
1984	Mark Schultz(USA)	Hideyuki Nagashima(JPN)	Chris Rinke(CAN)
1988	Myung-Woo Han(KOR)	Necmi Gencalp(TUR)	Josef Lohyna(TCH)
1992	Kevin Jackson(USA)	Elmadi Zhabraylov(EUN)	Razul Khadem Azghadi(IRI)
1996	Khadshimurad Magomedov(RUS)	Hyun-Mo Yang(KOR)	Amir Khadem Azghadi(IRI)
2000	Adam Saityev(RUS)	Yoel Romero(CUB)	Mogamed Ibragimov(MKD)
2004	Cael Sanderson(USA)	Eui-Jae Moon(KOR)	Sazhid Sazhidov(RUS)

1896–1906, 1912 Event not held

Freestyle up to 82.5kg 1920; up to 87kg 1924–60; up to 97kg 1964–68; up to 90kg 1972–96; up to 97kg 2000 – Men

	GOLD	SILVER	BRONZE
1920	Anders Larsson(SWE)	Charles Courant(SUI)	Walter Maurer(USA)
1924	John Spellman(USA)	Rudolf Svensson(SWE)	Charles Courant(FRA)
1928	Thure Sjöstedt(SWE)	Anton Bögli(SUI)	Henri Lefebre(FRA)
1932	Peter Mehringer(USA)	Thure Sjöstedt(SWE)	Eddie Scarf(AUS)
1936	Knut Fridell(SWE)	August Neo(EST)	Erich Siebert(GER)
1948	Henry Wittenberg(USA)	Fritz Stöckli(SUI)	Bengt Fahlkvist(SWE)
1952	Wiking Palm(SWE)	Henry Wittenberg(USA)	Adil Atan(TUR)
1956	Gholam Reza Tahkti(IRI)	Boris Kulayev(URS)	Peter Blair(USA)
1960	Ismet Atli(TUR)	Gholam Reza Tahkti(IRI)`	Anatoli Albul(URS)
1964	Alexander Medved(URS)	Ahmet Ayik(TUR)	Said Mustafafov(BUL)
1968	Ahmet Ayik(TUR)	Shota Lomidze(URS)	József Csatári(HUN)
1972	Ben Peterson(USA)	Gennadi Strakhov(URS)	Károly Bajkó(HUN)
1976	Levan Tediashvili(URS)	Ben Peterson(USA)	Stelica Morcov(ROM)
1980	Sanasar Oganesyan(URS)	Uwe Neupert(GDR)	Aleksandr Cichon(POL)
1984	Ed Banach(USA)	Akira Ota(JPN)	Noel Loban(GBR)
1988	Makharbek Khadartsev(URS)	Akira Ota(JPN)	Tae-Woo Kim(KOR)
1992	Makharbek Khadartsev(EUN)	Kenan Simsek(TUR)	Christopher Campbell(USA)
1996	Rasul Khadem Azghadi(IRI)	Makharbek Khadartsev(RUS)	Eldar Kurtanidze(GEO)
2000	Saghid Murtasaliyev(RUS)	Islam Bairamukov(KAZ)	Eldar Kurtanidze(GEO)
2004	Khadjimourat Gatsalov(RUS)	Magomed Ibragimov(UZB)	Alireza Heidari(IRI)

1896–1912 Event not held

Freestyle up to 158lb (71.6kg) 1904; over 73kg 1908; over 82.5kg 1920; over 87kg 1924–60; over 97kg 1964–68; up to 100kg 1972–96 – Men

	GOLD	SILVER	BRONZE
1904	Bernhuff Hansen(USA)	Frank Kungler(USA)	Fred Warmbold(USA)
1908	George O'Kelly(GBR)	Jacob Gundersen(NOR)	Edmond Barrett(GBR)
1920	Robert Roth(SUI)	Nathan Pendleton(USA)	Ernst Nilsson(SWE) (1)
			Frederick Meyer(USA) (1)
1924	Harry Steele(USA)	Henry Wernli(SUI)	Andrew McDonald(GBR)
1928	Johan Richthoff(SWE)	Aukusti Sihovlla(FIN)	Edmond Dame(FRA)
1932	Johan Richthoff(SWE)	Joh Riley(USA)	Nikolaus Hirschl(AUT)
1936	Kristjan Palusalu(EST)	Josef Klapuch(TCH)	Hjalmar Nyström(FIN)
1948	Gyula Bóbis(HUN)	Bertil Antonsson(SWE)	Joseph Armstrong(AUS)
1952	Arsen Mekokishvili(URS)	Bertil Antonsson(SWE)	Kenneth Richmond(GBR)
1956	Hamit Kaplan(TUR)	Hussein Mekhmedov(BUL)	Taisto Kangasniemi(FIN)
1960	Wilfried Dietrich(GER)	Hamit Kaplan(TUR)	Savkus Dzarassov(URS)
1964	Alexander Ivanitsky(URS)	Liutvi Djiber(BUL)	Hamit Kaplan(TUR)
1968	Alexander Medved(URS)	Osman Duraliev(BUL)	Wilfried Dietrich(FRG)
1972	Ivan Yaragin(URS)	Khorloo Baianmunkh(MGL)	József Csatári(HUN)
1976	Ivan Yaragin(URS)	Russell Helickson(USA)	Dimo Kostov(BUL)
1980	Ilya Mate(URS)	Slavtcho Tchervenkov(BUL)	Julius Strnisko(TCH)
1984	Lou Banach(USA)	Joseph Atiyeh(SYR)	Vasile Pascasu(ROM)
1988	Vasile Pascasu(ROM)	Leri Khabelov(URS)	William Scherr(USA)
1992	Leri Khabelov(EUN)	Heiko Balz(GER)	Ali Kayali(TUR)
1996	Kurt Angle(USA)	Abbas Jadidi(IRI)	Arwat Sabejew(GER)

1896–1900, 1906, 1912, 2000, 2004 Event not held
(1) Third-place tie

Freestyle over 100kg 1972–96; up to 130kg 2000 – Men

	GOLD	SILVER	BRONZE
1972	Alexander Medved(URS)	Osman Duraliev(BUL)	Chris Taylor(USA)
1976	Soslan Andiev(URS)	Jozsef Balla(HUN)	Ladislau Simon(ROM)
1980	Soslan Andiev(URS)	Jozsef Balla(HUN)	Adam Sandurski(POL)
1984	Bruce Baumgartner(USA)	Bob Molle(CAN)	Ayhan Taskin(TUR)
1988	David Gobedjichvili(URS)	Bruce Baumgartner(USA)	Andreas Schröder(GDR)
1992	Bruce Baumgartner(USA)	Jeff Thue(CAN)	David Gobedjichvili(EUN)
1996	Mahmut Demir(TUR)	Alexei Medvedev(BUL)	Bruce Baumgartner(USA)
2000	David Mousoulbes(RUS)	Artur Taymazov(UZB)	Alexis Rodriguez(CUB)
2004	Artur Taymazov(UZB)	Alireza Rezaei(IRI)	Aydin Polatci(TUR)

1896–1968 Event not held

Greco-Roman Style up to 48kg – Men

	GOLD	SILVER	BRONZE
1972	Gheorghe Berceanu(ROM)	Rahim Ahabadi(IRI)	Stefan Anghelov(BUL)
1976	Aleksey Shumanov(URS)	Gheorghe Berceanu(ROM)	Stefan Anghelov(BUL)
1980	Zaksylik Ushkempirov(URS)	Constantin Alexandru(ROM)	Ferenc Seres(HUN)
1984	Vincenzo Maenza(ITA)	Markus Scherer(FRG)	Ikuzo Saito(JPN)
1988	Vincenzo Maenza(ITA)	Andrzej Glab(POL)	Bratan Tzenov(BUL)
1992	Oleg Kutcherenko(EUN)	Vincenzo Maenza(ITA)	Wiber Sanchez(CUB)
1996	Kwon-Ho Sim(KOR)	Alexander Pavlov(BLR)	Zafar Gulyov(RUS)

1896–1968, 2000, 2004 Event not held

Greco-Roman up to 52kg 1948–96; up to 54kg 2000 – Men

	GOLD	SILVER	BRONZE
1948	Pietro Lombardi(ITA)	Kenan Olcay(TUR)	Reino Kangasmäki(FIN)
1952	Boris Maksimovich Gurevich(URS)	Iganzio Fabra(ITA)	Leo Honkala(FIN)
1956	Nikolai Solovyov(URS)	Ignazio Fabra(ITA)	Durum Ali Egribas(TUR)
1960	Dumitru Pirvulescu(ROM)	Osman Sayed(UAR)	Mohamad Paziraye(IRI)
1964	Tsutomu Hanahara(JPN)	Angel Kerezov(BUL)	Dumitru Pirvulescu(ROM)
1968	Petar Kirov(BUL)	Vladimir Bakulin(URS)	Miroslav Zeman(TCH)
1972	Petar Kirov(BUL)	Koichiro Hirayama(JPN)	Giuseppe Bognanni(ITA)
1976	Vitaliy Konstantinov(URS)	Nicu Ginga(ROM)	Koichiro Kirayama(JPN)
1980	Vakhtang Blagidze(URS)	Lajos Racz(HUN)	Mladen Mladenov(BUL)
1984	Atsuji Miyahama(JPN)	Daniel Aceves(MEX)	Dae-Du Bang(KOR)
1988	Jon Ronningen(NOR)	Atsuji Miyahama(JPN)	Jae-Suk Lee(KOR)
1992	Jon Ronningen(NOR)	Alfred Ter-Mkrttchian(EUN)	Kyung-Kap Min(KOR)
1996	Arman Nazaryan(ARM)	Brandon Paulson(USA)	Andrei Kalashnikov(UKR)
2000	Kwon-Ho Sim(KOR)	Lazaro Rivas(CUB)	Yong-Gyun Kang(PRK)

1896–1936, 2004 Event not held

Greco-Roman up to 58kg 1924–28; up to 56kg 1932–36; up to 57kg 1948–96; up to 58kg 2000 – Men

	GOLD	SILVER	BRONZE
1924	Eduard Pütsep(EST)	Anselm Ahlfors(FIN)	Väinö Ikonen(FIN)

1928	Kurt Leucht(GER)	Jindrich Maudr(TCH)	Giovanni Gozzi(ITA)
1932	Jakob Brendel(GER)	Marcello Nizzola(ITA)	Louis François(FRA)
1936	Márton Lörincz(HUN)	Egon Svensson(SWE)	Jakob Brendel(GER)
1948	Kurt Pettersén(SWE)	Aly Mahmoud Hassan(EGY)	Habil Kaya(TUR)
1952	Imre Hódos(HUN)	Zakaria Chihab(LIB)	Artem Teryan(URS)
1956	Konstantin Vyrupayev(URS)	Evdin Vesterby(SWE)	Francisco Horvat(ROM)
1960	Oleg Karavayev(URS)	Ion Cernea(ROM)	Petrov Dinko(BUL)
1964	Masamitsu Ichiguchi(JPN)	Vladen Trostiansky(URS)	Ion Cernea(ROM)
1968	János Varga(HUN)	Ion Baciu(ROM)	Ivan Kochergin(URS)
1972	Rustem Kazakov(URS)	Hans-Jürgen Veil(FRG)	Risto Björlin(FIN)
1976	Pertti Ukkola(FIN)	Iván Frgic(YUG)	Farhat Mustafin(URS)
1980	Shamil Serikov(URS)	Jozef Lipien(POL)	Benni Ljungbeck(SWE)
1984	Pasquale Passarelli(FRG)	Masaki Eto(JPN)	Haralambos Holidis(GRE)
1988	Andras Sike(HUN)	Stoyan Balov(BUL)	Haralambos Holidis(GRE)
1992	Han-Bong An(KOR)	Rifat Yildiz(GER)	Zetian Sheng(CHN)
1996	Yovei Melnichenko(KAZ)	Denis Hall(USA)	Zetian Sheng(CHN)
2000	Armen Nazaryan(BUL)	In-Sub Kim(KOR)	Zetian Sheng(CHN)
2004	Istvan Majoros(HUN)	Geydar Mamedalyev(RUS)	Artiom Kiouregkian(GRE)

1896–1920 Event not held

Greco-Roman up to 60kg 1912–20; up to 62kg 1924–28, up to 61kg 1932–36; up to 62kg 1948–60; up to 63kg 1964–68; up to 62kg 1972–96; up to 63kg 2000 – Men

	GOLD	SILVER	BRONZE
1912	Kaarlo Koskelo(FIN)	Georg Gerstacker(GER)	Otto Lasanen(FIN)
1920	Oskari Friman(FIN)	Hekki Kähkönen(FIN)	Fridtjof Svensson(SWE)
1924	Kalle Antila(FIN)	Aleksanteri Toivola(FIN)	Erik Malmberg(SWE)
1928	Voldemar Väli(EST)	Erik Malmberg(SWE)	Giacomo Quaglia(ITA)
1932	Giovanni Gozzi(ITA)	Wolfgang Ehrl(GER)	Lauri Koskela(FIN)
1936	Yasar Erkan(TUR)	Aarne Reini(FIN)	Einar Karlsson(SWE)
1948	Mehmet Oktav(TUR)	Olle Anderberg(SWE)	Ferenc Tóth(HUN)
1952	Yakov Punkin(URS)	Imre Polyák(HUN)	Abdel Rashed(EGY)
1956	Rauno Mäkinen(FIN)	Imre Polyák(HUN)	Roman Dzneladze(URS)
1960	Muzahir Sille(TUR)	Imre Polyák(HUN)	Konstantin Vyrupayev(URS)
1964	Imre Polyák(HUN)	Roman Rurua(URS)	Branko Marttinovic(YUG)
1968	Roman Rurua(URS)	Hideo Fujimoto(JPN)	Simeon Popescu(ROM)
1972	Gheorghi Markov(BUL)	Heniz-Helmut Wehling(GDR)	Kazimierz Lipien(POL)
1976	Kazimierz Lipien(POL)	Nelson Davidian(URS)	László Réczi(HUN)
1980	Stilianos Migiakis(GRE)	István Tóth(HUN)	Boris Kramorenko(URS)
1984	Weon-Kee Kim(KOR)	Kent-Olle Johansson(SWE)	Hugo Dietsche(SUI)
1988	Kamandar Madjidov(URS)	Jivko Vanguelov(BUL)	Dae-Hyun An(KOR)
1992	Akif Pirim(TUR)	Sergei Martynov(EUN)	Juan Maren(CUB)
1996	Wlodzimierz Zawadzki(POL)	Juan Delis(CUB)	Akif Pirim(TUR)
2000	Varteres Samourgachev(RUS)	Juan Luis Maren(CUB)	Akaki Chachua(GEO)
2004	Ji Hyun Jung(KOR)	Roberto Monzon(CUB)	Armen Nazarian(BUL)

1896–1908 Event not held

Greco-Roman up to 75kg 1906; up to 66.6kg 1912; up to 67.5kg 1912–28; up to 66kg 1932–36; up to 67kg 1948–60; up to 70kg 1964–68; up to 68kg 1972–96; up to 69kg 2000 – Men

	GOLD	SILVER	BRONZE
1906	Rudolf Watzl(AUT)	Karl Karlsen(DEN)	Ferenc Holuban(HUN)
1908	Enrico Porro(ITA)	Nikolav Orlov(URS0	Avid Lindén-Linko(FIN)
1912	Eemil Wäre(FIN)	Gustaf Malmström(SWE)	Edvin Matiasson(SWE)
1920	Eemil Wäre(FIN)	Taavi Tamminen(FIN)	Fritjof Andersen(NOR)
1924	Oskari Friman(FIN)	Lajos Keresztes(HUN)	Kalle Westerlund(FIN)
1928	Lajos Keresztes(HUN)	Eduard Sperling(GER)	Eduard Westerlund(FIN)
1932	Erik Malmberg(SWE)	Abraham Kurland(DEN)	Eduard Sperling(GER)
1936	Lauri Koskela(FIN)	Josef Herda(TCH)	Voldemar Väli(EST)
1948	Gustaf Freij(SWE)	Aage Eriksen(NOR)	Károly Ferencz(HUN)
1952	Shazam Safim(URS)	Gustaf Freij(SWE)	Mikulás Athanasov(TCH)
1956	Kyösti Lentonen(FIN)	Riza Dogan(TUR)	Gyula Tóth(HUN)
1960	Avtandil Koridza(URS)	Branislav Martinovic(YUG)	Gustaf Freij(SWE)
1964	Kazim Avvaz(TUR)	Valeriu Bularca(ROM)	David Gvantseladze(URS)
1968	Munji Mumemura(JPN)	Stevan Horvat(YUG)	Petros Galaktopoulos(GRE)
1972	Shamii Khisamutdinov(URS)	Stoyan Apostolov(BUL)	Gian Matteo Ranzi(ITA)
1976	Suren Nalbandyan(URS)	Stefan Rusu(ROM)	Heinz-Helmut Wehling(GDR)
1980	Stefan Rusu(ROM)	Andrzej Supron(POL)	Lars-Erik Skiold(SWE)
1984	Vlado Lisjak(YUG)	Tapio Sipila(FIN)	James Martinez(USA)
1988	Levon Djoulfalakian(URS)	Sung-Moon Kim(KOR)	Tapio Sipila(FIN)
1992	Attila Repka(HUN)	Islam Dougutchyev(EUN)	Rodney Smith(USA)
1996	Ryzsard Wolny(POL)	Ghani Yalouz(FRA)	Alexander Tretyakov(RUS)
2000	Filberto Azcuy(CUB)	Katsuhiko Nagata(JPN)	Alexei Glouchkov(RUS)
2004	Farid Mansurov(AZE)	Seref Eroglu(TUR)	Mkhitar Manukyan(KAZ)

1896–1904 Event not held

Greco-Roman up to 73kg 1932–36; up to 73kg 1948–60; up to 78kg 1964–68; up to 74kg 1972–96; up to 76kg 2000 – Men

	GOLD	SILVER	BRONZE
1932	Ivar Johansson(SWE)	Väinö Kajander(FIN)	Ercole Gallegatti(ITA)
1936	Rudolf Svedberg(SWE)	Fritz Schäfer(GER)	Eino Virtanen(FIN)
1948	Gösta Andersson(SWE)	Miklós Szilvási(HUN)	Henrik Hansen(DEN)
1952	Miklós Szilvási(HUN)	Gösta Andersson(SWE)	Khalil Taha(LIB)
1956	Mithat Bayrak(TUR)	Vladimir Maneyev(URS)	Per Berlin(SWE)
1960	Mithat Bayrak(TUR)	Günther Maritschnigg(GER)	René Schiermeyer(FRA)
1964	Anatoli Kolesov(URS)	Cyril Todorov(BUL)	Bertil Nyström(SWE)
1968	Rudolf Vesper(GDR)	Daniel Robin(FRA)	Károly Bajkó(HUN)
1972	Vitezslav Macha(TCH)	Petros Galaktopoulos(GRE)	Jan Karlsson(SWE)
1976	Anatoli Kykov(URS)	Vitezslav Macha(TCH)	Karlhienz Helbing(FRG)
1980	Ferenc Kocsis(HUN)	Anatoli Bykov(URS)	Mikko Huhtala(FIN)
1984	Jonko Salomaki(FIN)	Roger Tallroth(SWE)	Stefan Rusu(ROM)
1988	Young-Nam Kim(KOR)	Daoulet Tourlykhanov(URS)	Jozef Tracz(POL)
1992	Mnatsakan Iskandaryan(EUN)	Jozef Tracz(POL)	Torbjörn Kornbakk(SWE)
1996	Feliberto Aguilera(CUB)	Marko Asell(FIN)	Jozef Tracz(POL)
2000	Muray Kardanov(RUS)	Matt Lindland(USA)	Marko Yli-Hannukselä(FIN)
2004	Alexandr Dokturishvili(UZB)	Marko Yli-Hannukselä(FIN)	Varteres Samourgachev(RUS)

1896–1928 Event not held

Greco-Roman up to 85kg 1906; up to 73kg 1908; up to 75kg 1912–28; up to 79kg 1932–60; up to 87kg 1964–68; up to 82kg 1972–96; up to 85kg 2000 – Men

	GOLD	SILVER	BRONZE
1906	Verner Weckman(FIN)	Rudolf Lindmayer(AUT)	Robert Bebrens(USA)
1908	Frithiof Märtensson(SWE)	Mauritz Andersson(SWE)	Anders Andersen(DEN)
1912	Claes Johansson(SWE)	Martin Klein(URS)	Alfred Asikainen(FIN)
1920	Carl Westergren(SWE)	Artur Lindfors(FIN)	Matti Perttilä(FIN)
1924	Eduard Westerlund(SWE)	Artur Lindfors(FIN)	Roman Steinberg(EST)
1928	Väinö Kokkinen(FIN)	László Papp(HUN)	Albert Kusnetz(EST)
1932	Väinö Kokkinen(FIN)	Jean Földeák(GER)	Axel Cadier(SWE)
1936	Ivar Johansson(SWE)	Ludwig Schweikert(GER)	József Palotás(HUN)
1948	Axel Grönberg(SWE)	Muhlis Tayfur(TUR)	Ercole Gallegatti(ITA)
1952	Axel Grönberg(SWE)	Kalervo Rauhala(FIN)	Nikolai Belov(URS)
1956	Givi Kartiziya(URS)	Dimiter Dobrev(BUL)	Rune Jansson(SWE)
1960	Dimiter Dobrev(BUL)	Lothar Metz(GER)	Ion Taranu(ROM)
1964	Branislav Simic(YUG)	Jiri Kormanik(TCH)	Lothar Metz(GER)
1968	Lothar Metz(GDR)	Valentin Olenik(URS)	Branislav Simic(YUG)
1972	Csaba Hegedus(HUN)	Anatoli Nazarenko(URS)	Milan Nenadic(YUG)
1976	Momir Petkovic(YUG)	Vladimir Cheboksarov(URS)	Ivan Kolev(BUL)
1980	Gennadi Korban(URS)	Jan Polgowicz(POL)	Pavel Pavlov(BUL)
1984	Ion Draica(ROM)	Dimitrios Thanapoulos(GRE)	Soren Claeson(SWE)
1988	Mikhail Mamiachvili(URS)	Tibor Komaromi(HUN)	Sang-Kyu Kim(KOR)
1992	Peter Farkas(HUN)	Piotr Stepien(POL)	Daoulet Tourlykhanov(EUN)
1996	Hamza Yerlikaya(TUR)	Thomas Zander(GER)	Valeri Tsilent(BLR)
2000	Hamza Yerlikaya(TUR)	Sandor Bardosi(HUN)	Muchran Vakhtangadze(GEO)
2004	Aleksei Michine(RUS)	Ara Abrahamian(SWE)	Vyachaslav Makarenko(BLR)

1896–1904 Event not held

Greco-Roman up to 93kg 1908; up to 82.5kg 1912–28; up to 87kg 1932–60; up to 97kg 1964–68; up to 90kg 1972–96; up to 97kg 2000 – Men

	GOLD	SILVER	BRONZE
1908	Verner Weckman(FIN)	Yrjö Saarala(FIN)	Carl Jensen(DEN)
1912	– (1)	Anders Ahlgren(SWE) Ivor Böhling(FIN)	Béla Varga(HUN)
1920	Claes Johansson(SWE)	Edil Rosenqvist(SWE)	Johannes Eriksen(DEN)
1924	Carl Westergren(SWE)	Rudolf Svensson(SWE)	Onni Pellinen(FIN)
1928	Ibrahim Moustafa(EGY)	Adolf Rieger(GER)	Onni Pellinen(FIN)
1932	Rudolf Svensson(SWE)	Onni Pellinen(FIN)	Mario Gruppioni(ITA)
1936	Axel Cadier(SWE)	Edwins Bietags(LAT)	August Néo(EST)
1948	Karl-Erik Nilsson(SWE)	Kaelpo Gröndahl(FIN)	Ibrahim Orabi(EGY)
1952	Kaelpo Gröndahl(FIN)	Shalva Shikhladze(URS)	Karl-Erik Nilsson(SWE)
1956	Valentin Nikolayev(URS)	Petko Sirakov(BUL)	Karl-Erik Nilsson(SWE)
1960	Tevfik Kis(TUR)	Krali Bimbalov(BUL)	Givi Kartoziya(URS)
1964	Boyan Radev(BUL)	Per Svensson(SWE)	Heinz Kiehl(GER)
1968	Boyan Radev(BUL)	Nikolai Yakovenko(URS)	Nicolae Martinescu(ROM)
1972	Valeri Rezantsky(URS)	Josip Corak(YUG)	Czeslaw Kwiecinski(POL)
1976	Valeri Rezantsky(URS)	Stoyan Ivanov(BUL)	Czesalw Kwiecinski(POL)
1980	Norbert Nottny(HUN)	Igor Kanygin(URS)	Petre Disu(ROM)
1984	Steven Fraser(USA)	Ilie Matei(ROM)	Frank Andersson(SWE)
1988	Atanas Komchev(BUL)	Harri Koskela(FIN)	Vladimir Popov(URS)
1992	Maik Bullmann(GER)	Hakki Basar(TUR)	Gogui Kogouachvili(EUN)
1996	Vyachetslav Oleynik(UKR)	Jacek Fafinski(POL)	Maik Bullmann(GER)
2000	Mikael Ljungberg(SWE)	David Saldadze(UKR)	Garrett Lowney(USA)

| 2004 | Karim Ibrahim(EGY) | Ramaz Nozadze(GEO) | Mehmet Ozal(TUR) |

1896–1906 Event not held
(1) No winner, Ahlgren and Böhling equal second

Greco-Roman open in 1896; over 85kg 1906; over 93kg 1908; over 82.5kg 1912–28; over 81kg 1932–60; over 91kg 1964–68; up to 100kg 1972–96 – Men

	GOLD	SILVER	BRONZE
1896	Carl Schuhmann(GER)	Georgios Tsitas(GRE)	Stephanos Christopoulos(GRE)
1906	Sören Jensen(DEN)	Henri Baur(AUT)	Marcel Dubois(BEL)
1908	Richard Weisz(HUN)	Alexander Petrov(RUS)	Sören Jensen(DEN)
1912	Yrjö Saarela(FIN)	Johan Olin(FIN)	Sören Jensen(DEN)
1920	Adolf Lindfors(FIN)	Poul Hansen(DEN)	Martti Nieminen(FIN)
1924	Henri Deglane(FRA)	Edil Rosenqvist(FIN)	Raymund Badó(HUN)
1928	Rudolf Svensson(SWE)	Hjalmar Nyström(FIN)	Georg Gehring(GER)
1932	Carl Westergren(SWE)	Josef Urban(TCH)	Nikolaus Hirschl(AUT)
1936	Kristjan Palusalu(EST)	John Nyman(SWE)	Kurt Hornfischer(GER)
1948	Ahmet Kireçci(TUR)	Tor Nilsson(SWE)	Guido Fantoni(ITA)
1952	Johannes Kotkas(URS)	Josef Ruzicka(TCH)	Tauno Kovanen(FIN)
1956	Anatoliy Parfenov(URS)	Wilfried Dietrich(GER)	Adelmo Bulgarelli(ITA)
1960	Ivan Bogdan(URS)	Wilfried Dietrich(GER)	Bohumil Kubat(TCH)
1964	István Kozma(HUN)	Anatoliy Roschin(URS)	Wilfried Dietrich(GER)
1968	István Kozma(HUN)	Anatoliy Roschin(URS)	Petr Kment(TCH)
1972	Nicolae Martinescu(ROM)	Nikolai Yakovenko(URS)	Ferenc Kiss(HUN)
1976	Nikolai Bolboshin(URS)	Kamen Goranov(BUL)	Andrzej Skrzylewski(POL)
1980	Gheorghi Raikov(BUL)	Roman Bierla(POL)	Vasile Andrei(ROM)
1984	Vasile Andrei(ROM)	Greg Gibson(USA)	Jozef Tertelje(YUG)
1988	Andrzej Wronski(POL)	Gerhard Himmel(FRG)	Dennis Koslowski(USA)
1992	Hector Milian(CUB)	Dennis Koslowski(USA)	Sergei Demyashkevich(EUN)
1996	Andreas Wronski(POL)	Sergei Lishvan(BLR)	Mikael Ljungberg(SWE)

1900–04, 2000, 2004 Event not held

Greco-Roman over 100kg (since 1988 a maximum of 130kg has been imposed) – Men

	GOLD	SILVER	BRONZE
1972	Anatoli Roschin(URS)	Alexandre Tomov(BUL)	Victor Dolipschi(ROM)
1976	Alexander Kolchinsky(URS)	Alexandre Tomov(BUL)	Roman Codreanu(ROM)
1980	Alexander Kolchinsky(URS)	Alexandre Tomov(BUL)	Hassan Bchara(LIB)
1984	Jeffrey Blatnick(USA)	Refik Memisevic(YUG)	Victor Dolipschi(ROM)
1988	Alexander Karelin(URS)	Ranguel Guerovski(BUL)	Tomas Johansson(SWE)
1992	Alexander Karelin(URS)	Tomas Johansson(SWE)	Ioan Grigoras(ROM)
1996	Alexander Karelin(URS)	Matt Ghaffari(USA)	Sergei Moureiko(MDA)
2000	Rulon Gardner(USA)	Alexander Karelin(RUS)	Dmitri Debelka(BLR)
2004	Khasan Baroyev(RUS)	Georgi Tsurtsumia(KAZ)	Rulon Gardner(USA)

1896–1968 Event not held

Freestyle up to 48kg – Women

	GOLD	SILVER	BRONZE
2004	Irini Merleni(UKR)	Chiharu Icho(JPN)	Patricia Miranda(USA)

1896–2000 Event not held

Freestyle up to 55kg – Women

	GOLD	SILVER	BRONZE
2004	Saori Yoshida(JPN)	Tonya Verbeek(CAN)	Anna Gomis(FRA)

1896–2000 Event not held

Freestyle up to 63kg – Women

	GOLD	SILVER	BRONZE
2004	Kaori Icho(JPN)	Sara McMann(USA)	Lise Legrand(FRA)

1896–2000 Event not held

Freestyle up to 72kg – Women

	GOLD	SILVER	BRONZE
2004	Xu Wang(CHN)	Gouzel Manyourova(RUS)	Kyoko Hamaguchi(JPN))

1896–2000 Event not held

WRESTLING – DISCONTINUED EVENT

	GOLD	SILVER	BRONZE
Greco-Roman all-around			
1906	Sören Jensen(DEN)	Verner Weckmann(FIN)	Rudolf Watzl(AUT)

DISCONTINUED OLYMPIC SPORTS

CRICKET

	GOLD	SILVER	BRONZE
1900	GREAT BRITAIN	FRANCE	-

CROQUET

	GOLD	SILVER	BRONZE

Simple à la boule

1900	Aumoitte(FRA)	Johin(FRA)	Waydelich(FRA)

Simple à deux boules

1900	Waydelich(FRA)	Vignerot(FRA)	Sautereau(FRA)

Doubles

1900	FRANCE	–	–

GOLF

	GOLD	SILVER	BRONZE

Singles – Men

1900	Charles Sands(USA)	Walter Rutherford(GBR)	David Robertson(GBR)
1904	George Lyon(CAN)	Chandler Egan(USA)	Burt McKinnie(USA)

Team – Men

1904	UNITED STATES	UNITED STATES	–

Singles – Women

1900	Margaret Abbott(USA)	Pauline Whittier(USA)	Daria Pratt(USA)

JEU DE PAUME

	GOLD	SILVER	BRONZE
1908	Jay Gould(USA)	Eustace Mills(GBR)	Neville Lytton(GBR)

LACROSSE

	GOLD	SILVER	BRONZE
1904	CANADA	UNITED STATES	CANADA
1908	CANADA	GREAT BRITAIN	–

MOTORBOATING

	GOLD	SILVER	BRONZE

Open Class

1908	FRANCE	–	–

60-Foot Class

1908	GREAT BRITAIN	–	–

8-Metre Class

1908	GREAT BRITAIN	–	–

POLO

	GOLD	SILVER	BRONZE
1900	GREAT BRITAIN	GREAT BRITAIN	FRANCE
1908	GREAT BRITAIN	GREAT BRITAIN	GREAT BRITAIN
1920	GREAT BRITAIN	SPAIN	UNITED STATES
1924	ARGENTINA	UNITED STATES	GREAT BRITAIN
1936	ARGENTINA	GREAT BRITAIN	MEXICO

ROQUE

	GOLD	SILVER	BRONZE
1904	Charles Jacobus(USA)	Smith Streeter(USA)	Charles Brown(USA)

RACKETS

	GOLD	SILVER	BRONZE

Singles

1908	Evan Noel(GBR)	Henry Leaf(GBR)	John Jacob Astor(GBR)

Doubles

| 1908 | GREAT BRITAIN | GREAT BRITAIN | GREAT BRITAIN |

RUGBY UNION

	GOLD	SILVER	BRONZE
1900	FRANCE	GERMANY	GREAT BRITAIN
1908	AUSTRALIA	GREAT BRITAIN	–
1920	UNITED STATES	FRANCE	–
1924	UNITED STATES	FRANCE	ROMANIA

TUG OF WAR

	GOLD	SILVER	BRONZE
1900	SWEDEN/DENMARK (1)	FRANCE	–
1904	UNITED STATES	UNITED STATES	UNITED STATES
1906	GERMANY	GREECE	SWEDEN
1908	GREAT BRITAIN	GREAT BRITAIN	GREAT BRITAIN
1912	SWEDEN	GREAT BRITAIN	–
1920	GREAT BRITAIN	NETHERLANDS	BELGIUM

(1) Combined team

Olympic Winter Games Results

ALPINE SKIING

Downhill – Men

	GOLD	SILVER	BRONZE
1948	Henri Oreiller(FRA) 2:55.0	Franz Gabl(AUT) 2:59.1	Karl Molitor(SUI) 3:00.3
			Rolf Olinger(SUI) 3:00.3
1952	Zeno Colò(ITA) 2:30.8	Othmar Schneider(AUT) 2:32.0	Christian Pravda(AUT) 2:32.4
1956	Anton Sailer(AUT) 2:52.2	Raymond Fellay(SUI) 2:55.7	Andreas Molterer(AUT) 2:56.2
1960	Jean Vuarnet(FRA) 2:06.0	Hans-Peter Lanig(GER) 2:06.5	Guy Périllat(FRA) 2:06.9
1964	Egon Zimmerman(AUT) 2:18.16	Léo Lacroix(FRA) 2:18.90	Wolfgang Bartels(GER) 2:19.48
1968	Jean-Claude Killy(FRA) 1:59.85	Guy Périllat(FRA) 1:59.93	Jean-Daniel Dätwyler(SUI) 2:00.32
1972	Bernhard Russi(SUI) 1:51.43	Roland Collombin(SUI) 1:52.07	Heinrich Messner(AUT) 1:52.40
1976	Franz Klammer(AUT) 1:45.73	Bernhard Russi(SUI) 1:46.06	Herbert Plank(ITA) 1:46.59
1980	Leonhard Stock(AUT) 1:45.50	Peter Wirnsberger(AUT) 1:46.12	Steve Podborski(CAN) 1:46.62
1984	BIll Johnson(USA) 1:45.59	Peter Müller(SUI) 1:45.86	Anton Steiner(AUT) 1:45.95
1988	Pirmin Zurbriggen(AUT) 1:59.63	Peter Müller(SUI) 2:00.14	Franck Piccard(FRA) 2:01.24
1992	Patrick Ortlieb(AUT) 1:50.37	Franck Piccard(FRA) 1:50.42	Günther Mader(AUT) 1:50.47
1994	Tommy Moe(USA) 1:45.75	Kjetil-André Aamodt(NOR) 1:45.79	Edward Podivinsky(CAN) 1:45.87
1998	Jean Luc Cretier(FRA) 1:50.11	Lasse Kjus(NOR) 1:50.51	Hannes Trinkl(AUT) 1:50.63
2002	Fritz Strobl(AUT) 1:39.13	Lasse Kjus(NOR) 1:39.35	Stephan Eberharter(AUT) 1:39.41
2006	Antoine Deneriaz(FRA) 1:48.80	Michael Walchhofer(AUT) 1:49.52	Bruno Kernen(SUI) 1:49.82

1924–36 Event not held

Slalom – Men

	GOLD	SILVER	BRONZE
1948	Edi Reinalter(SUI) 2:10.3	James Couttret(FRA) 2:10.8	Henri Oreiller(FRA) 2:12.8
1952	Othmar Schneider(AUT) 2:00.0	Stein Eriksen(NOR) 2:01.2	Guttorm Berge(NOR) 2:01.7
1956	Anton Sailer(AUT) 3:14.7	Chiharu Igaya(JPN) 3:18.7	Stig Sollander(SWE) 3:20.2
1960	Ernst Hinterseer(AUT) 2:08.9	Matthias Leitner(AUT) 2:10.3	Charles Bozon(FRA) 2:10.4
1964	Josef Stiegler(AUT) 2:21.13	William Kidd(USA) 2:21.27	James Hengu(USA) 2:21.52
1968	Jean-Claude Killy(FRA) 1:39.73	Herbert Huber(AUT) 1:39.82	Alfred Matt(AUT) 1:40.09
1972	Francisco Fernández Ochoa(ESP) 1:49.27	Gustavo Thöni(ITA) 1:50.28	Rolando Thöni(ITA) 1:50.30
1976	Piero Gros(ITA) 2:03.29	Gustavo Thöni(ITA) 2:03.73	Willy Frommelt(LIE) 2:04.28
1980	Ingemar Stenmark(SWE) 1:44.26	Phil Mahre(USA) 1:44.76	Jacques Lüthy(SUI) 1:45.06
1984	Phil Mahre(USA) 1:39.21	Steve Mahre(USA) 1:39.62	Didier Bouvet(FRA) 1:40.20
1988	Alberto Tomba(ITA) 1:39.47	Frank Wörndl(FRG) 1:39.53	Paul Frommelt(LIE) 1:39.84
1992	Finn Christian Jagge(NOR) 1:44.39	Alberto Tomba(ITA) 1:44.67	Michael Tritscher(AUT) 1:44.85
1994	Thomas Stangassinger(AUT) 2:02.02	Alberto Tomba(ITA) 2:02.17	Jure Kosir(SLO) 2:02.5
1998	Hans Petter Buraas(NOR) 1:49.31	Ole Christian Furuseth(NOR) 1:50.64	Thomas Sykora(AUT) 1:50.68
2002	Jean-Pierre Vidal(FRA) 1:41.06	Sebastien Amiez(FRA) 1:41.76	Benjamin Raich(AUT) 1:42.41 (1)
2006	Benjamin Raich(AUT) 1:43.14s	Reinfried Herbst(AUT) 1:43.97	Rainer Schönfelder(AUT) 1:44.15

1924–36 Event not held

(1) Alain Baxter (GBR) finished third but was disqualified

Giant Slalom – Men

	GOLD	SILVER	BRONZE
1952	Stein Eriksen(NOR) 2:25.0	Christian Pravda(AUT) 2:26.9	Toni Spiss(AUT) 2:28.8
1956	Anton Sailer(AUT) 3:00.1	Andreas Molterer(AUT) 3:06.3	Walter Schuster(AUT) 3:07.2
1960	Roger Staub(SUI) 1:48.3	Josef Stiegler(AUT) 1:48.7	Ernst Hinterseer(AUT) 1:49.1
1964	François Bonlieu(FRA) 1:46.71	Karl Schranz(AUT) 1:47.09	Josef Steigler(AUT) 1:48.05

1968	Jean-Claude Killy(FRA) 3:29.28	WIlly Favre(SUI) 3:31.50	Heinrich Messner(AUT) 3:31.83
1972	Gustavo Thöni(ITA) 3:09.62	Edmund Bruggmann(SUI) 3:10.75	Werner Mattle(SUI) 3:10.99
1976	Heini Hemmi(SUI) 3:26.97	Ernst Good(SUI) 3:27.17	Ingemar Stenmark(SWE) 3:27.41
1980	Ingemar Stenmark(SWE) 2:40.74	Andreas Wenzel(LIE) 2:41.49	Hans Enn(AUT) 2:42.51
1984	Max Julen(SUI) 2:41.18	Jure Franko(YUG) 2:41.41	Andreas Wenzel(LIE) 2:41.75
1988	Alberto Tomba(ITA) 2:06.37	Hubert Strolz(AUT) 2:07.41	Pirmin Zurbriggen(SUI) 2:08.39
1992	Alberto Tomba(ITA) 2:06.98	Marc Girardelli(LUX) 2:07.30	Kjetil-André Aamodt(NOR) 2:07.82
1994	Markus Wasmeier(GER) 2:52.46	Urs Kälin(SUI) 2:52.48	Christian Mayer(AUT) 2:52.58
1998	Hans Petter Buraas(NOR) 1:49.31	Ole Christian Furuseth(NOR) 1:50.64	Thomas Sykora(AUT) 1:50.68
2002	Stephan Eberhalter(AUT) 2:23.28	Bode Miller(USA) 2:24.16	Lasse Kjus(NOR) 2:24.32
2006	Benjamin Raich(AUT) 2:35.00	Joel Chenal(FRA) 2:35.07	Hermann Maier(AUT) 2:35.16

1924–48 Event not held

Super Giant Slalom – Men

	GOLD	SILVER	BRONZE
1988	Franck Piccard(FRA) 1:39.66	Helmut Mayer(AUT) 1:40.96	Lars-Börje Eriksson(SWE) 1:41.08
1992	Kjetil-André Aamodt(NOR) 1:13.04	Marc Girardelli(LUX) 1:13.77	Jan Einar Thorsen(NOR) 1:13.83
1994	Markus Wasmeier(GER) 1:32.53	Tommy Moe(USA) 1:32.61	Kjetil-André Aamodt(NOR) 1:32.93
1998	Hermann Maier(AUT) 1:34.82	Hans Knauss(AUT) 1:35.43	–
		Didier Cuche(SUI) 1:35.43	
2002	Kjetil-André Aamodt(NOR) 1:21.58	Stephan Eberhalter(AUT) 1:21.68	Andreas Schifferer(AUT) 1:21.83
2006	Kjetil André Aamodt(NOR) 1:30.65	Hermann Maier(AUT) 1:30.78	Ambrosi Hoffmann(SUI) 1:30.98

1924–84 Event not held

Alpine Combination (Downhill and Slalom) – Men

	GOLD	SILVER	BRONZE
1936	Franz Pfnür(GER) 99.25pts	Gustav Lantschner(GER) 96.26pts	Emile Allais(FRA) 94.69pts
1948	Henri Orellier(FRA) 3.27pts	Karl Molitor(SUI) 6.44pts	James Couttet(FRA) 6.95pts
1988	Hubert Strolz(AUT) 36.55pts	Bernhard Gstrein(AUT) 43.45pts	Paul Accola(SUI) 48.24pts
1992	Josef Polig(ITA) 14.58pts	Gianfranco Martin(ITA) 14.90pts	Steve Locher(SUI) 18.16pts
1994	Lasse Kjus(NOR) 3:17.53	Kjetil-André Aamodt(NOR) 3:18.55	Harald Strand Nielsen(NOR) 3:19.14
1998	Mario Reiter(AUT) 3:08.06	Lasse Kjus(NOR) 3:08.65	Christian Mayer(AUT) 3:10.11
2002	Kjetil-André Aamodt(NOR) 3:17.56	Bode Miller(USA) 3:17.84	Benjamin Raich(AUT) 3:18.26
2006	Ted Ligety(USA) 3:09.35	Ivica Kostelic(CRO) 3:09.88	Rainer Schönfelder(AUT) 3:10.67

1924–32,1952–84 Event not held

Downhill – Women

	GOLD	SILVER	BRONZE
1948	Hedy Schlunegger(SUI) 2:28.3	Trude Beiser(AUT) 2:29.1	Resi Hammerer(AUT) 2:30.2
1952	Trude Jochum-Beiser(AUT) 1:47.1	Annemarie Buchner(GER) 1:48.0	Giuliana Mimuzzo(ITA) 1:49.0
1956	Madeleine Berthod(SUI) 1:40.7	Frieda Dänzer(SUI) 1:45.4	Lucile Wheeler(CAN) 1:45.9
1960	Heidi Beibl(GER) 1:37.6	Penelope Pitou(USA) 1:38.6	Traudl Hecher(AUT) 1:38.9
1964	Christl Haas(AUT) 1:55.39	Edith Zimmerman(AUT) 1:56.42	Traudl Hecher(AUT) 1:56.66
1968	Olga Pall(AUT) 1:40.87	Isabelle Mir(FRA) 1:41.33	Christl Haas(AUT) 1:41.41
1972	Marie-Thérèse Nadig(SUI) 1:36.68	Annemarie Pröll(AUT) 1:37.00	Susan Corrock(USA) 1:37.68
1976	Rosi Mittermaier(FRG) 1:46.16	Brigitte Totschnig(AUT) 1:46.68	Cindy Nelson(USA) 1:47.50
1980	Annemarie Pröll(AUT) 1:37.52	Hanni Wenzel(LIE) 1:38.22	Marie-Thérèse Nadig(SUI) 1:38.36
1984	Michela Figini(SUI) 1:13.36	Maria Walliser(SUI) 1:13.41	Olga Charvátová(TCH) 1:13.53
1988	Marina Kiehl(FRG) 1:25.86	Brigitte Oertli(SUI) 1:26.61	Karen Percy(CAN) 1:26.62
1992	Kerin Lee-Gartner(CAN) 1:52.55	Hilary Lindh(USA) 1:52.61	Veronika Wallinger(AUT) 1:52.64
1994	Katja Seizinger(GER) 1:35.93	Picabo Street(USA) 1:36.59	Isolde Kostner(ITA) 1:36.85
1998	Katja Seizinger(GER) 1:28.89	Pernilla Wiberg(SWE) 1:29.18	Florence Masnada(FRA) 1:29.37
2002	Carole Montillet(FRA) 1:39.56	Isolde Kostner(ITA) 1:40.01	Renate Götschil(AUT) 1:40.39
2006	Michaela Dorfmeister(AUT) 1:56.49	Martina Schlid(SUI) 1:56.86	Anja Pärson(SWE) 1:57.13

1924–36 Event not held

Slalom – Women

	GOLD	SILVER	BRONZE
1948	Gretchen Fraser(USA) 1:57.2	Antoinette Meyer(SUI) 1:57.7	Erika Mahringer(AUT) 1:58.0
1952	Andrea Mead-Lawrence(USA) 2:10.6	Ossi Reichert(GER) 2:11.4	Annemarie Buchner(GER) 2:13.3
1956	Renée Colliard(SUI) 1:52.3	Regina Schöpf(AUT) 1:55.4	Yevgeniya Sidorova(URS) 1:56.7
1960	Anne Heggtveit(CAN) 1:49.6	Betsy Snite(USA) 1:52.9	Barbara Henneberger(GER) 1:56.6
1964	Christine Goitschel(FRA) 1:29.86	Marielle Goitschel(FRA) 1:30.77	Jean Saubert(USA) 1:31.36
1968	Marielle Goitschel(FRA) 1:25.86	Nancy Greene(CAN) 1:26.15	Annie Famose(FRA) 1:27.89
1972	Barbara Cochran(USA) 1:31.24	Danièlle Debernard(FRA) 1:31.26	Florence Steurer(FRA) 1:32.69
1976	Rosi Mittermaier(FRG) 1:30.54	Claudia Giordani(ITA) 1:30.87	Hanni Wenzel(LIE) 1:32.20
1980	Hanni Wenzel(LIE) 1;25.09	Christa Kinshofer(FRG) 1:26.50	Erika Hess(SUI) 1:27.89
1984	Paolette Magoin(ITA) 1:36.47	Perrine Pelen(FRA) 1:37.38	Ursula Konsett(LIE) 1:37.50
1988	Vreni Schneider(SUI) 1:36.69	Mateja Svet(YUG) 1:38.37	Christa Kinshofer-Güthlein(FRG) 1:38.40
1992	Petra Kronberger(AUT) 1:32.68	Annelise Coberger(NZL) 1:33.10	Bianca Fernández-Ochoa(ESP) 1:33.35
1994	Vreni Schneider(SUI) 1:56.01	Elfi Eder(AUT) 1:56.36	Katja Koren(SLO) 1:56.61
1998	Hilde Gerg(GER) 1:32.40	Deboarah Compagnoni(ITA) 1:32.46	Zali Steggall(AUS) 1:32.67

2002	Janica Kostelic(CRO) 1:46.10	Laure Pequegnot(FRA) 1:46.17	Anja Pärson(SWE) 1:47.09
2006	Anja Pärson(SWE) 1:29.04	Nicole Hosp(AUT) 1:29.33	Marlies Schild(AUT) 1:29.79

1924–36 Event not held

Giant Slalom – Women

	GOLD	SILVER	BRONZE
1952	Andrea Mead-Lawrence(USA) 2:06.8	Dagmar Rom(AUT) 2:09.0	Annemarie Buchner(GER) 2:10.0
1956	Ossi Reichert(GER) 1:56.5	Josefine Frandl(AUT) 1:57.8	Dorothea Hochleitner(AUT) 1:58.2
1960	Yvonne Rüegg(SUI) 1:39.9	Penelope Pitou(USA) 1:40.0	Giuliana Chenal-Minuzzo(ITA) 1:40.2
1964	Marielle Goitschel(FRA) 1:52.24	Christine Goitschel(FRA) 1:53.11 Jean Saubert(USA) 1:53.11	–
1968	Nancy Greene(CAN) 1:51.97	Annie Famose(FRA) 1:54.61	Fernande Bochatay(SUI) 1:54.74
1972	Marie-Thérèse Nadig(SUI) 1:29.90	Annemarie Pröll(AUT) 1:30.75	Wiltrud Drexel(AUT) 1:32.35
1976	Kathy Kreiner(CAN) 1:29.13	Rosi Mittermaier(FRG) 1:29.25	Danièlle Debernard(FRA) 1:29.95
1980	Hanni Wenzel(LIE) 2:41.66	Irene Epple(FRG) 2:42.12	Perrine Pelen(FRA) 2:42.41
1984	Debbie Armstrong(USA) 2:20.98	Christin Cooper(USA) 2:21.38	Perrine Pelen(FRA) 2:21.40
1988	Vreni Schneider(SUI) 2:06.49	Christa Kinshofer-Güthlein(FRG) 2:07.42	Maria Walliser(SUI) 2:07.72
1992	Pernilla Wiberg(SWE) 2:12.74	Diann Roffe(USA) 2:13.71 Anita Wachter(AUT) 2:13.71	–
1994	Deborah Compagnoni(ITA) 2:30.47	Martina Ertl(GER) 2:32.19	Vreni Schneider(SUI) 2:32.97
1998	Deborah Compagnoni(ITA) 2:50.59	Alexandra Meissnitzer(AUT) 2:52.39	Katja Seizinger(GER) 2:52.61
2002	Janica Kostelic(CRO) 2:30.01	Anja Pärson(SWE) 2:31.33	Sonja Nef(SUI) 2:31.67
2006	Julia Mancuso(USA) 2:09.19	Tanja Poutiainen(FIN) 2:09.86	Anna Ottosson(SWE) 2:10.33

1924–48 Event not held

Super Giant Slalom – Women

	GOLD	SILVER	BRONZE
1988	Sigrid Wolf(AUT) 1:19.03	Michela Figini(SUI) 1:20.03	Karen Percy(CAN) 1:20.29
1992	Deborah Compagnoni(ITA) 1:21.22	Carole Merle(FRA) 1:22.63	Katja Seizinger(GER) 1:23.19
1994	Diann Roffe(USA) 1:22.15	Svetlana Gladischeva(RUS) 1:22.44	Isolde Kostner(ITA) 1:22.45
1998	Picabo Street(USA) 1:18.02	Michaela Dorfmeister(AUT) 1:18.03	Alexandra Meissnitzer(AUT) 1:18.09
2002	Daniela Ceccarelli(ITA) 1:13.59	Janica Kostelic(CRO) 1:13.64	Karen Putzer(ITA) 1:13.86
2006	Michaela Dorfmeister(AUT) 1:32.47	Janica Kostelic(CRO) 1:32.74	Alexandra Meissnitzer(AUT) 1:33.06

1924–84 Event not held

Alpine Combination (Downhill and Slalom) – Women

	GOLD	SILVER	BRONZE
1936	Christel Cranz(GER) 97.06pts	Käthe Grasegger(GER) 95.26pts	Laila Schou Nilsen(NOR) 93.48pts
1948	Trude Beiser(AUT) 6.58pts	Gretchen Fraser(USA) 6.95pts	Erika Mahringer(AUT) 7.04pts
1988	Anita Wachter(AUT) 29.25pts	Brigitte Oertli(SUI) 29.48pts	Maria Walliser(SUI) 51.28pts
1992	Petra Kronberger(AUT) 2.55pts	Anita Wachter(AUT) 19.39pts	Florence Masnada(FRA) 21.38pts
1994	Pernilla Wiberg(SWE) 3:05.16	Vreni Schneider(SUI) 3:05.29	Alenka Dovzan(SLO) 3:06.64
1998	Katja Seizinger(GER) 2:40.74	Martina Ertl(GER) 2:40.92	Hilde Gerg(GER) 2:41.50
2002	Janica Kostelic(CRO) 2:43.28	Renate Götschil(AUT) 2:44.77	Martina Ertl(GER) 2:45.16
2006	Janica Kostelic(CRO) 2:51.08	Marlies Schild(AUT) 2:51.58	Anja Pärson(SWE) 2:51.63

1924–32, 1952–84 Event not held

BOBSLEIGH

2-Man Bob

	GOLD	SILVER	BRONZE
1932	UNITED STATES I 8:14.14	SWITZERLAND II 8:16.28	UNITED STATES II 8:29.15
1936	UNITED STATES I 5:29.29	SWITZERLAND II 5:30.64	UNITED STATES II 5:33.96
1948	SWITZERLAND II 5:29.2	SWITZERLAND I 5:30.4	UNITED STATES II 5:35.3
1952	GERMANY I 5:24.54	UNITED STATES I 5:26.89	SWITZERLAND I 5:27.71
1956	ITALY I 5:39.14	ITALY II 5:31.45	SWITZERLAND I 5:37.46
1964	GREAT BRITAIN I 4:21.90	ITALY II 4:22.02	ITALY I 4:22.63
1968	ITALY I 4:41.54 (1)	FRG I 4:41.54	ROMANIA 4:44.46
1972	FRG II 4:47.07	FRG I 4:58.84	SWITZERLAND I 4:59.33
1976	GDR II 3:44.42	FRG I 3:44.99	SWITZERLAND I 3:45.70
1980	SWITZERLAND II 4:09.36	GDR II 4:10.93	GDR I 4:11.08
1984	GDR II 3:28.56	GDR I 3:26.04	SOVIET UNION II 3:26.16
1988	SOVIET UNION I 3:53.48	GDR I 3:54.19	GDR II 3:54.64
1992	SWITZERLAND I 4:03.26	GERMANY I 4:03.55	GERMANY II 4:03.63
1994	SWITZERLAND I 3:30.81	SWITZERLAND II 3:30.86	ITALY I 3:31.01
1998	ITALY I 3:37.24 CANADA I 3:27.24	-	GERMANY I 3:37.89
2002	GERMANY I 3:10.11	SWITZERLAND I 3:10.20	SWITZERLAND II 3:10.62
2006	GERMANY I 3:43.38	CANADA 3:43.59	SWITZERLAND 3:43.73

1924–28,1960 Event not held
(1) Italy had fastest single run

4-Man Bob
(Five man teams allowed until 1932)

	GOLD	SILVER	BRONZE
1924	SWITZERLAND I 5:45.54	GREAT BRITAIN II 5:48.83	BELGIUM I 6:02.29
1928(1)	UNITED STATES II 3:20.5	UNITED STATES I 3:21.0	GERMANY II 3:21.9
1932	UNITED STATES I 7:53.68	UNITED STATES II 7:55.70	GERMANY I 8:00.04
1936	SWITZERLAND II 5:19.85	SWITZERLAND I 5:22.73	GREAT BRITAIN I 5:23.41
1948	UNITED STATES II 5:20.1	BELGIUM 5:21.3	UNITED STATES I 5:21.5
1952	GERMANY 5:07.84	UNITED STATES I 5:10.48	SWITZERLAND I 5:11.70
1956	SWITZERLAND I 5:10.44	ITALY II 5:12.10	UNITED STATES I 5:12.39
1964	CANADA 4:14.46	AUSTRIA 4:15.48	ITALY II 4:15.60
1968(1)	ITALY I 2:17.39	AUSTRIA I 2:17.48	SWITZERLAND I 2:18.04
1972	SWITZERLAND 4:43.07	ITALY I 4:43.83	FRG I 4:43.92
1976	GDR I 3:40.43	SWITZERLAND II 3:40.89	FRG I 3:41.37
1980	GDR I 3:59.92	SWITZERLAND I 4:00.87	GDR I 4:00.97
1984	GDR I 3:20.22	GDR II 3:20.78	SWITZERLAND I 3:21.39
1988	SWITZERLAND I 3:47.51	GDR I 3:47.58	SOVIET UNION II 3:48.26
1992	AUSTRIA I 3:53.90	GERMANY I 3:53.92	SWITZERLAND I 3:54.13
1994	GERMANY II 3:27.78	SWITZERLAND I 3:27.84	GERMANY I 3:28.01
1998(2)	GERMANY II 2:39.41	SWITZERLAND I 2:40.01	GREAT BRITAIN I 2:40.06 FRANCE 2:40.06
2002	GERMANY I 3:07.51	UNITED STATES I 3:07.81	UNITED STATES II 3:07.86
2006	GERMANY I 3:40.42	RUSSIA I 3:40.55	SWITZERLAND I 3:40.83

1960 Event not held
(1) Only two runs
(2) Only three runs

2-Woman

	GOLD	SILVER	BRONZE
2002	UNITED STATES II 1:37.76	GERMANY I 1:38.06	GERMANY II 1:38.29
2006	GERMANY 3:49.98	UNITED STATES 3:50.69s	ITALY 3:51.01

1924–98 Event not held

CURLING

Men

	GOLD	SILVER	BRONZE
1998	SWITZERLAND	CANADA	NORWAY
2002	NORWAY	CANADA	SWITZERLAND
2006	CANADA	FINLAND	UNITED STATES

1924–94 Event not held

Women

	GOLD	SILVER	BRONZE
1998	CANADA	DENMARK	SWEDEN
2002	GREAT BRITAIN	SWITZERLAND	CANADA
2006	SWEDEN	SWITZERLAND	CANADA

1924–94 Event not held

FIGURE SKATING

Men

	GOLD	SILVER	BRONZE
1908(1)	Nikolai Panin(RUS) 219pts	Arthur Cumming(GBR) 164pts	George Hall-Say(GBR) 104pts
1908	Ulrich Salchow(SWE) 1886.5pts	Richard Johansson(SWE) 1826.0pts	Per Thorén(SWE) 1787.0pts
1920	Gillis Grafström(SWE) 2838.5pts	Andreas Krogh(NOR) 2634pts	Martin Stixrud(NOR) 2561.5pts
1924	Gillis Grafström(SWE) 2757.2pts	Willy Böckl(AUT) 2518.75pts	Georges Gautschi(SUI) 2233.5pts
1928	Gillis Grafström(SWE) 2698.25pts	Willy Böckl(AUT) 2682.50 pts	Robert Van Zeebroeck (BEL) 2578.75 pts
1932	Karl Schäfer(AUT) 2602.0pts	Gillis Grafström(SWE) 2514.5pts	Montgomery Wilson(CAN) 2448.3pts
1936	Karl Schäfer(AUT) 2959.0pts	Ernst Baier(GER) 2805.3pts	Felix Kaspar(AUT) 2801.0pts
1948	Richard Button(USA) 1720pts	Hans Gerschwiler(SUI) 1630.1pts	Edi Rada(AUT) 1603.2pts
1952	Richard Button(USA) 1730.3pts	Helmut Seibt(AUT) 1621.3pts	James Grogan(USA) 1627.4pts
1956	Hayes Alan Jenkins(USA) 1497.95pts	Ronald Robertson(USA) 1492.1pts	David Jenkins(USA) 1465.41pts
1960	David Jenkins(USA) 1440.2pts	Karol Divin(TCH) 141.3pts	Donald Jackson(CAN) 1401.0pts
1964	Manfred Schnelldorfer(GER) 1916.9pts	Alain Calmar(FRA) 1876.5pts	Scott Allen(USA) 1873.6pts
1968	Wolfgang Schwarz(AUT) 1894.1pts	Tim Woods(USA) 1891.6pts	Patrick Péra(FRA) 1864.5pts
1972	Ondrej Nepela(TCH) 2739.1pts	Sergey Tchetveroukhin(URS) 2672.4pts	Patrick Péra(FRA) 2653.1pts
1976	John Curry(GBR) 192.74pts	Vladimir Kovalev(URS) 187.64pts	Toller Cranston(CAN) 187.38pts

1980	Robin Cousins(GBR) 189.48pts (2)	Jan Hoffmann(GDR) 189.72pts (2)	Charles Tickner(USA) 187.06pts
1984	Scott Hamilton(USA) 3.4pl	Brian Orser(CAN) 5.6pl	Jozef Sabovtchik(TCH) 7.4pl
1988	Brian Boitano(USA) 3.0pl	Brian Orser(CAN) 4.2pl	Viktor Petrenko(URS) 7.8pl
1992	Viktor Petrenko(EUN) 1.5	Paul Wylie(USA) 3.5	Petr Barna(TCH) 4.0
1994	Alexei Urmanov(RUS) 1.5	Elvis Stojko(CAN) 3.0	Philippe Candeloro(FRA) 6.5
1998	Ilya Kulik(RUS) 1.5	Elvis Stojko(CAN) 4.0	Philippe Candeloro(FRA) 4.5
2002	Alexei Yagudin(RUS) 1.5	Yevgeni Pluschenko(RUS) 4.0	Timothy Goebel(USA) 4.5
2006	Evgeni Plushenko(RUS) 258.33	Stéphane Lambiel(SUI) 231.21	Jeffrey Buttle(CAN) 227.59

1912 Event not held
(1) Special figures competition
(2) Most judges favoured Cousins; all medallists since are decided by judges' placements

Women

	GOLD	SILVER	BRONZE
1908	Madge Syers(GBR) 1262.5pts	Elsa Rendschmidt(GER) 1055.0pts	Dorothy Greenhough-Smith(GBR) 960.0pts
1920	Magda Mauroy-Julin(SWE) 913.5pts	Svea Norén(SWE) 887.75pts	Theresa Weld(USA) 898.0pts
1924	Herma Planck-Szabó(AUT) 2094.25pts	Beatrix Loughran(USA) 1959.0pts	Ethel Muckelt(GBR) 1750.50pts
1928	Sonja Henie(NOR) 2452.25pts	Fritzi Burger(AUT) 2248.50pts	Beatrix Loughran(USA) 2254.50pts
1932	Sonja Henie(NOR) 2302.5pts	Fritzi Burger(AUT) 2167.1pts	Maribel Vinson(USA) 2158.5pts
1936	Sonja Henie(NOR) 2971.4pts	Cecilia Colledge(GBR) 2926.8pts	Vivi-Anne Hultén(SWE) 2763.2pts
1948	Barbara-Ann Scott(CAN) 1467.7pts	Eva Pawlik(AUT) 1418.3pts	Jeanette Altwegg(GBR) 1405.5pts
1952	Jeanette Altwegg(GBR) 1455.8pts	Tenley Albright(USA) 1432.2pts	Jacqueline du Bief(FRA) 1422.0pts
1956	Tenley Albright(USA) 1866.30pts	Carol Heiss(USA) 1848.24pts	Ingrid Wendl(AUT) 1753.91pts
1960	Carol Heiss(USA) 1490.1pts	Sjoukje Dijkstra(NED) 1424.8pts	Barbara Roles(USA) 1414.8pts
1964	Sjoukje Dijkstra(NED) 20.18.5pts	Regine Heitzer(AUT) 1945.5pts	Petra Burka(CAN) 1940.0pts
1968	Peggy Fleming(USA) 1970.5pts	Gabrielle Seyfert(GDR) 1882.3pts	Hana Maskova(TCH) 1828.8pts
1972	Beatrix Schuba(AUT) 2751.5pts	Karen Magnussen(CAN) 2763.2pts	Janet Lynn(USA) 2663.1pts
1976	Dorothy Hamill(USA) 193.80pts	Dianne De Leeuw(NED) 190.24pts	Christine Errath(GDR) 188.16pts
1980	Anett Pötzsch(GDR) 189.00pts	Linda Fratianne(USA) 188.30pts	Dagmar Lurz(FRG) 183.04pts
1984	Katarina Witt(GDR) 3.2pl	Rosalyn Sumners(USA) 4.6pl	Kira Ivanova(URS) 9.2pl
1988	Katarina Witt(GDR) 4.2pl	Elizabeth Manley(CAN) 4.6pl	Debra Thomas(USA) 6.0pl
1992	Kristi Yamaguchi(USA) 1.5	Midori Ito(JPN) 4.0	Nancy Kerrigan(USA) 4.0
1994	Oksana Baiul(UKR) 2.0	Nancy Kerrigan(USA) 2.5	Chen Lu(CHN) 5.0
1998	Tara Lipinski(USA) 2.0	Michelle Kwan(USA) 2.5	Chen Lu(CHN) 5.0
2002	Sarah Hughes(USA) 3.0	Irina Slutskaya(RUS) 3.0	Michelle Kwan(USA) 3.5
2006	Shizuka Arakawa(JPN) 191.34	Sasha Cohen(USA) 183.36	Irina Slutskaya(RUS) 181.44

1912 Event not held

Pairs

	GOLD	SILVER	BRONZE
1908	GERMANY 56.0pts	GREAT BRITAIN 51.5pts	GREAT BRITAIN 48.0pts
1920	FINLAND 80.75pts	NORWAY 72.75pts	GREAT BRITAIN 66.25pts
1924	AUSTRIA 74.50pts	FINLAND 71.75pts	FRANCE 69.25pts
1928	FRANCE 100.50pts	AUSTRIA 99.25pts	AUSTRIA 93.25pts
1932	FRANCE 76.7pts	UNITED STATES 77.5pts	HUNGARY 76.4pts
1936	GERMANY 103.0pts	AUSTRIA 102.7pts	HUNGARY 97.6pts
1948	BELGIUM 123.5pts	HUNGARY 122.2pts	CANADA 121.0pts
1952	GERMANY 102.6pts	UNITED STATES 100.6pts	HUNGARY 97.4pts
1956	AUSTRIA 101.8pts	CANADA 101.9pts	HUNGARY 99.3pts
1960	CANADA 80.4pts	GERMANY 76.8pts	UNITED STATES 76.2pts
1964	SOVIET UNION 104.4pts	GERMANY 103.6pts (1)	CANADA 98.5pts
1968	SOVIET UNION 315.2pts	SOVIET UNION 312.3pts	FRG 304.4pts
1972	SOVIET UNION 420.4pts	SOVIET UNION 419.4pts	GDR 411.8pts
1976	SOVIET UNION 140.54pts	GDR 136.35pts	GDR 134.57pts
1980	SOVIET UNION 147.26pts	SOVIET UNION 143.80pts	GDR 140.52pts
1984	SOVIET UNION 1.4pl	UNITED STATES 2.8pl	SOVIET UNION 3.8pl
1988	SOVIET UNION 1.4pl	SOVIET UNION 2.8pl	UNITED STATES 4.2pl
1992	UNIFIED TEAM 1.5	UNIFIED TEAM 3.0	CANADA 4.5
1994	RUSSIA 1.5	RUSSIA 3.0	CANADA 4.5
1998	RUSSIA 2.0	RUSSIA 3.5	GERMANY 6.0
2002	RUSSIA 1.5		
	CANADA (2)	–	CHINA 4.5
2006	RUSSIA 204.48	CHINA 189.73	CHINA 186.91

1912 Event not held
(1) German pair finished second, but were first disqualified, and later reinstated
(2) Canada originally placed second, but placed equal first after protest about a judge

Ice Dance

	GOLD	SILVER	BRONZE
1976	SOVIET UNION 209.92pts	SOVIET UNION 204.88pts	UNITED STATES 202.64pts
1980	SOVIET UNION 205.48pts	HUNGARY 204.52pts	SOVIET UNION 201.86pts
1984	GREAT BRITAIN 2.0pl	SOVIET UNION 4.0pl	SOVIET UNION 7.0pl

1988	SOVIET UNION 2.0pl	SOVIET UNION 4.0pl	CANADA 6.0pl
1992	UNIFIED TEAM 2.0	FRANCE 4.4	UNIFIED TEAM 5.6
1994	RUSSIA 3.4	RUSSIA 3.8	GREAT BRITAIN 4.8
1998	RUSSIA 2.0	RUSSIA 4.0	FRANCE 7.0
2002	FRANCE 2.0	RUSSIA 4.0	ITALY 6.0
2006	RUSSIA 200.64	UNITED STATES 196.06	UKRAINE 195.85

1908–72 Event not held

FREESTYLE SKIING

Moguls – Men

	GOLD	SILVER	BRONZE
1992	Edgar Grospiron(FRA) 25.81pts	Olivier Allamand(FRA) 24.87	Nelson Carmichael(USA) 24.82
1994	Jean-Luc Brassard(CAN) 27.74pts	Sergei Shoupletsov(RUS) 26.90	Edgar Grospiron(FRA) 26.64
1998	Jonny Moseley(USA) 26.93pts	Janne Lahtela(FIN) 26.01	Sami Mustonen(FIN) 25.76
2002	Janne Lahtela(FIN) 27.97pts	Travis Mayer(USA) 27.59	Richard Gay(FRA) 26.91
2006	Dale Begg-Smith(AUS) 26.77	Mikko Ronkainen(FIN) 26.62	Toby Dawson(USA) 26.30

1924–88 Event not held

Aerials – Men

	GOLD	SILVER	BRONZE
1994	Andreas Schönbächler(SUI) 234.67pts	Phillippe Laroche(CAN) 228.23	Lloyd Langlois(CAN) 222.44
1998	Eric Bergoust(USA) 255.64pts	Sebastien Foucras(FRA) 248.79	Dmitri Daschinsky(BLR) 240.79
2002	Ales Valenta(CZE) 257.02pts	Joe Pack(USA) 251.64	Alexei Grichin(BLR) 251.19
2006	Xiaopeng Han(CHN) 250.77	Dmitri Dashinski(BLR) 248.68	Vladimir Lebedyev(RUS) 246.76

1924–92 Event not held

Moguls – Women

	GOLD	SILVER	BRONZE
1992	Donna Weinbrecht(USA) 23.69pts	Yelizaveta Kozhevnikova(EUN) 23.50	Stine Lise Hattestad(NOR) 23.04
1994	Stine Lise Hattestad(NOR) 25.97pts	Elizabeth McIntyre(USA) 25.89	Yelizaveta Kozhevnikova(EUN) 25.81
1998	Tae Satoya(JPN) 25.06pts	Tatyana Mittermayer(GER) 24.62	Kari Traa(NOR) 24.09
2002	Kari Traa(NOR) 25.94pts	Shannon Bahrke(USA) 25.06	Tae Satoya(JPN) 24.85
2006	Jennifer Heil(CAN) 26.50	Kari Traa(NOR) 25.65	Sandra Laoura(FRA) 25.37

1924–88 Event not held

Aerials – Women

	GOLD	SILVER	BRONZE
1994	Lina Cheryasova(UZB) 166.84pts	Marie Lindgren(SWE) 165.88	Hilde Synnøve Lid(NOR) 164.13
1998	Nikki Stone(USA) 193.00pts	Nannan Xu(CHN) 186.97	Colette Brand(SUI) 171.83
2002	Alisa Camplin(AUS) 193.47pts	Veronica Brenner(CAN) 190.02	Deidra Dionne(CAN) 189.26
2006	Evelyne Leu(SUI) 202.55	Nina Li (CHN) 197.39	Alisa Camplin(AUS) 191.39

1924–92 Event not held

ICE HOCKEY

Men

	GOLD	SILVER	BRONZE
1920	CANADA	UNITED STATES	CZECHOSLOVAKIA
1924	CANADA	UNITED STATES	GREAT BRITAIN
1928	CANADA	SWEDEN	SWITZERLAND
1932	CANADA	UNITED STATES	GERMANY
1936	GREAT BRITAIN	CANADA	UNITED STATES
1948	CANADA	CZECHOSLOVAKIA	SWITZERLAND
1952	CANADA	UNITED STATES	SWEDEN
1956	SOVIET UNION	UNITED STATES	CANADA
1960	UNITED STATES	CANADA	SOVIET UNION
1964	SOVIET UNION	SWEDEN	CZECHOSLOVAKIA
1968	SOVIET UNION	CZECHOSLOVAKIA	CANADA
1972	SOVIET UNION	UNITED STATES	CZECHOSLOVAKIA
1976	SOVIET UNION	CZECHOSLOVAKIA	FRG (1)
1980	UNITED STATES	SOVIET UNION	SWEDEN
1984	SOVIET UNION	CZECHOSLOVAKIA	SWEDEN
1988	SOVIET UNION	FINLAND	SWEDEN
1992	UNIFIED TEAM	CANADA	CZECHOSLOVAKIA
1994	SWEDEN	CANADA	FINLAND
1998	CZECH REPUBLIC	RUSSIA	FINLAND
2002	CANADA	UNITED STATES	RUSSIA

2006	SWEDEN	FINLAND	CZECH REPUBLIC

(1) Third-place tie (with USA and Finland) decided on goal average

Women

	GOLD	SILVER	BRONZE
1998	UNITED STATES	CANADA	FINLAND
2002	CANADA	UNITED STATES	SWEDEN
2006	CANADA	SWEDEN	UNITED STATES

1924–94 Event not held

LUGEING

Singles – Men

	GOLD	SILVER	BRONZE
1964	Thomas Köhler(GER) 3:26.77	Klaus Bonsack(GER) 3:27.04	Hans Plenk(GER) 3:30.15
1968	Manfred Schmid(AUT) 2:52.48	Thomas Köhler(GDR) 2:52.66	Klaus Bonsack(GDR) 2:55.33
1972	Wolfgang Scheidel(GDR) 3:27.58	Harald Ehrig(GDR) 3:28.39	Wolfram Fiedler(GDR) 3:28.73
1976	Detlef Günther(GDR) 3:27.688	Josef Fendt(FRG) 3:28.196	Hans Rinn(GDR) 3:28.574
1980	Bernhard Glass(GDR) 2:54.796	Paul Hildgartner(ITA) 2:55.372	Anton Winkler(FRG) 2:56.545
1984	Paul Hildgartner(ITA) 3:04.258	Sergey Danilin(URS) 3:04.962	Valeriy Dudin(URS) 3:05.012
1988	Jens Müller(GDR) 3:05.548	Georg Hackl(FRG) 3:05.916	Yuriy Khartchenko(URS) 3:06.274
1992	Georg Hackl(GER) 3:02.363	Markus Prock(AUT) 3:02.669	Markus Schmidt(AUT) 3:02.942
1994	Georg Hackl(GER) 3:21.571	Markus Prock(AUT) 3:21.584	Armin Zöggeler(ITA) 3:21.833
1998	Georg Hackl(GER) 3:18.436	Armin Zöggeler(ITA) 3:18.939	Jens Müller(GER) 3:19.093
2002	Armin Zöggeler(ITA) 2:57.941	Georg Hackl(GER) 2:58.270	Markus Prock(AUT) 2:58.283
2006	Armin Zöggeler(ITA) 3:26.088s	Albert Demtschenko(RUS) 3:26.198	Martins Rubenis(LAT) 3:26.445

1924–60 Event not held

2-Man

(Since 1992 this has been designated a mixed event)

	GOLD	SILVER	BRONZE
1964	AUSTRIA 1:41.62	AUSTRIA 1:41.91	ITALY 1:42.87
1968	GDR 1:35.85	AUSTRIA 1:36.34	FRG 1:37.29
1972	ITALY 1:28.35	–	GDR 1:29.16
	GDR 1:28.35		
1976	GDR 1:25.604	FRG 1:25.889	AUSTRIA 1:25.919
1980	GDR 1:19.331	ITALY 1:19.606	AUSTRIA 1:19.795
1984	FRG 1:23.620	SOVIET UNION 1:23.660	GDR 1:23.887
1988	GDR 1:31.940	GDR 1:32.039	FRG 1:32.274
1992	GERMANY 1:32.053	GERMANY 1:32.239	ITALY 1:32.298
1994	ITALY 1:36.720	ITALY II 1:36.769	GERMANY 1:36.945
1998	GERMANY 1:41.105	UNITED STATES 1:41.127	UNITED STATES 1:41.217
2002	GERMANY 1:26.082	UNITED STATES 1:26.216	UNITED STATES 1:26.220
2006	AUSTRIA 1:34.497	GERMANY 1:34.807	ITALY 1:34.930

192–60 Event not held

Skeleton Sled – Men

	GOLD	SILVER	BRONZE
1928(1)	Jennison Heaton(USA) 3:01.8	John Heaton(USA) 3:02.8	Earl of Northesk(GBR) 3:05.1
1948(2)	Nino Bibbia(ITA) 5:23.2	John Heaton(USA) 5:24.6	John Crammond(GBR) 5:25.1
2002	Jim Shea(USA) 1:41.96	Martin Rettl(AUT) 1:42.01	Gregor Stähli(SUI) 1:42.15
2006	Duff Gibson(CAN) 1:55.88	Jeffery Pain(CAN) 1:56.14s	Gregor Stähli(SUI) 1:56.80

1924,1932–36, 1952–98 Event not held
(1) Total of three runs
(2) Total of six runs

Singles – Women

	GOLD	SILVER	BRONZE
1964	Ortrun Enderlein(GER) 3:24.67	Ilse Geisler(GER) 3:27.42	Helene Thurner(AUT) 3:29.06
1968	Erica Lechner(ITA) 2:28.66	Christa Schmuck(FRG) 2:29.37	Angelika Dünhaupt(FRG) 2:29.56
1972	Anna-Maria Müller(GDR) 2:59.18	Ute Rührold(GDR) 2:59.49	Margit Schumann(GDR) 2:59.54
1976	Margit Schumann(GDR) 2:50.621	Ute Rührold(GDR) 2:50.846	Elisabeth Demleitner(FRG) 2:51.056
1980	Vera Sosulya(URS) 2:36.537	Melitta Sollmann(GDR) 2:37.657	Ingrida Amantova(URS) 2:37.817
1984	Steffi Martin(GDR) 2:46.570	Bettine Schmidt(GDR) 2:46.873	Ute Weiss(GDR) 2:47.248
1988	Steffi Martin-Walter(GDR) 3:03.973	Ute Weiss-Oberhoffner(GDR) 3:04.105	Cerstin Schmidt(GDR) 3:04.181
1992	Doris Neuner(AUT) 3:06.696	Angelika Neuner(AUT) 3:06.769	Susi Erdmann(GER) 3:07.115
1998	Silke Kraushaar(GER) 3:23.779	Barbara Niedernhuber(GER) 3:23.781	Angelika Neuner(AUT) 3:24.253
2002	Sylke Otto(GER) 2:52.464	Barbara Niedernhuber(GER) 2:52.785	Silke Kraushaar(GER) 2:52.865
2006	Sylke Otto(GER) 3:07.979	Silke Kraushaar(GER) 3:08.115	Tatjana Hüfner(GER) 3:08.460

1924–60 Event not held

Skeleton Sled – Women

2002	Tristan Gale(USA) 1:45.11	Lea Ann Parsley(USA) 1:45.21	Alex Coomber(GBR) 1:45.37
2006	Maya Pedersen(SUI) 1:59.83s	Shelley Rudman(GBR) 2:01.06	Melissa Hollingsworth-Richards(CAN) 2:01.41

1924–98 Event not held

NORDIC SKIING

1,500m – Men

	GOLD	SILVER	BRONZE
2002	Tor Arne Hetland(NOR) 2:56.9	Peter Schlikenrieder(GER) 2:57.0	Cristian Zorzi(ITA) 2:57.2
2006	Björn Lind(SWE) 2:26.5	Roddy Darragon(FRA) 2:27.1	Thobias Fredriksson(SWE) 2:27.8

1924–98 Event not held

10,000m Classical – Men

	GOLD	SILVER	BRONZE
1992	Vegard Ulvang(NOR) 27:36.0	Marco Alberello(ITA) 27:55.2	Christer Majbäck(SWE) 27:56.4
1994	Bjørn Daehlie(NOR) 24:20.1	Vladimir Smirnov(KZK) 24:38.3	Marco Alberello(ITA) 24:42.3
1998	Bjørn Daehlie(NOR) 27:24.5	Markus Gander(AUT) 27:32.5	Mika Myllylä(FIN) 27:40.1

1924–88, 2002, 2006 Event not held

15,000m Classical – Men

	GOLD	SILVER	BRONZE
1924(1)	Thorleif Haug(NOR) 1h 14:31.0	Johan Gröttumsbraaten(NOR) 1h 15.51.0	Tipani Niku(FIN) 1h 16:26.0
1928(2)	Johan Gröttumsbraaten(NOR) 1h 37:01.0	Ole Hegge(NOR) 1h 39:01.0	Reidar Ödegaard(NOR) 1h 40:11.0
1932(3)	Sven Utterström(SWE) 1h 23:07.0	Axel Wikström(SWE) 1h 25:07.0	Veli Saarinen(FIN) 1h 25:24.0
1936(1)	Erik-August Larsson(SWE) 1h 14:38.0	Oddbjörn Hagen(NOR) 1h 15:33.0	Pekka Niemi(FIN) 1h 16:59.0
1948(1)	Martin Lundström(SWE) 1h 13:50.0	Nils Östensson(SWE) 1h 14:22.0	Gunnar Eriksson(SWE) 1h 16:06.6
1952(1)	Hallgeir Brenden(NOR) 1h 1:34.0	Tapio Mäkelä(FIN) 1h 2:09.0	Paavo Lonkila(FIN) 1h 2:20.0
1956	Hallgeir Brenden(NOR) 49:39.0	Sixten Jernberg(SWE) 50:14.0	Pavel Koltschin(URS) 50:17.0
1960	Haakon Brusveen(NOR) 51:55.5	Sixten Jernberg(SWE) 51:58.6	Veikko Hakulinen(FIN) 52:03.0
1964	Eero Mäntyranta(FIN) 50:54.1	Harald Grönningen(NOR) 51:34.8	Sixten Jernberg(SWE) 51:42.2
1968	Harald Grönningen(NOR) 47:54.2	Eero Mäntyranta(FIN) 47:56.1	Gunnar Larsson(SWE) 48:33.7
1972	Sven-Ake Lundback(SWE) 45:28.24	Fedor Simsachov(URS) 46:00.84	Ivar Koivisto(FIN) 44:19.25
1976	Nikolai Bayukov(URS) 43:58.47	Yevgeni Belyayev(URS) 44:01.10	Arto Koivisto(FIN) 44:19.25
1980	Thomas Wassberg(SWE) 41:25.63	Juha Mieto(FIN) 41:57.64	Ove Aunli(NOR) 452:28.62
1984	Gunde Swan(SWE) 41:25.6	Aki Karvonen(FIN) 41:34.9	Harri Kirvesniemi(FIN) 41:45.6
1988	Michael Deviatyarov(URS) 41:18.9	Pal Mikkelsplass(NOR) 41:33.4	Vladimir Smirnov(URS) 41:48.5
2002	Andrus Veerpalu(EST) 37:07.4	Frode Estil(NOR) 37:43.4	Jaak Mae(EST) 37:50.8
2006	Andrus Veerpalu(EST) 38:01.3	Lukas Bauer(CZE) 38:15.8	Tobias Angerer(GER) 38:20.5

1992–98 Event not held
(1) Distance 18km
(2) Distance 19.7km
(3) Distance 18.2km

Combined Pursuit – Men
(10km classical plus 15km freestyle 1992–98)

	GOLD	SILVER	BRONZE
1992	Bjørn Daehlie(NOR) 1h 05:37.9	Vegard Ulvang(NOR) 1h 06:31.3	Giorgio Vanzetta(ITA) 1h 06:31.2
1994	Bjørn Daehlie(NOR) 1h 00:08.8	Vladimir Smirnov(KZK) 1h 00:38.0	Silvio Fauner(ITA) 1h 01:48.6
1998	Thomas Alsgaard(NOR) 1h 07:01.7	Bjørn Daehlie(NOR) 1h 07:02.8	Vladimir Smirnov(URS) 1h 07:31.5
2002(1)	Johann Mühlegg(ESP) 49:20.4	Frode Estil(NOR) 49:48.9 Thomas Alsgaard(NOR) 49:48.9	–
2006(2)	Eugeni Dementiev(RUS) 1h 17:00.8	Frode Estil(NOR) 1h 17:01.4	Pietro Piller Cottrer(ITA) 1h 17:01.7

1924–88 Event not held
(1) 10km classical plus 10km freestyle
(2) 15km classical plus 15km freestyle

30,000m – Men
(Classical style 1956–92 and 1998; 1994 and 2002 freestyle)

	GOLD	SILVER	BRONZE
1956	Veikko Hakulinen(FIN) 1h 44:06.0	Sixten Jernberg(SWE) 1h 44:30.0	Pavel Koltschin(URS) 1h 45:45.0
1960	Sixten Jernberg(SWE) 1h 56:03.9	Rolf Rämgard(SWE) 1h 51:16.9	Nikolai Anikin(URS) 1h 52:28.2
1964	Eero Mäntyranta(FIN) 1h 30:50.7	Harald Grönningen(NOR) 1h 32:02.3	Igor Voronchikin(URS) 1h 32:15.8
1968	Franco Nones(ITA) 1h 35:29.2	Odd Martinsen(NOR) 1h 36:28.9	Eero Mäntyranta(FIN) 1h 36:55.3
1972	Vyacheslav Vedenine(URS) 1h 36:31.2	Paal Tyldum(NOR) 1h 37:25.3	Johs Harviken(NOR) 1h 37:32.4
1976	Sergei Savelyev(URS) 1h 30:29.38	William Koch(USA) 1h 30:57.84	Ivan Garanin(URS) 1h 31:09.29
1980	Nikolai Simyatov(URS) 1h 27:02.80	Vassili Rochev(URS) 1h 27:34.22	Ivan Lebanov(BUL) 1h 28:03.87
1984	Nikolai Simyatov(URS) 1h 28:56.3	Alexander Zavialov(URS) 1h 24:35.1	Gunde Svan(SWE) 1h 29:35.7
1988	Alexei Prokurorov(URS) 1h 24:26.3	Vladimir Smirnov(URS) 1h 24:35.1	Vegard Ulvang(NOR) 1h 25:11.6

1992	Vegard Ulvang(NOR) 1h 22:27.8	Bjørn Daehlie(NOR) 1h 23:14.0	Terje Langli(NOR) 1h 23:42.5
1994	Thomas Alsgaard(NOR) 1h 12:26.4	Bjørn Daehlie(NOR) 1h 13:13.6	Mika Myllylä(FIN) 1h 14:14.0
1998	Mika Myllylä(FIN) 1h 33:55.8	Erling Jeune(NOR) 1h 35:27.1	Silvio Fauner(ITA) 1h 36:08.5
2002	Johann Mühlegg(ESP) 1h 09:28.9	Christian Hoffmann(AUT) 1h 11:31.0	Mikhail Botvinov(AUT) 1h 11:32.3

1924–52, 2006 Event not held

50,000m Classical – Men

	GOLD	SILVER	BRONZE
1924	Thorleif Haug(NOR) 3h 44:32.0	Thoralf Strömstad(NOR) 3h 46:23.0	Johan Gröttumsbraaten(NOR) 3h 47:46.0
1928	Per Erik Hedlund(SWE) 4h 52:03.0	Gustaf Jonsson(SWE) 5h 05:30.0	Volger Andersson(SWE) 5h 05:46.0
1932	Veli Saarinen(FIN) 4h 28:00.0	Väinö Likkanen(FIN) 4h 28:20.0	Arne Rustadstuen(NOR) 4h 31:53.0
1936	Elis Wiklung(SWE) 3h 30:11.1	Axel Wikström(SWE) 3h 33:20.0	Nils-Joel Englund(SWE) 3h 34:10.0
1948	Nils Karlsson(SWE) 3h 47:48.0	Harald Eriksson(SWE) 3h 52:20.0	Benjamin Vanninen(FIN) 3h 38:28.0
1952	Veikko Hakulinen(FIN) 3h 33:33.0	Eero Kolehmainen(FIN) 3h 38:11.0	Magnar Estenstad(NOR) 3h 57:28.0
1956	Sixten Jernberg(SWE) 2h 50:27.0	Veikko Hakulinen(FIN) 2h 51:45.0	Fedor Terentyev(URS) 2h 53:32.0
1960	Kalevi Hämäläinen(FIN) 2h 59:06.3	Veikko Hakulinen(FIN) 2h 59:26.7	Rolf Rämgard(SWE) 3h 02:46.7
1964	Sixten Jernberg(SWE) 2h 43:52.6	Assar Rönnlund(SWE) 2h 44:58.2	Arto Tiainen(FIN) 2h 45:30.4
1968	Olle Ellefsäter(NOR) 2h 28:45.8	Vyacheslav Vedenine(URS) 2h 29:02.5	Josef Haas(SUI) 2h 29:14.8
1972	Paal Tyldrum(NOR) 2h 43:14.75	Magne Myrmo(NOR) 2h 43:29.45	Vyacheslav Vedenine(URS) 2h 44:00.19
1976	Ivar Formo(NOR) 2h 37:30.50	Gert-Dietmar Klause(GDR) 2h 38:13.21	Benny Södergren(SWE) 2h 39:39.21
1980	Nikolai Simyatov(URS) 2h 27:24.60	Juha Mieto(FIN) 2h 30:20.52	Alexander Savyalov(URS) 2h 30:51.52
1984	Thomas Wassberg(SWE) 2h 15:55.8	Gunde Svan(SWE) 2h 16:00.7	Aki Karvonen(FIN) 2h 17:04.7
1988	Gunde Svan(SWE) 2h 04:30.9	Maurilio De Zolt(ITA) 2h 05:36.4	Andy Grünenfelder(SUI) 2h 06:01.9
1992	Bjørn Daehlie(NOR) 2h 03:41.5	Maurilio De Zolt(ITA) 2h 04:39.1	Giorgio Vanzetta(ITA) 2h 06:42.1
1994	Vladimir Smirnov(KZK) 2h 07:20.0	Myka Myllylä(FIN) 2h 08:41.9	Sture Sivertsen(NOR) 2h 08:49.0
1998	Bjørn Daehlie(NOR) 2h 05:08.2	Niklas Jonsson(SWE) 2h 05:16.3	Christian Hoffmann(AUT) 2h 06:01.8
2002	Mikhail Ivanov(RUS) 2h 06:20.8 (1)	Andrus Veerpalu(EST) 2h 06:44.5	Odd-Björn Hjelmeset(NOR) 2h 08:41.5

2006 Event not held

(1) Johann Mühlegg (ESP) finished first in 2h 06:05.9 but was disqualified

4 x 10,000m Relay – Men

	GOLD	SILVER	BRONZE
1936	FINLAND 2h 41:33.0	NORWAY 2h 41:39.0	SWEDEN 2h 43:03.0
1948	SWEDEN 2h 32:08.0	FINLAND 2h 41:06.0	NORWAY 2h 44:33.0
1952	FINLAND 2h 20:16.0	NORWAY 2h 23:13.0	SWEDEN 2h 24:13.0
1956	SOVIET UNION 2h 15:30.0	FINLAND 2h 16:31.0	SWEDEN 2h 17:42.0
1960	FINLAND 2h 18:45.6	NORWAY 2h 18:46.4	SOVIET UNION 2h 21:21.6
1964	SWEDEN 2h 18:34.6	FINLAND 2h 18:42.4	SOVIET UNION 2h 18:46.9
1968	NORWAY 2h 08:33.5	SWEDEN 2h 10:13.2	FINLAND 2h 10:56.7
1972	SOVIET UNION 2h 04:47.94	NORWAY 2h 04:57.6	SWITZERLAND 2h 07:00.06
1976	FINLAND 2h 07:59.72	NORWAY 2h 09:58.36	SOVIET UNION 2h 10:51.46
1980	SOVIET UNION 1h 57:03.6	NORWAY 1h 58:45.77	FINLAND 2h 00:00.18
1984	SWEDEN 1h 55:06.3	SOVIET UNION 1h 55:16.5	FINLAND 1h 56:31.4
1988	SWEDEN 1h 43:58.6	SOVIET UNION 1h 44:11.3	CZECHOSLOVAKIA 1h 45:22.7
1992	NORWAY 1h 39:26.0	ITALY 1h 40:52.7	FINLAND 1h 41:22.9
1994	ITALY 1h 41:15.0	NORWAY 1h 41:15.4	FINLAND 1h 42:15.6
1998	NORWAY 1h 40:55.7	ITALY 1h 40:55.9	FINLAND 1h 42:15.5
2002	NORWAY 1h 32:45.5	ITALY 1h 32:45.8	GERMANY 1h 33:34.5
2006	ITALY 1h 43:45.7	GERMANY 1h 44:01.4	SWEDEN 1h 44:01.7

1924–32 Event not held

50,0000m Mass Start – Men

	GOLD	SILVER	BRONZE
2006	Georgio Di Centa(ITA) 2h 06:11.8	Eugeni Dementiev(RUS) 2h 06:12.6	Mikhail Botvinov(AUT) 2h 06:12.7

1924–2006 Event not held

Team Sprint – Men

	GOLD	SILVER	BRONZE
2006	SWEDEN 17:02.9	NORWAY 17:03.5	RUSSIA 17:05.2

1924–2006 Event not held

1,500m – Women

	GOLD	SILVER	BRONZE
2002	Yulia Tchepalova(RUS) 3:10.6	Evi Sachenbacher(GER) 3:12.2	Anita Moen (NOR)3:12.7
2006	Chandra Crawford(CAN) 2:12.3	Claudia Künzel(GER) 2:13.0	Alena Sidko(RUS) 2:13.2

1924–98 Event not held

5,000m Classical – Women

	GOLD	SILVER	BRONZE
1964	Klaudia Boyarskikh(URS) 17:50.5	Mirja Lehtonen(FIN) 17:52.9	Alevtina Koltschina(URS) 18:08.4
1968	Toini Gustafsson(SWE) 16:45.2	Galina Kulakova(URS) 16:48.4	Alevtina Koltschina(URS) 16:51.6
1972	Galina Kulakova(URS) 17:00.50	Marjatta Kajosmaa(FIN) 17:05.50	Helena Sikolova(TCH) 17:07.32
1976	Helena Takalo(FIN) 15:48.69	Raisa Smetanina(URS) 15:49.73	Nina Baldycheva(URS) 16:12.82 (1)

1980	Raisa Smetanina(URS) 15:06.92	Hikka Riihivuori(FIN) 15:11.96	Kvetoslava Jeriová(TCH) 15:23.44
1984	Marja-Liisa Hämäläinen(FIN) 17:04.0	Berit Aunli(NOR) 17:41.1	Kvetoslava Jeriová(TCH) 17:18.3
1988	Marjo Matikainen(FIN) 15:04.0	Tamara Tikhonova(URS) 15:05.3	Vida Ventsene(URS) 15:11.1
1992	Marjut Lukkarinen(FIN) 14:13.8	Lyubov Yegorova(EUN) 14:14.7	Yelena Valbe(EUN) 14:22.7
1994	Lyubov Yegorova(RUS) 14:08.8	Manuela Di Centa(ITA) 14:28.3	Marja-Liisa Kirvesniemi(FIN) 14:36.0
1998	Larissa Lazutina(RUS) 17:37.9	Katerina Neumannova(CZE) 17:42.7	Bente Martinsen(NOR) 17:49.4

1924–60, 2002–06 Event not held
(1) Galina Kulakova (URS) finished third but was disqualified

10,000m Classical – Women

	GOLD	SILVER	BRONZE
1952	Lydia Wideman(FIN) 41:40.0	Mirja Hietamies(FIN) 42:39.0	Siiri Rantanen(FIN) 42:50.0
1956	Lyubov Kozyreva(URS) 38:11.0	Radya Yeroschina(URS) 38:16.0	Sonja Edström(SWE) 38:23.0
1960	Maria Gusakova(URS) 39:46.6	Lyubov Baranova-Kozyreva(URS) 40:04.2	Radya Yeroschina(URS) 40:06.0
1964	Klaudia Boyarskikh(URS) 40:24.3	Yevdokia Mekshilo(URS) 40:26.6	Maria Gusakova(URS) 40:46.6
1968	Toini Gustafsson(SWE) 36:46.5	Berit Mördre(NOR) 37:54.6	Inger Aufles(NOR) 37:59.9
1972	Galina Kulakova(URS) 34:17.8	Alevtina Olunina(URS) 34:54.1	Marjatta Kajosmaa(FIN) 34:56.5
1976	Raisa Smetanina(URS) 30:13.41	Helena Takalo(FIN) 30:14.28	Galina Kulalkova(URS) 30:38.61
1980	Barbara Petzold(GDR) 30:31.54	Hilkka Riihivuori(FIN) 30:35.05	Helena Takalo(FIN) 30:45.25
1984	Marja-Liisa Hämäläinen(FIN) 31:44.2	Raisa Smetanina(URS) 32:02.9	Brit Petersen(NOR) 32:12.7
1988	Vida Ventsene(URS) 30:08.3	Raisa Smetanina(URS) 30:17.0	Marjo Matikainen(FIN) 30:20.5
2002	Bente Skari(NOR) 28:05.6	Olga Danilova(RUS) 28:08.1	Yulia Tchepalova(RUS) 28:09.9
2006	Kristina Smigun(EST) 27:51.4	Marit Bjørgen(NOR) 28:12.7	Hilde Pedersen(NOR) 28:14.0

1924–48 Event not held; discontinued after 1988

Combined Pursuit –Women
(5km classical plus 10km freestyle)

	GOLD	SILVER	BRONZE
1992	Lyubov Yegorova(EUN) 42:20.8	Marjut Lukkavinen(FIN) 43:29.9	Yelena Välbe(EUN) 43:42.3
1994	Manuela Di Centa(ITA) 39:44.6	Lyubov Yegorova(RUS) 41:03.0	Nina Gavvilyuk(RUS) 41:10.4
1998	Larissa Lazutina(RUS) 46:06.9	Olga Danilova(RUS) 46:13.4	Katerina Neumannova(CZE) 46:14.2
2002(1)	Olga Danilova(RUS) 24:52.1	Larissa Lazutina(RUS) 24:59.0	Beckie Scott(CAN) 25:09.9
2006(2)	Kristina Smigun(EST) 42:48.7	Katerina Neumannova(CZE) 42:50.6	Evgenia Medvedyeva-Abruzova(RUS) 43:03.2

1924–88 Event not held
(1) 5km classical plus 5km freestyle
(2) 7.5km classical plus 7.5 km freestyle

15,000m Freestyle – Women

	GOLD	SILVER	BRONZE
1992	Lyubov Yegorova(EUN) 40:07.7	Stefania Belmondo(ITA) 40:31.8	Yelena Välbe(EUN) 40:51.7
1994	Lyubov Yegorova(RUS) 41:38.9	Manuela Di Centa(ITA) 41:46.7	Stefania Belmondo(ITA) 42:21.1
1998	Olga Danilova(RUS) 46:55.4	Larissa Lazutina(RUS) 47:01.0	Anita Moen-Guidon(NOR) 47:52.6
2002	Stefania Belmondo(ITA) 39:54.4	Larissa Lazutina(RUS) 39:56.2	Katerina Neumannova(CZE) 40:01.5

1924–88, 2006 Event not held

30,000m Classical – Women
(1984–92 freestyle; 1984–88 distance 20km)

	GOLD	SILVER	BRONZE
1984	Marja-Liisa Hämäläinen(FIN) 1h 01:45.0	Raisa Smetanina(URS) 1h 02:26.7	Anne Jahren(NOR) 1h 03:13.06
1988	Tamara Tikhonova(URS) 55:53.6	Anfissa Reztsov(URS) 56:12.8	Raisa Smetanina(URS) 57:22.1
1992	Stefania Belmondo(ITA) 1h 22:30.1	Lyobov Yegorova(EUN) 1h 22:52.0	Yelena Välbe(EUN) 1h 24:13.9
1994	Manuela Di Centa(ITA) 1h 25:41.6	Marit Wold(NOR) 1h 25:57.8	Marja-Liisa Hämäläinen(FIN) 1h 26:13.6
1998	Yulia Chepalova(RUS) 1h 22:01.5	Stefania Belmondo(ITA) 1h 22:11.7	Larissa Lazutina(RUS) 1h 23:15.7
2002	Gabrielle Paruzzi(ITA) 1h 30:57.1 (1)	Stefania Belmondo(ITA) 1h 31:01.6	Bente Skari(NOR) 1h 31:36.3

1924–80, 2006 Event not held
(1) Larissa Lazutina (RUS) finished first in 1h 29:09.0 but was disqualified

4 x 5,000m Relay – Women
(Only three stages before 1976)

	GOLD	SILVER	BRONZE
1956	FINLAND 1h 09:01.0	SOVIET UNION 1h 09:28.0	SWEDEN 1h 09:48.0
1960	SWEDEN 1h 04:21.4	SOVIET UNION 1h 05:02.6	FINLAND 1h 06:27.5
1964	SOVIET UNION 59:20.2	SWEDEN 1h 01:27.0	FINLAND 1h 02:45.1
1968	NORWAY 57:30.0	SWEDEN 57:51.0	SOVIET UNION 58:13.6
1972	SOVIET UNION 48:46.15	FINLAND 49:19.37	NORWAY 49:51.49
1976	SOVIET UNION 1h 07:49.75	FINLAND 1h 08:36.57	GDR 1h 09:57.95
1980	GDR 1h 02:11.10	SOVIET UNION 1h 03:18.30	NORWAY 1h 04:13.50
1984	NORWAY 1h 06:49.7	CZECHOSLOVAKIA 1h 01:33.0	FINLAND 1h 07:36.7
1988	SOVIET UNION 59:51.1	NORWAY 1h 01:33.0	FINLAND 1h 01:53.8

1992	UNIFIED TEAM 59:34.8	NORWAY 59:56.4	ITALY 1h 00:25.9
1994	RUSSIA 57:12.5	NORWAY 57:42.6	ITALY 58:42.6
1998	RUSSIA 55:33.5	NORWAY 55:38.0	ITALY 56:53.3
2002	GERMANY 49:30.6	NORWAY 49:31.9	SWITZERLAND 50:03.6
2006	RUSSIA 54:47.7	GERMANY 54:57.7	ITALY 54:58.7

1924–52 Event not held

30,000m Mass Start – Women

	GOLD	SILVER	BRONZE
2006	Katerina Neumannova(CZE) 1:22:25.4	Julija Tchepalova(RUS) 1:22:26.8	Justyna Kowalcyzk(POL) 1:22:27.5

1924–2006 Event not held

Team Classic Sprint – Women

	GOLD	SILVER	BRONZE
2006	SWEDEN 16:36.9	CANADA 16:37.5	FINLAND 16:39.2

1924–2006 Event not held

BIATHLON

10,000m – Men

	GOLD	SILVER	BRONZE
1980	Frank Ulrich(GDR) 32:10.69	Vladimir Alikin(URS) 32:53.10	Anatoliy Alyabiev(URS) 33:09.16
1984	Eirik Kvalfoss(NOR) 30:53.8	Peter Angerer(FRG) 31:02.4	Matthias Jacob(GDR) 31:10.5
1988	Frank-Peter Roetsch(GDR) 25:08.1	Valeri Medvedtsev(URS) 25:23.7	Sergei Tchepikov(URS) 25:29.4
1992	Mark Kirchner(GER) 26:02.3	Ricco Gross(GER) 26:18.0	Harri Eloranta(FIN) 26:26.6
1994	Sergei Chepikov(RUS) 28:07.0	Ricco Gross(GER) 28:13.0	Sergei Tarasov(RUS) 28:27.4
1998	Ole Björndalen(NOR) 27:16.2	Frode Andersson(NOR) 28:17.8	Ville Raikkonen(FIN) 28:21.7
2002	Ole Einar Björndalen(NOR) 24:51.3	Sven Fischer(GER) 25:20.5	Wolfgang Perner(AUT) 25:44.4
2006	Sven Fischer(GER) 26:11.6	Halvard Hanevold(NOR) 26:19.8	Frode Andresen(NOR) 26:31.3

1924–76 Event not held

Combined Pursuit – Men
(Times from previous 10km race added to a 12.5km race)

	GOLD	SILVER	BRONZE
2002	Ole Einar Björndalen(NOR) 32:34.6	Raphael Poiree(FRA) 33:17.6	Ricco Gross(GER) 33:30.6
2006	Vincent Defrasne(FRA) 35:20.2	Ole Einar Bjørndalen(NOR) 35 22.9	Sven Fischer(GER) 35:35.8

1924–98 Event not held

20,000m – Men

	GOLD	SILVER	BRONZE
1960	Klas Lestander(SWE) 1h 33:21.6	Antii Tyrväinen(FIN) 1h 33:57.7	Aleksandr Privalov(URS) 1h 34:54.2
1964	Vladimir Melyanin(URS) 1h 20:26.8	Alexander Privalov(URS) 1h 23:42.5	Olav Jordet(NOR) 1h 24:38.8
1968	Magnar Solberg(NOR) 1h 13:45.9	Alexander Tikhonov(URS) 1h 14:40.4	Vladimir Gundartsev(URS) 1h 18:27.4
1972	Magnar Solberg(NOR) 1h 15:55.5	Hans-Jörg Knauthe(GDR) 1h 16:07.6	Lars Arvidsson(SWE) 1h 16:27.03
1976	Nikolai Kruglov(URS) 1h 14:12.26	Heikki Ikola(FIN) 1h 15:54.10	Alexander Elizarov(URS) 1h 16:05.57
1980	Anatoli Alyabiev(URS) 1h 08:16.31	Frank Ullrich(GDR) 1h 13:21.4	Eberhard Rösch(GDR) 1h 11:11.73
1984	Peter Angerer(FRG) 1h 11:52.7	Frank-Peter Roetsch(GDR) 1h 13:21.4	Eirik Kvalfoss(NOR) 1h 14:02.4
1988	Frank-Peter Roetsch(GDR) 56:33.3	Valeri Medvedtsev(URS) 56:54.6	Johann Pasler(ITA) 57:10.1
1992	Yevgeni Redkine(EUN) 57:34.4	Mark Kirchner(GER) 57:40.8	Mikael Löfgren(SWE) 57:59.4
1994	Sergei Tarasov(RUS) 57:25.3	Frank Luck(GER) 57:28.7	Sven Fischer(GER) 57:41.9
1998	Halvard Hanevold(NOR) 56:16.4	Pier Carrara(ITA) 56:21.9	Alexei Aidarov(BLR) 56:46.5
2002	Ole Einar Björndalen(NOR) 51:03.3	Frank Luck(GER) 51:39.4	Viktor Maigovrov(RUS) 51:40.6
2006	Michael Greis(GER) 54:23.0	Ole Einar Bjørndalen(NOR) 54:39.0	Halvard Hanevold(NOR) 55:31.9

1924–56 Event not held

Relay (4 x 7,500m) – Men

	GOLD	SILVER	BRONZE
1968	SOVIET UNION 2h 13:02.4	NORWAY 2h 14:50.2	SWEDEN 2h 17:26.3
1972	SOVIET UNION 1h 51:44.92	FINLAND 1h 54:37.22	GDR 1h 54:57.67
1976	SOVIET UNION 1h 57:55.64	FINLAND 2h 01:45.58	GDR 2h 04:08.61
1980	SOVIET UNION 1h 34:03.27	GDR 1h 34:56.99	FRG 1h 37:30.26
1984	SOVIET UNION 1h 38:51.7	NORWAY 1h 39:03.9	FRG 1h 39:05.1
1988	SOVIET UNION 1h 22:30.0	FRG 1h 23:37.4	ITALY 1h 23:51.5
1992	GERMANY 1h 24:43.5	UNIFIED TEAM 1h 25:06.3	SWEDEN 1h 25:38.2
1994	GERMANY 1h 30:22.1	RUSSIA 1h 31:23.6	FRANCE 1h 32:31.3
1998	GERMANY 1h 21:36.2	NORWAY 1h 21:56.3	RUSSIA 1h 22:19.3
2002	NORWAY 1h 23:42.3	GERMANY 1h 24:27.6	FRANCE 1h 24:36.6
2006	GERMANY 1h 21:51.5	RUSSIA 1h 22:12.4	FRANCE 1h 22:35.1

1924–64 Event not held

12,500m Pursuit – Men

	GOLD	SILVER	BRONZE
2006	Vincent Defrasne(FRA) 35:20.2	Ole Einar Bjørndalen(NOR) 35:22.9	Sven Fischer(GER) 35:35.8

1924–2002 Event not held

15,000m Mass Start – Men

	GOLD	SILVER	BRONZE
2006	Michael Greis(GER) 47:20.0	Tomasz Sikora(POL) 47:26.3	Ole Einar Bjørndalen(NOR) 47:32.3

1924–2002 Event not held

7,500m – Women

	GOLD	SILVER	BRONZE
1992	Anfissa Reztsova(EUN) 24:29.2	Antje Misersky(GER) 24:45.1	Yelena Belova(EUN) 24:50.8
1994	Myriam Bédard(CAN) 26:08.8	Svetlana Paramygina(BLR) 26:09.9	Valentina Tserbe(UKR) 26:10.0
1998	Galina Kukleva(RUS) 23:08.0	Uschi Disl(GER) 23:08.7	Katrin Apel(GER) 23:32.4
2002	Kati Wilhelm(GER) 20:41.4	Uschi Disl(GER) 20:57.0	Magdalena Forsberg(SWE) 21:20.4
2006	Florence Baverel-Robert(FRA) 22:31.4	Anna Olofsson(SWE) 22:33.8	Lilia Efremova(UKR) 22:38.0

1924–88 Event not held

Combined Pursuit – Women

(Times from previous 7.5km race added to a 10km race)

	GOLD	SILVER	BRONZE
2002	Olga Pyleva(RUS) 31:07.7	Kati Wilhelm(GER) 31:13.0	Irina Nikoultina(BUL) 31:15.8

1924–98, 2006 Event not held

10,000m Pursuit – Women

	GOLD	SILVER	BRONZE
2006	Kati Wilhelm(GER) 36:43.6	Martina Glagow(GER) 37:57.2	Albina Akhatova(RUS) 38:05.0

1924–2002 Event not held

15,000m – Women

	GOLD	SILVER	BRONZE
1992	Antje Misersky(GER) 51:47.2	Svetlana Paramygina(EUN) 51:58.5	Myriam Bédard(CAN) 52:15.0
1994	Myriam Bédard(CAN) 52:06.6	Anne Briand(FRA) 52:53.3	Ursula Disl(GER) 53:15.3
1998	Ekaterina Dafovska(BUL) 54:52.0	Olena Petrova(UKR) 55:09.8	Ursula Disl(GER) 55:17.9
2002	Andrea Henkel(GER) 47:29.1	Liv Grete Poiree(NOR) 47:37.0	Magdalena Forsberg(SWE) 48:08.3
2006	Svetlana Ishmouratova(RUS) 49:24.1	Martina Glagow(GER) 50: 34.9 (1)	Albina Akhatova(RUS) 50:55.0

1924–64 Event not held

(1) Olga Pyleva (RUS) finished second in 50:09.6 but was disqualified

Relay (4 x 7,500m) – Women

	GOLD	SILVER	BRONZE
1992(1)	FRANCE 1h 15:55.6	GERMANY 1h 16:18.4	UNIFIED TEAM 1h 16:54.6
1994	RUSSIA 1h 47:19.5	GERMANY 1h 51:16.5	FRANCE 1h 52:28.1
1998	GERMANY 1h 40:13.6	RUSSIA 1h 40:25.2	NORWAY 1h 40:37.3
2002	GERMANY 1h 27:55.0	NORWAY 1h 28:25.6	RUSSIA 1h 19:19.7
2006(2)	RUSSIA 1h:16:12.5	GERMANY 1h:17:03.2	FRANCE 1h:18:38.7

1924–88 Event not held
(1) 4,500m in 1992
(2) 4 x 6,000m in 2006

12,500m Mass Start – Women

	GOLD	SILVER	BRONZE
2006	Anna Carin Olofsson(SWE) 40:36.5	Kati Wilhelm(GER) 40:55.3	Uschi Disl(GER) 41:18.4

1924–2002 Event not held

NORDIC COMBINED

Individual

(Distance 18km 1924–52; since then 15km)

	GOLD	SILVER	BRONZE
1924(1)	Thorleif Haug(NOR)	Thoralf Strömstad(NOR)	Johan Gröttumsbraaten(NOR)
1928(1)	Johan Grötttumsbraaten(NOR)	Hans Vinjarengen(NOR)	John Snersrud(NOR)
1932	Johan Gröttumsbraaten(NOR) 446.00pts	Ole Stenen(NOR) 436.05pts	Hans Vinjarengen(NOR) 434.60pts
1936	Oddbjörn Hagen(NOR) 430.30pts	Olaf Hoffsbakken(NOR) 419.80pts	Sverre Brodahl(NOR) 408.10pts
1948	Heikki Hasu(FIN) 448.80pts	Martti Huhtala(FIN) 433.65pts	Sven Israelsson(SWE) 433.40pts
1952	Simon Slåttvik(NOR) 431.621pts	Heikki Hasu(FIN) 447.50pts	Sverre Stenersen(NOR) 436.355pts
1956	Sverre Stenersen(NOR) 455.00pts	Bengt Eriksson(SWE) 437.4pts	Franciszek Gron-Gasienica(POL) 436.8pts
1960	Georg Thoma(GER) 457.952pts	Tormod Knutsen(NOR) 453.000pts	Nikolai Gusakow(URS) 452.000pts
1964	Tormod Knutsen(NOR) 469.28pts	Nikolai Kiselyev(URS) 453.04pts	Georg Thoma(GER) 452.88pts

1968	Frantz Keller(FRG) 449.04pts	Alois Kälin(SUI) 447.94pts	Andreas Kunz(GDR) 444.10pts
1972	Ulrich Wehling(GDR) 413.34pts	Rauno Miettinen(FIN) 405.55pts	Karl-Heinz Luck(GDR) 398.80pts
1976	Ulrich Wehling(GDR) 423.39pts	Urban Hettich(FRG) 418.90pts	Konrad Winkler(GDR) 417.47pts
1980	Ulrich Wehling(GDR) 432.20pts	Jouko Karjalainen(FIN) 429.50pts	Konrad Winkler(GDR) 425.32pts
1984	Tom Sandberg(NOR) 422.595pts	Jouko Karjalainen(FIN) 416.900pts	Jukka Ylipulli(FIN) 410.825pts
1988	Hippolyt Kempt(SUI)	Klaus Sulzenbacher(AUT)	Allar Levandi(URS)
1992	Fabrice Guy(FRA)	Sylvain Guillaume(FRA)	Klaus Sulzenbacher(AUT)
1994	Fred Børre Lunberg(NOR)	Takanori Kono(JPN)	Bjarte Engen Vik(NOR)
1998	Bjarte Engen Vik(NOR)	Samppa Lajunen(FIN)	Valeri Stolyarov(RUS)
2002	Samppa Lajunen(FIN) 39:11.7	Jaakko Tallus(FIN) 39:36.4	Felix Gottwald(AUT) 40:06.5
2006	Georg Hettich(GER) 39:11.7	Felix Gottwald(AUT) 39:21.5	Magnus Moan(NOR) 39:27.9

(1) 1924 and 1928 scored differently to that from 1932 onwards

Sprint
(Single jump plus 7.5km race)

	GOLD	SILVER	BRONZE
2002	Samppa Lajunen(FIN) 16:40.1	Ronny Ackermann(GER) 16:49.1	Felix Gottwald(AUT) 17:20.3
2006	Felix Gottwald(AUT) 17:35.0	Magnus Moan(NOR) 17:40.4	Georg Hettich(GER) 17:44.6

1924–98 Event not held

Team

	GOLD	SILVER	BRONZE
1988	FRG	SWITZERLAND	AUSTRIA
1992	JAPAN	NORWAY	AUSTRIA
1994	JAPAN	NORWAY	SWITZERLAND
1998	NORWAY	FINLAND	FRANCE
2002	FINLAND	GERMANY	AUSTRIA

1924–84, 2006 Event not held

4 x 5,000m Relay

	GOLD	SILVER	BRONZE
2006	AUSTRIA	GERMANY	FINLAND

1924–2002 Event not held

SKI-JUMPING

Normal Hill (70m 1924–88; 90m from 1992)

	GOLD	SILVER	BRONZE
1924	Jacob Tullin Thams(NOR) 18 960pts	Narve Bonna(NOR) 18 689pts	Anders Haugen(USA) 17 916pts (1)
1928	Alf Andersen(NOR) 19 208pts	Sigmund Ruud(NOR) 18 542pts	Rudolf Burkert(TCH) 17 937pts
1932	Birger Ruud(NOR) 228.1pts	Hans Beck(NOR) 227.0pts	Kaare Wahlberg(NOR) 219.5pts
1936	Birger Ruud(NOR) 232.0pts	Sven Eriksson(SWE) 230.5pts	Reidar Andersen(NOR) 228.9pts
1948	Petter Hugsted(NOR) 228.1pts	Birger Ruud(NOR) 226.6pts	Thorleif Schjeldrup(NOR) 225.1pts
1952	Arnfinn Bergmann(NOR) 226.0pts	Torbjörn Falkangar(NOR) 221.5pts	Karl Holmström(SWE) 219.5pts
1956	Antti Hyvärinen(FIN) 229.9pts	Aulis Kallakorpi(FIN) 225.0pts	Harry Glass(GER) 224.5pts
1960	Helmut Recknagel(GER) 227.2pts	Niilio Halonen(FIN) 222.6pts	Otto Leodolter(AUT) 219.4pts
1964	Veikko Kankkonen(FIN) 229.9pts	Toralf Engan(NOR) 226.3pts	Torgeir Brandtzäg(NOR) 222.9pts
1968	Jiri Taska(TCH) 216.5pts	Reinhold Bachler(AUT) 214.2pts	Baldur Preiml(AUT) 212.6pts
1972	Yukio Kasaya(JPN) 244.2pts	Akitsugu Konno(JPN) 234.8pts	Seiji Aochi(JPN) 229.5pts
1976	Hans-Georg Aschenbach(GDR) 252.0pts	Jochen Danneberg(GDR) 246.2pts	Karl Schnabl(AUT) 242.0pts
1980	Toni Innauer(AUT) 266.3pts	Manfred Dekker(GDR) 268.0pts Hirokazu Yagi(JPN) 249.2pts	–
1984	Jens Weissflog(GDR) 215.2pts	Matti Nykänen(FIN) 214.0pts	Jari Puikkonen(FIN) 212.8pts
1988	Matti Nykänen(FIN) 229.1pts	Pavel Ploc(TCH) 212.1pts	Jiri Malec(TCH) 211.8pts
1992	Ernst Vettori(AUT) 222.8pts	Martin Höllwarth(AUT) 218.1pts	Toni Nieminen(FIN) 217.0pts
1994	Espen Bredesen(NOR) 282.0pts	Lasse Ottesen(NOR) 268.0pts	Dieter Thoma(GER) 260.5pts
1998	Jani Soininen(FIN) 234.5pts	Kazuyoshi Funaki(JPN) 233.5pts	Andreas Wiidhöelz(AUT) 232.5pts
2002	Simon Ammann(SUI) 269.0pts	Sven Hannawald(GER) 267.5pts	Adam Malysz(POL) 263.0pts
2006	Lars Bystøl(NOR) 266.5pts	Matti Hautamäki(FIN) 265.5pts	Roar Ljøkelsøy(NOR) 264.5pts

(1) Due to wrong calculations Thorleif Haug (NOR) originally was third, but in 1974 the error was corrected

Large Hill (90m 1964–88; 120m from 1992)

	GOLD	SILVER	BRONZE
1964	Toralf Engan(NOR) 230.7pts	Veikko Kankkonen(FIN) 228.9pts	Torgeir Brandtzaeg(NOR) 227.2pts
1968	Vladimir Belousov(URS) 231.3pts	Jiri Raska(TCH) 229.4pts	Lars Grini(NOR) 214.3pts
1972	Wojciech Fortuna(POL) 219.9pts	Walter Steiner(SUI) 219.8pts	Rainer Schmidt(GDR) 219.3pts
1976	Karl Schnabl(AUT) 234.8pts	Toni Innauer(AUT) 232.9pts	Henry Glass(GDR) 221.7pts
1980	Jouko Törmäinen(FIN) 271.0pts	Hubert Neuper(AUT) 262.4pts	Jari Puikkonen(FIN) 248.5pts
1984	Matti Nykänen(FIN) 232.2pts	Jens Weissflog(GDR) 213.7pts	Pavel Ploc(TCH) 202.9pts
1988	Matti Nykänen(FIN) 224.0pts	Erik Johnsen(NOR) 207.9pts	Matjaz Debelak(YUG) 207.7pts
1992	Toni Nieminen(FIN) 239.5pts	Martin Höllwarth(AUT) 227.3pts	Heinz Kuttin(AUT) 214.8pts

1994	Jens Weissflog(GER) 274.5pts	Espen Bredesen(NOR) 266.5pts	Andreas Goldberger(AUT) 255.0pts
1998	Kazuyoshi Funaki(JPN) 272.3pts	Jani Soininen(FIN) 260.8pts	Mashiko Harada(JPN) 258.3pts
2002	Simon Ammann(SUI) 281.4pts	Adam Malysz(POL) 267.9pts	Matti Hautamäki(FIN) 256.0pts
2006	Thomas Morgenstern(AUT) 276.9pts	Andreas Kofler(AUT) 276.8pts	Lars Bystøl(NOR) 250.7pts

1924–60 Event not held

Large Hill Team

	GOLD	SILVER	BRONZE
1988	FINLAND 634.4pts	YUGOSLAVIA 625.5pts	NORWAY 596.1pts
1992	FINLAND 644.4pts	AUSTRIA 642.9pts	CZECHOSLOVAKIA 620.1pts
1994	GERMANY 970.1	JAPAN 956.9pts	AUSTRIA 918.9pts
1998	JAPAN 933.0pts	GERMANY 897.4pts	AUSTRIA 881.5pts
2002	GERMANY 974.1pts	FINLAND 974.0pts	SLOVENIA 946.3pts
2006	AUSTRIA 984.0pts	FINLAND 976.6pts	NORWAY 950.1pts

1924–84 Event not held

SNOWBOARDING

Halfpipe – Men

	GOLD	SILVER	BRONZE
1998	Gian Simmen(SUI) 85.2pts	Daniel Franck(NOR) 82.4	Ross Powers(USA) 82.1
2002	Ross Powers(USA) 46.1pts	Danny Kass(USA) 42.5	Jarred Thomas(USA) 42.1
2006	Shaun White(USA) 46.8	Daniel Kass(USA) 44.0	Markku Koski(FIN) 41.5

1924–94 Event not held

Giant Slalom – Men
(In 2002 the event consisted of parallel runs against another competitor)

	GOLD	SILVER	BRONZE
1998	Ross Rebagliati(CAN) 2:03.96	Thomas Prugger(ITA) 2:03.98	Ueli Kestenholz(SUI) 2:04.08
2002	Philipp Schjoch(SUI)	Richard Richardsson(SWE)	Chris Klug(USA)
2006	Phillip Schoch(SUI)	Simon Schoch(SUI)	Siegfried Grabner(AUT)

1924–94 Event not held

Cross – Men

	GOLD	SILVER	BRONZE
2006	Seth Westcott(USA)	Radoslav Zidek(SVK)	Paul-Henri Delerue(FRA)

1924–2002 Event not held

Halfpipe – Women

	GOLD	SILVER	BRONZE
1998	Nicola Thost(GER) 74.6pts	Stine Brun Kjeldaas(NOR) 74.2	Shannon Dunn(USA) 72.8
2002	Kelly Clark(USA) 47.9pts	Doriane Vidal(FRA) 43.0	Fabienne Reuteler(SUI) 39.7
2006	Hannah Teter(USA) 46.4	Gretchen Bleiler(USA) 43.4	Kjersti Buaas(NOR) 42.0

1924–94 Event not held

Giant Slalom – Women
(In 2002 the event consisted of parallel runs against another competitor)

1998	Karine Ruby(FRA) 2:17.34	Heidi Renoth(GER) 2:19.17	Brigitte Koeck(AUT) 2:19.42
2002	Isabelle Blanc(FRA)	Karine Ruby(FRA)	Lidia Trettel(ITA)
2006	Daniela Meuli(SUI)	Amelie Kober(GER)	Rosey Fletcher(USA)

1924–94 Event not held

Cross – Women

	GOLD	SILVER	BRONZE
2006	Tanja Frieden(SUI)	Lindsey Jacobellis(USA)	Dominique Maltais(CAN)

1924–2002 Event not held

SPEED SKATING

500m – Men

	GOLD	SILVER	BRONZE
1924	Charles Jewtraw(USA) 44.0	Oskar Olsen(NOR) 44.2	Roald Larsen(NOR) 44.8
			Clas Thunberg(FIN) 44.8
1928	Clas Thunberg(FIN) 43.4	–	John Farrrell(USA) 43.6
	Bernt Evensen(NOR) 43.4		Roald Larsen(NOR) 43.6
			Jaako Friman(FIN) 43.6
1932	Jack Shea(USA) 43.4	Bernt Evensen(NOR) 5m	Alexander Hurd(CAN) 8m
1936	Ivar Ballandgrud(NOR) 43.4	Georg Krog(NOR) 43.5	Leo Friesinger(USA) 44.0
1948	Finn Helgesen(NOR) 43.1	Kenneth Bartholomew(USA) 43.2	–
		Thomas Byberg(NOR) 43.2	
		Robert Fitzgerald(USA) 43.2	

1952	Kenneth Henry(USA) 43.2	Donald McDermott(USA) 43.9	Arne Johansen(NOR) 44.0

	GOLD	SILVER	BRONZE
1952	Kenneth Henry(USA) 43.2	Donald McDermott(USA) 43.9	Arne Johansen(NOR) 44.0
			Gordon Audley(CAN) 44.0
1956	Yevgeni Grishin(URS) 40.2	Rafael Gratsch(URS) 40.8	Alv Gjestvang(NOR) 41.0
1960	Yevgeni Grishin(URS) 40.2	William Disney(USA) 40.3	Rafael Gratsch(URS) 40.4
1964	Richard McDermott(USA) 40.1	Yevgeni Grishin(URS) 40.6	–
		Vladimir Orlov(URS) 40.6	
		Alv Gjestvang(NOR) 40.6	
1968	Erhard Keller(FRG) 40.3	Richard McDermott(USA) 40.5	–
		Magne Thomassen(NOR) 40.5	
1972	Erhard Keller(FRG) 39.44	Hasse Börjes(SWE) 39.69	Valeri Muratov(URS) 39.80
1976	Yevgeni Kulikov(URS) 39.17	Valeri Muratov(URS) 39.25	Daniel Immerfall(USA) 39.54
1980	Eric Heiden(USA) 38.03	Yevgeni Kulikov(URS) 38.37	Lieuwe de Boer(NED) 38.48
1984	Sergei Fokitchev(URS) 38.19	Yoshihiro Kitazawa(JPN) 38.30	Gaétan Boucher(CAN) 38.39
1988	Uwe-Jens Mey(GDR) 36.45	Jan Ykema(NED) 36.76	Akira Kuriowa(JPN) 36.77
1992	Uwe-Jens Mey(GER) 37.14	Toshiyuki Kuriowa(JPN) 37.18	Junichi Inoue(JPN) 37.26
1994	Alexander Golubyev(RUS) 36.33	Sergei Klevchenya(RUS) 36.39	Manabu Horii(JPN) 36.53
1998(1)	Hiroyasu Shimizu(JPN) 1:11.35	Jeremy Wotherspoon(CAN) 1:11.84	Kevin Overland(CAN) 1:11.86
2002	Casey FitzRandolph(USA) 1:09.23	Hiroyasu Shimizu(JPN) 1:09.26	Kip Carpenter(USA) 1:09.47
2006	Joey Cheek(USA) 1:09.76	Dmitri Dorofeyev(RUS) 1:10.41	Kang Seok Lee(KOR) 1:10.43

(1) Since 1998 the result is based on the combined times of two races

1,000m – Men

	GOLD	SILVER	BRONZE
1976	Peter Müller(USA) 1:19.32	Jörn Didriksen(NOR) 1:20.45	Valeri Muratov(URS) 1:20.57
1980	Eric Heiden(USA) 1:15.18	Gaétan Boucher(CAN) 1:16.68	Frode Rönning(NOR) 1:16.91
			Vladimir Lobanov(URS) 1:16.91
1984	Gaétan Boucher(CAN) 1:15.80	Sergei Khlebnikov(URS) 1:16.63	Kai Arne Engelstad(NOR) 1:16.75
1988	Nikolai Gulyayev(URS) 1:13.03	Uwe-Jens Mey(GDR) 1:13.11	Igor Gelezovsky(URS) 1:13.19
1992	Olaf Zinke(GER) 1:14.85	Moon-Yan Kim(KOR) 1:14.86	Yukinori Miyabe(JPN) 1:14.92
1994	Dan Jansen(USA) 1:12.43	Igor Zhelezovsky(BLS) 1:12.72	Sergei Klevchenya(RUS) 1:12.85
1998	Ids Postma(NED) 1:10.64	Jan Bos(NED) 1:10.71	Hiroyasu Shimizu(JPN) 1:11.00
2002	Gerard van Velde(NED) 1:07.18	Jan Bos(NED) 1:07.53	Joey Cheek(USA) 1:07.61
2006	Shani Davis(USA) 1:08.89	Joey Cheek(USA) 1:09.16	Erben Wennemars(NED) 1:09.32

1924–72 Event not held

1,500m – Men

	GOLD	SILVER	BRONZE
1924	Clas Thunberg(FIN) 2:20.8	Roald Larsen(NOR) 2:20.0	Sigurd Moen(NOR) 2:25.6
1928	Clas Thunberg(FIN) 2:21.1	Bernt Evensen(NOR) 2:21.9	Ivar Ballangrud(NOR) 2:22.6
1932	Jack Shea(USA) 2:57.5	Alexander Hurd(CAN) 5m	William Logan(CAN) 6m
1936	Charles Mathiesen(NOR) 2:19.2	Ivar Ballangrud(NOR) 2:20.2	Birger Wasenius(FIN) 2:20.9
1948	Sverre Farstad(NOR) 2:17.6	Ake Seyffarth(SWE) 2:18.1	Odd Lundberg(NOR) 2:18.9
1952	Hjalmar Andersen(NOR) 2:20.4	Willem van der Voort(NED) 2:20.6	Roald Aas(NOR) 2:21.6
1956	Yevgeni Grischin(URS) 2:08.6	–	Tiovo Salonen(FIN) 2:09.4
	Yuri Mikhailov(URS) 2:08.6		
1960	Roald Aas(NOR) 2:10.4	–	Boris Stenin(URS) 2:11.5
	Yevgeni Grishin(URS) 2:10.4		
1964	Ants Antson(URS) 2:10.3	Cornelis Verkerk(NED) 2:10.6	Villy Haugen(NOR) 2:11.25
1968	Cornelis Verkerk(NED) 2:03.4	Ard Schenk(NED) 2:05.0	–
		Ivar Eriksen(NOR) 2:05.0	
1972	Ard Schenk(NED) 2:02.96	Roar Grönvold(NOR) 2:04.26	Göran Claeson(SWE) 2:05.89
1976	Jan Egil Storholt(NOR) 1:59.38	Yuri Kondakov(URS) 1:59.97	Hans Van Helden(NED) 2:00.87
1980	Eric Heiden(USA) 1:55.44	Kai Stenshjemmet(NOR) 1:56.81	Terje Andersen(NOR) 1:56.92
1984	Gaétan Boucher(CAN) 1:58.36	Sergei Khlebnikov(URS) 1:58.83	Oleg Bogyev(URS) 1:58.89
1988	André Hoffmann(GDR) 1:52.06	Eric Flaim(USA) 1:52.12	Michael Hadschieff(AUT) 1:52.31
1992	Johann Olav Koss(NOR) 1:54.81	Adne Sønderal(NOR) 1:54.85	Leo Visser(NED) 1:54.90
1994	Johann Olav Koss(NOR) 1:51.29	Rintje Ritsma(NED) 1:51.99	Falko Zandstra(NED) 1:52.38
1998	Adne Sønderal(NOR) 1:47.87	Ids Postma(NED) 1:48.13	Rintje Ritsma(NED) 1:48.52
2002	Derek Parra(USA) 1:43.85	Jochen Uytdehaage(NED) 1:44.57	Adne Sondral(NED) 1:45.26
2006	Enrico Fabris(ITA) 1:45.97	Shani Davis(USA) 1:46.13	Chad Hedrick(USA) 1:46.22

5,000m – Men

	GOLD	SILVER	BRONZE
1924	Clas Thunberg(FIN) 8:39.0	Julius Skutnabb(FIN) 8:48.4	Roald Larsen(NOR) 2:00.87
1928	Ivar Ballangrud(NOR) 8:50.5	Julius Skutnabb(FIN) 8:59.1	Bernt Evensen(NOR) 9:01.1
1932	Irving Jaffee(USA) 9:40.8	Edward Murphy(USA) 2m	William Logan(CAN) 4m
1936	Ivar Ballangrud(NOR) 8:19.6	Birger Wasenius(FIN) 8:23.3	Antero Ojala(FIN) 8:30.1
1948	Reidar Liaklev(NOR) 8:29.4	Odd Lundberg(NOR) 8:32.7	Göthe Hedlund(SWE) 8:34.8
1952	Hjalmar Andersen(NOR) 8:10.6	Kees Broekman(NED) 8:21.6	Sverre Haugli(NOR) 8:22.4
1956	Boris Schilkov(URS) 7:48.7	Sigvard Ericsson(SWE) 7:56.7	Oleg Gontscharenko(URS) 7:57.5
1960	Viktor Kositschkin(URS) 7:51.3	Knut Johannesen(NOR) 8:00.8	Jan Pesman(NED) 8:05.1
1964	Knut Johannesen(NOR) 7:38.4	Per Moe(NOR) 7:38.6	Anton Maier(NOR) 7:42.0

	GOLD	SILVER	BRONZE
1968	Anton Maier(NOR) 7:22.4	Cornelis Verkerk(NED) 7:23.2	Petrus Nottet(NED) 7:25.5
1972	Ard Schenk(NED) 7:23.6	Roar Grönvald(NOR) 7:28.18	Sten Stensen(NOR) 7:33.39
1976	Sten Stensen(NOR) 7:24.48	Piet Kleine(NED) 7:26.47	Hans Van Helden(NED) 7:26.54
1980	Eric Heiden(USA) 7:02.29	Kai Stenshjammet(NOR) 7:03.28	Tom Oxholm(NOR) 7:05.59
1984	Tomas Gustafson(SWE) 7:12.28	Igor Malkov(URS) 7:12.30	René Schöfisch(GDR) 7:17.49
1988	Tomas Gustafson(SWE) 6:44.63	Leendert Visser(NED) 6:44.98	Gerard Kemkers(NED) 6:45.92
1992	Geir Karlstad(NOR) 6:59.97	Falko Zandstra(NED) 7:02.28	Leo Visser(NED) 7:04.96
1994	Johann Olav Koss(NOR) 6:34.96	Kjell Storelid(NOR) 6:42.68	Rintje Ritsma(NED) 6:43.94
1998	Gianni Romme(NED) 6:22.20	Rintje Ritsma(NED) 6:28.24	Bart Veldkamp(BEL) 6:28.31
2002	Jochen Uytdehaage(NED) 6:14.66	Derek Parra(USA) 6:17.98	Jens Boden(GER) 6:21.73
2006	Chad Hedrick(USA) 6:14.68	Sven Kramer(NED) 6:16.40	Enrico Fabris(ITA) 6:18.25

10,000m – Men

	GOLD	SILVER	BRONZE
1924	Julius Skutnabb(FIN) 18:04.8	Clas Thunberg(FIN) 18:97.8	Roald Larsen(NOR) 18:12.2
1932	Irving Jaffee(USA) 19:13.6	Ivar Ballangrud(NOR) 5m	Frank Stack(CAN) 6m
1936	Ivar Ballangrud(NOR) 17:24.3	Birger Wasenius(FIN) 17:28.2	Max Stiepl(AUT) 17:30.0
1948	Ake Seyffarth(SWE) 17:26.3	Lauri Parkkinen(FIN) 17:36.0	Pentti Lammio(FIN) 17:42.7
1952	Hjalmar Andersen(NOR) 16:45.8	Kees Broekman(NED) 17:10.6	Carl-Erik Asplund(SWE) 17:16.6
1956	Sigvard Ericsson(SWE) 16:35.9	Knut Johannesen(NOR) 16:36.9	Oleg Gontscharenko(URS) 16:42.3
1960	Knut Johannesen(NOR) 15:46.6	Viktor Kositschkin(URS) 15:49.2	Kjell Bäckman(SWE) 16:14.2
1964	Jonny Nilsson(SWE) 15:50.1	Anton Maier(NOR) 16:06.0	Knut Johannesen(NOR) 16:06.3
1968	Johnny Höglin(SWE) 15:23.6	Anton Maier(NOR) 15:23.9	Orjan Sandler(SWE) 15:31.8
1972	Ard Schenk(NED) 15:01.35	Cornelis Verkerk(NED) 15:04.70	Sten Stensen(NOR) 15:07.08
1976	Piet Kleine(NED) 14:50.59	Sten Stensen(NOR) 14:53.30	Hans Van Helden(NED) 15:02.02
1980	Eric Heiden(USA) 14:28.13	Piet Kleine(NED) 14:36.03	Tom Oxholm(NOR) 14:36.60
1984	Igor Malkov(URS) 14:39.90	Tomas Gustafson(SWE) 14:39.95	René Schöfisch(GDR) 14:46.91
1988	Tomas Gustafson(SWE) 13:48.20	Michael Hadschieff(AUT) 13:56.11	Leendert Visser(NED) 14:00.55
1992	Bart Veldkamp(NED) 14:12.12	Johann Olav Koss(NOR) 14:14.58	Geir Karlstad(NOR) 14:18.13
1994	Johann Olav Koss(NOR) 13:30.55	Kjell Storelid(NOR) 13:49.25	Bart Veldkamp(NED) 13:56.73
1998	Gianni Romme(NED) 13:15.33	Bob de Jong(NED) 13:25.76	Rintje Ritsma(NED) 13:28.19
2002	Jochen Uytdehaage(NED) 12:58.92	Gianni Romme(NED) 13:10.03	Lasse Saetre(NOR) 13:16.92
2006	Bob de Jong(NED) 13:01.57	Chad Hedrick(USA) 13:05.40	Carl Verheijen(NED) 13:08.80

1928 Event abandoned

Team Pursuit – Men

	GOLD	SILVER	BRONZE
2006	ITALY	CANADA	NETHERLANDS(1)

1924–2002 Event not held
(1) Winner of B final

500m – Women

	GOLD	SILVER	BRONZE
1960	Helga Haase(GER) 45.9	Natalya Donchenko(URS) 46.0	Jeanne Ashworth(USA) 46.1
1964	Lydia Skoblikova(URS) 45.0	Irina Yegorova(URS) 45.4	Tatyana Sidorova(URS) 45.5
1968	Ludmila Titova(URS) 46.1	Mary Meyers(USA) 46.3	–
		Dianne Holum(USA) 46.3	
		Jennifer Fish(USA) 46.3	
1972	Anne Henning(USA) 43.33	Vera Krasnova(URS) 44.01	Ludmila Titova(URS) 44.45
1976	Sheila Young(USA) 42.76	Catherine Priestner(CAN) 43.12	Tatyana Averina(URS) 43.17
1980	Karin Enke(GDR) 41.78	Leah Poulos-Mueller(USA) 42.26	Natalya Petruseva(URS) 42.42
1984	Christa Rothenburger(GDR) 41.02	Karin Enke(GDR) 41.28	Natalya Chive(URS) 41.50
1988	Bonnie Blair(USA) 39.10	Christa Rothenburger(GDR) 39.12	Karin Enke-Kania(GDR) 39.24
1992	Bonnie Blair(USA) 40.33	Qiaobo Ye(CHN) 40.51	Christa Rothenburger-Luding(GER) 40.57
1994	Bonnie Blair(USA) 39.25	Susan Auch(CAN) 39.61	Franziska Schenk(GER) 39.70
1998(1)	Catriona LeMay-Doan(CAN) 1:16.60	Susan Auch(CAN) 1:16.93	Tomomi Okazaki(JPN) 1:17.10
2002	Catriona LeMay-Doan(CAN) 1:14.75	Monique Garbrecht-Enfieldt(GER) 1:14.94	Sabine Völker(GER) 1:15.19
2006	Svetlana Zhurova(RUS) 1:16.57	Manli Wang(CHN) 1:16.78	Hui Ren(CHN) 1:16.87

(1) Since 1998 the result is based on the combined times of two races

1,000m – Women

	GOLD	SILVER	BRONZE
1960	Klara Guseva(URS) 1:34.1	Helga Haase(GER) 1:34.3	Tamara Rylova(URS) 1:34.8
1964	Lydia Skoblikova(URS) 1:33.2	Irina Yegorova(URS) 1:34.3	Kaija Mustonen(FIN) 1:34.8
1968	Carolina Geijssen(NED) 1:32.6	Ludmila Titova(URS) 1:32.9	Dianne Holum(USA) 1:33.4
1972	Monika Pflug(FRG) 1:31.40	Atje Keulen-Deelstra(NED) 1:31.61	Anne Henning(USA) 1:31.62
1976	Tatyana Averina(URS) 1:28.43	Leah Poulos(USA) 1:28.57	Sheila Young(USA) 1:29.14
1980	Natalya Petruseva(URS) 1:24.10	Leah Poulos-Mueller(USA) 1:25.41	Sylvia Albrecht(GDR) 1:26.46
1984	Karin Enke(GDR) 1:21.61	Andrea Schöne(GDR) 1:22.83	Natalya Petruseva(URS) 1:23.21
1988	Christa Rothenburger(GDR) 1:17.65	Karin Enke-Kania(GDR) 1:17.70	Bonnie Blair(USA) 1:18.31
1992	Bonnie Blair(USA) 1:21.90	Qiaobo Ye(CHN) 1:21.92	Monique Garbrecht(GER) 1:22.10

1994	Bonnie Blair(USA) 1:18.74	Anke Baier(GER) 1:20.12	Qiaobo Ye(CHN) 1:20.22
1998	Marianne Timmer(NED) 1:16.51	Christine Witty(USA) 1:16.79	Catriona LeMay-Doan(CAN) 1:17.37
2002	Christine Witty(USA) 1:13.83	Sabine Völker(GER) 1:13.96	Jennifer Rodriguez(USA) 1:14.24
2006	Marianne Timmer(NED) 1:16.05	Cindy Klassen(CAN) 1:16.09	Anni Freisinger(GER) 1:16.11

1,500m – Women

	GOLD	SILVER	BRONZE
1960	Lydia Skoblikova(URS) 2:25.2	Elvira Seroczynska(POL) 2:25.7	Helena Pilejeyk(POL) 2:27.1
1964	Lydia Skoblikova(URS) 2:22.6	Kaija Mustonen(FIN) 2:25.5	Berta Kolokoltseva(URS) 2:27.1
1968	Kaija Mustonen(FIN) 2:22.4	Carolina Geijssen(NED) 2:22.7	Christina Kaiser(NED) 2:24.5
1972	Dianne Holum(USA) 2:20.85	Christina Baas-Kaiser(NED) 2:21.05	Atje Keulen-Deelstra(NED) 2:22.05
1976	Galina Stepanskaya(URS) 2:16.58	Sheila Young(USA) 2:17.06	Tatyana Averina(URS) 2:17.96
1980	Annie Borckink(NED) 2:10.95	Ria Visser(NED) 2:12.35	Sabine Becker(GDR) 2:12.38
1984	Karin Enke(GDR) 2:03.42	Andrea Schöne(GDR) 2:05.29	Natalya Petruseva(URS) 2:05.78
1988	Yvonne Van Gennip(NED) 2:00.68	Karin Enke-Kania(GDR) 2:00.82	Andrea Schöne-Ehrig(GDR) 2:01.49
1992	Jacqueline Börner(GER) 2:05.87	Gunda Niemann(GER) 2:05.92	Seiko Hashimoto(JPN) 2:06.88
1994	Emese Hunyady(AUT) 2:02.19	Svetlana Fedotkin(RUS) 2:02.69	Gunda Niemann(GER) 2:03.41
1998	Marianne Timmer(NED) 1:57.58	Gunda Niemann-Stirnemann(GER) 1:58.86	Christine Witty(USA) 1:58.97
2002	Ann Friesinger(GER) 1:54.02	Sabine Völker(GER) 1:54.97	Jennifer Rodriguez(USA) 1:55.32
2006	Cindy Klassen(CAN) 1:55.27	Kristina Groves(CAN) 1:56.74	Ireen Wust(NED) 1:56.90

3,000m – Women

	GOLD	SILVER	BRONZE
1960	Lydia Skobilova(URS) 5:14.3	Valentina Stenina(URS) 5:16.9	Eevi Huttunen(FIN) 5:21.0
1964	Lydia Skobilova(URS) 5:14.9	Valentina Stenina(URS) 5:18.5 Pil-Hwa Han(PRK) 5:18.5	–
1968	Johanna Schut(NED) 4:56.2	Kaija Mustonen(FIN) 5:01.0	Christina Kaiser(NED) 5:01.3
1972	Christina Baas-Kaiser(NED) 4:52.14	Dianne Holum(USA) 4:58.67	Atje Keulen-Deelstra(NED) 4:59.91
1976	Tatyana Averina(URS) 4:45.19	Andrea Mitscherlich(GDR) 4:45.23	Lisbeth Korsmo(NOR) 4:45.24
1980	Bjørg Eva Jensen(NOR) 4:32.13	Sabine Becker(GDR) 4:32.79	Beth Heiden(USA) 4:33.77
1984	Andrea Mitscherlich-Schöne(GDR) 4:24.79	Karin Enke(GDR) 4:26.33	Gabi Schönbrunn(GDR) 4:33.13
1988	Yvonne Van Gennip(NED) 4:11.94	Andrea Schöne-Ehrig(GDR) 4:12.09	Gabi Schönbrunn-Zange(GDR) 4:16.92
1992	Gunda Niemann(GER) 4:19.90	Heike Warnicke(GER) 4:22.88	Emese Hunyadi(AUT) 4:24.64
1994	Svetlana Bazhanova(RUS) 4:17.43	Emese Hunyadi(AUT) 4:18.14	Claudia Pechstein(GER) 4:18.34
1998	Gunda Niemann-Stirnemann(GER) 4:07.29	Claudia Pechstein(GER) 4:08.47	Anna Friesinger(GER) 4:09.44
2002	Claudia Pechstein(GER) 3:57.70	Renate Groenewold(NED) 3:58.94	Cindy Klassen(CAN) 3:58.97
2006	Ireen Wust(NED) 4:02.43	Renate Groenewold(NED) 4:03.48	Cindy Klassen(CAN) 4:04.37

5,000m – Women

	GOLD	SILVER	BRONZE
1988	Yvonne Van Gennip(NED) 7:14.13	Andrea Schöne-Ehrig(GDR) 7:17.2	Gabi Schönbrunn-Zange(GDR) 7:21.61
1992	Gunda Niemann(GER) 7:31.57	Heike Warnicke(GER) 7:37.59	Claudia Pechstein(GER) 7:39.80
1994	Claudia Pechstein(GER) 7:14.37	Gunda Niemann(GER) 7:14.88	Hiromi Yamamoto(JPN) 7:19.68
1998	Claudia Pechstein(GER) 6:59.61	Gunda Niemann-Stirnemann(GER) 6:59.65	Lyudmila Prokasheva(KZK) 7:11.14
2002	Claudia Pechstein(GER) 6:46.91	Gretha Smit(NED) 6:49.22	Clara Hughes(CAN) 6:53.53
2006	Clara Hughes(CAN) 6:59.07	Claudia Pechstein(GER) 7:00.08	Cindy Klassen(CAN) 7.00.57

1960–84 Event not held

Team Pursuit – Women

	GOLD	SILVER	BRONZE
2006	GERMANY	CANADA	USSIA

1924–2002 Event not held

SPEED SKATING – DISCONTINUED EVENT

All-Round Championship – Men
(Aggregate of placings in 500m, 1500m, 5km and 10km)

	GOLD	SILVER	BRONZE
1924	Clas Thunberg(FIN) 5.5pts	Roald Larsen(NOR) 9.5pts	Julius Skutnabb(FIN) 11pts

SHORT-TRACK SPEED SKATING

500m – Men
	GOLD	SILVER	BRONZE
1994	Ji-Hoon Chae(KOR) 43.45	Mirko Vuillermin(ITA) 43.47	Nicky Gooch(GBR) 43.68
1998	Takafuni Nishitani(JPN) 42.862	Yulong An(CHN) 43.022	Hitoshi Uematsu(JPN) 43.713
2002	Marc Gagnon(CAN) 41.802	Jonathan Guilmette(CAN) 41.994	Rusty Smith(USA) 42.027
2006	Apolo Anton Ohno(USA) 41.935	François-Louis Tremblay(CAN) 42.002	Hyun-Soo Ahn(KOR) 42.089

1924–92 Event not held

1,000m – Men
	GOLD	SILVER	BRONZE
1992	Ki-Hoon Kim(KOR) 1:30.76	Frederic Blackburn(CAN) 1:31.11	Joon-Ho Lee(KOR) 1:31.16
1994	Ki-Hoon Kim(KOR) 1:34.57	Ji-Hoon Chae(KOR) 1:34.92	Marc Gagnon(CAN) 1:33.03 (1)
1998	Dong-Sung Kim(KOR) 1:32.375	Jiajun Li(CHN) 1:32.428	Eric Bedard(CAN) 1:32.661
2002	Steven Bradbury(AUS) 1:29.109	Apolo Anton Ohno(USA) 1:30.160	Mathieu Turcotte(CAN) 1:30.563
2006	Hyun-Soo Ahn(KOR) 1:26:739	Ho-Suk Lee(KOR) 1:26.764	Apolo Anton Ohno(USA) 1:26.927

1924–88 Event not held
(1) No third finisher in 'A' final, so winner of 'B' final given bronze medal

1,500m – Men
	GOLD	SILVER	BRONZE
2002	Apolo Anton Ohno(USA) 2:18.541 (1)	Jiajun Li(CHN) 2:18.731	Marc Gagnon(CAN) 2:18.806
2006	Hyun-Soo Ahn(KOR) 2:25.341	Ho-Suk Lee(KOR) 2:25.600	Jia Jun Li(CHN) 2:26.005

1924–98 Event not held
(1) Dong-Sung Kim (KOR) finished first but was disqualified

5,000m Relay – Men
	GOLD	SILVER	BRONZE
1992	KOREA 7:14.02	CANADA 7:14.06	JAPAN 7:18.18
1994	ITALY 7:11.74	UNITED STATES 7:13.37	AUSTRALIA 7:13.68
1998	CANADA 7:32.075	KOREA 7:06.776	CHINA 7:11.559
2002	CANADA 6:51.579	ITALY 6:56.327	CHINA 6:59.633
2006	KOREA 6:43.376	CANADA 6:43.707	UNITED STATES 6:47.990

1924–88 Event not held

500m – Women
	GOLD	SILVER	BRONZE
1992	Cathy Turner(USA) 47.04	Yan Li(CHN) 47.08	Ok-Sil Hwang(PRK) 47.23
1994	Cathy Turner(USA) 45.98	Yanmei Zhang(CHN) 46.44	Amy Peterson(USA) 46.76
1998	Annie Perreault(CAN) 46.568	Yang (S) Yang(CHN) 46.627	Kyung-Chun Lee(KOR) 46.335 (1)
2002	Yang (A) Yang(CHN) 44.187	Yevgeniya Radanova(BUL) 44.252	Chunlu Wang(CHN) 44.272

1924–88 Event not held
(1) Isabelle Charest (CAN) disqualified so winner of 'B' final given bronze medal

1,000m – Women
	GOLD	SILVER	BRONZE
1994	Lee-Kyung Chun(KOR) 1:36.87	Nathalie Lambert(CAN) 1:36.97	So-Hee Kim(KOR) 1:37.09
1998	Lee-Kyung Chun(KOR) 1:42.776	Yang (S) Yang(CHN) 1:43.343	Hye-Kyung Won(KOR) 1:43.361
2002	Yang (A) Yang(CHN) 1:36.391	Gi-Hyun Ko(KOR) 1:36.427	Yang (S) Yang(CHN) 1:37.008
2006	Meng Wang(CHN) 44.345	Evgenia Radanova(BUL) 44.374	Anouk LeBlanc-Boucher(CAN) 44.759
2006	Sun-Yu Jin(KOR) 1:32.859	Meng Wang(CHN) 1:33.079	Yang Yang (A) (CHN) 1:33.937

1924–92 Event not held

1,500m – Women
	GOLD	SILVER	BRONZE
2002	Gi-Hyun Ko(KOR) 2:31.581	Eun-Kyung Choi(KOR) 2:31.610	Yevgeniya Radanova(BUL) 2:31.723
2006	Sun-Yu Jin(KOR) 2:23.494	Eun-Kyung Choi (KOR) 2:24.069	Meng Wang(CHN) 2:24.469

1924–98 Event not held

3,000m Relay – Women
	GOLD	SILVER	BRONZE
1992	CANADA 4:36.62	UNITED STATES 4:37.85	UNIFIED TEAM 4:42.69
1994	KOREA 4:26.64	CANADA 4:32.04	UNITED STATES 4:39.34
1998	KOREA 4:16.260	CHINA 4:16.383	CANADA 4:21.205
2002	KOREA 4:12.793	CHINA 4:13.236	CANADA 4:15.738
2006	KOREA 4:17.040	CANADA 4:17.336	ITALY 4:20.030

1924–88 Event not held

APPENDIX C

Olympic Games Medals Tables

ATHENS (I) 1896

	GOLD	SILVER	BRONZE	TOTAL
United States	11	7	1	19
Greece	10	19	18	47
Germany	7	5	2	14
France	5	4	2	11
Great Britain	3	3	1	7
Hungary	2	1	3	6
Austria	2	0	3	5
Australia	2	0	0	2
Denmark	1	2	4	7
Switzerland	1	2	0	3

PARIS (II) 1900

	GOLD	SILVER	BRONZE	TOTAL
France	27	39	34	100
Great Britain	17	9	12	38
United States	9	15	15	39
Switzerland	6	3	1	10
Belgium	5	5	3	13
Germany	3	2	2	8
Australia	2	0	4	6
Denmark	2	3	2	7
Italy	2	2	0	4
Netherlands	1	1	4	6
Hungary	1	2	2	5
Cuba	1	1	0	2
Canada	1	0	1	2
Sweden	1	0	1	2
Austria	0	3	3	6
Norway	0	2	3	5
Czechoslovakia	0	1	2	3

ST LOUIS (III) 1904

	GOLD	SILVER	BRONZE	TOTAL
United States	80	84	78	242
Germany	4	4	5	13
Canada	4	1	1	6
Cuba	4	0	0	4
Austria	2	1	1	4
Hungary	2	1	1	4
Great Britain	1	1	0	2
Greece	1	0	0	1
Switzerland	1	0	1	2
France	0	1	0	1

LONDON (IV) 1908

	GOLD	SILVER	BRONZE	TOTAL
Great Britain	56	50	39	145
United States	23	12	12	47
Sweden	8	6	11	25
France	5	5	9	19
Germany	3	5	5	11
Hungary	3	4	2	9
Canada	3	3	10	16
Norway	2	3	3	8
Italy	2	2	0	4
Belgium	1	5	2	8
Australia	1	2	1	4
Russia	1	2	0	3
Finland	1	1	3	5
South Africa	1	1	0	2
Greece	0	3	1	4
Denmark	0	2	3	5
Czechoslovakia	0	0	2	2
Netherlands	0	0	2	2
Austria	0	0	1	1
New Zealand	0	0	1	1

STOCKHOLM (V) 1912

	GOLD	SILVER	BRONZE	TOTAL
United States (1)	25	19	18	62
Sweden	24	24	16	64
Great Britain	10	15	16	31
Finland	9	8	9	26
France	7	4	3	14
Germany	5	13	7	25
South Africa	4	2	0	6
Norway	4	1	5	10
Hungary	3	2	3	8
Canada	3	2	2	7
Italy	3	1	2	6
Australia (2)	2	2	2	6
Belgium	2	1	3	6
Denmark	1	6	5	12
Greece	1	0	1	2
New Zealand (2)	1	0	1	2
Switzerland	1	0	0	1
Russia	0	2	3	5
Austria	0	2	2	4
Netherlands	0	0	3	3

(1) Adjusted by reinstatement of Jim Thorpe in 1982 (official medal records unaltered)

(2) Australia and New Zealand combined as Australasia

ANTWERP (VII) 1920

	GOLD	SILVER	BRONZE	TOTAL
United States	41	27	27	95
Sweden	19	20	25	64
Finland	15	10	9	34
Great Britain	14	15	13	42
Belgium	13	11	11	35
Norway	13	9	9	31
Italy	13	5	5	23
France	9	19	13	41
Netherlands	4	2	5	11
Denmark	3	9	1	13
South Africa	3	4	3	10
Canada	3	3	3	9
Switzerland	2	2	7	11
Estonia	1	2	0	3
Brazil	1	1	1	3
Australia	0	2	1	3
Japan	0	2	0	2
Spain	0	1	0	1
Greece	0	1	0	1
Luxembourg	0	1	0	1
Czechoslovakia	0	0	2	2
New Zealand	0	0	1	1

PARIS (VIII) 1924

	GOLD	SILVER	BRONZE	TOTAL
United States	45	27	27	99
Finland	14	13	10	37
France	13	15	10	38
Great Britain	9	13	12	34
Italy	8	3	5	16
Switzerland	7	8	10	25
Norway	5	2	3	10
Sweden	4	13	12	29
Netherlands	4	1	5	10
Belgium	3	7	3	13
Australia	3	1	2	6
Denmark	2	5	2	9
Hungary	2	3	4	9
Yugoslavia	2	0	0	2
Czechoslovakia	1	4	5	10
Argentina	1	3	2	6
Estonia	1	1	4	6
South Africa	1	1	1	3
Luxembourg	1	1	0	2
Greece	1	0	0	1
Uruguay	1	0	0	1
Austria	0	3	1	4
Canada	0	3	1	4
Ireland	0	1	1	2
Poland	0	1	1	2
Haiti	0	0	1	1
Japan	0	0	1	1
New Zealand	0	0	1	1
Portugal	0	0	1	1
Romania	0	0	1	1

AMSTERDAM (IX) 1928

	GOLD	SILVER	BRONZE	TOTAL
United States	22	18	16	56
Germany	10	7	14	31
Finland	8	8	9	25
Sweden	7	6	12	25
Italy	7	5	7	19
Switzerland	7	4	4	15
France	6	10	5	21
Netherlands	6	9	4	19
Hungary	4	5	0	9
Canada	4	4	7	15

AMSTERDAM (IX) 1928 CONTD

	GOLD	SILVER	BRONZE	TOTAL
Great Britain	3	10	7	20
Argentina	3	3	1	7
Denmark	3	1	2	6
Czechoslovakia	2	5	2	9
Japan	2	2	1	5
Estonia	2	1	2	5
Egypt	2	1	1	4
Austria	2	0	1	3
Australia	1	2	1	4
Norway	1	2	1	4
Poland	1	1	3	5
Yugoslavia	1	1	3	5
South Africa	1	0	2	3
India	1	0	0	1
Ireland	1	0	0	1
New Zealand	1	0	0	1
Spain	1	0	0	1
Uruguay	1	0	0	1
Belgium	0	1	2	3
Chile	0	1	0	1
Haiti	0	1	0	1
Philippines	0	0	1	1
Portugal	0	0	1	1

LOS ANGELES (X) 1932

	GOLD	SILVER	BRONZE	TOTAL
United States	41	32	30	103
Italy	12	12	12	36
France	10	5	4	19
Sweden	9	5	9	23
Japan	7	7	4	18
Hungary	6	4	5	15
Finland	5	8	12	25
Germany	3	12	5	20
Great Britain	4	7	5	16
Australia	3	1	1	5
Argentina	3	1	0	4
Canada	2	5	8	15
Netherlands	2	5	0	7
Poland	2	1	4	7
South Africa	2	0	3	5
Ireland	2	0	0	2
Czechoslovakia	1	2	1	4
Austria	1	1	3	5
India	1	0	0	1
Denmark	0	3	3	6
Mexico	0	2	0	2
Latvia	0	1	0	1
New Zealand	0	1	0	1
Switzerland	0	1	0	1
Philippines	0	0	3	3
Spain	0	0	1	1
Uruguay	0	0	1	1

BERLIN (XI) 1936

	GOLD	SILVER	BRONZE	TOTAL
Germany	33	26	30	89
United States	24	20	12	56
Hungary	10	1	5	16
Italy	8	9	5	22
Finland	7	6	6	19
France	7	6	6	19
Sweden	6	5	9	20
Japan	6	4	8	18
Netherlands	6	4	7	17
Great Britain	4	7	3	14
Austria	4	6	3	13
Czechoslovakia	3	5	0	8

BERLIN (XI) 1936 CONTD

	GOLD	SILVER	BRONZE	TOTAL
Argentina	2	2	3	7
Estonia	2	2	3	7
Egypt	2	1	2	5
Switzerland	1	9	5	15
Canada	1	3	5	9
Norway	1	3	2	6
Turkey	1	0	1	2
India	1	0	0	1
New Zealand	1	0	0	1
Poland	0	3	3	6
Denmark	0	2	3	5
Latvia	0	1	1	2
Romania	0	1	0	1
South Africa	0	1	0	1
Yugoslavia	0	1	0	1
Mexico	0	0	3	3
Belgium	0	0	2	2
Australia	0	0	1	1
Philippines	0	0	1	1
Portugal	0	0	1	1

LONDON (XIV) 1948

	GOLD	SILVER	BRONZE	TOTAL
United States	38	27	19	84
Sweden	16	11	17	44
France	10	6	13	29
Hungary	10	5	12	27
Italy	8	12	9	29
Finland	8	7	5	20
Turkey	6	4	2	12
Czechoslovakia	6	2	3	11
Switzerland	5	10	5	20
Denmark	5	7	8	20
Netherlands	5	2	9	16
Great Britain	3	14	6	23
Argentina	3	3	1	7
Australia	2	6	5	13
Belgium	2	2	3	7
Egypt	2	2	1	5
Mexico	2	1	2	5
South Africa	2	1	1	4
Norway	1	3	3	7
Jamaica	1	2	0	3
Austria	1	0	3	4
India	1	0	0	1
Peru	1	0	0	1
Yugoslavia	0	2	0	2
Canada	0	1	2	3
Portugal	0	1	1	2
Uruguay	0	1	1	2
Ceylon (now Sri Lanka)	0	1	0	1
Cuba	0	1	0	1
Spain	0	1	0	1
Trinidad	0	1	0	1
South Korea	0	0	2	2
Panama	0	0	2	2
Brazil	0	0	1	1
Iran	0	0	1	1
Poland	0	0	1	1
Puerto Rico	0	0	1	1

HELSINKI (XV) 1952

	GOLD	SILVER	BRONZE	TOTAL
United States	40	19	17	76
Soviet Union	22	30	19	71
Hungary	16	10	16	42
Sweden	12	13	10	35
Italy	8	9	4	21

HELSINKI (XV) 1952 CONTD

	GOLD	SILVER	BRONZE	TOTAL
Czechoslovakia	7	3	3	13
France	6	6	6	18
Finland	6	3	13	22
Australia	6	2	3	11
Norway	3	2	0	5
Switzerland	2	6	6	14
South Africa	2	4	4	10
Jamaica	2	3	0	5
Belgium	2	2	0	4
Denmark	2	1	3	6
Turkey	2	0	1	3
Japan	1	6	2	9
Great Britain	1	2	8	11
Argentina	1	2	2	5
Poland	1	2	1	4
Canada	1	2	0	3
Yugoslavia	1	2	0	3
Romania	1	1	2	4
Brazil	1	0	2	3
New Zealand	1	0	2	3
India	1	0	1	2
Luxembourg	1	0	0	1
Germany	0	7	17	24
Netherlands	0	5	0	5
Iran	0	3	4	7
Chile	0	2	0	2
Austria	0	1	1	2
Lebanon	0	1	1	2
Ireland	0	1	0	1
Mexico	0	1	0	1
Spain	0	1	0	1
South Korea	0	0	2	2
Trinidad	0	0	2	2
Uruguay	0	0	2	2
Bulgaria	0	0	1	1
Egypt	0	0	1	1
Portugal	0	0	1	1
Venezuela	0	0	1	1

MELBOURNE (XVI) 1956

	GOLD	SILVER	BRONZE	TOTAL
Soviet Union	37	29	32	98
United States	32	25	17	74
Australia	13	8	14	35
Hungary	9	10	7	26
Italy	8	8	9	25
Sweden	8	5	6	19
Germany	6	13	7	26
Great Britain	6	7	11	24
Romania	5	3	5	13
Japan	4	10	5	19
France	4	4	6	14
Turkey	3	2	2	8
Finland	3	1	11	15
Iran	2	2	1	5
Canada	2	1	3	6
New Zealand	2	0	0	2
Poland	1	4	4	9
Czechoslovakia	1	4	1	6
Bulgaria	1	3	1	5
Denmark	1	2	1	4
Ireland	1	1	3	5
Norway	1	0	2	3
Mexico	1	0	1	2
Brazil	1	0	0	1
India	1	0	0	1
Yugoslavia	0	3	0	3
Chile	0	2	2	4
Belgium	0	2	0	2

MELBOURNE (XVI) 1956 CONTD

	GOLD	SILVER	BRONZE	TOTAL
Argentina	0	1	1	2
South Korea	0	1	1	2
Iceland	0	1	0	1
Pakistan	0	1	0	1
South Africa	0	0	4	4
Austria	0	0	2	2
Bahamas	0	0	1	1
Greece	0	0	1	1
Switzerland	0	0	1	1
Uruguay	0	0	1	1

ROME (XVII) 1960

	GOLD	SILVER	BRONZE	TOTAL
Soviet Union	43	29	31	103
United States	34	21	16	71
Italy	13	10	13	36
Germany	12	19	11	42
Australia	8	8	6	22
Turkey	7	2	0	9
Hungary	6	8	7	21
Japan	4	7	7	18
Poland	4	6	11	21
Czechoslovakia	3	2	3	8
Romania	3	1	6	10
Great Britain	2	6	12	20
Denmark	2	3	1	6
New Zealand	2	0	1	3
Bulgaria	1	3	3	7
Sweden	1	2	3	6
Finland	1	1	3	5
Austria	1	1	0	2
Yugoslavia	1	1	0	2
Pakistan	1	0	1	2
Ethiopia	1	0	0	1
Greece	1	0	0	1
Norway	1	0	0	1
Switzerland	0	3	3	6
France	0	2	3	5
Belgium	0	2	2	4
Iran	0	1	3	4
Netherlands	0	1	2	3
South Africa	0	1	2	3
Argentina	0	1	1	2
Egypt (UAR)	0	1	1	2
Canada	0	1	0	1
Ghana	0	1	0	1
India	0	1	0	1
Morocco	0	1	0	1
Portugal	0	1	0	1
Singapore	0	1	0	1
Taiwan (Chinese Taipei)	0	1	0	1
Brazil	0	0	2	2
Jamaica(1)	0	0	2	2
Barbados(1)	0	0	1	1
Iraq	0	0	1	1
Mexico	0	0	1	1
Spain	0	0	1	1
Venezuela	0	0	1	1

(1) Double-counted, part of Antilles team

TOKYO (XVIII) 1964

	GOLD	SILVER	BRONZE	TOTAL
United States	36	26	28	90
Soviet Union	30	31	35	96
Japan	16	5	8	29
Germany	10	22	18	50
Italy	10	10	7	27
Hungary	10	7	5	22

TOKYO (XVIII) 1964 CONTD

	GOLD	SILVER	BRONZE	TOTAL
Poland	7	6	10	23
Australia	6	2	10	18
Czechoslovakia	5	6	3	14
Great Britain	4	12	2	18
Bulgaria	3	5	2	10
Finland	3	0	2	5
New Zealand	3	0	2	5
Romania	2	4	6	12
Netherlands	2	4	4	10
Turkey	2	3	1	6
Sweden	2	2	4	8
Denmark	2	1	3	6
Yugoslavia	2	1	2	5
Belgium	2	0	1	3
France	1	8	6	15
Canada	1	2	1	4
Switzerland	1	2	1	4
Bahamas	1	0	0	1
Ethiopia	1	0	0	1
India	1	0	0	1
South Korea	0	2	1	3
Trinidad	0	1	2	3
Tunisia	0	1	1	2
Argentina	0	1	0	1
Cuba	0	1	0	1
Pakistan	0	1	0	1
Philippines	0	1	0	1
Iran	0	0	2	2
Brazil	0	0	1	1
Ghana	0	0	1	1
Ireland	0	0	1	1
Kenya	0	0	1	1
Mexico	0	0	1	1
Nigeria	0	0	1	1
Uruguay	0	0	1	1

MEXICO (XIX) 1968

	GOLD	SILVER	BRONZE	TOTAL
United States	45	28	34	107
Soviet Union	29	32	30	91
Japan	11	7	7	25
Hungary	10	10	12	32
East Germany	9	9	7	25
France	7	3	5	15
Czechoslovakia	7	2	4	13
West Germany	5	11	10	26
Australia	5	7	5	17
Great Britain	5	5	3	13
Poland	5	2	11	18
Romania	4	6	5	15
Italy	3	4	9	16
Kenya	3	4	2	9
Mexico	3	3	3	9
Yugoslavia	3	3	2	8
Netherlands	3	3	1	7
Bulgaria	2	4	3	9
Iran	2	1	2	5
Sweden	2	1	1	4
Turkey	2	0	0	2
Denmark	1	4	3	8
Canada	1	2	1	4
Ethiopia	1	1	0	2
Norway	1	1	0	2
New Zealand	1	0	2	3
Tunisia	1	0	1	2
Pakistan	1	0	0	1
Venezuela	1	0	0	1
Cuba	0	4	0	4
Austria	0	2	2	4

MEXICO (XIX) 1968 CONTD

	GOLD	SILVER	BRONZE	TOTAL
Switzerland	0	1	4	5
Mongolia	0	1	3	4
Brazil	0	1	2	3
Belgium	0	1	1	2
South Korea	0	1	1	2
Uganda	0	1	1	2
Cameroon	0	1	0	1
Jamaica	0	1	0	1
Argentina	0	0	2	2
Greece	0	0	1	1
India	0	0	1	1
Taiwan (Chinese Taipei)	0	0	1	1

MUNICH (XX) 1972

	GOLD	SILVER	BRONZE	TOTAL
Soviet Union	50	27	22	99
United States	33	31	30	94
East Germany	20	23	23	66
West Germany	13	11	16	39
Japan	13	8	8	29
Australia	8	7	2	17
Poland	7	5	9	21
Hungary	6	13	16	35
Bulgaria	6	10	5	21
Italy	5	3	10	18
Sweden	4	6	6	16
Great Britain	4	5	9	18
Romania	3	6	7	16
Cuba	3	1	4	8
Finland	3	1	4	8
Netherlands	3	1	1	5
France	2	4	7	13
Czechoslovakia	2	4	2	8
Kenya	2	3	4	9
Yugoslavia	2	1	2	5
Norway	2	1	1	4
North Korea (PRK)	1	1	3	5
New Zealand	1	1	1	3
Uganda	1	1	0	2
Denmark	1	0	0	1
Switzerland	0	3	0	3
Canada	0	2	3	5
Iran	0	2	1	3
Belgium	0	2	0	2
Greece	0	2	0	2
Austria	0	1	2	3
Columbia	0	1	2	3
Argentina	0	1	0	1
South Korea	0	1	0	1
Lebanon	0	1	0	1
Mexico	0	1	0	1
Mongolia	0	1	0	1
Pakistan	0	1	0	1
Tunisia	0	1	0	1
Turkey	0	1	0	1
Brazil	0	0	2	2
Ethiopia	0	0	2	2
Ghana	0	0	1	1
India	0	0	1	1
Jamaica	0	0	1	1
Niger Republic	0	0	1	1
Nigeria	0	0	1	1
Spain	0	0	1	1

MONTREAL (XXI) 1976

	GOLD	SILVER	BRONZE	TOTAL
Soviet Union	49	41	35	125
East Germany	40	25	25	90

MONTREAL (XXI) 1976 CONTD

	GOLD	SILVER	BRONZE	TOTAL
United States	34	35	25	94
West Germany	10	12	17	39
Japan	9	6	10	25
Poland	7	6	13	26
Bulgaria	6	9	7	22
Cuba	6	4	3	13
Romania	4	9	14	27
Hungary	4	5	13	22
Finland	4	2	0	6
Sweden	4	1	0	5
Great Britain	3	5	5	13
Italy	2	7	4	13
France	2	3	4	9
Yugoslavia	2	3	3	8
Czechoslovakia	2	2	4	8
New Zealand	2	1	1	4
South Korea	1	1	4	6
Switzerland	1	1	2	4
Jamaica	1	1	0	2
North Korea (PRK)	1	1	0	2
Norway	1	1	0	2
Denmark	1	0	2	3
Mexico	1	0	1	2
Trinidad	1	0	0	1
Canada	0	5	6	11
Belgium	0	3	3	6
Netherlands	0	2	3	5
Portugal	0	2	0	2
Spain	0	2	0	2
Australia	0	1	4	5
Iran	0	1	1	2
Mongolia	0	1	0	1
Venezuela	0	1	0	1
Brazil	0	0	2	2
Austria	0	0	1	1
Bermuda	0	0	1	1
Pakistan	0	0	1	1
Puerto Rico	0	0	1	1
Thailand	0	0	1	1

MOSCOW (XXII) 1980

	GOLD	SILVER	BRONZE	TOTAL
Soviet Union	80	69	46	195
East Germany	47	37	42	126
Bulgaria	8	16	17	41
Cuba	8	7	5	20
Italy	8	3	4	15
Hungary	7	10	15	32
Romania	6	6	13	25
France	6	5	3	14
Great Britain	5	7	9	21
Poland	3	14	15	32
Sweden	3	3	6	12
Finland	3	1	4	8
Czechoslovakia	2	3	9	14
Yugoslavia	2	3	4	9
Australia	2	2	5	9
Denmark	2	1	2	5
Brazil	2	0	2	4
Ethiopia	2	0	2	4
Switzerland	2	0	0	2
Spain	1	3	2	6
Austria	1	2	1	4
Greece	1	0	2	3
Belgium	1	0	0	1
India	1	0	0	1
Zimbabwe	1	0	0	1
North Korea (PRK)	0	3	2	5
Mongolia	0	2	2	4

MOSCOW (XXII) 1980 CONTD

	GOLD	SILVER	BRONZE	TOTAL
Tanzania	0	2	0	2
Mexico	0	1	3	4
Netherlands	0	1	2	3
Ireland	0	1	1	2
Uganda	0	1	0	1
Venezuela	0	1	0	1
Jamaica	0	0	3	3
Guyana	0	0	1	1
Lebanon	0	0	1	1

LOS ANGELES (XXIII) 1984

	GOLD	SILVER	BRONZE	TOTAL
United States	83	61	30	172
Romania	20	16	17	53
West Germany	17	19	23	59
China	15	8	9	32
Italy	14	6	12	32
Canada	10	18	16	44
Japan	10	8	14	32
New Zealand	8	1	2	11
Yugoslavia	7	4	7	18
Great Britain	5	11	21	37
France	5	7	16	38
Netherlands	5	2	6	13
Australia	4	8	12	24
Finland	4	2	6	12
Sweden	2	11	6	19
Mexico	2	3	1	6
Brazil	1	5	2	8
Spain	1	2	2	5
Belgium	1	1	2	4
Austria	1	1	1	3
Kenya	1	0	2	3
Portugal	1	0	2	3
Pakistan	1	0	0	1
Switzerland	0	4	4	8
Denmark	0	3	3	6
Jamaica	0	1	2	3
Norway	0	1	2	3
Greece	0	1	1	2
Nigeria	0	1	1	2
Puerto Rico	0	1	1	2
Colombia	0	1	0	1
Egypt	0	1	0	1
Ireland	0	1	0	1
Ivory Coast	0	1	0	1
Peru	0	1	0	1
Syria	0	1	0	1
Thailand	0	1	0	1
Turkey	0	0	3	3
Venezuela	0	0	3	3
Algeria	0	0	2	2
Cameroon	0	0	1	1
Dominican Republic	0	0	1	1
Iceland	0	0	1	1
Taiwan (Chinese Taipei)	0	0	1	1
Zambia	0	0	1	1

SEOUL (XXIV) 1988

	GOLD	SILVER	BRONZE	TOTAL
Soviet Union	55	31	46	132
East Germany	37	35	30	102
United States	36	31	27	94
South Korea	12	10	11	33
West Germany	11	14	15	40
Hungary	11	6	6	23
Bulgaria	10	12	13	35

SEOUL (XXIV) 1988 CONTD

	GOLD	SILVER	BRONZE	TOTAL
Romania	7	11	6	24
France	6	4	6	16
Italy	6	4	4	14
China	5	11	12	28
Great Britain	5	10	9	24
Kenya	5	2	2	9
Japan	4	3	7	14
Australia	3	6	5	14
Yugoslavia	3	4	5	12
Czechoslovakia	3	3	2	8
New Zealand	3	2	8	13
Canada	3	2	5	10
Poland	2	5	9	16
Norway	2	3	0	5
Netherlands	2	2	5	9
Denmark	2	1	1	4
Brazil	1	2	3	6
Finland	1	1	2	4
Spain	1	1	2	4
Turkey	1	1	0	2
Morocco	1	0	2	3
Austria	1	0	0	1
Portugal	1	0	0	1
Surinam	1	0	0	1
Sweden	0	4	7	11
Switzerland	0	2	2	4
Jamaica	0	2	0	2
Argentina	0	1	1	2
Chile	0	1	0	1
Costa Rica	0	1	0	1
Indonesia	0	1	0	1
Iran	0	1	0	1
Netherlands Antilles	0	1	0	1
Peru	0	1	0	1
Senegal	0	1	0	1
Virgin Islands	0	1	0	1
Belgium	0	0	2	2
Mexico	0	0	2	2
Colombia	0	0	1	1
Djibouti	0	0	1	1
Greece	0	0	1	1
Mongolia	0	0	1	1
Pakistan	0	0	1	1
Philippines	0	0	1	1
Thailand	0	0	1	1

BARCELONA (XXV) 1992

	GOLD	SILVER	BRONZE	TOTAL
Unified Team	45	38	29	112
United States	37	34	37	108
Germany	33	21	28	82
China	16	22	16	54
Cuba	14	6	11	31
Spain	13	7	2	22
South Korea	12	5	12	29
Hungary	11	12	7	30
France	8	5	16	29
Australia	7	9	11	27
Canada	7	4	7	18
Italy	6	5	8	19
Great Britain	5	3	12	20
Romania	4	6	8	18
Czechoslovakia	4	2	1	7
North Korea (PRK)	4	0	5	9
Japan	3	8	11	22
Bulgaria	3	7	6	16
Poland	3	6	10	19
Netherlands	2	6	7	15

BARCELONA (XXV) 1992 CONTD

	GOLD	SILVER	BRONZE	TOTAL
Kenya	2	4	2	8
Norway	2	4	1	7
Turkey	2	2	2	6
Indonesia	2	2	1	5
Brazil	2	1	0	3
Greece	2	0	0	2
Sweden	1	7	4	12
New Zealand	1	4	5	10
Finland	1	2	2	5
Denmark	1	1	4	6
Morocco	1	1	1	3
Ireland	1	1	0	2
Ethiopia	1	0	2	3
Algeria	1	0	1	2
Estonia	1	0	1	2
Lithuania	1	0	1	2
Switzerland	1	0	0	1
Jamaica	0	3	1	4
Nigeria	0	3	1	4
Latvia	0	2	1	3
Austria	0	2	0	2
Namibia	0	2	0	2
South Africa	0	2	0	2
Belgium	0	1	2	3
Croatia	0	1	2	3
IOP	0	1	2	3
Iran	0	1	2	3
Israel	0	1	1	2
Taiwan (Chinese Taipei)	0	1	0	1
Mexico	0	1	0	1
Peru	0	1	0	1
Slovenia	0	0	2	2
Mongolia	0	0	2	2
Argentina	0	0	1	1
Bahamas	0	0	1	1
Colombia	0	0	1	1
Ghana	0	0	1	1
Malaysia	0	0	1	1
Pakistan	0	0	1	1
Philippines	0	0	1	1
Puerto Rico	0	0	1	1
Qatar	0	0	1	1
Surinam	0	0	1	1
Thailand	0	0	1	1

ATLANTA (XXVI) 1996

	GOLD	SILVER	BRONZE	TOTAL
United States	44	32	25	101
Russia	26	21	16	63
Germany	20	18	27	65
China	16	22	12	50
France	15	7	15	37
Italy	13	10	12	35
Australia	9	9	23	41
Cuba	9	8	8	25
Ukraine	9	2	12	23
South Korea	7	15	5	27
Poland	7	5	5	17
Hungary	7	4	10	21
Spain	5	6	6	17
Romania	4	7	9	20
Netherlands	4	5	10	19
Greece	4	4	0	8
Czech Republic	4	3	4	11
Switzerland	4	3	0	7
Denmark	4	1	1	6
Turkey	4	1	1	6
Canada	3	11	8	22

ATLANTA (XXVI) 1996 CONTD

	GOLD	SILVER	BRONZE	TOTAL
Bulgaria	3	7	5	15
Japan	3	6	5	14
Kazakhstan	3	4	4	11
Brazil	3	3	9	15
New Zealand	3	2	1	6
South Africa	3	1	1	5
Ireland	3	0	1	4
Sweden	2	4	2	8
Norway	2	2	3	7
Belgium	2	2	2	6
Nigeria	2	1	3	6
North Korea (PRK)	2	1	2	5
Algeria	2	0	1	3
Ethiopia	2	0	1	3
Great Britain	1	8	6	15
Belarus	1	6	8	15
Kenya	1	4	3	8
Jamaica	1	3	2	6
Finland	1	2	1	4
Indonesia	1	1	2	4
Yugoslavia	1	1	2	4
Iran	1	1	1	3
Slovakia	1	1	1	3
Armenia	1	1	0	2
Croatia	1	1	0	2
Portugal	1	0	1	2
Thailand	1	0	1	2
Syrian Arab Republic	1	0	0	1
Costa Rica	1	0	0	1
Burundi	1	0	0	1
Hong Kong	1	0	0	1
Ecuador	1	0	0	1
Argentina	0	2	1	3
Slovenia	0	2	0	2
Namibia	0	2	0	2
Austria	0	1	2	3
Malaysia	0	1	1	2
Moldova	0	1	1	2
Uzbekistan	0	1	1	2
Zambia	0	1	0	1
Tonga	0	1	0	1
Latvia	0	1	0	1
Philippines	0	1	0	1
Azerbaijan	0	1	0	1
Bahamas	0	1	0	1
Taiwan (Chinese Taipei)	0	1	0	1
Georgia	0	1	0	1
Morocco	0	0	2	2
Trinidad and Tobago	0	0	2	2
Tunisia	0	0	1	1
Uganda	0	0	1	1
Mongolia	0	0	1	1
Mexico	0	0	1	1
Lithuania	0	0	1	1
Israel	0	0	1	1
Mozambique	0	0	1	1
Puerto Rico	0	0	1	1
India	0	0	1	1

SYDNEY (XXVII) 2000

	GOLD	SILVER	BRONZE	TOTAL
United States	39	25	33	97
Russia	32	28	28	88
China	28	16	15	59
Australia	16	25	58	99
Germany	14	17	26	57

SYDNEY (XXVII) 2000 CONTD

	GOLD	SILVER	BRONZE	TOTAL
France	13	14	11	38
Italy	13	8	13	34
Netherlands	12	9	4	25
Cuba	11	11	7	29
Great Britain	11	10	7	28
Romania	11	6	9	26
South Korea	8	9	11	28
Hungary	8	6	3	17
Poland	6	5	3	14
Japan	5	8	5	18
Bulgaria	5	6	2	13
Greece	4	6	3	13
Sweden	4	5	3	12
Norway	4	3	3	10
Ethiopia	4	1	3	8
Ukraine	3	10	10	23
Kazakhstan	3	4	0	7
Belarus	3	3	11	17
Canada	3	3	8	14
Spain	3	3	5	11
Iran	3	0	1	4
Turkey	3	0	1	4
Czech Republic	2	3	3	8
Kenya	2	3	2	7
Denmark	2	3	1	6
Finland	2	1	1	4
Austria	2	1	0	3
Lithuania	2	0	3	5
Azerbaijan	2	0	1	3
Slovenia	2	0	0	2
Switzerland	1	6	2	9
Indonesia	1	3	2	6
Slovakia	1	3	1	5
Mexico	1	2	3	6
Algeria	1	1	3	5
Uzbekistan	1	1	2	4
Latvia	1	1	1	3
Yugoslavia	1	1	1	3
Bahamas	1	1	0	2
New Zealand	1	0	3	4
Estonia	1	0	2	3
Thailand	1	0	2	3
Croatia	1	0	1	2
Cameroon	1	0	0	1
Colombia	1	0	0	1
Mozambique	1	0	0	1
Brazil	0	6	6	12
Jamaica	0	4	3	7
Nigeria	0	3	0	3
Belgium	0	2	3	5
South Africa	0	2	3	5
Argentina	0	2	2	4
Morocco	0	1	4	5
Taiwan (Chinese Taipei)	0	1	4	5
North Korea (PRK)	0	1	3	4
Moldova	0	1	1	2
Saudi Arabia	0	1	1	2
Trinidad and Tobago	0	1	1	2
Ireland	0	1	0	1
Uruguay	0	1	0	1
Vietnam	0	1	0	1
Georgia	0	0	6	6
Costa Rica	0	0	2	2
Portugal	0	0	2	2
Armenia	0	0	1	1
Barbados	0	0	1	1
Chile	0	0	1	1
Iceland	0	0	1	1
India	0	0	1	1
Israel	0	0	1	1

SYDNEY (XXVII) 2000 CONTD

	GOLD	SILVER	BRONZE	TOTAL
Kyrgyzstan	0	0	1	1
Kuwait	0	0	1	1
Macedonia	0	0	1	1
Qatar	0	0	1	1
Sri Lanka	0	0	1	1

ATHENS (XXVIII) 2004

	GOLD	SILVER	BRONZE	TOTAL
United States	36	39	27	102
China	32	17	14	63
Russian Federation	27	27	38	92
Australia	17	16	16	49
Japan	16	9	12	37
Germany	13	16	20	49
France	11	9	13	33
Italy	10	11	11	32
Korea	9	12	9	30
Great Britain	9	9	12	30
Cuba	9	7	11	27
Ukraine	9	5	9	23
Hungary	8	6	3	17
Romania	8	5	6	19
Greece	6	6	4	16
Brazil	5	2	3	10
Norway	5	0	1	6
Netherlands	4	9	9	22
Sweden	4	2	1	7
Spain	3	11	5	19
Canada	3	6	3	12
Turkey	3	3	4	10
Poland	3	2	5	10
New Zealand	3	2	0	5
Thailand	3	1	4	8
Belarus	2	6	7	15
Austria	2	4	1	7
Ethiopia	2	3	2	7
Iran	2	2	2	6
Slovakia	2	2	2	6
Chinese Taipei	2	2	1	5
Georgia	2	2	0	4
Bulgaria	2	1	9	12
Jamaica	2	1	2	5
Uzbekistan	2	1	2	5
Morocco	2	1	0	3
Denmark	2	0	6	8
Argentina	2	0	4	6
Chile	2	0	1	3
Kazakhstan	1	4	3	8
Kenya	1	4	2	7
Czech Republic	1	3	4	8
South Africa	1	3	2	6
Croatia	1	2	2	5
Lithuania	1	2	0	3
Egypt	1	1	3	5
Switzerland	1	1	3	5
Indonesia	1	1	2	4
Zimbabwe	1	1	1	3
Azerbaijan	1	0	4	5
Belgium	1	0	2	3
Bahamas	1	0	1	2
Israel	1	0	1	2
Cameroon	1	0	0	1
Dominican Republic	1	0	0	1
United Arab Emirates	1	0	0	1
PR Korea	0	4	1	5
Latvia	0	4	0	4
Mexico	0	3	1	4
Portugal	0	2	1	3
Finland	0	2	0	2

ATHENS (XXVIII) 2004 CONTD

	GOLD	SILVER	BRONZE	TOTAL
Serbia-Montenegro	0	2	0	2
Slovenia	0	1	3	4
Estonia	0	1	2	3
Hong Kong	0	1	0	1
India	0	1	0	1
Paraguay	0	1	0	1
Colombia	0	0	2	2

ATHENS (XXVIII) 2004 CONTD

	GOLD	SILVER	BRONZE	TOTAL
Nigeria	0	0	2	2
Venezuela	0	0	2	2
Eritrea	0	0	1	1
Mongolia	0	0	1	1
Syria	0	0	1	1
Trinidad and Tobago	0	0	1	1

Olympic Winter Games Medals Tables

CHAMONIX (I) 1924

	GOLD	SILVER	BRONZE	TOTAL
Norway	4	7	6	17
Finland	4	3	3	10
Austria	2	1	0	3
United States	1	2	1	4
Switzerland	1	0	1	2
Canada	1	0	1	2
Sweden	1	0	0	1
Great Britain	0	1	2	3
Belgium	0	0	1	1
France	0	0	1	1

ST MORITZ (II) 1928

	GOLD	SILVER	BRONZE	TOTAL
Norway	6	4	5	15
United States	2	2	2	6
Sweden	2	2	1	5
Finland	2	1	1	4
Canada	1	0	0	1
France	1	0	0	1
Austria	0	3	1	4
Belgium	0	0	1	1
Czechoslovakia	0	0	1	1
Germany	0	0	1	1
Great Britain	0	0	1	1
Switzerland	0	0	1	1

LAKE PLACID (III) 1932

	GOLD	SILVER	BRONZE	TOTAL
United States	6	4	2	12
Norway	3	4	3	10
Sweden	1	2	0	3
Canada	1	1	5	7
Finland	1	1	1	3
Austria	1	1	0	2
France	1	0	0	1
Switzerland	0	1	0	1
Germany	0	0	2	2
Hungary	0	0	1	1

GARMISCH-PARTENKIRCHEN (IV) 1936

	GOLD	SILVER	BRONZE	TOTAL
Norway	7	5	3	15
Germany	3	3	0	6
Sweden	2	2	3	7
Finland	1	2	3	6

GARMISCH-PARTENKIRCHEN (IV) 1936 CONTD

	GOLD	SILVER	BRONZE	TOTAL
Austria	1	1	2	4
Switzerland	1	2	0	3
Great Britain	1	1	1	3
United States	1	0	3	4
Canada	0	1	0	1
France	0	0	1	1
Hungary	0	0	1	1

ST MORITZ (V) 1948

	GOLD	SILVER	BRONZE	TOTAL
Norway	4	3	3	10
Sweden	4	3	3	10
Switzerland	3	4	3	10
United States	3	4	2	9
France	2	1	2	5
Canada	2	0	1	3
Austria	1	3	4	8
Finland	1	3	2	6
Belgium	1	1	0	2
Italy	1	0	0	1
Czechoslovakia	0	1	0	1
Hungary	0	1	0	1
Great Britain	0	0	2	2

OLSO (VI) 1952

	GOLD	SILVER	BRONZE	TOTAL
Norway	7	3	6	16
United States	4	6	1	11
Finland	3	4	2	9
Germany	3	2	2	7
Austria	2	4	2	8
Canada	1	0	1	2
Italy	1	0	1	2
Great Britain	1	0	0	1
Netherlands	0	3	0	3
Sweden	0	0	4	4
Switzerland	0	0	2	2
France	0	0	1	1
Hungary	0	0	1	1

CORTINA D'AMPEZZO (VII) 1956

	GOLD	SILVER	BRONZE	TOTAL
Soviet Union	7	3	6	16
Austria	4	3	4	11
Finland	3	3	1	7

CORTINA D'AMPEZZO (VII) 1956 CONTD

	GOLD	SILVER	BRONZE	TOTAL
Switzerland	3	2	1	6
Sweden	2	4	4	10
United States	2	3	2	7
Norway	2	1	1	4
Italy	1	2	0	3
Germany	1	0	1	2
Canada	0	1	2	3
Japan	0	1	0	1
Hungary	0	0	1	1
Poland	0	0	1	1

SQUAW VALLEY (VIII) 1960

	GOLD	SILVER	BRONZE	TOTAL
Soviet Union	7	5	9	21
Germany	4	3	1	8
United States	3	4	3	10
Norway	3	3	0	6
Sweden	3	2	2	7
Finland	2	3	3	8
Canada	2	1	1	4
Switzerland	2	0	0	2
Austria	1	2	3	6
France	1	0	2	3
Netherlands	0	1	1	2
Poland	0	1	1	2
Czechoslovakia	0	1	0	1
Italy	0	0	1	1

INNSBRUCK (IX) 1964

	GOLD	SILVER	BRONZE	TOTAL
Soviet Union	11	8	6	25
Austria	4	5	3	12
Norway	3	6	6	15
Finland	3	4	3	10
France	3	4	0	7
Sweden	3	3	1	7
Germany	3	2	3	8
United States	1	2	4	7
Canada	1	1	1	3
Netherlands	1	1	0	2
Great Britain	1	0	0	1
Italy	0	1	3	4
North Korea (PRK)	0	1	0	1
Czechoslovakia	0	0	1	1

GRENOBLE (X) 1968

	GOLD	SILVER	BRONZE	TOTAL
Norway	6	6	2	14
Soviet Union	5	5	3	13
France	4	3	2	9
Italy	4	0	0	4
Austria	3	4	4	11
Netherlands	3	3	3	9
West Germany	2	2	3	7
United States	1	5	1	7
Finland	1	2	2	5
East Germany	1	2	2	5
Czechoslovakia	1	2	1	4
Canada	1	1	1	3
Switzerland	0	2	4	6
Romania	0	0	1	1

SAPPORO (XI) 1972

	GOLD	SILVER	BRONZE	TOTAL
Soviet Union	8	5	3	16
East Germany	4	3	7	14

SAPPORO (XI) 1972 CONTD

	GOLD	SILVER	BRONZE	TOTAL
Switzerland	4	3	3	10
Netherlands	4	3	2	9
United States	3	2	3	8
West Germany	3	1	1	5
Norway	2	5	5	12
Italy	2	2	1	5
Austria	1	2	2	5
Sweden	1	1	2	4
Japan	1	1	1	3
Czechoslovakia	1	0	2	3
Poland	1	0	0	1
Spain	1	0	0	1
Finland	0	4	1	5
France	0	1	2	3
Canada	0	1	0	1

INNSBRUCK (XII) 1976

	GOLD	SILVER	BRONZE	TOTAL
Soviet Union	13	6	8	27
East Germany	7	5	7	19
United States	3	3	4	10
Norway	3	3	1	9
West Germany	2	5	3	10
Finland	2	4	1	7
Austria	2	2	2	6
Switzerland	1	3	1	5
Netherlands	1	2	3	6
Italy	1	2	1	4
Canada	1	1	1	3
Great Britain	1	0	0	1
Czechoslovakia	0	1	0	1
Liechtenstein	0	0	2	2
Sweden	0	0	2	2
France	0	0	1	1

LAKE PLACID (XIII) 1980

	GOLD	SILVER	BRONZE	TOTAL
Soviet Union	10	6	6	22
East Germany	9	7	7	23
United States	6	4	2	12
Austria	3	2	2	7
Sweden	3	0	1	4
Liechtenstein	2	2	0	4
Finland	1	5	3	9
Norway	1	3	6	10
Netherlands	1	2	1	4
Switzerland	1	1	3	5
Great Britain	1	0	0	1
West Germany	0	2	3	5
Italy	0	2	0	2
Canada	0	1	1	2
Hungary	0	1	0	1
Japan	0	1	0	1
Bulgaria	0	0	1	1
Czechoslovakia	0	0	1	1
France	0	0	1	1

SARAJEVO (XIV) 1984

	GOLD	SILVER	BRONZE	TOTAL
East Germany	9	9	6	24
Soviet Union	6	10	9	25
United States	4	4	0	8
Finland	4	3	6	13
Sweden	4	2	2	8
Norway	3	2	4	9
Switzerland	2	2	1	5
Canada	2	1	1	4
West Germany	2	1	1	4

SARAJEVO (XIV) 1984 CONTD

	GOLD	SILVER	BRONZE	TOTAL
Italy	2	0	0	2
Great Britain	1	0	0	1
Czechoslovakia	0	2	4	6
France	0	1	2	3
Japan	0	1	0	1
Yugoslavia	0	1	0	1
Liechtenstein	0	0	2	2
Austria	0	0	1	1

CALGARY (XV) 1988

	GOLD	SILVER	BRONZE	TOTAL
Soviet Union	11	9	9	29
East Germany	9	10	6	25
Switzerland	5	5	5	15
Finland	4	1	2	7
Sweden	4	0	2	6
Austria	3	5	2	10
Netherlands	3	2	2	7
West Germany	2	4	2	8
United States	2	1	3	6
Italy	2	1	2	5
France	1	0	1	2
Norway	0	3	2	5
Canada	0	2	3	5
Yugoslavia	0	2	1	3
Czechoslovakia	0	1	2	3
Japan	0	0	1	1
Liechtenstein	0	0	1	1

ALBERTVILLE (XVI) 1992

	GOLD	SILVER	BRONZE	TOTAL
Germany	10	10	6	26
Unified	9	6	8	23
Norway	9	6	5	20
Austria	6	7	8	21
United States	5	4	2	11
Italy	4	6	4	14
France	3	5	1	9
Finland	3	1	3	7
Canada	2	3	2	7
South Korea	2	1	1	4
Japan	1	2	4	7
Netherlands	1	1	2	4
Sweden	1	0	3	4
Switzerland	1	0	2	3
China	0	3	0	3
Luxembourg	0	2	0	2
New Zealand	0	1	0	1
Czechoslovakia	0	0	3	3
North Korea (PRK)	0	0	1	1
Spain	0	0	1	1

NB: Two silvers in women's giant slalom

LILLEHAMMER (XVII) 1994

	GOLD	SILVER	BRONZE	TOTAL
Russia	11	8	4	23
Norway	10	11	5	26
Germany	9	7	8	24
Italy	7	5	8	20
United States	6	5	2	13
South Korea	4	1	1	6
Canada	3	6	4	13
Switzerland	3	4	2	9
Austria	2	3	4	9
Sweden	2	1	0	3
Japan	1	2	2	5
Kazakhstan	1	2	0	3

LILLEHAMMER (XVII) 1994 CONTD

	GOLD	SILVER	BRONZE	TOTAL
Ukraine	1	0	1	2
Uzbekistan	1	0	0	1
Belarus	0	2	0	2
Finland	0	1	5	6
France	0	1	4	5
Netherlands	0	1	3	4
China	0	1	2	3
Slovenia	0	0	3	3
Great Britain	0	0	2	2
Australia	0	0	1	1

NAGANO (XVIII) 1998

	GOLD	SILVER	BRONZE	TOTAL
Germany	12	9	8	29
Norway	10	10	5	25
Russia	9	6	3	18
Canada	6	5	4	15
United States	6	3	4	13
Netherlands	5	4	2	11
Japan	5	1	4	10
Austria	3	5	9	17
South Korea	3	1	2	6
Italy	2	6	2	10
Finland	2	4	6	12
Switzerland	2	2	3	7
France	2	1	5	8
Czech Republic	1	1	1	3
Bulgaria	1	0	0	1
China	0	6	2	8
Sweden	0	2	1	3
Ukraine	0	1	0	1
Denmark	0	1	0	1
Belarus	0	0	2	2
Kazakhstan	0	0	2	2
Great Britain	0	0	1	1
Belgium	0	0	1	1
Australia	0	0	1	1

SALT LAKE CITY (XIX) 2002

	GOLD	SILVER	BRONZE	TOTAL
Germany	12	16	7	35
Norway	11	7	7	25
United States	10	14	11	35
Russia	6	6	4	16
Canada	6	3	8	17
France	4	5	2	11
Italy	4	4	4	12
Finland	4	2	1	7
Netherlands	3	5	0	8
Austria	3	4	11	18
Switzerland	3	2	6	11
Croatia	3	1	0	4
China	2	2	4	8
South Korea	2	2	0	4
Australia	2	0	0	2
Spain	2	0	0	2
Estonia	1	1	1	3
Czech Republic	1	0	1	2
Great Britain	1	0	1	2
Sweden	0	2	4	6
Bulgaria	0	1	2	3
Japan	0	1	1	2
Poland	0	1	1	2
Slovenia	0	0	1	1
Belarus	0	0	1	1

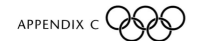

TURIN (XX) 2006

	GOLD	SILVER	BRONZE	TOTAL
Germany	11	12	6	29
United States	9	9	7	25
Austria	9	7	7	23
Russia	8	6	8	22
Canada	7	10	7	24
Sweden	7	2	5	14
Korea	6	3	2	11
Switzerland	5	4	5	14
Italy	5	0	6	11
France	3	2	4	9
Netherlands	3	2	4	9
Estonia	3	0	0	3
Norway	2	8	9	19

TURIN (XX) 2006 CONTD

	GOLD	SILVER	BRONZE	TOTAL
China	2	4	5	11
Czech Republic	1	2	1	4
Croatia	1	2	0	3
Australia	1	0	1	2
Japan	1	0	0	1
Finland	0	6	3	9
Poland	0	1	1	2
Belarus	0	1	0	1
Bulgaria	0	1	0	1
Great Britain	0	1	0	1
Slovakia	0	1	0	1
Ukraine	0	0	2	2
Latvia	0	0	1	1

APPENDIX D

List of Abbreviations

AGF	Asian Games Federation
AIBA	* International Amateur Boxing Association
AIPS	Association of International Sports Press
AIOWF	Association of International Olympic Winter Sports Federations
ANOC	Association of National Olympic Committees
ANOCA	Association of National Olympic Committees of Africa
ARISF	Association of (IOC) Recognised International Sports Federations
ASOIF	Association of Summer Olympic International Federations
BALCO	Bay Area Laboratory Cooperative
BOA	British Olympic Association
CAF	African Football Confederation
CAS	Court of Arbitration for Sport
CGF	Commonwealth Games Federation
CISM	International Military Sports Council
CONI	Italian National Olympic Committee
EBU	European Broadcasting Union
EOC	European Olympic Committees
FEI	*Fédération Equestre Internationale
FIBA	*International Basketball Federation
FIBT	*International Bobsleigh and Tobogganing Federation
FIE	*International Fencing (Escrime) Federation
FIFA	*Federation of International Football Associations
FIG	*International Gymnastics Federation
FIH	*International Hockey Federation
FIL	*International Luge Federation
FILA	*International Federation of Associated Wrestling (Lutte) Styles
FIMS	International Federation of Sports Medicine
FINA	*International Swimming (Natation) Federation
FIS	*International Ski Federation
FISA	*International Rowing (Aviron) Federation
FISU	International Federation of University Sport
FITA	*International Archery (Tir à l'Arc) Federation
FIVB	*International Volleyball Federation
FSFI	International Federation of Women's Sports
GAISF	General Association of International Sports Federations
IAAF	*International Association of Athletic Federations (formerly International Amateur Athletic Federation)
IBAF	*International Baseball Federation
IBF	*International Badminton Federation
IBU	*International Biathlon Union
ICAS	International Council of Arbitration for Sport
ICF	*International Canoe Federation
IHF	*International Handball Federation
IIHF	*International Ice Hockey Federation
IJF	*International Judo Federation
IWGA	International World Games Association
IOA	International Olympic Academy
IPC	International Paralympic Committee
IRB	International Rugby Board
ISAF	*International Sailing Federation
ISF	*International Softball Federation
ISOH	International Society of Olympic Historians
ISSF	*International Shooting Sport Federation
ISU	*International Skating Union
ITF	*International Tennis Federation (formerly IL (Lawn) TF)
ITTF	*International Table Tennis Federation
ITU	*International Triathlon Union
IWF	*International Weightlifting Federation
NOCSA	National Olympic Committee of South Africa
OAU	Organisation of African Unity
OCA	Olympic Council of Asia
ODECABE	Central American and Caribbean Sports Organisation

ODEPA	Panamerican Sports Organisation	USATF	USA Track and Field
ODESUR	South American Sports Organisation	USFSR	Union des Sociétés Francais de Sports Athlétiques
ONOC	Oceania National Olympic Committees	USOC	United States Olympic Committee
RSI	Red Sport International	WADA	World Anti-Doping Agency
SANOC	South African (former) National Olympic Committee	WAGC	World Amateur Golf Council
		WCF	*World Curling Federation
SANROC	South African Non-Racial Olympic Committee	WOA	World Olympians Association
SCSA	Supreme Council for Sport in Africa	WSF	World Squash Federation
SWSI	Socialist Workers Sports International	WTF	*World Taekwondo Federation
UCI	*International Cycling Union		
UIPM	*International Union of Modern Pentathlon		

* Current Olympic sport

APPENDIX E

Current National Olympic Committees (per continent)

AFRICA (53)

Algeria	ALG
Angola	ANG
Benin	BEN
Botswana	BOT
Burkina Faso	BUR
Burundi	BDI
Cameroon	CMR
Cape Verde	CPV
Central African Republic	CAF
Chad	CHA
Comoros	COM
Congo	CGO
Democratic Republic of the Congo	COD
Djibouti	DJI
Egypt	EGY
Equatorial Guinea	GEQ
Eritrea	ERI
Ethiopia	ETH
Gabon	GAB
Gambia	GAM
Ghana	GHA
Guinea	GUI
Guinea-Bissau	GBS
Ivory Coast	CIV
Kenya	KEN
Lesotho	LES
Liberia	LBR
Libya	LBA
Madagascar	MAD
Malawi	MAW
Mali	MLI
Mauritania	MTN
Mauritius	MRI
Morocco	MAR
Mozambique	MOZ
Namibia	NAM
Niger	NIG
Nigeria	NGR
Rwanda	RWA
Sao Tome and Principe	STP
Senegal	SEN
Seychelles	SEY
Sierra Leone	SLE
Somalia	SOM
South Africa	RSA
Sudan	SUD
Swaziland	SWZ
United Republic of Tanzania	TAN
Togo	TOG

AFRICA (53) CONTD

Tunisia	TUN
Uganda	UGA
Zambia	ZAM
Zimbabwe	ZIM

THE AMERICAS (42)

Antigua and Barbuda	ANT
Argentina	ARG
Aruba	ARU
Bahamas	BAH
Barbados	BAR
Belize	BIZ
Bermuda	BER
Bolivia	BOL
Brazil	BRA
British Virgin Islands	IVB
Canada	CAN
Cayman Islands	CAY
Chile	CHI
Colombia	COL
Costa Rica	CRC
Cuba	CUB
Dominica	DMA
Dominican Republic	DOM
Ecuador	ECU
El Salvador	ESA
Grenada	GRN
Guatemala	GUA
Guyana	GUY
Haiti	HAI
Honduras	HON
Jamaica	JAM
Mexico	MEX
Netherlands Antilles	AHO
Nicaragua	NCA
Panama	PAN
Paraguay	PAR
Peru	PER
Puerto Rico	PUR
Saint Kitts and Nevis	SKN
Saint Lucia	LCA
Saint Vincent and the Grenadines	VIN
Surinam	SUR
Trinidad and Tobago	TRI
United States of America	USA
Uruguay	URU
Venezuela	VEN
Virgin Islands	ISV

ASIA (44)

Afghanistan	AFG
Bahrain	BRN
Bangladesh	BAN
Bhutan	BHU
Brunei Darussalam	BRU
Cambodia	CAM
People's Republic of China	CHN
East Timor	TLS
Hong Kong, China	HKG
India	IND
Indonesia	INA
Islamic Republic of Iran	IRI
Iraq	IRQ
Japan	JPN
Jordan	JOR
Kazakhstan	KAZ
(South) Korea	KOR
Democratic People's Republic of Korea	PRK
Kyrgyzstan	KGZ
Kuwait	KUW
Laos People's Democratic Republic	LAO
Lebanon	LIB
Malaysia	MAS
Maldives	MDV
Mongolia	MGL
Myanmar	MYA
Nepal	NEP
Oman	OMA
Pakistan	PAK
Palestine	PLE
Philippines	PHI
Qatar	QAT
Saudi Arabia	KSA
Singapore	SIN
Sri Lanka	SRI
Syrian Arab Republic	SYR
Tajikistan	TJK
Chinese Taipei (Taiwan)	TPE
Thailand	THA
Turkmenistan	TKM
United Arab Emirates	UAE
Uzbekistan	UZB
Vietnam	VIE
Yemen	YEM

EUROPE (49)

Albania	ALB
Andorra	AND
Armenia	ARM
Austria	AUT
Azerbaijan	AZE
Belarus	BLR
Belgium	BEL
Bosnia and Herzegovina	BIH
Bulgaria	BUL
Croatia	CRO
Cyprus	CYP

EUROPE (49) CONTD

Czech Republic	CZE
Denmark	DEN
Estonia	EST
Finland	FIN
France	FRA
Georgia	GEO
Germany	GER
Great Britain	GBR
Greece	GRE
Hungary	HUN
Iceland	ISL
Ireland	IRL
Israel	ISR
Italy	ITA
Latvia	LAT
Liechtenstein	LIE
Lithuania	LTU
Luxembourg	LUX
Former Yugoslavia Republic of Macedonia	MKD
Malta	MLT
Republic of Moldova	MDA
Monaco	MON
Montenegro	MNE
Netherlands	NED
Norway	NOR
Poland	POL
Portugal	POR
Romania	ROM
Russian Federation	RUS
San Marino	SMR
Serbia	SRB
Slovakia	SVK
Slovenia	SLO
Spain	ESP
Sweden	SWE
Switzerland	SUI
Turkey	TUR
Ukraine	UKR

OCEANIA (17)

American Samoa	ASA
Australia	AUS
Cook Islands	COK
Fiji	FIJ
Guam	GUM
Kiribati	KIR
Marshall Islands	MHL
Federated States of Micronesia	FSM
Nauru	NRU
New Zealand	NZL
Palau	PLW
Papua New Guinea	PNG
Samoa	SAM
Solomon Islands	SOL
Tonga	TGA
Tuvalu	TUV
Vanuatu	VAN

APPENDIX F

Summer and Winter Games: dates and statistics

SUMMER GAMES

	YEAR	NOCs	MALE ATHLETES	FEMALE ATHLETES	SPORTS	EVENTS
Athens	1896	14	245	0	9	43
Paris	1900	19	1,066	12	17	86
St Louis	1904	13	681	6	14	89
London	1908	22	1,999	36	20	107
Stockholm	1912	28	2,382	55	13	102
Antwerp	1920	29	2,543	64	19	152
Paris	1924	44	2,941	131	17	126
Amsterdam	1928	46	2,611	273	14	109
Los Angeles	1932	37	1,209	124	14	117
Berlin	1936	49	3,606	330	19	129
London	1948	59	3,702	390	17	136
Helsinki	1952	69	4,922	507	17	149
Melbourne	1956	67	3,184	363	16	145
(Stockholm/Equestrian)	1956	29	147	12	1	6
Rome	1960	83	4,717	596	17	150
Tokyo	1964	93	4,451	682	19	163
Mexico	1968	112	4,724	774	18	172
Munich	1972	121	6,062	1,059	21	195
Montreal	1976	92	4,785	1,258	21	198
Moscow	1980	80	4,149	1,134	21	203
Los Angeles	1984	140	5,233	1,569	21	221
Seoul	1988	159	6,259	2,214	23	237
Barcelona	1992	169	6,656	2,712	25	257
Atlanta	1996	197	6,797	3,523	26	271
Sydney	2000	200	6,582	4,069	28	272
Athens	2004	201	6,296	4,329	28	301

WINTER GAMES

	YEAR	NOCs	MALE ATHLETES	FEMALE ATHLETES	SPORTS	EVENTS
Chamonix	1924	16	245	13	6	14
St Mortiz	1928	25	438	26	5	13
Lake Placid	1932	17	231	21	4	14
Garmisch-Partenkirchen	1936	28	588	80	4	17
St Moritz	1948	28	592	77	5	22
Oslo	1952	30	585	109	4	22
Cortina D'Ampezzo	1956	32	688	132	4	24
Squaw Valley	1960	30	522	143	4	27
Innsbruck	1964	36	891	200	6	34
Grenoble	1968	37	947	211	6	35
Sapporo	1972	35	800	206	6	35
Innsbruck	1976	37	892	231	6	37
Lake Placid	1980	37	839	233	6	38
Sarajevo	1984	49	1,000	274	6	39
Calgary	1988	57	1,110	313	6	46
Albertville	1992	64	1,313	488	6	57
Lillehammer	1994	67	1,216	523	6	61
Nagano	1998	72	1,412	827	7	68
Salt Lake City	2002	77	1,513	886	8	78
Turin	2006	80	1,548	960	7	84

APPENDIX G

IOC Sessions

YEAR	CITY	NO.	MEMBERS PRESENT	YEAR	CITY	NO.	MEMBERS PRESENT
1894	Paris	1	6	1953	Mexico City	49	35
1896	Athens	2	7	1954	Athens	50	48
1897	Le Havre	3	9	1955	Paris	51	62
1901	Paris	4	11	1956	Cortina D'Ampezzo	52	43
1902	Paris	5	8	1956	Melbourne	53	38
1903	Paris	6	–	1957	Sofia	54	36
1904	London	7	11	1958	Tokyo	55	31
1905	Brussels	8	15	1959	Munich	56	60
1906	Athens	9	8	1960	San Francisco	57	25
1907	La Haye	10	14	1960	Rome	58	63
1908	London	11	16	1961	Athens	59	43
1909	Berlin	12	22	1962	Moscow	60	44
1910	Luxembourg	13	16	1963	Baden-Baden	61	62
1911	Budapest	14	20	1964	Innsbruck	62	52
1912	Stockholm	15	31	1964	Tokyo	63	59
1913	Lausanne	16	23	1965	Madrid	64	63
1914	Paris	17	41	1966	Rome	65	64
1919	Lausanne	18	37	1967	Tehran	66	57
1920	Antwerp	19	30	1968	Grenoble	67	50
1921	Lausanne	20	24	1968	Mexico City	68	58
1922	Paris	21	27	1969	Warsaw	69	57
1923	Rome	22	29	1970	Amsterdam	70	62
1924	Paris	23	39	1971	Luxembourg	71	62
1925	Prague	24	30	1972	Sapporo	72	42
1926	Lisbon	25	24	1972	Munich	73	73
1927	Monaco	26	36	1973	Varna	74	61
1928	Amsterdam	27	39	1974	Vienna	75	64
1929	Lausanne	28	24	1975	Lausanne	76	70
1930	Berlin	29	32	1976	Innsbruck	77	56
1931	Barcelona	30	19	1976	Montreal	78	65
1932	Los Angeles	31	18	1977	Prague	79	69
1933	Vienna	32	29	1978	Athens	80	79
1934	Athens	33	22	1979	Montevideo	81	74
1935	Oslo	34	23	1980	Lake Placid	82	73
1936	Garmisch-Partenkirchen	35	15	1980	Moscow	83	77
1936	Berlin	36	50	1981	Baden-Baden	84	81
1937	Warsaw	37	26	1982	Rome	85	78
1938	Cairo	38	26	1983	New Delhi	86	78
1939	London	39	35	1984	Sarajevo	87	74
1946	Lausanne	40	26	1984	Los Angeles	88	85
1947	Stockholm	41	28	1984	Lausanne	89	79
1948	St Moritz	42	26	1985	Berlin	90	80
1948	London	43	44	1986	Lausanne	91	85
1949	Rome	44	41	1987	Istanbul	92	84
1950	Copenhagen	45	32	1988	Calgary	93	77
1951	Vienna	46	38	1988	Seoul	94	87
1952	Oslo	47	34	1989	Puerto Rico	95	84
1952	Helsinki	48	57	1990	Tokyo	96	87

YEAR	CITY	NO.	MEMBERS PRESENT	YEAR	CITY	NO.	MEMBERS PRESENT
1991	Birmingham	97	89	1999	Seoul	109	92
1992	Albertville	98	86	1999	Lausanne	110	92
1992	Barcelona	99	91	2000	Sydney	111	107
1993	Lausanne	100	86	2001	Moscow	112	118
1993	Monaco	101	90	2002	Salt Lake City	113	105
1994	Lillehammer	102	83	2002	Mexico City	114	115
1994	Paris	103	85	2003	Prague	115	118
1995	Budapest	104	93	2004	Athens	116	120
1996	Atlanta	105	102	2005	Singapore	117	116
1997	Lausanne	106	109	2006	Turin	118	107
1998	Nagano	107	99	2007	Guatemala City	119	117
1999	Lausanne	108	95	2008	Beijing	120	

APPENDIX H

Olympic Congresses

YEAR	CITY	THEME
1894	Paris	Re-establishment of the Olympic Games
1897	Le Havre	Sports hygiene and pedagogy
1905	Brussels	Sport and physical education
1906	Paris	Arts, literature and sport
1913	Lausanne	Sports psychology and physiology
1914	Paris	Olympic regulations
1921	Lausanne	Olympic regulations
1925	Prague	Sports pedagogy
		Olympic regulations
1930	Berlin	Olympic regulations
1973	Varna	Sport for a world of peace
		The Olympic Movement and its future
1981	Baden-Baden	United by and for sport
		1. The future of the Olympic Games
		2. International cooperation
		3. The future Olympic Movement
1994	Paris	Centennial Olympic Congress, Congress of Unity
		1. The Olympic Movement's contribution to modern society
		2. The contemporary athlete
		3. Sport in its social context
		4. Sport and the mass media
2009	Copenhagen	The Role of the Olympic Movement in Society
		1. The athletes
		2. The Olympic Games
		3. The structure of the Olympic Movement
		4. Olympism and youth
		5. The digital revolution

APPENDIX I

Distribution of Olympic Revenue

DIAGRAM A

NOC Revenue from the IOC: Quadrennium Comparison (US $ million)

OLYMPIC QUADRENNIUM	OLYMPIC SOLIDARITY BROADCAST REVENUE	TOP REVENUE*	TOTAL CONTRIBUTION
1989–92 (Albertville/Barcelona)	51.6	35	86.6
1993–96 (Lillehammer/Atlanta)	80.9	57	37.9
1997–2000 (Nagano/Sydney)	118.7	80	198.7
2001–04 (Salt Lake/Athens)	209.5	95	304.5
2005–08 (Athens/Turin)	244.0		

* excluding United States Olympic Committee (USOC) and Host Country NOCs

N.B. Substantial additional indirect financial support is provided to the NOCs through the provision of a free athletes' village and travel grants to the Olympic Games

DIAGRAM B

Olympic Solidarity Programme (US $000)

	2006	2005
Previous years' programme	937	3,227
Current year programme Programme managed by continental associations	23,389	22,289
World Programme managed by Olympic Solidarity		
NOC preparation programme	490	1,512
Scholarships for athletes	6,024	1,364
Regional and Continental Games – NOC preparation	3,111	1,178
Youth development programme	1,945	1,533
Technical courses	3,334	2,123
Scholarships for coaches	1,446	1,208
Development of national coaching structure	1,074	931
NOC infrastructure	5,501	5,175
Sports administrators programme	391	553
High-level education for sports administrators	453	352
Sports medicine	558	430
Sport and environment	190	252
Women and sport	287	249
International Olympic Academy	471	493
Sport for All	637	598
Culture and education	527	365
NOC's heritage	433	480
	26,872	18,796
Forums	570	606
Total current year programme	50,831	41,691
Total current and prior years' programme costs	51,786	44,918

DIAGRAM C

Television Broadcasting Rights Revenues and Distribution (US $000)

	2006	2005
Source of rights revenues by continent		
America	643,213	–
Europe	133,667	–
Africa	615	–
Asia	40,205	–
Oceania	13,144	–
Total revenues from television broadcasting rights	830,844	–
Use and distribution of revenues		
Insurance premium for Games cancellation	3,308	–
Organising committee of the XX Olympic WInter Games	406,071	–
United States Olympic Committee	78,209	–
Special marketing renumeration to international federations	52,654	–
International federations	73,346	–
Use and distribution of television broadcasting rights to OCOG, USOC and IF	613,588	–
Allocation to IS	73,346	–
Total use and distribution of television broadcasting rights	686,934	–

DIAGRAM D

TOP Programme Marketing Rights Revenues and Distribution (US $000)

	2006	2005
Total revenues from the TOP marketing programme	268,390	176,237
Use and distribution of revenues		
Organising committees of the Games of the Olympiad and of the Olympic Winter Games	171,915	48,445
United States Olympic Committee	23,932	33,854
National Olympic committees	33,206	48,667
Other programme costs	9,700	6,104
Total use and distribution of programme TOP revenues	238,753	137,070

Bibliography

100 Years of the Olympic Games (ed. Willi Knecht, OSB, 8 vol., Munich, 1990)

1894–1994, The International Olympic Committe: One Hundred Years (edited, 3 vol. IOC, Lausanne, 1993)

African Running Revolution, The (ed. Dave Prokop, Runner's World Publications, Mountain View, CA, 1975)

Albertville '92 (David Miller, IMS/Studio 6, Lausanne, 1992)

Athletic World Records in the 20th Century (Lionel Blackman, The Book Guild, Lewes, 1988)

Atlanta '96 (David Miller, IMS/Studio 6, Lausanne, 1996)

Babe: Life and Legend (Susan Cayleff, University of Illinois, Urbana, 1995)

Barcelona '92 (Stephen Woodward, IMS/Studio 6, Lausanne, 1992)

Behind the Olympic Rings (Geoffrey Miller, H.O. Zimman, Massachusetts, 1979)

Bid, The. How Australia Won the 2000 Games (Rod McGeoch with Glenda Korporaal, Heinemann, Melbourne, 1994)

Born to Run (David Miller with Sebastian Coe, Pavilion, London, 1992)

Brendan Foster (Cliff Temple, Heinemann, London, 1978)

British Olympians (Ian Buchanan, Guinness, London, 1991)

Calgary '88 (edited, IMS/Studio 6, Lausanne, 1988)

Campagne de 21 ans (1887–1908), Une (Pierre de Coubertin, Education Physique, Paris, 1909)

Coe and Ovett File (ed. Mel Watman, Athletics Weekly, Rochester, 1982)

Coming Back (David Miller, Sidgwick & Jackson, London, 1984)

Commonwealth Games, The (Cleve Dheenshaw, Q.A.P., Victoria BC, 1994)

Complete Book of the Summer Olympics, The (David Wallechinsky, Overlook Press, NY, 2000)

Complete Book of the Winter Olympics, The (David Wallechinsky, Aurum, London, 2002)

Daley Thompson: The Subject is Winning (Skip Rozin, Stanley Paul, London, 1983)

Dunlop Book of the Olympics (David Guiney, Eastland, London, 1960)

Encyclopaedia of Track and Field Athletics (Mel Watman, Hale, London, 1981)

Essays and Studies on Olympic Problems (Nadejda Lekarska, Medicina & Fitzcultura, Sofia, 1973)

Fabulous 100 Years of the IOC (Wolf Lyberg, IOC, Lausanne, 1996)

Fair Game: Myth and Reality in Sport (Eric Midwinter, Allen & Unwin, London, 1986)

Female Runner, The (edited, Runner's World Publications, Mountain View, CA, 1974)

First Four Minutes (Roger Bannister, Putnam, London, 1955)

Five Ring Circus (ed. Tomlinson & Whannel, Pluto, London, 1984)

Five Rings over Korea (Richard Pound, Little Brown, Toronto, 1994)

4-Minute Smiler: The Derek Ibbotson Story (Terry O'Connor, Stanley Paul, London, 1960)

Future of the Olympic Games (John Lucas, Human Kinetics, Champaign, Illinois, 1992)

Game, The (112-part, 8 vol. encyclopaedia, Marshall Cavendish, London, 1971)

Game of Shadows: Barry Bonds, Balco, and the Steroids Scandal That Rocked Professional Sports (Mark Fainaru-Wada and Lance Williams, Gotham, NY, 2006)

Games of the XXIII Olympiad, LA 1984 (edited, International Sports Pub. Inc., LA, 1984)

Games War, The (Christopher Booker, Faber, London, 1981)

Games Within the Games, The (Vincent Ricquart, Hantong, Seoul, 1988)

General, The (Anton Antonovic, Sofia Press, 1981)

Get to Your Marks (Ross and Norris McWhirter, Nicholas Kaye, London, 1951)

Golden Age, A (Steve Redgrave, BBC, London, 2000)

Great Men and Moments in Sport (Esquire, ed., Harper, NY, 1934)

Great Olympic Swindle, The (Andrew Jennings and Clare Sambrook, Simon & Schuster, London, 2000)

Great Symbol, The (John MacAloon, Chicago Press, 1981)

Greatest Olympics, The (Kim Un Yong, Si-sa-yong-o-sa, Seoul, 1990)

Guinness International Who's Who of Sport (Peter Matthews, Ian Buchanan and Bill Mallon, Guinness, London, 1993)

Highlights of the Olympics (John Durant, Arco, London, 1961)

Historical Dictionary of the Modern Olympic Movement (ed. John Findling and Kimberley Pelle, Greenwood Press, London, 1996)

History of British Athletics (Mel Watman, Robert Hale, London, 1968)

History of Modern Track and Field Athletics (Roberto Quercetani, SEP, Milan, 2000)

History of the Olympics (James Coote, Tom Stacey, Verona, 1972)

History of the Olympics (Tyler & Soar, Marshall Cavendish, London, 1975)

Hitler's Olympics: The 1936 Games (Duff Hart-Davis, Coronet, London, 1988)

Hitler's Olympics: The Story of the 1936 Nazi Games (Anton Rippon, Pen & Sword, Barnsley, 2006)

Human Performance in Athletics (edited, International Athletic Foundation, Monaco, 1998)

IIIrd Olympiad: St Louis 1904 (Official Report, Amateur Athletic Union US, 1904)

Illustrated History of the Olympics (Dick Schaap, Ballantyne, NY, 1963)

In Black and White: The Untold Story of Joe Louis and Jesse Owens (Donald McRae, Scribner, London, 2002)

Inside the Olympics: A Behind-the-Scenes Look at the Politics, the Scandals, and the Glory of the Games (Dick Pound, Wiley, Canada, 2004)

Introduction to Sportology (Vladimir Rodichenko, Sovetsky Sport, Moscow, 2001)

IOC and South Africa, The (Keba M'Baye, IOC, Lausanne, 1995)

Jesse (Jesse Owens with Paul Neimark, Fawcett, NY, 1978)

Jesse Owens: An American Life (William J. Baker, The Free Press, NY, 1986)

Jim Thorpe's History of the Olympics (Jim Thorpe with Thomas Collison, Wetzel, LA, 1932)

Journal of Olympic History (current periodical, International Society of Olympic Historians, Fochteloo, Netherlands)

Leon Stukelj: 100 (Ivo Kuljaj, Magnolia, Ljubljiana, 1998)

Lillehammer '94 (David Miller, IMS/Studio 6, Lausanne, 1994)

Lords of the Rings, The (Vyv Simson and Andrew Jennings, Simon & Schuster, London, 1992)

Made in America (Peter Ueberroth, William Morrow, NY, 1985)

Magic of Athletics, The (Alain Billouin, Roberto Quercetani. Mel Watman, IAAF, Monaco, 1999)

Making it Happen (Kenneth Reich, Capra Press, Santa Barbara, CA, 1986)

Mémoirs Olympiques (Pierre de Coubertin, IOC, Lausanne, 1997)

Mexico 1968 (Christopher Brasher, Stanley Paul, London, 1968)

Miracle Machine, The (Doug Gilbert, Coward McCann, Geoghegan, NY, 1980)

Munich '72 (edited, German Sport Aid Foundation, Munich, 1972)

My Olympic Years, 1972–80 (Lord Killanin, Secker & Warburg, London, 1983)

Nagano '98 (David Miller, IMS/Studio 6, Lausanne, 1998)

Nazi Olympics, The (Richard Mandell, Souvenir, London, 1971)

Official Reports of the Olympic Games 1960/1964/1968 (World Sports Magazine, UK)

Olympia: Gods, Artists and Athletes (Ludwig Drees, Pall Mall, London, 1968)

Olympic Century, The (ed. Christian D. Kinney, 24 vol., World Sport Research and Pub. Inc., LA, 2000)

Olympic Diary, 1964 (Neil Allen, Nicholas Kaye, London, 1965)

Olympic Facts and Feats (Stan Greenberg, Guinness, London, 1996)

Olympic Life, An (Kevan Gosper and Glenda Korporaal, Allen & Unwin, St Leonards NSW, 2000)

Olympic Games, The (ed. Lord Killanin with John Rodda, Barrie & Jenkins, London, 1976)

Olympic Games 1976 (edited, Runner's World Magazine, NY, 1976)

Olympic Games Companion (ed. Caroline Searle and Bryn Vaile, Brassey's, London, 1998)

Olympic Idea, The (Karl Hofman, Carl Diem Institute, Stuttgart, 1970)

Olympic Memoirs (Pierre de Coubertin, Bureau International de Pedagogie Sportive, Paris, 1931)

Olympic Message (periodical, IOC, Lausanne, 1980–96)

Olympic Politics (Christopher Hill, Manchester University Press, 1992)

Olympic Report '76 (James Coote and John Goodbody, Kemps, London, 1976)

Olympic Review (current periodical, IOC, Lausanne)

Olympic Revolution (David Miller, Pavilion, London, 1992)

Olympic Turnaround (Michael Payne, London Business Press, Twyford, 2006)

Olympics, The. History of the Modern Games (Allen Guttmann, University of Illinois, Chicago, 1992)

Olympics, The (William Oscar Johnson, *Sports Illustrated/Time* Inc., Birmingham, Alabama, 1992)

Olympics Factbook, The (Martin Connors, Diane Dupuis and Brad Morgan, Visible Ink, Detroit, 1984)

Olympism in Antiquity (edited, IOC, Lausanne, 1993)

One Is My Lucky Number (Daley Thompson, W.H. Allen, London, 1980)

Our Sporting Times (David Miller, Pavilion, London, 1996)

Ovett: An Autobiography (Steve Ovett with John Rodda, Collins Willow, London, 1984)

Paavo Nurmi: The Flying Finn (Sulo Kolkka and Helge Nygren, Otava, 1974)

Pascoe: The Story of an Athlete (Alan Hubbard, Stanley Paul, London, 1979)

Pathway to Glory (Robert W. Wheeler, Carlton Press, NY, 1975)

Philosophy of Sport, The (ed., Robert G. Osterhoudt, Charles C. Thomas, Springfield, Illinois, 1973)

Race for the 2012 Olympics, The (Mike Lee, Virgin, London, 2006)

Running, The Power and Glory (ed. Norman Harris, Partridge Press, Hayward's Heath, 1986)

Running Commentary (David Moorcroft with Cliff Temple, Stanley Paul, London, 1984)

Running Free (David Miller with Sebastian Coe, Sidgwick & Jackson, London, 1981)

Saga of the Modern Olympic Games (John Lucas, New Brunswick, NJ, 1980)

Sapporo '72 (edited, German Sport Aid Foundation, Munich, 1972)

Science of Track and Field Athletics (Howard and Rosemary Payne, Pelham, London, 1981)

Seoul '88 (David Miller, IMS/Studio 6, Lausanne, 1988)

Seoul Olympics, The (Park Seh-Jik, Bellew, London, 1991)

Seventh President of the IOC, 1980–2001, The (Wolf Lyberg, IOC, Lausanne, 2001)

Seventh President, The (Alex Ratner, Olympic Panorama, Moscow, 2001)

Sixty Olympic Years (Artur Takac with John Rodda, IOC, Lausanne, 1998)

Soviet Sport (James Riordan, Blackwell, Oxford, 1980)

Spalding's Official Athletic Almanac, 1905 (James E. Sullivan, American Publishing Co., NY, 1905)

Sport and The British (Richard Holt, Clarendon, Oxford, 1995)

Sport Ethics (David Malloy, Saul Ross and Dwight Zakus, TEP Inc., NY, 2000)

Sport Intern (current news circular, Karl Heinz Huba, Inside Sports Media, Lorsch, Germany)

Sport and Politics (Neil Macfarlane, Collins Willow, 1986)

Sport under Communism (James Riordan, C. Hurst, London 1978)

Sporting Excellence (David Hemery, Collins Willow, 1986)

Sports Book, The (ed. James Rivers, Macdonald, London, 1946)

Sports Illustrated (periodical, Olympic Games issues, Time Life, 1976–2002)

Sports Immortals, The (ed. Will Grimsley, Prentice Hall Inc., NJ, 1972)

Steve Cram (Norman Barrett and Mel Watman, Virgin, London, 1984)

Steve Cram: The Making of an Athlete (Roger Tanes, W.H. Allen, London, 1984)

Steve Ovett: Portrait of an Athlete (Simon Turnbull, W.H. Allen, London, 1982)

Strategy for British Sports (Don Anthony, Hurst, London, 1980)

Sydney Passion (ed. Nancy Dorking, Hachette, Luçon, 2000)

This Life I've Led (Babe Didriksen with Harry Paxton, Barnes, NJ, 1955)

Torino 2006 (Erwin Roth, OSB, Munich, 2006)

Unfriendly Games, 1986, The (Derek Bateman and Derek Douglas, Mainstream, Edinburgh, 1986)

What They Don't Teach You At Harvard Business School (Mark McCormack, Collins, London, 1984)

What's Wrong with Sports? (Howard Cosell, Simon & Schuster, London, 1991)

Whitaker's Olympic Almanack (Stan Greenberg, Stationery Office, London, 2000)

Wings on my Feet (Sonja Henie, Prentice Hall Inc., NJ, 1940)

Wizards of the Middle Distances (Roberto Quercetani and Nejat Kök, Vallardi, Milan, 1992)

World Sports Magazine (UK, 1948–76)

XVII Olympiad, Rome 1960 (Harold Abrahams, Cassell, London, 1960)

Zola: The Official Biography (Brian Vine, Stanley Paul, London, 1984)

Index